MANAGING MARKETING IN THE 21ST CENTURY:

Developing & Implementing The Market Strategy

3rd edition

v001

www.axcesscapon.com

To access O-codes, go to **www.ocodes.com**

MANAGING MARKETING IN THE 21ST CENTURY:

Developing & Implementing The Market Strategy

3rd edition

Noel Capon

Graduate School of Business

Columbia University

New York, NY

Library of Congress Cataloging-in-Publication Data

Capon, Noel
    Managing Marketing in the 21st Century / Noel Capon — 3rd edition
        p. cm.
    Includes index
    ISBN 978-0-9833300-4-2
        1. Managing—Marketing.   I. Title: Managing marketing in the twenty-first century.

Copy Editor: Christy Goldfinch
Permissions Editor: Sandra Lord
Book / Cover Design: Anna Botelho
Indexer: Judi Gibbs

Credits and acknowledgments are a continuation of the copyright page; they are on pages xxix, xxx, C1 and C2.

This book contains references to the products of SAP AG, Dietmar-Hopp-allee 16, 69190 Walldorf, Germany. The names of these products are registered and/or unregistered trademarks of SAP AG. SAP AG is neither the author nor the publisher of this book and is not responsible for its content.

DEDICATION

To Deanna Kuhn

ABOUT THE AUTHOR

NOEL CAPON is the R. C. Kopf Professor of International Marketing and past Chair of the Marketing Division at the Graduate School of Business, Columbia University. Educated primarily in Great Britain, Professor Capon earned B.Sc. and Ph.D. degrees in Chemistry from University College, London University. He also received degrees in Business Administration from Manchester (Dip. BA), Harvard (MBA), and Columbia Business School (Ph.D.).

Professor Capon joined the Columbia Business School faculty in 1979. Previously he served on the faculty of, and received tenure from, the University of California – Graduate School of Management, UCLA. He has taught and held faculty positions at Harvard Business School; Australia — Monash University; England — Bradford Management Centre and Manchester Business School; France — INSEAD; Hong Kong — The Hong Kong University of Science and Technology (HKUST); China — China European International Business School (CEIBS — Shanghai); and India — Indian School of Business (ISB — Hyderabad). Professor Capon currently holds the position of Distinguished Visiting Professor at Manchester Business School.

Professor Capon has published more than 60 refereed articles and book chapters, and is editor for sections on Marketing, and Sales Management and Distribution, in the *AMA Management Handbook* (1994). He has published more than 20 books, including *Corporate Strategic Planning*, a major study of the planning practices of major U.S. manufacturing corporations (Columbia University Press 1988); *The Marketing of Financial Services: A Book of Cases* (Prentice-Hall 1992); *Planning the Development of Builders, Leaders, and Managers of Twenty First Century Business* (Kluwer Academic Publishers 1996) on the curriculum review process at Columbia Business School; *Why Some Firms Perform Better than Others: Towards a More Integrative Explanation* (Kluwer Academic Publishers 1996) on the underpinnings of superior corporate financial performance; *The Asian Marketing Case Book* (Prentice Hall 1999); *Marketing Management in the 21st Century* (Prentice Hall 2001); *Key Account Management and Planning* (Free Press 2001); *Total Integrated Marketing* (Free Press 2003); *The Marketing Mavens* (Crown Business 2007); *Managing Global Accounts* (Wessex 2008); *Strategic Account Strategy* (Wessex 2011); and *Sales Eats First* (Wessex 2011).

In addition to *Managing Marketing in the 21st Century* (U.S. and European versions), Professor Capon's textbook publications include *Capon's Marketing Framework* (Wessex 2009); a companion marketing planning workbook, *The Virgin Marketer* (Wessex 2007); and several Student Study Guides. Professor Capon's textbooks are also published in Chinese, Russian, and Spanish.

Professor Capon contributes extensively to Columbia Business School's Executive Education. He is the Founding Director of *Managing Strategic Accounts* and the *Global Account Manager Certification* program in conjunction with St. Gallen University (Switzerland). He teaches on Columbia's *Full-time MBA and Executive MBA* (EMBA) programs and its partner program with London Business School. He founded and directs the Advanced Marketing Management Program in conjunction with the Chinese European International Business School (CEIBS — Shanghai). He also designs, directs, and teaches in numerous custom programs for major corporations globally. In 2001, Professor Capon co-founded *The Chief Sales Executive Forum*, offering multiple educational opportunities for sales leaders.

FOREWORD

Having been active in business education for more than three decades, I believe that the traditional textbook system must change, and must change radically. *Managing Marketing in the 21st Century* is my attempt to usher in a new model and bring considerable additional value to both marketing instructors and their students.

Whether you are an instructor or student, I encourage you to search *amazon.com* or *barnesandnoble.com* for a marketing textbook for your graduate or senior undergraduate marketing course. Or just go to your college bookstore. You will find no suitable textbook for under $100, and several priced more than $150. Of course, pre-owned books are somewhat cheaper, but these rapidly become out of date in the three-year new-edition cycle.

Even for students in the U.S. and advanced western countries, $100 to $150 per textbook is a pretty big nut to swallow. When we consider less-developed countries, a new marketing textbook is far out of reach for the average student. Such high prices are not only an issue for individual faculty members and their students. There is, perhaps, a more basic societal issue. Many political scientists believe that, over the long run, there is a strong relationship between market freedom and political freedom. What could be more fundamental to learning how to participate in free markets than a marketing textbook? Excessively priced marketing textbooks deprive people all over the world from learning about the tools they need to operate in free-market economies. Arguably, they also inhibit the growth of political freedom.

I have spent most of my career at Columba Business School in Manhattan, New York. Situated in the world's financial capital, Columbia University has long played a global role in creating and disseminating knowledge. I have spent time at major business schools around the world, and have worked with corporations large and small in several continents and many countries. These experiences have helped me accumulate the ability to bridge theory and practice. I also firmly believe I have a professional responsibility to deliver the intellectual capital expressed in this volume to faculty and students, no matter where they are located.

Please do not misunderstand; many conventional marketing textbooks have fine content. Indeed, my friends and professional colleagues wrote these books. But the traditional textbook model must change. There is simply no reason why students should pay such excessive prices for their textbooks, nor why publishers should earn gross margins in excess of 75 percent.

Wessex Press offers the third edition of *Managing Marketing in the 21st Century* at a fraction of the price of traditional textbooks. This state-of-the-art marketing textbook is available to you as a printed book; a downloadable pdf; or in electronic form to read online for a FREE trial period, then *pay what you think it's worth*. Just go to the website — *www.axcesscapon.com* — and you will find out how to secure the version that best suits your needs. To assist your learning, Wessex also provides a student study guide and a series of flash cards.

Managing Marketing in the 21ˢᵗ Century

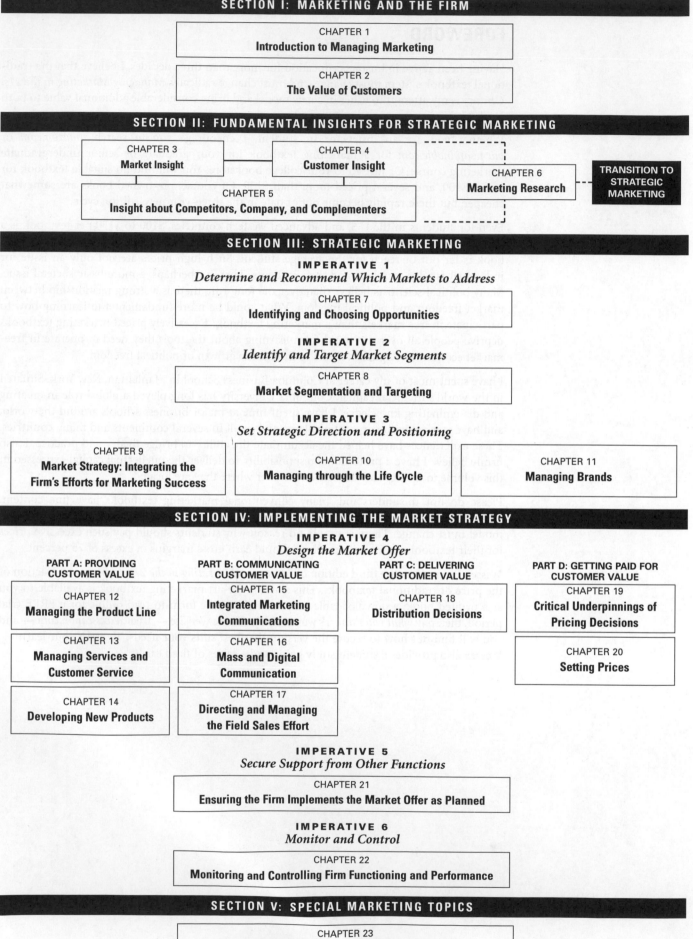

SECTION I: MARKETING AND THE FIRM

CHAPTER 1
Introduction to Managing Marketing

CHAPTER 2
The Value of Customers

SECTION II: FUNDAMENTAL INSIGHTS FOR STRATEGIC MARKETING

CHAPTER 3
Market Insight

CHAPTER 4
Customer Insight

CHAPTER 5
Insight about Competitors, Company, and Complementers

CHAPTER 6
Marketing Research

TRANSITION TO STRATEGIC MARKETING

SECTION III: STRATEGIC MARKETING

IMPERATIVE 1
Determine and Recommend Which Markets to Address

CHAPTER 7
Identifying and Choosing Opportunities

IMPERATIVE 2
Identify and Target Market Segments

CHAPTER 8
Market Segmentation and Targeting

IMPERATIVE 3
Set Strategic Direction and Positioning

CHAPTER 9
Market Strategy: Integrating the Firm's Efforts for Marketing Success

CHAPTER 10
Managing through the Life Cycle

CHAPTER 11
Managing Brands

SECTION IV: IMPLEMENTING THE MARKET STRATEGY

IMPERATIVE 4
Design the Market Offer

PART A: PROVIDING CUSTOMER VALUE

PART B: COMMUNICATING CUSTOMER VALUE

PART C: DELIVERING CUSTOMER VALUE

PART D: GETTING PAID FOR CUSTOMER VALUE

CHAPTER 12
Managing the Product Line

CHAPTER 15
Integrated Marketing Communications

CHAPTER 18
Distribution Decisions

CHAPTER 19
Critical Underpinnings of Pricing Decisions

CHAPTER 13
Managing Services and Customer Service

CHAPTER 16
Mass and Digital Communication

CHAPTER 20
Setting Prices

CHAPTER 14
Developing New Products

CHAPTER 17
Directing and Managing the Field Sales Effort

IMPERATIVE 5
Secure Support from Other Functions

CHAPTER 21
Ensuring the Firm Implements the Market Offer as Planned

IMPERATIVE 6
Monitor and Control

CHAPTER 22
Monitoring and Controlling Firm Functioning and Performance

SECTION V: SPECIAL MARKETING TOPICS

CHAPTER 23
International, Regional, and Global Marketing

TABLE OF CONTENTS IN BRIEF

TABLE OF CONTENTS IN DETAIL

PREFACE

In *Managing Marketing in the 21st Century* you will learn about marketing language, logic, strategy, and implementation. To get us off to a good start, we'll begin by providing you the book's positioning.

POSITIONING

As you will learn in Chapter 9, positioning comprises four elements — customer targets, competitor targets, value proposition, and reasons to believe. The positioning for *Managing Marketing in the 21st Century* is:

- **Customer targets.** Marketing instructors who specify texts for graduate and senior undergraduate marketing courses, and the students who will learn to practice marketing in these courses.

- **Competitor targets.** All textbooks entitled *Marketing Management*, or some close approximation, for use in graduate and senior undergraduate marketing courses.

- **Value proposition.** *Managing Marketing in the 21st Century* supports instructors in their quest to enhance students' grasp of marketing. Students learn how to successfully address simple and complex marketing problems. They learn *what to do* and *how to do it*, and how to infuse the organizations in which they work with a customer-focused view of business. And they pay a fraction of the price of traditional textbooks.

- **Reason to believe.** Professor Capon is among the world's most experienced marketing educators, from one of the world's leading business schools. The author has extensive experience educating students at all levels of business degree programs, as well as senior and mid-level executives in major corporations globally.

PURPOSE

Managing Marketing in the 21st Century is about understanding how to develop market strategy, implement market offers, and manage the marketing process. This is not a book that attempts to describe all there is to know about marketing, but focuses on what the prospective manager needs to know. *Managing Marketing in the 21st Century* differs from other senior undergraduate and introductory graduate marketing texts. The author takes a position on what he believes is a better or worse course of action for marketers. Marketing is an applied field; the author believes he should provide guidance for good marketing practice.

Furthermore, *Managing Marketing in the 21st Century* focuses on the manager, not just the marketer. For readers committed to a career in marketing (and we hope there are many), this book will form a solid foundation as you study marketing further and deeper. But the vast majority of you will not work in marketing departments, but will instead become senior executives, general managers, CFOs, and CEOs. This book is also for you because an understanding and appreciation of marketing is central to virtually every important decision that senior managers make. Because this may be the only marketing course many of you will take, *Managing Marketing in the 21st Century* provides what every general manager and senior executive must know about marketing.

Marketing activity lies at the core of leading and managing a business by providing the focus for interfacing with customers. Marketing is also the source of insight about the market, customers, competitors, and complementers, and the business environment in general. Marketing is concerned with the firm's long-run relationships with customers as well as its short-run sales activity. Marketing must be a major organizational thrust, not just a responsibility assigned to a single functional department. For this reason, *Managing Marketing in the 21st Century* emphasizes the role of marketing in creating value for customers — this leads to the creation of value for other firm stakeholders, including shareholders and employees.

CUSTOMERS: STUDENTS

To better understand how marketing fits into the broader challenge of leading and managing a corporation, we address marketing at the firm/business-unit level, as well as in the marketing function. *Managing Marketing in the 21st Century* provides you with a set of concepts and ideas for approaching marketing decisions. The book also gives you a common language for thinking about marketing issues. You will learn to structure and analyze managerial problems in marketing. *Managing Marketing in the 21st Century* prepares you to deal with core marketing issues that future marketers, senior executives, general managers, and CEOs will have to face. The book will also help you think strategically about your firm's markets, products, and services so that you can:

- Develop frameworks for approaching simple and complex marketing problems.
- Analyze markets, customers, competitors, your company, and complementers.
- Identify and assess market opportunities and develop market strategy.
- Prepare strategic marketing plans.
- Design implementation programs comprising product, promotion, distribution, and price, otherwise known as the marketing mix.
- Understand the importance of working across organizational boundaries to align all of the firm's capabilities.
- Assess the success of your marketing initiatives.
- Gain practical experience in addressing marketing issues in a variety of contexts — domestic and international, entrepreneurial startups and established corporations, business (B2B) and consumer (B2C) markets, products and services, and private and public and not-for-profit sectors.

As you work your way through *Managing Marketing in the 21st Century* you will develop a high tolerance for ambiguity — a quality of all successful senior executives, general managers, and CEOs. You will learn that there are no right or wrong answers to marketing problems, just some answers that are better than others. There are no simple — or even complex — formulae in which to plug a set of numbers and find the *right* answer. Rather, you must learn to approach complex and unstructured marketing problems in a creative and measured way. Throughout the book, and at the end of each chapter, are questions and exercises that can help you dig deeper. When appropriate, we urge you to use secondary sources, especially the Internet, to address these issues.

CUSTOMERS: MARKETING FACULTY

For marketing instructors, *Managing Marketing in the 21st Century* provides an opportunity to support your efforts in the classroom by presenting a contemporary perspective on how marketing works within the modern corporation. The book not only offers a firm basis on which to ground a first graduate or senior undergraduate marketing course, but will also challenge your students by including material and ideas not typically covered in marketing texts. Of course, *Managing Marketing in the 21st Century* focuses on how marketing should address customer needs, but it also emphasizes marketing's *bottom line* — shareholder value. By understanding and acting upon the principles and frameworks in this book, students will avoid the many pitfalls of operating in an increasingly complex, competitive, and global environment.

In order to learn how to think appropriately about marketing problems, students must develop skills in marketing problem-solving and analysis. We recommend that your course also use marketing cases and/or simulations in context with this text.[1] Rather than write or include lengthy

---

[1] We have had very good experience with Markstrat, www.stratxsimulations.com/.

cases in the text, the Instructor's Manual and website <*www.axcesscapon.com*> provide numerous suggestions for course outlines, cases, and other activities linked to topics in the text. The website also shows ways to approach case analysis.

DIFFERENTIAL ADVANTAGE

As indicated in the foreword, many good marketing textbooks have been published over the years, but they can grow into comprehensive tomes or reference books. Further, they often contain excessive descriptive data and lots of pictures as they move from edition to edition. *Managing Marketing in the 21st Century* has a fresh look and feel for how marketing really works, and offers instructors and students many compelling benefits and values that clearly differentiate this book from others:

1. **More useful and less costly.** When students access *Managing Marketing in the 21st Century*, they pay a fraction of the price of traditional marketing textbooks. Students have three options: printed book, pdf e-book for downloading, and an electronic file to read online — for this option students have a FREE trial, then *pay what you think it's worth*. Quite simply, students who use this book will also be able to afford lunch.

2. **Improving shareholder value.** Business is ever more complex. Students learn the important link between success in delivering value to customers and success in improving shareholder value. This relationship is explicit and shows how world-class marketing decision-making must always consider the impact on shareholders.

3. **Normative focus.** *Managing Marketing in the 21st Century* takes a position on what are appropriate courses of action. Readers should know where the author stands and what he believes. Chapter 1 identifies a set of Marketing Imperatives and a set of Marketing Principles as guides for developing market strategy. The Marketing Imperatives form the basis for the book's macro-organization. Chapter 9 lays out core elements of a market strategy; a strategy that does not include these elements is incomplete.

4. **New ideas relevant to modern marketing environments.** *Managing Marketing in the 21st Century* introduces several genuinely new ideas drawn from personal research and writings and helps students develop critical thinking and problem-solving skills to use them. A textbook should present established procedures, processes, and generalized norms, but such a narrow mandate would perform a disservice to readers. Changes taking place in marketing are dramatic and rapid. They require good problem-solving and analytic skills, as well as sound understanding of principles and practice.

5. **Applying the marketing mix** — as the means of **implementing the firm's market strategy.** For far too long, marketing students have completed their introductory marketing courses believing that marketing equals the marketing mix — product, promotion, distribution, and price. Other critical questions must necessarily precede decisions about marketing mix elements. For example:

   - What is the essential role of marketing?

   - How does marketing increase shareholder value?

   - What is a market strategy? How do you know if your market strategy is complete?

   - Why are brands important? What are key issues for developing a branding strategy?

   Only after these and other questions have been resolved should the firm make marketing-mix decisions.

6. **Balance between B2C and B2B marketing** is critically important. In chapter discussions, sometimes customers are consumers; other times they are organizations. *Managing Marketing in the 21st Century* favors neither one nor the other, but puts significant effort in both B2C and B2B marketing to address key developments in marketing practice today.

7. **Branding and marketing metrics** are increasingly important strategic issues for firms — the book devotes full chapters to each.

8. **International, regional, and global marketing.** The world is fast globalizing and firms increasingly seek opportunities outside their domestic markets. They face new and complex issues; hence this chapter focuses exclusively on international, regional, and global marketing.

9. **Public and not-for-profit marketing.** This book focuses squarely on marketing challenges facing managers in for-profit businesses. But it will also prove useful for those students interested in not-for-profit and public-sector marketing. First, the vast majority of concepts are readily transferable to these sectors — major differences concern organizational objectives. In the for-profit sector, objectives are unambiguously concerned with profit and shareholder value — in the not-for-profit and public sectors, setting objectives is often a complex undertaking. Second, experience shows that students who develop a firm grounding in for-profit marketing are better prepared for the challenges of not-for-profit and public-sector marketing.

A PEDAGOGICAL FRAMEWORK FOR STUDYING AND LEARNING

The book includes several features to enhance your learning experience:

- **Video Introduction.** The author delivers a short overview of what to expect in the chapter.

- **Learning Objectives.** These highlight the learning you will gain from diligently studying material in each chapter.

- **Opening Case.** To bring the book to life, each chapter opens with a real-life example of an organization that helps focus the upcoming material.

- **The Changing View.** The Old Way/New Way device shows the direction of change regarding the upcoming material.

- **Examples.** The book showcases examples to illustrate specific ideas in each chapter.

- **Key Ideas.** Key ideas are distributed throughout the book and highlighted in the margins for easy reference.

- **Marketing Questions/Marketing Exercises.** To engage you with the text and deepen your understanding. Questions/exercises about the material are in the margins.

- **Special Topics.** Several chapters contain special-topic material highlighted in boxes.

- **Marketing Enrichment.** *Managing Marketing in the 21st Century* has no appendices. Rather, additional material is clearly noted and easily accessible (FREE) via O-codes and QR codes (below).

- **Key Messages.** This section concisely identifies the key learning points in the chapter

- **Videos and Audios.** Many chapters offer video interviews of the author with marketing leaders and audio interviews with the author. Students may access these material via cell phone or personal computer using O-codes and QR codes (below).

- **Questions for Study and Discussion.** Each chapter concludes with questions to help you reflect on the chapter material and gain deeper insight.

- **Glossary.** At the end of the book, we gather together and provide an explanation of key marketing terms.

Managing Marketing in the 21st Century is pretty light on pictures, fluff, and entertainment value. After all, marketing is a serious business.

ORGANIZATION OF THE BOOK

As laid out in the Table of Contents, *Managing Marketing in the 21st Century* addresses the challenge of *managing marketing in the 21st century* in five sections and 23 chapters. Briefly:

SECTION I — MARKETING AND THE FIRM

SECTION II — FUNDAMENTAL INSIGHTS FOR STRATEGIC MARKETING

SECTION III — STRATEGIC MARKETING
SECTION IV — IMPLEMENTING THE MARKET STRATEGY
SECTION V — SPECIAL MARKETING TOPICS

SECTION 1 — MARKETING AND THE FIRM. This section introduces fundamental concepts in marketing and emphasizes the importance of customers. The section comprises two chapters:

- Chapter 1, *Introduction to Managing Marketing*, provides an introduction to the book. This chapter makes the case for the critical importance of marketing in the modern corporation. The chapter describes two key meanings of marketing — **marketing as a philosophy** and **six marketing imperatives** that encompass the tasks of strategic marketing. Chapter 1 also introduces four principles that should form the basis for all marketing decision-making — they continue thematically throughout the book.

- Chapter 2, *The Value of Customers: Optimizing Shareholder Value* delves into the notion of customers as critical firm assets. This chapter introduces the concept of customer lifetime value (CLV) and emphasizes the importance of customer retention. The chapter also shows that, in addition to measuring product profitability, the firm should measure customer profitability. The second part of the chapter focuses on actions designed to bind customers closer to the firm, notably customer relationship management (CRM) and customer loyalty programs.

SECTION II — FUNDAMENTAL INSIGHTS FOR STRATEGIC MARKETING. The four chapters in this section focus on securing insight — situation analysis — that lays the foundation for developing market strategy.

- Chapter 3, *Market Insight*, focuses on understanding the market. The chapter framework embraces market structure, market and product evolution, industry forces, and environmental forces.

- Chapter 4, *Customer Insight*, focuses on customers — consumers and organizations. This chapter addresses three main questions: Who are the customers? What do customers need? How do customers buy?

- Chapter 5, *Insight about Competitors, Company, and Complementers*, focuses on each area. This chapter offers an extended section on competitors and presents a five-step process — identify, describe, evaluate, project, and manage.

- Chapter 6, *Marketing Research*, focuses on marketing research methodologies to gain insight relative to markets, customers, competitors, company, and complementers.

TRANSITION TO STRATEGIC MARKETING. This material shows how planning assumptions form the supporting pillars for strategic marketing and implementation.

SECTION III — STRATEGIC MARKETING. Marketing Imperatives 1, 2, 3 are the *to dos* of marketing: when and how to apply the four marketing principles. **Strategic marketing** embraces the first three of six imperatives; these imperatives address issues the firm must consider in building the strategic market plan from the foundation of fundamental insights in the situation analysis — Section II.

Marketing Imperative 1 — Determine and Recommend Which Markets to Address

- Chapter 7, *Identifying and Choosing Opportunities*. This chapter focuses on growth opportunities. The chapter develops growth strategy frameworks, introduces the venture portfolio, explores criteria to evaluate growth opportunities, and identifies implementation methods.

Marketing Imperative 2 — Identify and Target Market Segments

- Chapter 8, *Market Segmentation and Targeting*. This chapter covers two basic topics: methods of grouping customers into market segments, and targeting — the process of deciding which segments to address.

Both Imperatives 1 and 2 exemplify the *Principle of Selectivity and Concentration*.

Marketing Imperative 3 — Set Strategic Direction and Positioning

This imperative comprises three separate chapters and advances the concept of market strategy as a fundamental integrating force.

- Chapter 9, *Market Strategy — Integrating the Firm's Efforts for Marketing Success*. This chapter presents critical market strategy components in some depth and shows how they play an integrating role for the marketing mix and other functional programs. In particular, the chapter illustrates applying the *Principles of Differential Advantage, Customer Value, and Integration*.

- Chapter 10, *Managing through the Life Cycle*, uses the product life cycle to focus on the competitive aspects of market strategy. This chapter adopts a scenario approach to developing strategic options for different competitive and life-cycle situations.

- Chapter 11, *Managing Brands*. This chapter addresses the management of brands and the increasingly important brand equity concept. Specific issues addressed in this chapter are developing and sustaining a strong brand and managing brand architecture.

SECTION IV — IMPLEMENTING THE MARKET STRATEGY: Marketing Imperatives 4, 5, and 6
focus on implementing the market strategy.

Marketing Imperative 4 — Design the Market Offer

Eight chapters address Imperative 4; they describe the marketing mix and when and how to manage each component in a way that reinforces and implements the market strategy. Appropriately designing the firm's offer is a critical component of the marketing plan.

Each marketing mix element may bestow value on customers, but our fourfold framework focuses on the major role of each element. Part A — *Providing Customer Value*; Part B — *Communicating Customer Value*; Part C — *Delivering Customer Value*; and Part 4 — *Getting Paid for Customer Value*.

PART A. PROVIDING CUSTOMER VALUE

Three chapters focus on managing and developing product and services:

- Chapter 12, *Managing the Product Line*, concerns managing product line composition. This chapter leans heavily on strategic portfolio frameworks to complement traditional financial analysis methods. The chapter also addresses complementarity, product line breadth (including trade-offs between product proliferation and simplification), bundling, counterfeiting, evolving the product line, extending product life, product quality, product safety, secondary markets, packaging, and product and packaging disposal.

- Chapter 13, *Managing Services and Customer Service*. Services are important factors in all advanced economies yet they display important differences from physical products. Furthermore, as product quality has improved across the board, customer service has become an increasingly important competitive weapon.

- Chapter 14, *Developing New Products*, discusses success factors for innovative companies and different ways to approach the innovation challenge. This chapter also describes the evolving stage-gate new-product-development process and the new product development portfolio.

PART B. COMMUNICATING CUSTOMER VALUE

Three chapters focus on personal and impersonal communications:

- Chapter 15, *Integrated Marketing Communications*, presents an integrated communications framework for developing communications strategy in the context of external and internal challenges.

- Chapter 16, *Mass and Digital Communication*, focuses on impersonal communication, specifically advertising, direct marketing, publicity and public relations, sales promotion, and the variety of communications opportunities spawned by the Internet and mobile marketing.

- Chapter 17, *Directing and Managing the Field Sales Effort*, deals with personal selling efforts and highlights critical issues in managing the field sales effort. This chapter presents six tasks for developing sales strategy and organization, and addresses contemporary challenges of managing strategic (key) and global accounts.

PART C. DELIVERING CUSTOMER VALUE

- Chapter 18, *Distribution Decisions*, focuses on providing customers with products and services, when and where they want them. The chapter discusses choosing and managing channel relationships, an area of substantial innovation where the Internet is playing a critical role.

PART D. GETTING PAID FOR CUSTOMER VALUE

- Chapter 19, *Critical Underpinnings of Pricing Decisions*, highlights the tremendous revenue and profit implications of pricing decisions. The chapter focuses on critical factors in developing pricing strategy — customer value, costs, competition, and the firm's strategic objectives.

- Chapter 20, *Setting Prices*, shows how to both set actual prices and avoid price changes. The chapter highlights the pricing toolkit and illustrates various pricing approaches.

Imperatives 3 and 4 draw heavily on the *Principles of Customer Value and Differential Advantage*.

Marketing Imperative 5 — Secure Support from Other Functions

- Chapter 21, *Ensuring the Firm Implements the Market Offer as Planned*, returns to the distinction between marketing as a philosophy and marketing as a function. The chapter highlights successful externally oriented firms and develops a system for making the firm externally oriented and customer-focused so that the various functions support the marketing effort.

Marketing Imperative 6 — Monitor and Control

- Chapter 22, *Monitoring and Controlling Firm Functioning and Performance*, discusses ways of ensuring the firm implements its planned marketing effort and achieves desired results.

Both Imperatives 5 and 6 rest on the *Principle of Integration*.

SECTION V — SPECIAL MARKETING TOPICS.

- Chapter 23, *International, Regional, and Global Marketing*, focuses on marketing activity outside the firm's domestic market. This chapter addresses foreign market entry — how to select countries and how to enter. The chapter also addresses alternative international marketing strategies and options for marketing organization.

SUPPLEMENTAL MATERIAL FOR TEACHING AND LEARNING

Managing Marketing in the 21st Century is a standalone book, but several additional materials can help instructors design courses and make the learning experience more meaningful for students. Instructors can access these materials in a protected area at *www.axcesscapon.com*.

- **Instructor's manual:** The manual employs a consistent format, chapter by chapter. Essentially, the manual summarizes critical learning points in each chapter and provides approaches to address *Marketing Questions and Exercises* distributed throughout the text. For the *Questions for Study and Discussion* at the end of each chapter, the manual offers answers or suggestions for managing class discussion.

- **Test item file:** Prepared by experienced test developer Andrew Yap this file contains well over 1,000 multiple choice and essay questions for use by instructors in setting tests and examinations. Organized by chapter, the file links each question to relevant pages in the textbook.

- **PowerPoint files:** Each chapter comes with a set of teaching materials in the form of PowerPoint files. Each slide has a *notes* page that suggests how the instructor may use that particular slide for teaching purposes.

- **Case studies:** Two sets of materials are available: a list and short descriptions of many traditional marketing case studies, and a large number of short case studies for FREE pdf download. In both cases, organization is by book chapter. This material also includes two approaches to studying marketing cases — a faculty perspective developed at Columbia Business School and an approach prepared by Mary Cunningham Agee, then a Harvard Business School student, to help fellow students.

Additional study aids for students are accessible from *www.axcesscapon.com.*

- **Student study guide:** The purpose of this publication is to help students in their marketing studies. The guide is structured in the same way as the textbook so that students can easily work back and forth between the two volumes. Available as a printed book and e-book.

- **Electronic flash cards:** Similar in concept to traditional flash cards, electronic flash cards are designed to improve students' marketing expertise.

- **Financial analysis for marketing decisions:** A good understanding of financial analysis is critical for sound marketing decision making. Financial analysis comes in many shapes and forms; students should understand the specific issues that concern marketers. We discuss financial issue throughout *Managing Marketing in the 21st Century,* but do not have space to lay the groundwork. Hence, we have prepared the Marketing Enrichment me01 document that we hope you will find useful. Feel free to download the file and use it as a handy reference.

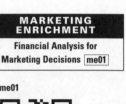

me01

Finally, students have access to three other leaning sources via the Internet:

- **Marketing Enrichment.** A difficult problem for textbook authors is what material to put in the book and what to leave out. We have tried to alleviate this problem by adding a new *Marketing Enrichment* feature. From time to time throughout *Managing Marketing in the 21st Century,* we have developed additional material. We note each Marketing Enrichment item in the text and in the margin; students can easily access this material via an O-code or QR code (next section).

- **Videos.** Each section and chapter has a short introductory video. We note these files with a video icon 🎥 and both an O-code and QR code (next section). Videos of the author interviewing marketing experts are at the end of each chapter.

- **Audios.** The author speaks with Dave Basarab about Marketing Mastery. We list these files with an audio icon 🎧 at the end of appropriate chapters, noted by O-codes and QR codes.

We may add to these items from time to time, so please check the appropriate Marketing Enrichment list.

O-CODES AND QR CODES

An innovative feature of the third edition of *Managing Marketing in the 21ˢᵗ Century* is the addition of O-codes and QR codes. The purpose of O-codes and QR codes is to link items in the text to additional material you may find interesting, in an easy way. O-codes and QR codes act as hot-links in the book's e-versions but, perhaps more importantly, O-codes and QR codes operate as simple links between the printed version and the Internet. Right now, with any printed book, if you want to follow up on some item, like a reference, you have to complete a painful search to find the book or article in question. With O-codes, you text a simple code on your mobile phone, or enter that code into a special field at *www.ocodes.com;* with QR codes, you just scan the item with your cell phone, using any QR code scanning app. In either case, you are instantly linked to the content related to that code.

me02

me03

v01

MARKETING
ENRICHMENT

Marketing Enrichments `me02`

MARKETING
ENRICHMENT

Interview Vidoes `me03`

MARKETING
ENRICHMENT

Audios `me04`

MARKETING
ENRICHMENT

QR Codes for
*Managing Marketing in
the 21st Century* `me05`

me04

me05

Each O-code you text *from* your phone (or QR code you scan *with* your phone) is automatically saved online for future reference. O-codes are stored in a free account at *www.ocodes.com*, linked to your mobile number. You don't need to create an account before using *Managing Marketing in the 21st Century* O-codes. But if you do create an account (FREE), you may share content by linking to Twitter, Facebook, or Evernote. QR codes are typically saved inside most QR scanning apps; some may also have sharing functionality.

The O-code phone number for *Managing Marketing in the 21st Century* is 347-609-0751. Add this number to your contact list and simply text any O-code to that number. You can test the link quickly right now by texting the O-code "v01," or scanning the QR code in the adjacent column. You will link directly to a video introducing *Managing Marketing in the 21st Century*. AxcessCapon does not charge for using O-codes or QR codes. Regardless, when using text messages, QR codes, or accessing online content, your wireless carrier will apply standard text message and data rates. At the time of publication, phone access to O-codes is limited to the U.S. (and some Canadian locations).

Alternatively, you may also test the link using your computer by typing "v01" into the field on the *www.ocodes.com* home page. No charges apply to computer access.

CHAPTER TEXT. The chapter text contains three item types. Each item has both an O-code and a QR code:

- **Marketing Enrichment.** Each Marketing Enrichment O-code begins with *me*. The first item in Chapter 2 is `me201`; the fourth item `me204`. For a full list of Marketing Enrichments see `me02`.

- **Videos.** We identify each video item with a video icon 🎥. Each video O-code begins with the letter *v*. Hence, the introductory video for Chapter 12 is `v1201`. The O-code for the first end-of-chapter video for Chapter 16 is `v1602`. The set of videos is available as a Marketing Enrichment `me03`.

- **Audios.** We identify audio files with an audio icon 🎧. Each audio icon begins with the letter *a*. Hence, the first audio file for Chapter 5 is `a501`. The set of audios is available as a Marketing Enrichment `me04`.

A complete set of QR codes is in Marketing Enrichment `me05`.

ENDNOTES. O-codes appearing in the endnotes are related to each endnote number, and begin with the letter *e* to designate them as endnote O-codes. (Endnotes do not have associated QR codes.) Endnotes containing more than one reference have an additional letter. Hence the O-code `e1523c` is the third reference in endnote 23, Chapter 15. (Disclaimer: All Endnote O-code links are active at the time of publication. Inevitably, some links may be taken down; we apologize in advance for this eventuality which is beyond our control.)

THE VIRGIN MARKETER

No matter how well-written a textbook, the only way to really learn marketing is by doing it. You simply have to take the ideas, concepts, and frameworks and put them into practice. *The Virgin Marketer* is a companion volume to *Managing Marketing in the 21st Century*. *The Virgin Marketer's* 23 chapters correspond to the 23 chapters in the textbook. Each chapter contains a set of tried-and-true experiential exercises designed to help the user prepare a strategic marketing plan — analyze a marketing situation, develop a market strategy, and design a series of implementation programs.

The best approach is for you to select a product or service as your *marketing case*. Your instructor may assign the case — perhaps a local firm or an entrepreneurial startup. Alternatively, you may select your own product or service. The ideal way to *learn by doing* is to complete each chapter of *The Virgin Marketer* right after you have completed a chapter of this book. Then you use the ideas, concepts, and frameworks while they are fresh in your mind. If you work through your marketing case assiduously, you will finish the book with an operating marketing plan. Examples of strategic marketing plans using *The Virgin Marketer* are in Marketing Enrichment me06.

MARKETING ENRICHMENT

Sample Marketing Plans using *The Virgin Marketer* me06

me06

ACKNOWLEDGMENTS

Many individuals contributed to *Managing Marketing in the 21st Century* in this and earlier editions. I thank them for their continued support. Here I want to recognize four special groups of people for their roles in bringing this third edition to fruition: current and former colleagues at Columbia Business School; marketing instructors at other business schools including the many adopters of my textbooks; my MBA and EMBA students; and participants in my various educational and consulting engagements with corporations around the world. In various ways you have stimulated and challenged my thinking: I thank you for that. I also thank all members of Wessex Press' production team. I specially recognize my long-time co-author, Mac Hulbert, now Emeritus Professor at Columbia Business School. Mac contributed to previous editions of *Managing Marketing in the 21st Century* and has been a friend and collaborator for more than 40 years: Mac, many thanks. Finally, I acknowledge the contributions of the business press; several publications provided many of the examples that make *Managing Marketing in the 21st Century* fresh and relevant.

CONCLUDING STATEMENT

The extensive experience the author brings to *Managing Marketing in the 21st Century* has infused the book with the very real marketing challenges that face corporations daily around the world. The author writes from the standpoint of a marketing academic with a deep commitment to helping corporations improve their marketing practice and imparting his knowledge and expertise to students at the dawn of their careers.

The material in *Managing Marketing in the 21st Century* will help you to learn about marketing. It will equip you to survive and prosper in your careers as marketers, senior executives, general managers, and CEOs. All those who have helped bring this book to fruition wish you well as you develop your careers.

Managing Marketing in the 21st Century is also a reference for future use. If you become an entrepreneur, this book will help you launch and manage your new business. If you join a firm's marketing department, you will never have enough books on the subject; hopefully this will be one of your favorite reference guides. And, if you find yourself in another function where you work with marketing, you will be equipped to ask your marketing colleagues the right questions.

Good luck!

Noel Capon

R. C. Kopf Professor of International Marketing

Graduate School of Business

Columbia University, New York, New York

ABBREVIATIONS GLOSSARY

To improve readability we avoid spelling out the full names of organizations in examples. Rather, we use the shortened versions or mnemonics by which they are typically known.

Corporations

Advanced Micro Devices	AMD
American Express	AmEx
Barnes & Noble	B&N
Bausch & Lomb	B&L
Black & Decker	B&D
Boston Consulting Group	BCG
Bristol-Myers Squibb	BMS
British Airways	BA
General Electric	GE
General Motors	GM
GlaxoSmithKline	GSK
Hewlett Packard	HP
Home Box Office	HBO
International Business Machines	IBM
International Paper	IP
Johnson & Johnson	J&J
Procter & Gamble	P&G
Texas Instruments	TI
Volkswagen	VW

General Business Terms

Chief executive officer	CEO
Chief financial officer	CFO
Chief marketing officer	CMO
Customer relationship management	CRM
Fast moving consumer goods	FMCG
Personal computer	PC
Research and development	R&D
Senior vice president	SVP

U.S. Government Departments

Consumer Product Safety Commission	CPSC
Environmental Protection Agency	EPA
Federal Communications Commission	FCC
Federal Drug Administration	FDA
Federal Trade Commission	FTC
National Transportation Safety Board	NTSB
Securities and Exchange Commission	SEC

International Organizations

European Union	EU
International Monetary Fund	IMF
United Nations	UN
United Nations Educational, Scientific and Cultural Organization	UNESCO
United States	U.S.
World Trade Organization	WTO

SECTION I
MARKETING
AND THE FIRM

To access O-codes, go to **www.ocodes.com**

SECTION I — MARKETING AND THE FIRM — COMPRISES TWO CHAPTERS: Marketing and the Firm — Chapter 1, and The Value of Customers: Optimizing Shareholder Value — Chapter 2.

Chapter 1 introduces two marketing concepts that form the basis for *Managing Marketing in the 21st Century* — marketing as a **philosophy**, and marketing as **six imperatives** — the *must-do* activities the firm performs in marketing. Chapter 1 also presents four marketing principles and shows the relationship between customer value and shareholder value.

Chapter 2 focuses on the value of customers to the firm and introduces the customer-lifetime-value (CLV) concept. The chapter discusses various ways to enhance CLV, paying special attention to customer retention. The chapter concludes with the role of customer relationship management (CRM) systems in driving customer loyalty.

Managing Marketing in the 21ˢᵗ Century

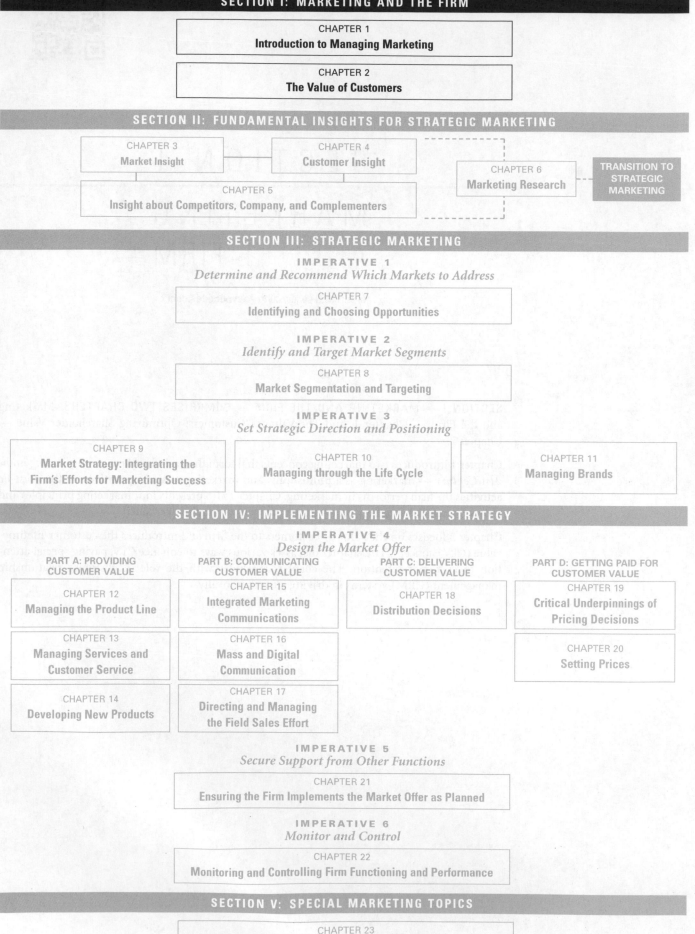

SECTION I: MARKETING AND THE FIRM

CHAPTER 1
Introduction to Managing Marketing

CHAPTER 2
The Value of Customers

SECTION II: FUNDAMENTAL INSIGHTS FOR STRATEGIC MARKETING

CHAPTER 3
Market Insight

CHAPTER 4
Customer Insight

CHAPTER 5
Insight about Competitors, Company, and Complementers

CHAPTER 6
Marketing Research

TRANSITION TO STRATEGIC MARKETING

SECTION III: STRATEGIC MARKETING

IMPERATIVE 1
Determine and Recommend Which Markets to Address

CHAPTER 7
Identifying and Choosing Opportunities

IMPERATIVE 2
Identify and Target Market Segments

CHAPTER 8
Market Segmentation and Targeting

IMPERATIVE 3
Set Strategic Direction and Positioning

CHAPTER 9
Market Strategy: Integrating the Firm's Efforts for Marketing Success

CHAPTER 10
Managing through the Life Cycle

CHAPTER 11
Managing Brands

SECTION IV: IMPLEMENTING THE MARKET STRATEGY

IMPERATIVE 4
Design the Market Offer

PART A: PROVIDING CUSTOMER VALUE

PART B: COMMUNICATING CUSTOMER VALUE

PART C: DELIVERING CUSTOMER VALUE

PART D: GETTING PAID FOR CUSTOMER VALUE

CHAPTER 12
Managing the Product Line

CHAPTER 15
Integrated Marketing Communications

CHAPTER 18
Distribution Decisions

CHAPTER 19
Critical Underpinnings of Pricing Decisions

CHAPTER 13
Managing Services and Customer Service

CHAPTER 16
Mass and Digital Communication

CHAPTER 20
Setting Prices

CHAPTER 14
Developing New Products

CHAPTER 17
Directing and Managing the Field Sales Effort

IMPERATIVE 5
Secure Support from Other Functions

CHAPTER 21
Ensuring the Firm Implements the Market Offer as Planned

IMPERATIVE 6
Monitor and Control

CHAPTER 22
Monitoring and Controlling Firm Functioning and Performance

SECTION V: SPECIAL MARKETING TOPICS

CHAPTER 23
International, Regional, and Global Marketing

CHAPTER 1

INTRODUCTION TO MANAGING MARKETING v101 📽

LEARNING OBJECTIVES

When you have completed this chapter, you will be able to:

- Define the term *marketing*.
- Explain the fundamental business model.
- Articulate why marketing is so important for business organizations.
- Explain how success in attracting, retaining, and growing customers improves shareholder value.
- Articulate how marketing as a philosophy embraces an external orientation.
- Understand how an external orientation differs from various internal orientations.
- Be ready to act on the six marketing imperatives.
- Identify the four marketing principles.
- Understand the book's structure and additional features to enhance learning.

OPENING CASE: STARBUCKS

In 1982, 28-year-old Howard Schultz joined Seattle's specialty coffee emporium, Starbucks Coffee, Tea & Spice (formed 1971), as director of retail operations and marketing — selling coffee beans to coffee aficionados. In 1983, while on a buying trip to Milan, Schultz became fascinated by Italy's espresso bars — people gathered to read newspapers, converse, and socialize while drinking coffee. Schultz persuaded Starbucks' owners to transplant the concept to downtown Seattle; it was wildly successful. Schultz left Starbucks to form his own firm but, in 1987, together with local investors, purchased Starbucks and renamed the firm Starbucks Coffee Company. Starbucks began a major store expansion: In 1992, when Starbucks went public, it had 140 stores in the northwest and

Chicago. By 2006, Starbucks was the world's leading retailer, roaster, and brand of specialty coffee with 7,950 stores in the U.S. and over 11,000 globally.

To fulfill its primary goal of providing high-quality coffee to customers, Starbucks purchases coffee direct from growers, roasts all its coffee, and distributes to its stores. Howard Schultz commented: "We own and operate almost all our own stores — the only exceptions are in foreign countries, where we have partnership and licensing agreements with local business people, and in licensed locations in the U.S., such as campus bookstores and airports, where we cannot own and operate the store outright. All people in company-owned stores work for Starbucks.[1]

Schultz continued: "Starbucks is one of the world's great experience brands … . All the stores are similar, yet they're also all different. A Starbucks on Wall Street in downtown Manhattan doesn't look exactly like one in Berkeley, or in Barcelona, but they all have the same spirit." He added, "In 1989, when we had only 50 stores, we decided to bring all of our architecture and design work in-house. We have over 200 architects … and more people in our own design studio."

Schultz talked about the meaning of the Starbucks brand: "We decided early on that the equity of the brand is linked to all of the cues of the brand experience, from the overall look of the store and subtle visual cues, to the senses of aroma and the sound of the music that we have playing … . [They are] a very significant component of the customer's experience. And that became a very, very large competitive advantage, because there wasn't a competitor around that was willing or able to spend the amount of money that we spent on these things and that we continue to spend."

For Schultz, Starbucks should be its customers' third place — after home and work. "As a customer, I walk into the store and I'm swept away for a minute, even if I get a coffee to go, because I'm part of this experience that makes me feel better. A missing part of our lives as consumers is that we don't feel valued. So we really take notice when someone touches us and says, 'I appreciate you, I respect you, and I can help you.' … We have to ensure that there's incredible consistency without having every location seem like a fast-food franchise. That is part of the genius of Starbucks."

Starbucks enhances customer experience value by focusing on its employees — partners. Schultz observed: "The keys are the culture and values of our company that allow our people to feel the way they do about Starbucks, so that they genuinely want to convey the attributes, the characteristics, the aspirational qualities of what we offer the customer … . We've made a very large investment over the last 20 years in training. We've spent more money every year on training than we do on advertising." Early on, Starbucks did no advertising, preferring to let its clusters of stores fulfill the communications function. Schultz went on: "Starbucks has the lowest attrition of any retail restaurant in North America. We do a cultural, internal audit every year where we go to our people, and we ask them to evaluate our behavior and practices and their trust and confidence in management. And we share those scores with the company.

"The training is twofold. One path is on the fundamentals of what we do — how to make great coffee; how to explain the differences in features and benefits between different coffee makers, different coffees, all that stuff. The other piece is who we are, what we expect, how customers experience the store … . [We work on] hiring the right kind of people and not just filling shifts. A colleague said it best: 'We're not in the coffee business; we're in the people business serving coffee.' … People recognize when they get in the company that this is a special place and they want to protect it, so … good people are hired and developed." Starbucks offers comprehensive healthcare and stock options to all employees, including part-timers. Said Schultz, "That was the transformational event, where everyone then had a stake in the company. This brought all employees into one company-wide conversation about serving customers better."

Starbucks continues to look for new market segments. Schultz explained: "Several years ago we were in the morning day-part business.[2] And we had no business to speak of in the afternoon. Our stores closed at seven at night, and we were done for the day. Customers started driving a new business for us by using our stores in multiple day-parts … We had to create an afternoon beverage business and an after-dinner dessert business." Product innovation is also very important to Starbucks — it has introduced many new products, some not related to coffee. A major success is Frappuccino, sold widely in supermarkets under an agreement with PepsiCo. Starbucks also added recorded music and occasional events to the store experience.

Starbucks works hard to transfer best practice. Said Schultz: "At our first global conference, it was like the United Nations at Starbucks — 30 countries ... we had a mini Starbucks trade show with booths for every country to show their best practices. The people from Japan showed us how to utilize small spaces. The people from the Philippines, our best food market, shared how they achieve such high-quality food."

Seeking fast growth, by the mid-2000s Starbucks made a series of decisions that harmed the brand. Starbucks relaxed location criteria and over-expanded, introduced drive-through windows, added breakfast sandwiches, put in automated espresso machines, ceased coffee grinding, and made the stores less comfy. Strong competitors emerged — Dunkin' Donuts and McDonalds, and as its stock price plunged in the 2008 recession, Starbucks fired its CEO and Howard Schultz returned. Schultz took several actions — gave stores more local-ness; closed under-performing stores; refocused on the customer experience; introduced Via instant coffee in Starbucks' outlets, supermarkets, and mass merchandisers; undertook disciplined expansion in Asia; slimmed the supply chain; and reinvigorated a second brand, Seattle's Best.

CASE QUESTIONS

What other firms have grown as successfully as Starbucks?

What accounts for their successes?

More than 40 million customers monthly frequent Starbucks locations around the world. The most loyal customers visit Starbucks an average of 18 times a month. Starbucks' customer loyalty has brought significant financial success. In 2010, revenues were $10.7 billion; net profits were $946 million (up from $316 million in 2008) and the share price had tripled from its early 2009 low.

WHAT DOES MARKETING MEAN TODAY?

Marketing plays a critical role in today's business environment, where maximizing **shareholder value** is an increasingly important goal. The essence of marketing focuses on how firms attract, retain, and enhance their relationships with customers. Success in delivering **customer value** leads directly to improving shareholder value and long-run firm prosperity. In *Managing Marketing in the 21st Century*, we explore both the strategic aspects of marketing and the tactical decisions that marketers make every day. But first, we investigate two quite different but related meanings of marketing.

KEY IDEA

➤ Marketing is a guiding philosophy for the firm as a whole.

MARKETING AS A PHILOSOPHY embraces the view that marketing is the guiding force or orientation for the entire organization. Firms with a marketing philosophy operate with an external orientation. Such firms focus their attention and resources *outside* the corporation — to acquire, retain, and grow customers, but take careful account of competitors and the broader external environment. By contrast, internally oriented firms focus largely on internal issues like products, services, and processes.[3] *Managing Marketing in the 21st Century* embraces the *marketing-as-philosophy* perspective. The author believes, and has seen in his own career, how powerful and effective a business can be when the entire organization is attuned to the external world. Such agile firms not only sense critical environmental factors but also adapt and change to address them.

In addition to the philosophical perspective, marketers must possess the tools and decision-making skills to get the marketing job done. Effective marketers implement six marketing imperatives.

MARKETING IMPERATIVES describe the specifics of the marketing job. Executives with marketing and product management titles generally focus on these *must dos* of marketing. We identify two groups:

STRATEGIC MARKETING

- Imperative 1: Determine and recommend which markets to address.
- Imperative 2: Identify and target market segments.
- Imperative 3: Set strategic direction and positioning.

IMPLEMENTING THE MARKET STRATEGY

- Imperative 4: Design the market offer.
- Imperative 5: Secure support from other functions.
- Imperative 6: Monitor and control execution and performance.

As a broader framework when thinking about markets and marketing, marketers must also consider the **four principles** of marketing. These principles should form the basis of marketing decision-making. They act as guidelines for acting on the six imperatives:

- Principle 1: Selectivity and Concentration
- Principle 2: Customer Value
- Principle 3: Differential Advantage
- Principle 4: Integration

Chapter 1's discussion of these issues sets the stage for the entire book.

THE CHANGING VIEW

OLD WAY	NEW WAY
Accounting profit is critical	Shareholder value is critical
Core of marketing job is the marketing mix	The marketing job encompasses six marketing imperatives
Customers are a *necessary evil*	Customers are the firm's *core assets*
Firm must manage the *status quo*	Firm must manage change
Firm operates to suit managers' goals	Firm operates to deliver value to customers
Internal orientations are acceptable	An external orientation is critical for success
Marketing department does the marketing	All firm employees have a marketing orientation
Marketing is one of the firm's functions	Marketing is a philosophy as well as a function
Organizational survival is a major firm objective	Shareholder value is the major firm objective
Seller power dominates	Customer power dominates
Shareholder value is an issue for finance	Shareholder value is an issue for marketing
Suppliers choose options	Customers choose options

KEY IDEA

➤ Marketing is a set of six imperatives — the *must dos* of marketing.

➤ Four marketing principles guide execution of the six marketing imperatives.

Marketing Question

Choose two familiar firms, one that exemplifies the *old way* and one that exemplifies the *new way*. What criteria led you to identify these firms? Why?

THE MARKETING JOB

William Rosenberg, Dunkin' Donuts' (DD) pioneering entrepreneur, had a very simple philosophy: "The boss is the customer." To find out how to make his customer "the boss," Rosenberg and his wife drove all around the country visiting every donut shop they could find. By implementing Rosenberg's philosophy, DD's franchise operates about 9,000 outlets in 30 countries and sells 4 million donuts and 3 million cups of coffee daily. Echoing Rosenberg, P&G CEO Art Laffley commented: "Everywhere I go, I try to hammer home the simple message that the consumer is boss."[4]

Target has grown successfully for many years while competitor Kmart has struggled. Target understands and addresses customer needs in a compelling manner — Target has a cool brand, the right product mix, and excellent service. Target illustrates the essence of effective marketing.

Marketing Question

What marketing question would you like to ask your favorite CEO? How do you think the CEO would answer?

Many executives are confused about marketing.[5] It seems so intuitive. Can't anybody be a marketer? Real people at real companies told us:

- "Marketing is just advertising."
- "Marketing is giving away tee-shirts, products, and concert tickets to potential clients."
- "Marketing's job is to support our sales force."
- "Marketing is what consumers do at the supermarket on a Saturday morning."

These activities relate to the two broader meanings of marketing that we just discussed — **marketing as a philosophy**, and **marketing as six imperatives**, but none really captures the true essence of marketing.

FIGURE 1.1

THE FUNDAMENTAL BUSINESS MODEL

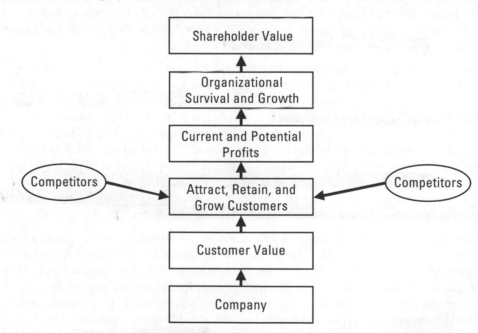

Marketing Question

Pluto Inc. (fictional electronics firm) spends $100 million annually on R&D. Pluto management believes that eliminating all R&D will increase profits by $80 million in the current year. What would happen to Pluto's stock price? Why?

Figure 1.1 demonstrates that marketing's focus on customers makes it the firm's fundamental activity.[6] When marketing delivers *customer value* to satisfy customer needs, the firm *attracts, retains, and grows customers*.[7] If costs are in line, *profits* follow. Profits help the firm *survive* as an independent entity and secure resources to *grow*. Of course, if the firm does not earn profits consistently, it will go bankrupt; over 100,000 entities go out of business annually in the U.S. Survival and growth are the critical links between earning profits and enhancing *shareholder value* by increasing stock price.[8,9] Enhanced shareholder value makes funds available for investment.[10]

Marketing's role includes identifying opportunities, figuring out customer needs, understanding the competition, developing appealing products and services, and communicating value to potential customers. When these tasks are done well, shareholder value increases. Re-read the Opening Case to see how Howard Schultz accomplished these tasks at Starbucks and the success he achieved. Well-known authors Tracy and Wiersema state that "Creating shareholder wealth is not the purpose of the business. It is the reward for creating customer value."[11] And Alibaba (successful Chinese e-commerce firm) CEO Jack Ma emphasizes that customers come first and owners come last: "You don't have to invest in Alibaba."[12]

Figure 1.1 also demonstrates the process for achieving the firm's goal of enhancing shareholder value, both for private firms with few shareholders and public firms with many. Growth and long-run profits are the means. Increasing profits in the short run is easy: Just reduce R&D (research and development), cut advertising, and fire half the sales force — but such decisions typically lead to long-run problems. For forward-looking businesses seeking long-run profits, customers are the core assets. Of course, *competitors* seek these same customers. The competitive battle to attract, retain, and grow customers is central to all business activity.

The critical weapon in the battle for customers is straightforward in concept, but may be complex and difficult in execution. Quite simply, the firm must deliver to customers greater value than competitors. Customers reward firms that deliver greater value by purchasing their products and services, today and tomorrow. This **exchange** is the basis of all markets. Customers prefer the value inherent in the firm's products and services to their own money or other resources: The firm prefers the customer's money or other resources to its own products and services.[13]

In sum, when the firm delivers greater customer value than competitors, it should earn profits, survive and grow, and make shareholders very happy. If customers perceive that competitors deliver greater value, ultimately the firm will perish. Don't just take the author's word for the power of this framework. Lou Gerstner, who led IBM's rejuvenation from a near-death experience, stated, "Everything starts with the customer."[14]

Pre-eminent management theorist, the late Peter Drucker, is generally credited with developing the customer orientation and modern marketing perspective.[15] Drucker stated, "If we want to know what a business is, we have to start with its purpose. There is only one valid definition of business purpose — *to create a customer.* It is the customer who determines what a business is. For it is the customer, and he alone, who through being willing to pay for a good or service, converts economic resources into wealth, things into goods." Drucker added, "What the business thinks it produces is not of first importance — especially not to the future of the business and its success. What the customer thinks he is buying, what he considers 'value' is decisive ... . Because it is [the purpose of a business] to create a customer, [the] business enterprise has two — and only these two, basic functions — marketing and innovation."[16]

In addition, today's customers are the firm's core assets — attracting, retaining, and growing customers is critical to firm health.[17] But this task is ever more difficult. Competition is growing in depth and scope as the firm's environment becomes increasingly more complex and changes more quickly. Globalization, the rise of BRICI (Brazil, Russia, India, China, Indonesia) and other national economies, Internet-based and mobile solutions, and deep structural changes in the world economy are driving increased competition.[18] Many countries and industries are shifting from *scarcity of supply* to *scarcity of demand.* When supply is scarce, the firm's critical skill is production; when demand is scarce, the firm's critical skill is marketing.

Notwithstanding increased competition, today's customers are more aware and knowledgeable about competitive offers and prices, in part because of the Internet. Airline travelers can easily compare prices on Expedia, Travelocity, Orbitz, and the airlines' own websites. Consumers in advanced affluent societies have ever-increasing numbers of discretionary product and service options and may choose among expensive clothes, an iPad, or a European vacation. And, in future, intelligent agents may make buying decisions and shop for us.

KEY IDEA

➤ The firm's major task is to attract, retain, and grow customers by developing and delivering valued offers.

➤ The firm enhances shareholder value by successfully attracting, retaining, and growing customers.

KEY IDEA

➤ The firm has two basic functions:
- Marketing
- Innovation

KEY IDEA

➤ Marketing is critical for the firm's success in today's increasingly complex and fast-changing environment.

Marketing encompasses a wide variety of activities the firm undertakes to attract, retain, and grow customers — of course, competitors are trying to do the same thing. If the firm is more successful than its competitors in creating customer value, it will make profits, survive and grow, and enhance shareholder value.[19]

MARKETING AND SHAREHOLDER VALUE

Electronic Accounting Systems (EAS) successfully sold payroll services to firms with 50 to 100 employees; customers filled in payroll sheets and EAS arranged courier pickup. But EAS could not serve smaller customers profitably. Former EAS employee Tom Golisano founded Paychex to serve smaller businesses. Paychex's prices were lower than EAS's — partly because customers phoned in payroll information; Paychex also provided a payroll tax return service. Golisano became a billionaire and created significant value for Paychex's shareholders.

Progressive identified a relationship between people's credit history and driving record, then used this insight to profitably insure customers rejected by mainstream insurers — mainly young drivers and those with poor driving records. Progressive is now a leading U.S. insurer and has considerably enhanced shareholder value.

The central focus on shareholder value is deeply rooted in many capitalist countries — particularly the U.S. The **shareholder-value perspective** defines management's job as maximizing returns for the firm's owners — its shareholders.[20] When this perspective dominates, government regulations tend to favor owners. Active shareholder opposition, CEO departures, and unfriendly takeover bids, tend to occur when the firm underperforms in shareholder value.[21]

KEY IDEA

➤ The shareholder-value perspective is increasingly widespread around the world.

The firm also has other *stakeholders,* like management, labor, and the public at large. In some countries, these stakeholders are more favored than shareholders. Regulation in these countries generally favors managers and protects them from unwelcome mergers and acquisitions. The stakeholder view is particularly popular in Asia, where many firms and politicians are ardent advocates of managerial power.

In recent years, developing global capital markets have favored the shareholder-value perspective. Conservative Japanese electronics giant Panasonic has share-repurchase plans, provides stock options for senior executives, and links managers' salaries to stock market performance.[22] Even in China, stock markets are now firmly established. The shareholder-value perspective is also having a significant impact on public companies in France, Italy, the Netherlands, and Germany. Restrictions on corporate acquisitions have diminished, and when new owners take control, significant corporate restructuring often occurs.

Rheinmetall (RM), a family-controlled Düsseldorf-based industrial conglomerate, had $4 billion revenues; but stock-market value was only $300 million! A New York investment group purchased 7.8 percent ownership and demanded improved profits. Management took strategic action by shedding many peripheral businesses and making several global alliances for its three main divisions. Shareholder value increased significantly.

Marketing Question

Can you identify some firms that work especially hard to enhance shareholder value by focusing on creating customer value? Specifically, what do they do?

Increased globalization will inevitably spread the shareholder-value perspective. Enhanced share ownership will give shareholders greater political power — both directly as individual investors and indirectly via third-party investment vehicles like mutual funds.

Earlier, we asserted that customers are the firm's core assets. Traditionally, we find assets on the firm's balance sheet. Balance-sheet assets (current and fixed) include cash, accounts receivable, inventory, land, and plant and equipment — they do not include customers! Balance-sheet assets may be important, but none is absolutely crucial! The only critical asset the firm has to have is paying customers. Customers are the sole source of firm revenues; all firm activities are costs. Balance-sheet assets are only assets because they contribute to attracting, retaining, and growing customers.

But what if balance-sheet assets are not *assets*? What if they are really *strategic liabilities*? Consider the following: Firm A builds a factory to meet market demand for its *swish* product. Later, customers shift their preferences to *twish*. Firm A focuses its efforts on trying to persuade customers that they really need *swish*. By contrast, competitors B and C each develop their own versions of *twish*. Firm A's factory investment constrains its actions — it fails to invest to meet customer needs for *twish*. The *swish* factory was not a real asset — it was a *strategic liability*.[23] The retail book industry provides a good illustration. In the 1980s, Barnes & Noble became the dominant U.S. bookseller using a bricks-and-mortar strategy. But as the Internet grew, B&N was slow to embrace purchasing books online. Seeing an opportunity, Jeff Bezos launched Amazon.com. Amazon is the premier online bookseller and has developed online businesses far beyond books. B&N eventually reacted and now has a decent online book business, but is a distant second to Amazon.

The firm only increases shareholder value if incoming cash flows earn a return on investment at least equal to its **cost of capital** (the weighted average of the firm's cost of equity and cost of debt).[24] When the firm fails to earn its cost of capital, it destroys shareholder value. Unfortunately, managers sometimes forget that the only source of firm cash flows (except new debt and equity) comes from attracting, retaining, and growing customers. Customers provide revenues and cash flow when they believe the firm's products and services offer better value than competitive alternatives.

Of course, the firm's strategy and operations must conform to a business model that allows it to earn its cost of capital.[25] Many Internet organizations have secured large numbers of customers but do not have such models. When eBay acquired Skype (2005) for $2.6 billion, it had 54 million users and $60 million revenues, but in 2007 eBay wrote down its investment by more than $1 billion. In 2009, Skype had 500 million users and over $500 million in revenues, but eBay decided to divest (to Microsoft).

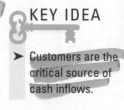

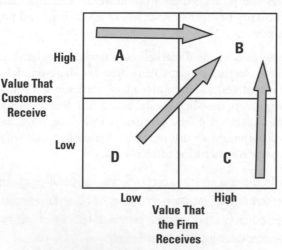

KEY IDEA

➤ Customers are the sole source of firm revenues; relatedly, all firm activities are costs.

➤ Customers are the firm's core assets, yet they do not appear on the balance sheet.

➤ Some balance-sheet assets act as strategic liabilities.

KEY IDEA

➤ Customers are the critical source of cash inflows.

FIGURE 1.2

VALUE THAT CUSTOMERS RECEIVE; VALUE THAT THE FIRM RECEIVES

Marketing Question

LinkedIn is a publicly traded social networking firm. What value does LinkedIn provide for customers? What value do customers provide LinkedIn's shareholders?

Figure 1.2 shows the relationship between the *value that customers receive* and the *value that the firm receives* as revenues and profits. Cells B and D represent stable situations:

CELL B. Customers receive high value. The firm attracts, retains, and grows these customers — it also receives high value. The firm should continue to deliver significant customer value by innovating new products and services and enhancing its offers.

CELL D. Both customers and the firm receive low value. Perhaps the firm's resources are poorly matched to customer needs. Better alignment can move the firm to Cell B, but these may not be good customers for the firm to serve.

KEY IDEA

➤ Value has two sides:
- When the firm delivers high customer value, it attracts, retains, and grows customers.
- When the firm attracts, retains, and grows customers, it earns high value for shareholders.

The other two cells are essentially unstable positions:

CELL C. Customers receive low value but the firm receives high value, perhaps because of long-term relationships. Ultimately, competitors will offer greater value and customers will switch suppliers.

CELL A. Customers receive high value from the firm, but the firm receives low value. Perhaps prices are too low — the firm should convince customers of its value or possibly reduce service.

If customers believe competitors offer greater value they will simply take their business elsewhere. If marketing fails to deliver superior value, the firm will go out of business — by bankruptcy, merger, or acquisition. Today, more than ever, customer value and shareholder value are closely intertwined. Increased acceptance of the shareholder-value perspective has raised the stakes considerably. Quite simply, if marketing does not perform consistently well, the firm should anticipate a bleak future.

MARKETING AS A PHILOSOPHY: EXTERNAL AND INTERNAL ORIENTATIONS

KEY IDEA

➤ *External* and *internal* orientations are core concepts for examining the firm's basic philosophy.

You just learned that the firm enhances shareholder value by attracting, retaining, and growing customers. At a *philosophical* level, each employee has some responsibility and marketing is *everybody's* business. At a personal level, because customers are the firm's only revenue source, they also pay everyone's salary! To quote Drucker again, "Marketing is so basic that it cannot be considered a separate function (i.e., a separate skill or work) within the business ... it is, first, a central dimension of the entire business. It is the whole business ... seen from the customer's point of view. Concern and responsibility for marketing must, therefore, permeate all areas of the enterprise."[26] More recently, David Haines, brand czar of Vodafone, the world's largest cell phone service provider, said, "Marketing is too important to be left to the marketers. It's the obligation of every single individual in the company, whether you're a phone operator, the CEO, or anyone else in the company."[27]

Marketing as a philosophy concerns the firm's entire *orientation*. A firm embracing marketing as a philosophy has an **external orientation**. Other firms focusing on internal business drivers have one of several **internal orientations**.

THE EXTERNAL ORIENTATION

Lou Gerstner described the IBM he inherited as CEO: "[IBM had a] ... general disinterest in customer needs, accompanied by a preoccupation with internal politics ... a bureaucratic infrastructure that defended turf instead of promoting collaboration, and a management class that presided rather than acted."[28] Gerstner described one of his key strategic decisions: "Drive all we did from the customer back, and turn IBM into a market-driven rather than an internally focused, process-driven enterprise"[29]

The externally oriented firm looks outward to the environment and knows that customers are central to its future — Gerstner really understood this aspect of marketing. Marketing is the *point person*[30] — and marketing must gain insight into customers, competitors, and broader environmental factors. The externally oriented firm knows that its current products, services, and processes are the reasons for past and present success. It also knows that as the external environment changes, its products, services, and processes must also change. The externally oriented firm does not fear change — it knows that change is inevitable and that new opportunities are its *lifeblood*. The externally oriented firm invests in new capabilities and competencies to exploit opportunities and create and serve customers.[31] (See Marketing Enrichment me101 for a measurement approach.)

In difficult economic times, when profits are under pressure, many firms cut spending and investment. The externally oriented firm invests. It may increase its marketing budget, acquire weaker rivals, and/or cut prices. In recent recessions, several firms invested in customers and markets and swept past more internally oriented competitors[32]:

- Best Buy acquired the 91-store Future Shop chain and quadrupled its Canadian presence.

- Cisco invested in Asia as competitors were contracting. Within one year Cisco had lead market share in many countries.

- Coca-Cola CEO Muhtar Kent said, "We don't cut marketing in this crisis around the world. We make sure our brands stay healthy and that we exit this tunnel with more market share than when we went in."[33]

- Intel maintained R&D and production spending. Said then Intel CEO Craig Barrett: "You never save your way out of a recession. The only way to get out of a recession stronger than when you went in is to have great new products."[34]

- Kohl's continued new store expansion and old store refurbishing; Sara Lee increased advertising by 25 percent[35]; Starbucks aggressively expanded internationally; Walmart increased capital spending to $10 billion annually.

- Said then Xerox CEO Anne Mulcahy, "Everywhere I went, lenders and investors were demanding I cut R&D spending. But Xerox innovation is sacred … investing in innovation was the best decision I ever made."[36]

Spending on Marketing — Investment or Expense?

A graduating Columbia MBA joined an FMCG firm. Her first job was to shepherd a new product from development to launch. The firm believed it had one year's lead time over competitors. As she developed her launch plan, the MBA realized the sales force was working at capacity. The new product would get insufficient attention and would not secure adequate retail distribution. Her innovative solution was to hire a temporary sales force. These salespeople would gain distribution; the regular sales force would later perform maintenance. Her financials showed a first-year loss, but then profits rose steadily. She presented her launch plan to senior management.

Senior managers were unhappy about the first-year loss. But, by eliminating the temporary sales force and using the regular sales force, the financials worked. The firm launched on this basis, and the first year showed a modest profit. Unexpectedly, the first competitor entered after six months, and within one year, the firm had three competitors. Two years after launch, the firm exited the market.

CEOs and top managers are generally responsible for establishing an external orientation as the overarching corporate thrust. Leaders of firms like Amazon, Google, P&G, and Starbucks understand this; they really *get it*.[37] Only a CEO like former Wachovia banker John Medlin can dismiss the *tyranny of the quarterly earnings statement* and say, "You've got to expect a down quarter from time to time."[38] Only a CEO like James Burke (J&J) can make customer concerns central to the firm. In the 1982 Tylenol cyanide-lacing crisis, J&J immediately withdrew Tylenol capsules until it developed fail-safe packaging.[39] J&J's $250 million write-off demonstrated a long-term investment in customers, and it quickly returned to market leadership.

Some of the world's most successful companies practice marketing as a philosophy. P&G spends $350 million annually seeking customer and market insight. A senior Pfizer executive asserted: "Our strong belief at Pfizer is that marketing is really an investment, not an expense. Our most recent former CEO believed it was important to invest in R&D. He also believed it was equally important to invest in marketing. He said if you are best at both, there's no way you can be beat! We invest billions and billions of dollars in R&D to have better science and develop innovative products. We have always had the leading industry investment in marketing. We parallel our R&D spending with a similar investment in research about markets and customers. What separates us from competitors is an assiduous pursuit of information, knowledge, and understanding of our customer."[40]

Marketing Question

How did senior managers view the temporary sales force? Did they view these expenditures as an investment — returns expected in the future? Or, did they think of them as expenses — returns expected in the short term?

KEY IDEA

➤ The firm should view marketing expenditures as an *investment*, NOT as an *expense*.

Table 1.1 shows general characteristics of internal and external orientations.[41]

TABLE 1.1

**GENERAL
CHARACTERISTICS
OF INTERNAL
AND EXTERNAL
ORIENTATIONS**[42]

Dimension	Internal	External
Customer perspective	Transactional	Relational
Focus	Products	Markets
Know-how	Inherent in patents, machinery	Inherent in people, processes
Measurement	Profit, margin, volume	Customer value, satisfaction, retention
Organizational philosophy	Bureaucracy	Adhocracy
Priorities	Efficiency and productivity	Flexibility and responsiveness
Process	Mass production	Mass customization

INTERNAL ORIENTATIONS

J&J pioneered the stent — a metal scaffold that holds open human arteries to allow blood flow. Two years later, J&J had 91 percent market share and $1 billion revenues. Five years after entry, J&J's market share was 8 percent! What happened? Competitors responded to physicians' newfound needs for different sizes and materials; J&J ignored these concerns. J&J's internal orientation had a direct and negative impact on profits and shareholder value.[43]

In a small and simply organized firm, the sole proprietor (SP) or owner conducts most activities. The SP seeks and serves customers, arranges financing, performs operational functions, and manages the payroll. At a visceral level, the SP knows that customers are critical assets and operates with an external orientation almost by instinct. Can you recall an occasion when your local garage, dry cleaner, hardware store, or other small business treated you personally as an important and valuable asset?[44]

As firms grow, they seek efficiency through specialization and differentiation — operations, sales, product design, finance, legal, technology, and other functions have specific responsibilities. Typically, these functions develop their own missions, objectives, systems and processes, and business philosophies. Rather than work together to deliver customer value, they may pursue their own agendas, spurred by local cultural norms, and management systems that measure, motivate, and reward securing departmental objectives. Nonproductive differentiation that history and internal political rivalries exacerbate may trump a customer focus.

KEY IDEA

➤ An externally oriented firm goes beyond customer focus. This firm works hard to understand competitors, markets, and environmental forces in general.

Frequently, internal functions act in mutually inconsistent ways. The sales department tries to increase sales, but operations, working to produce acceptable-quality products at low cost, cuts down on product varieties; and R&D sees no reason to hurry the new product development process. Marketing wants to increase advertising spending, but finance reduces budgets to meet financial targets. These individual functions are often important strengths for the firm, but some, like accounting and R&D, are organizationally distant from customers. Focusing too heavily on one function versus another often leads to problems. The common denominator when firms operate in silos (stovepipes) is that delivering customer value often takes a back seat. These firms follow an **internal orientation**.

A former Microsoft vice president described difficulties in securing in-house acceptance of ClearType, a broadly applicable, innovative way to display text on a screen that received much public praise, internal promotions, and patents. "It annoyed other Microsoft groups that felt threatened by our success. Engineers in the Windows group falsely claimed it made the display go haywire when certain colors were used. The head of Office Products said it was fuzzy and gave him headaches. The vice president for Pocket Devices was blunter: He'd support ClearType and use it, but only if I transferred the program and the programmers to his control."[45]

At internally oriented firms, you often hear the statement, "That's the way we do things around here." Regardless of changes in customer needs, competitor actions, and/or the external environment in general, the firm continues on its current course. We discuss several internal orientations — operations, sales, finance, and technology.

> Wholly owned by its growers, Zespri is New Zealand's sole kiwifruit exporter. Many Zespri customers requested fruit with higher proportions of pulp to liquid. But growers were highly reluctant to change agricultural practices to produce these products.

OPERATIONS ORIENTATION. The firm with an **operations orientation** typically focuses on reducing unit costs. There is nothing wrong with cutting costs — indeed, low costs allow firms to reduce prices and/or earn higher profit margins. Cutting costs is particularly important when customers are price-sensitive and/or competitors compete on price. But cost-cutting should not be a priority when the firm introduces new products or when product varieties, promotional effort, and short delivery times are crucial for attracting, retaining, and growing customers.

The problem occurs when the firm fails to think through its cost-cutting program. Pruning the product line, taking design shortcuts, reducing customer service, curbing promotional spending, and/or lengthening delivery times typically reduce costs. But they do not deliver greater customer value — they may create dissatisfaction. Union Pacific Railroad employees met operating budgets by canceling cargo pickups and sending out trains with insufficient locomotive power! The plant manager at a leading cell phone supplier replaced a crucial part with a cheaper alternative; the phone failed.

> Nabisco developed a new corporate policy. Regardless of where products were made and sold, recipes, raw materials, process control, and quality standards were identical to the U.S. But in China, market conditions were very different. Nabisco did not focus on customer needs, made overly optimistic forecasts, had significant excess capacity, and suffered major losses. Said a spokesperson for competitor Danone: "I'm grateful to Nabisco. Their actions have strengthened our position!"[46]

SALES ORIENTATION. Increasing sales is a worthy objective. After all, sales revenues and cash flow are critical for enhancing shareholder value. The problem: Firms with a **sales orientation** focus on short-term sales volume. They are less concerned with profits and long-run customer relationships. They set prices too low and offer excessive discounts and/or too-favorable credit terms — and may create a perception of low quality. They spend little on marketing research and planning, target customers indiscriminately, offer too many products, and over-invest in finished-goods inventories. Taiwan-based Chi Mei was this sort of firm — but became very profitable by abandoning its sales orientation:

> Chi Mei's Chairman Wu made a plant visit. In the warehouse, he found many acrylic sheets, cut to various sizes — *excessive* attention to customer needs. Wu ordered the plant to refocus on four types of sheets, accounting for 70 percent of sales — and set premium prices for special sheet sizes. As production and inventory costs dropped, Chi Mei reduced prices. Market share and profits increased dramatically. Chi Mei is now one of the world's largest plastics producers.

The sales-oriented firm places excessive effort on *getting customers to buy what the firm has to offer*; the externally oriented firm focuses on *getting the firm to offer what customers want to buy*.

FINANCE ORIENTATION. The firm with a **finance orientation** focuses too heavily on short-term profits. When a firm *manages by the numbers*, it tends to avoid expenditures with long-term payoff. The finance-oriented firm mortgages its future by indiscriminately cutting back on R&D, capital investment, marketing research, and/or advertising. Pricing focuses on short-term profits, and planning processes are weak or nonexistent.[47] Sometimes a single-minded focus on short-term profits and cash flow is the right approach — if the firm consistently loses money or makes marginal profits. In other cases, the finance-oriented firm makes insufficient long-term invest-

KEY IDEA

➤ Long-run success is difficult for internally oriented firms.

➤ Internal orientations often focus on operations, sales, finance, and/or technology.

Marketing Exercise

Interview an executive. Identify examples where functional silos hurt performance — and where different functions worked well together. Why did these different behaviors occur?

ments and is vulnerable to competitors.[48] J&J's stents (p. 13) exemplifies a firm that focused on short-term profits and paid a heavy long-term price. Dunlap is another example:

> Scott Paper CEO "Chainsaw" Al Dunlap laid off 35,000 people (11 percent of the workforce) and sold $3.5 billion worth of assets. Return on investment and shareholder value increased. Kimberly-Clark purchased Scott Paper and Dunlap became CEO of small-appliance manufacturer Sunbeam. Dunlap applied the same approach but major problems soon emerged. As Sunbeam's share price dropped precipitously, Dunlap was unceremoniously fired.[49]

Marketing Question

Name some firms you believe are internally oriented; name some firms you believe are externally oriented. Why did you select the ones you did?

TECHNOLOGY ORIENTATION. Bill Joy, often called the "Edison of the Internet," said, "My own biggest mistake in the last 20 years was that sometimes I designed solutions for problems that people didn't yet know they had. That's why some of the things that could've made a difference couldn't find a market." A firm with a **technology orientation** focuses on RD&E (research, development, and engineering) and pays little attention to customer value. Engineering and manufacturing make new product and facility decisions; marketing has little role in product development and product planning is inadequate.[50] The firm's products are often over-engineered, but customers will not pay for unneeded features. First-class products are critical for attracting, retaining, and growing customers, but the firm's product development efforts must center on customer requirements.[51] Panasonic learned this lesson:

> Panasonic engineers believed that lots of buttons and technical gadgets would add value to camcorders and increase market share. Sales stagnated because customers wanted easy-to-use products and manuals in everyday language. Philips had a similar orientation but conducted more than 200,000 customer interviews and refocused on what they wanted — sense and simplicity.

THE SIX MARKETING IMPERATIVES

The job of putting the marketing philosophy into practice normally falls to people with marketing and/or product-management titles.[52] These people tend to engage in many marketing activities, like securing data on customers and competitors, developing advertising campaigns, designing direct-mail brochures, meeting with R&D on new products, devising Internet and mobile strategies, setting prices, and/or preparing persuasive messages for the sales force. Certainly these activities often enhance the firm's market position, but deciding how to allocate marketers' time and/or other resources requires answers to several questions:

- Which of these activities is critical?
- Do these activities represent the core elements of marketing?
- What critical tasks must the firm perform to truly accomplish its marketing agenda?
- In what order should the firm perform these tasks?

We now discuss the six marketing imperatives — the firm's *must dos* — these are core elements for *managing marketing in the 21st century*. The first three imperatives focus on **strategic marketing**; the second three imperatives zero in on **implementing the market strategy**.

The Six Marketing Imperatives

Strategic Marketing
- Imperative 1: Determine and recommend which markets to address.
- Imperative 2: Identify and target market segments.
- Imperative 3: Set strategic direction and positioning.

Implementing the Market Strategy
- Imperative 4: Design the market offer.
- Imperative 5: Secure support from other functions.
- Imperative 6: Monitor and control execution and performance.

STRATEGIC MARKETING — IMPERATIVE 1: DETERMINE AND RECOMMEND WHICH MARKETS TO ADDRESS

Until the late 1990s, the Japanese antidepressant market was untapped. To the Japanese, *depression* (*Utsubyo*) was a bad word — a social stigma. Other pharmaceutical firms avoided Japan, but GlaxoSmithKline (GSK) saw a market opportunity. Using a consistent message, GSK changed the way Japanese think about depression — "Does your soul have a cold (*Kokoro no Kaze*) ... depression is a disease that anyone can get. It can be cured by medicine. Early detection is important." For four years, 1,300 GSK salespeople visited selected doctors twice a week with this message. In three years, GSK's Paxil sales tripled — from $108 million to $298 million. GSK's message hit home — online bulletin boards had as many conversations about depression as performance!

Simply put, the firm must choose those markets where it will compete — as GSK chose the Japanese antidepressant market. To help make these choices, the firm should ask: What businesses are we in? What businesses do we want to be in? Market-choice decisions are typically strategic for the firm, or at least for individual business units. Choosing markets is often more important than choosing technologies and/or products. Given the choice of owning a market or owning a factory, most senior executives would prefer owning a market.

The firm must continually make market-choice decisions. Faster environmental change opens up new market opportunities but may also lead the firm to exit current markets. IBM has been very successful in the information-technology services market — but exited PCs by divesting to China's Lenovo. Market-choice decisions can totally transform a corporation. Nokia exited its traditional paper-making, rubber-goods, and electric-cable markets as it evolved from a diversified conglomerate to global leadership in wireless communication (but is a follower in smart phones):

To comprehend the magnitude of Nokia's transformation, conduct the following thought experiment. It is 1990: Someone tells you about a soon-to-be-launched technology called *cell phones*. They anticipate fast growth and tell you that ten years after launch, one firm will be the global market leader. They ask you the following question: What country will spawn this global leader? What will you answer? Finland!

The firm must decide where to invest — to compete or not, in various markets, and decide how much to invest. The firm must answer critical questions about its business and market portfolio:

- In which new businesses and markets shall we invest — people, time, dollars?
- From which businesses and markets shall we withdraw?
- In which current businesses and markets shall we continue to invest?
- How much investment shall we make in these various businesses and markets?

Typically, marketing does not make these decisions. Top management has this responsibility but marketing must provide good advice. For Imperative 1, marketing plays two key roles:

- **Identify opportunities.** Marketing is the only function with explicit responsibility to focus attention outside the firm. Marketing personnel should research the environment to identify potential opportunities and bring these to top management's attention. They should also collect and analyze data that bear on entry decisions. Marketing should be intimately involved with the firm's current markets and businesses and advise on investment and exit decisions.

- **Advise on proposed strategic actions.** Many firm functions develop strategic initiatives. Finance may suggest acquisitions and divestitures; R&D may propose strategic alliances; and the sales force may champion a new distribution system. Marketing has the responsibility to insert itself into these decisions. The firm should fully explore the marketing ramifications of its decisions or disaster may ensue. Most observers believe the AOL/Time

KEY IDEA

➤ **Imperative 1.** Marketing should identify market opportunities and advise top management on potential strategic actions.

Marketing Question

In recent years P&G has divested and acquired several businesses. How do you assess P&G's choices regarding Marketing Imperative 1?

Warner and Quaker/Snapple acquisitions were failures. Perhaps the acquirers would have made superior decisions with better marketing advice!

STRATEGIC MARKETING — IMPERATIVE 2: IDENTIFY AND TARGET MARKET SEGMENTS

Boeing purchased de Havilland Canada (DHC) to address the market segment for smaller, regional aircraft (under 20 to 90 seats). Boeing believed DHC's family of Dash 8 turbo-prop planes satisfied customer needs. During the following six years, Boeing lost nearly $1 billion on the DHC acquisition, then sold DHC to Bombardier. Potential customers for Dash 8 planes were new to Boeing, but Bombardier already operated in this segment. Bombardier tripled the Dash 8 family's turbo-prop market share to 35 percent — Dash 8 then accounted for two-thirds of regional planes sold worldwide.

KEY IDEA

➤ **Imperative 2.** Marketing must identify market segments — groups of customers with similar needs that value similar benefits, with similar levels of priority.

➤ The firm should target those market segments where it can best use its strengths and exploit competitor weakness.

In any **B2B** or **B2C** market, customers have a diverse set of needs. A single offer directed at the overall market may satisfy some customers, but typically many customers are dissatisfied. Imperative 2 states that marketing must identify **market segments** — groups of customers with similar needs that value similar benefits, with similar levels of priority. When the firm does **market segmentation** well, the needs, benefits, and values that define one segment are quite different from the needs, benefits, and values that define other segments. Once the firm has identified market segments, it must decide which to target.

Note the two elements of Imperative 2: A *creative and analytic* part — identifying market segments; and a *decision-making* part — choosing which segments to target, based on the firm's ability to deliver customer value. The Dash 8 example demonstrates both elements quite clearly. Both Boeing and Bombardier did a good job of identifying the small, regional segment of the overall aircraft market. Bombardier had the appropriate skills and resources to target this market segment; Boeing did not. This lesson is important — a market segment may be attractive to one firm but unattractive to another.

Figure 1.3 illustrates segmentation and targeting by noting several segments, then showing a firm targeting a subset of those segments. Once top management has decided which markets to address (Imperative 1), market segmentation and targeting is arguably the most critical imperative. Effective segmentation and targeting drive profits.

FIGURE 1.3

MARKET SEGMENTATION AND TARGETING

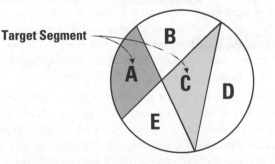

Note: The entire *pie* represents the population of existing and potential customers. Each *slice* or target segment — A,B,C,D,E — reflects specific needs and required benefits of customers in that segment. Note that each segment may contain *sub-segments*.

STRATEGIC MARKETING — IMPERATIVE 3: SET STRATEGIC DIRECTION AND POSITIONING

P&G's Gillette brand is the global leader in both men's and women's shaving markets. Gillette continually introduces higher-value products in advanced countries. In the U.S., it offers Trac II, Atra, and Sensor brands (two blades), Mach3 and the battery-operated M3Power (three blades), and Fusion and Fusion Power (five blades). In less-developed countries, Gillette offers double-edge blades, twin- and four-blade shaving systems, and disposable razors.

In Imperative 3, the firm decides how to compete in those market segments it has targeted. For each target segment, marketing must formulate performance objectives. These objectives guide the firm's strategic decisions in the target segments. Second, the firm must decide on its positioning for each segment. It must identify target customers and target competitors, design a more persuasive value proposition than competitors, and provide reasons for customers to believe the firm can deliver that value. Together with Imperative 2, positioning completes the critical STP triumvirate — segmentation, targeting, and positioning.

Typically, individual market segments are at different developmental stages and hence require different approaches. The appropriate way to address a growing market segment is quite different from a mature or declining segment. In addition, decisions about strategic direction also include questions of branding — how the firm wants customers to view the corporate entity and its products. Top management increasingly views the firm's brands as major corporate assets; hence, branding issues are among its most important strategic decisions.

Of course, the firm does not make these decisions only once. It faces an ever-changing environmental landscape: Customer needs evolve and competitors enter, exit, and adopt different strategies. The firm's products also evolve as target segments grow, mature, and decline. The firm must continually assess its strategic direction and make necessary course corrections.

KEY IDEA

➤ **Imperative 3.** Marketing should fix the firm's strategic direction and positioning. These decisions set the stage for designing the market offer.

IMPLEMENTING THE MARKET STRATEGY — IMPERATIVE 4: DESIGN THE MARKET OFFER

The elements of Steuben Glass' market offer are closely integrated and mutually supportive. Many customers buy Steuben glass objects as gifts. Products are very high quality — tough quality control standards demand that objects with the slightest imperfection be destroyed: You cannot buy Steuben seconds! Steuben distributes its products only in high quality retail outlets — upmarket department stores like Bloomingdale's and Macy's, and specialty stores — where salespeople are very knowledgeable and presentable and provide high service levels. Advertising is confined to high quality shelter magazines like *Good Housekeeping* and *Town & Country*. These elements of the market offer develop a *status-like* brand identity that supports a high price.

Imperative 4 focuses on design of the **market offer**. The market offer is the total benefit package the firm provides customers. Tools for designing the offer are the most well-known part of marketing. If you took a previous marketing course, the professor probably spent significant time talking about the **marketing mix** (aka the **4Ps**). The marketing mix is an important part of marketing, but note: the marketing mix represents just *one* out of *six* marketing imperatives. Marketing-mix elements comprise the basic building blocks of the firm's offer:

- **Product.** In general, the product embodies the major benefits the firm offers to satisfy customer needs — these benefits provide value to customers. If the firm offers greater value than its competitors, customer purchases increase. The term *product* typically embraces both physical products and services — like airline travel, packaging, and additional customer service. Hence, FedEx's core offering is overnight package delivery — but special handling, insurance, tracking, and other customer services are important competitive weapons.[53]

- **Promotion.** Promotion embraces the various ways the firm communicates with customers — informing and persuading them to purchase its products. Promotion includes *impersonal communications* like advertising and sales promotions, and *personal communications* like the sales force. In addition to informing and persuading, communications may add customer value directly by providing imagery, status, and reassurance.[54]

- **Distribution.** Distribution focuses on how and where customers secure the product. To conform to the 4Ps framework, marketers sometimes refer to *distribution* as **place**.

- **Price.** Price is what customers pay. The firm establishes the feasible price by the equivalent amount of value it offers through its product, promotion, distribution, and service.

Marketing Exercise

Identify three examples each of well-integrated and poorly integrated market offers.

KEY IDEA

➤ **Imperative 4.** The firm designs the market offer using the tools of the marketing mix:

- Product
- Promotion
- Distribution (Place)
- Price

The Steuben example shows marketing design elements' many interrelationships. If the firm offers significant benefits and high customer value from its product, communications, distribution, and customer service, it can set a high price. But if customer benefits and value are low, price must also be low. When the firm designs good market offers, customers purchase its products.

When the firm targets multiple market segments, it should design multiple offers. Toyota offers the Camry for one segment and the Lexus for a quite different segment. These cars have different physical designs and customers have different buying experiences. Even the type and location of dealerships is different. Customers receive different values and, accordingly, pay different prices. When targeting a market segment, the firm can combine marketing-mix elements in an infinite number of ways. Creativity, imagination, innovation, and capability are core ingredients.

Marketing and Other Functions: The Architect and the Builder

A useful metaphor for capturing marketing's organizational role is *architect* and *builder*. Marketing is the architect — designs the house. The other functions represent the builder — build the house. Certainly, builders could build houses on their own but the architect provides significant design value. Similarly, in the firm marketing designs the offer; other functions implement the offer.

IMPLEMENTING THE MARKET STRATEGY — IMPERATIVE 5: SECURE SUPPORT FROM OTHER FUNCTIONS

Integrating across firm functions is a critical organizational value at Valeo, a major French car-parts manufacturer. Said a senior executive, "Customers expect seamless delivery, and they don't care how we're organized. We have to work as a team and forget our internal battles." Valeo bases its organization on seven principal *domains* — broad product areas that have separate functions inside a car.[55]

KEY IDEA

➤ **Imperative 5**. Marketing must keep the firm focused on customer needs, regardless of current feasibility.

➤ Marketing must exercise leadership to encourage cooperation across multiple functions.

Imperatives 1, 2, 3, and 4 concern *where* and *how* questions. Imperatives 1, 2, and 3 focus on *where* the firm will place its resources. Imperative 4 concerns *how* the firm will use its resources to design the market offer. Imperative 5 focuses on how firm functions work together to ensure the firm executes the market offer as designed. Marketing requires two very different types of support:

• **Support for design** — relates to technical, operational, and economic feasibility.
• **Support for implementation** — assumes the design is agreed upon and fixed.

SUPPORT FOR DESIGN. Imperative 4 focuses on designing the market offer that best meets customer needs in a target segment. The firm's ability to deliver the market offer depends on its abilities and resources. The *best* design for customers may require a product feature the firm cannot make. When the best design is not feasible, marketing must develop extraordinary strength to keep the firm focused on satisfying customer needs — and push specific functions to evolve their capabilities.[56] In the face of short-run pressures for a less demanding route, marketing must commit to this long-run task.

Pete Swenson, new product head at leading industrial floor cleaner Tennant, developed a new carpet scrubber using innovative cleaning technology. A major customer and four senior executives including Swenson's boss told him to kill the project. Swenson persevered and ReadySpace became Tennant's best selling carpet cleaner.

SUPPORT FOR IMPLEMENTATION. We often call this support *internal marketing*, or getting *buy-in*. In many firms, marketing designs the offer — but has little authority to implement the design. Marketers must possess the leadership and interpersonal skills to encourage and stimulate cooperation across multiple functions. After all, *the chain is only as strong as its weakest link*. If a key function does not perform, other functions may waste their efforts.

We should not underestimate the importance of Imperative 5. Many firms suffer from inter-departmental strife and rivalry driven by *silo thinking*. Destructive internal conflicts siphon off precious management time the firm could spend addressing external opportunities and threats. Some firms address the *silo* problem head-on by forming cross-functional teams — like marketing, operations, and R&D. Others redesign their organizations. At GE, CEO Jack Welch introduced the *boundaryless* organization and boundarylessness became a core value.[57] Most approaches use some form of team-based evaluation to encourage cooperation.

IMPLEMENTING THE MARKET STRATEGY — IMPERATIVE 6: MONITOR AND CONTROL EXECUTION AND PERFORMANCE

> Pfizer has a strong reputation for optimizing spending on the marketing mix. Pfizer continually tests different budgets for selling effort and advertising and promotion. Says a senior Pfizer executive, "We're measurement-intense. So 'metrics are us.' We believe in it. We measure everything. That is the root of our business.[58]

It's one thing to plan and implement, but figuring out the firm's performance is quite another. Imperative 6 focuses on *monitor and control* — is the firm achieving its desired results? All things equal, if the firm is successful, it should keep on truckin'; otherwise, it should make changes.

Essentially, marketing should continually secure answers to three questions and act accordingly:

- Are the firm's various functions and departments *implementing* the market offer?
- Are the firm's market and financial *performance* reaching planned objectives?
- Based on the current *environment*, are the firm's objectives, strategies, and implementation plans on track, or should it make changes?

IMPLEMENTATION. The firm may have many implementation problems — like lack of buy-in, Imperative 5. But even with excellent buy-in, antiquated or inappropriate management systems create implementation difficulties. For example, if the firm sets unrealistic sales force objectives, salespeople may be unmotivated and lack effort. Ratchet-based compensation systems — success in one year leads automatically to higher sales targets for the following year — are a prime example. In mature and declining markets, ratchet-based systems generate significant dissatisfaction and low motivation.

POOR PERFORMANCE. If the firm is not achieving market and/or financial performance objectives, marketing may require more data and further analysis. If environmental change is low, marketing should focus on course corrections by fine-tuning its strategy and/or modifying implementation plans.

ENVIRONMENTAL CHANGE. The firm bases objectives, strategy, and implementation on its best insight into customer needs, competitive offers, and the external environment. A good strategy should accommodate evolutionary changes — more significant change may require new objectives and strategies.

KEY IDEA

➤ **Imperative 6.** Marketing must monitor and control the firm's actions and performance to keep it on track.

Marketing Question

How good a job has Google done in implementing the six marketing imperatives?

THE FOUR PRINCIPLES OF MARKETING

You just learned that six imperatives are the *must dos* of marketing. Four marketing principles serve as guidelines for implementing these imperatives:

The Four Principles of Marketing

- Principle 1: Selectivity and Concentration
- Principle 2: Customer Value
- Principle 3: Differential Advantage
- Principle 4: Integration

PRINCIPLE 1: SELECTIVITY AND CONCENTRATION

Retail stockbroker Edward D. Jones consistently earns among the highest financial returns in its industry. Jones has successfully expanded its geographic focus from rural and small-town America to most major U.S., Canadian, and British cities. Jones' approach remains consistent — a focus on customers who want personal service. Jones has expanded, while being *selective and concentrating* its resources.

Providing advice on market selection (Imperative 1) and deciding which market segments to target (Imperative 2) are among marketing's primary responsibilities. The basic principle underlying these imperatives is the **Principle of Selectivity and Concentration**.[59]

Two aspects comprise the Selectivity and Concentration principle:

- **Selectivity.** Marketing must carefully choose targets for the firm's efforts.
- **Concentration.** The firm should concentrate resources against those targets.

This principle is about choosing the firm's battles. It is dangerous to dissipate limited resources over too many alternatives by trying to do too much. No organization, no matter how large or successful, has infinite resources. Each must make timely choices. The selectivity element is fundamental to recommending which markets to target — Imperative 1, but the best-known manifestation is identifying and targeting market segments — Imperative 2. Market segmentation is a fundamental topic in marketing, but we repeat the distinction between two related, but quite different, issues:

- **Market segmentation process.** The firm divides the market into groups of customers — segments. In each segment, customers have similar needs and value similar benefits with similar levels of priority.
- **Targeting market segments.** Good segmentation only *allows* for better strategic decisions; it does not guarantee them — *selectivity* is crucial. Which segment(s) should the firm select for effort? Which should it *target*?[60] The firm that skillfully implements this principle probes selected segment(s) in greater depth and uncovers hidden opportunities.

Small firms that concentrate their slender resources on specific market segments often gain leverage over larger competitors, like eBay and Google did in their early years. Small firms concentrate their limited resources by default. Large firms have greater resources but often spread themselves too thin because they have difficulty concentrating.

Of course, concentration involves risk. When the firm concentrates resources on some opportunities, it forgoes others.[61] The firm will fail with some chosen options — and options it does not choose will be successful for others. Get used to this fact: As a marketer, you are a gambler. You make bets on markets and segments — your reward is market share and profit. Gamblers in Atlantic City, Macau, Monte Carlo, and Las Vegas play against an impersonal house and win only by chance. You play against living, breathing, unpredictable competitors and shift the odds in your favor by practicing your marketing craft well.

KEY IDEA

➤ **Principle 1: Selectivity and Concentration:**

- **Selectivity.** Marketing must carefully choose targets for the firm's efforts.
- **Concentration.** The firm should concentrate its resources against those targets.

As markets become increasingly competitive, hedging bets by allocating small amounts of resources to a broad set of options will certainly fail. For this reason, some experts have relabeled this principle *Concentration and Concession.* Not only must the firm concentrate its resources in chosen segments, it should affirmatively concede other segments to competitors:

> Samsung is a highly successful electronics firm — it ruthlessly practices selectivity and concentration. Said a senior marketing executive, "We had an explicit strategy to get out of low-end commodity-oriented channels. We actually withdrew from places like Walmart and Kmart, even though these were a big source of revenues. Instead, we focused on channels like Best Buy, Sears, and several regional electronics specialists. We establish deep relationships with our true value-added channel partners. This focus provides them direct benefits from our marketing."[62]

PRINCIPLE 2: CUSTOMER VALUE

> Dell focuses on delivering high levels of customer value. Said a senior marketing executive, "We're very centered on truly understanding customer behavior and having a deep level of customer insights. We use those insights and customer access to align the entire organization. We're really the only major player with a totally seamless link from the customer back to the component manufacturer, so we're the best placed to really deliver customer value. We have a knowledge base that enables us to meet customer needs better than anyone else. At the highest level, we understand what customers want. We tailor our product offerings and our suppliers' product offerings to what customers want. We have a pretty tight set of feedback loops. Our account executives talk to customers regularly and feed that back. Our Platinum Council (Customer Advisory Board) of our best customers meets periodically and looks at our forward-looking product roadmaps. The members give us feedback on whether these product development plans are geared to their needs. In a very real sense, the Council is part of a virtual product development organization — they really shape our priorities at a fairly early stage and enable us to ratchet up our ability to deliver customer value."[63]

According to the **Principle of Customer Value,** the firm's marketplace success depends on providing value to customers. This principle is central to marketing's job. Customer insight should drive design and implementation of market offers. Customer value should drive the firm's product and investment decisions — and its performance evaluations. The firm develops, produces, and delivers products and services, but customers perceive value only in the benefits these products and services provide. To be very clear: Customers *do not want* the firm's products; they only want *the value* those products deliver.

Customer value is a moving target. As the environment changes, customers accumulate experience and their needs evolve — the values they seek evolve also. World-class companies continuously invest in marketing research to probe deeply into customer needs, priorities, expectations, and experiences. They feed these results into the product development process to produce greater value for customers.

Cisco continues to be the market-share leader and a major force in high technology. Said an important Wall Street analyst, "They [Cisco] don't have the best technology, but they do have the best [customer] relationships."[64] Dell also has an extraordinary focus on customer value. Firms that take their eye off the *customer ball* can get into serious trouble. Sears and Kmart (U.S.) and Sainsbury's and Marks & Spencer (Great Britain) were once powerful and successful retailers. In recent years, each has been in crisis.

We reinforce the point by adapting from U.S. presidential politics: "It's the customer, stupid!"[65]

KEY IDEA

➤ **Principle 2: Customer Value:**

- The firm earns success by providing value to customers.

- The firm develops, produces, and delivers products and services, but customers perceive value only in the benefits these products and services provide.

PRINCIPLE 3: DIFFERENTIAL ADVANTAGE

A senior executive explained ExxonMobil's efforts to secure differential advantage. "We woke up and realized that people didn't care about our product. The government wrote standards for fuel specification, so the consumer said 'hey, fuel is fuel.' We started to think, not about the product, but about people's experience. All of our research around the world confirmed the same thing. It's a mobile society, everybody's in a rush. We moved from being auto-centric — we're here to serve the car, tires, batteries, and fan belts, to driver-centric — we'll give you gas and fuel, but we'll give you clean restrooms, telephones, the things you need to enhance your life on the move .... Our convenience stores were the same as competitors', nice designs and colors — everything inside is great, but it's a box. And the stuff we sell is the same. What we bring to the party is location — we make it convenient and give you the right experience. If you just want gasoline and are in a hurry, use your speed pass, pay at the pump, get in and get out. If you want to get out of traffic for a minute, or feel like a cup of coffee, need a restroom, then we welcome you inside. We will take as good care of you inside the store as when you are outside."[66]

The **Principle of Differential Advantage** is closely related to the Principle of Customer Value. Differential advantage is similar to having a *competitive advantage,* a *unique selling proposition (USP),* or an *edge.* Differential advantage lies at the heart of every successful market strategy. The Principle of Differential Advantage asserts that the firm should offer customers something they value but cannot get elsewhere.

More formally, *a differential advantage is a net benefit or cluster of benefits, offered to a sizable group of customers, which they value and are willing to pay for but cannot get, or believe they cannot get, elsewhere.* To implement this principle, the firm must develop well-designed market offers based on the marketing-mix elements we discussed earlier. If the firm achieves a differential advantage, it should secure improved prices.[67] This principle leads to several implications:

- **Competition.** The principle emphasizes competition. Offering customer value is not enough. To avoid competitive parity, the firm must offer greater value than competitors. The firm must create and re-create its differential advantage to beat competitors.

- **Superiority of differential advantages.** Some differential advantages are better than others. A differential advantage based on product design or product availability may be more sustainable than one based on communications. A differential advantage based on an organizational process like Dell's low-cost, made-to-order manufacturing systems — or parts delivery, good customer relationships, qualified technicians, and/or a willingness-to-serve culture may be even more sustainable.[68] But in an increasingly complex, competitive, and changing world, the firm's true differential advantage may belong in a meta-level adaptive ability to create a series of differential advantages over time.[69]

- **Eroding differential advantages.** Competition will eventually erode away even the apparently most sustainable differential advantage.[70] Motorola had a 2004 hit with the superthin RAZR phone but lost market share when it failed to produce a follow-up advantage. Maintaining differential advantage is marketing's most fundamental challenge, and the search for differential advantage must be ongoing. Ideally, the firm should have a hidden differential advantage, ready to trump the competitor's ace![71]

- **Cannibalizing a differential advantage.** To stay ahead of competition, the firm must be willing to cannibalize its own offers. Many firms will not do so, in part because of strong political constituencies for the status quo. Adhering to the sentiment "If it ain't broke, don't fix it" runs the risk of passing marketplace initiative to a competitor.[72]

- **Differential advantage and difference.** A *differential advantage* is not the same as a *difference.* To develop a different market offer may not be difficult. The firm's differences must create benefits that customers recognize, value, and are willing to pay for.[73]

KEY IDEA

➤ **Principle 3: Differential Advantage:**

- To secure differential advantage, customers must perceive greater value in the firm's offer than in competitor offers.

Marketing Question

Groupon and OpenTable each target restaurants and have similar business models. Suppose you were able to invest $5,000 in either Groupon or OpenTable. Which would you choose? Why?

PRINCIPLE 4: INTEGRATION

Integration is critical to Target's success. "Every one of us, in every functional group, from Stores to Merchandising, from Logistics to Support, identifies with the role as marketing. We're all attempting to build better relationships with our guest [Target's term for customer]. And every decision starts with the guest, so everyone becomes a marketer. We instill that attitude with evangelical passion and great consistency — the evangelizing starts at the top with our Chairman and CEO. Our core brand promise since 1962 has been 'Expect more, pay less.' We live it — every single function of this company lives it. We search the globe for the best products to serve our guest needs and everyone in the store is hard-wired to meet guest expectations at all times."[74]

Successful integration — critical for all marketing efforts — has two dimensions:

- **At the customer.** The firm must carefully integrate and coordinate all design and executional elements of the offer it makes to customers. Poor advertising can ruin an excellent product; delayed promotional materials can doom a product launch; and improper pricing can cause havoc with sales forecasts. *New York Magazine* designed a new-subscriber promotion — offer free magazines for six weeks and then follow with a subscription request. Unfortunately, the subscription request arrived before the first free magazine!

- **In the firm.** To achieve integration at the customer, the firm must carefully integrate and coordinate all internal functional activities — this is often very difficult.[75] Different functions and/or departments often squabble over priorities — and senior management may send ambiguous messages. A senior executive at a well-known multinational described the situation to his incoming superior: "There have been too many years of business units versus corporate, too many years of control versus trust, too many years of operating in silos, too many years of manipulating the facts to serve personal interests, and too many years of defending internal turf at the expense of market share and position."[76]

Examples of insufficient integration are legion. Consider the following dialogue involving the author, at an in-house seminar for a major U.S. computer firm. During the presentation, a participant asked several questions about sales forecasting. The following exchange occurred:

> **AUTHOR:** "How come you're so interested in sales forecasting?"
>
> **PARTICIPANT:** "Well, I have a sales forecasting department, and since you were here, I thought I might learn something."
>
> **AUTHOR:** "That's fine, but tell me, what's your position in the firm?"
>
> **PARTICIPANT:** I'm the production director."
>
> **AUTHOR:** "Oh! That's a little unusual. I'd have thought the sales forecasting department might have been in marketing, or in sales."
>
> **PARTICIPANT:** "Sure, they have one too. But we can't believe a word they say, so we have to have our own."

Or consider this scenario in a major electronics firm: Business unit (A) shared salespeople with a sister business unit (B). But senior managers in business unit (B) would not allow these salespeople or their managers to attend business unit (A)'s annual strategy conference!

Firms with an external orientation are more likely to achieve integration because the shared value of serving customers promotes a common purpose. Sharing responsibility for designing and implementing market offers drives agreement on priorities, together with close and cooperative working relationships.

Marketing Question

Apple's success has made it one of the world's most admired firms. How do you assess Apple's adherence to the four marketing principles?

KEY IDEA

➤ **Principle 4: Integration:**

- The firm must carefully integrate all elements in the design and execution of its market offer.

- To achieve integration at customers, the firm must coordinate and integrate internal functional activities.

Marketing Question

What other messages did you glean from this chapter?

v102

v103

a101

a102

a103

KEY MESSAGES

- Firms that deliver greater customer value than competitors are more successful in attracting, retaining, and growing customers.

- Firms that successfully attract, retain, and grow customers earn profits. They are more likely to survive and grow, and enhance shareholder value.

- Value has two sides. When firms deliver significant customer value, they attract, retain, and grow customers. When firms attract, retain, and grow customers, they create value for shareholders.

- Marketing as a philosophy embraces an external orientation — all organizational members have a responsibility for delivering customer value.

- Six marketing imperatives are *must dos* for the firm.

- Four marketing principles provide the guiding framework within which the firm implements the six marketing imperatives.

VIDEOS AND AUDIOS

Marketing Careers	v102	Ellen	Columbia Business School
Pharmaceutical Marketing	v103	Robert Essner	Wyeth; Columbia Business School
The Role of Marketing	a101		
The Externally Oriented Firm	a102		
Four Marketing Principles	a103		

QUESTIONS FOR STUDY AND DISCUSSION

Can you answer the questions implied by this chapter's learning objectives? Check!

1. Select a well-known FMCG firm. From its financial statements, identify the book value of its assets. Also identify the firm's market value based on its stock price. Is there a difference? What accounts for this difference? Do these findings change the way you think about marketing's role in delivering value?

2. The chapter describes how Barnes & Noble's balance-sheet assets became strategic liabilities. Describe another example. What was the outcome? What would you have done differently? Would it have been easy to implement your decisions? Why or why not? How would your decisions have affected firm employees? Can you identify firms facing similar challenges?

3. Does your school approach the market for new students in a systematic way? How could it use the six marketing imperatives to improve its efforts?

4. Identify a successful local merchant. Use the six marketing imperatives to explain its success.

5. Why did Kmart decline? Which marketing principle(s) did it neglect? What would you have done differently? How do you assess Kmart's merger with Sears? Compare Kmart's performance with Target's — what accounts for the performance differences?

6. How has the Internet and mobile marketing affected marketing practice?

7. Describe the challenges and opportunities that marketing faces in your school or firm.

CHAPTER 2

THE VALUE
OF CUSTOMERS v201

To access O-codes, go to **www.ocodes.com**

Success is getting the right customers ... and keeping them.

— Charles Cawley, founder of credit card giant MBNA

LEARNING OBJECTIVES

When you have completed this chapter, you will be able to:

- Identify the critical elements that define customer lifetime value.
- Calculate customer profitability and customer lifetime value.
- Recognize the importance of investing in, and retaining, the *right* customers.
- Relate delivering customer value to generating long-term customer loyalty.
- Explain the importance of measuring customer profitability.
- Make tough decisions on dealing with unprofitable current customers.
- Make tough decisions about accepting/rejecting potential customers.
- Establish a customer relationship management (CRM) program.
- Design customer loyalty programs.

OPENING CASE: ROYAL BANK OF CANADA

Toronto-based Royal Bank of Canada (RBC) serves over 14 million personal, business, and public-sector customers via offices in North America and 30 other countries. RBC is Canada's leading bank, with more than 1,700 offices and 5,000 banking machines. What sets RBC apart from competitors is its focus on customer profitability. In RBC's retail business, 17 percent of customers account for 93 percent of profits — an extreme version of the 80/20 rule at 93/17. RBC concentrates on this 17 percent and discourages, or even discards, its least profitable and loss-making customers.

RBC calculates economic profit by customer.[1] Identifying revenue, product profit margins (spreads), and invested capital is easy. RBC tracks labor costs via activity-based costing. RBC monitors costs for back office processing, call centers, serving customers through various channels, and other activities. RBC calculates labor costs per customer, based on product portfolios and monthly transactions.

Because RBC knows which customers earn it economic profit (loss), it can take actions other firms cannot. RBC determines the shareholder value each individual customer or segment creates. RBC also calculates an intrinsic price/earnings (P/E) multiple and compares this P/E ratio to the market average. Golden customer segments — higher than average P/E ratios — are profitable investment opportunities. RBC rationalizes, closes, or sells off customer segments with low P/E ratios.

RBC's retail bank has nine customer segment managers and many product managers. Each segment/ product manager has individual and primary responsibility for strategy and profit and loss (P&L), for their segment/product. They compete with functional managers — marketing, human resources, facilities — for bank resources. This matrix organization encourages collaboration; it works because RBC's culture has always been customer-centric and consensus driven. Also, senior management has clearly signaled that managing for team success is important for career advancement.

RBC'S NEW APPROACH. *RBC traditionally ran mortgage promotions in the spring home-buying season, emphasizing RBC's rates. Competitor banks operated similarly. But Louise Mitchell, RBC's leader for the builders and borrowers segment, pursued a different approach — she targeted the life event of a first home purchase. Mitchell created a value proposition to serve the total needs of first-time home buyers, and add significant value to RBC's shareholders:*

- *First-time home buyers have most of their financial lives ahead of them. Attracting these customers promises long-term banking relationships, with significant growth prospects.*

- *On average, first-time home buyers borrow larger amounts for longer terms than other buyers and are less sensitive to rates. They promise larger investment opportunities, longer-term relationships, and higher returns on invested capital than other customers.*

RBC distributed (direct mail and e-mail) a freestanding newspaper insert — First Time Home Buyers' Guide — full of information and expert advice. RBC's offer included the mortgage and a $500 savings deposit and free financial review (annually for the first five years). Customers also received six months free online banking, one year free Internet service, and a no-fee Visa card.

RBC's product-centric organization could not have executed this promotion; the promotion required coordination among managers responsible for mortgages, savings accounts, financial advice, and marketing. As segment leader, Mitchell was a powerful catalyst. She stated: "Looking through the customer lens," the promotional ideas "jump right out at you."

RBC's customer-focused strategy delivered impressive results: First-time mortgage share grew significantly, particularly in the longest, most profitable (for RBC) terms. Although 2008 was difficult, from 1994 to 2010, RBC earned several increases: revenues — $7.39 billion to $40+ billion; profits — $1.17 billion to $6+ billion; year-end market value — $8.9 billion to $70+ billion; and P/E ratio — 8 to 15.

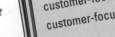

CASE QUESTION

What challenges do firms face in securing customer-focused data and implementing customer-focused strategies like RBC?

Chapter 1 discusses the critical role customers play for the firm's well-being. By attracting, retaining, and growing customers, the firm makes profits today and promises profits tomorrow. Profits allow the firm to survive and grow, and enhance shareholder value. Because of these relationships, customers are the firm's core assets.[2] More precisely, customers are core assets because of two sides of the concept of value. When the firm creates value for customers, it successfully attracts, retains, and grows those customers. By being attracted, retained, and grown, customers create value for the firm and its shareholders.[3]

A retained customer returns to buy more products and services. If your local coffee shop provides good value, like a tasty cup of coffee and a fresh snack for a reasonable price, you will keep going back, morning after morning. The value you bring to the coffee shop is more than just one morning's purchases. You make a stream of purchases because the coffee shop gives you value. By delivering customer value, the firm generates customer loyalty. This relationship applies to all customers regardless of product — automobiles, credit cards, haircuts, jet engines, or TVs.

The first part of this chapter moves beyond the customers-as-assets concept to measuring the value that customers bring to the firm. The critical concept is **customer lifetime value (CLV)** — what the customer is worth. CLV is the discounted future stream of profits the customer generates over the life of its relationship with the firm. CLV is the crucial link between the value the firm delivers to customers and the value customers deliver to the firm. Increasing CLV enhances shareholder value. This chapter shows how to use CLV to increase the value customers bring to the firm; both current customers and potential new customers. The chapter also identifies the *right* customers and shows that some customers are undesirable.

Specifically, we address two questions:

• How can we put a monetary value on the firm's current customers and on potential customers it may acquire? This monetary value is CLV.

• How can we use the CLV concept to help the firm enhance shareholder value?

In the second part of this chapter, we examine practical ways in which firms use the CLV concept to bind customers closer to the firm. Specifically, we address customer relationship management (CRM systems and customer loyalty programs.

THE CHANGING VIEW

Accept that some customers are difficult to address	Strive to give customers consistently good experiences
Acquiring customers is critical	Retaining and growing profitable customers and acquiring new customers are critical
Customer databases nonexistent	Customer databases pivotal
Firm manages products	Firm manages customers
Firm should attract, retain, and grow all customers	Firm should *fire* some current customers and be selective in acquiring new customers
Fragmented information on customers	Sophisticated CRM systems and data mining
Measure product profitability	Measure customer profitability and customer lifetime value
Plant and equipment are the firm's core assets	Customers are the firm's core assets
Product profitability drives incentive systems	Customer profitability drives incentive systems
Product and sales territory considerations dominate resource allocation	Customer and customer segment considerations dominate resource allocation
Products are at the heart of firm decision-making	Customers are at the heart of firm decision-making
Zero or negative reward for customer loyalty	Loyalty incentives very common

Why Customers Are So Important for the Firm

CUSTOMER LIFETIME VALUE (CLV)

Several local, regional, and national electronics retail chains have suffered, giving manufacturers like Sony a serious problem — a long-term customer could go out of business. Sony uses CLV to decide whether, and how much, to invest in a troubled retailer. Said a senior Sony executive: "We sometimes invest in these customers to try to help them stay healthy. We actually hire outside consultants to work with them on process re-engineering. We're working on advertising productivity. We're working on supply-chain management. If we invest and that customer somehow turns, we're not going to take credit for it, but we certainly didn't help them go down."[4]

When customers purchase the firm's products and services, the firm earns sales revenues; it also accrues costs. If sales revenues are greater than costs, the firm earns a profit. The profit earned from an individual customer during a single time period (year) is the **profit margin** — the annual value the customer brings to the firm.[5]

Of course, many customers, both consumers (B2C) and partners, distributors, and resellers (B2B) often purchase the firm's products for several successive years. Each year, the firm receives sales revenues, accrues costs, and earns a profit margin. CLV takes into account profit margins the firm earns in each of these years by using a **discount rate**.[6] Pharmaceutical firms traditionally focused sales efforts on mature, high-prescribing physicians; some firms now place more effort on young physicians (currently low prescribers) with many more prescribing years ahead of them.

Some firm customers this year will not be customers next year. They may defect to competitors, or stop buying the types of products the firm offers.[7] In calculating CLV, we must consider customer *defection* and customer *retention*. **Retention rate** is simply the number of customers at the end of the year, divided by the number of customers at the start of the year. If the firm starts the year with 100 customers and ends the year with 80 of these same customers, its retention rate is 80 percent. Retention is the inverse of defection or *churn*. In this illustration, the **defection rate** is 20 percent (100 percent minus 80 percent).[8] Understanding CLV allows the firm to better manage its customer base.

CALCULATING CLV

In each year, the firm earns a portion of its CLV. In the first year, it earns CLV (1)[9]:

$$\text{CLV (1)} = m \times r/(1 + d)$$

Restating this simple expression in words, CLV (1) is:

- The *profit margin (m)* the firm earns in year 1,[10]
- Multiplied by the *retention rate (r)* — the probability that a customer at the start of the year will still be a customer at the end of the year,
- *Discounted* back to the start of the year, using the term **1/(1+d)**. The *discount rate (d)* is the firm's *cost of capital* — typically provided by the firm's chief financial officer (CFO).

To calculate a customer's total CLV, we simply add up the CLV contributions for each successive year.[11] This is complicated mathematically. We simplify the calculation by assuming that each term — profit margin (m), discount rate (d), retention rate (r) — is constant year to year.

With these assumptions, CLV equals the profit margin (m) multiplied by the **margin multiple**. (For interested readers, Marketing Enrichment me201 derives the margin-multiple formula.)

KEY IDEA

➤ CLV depends on three factors:
- Profit margin
- Retention rate
- Discount rate

Marketing Question

What question about the firm's customers would you like to ask your favorite CEO? How do you think the CEO would answer?

KEY IDEA

➤ The margin multiple is a handy way to calculate customer lifetime value.

MARKETING ENRICHMENT

Derivation of Customer Lifetime Value (CLV) Formula me201

me201

The margin multiple = r/(1 + d − r), so that:

$$\textbf{CLV} = \textbf{m} \times \textbf{r}/(\textbf{1} + \textbf{d} - \textbf{r})$$

Calculating CLV is quite straightforward using this formula.[12] Table 2.1 makes it easier by providing margin multiple values for different retention rates (r) and discount rates (d).

TABLE 2.1

THE MARGIN
MULTIPLE =
r/(1+d−r)

Retention Rate (r)	Discount Rate (d)			
	8%	12%	16%	20%
60%	1.25	1.15	1.07	1.00
70%	1.84	1.67	1.52	1.40
80%	2.86	2.50	2.22	2.00
90%	5.00	4.09	3.46	3.00
95%	7.31	5.59	4.52	3.80

Suppose the firm earns an annual profit margin of $500,000, customer retention rate is 70 percent, and the firm's discount rate is 12 percent. From Table 2.1, the margin multiple is 1.67. Hence, CLV = **$500,000** × **1.67** = **$835,000**. Of course, we lose some precision with these assumptions, but, in most cases, putting us in the right ballpark is sufficient.

Note several things about Table 2.1:

1. The ranges of values for discount rate (d) (8 percent to 20 percent) and retention rate (r) (60 percent to 95 percent) are quite large. They cover most cases for most firms — the margin multiple value spans 1.00 to 7.31.

2. The median value of the margin multiple is around 2.5.

3. Improving retention rate (r) has a greater impact on the margin multiple than reducing discount rate (d):

    a. When retention rate (r) is 90 percent, reducing discount rate (d) from 20 percent to 8 percent improves the margin multiple from 3.00 to 5.00 — 67 percent.

    b. When discount rate (d) is 12 percent, increasing retention rate (r) from 60 percent to 90 percent increases the margin multiple from 1.15 to 4.09 — well over three times! It follows that:

4. All things equal, the firm is better off increasing retention rate (r) than reducing discount rate (d) — cost of capital — by financial engineering. Finance students, please note!

5. Customer retention is a big deal. More on this later.

Here's how we use the margin multiple to calculate CLV for a FedEx customer:

KEY IDEA

➤ Increasing customer retention rate has greater leverage on customer lifetime value than reducing the discount rate.

Example: Lifetime Value of a FedEx Customer

FedEx has identified a market segment — these data apply to FedEx's customers in that segment:

Assumptions

- Total FedEx letters shipped per month = 2,285
- Number of FedEx customers = 140
- FedEx profit margin per letter (m) = $8.25
- Discount rate (cost of capital) (d) = 12%
- Annual retention rate (r) = 90%

We assume these numbers remain constant year to year.

CONTINUES ON NEXT PAGE

*Marketing
Question*

How do you assess CLV for customers of Apple, Facebook. Google, Hershey, Nokia, Pfizer, and Walmart? If CLV is high — why? If CLV is low — why?

Customer lifetime value calculation:

Number of FedEx letters per customer per annum = 2,285 × 12/140 = 195.8

FedEx profit margin per customer per annum = $8.25 × 195.8 = $1,616

Discount rate (d) = 12%

Retention rate (r) = 90%

From Table 2.1, the **margin multiple** = 4.09

CLV = FedEx profit margin per customer per annum × margin multiple = $1,616 × 4.09 = **$6,609**

Marketing Enrichment me202 shows an alternate way to calculate CLV for FedEx. (CLV can also be used to calculate shareholder value me203.)

MARKETING
ENRICHMENT

Alternate Way to Calculate CLV
for a FedEx Customer me202

me202

MARKETING
ENRICHMENT

Customer Lifetime Value (CLV)
and Shareholder Value me203

me203

INCREASING CUSTOMER LIFETIME VALUE

We now explore ways to increase CLV. Restating the CLV formula:

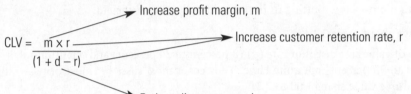

Quite simply, the firm has three, and only three, ways to increase CLV:

- Increase profit margin (m) the firm earns from customers
- Increase customer retention rate (r) (reduce customer defection rate)
- Reduce discount rate (d)

If the firm spends resources to increase customer retention (r), it reduces profit margin (m). Or the firm may increase profit margin (m) by raising prices — but customer retention (r) may fall. Nonetheless, we consider these approaches separately. The third item — discount rate (d) — is the firm's cost of capital, the CFO's responsibility. As marketers, we encourage CFOs to reduce the firm's cost of capital, but marketing can do little to help. Hence, we drop further discussion of discount rate and focus on increasing profit margin and customer retention.[13]

INCREASE THE PROFIT MARGIN THE FIRM EARNS FROM CUSTOMERS

The firm has several options for raising CLV by increasing profit margins from current customers:

- **Customer selection.** Well-selected current customers provide a base level of profit margin.
- **Customer satisfaction and loyalty.** Well-served customers increase purchases over time. Hence, revenues and profit margins increase.[14]
- **Customization.** Targeted offers to defined segments provide greater customer value.
- **Raise prices.** If customer satisfaction is high, the firm may be able to set higher prices.
- **Reduce operating costs.** As the firm learns to serve customers, it reduces operating costs and may reap scale economies with individual customers.

In addition, satisfied customers may help the firm to secure revenues from other customers:

- **Learning.** The firm learns by working closely with customers and becomes better able to attract new customers.

- **Network externalities.** In some markets, customers bring value to other customers. The more *sellers* eBay attracts, the more valuable is eBay's service to *buyers*. The more *buyers* eBay attracts, the more valuable it is to *sellers*. Television, some printed media, and websites are free, yet their customer traffic has value to advertisers. Deciding what marketing resources to allocate for securing *free* customers may be a crucial firm decision.[15]

- **Positive word of mouth and referrals.** Satisfied customers generate positive word of mouth and provide referrals to potential customers. Lexus secures more new customers from referrals than any other source.[16]

- **Signals.** Securing a high-profile customer may provide the firm with credibility among other potential customers.

Marketing Question

Do you tend to increase your purchases from firms that treat you well? Have you told others about these experiences?

Figure 2.1 shows annual profit margin per customer in the U.S. credit card industry. In year 1, by incurring customer acquisition and start-up costs, the average credit card issuer loses $80; in year 2, the customer earns the firm $40. Profit margin per customer increases steadily with customer longevity.[17]

FIGURE 2.1

PROFIT MARGIN IN THE U.S. CREDIT CARD INDUSTRY BY LENGTH OF CUSTOMER RELATIONSHIP

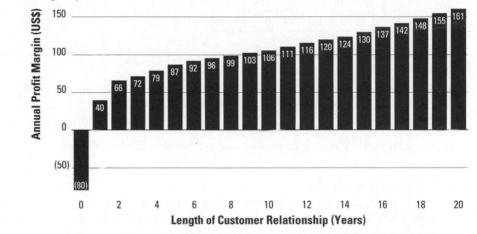

Figure 2.2 shows how customer retention relates to profit patterns in several other industries.[18]

FIGURE 2.2

PROFIT MARGINS IN SEVERAL INDUSTRIES BY LENGTH OF CUSTOMER RELATIONSHIP

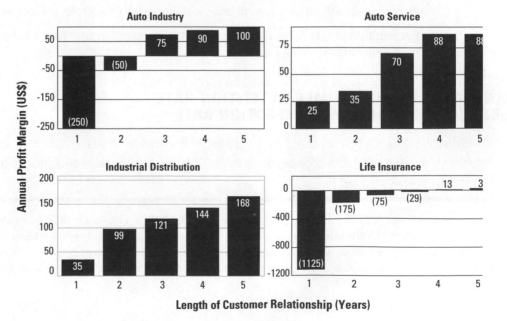

me204

Increasing the profit margin the firm earns from customers has an important impact on CLV.[19] The impact is simply the *profit margin* multiplied by the *margin multiple*. Previously, we showed that the margin multiple with constant profit margin, retention rate, and discount rate was:

$$CLV = m \times r/(1 + d - r)$$

If profit margin grows at a constant rate (g), then:

$$CLV = m \times r/(1 + d - r [1 + g])$$

As **g** increases, **r [1 + g]** also increases, but the entire denominator **(1 + d − r [1 + g])** decreases; hence CLV increases. Table 2.2 shows the margin multiples for different profit margin growth rates, assuming a 12 percent discount rate (**d**). (For formula derivation, see Marketing Enrichment me204.)

Retention Rate (r)	Profit Margin Growth (g)				
	0%	2%	4%	6%	8%
60%	1.15	1.18	1.21	1.24	1.27
70%	1.67	1.72	1.79	1.85	1.92
80%	2.50	2.63	2.78	2.94	3.13
90%	4.09	4.46	4.89	5.42	6.08

Because we selected a 12 percent discount rate, the first column of Table 2.2 is identical to the "12%" column in Table 2.1. Note two items from Table 2.2:

- Regardless of retention rate, higher profit margin growth gives higher margin multiples. For example, when the retention rate is 80 percent:
  - At 0 percent profit margin growth, the margin multiple is 2.50.
  - At 6 percent profit margin growth, the margin multiple is 2.94.
- As retention rate increases, higher profit margin growth has greater impact:
  - At 70 percent retention rate:
    - Profit margin growth rate = 0 percent, margin multiple = 1.67
    - Profit margin growth rate = 8 percent, margin multiple = 1.92 – 15 percent increase
  - At 90 percent retention rate:
    - Profit margin growth rate = 0 percent, margin multiple = 4.09
    - Profit margin growth rate = 8 percent, margin multiple = 6.08 – 50 percent increase

Of course, this last result is not surprising. Customers with higher retention rates have a longer time period to provide the firm with higher profit margins.[20]

INCREASE THE CUSTOMER RETENTION RATE — REDUCE THE CUSTOMER DEFECTION RATE

Medco Health Solutions (MHS) provides pharmacy services to 60 million Americans. In 2003, MHS secured independence from Merck with a $12 stock price (adjusted). By 2010, MHS's retention rate among corporate customers rose to 98 percent; stock price reached $63.

We just showed that a profit margin (m) increase leads to CLV increase. Of course, profit margin is only relevant if the customer continues to be a customer! Figure 2.3 shows retention/defection patterns based on customer tenure — for 90 percent and 80 percent retention rates; of course, defection is greater at 80 percent retention rate than 90 percent. Regardless, the

MARKETING ENRICHMENT

Derivation of Customer Lifetime Value (CLV) Formula with Constant Annual Profit Margin Growth me204

TABLE 2.2

THE MARGIN MULTIPLE WITH PROFIT MARGIN GROWTH = r/(1+d−r [1 + g])

KEY IDEA

➤ The profit margin the firm earns from a customer tends to increase over time.

Marketing Question

Suppose you were advising a local restaurant located on a busy street. The owner tells you she receives plenty of walk-in traffic but has few returning customers. What options can you suggest?

number of customers defecting is greatest in the first year — as time goes on, fewer customers defect. Assume the firm acquires 1,000 new customers at the beginning of year 1:

- 90% retention: Start — 1,000 customers
  - 1st year — Lose 100 customers; 900 remain
  - 2nd year — Lose 90 customers; 810 remain
  - 3rd year — Lose 81 customers; 729 remain

- 80% retention: Start — 1,000 customers
  - 1st year — Lose 200 customers; 800 remain
  - 2nd year — Lose 160 customers; 640 remain
  - 3rd year — Lose 128 customers; 512 remain

These data tell us that customer retention rate has an important impact on CLV. Figure 2.4 shows that a 5 percent increase in customer retention rate enhances customer CLV by over 50 percent in several industries.[21] Figures differ by industry because of different profit patterns — and different retention/defection rates. We discuss customer relationship management (CRM) and specific programs to encourage customer loyalty later in the chapter.

FIGURE 2.3

RETENTION/DEFECTION PATTERNS — PERCENT OF STARTING CUSTOMERS REMAINING BY LENGTH OF CUSTOMER RELATIONSHIP — 80% AND 90% RETENTION RATES

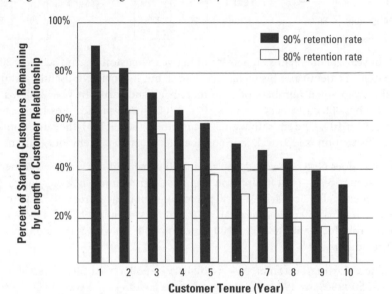

FIGURE 2.4

INCREASE IN CUSTOMER LIFETIME VALUE BY IMPROVING CUSTOMER RETENTION 5% IN SELECTED INDUSTRIES

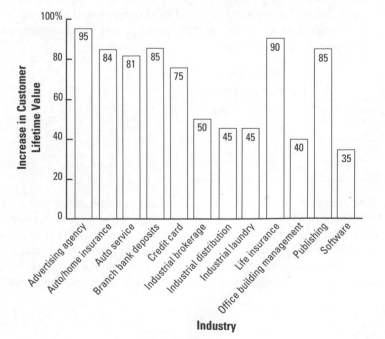

KEY IDEA

➤ Small increases in customer retention can dramatically improve CLV.

HOW CUSTOMER RETENTION WORKS

We just saw that customer retention rate is an important CLV driver. We now show how small differences in customer retention lead, over time, to major differences in sales and market share. Figure 2.5 shows three hypothetical scenarios — A, B, C — each with two firms, Jane's Makeup Emporium and Joe's Beauty Aids, and two time periods, year 1 and year 2. Each scenario shows patterns of customer retention (defection), and customer acquisition. To keep things simple, we assume 1,000 customers in total and that Jane and Joe each start with 500. Our task is to figure out the number of customers that Jane and Joe eventually secure in each scenario, and their steady-state market shares.

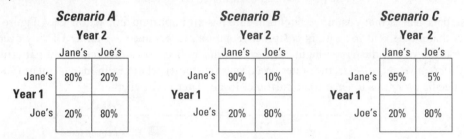

FIGURE 2.5

ILLUSTRATIVE
LONG-RUN
MARKET-SHARE
SCENARIOS

Scenario A. In year 2, Jane retains 80 percent of her year-1 customers and acquires 20 percent of Joe's. Joe's pattern is identical. This scenario is trivial, but it provides a useful baseline. Jane and Joe essentially swap equal numbers of customers back and forth. In year 2, Jane's 80 percent retention yields her 400 customers — 500 × 80% = 400 — and she acquires 100 customers from Joe — 500 × 20% = 100. Jane ends up with 500 customers (400 + 100), the same number she had originally. Joe's situation is identical. Jane and Joe each earn 50 percent long-run market share.

Scenario B. Jane does better. In year 2, she retains 90 percent of her year-1 customers — versus 80 percent in scenario A — but again, Jane acquires 20 percent of Joe's customers. Joe's retention pattern is identical to Scenario A — 80 percent — but he acquires only 10 percent of Jane's customers. Jane retains 450 of her original 500 customers — 500 × 90% = 450 — and acquires 100 customers from Joe — 500 × 20% = 100. Jane now ends up with 550 customers (450 + 100). Joe has 450 customers.

In year 3, Jane's starting customer base is higher — 550 versus 500 — so she retains 495 customers — 550 × 90% = 495. Joe's starting base is lower — 450 versus 500 — so Jane only acquires 90 of his customers — 450 × 20% = 90. But the combination of acquisition and retention increases Jane's customers from 550 to 585 (495 + 90). Joe has 415 customers. These numbers converge to a steady state where Jane and Joe have 670 and 330 customers, respectively — 67 percent and 33 percent market shares.

Jane's Retention Rate	Steady-State Market Shares	
	Jane	Joe
80%	50%	50%
90%	67%	33%
95%	80%	20%

Scenario C. Jane does even better. In year 2, she retains 95 percent of her year-1 customers and again acquires 20 percent of Joe's. Joe's retention pattern is the same as previously — 80 percent — but he acquires only 5 percent of Jane's customers. Using the same process as before, the steady-state customer numbers are 800 for Jane and 200 for Joe — 80 percent and 20 percent market shares, respectively — Table 2.3. (You may want to confirm this result for yourself. For the formula to calculate steady-state market share, see Marketing Enrichment me205.)

Marketing Question

Suppose a firm's annual revenue growth goal was 15 percent. Consider two situations:

- Customer retention rate = 80 percent
- Customer retention rate = 95 percent

What would the firm's customer acquisition rate have to be in each case? What would be the implications for the firm?

TABLE 2.3

ILLUSTRATIVE STEADY-STATE MARKET SHARES[22]

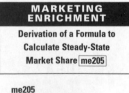

MARKETING ENRICHMENT

Derivation of a Formula to Calculate Steady-State Market Share me205

me205

To summarize:

- As retention rate increases, steady-state market share increases;
- The higher the retention rate, the greater is the impact on market share for a given increase in retention rate. For example:
  - When Jane's retention rate is 80 percent, a 10 percent increase — to 90 percent — increases her market share by 17 points — from 50 percent to 67 percent; but,
  - When Jane's retention rate is 90 percent, a 5 percent increase — to 95 percent — increases her market share by 13 points — from 67 percent to 80 percent.

Of course, it may be more expensive to improve retention rate from 90 percent to 95 percent than from 80 percent to 90 percent!

This simple exercise demonstrates an important truth — customer retention is a big deal! Relatively small differences in customer retention lead to large differences in long-run market share. Table 2.4 shows steady-state market shares for various retention and acquisition rates.

TABLE 2.4

STEADY-STATE MARKET SHARES FOR VARIOUS ACQUISITION RATES AND RETENTION RATES

Retention Rate (r)	Acquisition Rate (a)					
	5	10	15	20	25	30
60	11.1	20.0	27.3	33.3	38.5	42.9
70	14.2	25.0	33.3	40.0	45.5	50.0
80	20.0	33.3	42.9	50.0	55.6	60.0
90	33.3	50.0	60.0	66.7	71.4	75.0
95	50.0	66.7	75.0	80.0	83.3	85.7

The key implication of increased retention rate is longer customer tenure — individual customers provide sales revenues and profit margins for longer periods.[23] Table 2.5 shows this **duration effect**. Note that at high retention rates, small retention rate increases have a disproportionate impact on average customer tenure:

- When customer retention rate is 50 percent, a 30-point increase in retention rate — to 80 percent — increases average customer tenure by 3 years — from 2 years to 5 years; but,
- When customer retention rate is 90 percent, a 5-point increase in retention rate — to 95 percent — increases average customer tenure by 10 years — from 10 years to 20 years.

Boeing's relationship with Southwest Airlines (SWA) is a good example. In the early 1970s, SWA was a startup airline serving Dallas, Houston, and San Antonio, but later became the U.S.'s largest domestic airline. Boeing supplied SWA's original planes — SWA has never purchased planes from any other supplier!

TABLE 2.5

THE DURATION EFFECT: RETENTION RATE AND AVERAGE CUSTOMER TENURE

Customer Retention Rate	Average Customer Tenure
50%	2 years
75%	4 years
80%	5 years
90%	10 years
95%	20 years

PROFIT MARGINS AND CUSTOMER RETENTION

Table 2.6 combines credit card profit margin data — Figure 2.1, with customer retention data — Figure 2.3, assuming a 10 percent discount rate. We see the effect of increased profit margin over the length of the customer relationship, based on two different retention rates. Table 2.6 shows:

- When retention rate is 90 percent, total annual profit peaks at $53,460 (year 2), then declines annually. Ten-year discounted profits are **$205,721**.

- When retention rate is 80 percent, total annual profit also peaks in year 2, but at a lower figure — $42,240. Ten-year discounted profits are **$93,475**.

The 90 percent to 80 percent retention rate difference leads to a CLV difference of **$112,246** ($205,721 – $93,475).

Age of Account	Annual Profit Margin per Customer by Age of Account	90% Retention Rate			80% Retention Rate		
		Number of Customers Remaining	Total Annual Customer Profit Margin by Age of Account	Total Discounted Annual Customer Profit Margin by Age of Account	Number of Customers Remaining	Total Annual Customer Profit Margin by Age of Account	Total Discounted Annual Customer Profit Margin by Age of Account
0	–$80	1000	–$80,000	–$80,000	1000	–$80,000	–$80,000
1	$40	900	$36,000	$32,727	800	$32,000	$29,091
2	$66	810	$53,460	$44,182	640	$42,240	$34,910
3	$72	729	$52,488	$39,435	512	$36,864	$27,696
4	$79	656	$51,824	$35,396	410	$32,390	$22,123
5	$87	590	$51,330	$31,872	328	$28,536	$17,719
6	$92	531	$48,852	$27,576	262	$24,104	$13,606
7	$96	478	$45,888	$23,548	210	$20,160	$10,345
8	$99	430	$42,570	$19,859	168	$16,632	$ 7,759
9	$103	387	$39,861	$16,905	134	$13,802	$ 5,853
10	$106	348	$36,888	$14,221	107	$11,342	$ 4,373
			Total CLV	**$205,721**		**Total CLV**	**$93,475**

TABLE 2.6

PROFITS IN THE U.S. CREDIT CARD INDUSTRY AT DIFFERENT CUSTOMER RETENTION RATES

Marketing Question

Suppose a firm can sustain a 15 percent customer acquisition rate; its goal is to double the customer base. Consider two situations:

- Customer retention rate = 90 percent
- Customer retention rate = 95 percent

In each case, how many years will it take for the firm to reach its goal?

Marketing Question

What is the source of CLV for: Capital One, Domino's Pizza, Potemkin automobile dealership, and Rolls-Royce aero engines?

ACQUIRING NEW CUSTOMERS

So far, we used CLV to focus on the firm's current customers. We showed that increasing both profit margin and customer retention rate raises CLV. But what about potential future customers? How valuable are they? We can use the same approach to consider potential customers. The biggest difference is that, right now, the firm earns no revenues from these potential customers and, to attract them, it must incur an **acquisition cost (AC)**. Using the same approach as before, we include the cost to acquire these new customers:

$$CLV = m \times r/(1 + d - r) - AC$$

We now have a useful way to think about new customers. All thing equal, the firm should acquire a customer if the first term in the CLV expression, $m \times r/(1 + d - r)$, is greater than the acquisition cost (AC). If the customer acquisition cost were greater, the firm would lose money.

The actual cost to acquire new customers varies widely by company and industry. Table 2.7 shows public data on company experience in acquiring customers.

Customer acquisition costs in a petroleum industry study varied by acquisition method: personal selling — $500, direct mail — $115, telesales — $95, and e-mail and websites — $30.[24] The firm should assess acquisition costs for the various ways it secures new customers and redesign its processes accordingly. One firm found the typical sales rep's time allocation was selling — 45 percent, lead qualification — 40 percent, and administration — 15 percent. Adding telesales to supplement personal selling lowered the small-customer-acquisition cost.[25]

KEY IDEA

➤ The firm should try to acquire customers whose expected CLV is greater than the acquisition cost.

TABLE 2.7

SELECTED DATA
ON CUSTOMER
ACQUISITION COSTS

Industry	Firm	Acquisition Cost per Customer
Financial	Ameritrade	$202
	Credit card	$25 – $35 (sub-prime)
	Credit card	$75 – $150 (platinum)
	E-Trade	$475
	Lending Tree	$ 28
	Mortgage	$300 – $700
Satellite/Cable	Cable companies	$150
	Direct satellite broadcasting companies	$400
	DirecTV	$550 $670 $758 $894
	XM Satellite Radio	$123
Telecom	Nextel	$430
	Sprint	$315
Travel	Priceline.com	$8.66

* Adapted from Table 3.2, pp 54–55, S. Gupta and D.R. Lehmann, *Managing Customers as Investments*, Philadelphia, PA: Wharton, 2005.

OPTIONS FOR ADDRESSING CUSTOMERS

Much of *Managing Marketing in the 21st Century* focuses on increasing CLV from current customers and acquiring profitable new customers. From Chapter 7 on, we elaborate on the six marketing imperatives that encapsulate approaches for achieving these goals. Here, we identify a broad set of options for addressing current and potential customers — Figure 2.6.[26]

FIGURE 2.6

APPROACHES
TO IMPROVING
CUSTOMER
LIFETIME VALUE

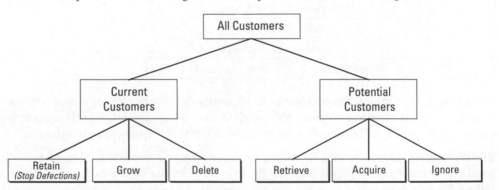

When asked to divide promotional expenses into two buckets — one for retaining current customers and one for attracting new customers — most executives report a focus on attracting new customers. Of course, new customers are critical for firm growth: The issue is one of balance. Far too often, the firm takes current customers for granted and spends too little on customer retention. Further, retaining current customers is generally less costly than acquiring new customers! We do not suggest that current customers are more important than new customers. After all, new customers may have greater growth potential. But we do believe the firm should make customer investment decisions carefully and deliberately.[27]

British cell phone operator O2 outperformed its peers, and reduced customer churn by half, in part by encouraging renewals and placing equal effort on retention and acquisition.

CURRENT CUSTOMERS

Figure 2.6 shows three firm options for addressing current customers — retain, grow, and delete.

RETAIN. The firm's customer base is like a leaky bucket; the firm should plug its holes. By updating products and services to meet evolving customer needs and taking other actions to bind customers more closely, the firm enhances customer satisfaction, increases loyalty, and reduces defections.[28] Satisfied and delighted customers are more likely to continue buying than dissatisfied customers. For its most loyal fans, The Grateful Dead's telephone hot line provided its touring schedule before any public announcement, reserved some of the best seats, and distributed tickets through a proprietary mail-order house. Wachovia Bank's (now Wells Fargo) customer satisfaction scores improved from 5.5 to 6.5 (1 to 7 scale — Gallup) over a five-year period; annual customer defection declined from 20 percent to 11 percent. In the insurance and mutual fund industries, firms try to sell extra products to existing single-product customers; increased reliance on the firm creates **lock-in.**[29] Table 2.8 shows that monthly churn for cable firm Cox Communications is less for multiple-product customers. Some firms conduct lost-customer research to identify and repair the reasons for defection. Others implement early warning systems to identify potential defectors:

> OfficeMax has a *defection detector.* Said a senior executive: "We have automatic warning signs that apply to all major customers, and then for each one there are also special warning signs that we enter manually. Has the customer gone more than 12 weeks without placing an order? Are orders becoming less frequent? Has the buyer or purchasing manager changed? Has the content or size of the average order decreased? Has the sales rep changed? There may be eight warning signs for a customer, and if five of them go off that's when our CEO gets on the plane and pays a call to see what's going on and make sure we don't lose a valuable account."[30]

Number of Products per Customer	Products Purchased	Monthly Churn Rate
1	Video only	3.0%
2	Video plus high-speed Internet	2.3%
2	Video plus phone	2.2%
2	High-speed Internet plus phone	1.9%
3	Video plus high-speed Internet plus phone	1.4%

Some firms budget **maintenance expenses** as a retention strategy by offering current customers extra services. Maintenance expenses are not trivial; they reduce the firm's profit margin from current customers. But they are often more cost-effective than having customers defect.

GROW. Satisfied customers may be willing to increase current purchases. Also, by providing good information and employee training, the firm may increase customer revenues by **cross-selling**. Your cable company provides basic channels for a standard fee, but offers *higher-value* channels like HBO and special sports events for extra fees. Amazon is a good Internet example of increasing revenues via cross-selling. Initially, Amazon offered books, then CDs, and now sells a vast array of different products, enabling and personalizing one-stop shopping. Actually, Amazon has two types of marketing effort: Type 1 attracts customers to its website through targeted offerings; type 2 encourages visitors to explore the site for new items, driving multiple purchases and enhanced customer satisfaction.[31]

DELETE. Generally, the firm tries to retain and grow current customers so as to increase profit margins. But some customers are not worth having. Sprint Nextel disconnected 1,000 subscribers who called customer service excessively; Marsh & McLennan (insurance brokers) terminated thousands of clients; and many local newspapers, like the *Atlanta Journal-*

Marketing Question

Suppose your research for the local restaurant (Marketing Question, p. 35) reveals that customer retention is suffering because the restaurant is too crowded. What options would you suggest to reduce the number of walk-in customers?

TABLE 2.8

CHURN RATES FOR COX COMMUNICATIONS

KEY IDEA

➤ The firm's options for addressing current customers are:
- Retain
- Grow
- Delete

Constitution, reduced geographic delivery footprints. Most firms have unprofitable customers and should seriously evaluate ending these relationships, taking care to avoid potentially negative word of mouth. We address customer deletion in the next section.

POTENTIAL CUSTOMERS

Potential customers offer an excellent way for the firm to grow. But as we learned earlier, not all customers are alike. Returning to Figure 2.6, we discuss three broad options for addressing potential customers — retrieve, acquire, and ignore.

RETRIEVE. All firms have customers that defect; the prior relationship makes them *winback* opportunities. These customers are a special category because the firm often has more information about them than about other potential customers. The firm knows (or can find out) what they purchased, what they spent, how they make decisions, why they left, and other data that can help the firm serve them again. The video rental firm Netflix has a targeted **winback** program. If the firm understands why customers defect, winbacks can improve.

ACQUIRE. To reach sales and profit goals, most firms must acquire profitable new customers. Sometimes the firm seeks customers with similar characteristics to current customers — other times it wants very different customers. Regardless, the firm should be selective in its marketing efforts so as to acquire the *right* customers — customers with positive CLV.[32]

Some firms have well-developed systems for accepting/rejecting customers. In the credit card and insurance industries, firms use extensive databases on customer demographics and past behavior to make accept/reject decisions.[33] Most venture capital firms conduct extensive analyses of potential investment opportunities, accepting only a small fraction. Flextronics (leading electronics contract manufacturer) conducts similarly detailed analyses to select the few customers it believes will be successful.

Four major approaches for acquiring customers are:

- **Independent marketing activities.** Most firms use communications to reach potential customers and persuade them to buy products and services. AT&T, GM, P&G, Time Warner, and others spend immense sums on advertising; life insurance firms like AXA and New York Life place major resources into personal selling. So do FedEx, Xerox, and many others. We discuss these and other approaches later in the book.

- **Affiliations.** The firm makes formal or informal relationships with individuals or other organizations to feed it customers. Informal relationships are very common in the service sector. General medical practitioners feed patients to specialist physicians; specialist consulting firms feed clients to consultants with different specialties. Some firms formalize this process by paying directly for delivered customers. Amazon has more than one million *affiliate* relationships that send customers to its website.

- **Channel strategies.** Rather than approach potential customers directly, the firm works through third parties like agents, brokers, and distributors. In the late 1990s, Cisco made 85 percent of sales direct to customers; today, it makes 85 percent of sales though distributors and value-added resellers (Opening Case Chapter 18).

- **Firm and business-unit acquisitions.** Regardless of purpose, whenever the firm completes a merger or acquisition, it acquires customers. But firms make some acquisitions — like cable TV franchises and credit card portfolios (Bank of America's MBNA acquisition) — for this specific purpose.

IGNORE. The firm must decide on desirable customer characteristics and make investments in potential customers that bring value. By the same token, it should ignore customers that do not possess these favorable characteristics. Bottom line: The firm must be selective in making investments to secure potential customers.

KEY IDEA

➤ The firm's options for addressing potential customers are:
- Retrieve
- Acquire
- Ignore

Marketing Question

Think of a local business. What approaches does it use to acquire customers? What alternative approaches could it implement?

BEING SELECTIVE ABOUT CUSTOMERS

Many customers bring value to the firm, but some do not. Quantifying customer value is important in understanding how to identify customers the firm wants to serve, and develop options for addressing unwelcome customers.[34]

CUSTOMER PROFITABILITY

Most firms understand and measure product profitability — revenues minus costs for individual products. Product profit is a key metric for most product managers. Many firms invest heavily in sophisticated accounting systems and data analysis tools that help answer questions like:

- Are our current products profitable?
- Shall we discontinue this old product and, if so, when?
- Shall we introduce a new product?[35]

By contrast, few firms can answer equivalent questions about customers. This failure is especially critical in multi-business and multinational firms. Profitability data typically reside in individual businesses and geographies whose systems do not interface with one another. Hence, there is no easy way to extract and integrate sales and profit data for individual customers across businesses and geographies.

Indeed, several different businesses and/or geographies may have the same customer, but not know it! Full-line insurance companies are a good example. If you or your parents have automobile, homeowner's, and life insurance from the same firm, try getting a single annual bill. Impossible! Each business typically acts independently and does not share customer data. Consider the following: A business executive regularly entertained clients at a top-level restaurant in his home city. He called the restaurant's catering division to arrange for his daughter's wedding. Catering did not know who he was and gave him no special consideration. Unsurprisingly, he started to take his clients elsewhere!

The firm's inability to measure **customer profitability** stands in sharp contrast to treating customers as assets and CLV. Product profitability is important, but products and services are only a means to attract, retain, and grow customers. To paraphrase an old management saying: "If you can't measure it, you can't manage it!"

> At TreeCo Paper (disguised name) the top ten customers generated 70 percent of revenues. Detailed analysis showed that three of these customers were unprofitable. At contract renewal time, TreeCo offered sales incentives to *lose* contracts with these customers. Six months later, senior management said: "Revenues are down, but profits are way up."[36]

When customers purchase products and services, the firm earns sales revenues; unfortunately, most firms have some unprofitable customers. The firm must examine the relevant metrics across products to assess whether or not customers are profitable. In other words, are revenues greater than costs?

Firms use a variety of methods to gather and assess data relevant to customer activity and profitability, notably via CRM systems. We explore CRM later in the chapter.

When firms examine revenues, costs, and profits by customer, they often find an **80:20 rule**: 80 percent of revenues come from 20 percent of customers. Of course, this rule is not absolute, but is a better working hypothesis than assuming all customers have similar revenue/profit relationships. Some firms have even more skewed revenue distributions. A major magazine publisher found a 90:10 pattern: 90 percent of revenues from 10 percent of customers! We have even seen 95:5 ratios. The firm's strategic (key) accounts can be very profitable and many firms have installed account management systems to serve them — Chapter 17. Losing a strategic account to a competitor or from bankruptcy can be serious. When $9.5 billion hedge fund Amaranth

KEY IDEA

➤ Measuring product profitability is insufficient; the firm should develop systems for measuring customer profitability.

Demonstrating Customer Profitability

Table 2.9 shows how to convert product profits into customer profits. Suppose the firm's three businesses, each with its own sales and service operation, sell three products (X, Y, and Z) to a large customer:

- **Sales revenues.** Sales revenues for products X, Y, and Z are respectively $4M, $5M, and $6M — total sales revenues = $15M.

- **Gross margin.** The firm makes a positive gross margin of $1.5 million on each product — total gross margin = $4.5 million.

- **Profits.** The firm makes profits of $125K and $50K respectively on products Y and Z — it loses $500K on product X. Overall, the firm loses $325K on this customer, despite $15M sales revenues.[37]

TABLE 2.9

FROM PRODUCT PROFITS TO CUSTOMER PROFITS ($000s)

	Product X	Product Y	Product Z	Total
Sales revenues	4,000	5,000	6,000	15,000
Cost of goods sold	2,500	3,500	4,500	10,500
Gross margin	1,500	1,500	1,500	4,500
Selling expenses	750	275	150	1,175
Service expenses	500	600	700	1,800
Additional expenses	750	500	600	1,850
Profit	(500)	125	50	(325)

Note that these same products may be more profitable with other customers: Production lot sizes may be larger, prices may be higher, and selling, service, and/or additional expenses may be lower.

Advisors closed, it voided contracts on 221 Bloomberg terminals, an expensive loss for Bloomberg.

In the ten years after 1995, Illinois Tool Works (ITW) acquired more than 200 firms. ITW developed and successfully implemented an 80:20 process — each business-unit manager focused exclusively on the 20 percent of customers providing 80 percent of revenues. From 2000 to 2005, ITW increased the average operating margin of its acquired firms from 9 percent to 19 percent; revenue per employee increased 50 percent, and net income doubled.

BrainQUICKEN (online sports-nutrition supplements) sold products through 120 wholesalers. Founder Tim Ferriss discovered that 5 wholesalers produced more than 90 percent of profits, yet he was spending 90 percent of effort on the other 115. Ferriss switched effort to his profitable five and added several others with similar profitability profiles.

KEY IDEA

➤ At many firms, 20 percent of customers provide 80 percent of revenues and 120 percent of profits.

➤ At these same firms, 80 percent of customers provide 20 percent of revenues and reduce profits by 20 percent.

Returning to the 80:20 rule, the converse analogue is the **20:80 rule**; 20 percent of revenues from 80 percent of customers. This rule raises two critical yet related questions:

- What does it cost the firm to serve these customers?
- Is it profitable to serve these customers? If not, what action should the firm take?

Frequently, firms find that these costs are very high and many customers are unprofitable. Some firms use extended rules — the **80:20:120 rule** and the **20:80:20 rule**!

- **80:20:120** — 80 percent of revenues from 20 percent of customers; these customers provide 120 percent of firm profits.
- **20:80:20** — 20 percent of revenues from 80 percent of customers; these customers reduce firm profits by 20 percent.

Some examples: In the Opening Case, 17 percent of RBC's customers accounted for 93 percent of profits[38]; at a major media company, 17 of 1,017 advertisers accounted for *all* profits; a major software company found only 7 of 307 customers were profitable; and Marsh & McLennan's insurance brokerage unit lost money on about a quarter of its clients. One study found similar CLV distributions for B2B and B2C firms — Figure 2.7.[39]

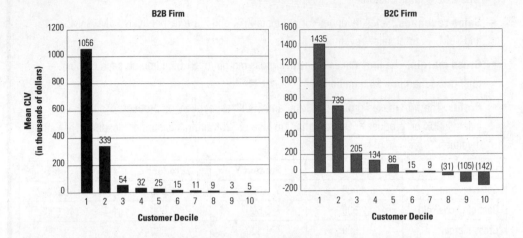

FIGURE 2.7

CUSTOMER LIFETIME VALUE DISTRIBUTIONS FOR B2B AND B2C FIRMS BY CUSTOMER DECILE

We should not forget that unprofitable customers may be small or large. Unprofitable small customers typically provide insufficient revenues to offset the costs to serve. By contrast, revenues from large customers may be high, but they require expensive customization and/or service support. They may also bargain down prices below sustainable levels.

The firm has two broad options for addressing currently low-profit or unprofitable customers — invest for the future or reduce resource commitment:

- **Invest for the future.** Two types of customer may have significant potential: small organizations that may grow — think Google in 1995; and large organizations where the firm is currently unsuccessful. Citicorp consistently targets a few large firms like these; each receives a structured two-year program for attempted conversion into a profitable customer.

- **Reduce resource commitment.** Essentially, the firm has two options:

  - **New communications strategy.** The firm may switch an on-the-road sales force to telesales. In Scandinavia, Reebok made this change to address *mom-and-pop* shoe retailers. Regular contact became weekly (versus monthly); the tele-salesperson was always available to answer questions; customer satisfaction improved; and Reebok cut costs. Internet and e-mail approaches also reduce costs, and combination Internet and telesales that direct website visitors to a salesperson can be especially effective.

  - **Hand-off to third parties.** In many industries, third parties like agents, brokers, contract sales forces, distributors, and value-added resellers conduct the firm's selling efforts. They often have lower fixed costs such that unprofitable customers for the firm become profitable for third parties. But,

    - Customers that object to losing field salespeople may shift business to competitors.

    - Over time the firm's third-party organization may grow customer revenues. The now-successful customer wants a direct relationship with the firm. Yet this switch would cut out the third party and negatively affect its relationship with the firm.

- **Fire customers.** The firm stops selling to loss-making customers with little potential.[40] Profitability may increase, but firing customers may generate negative word of mouth.

A critical firm challenge is to correctly identify the *right* customers. After all, today's unprofitable customers could be tomorrow's big winners. Also, unprofitable large customers may carry significant overhead allocations; eliminating them lowers overall profits because the overhead remains.[41]

> ### Marketing Question
>
> You learn from an internal report that 20 percent of your firm's customers provide 80 percent of profits but that these customers' retention rate is slipping. Can you develop a list of potential actions to halt these defections?

Deciding how to deal with today's unprofitable and least profitable customers is a tricky matter. Creative approaches may increase current profits and/or generate profitable future customers. The following boxed insert and Figure 2.8 show how changes in customer classification helped a financial services firm to better isolate customer profitability and improve overall profits.[42]

A Financial Services Firm Classifies Customers by Profitability

Simpson Inc. (fictional financial services firm) traditionally classified customers by account balances and demographic characteristics. Simpson developed four different customer groups: *upscale* — age over 45 years, balances more than $60K; *prime* — age over 45 years; *emergent* — balances less than $60K, age under 45 years; and *small business*. Simpson based its marketing efforts on these groups.

The incoming marketing director believed that this classification provided few insights into customer buying behavior. Figure 2.8 shows that each group was profitable, but the director believed that some customers were unprofitable.

The director developed a totally new classification that also contained four groups: *heavy hitters* — long-term customers with high balances and high activity; *comfortables* — long-term customers with high balances and low activity; *growers* — newer customers with low activity; and *movers* — newer customers with high activity. Figure 2.8 shows a markedly different profitability pattern. In particular, *movers* were unprofitable.

Simpson implemented two key decisions. First, it raised prices for products purchased largely by *movers*. It reduced the number of high-activity customers — the remaining movers were profitable. Second, it developed a targeting scheme to acquire more *heavy hitters*.

FIGURE 2.8

CUSTOMER CLASSIFICATION BY A FINANCIAL SERVICES FIRM

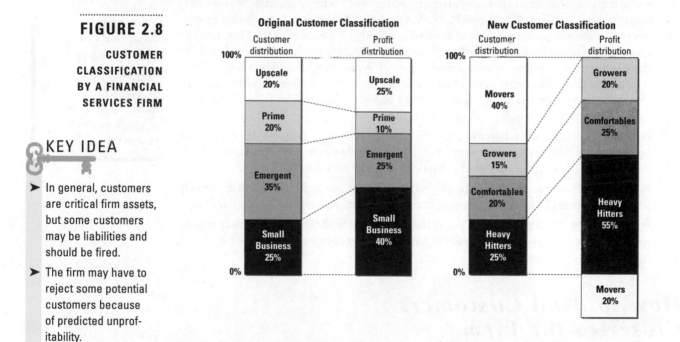

KEY IDEA

➤ In general, customers are critical firm assets, but some customers may be liabilities and should be fired.

➤ The firm may have to reject some potential customers because of predicted unprofitability.

CUSTOMER SUITABILITY

Best Buy (BB) implemented a strategy to avoid several types of undesirable customers. According to CEO Brad Anderson, BB's worst customers "can wreak enormous economic havoc." These customers follow various strategies. They buy products, apply for rebates, return purchases, and then buy back the products at returned-merchandise discounts. They purchase large quantities of loss leaders and clearance items, then resell them on eBay. They also secure the lowest price quotes from websites, then demand that Best Buy honor its lowest-price pledge.[43]

Unprofitable customers do not deliver value. But the firm may cease doing business with a current customer or forgo a potential customer for other reasons:

- **Capacity constraints.** The firm may have insufficient ability — expertise, financial resources, physical capacity — to serve all its customers. When the Sarbanes-Oxley Act vastly increased compliance requirements for large public companies, some accounting firms dropped many smaller clients.[44] Failure to match firm resources to customer needs can lead to dissatisfaction, monetary losses, and harmful word of mouth.[45] EDS (now part of HP) had great difficulty performing on an $8.8 billion computer modernization contract with the U.S. Navy, resulting in significant losses.

- **Competition.** The customer is a current or potential competitor that could reverse engineer the firm's product, then launch its own. Hi-tech firms often refuse to sell to competitors; they also stop customers from passing on their products.

- **Evolving strategy.** If the firm shifts direction, drops products, or divests a business, it sheds customers as a byproduct of strategic change.

- **Foreclosing options.** The customer prohibits the firm from serving other customers. A P&G advertising agency is unlikely to work for Colgate or Unilever![46]

- **Impact on the firm's reputation.** A firm/customer relationship negatively affects the firm's brand image: Can you find Gucci in Kmart? Or the customer may use the firm's product inappropriately, leading to aggravation, negative word of mouth, and/or financial loss.

- **Impact on the offer.** In many service businesses, fellow customers are integral to the offer. Bad behavior by some customers reduces the value for all customers and can negatively affect employee morale. Rowdy sports fans negatively affect the ambiance in expensive restaurants; college admissions departments screen out many applicants. Specific customer profiles the firm should avoid include: *cheats* — like Best Buy faces (boxed insert); *thieves* — like pickpockets and shoplifters who rob other customers or the firm; *belligerents* — like diners who display insufficient patience in waiting for their meals and verbally abuse waiters; *family feuders* — a sub-category of *belligerents* who fight among themselves; *vandals* — who destroy equipment; and *rule breakers* — like unruly airline passengers who pose a physical danger and affect the service experience for fellow customers. Customers who behave badly also raise firm costs.[47]

- **Instability.** The customer may be profitable but too unstable. People-intensive service businesses like advertising or PR agencies often add employees to serve new customers. If those customers left, necessary staff reductions could be very difficult.

- **Non-payer.** This customer would be profitable if it paid, but it doesn't! Or it eventually pays, but the collection costs — money, human resources, aggravation — are too high.

- **Potential costs.** The future costs of doing business are too high. The customer may require costly customization, or the firm believes future servicing costs will be prohibitive.

How to Bind Customers Closer to the Firm

CUSTOMER RELATIONSHIP MANAGEMENT

A customer relationship comprises the series of over-time interactions or *touch points* between the customer and the firm. **Customer relationship management (CRM)** (relationship marketing) manages these *touch points*. More precisely, CRM is *the ongoing process of identifying and creating new value with individual customers and sharing these benefits over a lifetime of association with them*.[48] CRM helps the firm *know* its customers better. In B2C, mom-and-pop stores often form personal relationships with customers; CRM helps large firms build relationships in

Marketing Question

Which companies do you believe affirmatively seek to fire and/or reject customers? Are they successful in pursuing these activities? What firms inadvertently fire and/or reject *good* customers?

KEY IDEA

➤ Poor profitability is not the only reason to fire current customers or reject potential customers.

Marketing Question

What economic value do you offer to your educational institution? How might the institution enhance this value?

a systematic way. Strong relationships should drive customer purchases over a long time period. Tesco, the leading British supermarket, has a very successful CRM program:

Tesco has 2,700 stores in Britain (5,400 worldwide) — more than 30 percent market share of retail food sales and 13 percent market share of all retail sales. Tesco lives its catch phrase — "every little helps" — by removing irritants in the shopping experience. Tesco tackled queues, improved product availability, introduced a *Value* product line, and refurbished stores. A critical element in Tesco's success is Clubcard: Tesco collects data on customer purchases, then makes highly segmented offers based on customer needs. Said Tesco CEO Sir Terry Leahy, "The customers get what they want, not what some 'bod' in head office wants."[49]

CRM's underlying rationale is CLV — forming *mutually beneficial relationships* is crucial. CRM systems are only really successful in firms with a true external orientation.[50] Unfortunately, many firms invest millions of dollars in CRM programs but do not realize the promised benefits. Three issues are crucial for success:

- **Objectives.** The firm must be clear about CRM system objectives. Without good direction, the firm cannot select from myriad initiatives, and costs can easily spiral out of control.[51]
- **Customer benefits.** The CRM system must provide benefits and value to customers — new products and services, attractive offers, high customer service levels — and to the firm. Many firms focus on firm value, often by cutting costs, but give short shrift to customer value. The CRM system must drive *mutually* beneficial relationships with customers.
- **Technology.** Many people believe extensive databases and advanced information technology underpin CRM systems. Of course, technology, customer databases, and **data-mining** often play important roles. But CRM is not about technology. To repeat, CRM is about forming *mutually beneficial relationships* with customers.[52]

DEVELOPING A CRM SYSTEM

Customer databases for effective CRM systems must be accessible, accurate, complete, consistent, current, relevant, secure, and structured. According to one expert, "To implement CRM, a firm must have an integrated database available at every customer *touch point* and analyze that data well. ... [CRM] allows companies to automate the way they interact with their customers and to communicate with relevant, timely messages."[53] A large firm's database contains longitudinal (overtime) data, including responses to promotional campaigns, on millions of customers — even prospective customers. Royal Bank of Canada maintains data on rejected loan applicants, periodically reviews credit status, and offers credit when improvement is significant.

Adding state-of-the-art **data-mining** technology in the context of a *test-and-learn* culture secures and manipulates these data to yield marketing insight. Capital One's expertise has shaken up the credit card industry, and Harrah's (casinos and hotels) has achieved marked success. Communications with customers are more personal, and the firm can mass-customize its offers. Direct marketer Fingerhut maintains 100 pages of data per customer, mostly about buying habits.[54] Customer data is equally important for firms with few customers, like your local dry cleaner or garage — paper and pencil may be adequate technology.

The firm must identify each customer. In some service industries, customer databases are fundamental to formal relationships, like bank accounts, insurance policies, and telephone service. But these firms often collect and store data by account or policy number, rather than by customer. Hence, the best customers — those who buy multiple services — escape firm attention. Many firms neither collect a full set of customer data nor use it for building long-term relationships. At other firms, marketing data resides in the transactional sales/invoice system, not in a longitudinal and relationship-based form. Many retailers do not know who buys their products — hence, the introduction of customer value cards:

Smitty's Super Value (SSV) is a Phoenix-based regional hypermarket chain. SSV offers a full range of grocery, clothing, electrical, and household goods in a very competitive market. *Smitty's Shoppers Passport* is a magnetic card swiped at checkout. On average, 60 percent of SSV's 750,000 cardholders use their cards every six weeks, earning points they can redeem from SSV's gift catalog. SSV uses *Shoppers Passport* data to selectively mail customers coupons, magazines, and other information. Families with children under 13 receive coupons for toys, videos, clothes, and cakes three weeks before the child's birthday. Customers whose purchases change or decline receive special mailings. The *Shoppers Passport* is fully integrated into the business; startup costs were 20 percent of sales, but maintenance costs are less than 1 percent of sales. Results are spectacular. Cardholders account for 70 percent of sales — purchases are 50 percent higher than for non-cardholders.[55]

For suppliers, identifying customers that purchase from intermediaries like distributors or retailers can be difficult. Indirect methods include customer-get-customer campaigns, customer value cards, factory warranties, loyalty cards, mail inserts, special events, syndicated questionnaires, telephone help lines, third-party lifestyle databases, and websites — supplemented by data from marketing information firms. Many firms spend highly to develop customer databases. Table 2.10 identifies the sorts of data required[56]:

- **Customer characteristics.** Demographic data independent of the firm: B2C — name, gender, age, family size (birth dates), address; B2B — sales revenues, number of employees, age of organization, industry, decision-makers, influencers.

- **Customer responses to firm decisions.** Purchases following sales promotions, direct marketing offers, price changes — also perceptions and preferences (from research).

- **Customer contact history.** B2C — phone calls for product information, customer service requests; B2B — deliveries, sales calls, technical service.

- **Customer purchase history.** What was purchased — by SKU; when; by what method — cash or credit; through what intermediary (if any); what price and/or discounts; how and when delivered. Data should include firm profit margins per purchase.

- **Customer value to the firm.** Data for assessing CLV, like purchase history.

Customer Identifier	Customer Characteristics	Customer Responses to Firm Decisions	Customer Contact History	Customer Purchase History	Customer Value to the Firm
Jane Doe					
John Smith					
Name					
Name					
Name					
XYZ Inc.					
DEF Inc.					
Company					
Company					
Company					

TABLE 2.10

THE CUSTOMER DATABASE

Marketing Question

CVS/Caremart (CC) is the U.S.'s largest single buyer and dispenser of prescription drugs. What actions could CC take to help reduce national healthcare costs?

The database should be sufficiently flexible to follow individuals and track life changes. In B2C, consumers move houses and cities, and change jobs, marital status, names, and family size; needs also change.[57] In B2B, employees change jobs within firms, change firms, and have changing business and individual needs. Every customer response, contact, and purchase deserves an entry. But the firm should not limit itself to data on its own customer relationships; it should also seek data on its customers' relationships with its competitors. An equipment provider should know the age and equipment types installed at the customer by *all* providers. A financial services firm should collect data on its customers' relationships with other suppliers. These data may be available direct from customers or from third-party data providers.

FinSer Inc. (FI) (disguised name) became market leader in cross-selling. FI developed new lead-identification guidelines for service reps (SR); SRs entered leads into a lead-tracking system that routed them to the appropriate sales reps.

Cell Inc.'s (CI) (disguised name) website received five million unique visitors monthly; 10,000 purchased cell phones, but 27,000 started a purchase process, then quit. By collecting and passing these data to sales teams, CI secured 8,000 additional subscribers per month. CI also followed up on the 20 percent of visitors who left contact information; CI added an additional 35,000 new subscribers monthly.

CONTROL OF, AND ACCESS TO, THE CUSTOMER DATABASE

KEY IDEA

➤ Superior customer databases are accessible, accurate, complete, consistent, current, relevant, secure, and structured.

➤ The customer database should distinguish among customers on behavioral measures and value to the firm.

➤ Customer databases are more valuable when they also contain data about relationships with competitors.

Control of, and access to, the customer database are critical issues. Consider a firm with several businesses — each product group or business may have its own customer database. When there is little customer overlap across product groups/businesses, independent databases work fine. But when customer overlap is considerable, a corporate-level database that integrates all customer information makes more sense. Regardless, individual businesses may not be pleased. They may fear competition from sister businesses and/or be concerned how other businesses may use their valuable data: Internecine territorial disputes often impede cross-selling initiatives. Top managers must strongly support the corporate-level database; they must also gain agreement on use — for sales, customer service, or collections; on control; and on access at the appropriately aggregated level.[58] If building a corporate-level database is infeasible, the firm should at least implement processes that cross organizational boundaries.

A well-developed customer database is valuable to the firm and others. Many firms earn significant revenues by selling customer data to non-competitors. But privacy is a serious concern: jetBlue, Northwest, and American Airlines provided passenger records to firms with U.S. government contracts, causing an outcry of negative publicity. Personal data theft is also an issue: Sony's PlayStation network suffered an "unauthorized and illegal intrusion," potentially affecting millions of customers.

The firm must carefully think through its privacy policy. Some firms like Amazon and UPS absolutely refuse to sell customer data. Said an Amazon spokesperson, "We don't want to create an enormous database that becomes a public relations risk or something that offends our customers. We believe that we have done well because of the trust customers have for Amazon and their belief that our privacy policies are taken very seriously. It's partly a moral point of view, but it's also a sensible business decision."[59]

19th-Century National Politics

Foreign Affairs Minister, Austro-Hungarian Empire — Klemens Furst Von Metternich: "I don't care who the King is as long as I control the purse strings."

21st-Century IBM Politics

Senior IBM Executive: "I don't care who the CEO is, as long as I control the customer databases."

ASSESSING THE VALUE OF CUSTOMERS AND DESIGNING FIRM ACTIONS

The firm implementing CRM well acts with significantly greater focus. The firm estimates profitability and CLV by customer, anticipates key customer events, and initiates action. A B2C firm may send consumers vacation ideas; a B2B firm may alert customers that ordering seasonal stock can add value. The more comprehensive the customer database, and the more creative the firm, the more valuable will be its initiatives. The firm can offer new products and services and give greater customer service to its more valuable and loyal customers. In making offers, the firm must be concerned about the **communications tipping point** — the level after which communications create customer resentment. Amazon spends significant effort to identify its tipping point. Figure 2.9 suggests firm objectives and actions, based on customer value and loyalty.

Customer Value

High	**Objective:** Switch customers from competitors to high-value/high-loyalty group **Action:** Sampling and targeted sales promotion to gain trial, then loyalty/reward programs	**Objective:** Customer retention **Action:** Targeted customer loyalty/reward programs
Low	**Objective:** No special objective **Action:** No special effort	**Objective:** Increase purchases **Action:** Cross-sell other products
	Low	**High**

Customer Loyalty

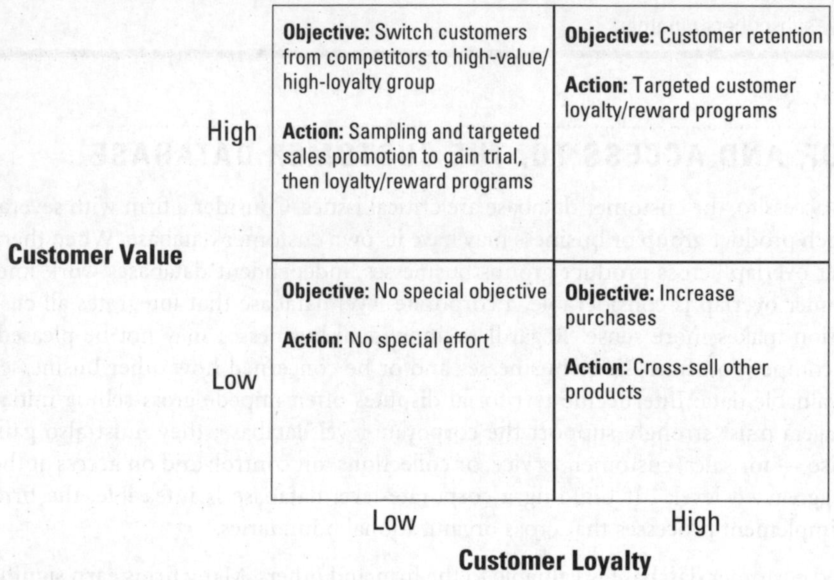

FIGURE 2.9

CUSTOMER VALUE AND LOYALTY

High-value, high-loyalty customers are very important, yet some firms offer better service to low-value customers. Express checkout lanes in supermarkets often reward customers who make few purchases. The Fairway supermarket on New York's Upper West Side strives to cut waiting time for all customers.

EVENT-DRIVEN MARKETING[60]

Firms experienced in CRM identify events in their customers' lives that provide communication opportunities to enhance the relationship and/or make sales. A simple threefold classification comprises triggers, scheduled events, and significant events.[61]

- **Triggers.** Do not require a customer decision but are often valuable for activating straightforward business processes, like credit card expiry (send a new card) or reaching a pre-determined inventory level (reorder).

- **Scheduled events.** Provide the firm communication opportunities, like the end of a contract (offer/negotiate new contract), birthdays and anniversaries (congratulatory communications), and graduation. They provide sales opportunities for some firms — Hallmark develops/maintains birthday/anniversary data for offering customers greeting cards and e-cards.

- **Significant events.** Represent significant changes in customer life stage, like marriage, divorce, first child, first job, first apartment, and relocation. Customers are often responsive to receiving communications when these events occur but firms have difficulty identifying them.

Austra Bank (disguised name) uses high-powered CRM systems to identify indicators of significant events. Twice daily, Austra examines its five-million-consumer database against a set of predefined criteria like exceptionally large deposits, salary cessation, and criteria combinations. A four-person call center makes telephone calls to identified customers. Austra claims that over 50 percent of calls lead to sales and that all customers value the personal contact.[62] For Bunca Bank (disguised name), many middle-market firms are potential customers, but they are reluctant to switch banks because of administrative hassle. Bunca identified three events that increase the probability of a firm switching banks: The current bank merges and the firm anticipates painful bank integration; the firm has rapid growth and requires new and better services; and a new leadership team wants to make its mark.[63]

Centura Banks (Raleigh, NC) rates two million customers on a 1-to-5 profitability scale. High-value customers receive several service calls annually, plus a *happy holidays* call from the CEO. In four years, customer attrition dropped 50 percent. Less-valued customers receive less service — unprofitable customers dropped from 27 to 21 percent.

CUSTOMER LOYALTY PROGRAMS

Loyalty is a customer's sustained commitment to the firm demonstrated by repeat purchase and positive word of mouth. **Loyalty programs**, designed to retain customers and improve loyalty, are a central part of many CRM systems. All loyalty programs have a similar structure: Customers earn rewards by purchasing goods and services (examples below). Some programs are simple, like JCPenney's *baker's dozen: Buy 12 panties, get the 13th free*. Other programs, like airline frequent flier and hotel and credit card loyalty, involve complex, multi-tiered incentives;[64] higher tiers earn greater rewards, but customer demotion to lower tiers may jeopardize loyalty.[65] Complex programs use currencies such as *points* that customers exchange for various rewards. Some programs, like AmEx's Membership Rewards, are well designed; others fail — like an AT&T points program for consumer long distance — or are too generous.[66] Program designers must consider value both for the customer and the firm to establish successful programs.[67]

Examples of Loyalty Programs

King Soopers — Consumers automatically earn members-only discounts when they pay with the 1-2-3 Rewards Visa card. They also earn points towards free groceries.

Recyclebank — Members act *green*, like pledging to recycle beverage containers and sell or recycle used electronic products. They receive free offers, and earn points to apply to grocery and entertainment purchases and discounts at various retailers.

Saks Fifth Avenue's — *SaksFirst*. Members earn points for each $1 charged on Saks Fifth Avenue MasterCard at Saks stores, Folio catalog, and *www.saksfifthavenue.com*. They earn double points for dining and essentials like groceries and gasoline, and triple points for purchases at salons and spas.

Tesco — *Club Card Loyalty Program*. All Internet customers and 90 percent of store customers belong. Tesco uses 13 market segments to tailor store inventory and creates up to eight million coupon variations for Club Card mailings.

United Airlines — *MileagePlus Program*. Members earn award miles by flying on United and companion airlines, and by purchasing products and services from partners worldwide. Members use award miles for travel, hotel and car rental, plus a wide variety of everyday purchases and activities.

VALUE OF REWARDS PROGRAMS TO CUSTOMERS

Designing a customer-loyalty program can be complicated. Design considerations include:

- **Rate of earning?** Should the reward design be *equal* or *accelerated* earning? For a vacation package reward, should the customer earn the same *points* for each dollar spent? Or should she earn more points per dollar the closer she is to the goal?

- **Aspirational value of the reward.** Two rewards can have the same cash value but different psychological value — like groceries versus vacation travel. Consumers engage in **mental accounting** by placing funds and resources in different mental accounts — Chapter 4. AmEx Membership Rewards program offers airline travel, cruises, hotel stays, and many luxury products.

- **Cash value of the reward.** The reward should offer real economic value. Some programs, like the Discover card, pay cash; airline frequent flier programs provide free travel.

- **Deterministic or probabilistic rewards.** Many reward programs are **deterministic** — the customer accumulates *points*, then collects the reward. In **probabilistic** programs, the customer wins a large reward, or nothing. Internet portal *iWon* used sweepstakes entries. *McDonald's monopoly game* had both reward types. Customers won sweepstakes prizes but could also exchange *Collect & Win Game Stamps* for certain rewards.

- **Ease of collecting the reward.** The customer must be able to redeem the reward. Airlines face criticism for blocking rewards on some routes. On other routes they offer so few reward seats that large families cannot travel together.

- **Length of time to earn the reward.** Many consumers engage in **hyperbolic discounting** — Chapter 4. The design question for reward programs is: Should the program have smaller rewards earned frequently or larger, delayed rewards? Many airlines and AmEx Membership Rewards program alleviate the problem by providing data on progress to the reward goal. The firm can also use reminders, or periodically provide small rewards to keep customers engaged.

- **Rewards based on the firm's product and services, or a broad variety.** Some programs reward customers with their own products and services. *Buy X, get one free* programs are ubiquitous — BestBuy and Subway. Many small firms use these programs, often by punching out a card with each purchase. The alternative is to partner and offer many different rewards, like AmEx Membership Rewards program.

- **Soft versus hard rewards. Hard rewards** are denominated in dollars and cents or translatable points. **Soft rewards** include toll-free information numbers, restaurant seating, theater ticket availability, and hotel room and airline seat upgrades.

- **Type of reward.** Should the reward be *cash* or *products and services*? The Discover program now includes frequent flier miles and goods and services. Should entry into the reward program be free? A fee may discourage entry, but encourage commitment.

VALUE OF THE REWARDS PROGRAM TO THE FIRM

A well-designed loyalty program decreases customer defection, increases customer retention, and enhances share of wallet. Specific benefits for the firm include:

- Creates barriers for competitors.
- Gains insight into customer behavior.
- Lowers costs to serve loyal customers.
- Makes loyal customers less price sensitive.
- Encourages loyal customers to spend more.
- Stimulates loyal customers to spread positive word of mouth.
- Increases sales via purchase acceleration as customers approach the goal.[68]

Marketing Question

Go to *www.colloquy.com* to learn more about loyalty programs. You have to register, but it's free. Which loyalty programs are especially good deals for customers? Why?

Marketing Question

Many students have low incomes. But your educational investment may lead to high future income. Which firms understand that and actively seek your business with an eye to your future? How do they do so? Which firms seem oblivious?

KEY IDEA

➤ The firm should examine its privacy policy for the impact on customer relationships.

➤ Customer loyalty programs have many design parameters.

The firm should assess loyalty programs via hard-nosed financial analysis, but this can be difficult. First, assessing potential revenues is not simple. Second, some costs — like launching, creating, and maintaining the database; issuing status reports on earned rewards; and the cost of rewards — are highly visible. But managerial opportunity costs versus other activities are less easy to identify. Further, the firm should consider both purchase quantity and loyalty: A totally loyal customer who buys infrequently may not be very valuable. The firm should evaluate loyalty programs against alternative spending like increased advertising, better customer service, and/or lower prices. Loyalty programs have value, but are just one of many revenue-generating tools at the firm's disposal.[69]

Marketing Question

What other messages did you glean from this chapter?

KEY MESSAGES

- Customer lifetime value (CLV) is the critical link between delivering value to customers and creating value for the firm and its shareholders.
- The firm improves CLV by increasing profit margin (m) and customer retention rate (r), and decreasing discount rate (d).
- Increasing customer retention rate (r) has greater leverage on CLV than decreasing discount rate (d).
- The firm has three broad options for addressing current customers — retain, grow, and delete.
- The firm has three broad options for addressing potential customers — retrieve, acquire, and ignore.
- The firm should strive to understand the reasons for customer retention and defection and act accordingly.
- Some of the firm's current customers are probably unprofitable — but a fraction of these may present future opportunities.
- The firm may forgo a customer relationship for reasons other than poor profitability.
- A well-designed customer relationship management (CRM) system deepen the firm's knowledge about its customers.
- Understanding customer value to the firm and customer loyalty allows the firm to design effective loyalty programs.

VIDEOS AND AUDIOS

Loyalty Programs   v202 🎥   Ran Kivetz   Columbia Business School

v202

QUESTIONS FOR STUDY AND DISCUSSION

Can you answer the questions implied by this chapter's learning objectives? Check!

1. A cable company spends on average $600 to acquire a customer. Annual maintenance costs per customer — $45; record-keeping and billing costs — $30 per customer per annum. Price of a basic service package — $30 per month. Typically, 40 percent of customers buy a premium package — $50 per month; 10 percent buy the super-premium package — $80 per month. Over time, 80 percent of customers remain with the company from one year to the next.

   - What is the average CLV for all customers?

   - What is the CLV of a super-premium customer?

2. Chapter 11 introduces *brand equity*. What is the relationship between CLV and brand equity?

3. Which firms do a good job of retaining and growing current customers, while simultaneously acquiring new customers? What has made these firms successful?

4. Sonik CD (disguised name) was a wholesale buying club for classical, jazz, and blues enthusiasts — annual membership fee $40. Sonik scoured distributors and independent retailers for hard-to-get and out-of-print releases. Sonik's price of $10.95 per CD was lower than average retail price; average Sonik cost — $10.50 per CD. Shipping and handling price — $4.00 per package; average cost — $0.50. Subscribers purchased 19.9 CDs annually, mostly at Sonik's website; annual retention rate — 90 percent. Sonik fulfilled all orders — annual fixed cost, $400,000; shipments averaged 3.7 CDs per package. Annual marketing expenses — $230,000; 90 percent for new subscribers, 5 percent for retention. Sonik's cost of capital was 12 percent. Three growth options were:

   a. **Continue niche strategy:** Sonik anticipated acquiring 20,000–30,000 new customers annually for several years without major new investment. Spending $0.5 million annually would increase customer retention to 95 percent.

   b. **Mass-market strategy:** Abandon the subscription model; add many music genres; build a mass-market brand. An initial $1 million to $2 million investment would build brand awareness; distribution and warehousing would require $0.5 million annually. Sonik estimated adding 40,000–50,000 new subscribers per quarter for $12.50 acquisition cost; annual profit margin — $15; retention rate — 60 percent.

   c. **Distribution strategy:** Sonik also distributed products for other online retailers. AmeriNet Radio (ANR) operated 43 radio stations (southeast U.S., 25 million listeners); ANR sold CDs through station websites. ANR asked Sonik for an exclusive arrangement: Sonik would close retail operations; it would become sole distributor for all ANR CD sales, charging its normal handling fee. Sonik's CD price — $13.25; Sonik would pay ANR $1.50 per CD. Research suggested: 5 percent ANR listeners bought CDs online; 10 percent would buy from Sonik; a typical customer would buy twice a year, averaging two CDs per order. Sonik's additional fixed costs — $0.5 million annually.

   Which option should Sonik choose?[70]

5. Develop a loyalty program for your favorite restaurant. Justify the variables — used/omitted.

6. Select a firm and one of its products. Alternatively, consider this book — *Managing Marketing in the 21st Century*. Who are the customers? Use the Figure 2.6 framework to suggest how you would address customers. Then, design a CRM program.

SECTION II

FUNDAMENTAL INSIGHTS FOR STRATEGIC MARKETING vs2

To access O-codes, go to **www.ocodes.com**

SECTION II — FUNDAMENTAL INSIGHTS FOR STRATEGIC MARKETING — comprises four chapters, Chapter 3 through Chapter 6. These chapters focus on the data, knowledge, and insight the firm must secure to make effective marketing decisions. Data are facts about a particular topic, like a customer's demographic characteristics and purchasing data. Knowledge is the meaning the firm gains from combining data as in a customer profile. Insight results from further knowledge combinations that provide ideas for action, like linking a customer profile to an R&D project. The firm needs data and knowledge, but should strive for insight.

To build a strong foundation for developing market strategy, the firm must secure insight in several core areas — market; customers; and competitors, company, and complementers — the M4Cs. This insight is the *situation analysis* for the market plan.

- **Market.** Good market insight helps the firm decide what parts of the market to address. The firm must understand market demand, today's participants and the pressures they face, and how each may evolve over time — Chapter 3.

- **Customers.** The firm tries to satisfy customer needs through market offers. The firm must identify customers, and gain insight into their needs and the processes they use to make purchase decisions — Chapter 4.

- **Competitors, company, and complementers.** Both the firm and competitors seek to attract, retain, and grow customers. As the firm secures *competitive* insight, it also learns about its own *company* capabilities and how to win in the market. We also discuss firm *complementers* — organizations that help the firm achieve its objectives — Chapter 5.

Chapter 6 addresses approaches to securing insight via *marketing research*. Following Chapter 6, we show how to use insight from the situation analysis to construct assumptions that form the foundation of the market plan.

KEY IDEA

➤ The firm must secure insight in three broad areas:

- Market
- Customers
- Competitors, the company, and complementers

— the M4Cs.

Managing Marketing in the 21st Century

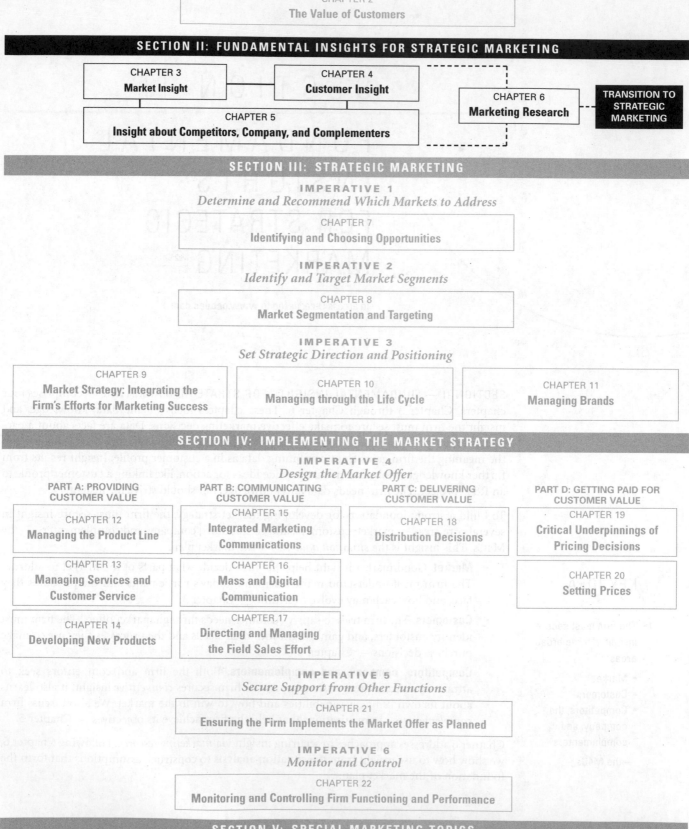

SECTION I: MARKETING AND THE FIRM

CHAPTER 1
Introduction to Managing Marketing

CHAPTER 2
The Value of Customers

SECTION II: FUNDAMENTAL INSIGHTS FOR STRATEGIC MARKETING

CHAPTER 3
Market Insight

CHAPTER 4
Customer Insight

CHAPTER 5
Insight about Competitors, Company, and Complementers

CHAPTER 6
Marketing Research

TRANSITION TO STRATEGIC MARKETING

SECTION III: STRATEGIC MARKETING

IMPERATIVE 1
Determine and Recommend Which Markets to Address

CHAPTER 7
Identifying and Choosing Opportunities

IMPERATIVE 2
Identify and Target Market Segments

CHAPTER 8
Market Segmentation and Targeting

IMPERATIVE 3
Set Strategic Direction and Positioning

CHAPTER 9
Market Strategy: Integrating the Firm's Efforts for Marketing Success

CHAPTER 10
Managing through the Life Cycle

CHAPTER 11
Managing Brands

SECTION IV: IMPLEMENTING THE MARKET STRATEGY

IMPERATIVE 4
Design the Market Offer

PART A: PROVIDING CUSTOMER VALUE

PART B: COMMUNICATING CUSTOMER VALUE

PART C: DELIVERING CUSTOMER VALUE

PART D: GETTING PAID FOR CUSTOMER VALUE

CHAPTER 12
Managing the Product Line

CHAPTER 15
Integrated Marketing Communications

CHAPTER 18
Distribution Decisions

CHAPTER 19
Critical Underpinnings of Pricing Decisions

CHAPTER 13
Managing Services and Customer Service

CHAPTER 16
Mass and Digital Communication

CHAPTER 20
Setting Prices

CHAPTER 14
Developing New Products

CHAPTER 17
Directing and Managing the Field Sales Effort

IMPERATIVE 5
Secure Support from Other Functions

CHAPTER 21
Ensuring the Firm Implements the Market Offer as Planned

IMPERATIVE 6
Monitor and Control

CHAPTER 22
Monitoring and Controlling Firm Functioning and Performance

SECTION V: SPECIAL MARKETING TOPICS

CHAPTER 23
International, Regional, and Global Marketing

CHAPTER 3

MARKET INSIGHT v301 📺

Why am I a great player? Because I go to where the puck will be.

— Wayne Gretzky

LEARNING OBJECTIVES

When you have completed this chapter, you will be able to:

- Analyze and understand market structure.
- Understand alternative ways of thinking about products that firms offer.
- Distinguish among product class, product form, product line, and product item.
- Forecast market and product evolution using a life-cycle framework.
- Summarize industry forces exerting pressure on the firm.
- Recognize major environmental forces affecting the firm and industry.
- Show how industry and environmental forces interact.

OPENING CASE: NETFLIX

Since the mid-1970s, when Sony introduced Betamax technology, watching videos at home, typically on TV, has become a major sociocultural trend. VHS eclipsed Betamax, and consumers used videotape recorders/players to record and play back TV programs, and play movies secured from retailers. Initially, most retailers were small local stores, but many went out of business in the 1990s as Blockbuster became dominant, in part because of larger inventories.

When DVDs replaced VHS, California entrepreneur Reed Hastings founded Netflix, an online DVD-rental service, www.netflix.com. Netflix subscribers create a list of videos they want to rent, selecting from more than 100,000 movies and TV programs. DVDs arrive by U.S. Mail in distinctive red envelopes. When a subscriber returns a movie in a prepaid envelope, Netflix sends another. There are no due dates, no late fees, and no shipping charges. Netflix analyzes subscribers' choices and their recommendations; subscribers may search by actor, critic, customer recommendation, decade, director, genre, new releases, studio, and title! Subscribers may request movies not yet released on video; Netflix sends them out as available. On any given day, more than 50,000 Netflix titles are in distribution.

For its DVD offerings, Netflix maintains about 60 warehouses in major metropolitan areas. Employees pick up returning DVD envelopes from post offices in the early morning. By mid-afternoon, Netflix has sorted returned DVDs and delivered ordered DVDs to post offices. Subscribers living within 50 miles of a warehouse typically receive delivery in one business day. Netflix provides customer service from U.S.-based telephone operators. Netflix ships roughly 2 million DVDs daily; and spends $600 million annually on postage. Netflix faces competition from bricks-and-mortar video stores, notably Blockbuster (filed for bankruptcy in 2010). Redbox and Blockbuster also offer standalone kiosks containing relatively few popular DVDs in supermarkets, drugstores, and fast-food restaurants for $1 overnight.

In 2007, Netflix started streaming movies and TV episodes for viewing on various devices: personal computers; TVs; Xbox 360 (Microsoft), PS3 (Sony) and Wii (Nintendo) game consoles; Blu-ray disc players (Samsung, LG, Insignia); "smart" (Internet-connected) TVs (LG, Sony, Vizio); digital video players (Roku [Netflix has minority stake]), and TiVo digital video recorders. Netflix faces current and potential competition from Apple, Amazon, Blockbuster, Google, and Hulu.

Netflix offers various subscriber plans. Customers may select DVD-only, steaming-only, or combination DVD/streaming plans. In 2012, new subscribers paid $7.99, $11.99, or $15.99 for one, two, or three DVDs in circulation, respectively. Streaming service cost an additional $7.99; that was also the price for streaming-only service. In 2012, Netflix had roughly 35 million subscribers: 3 million DVD-only, 12 million DVD and streaming, and 10 million streaming-only.

A critical competitive area is the ability to secure rights to recently released movies from movie studios, and length of the movie-house-only window (traditionally averaging 120 days). In 2011, Netflix announced distribution of original programming, but received significant negative publicity when it sharply increased prices for customers who subscribed for both DVDs and streaming video.

Netflix's 2011 revenues exceeded $3 billion; profits were $226 million. Originally priced at around $15, in mid-2011 Netflix's share price reached $298 but later dropped to less than $100 ⟨302⟩.[1]

CASE QUESTIONS

What environmental changes enabled Netflix to successfully innovate in the home video market? How do you assess Netflix's decision to offer streaming videos? Why did Netflix stock price drop so significantly?

In 2010, Nokia was the acknowledged market share leader in cell phones globally — 450 million sold. But Nokia faced fierce price competition from Asian producers for basic cell phones; also, Nokia's market share of smart phones dropped considerably as Apple's iPhone and phones running Google's Android software gained strength. In 2011, Nokia's stock price dropped 80 percent from a 2008 high. Significant events in 2011 were: Google acquired Motorola Mobility; Nokia abandoned its smart phone operating systems, agreeing to base future models on Microsoft's Windows Phone 7.

Defining the market is a fundamental but tricky marketing challenge. If the firm defines the market too narrowly, it risks being blindsided by competitors (Netscape's experience in browsers). If the firm defines the market too broadly, it will not allocate resources effectively. The firm must also understand the market's evolutionary patterns and the forces that drive this process. Because most forces are external in nature, the firm that embraces an external orientation, with customers and competitors in mind, generally understands markets better than firms with internal orientations.

Figure 3.1 shows four aspects of **market insight** this chapter covers, each equally important. Each aspect provides a different window on the market and lays a foundation for developing the market strategy. Together they help the firm anticipate market change, and identify and size new opportunities:

KEY IDEA

➤ Market insight comprises four separate aspects:
- Market structure
- Market and product evolution
- Industry forces
- Environmental forces

- **Market structure.** We define the market and show that effective market partitioning helps the firm identify opportunities and gain differential advantage. The chapter shows how different product classes and product forms serve customer needs, and explores factors affecting market size.

- **Market and product evolution.** Markets evolve over time. Sometimes evolutionary patterns are predictable, like the market for geriatric healthcare — easily knowable from age-distribution demographics. Other markets are unpredictable, like demand for home-rebuilding products in hurricane-prone areas. Products also evolve over time as customers refine their needs and competitors compete for their business. Technological evolution can also drive market evolution. We use a life-cycle framework to show how markets and products evolve.

- **Industry forces.** Industry forces include various competitive and supply-chain pressures. The *five forces* we identify impinge directly on the firm.

- **Environmental forces.** These broad-scale environmental forces impact both the firm and other industry participants. We use the PESTLE framework — political, economic, sociocultural, technological, legal/regulatory, and environmental (physical) to gain insight.

FIGURE 3.1

CRITICAL BUILDING BLOCKS FOR SECURING MARKET INSIGHT

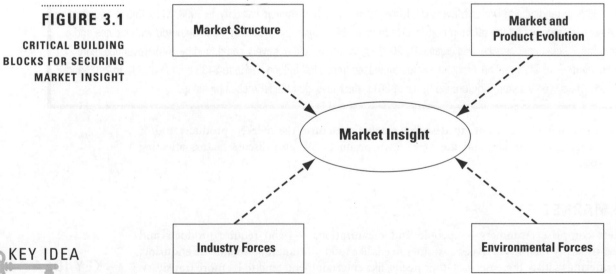

The firm must keep two things squarely in mind when seeking insight into these four aspects:
- **State of nature.** The firm must understand the current state of nature. For example: What competitors does the firm face today? How many baby boomers are in its target market?
- **Trends.** The firm must also identify trends. For example: What additional direct competitors will it face in two years' time? How will demographic changes affect the market?

KEY IDEA

➤ When firms secure good market insight, they do a better job of identifying and sizing opportunities and gaining differential advantage.

Good market insight can put the firm ahead and provide significant competitive advantage. Post-September 11, 2001, Alcoa predicted significant demand for secure cockpit doors on passenger aircraft and won a commanding share of the retrofit market.

THE CHANGING VIEW

OLD WAY	NEW WAY
Change as evolutionary	Change as revolutionary
Change is a problem	Change is an opportunity
Competitive advantages are long-lasting	Competitive advantages are quickly dissipated
Firms operate independently	Firms are networked
Focus on national and regional economies	Understand the integrated global economy
Future predictable — all that's needed is good forecasting	Future not completely predictable — need to be flexible
Imitation is common	Innovation is essential
Life cycles are fixed and constrained	Life cycles are dynamic and subject to firm influence
Reacting to environmental change is sufficient	Proactively influencing environmental change is a reasonable goal
The firm has ample time to recoup front-end investment	Peak profit-margin period arrives sooner, and disappears earlier

MARKET STRUCTURE

In the 1990s, attendance at Dallas Mavericks' (Mavs) games was half stadium capacity. In 2000, Mark Cuban bought the Mavs and transitioned the offering from *sports team* to *entertainment*. The Mavs then competed with movies and restaurants — customer service was crucial. By 2002–3, the Mavs sold out every game, and by 2005, revenues more than doubled — to $124 million. Franchise value increased from $167 million (1999) to $438 million (2011). In 2006 and 2011, the Mavs won Western Conference titles; in 2011, the Mavs won the NBA championship.

We use three separate concepts to describe **market structure**: the market; products and/or services serving the market; and the firm's own products. We also discuss factors affecting market size.

THE MARKET

Markets comprise customers — people and organizations — who require products and services to satisfy their needs. Basic customer needs like food, clothing, and shelter are enduring; many offerings satisfy these needs. Other needs, like entertainment, tend to be more transitory. Of course, to be in the market, customers must also possess sufficient purchasing power — and interest, to buy what firms are offering.[2]

The concept of a *market* is slippery because we can identify a market at several different levels. The transportation market is the basic need to move people and things from point A to point B. In turn, the transportation market comprises several more narrowly defined markets — ground, air, and water transportation. Even more narrowly, we can define the automobile market and, more narrowly still, the market for particular types of automobiles like SUVs and hybrids. Good market definition drove the Dallas Mavericks' marketing success.

KEY IDEA

➤ Markets comprise people and organizations that require goods and services to satisfy their needs, and are willing and able to pay.

We can partition all broadly defined markets. Figure 3.2 shows market partitions for endovascular products that treat aneurysms (expansions in the walls of blood vessels like arteries).

FIGURE 3.2

EXAMPLE OF MARKET STRUCTURE FOR TREATING ANEURYSMS

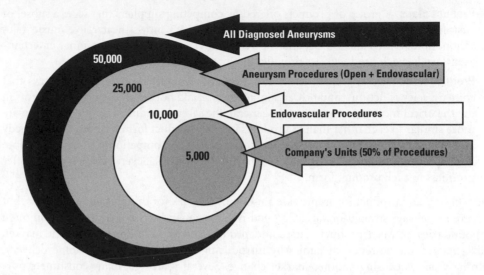

Marketing Question

Select a product and industry with which you are familiar. Define the market at different levels. How much more broadly could you go (as Mark Cuban with the Mavs) and still maintain a focus? Illustrate your answer similarly to Figure 3.2.

In defining a market, it's best to start broad, and then focus as necessary. A broad approach ensures against **marketing myopia**,[3] missing opportunities by defining a market too narrowly — Chapter 7.[4] Hence, in the aneurysm illustration, the firm's 50 percent share of endovascular procedures (5,000/10,000) suggests limited opportunity. But viewed as 20 percent share of all procedures (5,000/25,000), 10 percent share (5,000/50,000) of all diagnosed aneurysms, or an unknown share of all aneurysms (diagnosed and undiagnosed), the opportunity is much greater.

Unfortunately, biases, insufficient data, and/or measurement systems can narrow market definitions. At GE, Jack Welch's (CEO) initial approach was to retain GE businesses whose market share was #1 or #2; GE sold other businesses. After early success, managers began to define markets narrowly to ensure high market share. To spur opportunity search, Welch told managers in each business that actual market share was less than 10 percent; managers had to redefine their businesses to seek growth opportunities.

For more than 90 years Smith-Corona (SC) was a market leader in typewriters. In the 1970s and 1980s, SC continued to define its market as typewriters. Because of this narrow definition, SC was late entering word-processing, computer hardware and software, and document processing. SC now serves only a very small part of a redefined market.

Marketing Question

Suppose you had been a senior marketing executive at Kodak in the mid-1990s; how would you have defined Kodak's market? How would you change this definition today?

More generally, a market definition that focuses on customer needs reinforces an external orientation and offsets tendencies toward internal orientations. But working with a broad market definition is not easy. The broader the market definition — especially regional (multi-country) or global — the greater the challenge of gathering data.

PRODUCTS SERVING THE MARKET

Both the firm and competitors provide products and services to the market. A useful categorization of product offerings is **product class**, **product form**, **product line**, and **product item**.[5] These distinctions help the firm identify opportunities and/or emerging competitors. When P&G launched Whitestrips for teeth whitening, consumer options included toothpaste, bleaches, gels, and professional dental procedures. Because P&G focused on customer needs for convenience, ease of use, safety, and economy, sales quickly reached $50 million annually with this new product form, in a seemingly mature market. (Note: *Product* is anything a firm offers for sale, both physical products and services.) Figure 3.3 shows a hierarchical decomposition of the entertainment market, illustrating relationships among market, product class, product form, and product item, based on established customer preferences.

- **Product class.** A group of products offered by competing suppliers that serve a subset of customer needs in a roughly similar manner. Figure 3.3 shows theater, live music, television, home video and DVDs, and theatrical movies each serving consumer entertainment needs. Each product class provides distinct customer benefits.

- **Product form.** Several *product forms* comprise each *product class*. Figure 3.3 shows that comedy, science fiction, romance, action/adventure, and horror are each product forms in the theatrical movies product class. In general, the several products in a product form are more similar to each other than to products in other product forms; for example, comedy and science-fiction movies versus live theater. Hence, competition is typically more intense among product forms than among product classes. Several firms typically offer products in each product form.

Product classes and product forms provide a useful framework for thinking about markets, but things are not always straightforward. Competitive changes and technological evolution often blur boundaries between product classes and product forms. In the entertainment market, Netflix changed movie-rental dynamics by introducing online ordering and home delivery; streaming video is causing another market change. Several years ago, many consumers purchased cash management, life insurance, property and casualty insurance, and investments from different firms. Deregulation has led to a single *financial services* market that offers many consumers *one-stop* shopping.[6] Similarly, engineering plastics now compete with metal in many applications. Previously, your automobile's oil pan and fuel tank were made of metal; today, they are probably made of plastic. (The PAM, TAM, SAM framework, Marketing Enrichment ⬚me301, offers useful insight for market opportunities.)

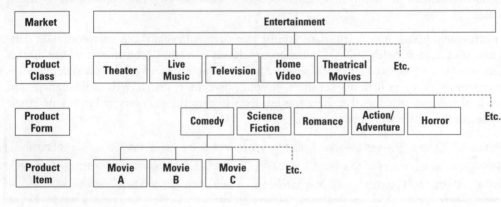

THE FIRM'S PRODUCTS

Product classes and product forms embrace products from all competitors. One firm may offer products in multiple product classes; another may specialize in just one or two product forms. IBM offers products in many (but not all) product forms in the information systems product class. By contrast, Gateway offers only PCs (IBM no longer offers PCs). When we consider individual firms, we speak of product lines and product items.

- **Product line.** A group of related products that a single firm offers. Gateway offers a product line of desktop PCs and a product line of laptop PCs.

- **Product item.** A subset of the product line. A product item is uniquely identified, like having a specific size and color. The firm offers various product items to meet different customer needs. Gateway offers several desktops, each with a unique item (model) number; laptops (notebooks and netbooks) are available in various colors.

KEY IDEA

➤ We can view any market as comprising several different areas.

➤ The firm avoids *marketing myopia* by using a broad market definition.

me301

MARKETING ENRICHMENT
PAM, TAM, and SAM ⬚me301

FIGURE 3.3

HIERARCHICAL DECOMPOSITION OF THE ENTERTAINMENT MARKET

KEY IDEA

➤ A useful way of categorizing products in a market is:

- Product class
- Product form
- Product line
- Product item

FACTORS AFFECTING MARKET SIZE

Current and potential market sizes are important data for evaluating the firm's opportunities. Before entering a market, the firm should know the numbers of current and potential customers and their purchasing power. For B2C markets, the firm should consider factors like population size, population mix, geographic population shifts, income and income distribution, and age distribution.[7] (Of course, B2B market sizes are typically driven by underlying consumer demand: Demand for automobiles [B2C] drives demand for steering wheels by automobile firms [B2B]; demand for medical procedures [B2C] drives demand for sutures by hospitals [B2B]).

POPULATION SIZE. World population exceeds 7 billion (versus 1960: 3 billion). Increasing by 200,000 people daily, by 2030, population will exceed 8 billion.[8] Population is unevenly distributed across nations — from highs of 1.3 billion in China and 1.2 billion in India to lows of 9,000 in Nauru and 10,000 in Tuvalu: Table 3.1 for 2006 and 2015-predicted populations in selected countries.

Population growth rates also differ markedly across nations and are falling globally. In many developed nations, annual growth rates are less than 1 percent, and some are negative, leading to population declines.[9] Important drivers are social norms promoting education, work opportunities for women, and greater access to birth control. Conversely, in many less-developed countries, particularly in Latin America, population growth is well over 2 percent. Population control programs are successful in some countries like Bangladesh; China enforces a one-child policy. In some African countries, birth rates are high, but AIDS is taking a heavy toll.

TABLE 3.1

POPULATION SIZE IN SELECTED COUNTRIES (MILLIONS)[10]

Country	2010 Population	2020 Population (est.)	Country	2020 Population	2020 Population (est.)
Argentina	41	45	Malaysia	28	33
Australia	22	24	Mexico	112	125
Bangladesh	156	183	Nigeria	162	208
Brazil	201	222	Paraguay	6	7
Colombia	44	49	Pakistan	184	214
Chile	17	18	Poland	38	38
China	1,330	1,385	Russia	139	132
Egypt	80	96	Saudi Arabia	26	30
France	65	68	Singapore	5	6
Germany	82	80	South Africa	49	49
Great Britain	62	66	South Korea	49	49
Greece	11	11	Spain	47	50
India	1,173	1,326	Sweden	9	9
Indonesia	243	268	Thailand	66	70
Iran	77	87	Turkey	78	87
Israel	7	9	Ukraine	45	43
Italy	61	62	U.S.	308	337
Japan	128	126	Venezuela	27	31
Kenya	41	50	Vietnam	90	99

Marketing Question

Consider Tables 3.1, 3.2, 3.3 and other data you can secure. What are the pros and cons of entering either the Brazilian or Japanese markets with a new line of bicycles?

POPULATION MIX. In many developed countries, immigration drives population-mix changes. Of the world's 200 million immigrants (foreign-born residents), the U.S. leads with 35 million. Other countries with large immigrant populations are Russia (13 million); Germany and Ukraine (7 million); France, India, and Canada (6 million); and Saudi Arabia (5 million). Most labor migration, legal and illegal, is from less-developed countries to more-developed countries. Frequently, provider and receiver countries are geographically close like Mexico and the U.S. and Turkey and Germany. Reduced mobility barriers in the European Union (EU) increase population shifts; and the long-standing pattern of Asian workers in Middle Eastern countries continues apace.[11] Foreign workers have a major impact on home-country economies via remittances, sending back well over $300 billion (more than twice the official aid received by OECD members):

> Goya Foods, the largest Hispanic family-owned U.S. food firm (fourth-largest Hispanic firm overall) has revenues exceeding $1 billion. In many grocery stores, Goya has its own shop within a shop. Goya offers a broad range of imported products including Spanish olive oil, seasonings like Mexican chiles, and Caribbean fruit juices.

In some ethnic and/or language groups, immigrants and offspring represent significant marketing opportunities — see the Goya example. In the U.S., more than 10 percent of Americans speak Spanish at home, versus 3.8 and 2.7 percent, respectively, for European and Asian languages. More than 100 U.S. television stations broadcast Spanish-language programs, and growth in Hispanic advertising outpaces overall advertising growth.[12] Some firms target sub-segments of the Hispanic market based on national origin — Dominican Republic, Guatemala, Mexico, Puerto Rico; others focus on purchasing tendencies, cultural influences, and affordability.

GEOGRAPHIC POPULATION SHIFTS. Generally, as national income grows, people leave rural areas for urban areas. Then urban areas become overcrowded — Mumbai (India) 14 million and Sao Paulo (Brazil) 11 million. China predicts 500 million people will move from rural to urban areas by 2050. In developed countries, a more recent trend is *exurban* growth — return to rural communities. Desire for less crowding, a slower life pace, and advances in information technology are enabling this trend. In contrast, some affluent empty-nester baby boomers are returning to regenerate city centers.

Population shifts often follow the sun. In the U.S., the Northeast is losing population to the Southeast and Southwest. From 2000 to 2010, the U.S. population grew by 9.7 percent, but several states grew much faster — Nevada (35 percent), Arizona (25 percent), Utah (24 percent), Idaho (21 percent), and Texas (21 percent). States growing less than half the national average were North Dakota (4.7 percent), New Jersey (4.5 percent), Mississippi (4.3 percent), Maine (4.2 percent), Iowa (4.1 percent), Vermont (3.8 percent), West Virginia (3.5 percent), Pennsylvania (3.4 percent), Illinois (3.3 percent), Massachusetts (3.1 percent), Vermont (2.8 percent), West Virginia (2.5 percent), New York (2.1 percent), Ohio (1.6 percent), Louisiana (1.4 percent), Rhode Island (0.4 percent), and Michigan (0.6 percent decline). Similarly, in Europe, many Northern Europeans move to Croatia, southern France, Italy's Tuscan region, Portugal, and Spain.

INCOME AND INCOME DISTRIBUTION. Table 3.2 shows the world's richest countries. Several countries now surpass the U.S. in per capita income. Most countries are far less wealthy than those in Table 3.2. Thirty-seven countries have GDP per capita between $10,000 and $20,000; 67 countries have GDP per capita less than $5,000; the largest group of countries has GDP per capita under $1,000 per annum.

Country	GDP/Capita	Country	GDP/Capita	Country	GDP/Capita
Qatar	88	Austria	40	Finland	34
Luxembourg	81	Canada	39	France	34
Singapore	56	Ireland	39	Israel	30
Norway	52	Kuwait	39	South Korea	30
UAE	47	Sweden	38	Spain	30
U.S.	47	Belgium	36	Cyprus	29
Hong Kong	46	Denmark	36	Italy	29
Switzerland	42	Germany	36	Slovenia	29
Netherlands	41	Japan	36	Greece	28
Australia	40	Great Britain	35	New Zealand	27

Marketing Question

Cold Stone Creamery (CSC) offers freshly made ice cream, Italian sorbet, and yogurt. CSC blends products to order on a frozen granite stone with the consumer's choice of mix-ins. CSC (formed 1988) has well over 1,400 stores in the U.S., Japan, and Korea. If you were advising CSC, how might U.S. population shifts affect your recommendations for seeking new franchisees?

Marketing Question

How would an analysis of population, income, and income distribution help Pepsi-Cola defeat Coca-Cola in developing countries?

TABLE 3.2

GROSS DOMESTIC PRODUCT PER CAPITA (GDP) PURCHASING POWER PARITY (PPP) FOR SELECTED WEALTHY COUNTRIES ($000s)[13]

In many poor countries, small elite minorities enjoy most national wealth. The elite-population-income ratio (EPIR) (top 20 percent income divided by bottom 20 percent income) is frequently very high and exceeds 25 in Botswana, Central African Republic, Colombia, Ethiopia, Guatemala, Lesotho, Namibia, Nicaragua, Paraguay, Sierra Leone, and South Africa. By contrast, ratios for wealthy countries like Great Britain, Japan, and Sweden are well under 10.[14]

Population, income, and income distribution influence the size of many markets. Economic development and demographic changes are shifting opportunities from traditional markets to emerging markets. Especially important growing markets are BRICI countries — Brazil, Russia, India, China, and Indonesia. Western firms like CitiCorp, ExxonMobil, GE, Nestlé, and P&G continually develop their global organizations to tap this potential. Additionally, emerging-market countries are generating their own multinationals like Brazil (Embraer), China (Haier, Lenovo), and India (Tata Motors, Wipro).

AGE DISTRIBUTION. Table 3.3 shows increasing median ages in selected developed and developing countries. Major drivers are decreasing birth rates and family size and increasing life expectancy. These shifts have enormous implications for B2C marketers. In developed countries, large numbers of retirement-age consumers (baby boomers) are active, have significant discretionary income, and are sophisticated buyers — cruises and assisted-living facilities are growth markets. By contrast, countries with median ages in the mid-20s — Mexico, Brazil, Indonesia — offer opportunities for Coke, Pepsi, McDonald's, Kentucky Fried Chicken, and other marketers whose products appeal to a younger demographic.

TABLE 3.3

MEDIAN AGES IN SELECTED COUNTRIES[15]

Country	Median Age, 2000	Projected Median Age, 2040
Japan	41.3	54.2
Spain	37.4	52.3
Australia	35.2	43.3
U.S.	35.2	39.0
Brazil	25.4	38.8
Indonesia	24.6	37.4
Mexico	22.9	38.7
Niger	15.1	17.8

Marketing Question

Think about the firm and product you selected earlier (p. 61). What factors help determine market size — population (size, mix, geographic shift), income distribution, and/or age distribution? What other factors help determine market size in three to five years?

Other important market-size drivers include marriage, marrying age, divorce and remarriage, same-sex households, infant and adult mortality, and work force composition. These variables often help the firm make good market-size predictions — birth rates and infant mortality influence demand for products like diapers and car seats.

MARKET AND PRODUCT EVOLUTION

In the mid-1990s Canon, Fuji, Kodak, Minolta, and Nikon together invested around $1 billion to develop the Advanced Photo System (APS). Several firms introduced APS cameras, but sales lagged expectations. Question: Why isn't APS widely used today? Answer: The APS life cycle was cut unexpectedly short by the introduction of digital cameras.

Life cycles are the most common means for describing the evolution of markets and products — product classes, product forms, product lines, and product items.[16] Figure 3.4 shows a classic S-shaped curve depicting the sales trajectory. Understanding life-cycle phenomena helps the firm predict future market conditions and develop robust strategies.[17] Typically, we partition life cycles into five stages (phases) — introduction, early growth, late growth, maturity, and decline.

KEY IDEA

➤ Critical variables affecting market size include:
- Population size
- Population mix
- Geographic population shifts
- Income and income distribution
- Age distribution

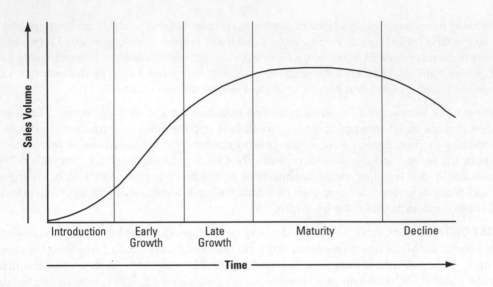

FIGURE 3.4

THE CLASSIC LIFE CYCLE

THE FAMILY OF LIFE CYCLES

The several life cycles fall into a simple hierarchy based on longevity and demand. *Market life cycles* last longest — generally, the firm has little impact on market life cycles. *Product-class* and *product-form* life cycles are each shorter than the market life cycle — understanding these two life cycles is helpful in developing market strategy. Several product-class life cycles typically comprise a market life cycle. Figure 3.5 shows several product-form life cycles, each starting at a different time, and coexisting within one product-class life cycle. By developing and launching products, the firm affects the trajectory of these life cycles.[18]

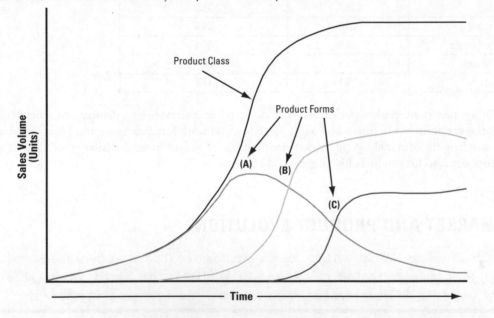

FIGURE 3.5

PRODUCT-CLASS AND PRODUCT-FORM LIFE CYCLES

Product-line and *product-item* life cycles are critical for product and brand managers — they significantly influence product line and product item performance. Firm actions greatly impact these life cycles; they are shorter than product-class and product-form life cycles and come in many different shapes. But because they provide little insight into competitor activity, they are not very helpful for drawing strategic implications.

PRODUCT-FORM LIFE CYCLES

The firm gains the greatest insight into market and product evolution by examining product forms. Although product classes compete with one another, competition both within and across product forms is typically more intense. For example, although desktop PCs compete with laptops, the various brands of laptop PCs compete more fiercely with one another. Although actual life-cycle curves often depart from the idealized shape in Figure 3.4, across product forms, life-cycle stages follow one another in a remarkably consistent fashion. Hence, product-form lifecycles can provide important strategic insights.

As Figure 3.4 shows, we typically categorize product-form life cycles into five stages:

- **Introduction**. Sales volume is initially low.
- **Early growth**. Sales volume grows at an increasing rate.
- **Late growth**. Sales volume grows, but at a decreasing rate.
- **Maturity**. Sales volume grows at about the same rate as GNP.
- **Decline**. Sales volume eventually declines.

STAGE 1: INTRODUCTION. Product introduction frequently follows many years of R&D and reflects the first market entry/entries by leading firms. Honda launched the first gasoline/electric hybrid car in 1999, but modern-day research started in the mid-1970s.[19] Uncertainty characterizes introduction. The firm explores questions like: Will the product perform adequately? What is the best technology? What is the optimal market strategy? Will customer demand be sufficient? What specific benefits do customers require? Which competitors will enter? When? What resources will be necessary? What are our chances of success? Products currently in introduction include implantable ID chips for humans and RFID (radio frequency identification) chips for identifying products.

In the introduction stage, suppliers struggle to build profitable volume. Typically, the firm offers a single product design, but prices may not cover total costs. Managers expect that unit costs will fall as sales increase over time and ultimately the firm will earn profits. Introduction requires significant educational effort. Firms use advertising and/or personal selling to show product value to customers and distributors. But production problems, product failures, and/or an inability to expand capacity may cause delays.[20] Sometimes the first product version has low quality and performs poorly, yet may possess the seeds of an important breakthrough.[21] The BlackBerry, iPad, and other hand-held electronic devices are now widely popular, but their success was built in part on the Apple Newton, the failed pioneer (launched 1993/withdrawn 1998). The introduction stage may last many years. But fierce competition, increased innovation, and customer willingness to try new products are shortening this stage.

STAGE 2: EARLY GROWTH. Many products do not reach early growth, but survivors' sales revenues grow at an increasing rate. Hybrid cars and tablet computers are in early growth — cellular phones with built-in cameras have moved from early growth into late growth. Increasing sales and high profit margins attract other entrants. New players often bring capacity, resources, and a loyal customer base to fuel market growth. As competitors struggle for market position, new distribution channels open up, and promotional effort remains high. Previously, advertising and promotion emphasized generating primary demand — *buy a hybrid car*. Now the focus shifts to differentiation and selective demand based on features, functionality, and customer perceptions — *buy a Ford Fusion hybrid*. Firms secure production and marketing efficiencies, and price becomes a competitive weapon. In early growth, many firms increase sales volume and work at managing costs. One caution: While the firm's sales can increase, market share *decreases* if competitors grow faster!

STAGE 3: LATE GROWTH. By late growth, many uncertainties that dominated introduction and early growth are largely resolved. Sales continue to increase, but the growth rate slows. Strong competitors initiate tough actions to maintain the growth rates, and force weaker entrants to

KEY IDEA

➤ The product life cycle comprises several stages:
- Introduction
- Early growth
- Late growth
- Maturity
- Decline

withdraw. Laptop computers are now in late growth. Customers' product experiences reveal more specific needs and market segmentation opportunities. Firms differentiate products by introducing and promoting design and packaging variations. The distribution infrastructure is usually well developed, but outlets are more selective about brands and product lines. Price is a major competitive weapon, squeezing distributor margins. Purchase terms like credit, warranties, and customer service become more favorable to purchasers.

STAGE 4: MATURITY. Slow growth or flat year-to-year sales characterize maturity. Most sales are to repeat and loyal users. Examples include everyday products like detergents and kitchen appliances. Because competitive situations vary widely, the firm must secure deep market insight. Some markets are concentrated, others are fragmented:

- **Concentrated markets.** Economists use the term *oligopoly* to describe concentrated markets. The few major players that together make most sales often coexist with a few niche firms. Market leaders often enjoy entry barriers like economies of scale, brand preference, and/or distribution-channel dominance. Market positions that firms achieve by early maturity often survive for many years. Examples include IBM in mainframe computers, GE in steam turbine generators, and Gillette in shaving products.

  Many firms pursue product differentiation approaches, but competitors that quickly offer *me-too* products can cause problems. Increasingly, firms focus on value-added services, packaging, distribution, and branding and promotion. They streamline operations and distribution to reduce costs, and pricing is often competitive. Leaders get in trouble when they fail to innovate new products and processes and do not reduce costs. Xerox's experience is a strong caution:

Xerox, the pioneer and market leader in dry copying, was slower than Canon and Savin to introduce small copiers. Xerox has almost failed several times and narrowly avoided bankruptcy in 2001. At one point, Japanese producers had a 40 to 50 percent cost advantage; U.S. prices approximated Xerox's manufacturing costs![22]

- **Fragmented markets.** No firm has a large market share. Fragmentation generally occurs because of some combination of low entry barriers, high exit barriers, regulation,[23] diverse market needs, and high transportation costs. Examples include personal services like dentistry, education, home plumbing, and electrical contracting.[24]

STAGE 5: DECLINE. Maturity may last many years, but eventually sales turn down. Products in decline include carbon paper, chemical-film cameras, and videotapes. Sometimes decline is slow — payphones; but it may also be precipitous — vinyl records. When decline is swift, overcapacity often leads to fierce price competition. Managing costs is a high priority — firms prune product lines and reduce inventory and marketing expenses. Strong firms may increase sales as weaker competitors exit. Firms often raise prices to cover costs as sales drop, but sales decline further in a vicious cycle. Marketing efforts should target remaining customers. Firms with good cost management and a core of loyal price-insensitive buyers can be quite profitable.

Sometimes products in decline enjoy resurgence. In the 1990s, creative marketing led to growth in cigar smoking in the U.S. Improved technology has made yo-yo tricks easier; the product is now more attractive to young consumers and sales have increased.

The product-form life cycle is a useful framework, but two points are important:

- **Life-cycle shape.** A product's sales trajectory depends on several factors — underlying customer demand, product quality and consistency, and overall resource commitments by participating firms. In general, life cycles are shortening.[25]
- **Profit curves.** Profit curves do not mirror sales life cycles. Figure 3.6 shows that, on average, profit margins are greatest in early growth — then drop in late growth and maturity. Do not confuse profit margin with gross profit. Gross profit may be greater later in the cycle — lower profit margins, but higher volume.

KEY IDEA

➤ Markets and products generally evolve in a consistent manner over time.

➤ The life-cycle framework is useful for describing market and product evolution.

KEY IDEA

➤ Product-form life-cycle stages have consistent characteristics across products and services.

➤ Profit-margin life cycles do *not* mirror sales life cycles.

Marketing Question

Think about the firm and product you selected earlier (p. 61). In what life-cycle stage is the product form? How did you make this assessment? What are the implications for the firm's product strategy in the next three to five years?

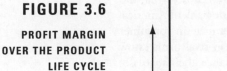

FIGURE 3.6

PROFIT MARGIN
OVER THE PRODUCT
LIFE CYCLE

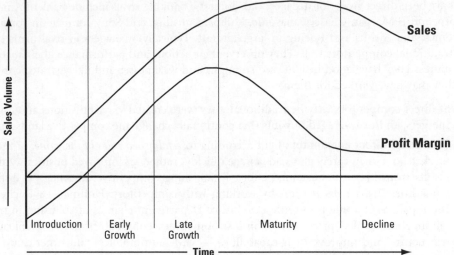

INDUSTRY FORCES

United Airlines (UA) battles daily with peer carriers like Delta and American Airlines. But Southwest Airlines and newer entrants like jetBlue are also strong competitors. On short-haul U.S. routes, customers may drive or take the train. UA must also contend with rising fuel prices and corporate travel offices pushing hard for lower prices.

Figure 3.7 shows the **five-forces model** used by marketing professionals to identify the several industry forces firms face — current direct competitors, new direct entrants, indirect competitors, suppliers, and buyers.[26] Some forces affect the firm specifically; others may impact the entire industry, like fuel prices for airlines. Strong industry forces may produce many unprofitable or marginally profitable firms, as in the airline and worldwide paper industries.[27] The firm must develop a good understanding of these forces and their implications.

FIGURE 3.7

INDUSTRY FORCES —
THE FIVE-FORCES MODEL

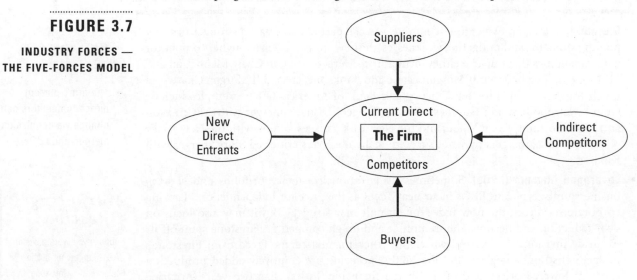

CURRENT DIRECT COMPETITORS

A firm's **current direct competitors** offer customers similar benefits with similar products, technology, and/or business models. Current direct competitors are the competitive *status quo*, the traditional rivalry between established players. In the automobile industry, GM, Toyota, and Ford have been direct rivals for decades; U.S. domestic banking rivals include Bank of America, Citicorp, and JPMorgan Chase; Panasonic, Philips, Samsung, and Sony compete in consumer electronics; and Airbus and Boeing in large aircraft. Typically, managers in rival firms know their traditional competitors well. They observe their actions and performance, their successes and failures. They have good insight into strengths and weaknesses and likely strategic moves. And they may have worked for them!

Current direct competitors may be traditional; they were created via acquisitions and divestitures, mergers, and/or leveraged buyouts that continually change the competitive landscape.

- **Traditional direct competitors** fight according to *established rules of the game*. In mature markets, one firm rarely gains advantage quickly; rather, an improved position typically results from long-run sustained effort. Establishing competitive advantage is difficult. Sometimes firms *cross the line* by working with competitors: Hoffman-La Roche and BASF paid $725 million to settle U.S. Justice Department charges of collusion in maintaining high global prices for vitamins. Sometimes competitors declare bankruptcy, restructure, and improve their capabilities — GM (automobiles) and American, Delta, and United (airlines). Or employees bolster competitors — most employees of failed investment bank Lehman Brothers joined either Barclays or Nomura.

    Globalization and industry concentration affect direct competition in many markets. Consolidation leads to global oligopoly, where a few firms mostly share the global market.[28] In large commercial aircraft, only Airbus and Boeing remain. In passenger tires, Bridgestone, Continental, Goodyear, and Michelin together enjoy over 80 percent global market share.

- **Acquisitions and divestitures.** Suppose one of your competitors or an outside firm acquires a second competitor — an independent firm or a divestiture. Your competitor has changed. Its objectives, strategy, action programs, and available resources will most likely all be different.

> Miller Brewing was No. 2 to Anheuser-Busch (AB) among U.S. brewers. South African Breweries acquired Miller to create SABMiller (SABM), the No. 2 brewer worldwide. Among SABM's strategic changes at Miller were redesigning packaging; importing Chinese, Polish, and Czech Republic brands into the U.S.; and exporting Miller overseas.[29]

- **Merger.** In a merger, two entities combine as *equal* partners to create a stronger firm. By pooling strengths and mitigating weaknesses, the new entity is often a tougher competitor with capabilities that outstrip either former firm. Mergers between Chase Manhattan and J.P. Morgan, then between JPMorgan Chase and Bank One, created JPMorgan Chase — a much tougher competitor for Citicorp and Bank of America. Other examples include Grand Metropolitan and Guinness to form Diageo; Disney's merger with ABC; Exxon and Mobil forming ExxonMobil; and the New York Yankees joining with the New Jersey Nets. Of course, mergers may not succeed; many observers criticized Sears' merger with Kmart.

- **Leveraged buyouts (LBOs).** Sometimes firms rationalize their portfolios and *spin off* business units; typically, LBOs incur heavy debt as the price for independence.[30] Lacking corporate resources, the now-independent unit may struggle. But it may also focus on debt reduction and become a more nimble and tough competitor. Firestone spun off its Accuride division — rims and wheels for truck manufacturers. Freed from Firestone's budget constraints, neglect, and low status, Accuride pre-emptively added production capacity, lowered prices, and offered better financing. In less than two years, Accuride doubled market share and increased profits 66 percent.[31] Other spinoffs include Ciba Specialty Chemicals from Ciba Geigy; Cytec from American Cyanamid; Praxair from Union Carbide; Clariant from Sandoz; Rhodia from Rhone Poulenc; Solutia from Monsanto; Zeneca from ICI; and Quest Diagnostics from Corning. Sometimes the new firm, freed from corporate restraints, performs better than its former parent!

KEY IDEA

➤ The firm faces many external forces:
- Current direct competitors
- New direct entrants
- Indirect competitors
- Suppliers
- Buyers

These forces can frustrate its ability to earn profits and seize new opportunities.

KEY IDEA

➤ The firm's current direct competitors can change via acquisition, merger, and LBOs.

Marketing Question

Suppose you were advising SABMiller, owner of the Miller brand. How would you react to the joining together of AmBev, Interbrew, and Anheuser-Busch to form Anheuser-Busch InBev (ABI)?

NEW DIRECT ENTRANTS

New direct entrants offer products and services similar to the firm, but previously they did not compete. Historically, Nintendo and Sega dominated electronic games; Sony's PlayStation and Microsoft's Xbox were new direct entrants. Entry barriers significantly affect market entry by new firms, but new entrants may emerge from many sources.

- **Firm employees.** In some industries, firm employees pose a significant competitive threat. They may develop new business ideas and/or technologies the firm will not fund and leave to pursue them. Frequently, they set up shop locally; hence, Silicon Valley for Hi Tech and Warsaw, Ind. for orthopedic devices. Several former Fairchild Semiconductor employees founded Intel. Potential competition from employees is greatest when the firm's core asset is intellectual capital as in financial services, advertising, and consulting. Credit Suisse First Boston hired Deutsche Bank's entire 132-person technology group. When *the firm's major assets arrive at 9 a.m. and leave at 5 p.m.*, retaining them is crucial.

- **Geographic expansion.** New direct entrants are often profitable, well-capitalized firms from a different geography. They have solid strengths and cost advantages but may lack market knowledge and customer relationships. They may use superior cost positions to support low price strategies and aggressively seek market share. Many Asian firms entered U.S. and European markets to devastating effect: Panasonic, Samsung, and Sony in consumer electronics; Canon in high-speed copying; Nissan and Toyota in automobiles; and LG and Samsung in cell phones.[32]

- **Networks.** A network is a group of firms and/or individuals that collaborate using their combined talents and resources. Networks are very flexible and change composition as requirements evolve.[33] *Managing Marketing in the 21st Century* competes with traditional textbooks, but a network made it possible. Critical components were an author; reviewers; developmental, copy, and permissions editors; book, cover, and website designers; testbank, caselet, and instructor manual developers; video technicians; credit card processors; and for the printed version, a pre-publication service provider, printer, fulfillment house, wholesaler, bricks-and-mortar and Internet retailers, and package delivery services.

KEY IDEA

➤ The firm may face competition from new direct entrants:

- Firm employees
- Geographic expansion
- Networks
- New sales and distribution channels
- Startup entry
- Strategic alliances

- **New sales and distribution channels.** Firms that develop new distribution channels can pose significant challenges to traditional players. Direct marketers L.L. Bean and Lands' End are tough competitors for department stores. Amazon competes with traditional distribution via the Internet. And pyramid sales forces like Amway (consumer goods) and Primerica (life insurance) are tough competitors.[34] Strong firms that add channels also heighten competition. Avon became more competitive with cosmetics firms by adding department store distribution to traditional door-to-door Avon Ladies.

- **Startup entry.** A startup is unencumbered by the *status quo*; flexibility can make startups potent competitors. By contrast, the incumbent firm may have old facilities, old technology, old processes, and/or an established organization and personnel set in their ways. Successful airline startups include JetBlue (U.S.) and easyJet and Ryanair (Europe).

- **Strategic alliances.** Some firms will not assume the risks and costs of new market entry. They may lack critical assets like capital, skills, technology, or market access. When two firms pool resources, the **strategic alliance** may be stronger than either firm separately. Many U.S. and European firms enter Asian markets with local partners. Of course, partnerships often fail — partners' objectives diverge, and/or one partner fails to provide agreed-upon resources.

INDIRECT COMPETITORS

Indirect competitors and the firm offer customers similar *benefits*, but indirect competitors *provide them in a significantly different way*. These *functional substitutes* often appear as different product forms or product classes. Xerox copiers convey information — they compete with computers, fax machines, video conferencing, and the Internet; e-books compete with physical books from bricks-and-mortar and Internet booksellers. Indirect competitors may redefine the industry by using different suppliers, technologies, distribution methods and/or business models. Netflix customers pay monthly subscription fees and receive their selections by mail and/or streaming video (Opening Case); Redbox offers vastly fewer DVDs from vending machines in supermarkets, drug stores, and fast food restaurants — $1 overnight. More broadly, cruise lines compete with automobile and clothing manufacturers — each seeks consumers' discretionary income. Movie theaters compete with cable TV, online and retail video rental, restaurants, sporting events, and other entertainment.

> The New York Knicks is a professional basketball team. The Knicks competes for spectators and TV viewers against many other sports teams like the New York Rangers (professional ice hockey), the New York Jets (football), the New York Yankees (baseball), and other entertainment.

Indirect competitors often attack from different industry sectors; incumbents sometimes ignore them. International Paper's market share in paper cups increased, but sales declined as plastic replaced paper. Sometimes regulations prohibit responding to indirect competitors. For many years, U.S. commercial banks could not offer money-market and mutual funds to compete with Fidelity and Vanguard. Changes in the law removed this restriction.[35]

SUPPLIERS

Suppliers provide the firm's inputs. Typically, pressure on the firm increases as supplier importance increases — like providing a critical product or a large percentage of purchases. Periodically, Apple faces pressure from music labels unhappy with iTunes' sales terms. Extreme pressure can send firms into bankruptcy: Business-class-only airlines Eos, MAXjet, and Silverjet each failed when fuel prices rose.[36] Pressure may also arise if the supplier's brand is attractive to the firm's customers: PC buyers value the Intel brand; PC manufacturers feel pressure from Intel and Intel earns high profit margins. Pressure is strongest when the supplier is a monopoly like local telephone firms, government services, and railroads; the firm may also have to accept poor service and/or delivery. Sometimes multiple suppliers form *cartels*, like oil (OPEC) and diamonds (De Beers), to manage production volumes and hence prices.

Of course, a supplier's most important job is to supply! Supplier failure to honor commitments can play havoc with the firm's operations. Nissan cut its steel supplier base from five to two — Nippon Steel and JFE. When these firms could not meet its needs, Nissan had to close plants and slash automobile output by tens of thousands. To produce the Dreamliner, Boeing modified its traditional production system to rely more heavily on suppliers; supplier-management problems caused significant delays. GM and Ford acquired plants from Delphi and Visteon, respectively, to assure parts supplies for automobile production. Sometimes firms seek supply guarantees; hence, Toyota invested in lithium extraction so as to control supply of a critical raw material for car batteries. Many firms form supplier partnerships to ensure security of supply: The firm and its supplier set joint long-term goals, engage in equitable value-sharing, and cooperate in investment decisions and technological development.

The most severe supplier threat is **forward integration** — the supplier becomes a direct competitor by conducting operations the firm currently performs.[37] Boeing suppliers gained expertise that could benefit Boeing's competitors. Many firms in less-developed countries are outsourced manufacturers for U.S. and European firms; but they also develop the skills for future forward integration. Indian diamond jewelry makers now sell branded products that compete with former customers. Some firms work hard to inhibit such forward integration: One firm relabeled and repainted supplier components to disguise their origin; another designed products to be incompatible with component suppliers.[38]

Marketing Question

Think about the firm and product you selected earlier, p. 61. Identify: (1) current direct competitors, (2) potential new direct entrants, (3) indirect competitors, (4) suppliers, and (5) buyers. In the next few years:
(a) What changes do you expect in current direct competitors?
(b) What positive and negative implications for the firm may occur from acquisitions, mergers, and leveraged buyouts?
(c) How should relationships with the firm's suppliers and buyers affect its strategy?

KEY IDEA

➤ The most significant threats from suppliers and buyers are, respectively:

• Forward integration
• Backward integration

BUYERS

Buyers purchase the firm's products. A firm with many small customers faces little buyer pressure, but a small number of large customers can exert tremendous pressure. Buyer pressure typically increases as its market share increases. The firm's margins shrink when powerful customers demand price discounts and expensive services. In 2010, Cablevision blacked out ABC channels less than 24 hours before the Academy Awards over a fee dispute. De Beers sets the price for diamonds; suppliers can take it or leave it! Walmart demands, and receives, many supplier concessions, and leading automobile firms secure large concessions from parts suppliers. Buyer pressure may ease if some suppliers go out of business and the remainder refuse to submit.

The most severe buyer threat is **backward integration** — the buyer becomes a new direct competitor by conducting operations the firm currently performs. Competition from backward-integrating buyers is especially difficult to address as they often enjoy better relationships with end customers. The fertilizer example illustrates the supplier's dilemma:

FD (fertilizer distributor) (disguised name) purchased bags of fertilizer from the manufacturer and resold them to farmers. FD believed it could increase profits by buying fertilizer in bulk and doing the bagging itself; FD planned to erect a small bagging plant in its parking lot. FD asked the manufacturer to supply fertilizer in bulk rather than in bags. The supplier was unwilling to give up margin on bagging and refused. FD secured bulk fertilizer elsewhere and entered the bagging business.

MULTIPLE INDUSTRY FORCES

Of course, multi-business firms face multiple industry forces, but their individual businesses may also face multiple industry forces, notably when they participate in *two-sided markets* — the firm faces two or more distinct buyer groups. The firm's ability to attract, retain, and grow customers in one buyer group depends on its success in attracting, retaining, and growing customers in a second buyer group. Examples include: TV stations — viewers and advertisers; recruitment agencies — job seekers and employers; video game hardware firms — players and developers; and HMOs — patients and doctors.[39] The firm faces a separate set of industry forces in each of the two markets.

Relatedly, in a simpler world, the firm may have been a direct competitor, indirect competitor, supplier, *or* buyer to another organization. With increased environmental complexity, the firm may today play multiple roles at that same organization. Samsung not only makes and sells consumer electronic products like TVs, cell phones, computers, printers, and cameras, it also makes components of these products for other firms; hence, Samsung is both supplier and direct competitor.[40]

KEY IDEA

➤ The firm faces a broad set of environmental forces — PESTLE:

- Political
- Economic
- Sociocultural
- Technological
- Legal/regulatory
- Environmental (physical)

ENVIRONMENTAL FORCES[41]

Environmental forces affect the firm and other industry participants. Figure 3.8 shows how these **PESTLE** forces — *political, economic, sociocultural, technological, legal/regulatory* and *environmental (physical)* — and industry forces relate to one another. Some PESTLE forces affect individual businesses. Other PESTLE forces like the World Trade Organization (WTO) (political), exchange rate movements (economic), and the Internet (technological) impact individual businesses but also a multi-business firm as a whole. Most observers believe that environmental change overall is much greater than at any time in the past. Hence, current businesses may be threatened but, correspondingly, entrepreneurial thinking can identify new opportunities.

Forward-thinking firms seek out leading indicators of environmental trends: Many firms are now developing *green* products that appeal to environmentally concerned customers. Germany leads in environmental legislation and related political activism; California spawns many youth-oriented trends; African-American male teenagers are a leading fashion influence; and research at universities like MIT, Cambridge, Columbia, and Stanford often leads the way in biotechnology, computers, medicine, and telecommunications. Siemens has identified and organized around four megatrends — climate change, demographic change, globalization, and urbanization.

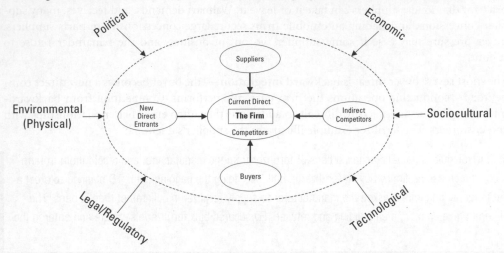

FIGURE 3.8

THE PESTLE MODEL — ENVIRONMENTAL FORCES ACTING ON THE INDUSTRY

POLITICAL

Governments set the frameworks for regulators to develop the rules for business. Table 3.4 identifies several policy variables and their general goals. Separate government departments at different levels (federal, state, local) are also often large purchasers, in part to make investments for the public good, and sometimes are sellers — like the U.S. Postal Service.

Policy Variable	General Goal
Competition policy	Enhance competition
Employment law	Protect employees
Government spending	Implement government policy
Multinational agreements	Enhance trade and investment
Political stability	Enhance investment
Privatization	Enhance competition
Regulation of financial markets	Protect investors
Taxation policy	Redistribute income

TABLE 3.4

SELECTED POLITICAL VARIABLES

Marketing Question

Google took several actions related to disagreements with the Chinese government over censorship. Research these. Do you agree with Google's actions? Why or why not?

Typically, governments intervene in economies via monetary and fiscal policy to pursue political ends and enhance consumer welfare by creating a *level playing field*. But they may also intervene to assist preferred local firms, like the U.S. favoring (allegedly) Boeing over EADS (Europe) for the next-generation aerial-refueling planes. In recent years, many national governments realized that regulations designed to protect consumers locked in competitive structures, restricted competitive entry, and stifled innovation, contrary to intended results; governments cut back regulations and placed greater reliance on the market. Regardless, many countries continue to regulate consumer protection, competitive entry, imports (tariffs and quotas), and exports, product performance, price-setting, distribution, and advertising. India and Japan no longer focus so heavily on import substitution and increasing exports, and some countries privatized state-owned enterprises. In a reversal of this trend in the 2008–9 financial crisis, the U.S. government took significant ownership in Citibank, AIG, and GM, and the British government in The Royal Bank of Scotland.

Governments sometimes intervene directly in the market. During the early 21st century anthrax scare, the Canadian government pressured Bayer to supply one million anthrax-fighting Cipro tablets at a *special price*, by threatening to invalidate its patent. Countries like India and Brazil sometimes threaten compulsory licenses unless drug prices fall, or they ignore drug patents. As a result, in Brazil, Roche priced Viracept, an AIDS drug, at 30 percent of the U.S. price.

Firms try to influence political actions by contributing to political campaigns and hiring lobbyists to influence legislation and the rule-making process. Sometimes trade associations undertake these actions. Four U.S. insurance firms — Chubb, Hartford, Kemper, and Liberty Mutual, lobbied the U.S. Congress (unsuccessfully) to close an income-tax loophole that they believed disadvantaged U.S. firms. Political action committees (PACs) and special-interest groups, like environmentalists, consumerists, and disease-related advocacy groups (breast cancer and obesity), also try to influence the political process. Some special-interest groups try to affect firms directly. PETA (People for the Ethical Treatment of Animals) has caused over 30 firms to ban wool from mulesed merino sheep.[42]

ECONOMIC

> ### Marketing Question
>
> In difficult economic times many firms suffer, but others prosper. Name some firms that prosper. Why are they successful?

The country's economic well-being influences market demand. High inflation, high and rising interest rates, falling share prices, and a depreciating currency point to an unhealthy economy. But some measures can be ambiguous. High inflation rates, like those in 1980s Latin America, are generally a negative indicator; but very low and below zero inflation rates, like in 1990s Japan, are also negative. High savings rates are generally positive, but too high rates lower consumption. Because *expectations* influence spending patterns, evaluating direction and rate of change are critical. China's GDP is quite low, but GDP growth is high, and China is now a major market. Table 3.5 shows several economic variables and their general impact on economic well-being.

TABLE 3.5

SELECTED ECONOMIC VARIABLES

Economic Variable	Impact on Economic Well-Being
Balance of payments	Negative balance of payments means government must borrow — increased pressure for higher taxes.
Exchange rates	Value of national currencies. Low exchange rates help exports; high exchange rates are better for purchasing foreign goods.
Disposable income	An individual's income after paying taxes — available for spending and saving. Higher is better.
GDP or GDP per capita	The measure of a nation's output, or output per person. Higher is better.
Inflation	Rate of price increases. Lower is better, but too low means deflation.
Interest rates	Affect customer spending — especially for durables and business investment. Lower is better, but too low may fuel deflation.
Savings rate	Affects interest rates and consumer spending. Higher is better, but too high means insufficient consumption.
Unemployment	Population out of work. Lower is better, but too low and labor costs increase.

Per capita GDP and disposable income are generally good indicators of market demand, but the firm must also consider distribution across the population and population size. Average incomes in India and China are low, but India's middle class exceeds 200 million. Residents of Shanghai, Beijing, and other Chinese cities have significant income, and SUVs are popular among middle-class Chinese!

Of course, most firms suffer in poor economies but some may prosper. In the 2008–9 recession, Campbell's soup and private-label sales increased significantly, and firms like Dollar General

(25 percent of products sell for $1 or less) and Walmart performed well — Walmart even earned profits in Japan for the first time. In Europe, sales at German discounters Lidl and Aldi grew fast.[43] U.S. toy industry sales declined by 5 percent but Lego sales increased almost 20 percent — based on a strong brand, entry into new market segments, high product quality, and operational efficiency.

Increased globalization has led to more closely integrated individual country economies. An economic downturn in one country can affect many others. In the early 21st century, no country escaped the U.S.-led recession. Furthermore, global firms must be concerned about exchange rate movements — they often incur costs in currency A but earn revenues in currency B. In Europe, the euro introduction has eased this problem.

SOCIOCULTURAL

Culture is "the distinctive customs, achievements, products, outlook, etc., of a society or group; the way of life of a society or group."[44] Culture is learned early in life, largely by influence from family, schools, and religious institutions. Cultural norms are resistant to change but do evolve; one example is the switch from traditional burial to cremation in western cultures. Generally, people do not notice culture in their everyday lives, but recognize cultural values by comparison with different cultures.

> Hispanics in the southeastern U.S. suffer from different diseases and make healthcare decisions differently from other cultural groups. Community and family are central to the buying process. Pfizer created market managers for Hispanics, assigning them the task of determining how Pfizer's drugs could best meet Hispanics' specific cultural needs.

What is normal in one culture may appear odd in another. Most cultures give gifts but meanings can differ widely. Chinese associate white, blue, and black gifts with funerals; sharp objects like knives, scissors, and letter-openers symbolize cutting off a friendship. In Germany, an even number of flowers is bad luck, but red roses suggest a strong romantic interest![45] For cleaning products, Americans value labor-saving convenience, but Italians want tough cleaners, not timesavers. Placing condoms in workplace bathrooms is fine in France and Scandinavia, and on-the-job flirting is normal. In the U.S., flirting may lead to termination of employment. Acquiring pirated products is acceptable in some cultures but viewed as stealing in others.

CULTURAL GROUPS. A cultural group may inhabit a nation-state, like Brazil or Iran; a geographic region within a nation, like the South or Midwest in the U.S.[46]; a multinational region, like Latin America or Southeast Asia; or it may comprise a people, regardless of geographic location, like the Armenian, Jewish, and Kurdish diasporas. A person may belong to several cultural groups, such as a Turkish immigrant in Germany. Table 3.6 outlines cultural variables.

Marketing Question

Suppose your firm transfers you to a marketing position in Brazil (France, Japan, Saudi Arabia, or your choice). What issues will you focus on to avoid professional and personal missteps?

TABLE 3.6

SELECTED SOCIOCULTURAL VARIABLES[47]

Cultural Dimension	Elements of Cultural Dimensions
Aesthetics	Beauty, good taste, color, music, brand names, architecture
Education	Formal, vocational, primary, secondary, higher, literacy, human resources planning
Language	Spoken, written, official, linguistic pluralism, hierarchy, international, mass media
Law	Common, code, foreign, home country antitrust policy, international, regulation
Politics	Nationalism, sovereignty, imperialism, power, national interests, ideologies, political risk
Religion	Sacred objects, philosophical systems, beliefs and norms, prayer, taboos, holidays, rituals
Social organization	Kinship, institutions, authority structures, interest groups, mobility, stratification, status systems
Technical and material	Transportation, energy systems, tools and objects, communications, urbanization, science, invention
Values and attitudes	Time, achievement, work, wealth, change, scientific method, risk-taking, community involvement

A cultural group may comprise different subcultures, each reflecting both group-culture and sub-cultural elements. Three important U.S. subcultures are Baby Boomers, Generation X, and Generation Y; each represents a different marketing opportunity.[48] Consider music: Baby Boomers — Simon and Garfunkel; Generation X — Nirvana; and Generation Y — Tupac Shakur. Of course, subcultures evolve; perhaps, in 20 years, today's Generation Y will appreciate Simon and Garfunkel? Religious and social-issue groups may also play a critical role by pressuring firms to behave in ways they view as appropriate: Several groups target Walmart for various reasons, and religious and family groups boycotted Ford for sponsoring gay rights parades.

> Intel's ethnographers visited people at home, focusing on their lives and computer needs. Chinese parents worried that computers would distract children from schoolwork. Intel changed its design to include several education applications and a lock. Chinese parents could help children with schoolwork and stop them *wasting time* on the Web.

Marketing Question

Nestlé Prepared Foods (NPF) identified several trends — increasing time pressure on dual-income households, sharpening decline in culinary skills, growth of empty-nester households, increasing belief that good food equals good health, and growing concern with obesity. How would you advise NPF?

LOCALIZATION AND GLOBALIZATION. An important contemporary cultural issue is the tension between localization and globalization. Some groups seek identities based on religion — Muslim fundamentalism in the Middle East and North Africa, and Hindu fundamentalism in India. Other groups focus on ethnicity — Kurds (Iraq, Iran, and Turkey), the Welsh, and Basques (France and Spain). By contrast, organizations like the UN, WTO, and UNESCO promote globalism.[49] Enhanced travel, improved communications and transportation, the Internet, and globally available television and movies are ready lubricants. Indeed, Levi's jeans and Marlboro cigarettes benefited from scores of cowboy movies distributed around the world. But many individuals and groups resist globalization in general, and U.S. and Western influence in particular. Protesters routinely disrupt WTO meetings; the Iraq war spurred global boycotts of U.S. products, and French products have been boycotted in the U.S.[50] European countries banned genetically altered foods,[51] Muslims boycotted Danish products after a Danish newspaper published unflattering cartoons of the Prophet Muhammad, and Saudi Arabia banned Barbie dolls — a symbol of *Western decadence*. Global and local trends have a profound impact on firms and the products they produce and sell. For the 1.4 billion Muslims worldwide, Dubai-based Ilkone Mobile Telecommunications designed a mobile phone, loaded with the Koran, that alerts owners to prayer times and has a compass that points toward Mecca. Relatedly, major western banks now offer Islamic banking products (no interest charges) like Islamic loans, Islamic bonds, Islamic credit cards, and even Islamic derivatives!

TECHNOLOGICAL

Since World War II, technological innovation has produced many products and services we now take for granted. A partial list includes color television, dry copiers, synthetic and optical fibers, cellular telephones, computers, integrated circuits, microwave ovens, passenger jet aircraft, communication satellites, ATMs, virtually all plastics, and antibiotic drugs. These innovations changed individual, household, and organizational life; restructured industries; and drove economic growth.

Marketing Question

Select an industry you are considering as a career. How has technological change affected leading firms in this industry during the past ten years? How do you think technological change will affect leading firms during the next ten years?

Today, the pace of technological change continues to accelerate. In the 20 years between 1970 and 1990, six product classes in consumer electronics achieved mass acceptance — video recorders, video cameras, videogame consoles, CD players, telephone answering machines, and cordless telephones. Since the mid-1990s, widely adopted products include personal computers, personal digital assistants (PDAs), digital cameras, DVD players, MP3 players, and digital video recorders (DVRs). The Internet (box p. 79) is changing the way entire industries compete and offering previously unimaginable customer benefits. eBay affects the way many people buy and sell products — half a million U.S. residents now make their living selling products on eBay. South Korea plans that by the end of 2012, every household will be connected to the Internet at one gigabyte per second, 200 times faster than the average U.S. connection.

Some technological innovations are industry-specific; others, like the shift in payment methods from cash to checks to credit/debit cards to cell phones, affect the entire economy. Moore's law states that transistor density on computer chips and microprocessor speed double every 18 to 24 months; improving price/performance ratios — Table 3.7 — are transforming industry and commerce. Access to computers and cell phones continues to increase, and computing power infuses increasing numbers of products. Automobiles, aircraft, surgical equipment, and elevators already use computer technology to operate more efficiently, predictably, and safely. Experts believe genetic engineering and nanotechnology will have similarly broad impact.

Year	Cost	Power
1967	$10,000,000	1
2002	$7.0	1,500,000
2007	$0.7	11,000,000
2017 (forecast)	$0.01	67,000,000

TABLE 3.7

IMPLICATIONS OF MOORE'S LAW[52]

Technological change can be either sustaining or disruptive[53]:

- **Sustaining technologies** are often incremental. They improve performance for *current* products on dimensions that *existing* customers value. Included are *cordless* vacuum cleaners, *power* drills, and *mobile* telephones versus *plugged-in* products.

- **Disruptive technologies** bring new and very different value propositions. They change customer behavior by finding new applications and initially a few new-to-the-market customers. Included are PCs versus typewriters, digital music downloads to iPods and other devices versus store-bought CDs, and voice-over-Internet protocol (VOIP) versus long-distance telephone. Disruptive technologies spawn products that threaten and change entire industries. For existing customers, early product versions are typically inferior, like the first digital cameras — more expensive and complicated than chemical-film cameras. But as cost-benefit ratios improve, the disruptive technology surpasses the old technology. When disruptive technology becomes mainstream, it threatens old technology firms that do not adapt. Examples: Digital cameras and discount brokerages significantly affected market leaders Kodak and Merrill Lynch, respectively, and changed their industries.[54]

KEY IDEA

➤ Technological innovation can be:
- Sustaining — improving performance of established products
- Disruptive — offering new value propositions

Generally, current suppliers develop sustaining technologies to serve the needs of current customers; new entrants introduce disruptive technologies that initially satisfy new and different customers. In the disk-drive industry, current disk-drive suppliers pioneered 14-inch Winchester and 2.5-inch drives — sustaining innovations for mainframe and laptop computers, respectively. By contrast, 8.5-, 5.25-, 3.5-, and 1.8-inch drives were disruptive technologies. Initially, each innovation satisfied the needs of different customers — respectively, manufacturers of minicomputers, desktop PCs, laptops, and portable heart-monitoring devices.[55]

Current suppliers tend to ignore disruptive technologies, or at least underfund them. Two factors seem crucial:

- **Inferior performance.** Early on, the disruptive technology's performance is inferior to current technology, and products lack critical attributes current customers require.

- **Firm rewards.** Initial expectations of sales and profit in the disruptive technology are less attractive than continued investment to serve current customers.

To escape this trap, the firm should manage sustaining and disruptive technologies in separate organizations. For a disruptive technology, the firm could set up an independent unit or take an equity stake in a specially formed organization for developing the new technology.

Much new technology emerges from corporate R&D laboratories. But individual entrepreneurs are very influential; consider the births of Acer, Apple, HP, Intel, Microsoft, TI, Sony, and Xerox. Some inventors are very prolific. Jerome Murray held 75 patents on a diverse range of

The Internet

The Internet is a *killer app.*[56] Like movable type, the telephone, and the automobile, the Internet is changing the way society works and functions. The automobile changed the way people live, shop, work, and spend leisure time — the Internet is doing the same.

The Internet is an efficient distribution channel, interactive communications tool, marketplace, and information system. Firms communicate with customers and suppliers in new ways; customers communicate with each other and with product/service suppliers via social networking. Increasing interconnectedness via publicly available Wi-Fi and mobile devices, open standards, and new protocols will further ease information flow.[57] The type and quantity of data the firm collects, stores, and distributes is also changing. Many retailers transmit cash register data direct to suppliers. The ratio of goods shipped to goods in inventory has dropped from 1:2 in 1970 to 1:1.2, driving down inventory costs. Firms can also collect and manage data about current and potential customers and take action in real time.

The Internet reduces transactions costs; Table 3.8 shows the dramatic impact on personal financial services. When insurance buyers and sellers meet on the Internet, they eliminate agents and brokers — and their fees. Internet purchases are common for financial instruments, airline travel, and hotel reservations.

TABLE 3.8

AVERAGE COST PER TRANSACTION IN RETAIL BANKING[58]

Mode	Cost / Transaction
Branch teller	$2.50
Telephone	$1.00
ATM	$0.40
Voice response	$0.24
Internet	$0.10

Lead generation and advertising for small businesses is shifting from the Yellow Pages to real-time, adaptable, adjustable text ads spread across thousands of web pages. No longer must consumer "fingers do the walking." Google Adwords and Facebook ensure that contextually appropriate ads reach targeted customers.

Sellers reach more buyers on the Internet; buyers access more suppliers. eBay benefits from this *network effect.* As more sellers post products on eBay, eBay buyers receive greater value. As more buyers purchase on eBay, eBay sellers receive greater value![59]

B2B exchanges are popular. Firms like GE post requirements, and pre-approved suppliers bid in a *reverse auction.* (Note: In reverse auctions, prices go down, not up, as in traditional English auctions.) Some firms form B2B-exchange alliances with competitors to develop reverse auctions. Ford, GM, and DaimlerChrysler formed the Covisint exchange (since sold).

Perhaps the Internet's greatest impact will be in industries where products can be digitized. Recorded music has seen significant turmoil, including widespread piracy — iTunes has brought some stability. Movies and other videos may enter a turbulent phase as transmission capacity increases. Many Internet sites provide content — Google and Yahoo! — news, and interaction via chat rooms and bulletin boards, with suppliers, vendors, and customers.

Interactivity and accessibility of online content has upended the media industry. User-generated content and meta-data created by communities are watchwords for the next generation of Internet media firms. YouTube, Blogger, Wikipedia, and others have based their success on user-generated journals, videos, and other data.

Perhaps the most important recent trends are the growth of Facebook, LinkedIn, Twitter, and others, and the Internet's interface with mobile devices like cell phones and tablet computers. The emerging managerial role is to be fully aware of the various developments and to take advantage of the firm's emerging options.

new products — electric carving knife, audible pressure cooker, passenger aircraft-boarding ramp, and a pump for open-heart surgery. Leading firms do not always appreciate independent inventors' discoveries: 3M, A.B. Dick, IBM, Kodak, and RCA each rejected Chester Carlson's xerography invention.[60] All major appliance manufacturers declined James Dyson's vacuum cleaner; Dyson launched it himself and now has a net worth close to $1 billion.[61] Trevor Baylis, inventor of the Freeplay wind-up radio, had a similar experience.[62]

> Steve Jobs reflected on his and Steve Wozniak's experience with the personal computer: "So we went to Atari and said, 'Hey, we've got this amazing thing, even built it with some of your parts, and what do you think about funding us? Or we'll give it to you. We just want to do it. Pay our salary, we'll come work for you.' And they said 'No.' So, then we went to Hewlett-Packard, and they said 'Hey, we don't need you. You haven't gone through college yet.'"

LEGAL/REGULATORY

The legal framework (LF) is the rules for business. LF aims to protect societal interests, regulate market power, hinder collusion, and stop deceptive practices. LFs differ across countries, but generally govern mergers and acquisitions, capital movements, consumer protection, and employment conditions. The U.S. and Britain have well-developed systems based on statute and case law; the Napoleonic Code generally forms the LF in continental Europe. By contrast, poorly developed systems of commercial law in Russia and China cause major problems for foreign firms. In China, product copying and illegal use of brand names is rampant, despite China's WTO membership.

Individuals, firms, and governments use LFs to advance their interests. Individuals file lawsuits about poorly designed or manufactured products. Firms sue suppliers, customers, and competitors, and governments bring lawsuits. Regulation operates at various governmental levels. Successive New York Attorneys General Elliot Spitzer and Andrew Cuomo sued many financial service firms and their senior executives. And local regulations have often stopped Walmart from opening new stores.

Typically, legislation drives regulation. Powerful regulatory bodies, like the EPA, FCC, FDA, FTC, and NTSB in the U.S. and their equivalents in other countries, enact rules embodying legislation. The FDA decides what drugs pharmaceutical firms can make and sell, what diseases they can treat, and what data they can provide, and to whom. After Enron's collapse, the SEC acted to reduce conflicts of interest. Investment banks made greater separations between research and investment banking; accounting firms separated auditing from consulting, sometimes by divestiture.

International agreements developed via supra-national organizations like the EU, IMF, UN, and WTO also lead to regulation. China's WTO entry may someday ameliorate the copying problem. The U.S. government sued Microsoft for antitrust violations and in 2002 signed a *consent decree*; but in 2007, Microsoft suffered a major defeat by losing a related EU lawsuit.

ENVIRONMENTAL (PHYSICAL)

Natural and man-made forces coexist in an uneasy equilibrium. Humans have little or no control over natural phenomena like asteroids hitting the earth, earthquakes, erupting volcanoes, hurricanes and tornadoes, monsoons, tsunamis, and everyday weather patterns. In 2010 and 2011, volcanic ash from Iceland and Chile, respectively, upset European air travel for several days and devastated the Bariloche, Argentina, tourist industry. Forces like Japan's tsunami and Thailand's floods (2011) highlight the fragility of increasingly decentralized yet tightly integrated global supply chains — production of many products (especially automobiles) suffered from these events in many parts of the world. By contrast, human action is driving rain-forest and wetland destruction, global warming,[63] retreating coastlines, pollution, raw material

Marketing Question

Many specific environmental forces seem to take firms by surprise. How would you prepare your firm to deal with unexpected environmental shocks?

Marketing Question

Consider the firm/product you selected earlier, p. 61. How does each PESTLE force — political, economic, sociocultural, technological, legal/regulatory, and environmental (physical) — affect the product or market? What changes do you expect in the next three to five years? Will these be positive or negative for the firm?

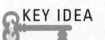

KEY IDEA

➤ Environmental forces are constantly in flux; they also interact with each other.

shortages, and the shrinking ozone layer. Damage and climate change to the natural environment has spawned demand for pollution control and renewable energy products; climate influences demand for beer, soft drinks, umbrellas, and pantyhose. Man-made modifications to the physical environment, typically involving large government investment, often have an important impact on commerce. The openings of the Suez (mid-19th century) and Panama (early 20th century) Canals cut costs and transit time for much international trade; the new Panama Canal widening (completion 2014) will permit much larger ships. The planned Central Bioceanic Corridor (rail) across the Andes between Argentina and Chile will have a similar impact in southern South America. Water diversion and other irrigation projects create and/or sustain farmland, and river modification allows electricity production via hydroelectricity.

Firms face increasing pressure from governments, environmentalists, single-issue advocacy groups, and the public at large to provide increased transparency and assume greater environmental responsibility for products, packaging, and production systems. In Germany, disposable packaging use has decreased substantially.[64] European automakers will soon have to re-use 80 percent of a car's weight, or pay for recycling.[65] Some firms are aggressively enacting *green* strategies. HP recycles 70,000 tons annually (about 10 percent of sales); Best Buy accepts virtually any junk electronic product from customers and directs its own recycling program; Walmart sells environmentally friendly products like concentrated laundry detergent and fluorescent bulbs; and Philips is investing heavily in LED (light-emitting diodes) — 98 percent more efficient than some incandescent bulbs.

Natural resource availability is a significant environmental issue. Oil is the basic raw material for energy, plastics, synthetic fibers, transportation, and other industries, yet new supplies are increasingly scarce. New industries like fuel cells, solar power, and wind power are starting to address this problem, and sales of hybrid cars are fast increasing. U.S. paper companies plant trees in the southern U.S., where they mature faster. Bamboo flooring use is also expanding; bamboo matures faster than trees.

INTERACTIONS AMONG PESTLE FORCES

Figure 3.9 shows each PESTLE force — political, economic, sociocultural, technological, legal/regulatory, and environmental (physical) — interacting with its sister forces. These interconnected forces form the firm's environmental panorama and in turn act on industry forces. The Internet (technological) has major implications for sociocultural and political forces, especially in countries with little political freedom, and has major implications for industry forces. In South Korea, huge government investment in broadband infrastructure (political) is spurring domestic innovation (technological).[66] In Germany, recycling has vital economic, environmental (physical) and political dimensions. As environmental change and turbulence grow, environmental interconnectedness will increase.

FIGURE 3.9

THE AUGMENTED INDUSTRY ENVIRONMENT

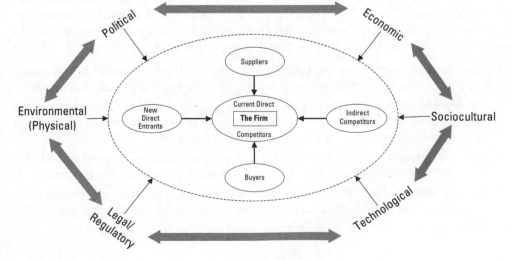

THE MANAGERIAL PROCESS ENVIRONMENT

Executives use *intellectual capital* (IC) — concepts, frameworks, tools, and ideas — to lead and manage their firms. IC evolves via research efforts at business schools, culling of consulting experience, and learning by practicing managers. Consider how the dominant view on corporate strategy has changed over the years. In the 1960s and 1970s, *conglomeration* was the received wisdom. The co-joining of many disparate businesses formed major firms like ITT, Gulf & Western, and Litton Industries in the U.S. and Slater Walker and the Hanson Trust in Britain. The underlying rationale was risk diversification, similar to how individuals construct personal financial portfolios.

In today's dominant view, investors can diversify more efficiently by investing in multiple single business firms, or buying diversified mutual funds.[67] The watchword for executives is *focus*. Firms should *stick to their knitting*, base strategies on core competence, and divest businesses unrelated to a common strength or purpose. PepsiCo divested Kentucky Fried Chicken, Taco Bell, and Pizza Hut; food and drinks giant Diageo divested Häagen-Dazs and Pillsbury; and British conglomerate, Unigate, sold its dairy, logistics, and bacon manufacturing to focus on fresh convenience foods, as Uniq Foods.[68]

IC spreads through the business environment much like other innovations and enters the modern manager's *kit bag*.[69] In recent years, firms have adopted benchmarking, best practice sharing, branding, customer relationship management (CRM), experience curves, market share/profitability relationships, outsourcing, policy matrices, portfolio models, positioning, strategic objectives, re-engineering, shareholder value, and total quality management (TQM).[70] We discuss some of these in this book.

We do not suggest that each new *buzzword* has value. Rather, your challenge is to distinguish fads from new concepts that add to your personal IC. In this book, we offer the latest thinking on marketing, but marketing will continue to evolve during your careers. Learning is a lifelong commitment. We hope that you will invest the effort to stay current with the evolving managerial process environment.[71]

PULLING IT ALL TOGETHER

The previous sections present four different facets for understanding the firm's current and/or anticipated markets. The managerial task is making sense of the variety of disparate data and turn them into information and insight. The critical problem that firms face is increasing change and turbulence, and hence uncertainty and surprises regarding the various factors we discussed, and their growing interdependence. Many experts converge on several mega trends — continuing technological advances, growth in emerging markets, aging in developed countries, globalization, spikes and spot shortages in commodities, and continuing pressure on prices and costs. Hence, simple extrapolation of the past into the future is increasingly likely to lead to false conclusions. The preferred approach is *scenario planning*.

Traditional uni-dimensional planning prepared the firm for a single future; scenario planning (SP) prepares the firm for multiple potential futures. SP comprises three essential elements:

- **Construct scenarios.** By reflecting on trends, distinguishing between those that are certain and uncertain, and analyzing the development of uncertain trends, the firm develops several internally consistent and mutually exclusive scenarios.

- **Form assumptions.** For each scenario, the firm develops a series of external and internal assumptions that form the building blocks of strategy development for each scenario.

- **Prepare strategy.** The firm tests its current strategy in each scenario and develops more appropriate strategies as necessary.[72] (Chapter 5 shows how to develop competitive scenarios.)

For any market where the firm competes or could compete, management must develop workable estimates of current and potential market size. The factors Chapter 3 discusses are critical influences on market size, and form the intellectual raw material for market-size forecasts. Chapter 6 discusses specific methodologies that can help the firm develop *good* forecasts.

Marketing Question

What other messages did you glean from this chapter?

KEY MESSAGES

To gain market insight, the firm should focus on four broad areas — market structure, market and product evolution, industry forces, and environmental forces:

Market Structure:

- The *market* comprises customers requiring goods and services to satisfy their needs.
- The firm should define the market at several levels.
- *Product class* and *product form* refer to products that all suppliers offer. Product class is a broader level of aggregation than product form.
- Firms offer *product items* to the market — a *product line* consists of multiple product items.
- Fundamental drivers of market size are population and purchasing power.

Market and Product Evolution:

- The life-cycle framework is a good way to think about market and product evolution.
- Life-cycle length is ordered: Market > product class > product form.
- Life cycles have several stages — *introduction, early growth, late growth, maturity, decline* — each with distinguishing characteristics.
- Profit-margin life cycles do not mirror sales life cycles.

Industry Forces:

- The *five-forces model* is a useful way of examining pressures on the firm.
- The five forces are *current direct competitors, new direct entrants, indirect competitors, suppliers,* and *buyers.* Each force affects the firm in a different way.

Environmental Forces:

- Environmental forces impact both the firm and other industry players.
- Environmental forces are *political, economic, sociocultural, technological, legal/ regulatory,* and *environmental (physical)* — PESTLE.
- The PESTLE forces are in a continuous state of flux and are increasingly interconnected.
- The *managerial process* environment is the intellectual capital for leading and managing firms.

Scenario planning is a useful approach for pulling together the various market-insight elements and predicting the future. Various approaches are available for forecasting market size — Chapter 6.

VIDEOS AND AUDIOS

Market Insight   a301 🎧

a301

QUESTIONS FOR STUDY AND DISCUSSION

Can you answer the questions implied by this chapter's learning objectives? Check!

1. In the early 2000s, Krispy Kreme Doughnuts (KKD) was one of the U.S.'s fastest-growing firms. Then the widely publicized Atkins low-carb diet changed consumer attitudes toward food. Some food firms quickly offered low-carb options; others repositioned their products. KKD did not address the low-carb trend. Rather, it manipulated financial results, and shareholder value collapsed. If you had been KKD's marketing director, how would you have addressed the low-carb trend?

2. Interpersonal communication is fundamental to the human condition. Develop life cycles for this market and the various product classes and product forms that satisfy this customer need.

3. For many years, Kodak has been a leading U.S. company. Use the five-forces model to assess the industry forces Kodak faces.

4. American Airlines (AA) is a major U.S. carrier. Use the five-forces and PESTLE models to scope out the various external forces AA faces.

5. Identify and classify environmental pressures that Walmart faces. Why does Walmart face these pressures? How do you assess Walmart's performance in addressing them?

6. Select a product in which you are interested. Alternatively, consider this book — *Managing Marketing in the 21st Century*. What are the direct and indirect competitors? What competitors do you expect tomorrow? How would you compete against direct competitors? Indirect competitors? How would you prepare for tomorrow's competition?

CHAPTER 4
CUSTOMER
INSIGHT v401 📹

To access O-codes, go to **www.ocodes.com**

LEARNING OBJECTIVES

When you have completed this chapter, you will be able to:

- Define and describe customer insight.
- Identify customers, and distinguish between macro and micro customers and between direct and indirect customers.
- Identify the various roles people play in the purchase-decision process.
- Use several frameworks to understand customer value.
- Analyze critical stages in the purchase-decision process.
- Highlight how customers choose among purchase alternatives.
- Classify customer purchasing processes to help develop market strategies.
- Understand the key influences on consumer (B2C) and organizational (B2B) purchases.

OPENING CASE: IKEA

IKEA is the world's most successful global retailer. All IKEA stores operate under a franchise from IKEA Systems B.V. The first IKEA store opened in Almhult, Sweden, in 1958. IKEA's vision is "to create a better everyday life for many people." IKEA is not just another furniture retailer; franchising supports IKEA's vision by easing market expansion. IKEA provides designers with customer insight for fashioning many different types of value.

In 2011, revenues for the 320 IKEA stores in more than 40 countries exceeded €25 billion. Targeting middle-class customers, IKEA offers a broad range of affordable, IKEA-designed, contemporary home-furnishing products. IKEA's immense product line spans 20 different categories including bathroom, beds and mattresses, bookcases and storage, pet products, lighting, TV and media solutions, tables and chairs, and work areas. Many IKEA stores also offer food products.

What makes IKEA such a different firm is the IKEA Concept, an obsessive drive for low costs via focus on design and function. For each product, IKEA designers start with a functional need and a price. They avoid non-value features like expensive finishes on shelf-backs or table undersides. Rather, design expertise and low-cost manufacturing lets IKEA develop products that suppliers can produce at the lowest possible cost.

Low costs and high volumes push prices down even further. To reduce transportation costs, IKEA designs and ships most products in flat packs. *Customers purchase products in the store, pick them up at the warehouse, then drive them home. Customers do simple assembly, with an IKEA-provided wrench and instructions. IKEA's mantra, "You do your part. We do our part. Together we save money," supports its low-price approach.*

By close attention to customer needs, IKEA has become a home furnishings icon. IKEA distributes millions of catalogs, printed in multiple languages, free to households in its primary market areas around the world. The catalog, also available online, offers solutions, inspiration, and low-price products. Prices are valid for 12 months.

Each IKEA store is a large blue and yellow building averaging 300,000 square feet. IKEA wants customers to become comfortable with its home furnishing solutions. Hence, IKEA displays products in realistic room settings and encourages customers to sit, lie down, open and close drawers, compare styles, compare prices, and imagine the possibilities.

A typical IKEA store displays up to 10,000 individual items. IKEA makes life easy for shoppers by laying out a unidirectional marked path through the store's many showrooms. Each store has a playroom at the entrance where parents can drop off children for more leisurely shopping, and a restaurant for shopping breaks. In 2010, IKEA stores had 700 million visitors!

CASE QUESTION

What value elements does IKEA deliver to customers? How do you assess the introduction of food products in IKEA stores?

IKEA strives to deliver great customer value. Customers are the firm's core assets. When the firm does a good job of delivering customer value, it attracts, retains, and grows customers, makes profits today and tomorrow, survives and grows, and enhances shareholder value. To succeed in the customer-value challenge, the firm must develop good **customer insight**, based on deep customer understanding. This chapter focuses on securing customer insight.

To deliver customer value, the firm must answer the three core questions in Figure 4.1:

- **Who are the customers?** So far, we have used the term *customer* fairly loosely. Now we sharpen focus by considering direct and indirect customers, and current and potential customers. The firm must know who is involved in the purchase decision, and the various roles individuals play in the **decision-making unit** (DMU).

- **What do customers need and want?** Understanding customer needs is critical for delivering benefits and values. Securing customer insight may require in-depth customer research and a deep understanding of customer value.

- **How do customers buy?** The firm must know the intricacies of the customer **decision-making process (DMP)**, and the various influencing factors. We consider consumer (B2C) and organizational (B2B) purchase decisions separately.

FIGURE 4.1

CUSTOMER INSIGHT

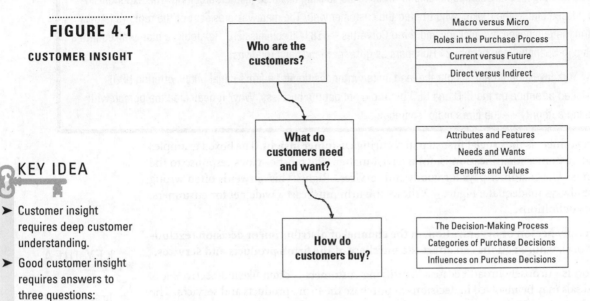

KEY IDEA

➤ Customer insight requires deep customer understanding.

➤ Good customer insight requires answers to three questions:

  • Who are the customers?
  • What do customers need and want?
  • How do customers buy?

THE CHANGING VIEW

OLD WAY	NEW WAY
Basic customer understanding is sufficient	Sophisticated and timely customer insight is critical
Cognitive bias regarding customer insight	Broader view of customer behavior
Customer insight mainly applied in consumer packaged goods	Customer insight applied in many domains: product and service, public and nonprofit, nation states, politics, and personal careers
Customers passive	Customers pro-active and interactive; want to be informed and engaged
Customers uninformed and accepting	Customers well-informed and demanding
Domestic view of customers is sufficient	Global view of customers essential
Focus on customers only	Focus also on organizational stakeholders and other influencers
Marketing concepts apply to consumers as buyers	Marketing concepts apply both to consumers and organizations as buyers
Narrow view of customers — like direct customers only, or consumers only	Multi-tiered, more complex view of customers
Supplier power dominates	Customer power dominates

WHO ARE THE CUSTOMERS?

A contact lens salesperson waited to see an eye doctor. The receptionist asked how his products compared with the doctor's current purchases. The salesperson patiently answered all her questions and left with an order. What he did not initially know: The receptionist was the doctor's wife and made most purchasing decisions.

A man entered the largest Chevrolet dealership in West Texas, looking like he'd just left an oil rig. The experienced salespeople passed him to the rookie, who treated the customer well. The man was president of the region's largest oil-drilling firm; he purchased two pickups and three Corvettes — $8,000 commission.[1] Relatedly, a man walked into a GM dealership in Shanghai and bought 24 Hummers as gifts for friends and relatives!

A major New York investment bank sought the lead underwriter position for a firm's initial public offering (IPO). The bank lavished attention on the CFO and CEO but it did not get the business. Why? It neglected the person with decision-making authority — the firm's major shareholder!

Identifying customers is the crucial first step in securing **customer insight**. The boxed examples highlight that customer identification is not a trivial matter. The most obvious response to the *who* question is: The customer pays for goods and services.[2] Right? This answer is often wrong and is almost always inadequate. Figure 4.2 shows the firm must cast a wide net for customers. We prefer this definition:

A customer is any person or organization, in the channel of distribution or decision (excluding competitors), whose actions can affect the purchase of the firm's products and services.[3]

This definition is purposely broad because identifying customers is often like a detective's job. Many individuals may be involved in decisions to purchase the firm's products and services. The definition reflects the fact that:

- Both organizations — **macro level** — and individuals — **micro level** — are customers.
- **Customer** roles in purchase decisions include influencers and decision-makers.
- The firm should consider both **current customers** and **potential customers**.
- **Direct customers** pay the firm for products and services, but **indirect customers** — customers of direct customers (and of other indirect customers) — frequently influence purchases.[4]
- Some **two-sided markets** comprise customers that **pay** for products, and customers that receive **free** products. Sellers pay auction houses, buyers receive services free; advertisers pay TV stations, consumers watch free; companies pay employment agencies, job seekers use services free.[5]

FIGURE 4.2

IDENTIFYING CUSTOMERS

Marketing Question

UPS makes offers to mailroom personnel; shipping, customer service, and logistics managers; CFOs; and CEOs. If you were developing a message for the CFO, what needs would you highlight? If you focused on the shipping manager, how might your message differ?

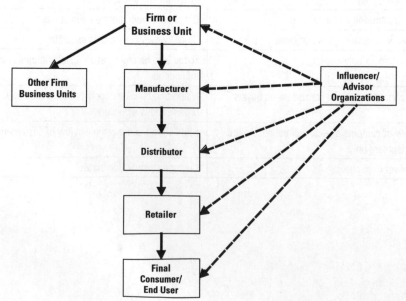

KEY IDEA

➤ Macro-level customers are organizations; micro-level customers are individuals.

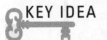

KEY IDEA

➤ Organizations do not make decisions; people in organizations make decisions.

KEY IDEA

➤ Purchase decisions involve many customer roles:
• Buyer
• Coach
• Decision-maker
• Gatekeeper
• Influencer:
 – Champion/Sponsor
 – Spoiler
• Information provider
• Initiator
• Specifier
• User

MACRO-LEVEL CUSTOMERS AND MICRO-LEVEL CUSTOMERS

To gain customer insight, the firm must understand how various customer types fit into the buying process. **Macro-level customers** are the organizational units — manufacturers, wholesalers, retailers, government entities (B2B)[6] and families (B2C) that purchase products and services. **Micro-level customers** are individuals within the macro-level customer that influence purchase or have decision-making authority. Let us be very clear: Organizations do not make decisions; people in organizations make decisions. When micro-level customers jointly make a purchase decision, they act as a **decision-making unit** (**DMU**).[7] Consider two situations — the purchase of a single product and purchases of multiple products.

- **Purchasing a single product.** Individual micro-level customers have specific needs and typically focus on different elements of suppliers' offers. Suppose Intel is buying nitrogen gas for making computer chips. Design engineers want product purity; operations personnel focus on delivery and establishing nitrogen plants on-site; and procurement managers are concerned about price. DMU members want offers that meet their needs but are typically also concerned that the purchase satisfies their colleagues' needs. AT&T won a global deal with Monsanto by meeting face-to-face with Monsanto's geographic regional heads around the world.

- **Purchasing multiple products.** The broad needs of a macro-level customer give the firm an opportunity to sell multiple (often complementary) products and services to a single customer. One of IBM's macro-level information-systems customers may purchase several hardware products, software, and consulting services. UPS makes specific offers to mailroom personnel; shipping, customer service, and logistics managers; CFOs; and CEOs.[8]

Individual micro-level customers sometimes make purchase decisions as members of several macro-level customers — most commonly as an executive (B2B) or as a family member (B2C). The executive may be a micro-level B2B customer for car rental, airline flight, personal computer, and cell phone, and similarly partake in many B2C household decisions.

ROLES IN THE PURCHASE DECISION

Both macro-level and micro-level customers may play several different roles in purchase decisions. *Macro-level customers* like distributors and retailers *purchase* the firm's products; they also *sell, deliver, store,* and/or *service* them. Customers like governments, standards bodies, and consulting firms may *influence* other *macro-level customers* to buy the firm's products.

Micro-level customers play similar roles in both B2C and B2B purchase decisions:

- **Buyer.** Has formal power to execute the purchase, like company purchasing agents.
- **Coach.** Helps the firm navigate the customer's organization and advises how to address influencers and decision-makers.
- **Decision-maker.** Has the formal power to make the purchase decision.
- **Gatekeeper.** Has the power to impede access to decision-makers and influencers. Secretaries, administrative assistants, and purchasing agents often play this role.
- **Influencer.** The decision-maker values the influencer's opinion. In family purchases, the influencer may be a friend, colleague, spouse, child, or grandparent. Organizational influencers include operations, engineering, marketing, and/or general management. Two special types of influencer are champions/sponsors and spoilers.
  - **Champions/Sponsors** promote the firm's interests, based on positive experiences with the supplier and/or personal relationships.
  - **Spoilers**, like disgruntled former employees, try to prevent the customer from purchasing the firm's products.
- **Information provider.** Provides the firm with important information about the customer.

- **Initiator.** Recognizes a problem and sets the purchase process in motion.
- **Specifier.** Exercises influence indirectly by providing expertise like setting specifications. Examples include an architect for a family house purchase or a customer's design engineer.
- **User.** Has little direct role in the purchase decision but may have veto power. Young children often have strong opinions about breakfast cereal, and the factory worker who says, "I'm not working with that red stuff," can be very influential.

Table 4.1 illustrates these various roles in B2C and B2B purchase decisions.

Purchase-Decision Roles	Organizational — B2B	Consumer — B2C
	Multinational firm seeks supplier for marketing training programs	Family is deciding whether to take a cruise for the family vacation
Buyer	Purchasing officer	Father
Coach	Consultant to firm; previously Columbia faculty member	Neighbor — takes three cruises annually
Decision-maker	CEO	Mother
Gatekeeper	Senior HR personnel	Live-in housekeeper
Influencer	Senior line executives	Children
Champion/sponsor	Senior executives committed to Columbia Business School	Second cousin (works for cruise line)
Spoiler	Two senior line executives with MBAs from Harvard and Wharton	Daughter's boyfriend — has summer job at a Caribbean resort
Information provider	Bricker's — good source on executive education	Travel agent
Initiator	Head of HR	Family physician — advises family to take vacation for mother's health
Specifier	Junior human resource (HR) personnel who develop the program	Grandmother (has basic requirements that must be met)
User	Middle managers	Mother, father, children, grandparents

TABLE 4.1

ILLUSTRATION OF ROLES IN B2B AND B2C PURCHASE DECISIONS[9]

Marketing Question

Think of when you were selling something — a product, an idea, or yourself for a job. Who played what roles in the decision? Hint: Don't underestimate gatekeepers, influencers, spoilers, or champions who may have worked in the background.

The Importance of Users

Venice (disguised names) was a large industrial manufacturer working directly with Baltimore Plastics on product development. Venice purchased large quantities of Baltimore's tapes on annual contracts from Gary Ludlow's brokerage firm. Ludlow had sold Baltimore products since Venice was a small customer; he had many close, first-name relationships with Venice personnel, both factory managers and shop-floor workers. Gary was well known for arriving at Venice factories with boxes of donuts that he distributed widely.

Venice owners replaced top management. Venice's new procurement strategy required cutting out middlemen like Ludlow and dealing directly with manufacturing suppliers. Venice put its Baltimore-Ludlow tape business out to competitive bid. Baltimore refused to bid, citing its long-standing Ludlow relationship. Washington, one of Baltimore's toughest competitors, won all the former Baltimore-Ludlow business.

Washington made several sample tape deliveries to Venice where they comfortably met Venice's rigorous testing standards. But the Washington tapes failed in production. Venice managers worked hard with shop-floor personnel, but the tapes would just not work! Shop-floor workers gave many reasons. Ultimately, Venice canceled the Washington contract and ordered Baltimore products from Ludlow. Venice had no further problems!

KEY IDEA

➤ In both B2B and B2C, the roles individuals play vary from purchase decision to purchase decision.

VARIETY AND EVOLUTION OF PURCHASE DECISION ROLES. Because macro-level customers make many different types of purchases, DMU composition typically varies markedly from one decision to another.

- **B2C decisions.** Roles for two typical household (B2C) decisions may be:
  - Home purchase — decision maker, wife; influencers, many family members; buyer, husband
  - Family movie trip — decision makers, children; influencer, father; buyer, mother

Generally speaking, influence by U.S. mothers and children is increasing and by fathers is declining: Women are *buyers* for more than 80 percent of discretionary purchases. These dynamics are driving marketing changes for many products — from automobiles to breakfast cereal. Of course, significant family events, like divorce, remarriage, and death, change family purchasing patterns.

- **B2B decisions.** Organizations use many different DMU constellations for their various purchases. These constellations evolve; suppliers should anticipate that an individual customer employee may — before, during, or after the purchase process:
  - Change roles and responsibilities
  - Enter/leave the DMU
  - Resign from the customer and join a different organization (maybe another customer)

In difficult economic times, purchasing decisions may escalate to the CFO, senior management committee, or even the board of directors for large dollar purchases. The firm may also drive change in customer DMUs by modifying its offer. When high-end supplier Hilti shifted focus from *selling power tools* to *providing a tool management program*, customer decision-making evolved from construction-site crew leaders and purchasing managers to CFOs and CEOs. Roles also change as customer organizations evolve from low-status *purchasing* to high-status *procurement*, or even more broadly into managing the entire *supply chain*. Corporate events like mergers and acquisitions frequently drive changes in the purchasing process. The firm should anticipate change.

CURRENT CUSTOMERS AND POTENTIAL CUSTOMERS

Current customers provide revenues and profits today; Chapter 2 highlighted the role of customer retention for future revenues and profits. But the firm must also identify potential customers. Alcoa and McKinsey devote major efforts to identifying and creating **tomorrow's customers:**

KEY IDEA

➤ The firm must pay attention to both:
- Current customers
- Potential customers

"In our aerospace system, senior Alcoa executives spend extensive time creating an environment to make customers open to innovation. We interact with the top universities that train aerospace and aeronautical engineers.[10] We help design curricula, teach classes, have design contests, and offer internships and jobs. We show students and faculty the latest and greatest in metals. These kids are going to be designing airplanes over the next 20 years — they know Alcoa, they know metals, and they feel pretty good about it. We also do opinion work with the other influential groups — airline executives, pilots, mechanics, and frequent travelers. We are creating a very favorable climate for demanding metallics in airplanes, particularly Alcoa metallics."[11]

McKinsey is a world-leading consulting firm that many business students aspire to join. McKinsey expects newly hired consultants to stay about six to ten years. McKinsey is quite willing to lose its consultants to high-level jobs at client companies, but it works hard to maintain contact with them — it even publishes an alumni magazine. When the former employees' new employer wants advice, which consulting firm will it call?

DIRECT CUSTOMERS AND INDIRECT CUSTOMERS

Typically, the firm's direct customers exchange money for products and services. Many indirect customers buy the firm's products from these direct customers or from other indirect customers. Sometimes direct customers are distributors or retailers (like supermarkets), or end users that buy and use the firm's finished products. In other cases, direct customers transform the firm's product before their own products reach their customers:

A sales team from packaging firm Mead Westvaco (MW) found that a potential direct customer's food products spoiled in the freezers of a potential indirect customer — supermarkets. The direct customer accepted MV's redesigned package; sales and profits increased.

A small German producer sold sheet zinc for the building trade to fabricators — direct customers. The fabricators sold roofing sheets and drainpipes to builders and roofers — indirect customers. Research with builders, roofers, and consumers led the zinc producer to develop a new alloy with better durability and color fastness. Sales soared.[12]

The direct-versus-indirect customer distinction is very important. The firm has a business relationship with direct customers but *may not know* its indirect customers, and hence have little insight into the benefits and values they seek. Until **customer relationship management (CRM)** technology became widely available, FMCG firms like P&G typically could not identify indirect customers — consumers purchasing their products. Today, FMCG firms learn via contests, promotions, and websites. Stouffer's encourages website registration to learn about recipes and menu items; correspondingly, Stouffer gains better insight into consumer needs.

Two examples show the importance of a broad customer view and indirect customers:

KEY IDEA

➤ *Indirect* customers may be more important than *direct* customers — they are often final users and ultimately drive product demand.

Intel traditionally focused efforts on direct customers — computer manufacturers. Much Intel success resulted from the *intel inside* campaign that placed emphasis on indirect customers — consumers, distributors, and retailers.[13]

Agricultural conglomerate Monsanto spent heavily to develop genetically modified seeds that improved yields for direct customers — farmers, but offered no visible benefit for indirect customers — consumers. Monsanto faced enormous criticism and product boycotts from European consumers.

To reinforce the importance of indirect customers, consider what a senior UPS executive told us: "As a company we are very focused, not just on our customers and what we do that helps them, but on what we do that helps their customer. We're always looking through our customer to their customer. We continually ask ourselves ... how does our technology, our products/services and opportunities transcend our customer's relationship with their customers. If they provide better customer service, and achieve lower costs, and really achieve their business vision, and help their customer be successful ... we have a stronger relationship than if we just focus on our relationship with our customer."[14]

WHAT DO CUSTOMERS NEED AND WANT?

The firm attracts, retains, and grows customers by delivering value to satisfy their needs. **Customer value** equates to the value in the firm's offer less the customer's monetary, time, effort, and emotional costs.[15] Two sorts of firm action are crucial:

- Make offers of value to satisfy customer needs
- Communicate the value of those offers to customers.[16]

The Opening Case shows that IKEA both provides customer value and communicates customer value. If the firm offers value, but customers don't know about it, they will not purchase. If the firm communicates its offer extensively, but customers don't perceive value (like GM advertis-

KEY IDEA

➤ To *attract, retain,* and
grow customers, the
firm must:
• Develop offers of
  value to satisfy
  customer needs
• Communicate the
  value of those offers
  to customers

ing the Hummer as gasoline prices rise), they will not purchase. We discuss customer needs, how they relate to product attributes/features, and the benefits and values customers receive.

RECOGNIZED NEEDS VERSUS LATENT NEEDS

Sometimes customers understand their needs — **recognized needs**; sometimes they don't — **latent needs**. Recognized needs may be expressed or non-expressed:

• **Expressed needs.** Customers often ask for advice on how to satisfy their needs.

• **Non-expressed needs.** Customers do not express their needs, like teenage girls contemplating condom purchases.

Customers may have a recognized need but not associate the firm with satisfying that need. Henry Ford said: "If I'd asked my customers what they wanted, they'd have said a faster horse!" Indeed, one of marketing's core jobs is to identify value that customers are not expecting. In the 2008–9 recession, Hyundai successfully offered unexpected value; car buyers could return vehicles at no cost nor credit-rating impact if they lost jobs/income within one year. When a Wipro (Indian outsourcing firm) salesperson asked a *Fortune 500* IT decision-maker how Wipro could earn outsourcing business, the executive replied: "Surprise me!" He meant, "Show how you can deliver value I'm not expecting."

KEY IDEA

➤ Customer needs are
recognized or *latent.*
Recognized needs
may be *expressed* or
non-expressed.

Customers are not consciously aware of *latent needs.* These needs may surface as technological innovation raises awareness and customers require benefits/values they could not previously express. Some people suggest that marketing *creates* customer needs; surfacing and satisfying latent needs is a more parsimonious explanation for customer behavior. A few years ago, few consumers could have articulated a need for cell phones. But widespread availability surfaced a latent need of wanting to stay in constant contact.

Watermelons are a traditional fruit. Technological advances address *recognized needs* and *latent needs.* Figure 4.3A shows watermelons that address *recognized needs* for display and refrigerator storage. Figure 4.3B shows a *personal* watermelon that satisfies the *latent need* for a one- or two-person product.[17]

FIGURE 4.3A (LEFT)

SATISFYING A
RECOGNIZED NEED:
CUBIC WATERMELONS

FIGURE 4.3B (RIGHT)

SATISFYING A LATENT
NEED: *PERSONAL*
WATERMELONS

ATTRIBUTES AND FEATURES VERSUS BENEFITS AND VALUES

Many firms define their products and services in terms of **attributes** and **features**. Think about television advertising touting *new and improved.* Now read very carefully: Customers *do not care about your products and services* — they are not interested in the attributes and features. Customers *do care* about satisfying *their needs* and the *benefits and values* your products and services provide. You must communicate these clearly. Let us be very clear about these terms:

• **Attributes and features.** Design elements or functions the firm builds into its products and services — typically of great concern to design engineers.

- **Benefit.** Something the product or service delivers that satisfies a customer need.
- **Value.** Something the product or service provides that has broader scope than a benefit.

The B&D example exemplifies attributes/features, benefits, and values:

> B&D makes hand-held electric drills. *Attributes/features* include color, drill speed, bit hardness, drill bit gauge, drill weight, presence/absence of battery, battery life, and the ability to use other tools like sanders. The statement "Last year we sold 40 million drill bits that nobody wanted"[18] captures the irrelevance of attributes/features to the customer. But B&D drills provide *benefits* to customers; they can make holes easily. *Values* that the B&D drill enables might be improving a living room, by hanging pictures and ornaments, or building a tree house and having fun with the children.
>
> Marty Homlish, president and CEO of SAP Global Marketing, explained the transformation from attributes/features to benefits and values that he directed. "We used to talk about successful implementation like this: 'Customer XYZ implemented SAP Supply Chain Management. They had to do it in 100 days, but they went live in 99 days and only had one critical crisis.' But that was not the issue. The real story was, 'Customer XYZ implemented SAP Supply Chain Management. As a result, it reduced its on-hand inventory from 2.8 months' supply to 2.1 months' and its on-the-water inventory from one month to two weeks. And XYZ saved $500 million.'"[19]

The firm should relate product attributes and features to customer benefits and values, then identify strong ties, weak ties, and orphans:

- **Strong ties.** The attribute is strongly related to a value, in fact and in the customer's mind. Generally, the firm should strive to enhance strong ties.
- **Weak ties.** The attribute is weakly related to a value. The firm should enhance the attribute to strengthen the tie or, if the tie is in fact strong, improve communications.
- **Orphan attributes.** The attribute is unrelated to a customer value. Product redesign to remove the attribute may reduce costs.
- **Orphan values.** The firm does not provide an attribute to deliver required customer value. Product redesign should add the required attribute.

> ### Marketing Question
>
> Select a product. What are its *strong ties* and *weak ties*? Can you identify *orphan attributes* and/or *orphan values*?

Most firms sell products and services that in turn provide benefits and values. Recently, some firms have begun selling benefits and values directly to customers. IBM's *on-demand computing* customers do not pay for hardware and software; they only pay for the computing power they use. Similarly, some airlines pay for airplane engines per hour of operating life.

HIERARCHIES OF NEEDS, FEATURES, BENEFITS, AND VALUES

Psychologists have studied individual needs extensively. We explore a popular need framework developed by psychologist Abraham Maslow that marketers often use. Maslow's ideas form the basis of the feature/benefit/value ladder.

MASLOW'S HIERARCHY OF NEEDS. Maslow's classic framework identifies five major groups of needs: *physiological, safety and security, social, ego,* and *self-actualization* — ordered low to high.[20] Generally, we expect individuals to satisfy lower-level *physiological, safety and security* needs before higher-level needs like *ego* and *self-actualization*.

Products like groceries, clothing, and housing satisfy lower-level *physiological needs*; sports equipment and educational services satisfy higher-level *social, ego,* and *self-actualization* needs. But firms can design market offers (products, advertising and promotion, distribution, and price) for groceries, clothing, and housing to also satisfy higher-level *social* and *ego* needs. Examples, respectively: organic food, designer fashions, and neighborhood location. Satisfying both *higher-level needs* and *lower-level needs* should provide greater customer value than satisfying *lower-level needs* alone. A woman is more likely to buy hair shampoo she believes will make her attractive (*ego* need) than if it just cleans her hair (*physiological* need). Table 4.2 applies Maslow's framework to two purchasing decisions.

KEY IDEA

➤ Maslow's approach places a person's needs in an ordered hierarchy.

TABLE 4.2

**USING MASLOW'S
HIERARCHY OF NEEDS
TO GAIN INSIGHT
INTO TWO CONSUMER
PURCHASES**

Product \\ Need	Folgers Coffee	Krispy Kreme Donuts
Self-Actualization (self-fulfillment)	Savoring	Be part of a cultural phenomenon
Ego (prestige, success, self-respect)	Confidence, achievement	Be in vogue (especially among Gen-Xers)
Social (love, affection, friendship, belonging)	Togetherness, freshness, taste	Eating donuts is a group experience that creates a sense of *togetherness*
Safety & Security (protection, order, security)	Easy on the stomach, no jitters	Safe, easy for kids to eat — and no mess
Physiological (food, drink, air, shelter, sex)	Satisfies thirst, keeps you alert, keeps you warm	Satisfies hunger and the sweet tooth

*Marketing
Exercise*

Develop a feature/benefit/
value ladder for the marketing course you are taking
right now.

LADDERING FEATURES, BENEFITS, AND VALUES. Many marketers meld Maslow's hierarchical approach to individual needs with the feature/benefit/value distinction to form a **feature/benefit/value ladder.**[21] Figure 4.4 demonstrates the ladder's three main characteristics:

- **Focuses attention on customer value.** Firms typically design attributes/features into their products and services. The feature/benefit/value ladder forces a translation into benefits and values for customers. B&D's drills deliver many benefits and values.

- **Provides alternatives for communicating with customers.** The variety of benefits and values broadens the firm's options for communicating with customers. The best communications depend on factors like stage of market development and competitive threats. Potential B&D communications like *drill speed and bit hardness*, *makes holes easily*, and *supports do-it-yourself activity* are quite different each from the other.

- **Broadens the view of competition.** When the firm focuses on attributes/features, its scope is direct competitors; a focus on customer benefits and values broadens this scope. With an attributes/features focus, B&D's competitors are electric drill manufacturers. Focusing on Benefit A — makes holes easily — introduces competitors like explosives, nails, lasers, water drills, and woodpeckers(!). Higher-level benefits broaden competitive scope even further.[22]

FIGURE 4.4

**FEATURE/BENEFIT/VALUE
LADDERS FOR BLACK &
DECKER ELECTRIC DRILLS
AND NIVEA SKIN CREAM**

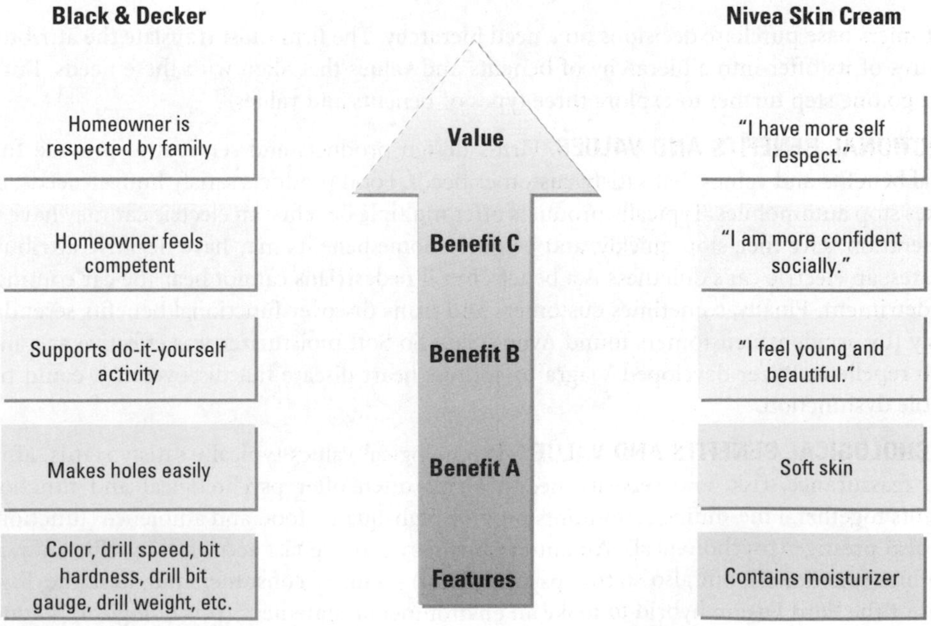

KEY IDEA

➤ The feature/benefit/
value ladder ensures
that the firm:

- Focuses on providing
value to customers
- Offers communication
options
- Broadens the view of
competition

Black & Decker		Nivea Skin Cream
Homeowner is respected by family	**Value**	"I have more self respect."
Homeowner feels competent	**Benefit C**	"I am more confident socially."
Supports do-it-yourself activity	**Benefit B**	"I feel young and beautiful."
Makes holes easily	**Benefit A**	Soft skin
Color, drill speed, bit hardness, drill bit gauge, drill weight, etc.	**Features**	Contains moisturizer

Excedrin contains aspirin, caffeine, and acetaminophen. Sales of a companion product, advertised as *aspirin-free* Excedrin, were declining. A new advertising message focused on *treating tension headaches*. The messaging switch from attributes/features — *aspirin-free*, to benefits — *treating tension headaches*, led to significant sales increase.

Xerox supplied about 10 percent of AT&T's more than 60,000 copiers (mostly black and white). Traditionally, copier suppliers competed on *feeds* and *speeds*, but Xerox knew AT&T liked its 5,000 color machines. Xerox conducted a multi-month study of AT&T's copier use and proposed a replacement program requiring 40,000 color copiers. AT&T agreed and Xerox became AT&T's sole supplier.

In general, customers using the firm's products and services focus on the benefits and values they provide. By contrast, resellers like distributors, retailers, and wholesalers are more interested in economic benefits like profit margins, net profit, and return on investment. Different customer types seek different benefits and values, so the firm should develop several feature/benefit/value ladders.[23] In practice, the firm may identify multiple feature/benefit value ladders for a single offer. Figure 4.5 shows how three Volvo attributes provide a major benefit — *safe car* — that in turn delivers three higher-level values.[24]

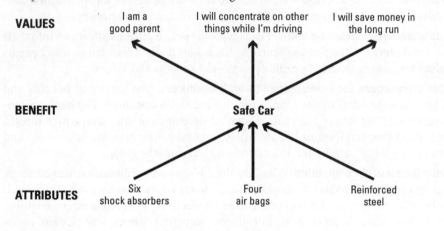

FIGURE 4.5

FEATURE/BENEFIT/VALUE LADDER FOR VOLVO

Marketing Question

The three major overnight shipping firms offer various benefits and values. Do you agree with these category assignments, based on their slogans?

Functional Provider: UPS – "Moving at the speed of business" and "See what Brown can do for you."

Psychological Provider: FedEx – "Be absolutely sure" (that is, don't get fired).

Economic Provider: United States Postal Service (USPS) – "We deliver." USPS's prices are lower than UPS and FedEx.

FUNCTIONAL, PSYCHOLOGICAL, AND ECONOMIC BENEFITS AND VALUES

Customers base purchase decisions on a need hierarchy. The firm must translate the attributes/features of its offer into a hierarchy of benefits and values that align with these needs. But we must go one step further to explore three types of benefits and values.[25]

FUNCTIONAL BENEFITS AND VALUES. Firms design products and services to provide functional benefits and values that satisfy customer needs. Food products satisfy hunger needs; disc brakes stop automobiles. Typically products offer multiple benefits: an electric car may have fast acceleration, save fuel, stop quickly, and be quiet. Some benefits may have negative attributes/features; an electric car's quietness is a benefit but if pedestrians cannot hear the car coming, it is a detriment. Finally, sometimes customers and firms discover functional benefits serendipitously (by accident); customers found Avon's Skin So Soft moisturizer was effective as a mosquito repellent; Pfizer developed Viagra to address heart disease but discovered it could treat erectile dysfunction.

PSYCHOLOGICAL BENEFITS AND VALUES. Psychological values typically satisfy status, affiliation, reassurance, risk, and security needs. Firms often offer psychological and functional benefits together. Fine-dining restaurants provide high-quality food and ambience (functional) and also prestige (psychological). An automobile may provide fast acceleration, efficiency, and comfort (functional), but also status (psychological) — many consumers purchase the Toyota Prius or the Ford Fusion hybrid to make an environmental statement (psychological). Laundry detergents clean clothes and make them soft and nice smelling (functional); they also provide

Marketing Question

Think about one of your favorite products. What *functional* benefits does it provide? What *psychological* benefits does it provide? Be creative!

self-confidence and reinforce caring for the family (psychological). Generally, psychological values transcend functional benefits and appear higher up the feature/benefit/ value ladder.[26]

ECONOMIC BENEFITS AND VALUES. Economic benefits and values concern financial aspects like price and credit terms. Price is often the primary purchase driver, especially in tough economies when customers trade off functional and psychological benefits to secure low prices. Walmart, purchasing clubs, dollar stores,[27] discount airlines, and generic drug producers provide economic benefits via lower prices. Similarly, many FMCG firms offer *everyday low pricing*. In B2B markets, price is often critical,[28] but sometimes firms deliver cost-cutting economic benefits and *lower total cost of ownership* at higher prices by providing greater functional benefits (Haworth and Jackson examples in the boxed insert). GE strengthens customer relationships by helping customers improve operational effectiveness.[29] The firm may also provide economic value by reducing customer transactions, usage, maintenance, ownership, and disposal costs and investment.[30]

The Jackson example shows the importance of assessing the customer's economic benefit. **Economic value for the customer** (EVC) is the competitive product's price, plus the net added value (positive differentiation value less negative differentiation value) from the firm's product. We show the EVC calculation for a polyester product used in making conveyor belts.[31]

U.S. furniture manufacturer Haworth competes successfully in China against fierce local price competition. Teams of Haworth designers and psychologists develop complete workplace environments for multinational and Chinese firms anxious to retain talent. The design service is free, but Haworth's furniture prices are 30 to 50 percent above local suppliers.

Traditionally, lumber firms used wood waste at zero cost to heat their drying kilns. Jackson (natural gas supplier) identified several sources of savings from switching to natural gas — labor costs to fuel and maintain the kilns, production losses from closing kilns to clean out ash residue, and EPA compliance problems. When a firm switched to natural gas, Jackson helped identify revenue-producing markets for its wood waste.[32]

Illustration of Economic Value to the Customer (EVC)

Industrial-strength conveyor belts are made by covering a textile fabric core with rubber; textile fiber strength is crucial for conveyor belt life. Traditionally, *sevens** cotton yarn was the core; polyester yarn was a potential replacement. Critical data for calculating the value of polyester in conveyor belts are:

- Price of sevens cotton is 90 cents per lb.
- 750 denier polyester yarn is four times stronger than cotton — 8 versus 2 grams per denier (g.p.d.)
- Extra cost of processing polyester yarn is 30 cents per lb.

EVC answers the question: What is the maximum price a conveyor belt manufacturer will pay for polyester yarn? (We assume that conveyor belt life does not change when polyester replaces cotton.) Since polyester is four times stronger than cotton, customers can use four pounds of cotton or one pound of polyester — Figure 4.6:

- Cotton: sevens cotton yarn @ 90 cents per lb. — reference value
- Polyester equivalence: 1 lb. of 750 denier polyester yarn or 4 lbs. of sevens cotton = $3.60 — reference value plus positive differentiation value
- Extra cost to process polyester fiber = 30 cents per lb. — negative differentiation value
- Net polyester equivalence = $3.60 less $0.30 = $3.30 — total economic value[33]

In sum, based on the economic value analysis, conveyor belt manufacturers should be indifferent between:

a. Sevens cotton @ 90 cents per lb. and

b. 750 denier polyester @ $3.30 per lb.

Hence, the maximum polyester price is $3.30 per lb. At any price above $3.30 per lb., conveyor belt manufacturers would be better off sticking with cotton.

*Sevens cotton is the standard type of cotton yarn used in industrial applications.

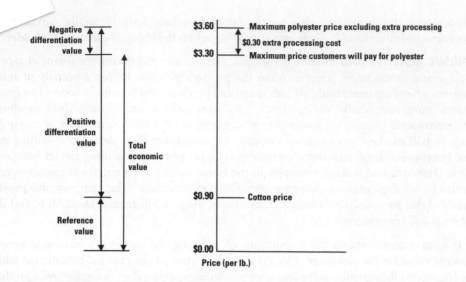

FIGURE 4.6

ILLUSTRATION OF
ECONOMIC VALUE
TO THE CUSTOMER

Many EVC calculations are more complex than this simple illustration.[34] Factors for inclusion are customer financing, maintenance, and operating costs plus revenue changes. International Paper (IP) developed new packaging for fresh fruit that reduced costs for its customers (supermarkets); by enhancing display, IP also increased customer revenues.

The firm's challenge is to deliver the *right* combination of functional, psychological, and economic benefits and values to those customers it wants to attract, retain, and grow. Figure 4.7 shows the mix of benefits and values a pharmaceutical firm might deliver to a physician.

Psychological
- Enhanced status
- Sense of belonging
- Sense of assurance
- Reduced risk

Functional
- Improved efficacy
- Less side effects
- Lower drug interactions

Economic
- Reduced input costs
- Increased reimbursements

FIGURE 4.7

FUNCTIONAL,
PSYCHOLOGICAL,
AND ECONOMIC
BENEFITS FOR A
PHYSICIAN

KEY IDEA

➤ For customers the firm wants to attract, retain, and grow, it must deliver the *right* combination of three types of benefits and values:

- Functional
- Psychological
- Economic

CHARACTERISTICS OF BENEFITS AND VALUES

ACTUAL VALUE VERSUS POTENTIAL VALUE. The critical value the firm offers may lie not in the product itself, but in the customer's ability to secure additional value if and when needed. The AmEx Platinum Card's Concierge program locates hard-to-find items, delivers gifts, provides secretarial services in remote areas, and offers secure reservations in upscale restaurants. Most cardholders rarely use these services but their availability has high value.[35] Insurance companies offer Mayo Clinic as a benefit on their policies, but relatively few patients assume the extra travel, hotel, and other out-of-pocket expenses to visit Mayo.

Marketing Question

How do decision-makers evaluate the success (or failure) of their purchases?

FUTURE VALUE. Generally, customers purchase products and services for benefits and values they expect to receive directly. But they may also purchase today for expected future benefits and values. When a B2B customer purchases from a technology firm, a key factor may be benefits inherent in the supplier relationship like preferential access to *beta* (pre-release) versions of future technology. Dell buys most computer chips from Intel (versus AMD) in part because Intel gives Dell early insight into new technologies.

PRESENCE VALUE. The firm may provide considerable customer value just by being a supplier, so long as its products are acceptable and prices are reasonable. When a customer has one strong and one weak supplier, the weak supplier's presence keeps the strong supplier *honest* and inhibits the exercise of monopoly power. For many years, Airbus played this role versus Boeing in passenger aircraft; AMD plays this role versus Intel in computer chips.

SCARCITY VALUE. Some firms like fashion retailer Zara deliberately make small product volumes to provide scarcity value. Beanie Babies limited production runs and ruthlessly retired prized stuffed animals; many Harley-Davidson models have long wait times.[36] Nike Air Force 1 sneakers have been market leaders for a quarter-century. Nike launches a new version every couple of months, but deliberately keeps supplies tight to develop scarcity value and create pent-up demand.

VALUE FOR WHOM. Consumers (B2C) typically make purchases for themselves, a friend, colleague, family member, or a group like the family. A B2B purchase may satisfy either organizational or individual needs. For the customer organization's well-being, the purchase value should be for the organization, but this is not always the case:

> A large British mail order firm was purchasing a new computer system. The management services head steered the purchase to his favored supplier. "[By sitting] ... at the junction of the communication channels between his subordinates, the manufacturers, and the board [of directors] ... he was able to exert biases in favor of his own demands and at the same time feed the board negative information about the demands of his opponents."[37]

Some suppliers have large budgets for entertaining customer employees and providing personal items to those with significant influence and/or decision-making power — like hospital physicians and radio disc jockeys. Individual benefits can be ethically questionable and even illegal — like *facilitation payments* (*kickbacks*). U.S. and European authorities fined German engineering giant Siemens a record $1.6 billion to settle allegations that it won lucrative overseas power and telecom contracts via bribery.

Some firms work hard to ensure their employees do not benefit personally from suppliers. Walmart prohibits employees from accepting gifts, trips, meals, or other items of value. Sometimes suppliers take advantage of customer processes to provide individual value. Suppose a customer firm pays purchasing agents (PA) bonuses based on the difference between the final negotiated price and the initial offering price. Suppliers that initially price high, then offer large discounts, may enhance their chances of winning by helping PAs earn bonuses.

WHEN CUSTOMERS RECOGNIZE VALUE. Sometimes customers have good data about the benefits and values a product provides; other times they are uncertain and cannot assess value until long after purchase. **Search**, **use**, and **credence** benefits capture this uncertainty and may offer important insight:

- **Search benefits.** Significant product and service data from the firm and/or independent sources like *Consumer Reports*. Customers may even inspect and try products, like test-driving a car.
- **Use benefits.** Relatively little data on customer value before purchase, like many services. Value is revealed when the product or service is consumed, like a concert performance, or an expensive restaurant meal.

Marketing Question

What products can you think of that have *potential value*, *future value*, *presence value*, and/or *scarcity value*?

KEY IDEA

➤ To gain greater customer insight, the firm must ask: "What motivates people in customer roles to behave the way they do?"

Marketing Question

Choose one product each that offers mainly *search*, *use*, and *credence* benefits and values. How would your communications to customers differ?

- **Credence benefits.** Impossible to assess value until long after purchase. Examples include an investment's economic benefits and health benefits from some medical procedures.

BEYOND CUSTOMER BENEFITS AND VALUES – CUSTOMER EXPERIENCES

As competition increases, growing numbers of firms focus on providing customer **experiences** (brand, consumption, product, shopping, and service) — conditions, events, or states that consciously affect buying behavior. Table 4.3 categorizes these experiences as *real* (experienced directly),[38] *anticipatory* (looking forward to), or *vicarious* (experienced through someone else). Experiences are an important factor in gaining insight into customer behavior and how and why customers value market offers.[39] Using a TV remote is a superior experience to dialing controls on the TV set; changing channels by simple hand gestures will be even better. Consider the value one customer group receives from Napa Valley Reserve:

> **Napa Valley Reserve**
>
> Most wineries offer value based on the wine quality, but not Napa Valley Reserve (NVR). NVR offers the Napa Valley experience "by invitation only" for a membership fee of $145,000. The NVR experience includes use of facilities to have dinner, host guest receptions, make wine supervised by an experienced wine maker, and bottle five barrels of wine, each at extra cost; members can buy the wine they make at $55 per bottle. NVR has about 300 members.[40]

Type of Experience	Example of the Experience
Real	Go to see a movie
Anticipatory	See an advertisement for the movie
Vicarious	Send a daughter to the movie

TABLE 4.3

TYPES OF CUSTOMER EXPERIENCES

A single event can create many different experiences. A New York City ballet aficionado experiences a touring Bolshoi performance differently from someone seeing their first ballet. Also, the experience may have more value than the product. Many cafes sell coffee for around $1 per cup; Starbucks coffee is several dollars per cup but it also offers a personal and memorable experience[41] — the language of the *baristas*, the noise of the grinders and espresso machines, the sight of scores of coffee varieties and products, the feel of hot coffee in the hand, and an atmosphere permeated by coffee aroma.[42] Many Starbucks customers continually return because they feel good when drinking their coffee.

Five modes of customer experience are[43]:

- **Sense.** Creates sensory experiences through sight, sound, touch, taste, and smell.
- **Feel.** Appeals to inner feelings and emotions. Attempts to create affective experiences, ranging from mildly positive to strong emotions of joy and pride.
- **Think.** Appeals to the intellect. Creates problem-solving experiences that engage creatively.
- **Act.** Enriches by showing alternative ways of doing things, alternative lifestyles and interactions.
- **Relate.** Contains aspects of sense, feel, think, and act, but reaches beyond individual personal, private feelings to something outside his/her private state.

Schmitt's framework offers a methodical way of determining those experiences the firm wants customers to associate with its products. Are you familiar with any of the examples in Table 4.4?

> ### *Marketing Question*
>
> Think about your favorite entertainment — theater, restaurant, concert, or sports event. Which mode(s) — sense, feel, think, act, relate — best describes your experience? Did the provider consciously create this experience? How?

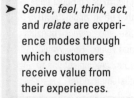

KEY IDEA

➤ *Sense, feel, think, act,* and *relate* are experience modes through which customers receive value from their experiences.

TABLE 4.4

CUSTOMER
EXPERIENCE
EXAMPLES

Experience Mode	Company/Brand	Example
Sense	P&G	"Tide Mountain Fresh"
Feel	Campbell's Soup	"Mmm, Mmm! Good for the body, good for the soul"
Think	Apple Computer	"Think Different"
Act	Nike	"Just do it"
Relate	Harley-Davidson	"Harley is a way of life"

By 2030, the U.S. population aged 65 and older will exceed 70 million. Kimberly-Clark educates retail executives about senior citizens' shopping experiences by simulating common vision impairments like glaucoma, cataracts, macular degeneration, and eye lens yellowing via cardboard glasses; and limited manual dexterity from arthritis via large rubber gloves. Walgreen and Rite Aid are also investing to improve the elderly's shopping experience.

HOW DO CUSTOMERS BUY?

Diesel makes high-priced denim jeans — $150 to $350 per pair. Diesel deliberately designs stores to *intimidate* shoppers, frequently inexperienced young men. Diesel salespeople *rescue* shoppers and *shepherd* them through the buying process.

KEY IDEA

➤ The firm must identify the customer's decision-making process (DMP).

The purchase **decision-making process (DMP)** ranges from the relatively simple — buying a mid-morning snack, to highly complex — the U.S. government purchasing a new fighter jet. The DMP can be as quick as an impulse purchase or take months/or even years.[44] Marketers must understand how customers move through the process and identify the various options for influence.

PURCHASE-DECISION STAGES

Figure 4.8 shows the DMP as a robust purchase model with five stages.[45] Each DMP may involve multiple feedback loops both within and among stages. The customer may identify a need or problem early on and then elaborate that need as she secures information and evaluates alternatives. Some purchases are *planned*, like the Table 4.5 example; others are *unplanned* (made spontaneously during a shopping trip).

FIGURE 4.8

THE PURCHASE
DECISION PROCESS

| 1 Recognizing Problems | 2 Acquiring Information | 3 Evaluating Alternatives | 4 Making a Choice | 5 Post-Purchase Processes |

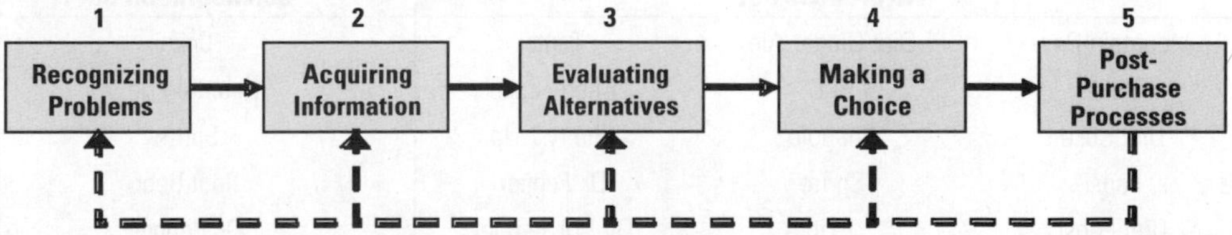

TABLE 4.5

AN INDIVIDUAL'S
PURCHASE DECISION
PROCESS FOR A
DVD PLAYER

Decision Process Stage	Customer Action and Cognitions
1. Recognizing problems	Sees advertisement: "That looks cool and I don't have one."
2. Acquiring information	Demonstration in store: "What is this thing?" "What does it do?" "What does multi-format mean?" "What is the price?"
3. Evaluating alternatives	Examine various options: "Is Sony better than Toshiba and Philips?"
4. Making a choice	"I am going to buy Sony."
5. Post-purchase processes	"How do I hook this up?" "Where do I get service?"

STAGE 1 – RECOGNIZING PROBLEMS. Some customer needs are critical to system functioning: food and drink for individuals, and raw materials and capital equipment for firms. The firm should keep good records of customer contract-expiry and capital equipment replacement dates for its own and competitor products so as to recognize problems early. Other needs are discretionary. Should I buy a vacation package? Should the firm lease a corporate jet? Some product needs are, or may become, habitual like toothpaste, chewing gum, smoking, air fresheners, and health snacks. The customer may recognize a need independently, or a potential supplier may point it out.

> In Ghana, only four percent of the population washed hands with soap and water after using the restroom; by comparison 50 percent washed hands when they believed they were dirty. Advertising messages associated bathroom visits with feelings of disgust; post-bathroom hand-washing increased sharply.
>
> P&G introduced Febreze for removing bad smells from smelly clothes but was initially unsuccessful. Advertising that associated Febreze with the finishing touch of cleaning a living room, kitchen, and laundry created a habit and generated significant revenues.

STAGE 2 – ACQUIRING INFORMATION. After recognizing a problem, customers generally seek information to help identify:

- The *feature* set — attributes/features that may satisfy the need.
- Criteria for evaluating satisfactory performance by the attributes/features.
- The *awareness* set — alternatives that may satisfy the need.
- The degree to which each alternative meets the attribute/feature criteria.

Customers may acquire information *externally* and/or *internally*. External information comes from: *personal sources* like colleagues, family, friends, social media, and salespeople; and from *impersonal sources* like advertising, the press, blogs, or other Internet sources. The degree of external search relates to current knowledge, involvement in the purchase, and perceived risk. Internal information derives from the customer's perceptual information store, including memory. Of course distinguishing between fact and opinion is critical for the evaluation stage.[46]

STAGES 3 AND 4 – EVALUATING ALTERNATIVES AND MAKING A CHOICE. Customers evaluate alternatives based on information they acquire in Stage 2.[47] Frequently, customers exclude several alternatives in the *awareness set* with little evaluation by forming a short list — *consideration set*, based on purchase criteria — Table 4.6. Membership in the *consideration set* is crucial as customers choose among this restricted number of alternatives.

Awareness Set			Consideration Set
Mountain Dew	Diet Ginger Ale	Fanta	Coke
Coke	Hi-C	Cherry Coke	Mountain Dew
Diet Coke	Snapple	Cherry 7-Up	Sprite
Pepsi	Sprite	Dr. Pepper	Root Beer
Diet Pepsi	7-Up	Diet Dr. Pepper	Dr. Pepper
Root Beer	Diet 7-Up	Mr. Pibb	
Ginger Ale	Orange Slice	Caffeine-free Coke	

Customer choices from the consideration set may be rational, or may deviate from rationality. By understanding the customer evaluation process, the firm can influence the purchase decision in its favor. We examine one rational approach,[49] and others that deviate from rationality:

A. Rational approach. In Table 4.7 a business traveler is choosing an airline to fly to London. We assume the customer:

- Identifies attributes/features that deliver required benefits and values — **attributes/features**.
- Decides on the relative importance of these benefits and values — **column A (sum to 100)**.

KEY IDEA

➤ The firm should try to understand customers' evaluation processes.

• Forms a belief about how well the attributes/features of each alternative deliver these benefits and values — **three B columns (1–10 scale)**.

The **linear compensatory** model is the most studied approach to evaluation and choice. An alternative's overall value comprises contributions from each attribute — good performance on one attribute balances out poor performance on another.[50] We consider each alternative separately. For each attribute, we multiply the relative importance **A** by the belief **B**; we then add the resulting **A × B** product terms. Table 4.7's totals are: British Airways (BA) — 670, American Airlines (AA) — 450, and United Airlines (UA) — 730. The traveler chooses UA.

TABLE 4.7

A BUSINESS TRAVELER'S EVALUATION OF AIRLINES FOR A LONDON – NEW YORK TRIP

Attributes/features	Relative Importance A (1–100)	British Airways (BA)		American Airlines (AA)		United Airlines (UA)	
		Belief B (1–10)	A × B	Belief B (1–10)	A × B	Belief B (1–10)	A × B
Frequent-flier program	30	9	270	2	60	8	240
Price	20	6	120	6	120	6	120
Schedule	20	8	160	5	100	6	120
Service level	20	5	100	7	140	9	180
Upgrade probability	10	2	20	3	30	7	70
Total	100		670		450		730

KEY IDEA

➤ The *linear-compensatory* approach to evaluation and choice balances firm performance on the relevant attributes.

The firm can take several actions to improve the value it offers customers:

• Improve perceived performance on important attributes.

• Add new valued attributes, especially important ones.

• Show customers that it performs better than competitors on important attributes.

• Show that the attributes where it performs really well are highly important.

Some attributes may be baseline requirements or *antes*; only alternatives scoring sufficiently well enter the consideration set. Safety is often an *ante* for airline travel; customers do not trade off schedule or frequent-flier miles for safety.[51,52] For other rational evaluation and choice processes based on *cognitive algebra*, see Marketing Enrichment me401 .

MARKETING ENRICHMENT

Rational Evaluation and Choice Processes me401

me401

Sometimes customer effort is an important decision factor. When the customer makes a choice, the firm may present several alternatives, or provide a default. Customers often *opt out* and select the default since *opting in* takes effort. Organ donation research shows much higher donation rates in countries with *opt-out* versus *opt-in* systems. Also, the U.S. government seeks to increase worker savings by automatic enrollment unless individuals opt out.[53]

B. Deviations from rationality. *Behavioral decision theory* and *behavioral economics* researchers have identified many purchase processes that seem *irrational* in both B2C and B2B markets; customers seem to base their choices on irrelevant factors. Consider the following scenario: Many consumers would travel for the book, but not for the home entertainment system, yet they would save the same amount in each case!

You are in a store about to buy a $25 book. Your friend walks by and says you can buy the same book a couple of blocks away for $10. Would you walk two blocks to save $15 ($25–$10)? Now, suppose you are in a store about to buy a home-entertainment system for $765. Your friend appears. He says you can buy the same system a couple of blocks away for $750. Would you walk two blocks to save $15 ($765–$750)?[54]

Marketing Question

Do you always act rationally in your purchase decisions? Identify situations where you have behaved less than rationally.

Other deviations from rationality in purchasing decisions include[55]:

• **Compromise effect.** Customers tend to avoid extreme price/value options in favor of intermediates. Given the choice between two microwave ovens, low price — $109.99 and medium price — $179.99, forty-three percent chose the medium-price oven. When customers chose among three ovens, the original two ovens plus a high-price oven —

$199.99, they chose the $179.99 more than 60 percent of the time.[56] How many drink-size choices do you have at McDonald's or Starbucks?

- **Decoy (asymmetric dominance) effect.** Customer choice among alternatives is affected by adding another option acting as a *decoy*. Suppose options A and B have two attributes — quality and price: option A (high quality, $50); option B (low quality, $35). Some customers prefer option A — high quality better than low quality; others prefer option B — $35 better than $50. Suppose a third option C (medium quality, $55) is added. Option A dominates C (*decoy*) on both quality and price: Customer preference shifts toward option A.[57]

- **Describing alternatives.** Researchers asked customers to choose between ground beef that was *75 percent lean* and ground beef that was *25 percent fat*. After tasting the *identical* products, customers preferred the *75 percent lean* ground beef![58]

- **Features of alternatives.** Customers chose between two purchase options for 35 mm film:
  - Option 1. Just the film.
  - Option 2. The film along with an offer to buy a golf umbrella for $8.29 (viewed as unattractive).

  Adding the golf umbrella offer led to a market share decrease.[59]

- **How customers evaluate alternatives.** Many factors affect how people evaluate alternatives, even just focusing attention on an alternative. Suppose a waiter offers the diner a choice between yogurt and fruit salad, then says, "How much more or less attractive to you is yogurt?" The probability of choosing yogurt increases![60] Even store organization has an impact:
  - Display A. Each display has several brands of a similar model
  - Display B. Each display has several models of a single brand.

  With Display A, customers are less likely to choose the lower-priced alternative.[61]

- **When customers evaluate alternatives.** Time of purchase may be rational — we buy Coke and Pepsi when it's hot and we are thirsty. But researchers found that eBay prices for weekend purchases were 2 percent higher than during the week. (For more deviations from rationality, see Marketing Enrichment me402 .)

STAGE 5 – POST-PURCHASE PROCESSES. Customers typically engage in several post-purchase processes. These can affect future purchases — for customers and others they influence[62]:

- **Communications with customers/potential customers.** Word of mouth (WOM) has always been an important post-purchase process; many firms hire people to stimulate WOM. Social networking on the Internet has increased its importance. Anti-firm websites like *chase-sucks.com* and *walmart-blows.com* can be a significant firm issue.[63]

- **Comparison with others.** Consumers modify consumption when they learn that neighbors' behavior is more socially acceptable. Electricity consumption decreases when utilities tell customers that neighbors with similar-size homes are more frugal.

- **Dissonance reduction.** If the product/service does not meet expectations, customers may reduce dissonance by seeking information and/or recalibrating product performance.[64] Most dissonance reduction occurs when customers expend significant time and/or money to acquire the product.

- **Product and packaging disposal.** Environmental advocates pay increasing attention to disposal. Many jurisdictions require customers to separate garbage into different categories. In France and Germany, firms must recover packaging and used products! HP and Kodak encourage returning used printer cartridges and disposable cameras, respectively.

- **Repurchase.** Repurchase drives customer lifetime value. All things equal, high customer satisfaction increases customer loyalty and repurchase.

- **Use.** For some products the firm may only be concerned with sales; for others, like credit cards, use is important. Use is particularly critical in pharmaceuticals; compliance failure causes 125,000 U.S. deaths annually. Hospital/nursing home costs and lost pharmaceutical revenues amount to tens of billions of dollars annually. Compliance failure includes failure to fill prescription and to take medicines.

- **Use experience.** The customer may be satisfied/dissatisfied with the product, and hence develop/diminish the firm/brand-customer relationship.

By mapping the customer DMP for B2C and/or B2B decisions, the firm learns how and when to influence the purchasing process. At the DMP front end, the firm may help a customer identify needs and understand options. At the back end, the firm may make it easy for the customer to pay, store, move, use, return and exchange, repair and service, and dispose of the product.[65]

PURCHASE-DECISION CATEGORIES

Madden Graphics (Chicago) earned thin margins selling printing services to purchasing departments. At a supermarket customer that Madden served with printed displays and sales promotion materials, it identified great inefficiency and waste. Madden developed a direct-to-store printing and shipping program, integrating construction design, manufacturing, assembly, and distribution of point-of-sale materials. Madden also developed direct relationships with the supermarket's sales, marketing, and product-promotion executives. In seven years, Madden's revenues from the supermarket increased twelvefold.[66]

Marketing Question

What type of purchase decision did Madden Graphics' customer make previously? What type of decision did customer make in its new approach?

We can usefully categorize purchases into three categories: **routinized-response behavior**, **limited problem-solving**, and **extended problem-solving**.[67]

ROUTINIZED-RESPONSE BEHAVIOR (RRB). The customer has well-defined purchase criteria and frequently makes similar purchases. The customer must choose among several familiar suppliers; the offers are well known and very similar. The customer makes choices rapidly with little effort, often based on brand loyalty, like B2C purchases of FMCG products and B2B firm purchases of raw materials and supplies. Frequently, a single individual makes RRB decisions. Established behavior patterns are typically resistant to change. The supplier must demonstrate superiority by promoting its *net competitive advantage*.

LIMITED PROBLEM-SOLVING (LPS). The customer has well-defined purchase criteria but one (or more) purchase alternatives is novel, and performance is uncertain. The customer may have to test the alternative and/or gather new data. Examples include evaluating a potential new supplier or replacing traditional purchases with a new material — like substituting plastics for metal, or replacing traditional seeds with genetically altered varieties. Typically, LPS decisions involve several influencers/decision-makers. The supplier must make the customer comfortable and reduce uncertainty by addressing specific concerns.

EXTENDED PROBLEM-SOLVING (EPS). The purchase is novel and the alternative(s) and potential supplier(s) are often new to the customer. Purchase criteria are not well-developed and the customer expends time and effort resolving uncertainty and reducing risk. If the customer purchases, other behaviors will probably also change. Examples include first purchase of a house or video-conferencing facilities and the first outsourcing of work previously done internally. In B2B, these purchases often affect several departments and/or management systems. Because of their broad impact many people are involved in EPS decisions. The supplier must help the customer decide and reduce its perceived risk.

KEY IDEA

➤ Three categories of purchase decisions are:
- Routinized-response behavior
- Limited problem-solving
- Extended problem-solving

Morgan Stanley (MS) successfully won a lucrative contract to broker the sale of Hughes Aircraft. Observers believed Hughes trustees selected MS because of Robert Greenhill's presentation. He focused on the problems of being a trustee, developed a vision of how the trustees should decide, then laid out their goals and alternatives.

These three purchase categories have important implications:

- **DMU varies by type of purchase.** Extended problem-solving typically involves more individuals and more senior individuals. Extended-family members often guide newlyweds buying their first home. Middle managers may work on an *extended problem-solving* purchase, but senior managers make the final decision. Firms often program *routinized response-behavior* decisions as a set of rules that mid- and low-level purchasing executives implement — in households, children may make these sorts of purchases.

- **Purchase categories depend on the customer, not on the product.** Different customers use different purchase criteria and purchase processes for identical products. A new-home purchase for young newlyweds is probably *extended problem-solving*; for a family that moves frequently, it's *limited problem-solving*. Purchasing video-conferencing is *extended problem-solving* for a first-time buyer, but may approach *routinized-response behavior* for an experienced firm. In purchasing complex products, customers gain experience; onetime *extended problem-solving* purchase shifts to *limited problem-solving* and may reach *routinized-response behavior*.

- **Suppliers should consider shifting decision-making from simple to complex.** This is the message from Madden Graphics. *Routinized-response behavior* often favors established suppliers. For *limited problem-solving* and *extended problem-solving*, customers must reframe the decision. Reframing typically shifts the decision from purchasing agent to a larger decision-making unit. The challenger's job is motivating the customer to reframe the decision, and so enter its consideration set.

INFLUENCES ON CONSUMER PURCHASE PROCESSES

We explore several influences on consumer purchase processes (B2C).[68] Deep understanding of *environmental* and *individual* factors can help the firm be proactive in strategy development.

ENVIRONMENTAL FACTORS

Figure 4.9 shows **environmental influences** ranging from broad to narrow: culture, social class, other people, family, and the situation.

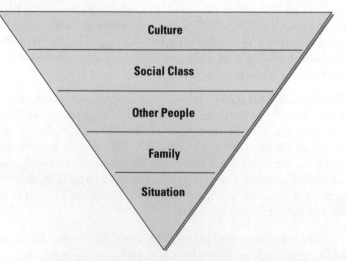

FIGURE 4.9

ENVIRONMENTAL INFLUENCES ON CONSUMER PURCHASE PROCESSES (B2C)

CULTURE. Consumer purchasing behavior and product preferences are conditioned by cultural and subcultural norms; the firm must be careful not to violate these norms, especially abroad — Chapter 3.[69] In the West, the female head of household traditionally does the weekly shopping; in rural Bangladesh, men do the shopping. Indonesians smoke more than 200 billion cigarettes annually, but only 10 percent are the standard "white variety"; 90 percent are kreteks, a clove cigarette that adds chocolate, cinnamon, coffee, licorice, and pineapple to tobacco.[70] In the U.S., business-casual dress has affected detergent, fiber, garment, and washing machine manufacturers. Increasing life spans that focus baby boomers' attention on saving for old age have important implications for life insurance and mutual funds. Because cultural influences are so deeply seated, many firms develop separate marketing programs for cultural groups, like Asian-American and Hispanic groups in the U.S. Some consumers purchase to emulate cultural and subcultural norms: White middle-class teenagers adopt dress styles from inner-city African-Americans; most Japanese eat raw fish, but Japan is also an attractive market for Levi's, Marlboro, McDonald's, and Starbucks. The Internet has spawned a global tech-savvy youth culture addressed by brands like Unilever's Axe deodorant (Bom Chika Wah Wah).

Cosmopolitan, the sex-oriented women's magazine, appears in almost 50 countries. Local editions consider cultural sensitivities and legal realities. Indian editions have no articles on sexual positions; sex is rarely explicitly mentioned in China; and Swedish society is so open that sex receives little attention. In Hong Kong, most models are local Asian celebrities, but in the PRC most models are Western.

Cemex, the Mexican cement producer, tapped into *tandas*, a traditional community savings scheme. In Cemex's *Patrimonio Hoy* program, groups of 70 persons contribute about 120 pesos per week for 70 weeks. Each week, the program selects a *winner* who receives sufficient materials to build an extra room onto his/her home. Cemex also provides technical building assistance. Cemex's cement consumption by do-it-yourself homebuilders tripled.[71]

SOCIAL CLASS. All societies have hierarchically ordered groupings or social classes. Wealth and income are key discriminators, but occupation, residential location, and education also matter. Sometimes individuals migrate across classes. Values and interests, and purchases like clothing and leisure activities, are often similar within a social class — Table 4.8 shows a U.S. scheme.

TABLE 4.8

SOCIAL CLASSES IN AMERICA[72]

Broad Category	Narrower Category	Description
Upper Americans	Upper-upper (0.3%)	Inherited wealth, aristocratic names
	Lower-upper (1.2%)	Newer social elite, corporate leadership
	Upper-middle (12.5%)	Managers and professionals
Middle Americans	Middle class (32%)	Average pay white-collar workers
	Working class (38%)	Average pay blue-collar workers
Lower Americans	Lower (9%)	Working, living standards just above poverty
	Real lower-lower (7%)	On public assistance, poverty-stricken, often without work

OTHER PEOPLE. Other people and groups influence consumers. Individuals have frequent face-to-face contact with **primary reference groups** — family members and organizational work groups. **Secondary reference groups** include club and church members and professional organizations. **Aspirational groups** are those a person would like to join for reasons like prestige.[73] People with expertise are particularly influential if they belong to attractive reference groups. Soccer player David Beckham is influential with many teenagers; he has significant expertise and style and belongs to an aspirational reference group — professional soccer players. Sometimes individuals join groups for influence and purchase — medical advocacy groups pressure drug companies and the FDA for speedier trials of promising drugs. In China, *tuangou* groups, formed on the Internet, bargain *en masse* with retailers for special deals.

FAMILY. The *nuclear family* (father, mother, children) and/or *extended family* (grandparents, aunts, uncles, cousins, in-laws) may exert considerable influence. The relative nuclear family versus the extended family influence is culturally determined. Nuclear family influence predominates in the West; extended family influence is very important in many Asian countries. In nuclear families, the wife and/or husband typically make family purchase decisions, often based

KEY IDEA

➤ A variety of environmental factors affect consumer purchasing decisions:

- Culture
- Social class
- Other people
- Family
- Situation

on product type — but children may be important influencers. In the U.S., husbands generally make major financial decisions; wives make most shopping decisions, including 60 percent of auto buying. Decision-making in nuclear families is changing in many societies:

- High divorce rates lead to increased numbers of single-parent and reconstructed families.

- Young people delay marriage, wait longer for children, and limit family size.

- Same-sex partnerships redefine the nature of couples and marriage.

- Women's roles change as they increasingly demand, and receive, equality.

SITUATION. Consumers face situational influences daily — presentations and displays, and time constraints. *Purchase location aesthetics* are also important: People purchase real estate on vacation while enjoying free meals and other perks. U.S. college students purchase and consume more alcohol at football games, parties, and spring break than other times.

> A Korean firm was considering Britain for a new European factory. When its delegation visited a potential supplier, the Korean flag was flying. This thoughtfulness and attention to detail was a key factor in the decision to build in Britain.

INDIVIDUAL FACTORS

Several individual factors also influence purchase decisions. We commence with resources:

COGNITIVE. Consumers need cognitive resources to process information. The firm must secure *direction of attention* to break through the *clutter* of thousands of messages per day people receive. *Intensity of attention* affects the ability to process the received information. Consumers often minimize cognitive effort and require reminders, or brand name cues, to access stored associations. Better education, government action, and increased competition are making consumers more sophisticated buyers.

ECONOMIC. Economic resources are necessary for purchase. When people have fewer resources — at the end of the month (versus beginning) and in recessions, purchasing behavior changes. Developed countries have most global resources, but purchasing power is increasing in emerging economies. Malaysia, Singapore, and South Korea grew rapidly in the 1990s; in the 2000s, Chinese and Indian middle classes are growing fast. Access to credit increases purchasing ability; the U.S. has highly sophisticated credit systems, but other countries less so.

TECHNOLOGICAL COMPETENCE. Internet websites offer consumers immediate access to many options — and are changing shopping patterns. Amazon and other websites feature wide varieties of product categories. Online supermarkets, like FreshDirect (U.S.) and Tesco (Britain), are quite successful. Using eBay and other sites, people transact commerce worldwide.[74] These trends will increase as young, technologically literate consumers age.

TIME. In many societies, time is an increasingly scarce resource — hence, fast-food restaurants, prepared meals, in-home medical test kits, and robotic vacuum cleaners. Less time to search for information, evaluate alternatives, and make purchases fueled the growth of direct marketing and Internet shopping. Time-saving requirements also led to service innovations like express checkout in hotels, single queue/multiple checkouts in supermarkets like Whole Foods, and speedy car rental at airports.[75]

Other individual factors are:

PHYSICAL AND MENTAL HEALTH. The ability of individuals to present themselves and function as desired has a major impact on many purchasing decisions — prescription-pharmaceutical, health and beauty products, and health services. These factors also drive decisions like sports and exercise equipment, and related services.

Marketing Question

The last time you purchased a ticket for long-distance air travel, what critical resource most influenced your decision?

KEY IDEA

➤ Individual factors that affect purchase decisions include several types of resources:

- Cognitive
- Economic
- Technological competence
- Time

Other factors include:

- Physical and mental health
- Should/want conflicts
- Life-cycle stage
- Lifestyle

SHOULD/WANT CONFLICTS. Individuals often face should/want conflicts: an option that brings short-term-pleasure — *want* versus a long-term-best-interest option — *should*. Restaurant choice — pepperoni pizza or healthy salad? Movie choice — action-adventure or Holocaust documentary?[76]

LIFE-CYCLE STAGE. Age, family size, and marital status are critical elements in the consumer life cycle. Life-cycle stage often influences purchasing behavior; Table 4.9 shows one version[77]:

TABLE 4.9

STAGES IN THE HUMAN LIFE CYCLE

Infant and pre-school — parents make all purchase decisions
School age — may influence parents making purchase decisions
Teenager, living at home — purchases from allowance, gifts, part-time jobs
Young, single, head of household, no children
Married, no children
Married, young children
Married, teenage children
Married, second family, young children
Married, no children, empty-nesters
Single, widow/widower

LIFESTYLE. Lifestyle embraces how people live their lives and spend their time. The **VALS** lifestyle framework integrates several foregoing factors and is the most influential approach to categorizing lifestyles. VALS recognizes two major lifestyle dimensions — *self-orientation* and *resources*:

- **Self-orientation** comprises three ways that consumers pursue and acquire products, services, and experiences to give their identities "shape, substance, and character":
  - **Action orientation** — guided by a desire for social/physical activity and risk-taking. These people purchase fast cars and take physically exacting vacations.
  - **Principle orientation** — guided by abstract idealized criteria. Environmental advocates purchase hybrid automobiles to reduce pollution; educational advocates support school-related causes and products.
  - **Status orientation** — guided by a desire for approval and the opinions of others. Brand name products are important to these people.
- **Resources** encompass the full range of psychological, physical, demographic, and material assets, including education, income, health, eagerness to buy, and energy. Resources both allow and constrain purchases and range from minimal to abundant.

Table 4.10 shows how these dimensions form the eight lifestyles[78]:

Marketing Question

Take the VALS survey. What VALS type are you? Do you agree with this assessment? How does your VALS type compare with the VALS types for your friends and family members? Can you identify a person for each of VALS' eight lifestyles? Can the VALS types explain differential preferences for breakfast cereal, cars, leisure activities, or vacation preferences? How?

TABLE 4.10

THE VALS LIFESTYLE FRAMEWORK

High Resources	
1. Innovators	Successful, active, sophisticated, take-charge — high self-esteem and abundant resources; seek to develop, explore, and express themselves in a variety of ways. Eager to try new products.
Moderately High Resources	
2. Thinkers (principle-oriented)	Mature, satisfied, comfortable, well-educated, reflective — value order, knowledge, and responsibility; tend to base decisions on strongly held principles; seem calm and self-assured; focus leisure activities on the home.
3. Achievers (status-oriented)	Successful career and work-oriented — feel in control of their lives; value structure, predictability, and stability; are deeply committed to work and family. Social life is structured around family, church, and business.
4. Experiencers (action-oriented)	Young, vital, enthusiastic, impulsive, and rebellious — seek variety and excitement; quickly become enthusiastic about new possibilities, but are equally quick to cool; energy finds an outlet in exercise, outdoor recreation, sports, and social activities.

Moderately Low Resources	
5. Believers (principle-oriented)	Conservative and conventional — concrete beliefs based on traditional established codes such as family, church, community, and nation; follow established routines largely structured around homes, families, social, and religious organizations.
6. Strivers (status-oriented)	Seek motivation, self-definition, and approval from their world — unsure of themselves and low on economic, social, and psychological resources; deeply concerned with the opinions and approval of others.
7. Makers (action-oriented)	Practical with constructive skills; value self-sufficiency — live in traditional contexts of family, practical work, and physical recreation; unimpressed by material possessions, except with a practical purpose.
Low Resources	
8. Survivors	Have limited economic, social, and emotional resources — the world is pressing and difficult; focus on the needs of the moment.

TABLE 4.10

(CONTINUED)

INFLUENCES ON ORGANIZATIONAL PURCHASE PROCESSES

Organizational buying generally concerns larger sums of money than consumer purchases, is often more protracted and complex, engages more people, and may involve company politics.[79,80] Processes and/or rules often govern organizational purchasing or *procurement* and interfacing with suppliers.[81]

CHANGES IN THE PROCUREMENT PROCESS

Important changes include:

BROADER SCOPE OF PROCUREMENT RESPONSIBILITIES. Historically, purchasing departments focused on buying factory inputs. Today, procurement is often also responsible for spending categories like auto rental, consulting services, and travel.

CENTRALIZATION. Technological advances in telecommunications, computers, and the Internet provide corporate buyers with greater leverage. They secure complete, accurate, and timely purchasing data on individual suppliers from the firm's decentralized units and track purchasing performance against benchmark databases. Home Depot centralized purchasing and cut costs significantly. Some customers demand a single supplier interface to avoid dealing with multiple salespeople. Previously, many P&G salespeople, each responsible for a product group like laundry detergent, toothpaste, or deodorants, visited Walmart. Today P&G's Walmart account executive directs a dedicated team of more than 400 employees, including specialists in various products, logistics, finance, and transportation.

> A hardware-products salesperson described his experience with a large customer. "They asked us to arrive in the late afternoon to negotiate next year's contract. They gave us a room, then called us to make our proposal. When we went back to our room, they called in our major competitor — from a similar room. A couple of hours later, they called us back and told us where the competitor had lower prices. They asked us to go to our room and return with a better offer. After we rebid, they did the same to the competitor. We left at 10 a.m. the next morning. It was brutal; we were in prison and just couldn't leave."[82]

GLOBALIZATION. The centralizing trend just discussed is expanding globally as multinational firms broaden supplier searches. They want global contracts and are increasingly ready to switch suppliers as price differentials appear and disappear.

INTERNET. Using *reverse auctions*, Internet-based B2B exchanges significantly affect the purchase of standard products. Buyers have better (and cheaper) access to information to drive out market inefficiencies and price differentials.

PROCUREMENT EXPERTISE.[83] Skilled procurement staffs introduce new strategies like **strategic sourcing** to reduce costs, improve quality, and increase efficiency. To become a *preferred supplier*, the firm must complete an extensive *request for information* (RFI); only then can it respond to a detailed *request for proposal* (RFP). Long-standing relationships mean little as procurement personnel gain deep insight into supplier cost structures and aggressively negotiate prices.[84] Some buyers, like Honda, assign efficiency consultants to supplier plants. Others go to great lengths to get secure low prices.

EVOLUTION IN BUYER-SELLER RELATIONSHIPS

Some firms evolve relationships with selected customers from vendor to quality supplier, and even to partner.[85]

VENDOR. Customer and supplier operate at *arm's length* in this traditional adversarial relationship. Contracts are typically short term with frequent re-bidding. Price is critical; buyers switch suppliers for small price differentials and/or better delivery. Salespeople meet with purchasing agents who restrict the information they provide suppliers to maintain negotiating positions.

QUALITY SUPPLIER. Both supplier and customer believe they receive value — like high-quality products — from a close long-term relationship. Each firm plans for continuous quality improvement. The supplier secures advantage by providing greater value than competitors.

PARTNER. Both firms share (or jointly develop) future strategies, technologies, and resources, and focus on the entire value chain. The customer bases critical buying decisions on value versus price. Each firm is deeply involved in the other's product-development cycles. Routine and sensitive information flows freely, as the supplier learns about/solves important customer problems. Partnerships involve multi-functional, multi-level interactions, joint quality control, and joint project teams. The supplier helps the customer achieve its objectives and undertakes many activities a *quality supplier* or *vendor* would not contemplate.[86] Armstrong World Industries runs a management development program for partners. When a supplier realized its distributor-partner often requested rush orders, yet later *discovered* lost inventory, it installed an inventory control system.

INCREASED CORPORATE ATTENTION TO PROCUREMENT

At many firms, the *procurement-spend/company-revenue ratio* has increased dramatically. Traditional *purchasing* is evolving from an unimportant managerial backwater to highly strategic *procurement*. High-quality, fast-track managers reduce procurement costs — by $1.5 billion at a $10 billion pharma firm! Several factors are responsible:

BRANDING. The rising importance of branding allows many firms to resell products made by others. The author is writing this book on a MacBook Pro; Apple did not manufacture the computer, carrying case, or power cord, but the complete package arrived ready to use.

ORGANIZATIONAL DOWNSIZING. Many firms are downsizing by replacing labor with capital. Equipment, raw material, and supply expenses have increased, relative to other costs.

OUTSOURCING. Outsourcing allows firms to reduce balance-sheet assets and fixed costs while increasing productivity, functional expertise, and flexibility. Many major firms outsource data centers and other business processes to IBM, HP, and Accenture. Others outsource software development, human resource and accounting functions, and call centers to India.

REDUCING THE NUMBER OF SUPPLIERS

Traditional purchasing departments sent specifications to many potential suppliers, then chose on criteria like price and delivery. Because streamlined supply-chains improve efficiency and effectiveness in converting raw materials to finished products, many firms are forging closer relationships with fewer suppliers. Table 4.11 shows several examples. Factors driving this trend include attempts to:

- Address increased purchase complexity involving multiple technologies.
- Improve product quality by securing tighter control over raw material inputs.
- Move closer to suppliers and enjoy better communications, greater transparency, improved operational excellence like just-in-time (JIT) inventory systems, and greater control.
- Reduce input costs via
  - Increased procurement effectiveness.[87]
  - Purchase assemblies versus parts.
  - Secure lower prices by letting selected suppliers gain economies of scale.
- Secure better and more consistent service in multiple geographies.

Company	Previous number of suppliers	New number of suppliers	Reduction (%) in number of suppliers
Airbus	3,000	500	83%
BAA Airports	11,500	3,000	74%
Barclay's Bank	2,000	180	91%
Boeing	30,000	10,000	67%
Motorola	10,000	3,000	70%
Texas Instruments	22,000	14,000	36%
Volkswagen	2,000	200	90%
Xerox	5,000	500	90%

TABLE 4.11

REDUCING THE NUMBER OF SUPPLIERS

Marketing Question

What other messages did you glean from this chapter?

KEY MESSAGES

To attract, retain, and grow customers, the firm gains deep customer insight by answering three critical questions:

Who are the customers? The firm should explore several issues:

- Macro-level customers — organizations; and micro-level customers — individuals.
- The many different roles individuals play in the purchase process.
- Current customers and future customers.
- Direct customers that exchange money for the firm's products and services, and indirect customers that receive value from the firm's products and services through intermediaries.

What do customers need and want? The firm satisfies customers' needs by making value offers. The firm should gain customer insight into:

- Recognized needs that customers express — expressed needs; latent needs: that they do not express — non-expressed needs.
- Who receives the firm's value — the customer organization or an individual in the organization.
- Attributes and features comprising the firm's product; benefits and values the firm offers customers.
- Hierarchies of needs, attributes/features, benefits, and values.
- Different types of value, including functional, psychological, and economic.
- Customer experiences that transcend customer benefits and values.

How do customers buy? The firm gains insight from the customer's purchase-decision process:

- The process comprises five stages — recognizing problems, acquiring information, evaluating alternatives, making a choice, and engaging in post-purchase processes.
- The dominant way customers evaluate alternatives is the linear-compensatory approach.
- Customers may deviate from rationality in their purchase decisions.
- We can usefully categorize purchase decisions into three types: routinized-response behavior, limited problem-solving, and extended problem-solving.
- Environmental factors that influence consumer purchase decisions include culture, social class, other people, family, and the situation.
- Individual influences like various types of resources, life-cycle stage, lifestyle, physical and mental health, and should/want conflicts influence the consumer purchase decision.
- Key factors influencing organizational purchase decisions are changes in the procurement process, evolution in buyer-seller relationships, increased corporate attention to procurement, and reducing the number of suppliers.

VIDEOS AND AUDIOS

Procurement at Merck	v402 🎥	Howard Richman	Merck
Customer Insight	a401 🎧		

v402

a401

QUESTIONS FOR STUDY AND DISCUSSION

Can you answer the questions implied by this chapter's learning objectives? Check!

1. a. Airbus developed the A380, a jet aircraft with more than 500 seats. Other than the airlines, what organizations should Airbus consider as macro-customers? Why did you select them?

    b. Suppose your job was to sell a fleet of A380s to Singapore Airlines. Who would you target for effort? What issues would you focus on for each of these targets?

2. Many teenagers have smart phones. Use the feature/benefit/value ladder to identify the benefits and values that smart phones deliver. Suppose you were advising Nokia on new products — what benefits and values could smart phones offer teenagers that they are currently not receiving? How would these benefits and values differ for adults?

3. All credit cards provide transaction value. What value(s) differentiates one card from another?

4. Motorco (fictional firm) is launching a new synthetic motor oil. The primary benefit is less-frequent need for changing — once every two years, regardless of mileage. Assume a car owner changes oil every 6,000 miles and keeps the car at least two years. Current oil-change cost = $50 (5 quarts @ $5/quart = $25, labor = $20, used oil disposal = $5). What is the new oil's EVC for a car owner who drives 15,000 miles per year?

5. a. Suppose you are going to take a two-week vacation when you graduate. How will you decide on your destination? Use the five-stage purchase-decision process to structure your answer.

    b. Based on your answer to 5a, what marketing program would you suggest for a vacation company targeting graduating students like you?

6. Select a product in which you are interested. Alternatively, consider this book — *Managing Marketing in the 21st Century*. Identify customers. What are their needs? What are their DMPs?

CHAPTER 5

INSIGHT ABOUT COMPETITORS, COMPANY, AND COMPLEMENTERS v501

To access O-codes, go to **www.ocodes.com**

The ability to learn faster than your competitors may be the only sustainable competitive advantage.

— Arie de Gues

LEARNING OBJECTIVES

When you have completed this chapter you will be able to:

- Articulate the importance of gaining *competitor* insight.
- Identify the firm's current (today) competitors and potential (tomorrow) competitors.
- Identify the firm's direct and indirect competitors.
- Describe competitors' capabilities and difficulties.
- Evaluate competitors by identifying their strategic options.
- Project competitors' objectives and future actions.
- Manage competitors' behavior.
- Assess the firm's competitive position.
- Understand the various sources and types of complementarity.

OPENING CASE: BOEING AND AIRBUS

Boeing and Airbus — headquartered in Chicago and Toulouse, France, respectively — compete intensely in the large passenger jet aircraft market.[1] Boeing launched modern jet aircraft in 1958 and has close to 25,000 planes in service; Airbus started in 1972 and has more than 5,000 planes flying. Boeing was market leader for several decades but recently Airbus has challenged its position. In 2003, for the first time, Airbus delivered more aircraft than Boeing; Airbus also secured more aircraft orders:

Year	Airbus Orders	Boeing Orders	Year	Airbus Orders	Boeing Orders
2002	300	251	2007	1341	1413
2003	284	239	2008	777	662
2004	370	272	2009	271	142
2005	1055	1002	2010	574	530
2006	790	1044	2011	1419	805

Although Airbus wins on annual plane sales, Boeing earns up to 55 percent of aircraft value because its 747 dominates in the wide-body market. The Boeing 737 and Airbus 320 account for about 80 percent of unit sales. Airbus' A380 threatens Boeing's position in wide-body jets, but Boeing's 787 fuel-efficient Dreamliner competes strongly in shorter-haul markets.

There is no love lost between Boeing and Airbus. Rival executives commonly denigrate each other's products, and the firms have a long-standing dispute over government subsidies. The World Trade Organization supported Boeing's claims that Airbus received illegal subsidies from European governments for developing the A380 and other planes. The WTO supported Airbus claims that Boeing received illegal subsidies via U.S. government tax breaks and defense and research contracts. The EU also claims Boeing receives investment subsidies from Japanese airlines related to its close relationships with Japanese consortia, notably for 787 wing production.

So far this century, Boeing has had other troubles. CEO Phil Condit resigned in fallout from unethical conduct by a U.S. Air Force procurement officer who favored Boeing, her soon-to-be new employer. The Boeing board forced out replacement CEO Harry Stonecipher because of a consensual relationship with a female executive. And the U.S. government transferred $1 billion of Boeing contracts to Lockheed Martin following allegations of industrial espionage.

Airbus was formed in the 1960s as a consortium of European aviation firms to compete with the U.S. In 2001, this loose alliance evolved into the European Aeronautic Defence and Space Company (EADS) when three Continental European firms merged. EADS (80 percent) and BAE Systems (formerly British Aerospace) (20 percent) owned the new Airbus. From the start, conflicts between French and German shareholders troubled EADS. In 2006, BAE Systems sold its 20 percent ownership, and EADS and Airbus CEOs resigned amid allegations of insider trading.

For the past several years, Boeing (2010 revenues $64 billion; 157,000 employees) has been integrating McDonnell Douglas (MD), acquired in 1997, into its operations. Boeing retired some MD aircraft, along with the Boeing 757 and now offers the following models:

- *Boeing 737: twin-engine narrow-body, 85–215 passengers, short-medium range, 1966**
- *Boeing 747: quad-engine large wide-body, 85–524 passengers, long haul, 1969**
- *Boeing 767: twin-engine small narrow-body, 180–375 passengers, short-medium range, 1981**
- *Boeing 777: twin-engine medium wide-body, 330–550 passengers, long haul, 1996**

Boeing's newest aircraft is the twin-engine medium wide-body 787 — Dreamliner, seating 210–330 passengers. Boeing claims the Dreamliner is 20 percent more fuel efficient than comparable planes — from engine (GE and Rolls-Royce) and aerodynamic improvements, greater use of lighter-

*first flight

weight composites, and advanced systems. But supply-chain problems delayed the Dreamliner's introduction by several years.[2] Boeing has more than 800 firm orders.

Airbus (2009 revenues € 43.3 billion, 57,000 employees) offers several passenger models:

- *Airbus A320: twin-engine single aisle, seating 180 passengers, short-medium range, 1987**
- *Airbus A318 (shortened A320): twin-engine twin aisle, seating 107 passengers, 2002**
- *Airbus A319 (shortened A320): twin-engine single aisle, seating 145 passengers, 1995**
- *Airbus A321 (stretched A320): twin-engine single aisle, seating 220 passengers, long haul, 1993**
- *Airbus A330: twin-engine twin aisle, seating 253–440 passengers, 1992**
- *Airbus A340: quad-engine twin aisle, seating 261–440 passengers, long haul, 1991**
- *Airbus A380: quad-engine twin aisle, seating 555–840 passengers, long haul, 2006**

Airbus also is developing the 250–350 passenger, twin-engine, twin-aisle A350, derived from the A330, to compete with Boeing's Dreamliner.

CASE QUESTION

As competitor research analyst at Boeing (Airbus), what insight would you want on Airbus (Boeing)? How would you secure it? Bombardier's CSeries and the planned C919 from Commercial Aircraft Corp. of China (planned launch 2014) will compete with the Airbus A320 and Boeing 737. How would you address these threats?

*first flight

Chapter 5 builds on the five-forces model from Chapter 3 to discuss the firm's competitive challenges. We *identify* specific competitors and present a process for gaining competitor insight. **Competitive insight** is securing deep understanding of competitors to provide a unique strategic perspective. Ultimately, we would like to know what competitors *cannot do*; what competitors *will not do*; and what will *put competitors at a disadvantage if they do.* Specifically, we develop a competitive insight framework by exploring how to *identify* competitors; *describe* competitors — their capabilities and difficulties (strengths and weaknesses); *evaluate* competitors — their strategic options; *project* competitors' actions — figure out what they will do; and *manage* competitors — influence their behavior to benefit the firm. As the firm gains insight into competitors, it also gains insight into itself — **company insight**. We also explore complementers: organizations that can help the firm achieve its objectives — **complementer insight**.

THE CHANGING VIEW

OLD WAY	NEW WAY
Competitive analysis concerns sales and marketing	Multifunctional involvement
Competitive consolidation nationally	Competitive consolidation globally
Competitive focus local/regional/national	Competitive focus regional/multinational/global
Competitive strategy a low priority	Competitive strategy a high priority
Competitor description only	Competitor evaluation and projection widespread
Conflict-based views of competition	Collaborative arrangements more common
Customers purchase the firm's products	Customers as potential competitors — backward integration
Ethical considerations often ignored	Ethical considerations becoming more salient
Examine competition at the firm level	Examine competition by brand and market segment
Focus only on direct competitors	Focus on a broad competitor set — indirect and supply-chain competitors, current and potential competitors, and competitive networks
Industry structure fixed	Industry structure evolves
Limited attention to gaining competitor insight	Increased emphasis on gaining competitor insight
Passive and reactive competitive strategy	Active and proactive competitive strategy
Suppliers supply raw materials	Suppliers as potential competitors — forward integration
The firm operates independently	The firm operates interdependently

Competitors

DEVELOPING COMPETITIVE INSIGHT

Dell's chief marketing officer said: "We have a wonderful healthy paranoia. At one level, we watch the competition like a hawk and we watch everything they do. And we watch the global competition, 'cause we fully recognize that tomorrow's fight may be with the guy that's today a small local, low-cost player in some remote region."[3] Dell knows the value of competitive insight.

Competitive intensity is increasing across the board in virtually all industries. Any executive will tell you that increased competition is a global phenomenon. Competition is especially tough where: industries are deregulating, rapid changes are occurring in product and/or process technology, state-owned enterprises are privatizing, and governments are reducing or removing tariffs, quotas, and other competitive barriers. Competition is also challenging in industries where regulatory restrictions are increasing, like financial services and pharmaceuticals. The firm must work harder and smarter to attain in-depth competitive insight and build that insight into strategic marketing decision-making. Only then will the firm develop the differential advantage it requires to attract, retain, and grow customers. Failure to gain good competitor insight can be serious, as Jaguar discovered:

> Discussing Jaguar's failure to meet the goals that Ford established, Joe Greenwell, Jaguar's new chairman, said, "We were over-optimistic, and we underestimated the amount of competitive activity, which is a typical and dangerous assumption to make when you are in management."[4]

Many firms put too little emphasis on gaining competitive insight. They may claim lack of time or resources, or simply be myopic, perhaps paralyzed by *groupthink*,[5] and not understand the competitive threat. Good competitor insight reduces decision-making uncertainty. The fundamental marketing job is to attract, retain, and grow customers, but other guys are trying to do the same thing! The firm should always know who competitors are today and who they will be tomorrow; what they are doing now and what they may do in the future. This chapter shows that developing good competitive insight has major firm value.

Gaining sound competitive insight is not easy, but most leading firms like IBM, Xerox, and Citibank put in significant effort. Firms often face internal challenges in securing and acting on competitive insight. The firm:

- Bases insight on out-of-date data from tired sources.
- Claims the cost of securing good competitive data is too high.
- Fails to go beyond basic description of competitors.
- Focuses on current competitors but ignores potential competitors.
- Gains good insight but does not take action:
- Does not commit the necessary resources.

A competitive intelligence professional presented the following data to top management[6]:

- A Japanese competitor is building a U.S. plant.
- The Japanese firm intends to penetrate the U.S. market via low price, high advertising and a large sales force.
- The Japanese firm has a history of sacrificing short-term profits for long-term gain.
- The Japanese firm hired salespeople from our firm and our domestic competitors.
- We have just lost one of our largest customers to the Japanese firm.

Top managers did not accept the analysis and ignored these warning signs!

Good competitive insight can be invaluable. By 1999, Google had the best search engine and had raised $25 million venture capital, but did not have a financially viable business model. Sergey Brin and Larry Page studied competitors including GoTo.com (renamed Overture). GoTo made money selling advertisements to accompany search results. Google introduced Adwords — the rest is history.[7]

Figure 5.1 shows a five-step framework for gaining competitor insight. Steps 1 and 2, *identifying* and *describing* competitors, are critical but insufficient; unfortunately, many firms stop right here. Identifying and describing competitors are the foundation for *evaluating* — step 3, *projecting* — step 4, and *managing* — step 5. To gain superior competitor insight, the firm must excel at each step and be very clear about what it does and does not know.[8]

> **Marketing Question**
>
> As a Starbucks competitive analyst, what information would help you complete the competitive insight framework in Figure 5.1?

FIGURE 5.1

A FRAMEWORK FOR GAINING COMPETITIVE INSIGHT

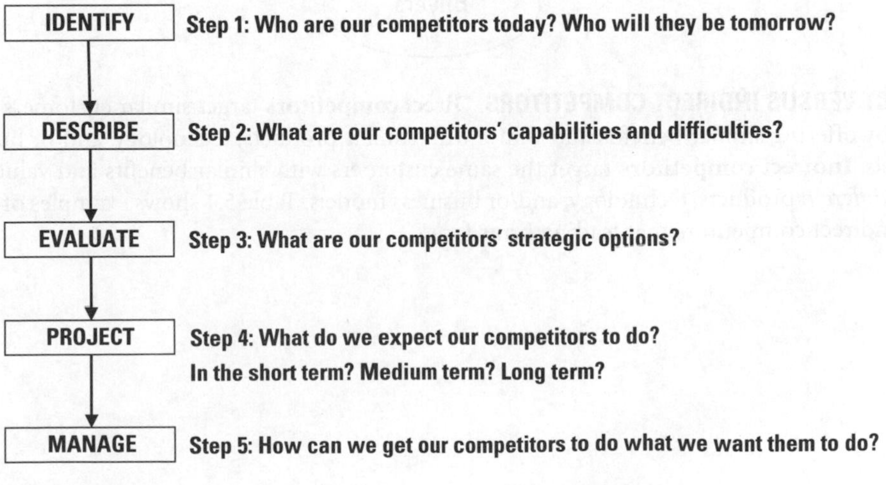

IDENTIFY	Step 1: Who are our competitors today? Who will they be tomorrow?
DESCRIBE	Step 2: What are our competitors' capabilities and difficulties?
EVALUATE	Step 3: What are our competitors' strategic options?
PROJECT	Step 4: What do we expect our competitors to do? In the short term? Medium term? Long term?
MANAGE	Step 5: How can we get our competitors to do what we want them to do?

IDENTIFYING COMPETITORS

A **competitor** is any organization whose products and services provide similar or superior benefits and values to the same customers the firm seeks to attract, retain, and grow. Of course, by making purchases, customers decide who competes with whom. Today the firm faces **current competitors**; tomorrow it may face **potential competitors**. Chapter 5 argues for a broad view of competitors, just as Chapter 4 argues for a broad view of customers. Many firms view competition too narrowly, focusing only on firms like themselves. For years, Hollywood did not realize television was a competitor; paper cup manufacturers did not address competition from plastic cups.[9] When the firm views competition too narrowly, it fails to identify many medium- and long-term threats. The firm should consider three key areas:

- Structure of competition
- Competitive dynamics
- The firm as competitor

STRUCTURE OF COMPETITION

Figure 5.2 reprises the *five-forces model* — Chapter 3. Three of the five forces represent competition: *current direct competitors*, *new direct entrants*, and *indirect competitors*. The two other forces are *suppliers* and *buyers*. We learned earlier that extreme forms of supplier and buyer pressure are, respectively, *forward* and *backward integration*; by undertaking operations the firm currently conducts, they become *direct competitors*. We simplify the *five-forces* approach and develop two identifying dimensions that help evaluate competitors and gain deep insight.

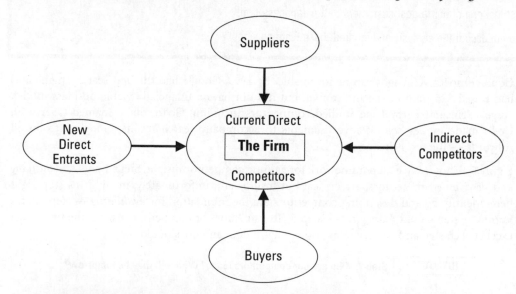

DIRECT VERSUS INDIRECT COMPETITORS. **Direct competitors** target similar customers to the firm by offering similar benefits and values with similar products, technology, and/or business models. **Indirect competitors** target the same customers with similar benefits and values, but have *different* products, technology, and/or business models. Table 5.1 shows examples of direct and indirect competitors that leading firms face.

TABLE 5.1

EXAMPLES OF
DIRECT AND
INDIRECT
COMPETITORS

Firm	Customer Benefits and Values	Direct Competitors	Indirect Competitors
BusinessWeek	Business information	*Fortune, Forbes*	MSNBC, Yahoo! News
Citibank (retail)	Financial deposits	JPMorgan Chase, Bank of New York	Vanguard, Merrill Lynch, T. Rowe Price
Disney World	Family fun	Universal Studios, Busch Gardens	Beach or ski vacation; home-entertainment system (for disposable income)
ESPN	Men (to advertisers as customers)	CBS, Fox, NBC, Fox SportsNet	Comedy Central, Discovery Channel
Monster	Employee recruiting	CareerBuilder, Yahoo!, Hot Jobs	LinkedIn, Facebook, Twitter
Home builders	New homes	Other builders	Foreclosed homes
Kodak	Images	Fuji, Agfa	HP, Sony
Metropolitan Museum of Art	Spending leisure time	Museum of Modern Art, Whitney Museum	Broadway plays, movies, Central Park
Professional sports	Live sports entertainment	Other professional sports	Movie theaters, restaurants, TV

⚷ **KEY IDEA**

➤ The firm's most serious competitive threats may be the least obvious.

CURRENT VERSUS POTENTIAL COMPETITORS. Today the firm faces **current competitors**; tomorrow it may face **potential competitors** — some may not even be around today. Potential competitors may even be firm employees who take intellectual capital developed at the firm and set up business on their own.

HP executive Karl Lamb formed a flat-panel TV firm at the same time as he worked on a flat-panel TV project for HP.

In March 2007, as Bear Stearns was collapsing, star broker Douglas Sharon joined Morgan Stanley; almost all his 90 customers and $1 billion investment moved also.

Star lawyer David Boies resigned from Cravath, Swaine & Moore; within a few days his new firm had four former Cravath clients including DuPont and Georgia-Pacific.

The Figure 5.3 framework identifies four types of competitive threat. It helps the firm decide which threats are most serious and where it should deploy resources:

- **Current direct competitors, cell A.** The competitive *status quo* — the traditional rivalry between established firms.
- **Current indirect competitors, cell B.** More difficult to identify than cell A competitors. They act differently and develop customer benefits and values differently.
- **Potential direct competitors, cell C.** Behave like Cell A competitors, but may emerge from a different industry or geography.
- **Potential indirect competitors, cell D.** The most difficult competitors to identify. They do not compete today, and it is unclear when and where they will emerge.

Marketing Question

Consider your most common mode of transportation — bicycle, automobile, train. Who are:
- Current direct competitors?
- Current indirect competitors?
- Potential direct competitors?
- Potential indirect competitors?

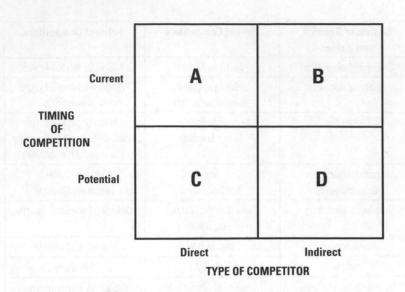

FIGURE 5.3

**A FRAMEWORK
FOR IDENTIFYING
COMPETITIVE THREATS**

Sometimes, the distinction between direct and indirect competitors is not very clear. Figure 5.4 shows a spectrum of direct versus indirect competitors. For United Airlines, Amtrak rail is a very different indirect competitor from video-conferencing.

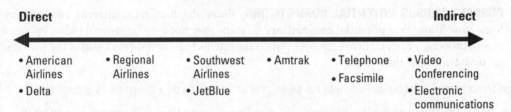

FIGURE 5.4

**THE SPECTRUM OF
DIRECT/INDIRECT
COMPETITION: UNITED
AIRLINES EXAMPLE**[10]

In mature, low-profit industries, new direct competition is unlikely. Consequently, firms in such industries should focus on identifying current and potential indirect competitors. Few firms enter the paper industry to compete with International Paper and Boise Cascade, but plastics and imaging solutions are replacing paper in some markets. By contrast, new firms have significant incentive to enter profitable and growing industries like digital document and knowledge management solutions; hence, new direct competitors are more likely.

COMPETITIVE DYNAMICS

We can extend Figure 5.3 to show competitive evolution. Dramatic changes may occur: New competitors may enter or local/regional competitors may become national/multinational. Figure 5.5 shows various paths competitors can take. These paths may help the firm forecast the competitive threat transitions. We identify eight transitions:

- **Transition I.** From *potential direct* competitor (C) to *current* direct competitor (A).

- **Transition II.** From *potential indirect* competitor (D) to *current* indirect competitor (B).

- **Transition III.** From *potential direct* competitor (C) to *withdrawal* — no longer a threat.

- **Transition IV.** From *potential indirect* competitor (D) to *withdrawal* — no longer a threat.

- **Transition V.** From *current direct* competitor (A) to *withdrawal* — no longer a threat.

- **Transition VI.** From *current indirect* competitor (B) to *withdrawal* — no longer a threat.

- **Transition VII.** From *current direct* competitor (A) to *current indirect* competitor (B). The direct competitor has developed some new approach to satisfy customer needs.

> ### Marketing Exercise
>
> Sony Music Entertainment (SME) is a world leader in recorded music. Use a direct/indirect competition spectrum like Figure 5.4 to identify SME's competitors.

- **Transition VIII.** From *current indirect* competitor (B) to *current direct competitor* (A). The indirect competitor has decided to compete on an *apples-to-apples* basis.

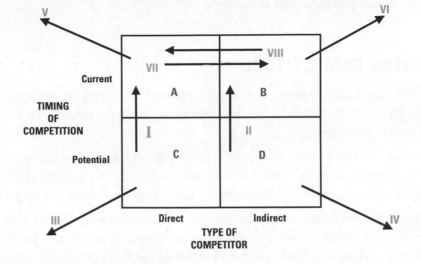

THE FIRM AS COMPETITOR

KEY IDEA

➤ Be aware of potential competition from within your own firm.

Our unstated assumption is that all competitors are other firms. But for product and brand managers, the toughest competition may be internal. Different businesses always compete for financial, human, and system resources and sales force time — but they may also compete for customers. The firm may encourage **intra-firm** competition, or it may occur by happenstance.

DELIBERATELY INDUCED INTERNAL COMPETITION. Motorola employees refer to its business units as *warring tribes*. Some firms foster Darwinian *internal* competition to improve effectiveness against *external* competitors. These firms believe increased competitiveness more than compensates for resource duplication, especially if customers tend to switch products and/or brands. P&G regularly mounts parallel product development efforts to produce better products and get to market faster.

Citibank undertook several parallel initiatives to develop electronic letters of credit for foreign trade. At one point, the successful Asia-Pacific Group was selling its new electronic system to customers of its sister North America Group. Simultaneously, Citibank North America was developing its own system![11]

When product technology changes, the firm may place responsibility for old and new products in different businesses.[12] At Microsoft, one unit supports Office, a different unit supports Windows; Microsoft also separates new Office versions from older versions.

INTERNAL COMPETITION BY HAPPENSTANCE. Internal competition often evolves. Suppose the firm targets two market segments — segment A with product I, and segment B with product II. Over time, these segments may merge, and/or the firm's products become more similar. Two originally independent approaches now become competitive:

Australian resources firm BHP's steel division found that, compared to other industrialized countries, Australian high-rise buildings used more reinforced concrete than structural steel.[13] Three BHP product groups funded the structural steel development group (SSDG) to increase use of structural steel; SSDG was quite successful. Later, one of the three groups discovered that structural steel used less of its products than reinforced concrete. The group withdrew from SSDG and helped form an industry group to support reinforced concrete technology in Australia.

In step 1 of the competitive insight framework, the firm probably identifies several external competitors. In steps 2 through 5, the firm should focus on the most serious competitive threats and develop deep competitive insight about them.

DESCRIBING COMPETITORS

Jackson and Walker (disguised names) are strategically important chemical subsidiaries of major U.S. multinationals operating in Asia/Pacific. Jackson has 60 percent market share and is highly profitable; Walker has 20 percent market share and is barely breaking even.

Jackson learns that Walker's president is retiring. Information on the new president is: male; early 40s; chemical engineer by training; 20+ years with Walker's parent; joined Walker's parent after graduate school; known as a turnaround manager; has just successfully completed a smaller turnaround; known as a *margin-raiser*.

Jackson's analysis and action: Jackson decided that, within reason, it wanted Walker to be successful — a successful competitor would take predictable actions; an unsuccessful competitor could be a *wild card*. Jackson knew that Walker would not leave the market and also knew the new president's *margin-raiser* reputation.

Jackson raised prices modestly. Because of its 60 percent market share, it would significantly increase profits if Walker followed suit. When Walker's president arrived, he also raised prices. Walker became moderately profitable. Jackson invested some of its increased profits in additional services to strengthen its position.

Jackson based its action on good competitor insight. By learning about Walker's new president, Jackson developed an innovative strategy that allowed it to *win*.

Describing competitors concerns four key areas:[14]

- What *competitor data* should the firm collect?
- What *sources* of competitor data are available?
- What *processes* should the firm use for competitive data-gathering?
- What *frameworks* can the firm use to describe competitors?

COLLECTING COMPETITOR DATA

To describe competitors effectively, the firm must decide what it wants to know, based on the sort of decisions it has to make. We consider **level of data** and **type of data**.

LEVEL OF DATA. The firm should consider several organizational levels like corporate, business unit, market, and market segment. A competitive data profile on GE by a home appliance firm might include answers to several types of question. To illustrate:

- **Corporate.** How does GE allocate resources across its major businesses like financial services, healthcare, home appliances, and jet engines? What are its acquisition and divestiture plans? What effort is GE placing on innovation versus increasing efficiency?

- **Business unit.** How does GE allocate resources across its home appliance portfolio: refrigerators, dishwashers, washers and driers, and ranges?

- **Market.** What is GE's strategy in the refrigerator market? How does GE segment the market? Where is GE focusing its efforts by segment? What is GE's R&D in refrigerators? What is GE's capacity and capacity utilization for refrigerator production?

- **Market segment.** For segments where the firm competes with GE: What brand(s) does GE offer? How does GE position these brands? What are GE's models? What are GE's prices? What are GE's credit terms? How do retailers display GE's products? What is GE's promotional emphasis: advertising, sales force, direct mail? What is GE's core message? How do target customers evaluate GE's offers? What is GE's refrigerator profitability by segment?

Responsibility for competitor data-gathering typically varies by data type and level. At corporate and the business units, a competitive intelligence group often has direct access to industry analysts and consulting firms. Product and market managers are generally responsible for market and market-segment data; they use these data to *reverse engineer* competitor market and market segment strategies. Responsible persons should develop their own data networks. Because the types of data vary by level, appropriate data-gathering approaches, analysis methods, and methodologies vary widely.

TYPE OF DATA. The firm should collect both quantitative and qualitative data. *Quantitative* data include measures like market share and profitability: SEC filings often provide these data for public companies; business data services supply profiles for private firms. *Qualitative* data include competitor manager expertise, commitment to various businesses, and anticipated strategic moves. The Internet offers many ways to obtain qualitative data. The data Jackson compiled on Walker's new president are in the qualitative category.

Competitive data-gathering should not focus solely on marketing issues. Information about products and services is crucial, but the firm should also seek data on costing systems, financial strength, logistics, operations, R&D, speed of action, and business philosophy (including willingness to innovate and take risks). In his early days in oil and gas, T Boone Pickens learned about a rival's drilling activity by having a spotter watch the drilling floor with binoculars from half a mile away. By counting the number of joints connecting 30-foot lengths of drill pipe, Pickens knew the depth of the competitor's wells.[15] Xerox purchases competitive products from dealers and assesses both customer value and manufacturing cost. Under severe price pressure from Schott Glass (Germany), Corning's competitive intelligence discovered Schott was implementing a deliberate strategy of taking losses in a specific product class to drive Corning from the market.[16] The firm should always be on the lookout for illegally acting competitors. Patent and trademark violations, predatory pricing, price fixing, and misleading advertising should be matters of concern.

> Cisco suspected that low-cost Chinese competitor Huawei Technologies was illegally using Cisco's copyrighted software in its routers. Cisco secured a Huawei router from a customer and confirmed the copyright infringement; Huawei's routers even had the same software bugs! Cisco filed charges. Huawei's subsequent legal problems compromised its ability to compete against Cisco.

SOURCES OF COMPETITIVE DATA

The firm probably already has some competitive data internally; it needs a process to make these data available to the analyst. The firm should also seek competitor data externally. For both internal and external data, there are two approaches:

- **Secondary data** are available in various reports, publications, and the Internet; the firm must collect, sort, and give them meaning, based on the questions it wants answered. According to McKinsey, the major sources of competitive secondary data are news reports, industry groups/conferences, annual reports, and CEO speeches.[17]

- **Primary data** require a focused acquisition effort like customer interviews and surveys. For important data, the analyst should seek multiple sources, filter for reliability, and cross-validate. Table 5.2 lists data sources for various competitive issues.

KEY IDEA

➤ Critical elements for gaining competitive insight are:

- Identify
- **Describe**
- Evaluate
- Project
- Manage

KEY IDEA

➤ The firm should seek competitive data at several levels:

- Corporate
- Business
- Market
- Market segment

These data may be:

- Primary
- Secondary

Generic Modes of Competition	Sample Internal Sources	Sample External Sources
Availability	• Distribution and logistics personnel • Sales force reports	• Customer satisfaction surveys • Third-party (industry analysts) studies • Distributor access
Features	• Sales, marketing, engineering personnel • Internal analyses and trials	• Trade publication product reviews • Competitor literature, consultants • Competitor websites
Functionality	• Competitor supplier analysis • Product comparison studies • Reverse engineering	• Customer reports • Specialist trade reports/industry observers

General information	• Senior firm executives	• The Internet, including
		  • Competitor websites
		  • Rumor sites, e.g., www.gawker.com
		  • Complaint sites, e.g.,
		    www.PayPalsucks.com
		  • Blogs and forums
		• Investment bankers/industry analysts
		• Media (local, national)
		• Annual reports, SEC filings, 10Ks
		• Suppliers

Image and reputation	• Marketing, sales, and advertising personnel • Tracking studies	• Customer perceptions, third-party studies • Competitor advertising, promotion, and public relations
Product line	• Sales, marketing, engineering personnel • Industry studies	• Competitor product catalogs • Trade shows • Trade associations, press, consultants • Regulatory and patent filings
Price	• Marketing, sales, and service personnel • Sales force reports	• Competitor price lists • Interviews with end customers
Selling and relationships	• Sales force reports • Managerial assessments	• Interviews with customers and channel members
Service	• Service personnel comparisons • Comparative studies	• Customer, third-party assessments • Mystery shopper reports

TABLE 5.2

SAMPLE INTERNAL AND EXTERNAL DATA SOURCES[18]

> ### Marketing Question
>
> Returning from an industry conference, the attractive young woman took her seat on the plane. The middle-aged man in the next seat glanced at her reading material, noting they had both attended the same conference. He introduced himself as marketing VP of a major pharmaceutical firm. She introduced herself as a product manager for its chief competitor. Trying to impress, the VP discussed, at length, his firm's marketing plans. The young woman listened attentively!
>
> Did the young woman behave ethically? Would your answer change if she had not indicated her employment status? What do you think of the VP's behavior?

INTERNAL PROCESSES FOR SECURING COMPETITIVE DATA

Many competitive data-gathering efforts fail because of poor processes — too few sources, failure to cross-validate, and/or short-term focused when the firm needs a longer-term view. Competitive data-gathering options differ by focus and required resources:

- **Competing.** Sometimes the best way to learn about competitors is just to observe them. By operating in the marketplace day-by-day, an observant firm can gain significant competitive insight. Many automobile firms compete vigorously in Chile, a country where import duties are low or zero. Many firms from developing nations compete directly with established players; the opportunities for competitive learning are enormous.

- **Competitive intelligence system.** The firm builds a culture where all employees are responsible for competitive intelligence. They come across competitive data daily; the critical step is to share these data with a competitor intelligence group. Group members

KEY IDEA

➤ The firm can secure timely and relevant competitive information from many internal and external sources.

check, sort, and digest the data they receive, then send it to those who need it. This approach is relatively inexpensive, but is relatively unfocused.

- **Competitive intelligence department (CID).** The CID is responsible for collecting, analyzing, and distributing competitive information.[19] The CID can be highly focused but is expensive.

- **Formal development of strategic plans.** When the firm has few major competitors, it can develop strategic plans as though it were the competitor. This highly focused approach is usually only practical for one or two competitors. Boeing may use it (and the following approach) for Airbus, and AMD for Intel, and vice versa.

- **Gaming with multifunctional teams.** In these *war games*, executive teams play one of two roles: the firm or competitor. Each team develops and presents its strategy and action plans; the *firm* and *competitor* then develop counter-strategies and action plans. Conducted at one- or two-day offsite meetings, this process often generates important insights.[20]

- **Review of business lost and business gained.** When the firm wins or loses a sale it should find out why it won or lost.[21] In well-managed firms, this process is standard operating procedure. Typically, customers are willing to share this sort of information.

- **Shadow system.** Individual executives or teams *shadow* specific competitors, either as a full- or part-time job. When shadowing is an extra responsibility, it can be an effective way of focusing attention on specific competitors, at relatively low cost.

Marketing Question

Which data-gathering process did Surgical use? Considering Surgical's strategic position, was this a wise decision?

Surgical's (disguised names) products were used in hospitals throughout the U.S.; Surgical enjoyed over 60 percent market share. Hove was Surgical's largest competitor. Hove grew by acquiring several small players and became a significant threat to Surgical. Surgical executives were unclear about Hove's future objectives and strategy. During a two-day offsite meeting, teams of Surgical executives played Hove and Surgical roles. Surgical gained significant insight about Hove's potential actions.

KEY IDEA

➤ The firm should develop formal processes to secure timely and relevant competitive information.

Students and executives are often concerned about the ethics and legality of competitor data-gathering. Our position is clear: There are many ethical and legal approaches to securing competitor data; the firm should not use unethical or illegal methods like bribery, covert recording, knowingly jeopardizing someone's job, misrepresentation (including pretexting [gaining phone records]), placing *moles* at competitors, setting up fake job interviews to trawl for competitive data when no jobs are available, or theft (including hiring employees who steal data from former employers). Some firms have specific policies: HP prohibits examining "information about competitive proposals or products that was submitted to customers, channel partners, suppliers, other business partners, or anyone else with the understanding they would treat it as confidential."[22] The firm must ensure it enforces data-gathering policies, especially if agents are responsible; P&G's experience is instructive[23]:

P&G hired agents to secure competitive data about Unilever. The agents secured 80 documents from trash bins, on public property, outside Unilever's Chicago offices. The documents laid out Unilever's long-term hair-care strategy. P&G possession of these documents was not illegal, but the data-gathering process breached its ethics policy. P&G agreed to a third-party audit and paid Unilever $10 million compensation. P&G fired three executives.

A widespread perception of industrial espionage by foreign governments led the U.S. Congress to pass the 1996 Economic Espionage Act making the theft or misappropriation of trade secrets a federal crime.[24]

Firms can secure good competitive data without breaking any rules — most organizations are *leaky*. When the firm's competitive data-gathering efforts fail, the reason is usually insufficient resources and/or unfocused efforts. But, if competitors are leaky, your firm may also be leaky! Counter-intelligence is vital. The firm should take affirmative steps to protect its data:

- Classify information according to the degree of secrecy warranted.

- Execute employee **non-compete agreements** to prohibit former employees from working for competitors for a defined time period.

- Train employees on the danger of loose tongues, especially when attending industry meetings and social events. Teach them to be good listeners — ears open and mouths shut!

- Use **nondisclosure agreements (NDAs)** to prohibit revealing information to third parties. NDAs are standard for consultants and others working on a contract basis.

FRAMEWORKS TO DESCRIBE COMPETITORS

To gain insight, the firm must organize competitive data into a useful framework. Good competitive insight often results from a *differential diagnosis* of the firm versus competitors. We use four basic building blocks: *competitor's organization, strengths and vulnerabilities, firm in the environment*, and *mind-set*. These analytic guidelines help the firm understand the competitor's *current strategy and performance*. The firm also gains insight into the competitor's future strategy.[25] The firm should adapt the framework for the level of competitive insight it seeks — corporate, business unit, market, or market segment.

COMPETITOR'S ORGANIZATION. How the organization functions:

- **Culture.** The behaviors, norms, beliefs, and values that together describe what the competitor stands for and how its members operate and behave.

- **Infrastructure.** The line organization — basic responsibilities and reporting relationships.

- **Processes.** Accounting, information, control, and reward systems and processes.

STRENGTHS AND VULNERABILITIES. Assets, capabilities, competences, and failings. This part of the framework comprises the strengths and weakness elements of a SWOT analysis[26]:

- **Assets.** Financial, human, knowledge, organizational, perceptual, physical, and political assets that embrace the competitor's brand equity and customer loyalty — proprietary and non-proprietary. The firm should also evaluate competitor liabilities, emotional commitments or *blind spots* that sometimes compromise hard-headed business judgments.

- **Capabilities and competencies.** Activities the competitor does well, including *local* expertise and broad-scale abilities, and areas where it does poorly. Specific product-related abilities are: conceive and design, finance, produce, manage, and market. The competitor's approach to risk and speed of action may also be a competence — or not!

FIRM IN THE ENVIRONMENT. Embraces relationships with other organizations:

- **Value chain.** Major work activities the competitor conducts and how they connect to external entities like suppliers and customers — Figure 5.6.[27] The firm asks four questions:
  - Where does the competitor have a cost advantage?
  - Where is the competitor at a cost disadvantage?
  - Where does the competitor have a value advantage?
  - Where is the competitor at a value disadvantage?

Supporting activities	Infrastructure				
	Human resource management				
	Product and process development				
	Procurement				
Primary activities	Inbound logistics	Production	Outbound logistics	Sales and marketing	Service

FIGURE 5.6

THE VALUE CHAIN

- **Alliances and special relationships. Alliances** are formal economic relationships between the competitor and other entities (partners) — customers, distributors, and suppliers. **Special relationships** are informal and may embrace government agencies, political parties, and public interest groups — as well as customers and suppliers.
- **Networks.** Interconnected sets of alliances and relationships, each fulfilling a unique role. Rather than compete with a single competitor, the firm may compete with a network.

MIND-SET. How the competitor thinks and the bases for its decisions. What are its *assumptions*? What does the competitor take for granted, or as a *given*? Assumptions are the outcomes of analysts' judgments, inferred from competitive data.

CURRENT STRATEGY AND PERFORMANCE. How the competitor behaves and its results:

- **Market strategy.** The firm observes the competitor's actions and infers its objectives, segment choices, and strategies.[28]
- **Other major resource commitments.** The competitor may build new factories, expand existing plants, and/or spend extensively on a particular type of R&D. The competitor may also display different levels of commitment to various businesses.
- **Performance.** Most performance measures are market-oriented or financially based. Market measures include market share and customer satisfaction. Financial measures range from product-line profitability to stock price performance.

Won't the firm using this framework collect a tremendous amount of information, and won't it be overwhelming? Right! Describing competitors is not for the faint-hearted. When the task seems too great, remember that competitors are trying to attract, retain, and grow the same customers as you. If they are successful, they will survive and grow, and your firm will not. And you will be out of a job. The best way to appreciate this framework is to use it. We suggest you answer the Marketing Question, p. 128.

PULLING IT ALL TOGETHER

Sometimes the firm gains competitive insight directly from the data it collects. Other times, it must integrate several data items. The firm can secure data on the competitor's advertising, distribution, price, product, service, and other factors — but does not *see* what was behind these actions. The firm must make inferences from these data. Table 5.3 illustrates making inferences from *indicator* data.

TABLE 5.3

DRAWING INFERENCES FROM COMPETITOR DATA[29]

me501

Indicators	Inferences
Hired new customer service manager	Competitor going to upgrade service quality
Reorganized customer support and service (CSS)	Initial confirmation of alerting signal
CSS now reports to VP of marketing (versus sales)	Signals increased importance of service
Initiating new training programs for sales force	Enhancing service for all key customer segments
Emphasizes customer service in advertising	Service valuable to attract, retain, and grow customers
CEO comments: "Customers expect quality in services as well as in the product."	Service is becoming part of the competitor's mind-set — will be institutionalized
Customer to our salesperson: "ABC is now doing things for us they never did before."	Confirms competitor is institutionalizing and leveraging service

Finally, competitors *do not make* decisions: People working for competitors make decisions. The firm should identify competitors' decision-makers and influencers. The Jackson example (p. 124) shows that career backgrounds, successes, and failures provide good competitor insight. (More on competitive analysis frameworks in Marketing Enrichment me501.)

EVALUATING COMPETITORS

The reason for *evaluating* competitors is to generate their strategic options. Knowing these options allows the firm to *project* competitors' actions. Identifying competitors (step 1) and describing competitors (step 2) are fine, but these are just the building blocks of competitive insight. The firm can only justify competitive intelligence efforts if they provide insight into competitors' future actions. **Competitor assessment analysis** and **game theory** help answer three competitive evaluation questions[30]:

- What options does the competitor have to be successful?
- What would the competitor have to do to pursue each option?
- Is the competitor capable? (Does it have the resources to implement a particular option?)

COMPETITOR ASSESSMENT ANALYSIS

This powerful tool focuses on an individual competitor or group of similar competitors in a market or market segment and maps customer perspectives into required resources. The firm and competitors satisfy customer needs by delivering benefits and values. But they must possess resources to deliver these benefits and values. The competitor assessment analysis (CAA) allows the firm to identify where it has a *differential advantage* and where competitors have *differential advantages*. Recall from Chapter 1: *A differential advantage is a net benefit or cluster of benefits, offered to a sizable group of customers, which they value and are willing to pay for but cannot get, or believe they cannot get, elsewhere.* Identifying differential advantage has five stages. Table 5.4 illustrates CAA for one competitor in a market segment.

Customer Requirements: Needs, Benefits, Values A	Customer Importance Rank B	Necessary Capabilities / Resources C				
		Efficient Manufacturing	Good Distribution	Just-in-Time Delivery	Well-Funded R&D	Access to Low-Cost Materials
Easy product availability	1	* YN	* YYY			
Low prices	2	* YN				* YYN
Low inventories	3			* N		
Access to cutting-edge technology	4				* YYN	
Etc.						

TABLE 5.4

ILLUSTRATION OF COMPETITOR ASSESSMENT ANALYSIS

KEY IDEA

➤ Critical elements for gaining competitive insight are:
- Identify
- Describe
- **Evaluate**
- Project
- Manage

- **Stage 1 – Identify customer requirements in terms of needs, benefits, and values.** Brainstorm or use marketing research.
- **Stage 2 – Rank in order of importance.** Reduce the Stage 1 items to a manageable number, typically six to ten. Rank items in order of importance to customers — columns A and B.
- **Stage 3 – Determine necessary capabilities and resources.** Any firm would require these capabilities and resources to satisfy customer requirements in column A. Needs/benefits or values map directly into capabilities or resources. To satisfy the most important item, *easy product availability*, requires *efficient manufacturing* and *good distribution*. To offer *low prices* requires *efficient manufacturing* and *access to low-cost materials*. Enter capabilities and resources in row C.
- **Stage 4 – Identify the matches.** Place an asterisk (*) in each matrix cell where a customer need/benefit or value — column A, intersects with a firm capability or resource — row C. Typically, the result is a sparse matrix; for any particular customer need/benefit or value, some capabilities and resources are irrelevant. For customer requirement *easy product availability* — *just-in-time delivery*, *well-funded R&D*, and *access to low-cost materials* are

Marketing Question

Huawei is a major Chinese technology firm that frequently competes with Cisco. Write a short memorandum identifying the type and level of threat that Huawei poses for Cisco.

KEY IDEA

➤ Competitor assessment analysis (CAA) is a powerful tool for marketers. CAA maps customer requirements — needs/benefits or values — directly into necessary supplier capabilities or resources.

not decisive. Of course, sometimes a capability or resource addresses more than one customer need/benefit or value.

- **Stage 5 – Examine the matches.** Ask up to three questions of each asterisked matrix cell. Asking a subsequent question depends on the answer to a previous question:
  a. **Relevance.** Does the firm have the capabilities or resources necessary to address the customer need/benefit or value? If yes, enter **Y**; if no, enter **N**, and stop.
  b. **Superiority.** For each cell where you entered **Y**: Are the firm's capabilities or resources superior to the competitor? If yes, enter **Y**; if no, enter **N**, and stop.
  c. **Sustainability.** For each cell where you entered **YY**: Would it be difficult for the competitor to match the firm's capabilities or resources? If yes, enter **Y**; if no, enter **N**.

The meaning of the entries is:

- **YYY.** The firm has a sustainable *differential advantage*. The firm's capabilities or resources match customer needs/benefits or values; they are superior to the competitor; it would be difficult for the competitor to catch up.
- **YYN.** The firm's capabilities or resources match the customer needs/benefits or values; the firm has an advantage, but the competitor could match the firm relatively easily.
- **YN.** The firm's capabilities or resources match the customer needs/benefits or values, but are no better than the competitor.
- **N.** The firm has a significant weakness or gap. The competitor completing a similar analysis would likely show a **YYY** and have its own differential advantage.

Returning to Table 5.4, we explore competitor options by examining several cells:

- **YYY** – *easy product availability/good distribution system.* The firm has a differential advantage in the customers' most important requirement. If the competitor is serious about this market segment, it would expend significant resources to improve its distribution.
- **YYN** – *low prices/access to low-cost materials; access to cutting-edge technology/well-funded R&D.* The firm leads the competitor in the customer's second and fourth most important areas. The competitor may invest in procurement and/or increase R&D.
- **YN** – *easy product availability/efficient manufacturing; low prices/efficient manufacturing system.* The firm and competitor perform equally well in the customer's most and second most important areas. The competitor may work on improving manufacturing efficiency.
- **N** – *low inventories/just-in-time delivery systems.* The competitor dominates. It will probably focus customer communications on *low inventories* to make sure it stays ahead.

Now that the firm views the market segment from its competitor's perspective, it can project those options the competitor will pursue. It should repeat the analysis for another competitor.

GAME THEORY

KEY IDEA

➤ Game theory is a structured way of identifying options and evaluating consequences.

Game theory is a structured way of identifying options and evaluating consequences. Game theory helps marketers think through the impact of firm actions on competitors — and vice versa. Game theory helps assess consequences for the firm and competitor of pursuing each option.[31] In Figure 5.7, both the firm and competitor must make a pricing decision.

Columbia and Wharton (disguised names) are major players in a steel-pipe market segment. Each competitor sends a quarterly price list to customers on the last day of the preceding quarter — December 31 for quarter I, March 31 for quarter II, and so forth. These prices are effective for the quarter. In previous quarters, prices have been either $6 or $7 per yard. Sometimes Columbia is higher, sometimes Wharton is higher. Based on historical purchasing patterns, Columbia predicts sales volumes for itself and Wharton, for each of the four possible price configurations. Columbia uses its own costs and competitive data about Wharton's costs to predict each firm's profits.[32]

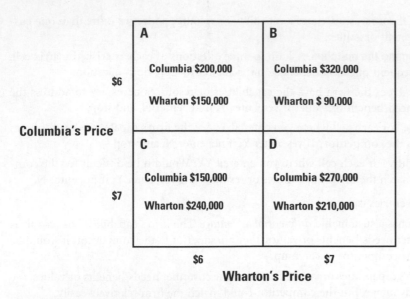

FIGURE 5.7

A GAME THEORY
APPROACH TO
EVALUATING
COMPETITORS:
PROJECTED PROFITS
FROM COMBINATIONS
OF PRICING ACTIONS

In cells D and A, Columbia and Wharton each set the same price:

- **Columbia $7, Wharton $7 – Cell D.** Profits are: Columbia $270,000, Wharton $210,000.
- **Columbia $6, Wharton $6 – Cell A.** Profits are: Columbia $200,000, Wharton $150,000.

In cells C and B, Columbia and Wharton each set different prices:

- **Columbia $7, Wharton $6 – Cell C.** Profits are: Columbia $150,000, Wharton $240,000.
- **Columbia $6, Wharton $7 – Cell B.** Profits are: Columbia $320,000, Wharton $90,000.

We draw several conclusions:

- When the firms set identical prices, Columbia is more profitable than Wharton.
- When the firms set identical prices, $7 prices earn greater profits than $6 prices.
- When the firms set different prices, the firm with the $6 price fares better.
- Columbia makes its greatest profit with a $6 price, but only if Wharton's price is $7.
- Wharton makes its greatest profit with a $6 price, but only if Columbia's price is $7.
- Columbia makes least profits when its price is $7 and Wharton's is $6.
- Wharton makes least profits when its price is $7 and Columbia's is $6.

The pricing decision is not trivial. Columbia should base its price on the best prediction of Wharton's price. Wharton should base its price on the best prediction of Columbia's price. One firm may try to signal an intended price of $7, but that could lead to price-fixing allegations.

PROJECTING COMPETITORS' ACTIONS

J&J's Tylenol was the leading over-the-counter analgesic. Bayer planned to launch Aleve as an indirect competitor, but J&J did not know when Bayer would receive final FDA approval. The Tylenol brand team monitored raw material shipments to Bayer's Aleve plant in Puerto Rico. J&J predicted Aleve's launch to within one week. Shortly before launch, J&J flooded the market with *two-for-one* coupons and took other competitive actions.[33]

The evaluation step generates a set of options for the competitor; the firm must assess which option the competitor will choose. Will it continue its current strategy? Or make a strategic

Marketing Exercise

Abu Dhabi, Dubai, and Qatar are investing substantially in new airports. Flagship carriers, respectively, Etihad Airways, Emirates, and Qatar Airways, are each growing at double-digit rates. As an airline industry analyst, identify three likely scenarios and implications for Lufthansa.

change — short term, medium term, or long term? What specific change(s) will the competitor make? To start: what is the competitor trying to achieve? Specific questions include:

- What are the competitor's objectives in the market? Understanding objectives can help predict resource allocations.
- What market segments will the competitor address? How will it try to achieve its objectives — price leadership, operational excellence, product leadership, distribution strength, or what? What customer behavior is the competitor seeking to address?
- What is the competitor's staying power? Is it committed for the long run, or will it withdraw if the going gets tough? Of course, sometimes withdrawal is not in the firm's best interest, as a competitor's divested unit may become a stronger and more difficult competitor.

Scenarios are a particularly effective way of evaluating competitor options; they help the firm understand and predict competitor action.[34] The scenario for a plausible option is a descriptive narrative of how the future may evolve; the firm should develop a scenario for each option. Based on various conditions and assumptions, the firm can compare and contrast the scenarios to gain insight into the competitor's possible actions. The firm projects competitor behavior by selecting the most probable action from the alternative scenarios. Three major scenario types are:

- **Emergent scenarios.** Start with the current strategy and consider what might emerge.
- **Unconstrained scenarios.** Based on open-ended *what-if* questions that suggest possible end states.
- **Constrained scenarios.** *What-if* scenarios that ask how the competitor may act under different market and/or industry conditions.

Effective scenarios have several important attributes:

- **Articulated plot and logic.** The *story* comprises a set of events and a coherent logic.
- **Internally consistent logic.** The *story* hangs together.
- **Specific time frame.** The *story* specifies a time element for key events, actions, and results.
- **Decision/action-oriented.** The firm can derive and demonstrate implications for its current and future decisions.

As the firm builds scenarios, it must incorporate:

- **An end state.** An outcome at some specific future point.
- **A plot.** What the competitor must do to get to the end state.
- **Driving forces.** The circumstances, conditions, events, and trends that shape or drive the story described in a particular plot.
- **Logics.** The evidence and rationale for the end state and plot.

This description of scenarios and their attributes is fairly abstract, so we show an illustration. Our fictional firm is a yogurt manufacturer — Sunshine. Sunshine's major competitor — Moonglow — is contemplating a low-price market entry. We start by elaborating Moonglow's *projected strategy alternative* — low-price entry. This option, together with *supporting logics for Moonglow* and *supporting logics for Moonglow's environment*, allow us to *identify consequences for Moonglow*. These *consequences* lead directly to *implications for Sunshine*.

MOONGLOW'S PROJECTED STRATEGY ALTERNATIVE. Key elements in the strategy are:

- Add a low-price product line aimed at customers for generic products.
- Use a different brand name.
- Maintain a high service level and use the same superior national distribution.
- Price similarly to low-end competitors and position against rivals' low-end products.
- Gain financial breakeven in one year and 10 percent low-end market share in three years.

⚷ KEY IDEA

➤ Critical elements for gaining competitive insight are:

- Identify
- Describe
- Evaluate
- **Project**
- Manage

⚷ KEY IDEA

➤ A good approach to projecting future competitor actions is to develop a set of robust scenarios that examine the competitor's strategic options.

SUPPORTING LOGICS FOR MOONGLOW.

- Moonglow must extend its product line to gain scope economies and pre-empt competition.
- Moonglow can acquire product supply from well-established vendors.
- Moonglow has demonstrated a capacity for building the required alliances.
- The entry fits Moonglow's apparent core assumptions that distinct market segments exist.
- The entry would leverage Moonglow's extensive marketing and sales capabilities.
- Moonglow's organizational culture — to be *the best in the industry* — supports the entry.

SUPPORTING LOGICS FOR MOONGLOW'S ENVIRONMENT.

- Growth rates in Moonglow's current segments do not support its announced revenue targets.
- Low-end segments have higher growth rates.
- The channels are demanding broad product coverage from suppliers.
- Successful competitors at the low end may be contemplating adding higher-end products.
- New vendors are specializing in providing products to branded competitors.
- The projected strategy could succeed if Moonglow can quickly establish a brand name, with a superior image, at a comparatively low price and with strong channel support.

CONSEQUENCES FOR MOONGLOW. Moonglow will have to:

- Determine product content.
- Secure vendors.
- Create marketing programs.
- Develop products.
- Establish its own manufacturing.
- Build trade relationships for the new product line.
- Organize its sales force.
- Moonglow could gain significant early market penetration.
- Moonglow will face significant issues on how best to differentiate its product line, build brand name image, and leverage distribution channels.
- Moonglow will need to monitor each execution step.

IMPLICATIONS FOR SUNSHINE. Moonglow's new market entry:

- Would pose a direct threat to Sunshine's current market strategy.
- Would radically change current market assumptions.
- May eliminate potential sources of supply.
- May jeopardize potential alliance partners.
- Similar products would address the same customers through the same channels.
- Sunshine's existing capabilities may be insufficient to sustain sales growth.
- Sunshine will need to introduce new options.
- Sunshine may need to introduce a new product line more quickly than planned.

Note how this scenario fulfills the conditions we outlined. The scenario has an *articulated plot and logic*, an *internally consistent logic*, a *specific time frame*, and is *decision/action-oriented*. Of course, this is just one possible scenario that Sunshine might develop for Moonglow. To predict what Moonglow will actually do, Sunshine must develop a scenario for each of Moonglow's plausible options. Sunshine then selects, from the various scenarios, what it believes is Moonglow's most likely course of action.

KEY IDEA

➤ The firm projects future competitor actions by identifying the most likely scenario from a set of alternative scenarios.

MANAGING COMPETITORS

Multinational electronics firm Colorado's (disguised name) corporate objective was to be the dominant producer in each product/market it entered. Colorado developed a four-part strategy to accomplish its objective: aggressive pricing to follow planned cost reductions, continued efforts to improve products and reduce costs, use experience with one product to improve performance in other products, and keep capacity growing ahead of demand. Colorado published its objectives and strategy in a shareholders' letter. The message to potential competitors was very clear: Enter our markets if you want. But the game will be tough. And we shall set the rules!

KEY IDEA

➤ Critical elements for gaining competitive insight are:
- Identify
- Describe
- Evaluate
- Project
- **Manage**

Identifying competitor options and projecting competitor strategies put the firm in good position. But shaping (or managing) competitor actions is even better! Before trying to get competitors to behave in beneficial ways, the firm must answer two questions:

- What actions does the firm want its competitor(s) to take?
- What actions does the firm prefer that its competitor(s) not take?

Ecolab and Diversey (disguised names) were leading suppliers of cleaning chemicals to U.S. hospitals, office buildings, restaurants, and schools. Ecolab *encouraged* Diversey to focus on smaller independent customers by raising prices modestly; Diversey *took the bait* and its gross margins improved. By contrast, Ecolab targeted large chain customers and won business with aggressive pricing. But Ecolab had thrown Diversey a *curveball*; higher gross margins did not offset increased costs-to-serve and Diversey lost money. By focusing on large customers, Ecolab reduced its costs-to-serve and profits improved.[35]

KEY IDEA

➤ The firm may be able to *manage* competitors by sending signals.

➤ The major signals available to the firm are:
- Pre-emptive
- Tit-for-tat
- Warning

➤ The firm may also send competitors misleading information.

SIGNALING[36]

Sometimes firms send **signals** to competitors, hoping they will process the information and act accordingly. The firm should ensure its signals are clear, believable, and have time to take effect. The firm should also ensure the signals do not violate antitrust laws.[37]

PRE-EMPTIVE SIGNALS. The firm sends *pre-emptive* signals so that competitors will make decisions favorable to the firm. In mature industries, market share often approximates production-capacity share. Hence, to hold market share, the firm tries to maintain capacity share by discouraging competitors from adding capacity and announcing its own capacity additions. In mid-2006, Daryl Ostrander, AMD's vice president of manufacturing, said, "We are fully positioned to service one-third of the market by 2008. We will manage, as we always do, these capacity additions. We aren't going to build too much, we aren't going to build too little."[38] The Colorado example above is an excellent illustration of pre-emptive signaling.

Sometimes, the firm must decide whether, and how, to *respond* to competitors. Many competitor moves do not require direct action, but the responding firm must make several decisions:

- Where should it respond? In the same market or in a different market?
- How fast should it respond — immediately or wait to assess market reaction?[39]
- How large should the response be? Match or outdo the competitor?

This chapter forms a solid foundation for these decisions. Two types of response signal are:

TIT-FOR-TAT SIGNALS. The firm designs tit-for-tat signals to bring competitors into line and stop them from making unilateral gains. The firm encourages the competitor to behave by matching (but not overreacting to) competitor actions. Sagebrush shows a *tit-for-tat* signal:

Sagebrush (disguised name) was the U.S. market-share leader. A new Japanese entrant sharply undercut Sagebrush prices. Sagebrush did not respond directly. Sagebrush's U.S. managers instructed its Japanese subsidiary to drastically cut prices in Japan immediately. The Japanese firm raised U.S. prices! The U.S. firm followed by raising prices in Japan.

WARNING SIGNALS. Warning signals tell competitors that if their actions reach certain thresholds, the firm will take serious steps. The firm makes sure that competitors can predict its responses. A senior executive from a toothpaste market leader stated, "We believe there is a place in the market for natural toothpaste. But if market share reached 3 percent, that could be a real problem! We would necessarily have to protect our market position!"[40] The warning: "Don't increase your market share over 3 percent."

MISINFORMATION

Misinformation is designed to mislead competitors. Relating to the capacity discussion above, capacity-increase announcements are relatively common in the chemical and other industries, but often new capacity is never added! Misinformation may buy time for a developing strategy, but overuse can cause credibility problems. Square D shows misinformation in practice[41]:

> Electrical component supplier Square D discovered that customers would pay price premiums for faster delivery. Square D sought distributors to implement a new system for order-taking, product design, and assembly; but it needed time to make the change. Square D leaked a fictitious story to an industry trade journal: Square D planned to shrink delivery time for circuit boards and other customized components from 10–12 weeks to one week. Square D would maintain large inventories and have employees work overtime. Square D's competitors knew the industry demanded customization and skilled labor and believed these actions were stupid. But the report convinced them that Square D was headed in the wrong direction, and Square D gained the head start it needed.

The Company

The starting point for developing good firm insight has three components: *intended* strategy — what the firm planned to do; *revealed* strategy — what the firm actually did; and *results* — what the firm achieved. (Chapter 22 discusses monitor-and-control procedures.) Understanding the firm's ability to implement planned actions (*revealed* versus *planned*), and the results of its actions provides excellent insight into firm competencies. The firm can secure additional insight by using two approaches previously discussed for gaining competitor insight — *company description* and *company assessment analysis.*

COMPANY DESCRIPTION

The four building blocks are *the firm's organization, strengths and vulnerabilities, firm in the environment*, and *mind-set* — just as previously used for describing competitors, pp. 128–129. These elements help show how the firm settled on its *current strategy* and achieved its *current performance.* To apply this framework, simply substitute *the firm* wherever *competitor* appears.

COMPANY ASSESSMENT ANALYSIS

Competitor assessment analysis (CAA) (pp. 130–131) identifies where the firm *possesses* a differential advantage, and where it might place resources to *secure* future differential advantage. We reproduce the analytic findings but now interpret them from the firm's perspective. Table 5.4 is the starting point:

- **YYY** — *easy product availability/good distribution system.* The firm has a differential advantage in the customers' most important requirement. The firm should maintain its position by making deliberate investments to continually enhance its distribution system.
- **YYN** — *low prices/access to low-cost materials; access to cutting-edge technology/well-funded R&D.* The firm leads the competitor in the customer's second and fourth most important

areas. It should keep a close eye on the competitor and make the necessary investments to maintain its leadership position.

- **YN** — *easy product availability/efficient manufacturing; low prices/efficient manufacturing system*. The firm has a significant vulnerability in the customer's second most and most important areas. The firm and its competitor perform equally well, but effective investment would put the competitor ahead. The firm cannot afford this to happen.
- **N** — *low inventories/just-in-time delivery systems*. The competitor dominates. It will probably focus customer communications on *low inventories* to make sure it stays ahead. The firm may find it difficult to achieve parity, but this is the customers' third most important area!

Company description and company assessment analysis give the firm invaluable insight into its own position versus competitors. For *company description*, the firm must gather a significant amount of data. For *company assessment analysis*, it simply reinterprets the CAA from the firm's perspective.

Complementers

We find the most obvious examples of complementary products in economics texts: bread and butter, coffee and cream. More modern examples are laboratory equipment and chemicals; printers and toners; and hardware and software (computers and video games).

> Microsoft and Intel — aka *Wintel* — have an exceptionally strong complementary relationship. PC sales depend jointly on Intel's advances in chip design and Microsoft's improved software. Each firm commits large employee teams to optimize their complementary strategies. Intel's share of PC processors is over 80 percent; Microsoft's share of PC operating software is 95 percent.

A **complementer** is any organization whose actions affect the firm's sales[42]; of course, we exclude purchasers. Both independent organizations and competitors can be complementers. The firm may also act as its own complementer — Chapter 12.

INDEPENDENT ORGANIZATIONS AS COMPLEMENTERS

When independent organizations develop mutually beneficial strategies, they frustrate competitors and help each other generate sales. IBM has a complementer relationship with software firm SAP. IBM and SAP cross-license and develop software to integrate each other's products; SAP also trains IBM service engineers on SAP products. SAP generates 25 percent of sales from its IBM relationship; SAP helps IBM sell several million dollars' worth of hardware annually.

Microsoft, Nintendo, and Sony successfully persuaded complementers to develop games for their consols. Likewise, Apple's iPhone has well over 125,000 complementary applications and accessories produced by thousands of developers; but the iPhone (and iPad) put tremendous pressure on its primary wireless complementer — AT&T's data network. In home laundry, design changes in washers and driers have major implications for detergent manufacturers; fabric designs have important implications for both appliance and detergent manufacturers. P&G and major appliance manufacturers work together to address new customer needs and align innovations across various industry sectors. Complementary relationships often drive major industry changes — rising oil prices have major implications for automobiles; indeed, electric utilities may switch to electric car fleets to spur market development.

CUSTOMERS AS COMPLEMENTERS. Customers act as complementers when they enhance the firm's offer. Comfort (disguised name) specializes in fraud detection systems based on statistical models. Customers supply data to Comfort's data consortium. Comfort uses these data to

KEY IDEA

➤ Independent organizations, including customers and suppliers, can be complementers for the firm.

improve its detection systems. Similarly, Google's advantage over Bing in search relates in part to its greater market share which provides more data to test hypotheses, leading to increased advertising effectiveness.

SUPPLIERS AS COMPLEMENTERS. Suppliers often complement firm actions to increase sales. Car makers expect suppliers to conduct R&D to improve automobile performance. McDonald's expects suppliers to contribute ideas and concepts to help grow McDonald's business — to be a *McPartner*, a supplier must do more than just deliver products!

COMPETITORS AS COMPLEMENTERS

As a general rule, competitors are the firm's nemesis. They try to attract, retain, and grow the same customers as the firm. But competitors can also act as complementers without getting into antitrust problems. We distinguish among strong, weak, and unwelcome complementarity.

STRONG COMPLEMENTARITY: MARKETPLACE (FRONT OFFICE). Sometimes competitors work together to better satisfy customer needs, like agreeing on technological standards. Verizon and other telephone firms agreed on standards for ultra-fast fiber optic lines that reduced costs, sped introduction, and helped each firm compete with cable companies. Without this type of cooperation, customers are often uncertain about which technology will succeed; they withhold purchases and the market develops more slowly.

A firm with new technology making a direct market entry essentially has two choices — go it alone or offer its technology to competitors. If the firm acts alone, it must shoulder the entire market development effort. When it decides on **cooperation**, the market develops faster, but the firm must accept a diminished position. This decision involves difficult trade-offs.

Apple chose to *go it alone* with Macintosh technology. Many observers believe this decision led to Apple's small market share in PCs; virtually all other firms settled on the DOS format championed by IBM and Microsoft. By contrast, Intel gave competitors AMD and Cyrix access to its MMX technology for graphics and video chips. For many years, Citibank successfully operated a proprietary ATM system, but when national and international networks like Cirrus, Maestro, and Star grew, Citibank eventually joined. At different times, Sony has used *go-it-alone* and *marketplace-cooperation*:

> Sony was first to enter consumer videotape with Betamax. Sony failed, in part because JVC provided its VHS format to competitors. JVC's licensees helped expand acceptance and Sony ultimately withdrew. By contrast, all major electronic firms adopted the DVD-replacing Blu-ray format championed by Sony.[43]

STRONG COMPLEMENTARITY: BACK OFFICE. Competitors may *compete* fiercely in the market, but their back offices *collaborate* extensively. **Back-office cooperation** in non-customer-facing activities reduces costs and improves efficiency for all firms. Examples include:

- General Mills, Columbo yogurt, and Land O'Lakes butter share delivery trucks.[44]
- Italian tile manufacturers jointly purchase freight to reduce international shipping costs.
- Major airlines collaborate in interline arrangements to move luggage among airlines.[45]
- Retail brokerage houses work closely with competitors to clear trades.
- U.S. paper makers routinely swap products at list price to save freight costs.

WEAK COMPLEMENTARITY. Marketplace and back-office complementarity generally require formal agreements. Other types of complementarity are weaker but may contribute positively:

- **Cost reduction.** When several competitors have common suppliers, one competitor's actions may affect the others. Dell and HP compete in PCs, but if either firm's sales expand total volume, joint purchases of computer chips increase. Chip suppliers achieve scale economies that reduce costs — ultimately, chip prices decline for all PC producers.

KEY IDEA

➤ Competitors can complement the firm in the marketplace (front office) or back office.

➤ Competitors may be *strong* or *weak* complementers.

Marketing Question

What organizations are complementers for NBC (U.S. television network)?

- **Greater customer value.** A firm's product may provide greater customer benefit when combined with a rival's product. Complementary drug regimens — *drug cocktails*, comprising products from different firms — are an increasing trend; they dominate AIDS treatment. BMS initially introduced blood-thinning product Plavix as a competitor to aspirin; today BMS positions Plavix and aspirin as complementers.

- **Increasing demand.** Competitors engage in joint advertising and other promotions so all firms benefit. Many shopping malls draw consumers from large distances; all stores gain.[46]

- **Keeping the firm sharp.** Tough competition keeps a firm on its toes. Some firms deliberately seek out tough competitors. One German engineering firm always launches new products in Japan.[47]

- **Market development.** Competitor market development actions may assist the firm. Apple's iPhone opened up the smart phone market; the BlackBerry (Research in Motion) was a major beneficiary. Monsanto's success with genetically modified seeds has helped competitor DuPont.

- **Political action.** Competitors join trade associations to lobby governments for favorable decisions.

UNWELCOME COMPLEMENTARITY. Sometimes firms do not want their products associated with other firms — unwelcome complementers. Automobile and aircraft manufacturers fight fiercely against unauthorized parts manufacturers; they believe these parts degrade their products. Callaway Golf is very successful with oversized Big Bertha golf clubs. Spalding advertised that its Top-Flite/Club System C balls improved play with Big Bertha clubs. Callaway sued Spalding for trademark infringement, false advertising, and unfair competition; the case was settled out of court. Callaway later launched a line of Callaway Rule 35 premium golf balls!

KEY IDEA

➤ A firm's complementary product activities may be unwelcome by competitors.

Marketing Question

What other messages did you glean from this chapter?

KEY MESSAGES

- The firm must gain deep competitor insight in pursuit of differential advantage.

- A structured competitor insight process asks several questions:
  - **Identify.** Who are the firm's competitors:
    - Current competitors — today?
    - Potential competitors — tomorrow?
    - Direct competitors?
    - Indirect competitors?
  - **Describe.** What are the competitors' capabilities and difficulties?
  - **Evaluate.** What are the competitors' strategic options?
  - **Project.** What do we expect the competitors to do?
  - **Manage.** How can we get the competitors to do what we want them to do?

- Answering these questions is not a simple matter but, for each question, several approaches help improve competitor insight.

- The firm must know itself —company insight — but this is a simpler task.

- The firm must understand its complementary relationships. Complementers can help the firm achieve its objectives.

- Both independent organizations and competitors can be complementers, each in different ways.

VIDEOS AND AUDIOS

Competitor Insight   a501 🎧

a501

QUESTIONS FOR STUDY AND DISCUSSION

Can you answer the questions implied by this chapter's learning objectives? Check!

1. Evidence suggests that large companies sometimes dismiss competitive threats. Do you believe this is true? Why or why not? How could you ensure that a successful large company retains a competitive outlook?

2. Many observers believe that competition between Microsoft and Google will increase. Microsoft has a large lead in operating systems, office suites, and browsers; Google leads in search. Identify one or two colleagues to act as Google's top managers; identify one or two colleagues to act as Microsoft's top managers. First, the Google team develops a market strategy for Google; the Microsoft team develops a market strategy for Microsoft. The two teams exchange strategies. Second, the Google team develops a market strategy to counteract Microsoft's strategy, and vice versa. How did you define the field of competition? What did you learn from this competitive-gaming exercise? (Feel free to substitute Facebook for Microsoft.)

3. In the hair-coloring market, L'Oreal competes with Clairol; in the men's shaving market, Gillette competes with Schick. Suppose you work for Clairol — use the competitor assessment analysis to evaluate L'Oreal and identify its strategic options. Or suppose you work for Gillette — use the competitor assessment analysis to evaluate Schick and identify its strategic options.

4. Southwest Airlines (SWA) carries more domestic passengers than any U.S. airline. Early in its history, SWA faced a difficult competitive situation with Braniff Airlines — a large domestic and international carrier. SWA operated three routes — Dallas–Houston, Houston–San Antonio, and Dallas–San Antonio. Overall, SWA was unprofitable. To increase volume on the Houston–San Antonio and Dallas–San Antonio routes, SWA reduced prices from $26 to $13 for a one-way trip. Braniff offered a sale on the Dallas–Houston route at $13. Dallas–Houston was the only profitable route for SWA. How would you have advised SWA?

5. Slovak Inc. (disguised name) hired Peter Fry for a summer internship. Peter arrived at Slovak's Budapest headquarters in late June. The CEO directed Peter to visit competitors in different European countries. Peter was to pose as a student seeking data for a term paper — Slovak would pay Peter's travel and accommodation. Peter was relying on income from Slovak to pay his MBA tuition. It was too late to secure another summer job. What would you have done in Peter's place? Why?

6. Explain the impact of oil prices on product design decisions for car manufacturers. Compare and contrast GM and Toyota.

7. Printers and ink account for over 50 percent of HP's profits, but less than 25 percent of HP's $127 billion revenues (2011). Fast-growing retailers like Cartridge World sell refills at one-half HP's prices. How should HP respond? Use scenario analysis to develop options for HP.

8. How would you define 7-Up's competitive landscape?

9. Select a product in which you are interested. Alternatively, consider this book — *Managing Marketing in the 21st Century*. From the competitors you identified in Chapter 3: What are their capabilities and difficulties? What are their strategic options? What do you expect them to do?

CHAPTER 6

MARKETING
RESEARCH v601

To access O-codes, go to **www.ocodes.com**

LEARNING OBJECTIVES

When you have completed this chapter, you will be able to:

- Translate your marketing problems and issues into actionable research questions.
- Think systematically about the marketing research process.
- Become familiar with the language and terminology of marketing research.
- Interact productively with specialist marketing researchers.
- Appreciate the advantages and disadvantages of several marketing research techniques.
- Use marketing research data to obtain greater customer insight.[1]
- Identify new marketing research techniques to help secure differential advantage.
- Assess market and sales potential, and make market and sales forecasts.
- Understand the category development index (CDI) and brand development index (BDI).
- Become a sophisticated user (and client) of marketing research.
- Recognize the limitations and drawbacks of marketing research.

OPENING CASE: THOMSON FINANCIAL

Thomson Financial (TF) provides information and decision analysis tools for the financial market and has evolved steadily in recent years via organic development and acquisition.[2] TF continually redefines offerings to keep pace with evolving market needs. TF focuses on helping organizations inform and build front-end customer strategy (FECS) by developing unique ways to gather, interpret, and disseminate customer insight. TF has a large customer base and many competitors; insight gleaned from customer experiences play a key role in differentiation and strategy development.

Warren Breakstone, TF COO for global sales, marketing, and services, realized the importance of measuring overall customer experience at all service touch-points — sales, account management, training, and help-desk support. Breakstone launched an annual global benchmarking satisfaction study, together with intermittent check-ups *on clients that recently used training or help-desk services. Breakstone said, "The most important result was a deeper understanding of customer satisfaction drivers; that helped priority-setting and framed resource allocation decisions. We began to understand the complex interplay between product satisfaction and customer services."*

Breakstone said customers might be very satisfied with a particular aspect of help-desk support. But that might not be a strong driver of customer satisfaction or increase likelihood of referrals (an important loyalty measure). Teasing out key customer-satisfaction drivers allowed TF to focus on actions generating the greatest impact. Breakstone said, "As the result of our studies, we have more discipline in resource allocation — dollars, personnel, and management focus." One high-end customer subgroup greatly valued TF's financial-modeling consulting service. TF doubled its modeling investment, and consulting services became more successful.

For Breakstone, gaining customer insight is more than executing quantitative benchmarking studies. "The key is to incorporate an understanding of how the data impact ongoing decisions. Customer satisfaction measures have allowed us to challenge assumptions and make more fact-based decisions. We introduce more data into our discussions of what we should do differently going forward. We are dedicated to linking customer research to day-to-day decisions. Many firms do not have this discipline; research reports lie dormant and they never explore their customer insights. The amount of unused or poorly used marketing research is astounding."

Kim Collins, SVP of marketing for TF's Corporate Services, builds client insight via structured monthly pulse *surveys measuring customer satisfaction with TF training and support functions. Collins said, "I believe that true* insight *is gleaned from comprehensive, detailed, and continual measurement of customer experiences with products and services at every touch-point with customers. Insight is the intelligence we gather when we stop to listen to clients. Only then do we begin to understand the impact, positive or negative, we're having on customer workflow."*

Collins' online surveys are briefer than annual benchmarking studies — only five to ten questions — but they deliver important data for trend analysis. They also alert Corporate Services to potential problems with customer experiences. TF's rapid response mitigates dissatisfaction, but also reminds customers that TF is listening to their concerns and cares about their experiences. By involving cross-functional teams in the pulse initiative, customer insight infiltrates important functional areas.

Collins said, "When product developers understand first-hand the frustrations or work-arounds that customers encounter with TF's products, they prioritize development efforts to address the key issues affecting customer satisfaction. When marketers understand how diverse customers use the same product for different purposes, they can more closely target key messages and product benefits."

CASE QUESTION

What insight about marketing research can you draw from Thomson Financial's experience?

Gaining customer insight is crucial for Thomson Financial. TF gains short-term and long-term insight, then applies this insight into its decision-making processes.

THOMSON™

I think one of the big dangers in today's marketing is that you get these big volumes of stuff, data, which mean nothing. In fact, I hate marketing research, but I love actionable customer insight. You have to work a bit harder. You have to apply your brain to really think through what questions you want to ask people. I think the issue is really thinking through what action you're going to take as a result of your study, rather than just producing a 150-page report that isn't actionable. What's important is research to take action, rather than research just to prove a point. We're not into that.

—David Haines, Director of Global Branding, Vodafone[3]

Marketing research is any process of data collection, analysis, and interpretation the firm adopts to improve the quality of its marketing efforts. The firm may conduct marketing research on actual and potential customers, but also on customer influencers like legislators and regulators. Sometimes marketing research focuses on behavior. Other times the concern is with mental states like awareness, perceptions, attitudes, and intentions — at any and all stages in the customer experience. Marketing research also subsumes activities like gathering competitive intelligence — Chapter 5, and measuring marketing effectiveness. The related term *market research* has a narrower focus — specifically gathering data about current and potential markets.

Chapter 6 is not designed to make you a marketing research expert. There are many fine books and courses to guide you toward that goal. But we do believe that astute marketers must become *intelligent customers* of marketing research. You need to know where marketing research can be helpful and where it cannot. You must learn what sorts of questions to ask your marketing research suppliers and how to interpret their answers. This chapter also addresses specific and very important topics for marketers: assessing market and sales potential and making sound marketing and sales forecasts.

THE CHANGING VIEW

OLD WAY	NEW WAY
Basic analysis (tabs, X-tabs, regression)	Sophisticated analysis (complex methods, choice models)
Customer market focus only	Research on multiple constituencies
Data scarce	Data plentiful
Descriptive orientation	Causal orientation
Direct elicitation techniques	Projective techniques
Focus groups and one-on-one interviews	Eclectic methodologies
Identify trends	Build trends into market strategy
Loose measurement technology	Careful measurement technology
Market research is unfamiliar to much of the public	Market research is familiar to much of the public but many people are unhappy with intrusive phone calls
Observational methods rare	Observational methods often employed
One major market research approach used	Combination of multiple research methodologies
Pencil and paper surveys	Web panels and online surveys
Quantitative results	Actionable results
Sometimes cavalier attitude to confidentiality	Much stricter observance of privacy rights
Strive to increase sample sizes	Strive to improve management of large databases
Typically instrumental	Purely investigative more common

THE MARKETING RESEARCH PROCESS

Bristol-Myers Squibb's (BMS) marketing research mission is "to ensure the superior use of information and analysis to objectively identify opportunities, frame and validate strategic options, monitor results, provide insight, and build cumulative knowledge." BMS believes that superior customer understanding provides critical insight for integrating into its decision-making processes. By championing industry-leading techniques, BMS' understanding and anticipation of market evolution provides critical insight into strategic issues. Insight from marketing research allow BMS to create leading programs, earn superior marketing and financial results, and develop and retain top business leaders. These lofty goals provide a window into the importance of timely and effective marketing research in developing the firm's future.

The purpose of marketing research is simply to help the firm make better marketing decisions. The marketing research process should follow a basic problem-solving approach. After all, without problems marketing research would be unnecessary. A critical element of success rests on the relationship between the manager and the researcher. Marketing research is a support function helping the firm to make decisions, but never forget: The manager is ultimately responsible for the decision and its outcomes. We know many cases where the manager, in effect, tossed the problem *over the wall* to marketing research with little guidance or direction, and then expected an answer. This is an especial problem when the firm outsources marketing research to one of many marketing research suppliers. Failure to define the research problem is an abdication of managerial responsibility, often leading to dissatisfaction and frustration for all involved. Absence of a clear problem statement does not lead to actionable marketing research.

Sometimes the marketing research department conducts studies for marketing managers. Other times, the marketing research departments helps frame individual studies, but specialist research suppliers provide data and/or conduct analyses. Indeed, marketing research is a major industry with many players; Nielsen (the largest) has annual revenues exceeding $4 billion.

Responsibility for marketing research often extends beyond the marketing research department, single manager, or business unit. At B2B firms, various individuals with customer relationships may meet periodically to discuss customer needs. Medical equipment firm Hill-Rom (HM) has various hospital contacts — senior administrators, purchasing, maintenance, nurses, and ward orderlies. Pooled insight led HM to redesign its beds to reduce nurse injuries, save time on non-nursing tasks, and cut hospital costs. When the firm has a few major customers, strategic (key) account managers orchestrate the search for insight — Chapter 17.

B2C firms have similar processes. A senior executive shared Target's approach: "We identify trends with a dedicated trend group that travels the world to find new trends in everything from apparel to home décor to food, and we use a tool called the trend curve to segment the life cycle of trends. This helps us determine when it will be hot, so we can get it into our stores at the right time for our guests. But we also involve the rest of the company. When anyone is traveling abroad, the expectation is that they will carve out time to go and understand what is happening in Antwerp, Berlin, London, Prague, Tokyo, or wherever they are. We want to know what's emerging? What is the cool restaurant? What are the teenagers wearing? What are the young artists showing? We have an excellent trend department, but we also have people in every area of the company who have carved out the niche of being trend czars, because everyone has that role to play. We expect everyone to cultivate an eye."[4]

To ensure that marketing research is tightly aligned with marketing decision-making, the marketing research process must follow a consistent methodology. Key elements are in Figure 6.1.

KEY IDEA

➤ The purpose of marketing research is to help the firm make better marketing decisions.

KEY IDEA

➤ The marketing research process comprises several sequential steps:
- Define the business issue
- Identify a researchable problem
- Formulate objectives and hypotheses
- Conduct a preliminary investigation
- Develop the research plan
- Collect and analyze data
- Prepare the report

Marketing Question

Suppose you were General Motors' Marketing VP. For what top 5 marketing research questions would you like answers?

DEFINE THE BUSINESS ISSUE

As a manager, you have primary responsibility for defining the business issue. Of course, marketing researchers (internal department or outsourced supplier) may encourage you to think more deeply about your concerns. Sometimes the *presenting* (or immediate) problem may actually be a symptom. You may believe that poor sales performance is due to lazy salespeople, but marketing research may suggest other potential causes like untrained first-line sales managers or unsatisfactory products. A Total Quality Management (TQM) methodology, illustrated in Table 6.1, asks five "Whys?" as it seeks the root cause of an issue. Of course, you may already have sufficient data to solve the problem. If not, you should state the issue as clearly, completely, and simply as possible, then call in the marketing researchers.

FIGURE 6.1

THE MARKETING RESEARCH PROCESS

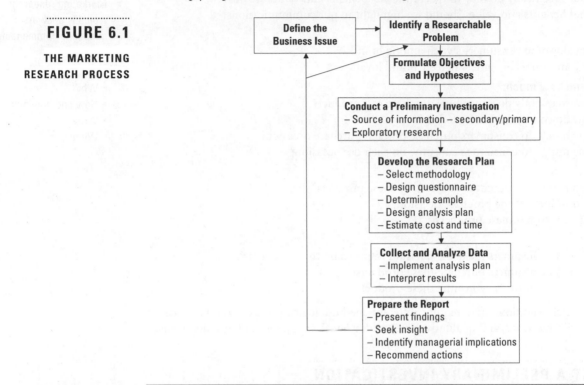

TABLE 6.1

AN ILLUSTRATION OF DEFINING THE BUSINESS ISSUE

Round	Apparent Business Issue (Symptom)	Question (Cause)
1	Our sales performance isn't up to par.	Why?
2	Salespeople aren't putting in enough effort.	Why?
3	It's hard to persuade customers to buy our products.	Why?
4	Our products don't really satisfy customer needs.	Why?
5	Our product design process is deficient on customer insight.	Why?

IDENTIFY A RESEARCHABLE PROBLEM

Marketing research may be unable to solve all your problems, but a good marketing researcher will help you frame the issues and problems so that research can be useful. (Sometimes managers expect too much, and exploratory research is necessary to frame the problem; a consultant's outside perspective may also be useful.) Good marketing research can highlight the facts, point you in the right direction, and help you reduce uncertainty. But there is always a time cost of completing marketing research — forgone revenues and/or competitor action. You should always weigh the value of reducing uncertainty against these costs, and collaborate with your researchers to define a researchable problem.

FORMULATE OBJECTIVES AND HYPOTHESES

Together with marketing researchers, you should agree upon research objectives and the hypotheses you will test. (You may revise the hypotheses after exploratory research.) Objectives and hypotheses are usually related, but hypotheses are always more specific. Suppose your objective is to identify a market opportunity for a new product. Specific hypotheses may relate to positioning alternatives, price points, and brand name. You should be very clear about what insight you are looking for. Examples are:

- **What:**
  - What do consumers think about our product versus competitor products?
  - What specifically do they think are the key benefits and values we offer?
  - What benefits and values should we highlight in our communications?

- **Why:**
  - Why do some consumers switch among brands?
  - Why are some consumers fiercely brand loyal?

- **How and how much:**
  - How frequently do consumers purchase our product?
  - How do consumers prefer to buy?
  - How much do consumers purchase on each purchase occasion?
  - How much do consumers consume on each use occasion?

- **Who:**
  - Who makes the purchase decision for these products?
  - Who influences the purchase decision?
  - Who consumes these products?

- **When:**
  - When do consumers make the decision to purchase these products?
  - When do consumers purchase these products?
  - When do consumers consume these products?

Different research questions may require different methodologies like exploratory or causal research for *why* questions, and qualitative research for *how, what, when*, and *who* questions.

> **KEY IDEA**
>
> ➤ Marketing research typically answers questions commencing with:
>
> - What
> - Why
> - How and how much
> - Who
> - When

CONDUCT A PRELIMINARY INVESTIGATION

Before conducting *primary* research directly with respondents, you should always evaluate *secondary* data. Secondary data or existing sources may be inside the firm, but are often outside. (We discuss distinctions between primary and secondary data, and qualitative and quantitative data, later in the chapter.) Secondary data may provide partial, or even complete, answers to your research questions more quickly and less expensively than primary data. In other cases, you may commence primary research by talking to colleagues — someone may have previously addressed a problem like yours in a former job or company. You may also conduct an exploratory *qualitative* study to secure preliminary insight. By these means, you may be able to narrow the scope of your enquiry and identify gaps between the data you need to meet your research objectives and the data you already have. Typically, this information gap is the basis for larger-scale and more *quantitative* research, where costs really mount. Skipping the preliminary stage can lead to heavy expenditures without commensurate insight.

DEVELOP THE RESEARCH PLAN

As your research blueprint, the more detailed research plan should include data-collection methodologies, including data collection instruments like questionnaires. The research plan should also contain a sampling plan identifying who will provide data. You must specify:

- The target group or universe for your study;
- The sample size for securing statistically significant results;
- The sampling method — how to chose your respondents.

Typically, you want to project study results to your universe; hence, you must ensure that the sample you select is random and unbiased. You have two options: Each universe member has an equal chance of being selected; or you divide the universe into mutually exclusive groups before random selection.[5] You should avoid non-randomly selected (biased) samples like *convenience samples* or allowing respondents to self-select. You must also rule out *non-response bias* — when responders are different from non-responders. The researcher's job is to make sure you get the right data from the right people at the right time.

You should also specify the analytic methods you anticipate using. This can be intellectually challenging, but you should never collect data and then scratch your head wondering how to analyze. Your research plan should also include time and cost estimates, both for management approval and negotiating contracts with outside suppliers. Experienced firms apply a similar discipline to internal research projects and suppliers.

Marketing Question

Your firm collects confidential consumer data via face-to-face interviews. You suspect one of your interviewers is lazy and is faking the data, yet he denies your accusations. How would you proceed?

COLLECT AND ANALYZE DATA

With a research plan in place, you are now ready to begin your research. There are many ways to collect data, so make sure you use the *right* method, not just one that's easy.[6] If you plan to collect survey data, make sure your subjects are representative of the target population. We reinforce the fact that you must not select respondents because they are easily available; and you must pay careful attention to response rates and implement procedures for dealing with non-responders. You should always be concerned with data integrity and make sure that data collectors act honestly. No matter how carefully you plan your analysis, additional follow-up analyses may seem appropriate. But these add time and expense, and you will need to weigh their anticipated value versus the scope of your research plan.

Dishonesty in Marketing Research

Early this century, Coca-Cola rigged a market test in several Burger King outlets. A Coke employee supposedly manipulated the popularity of Frozen Coke (FC) (a slushy drink), by hiring a consultant to buy value meals including FC for children. Coke paid $540,000 to a former auditor who claimed wrongful dismissal for exposing the scheme, and $21 million to Burger King.

The marketing manager and marketing researcher should collaborate in interpreting the results. Marketing researchers should serve as experts on questionnaire design, sampling methods, analytic techniques, and interpreting statistically significant results. But marketing managers are responsible for restricting researcher interpretations to these issues; after all, marketing researchers may lack insight into the problem context. Managers have ultimate decision-making responsibility and should not encourage researchers to make recommendations beyond their expertise. Correspondingly, the prudent researcher should always deflect such pressure.

PREPARE THE REPORT

As a marketing manager, you will often review marketing research reports that others prepare. They present findings, but your goal and responsibility is always to seek insight. Figure 6.2 illustrates distinctions among *data and information, knowledge,* and *insight.* Many firms are rich in data and information, but lack knowledge and may have little insight. Take seriously David Haines' comments, p. 143.

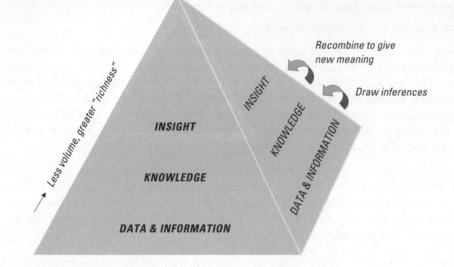

Reproduced by permission of the Impact Planning Group

FIGURE 6.2

DATA, KNOWLEDGE, AND INSIGHT

Accurate inferences drawn from raw data or processed information constitute knowledge. Many firms devote considerable effort to codifying knowledge and making it widely available (often with varying access); some firms even appoint *knowledge czars* (chief knowledge officers). Insight is different from knowledge. You develop insight by combining different knowledge elements, or using knowledge to create new meaning. Fred Smith's (FedEx) insight was that freight forwarders using passenger airlines could not provide reliable overnight package delivery. Other key insights that led to innovation and significant success include: Steve Jobs and Steve Wozniak — Apple and the PC industry; Jeff Bezos — Amazon; Howard Schultz — Starbucks; Sergey Brin and Larry Page — Google; Reed Hastings — Netflix; Mark Zuckerberg — Facebook; Jack Dorsey, Biz Stone, and Evan Williams — Twitter; and Andrew Mason — Groupon.

Make the assumptions in your research report transparent so they can be challenged and defended, clearly present the findings, and develop managerial implications. You may propose further research to clarify incompletely answered questions, but marketing research can only reduce uncertainty, never eliminate it entirely. A good report proposes alternative courses of action and makes specific recommendations; after all, the goal of any research project should be some change in practice. Changes may range from minor course corrections to major innovations. If the report recommends no change, at best you validated a current direction; at worst, you asked the wrong questions! Beware of research that is mere ritual or managers who ignore results, perhaps because they offend a comfortable status quo.

CRITICAL DISTINCTIONS IN MARKETING RESEARCH

As a marketing manager, you will be responsible for directing marketing researchers and the marketing research process. Here we make some critical distinctions that can help you devise marketing research plans.

PRIMARY AND SECONDARY RESEARCH

The researcher should assess available secondary data, then fill information *gaps* with primary data.

Marketing Exercise

It's the first day at your new job and your boss calls you into her office. "I want you to design a marketing research study to determine the reasons for customer loyalty." Prepare a response for your boss.

KEY IDEA

➤ *Secondary* marketing research uses data relevant to your research that some person or organization has already collected for another purpose.

➤ *Primary* marketing research requires that you collect new data.

Marketing Question

Suppose you require data on sales of a product class or product form. What secondary sources will provide these data?

KEY IDEA

➤ Key types of secondary data are:

• Company data
• Public data
• Technical analysis

SECONDARY RESEARCH. Some person or organization has already collected secondary data for another purpose. Three basic types of secondary data are:

- **Company data.** Comprises routinely generated data from transactions with customers and suppliers; information from internal databases on costs, production, and capacity; customer lists; salesperson call reports; delivery, maintenance, and servicing reports; customer purchases (what, when, how much, prices paid), complaints, information requests, payment history, service calls, and previously completed marketing research reports. Company data also includes data collected by the firm's customers, like bar code scanner data and RFID tracking data.

- **Public data.** Includes information about competitors, customers, and suppliers; industry trends; and technologies. Sources include competitors' annual reports; competitor and public domain websites; general business and industry-specific media and books; government and trade associations; government and published academic research; Internet sites (like dnb.com, Dialog.com, LexisNexis.com); legal and government filings; supplier white papers; trade show literature; and presentations. Public data also include semi-public data like syndicated research reports from firms like Nielsen and IRI, and reports from industry and financial analysts. Locating data is often a challenge, but subscription databases and Internet search engines have eased this task.

- **Technical analysis.** Includes objective, repeatable descriptions of products and services or production capacity collected by internal engineers or developers. Examples include benchmarking product design and reverse engineering competitor products to estimate manufacturing costs and supply-chain processes.

PRIMARY RESEARCH. Typically, **primary research** is more expensive than secondary research. The firm usually collects primary data for a specific purpose, often to close gaps between data required to make decisions and secondary research data. Primary data sources depend on the research problem but may include previous, current, and/or potential customers, especially people in various purchase and consumption roles; industry experts and trade association personnel; and channel members like agents, brokers, distributors, retailers, and wholesalers.

All primary research requires a stimulus, frequently a question the researcher wants answered. Sometimes the firm provides specific stimuli like advertising or positioning concepts, attribute lists or product profiles, advertising or sales messages, or competitive materials/products.

QUALITATIVE AND QUANTITATIVE RESEARCH

"We used to position Lean Cuisine as 'calorie control,' competing with Healthy Choice and Weight Watchers, then as 'great taste but low fat/low sodium.' Then we gained a key insight from qualitative marketing research with customers — one-on-ones and focus groups. Our new positioning is, 'it's easy to do something good for yourself because it tastes so good.' Now Lean Cuisine competes with all the junk in people's refrigerators, and we have double-digit growth."[7]

Two major approaches to marketing research are **qualitative** and **quantitative**.

KEY IDEA

➤ *Qualitative* research is not concerned with numbers.

➤ *Quantitative* research focuses on quantitative analysis.

QUALITATIVE RESEARCH. Qualitative research (QualR) is typically not concerned with numbers. QualR is generally flexible and versatile, but is rarely conclusive and does not project to a larger population. Firms often conduct QualR to pursue interesting questions, uncover customer needs, identify buyer behavior, gain a better understanding of business issues and the *language* people use, develop ideas, and help define and prioritize marketing research problems. QualR can help assess how customers *feel* about products and suppliers. Small-scale exploratory primary QualR often precedes large-scale quantitative data collection.

A particular issue in QualR is the difference between self-reported responses and data on actual behavior. Both can be valuable, but the researcher should always be skeptical about self-reports.

Just because a respondent says "I did X" or "I will do X" does not mean the respondent actually did, or will do, X. Respondents may purposely mislead researchers, but mismatches between self-reports and actual behavior are often due to poor memory, bias, and unclear questions. Researchers should seek convergence; the Kimberly-Clark example is instructive:

> Focus groups provided Kimberly-Clark (KC) with little insight into why Huggies baby wipes were losing sales. KC introduced a new observational technique, a camera mounted on a pair of glasses that consumers wore at home. In focus groups, mothers talked about changing babies on a diaper table. From the cameras, researchers saw that mothers changed babies on many surfaces, often in awkward positions, and struggled with containers requiring two hands. KC redesigned packages for wipes, shampoo, and lotions so mothers could easily dispense them with one hand.

QUANTITATIVE RESEARCH. Quantitative research (QuanR) uses numerical data and mathematical analyses, often from large representative samples. Marketing researchers use QuanR to test hypotheses formulated earlier in the research process. Some analyses are quite simple; others are highly complex. The researcher should ask three types of question about QuanR:

- **Internal validity.** Do these data measure what I want to be measuring?
- **Reliability.** If I repeat data collection, will I get the same results?
- **External validity.** Will the results I secure generalize to other populations?

Sometimes drawing the line between qualitative and quantitative research is difficult, as some types of qualitative data are amenable to quantitative analysis. Researchers are always pursuing new forms of quantitative analysis, but qualitative data gathering is also evolving. Firms striving for increased customer insight are driving these innovations.

Figure 6.3 shows how primary and secondary research can be either qualitative or quantitative. Generally, quantitative approaches to primary research data yield more insight than qualitative approaches. But with secondary research, the firm can often gain significant insight from the large amounts of qualitative data that are often available.

KEY IDEA

➤ Critical concerns in quantitative research are:

- Internal validity
- Reliability
- External validity

	Primary	Secondary
Qualitative	Small-group discussions with customers about product alternatives	Review of advertising campaigns from various product suppliers
Quantitative	Large-scale sample survey of customers about product alternatives; test hypotheses by quantitative methods	Secure independent research reports on customers' views of product alternatives; conduct quantitative analyses

FIGURE 6.3

ILLUSTRATION OF RESEARCH TYPES

SECURING QUALITATIVE RESEARCH DATA

The simplest form of QualR is informal — a marketing executive talks to a few customers, scans competitor advertisements, buys competitive products and/or calls competitors' employees and service centers, or visits distributors to see how they display products. Nine West (shoes) founder Vince Camuto said: "Listen to the consumer. I'm out every week in the stores, talking to women and the salespeople. What do people want? Where is their lifestyle going? Trends don't come from designers. They come from the consumers."[8] And while chatting to a call-center phone operator, J. Crew's CEO Mickey Drexler learned that women were placing multiple orders for a popular beach dress in different sizes. Within a few weeks, J. Crew was successfully offering bridesmaid's dresses. The firm may also invest in more formal qualitative data-gathering approaches for securing insight.

FOCUS GROUPS

Single-location **focus groups** are one of the most popular qualitative data-collection methods. Typically, focus groups comprise eight to 12 members (often paid for participation and selected for their interest, knowledge, and/or experience) moderated by a skilled facilitator. The facilitator asks carefully scripted probing questions, maintains good participant interaction, and tries to ensure comparable contribution per member. Focus groups have the advantage that one member's ideas can spark responses in another. Potential problems include strong individuals dominating the discussion, less than honest responses, psychologically defensive behavior, yea-saying (unreflective agreement), and a conservative bias in favor of the known versus the unknown. The requirement of a central location can also limit participation and skew results if the firm takes insufficient care with member selection. Managers and researchers often receive immediate feedback by watching focus group discussions through one-way glass. Typically, researchers record and transcribe focus group discussions. Effective focus groups require significant skill; indeed, Whirlpool gained differential advantage by developing a specific competency in running focus groups for trade partners. Brainstorming — Chapter 14, is a variant of traditional focus groups. Telephone and videoconference focus groups are newer alternatives. They reduce problems of dominating participants and travel costs, but limit the degree of participant interaction.

ONE-ON-ONE INTERVIEWS (OOOs)

One-on-one interviews (OOOs) combine direct and indirect questions asked of individuals to probe needs and underlying purchase motivations. Mostly, researchers conduct OOOs in person — in the respondent's home or office, in a public place like a shopping mall, or on the telephone. OOOs avoid the various biases sometimes found in focus groups and can address more sensitive topics. OOOs can also dig more deeply into issues by asking several "why" questions, but are generally more expensive and time-consuming. OOOs cannot build on ideas from others, but dialog can be more open and skilled interviewers secure significant insight.

A market researcher for Zachys (Z) (disguised name) fast-food restaurant discovered that Z sold 40 percent of daily milk shakes in the early morning; purchasers were mostly alone and bought nothing else. When she interviewed purchasers individually, most told her they bought milk shakes to make long boring commutes more palatable and stave off hunger until noon. Z took several actions: made thicker shakes (last longer); added tiny fruit chunks (unpredictability to offset monotony); put in counter-top dispensers; and introduced prepaid swipe cards (save time).[9]

INTERNET: BLOGS, FORUMS, SOCIAL NETWORKS, TWITTER, WIKIS, YOUTUBE

As this section demonstrates, securing customer data frequently requires significant firm effort and expense. The advent of the Internet has substantially changed the data dynamic and data acquisition is no longer such a significant impediment to securing insight. Using *cookies*, firms gain direct insight into customer *travel* patterns on the Internet. In this new world of *big data*, researchers are developing new methods to analyze the substantial quantities of customer data that are becoming available.

One specific feature of the online world is that customers are increasingly willing to post complimentary and/or critical comments about products, brands, and firms. By offering its own forum, the firm can receive valuable customer feedback. Del Monte maintains a 400-person "I Love My Dog" online network that responds to new product ideas. The firm must also be vigilant about other Internet postings; many bloggers develop significant followings and become very influential. Data-mining services capture consumer ratings on independent sites, and count and analyze web conversations for specific phrases about products, brands, and firms; hence, they quantify essentially qualitative data. Firms learn about performance perceptions, where to improve, and ideas for new product features and services. Dell's 40-person team engages with communities on Facebook, Twitter, and other social media to capture responses to products and services. Of course, because Internet posters are often anonymous, marketing researchers must carefully weigh the validity of these types of qualitative data.

PROJECTIVE TECHNIQUES

Researchers use projective techniques (aka motivation research) mainly to uncover latent customer needs. Developed by psychologists, projective techniques have a long history in marketing:

- **Constructing a collage.** The respondent collects pictures from newspapers and magazines that express his feeling about the topic:

> Researchers asked diabetes sufferers to make a collage expressing how they felt about diabetes. One respondent's collage showed images of doctor with patient, pills, fast-food logo and several cheeseburgers, and glasses of thick liquid. She explained, "It represents the foods I can't have anymore because they got me into trouble, trips to the doctor, testing, pills, and new foods I must learn to like." Key insights: The patient focused on inconvenience and medication more than its consequences; she blamed the disease on poor eating habits.[10]

- **Imagery.** The respondent draws a picture showing her interacting with the product, then interprets the picture.[11]
- **Role-playing.** Respondents pretend they are a brand's friend and write it a letter, or they explain why a neighbor/work colleague may like/dislike a particular product. Role-playing and storytelling (below) avoid arousing the respondent's subconscious defenses.
- **Sentence completion.** The respondent completes an incomplete sentence.
- **Storytelling.** The respondent receives a picture/description of a situation relevant to the topic. The respondent makes up a story about one or more characters in the stimulus.[12]
- **Word associations.** The researcher supplies a stimulus word. The respondent offers the first word that comes to mind. Applications include image studies and branding research.

OBSERVATION

> "You can see a lot just by looking." — Yogi Berra[13]

The firm gains insight just by observing. Broadly speaking, observational research falls into two categories — planned and unplanned:

PLANNED OBSERVATION. The firm does not ask questions, but secures insight by watching (sometimes using one-way mirrors) and recording behavior (often by video) in naturalistic settings. The researcher assesses subjects' behavior, including emotional responses, body language, and person-to-person interactions. General Mills observed children playing in school yards and developed Yoplait Go-Gurt — yogurt in a squeezable tube for kids on the go. Many FMCG firms use observational techniques in supermarkets to gain insight into consumer shopping behavior. P&G observes consumers in specially designed innovation laboratories like its Baby Discovery Center, typical middle-class homes, and grocery and drug stores. Observation is a reliable technique provided the researcher uses correct methods. Although difficult to code, observational data are objective, accurate, and unbiased by researcher intervention[14]:

KEY IDEA

➤ Approaches to securing qualitative data are:

- Focus groups
- One-on-one interviews
- Internet
- Projective techniques
- Observation
- Ethnographic research

Ralph Lauren observed mothers and daughters leaving a Lauren store in Connecticut — mothers with shopping bags, daughters without. Lauren developed *Rugby* to address the 14-to-29 demographic. Ritz-Carlton's *Mystique* system catalogs and shares employees' observations about guests among its 60 hotels. When a guest checks in to a Ritz-Carlton hotel, employees act on these observations to provide extra service.

Observational data may be more accurate than other types.[15] When PepsiCo surveyed owners/managers at 7,000 restaurants serving Pepsi, respondents said price was the critical decision variable in choosing between Coke and Pepsi. An observational study of 800 restaurant *switchers* (Coke to/from Pepsi) showed four highly correlated service variables: poor delivery, unreliable equipment, emergency shipments, and poor equipment maintenance.[16]

UNPLANNED OBSERVATION. Individuals may gain significant insight about markets, customers, and/or competitors without planning to do so. Simple observation may trigger an idea with tremendous pay off:

- On an Italian coffee-buying trip, Howard Schultz saw Italians at expresso bars, reading newspapers and meeting friends. He believed the U.S. was ready for coffee houses — Starbucks.

- On a Mumbai street corner, Ratan Tata saw scores of motor scooters precariously carrying entire families. Tata now offers a safer inexpensive alternative — the $2,500 Tata Nano.

- Former Virginia governor Gerald Baliles said: "When I was in China, I was struck by how often I encountered chicken feet in the soups, foods, and markets. When I got back, my people called the poultry industry to find out what they do with chicken feet. They were chopped off on the assembly lines and discarded. Today Virginia ships 40 tons a month of chicken feet to the Far East."

- Research in Motion (RIM) founders, Mike Lazaridis and Doug Fregin, watched Canadian students embrace e-mail; they believed written communication would shift to devices like phones — the BlackBerry.

ETHNOGRAPHIC RESEARCH

Derived from anthropology, **ethnographic research** is an observational method where researchers spend *a day in the life of (DILO)* their customers,[17] corresponding to the anthropologist *living with the tribe*. Observers gain insight into their subjects' culture and belief systems, uncover needs, and understand how customers integrate products into their daily lives. Intel's cultural anthropologists examine the interface of technology and humanity; Tom Katzen, responsible for marketing Levi's jeans to teenagers, spent Saturday mornings in ticket lines at San Francisco's Fillmore Auditorium, observing the way teenagers customized their blue jeans.[18] Many firms employ *cool hunters* to observe people's behavior and clothing in natural settings like inner-city basketball courts and fashionable nightclubs; and to hang out on social networking sites like Facebook. Relatedly, defense contractor employees embed with U.S. military forces in Afghanistan to identify unmet needs.

Before Toyota designed the Lexus LS 400 specifically for the U.S., the chief engineer and his team lived for several months in Southern California's upscale Laguna Hills. They visited many upscale metropolitan areas around the U.S. — Coral Gables, Miami; north Lake Shore Drive, Chicago; and Westchester County, New York. They learned how luxury car owners drive, treat their cars, and deal with valet parking. They learned the role cars played in these people's lives and product and service expectations. The Lexus has been an unqualified success.

Marketing Question

Go to your local supermarket and observe consumer behavior in the cereal aisle. What can you learn? What hypotheses can you develop that you could test by quantitative methods?

In the *Living It* program, P&G employees live with consumers for several days, following them shopping, running errands, and talking with peers. After one study, New Tide advertising differed sharply from the traditional cleaning power message — women could focus on their lives, because Tide was taking care of the laundry. In *Working It*, employees work behind the counters of small shops to gain insight about consumer purchasing behavior.[19]

SECURING QUANTITATIVE RESEARCH DATA

Alternative ways of securing data for quantitative analysis are:

SURVEYS

Sample **surveys** of the target population are the most common way to secure primary data for quantitative analysis. Selecting a sample reflecting the underlying population is critical. So is assessing the required sample size for estimating parameter(s) of interest at the desired accuracy level. Detailed discussion of both topics is beyond the scope of this chapter, but as a rule, there are critical trade-offs between cost, flexibility, and time.[20] Typically firms sponsor their own research but sometimes they can reduce costs by joining a marketing research firm's omnibus survey (serving multiple clients). Table 6.2 identifies advantages and disadvantages of alternative ways to collect survey data.

Technique	Advantages and Disadvantages
Face-to-face personal interviews (home, office, mall intercepts)	Advantages: High completion rates; high level of control; researcher knows who was present at the interview; missing data minimized; researcher can show exhibits and samples and probe more deeply with follow-up and branching questions. Disadvantages: Most expensive; time-consuming; difficult to supervise; interviewers can bias results; interviewers may cheat — fill in questionnaires without interviews.
Telephone interviewing	Advantages: Fairly quick completion; better response rates than mail surveys, significantly less costly than face-to-face interviews; less interviewer bias; likely better for sensitive questions; ability to clarify and follow up; easier supervision of interviewers; useful for existing customer relationships. Disadvantages: Refusal rates generally higher than personal interviews (U.S. households with *no call* restrictions are increasing); increasing population without landlines; limited to short interviews; cannot use complex questions; cannot show exhibits or samples; lack of control over the respondent's environment. Despite disadvantages, telephone interviewing will continue to be useful for existing consumer relationships and in B2B settings. (Some researchers collect simple survey data by text messaging [especially about TV programs]).
Mail surveys (paper and pencil, disk/CD)	Advantages: Inexpensive; no interviewer bias; okay for simple branching questions. Disadvantages: Response rates generally low; responses are delayed (follow-ups often needed); others may influence the respondent; the respondent can look forward and back on the questionnaire to inflate consistency; questionnaire must be short; cannot use probes or complex branching questions; missing data and confused responses frequently pose analytic problems.
Internet surveys	Advantages: Fast and easy to implement; can show exhibits; lower cost due to no printing or postage (or interviewers); software programming reduces incomplete answers; data fed directly into analysis programs and reviewed almost in real time. Disadvantages: May not be appropriate for some products and topics; possible non-representative samples because of limited computer use; low respondent patience for anything but very short questionnaires; limited attention to the task[21]; low response rates from questionnaires viewed as spam or lying dormant in an e-mail inbox. (Using a website survey tool can mitigate these problems.)

TABLE 6.2

TECHNIQUES FOR COLLECTING SURVEY DATA

Questionnaire design is critical to survey success and should involve both the marketing researcher and marketing manager. Development can be relatively unstructured and qualitative, but producing the final questionnaire requires much thought. The questionnaire should avoid biases from yea-saying and question order. Questions should not be vague, ambiguous, complex, difficult to answer, easily misinterpreted, or contain jargon. In good questionnaire design, some questions require closed-ended responses (all possible answers specified)[22]; other responses should be open-ended (respondents answer in their own words). The simplest types of question are dichotomous (e.g., yes/no) and multiple choice (select one or more from several options). Table 6.3 identifies several standard, yet more complex, approaches to asking questions. The firm should always pretest the questionnaire.

> When conducting survey research, Xerox always asks: 1. Does the question tie into the survey objectives? 2. Will data from the question be actionable? If either response is No, Xerox deletes the question.

TABLE 6.3

SELECTED STANDARD APPROACHES TO ASKING QUESTIONS

Approach	Example	Comments
Rank ordering	Put "1" for the brand you would most likely buy; "2" for the next most likely brand, etc., until you have ordered all brands: Dell, HP, Lenovo, Macintosh, VAIO	Rotate brand order. Secures ordinal measures (below).
Constant sum	Allocate 100 points among these benefits so that the more important benefits get the most points.	Secures ratio measures (below).[23]
Paired comparison	Circle the brand in each pair that you would most likely buy: Dell or HP Dell or Macintosh Lenovo or VAIO	Comparisons limited by respondent fatigue.[24] Secures interval measures (below).
Likert-type scales	Agree or disagree: Dell computers are easy to maintain: | 1 Strongly agree	2 Agree	3 Neutral	4 Disagree	5 Strongly disagree
---	---	---	---	---		Be careful of positivity bias. Use positively/negatively worded items. Use multiple items for reliability.
Semantic differential scales	Rate (focal object) on these scales by circling the number that best reflects your opinion. Dumb 1 2 3 4 5 6 7 8 9 10 Smart Weak 1 2 3 4 5 6 7 8 9 10 Strong Bad 1 2 3 4 5 6 7 8 9 10 Good Soft 1 2 3 4 5 6 7 8 9 10 Hard Easy 1 2 3 4 5 6 7 8 9 10 Difficult Fast 1 2 3 4 5 6 7 8 9 10 Slow	Use 7–12 sets of bipolar adjectives. Factor analyze to secure the underlying meaning.

KEY IDEA

➤ When designing a process to collect survey data, the firm must make several important trade-offs among, primarily:

- Cost
- Time
- Flexibility

PANELS

For many marketing research projects, securing survey data from different respondent samples is fine. But sometimes the firm wants to follow up on individual responses. In a **tracking (longitudinal) study**, the firm forms a panel of individuals who agree to provide responses periodically. Maintaining a panel is challenging, but judicious member replacement can keep a panel going almost indefinitely.[25] Panel data allows the firm to *keep its pulse* on customers, conduct more sophisticated analysis, and better identify causal relationships.[26] Because panels are expensive to maintain and administer, firms like Nielsen and IRI form and manage panels, and provide a sense of data independence; several user firms share the costs. Online marketing research firms like Greenfield Online and Harris Interactive maintain large panels from which firms can select sub-populations for specific surveys.

Panels provide data with varying degrees of intrusiveness. Panelists may commit to write down purchases, answer questionnaires, or accept a simple installation to monitor TV watching. Panelists may use supermarket value cards providing scanner data (below) on purchases. Combining self-reported panel data with actual use data may provide significant insight.

OBJECTIVE SALES DATA

The firm's sales reporting system can provide valuable quantitative data. But sales data to end-user customers may be difficult to secure when products move through distribution channels. In supermarkets, the widespread use of barcodes and retail scanners makes it easy to collect and store sales data by sku. IRI and Nielsen each secure scanner data from several thousand supermarkets in many urban markets; they aggregate and sell these data to manufacturers.[27] Collection and use of automatically collected sales data is likely to increase. By remotely monitoring vending machine sales, a firm can better schedule deliveries, adjust product mix, price dynamically, and make personalized offers for purchasing by cell phone.

Sales data organized by customer can provide significant insight. Supermarket loyalty cards allow consumer profiling for making targeted offers. Internet firms collect sales data directly by individual and, together with search data from *cookies*, develop buyer profiles for making purchase recommendations. EZ Pass systems automatically measure use of road services.

BEHAVIORAL MEASUREMENT

Increasingly, firms use technology for marketing research. *Infrared sensors*, *video cameras*, and *digital voice recorders* monitor supermarket aisle-traffic patterns; *checkout scanners* measure consumer purchases. Electronic metering systems capture radio listenership and TV viewing by channel; GPS-enabled *cell phones* identify consumer locations. Some researchers provide subjects with *digital cameras*, like Burger King — several dozen *SuperFans* recorded and photographed everything they ate for two weeks. Others use *galvanometers* to measure consumers' physiological changes to stimuli like questions, products, displays, and advertisements. *Tachistoscopes* (now mainly computer controlled) measure recognition speed by projecting images like package designs for short time-periods.

Advertising researchers often use *eye-movement* devices: A TiVo study found consumers focused attention on the center of the screen when fast-forwarding through commercials[28]; IBM and Cisco use *heatmapping* to track attention to elements of e-mail messages. Using *brain-scans*, Coke and Pepsi each activated the brain's reward system in a blind taste test — different brain regions, linked to brand preferences.[29]

> British retailer Tesco now accounts for one in eight of every pound sterling spent at retail. An important component of Tesco's success has been analysis of its massive household database of actual purchases to better understand customers, and make offers based on their preferences.

Although technological advances allow firms to secure increasing amounts of customer data, they raise serious privacy issues because of their potentially intrusive nature. Some technologies like video cameras in stores raise privacy issues but are quite legal when used on private property. Regardless, the firm should protect itself against misuse and serious PR problems by developing and implementing clear privacy policies. Privacy is an especially important issue on the Internet where both Facebook and Google have run afoul of government watchdogs.

EXPERIMENTS

Experiments allow researchers to definitively establish causal relationships like A → B. The researcher manipulates independent variables like advertising and price, and measures results (dependent variables) like awareness and sales. Superior experimental designs include a control group. Because many non-manipulated and unmeasured variables can affect results, researchers typically use random assignment for experimental and control groups. Experiments range between limited-scale laboratory studies and large field experiments.[30] The critical trade-off is typically between cost and researchers' ability to draw conclusions.

KEY IDEA

➤ Approaches to securing quantitative research data include:

- Surveys
- Panels
- Objective sales data
- Behavioral measurement
- Experiments
- Prediction markets

Marketing Question

How would you design an experiment to measure the impact of advertising spending and price on sales of your product? (Choose your own product.)

Relatively few firms conduct experiments and then mostly in the laboratory. FMCG firms often use field experiments for test marketing new products and assessing alternative promotional programs. Experiments are a serious business at Pfizer; Pfizer spends millions of dollars to test different promotional strategies and ways of allocating selling effort. Amazon continuously tests different e-mail messages.

What most firms fail to realize is that day-to-day business life can function as a **natural experiment**. Rather than manipulate independent variables, the firm can use the *natural* variability in its decisions to seek relationships with results. Costs of data storage and analysis are fast reducing and some firms evolve their actions in real time. Leading firms are becoming learning organizations by treating their entire set of marketing actions as data in natural experiments.[31]

PREDICTION MARKETS

In prediction markets, buyers and sellers trade assets whose cash value is tied to a particular event. Dating to the mid-1990s, public prediction markets have successfully predicted Oscar nominations and various economic events. Some firms like GE and Microsoft use employee prediction markets to improve decision making; Lloyds TSB assesses new product ideas. In its *TagTrade* market, Best Buy employees trade imaginary stocks for new service packages and sales forecasts. In many cases, prediction markets secure better results than experts.[32]

ANALYZING QUANTITATIVE RESEARCH DATA

MARKETING ENRICHMENT

Analyzing Quantitative Research Data me601

me601

Quantitative research data are amenable to a broad variety of statistical analyses. If the underlying assumptions are valid, quantitative methods can have significant predictive power and be very helpful to the firm in making marketing decisions. But this is a huge topic that we do not address in this chapter. Rather, we provide material on types of variables, and both simple and complex quantitative analysis techniques as Marketing Enrichment me601 .[33]

MARKET AND SALES POTENTIALS, MARKET AND SALES FORECASTS

> "It's tough to make predictions, especially about the future." — Yogi Berra[34]

Chapters 3, 4, 5, and now Chapter 6 have armed you with many approaches, concepts, ideas, and options for designing and conducting marketing research studies. You now have a solid base of knowledge for securing greater insight into markets, customers, competitors, and complementers. These insights will enable you to build more powerful market strategies and implementation plans, as you prepare to deliver customer value and secure differential advantage.

However, one item we deferred from securing market insight — Chapter 3 — is predicting market size and firm sales. These predictions are critical for many reasons — identifying attractiveness of a market opportunity, production planning, and budgeting the firm's financial, human, and other resources.

Two related concepts — *potentials* and *forecasts* — are important for understanding market demand and firm performance. Unfortunately, many managers are confused about these terms. Potentials and forecasts are quite different, but each has important quantitative aspects. *Potential* embraces having a *capability or future state*:

- **Market potential** — what market sales could become.
- **Sales potential** — what the firm's sales could become.

Marketing Question

In 1999, Airbus predicted demand for its superjumbo A380 jet aircraft at 1,440 planes and forecast that 10 U.S. airlines would buy 281. In spring 2007, with Airbus expected to deliver its first plane in October, Airbus had orders for 156 aircraft from 14 airlines, yet none were U.S.-based. How do you explain the discrepancies?

By contrast, *forecast* concerns *expectations*:

- **Forecast market size** — expected market sales in a given time period.
- **Sales forecast** — the firm's expected sales in a given time period.

We explore ways to assess potentials and forecasts, and conclude Chapter 6 by discussing *category development index (CDI)* and *brand development index (BDI)*.

ASSESSING MARKET POTENTIAL

Market potential is the *maximum market-level sales*, from all suppliers, that the firm believes could occur in a future time period. Since all markets go through life cycles, the firm wants to have some idea of market sales at various life-cycle stages. Market potential is an upper bound to actual sales, based on a set of assumptions about future market conditions. Market potential is especially important when contemplating entry in a new market.

To assess market potential, the firm should estimate the number of likely customers and the amounts they are likely to buy. These estimates are based in part on the potential aggregate marketing effort from the firm and its competitors. Of course, the identity of likely customers may change as the life cycle evolves; propensity to buy evolves also. The three steps are:

- **Identify likely market segments.** Most markets comprise several segments. The firm must understand these segments, even though some may not buy at each time period.
- **Estimate numbers of customers in each segment.** The firm estimates the number of customers likely to buy in the time period for which it seeks market potential.
- **Estimate the number of products to be purchased.** The firm estimates the number of products customers in each segment are likely to buy for the relevant time period.

Table 6.4 shows typical market potential calculations for a new consumer product — for three years, six years, and 10 years after launch. In this illustration, we assume three market segments.

Time Period	Market Segments	Total Number of Customers in Each Segment (millions) A	Percent Likely to Buy (%) B	Expected Number of Customers Likely to Buy C = A × B (millions)	Number of Units Those Purchasing are Likely to Buy D	Segment Potential Calculation E = C × D (million units)	Market Potential (million units): Sum of Es
3 years after launch	Seg. 1	10	50%	5	5	25	
	Seg. 2	6	20%	1.2	2	2.4	**27.4**
	Seg. 3	8	0%	0	0	0	
6 years after launch	Seg. 1	11	70%	7.7	6	46.2	
	Seg. 2	6	40%	2.4	4	9.6	**58.6**
	Seg. 3	7	10%	0.7	4	2.8	
10 years after launch	Seg. 1	12	70%	8.4	7	58.8	
	Seg. 2	6	50%	3.0	6	18	**93**
	Seg. 3	6	30%	1.8	9	16.2	

Several interesting points within this table are:

- The firm believes the numbers of customers in each segment will change over time. Segment 1 increases, segment 2 stays the same, and segment 3 decreases.
- The percentage of customers likely to buy also evolves. Segment 1 increases, then stays constant; segment 2 increases continuously; segment 3 is zero initially, then increases.

KEY IDEA

➤ In assessing the market, the firm should project:
- Market potential
- Market forecast

➤ In assessing firm possibilities, the firm should project:
- Sales potential
- Sales forecast

TABLE 6.4

MARKET POTENTIAL CALCULATIONS

KEY IDEA

➤ Market potential is the maximum sales the firm expects in the market in a given time period from all suppliers.

➤ Market forecast is the expected market size.

➤ Sales potential is the maximum sales the firm could achieve in a given time period.

➤ Sales forecast is the firm's expected sales.

- For each segment, the firm predicts only a fraction of customers will purchase.
- The amount purchased increases for each segment, quite dramatically for segment 3.
- For each time period, market potential is the sum of individual segment potentials.

The firm can estimate *market potential revenues* by multiplying *potential units* by the estimated price in each time period.

ASSESSING SALES POTENTIAL

Sales potential is the maximum sales the firm could achieve in a given time period. Of course, sales potential is conditioned on assumptions about market potential, the firm's likely efforts, and future market conditions like number and strength of competitors.

The firm can calculate sales potential directly from market potential by assessing potential market share. The firm's potential share depends both on the resources it could commit to the market and the actions it believes competitors will take. If the firm contemplates increasing resources over time (and/or believes that competitors will reduce commitments) estimated potential market share should also increase. Table 6.5 shows illustrative sales potential calculations based on market potential estimates from Table 6.4.

TABLE 6.5

SALES POTENTIAL CALCULATIONS[35]

Time Period	Market Potential (million units) A	Firm's Potential Market Share (%) B	Sales Potential (million units) C = A × B
3 years after launch	27.4	10%	2.74
6 years after launch	58.6	20%	11.72
10 years after launch	93	30%	27.9

FORECASTING MARKET SIZE

Market forecasts often focus on the short run, like the upcoming year, where the firm can assess market conditions with a fair degree of accuracy. To forecast market size, the firm may focus either on the overall market or on individual segments that it later aggregates. Generally, a segmented approach provides better forecasts (if data are available). Three broad approaches to assessing market size are:

JUDGMENTAL METHODS. These are the simplest methods for forecasting market size:

- **Executive judgment.** The responsible manager has deep familiarity with the product class, competitive offers, customer needs and satisfaction levels, current market size, and many environmental factors. She makes her own intuitive judgments.
- **Delphi method.** A valuable approach when several people have opinions about the market. Each person makes a market forecast and specifies the rationale. Each person then receives all forecasts and rationales, and revises their forecast. Forecasts often converge after a couple of rounds, but may require several rounds.

TIME-BASED METHODS. These methods use past sales to predict future sales directly:

- **Judgmental extrapolation.** A special case of executive judgment using history to predict the percentage change from the previous year. The basis could be the most recent year-to-year change, a simple average of the previous two (three, four, five) years' changes, or a weighted average of previous years' changes, with greater weight to more recent years.
- **Linear extrapolation.** Two-variable regression analysis me601 estimates year-by-year change in sales. Forecast sales for next year are last year sales plus an increment (or decrement) based on prior year sales. The forecaster calculates the extrapolation increment mathematically, but must decide how many prior years to use.

MARKETING EXERCISE

Form a group of five or six students. Each person in the group forecasts the Dow Jones average (or some other event) for the last day of class and provides a rationale. Team members exchange forecasts and rationales and repeat the process one or more times. On the last day of class, compare the forecast with the actual Dow Jones average.

- **Moving average.** The manager uses sales data from previous years to calculate an average; this average is the forecast. For each successive year, the manager drops the earliest sales datum and adds in the most recent datum. Hence, sales from several years ago do not weigh too heavily in the forecast. Once again, the manager must judge how many years to include.

- **Exponential smoothing (ES).** This method uses previous sales data in a slightly unusual way. Rather making the forecast based only on actual sales data from previous years, exponential smoothing uses both actual sales from last year and last year's forecast sales. ES calculates a smoothing parameter, "a," from previous sales data:

    Forecast sales$_{t+1}$ = a × actual sales$_t$ + (1 − a) × forecast sales$_t$

    The value of "a" depends on the relative weight given to the prior year's actual sales versus the prior year's forecast sales; "a" ranges from zero to one. If historic sales were fairly constant, forecast sales weigh quite heavily, and "a" is on the low side. If sales change substantially year by year, as in a growth market, "a" may be close to 1.

Table 6.6 shows how to use these methods to forecast global market size for consumer durable A. Column 2 shows actual sales; columns to the right show market size forecasts using judgmental extrapolation, linear extrapolation, moving average, and exponential smoothing. In each case, the first forecasts are for 2000. Forecasts by judgmental extrapolation are based on the actual percentage change in sales for the most recent year. For the other methods, forecasts are based on the previous five years' sales. For example, the forecasts for year 6 are based on data for years 1, 2, 3, 4, and 5; forecasts for year 9 are based on years 4, 5, 6, 7, and 8. We can make several inferences:

- Actual sales increase markedly in year 9 and subsequent years; deviations are mostly greater for later years for all forecasting methods.

- Because actual sales growth is high in later years, simple judgmental extrapolation does best. Other methods are handicapped, to a greater or lesser extent, by sales from earlier years. This finding is especially marked for the five-year moving average. (Moving-average forecasts with fewer years [not reported] do better.)

- For all years, the exponential smoothing forecast is the previous year's actual sales. Sales increased significantly and the smoothing constant, a, is equal to 1.

Year	Actual Sales	Judgmental Extrapolation Forecast Sales	Judgmental Extrapolation Deviation from Actual Sales	Linear Extrapolation Forecast Sales	Linear Extrapolation Deviation from Actual Sales	Moving Average Forecast Sales	Moving Average Deviation from Actual Sales	Exponential Smoothing Forecast Sales	Exponential Smoothing Deviation from Actual Sales
1	8,791	—	—	—	—	—	—	—	—
2	11,148	—	—	—	—	—	—	—	—
3	14,043	—	—	—	—	—	—	—	—
4	15,482	—	—	—	—	—	—	—	—
5	19,858	—	—	—	—	—	—	—	—
6	26,352	25,470	(882)	21,805	(4,547)	13,864	(12,488)	19,858	(6,494)
7	27,968	34,970	7,002	28,224	256	17,377	(10,591)	26,352	(1,616)
8	30,799	29,683	(1,116)	32,357	1,558	20,741	(10,058)	27,968	(2,831)
9	39,365	33,917	(5,448)	35,715	(3,650)	24,092	(15,273)	30,799	(8,566)
10	48,926	50,313	1,387	41,907	(7,019)	28,868	(20,058)	39,365	(9,561)
11	65,271	60,809	(4,462)	51,646	(13,625)	34,682	(30,589)	48,926	(16,345)
12	82,314	87,076	4,762	70,286	(12,028)	42,466	(39,848)	65,271	(17,043)

TABLE 6.6

PREDICTING GLOBAL MARKET SIZES FOR CONSUMER DURABLE A (000s)

KEY IDEA

➤ Two judgmental methods for forecasting are:
- Executive judgment
- Delphi method

➤ Time-based methods for forecasting are:
- Judgmental extrapolation
- Linear extrapolation
- Moving average
- Exponential smoothing

me601

CAUSAL-FACTOR METHODS. The most common causal-factor method for predicting market size is **multiple regression analysis**. The researcher selects several independent (predictor) variables that she believes could be related to market size, the dependent (criterion) variable. She uses historical data to determine the relationships, if any, between these predictor variables and market size. She then uses these relationships to predict future sales. (We discuss this process in somewhat more detail in Marketing Enrichment me601, pp. 9–10.)

MAKING THE SALES FORECAST

The sales forecast is the firm's expected sales in a future time period, often the upcoming year. The sales forecast is central to many day-by-day operating processes like financial budgeting and production planning. Of course, *actual* factors can cause *actual* firm sales to be quite different from *forecast* sales. The following dialog (from Chapter 1) reinforces the importance of sales forecasting and the difficulty many firms face in making sales forecasts; the dialog is part of a real conversation when the author gave an in-house seminar at a major U.S. computer firm. One participant asked several questions about sales forecasting, leading to the following exchange:

> *Author*: "How come you're so interested in sales forecasting?"
>
> *Participant*: "Well, I have a sales forecasting department, and since you were here, I thought I might learn something."
>
> *Author*: "That's fine, but tell me, what's your position in the firm?"
>
> *Participant*: "I'm the production director."
>
> *Author*: "Oh! That's a little unusual. I'd have thought the sales forecasting department might have been in marketing, or in sales."
>
> *Participant*: "Sure, they have one too. But we can't believe a word they say, so we have to have our own."

Many firms use three broad approaches to sales forecasting: *top-down*, *bottom-up*, and *synthetic*.

TOP-DOWN SALES FORECASTING. Top-down sales forecasts follow directly from analyses of market potential, market-size (or individual market segment) forecasts, and the firm's market share estimates — typically contained in the marketing plan. Calculations are relatively simple but the marketer must understand market subtleties and nuances:

Sales forecast = forecast market size × forecast market share

Table 6.7 illustrates a market-segment approach using market segment size and share forecasts:

TABLE 6.7

TOP-DOWN SALES FORECASTS

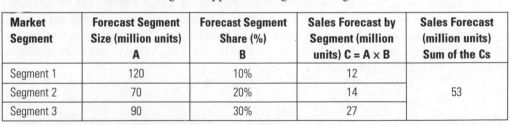

Market Segment	Forecast Segment Size (million units) A	Forecast Segment Share (%) B	Sales Forecast by Segment (million units) C = A × B	Sales Forecast (million units) Sum of the Cs
Segment 1	120	10%	12	
Segment 2	70	20%	14	53
Segment 3	90	30%	27	

KEY IDEA

➤ Many firms develop synthetic sales forecasts using a combination of *top-down* and *bottom-up* approaches.

BOTTOM-UP SALES FORECASTING. Bottom-up forecasts embrace the granularity (and reality) of sales by customer that is absent in top-down forecasts — salespeople can personally discuss customer requirements. The firm aggregates forecasts from individual salespeople to develop the bottom-up sales forecast. (In some firms, the sales forecast derives from a sales pipeline system — Chapter 17.) The downside of bottom-up forecasting is that salespeople may *lowball* estimates if the firm uses these forecasts to set sales quotas that affect take-home pay.

SYNTHETIC SALES FORECASTS. Synthetic sales forecasts combine the best features of top-down and bottom-up forecasting. The top-down forecast derives from the market planning process; the sales department independently prepares a bottom-up forecast. If these numbers are similar, the task is over. In most cases, the top-down sales forecast is higher, and sales managers and individual salespeople must re-examine their forecasts customer by customer to see where increases are possible. These reworked forecasts are the building blocks for a revised bottom-up sales forecast. Simultaneously, marketing reworks the top-down forecast. Hopefully, the revised forecasts agree. If not, senior management typically decides the forecast by executive decision, and sales managers apportions increases to individual salespeople.[36]

CATEGORY AND BRAND DEVELOPMENT INDICES

The category development index (CDI) and brand development index (BDI) are useful devices for assessing market and sales, potentials and forecasts. Each index relies on dividing the market into separate areas; CDI and BDI measure category and brand strengths in those areas. FMCG firms typically base CDIs and BDIs on geography:

- CDI — the percentage of category sales divided by the percentage of U.S. population, converted to a percentage.

- BDI — the percentage of brand sales divided by the percentage of U.S. population, converted to a percentage.

Table 6.8 illustrates CDI and BDI calculations for Brand X in Denver. The 90 percent CDI shows that the product category (class) is less developed in Denver than in the U.S. overall. By contrast, the 120 percent BDI shows that Brand X performed better than average in Denver. The firm can use market-area distributions of CDI and BDI (and over-time trends) to make market and sales, potentials and forecasts, and hence decide where to place marketing effort.

Market data	Firm data	Population data
Sales = $250 million	Sales = $50 million	U.S. = 300 million
Sales in Denver = $4.5 million	Sales in Denver = $1.2 million	Denver = 600,000
Denver percent of sales = 4.5/250 = **1.8 percent**	Denver percent of sales = 1.2/50 = **2.4 percent**	Denver population percent = 600,000/300 million = **2 percent**

Category development index (CDI) = Percent market sales/Percent population: Denver = 1.8/2 = **90 percent**

Brand development index (BDI) = Percent firm sales/Percent population: Denver = 2.4/2 = **120 percent**

TABLE 6.8

ILLUSTRATION OF CDI AND BDI CALCULATIONS

We covered a lot of ground in this chapter, but in many ways we have only scratched the surface of marketing research. We hope your key take-away is that marketing research can be very helpful in securing insight the firm requires to successfully execute the six marketing imperatives. But you should also realize that marketing research is no panacea. The manager and researcher must make many decisions before investing in a particular study. We have given you a glimpse of some of the available options.

KEY IDEA

➤ Important practical approaches for assessing market and sales potentials are:

- Category development index (CDI)
- Brand development index (BDI)

Marketing Question

What other messages did you glean from this chapter?

KEY MESSAGES

- Marketing research results should be actionable.

- Good marketing research can give the firm a differential advantage.

- Marketing researchers should provide analysis and insight; marketing managers make decisions.

- Marketing research studies should follow a rigorous process.

- Marketing researchers make critical distinctions between primary and secondary research, and qualitative and quantitative research.

- Both qualitative and quantitative research use several methodologies. Qualitative research is becoming more popular.

- The various techniques for collecting survey data have advantages and disadvantages.

- Methods of quantitative analysis range from simple to highly complex.

- Several methods are available for assessing market and sales potentials, and making market and sales forecasts.

VIDEOS AND AUDIOS

The Future of Marketing Research	v602 📹	Oded Netzer	Columbia Business School
Securing Insight	v603 📹	Spencer Pingel	Colgate-Palmolive

v602

v603

QUESTIONS FOR STUDY AND DISCUSSION

Can you answer the questions implied by this chapter's learning objectives? Check!

1. Suppose you are product manager for a pharmaceutical firm hoping to launch a new drug to treat schizophrenia. Identify the types of people from whom you would secure marketing-research data and the sorts of data you would seek.

2. As marketing director for a hotel chain, responsible for an observational technique to learn about customer needs and to provide data to individual hotels, you receive the following report from your San Francisco property. "Last night, one of our regular customers, Mr. Jackson, arrived to check in with a female companion. The desk clerk used the information system to greet the couple: 'Welcome back, Mr. and Mrs. Jackson, it's good to see you at the hotel again.' Apparently, the woman was not Mrs. Jackson, and Mr. Jackson had not told his companion he was married. The woman was furious with Mr. Jackson; Mr. Jackson was furious with us; they both stormed out of the hotel." How would this incident affect your observational program?

3. The table provides global market size data for consumer durable B. Select two forecasting methods that use past sales. Predict sales annually for years 6 though 12 using pre-year 6 data. How do the methods compare? Is one better than another? Why? How do your forecasts compare with consumer durable A predictions in Table 6.6? Are you more accurate? Why or why not?

Year	Actual Sales (000s)	Year	Actual Sales (000s)	Year	Actual Sales (000s)
1	50,003	5	98,5414	9	111,570
2	59,461	6	111,163	10	124,608
3	68,496	7	104,366	11	136,104
4	79,577	8	104,101	12	138,528

4. What secondary sources (including websites) would you use to find out how to best engage undergraduate college students for an innovative news website?

5. You are consulting for a local restaurant with strong brand recognition and loyalty that has many weekend customers; yet from Monday through Thursday, business is slow. Design a questionnaire to understand consumer behavior, lifestyle, and eating habits on weekdays. Your objective is to identify and address marketing opportunities during the week.

TRANSITION TO STRATEGIC MARKETING

➤ Insight developed from the situation analysis forms the foundation for developing planning assumptions.

➤ Planning assumptions are the critical supporting elements for developing market strategy and implementation plans.

CHAPTERS 3 THROUGH 6 FOCUS ON SECURING market, customer, competitor, company, and complementer insight. Some insight is fairly broad — like factors driving market growth or anticipated technological change; other insight is much narrower — like identifying new competitor entry or a specific competence the firm may secure. Regardless, the material in these chapters forms the basis for the *situation analysis* — the foundation for the market plan, leading to *Strategic Marketing* — Section III and *Implementing the Market Strategy* — Section IV in *Managing Marketing in the 21st Century*. An *effective* market plan provides the firm with a well-developed direction forward; an *ineffective* market plan, with a weak situation analysis, is prone to collapse at any time.

The best way to build a solid superstructure for market strategy and implementation is to transition from *insight* in the situation analysis to *assumptions* about the future. Planning assumptions help the firm anticipate the future, identify forces for change, and outline expected business conditions. Planning assumptions are critical supporting elements in the market plan — both three-year strategic market plans and one-year operational market plans. Drawing from the various insight elements — market, customer, competitor, company, and complementer — marketers should identify candidate planning assumptions on which to build market strategy and implementation. Table T.1 illustrates planning assumptions.

TABLE T.1

ILLUSTRATION OF PLANNING ASSUMPTIONS

1. The government will impose high import tariffs within the next two years.

2. Competitors will make a technological breakthrough that adds significant customer value.

3. The textile market will grow in excess of 3.5 percent annually.

4. By 20XY, Asian brands will gain at least 10 percent market share.

5. Consumers will not accept price increases greater than 1 percent annually.

6. E-commerce will capture greater than 15 percent of revenues for textile chemicals by 20XY.

7. New textile fibers will gain greater than 10 percent market share by 20XY+1.

8. Environmental regulations will significantly increase costs or cause the removal of major chemicals.

9. Our new plant will come on stream in summer 20XY.

10. The R&D department will successfully reduce our processing costs by 15 percent by early 20XY.

11. At least two major competitors will forward integrate to secure greater access to the industry value chain.

12. New local chemical suppliers will gain at least 8 percent market share.

Of course, planning assumptions vary on several dimensions; two of the most important are *magnitude of effect and probability of occurrence*. Figure T.1 plots the Table 1 planning assumptions on these two dimensions. Core assumptions for market plans are those with *high* magnitude of effect and *high* probability of occurrence — assumptions 3 through 9. Assumption 11 (low magnitude of effect, low probability of occurrence) is not worth worrying about. Neither is assumption 10; even though probability of occurrence is high, magnitude of effect is low. Assumption 12 falls outside the critical region but the firm should probably keep its eye on this issue. Assumptions 1 and 2 are unlikely to occur but the effect would be high if they did; these assumptions are good candidates for contingency plans.

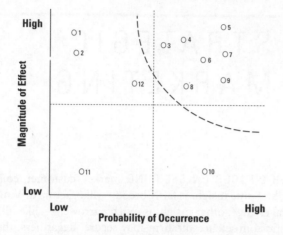

FIGURE T.1

PLANNING
ASSUMPTIONS

To complete the process, the marketer should identify implications for the firm of each high-magnitude-of-effect and high-probability-of-occurrence assumption, then turn these assumptions into "We believe…" statements. Drawing from Table T.1, examples are:

- We believe consumers will not accept price increases greater than 1 percent annually.
- We believe new textile fibers will gain greater than 10 percent market share by 20XY+1.

These assumptions are the pillars on which the firm builds market strategy and implementation.

A useful metaphor for illustrating the role of planning assumptions in the market plan is the *bridge* — Figure T.2. The bridge represents market strategy and implementation, taking the firm from *today* towards *tomorrow*. The bridge is built on pillars — the pillars represent *planning assumptions*, supported by a foundation — *situation analysis*. If the pillars are weak and/or the foundation is insecure, when the water rises the bridge will collapse and end up down the river. Correspondingly, if the situation analysis is weak and/or planning assumptions are ill developed, the market strategy and implementation will collapse. Section II teaches how to develop insight to construct a solid foundation of situation analysis; planning assumptions transition from that foundation into critical support for market strategy and implementation.

KEY IDEA

➤ The firm should assess each planning assumption on:
  • Probability of occurrence
  • Magnitude of effect

➤ The firm should develop market strategy and implementation plans on high probability of occurrence and high magnitude of effect assumptions.

➤ The firm should develop contingency plans for high magnitude of effect/low probability of occurrence assumptions.

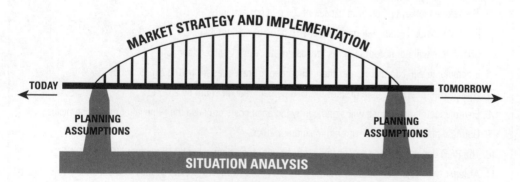

FIGURE T.2

PLANNING
ASSUMPTIONS —
THE BRIDGE
METAPHOR

SECTION III

STRATEGIC
MARKETING vs3

To access O-codes, go to **www.ocodes.com**

SECTION III — STRATEGIC MARKETING — COMPRISES FIVE CHAPTERS, Chapter 7 through Chapter 11. These chapters focus on the firm's critical strategic marketing decisions. The section embraces the first three Marketing Imperatives: Imperative 1 — Determine and Recommend Which Markets to Address, Imperative 2 — Identify and Target Market Segments, and Imperative 3 — Set Strategic Direction and Positioning.

Chapter 7, Identifying and Choosing Opportunities, addresses Imperative I. This chapter develops approaches for making market-choice decision — what markets to address and what markets not to address. Chapter 7 also offers various approaches for implementing the firm's market choices.

Chapter 8, Market Segmentation and Targeting, addresses Imperative 2. This chapter follows logically from market-choice decisions. Having selected markets, the firm must decide what parts of those markets to address. We shall see that the firm must engage in two processes: form market segments and then decide which of those segments to target for effort.

Chapters 9, 10, and 11 together address Imperative 3. Chapter 9, Market Strategy: Integrating the Firm's Efforts for Marketing Success, lays out the critical components of a market strategy; market strategies that omit any of these components are incomplete. The purpose of Chapter 10, Managing through the Life Cycle, is to help firms develop preemptive strategies by examining alternative scenarios based on life-cycle stage and competitive position. Finally, Chapter 11, Managing Brands, discusses the value of brands, key branding concepts, and approaches to building and maintaining strong brands.

Managing Marketing in the 21ˢᵗ Century

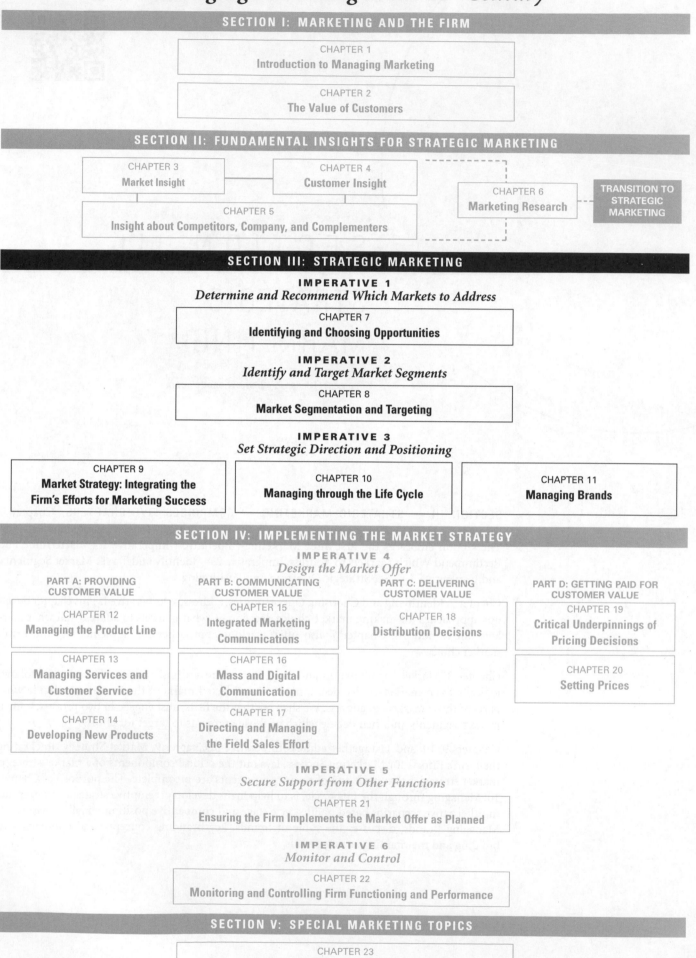

SECTION I: MARKETING AND THE FIRM

CHAPTER 1
Introduction to Managing Marketing

CHAPTER 2
The Value of Customers

SECTION II: FUNDAMENTAL INSIGHTS FOR STRATEGIC MARKETING

CHAPTER 3
Market Insight

CHAPTER 4
Customer Insight

CHAPTER 6
Marketing Research

TRANSITION TO
STRATEGIC
MARKETING

CHAPTER 5
Insight about Competitors, Company, and Complementers

SECTION III: STRATEGIC MARKETING

IMPERATIVE 1
Determine and Recommend Which Markets to Address

CHAPTER 7
Identifying and Choosing Opportunities

IMPERATIVE 2
Identify and Target Market Segments

CHAPTER 8
Market Segmentation and Targeting

IMPERATIVE 3
Set Strategic Direction and Positioning

CHAPTER 9
Market Strategy: Integrating the Firm's Efforts for Marketing Success

CHAPTER 10
Managing through the Life Cycle

CHAPTER 11
Managing Brands

SECTION IV: IMPLEMENTING THE MARKET STRATEGY

IMPERATIVE 4
Design the Market Offer

PART A: PROVIDING
CUSTOMER VALUE

PART B: COMMUNICATING
CUSTOMER VALUE

PART C: DELIVERING
CUSTOMER VALUE

PART D: GETTING PAID FOR
CUSTOMER VALUE

CHAPTER 12
Managing the Product Line

CHAPTER 15
Integrated Marketing Communications

CHAPTER 18
Distribution Decisions

CHAPTER 19
Critical Underpinnings of Pricing Decisions

CHAPTER 13
Managing Services and Customer Service

CHAPTER 16
Mass and Digital Communication

CHAPTER 20
Setting Prices

CHAPTER 14
Developing New Products

CHAPTER 17
Directing and Managing the Field Sales Effort

IMPERATIVE 5
Secure Support from Other Functions

CHAPTER 21
Ensuring the Firm Implements the Market Offer as Planned

IMPERATIVE 6
Monitor and Control

CHAPTER 22
Monitoring and Controlling Firm Functioning and Performance

SECTION V: SPECIAL MARKETING TOPICS

CHAPTER 23
International, Regional, and Global Marketing

IMPERATIVE 1
Determine and Recommend
Which Markets to Address

CHAPTER 7

IDENTIFYING AND CHOOSING OPPORTUNITIES v701

"I am going to wait for the next big thing."

— Steve Jobs[1]

LEARNING OBJECTIVES

When you have completed this chapter, you will be able to:

- Understand marketing's role in identifying new opportunities.
- Ensure the firm makes its strategic decisions with marketing input.
- Determine the fundamental elements that comprise a strategy for growth.
- Develop criteria for evaluating individual opportunities.
- Assess alternative ways to implement a strategy for growth.

OPENING CASE: ZIPCAR

Established nationwide firms in car-rental include Advantage, Alamo, Avis, Budget, Dollar, Enter-prise, Hertz, National, and Thrifty. Hertz, Avis, and National mainly compete on location and service, especially in airports. Advantage, Alamo, Budget, Dollar, and Thrifty compete on price. Enterprise became the leading car-rental firm overall by offering replacement cars for owners whose cars were being repaired. Surely the car-rental market is saturated? Not according to Zipcar, a car-sharing firm.

Car-sharing started in Germany in the 1980s, but Zipcar was first in the U.S.[2] Car-rental firms tra-ditionally offered minimum one-day rentals to customers with good driving and credit records and *meet age requirements. By contrast, Zipcar is a membership organization — customers pay an annual $50 membership fee and rent by the hour. The more than 50 cities with car-sharing service include Atlanta, Baltimore, Boston, Chicago, Gainesville, Los Angeles, New York, Philadelphia, Pittsburgh, Portland, San Diego, San Francisco, Seattle, Washington D.C., and Vancouver. In 2010, Zipcar entered Europe by acquiring London-based Streetcar.*

Zipcar members share cars; each Zipcar has a home location in a pay garage, street, or other designated location. Members can book 30 makes and models including hybrids, Smart cars, sedans, pickup trucks, SUVs, minivans, and sports cars online or by phone. They open the car with an access card (like a credit card), return the car to the same location, and check out with the card. Fees are around $10 per hour including gas and insurance; Zipcar also offers monthly arrangements for specified hours (like 6 p.m. to midnight, Monday to Friday) and daily commuting. Zipcar's small staff monitors cars via wireless and computer technologies. Some cities, hoping to ease congestion, provide free or subsidized parking.

City dwellers use Zipcars evenings and weekends; important customer groups for daily use are business and government. Portland uses car-sharing for its motor pool fleet, aiming to reduce annual operating, maintenance, and fuel costs by 25 percent and cut capital outlays. Discussing its business membership, mainly for hybrids, Starbucks' spokespeople said, "We need our partners [employees] to be able to take short trips to meetings and for other business purposes." And, "The Zipcar program and hybrid offering is a win-win for the environment and Starbucks. We reduce the number of vehicles ... and offer environmentally friendly, hassle-free mobility for our partners."

Zipcar also partners with university parking and transportation departments to offer car-sharing to students, faculty, and staff. Because many students are 18–20 and ineligible for car rentals, Zipcar has an under–21 program that offers special deals. In 2011, Zipcar agreed to use Ford cars at campus locations; Ford subsidizes student Zipcar membership and rental fees. Zipcar has 8,000 vehicles and 500,000 members and 80 percent market share; Hertz with Connect by Hertz, Enterprise, and U-Haul offer car sharing in some urban locations.[3]

CASE QUESTION

Do you think Zipcar will be successful in the long run? Why or why not? Do you think Connect by Hertz or Enterprise's *WeCar* will be successful? Why or why not? How do you assess Zipcar's arrangement with Ford?

zipcar. wheels when you want them

In Chapters 3 through 6, we learned to develop *insight* into the M4Cs — markets, customers, competitors, company, and complementers; and then made the transition to form *planning assumptions*. Now we shift direction to make *decisions* and focus on the six marketing imperatives. Marketing's first, and arguably most important, imperative is to influence firm decisions about which markets to address. **Market-choice decisions** are typically strategic for the firm or business unit. CEOs or general managers usually decide which opportunities are the most attractive, but marketing plays a critical role.

Growth is critical for injecting vigor into the firm, providing resources and rewards, keeping management on its toes, and retaining talent. Marketing should identify growth opportunities by systematically screening many alternatives. These opportunities may be in the firm's core business, in adjacencies close to the core, or further afield.[4] In consumer truck rental, U-Haul

Marketing Question

Can you identify examples of firms that have successfully entered *white spaces*?

was barely breaking even with an older truck fleet, higher maintenance costs, and lower prices than competition. But when No. 2 Ryder exited, U-Haul prospered by tapping an adjacent *profit pool* — accessories like boxes, insurance, trailer rental, and storage space.[5] Examples of successfully identifying opportunities in less-related areas like *white spaces* containing unsatisfied customer needs include Zipcar — automobile rental; Cirque du Soleil — neither traditional circus nor theater; NetJets — partial ownership of corporate jets, Starbucks; and Viagra.[6]

Marketing should play a key role in developing screening criteria for individual opportunities and helping make the business case for firm investments. Marketing should assess market potential, validate market size and growth, evaluate likely competitive challenges, and examine individual opportunity alignment with strategic initiatives. Marketing may act as internal entrepreneur, mobilizing resources like market development, R&D, strategic alliances, and acquisitions for developing opportunities.

Some opportunities may be unprofitable in the short run but offer significant long-run potential. Some opportunities surface in good times; others result directly from adverse economic circumstances.[7] Regardless, opportunities may originate in many places. R&D develops new technologies and/or product ideas it believes have market viability. Sales and engineering may propose strategic alliances or buying, selling, or licensing technology. When opportunities have marketing implications, marketing should be part of the discussion. The firm should make go/no-go decisions with the best available marketing insight — including voice-of-the-customer input. Unfortunately, in many firms, finance drives acquisition and divestiture decisions with little or no marketing input.

Figure 7.1 presents a systematic three-stage approach for developing, selecting, and implementing opportunities:

1. **Strategy for growth**: Provides guidance and analysis to generate opportunities.
2. **Screening criteria**: Used to evaluate and select individual opportunities.
3. **Implementation**: Specific actions the firm may take to achieve its objectives.

KEY IDEA

➤ A comprehensive approach for securing higher growth comprises:

- **Strategy for growth**
- Screening criteria
- Implementation

FIGURE 7.1

A COMPREHENSIVE APPROACH FOR SECURING HIGHER GROWTH

THE CHANGING VIEW

OLD WAY	NEW WAY
Competencies are fixed	Competencies are variable
Conglomeration is good	Conglomeration is bad
Firm goes it alone	Firm considers strategic alliances and other inter-organizational relationships
Growth is always desirable	*Right* and *timely* growth is desirable
Insourcing as a growth strategy	Insourcing and outsourcing as growth strategies
Organic growth by developing new products internally	Organic growth by expanding into global markets
Reinvest in historically profitable businesses	Prudent selection of appropriate growth ventures
Swift implementation of new opportunities desirable	Swift implementation of new opportunities critical

STRATEGY FOR GROWTH

Exiting the memory chip market was an agonizing decision for Andy Grove, founder and Intel CEO. Facing intense competition, Intel changed its mission and stopped selling the products on which it had been founded. Intel pursued growth in the microprocessor market and now has a commanding No. 1 position.[8]

Texas Instruments (TI) was a technology leader that lost out to Intel. In the 1980s, TI diversified widely but later divested from many markets, including chemicals, defense electronics, inspection equipment, memory chips, mold manufacturing, notebook computers, and software. TI is now market leader in chips for wireless phones, large-screen television processors, and many new electronic devices like the Slingbox (transfers TV programs from the user's home to a PC anywhere in the world), as it focuses on mobile TV service to cell phones and other devices. For the past several years TI has outgrown the semiconductor market.

Some pizza restaurant chains are highly profitable, but IBM does not make pizzas. Smart phones (like the iPhone) are fast growing and profitable, but Walmart does not produce them. Downloading music from the Internet is big business, but Carnival Cruise Lines does not offer this service. Each opportunity seems attractive, but these firms did not invest. Why not?

The reason is simple. Each of these firms has a **strategy for growth**; their strategies did not surface these options. A strategy for growth uses a set of frameworks to help the firm evaluate current businesses, decide which businesses *to be in*, and which businesses *not to be in*. Figure 7.2 shows that firms can generate attractive opportunities using four components: **vision**, **mission**, **growth path**, and **timing of entry**.

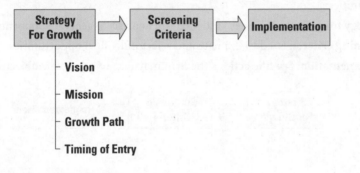

FIGURE 7.2

COMPONENTS OF A STRATEGY FOR GROWTH

VISION

Vision is a description of the firm's ideal future state — an impressionistic picture of what the future should be.[9] **Corporate** vision concerns the firm as a whole; **business-unit** vision focuses on an individual business. Good visions set a broad direction — they should inspire employees for the long run. A good vision is not too broad, nor too specific nor easily achievable.[10]

Visions

Ford Motor Company – circa 1920s – "A car in every garage."

Google – "To organize the world's information and make it universally accessible and useful."[11]

Komatsu – "Encircle Caterpillar."

Microsoft – 1980s and 1990s – "A personal computer on every desk"; 2000s – "To enable people and businesses throughout the world to realize their full potential"

Toyota – "Beat GM."

Marketing Question

How do you evaluate the following visions? Are they too broad? Are they too narrow? Are they inspiring?

• IBM (1990s) – "To lead big companies into the brave new networked world, IBM will devise their technology strategies, build and run their systems, and ultimately become the architect and repository for corporate computing, tying together not just companies, but entire industries."

• Merck – "We are in the business of preserving and improving human life."

These examples show the power of a good vision. Ford's vision led to the Model T, the production-line system, and continual price reductions. Ford's share of the U.S. automobile market reached over 50 percent by the mid-1920s. Microsoft had one vision for much of the 1980s and 1990s; when this became outmoded, Microsoft created a new, broader vision.

Marketing should make sure the vision is outward-looking. Without marketing input, vision can easily be too inwardly focused on what the firm does well. Of course, firm actions must support the vision — simply stating a goal doesn't mean you will achieve it. One CEO publicly announced his firm's vision — "to become our customers' most preferred supplier across all purchasing categories." This statement raised customer expectations far beyond the firm's ability to deliver, ultimately creating customer dissatisfaction. British Airways (BA) CEO made a similar mistake, publicly committing to "excellent customer service." He then single-mindedly pursued cost-cutting and outsourcing that alienated BA staff. The ensuing strike stranded tens of thousands very unhappy customers.

Developing a vision is one thing; having employees actively embrace the vision is another. When senior executives and consultants construct the firm's vision in isolation, employee buy-in may be minimal. Consider Oracle's experience:

> With little discussion, CEO Larry Ellison developed Oracle's new vision as an Internet-based company. He mandated that Oracle should convert all enterprise software to work as Web-based applications. Development would cease on client-server products, and the sales force would tell customers that Oracle was phasing them out. Several months later, Ellison discovered his product development directive being ignored and the sales force assuring customers that Oracle would not withdraw client-server products. Clearly, Ellison did not get employee buy-in!

When the firm involves employees, vision takes longer to develop. But broad participation and input lead to better visions. At Aramark, the large Philadelphia-based services firm, more than 8,500 employees participated directly in developing the new vision.

MISSION

The firm creates a vision to provide a lofty aspirational view of its overall direction. **Mission** guides the firm's search for market opportunities more directly.[12] A well-developed mission keeps the firm focused in a limited arena where success is likely. Mission avoids dispersing firm energy and resources in multiple directions. An ideal mission codifies opportunity areas where the firm does well or aspires to do well.[13] A firm with several business units should develop missions at both the corporate and business-unit levels; the corporate mission should encompass individual business missions.[14]

ARTICULATING THE MISSION. Mission states what the firm/business unit *will do*; by what it omits, mission also states what the firm/business unit *will not do*! (What business shall we be in? What business shall we *not* be in?) Three internal resource (IR) dimensions and two externally focused (EF) resource dimensions are critical:

- **IR — Core ingredient or natural resource.** The firm maximizes value from a core ingredient or natural resource. *We are a forest products company* implies the firm could make and sell products based on many technologies to many markets, so long as they were made from wood.

- **IR — Product/service.** This firm's mission focuses on a product/service. *We are an automobile firm* directs the firm to make cars that may use various fuels — alcohol, diesel, ethanol, gasoline, hydrogen, or natural gas, based on several technologies — electro-mechanical, fuel cell, gas-turbine, internal-combustion, hybrid, or steam.

 KEY IDEA

➤ The firm's *mission* should guide its search for opportunity.

➤ Five approaches to developing mission are:

Internally focused:
• Core ingredient or natural resource
• Product or service
• Technology

Externally focused:
• Customer needs
• Market or market segment

- **IR — Technology.** The firm focuses on a core technology. *We are an electronics firm* directs the search for opportunities to electronics, using any raw material and selling products into any market. China's BYD, a world leader in cell phone batteries, entered the automobile industry with the long-run goal of producing electric cars.[15]

- **EF — Customer needs.** This mission directs the firm to serve customers having a specific set of needs, with any product, using any technology. *We satisfy people's transportation needs* could embrace making bicycles, automobiles, trucks, helicopters, or airplanes.[16] Otis Elevator bases its mission on transportation — *to provide any customer a means of moving people and things up, down, and sideways over short distances with higher reliability than any similar enterprise in the world.*[17]

- **EF — Market/market segment.** A firm with this type of mission could make many products, using various raw materials and technologies. *Our markets are families with young children* is the mission for many FMCG firms like P&G and Unilever that offer household and personal-care products.

The firm/business unit can choose among these dimensions to develop missions, or may combine dimensions. Courtyard by Marriott's mission — *To provide economy and quality-minded frequent business travelers with a premier lodging facility, which is consistently perceived as clean, comfortable, well maintained, and attractive, staffed by friendly, attentive, and efficient people* — combines product/service and market/market segment.

To reiterate, every mission answers the question "What business are we in?" Mission states what the firm/business unit *will do* — externally focused missions also specify *for whom*. But by what it omits, a well-crafted mission also states what the firm/business unit *will not do*!

EVOLVING THE MISSION. Typically, successful firms evolve their missions. If opportunities are scarce with the current mission, or a target of opportunity appears, the firm should consider *broadening* the mission, but be cautious about the modified direction. Cannondale successfully expanded its mission from high-end bicycles to embrace dirt bikes and all-terrain vehicles, but Cisco's B2C entry with the Flip video camera was a failure. Successful mission broadenings include:

Amazon. Amazon's initial product-based mission focused on Internet book selling. As Amazon added many other products, its mission broadened to becoming an Internet retailer. Amazon has since added a search engine, video downloads, utility computing, and fulfillment services as it morphs into a firm that grows based on technology.

Apple. For many years Apple's mission focused on personal computers via continuous Macintosh upgrades. More recently, Apple's mission expanded to embrace digital music — iPod and iTunes, cell-phones — iPhone, and tablet computers — iPad.

Dell, HP, IBM, and Xerox each broadened its missions to embrace services, in part though acquisition; the firms acquired, respectively, Perot Systems, Electronic Data Systems (EDS), PricewaterhouseCoopers, and Affiliated Computer Services (ACS). By contrast, **Oracle** broadened into hardware by acquiring Sun Microsystems.

Google significantly broadened its mission by extending its software-led participation in cell phones (Android) to hardware and software by acquiring Motorola Mobility.

Pampers. P&G evolved its baby business mission from *We want the driest diapers* to *Helping moms with baby's development*. This change led to new products like Easy Ups training pants and Kandoo baby wipes.

ServiceMaster. For 40 years, ServiceMaster's (SM) compound annual growth rate and shareholder returns consistently exceeded 20 percent. Originally a mothproofing business, SM expanded into carpet cleaning, general household and commercial cleaning, and then to grounds management.

Faced with resources stretched too thin, poor financial performance, new/evolving competition, and/or a looming takeover threat, some firms *narrow* missions by dropping products and/or

---

KEY IDEA

➤ The firm's mission can use a single approach or combine approaches.

➤ The firm should proactively revise its mission.

Marketing Question

Based on your knowledge and/or Internet research, write one-sentence missions for AXA, Citigroup, Comcast, Disney, ExxonMobil, Facebook, Ford, GE, Groupon, Hitachi, IP, Morgan Stanley, Novartis, Siemens, Toyota, Twitter, Verizon, Yahoo!, and/or Xerox.

Marketing Question

In recent years, Google acquired YouTube, Double Click (online advertising network), Motorola Mobility, and Zagat (restaurant reviews). Write a mission for Google. As Google's CEO, where will you seek future growth?

divesting businesses. DuPont exited oil and textile fibers; Corning divested healthcare services and consumer products. Other firms *return to the core business* (*stick to the knitting*): Under CEO Art Laffley, P&G grew from its core — laundry products, baby diapers, feminine care, and hair care; built on strengths to enter new beauty and personal care categories; and expanded in developing markets. (P&G also divested less-strategic food and beverage brands [Crisco, Jif, Folgers], weak household and beauty brands [Comet, Noxzema], and exited pharmaceuticals.)

Some firms narrow product scope but place major effort on *expanding* geographic scope.

Guinness. Post-WWII, the Irish brewer launched a major diversification program, adding 250 businesses. As profitability declined, Guinness *aggressively divested* most of these businesses, rebuilt the Guinness brand, and *expanded internationally*. Guinness stock price increased nearly 10,000 times.

Knorr-Bremse. Munich-based Knorr-Bremse (KB) offered a diversified product line, mainly to German customers. After a management buyout, KB *narrowed its product line* to braking systems for trains and trucks, and *expanded geographic scope* globally. KB made 28 acquisitions and has 40 percent global market share.

Some firms totally change missions:

American Can. American Can (AC) was the U.S. No. 2 canning company. AC divested its entire canning operations and morphed, via acquisition, into Primerica, a financial services firm. Citibank later acquired Primerica.

Westinghouse Electric. Westinghouse acquired CBS, divested its electricity businesses, changed its name, and focused exclusively on media. CBS subsequently merged with media conglomerate Viacom.

Some firms narrow missions by breaking up into two or more parts — aka a *Starburst*. Each new firm has a narrower mission than the original company. Tyco split into three firms — Covidien (healthcare), TE Connectivity (electronics), and Tyco International (security, fire protection, flow control); Kraft split into two firms — grocery and snacks; McGraw-Hill split into McGraw-Hill Markets (business information) and McGraw-Hill Education; Motorola also split in two — Motorola Mobility (B2C) (acquired by Google) and Motorola Solutions (B2B); and Sara Lee split into a retail and food-service business and beverages.

GROWTH PATH

MARKETING
ENRICHMENT

Gap Analysis me701

me701

Mission provides a broad approach to identifying potential opportunities; **growth path** is more focused. (Gap Analysis, Marketing Enrichment me701, is a useful conceptual device for framing the growth-path challenge.) Growth path is specifically concerned with the trade-off between expected financial return and risk.[18] The firm should consider three factors:

- Revenue and profit potential of opportunities relative to the required investment
- Core competencies from its portfolio of businesses, technologies, products, and markets
- Assessment of risk[19]

The firm's expected financial returns, competencies, and risks from the opportunities it pursues coexist in a dynamic relationship. By investing in one opportunity, the firm may develop new competencies. These enhanced competencies may, in turn, make previously unattractive opportunities attractive. Expected financial returns and risks also change.

Figure 7.3 shows that the growth-path matrix uses two dimensions — *market* and *product/technology* — to analyze opportunities. We trisect each dimension — *existing, related*, and *new* — to develop nine matrix cells — A through I. Each cell represents a different type of opportunity. For ease of exposition, we combine individual cells to develop four broad approaches to growth: **market penetration, product growth, market growth**, and **product and market diversification.**[20]

FIGURE 7.3

THE GROWTH-PATH MATRIX

The matrix shows Market (vertical axis: New, Related, Existing) by Product or Technology (horizontal axis: Existing, Related, New (to firm)):

Market ↓ / Product →	Existing	Related	New (to firm)
New	Market Growth 2: Market Expansion (G)	Business Expansion: Concentric Products (H)	Conglomeration (I)
Related	Market Growth 1: Market Extension (D)	Business Extension (E)	Business Expansion: Concentric Markets (F)
Existing	Market Penetration (A)	Product Growth 1: Product Extension (B)	Product Growth 2: Product Expansion (C)

> **Marketing Question**
>
> Use the growth-path matrix to identify the growth trajectory of your favorite firm, or a firm for which you would like to work.

MARKET PENETRATION (CELL A). Most firms spend significant resources pursuing market-penetration strategies. The firm focuses effort on existing (or slightly modified) products in existing markets, but may also improve profits by increasing operational effectiveness. The firm bases growth on core competencies,[21] and has minimal *knowledge* risk. Of course, the firm may face significant risk from competitors and generally heightened environmental turbulence.[22]

PRODUCT GROWTH (CELLS B AND C). The firm brings new products to existing markets. A ski resort that adds ice-skating, downhill sledding, snowmobiling, and tubing pursues a product-growth strategy. VF Corporation acquired Timberland (boots) to add to its outdoor and action sports business brands like North Face and Eastpak. *Product growth 1 (product extension — cell B)* and *product growth 2 (product expansion — cell C)* differ in the degree of product newness. Product extensions relate to current products; product expansions are unrelated and hence more risky. For a bank skilled in making corporate loans, lock-box services are a product extension. Complex derivatives, requiring significant new technical expertise, are a product expansion.[23]

MARKET GROWTH (CELLS D AND G). The firm sells existing products to new markets via market development. *Market growth 1 (market extension — cell D)* and *market growth 2 (market expansion — cell G)* differ in degree of market newness. For the bank skilled in corporate loans, loans to public and/or nonprofit enterprises is a market extension. Loans to individuals is a market expansion. Generally, market expansions are more risky than market extensions.

> **KEY IDEA**
>
> ➤ The four fundamental *growth-path* directions are:
> - Market penetration
> - Product growth
> - Market growth
> - Product and market diversification
>
> These four growth directions comprise nine individual growth paths.

Porsche makes and sells automobiles — market penetration, but also pursues market growth. Porsche operates a highly profitable *rent-an-engineer* business to customers like Opel Zafira, Smart microcar, Linde forklifts, Airbus cockpit, and Harley-Davidson motorcycles. Porsche keeps its engineering team intact and also earns significant revenues.

Geographic expansion is a popular market growth option. Increasingly, firms are expanding to new countries. Readers will recognize that many large firms, headquartered in various countries, operate globally, including IBM (U.S), Pechiney (France), Sony (Japan), Samsung (Korea), Cemex (Mexico), South African Breweries, and British Airways.

Adjacencies

Adjacencies are special cases of product and market growth. Product and market growth 1 (extensions) (Cells B and D) are close to the firm's core competencies. Related technology products are less risky than new products. From a market perspective, a U.S. firm's geographic expansion to an English-speaking country with similar cultural values and legal system, like Australia, Britain, Canada, or South Africa, is much closer to the core than entry into China or Japan.

CONTINUES ON NEXT PAGE

Sometimes the firm bases *adjacent* growth on *hidden assets* — underutilized competencies, resources, or skills. De Beers shifted from a production focus to market focus by strengthening its brand and leveraging consumer, jeweler, and distributor relationships into new products. Marvel's comic-book franchise could not stave off bankruptcy but its 5,000-strong stable of characters (Green Goblin, Incredible Hulk, Spiderman, Wolverine) drove the turnaround via movies and merchandising. Internal functions may provide the basis for adjacent growth. American Airlines secured revenue from its Sabre reservation system (later spun off as a public company and developed as Travelocity); Disney Institute offers seminars based on Disney's brand building and service excellence; Zappos offers seminars and insight-videos about its unique culture; and IBM formed its highly successful Global Services from a subunit of the sales force.[24]

PRODUCT AND MARKET DIVERSIFICATION (CELLS E, F, H, AND I). A critical characteristic of *market penetration*, *product growth*, and *market growth* is that at least one of the two growth dimensions is *existing*, and just one changes. For product and market diversification, **both** *market and product/technology* change to either *related* or *new*. Opportunities are more risky, and the business as a whole shifts direction.

Business extension (cell E) requires moderate change for both *market* and *product/technology*. Nike made a product extension when it added athletic apparel to its core footwear line. By contrast, adding sporty street apparel was a business extension — *related* product to *related* market. *Business expansion* requires new products and related markets (*concentric markets — cell F*), or new markets and related products (*concentric products — cell H*).[25] Risk is greatest in *conglomeration (cell I)* — new products and new markets. Conglomeration by internal development is generally more risky than by acquisition, but many conglomerate acquisitions also fail. Quaker purchased Snapple from Triarc for $1.7 billion but made significant errors in distribution and promotion. Three years later, Triarc repurchased Snapple for $300 million.[26] Another conglomeration failure:

Under CEO Jean Paul Messier, a French water utility firm renamed itself Vivendi and began acquiring entertainment, media, and communications firms. Vivendi purchased the Seagram Company to secure Universal Studios and bought USA Networks' entertainment assets — it also began divesting water companies. When Vivendi faced bankruptcy, the board fired Messier and started selling assets. Vivendi exited water, and now focuses on media and telecommunications.

Marketing Question

Pick a country other than your own. Which firms from that country earn revenues from countries in more than three continents? What other diversification directions have these firms taken?

CHOOSING THE *RIGHT* GROWTH PATH. To identify and separate worthwhile opportunities from others typically requires significant marketing research and analysis. The firm should identify the scope of the opportunity, competition, and assess its ability to deliver the necessary customer value to secure differential advantage. More generally, the firm should evaluate its ability to be successful in various growth paths. For example, the firm may perform well with *market growth* but poorly with *product and market diversification*. If so, the firm should probably favor *market-growth* opportunities and set a higher bar for *product and market diversifications*.

Firms with technical expertise tend to choose product-focused growth; firms with market-development expertise select market-focused growth. By trial and error, the firm may discover it has greater competence in one growth area than another. Yet even firms with technical expertise need marketing expertise. Observers have often lauded Philips and Alcatel-Lucent for great technology but criticized them for not capitalizing on these strengths in their chosen markets. By contrast, Cisco has successfully acquired many technology firms and then introduced marketable products that customers value highly.

As a starting point for developing decision rules about new opportunities, the firm should conduct a retrospective growth-path analysis. It could go back, say, five years and classify each pursued opportunity into one of the nine cells, then assess success or failure. The firm may discover some areas where it generally performs well and others where it performs poorly.

TIMING OF ENTRY

Along with identifying the *right* growth path, when to seize an opportunity — **timing of entry** — is also crucial. Chapter 3 discusses five product life-cycle stages — *introduction, early growth, late growth, maturity,* and *decline.* Early stages have high uncertainty in both products and markets, but uncertainty decreases as the life cycle evolves. Correspondingly, competitive pressures typically increase. Figure 7.4 explores links between the first four life-cycle stages and specific strategic options for timing of market entry — **pioneer, follow-the-leader, segmenter,** and **me-too.**[27]

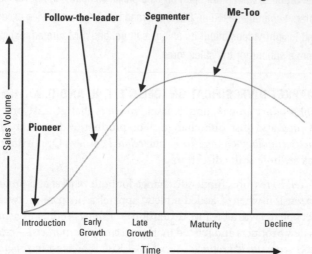

FIGURE 7.4

TIMING OF MARKET ENTRY

PIONEER. Pioneers blaze trails and create new markets via consistent and extensive R&D. Pioneers accept risk and understand that failure often accompanies success. Pioneers possess the R&D skills and internal processes to consistently develop new products/services, and the marketing capabilities to open up new markets. Pioneers have sufficient resources to support heavy R&D expenditures and fund market development; sometimes market-entry costs exceed R&D spending. Firms that commonly pioneer new products include Apple, DuPont, IBM, Intel, 3M, Monsanto, Sony, major pharmaceutical firms (like GSK, Novartis, and Pfizer), and biotech firms.

Of course, pioneers are not always successful, even when they bring products to market. Apple's experience illustrates the benefits and risks of pioneering:

> Founded by entrepreneurs Steve Jobs and Steve Wozniak, Apple pioneered personal computers, but the IBM PC and clones overtook it. Apple pioneered personal digital assistants (PDAs) with the Newton, but lost out to Palm. Apple pioneered paid-music downloading with iTunes and the iPod, smart phones with the iPhone, and tablet computers with the iPad. Will it sustain these early leads?

Successful pioneers often enjoy patent monopolies for limited time periods and related high margins. Pioneers protect intellectual property ferociously; they may also gain first-mover advantages and raise entry costs for followers. Some first-mover advantages are short-lived, but others can last for many years and pose difficult challenges for later entrants.

FOLLOW-THE-LEADER. Follow-the-leader firms enter rapidly growing markets on the heels of pioneers. Pioneers make large research investments to develop innovative new products/services; follow-the-leader firms focus on development. In what is sometimes called the used-apple policy, the *follower* lets the pioneer take the first bite. If the apple is fine, the follower enters; if not, it passes.[28] Follow-the-leader firms are happy for pioneers to invest heavily in R&D and market development — followers pursue the pioneer quickly with developmental R&D.

Market insight is critical; followers should enter as soon as possible after a successful pioneer. A successful follow-the-leader should have:

- Vision of serving a mass market
- Good competitive intelligence to develop products/services as soon as possible
- Good developmental engineers to leverage/enhance the pioneer's successful research
- Proactive patent lawyers to identify weak spots in pioneer patents
- Financial strength and commitment to outspend the pioneer
- Ability to differentiate offers and deliver superior customer value.
- Will and persistence to succeed[29]

Many industry leaders like FedEx (air package delivery), Gillette (razors), Google (search), Intel (microprocessors), Microsoft (operating system software, browsers, and search), Pampers (disposable diapers), and Xerox (copiers) entered their markets as follow-the-leader firms.[30] Ethicon (J&J) consistently follows medical device innovations from Covidien, typically 18 months later with better products at lower prices. Ford and Nissan both introduced hybrid cars many years after Toyota.

SEGMENTER. Segmenters enter established markets in late growth by adding value for specific segments. Segmenter strategies can be very effective in maturing markets. As customers gain knowledge and experience, their preferences typically become more specific. Using insightful marketing research, segmenters identify the unique needs of specific customer groups, then offer specially designed products/services.

Segmenter skill sets and competencies differ markedly from pioneers and follow-the-leaders. Technological expertise and innovation are no longer the driving forces. Segmenters require marketing research skills to identify unsatisfied customer needs, but also the flexibility to address narrow market niches. Segmenters often target several segments simultaneously, at low cost — perhaps using modular-design or platform engineering processes, combined with flexible operating systems.

Medical device maker Medtronics used successful segmentation and platform engineering to capture market share in cardiac pacemakers and implantable defibrillators.[31] Airbus and Boeing use modular design to produce commercial aircraft families — Boeing designed the 707, 727, 737, and 757 aircraft on the same fuselage platform. The automobile industry is a heavy user of these design and engineering approaches:

Automobile companies use segmentation to launch specialist vehicles that, for smaller firms, may be key to their survival. Chrysler minivans transformed its financial performance; the failing Mazda revived the sports-car market with the Miata (MX5). Daimler AG's Smart microcar is similarly aimed at a narrow group of urbanites.

ME-TOO. Me-too-ers enter mature markets with limited product lines. They base low-price/low-cost strategies on value engineering, efficient high-volume production (often in low-cost countries), low overhead, aggressive procurement, and great attention to detail. They spend little on R&D, have similar products to market leaders, are often leaders in process innovation, and have very focused marketing. Generic drug producers, notably Teva (Israel), are *poster children* for this strategy, although technological copying difficulties may cause problems. Me-too-ers can wreak havoc in segmented markets where firms compete with value-added offers; many Chinese firms pursue this approach:

Dell became the global PC market leader by continually reducing costs and putting enormous price pressure on competitors. Dell minimizes inventory, receives payment before production, and has negative working capital. Dell has lost ground to HP but Taiwan's Acer places huge price pressure on both rivals.[32]

CHOOSING THE *RIGHT* TIMING-OF-ENTRY STRATEGY. Similar to growth-path decisions, the firm should identify which *timing-of-entry* strategy best fits its capabilities, then match this strategy to market opportunities. Of course, as markets evolve, the firm must also evolve its capabilities.[33]

Discovery-Driven Growth

Discovery-driven growth addresses many firms' problem of unfocused growth. The starting point is to develop challenging and realistic goals for the firm/business unit. Then management examines current growth initiatives to assess whether they can meet these goals; if not, what are the gaps? Using, vision, mission, growth path, and timing of entry, the firm/business unit identifies the kinds of projects to close the gaps.

An important tool is the *reverse income statement* — starting with the bottom line, then working backwards to figure out what the firm/business unit must accomplish. Consider profit goals: return on sales (ROS) assumptions lead to revenue targets, which lead to volume and price targets, which lead to market share targets (via market size and growth assumptions), which lead to resource requirements like product development, sales force, and advertising. At each stage, the firm should test its assumptions for realism.[34]

SCREENING CRITERIA: EVALUATING OPPORTUNITIES

We showed how growth strategy helps the firm identify opportunities; but which specific opportunities should the firm pursue? Figure 7.5 shows four screening criteria — **objectives**, **compatibility (fit)**, **core competence**, and **synergy** — that help the firm evaluate opportunities and decide where to invest.

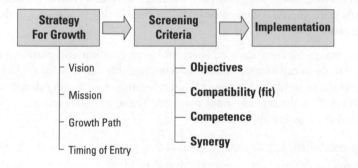

FIGURE 7.5

SCREENING CRITERIA

🔑 KEY IDEA

➤ A comprehensive approach for securing higher growth comprises:

• Strategy for growth
• **Screening criteria**
• Implementation

OBJECTIVES

The crucial first criterion for an investment opportunity is to satisfy firm objectives. Revenue and profit growth are critical for creating shareholder value, but unmitigated growth can be a real problem. The firm must temper its desire for growth with concern for risk, stability, and flexibility.

REVENUE AND PROFIT GROWTH. To assess revenue and profit potential, the firm should consider both financial and non-financial measures. Standard financial measures include timing of cash flows, payback, return on investment (ROI), profit margin, net present value (NPV), and internal rate of return (IRR). Leading indicators of profit performance embrace market size, expected market growth rate, market potential, forces driving market growth, number/strength of competitors, and market-share forecasts; these factors influence revenue, cost, and profit forecasts.[35]

Sometimes firms reject new opportunities because forecast performance is inferior to *historic* performance with some existing product(s). This comparison is incorrect. The firm should compare *forecast* market share, revenues, and profits from the new opportunity versus *forecast* market share, revenues, and profits without it. Despite a significant lead in expensive laser printers, HP added inexpensive inkjet printers (lower margins) to avoid losing market share.

RISK. The firm must weigh forecast revenues and profits against the risk and required investment. Risks the firm should consider include:

- **Demand risk.** Fundamental for every cell in the growth-path matrix: Is there an opportunity? Is there market demand?
- **Product/technology risk and market risk.** Generally, opportunities farther from *market-penetration* (cell A) of the growth-path matrix are more risky. The firm lacks experience with either the product/technology (cells B and C) or the market (cells D and G). Product and market diversification (cell I) is the most risky growth path — opportunities are very different from the firm's experience. Also, early life-cycle entries like *pioneer* and *follow-the-leader* may be more risky than later *segmenter* and *me-too* strategies. Critical questions: Will the technology work? Is there a viable market? Does (will) our product(s) satisfy customer needs?
- **Competitor risk.** In general, the lower the product/technology and market risk, the tougher the competition; hence, competitor risk is typically high for market penetration. By contrast, direct competition may be minimal for *pioneers.*

Other risks the firm should evaluate for each opportunity are:

- **Financial risk.** Is the opportunity sufficiently sustainable to justify the investment?
- **Firm risk.** Does the firm have the competencies, resources, and will to succeed?
- **Physical environment risk.** Are natural disasters likely to affect the opportunity?
- **Political risk.** How stable is the local government? Will it (or successors) take actions to make the market less attractive?

Opportunities differ in degree and type of risk; hence, the firm should set different profitability cut-offs. Generally, more-risky opportunities should offer higher potential returns than less-risky opportunities.[36,37]

TIMING. In addition to financial return and risk, when evaluating an opportunity the firm must consider the timing of contribution to profits. Depending on the firm's financial circumstances, a moderate return opportunity that delivers profits in the medium term may be more attractive than a higher return opportunity promising profits much later.

STABILITY. Suppose the firm must choose between two opportunities: A — high growth, significant profit variability; B — lower growth, low profit variability. The lower growth, low variability — higher *stability* option may be preferable. Schneider Electric Mexico focuses on markets it can serve through existing distributors. Schneider believes these revenues are more stable than revenues from potentially more profitable large electricity generation projects requiring major investments. Similarly:

A well-known ski resort had two investment options: develop ski trails on a neighboring hill or invest in mountain slides and outdoor concerts to attract summer visitors. The ski resort elected to develop summer facilities so as to even out annual revenue and profit streams.

FLEXIBILITY. All firms face increasing environmental change and complexity. No matter how good the firm's forecasting, it may be blindsided by unexpected events. *Insurance policies* give the firm *flexibility* to deal with changed circumstances:

- **Acquisition.** Intel, Microsoft, and Cisco acquire firms with positions in adjacent markets.
- **Joint technology agreements.** Oil companies often form partnerships for oil-drilling platforms and operations, like Texaco and Shell in the Gulf of Mexico.
- **Partial ownership.** Major drug companies frequently take this approach with biotechnology firms. BMS purchased shares in cancer-drug developer ImClone.

- **Research and development (R&D).** The firm hedges its bets by investing in competing fields. Car companies invest in hybrid, electric, and fuel cell technologies.
- **Venture capital.** The firm provides venture capital to startup companies but retains options to increase ownership. Cisco is a leader in this approach. Microsoft invests in firms that do spam marketing; it also invests in firms that develop anti-spam software.

Originally a textile power-loom producer, Toyota morphed into automobiles. Today its investments include prefabricated houses, resort development, helicopter operations and surveying, airport management, advertising agency, consulting, horticulture, golf course operations, and a professional soccer team. Some, but not all, have synergies with its automobile business.[38]

COMPATIBILITY (FIT)

Can the firm be successful in the opportunity? The firm should examine three core types of compatibility (fit): product-market fit, product-company fit, and company-market fit.

PRODUCT-MARKET FIT. Is the product appropriate for the market? Restated: Does the product satisfy customer needs in target market segments better than its competitors? Firms most often assess *product-market fit* through ongoing marketing research and market-testing. Timing is particularly important in assessing product-market fit as the firm and environment evolve.

PRODUCT-COMPANY FIT. Does the firm possess the financial, human, and other skills and resources to succeed? Can the firm successfully upgrade its efforts as the market evolves? British-based EMI's experience with the CAT scanner is a good example of insufficient *product-company fit*. Best known for recorded music (EMI launched the Beatles), EMI successfully pioneered the first CAT scanner in the U.S. EMI retained market leadership for several years, but continued pressure from major players in medical imaging — GE, Hitachi, Technicare — eventually forced its withdrawal.[39]

Sometimes a firm has great product-market fit but lacks distribution strength to reach customers. Independent inventors often have this problem — product-market fit is great, but product-company fit is poor. Un-du's experience is classic:

> Charles Foley developed Un-du (manufactured by Doumar Products) for removing oil-based stickers. The Business Product Industry Association gave Un-du its best-new-product award, but getting distribution was a major problem. Magic American introduced Sticker Lifter through established distribution and gained dominant market share.

COMPANY-MARKET FIT. Can the firm compete effectively in the market? Does it have sufficient customer insight, reputation, resources, and skills to defeat competitors? Product-market fit and product-company fit may both be fine, but poor *company-market fit* may lead to a reject decision. Geographic expansion offers many examples. Suppose a foreign market is attractive for the firm's product — good product-market fit, and the firm is skilled at producing, promoting, and distributing the product in its home market — good company-product fit. Little experience in the foreign market — poor company-market fit — may lead to opportunity rejection. Consider the different perspectives of Citibank and Capital One concerning credit cards in Asia:

> Citibank launched credit cards in several Asian countries. Because Citibank had operated in Asia for many years, credit cards in Asia were a good company-market fit. By contrast, Capital One is a strong U.S. competitor but has no operations in Asia. In considering an Asian entry, Capital One would have poor company-market fit.

RELATIONSHIPS AMONG THE THREE FORMS OF FIT. All three compatibility criteria are important for evaluating individual opportunities, but product-market fit is different from the others. If product-market fit is poor — the product does not satisfy customer needs — the firm

Marketing Question

Can you identify three examples of successful product-market fit? Can you identify three examples of failed product-market fit? What are the risks of unsuccessful product-market fit?

should dismiss the opportunity regardless of the other fits. If product-market fit is good, and either product-company fit or company-market fit is poor, the firm should consider options:

- **Poor product-company fit.** Divest the product/technology to a firm better suited to make and sell the product.[40] Many biotechnology firms and foreign pharmaceutical firms make these arrangements with U.S. pharmaceutical companies. BMS licenses its Plavix blood-thinning drug from Sanofi — a French pharmaceutical firm.

- **Poor company-market fit.** Form a strategic alliance with a better-positioned firm. General Mills — cereal expertise — and Nestlé — brand equity and distribution — formed Cereal Partners Worldwide (CPW) to produce and market cereals outside the U.S. At the time, Kellogg dominated the global market; now. CPW offers more than 50 brands in 130 markets worldwide and enjoys more than 20 percent market share in international cold cereals.

CORE COMPETENCE

Core competences are knowledge, skills, and other capabilities the firm possesses.[41] The **core-competence** criterion is straightforward: Does the firm *bring anything to the party*? Can the firm *take anything from the party*? More formally: Does this opportunity leverage the firm's core competencies or allow it to develop new ones? If the answer is *no* to both questions, the firm should probably reject the opportunity. But one *yes* may be sufficient to continue.

Generally, the firm is better off pursuing opportunities that use core competences. The firm can more easily gain differential advantage, like Coca-Cola introducing a new sports drink or Toyota launching a new automobile. Two Boston entrepreneurs developed a competence in buying common Internet domain names like beer.com, creditcards.com, and chocolate.com, developing sites, then selling. But core competence is not the only criterion — the opportunity must satisfy other criteria. Further, an opportunity may be attractive *even if the firm has little competence* — if it can *secure* competence by investing. Intel abandoned its core competence in memory chips, but gained competence in microprocessor technology and manufacturing.[42] When Jeff Bezos left New York for Seattle in his second-hand car, he had little competence for building Amazon, but it became the leading online retailer.[43] Also:

> Sir Richard Branson addressed Virgin's anticipated $300 million–$400 million investment in ethanol plants: "There were skeptics in the record business, but we built the biggest independent record company. With the airline, we've seen 13 competitors go bankrupt, and we've survived. We've built a successful mobile phone business. We're a slightly unusual company in that *we go into industries we know nothing about and immerse ourselves*" (emphasis added).[44]

SYNERGY

Synergy explores how an opportunity relates to the firm's existing capabilities/resources.[45] *Positive synergy* reflects the notion that 2+2 can be greater than 4! Synergy kicks in when the firm uses existing resources for an opportunity. If the firm sells a new product through existing distributors, like P&G or Unilever adding new products for supermarkets, it gains distribution synergy. If the firm makes the product in existing facilities, it gains manufacturing synergy. The firm should not decline an opportunity for lack of positive synergy — but positive synergy can enhance profits.

Sometimes the firm enjoys positive synergy by embarking on a new growth path. Dell employees are consultants on build-to-order manufacturing systems; Disney teaches firms to deliver top-notch customer service; Alcoa helps customers install and implement safety systems[46]; New York's Metro-North Railroad rents space in train stations for restaurants/cafés.

When 2+2 is less than 4, *negative synergy* is at work; pursuing a new opportunity may erode revenues and profits from existing products. Allergy-relief prescription drug Claritin was a major profit-maker for Schering Plough (SP); SP launched an over-the-counter version to reach the larger market for non-prescription allergy relief medicines. Prescription Claritin sales dropped more than 40 percent.

CONTRIBUTION TO THE VENTURE PORTFOLIO

In addition to considering opportunities individually, the firm should consider all opportunities as elements in its venture portfolio. A firm with good cash flow but few growth businesses may heavy-up on longer-term, higher-risk options. A firm with little cash may focus on short-term, low/moderate-risk opportunities. Generally, conservatively managed firms invest in low-risk opportunities that pay off quickly. Aggressive firms accept greater risk for potentially higher returns that pay off in the long term.[47] Novartis shifted R&D focus from drugs designed for major diseases where the underlying science was deficient (long term/high risk), to drugs backed by strong science even if potential markets were small (moderate term/moderate risk). Potential return and risk are typically correlated, but some opportunities may offer good returns at low risk.

INDEPENDENCE AND INTERDEPENDENCE. So far we assumed that opportunities are **independent**; but some opportunities may be **interdependent**. Suppose the firm is considering two opportunities, A and B. The firm may invest in A, in B, or in A plus B. The A plus B option has four potentially important interdependencies:

- **Costs.** Development and manufacturing costs are lower.
- **Marketing.** Sales of A may enhance or diminish sales of B.
- **Resources.** Uses fewer resources than A and B independently.
- **Technical.** Development success for A affects development success for B.

Understanding interdependencies complicates opportunity selection, but is critical for developing the venture portfolio. Hence, in the semiconductor and consumer electronics industries, firms often invest in multiple related opportunities.[48] The firm should consider the opportunity's return-risk profile and the impact each opportunity has on the venture portfolio.[49]

IMPLEMENTING GROWTH STRATEGIES

P&G funded a new group, Corporate New Ventures, with $250 million seed money. Using *My Idea*, a corporate collaboration network, P&G employees funnel ideas to an innovation panel. Accepted projects tap into P&G's entire global resource base. Within two years, P&G launched 58 new products. Swiffer, the successful new cleaning product, was launched in 10 months — half the normal time.

Figure 7.6 shows several options for implementing the firm's growth strategy.[50] Until recently, many firms would not have entertained several of these approaches. P&G's successful introduction of Crest SpinBrush was atypical; rather than an internal development, P&G purchased SpinBrush technology from an entrepreneur.

INTERNAL DEVELOPMENT

Many firms put significant effort into **internal development** of new products/services. Internal development is appropriate in all cells of the growth-path matrix and for all timing-of-entry options. Some evidence suggests a strong positive correlation between R&D spending and corporate profitability.[51]

FIGURE 7.6

IMPLEMENTING GROWTH STRATEGIES

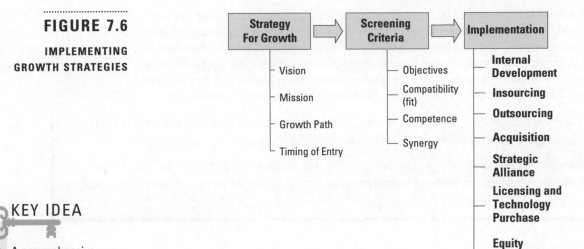

KEY IDEA

➤ A comprehensive approach for securing higher growth comprises:

• Strategy for growth
• Screening criteria
• **Implementation**

KEY IDEA

➤ Options for implementing a growth strategy include:

• Internal development
• Insourcing
• Outsourcing
• Acquisition
• Strategic alliance
• Licensing and technology purchase
• Equity investment

Many firms place internal development in business units (versus corporate) so as to get closer to the market. This location clarifies responsibility for R&D, but can *silo* development and minimize synergies among businesses. Properly harnessed, inter-business synergies can be extensive. P&G developed several products via inter-business unit collaboration: Actonel (osteoporosis drug); Crest Whitestrips (teeth whitener); Dawn Power Dissolver (pot and dish cleaner); Mr. Clean AutoDry (car-wash sprayer); and Olay Daily Facials (cleansing cloths).

Internal development is not just for technologists and engineers; marketing can play a major role in directing R&D efforts by infusing external insight at all developmental stages. Said a senior Pfizer executive, "We always have marketing people on our early product development teams. They interact with researchers from the first pre-clinical experiments in the laboratory. Before that, we have marketing people and researchers looking together at the drug market and asking, 'Where is the most potential to help a lot of people and sell a lot of medicine?'"[52]

Advantages of internal development over alternative growth modes are:

• **Control.** The firm has control over the entire development process. The firm purchases (or leases) required resources and makes all decisions about suppliers and distributors. The firm solves human-resource shortfalls by hiring and acculturating newcomers.[53]

• **Cost.** Internal development is typically less expensive than securing new products by acquisition and other means.

Disadvantages of internal development are:

• **Expertise.** The firm must successfully direct the R&D effort, or the resulting products may require commercialization skills the firm does not possess.

• **Resources.** Some resources may be unavailable, or too expensive to develop/ acquire.

• **Time.** Market windows are increasingly short; internal development takes time.[54]

To address these disadvantages, some firms modify internal development processes by streamlining bureaucracies and tapping employees' creative potential. They may reward employees based on the success of products their ideas generate — like P&G's *My Idea*.[55]

INSOURCING

The firm captures more added value in the supply chain by undertaking additional activities in developing, producing, marketing, distributing, and promoting. The firm can expand upstream by conducting supplier activities — *backward integration*, or downstream by conducting customer activities — *forward integration*.

Adjacencies (activities closely related to core competences) are prime insourcing candidates and may help develop new core competences. Prudential fired its advertising agencies and now develops all advertising in-house; Amazon launched several imprints like Montlake Romance to publish digital, physical, and audio books. Opportunities for insourcing evolve as profit pools in the supply-chain migrate. Managers should evaluate where to invest in building new competences.[56] Coca-Cola and Merck, respectively, show successful and unsuccessful insourcing:

> Historically, Coca-Cola focused on syrup manufacture and brand-building. More recently, Coca-Cola acquired bottlers. Forward integration provides increased flexibility and enables closer relationships with major customers.
>
> Merck insourced pharmaceutical distribution by acquiring Medco, the largest U.S. drug-benefits manager. Merck-Medco (MM) became a lightning rod for accusations that Medco favored Merck products over lower-priced competitor drugs. Ten years after acquisition, Merck dissolved MM.

OUTSOURCING

Outsourcing is the opposite of insourcing — the firm engages other firms to undertake activities it previously conducted in-house. With outsourcing, the firm can better focus resources on delivering customer value and securing differential advantage. Firms outsource a wide range of activities — managing information systems and technology infrastructure, accounts payable, benefits management and payroll, and procurement.

A common contemporary outsourcing aspect is *offshoring* — contracting with non-U.S-based firms. A common area is customer service operations. We're sure many readers have called a help desk and spoken with someone in India, Malaysia, or the Philippines. Cost reduction typically drives offshoring, but partners in different time zones can also provide scalable, flexible staffing. Quality control is important, especially when customer care is involved; Capital One dropped Wipro's outbound telemarketing service for quality reasons.[57]

Some home electronics firms like Apple and HP focus major internal efforts on R&D, design, and marketing, but outsource manufacturing. Boeing mainly assembles aircraft; contractors (often foreign) produce airplane parts like the fuselage and wings. Downsides include:

- **Manufacturing.** Outsourced suppliers may also outsource, leading to a difficult-to-manage fragmented supply chain; quality is a serious issue. Delivery delays for Boeing's Dreamliner was largely due to excessive outsourcing.
- **Marketing.** The outsourced supplier absorbs the firm's technological expertise; the supplier could supply a competitor, or itself become a strong competitor, like Taiwan's Acer and Asustek (PCs), and HTC (cell phones).[58]

ACQUISITION

We learned earlier that the firm can use **acquisitions** — individual business units or entire firms, to gain competences that provide customer value and secure differential advantage. Generally, growth by acquisition has a speed advantage — the firm gains immediate access to new products and/or markets. The firm also gains supporting infrastructure — human resources, operational capabilities, and systems and processes.[59] Firms that grow extensively by acquisition include Cisco, GE, J&J, Microsoft, and Oracle. Former IBM CEO Lou Gerstner said:

> *IBM made 90 acquisitions during my tenure. The most successful were those that fit neatly into an organic growth plan. IBM's purchase of Informix is a great example. We were neck-and-neck with Oracle in the database business, and Informix, another database company, had lost its momentum and market leadership. We didn't need to buy Informix to get into the database business or to shore up a weak position. However, we did acquire a set of customers more quickly and more efficiently than we could have following a go-it-alone strategy.*[60]

To broaden its product line, eBay made more than $6 billion of acquisitions — Baazee.com, Bill Me Later, Brands4friends, EachNet, GSI, Half.com, iBazar, Kurant (Prostores), Marktplaats.nl, Paypal, Rent.com, Shopping.com, Skype (acquired by Microsoft), Stubhub, Stumbleupon, and Tradera.[61] Pfizer acquired Warner-Lambert and its cholesterol-lowering drug Lipitor, taken daily by more than 10 million people in the U.S.[62]

But acquisitions are no panacea. Acquiring successful firms/business units can be expensive; marrying the cultures of acquired and acquiring firms/businesses may also be difficult, especially when the acquirer is well established and the acquiree is younger and entrepreneurial.[63] Uncertainty and delays can also diminish an acquisition's value:

> General Mills (GenM) took 18 months to complete its Pillsbury acquisition from Diageo. During this period, Diageo cut back marketing efforts; retailers complained about service reductions. Many Pillsbury salespeople resigned, unsure of their futures. By the time GenM completed the merger, rivals had cut severely into Pillsbury's market positions. While GenM was distracted, Kellogg launched many new cereal products and increased market share.

Acquisitions may improve margins via employee layoffs and other economies when integrating corporate staffs, purchasing, R&D, sales forces, warehousing, and other functions; Pfizer reduced costs by $1 billion following the Wyeth takeover. But losing employees at an acquired firm can be a significant issue. Credit Suisse First Boston (CSFB) acquired DLJ from AXA for $13 billion; rival Swiss bank UBS quickly hired away 20 percent of DLJ's Los Angeles-based investment bankers. Cisco believes employees are the most significant asset it acquires and works especially hard to retain them by offering opportunity and freedom for creativity.

Some acquisitions add value; some do not. Value creation depends on the specific acquisition, but we can usefully distinguish between two very different types:

Marketing Exercise

Develop a table in which you assess the pros and cons of each method of implementing a strategy for growth.

MAJOR ACQUISITIONS. These multi-million-dollar acquisitions often make the headlines: Alcan's acquisition of Pechiney (aluminum) and BHP's acquisition of Alcan; AOL/Time Warner; Daimler-Benz/Chrysler, Delta Airlines/Northwest, HP/Palm, United Airlines/Continental, and Boston Scientific's bidding war with J&J for Guidant. But bigger is not always better; many business leaders and scholars have spoken out against these types of acquisitions. They assert that CEO hubris often drives $100 million-plus acquisitions.[64] Academic studies suggest that 70 percent of acquisitions are dilutive for the acquiring firm's shareholders, and that *in the heat of the chase* acquirers typically overpay.[65] Sir George Bull (former Diageo CEO) asserts that **organic growth** (internal development) creates greater value for shareholders, and that acquisitions often destroy value. Eli Lilly (pharmaceuticals) reduced the accounting (book) value of its distribution arm (McKesson) by $2.4 billion; given the $4.1 billion acquisition price, this was a stark admission that Lilly had overpaid.

Government oversight on large acquisitions can cause major realignments of products and markets. Glaxo Wellcome (GW) and SmithKline Beecham (SKB) completed a $68 billion merger to form GlaxoSmithKline (GSK), the world's second-largest pharmaceutical firm. To pass *regulatory muster*, SKB sold rights to Kytril (chemotherapy) and Famvir (herpes). GSK also had to resolve its dominant market position for anti-smoking drugs — Nicorette gum, NicoDerm patches, and prescription drug Zyban.

Marketing Question

A startup biotech firm has a single R&D project that promises to produce a product that will significantly reduce the incidence of skin cancer. How would you advise this firm to proceed in drug development and marketing?

SMALL *FILL-IN* ACQUISITIONS. Small *fill-in* acquisitions complement an existing strategy. Amazon was unsuccessful in selling footwear online, so it acquired Zappos.com (leading online footwear retailer). IBM's experience (previous page) exemplifies this type of acquisition. Research suggests that modest acquisitions are the most successful[66]: Small acquisitions are easier to implement, and acquirers may get good deals. A firm making many small acquisitions gains experience; does a better job of identifying candidates, managing bids, and integrating acquired entities. Cisco and Oracle are other good examples of firms making many small acquisitions.

STRATEGIC ALLIANCE

Generally, **strategic alliances** address poor product-company fit and/or poor company-market fit without the capital investment and risks inherent in acquisitions. A good alliance partner complements firm strengths and/or compensates for firm weakness; the combined entity is stronger than either firm acting alone. Nokia formed a strategic partnership with Microsoft to use Windows 7 software as its smart phone platform. Other popular alliances are between small, innovative firms and well-established firms with strong marketing, good customer reputations, and deep pockets. BMS has several successful alliances: Other firms make basic drug discoveries; BMS conducts final development and marketing. IBM and P&G also have successful alliances:

> IBM's software group has many strategic alliances with application software specialists like Siebel Systems and SAP. Alliances add billions of dollars in incremental revenues from hardware, services, database programs, and middleware.[67]
>
> P&G has successfully launched several new products developed by strategic alliances and from buying/licensing technology. Included are Glad Press'n Seal (supersticky food wrap), Mr. Clean Magic Eraser (spot remover), Olay Regenerist (anti-aging cream), and Swiffer Duster (microfiber picker-upper).

Some alliances embrace many firms. Airline industry alliances allow travelers one-stop shopping for international trips; correspondingly, alliance members secure customers. Star Alliance comprises almost 30 airlines including Air Canada, Lufthansa, Singapore, and United; the somewhat smaller SkyTeam includes Aeroflot, Air France, Delta, and KLM; OneWorld members include American, British Airways, Cathay Pacific, Japan Airlines, and Quantas.

Strategic alliances can be an attractive way to secure needed resources. But like acquisitions, strategic alliances are no panacea; many fail due to changed objectives by one or more partners, incompatible organizational cultures, insufficient resources, lack of planning, and/or managerial attention.[68] What appears attractive in theory can be difficult to execute in practice.

LICENSING AND TECHNOLOGY PURCHASE

Licensing and technology purchase are alternative ways to access technology developed by others. Firms seeking technologies should execute a rigorous search process. In licensing, the licensor owns the technology; the licensee typically pays a minimum royalty (fixed payment regardless of use) plus an earned royalty rate based on volume (units/dollars) or profits. Technology purchasers typically pay a fixed price to own the technology. In both cases, the acquiring firm avoids the risks and expenses of R&D, but may pay a high price to secure successful new technology. Forest Laboratories employs a licensing strategy that enhances its product portfolio and market presence[69]:

> Forest Laboratories (FL) licenses, develops, and sells drugs developed by small pharmaceutical companies. FL's drug portfolio includes Aerobid (asthma), Celexa (depression), Infasurf (respiratory distress syndrome in premature babies), and Tiazac (angina and hypertension).

Conversely, the firm may grow revenues and profits by selling or licensing its technology. Sometimes firms sell products directly in favored markets but licence technology to gain market access for other uses, or for the same use in different geographies. Monsanto employs this approach for genetically modified seeds. Firms owning unexploited technologies can earn significant revenues from these unused assets. Alcatel-Lucent earns hundreds of millions of dollars annually from its patent portfolio; IBM earns billions.

EQUITY INVESTMENT

Many firms augment internal development efforts by making equity investments — taking partial ownership in startups. Sometimes firms form or *incubate* startups by spinning off their own successful product development efforts. Typically, the firm retains the ability to increase its equity position later. Xerox's program was highly successful:

In the 1970s and 1980s, Xerox's Palo Alto Research Center (PARC) developed many new technologies that Xerox failed to commercialize.[70] Xerox Technology Ventures (XTV) (formed 1989) invested in firms focusing on Xerox-related technologies — electronic publishing, document processing, electronic imaging, workstation and computer peripherals, software, and office automation. XTV earned a net internal rate of return greater than 50 percent.[71]

IMPLEMENTING GROWTH STRATEGIES IN THE MODERN CORPORATION

KEY IDEA

➤ Increasingly, firms employ multiple approaches for securing growth.

We learned that the components of a strategy for growth are *vision, mission, growth path*, and *timing of entry*. Together, these elements form a set of lenses the firm can use to approach markets and identify, generate, and decide to invest (or not) in opportunities. Each entry strategy demands quite different capabilities for success. Maintaining contrasting growth strategies in a single business unit is very difficult.[72] No full-service airline has operated a successful low-cost carrier! Discount broker Schwab stumbled badly when trying to serve both discount clients and high-net-worth clients through its U.S. Trust acquisition.

Today, leading firms use multiple approaches to implement growth strategies, often built on *repeatability*. These firms leverage skills in internal development, in/outsourcing, acquisitions, strategic alliances, and/or equity investment; hence, they are better able to address challenges and results are more predictable. P&G (p. 188) and J&J are good examples. J&J invests significantly in internal R&D and regularly introduces several hundred new products annually developed in its own laboratories. Yet, J&J purchased Cougar Biotechnology ($1 billion) and Pfizer's consumer health business ($16 billion), acquiring such brands as Listerine, Sudafed, Bengay, and Rolaids. J&J also paid well over $1 billion for research alliances with Elan Pharmaceuticals (Ireland) and Crucel (The Netherlands).

Marketing Question

What other messages did you glean from this chapter?

KEY MESSAGES

Marketing's first imperative is to determine and recommend which markets to address. A marketing perspective should infuse critical strategic decisions — marketing should focus on two areas:
- Identify potential opportunities.
- Provide marketing input for other strategic actions the firm is contemplating.

A systematic approach to developing, selecting, and implementing opportunities has four elements:
- Strategy for growth — frameworks to help the firm decide which businesses to be in/not in:
  - Vision — description of an ideal future state for the firm/business unit.
  - Mission — directly guides the firm's search for opportunity.
  - Growth path — a focused approach to identifying opportunities, trades off return and risk.
  - Timing of entry — market-entry options related to stage of the product life cycle.

- Screening criteria — a method for evaluating individual opportunities. Key considerations:
  - Objectives — including growth, risk, stability, and flexibility.
  - Compatibility (fit) — product-market fit, product-company fit, company-market fit.
  - Core competence — using special capabilities to achieve differential advantage.
  - Synergy — 2 + 2 = 5.
  - Contribution to the venture portfolio.

CONTINUES ON NEXT PAGE

- Implementation – specific actions to implement the firm's growth strategy:
  - Internal development — new products and services developed via firm efforts.
  - Insourcing — capturing greater value-added, either upstream or downstream.
  - Outsourcing — engaging other firms to conduct needed activities.
  - Acquisition — purchasing an entire firm or business unit.
  - Strategic alliance — an agreement with a partner firm to jointly exploit an opportunity.
  - Licensing and technology purchase — options to access technology developed by others.
  - Equity investment — taking ownership positions in startups.

VIDEOS AND AUDIOS

Marketing Imperative 1   a701 🎧

a701

QUESTIONS FOR STUDY AND DISCUSSION

Can you answer the questions implied by this chapter's learning objectives? Check!

1. Google raised large sums of money by going public and making a secondary equity offering. From publicly available data — using Google's search feature, develop a *strategy for growth* for Google. What should be Google's vision, mission, growth path, and timing of entry? Identify growth options for Google. Define and set standards for measuring Google's success.

2. From your knowledge of business, identify current-day examples of pioneer, follow-the-leader, segmenter, and me-too entry strategies.

3. In the 1950s, a small company named Haloid decided to back Chester Carlson, an inventor. His dry-copy invention — xerography — changed the world. IBM, 3M, and Kodak each turned down Carlson's proposal. As a 1950s corporate executive with one of these firms, using the concepts in this chapter, what decision would you have made? Why?

4. American, British Airways, Delta, United, and Virgin Atlantic compete on North Atlantic routes. Round-trip, business-class fares list for $8,000 to $9,000, but major corporate buyers may pay as little as $3,000. In late 2005, Eos and MAXJet started offering lower-priced, all-business-class, New York-to-London (Stansted Airport) flights. MAXJet priced its flights from $4,000 to $1,500 for bulk purchases, Eos prices were somewhat higher, but less than the majors. In 2008, both Eos and MAXJet filed for bankruptcy. Did Eos and MAXJet identify a market opportunity? How do you assess Eos' and MAXJet's strategies?

5. Founded in 1998, by 2008, eBay had merchandising volume of about $70 billion and profits approaching $2 billion. What accounts for eBay's success? How should eBay ensure continued growth and profits?

6. What is the marketing significance of the question, "What business are we in?" How does the answer help decide what markets to address?

7. Select a product in which you are interested. Alternatively, consider this book — *Managing Marketing in the 21st Century.* Lay out a strategy for growth — vision, mission, growth path, and timing of entry.

v801

IMPERATIVE 2

*Identify and Target
Market Segments*

CHAPTER 8

MARKET SEGMENTATION AND TARGETING v801 📺

To access O-codes, go to **www.ocodes.com**

LEARNING OBJECTIVES

When you have completed this chapter, you will be able to:

- Deconstruct a market into readily distinguishable customer groups.
- Recognize differences between market segments and customer segments.
- Select a market segmentation scheme to better understand market opportunities.
- Understand needs and preferences common to customers in each market segment.
- Develop criteria for constructing *good* market segments.
- Assess identifying characteristics for market segments.
- Address several complex issues in developing and engaging market segments.
- Decide which segments to target for marketing effort.
- Understand how different size firms should approach market segmentation.

OPENING CASE: MARRIOTT HOTELS, RESORTS, AND SUITES

In 1985, Marriott Hotels, Resorts, and Suites was a domestic (U.S.) mid- to large-size hotel chain, managing 67,034 rooms at 160 properties. Marriott decided to enhance traveler value by segmenting the market, then targeting selected segments each with a different brand. Then as now, Marriott was the flagship brand. Each new brand supports Marriott's overall brand identity — a commitment to superior customer service — and trains employees to have a passion for service. Employees:

- *Do whatever it takes to take care of customers.*
- *Pay extraordinary attention to detail.*
- *Take pride in their physical surroundings.*
- *Use their creativity to find new ways to meet the needs of customers.*

Marriott believes all customers require a base service level but that customers differ in their willingness to pay for different levels of comfort and luxury. Management also knows that many customers stay a few nights, but a growing number, like business people on assignment, require accommodations for several weeks. Recognizing the varying needs of hotel customers, Marriott was the first major hotel chain to base its strategy on market segmentation. Marriott grew new brands organically, but implemented its strategy in part by acquisition.

Marriott's flagship brand continues to target customers needing fine restaurants, meeting rooms, athletic facilities, and other upscale amenities.[1] But Marriott added several additional brands addressing different segments:

- **Courtyard** — *a moderately priced hotel providing some amenities, like an exercise room and a restaurant for breakfast for business travelers.*
- **Edition Hotels** — *a personal, intimate, individualized, and unique lodging experience.*
- **ExecuStay** — *furnished apartments for stays of 30 days or more.*
- **Fairfield Inn & Suites** — *an inexpensively priced, high quality hotel easily accessible by car, on or near the U.S. main interstate highway system.*
- **Renaissance Hotels** — *an international hotel with upscale amenities.*
- **Residence Inn** — *an extended-stay hotel for job relocation, job assignment, and government contracting.*
- **Ritz-Carlton** — *the ultimate in luxury hotels in urban centers.*
- **SpringHill Suites** — *an all-suites hotel at an upper-moderate price.*
- **TownePlace Suites** — *similar to Residence Inn, but lower priced.*

Each Marriott brand has a distinct personality and style. Marriott works hard to communicate the essence and strength of each brand so that target customers know what to expect. There is some customer crossover, but each brand focuses on a defined market segment. Internal competition is small.

CASE QUESTION

How do you assess Marriott's approach to segmenting the hotel market? Can you think of alternative approaches that may present marketing opportunities?

Marriott has achieved extraordinary results from its segmentation and targeting strategy. The Courtyard brand manages more rooms than the entire firm managed in 1985. Total number of rooms managed has increased to 600,000 rooms at 3,800 properties. About 20 percent of Marriott's rooms are outside the U.S. Marriott is a profitable firm with revenues well in excess of $10 billion.

Market segments and market segmentation are fundamental marketing concepts. Customers in a market either have a variety of different needs, or have similar needs with different priorities. A **market segment** is a subset of the total market that comprises a group of customers with similar (homogeneous) need profiles, seeking similar sets of benefits and values, with similar levels of priority. **Market segmentation** is the process of grouping together actual and potential customers in a market for the purpose of forming market segments.

A specifically designed market offer satisfies one market segment; a different market segment requires a different market offer. To design and produce effective market offers, the firm must understand each segment's need profile. A firm intent on serving a large market like snack foods must make several market offers, at least one per market segment, to meet varying customer preferences. Typically, a single offer, like potato chips, fails to satisfy the many diverse customers who purchase *snack foods*.

Because customers have different need profiles, marketers must complete three separate, but related, strategic marketing tasks:

Note an important distinction between these tasks. *Identifying* market segments is creative and analytic. *Targeting* market segments requires a strategic decision — the firm applies resources to some market segments and ignores others. Identifying and targeting the *right* market segments is a crucial strategic marketing task.

Section 4 — Chapters 12 through 21 — focuses on implementing the market strategy.

KEY IDEA

➤ Critical strategic marketing decisions are:
- Identify market segments
- Target market segments
- Develop market segment strategy

THE CHANGING VIEW

OLD WAY	NEW WAY
Crude segmentation	Precise segmentation
Databases poorly developed	Databases central to segmentation
Few large segments	Many small segments — tend to segments-of-one
Intuition-driven segmentation	Analytically driven segmentation
Low levels of analytic expertise	Increasingly sophisticated analyses
Market segments based mainly on demographics	Market segments based on many types of variables
Segmentation applied mainly in consumer packaged goods	Segmentation in B2B and B2C, public and non-profit, nation-states, politics, personal careers
Segmentation focused primarily on consumers	Segmentation extends to multiple customer levels and other company stakeholders

Two couples visit an electrical appliance superstore — each couple wants a kitchen range. Presumably they have similar needs — but let's look more closely. Couple A's new house will be built in six months — they are evaluating appliances to install in a high-tech kitchen. Couple B just received a call from the babysitter. A broken water pipe flooded the kitchen, the range is ruined, and what should she do about the children's dinner? These couples have different needs and priorities. Both need ranges, but there's a big difference between a dream home and an emergency replacement!

THE MARKET SEGMENTATION PROCESS

Most National car rental customers are corporate executives — most Alamo customers are leisure travelers. National and Alamo's parent company combined their operations — airport counters, buses, rental agents, and automobiles. Dual Alamo/National logos were ubiquitous. Customers had difficulty distinguishing the brands. Complaints doubled, especially from National's customers who paid 10 to 20 percent more than Alamo's customers.[2]

Market segmentation is a conceptual and analytic process critical for developing and implementing effective market strategies. In the market-segmentation process, the firm groups actual and potential customers in a market into various **market segments**. The firm then chooses which segments to **target** for effort. The firm must *position* itself in each target segment (segmentation, targeting, positioning [STP]) and develop a *market segment strategy*. When the segment strategy is set, the firm designs a suitable market offer.

Figure 8.1 describes the process of designing and implementing market offers for each target segment. By executing the process well, the firm:

- Secures better insight into the market, customers, competitors, company, and complementers — in particular, customer needs, and forms stronger planning assumptions.

- Develops a clearer focus on market strategy by targeting specific customer groups.

- Identifies opportunities to customize for target segments.

- Designs better offers comprising product, promotion, distribution, and price.

- Secures superior differential advantage and greater customer satisfaction and loyalty.

- Uses resources more efficiently and earns higher profitability.

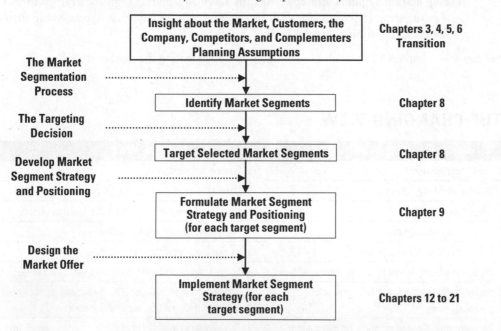

FIGURE 8.1

SEGMENTATION, TARGETING, AND POSITIONING

The fundamental premise underlying market segmentation is: In any broadly defined market, customer need profiles are heterogeneous (different).[3] Customers have different needs and/or different priorities of needs. They seek different benefits and values based on these differing need profiles. The segmentation task is to divide the market into several discrete groups of customers, each with relatively homogeneous (similar) need profiles. These customer need profiles differ from segment to segment, so an individual customer falls into one, but only one segment.[4] Customers requiring the rugged strength of a Panasonic Toughbook are quite different from those attracted to mini-laptops like Asustek's Eee PC! But Alamo/National's parent

KEY IDEA

➤ The market segmentation process identifies groups of customers. When segmentation is done well, customers within a segment have similar need profiles. Customers in different segments have different need profiles.

(previous boxed insert) does not seem to understand that its market comprises two quite different segments.[5]

Market segmentation is often a compromise. At one extreme, the firm develops one strategy, one positioning, and one offer for the entire market — mass marketing. This one-size-fits-all approach is the most efficient, lowest-cost way to address a broad market. But customer need profiles are typically heterogeneous, so many customers would be unsatisfied. At the other extreme, the firm develops a unique or specialized offer for each customer. Such customization ensures a good match between customer needs and the firm's market offer. But firms rarely earn sufficient revenues to offset development and implementation costs. Market segmentation operates between these extremes. The firm identifies homogeneous groups of customers — market segments, with similar need profiles: The firm targets one or more segments, and develops specific strategies, positionings, and offers to satisfy the needs of customers in those segments.

LEVELS OF SEGMENTATION

Are you a *Kinda*, *Sorta*, or *Alota*? San Francisco startup sock firm LittleMissMatched (LMM) identified a unique customer need in *tweens* (around 11 years old) — desire to resist fashion orthodoxy. LMM offers this segment color-drenched, mismatched socks in packs of three.

Within the *tweens* market segment, LMM identified and advises three finer-grained customer segments. *Kinda* customers are conservative — pick socks from the same color wave, creating a slightly off-kilter look. The *Alota* segment is wildest — mix and match colors, patterns, and styles. *Sortas* are in between. LMM's promotional book, *My MissMatched Life*, celebrates the joys of nonconformity.

Segmentation forms smaller, more discrete groups out of a whole. The firm chooses a broad market to address — Marketing Imperative 1 — then identifies several market segments. Within any single market segment, the firm may segment further, forming *customer* segments. Some practitioners define the first-level grouping as market segmentation, and the finer-grained, second-level segmentation as customer segmentation.

LMM identified the *tweens* market segment — the core need was a desire to resist fashion orthodoxy. LMM also identified three customer segments, defined by level of resistance, *Kinda*, *Sorta*, and *Alota*. The important idea: Segmentation can operate at different levels as the firm decides where to place its marketing efforts.

Marketing Question

Why would a startup like LMM create customer segments? Do its market segmentation and customer segmentation provide valuable insight?

We reinforce this idea with a simple example. Suppose half of the students in your class prefer *hot tea*, and half prefer *iced tea*. Figure 8.2 (top) shows a tea supplier that does not understand this segmentation and so offers the best *average* product — *warm tea*. Without alternatives, students wanting tea will purchase *warm tea*. They may desire *hot tea* or *iced tea*, but at least *warm tea* is tea!

Suppose a new supplier understands the segmentation. The supplier offers *hot tea* — the *hot-tea* students switch from *warm tea*. If a third supplier enters with *iced tea*, the *iced-tea* students also switch. The *warm-tea* supplier quickly loses customers because its competitors are more insightful about market segmentation.

How should the original supplier respond? The *hot-tea* and *iced-tea* suppliers focus on different segments and are doing just fine. One response is to segment at an even deeper level. Some students may like *sweetened tea*; others like *unsweetened* tea. Figure 8.2 (bottom) shows how to deconstruct the market into four segments — *hot sweetened tea*, *hot unsweetened tea*, *iced sweetened tea*, and *iced unsweetened tea*. A focus on one or more of these segments better satisfies customer needs. The firm may have to creatively segment the market at increasingly finer levels to beat competitors.

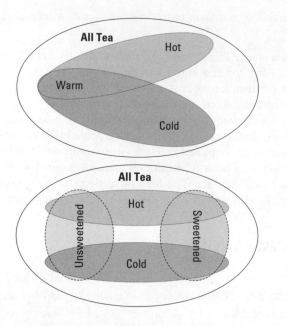

FIGURE 8.2

THE BENEFITS OF FINER-GRAINED SEGMENTATION: A TEA MARKET EXAMPLE

> ### Marketing Question
>
> What firms demonstrate the *warm-tea* syndrome — address markets generally, even though customer groups have different need profiles?

 KEY IDEA

> ➤ The best approach for forming market segments is to group customers based on need profiles. The firm should then use descriptor (segmentation) variables to identify different segments.

DEVELOPING MARKET SEGMENTS

The firm can approach the market segmentation process from two directions: **Customer needs** first or **candidate descriptor (segmentation) variables** first. The firm can also use *qualitative* or *quantitative* approaches.

CUSTOMER NEEDS FIRST. The firm identifies differing customer need profiles, then uses these profiles to form groups. Customers within each group have relatively homogeneous (similar) need profiles, but the various groups have heterogeneous (different) profiles. The firm's second task is to select descriptor (segmentation) variables that identify these groups.

> AT&T's data system organization identified three market segments based on complexity of customer communications needs:
>
> - Tier 1 segment — needs satisfied by common *off-the-shelf* products.
>
> - Tier 2 segment — needs satisfied by *off-the-shelf* products plus some options.
>
> - Tier 3 segment — requires tailored solutions.

AT&T's three segments seem sensible — each segment's needs differ from the other segments. AT&T's challenge is to identify distinguishing customer characteristics in each segment. Tier 1: What characteristics define customers that want *off-the-shelf* products? Are these small companies or large companies? Do they compete in specific industries? Are they located in specific geographic areas?

Sometimes the link between customer needs and distinguishing characteristics is straightforward. Table 8.1 shows that the benefits and values consumers want from skin-care products depends on their age.

> ### Marketing Question
>
> Review the data in Table 8.1. Suppose your firm decided to target the 14–18 and 40–49 market segments. How would you attract customers in each segment? How would the offers differ? How are the three over-40 segments similar?

TABLE 8.1

MARKET SEGMENTS
IN THE FEMALE
SKIN-CARE MARKET:
RANKING THE ORDER
OF IMPORTANCE OF
CUSTOMER NEED/
REQUIRED BENEFITS
AND VALUES BY
MARKET SEGMENT

Customer Need/Required Benefits and Values	Age-Based Market Segments					
	14-18	19-29	30-39	40-49	50-64	65 and over
Beauty	5	4	**1**	2	2	3
Confidence	2	2	3	3	3	4
Economy	4	5	7	7	6	5
Health	6	6	4	4	4	2
Sexual Allure	·3	**1**	2	5	5	6
Status	**1**	3	6	6	7	7
Youthfulness	7	7	5	**1**	**1**	**1**

CANDIDATE DESCRIPTOR (SEGMENTATION) VARIABLES FIRST. The firm uses candidate descriptor variables to construct customer groups. Then it searches for homogeneous (similar) need profiles within each group, and heterogeneous (different) need profiles across groups. If the firm cannot find *good* need profiles — similarity within groups and differences across groups, it tries again with different descriptors. Table 8.2 shows sample **candidate descriptor variables** in four categories — geographic, demographic, behavioral, and socio-psychological.

TABLE 8.2

EXAMPLES OF
CANDIDATE
DESCRIPTOR
(SEGMENTATION)
VARIABLES

Variable Type	Examples of Descriptor Variables
Geography	Country, region, county size, city or Standard Metropolitan Statistical Area (SMSA)[6] size, population density, climate
Demography	Consumers — age, education, family life-cycle stage, family size, gender, income, language, national origin, occupation, race, religion, social class, wealth Organizations — balance sheet items, firm size, growth, industry, profitability, legal entity, length of time at location, number of years in business
Behavioral	Composition/type of purchase decision, decision-making practice, decision-making unit, new or existing user, use occasion,[7] user situation. Specific organizational variables: procurement organization — centralized/decentralized, and power structure — like engineering dominated, financially dominated.
Socio-psychological	Consumers — attitudes; life stage; lifestyle characteristics like activities, interests, and opinions (AIO); personality (ambitiousness, authoritarianism, autonomy, compulsiveness, conservatism, gregariousness, leadership); sexual orientation. Organizations — inward/outward orientation and organizational climate and culture.

Table 8.3 shows examples of customer groups formed with these descriptor variables.

TABLE 8.3

EXAMPLES OF
DESCRIPTOR
(SEGMENTATION)
VARIABLES AND
GROUPS

Variable Type	Variable	Examples of Groups
Demography (consumer)	Education	Grade school or less, some high school, high school graduate, some college, college graduate
Demography (organization)	Firm size	*Fortune* 500, *Fortune* 501 to 1000, sales > $100 million, sales $50 to $100 million, sales < $50 million
Socio-psychological (consumer)	Life stage	Single, just married, married with children, divorced with children, empty-nester couple, empty-nesters with grandchildren, widow/widower[8]

Geography and demography are popular categories of descriptor (segmentation) variables.[9] Many retailers like Macy's cater to local tastes. MTV frequently uses country or geography when tailoring customer offers: MTV operates 38 separate nationally focused channels like MTV Romania and MTV Indonesia. In the Philippines, local hamburger chain Jollibee (69 percent market share) outsells McDonald's (16 percent) by using national origin and demographics to better meet Filipinos' needs. Jollibee's stores in Asia and California target customers of Filipino descent. Successful uses of geography, ethnic origin, and/or religion as descriptor (segmentation) variables include:

Geography, Ethnic Origin, and Religion as Descriptor (Segmentation) Variables

- Automobile distributor ACLN developed a $200 million business shipping used cars to North and West Africa.

- 65 percent of 35 million U.S. Hispanics are of Mexican descent. Banamex (Mexican bank) allows these customers to charge household appliances to U.S. credit cards for delivery in Mexico.

- P&G grew Gain to a $1 billion laundry detergent brand by recognizing the importance of fragrance to Hispanics.

- Pollo Campero is a Guatemalan fast-food franchise. At the Guatemala City airport, Guatemalan expatriates stock up before flying home, often buying hundreds of chicken pieces, sometimes for resale. Campero also has more than 300 stores in 13 countries (Latin America, Europe, India, Mid-East, China) and 15 U.S. states, to tap this market.

- SABMiller targets ethnic minorities by importing foreign brands to the U.S. In Chicago and other cities with large Polish communities, SABMiller offers the popular Polish beer, Tyskie.

- Samara Produce (SP) (southern California) grows high quality okra, chilies, opo squash, and daikon radishes. SP targets Indians, Pakistanis, and Bangladeshis in North America. SP ships vegetables to Chicago, New York, Toronto, Vancouver, and London.

- U.S. Muslims cluster in relatively few geographic areas. American Halal Meat (East Newark, NJ) slaughters animals according to Islamic teachings for butchers and restaurants serving Muslim customers.

Forming groups using geographic and demographic variables is relatively easy, but they may not be *good* market segments. Behavioral and socio-psychological variables are often more effective. Suppose a sneaker firm has four customers: male – 20 years, male – 40 years, female – 20 years, female – 40 years. How should the sneaker firm segment? By gender or by age? Neither may be effective. Suppose the 20-year-old male and the 40-year-old female exercise every day, but the 40-year-old male and the 20-year-old female exercise rarely. Grouping customers into two *lifestyle* segments — high exercise and low exercise may be far more effective. Figure 8.3 shows a pharmaceutical firm's attempt to segment the physician market using two variables. Each variable has two levels: *approach to treatment* — aggressive or conservative; *type of data* — relies on scientific evidence or relies on clinical experience. The firm formed four segments: *risk taker*, *hard headed*, *path finder*, and *tortoise*. The firm could easily identify physicians characterizing each segment; this approach and was far more effective than classifying by geography or demography.

The main problem of starting with candidate descriptor (segmentation) variables is that customer groups may not have distinct need profiles — descriptor variables do not produce segments at all. The marketer must repeat the process with other descriptor variable(s). The physician example shows that behavioral and/or socio-psychological variables may be more effective than geographic and demographic variables in forming *good* market segments. But assigning customers to market segments formed from behavioral and/or socio-psychological variables may be difficult. Generally, segmentation approaches that start with customer needs are preferable.

KEY IDEA

➤ Four categories of candidate descriptor (segmentation) variables can define market segments:

- Geographic
- Demographic
- Behavioral
- Socio-psychological

FIGURE 8.3

EXAMPLE OF
TWO-VARIABLE
SEGMENTATION
OF PHYSICIANS

Approach to Treatment

Type of Data	Aggressive	Conservative
Relies on scientific evidence	*Risk Taker*	*Hard Headed*
Relies on clinical experience	*Path Finder*	*Tortoise*

Marketing Question

How would you segment the market for dog food? Two possible approaches are:

1. Descriptors of dogs.
2. Need profiles of dog owners.

Which approach is easier? Which approach provides greater insight into the dog food market?

me601

METHODOLOGICAL APPROACHES TO FORMING SEGMENTS

Methodological approaches to forming market segments fall into two main categories:

QUALITATIVE. The segmentation task is highly judgmental, requiring significant conceptual skill. The firm's raw material is creative insight — Chapters 3, 4, 5, typically gained from field marketing research — Chapter 6, and/or customer relationship management (CRM) systems — Chapter 2. Table 8.1 shows a typical segmentation matrix formed in this manner.

QUANTITATIVE. Large-scale market segmentation studies use extensive customer survey data and sophisticated multivariate statistical techniques. A cluster analysis approach includes the following steps — Marketing Enrichment me601, pp. 8–9:

- Develop many statements (variables) about customer needs.
- Develop a set of questions (variables) that identify customers.
- Administer statements and questions to a random sample of current and potential customers.
- Analyze customer need responses by cluster analysis. Choose the number of clusters (segments) that form the *best* groupings of customer needs.
- Examine each customer cluster (segment) for identifying characteristics.

Mobil used a similar process to segment the gasoline market (pp. 202–203).[10]

The fundamental segmentation task is to link each segment's need profile to appropriate descriptor (segmentation) variables. If segmentation is done well, each segment has a well-defined need profile and is easily described by descriptor variables. Frequently, the firm makes several successive attempts to segment a market. As Figure 8.4 shows, each attempt uses customer need profiles and candidate descriptor variables; they converge somewhere in the middle.

Marketing Question

Many observers believe electric vehicles will gain a significant share of the automobile market. How would you segment the market for electric vehicles? What are the implications of your segmentation scheme for product design?

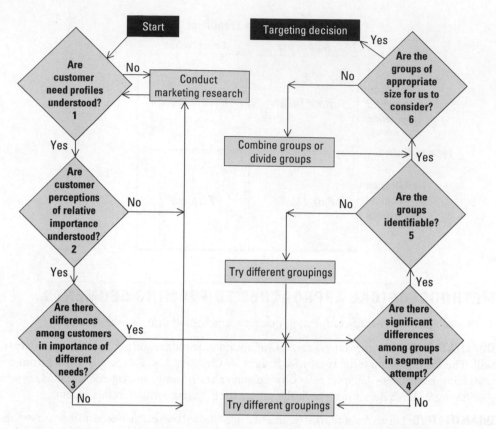

FIGURE 8.4

THE MARKET
SEGMENTATION
APPROACH

Market segmentation is a critical step in developing market strategy. Regardless, some firms approach the process as ritual, without a clear conviction of its strategic importance:

How *Not* to Approach Market Segmentation

That's the way we've always done it: Ignores market, customer, competitor, and complementer evolution. Because of change, segments that worked in the past may be obsolete.

That's the way data are available: Firms use secondary data from governments/trade associations. This approach implicitly assumes that the firm's segmentation method drove data-gathering: It did not. Also, because all competitors have access to the same data, the firm may not gain advantage through segmentation.

That's the way we're organized: Organization design often drives strategy for internally oriented firms. Externally oriented firms respond to environmental imperatives. Structure should follow strategy, not vice versa.

That's the way competitors do it: The firm accepts equivalence with competitors. Innovative segmentation can help achieve differential advantage. If the competitor's segmentation fits its capabilities, the firm is disadvantaged.

Segmentation at Thomson Financial

Traditionally, Thomson Financial (TF) segmented the information products market by sales channel — Figure 8.5A. A new end-user resegmentation, based on deeper customer insight, provided TF with a more actionable framework — Figure 8.5B. Figures 8.5A and 8.5B highlight TF's estimated competitive position by segment.[11]

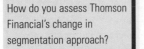

Marketing Question

How do you assess Thomson Financial's change in segmentation approach?

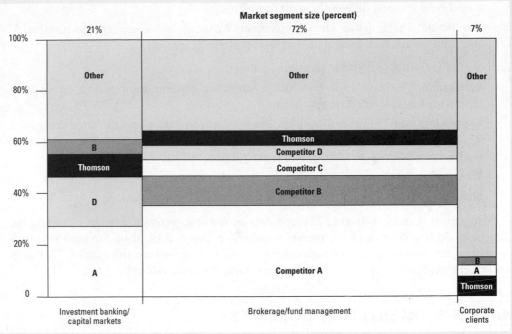

FIGURE 8.5A

THOMSON FINANCIAL: TRADITIONAL SEGMENTATION

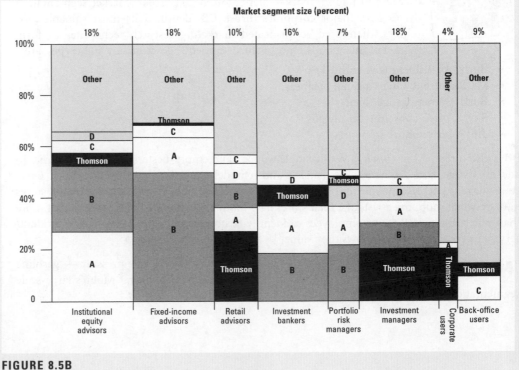

FIGURE 8.5B

THOMSON FINANCIAL: NEW END-USER SEGMENTATION

MARKET SEGMENTS

We just discussed the market segmentation process for developing market segments, but were we successful? **Good segments** are those the firm could target for marketing effort with a reasonable chance of success. So far, we focused on two important segmentation criteria:

- **Differentiated:** Customers in different segments have different need profiles. Accordingly, they should respond differently to market offers.
- **Identifiable:** The firm can identify customers by using descriptor (segmentation) variables and hence reach them with marketing offers.

Good market segments satisfy four additional criteria:

- **Accessible:** The firm can reach the segment via communications and distribution channels using cost-effective approaches.
- **Appropriate size:** Different firms like different size segments. Generally, large firms want large segments to justify their efforts and costs. By contrast, small firms like small segments so they can avoid large and powerful competitors.
- **Measurable:** The firm can measure important characteristics like size and growth.
- **Stable:** Customers stay in the segment for a reasonable period of time.

Marketers must remember that market segments are not *real, correct, incorrect,* or *unchanging.* Customers do not have market segment membership stamped on their foreheads! Market segments derive from appropriate data collection and analysis and creative insight. They help firms direct resources to those parts of the market where success is likely.

MARKET SEGMENTATION EXAMPLES

Segmentation schemes that major U.S. firms developed, and their targeting decisions include[13]:

 Best Buy (BB) is the leading U.S. consumer electronics retailer — revenues exceed $50 billion, market share around 20 percent. Market segmentation drives BB's major corporate thrust. BB identified its most valuable customers, then used sophisticated marketing research techniques to form market segments. BB's most valued segments, described by archetypes, are:

- **Barry:** An affluent tech enthusiast
- **Mr. Storefront:** Owns a small business
- **Buzz:** A young gadget fiend
- **Ray:** A price-conscious family guy
- **Jill:** A busy suburban mom

BB is also interested in *Carrie,* a young single woman, and empty-nesters *Helen* and *Charlie.* To address its five core segments, BB *centrizes* and remodels stores —about $600,000 per. *Barry* stores have expert salespeople and a separate department for home-theater systems; *Jill* stores have personal shopping assistants; *Buzz* stores have many video games. Some stores target more than one segment. BB trains employees to identify customers by segment and make product/service offers that research shows they value.[14]

Mobil Before the Exxon merger, Mobil's profits were under severe pressure — gasoline prices were low and Mobil was not the low-cost producer.[15] Mobil's large-scale segmentation study identified five segments of gasoline buyers — Table 8.4.

Marketing Question

When the magazine *Mirabella* ceased publication, *The New York Times* noted that *Mirabella* was aimed at "women who are no longer 24 years old, who care passionately about literary criticism and serious articles about, say, contemporary philosophers — and equally as passionately about where to buy those just adorable hot-pink leather pants."[12] Where did *Mirabella* fail in its segment criteria?

KEY IDEA

➤ Criteria for *good* segments:
- Differentiated
- Identifiable
- Accessible
- Appropriate size
- Measurable
- Stable

KEY IDEA

➤ The market segmentation process may combine creativity and sophisticated data analysis.

....

TABLE 8.4

MARKET SEGMENTS OF GASOLINE BUYERS IDENTIFIED BY MOBIL

Segment	Size (% of all buyers)	Description
Generation F3 — Food, Fuel, Fast	27	Upwardly mobile men and women; half under 25; constantly on the go; drive a lot and snack heavily from the convenience store.
Homebodies	21	Usually housewives shuttling children around during the day; use whatever gasoline station is in town or along their travel routes.
Price Shoppers	20	Generally neither loyal to a brand nor a gas station; rarely buy premium; frequently on tight budgets; historically Mobil's target customers.
Road Warriors	16	Generally higher-income, middle-aged men; drive 25,000 to 50,000 miles per year; buy premium gas with a credit card; purchase sandwiches and drinks from the convenience store, sometimes use the car wash.
True Blues	16	Usually men and women with moderate to high incomes; brand loyal and sometimes gas station loyal; frequently buy premium gasoline and pay cash.

These five segments satisfied criteria for *good* segments. Mobil targeted three segments — Road Warriors, True Blues, and Generation F3. Mobil's actions were:

- Upgrade convenience stores so they would become *destination* convenience stores.
- Speed up refueling by introducing the Mobil Speed Pass, based on new technology.
- Introduce widespread customer-service training for employees.
- Develop a direct marketing program to recognize and encourage customer loyalty.

Mobil improved market share and profits in a highly competitive mature market. When Exxon and Mobil merged, ExxonMobil adopted Mobil's pioneering approach.

 Ford uses birth year to form six truck-market segments — Table 8.5. Ford targeted baby boomers with its F-150 pick-up, narrowing and lengthening the cab so it was more comfortable to drive. Ford hit baby boomers' *hot buttons* — the F-150 was a best seller.

....

TABLE 8.5

MARKET SEGMENTS AT FORD MOTOR COMPANY

Segment	Born Between	Description
Depression Kids	1920-1934	Attitudes formed during the Depression and World War II — plan for a rainy day and are status-seekers.
Quiet Generation	1935-1945	Childhood of peace and prosperity made for an extended period of innocence; little parental pressure and lots of free time — like movies with humble heroes.
Baby Boomers	1946-1964	The first TV generation; indulged by parents and pushed to win — seek instant gratification; want an image of being smart purchasers.
Lost Generation	1965-1969	Disenfranchised; grew up in the boomers' shadow; hurt more by parental divorce — wait for life to get better and are not affluent.
Birth Dearth	1970-1977	Grew up in the rich 1980s and acquired a taste for excellence, but their jobs won't support it — practical, focused, and future-oriented.
Baby Boomlet	1978-present	Children of boomers — strong desire for the affluence of their parents' generation; unlikely to have as much money.

Marketing Question

Think about your grandparents, parents, peers, and other friends and acquaintances. Do Ford's segments describe them well? If not, how could Ford have segmented differently?

....

STANDARDIZED MARKET SEGMENTS

In the previous examples, individual firms identified and developed market segments. By contrast, some B2C firms competing in mature markets use **standardized segments** based on established buying trends, habits, and customer needs. The best-known approach is *PRIZM* (Nielsen Claritas), a U.S. segmentation system.

 The PRIZM scheme, based largely on income, urbanity, and life stage, comprises 66 clusters organized as 14 social groups: Affluentials, City Centers, Country Comfort, Elite Suburbs, Inner Suburbs, Landed

Gentry, Micro-City Blues, Middle America, Middleburbs, Midtown Mix, Rustic Living, Second City Society, Urban Uptown, and Urban Cores.[16]

We illustrate PRIZM's clusters with the Rustic Living social group — six mostly white clusters (some ethnic diversity), predominantly owners of single-family homes:

- **Back Country Folks.** Poor, over 55 years old, living in older, modest-sized homes and manufactured housing in remote farm communities.

- **Bedrock America.** Young, economically challenged, modestly educated, sprawling families with blue-collar jobs in small, isolated towns. One quarter live in mobile homes; one third hasn't finished high school. Spend time fishing, hunting, hiking, and camping.

- **Crossroads Villagers.** Middle-aged, blue-collar couples and families with rural lifestyles. High school-educated, with lower-middle incomes and modest housing; one-quarter live in mobile homes. Somewhat self-reliant; spend time fishing, gardening, and hunting.

- **Golden Ponds.** High school-educated seniors, singles, and couples, living in small apartments in small towns on less than $25,000 per annum; one in five resides in a nursing home. Daily life is often a succession of sedentary activities like reading, watching TV, playing bingo, and doing craft projects.

- **Old Milltowns.** Retired singles and couples from once-thriving mining and manufacturing towns living on downscale incomes in pre-1960 homes and apartments. Enjoy gardening, sewing, socializing at veterans clubs, or eating out at casual restaurants.

- **Young & Rustic.** Young, restless, lower-income, high-school-educated singles living in tiny apartments in exurban towns. Service industry jobs and modest incomes; fast-paced lifestyles center on sports, cars, and dating.

Using Standardized Segments

Ace Hardware launched its Helpful Hardware Club customer loyalty program by assigning a Claritas cluster code to each of seven million members. Twelve clusters generated most of Ace's business. Ace targeted female shoppers in those household clusters to buy Valentine's Day gifts for their husbands.

Hyundai identified high-potential clusters for purchasing automobiles. Hyundai selects ZIP codes with high cluster membership and sends test-drive offers. Results show more test drives, increased sales, and significantly lower marketing costs per vehicle sold.

The Base of the Pyramid

Around the world, four billion people live in poverty and many more have minimal economic resources, even in developed countries. But these people may represent attractive market opportunities.[17] Pfizer salespeople sell discounted brand name prescription drugs to clinics in Latin American's dangerous shanty towns. In rural India, Hindustan Unilever successfully offers cold-water shampoo sachets; it also sells a $43 water-purification system via a 45,000-women network.[18] Tata Motors' Nano automobile ($2,500) addresses this market and cell-phone sales are rising fast. Increasingly, banks are following Grameen Bank's (Bangladesh) example and making micro-loans to entrepreneurs (often women).[19]

In Kenya, PeePoople AB (Sweden) introduced the peepoo, a self-sanitizing biodegradable product sold by locals. Peepoo replaces *flying toilets* (plastic bags filled with human waste) for the extremely poor residents of informal settlements.

Many rural herdsmen face potential catastrophic drought-related losses when livestock (camels, cows, goats) die. Innovative weather-based index insurance pays out when real-time satellite images of grass and other vegetation show significant risk of animal death.[20]

KEY QUESTIONS ABOUT MARKET SEGMENTS

Managers often raise questions regarding their own approaches to market segments and the market segmentation process. Here are the most common[21]:

HOW MANY MARKET SEGMENTS ARE ENOUGH? How should the firm trade off enhancing customer satisfaction by defining large numbers of market segments, and seeking cost efficiency via few segments? Walmart faces this problem: Walmart's low-cost, low-price business model has brought great success; its current challenge is addressing segments defined by local needs without incurring significant cost penalties.[22] The core options are:

- **Large number of segments.** As the firm identifies increased numbers of segments in a market, the similarity of customer need profiles within each segment increases. Hence the firm can gain high customer satisfaction by targeting specialized groups. But product development, marketing costs, and other resource requirements are high and economies of scale are few. Also, managing many segments is a complex challenge.

- **Small number of segments.** When the firm develops fewer segments, customer needs are less granular and more diffuse. Customer satisfaction from addressing individual segments is necessarily lower, but costs are also lower and segment management is less difficult.

Marketing Question

In difficult economic times, most advanced Western countries have their own base-of-the-pyramid consumers. What opportunities can you identify for addressing them?

Firms experienced in market segmentation typically opt for a relatively small number of segments, often between five and eight. They may develop more discrete segments during the segmentation process, but include a rationalizing step to a smaller number.

In some industries, firms target several fine-grained segments via a **modularity** approach. Modularity speaks to product design, using individual components in multiple products to serve multiple segments.[23] Chapter 3 showed that Boeing and Airbus each use modular design, parts standardization, and advanced information technology in airplane manufacture. The Boeing 727, 737, and 757 serve different customer needs, yet some fuselage sections are identical, inherited from the 707.

Technological advances increase design and production flexibility. Computer-aided design (CAD) speeds development; computer-aided manufacturing (CAM) reduces set-up times. CAD/CAM innovations make product variations less expensive and allow customer personalization without the typical cost of making *one-offs*. Amazon.com is an excellent example of using information technology to personalize the user experience and reduce the cost of variety. Amazon uses recommendation systems, based on historic purchasing patterns, to advise customers of products meeting their preferences; they also remind customers of birthdays and other events that may trigger purchases.

CAN AN INDIVIDUAL CUSTOMER BE A MARKET SEGMENT? Firms that address B2B markets, or sell consumer goods through large retail chains, often focus their efforts on individual customers, known as **segments-of-one**. The firm treats an individual strategic (key) account as a market segment in its own right.

Historically, in B2C markets, individual artisans like custom tailors offered personally designed *bespoke* products to individuals, typically at high prices. Today, firms can integrate personally designed products with flexible mass production techniques — **mass customization**, and gain two advantages.[24] More precisely tailored products enhance customer satisfaction and loyalty, and the firm reduces finished-goods inventory throughout production and distribution.

KEY IDEA

➤ B2B firms often treat major customers as individual market segments. In B2C markets, many firms practice mass customization.

Panasonic retailers measure consumers for bicycles, just as tailors measure for suits. The retailer transmits measurements to the factory; custom-made bicycles are available in a few days. Similarly, Levi Strauss and Lands' End offer custom-made pants through Internet-based systems. Optical retailers like LensCrafters deliver individually fashioned spectacles within a few hours. At Callaway's *performance centers*, golfers receive computer analyses of their golf swing and place orders for clubs cut to a precise length and bent to a specific angle. Renault's goal is to build and deliver cars within 15 days of receiving a customer order.

Many Internet firms personalize products using *choiceboard* models.[25] Dell customers design their own PCs; Mattel customers design their own Barbie dolls. Hallmark sends personal e-mail reminders for birthdays and other anniversaries so customers can send cards that arrive on time.

DO MARKET SEGMENTS EVOLVE? We emphasized that market segmentation is critical to developing market strategy. If two firms are equally accomplished in designing market offers, the firm with better market segmentation will win. This firm's offers will be more precisely tailored to customer needs than those of competitors.

But customer need profiles are constantly evolving, so the firm's segmentation must also evolve, based on good market, customer, competitor, and complementer insight. When markets are young, early entrants are often successful providing basic functional benefits. Then, as the product life cycle evolves, competitors enter and basic functional benefits become the *cost of entry*. The firm achieves differential advantage by identifying customers with finer-grained needs and delivering appropriate benefits and values. Cell phones are a good example. Early in the product life cycle, the most important benefit was phone portability. Later, that benefit became less important in customer decision-making, and the need profiles of some market segments focused on additional functional benefits like e-mail, text messaging, and taking photos. Other segments focused on design and fashion statements.

Regardless, we should remember that many mature markets have segments requiring only basic functional benefits. easyHotels offers tiny rooms (cabins) at extremely low nightly rates; and discount airlines, netbooks, and many private-label supermarket products serve these segments.

HOW DO CUSTOMER LIFE CYCLES AFFECT MARKET SEGMENTS? Generally, promoting and selling products to current customers is less expensive than focusing on new customers. Firms increasingly recognize the lifetime value of current customers (CLV) and continually refocus their efforts to increase long-term customer loyalty — Chapter 2. B2B customers may continue indefinitely, but individual human consumers follow a predictable life cycle. B2C firms have two polar options:

- **Focus on a fixed age group.** The firm targets an age-defined segment, continually adding new consumers as current customers age and leave the market. Magazines often favor this approach — *Teen People, Time for Kids, Sports Illustrated for Kids*, and *Seventeen*.
- **Retain consumers as they age.** The firm evolves its offer to match changing customer need profiles and reaps the benefits of customer loyalty. But eventually, consumers stop buying. Daimler-Chrysler, Ford, and GM abandoned Plymouth, Mercury, and Oldsmobile respectively.

The Old Spice (OS) brand (aftershave and cologne) has followed both strategies. When Richardson Vicks owned OS, it was relatively successful targeting 18- to 25-year-old men as they aged but sales stagnated as product use declined. When P&G acquired OS, it retargeted the 18- to 25-year-old segment, now populated by new consumers. OS is the U.S. market leader.

DOES A *SEGMENT* OF CUSTOMERS DIFFER FROM A *GROUP* OF CUSTOMERS? We take a hard line on the definition of segments. Within a segment, customers have similar need profiles; these profiles differ from customers in other segments. By contrast, the firm can form groups in many ways: by degree of use, propensity to buy innovative products, and customer loyalty. Groups may be very important for understanding buyer behavior, but they may not be segments.

To illustrate, many firms group customers by level of use — heavy, medium, and light users. This grouping is often very useful for allocating marketing effort; generally, firms place more effort on heavy users than on light users. But the heavy user group is *not* a segment; customers may be heavy users for very different reasons. Consider frequent users of car rental: Two very different segments are traveling business people who want cars during the week, and city dwellers who want to leave town on the weekends; each segment has different needs.

KEY IDEA

➤ As customer need profiles evolve, the firm must continually evolve its segmentation.

McDonald's has a heavy-user group, but those customers fall into quite separate segments: families with young children, and single males in blue-collar jobs.[26] In general, the firm should develop groups *before* segments.

CAN WE DEVELOP SEGMENTS BASED ON JUST OUR CURRENT CUSTOMERS? Most firms segment the entire market, both current and potential customers. But when the firm has many current customers, it may use customer relationship management (CRM) approaches — Chapter 13π — to place purchase transactions in a **data warehouse**. The firm can then use **data mining** techniques to identify groups based on purchasing patterns and tailor offers to individual customers based on those patterns.[27]

Tesco (British supermarket) offers a good example of data mining in action. Tesco's loyalty card pays quarterly rebates based on cumulative customer purchases. Tesco has 16 million card users; ten million consumers use their cards weekly. Tesco analyzes data from over 600 million shopping baskets annually and places customers into roughly 40,000 groups. Tesco tailors rewards and incentives to consumers in these groups via 36 million personalized mailings annually.[28]

TARGETING MARKET SEGMENTS

> Chicago-based Seigle's operated many home centers in and around Chicago — 60 percent of sales to builders, 40 percent to consumers. Seigle's anticipated tough competition from Home Depot and focused its 33 on-the-road salespeople on the builder segment. Seigle's closed stores and reduced its product line from 7,000 to 1,500 items.[29]

The firm never has sufficient resources and/or abilities to address all segments in a market; hence, it must decide where to target its efforts. Some segments receive greater effort and resources; some segments receive little or no effort. By effective targeting, the firm better addresses customer needs and minimizes direct competition. When making targeting decisions, the firm should be conscious of the Principle of Selectivity and Concentration — Chapter 1.

- Marketing must carefully choose targets for the firm's efforts.
- The firm should concentrate its resources against those targets.

The Principle of Selectivity and Concentration governs both Marketing Imperative 1 and Marketing Imperative 2, but there is a difference. For Marketing Imperative 1, **Determine and Recommend Which Markets to Address**, marketing's role is *advisory*, helping the firm decide. For Marketing Imperative 2, **Identify and Target Market Segments**, marketing has a *decision-making* role. When the firm has chosen its markets, marketing has the explicit responsibility to identify and target segments.

KEY IDEA

➤ For each target market segment, the firm should develop a unique offer precisely tailored to the need profile of customers in that segment.

Whole Foods (WF) is a good example of successful segmentation and targeting in the competitive supermarket industry. WF targets the health-conscious segment with supermarket-style natural food stores, offering one-stop shopping and educational materials on its environmental practices. WF has grown from a single store (1980) to a $10+ billion, 300-store chain with 60,000 employees; average sales per square foot are close to twice that of regular supermarkets. Monsanto offers a second example. Faced with mounting criticism of its genetically modified seeds, Monsanto abandoned efforts on edible products like bananas, potatoes, tomatoes, and wheat, and successfully focused on four commodity crops — corn, soybean, cotton and canola. The Koss example shows precise targeting for a headphone producer:

> Koss is the leading U.S. headphone manufacturer. One target segment is the 1.3 million prison-inmate population. Special product features include: transparency so contraband cannot be hidden, plastic headbands that cannot be made into knives or other sharp objects, and weaker-than-normal cords that cannot strangle or restrain.

International document and package delivery firm DHL used successive approaches to targeting. Initially, DHL formed three segments based on customer needs:

- **Ad hoc** — small irregular shippers or occasional buyers
- **Regular** — high-volume shippers not requiring supply-chain solutions
- **Advantage** — shippers that need and want a supply-chain solution

The *advantage* segment offered DHL high revenue and profit potential and good partnership candidates. DHL also targeted the advantage segment because it could provide supply-chain solutions. DHL also selected 10 industry segments where it could offer industry-specific knowledge and solutions. Finally, DHL selected specific firms in those industries for selling effort.

> Netflix (Chapter 3 — Opening Case) has a successful DVD-rental subscription service offering more than 100,000 unique titles for mail delivery. Redbox targets a different segment via 20,000 kiosks in supermarkets, drugstores, and fast-food restaurants; each kiosk contains 600 discs/200 unique titles, for $1 overnight rental price.

Two separate approaches can help the firm decide which segments to target.

THE MULTIFACTOR MATRIX APPROACH TO TARGETING (STRATEGIC POSITION ANALYSIS)

The **multifactor matrix** (*strategic position analysis*) helps the firm decide which market segments to target.[30] For each candidate segment, the firm must answer two questions:

- How attractive is this segment? (Later, we discuss what makes a segment attractive.)
- Does the firm have the business strengths to win in this segment?

Figure 8.6 shows the conclusion of the analysis — a **market segment attractiveness** versus **business strengths** matrix. We trisect each axis — *high, medium, low* — and label the nine cells A through I. We illustrate by considering three cells:

- Cell C — high market attractiveness, high business strengths: A segment with these characteristics is a no-brainer; the firm should target this segment.
- Cell G — low market attractiveness, low business strengths: A segment with these characteristics is also a no-brainer, but the decision is very different; do not waste resources.
- Cell E — medium market attractiveness, medium business strengths: This decision is more difficult; the segment is somewhat attractive and the firm has some strengths.

Marketing Question

In recent years, newsstand sales and subscriptions declined for many news magazines — *Businessweek, Fortune, Newsweek, Time, U.S. News & World Report* — but *The Economist* has had significant increases. Why is *The Economist* successful? What market segment(s) does it target?

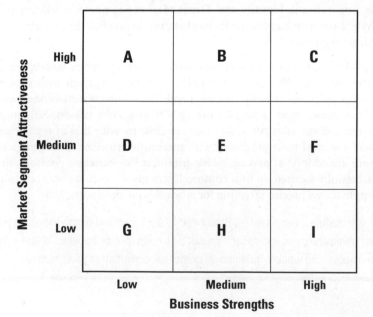

FIGURE 8.6

THE MULTIFACTOR MATRIX (STRATEGIC POSITION ANALYSIS) — MARKET SEGMENT ATTRACTIVENESS VERSUS BUSINESS STRENGTHS

More generally, the firm should seriously consider targeting market segments that fall in the top right corner — B, C, F, but avoid the bottom left corner — D, G, H. Segments in the diagonal cells — A, E, I — are more questionable; each has both positive and negative features.

We just discussed the conclusion of the analysis — the multifactor matrix. Now, we show (a) how to develop the matrix, and (b) how to make the most effective segment-targeting decisions. First, we identify two sets of criteria:

- **Market segment attractiveness.** Factors that make a market segment attractive to the firm.
- **Business strengths.** What any competitor would need to be successful in the segment.

Factors that make market segments attractive differ from firm to firm; business strengths needed to win differ from market segment to market segment. Table 8.6 identifies general factors to start an evaluation; actual factors are specific to the firm and candidate segments.

TABLE 8.6

TARGETING MARKET SEGMENTS: TYPICAL CRITERIA FOR ASSESSING SEGMENT ATTRACTIVENESS AND BUSINESS STRENGTHS NEEDED TO WIN

Market Segment Attractiveness	Business Strengths
Ability to use available resources	Brand value
Barriers to entry	Distribution facilities
Barriers to exit	Financial leverage
Customer service valued	Government relations
Degree of vertical integration	Liquidity
Likely competitor actions	Market segment share
Market segment growth rate	Marketing skills
Market segment potential	Modernity of plant and equipment
Market segment size	Production capacity
Potential profit margins	Profitability record
Regulatory constraints	Raw materials position
Social factors	Sales force
Technological change	Service levels
	Technological expertise

MARKET SEGMENT ATTRACTIVENESS. The firm should identify useful factors for evaluating many segments. Sometimes the firm considers corporate-level attractiveness factors; other times, it focuses on an individual business. A business with growth and market share objectives typically has different attractiveness factors than a business focused on improving cash flow.

For each attractiveness factor, the firm should also consider *direction*. Market segment size is a factor for many analysts. A large firm may prefer large segments; a smaller firm may prefer small segments. Michael Steinbeis, CEO of Steinbeis Holding, global leader in battery labels, says: "We want to be big in small markets. We may even pull out if a market becomes too large and, due to our size and resources, we can only be a small player" (more below).[31] Also, many firms view excessive government regulation as a negative factor. But for a firm with experience in dealing with regulatory bureaucracies, extensive regulation may be positive — as an entry barrier for potential competitors. Table 8.7 lays out a five-step process to score market segment attractiveness.

KEY IDEA

➤ In deciding which segments to target, the firm should ask two questions:

- How attractive is this segment?
- Does the firm have the business strengths to win?

Step Number	Step	Description
1	Identify factors	The firm seeks several factors (typically five to eight) according to the statement: "Given our history, objectives, culture, management style, successes, and failures, we like to be in market segments that offer ..."
2	Weight factors	Weight each factor by allocating 100 points based on its importance to the firm. Factor weights sum to 100.
3	Rate market segments	Rate each market segment according to how well it performs on each factor (1 = poor; 10 = excellent).
4	Develop factor scores	For each segment, form individual factor scores by multiplying the results of step 2 and step 3 for each factor. Factor score = Weighting x Rating.
5	Develop the market segment attractiveness score	Sum individual factor scores.

TABLE 8:7

SCORING THE ATTRACTIVENESS OF A MARKET SEGMENT

> **Marketing Exercise**
>
> Choose a firm that is a potential employer and a market segment that may be appropriate for that firm. Complete a market segment attractiveness analysis.

The firm completes Steps 1 and 2 once. These results are constant for all segments the firm is evaluating for which it has similar objectives. At Step 3, the analysis shifts to individual market segments. At Step 5, the firm develops a market segment attractiveness score — from 100 to 1,000. More attractive segments earn higher scores.[32] Table 8.8 shows how Robinson (fictional firm, plastics manufacturer) evaluated the plastic accessories segment — the segment scored 595 in attractiveness.

Factor	Robinson's Weighting	Plastic Accessories Segment Rating (1 to 10 scale)	Factor Score (weighting x rating)
Ability to build new strengths	10	6	60
Easy customer access	15	9	135
High market growth	20	7	140
Large potential size	20	5	100
Little regulation	10	8	80
Use excess resources	10	2	20
Weak competition	15	4	60
Total	100		**595**

TABLE 8.8

ASSESSING THE ATTRACTIVENESS OF THE PLASTIC ACCESSORIES MARKET SEGMENT TO ROBINSON

BUSINESS STRENGTHS. Required business strengths are specific to each market segment being evaluated. First, the firm must identify those strengths *any* competitor would require to be successful. Second, it must assess the firm's possession of those strengths. Table 8.9 lays out a five-step process to score the firm's business strengths for a market segment.

Step Number	Step	Description
1	Identify factors	For each segment, the firm selects several factors (typically five to eight) according to the statement: "To be successful in this market segment, any competitor must possess the following strengths ..."
2	Weight factors	Weight each factor by allocating 100 points based on its importance for being successful in the segment. Factor weights sum to 100.
3	Rate the firm	Rate the firm according to its possession of these strengths (1 = poor; 10 = excellent)
4	Develop factor scores	For each factor, form individual factor scores by multiplying the results of step 2 and step 3 for each factor. Factor score = Weighting x Rating.
5	Develop the business strengths score	Sum the individual factor scores.

TABLE 8.9

SCORING THE FIRM'S BUSINESS STRENGTHS

Steps 1 and 2 focus on the necessary strengths for being successful in the market segment. At Step 3, the analysis shifts to evaluating the degree to which the firm possesses these strengths. At Step 5, the firm develops a business strengths score — from 100 to 1,000. Higher scores demonstrate greater strengths for competing in the segment. Table 8.10 shows how Robinson assessed its strengths in the plastic accessories segment — it scored 645 on business strengths.

TABLE 8.10

ASSESSING ROBINSON'S
BUSINESS STRENGTHS
IN THE PLASTIC
ACCESSORIES
MARKET SEGMENT

Factor	Plastic Accessories Segment Weighting	Robinson's Rating (1 to 10 scale)	Factor Score (weighting × rating)
Deep pockets	10	9	90
Fast-moving organization	5	3	15
Good R&D	25	7	175
High-quality service	15	6	90
In-place distribution	20	5	100
Low-cost operations	10	4	40
Well-trained sales force	15	9	135
Total	100		**645**

Marketing Question

Review the Robinson example in Table 8.10. How could Robinson secure a better business strengths score?

The market segment attractiveness/business strengths analysis is a one-time snapshot; both market segments and the firm evolve. Segment attractiveness factors, importance weightings, and/or the assessment of individual segments will change. Similarly, business strength factors, importance weightings, and assessment of the firm will also change. This analysis is not a *one-time deal*; the firm should update periodically.

WHICH MARKET SEGMENTS TO TARGET? The multifactor matrix produces two index numbers per market segment: *attractiveness* and *business strengths*. In the Robinson example, index numbers are 595 and 645 respectively — the "X" point in Figure 8.7. The *cut points* — 400 and 700, discriminate low, medium, and high.[33]

FIGURE 8.7

ROBINSON'S
ASSESSMENT
OF THE PLASTIC
ACCESSORIES
MARKET SEGMENT

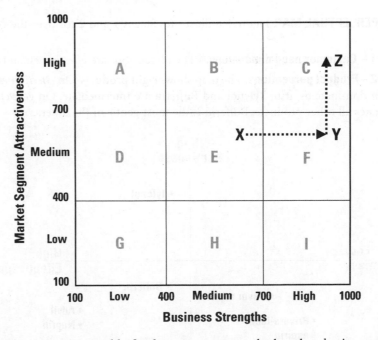

The "X" position is not immutably fixed; we must assess whether the plastics accessories segment can shift from cell E to cells B, C, or F. Robinson has two movement options — horizontal and vertical:

- **Horizontal:** To move from X to Y, Robinson must improve business strengths. Returning to Table 8.10, *Good R&D* (25) and *In-place distribution* (20) are most important; Robinson

Marketing Exercise

For the firm and market segment you selected on p. 210, conduct a business strengths analysis.

scored 7 and 5 respectively. Astute investment, acquisition, or forming an alliance may improve business strengths. Columbia Business School has alliances with the London Business School and Berkeley's Haas School to address separate Executive MBA segments; and a strategic alliance with CEIBS (Shanghai) to address the Chinese market for executive-level marketing education.

- **Vertical:** To move vertically — from Y to Z — is more subtle. This shift depends upon the plastic accessories segment being more attractive. Robinson should secure deeper market insight and refine its definition of this segment. With a modified segmentation approach, Robinson may identify a more attractive market segment.[34]

Of course, whether or not Robinson targets the plastic accessories segment depends on other alternatives and its investment resources.

PERCEPTUAL MAP APPROACH TO TARGETING

The **perceptual map** complements the multifactor matrix approach. The targeting process has four stages:

- **Stage 1 — Customer need dimensions.** Identify two key customer need dimensions for the perceptual map.
- **Stage 2 — Product perceptions.** Plot customer product perceptions on the map.
- **Stage 3 — Market segments.** Plot market segment ideal points and size on the map.
- **Stage 4 — Targeting decisions.** Use product data (stage 2) and segment data (stage 3) to target market segments.

We illustrate perceptual mapping using over-the-counter pain relievers and toy animals. Pain relievers show the basic perceptual map; toy animals show how to use the perceptual map for targeting decisions.

THE BASIC PERCEPTUAL MAP. Figure 8.8 illustrates Stages 1 and 2 for over-the-counter pain relievers.

- **Stage 1 – Customer need dimensions.**[35] The dimensions are *effectiveness* and *gentleness*.
- **Stage 2 – Product perceptions.** The map shows eight products. On *effectiveness*, Advil and Nuprin dominate aspirin; Tylenol and Bufferin are intermediate. On *gentleness*, Tylenol dominates all other products; Bufferin is the most gentle of the others.

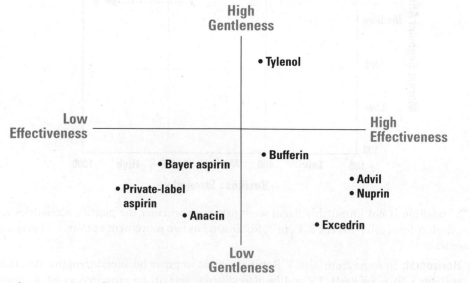

Source: Impact Planning Group

Marketing Question

For the firm and market segment you worked with on p. 210 and p. 211, plot its position on a market segment attractiveness/ business strengths matrix.

KEY IDEA

➤ A firm can improve market segment position by investing in those business strengths that determine success.

➤ A firm may identify more attractive market segments by refining its segmentation approach.

FIGURE 8.8

PERCEPTUAL MAP — PAIN RELIEVERS

The perceptual map provides additional interesting insight. Advil, Nuprin, and Excedrin compete closely with one another; Bayer aspirin, private-label aspirin, and Anacin are also closely competitive. Tylenol has no direct competitors. The map also shows unserved market areas. No product combines *high gentleness* and *high effectiveness*, nor *high gentleness* and *low effectiveness* but the map does not tell if customers require these need combinations.[36]

FIGURE 8.9

PERCEPTUAL MAP — TOY ANIMALS

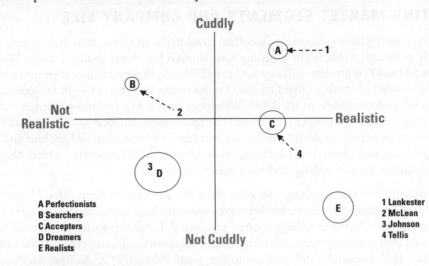

A Perfectionists
B Searchers
C Accepters
D Dreamers
E Realists

1 Lankester
2 McLean
3 Johnson
4 Tellis

USING THE PERCEPTUAL MAP FOR TARGETING DECISIONS. Figure 8.9 uses the toy animal market to illustrate all four stages of the targeting process:

- **Stage 1 – Customer need dimensions.** The dimensions are *cuddliness* and *realism*.[37]

- **Stage 2 – Product perceptions.** The four products are: Lankester, McLean, Johnson, and Tellis — 1, 2, 3, and 4 respectively.

- **Stage 3 – Market segments.** We have significant information:

  - There are five segments — *perfectionists*, *searchers*, *accepters*, *dreamers*, and *realists* — A, B, C, D, and E, respectively.

  - Specifically, A, B, C, D, and E represent market segment *ideal points*, the need profiles of customers in the segments.[38] Hence, *realists* (E) want highly realistic but not cuddly toys.

  - The size of the circle around each ideal point is proportional to market segment size, typically, revenues, units, or numbers of customers. *Dreamers* (D) is the largest segment; *searchers* (B) is the smallest segment.

  - Some segments are/are not well served by products. Product 3 — Johnson, satisfies the needs of *dreamers* — (D), but no product serves *realists* (E) very well.

- **Stage 4 – Targeting decisions.** Segment opportunities by enhancing the product and/or communications include:

  - *Perfectionists* (A). Lankester (1) has the highest segment share; it modifies customer perceptions to appear less realistic — it follows the arrow.

  - *Searchers* (B). McLean (2) is closest to the segment ideal point, but does not serve it well. McLean modifies customer perceptions — it follows the arrow to appear more cuddly and less realistic.

  - *Accepters* (C). McLean (2) probably captures some sales from this segment, but less than Tellis (4). Tellis follows the arrow to appear more cuddly and less realistic (but less so than McLean).

Options for new entries include:

- *Dreamers* (D). Johnson (3) seems secure, but this large segment may support another entrant, from Johnson or a competitor.

- *Realists* (E) represent an opportunity; no product serves this segment.[39]

KEY IDEA

➤ Perceptual maps show how various products serve market segment needs. Perceptual maps show market segment sizes and customer ideal points in each segment. These data help the firm make targeting decisions.

Perceptual maps can be helpful in targeting decisions, but have limitations:

- Maps show segment size, but not other characteristics like growth and profitability.
- Maps suggest unserved market areas but do not address required business strengths.

TARGETING MARKET SEGMENTS AND COMPANY SIZE

Large firms generally have greater resources than small firms, so a large firm that segments and targets well is difficult to beat. The Opening Case showed how hotel-industry leader Marriott targets several market segments with various brands. Marriott's performance is exemplary in its industry. Whirlpool is another large firm that targets multiple segments — in both developed and less-developed countries. In the latter, Whirlpool targets low-income customers with its Ideale washing machine; it makes minor design changes to appeal to local tastes. In Brazil, Ideale is white, has a transparent acrylic lid, and sits on four legs. In China, Ideale is light blue and gray, has a foldable top, and a heavy-duty cycle for *grease removal*. In India, Ideale is green, blue, and white; is on casters for easy rolling; and has a delicate *sari* cycle.[40]

Market segmentation and targeting can even the odds for smaller firms. Many large firms cannot achieve specialized focus on market segments — internal constituencies disagree about segment targets and decision-making is often protracted. Large firms may also spread themselves too thin over many segments, allowing smaller, more-focused, competitors to gain advantage. Startup Dell essentially defeated computer giant IBM in PCs. AirTran, jetBlue, and Southwest Airlines pressure airline majors like American, Delta, and United; and easyJet and Ryanair are winning in Europe.

Sometimes smaller firms win when larger firms ignore, reduce service to, or withdraw from less attractive (for them) market segments. In passenger aircraft, Bombardier Aerospace (Canada) and Embraer (Brazil) profitably produce *short-hop* planes designed to travel between main hubs and smaller regional airports. They avoid stiff competition from large plane builders Boeing and Airbus.

Small firms with limited resources enjoy focus advantages of targeting few segments and building strong customer relationships, almost by default. They don't *choose* to target fewer segments: they just don't have the resources to target more.[41] But successful small firms must understand their success is due to focus. When a small firm does not understand this reality it may expand into segments dominated by resource-rich competitors, like *www.Positively-You.com*:

Virtual bookstore *www.Positively-You.com* focused on self-help and motivational books and became profitable in six months! *New York Times* columnist Thomas Friedman wrote a highly complimentary op-ed piece, and website traffic increased dramatically. Positively-You expanded to compete more directly with Amazon.com — the result was a disaster, and within one year the store was out of business. Said owner Lyle Bowlin, "We were doing well as a small niche player, but when we decided to go after Amazon, we lost our way."[42]

Smaller firms face three other problems:

- **Demand shortage.** Of necessity small firms target few market segments. If demand drops, other segments cannot cushion the impact. Industry-wide recessions wreak havoc with specialized firms.
- **High costs.** Narrow focus implies high costs that cannot be offset by high prices.
- **Too successful.** The small firm is *too* successful and attracts the attention of major players. Startup Guiltless Gourmet (GG) grew its line of baked low-fat tortilla chips into a $23 million enterprise. When snacks giant Frito-Lay entered, GG's revenues fell precipitously.[43]

> ### *Marketing Question*
> Think of a small firm that failed. What role did segmentation and targeting play in its failure? Which pitfall(s) contributed to its failure? What could the firm have done better to understand the limitations of its market strategy?

> ### KEY IDEA
> ➤ Large firms and small firms each have advantages in targeting market segments. Missteps can cause each to lose a strong position.

Marketing Question

Are marketing instructors *the plumbers* of the marketing textbook market? How would you suggest Wessex segment and target the textbook market?

SEGMENT INTERRELATIONSHIPS IN TARGETING

Generally, the firm targets segments individually but sometimes it must target segment A to reach segment B. In many markets, like pharmaceuticals and medical diagnostics, the firm must successfully target a segment of influentials before addressing other segments.

In the British plumbing market, consumers typically rely on plumbers to advise on shower choice. Aquilisa developed the revolutionary, easy-to-install, electronic Quartz shower providing significant consumer value via consistent water pressure and temperature. But plumbers distrusted electronics and were very conservative; hence they did not recommend Quartz. Aquilisa achieved success by targeting showrooms where consumers selected showers and forced plumbers to install their choices. Plumbers learned Quartz's value and started recommending it to customers.[44] Similarly, target customers for *Managing Marketing in the 21st Century* are students in marketing courses, yet Wessex directs marketing effort at instructors.

Marketing Question

What other messages did you glean from this chapter?

KEY MESSAGES

- Market segmentation is fundamental to developing the market strategy. The firm has three separate, but related, strategic-level tasks:
  - Conduct a market segmentation process to identify market segments.
  - Decide which of the identified market segments to target for effort.
  - Develop a market segment strategy and positioning for each target segment.

  We discussed items 1 and 2 in this chapter; we take up item 3 in Chapter 9.

- Segmentation is a process for deconstructing the market into customer groups.

- Customers in a market segment have homogeneous (similar) need profiles; customers in other market segments have heterogeneous (different) need profiles.

- The firm can approach the segmentation process in two different ways:
  - Identifying groups of customers that differ in need profiles.
  - Using candidate descriptor (segmentation) variables to form groups, then seeing if need profiles differ.

- The firm should avoid ineffective ways of segmenting markets.

- Useful segments must satisfy six separate criteria: differentiated, identifiable, accessible, appropriate size, measurable, and stable.

- The segmentation process is creative and analytic, requiring good market, customer, competitor, and complementer insight. By contrast, targeting requires the firm to make decisions.

- Sometimes firms find commercially available standardized segmentation schemes useful.

- The *multifactor matrix* and *perceptual map* are alternative approaches for making targeting decisions.

- Large firms generally succeed by targeting multiple segments; small firms succeed by targeting few segments.

v802

a801

VIDEOS AND AUDIOS

Market Segmentation and Targeting	v802 📹	Ron Boire	Toys R Us
Marketing Imperative 2	a801 🎧		

QUESTIONS FOR STUDY AND DISCUSSION

Can you answer the questions implied by this chapter's learning objectives? Check!

1. Suppose your firm decides to address the human pain-relief market. How would you segment this market? What market segments can you identify? Can you identify both coarse- and fine-grained segments — market segments and customer segments?

2. Select a product/market with which you are familiar. Develop a segmentation matrix identifying the importance order of benefits and values for the various segments.

3. Assume you are marketing manager at a firm competing in the product/market you identified in Question 2. Select one or more segments to target by completing a multifactor matrix analysis.

4. Do politicians employ segmentation? Describe an example.

5. Describe a segment of the higher education market that includes you. Appraise this segment in terms of the criteria for *good* segments — differentiated, identifiable, accessible, appropriate size, measurable, and stable.

6. Visit retail outlets for Banana Republic, The Gap, and Old Navy. Observe customers and products. What do you infer about owner Gap Inc.'s segmentation and targeting?

7. Select a product in which you are interested. Alternatively, consider this book — *Managing Marketing in the 21st Century*. How would you segment the market? Describe the segments.

8. Select a market with which you are familiar. Develop a perceptual map by identifying two dimensions, product offerings, and your best guess at market segments.

9. What are the risks and limitations of a strategy based on market segmentation? How can you measure the effectiveness of a market segmentation approach?

10. Market segmentation raises serious ethical issues. Do you agree? Why or why not?

IMPERATIVE 3

Set Strategic Direction and Positioning

CHAPTER 9

MARKET STRATEGY— INTEGRATING THE FIRM'S EFFORTS FOR MARKETING SUCCESS v901

To access O-codes, go to **www.ocodes.com**

LEARNING OBJECTIVES

When you have completed this chapter, you will be able to:

- Articulate the purpose and functions of market and market-segment strategies.
- Provide direction to the firm and/or business unit.
- Know how to achieve differential advantage.
- Guide the effective allocation of scarce resources.
- Achieve cross-functional integration.
- Lay out the elements of a market-segment strategy.
- Select a strategic focus and design a positioning statement.
- Identify effective and ineffective market and market-segment strategies.
- Develop and manage market strategies targeted at multiple segments.

OPENING CASE: MAYO CLINIC

Mayo Clinic is the best known and most powerful healthcare brand in the world. Since the late 1880s, Mayo Clinic has delivered superb medical care to patients, provided value to many con-

stituencies, and wielded differential advantage over competitors. Mayo Clinic's history continues to define its differential advantage over other direct healthcare providers, even when every major hospital and medical institution has professional marketing and public relations staffs.

Mayo Clinic's market strategy has always had two core operating principles. First: "The best interest of the patient is the only interest to be considered." Second: "Two heads are better than one, and three are even better." Focused on these principles, Mayo Clinic has 50,000 employees serving more than 500,000 patients annually from the U.S. and around the world — at three clinic and hospital centers in Rochester, Minnesota; Jacksonville, Florida; and Scottsdale and Phoenix, Arizona. Mayo Clinic also maintains offices in Canada, Mexico, and the United Arab Emirates (UAE) to facilitate appointments, and provide hotel and visa assistance.

Mayo Clinic's brand awareness is extraordinary. The chair of Mayo Clinic's marketing division said, "Our research shows that in the U.S. we register over 1.8 billion consumer impressions a year — 90 percent of the population is aware of Mayo Clinic, 33 percent know someone who has been a Mayo Clinic patient, and 18 percent would make us their first choice for a serious health need if there were no financial barriers. Patients from all 50 U.S. states as well as from 150 countries typically visit each of our three clinics every year."[1]

Mayo Clinic is a multi-specialty clinic based on a collaborative practice model inaugurated by its founders. In most large healthcare institutions, physicians, nurses, and researchers are relatively isolated within their departments, laboratories, specialties, and sub-specialties. Not at Mayo Clinic; all caregivers serve as consultants to one another and as members of multiple-patient care teams led by the patient's primary physician. Mayo Clinic extends this collaboration to physicians and administrators. Said one administrator, "Mayo Clinic is run by physician leaders who implicitly and respectfully value the counsel and skills of the administrators they are paired with. The mutual respect flows both ways."

Mayo Clinic's model is difficult to maintain and even harder to duplicate. Despite several attempts, no other clinic has been able to fully copy its approach or success, and no competitor looks like Mayo Clinic. Part of Mayo Clinic's success results from its alignment of mission and organization. Hence, all employees receive salary checks from the same account, signed by the same person.

Mayo Clinic's collaborative model extends to patients' referring physicians. Mayo Clinic views other healthcare providers as potential collaborators. Mayo Clinic's chief marketer said, "Both the patients and Mayo Clinic need them to have a doctor back home, and our doctors will collaborate with their doctors in the best interests of the patient. When a physician or patient needs our specialty services, we're here for them. But because Mayo's market share is extremely small, it is rarely seen as a competitive threat."

Mayo Clinic has world-class facilities, staffed with the best and brightest, and the right organizational design, systems, and processes for its collaborative model. Mayo Clinic also communicates broadly to physicians, other healthcare professionals, and the general public. Clinicians and researchers publish several thousand articles, chapters, textbooks, and abstracts annually; and its peer-reviewed journal, Mayo Clinic Proceedings, has 150,000 physician subscribers. Mayo Clinic publishes a widely read newsletter, Clinical Update, for healthcare professionals. For the general public, Mayo Clinic offers Mayo Clinic Health Letter, published in four languages — 800,000 subscribers for the English edition, and the similarly successful Mayo Clinic Women's Health Source, both monthly newsletters. Mayo Clinic Family Health Book has sold over one million copies, and www.Mayoclinic.com is one of the most heavily visited health information sites on the Internet.

Mayo Clinic receives extensive public relations coverage when celebrities like entertainers, professional athletes, and government and business leaders visit for care. In small U.S. towns, word of mouth about someone's good experience at Mayo Clinic often leads to a local feature story in the newspaper, TV, or radio, and is frequently picked up by regional and national news services.

Communications about Mayo Clinic bring patient referrals from doctors and other healthcare providers. Word of mouth from active and former patients is also very strong. Ninety-five percent of *patients are very positive about Mayo Clinic; on average, each patient urges 20 others to go, and seven become new patients. In Rochester, Mayo Clinic cares for patients from nearly 40 percent of all U.S. residential zip codes, but few zip codes send ten or more patients. Demand typically outpaces available appointments, creating a significant patient-scheduling challenge.*

Mayo Clinic's tiny share of a huge market makes it attractive to many insurers. Research shows the greatest benefit from the Mayo brand is peace of mind — knowing it's there if you need it. Midwest U.S. consumers, in particular, find great value in insurance products that include Mayo Clinic.

CASE QUESTION

What are the critical elements in Mayo Clinic's market strategy?

Mayo Clinic grounds its market strategy in delivering customer value and securing differential advantage. Although a non-profit organization, Mayo Clinic's enormous financial success funds leading-edge research and hospital facilities, a medical school, high staff-per-patient ratio, and a roster of world-class physicians and researchers. All these constituents count on customer willingness to pay and to face the inconvenience of traveling to a Mayo Clinic for treatment.[2]

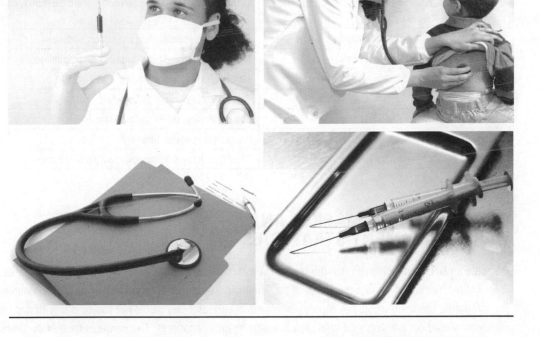

KEY IDEA

➤ The goal of market and market-segment strategies is very simple — *to attract, retain, and grow customers in the face of competitors trying to do the same thing.*

➤ The market strategy is the firm's game plan for addressing the market. The market strategy states:

• What the firm is trying to achieve

• What the firm will do

• What the firm will not do.

Chapter 7 discussed Imperative 1, Determine and Recommend Which Markets to Address. Chapter 8 discussed Imperative 2: Identify and Target Market Segments, addressing two separate, but related, strategic-level tasks. First, we learned how to conduct the *market segmentation process* and identify *market segments*. Second, we showed how the firm should decide which segments to *target* for marketing effort.

Chapter 9 is the first of three chapters that discuss separate aspects of Imperative 3: Set Strategic Direction and Positioning. Here we focus on developing **market strategy**, arguably one of marketing's most important roles and responsibilities. As we learned in earlier chapters, the market strategy goal is very simple — *to attract, retain, and grow customers, in the face of competitors trying to do the same thing.* The market strategy declares what the firm *will do* and what it *will not do.* Externally, a well-developed strategy reflects the common theme and emphasis of the firm's approach to the market. Internally, it coordinates the actions of many departments and people. An effective market strategy is crucial for success.[3]

The firm partitions each chosen market into several market segments; then decides which segment(s) to target for effort. If the firm's segmentation is effective, customers in each segment have homogeneous (similar) need profiles. But across segments, these profiles are heterogeneous (different). The extent and type of competition also varies by segment. Because of these differences, the firm must develop a separate strategy for each target segment; positioning is the heart of the *market-segment* strategy. The *market strategy* comprises one or more *market-segment* strategies.

THE CHANGING VIEW

OLD WAY	NEW WAY
Market strategy development done by marketing and general management	Cross-functional teamwork crucial in market strategy development
Competitor considerations ignored or demeaned	Competitor considerations play a major role
Compromise is common — fuzzy value propositions	Clarity is critical — value propositions are clear and differentiated
Internal and budgetary focus to market strategy	External and strategic focus to market strategy
Marketers focus on volume and share	Marketers concerned with creating shareholder value
Objectives uniform across products and markets	Objectives differ across products and markets
Positioning is poorly understood	Positioning is a crucial strategic element
Market strategy is the marketing mix	Market strategy drives the marketing mix
Integration is limited to the marketing mix	Integration spans all functions
Functional programs are poorly coordinated	Market strategy links together functional programs

MARKETING ENRICHMENT

Levels of Strategy me901

me901

THE PURPOSE OF MARKET AND MARKET-SEGMENT STRATEGIES

Imagine an NFL team going through the football season without a strategy. What are its chances of reaching the Super Bowl? Very slim — luck only goes so far. The team would lack direction and focus and be unable to leverage its strengths. The team would not deploy players effectively, and they would not coordinate with one another. In short, the team would not develop a differential advantage against opponents. ***The same is true in business. To be successful, a firm must have a clear market strategy to "win" in the marketplace.***

Strategy is one of the most abused and most misunderstood terms in business, yet important in any manager's vocabulary.[4] The market strategy builds on planning assumptions formed from market, customer, competitor, company, and complementer insight. The market strategy is the firm's game plan for the market, pointing the way to firm actions. The market strategy specifies what the firm is trying to achieve, which market segments it will target for effort, and how it will position itself in those segments.[5] The firm must make three types of decisions:

- **Results.** What the firm wants to achieve from addressing the market.
- **Resources.** Broadly, how the firm will deploy its resources to achieve these results.
- **Actions.** What specific actions the firm intends to take to be successful.[6]

KEY IDEA

➤ The market strategy requires decisions about:

- Results
- Resources
- Actions

KEY IDEA

➤ Well-developed market and market-segment strategies fulfill four purposes for the firm:

- Provide strategic direction in the market
- Show how to secure differential advantage
- Guide the effective allocation of scarce resources
- Achieve cross-functional integration

Well-developed market-segment and market strategies fulfill four purposes for the firm: Provide strategic direction in the market, show how to secure differential advantage, guide the effective allocation of scarce resources, and achieve cross-functional and cross-business integration.

PROVIDING STRATEGIC DIRECTION IN THE MARKET

Market and market-segment strategies provide strategic direction on how to attract, retain, and grow customers, in the face of competitors trying to do the same thing. We expect markets, customer needs, and competitive challenges to evolve and become more complex. The market strategy must guide the firm in the changing environment. Achieving this purpose is more difficult, yet more essential, the greater the complexity and change the firm faces.[7]

SECURING DIFFERENTIAL ADVANTAGE

Well-developed market-segment and market strategies must clarify why customers should buy from the firm rather than competitors. They also show how the firm will gain differential advantage. Recall from earlier chapters that a *differential advantage is a net benefit or cluster of benefits, offered to a sizable group of customers, which they value and are willing to pay for, but cannot get, or believe they cannot get, elsewhere.* Table 9.1 describes criteria for evaluating *good* market-segment and market strategies, and shows how Semic (fictional electronics firm) may attempt to secure differential advantage.[8]

The firm should reject any market-segment or market strategy that cannot withstand probable competitor responses.[9] The firm should also develop contingency plans, or *what if* responses, to possible competitor actions. Contingency planning leads to strategies that secure differential advantage, and helps the firm act pre-emptively — before competitors. (World-class chess players compete by identifying opponents' potential moves and thinking several moves ahead!)

TABLE 9.1

SECURING DIFFERENTIAL ADVANTAGE

Criteria	Strategy Description	Example
Competitors cannot do	The firm takes actions competitors cannot duplicate — typically they lack a key resource or competence.	Semic secures patent protection on a new discovery — competitors cannot copy.
Competitors will not do	Competitors could match the strategy, but are unlikely to do so. The firm needs significant competitive insight to make this judgment.	Semic enters a new distribution channel. The competitor's CEO tells an industry audience it will maintain its existing distribution strategy.
Competitors will be relatively disadvantaged if they do	The firm believes the competitor will duplicate its strategy — but the firm will receive a disproportionate benefit.	Semic launches a major advertising campaign aiming for market growth and larger market share. Semic expects the competitor to follow and increase sales, but believes Semic will improve market share in a larger market.[10]
Competitors and the firm will benefit	The firm believes its actions will be advantageous both to itself and competitors.	Semic joins with competitors to launch a major PR campaign to ward off adverse legislation, by showing the value all firms deliver to customers.

GUIDING THE EFFECTIVE ALLOCATION OF SCARCE RESOURCES

All firms have limited resources like capital, plant capacity, sales force time, and technological capability. These limitations apply at each organizational level and functional area — typically, some resources are more limited than others. The firm must allocate these scarce resources to secure differential advantage. A *good* market strategy considers resource limitations and defines, generally yet clearly, effective allocations to support the firm's strategic direction.

The firm must make two types of allocations. *Externally*, the firm allocates resources among target market segments, selecting the resources for securing differential advantage by segment. *Internally*, the firm allocates resources among activities like product development, advertising, and selling.

ACHIEVING CROSS-FUNCTIONAL INTEGRATION

Achieving integration across different parts of the firm and/or business unit is critical, yet often elusive. Sometimes critical integration is among different firm functions; other times different business units within the firm must work together.[11] The market strategy must coordinate the actions of various parts of the firm, so they all pull together to secure differential advantage. Without effective integration, significant internal conflict can arise.

Market-strategy owners must develop support throughout the firm. The various functions and/or business units likely have different opinions about the market strategy: The sales department wants to increase sales and operations wants to reduce costs, in part because that it what they are paid to do. But actions that seem reasonable from the perspective of a specific function may be inappropriate when market considerations are paramount. Well-managed contention is healthy, for it surfaces different perspectives on key issues.[12] But all parties must focus on external issues and take a holistic view on how the firm can win.[13]

ELEMENTS OF THE MARKET-SEGMENT STRATEGY

The Secrets of Samsung's Success

Samsung refocused semiconductor efforts from the mass PC market to niche segments with higher prices and fatter margins — game consoles, flash memory for handheld computers, and camcorders. In recent years, Samsung has shown impressive growth in sales and profits, the results of a successful market strategy.

A market is best viewed as a set of market segments. To be successful, the firm should target specific segments with strategies that create differential advantage. Generally, firms perform well when they focus on a few segments versus the market as a whole. Hertz, Alamo, and Enterprise are major players in car rental, but each focuses on a specific segment: Hertz — business travelers with speed and convenience; Alamo — vacation travelers with low-prices; and Enterprise — local convenience to drivers whose cars are being repaired.

Because of market segment differences, the basic market-strategy unit is the market-segment strategy — Figure 9.1: A market strategy frequently combines several interrelated market-segment strategies.

- **Performance objectives.** Stated as results the firm seeks; includes strategic objectives and operational objectives.
- **Strategic focus.** The broad direction of the strategy.
- **Positioning.** How the firm wants customers to view its offer; comprises *customer targets*, *competitor targets*, *value proposition*, and *reasons to believe*.[14]
- **Implementation programs.** How the firm should implement the strategy; includes the marketing mix and supporting functional programs.

KEY IDEA

➤ An effective market strategy helps the firm allocate resources.
- *Externally* — the firm allocates resources to target market segments so as to secure differential advantage.
- *Internally* — the firm allocates resources across internal activities.

Marketing Question

Your firm is launching a new product. You anticipate high short-run market growth and six months' competitive lead-time. How will these factors affect your marketing, sales, operations, R&D, human resources, and finance decisions?

KEY IDEA

➤ Inter-functional conflict is endemic. Formulating the market strategy should resolve this conflict and achieve cross-functional integration.

FIGURE 9.1

ELEMENTS OF THE MARKET-SEGMENT STRATEGY

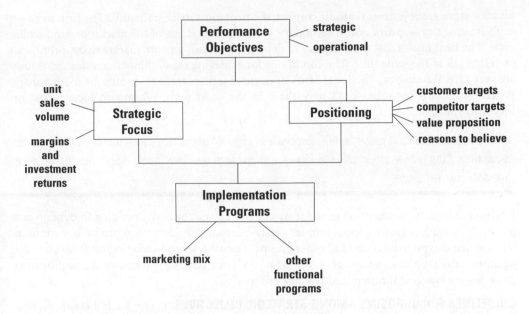

KEY IDEA

► The market segment strategy:

- **Performance objectives**
- Strategic focus
- Positioning
- Implementation programs

Performance objectives, *strategic focus*, and *positioning* are conceptual devices requiring creativity. Product and brand managers or marketing and business directors typically develop these elements based on planning assumptions formed from market, customer, competitor, company, and complementer insight. *Implementation programs* are more tangible. The firm secures integrated implementation by clearly articulating and gaining commitment to performance objectives, strategic focus, and positioning. Key executives must build relationships, manage group processes, and coordinate activities. By securing widespread cross-functional support early on, marketing sets the stage for successful design and implementation of the market-segment strategy.

PERFORMANCE OBJECTIVES

"If you don't know where you're going, any road will get you there."

— Lewis Carroll, *Alice in Wonderland*

Before the firm figures out what it will do, it must know where it's headed. **Performance objectives** articulate the firm's goals for the market segment. Two components state clearly and simply what the firm is trying to achieve: strategic objectives and operational objectives.

STRATEGIC OBJECTIVES

Strategic objectives establish the type of results the firm requires; they are qualitative and directional. Strategic objectives are not concerned with numbers, but declare, in general terms, how the firm will measure its success. Many people confuse strategic objectives with mission statements — Chapter 7. The difference is clear: Mission states where the firm will seek market opportunities; strategic objectives state the types of results the firm seeks.

The three broad categories of strategic objectives are growth and market share, profitability, and cash flow. Each strategic objective is attractive, but they often conflict. Many firms set growth and market share as key strategic objectives, but have to spend on fixed assets, working capital, and marketing expenses. These expenditures negatively affect short-term cash flow and profitability.[15]

Because strategic objectives typically conflict, the firm must make trade-offs. The firm must set explicit priorities — primary and secondary — for various stages of the market or product life cycle. The firm must resist the tendency to demand increased growth, market share, profit, *and* cash flow, all at the same time. The conditions for achieving on all dimensions simultaneously are very rare. Wheatcorn's (fictional firm) strategic objectives trade off profits for market share. Wheatcorn wants both, but can't have them in the short term; Wheatcorn focuses first on increasing profits:

> Wheatcorn targeted the *young family with children* segment of the cold-cereal market. Wheatcorn stated its strategic objectives: "Our primary objective is to *increase profits* from our *Cold Chunks* brand. Our secondary objective is to *maintain market share.*"

Reaching internal agreement on strategic objectives may not be easy. Spending to develop new products or exploit growth opportunities versus pressure for short-term profits is a common tension that can pit marketing (and other groups) against finance. Marketing must seek out and optimize opportunities, but also recognize that profits are necessary to maintain a healthy stock price, secure low-cost funding, and pay our salaries![16]

GUIDELINES FOR CHOOSING AMONG STRATEGIC OBJECTIVES. Figure 9.2 is a classic illustration of how strategic objectives evolve in a product life-cycle framework. In the introduction and early growth stages, firms often set priorities on growth and/or market share. These objectives shift to profit in late growth and for much of the maturity stage. Late in the maturity stage, especially if decline is imminent, cash flow predominates; hence the term *cash cow*.[17] Table 9.2 shows quantitative results from a PIMS (Profit Impact of Market Strategy) study supporting this pattern.[18] Sales growth is high in early life-cycle stages but is lower late in the life cycle. Return on investment and cash flow are often negative for startups but turn positive later.[19]

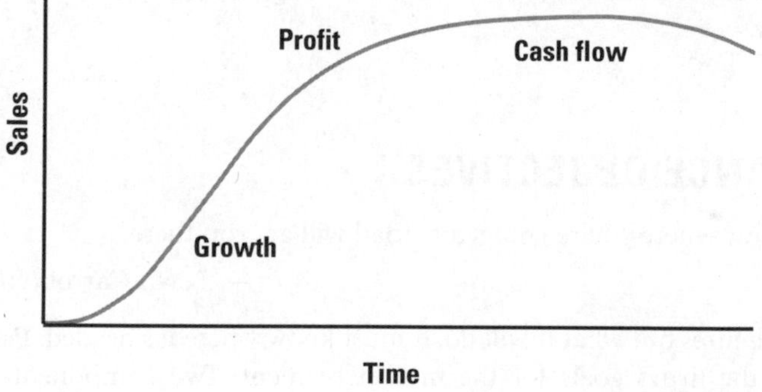

KEY IDEA

➤ The firm must make trade-offs among the three categories of strategic objectives:
- Growth and market share
- Profitability
- Cash flow

FIGURE 9.2

EVOLUTION OF STRATEGIC OBJECTIVES

Category	Measure	Life Cycle Stage			
		Startup	**Growth**	**Early Maturity**	**Late Maturity**
Market Performance	Sales Growth (%)	74	23	11	6
	Market Share (%)	8	25	24	24
Budget Levels	R&D/Sales (%)	10	3	2	1
	Marketing/Sales (%)	26	11	9	8
Financial Performance	ROI (%)	−19	25	22	17
	Net Income Growth (%)	7	20	15	11
	Investment Growth (%)	38	19	9	3
	Cash Flow/Investment (%)	−46	1	6	9

TABLE 9.2

OPERATING RESULTS OF PIMS BUSINESSES*

* Data are four-year average percentages, except growth rates; these are annual rates (current dollars); data in the *startup* column are medians. Figures (except net income growth) secured from The Strategic Planning Institute, Cambridge, MA.

Do not view these guidelines as prescriptions for choosing primary strategic objectives. Results simply show many firms' behavior, assuming results reflect original objectives (on average).

Examples of Setting Strategic Objectives

Growth: When economies enter recession, leading firms sometimes cut prices in attempts to increase growth and market share.

Profit: When Howard Schultz returned as Starbucks' CEO, strategic objectives shifted from growth to profit.

Cash flow: When patents protect products, major pharmaceutical firms generally make high operating profits. When patent protection ends and generics enter, leading firms often cut expenses to generate positive cash flow.

KEY IDEA

➤ Priorities for strategic objectives evolve during product life-cycle stages.

OPERATIONAL OBJECTIVES

Strategic objectives are qualitative and directional, but **operational objectives** are quantitative and time-bound. Operational objectives provide the numbers and time frame to attach to strategic objectives. What types of numbers? Operational objectives answer the following questions: How much is required, and when? Operational objectives should specify how much growth, market share, profit, and/or cash flow the firm should earn during a specific time frame.[20] Table 9.3 returns to Wheatcorn, showing operational objectives in context with each strategic objective.

TABLE 9.3

STRATEGIC AND OPERATIONAL OBJECTIVES

Typically, the firm sets operational objectives by year in the strategic marketing plan. In the annual marketing plan, the firm calendarizes these annual objectives by quarter or by month.

	Strategic Objectives	Operational Objectives*
Primary	*Increase profits* from our *Cold Chunks* brand	from: $12 million in 20XY to: $15 million in 20XY+1 $20 million in 20XY+2 $25 million in 20XY+3
Secondary	Maintain market share	at: 25% from 20XY through 20XY+3

The firm uses operational objectives to evaluate performance. Operational objectives should be **SMART** — **s**pecific, **m**easurable, **a**chievable, **r**ealistic, and **t**imely. Operational objectives should also be challenging, but not out of reach and demotivating. A particular problem is pursuing growth too aggressively. Starbucks — Chapter 1 Opening Case — had problems because it allowed growth objectives to override its rigorous location policies. The UBS example is cautionary:

Zurich-based UBS's investment-banking arm lagged competition in fixed-income products. UBS expanded quickly in structured credit and commodities, but emphasized revenue growth at the expense of risk. UBS focused on high-fee, but riskier (*mezzanine*), collateralized debt obligations of U.S. mortgage-backed securities, with minimal hedging. In the 2008–9 financial crisis, UBS lost $38 billion, significantly reducing its core capital and share price.

KEY IDEA

➤ Operational objectives provide the numbers to attach to the strategic objectives; they specify how much is needed and by when.

The firm should establish tentative short-term and long-term operational objectives early in the market-segment strategy development process. As it develops its strategy and implementation programs, the firm should continually assess budgetary implications. The firm should also revisit its operational objectives, ultimately freezing on them as finite expectations and targets.

SETTING PERFORMANCE OBJECTIVES

Sometimes managers fail to distinguish between strategic and operational objectives. Far too often, they state objectives in terms of profits, "Our profit target for 20XY is $45 million." In principle, setting a $45 million target is not wrong, but the problem is in not asking (yet alone answering) two basic questions. *How will achieving this profit objective affect the firm's overall objectives?* and *How shall we get there?*

Improving short-term profits is not that difficult. Just cut spending on new products, advertising, sales promotion, and salaries; raise prices; and tighten credit terms. The firm will quickly increase profits, but in time will lose market share and profitability. To avoid such results, the firm must articulate the trade-offs among the various strategic objectives. Managers from all functional areas should agree on appropriate strategic objectives for the firm's long-term health; only then should the firm insert numbers to form operational objectives.

Generally, strategic and operational objectives should not change during the operating period. But if significant environmental change occurs, adjusting performance objectives may be crucial. If the planning assumptions underlying market forecasts change substantially, then the forecasts and performance objectives should change also. Some firms fail to modify market forecasts and objectives in the face of significant environmental change:

🔑 **KEY IDEA**

➤ Managers should explicitly discuss trade-offs and expectations among strategic objectives before setting operational objectives.

Environmental Change and Performance Objectives

In recessions, many capital goods firms do not act on data that predict lower future sales:

- Sales taking longer to close.

- Sales for one-time infrastructure development likely to drop as the economy slows.

- Customers likely to cancel purchases based on venture capital when venture capital funding dries up.

- Sales projections possibly biased upwards: because some customers are ordering difficult-to-find products from several distributors and also direct from the manufacturer.

Of course, the firm may have specific marketing objectives like brand awareness and customer satisfaction that affect the strategic and operational objectives; we discuss these later.

STRATEGIC FOCUS

Once the firm has established performance objectives for its target market segment, it must decide where to allocate resources. The **strategic focus** does exactly that — Figure 9.1, p. 223. Figure 9.3 illustrates the firm's options using a **means/ends tree** to outline, assess, and choose among various alternatives for improving profits and return on investment (ROI).[21] The tree has two main branches: Branch A — *increase unit sales volume*; Branch B — *improve margins and investment returns*. The firm must select among the branches and sub-branches to create a focus that best helps achieve its strategic and operational performance objectives.

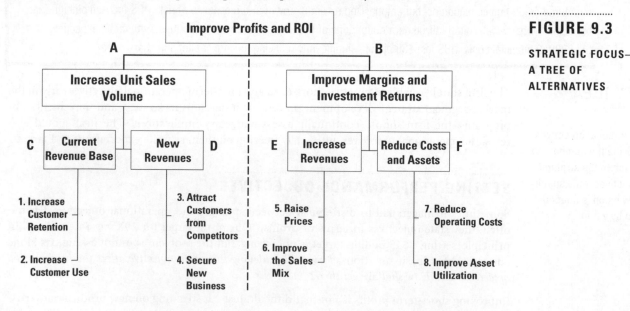

FIGURE 9.3

STRATEGIC FOCUS–
A TREE OF
ALTERNATIVES

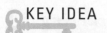
INCREASE UNIT SALES VOLUME (BRANCH A)

Branch A has two sub-branches, C and D, for increasing unit sales volume. Sub-branch C focuses on the firm's current revenue base; sub-branch D focuses on securing new revenues. Each sub-branch provides two alternatives. In sub-branch C, the firm enhances current revenues by *increasing customer retention* and *increasing customer use*. In sub-branch D, the firm secures new revenues by *attracting customers from competitors* and *securing new business* by identifying opportunities.

INCREASE CUSTOMER RETENTION, SUB-BRANCH C. A firm's customer base is like a leaky bucket. Some customers defect to competitors; others stop buying altogether. Chapter 2 shows that *plugging holes* by deploying approaches to reduce customer defection helps the firm retain customers longer and grow faster. This thinking also underpins customer relationship management (CRM). The New York Stock Exchange (NYSE) tries to persuade successful NASDAQ firms to join its exchange. NASDAQ's retention managers reduce defection and enhance loyalty via extensive contact with at-risk firms. Many firms have loyalty programs that reward customers for repeat business — we're all familiar with airline *frequent-flyer* programs, retail clubs, and supermarket loyalty cards. But many small retailers like your local dry cleaner or car wash also use loyalty programs, often via simple physical cards they *chop/nick* with each purchase.

INCREASE CUSTOMER USE, SUB-BRANCH C. The firm encourages customers to increase repeat purchases and/or buy other products. In B2C markets, the firm sells products in larger containers[22]; speeds up obsolescence by introducing new versions — like cars and software; finds new product uses — like Arm & Hammer's baking soda for cat litter, cleaning agent, deodorizer, toothpaste, and even cattle feed; provides price incentives for purchasing large quantities — like grocery store coupons[23]; and offers bundling opportunities like shampoo and conditioner, or durable goods with maintenance packages.

In B2B markets, many firms work with customers to engineer new product applications. Alcoa helps auto manufacturers reduce weight and increase gas mileage by replacing steel with aluminum. Helping customers grow their business is a powerful alternative. Xerox redesigned Citibank's monthly customer account statement to be more customer-friendly (easier to read/understand); Citibank gained banking clients.[24] Other approaches include distributor training, joint promotions, advertising and promotion allowances, guarantees and warranties, and *spiffs* — cash incentives for retailer and distributor salespeople.

Many firms incorporate their brands into other firms' products, then advertise directly to consumers. The *intel inside* advertising campaign increased sales of personal computers — and Intel chips. Other firms focus on cross-selling — selling multiple products to existing customers. Vanguard and Fidelity mutual fund customers can easily transfer deposits from fund to fund — and buy additional products like life insurance and annuities. This focus is easier to implement if the firm organizes around customers, rather than products or brands — Chapter 20.

ATTRACT CUSTOMERS FROM COMPETITORS, SUB-BRANCH D. There are two customer types in this category:

• Previous customers that defected to competitors.

• Customers that purchase exclusively from competitors.

These customer types are quite different. Type 1 previously had a relationship with the firm — the challenge is *win-back*. Type 2 have never had a relationship — the challenge is *switch* from competitors. In either case, the firm must offer significant customer value to be successful. Winning back and switching customers are especially important in mature markets like credit cards because there are fewer *new* customers. How many credit card offers did you receive last month? If you have a decent credit history, probably quite a few.

In many cases, like credit cards and other financial services, customers split purchases among several suppliers; the firm's task is to increase *share of wallet*. Failed competitors offer good opportunities for attracting customers: Macy's focused on fallen rivals like Fortunoff, Gottschalks, and Mervyn's; Westchester County's (New York) Phoenix gym made special offers when a neighboring gym closed.

SECURE NEW BUSINESS, SUB-BRANCH D. *Non-users* have never purchased this type of product — from the firm or competitors. In sub-branches A, B, and C, customers already had product experience; the firm's challenge was to beat competitors. In sub-branch D, the firm has a double selling task. First, it must convince *non-users* to buy this type of product. Second, it must convince them to purchase from the firm. Right now, firms making flat-screen plasma televisions must sell both the product's value and their brand.

BRANCH A — REPRISE. The firm has four alternatives to increase unit sales volume: *increase customer retention, increase customer use, attract customers from competitors*, and *secure new business*. Examples are in the boxed insert. How should the firm decide which alternative(s) to pursue? Two important factors are product life-cycle stage and the firm's competitive position. Early in the life cycle, few customers have tried the product and non-users make most purchases — the firm spends heavily on market development. Moving toward maturity, the proportion of non-users decreases, and focus shifts to retaining current customers and attracting competitor customers. Late in maturity when there are fewer non-users competitive position is particularly important. High-market-share leaders typically focus on retaining current customers and increasing their purchases — they are most of the market. Low-share firms focus on attracting competitor customers.

Examples of Increasing Unit Sales Volume — keyed to Figure 9.3

C1. Increase customer retention

To consumers who financed a new GM automobile, GM offered identical financing for a second new car purchased within the financing period.

C2. Increase customer use

Verizon cross-sells long distance, Internet access, and television services. Similarly, cable TV firms sell telephone service and Internet access. Often these firms make bundled offers.

D3. Attract customers from competitors

DirecTV explicitly targets the customers of cable TV firms; natural gas retailers target heating oil customers.

D4. Secure new business

Drug companies make *ask-your-physician* appeals, targeting *non-users* to generate interest, leading to trial. Examples include Plavix — blood thinner; Viagra — erectile dysfunction; and Wellbutrin — anxiety disorder.

IMPROVE MARGINS AND INVESTMENT RETURNS (BRANCH B)

Branch B has two sub-branches, E and F, for improving margins and investment returns, holding unit sales constant. Sub-branch E focuses on increasing the firm's revenues — sub-branch F focuses on reducing costs and assets. Each sub-branch provides two alternatives. In sub-branch E, the firm increases revenues by *raising prices* and *improving the sales mix*. In sub-branch F, the firm lowers costs and assets by *reducing operating costs* and *improving asset utilization*.

RAISE PRICES, SUB-BRANCH E. This option is straightforward: The firm increases revenues by raising prices. Chapter 20 shows many options like increasing list price, cutting discounts, and reducing trade allowances.

IMPROVE THE SALES MIX, SUB-BRANCH E. The firm sells more higher-profit products and fewer lower-profit products. Gillette pursued this strategy for many years with successively more

expensive two-blade shaving systems like Trac II, Atra, and Sensor. Then it introduced the three-blade Mach3, followed by the battery-operated M3Power, priced 67 percent higher than Mach3. Later, Gillette introduced the first five-blade razors, Fusion and Fusion Power, with refill prices one-third more than Mach3 Turbo and, in 2010, the Fusion ProGlide at a 15 percent price premium. The firm can also de-emphasize less-profitable customers and place more effort on higher-profit customers.

REDUCE OPERATING COSTS, SUB-BRANCH F. The firm has many options for reducing operating costs — related and/or unrelated to marketing. Marketing-related cost reductions include the sales force, promotion and advertising, administration and training, and new product development. The firm may also reduce operating costs by outsourcing, insourcing, and re-engineering work processes.

IMPROVE ASSET UTILIZATION, SUB-BRANCH F. Generally speaking, the firm has little asset investment in marketing — the closest are accounts receivable and finished-goods inventory. Marketing can reduce accounts receivable by implementing stiffer credit terms and insisting on faster payments. Supply-chain improvements can reduce the firm's inventory investment. In the Walmart and P&G relationship, marketing plays a major role getting retail store transaction data into the P&G system. These data help reduce inventory throughout the supply chain and benefits not only P&G, but also its suppliers and Walmart.

BRANCH B — REPRISE. The firm has four alternatives to *improve margins and investment returns: raise prices, improve the sales mix, reduce operating costs,* and *improve asset utilization.* Examples are in the boxed insert. The choice among these alternatives has a less sharp focus than Branch A. The firm should pursue alternatives providing the best financial returns.

Examples of Improving Margins and Investment Returns — keyed to Figure 9.3

E5. Raise prices
Firms with monopoly-like positions often use this approach — cable TV firms and their suppliers like ESPN and Disney; also, seasonal products like amusement parks and airline travel.

E6. Improve the sales mix
Many B2B firms add services or offer additional features, trying to persuade customers to trade up to more expensive offers with higher profit margins.

F7. Reduce operating costs
Many firms reduce costs by downsizing (firing workers), re-engineering processes, and outsourcing internal operations. Other approaches include cutting back on advertising, and other promotional and selling expenses.

F8. Improve asset utilization
Dell's make-to-order manufacturing system minimizes inventory investment. Also, by receiving payment before making the product, Dell operates with **negative working capital**.[25]

CHOOSING A STRATEGIC FOCUS: INCREASE UNIT SALES VOLUME OR IMPROVE MARGINS AND INVESTMENT RETURNS?

Question: How should the firm trade off alternatives in Branch A with alternatives in Branch B? After all, many are in conflict. Targeting competitor customers may be a viable option for increasing unit sales, but it won't be successful if the firm simultaneously cuts advertising and selling expenses!

Answer: The firm's choice of alternative(s) should closely parallel its primary strategic objective. For growth, the firm should focus on Branch A alternatives; but for increasing cash flow, it should focus on Branch B. If the primary strategic objective is improving profits, the firm should mix and match — select alternatives from both Branches A and B. What is very clear: The firm cannot pursue too many alternatives simultaneously without losing focus, and violating the Principle of Selectivity and Concentration.

POSITIONING

For many marketers and marketing faculty, **positioning** is the heart of the market-segment strategy — Figure 9.1, p. 223. The firm seeks to create a unique and favorable image for the firm's product in customers' minds. Clarity is key; confusion is positioning's enemy.

We must emphasize the critical distinction between *targeting* a market segment and *positioning* in a market segment. Chapter 8 discussed targeting market segments; Chapter 9 assumes the firm has made the targeting decision. Now we focus on developing a strategy to compete successfully in the target segment. Positioning requires four key decisions *within* the segment:

- Select customer targets.
- Frame competitor targets.
- Design the value proposition.
- Articulate reasons to believe.

We discuss these decisions sequentially but they are highly interrelated. Typically, the firm goes back and forth among these decisions until they form a coherent whole. Figure 9.4 breaks down the process by identifying considerations in selecting customer targets, framing competitor targets, and designing the value proposition.

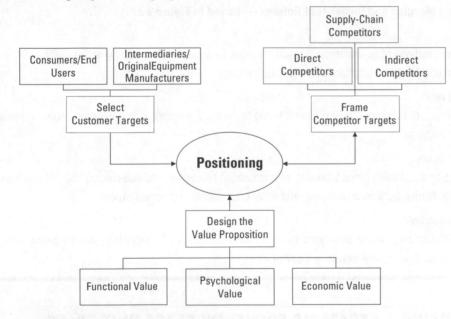

FIGURE 9.4

THE ELEMENTS OF POSITIONING

SELECTING CUSTOMER TARGETS

Customer targets are where the firm places the bulk of its marketing efforts. Unless you target the right customers, your chances of success are slim. Three issues are important:

- **Choosing the distribution system.** The firm must identify the appropriate distribution system — possibly comprising multiple levels — so its products reach end-user customers.
- **Targeting levels within the distribution system.** The firm must decide which level(s) in the distribution system should receive the most marketing effort.

➤ KEY IDEA

➤ Critical issues in selecting customer targets are:

• Choosing the distribution system
• Targeting levels within the distribution system
• Targeting specific person types/roles

Marketing Question

Pret a Manger (ready to eat), a British-based sandwich chain, entered the U.S. by opening stores in New York, Chicago, and Washington. Conduct research to identify Pret a Manger's positioning. How do you assess its chances for success in the U.S.?

• **Targeting specific person types/roles.** The firm must identify what specific person types/roles it should target for effort at the chosen distribution levels.

CHOOSING THE DISTRIBUTION SYSTEM. The firm's products (components, raw materials, or services) may reach end-user customers in many different ways — direct or via third-party organizations.[26] Examples for tangible products include:

• A component manufacturer sells products to finished-goods manufacturers.

• A component manufacturer sells products to sub-assembly manufacturers; in turn, they sell their products to finished-goods manufacturers.

• Products produced by finished-goods manufacturers pass through distributors, wholesalers, and/or retailers before reaching end-user customers.[27]

Many industries have well-established distribution systems whereby products travel *downstream* from level to level, ultimately reaching end-user customers. But the firm may develop innovative channels to gain differential advantage. Today, many firms avoid distributors, wholesalers, and retailers (and their margins) by targeting consumers directly via the Internet. Michael Dell believed that customer buying patterns would change as the PC market matured and that experienced users would no longer require retail salespeople to provide information and reassurance — Dell focused on direct distribution. Conversely, Apple developed its own extensive retail network to develop closer consumer relationships.

TARGETING LEVELS WITHIN THE DISTRIBUTION SYSTEM. With limited resources, the firm must decide which distribution levels to target for effort. Broad options are *push* and *pull* — Chapter 15:

• **Push strategy:** The firm places most marketing effort *upstream* on direct customers like manufacturers and distributors. A firm selling finished consumer products focuses on retailers; a raw material/component producer focuses on finished-goods manufacturers like original equipment manufacturers (OEMs). The firm expects these customers (and/or their customers) to promote its products to end users.

• **Pull strategy:** The firm places most marketing effort *downstream* on indirect customers — consumers/end users. FMCG firms focus on consumers; raw material/component manufacturers focus on end-user customers — like the *intel inside* campaign.

Typically, the firm cannot apply equal effort at all potential customer targets. The firm should designate primary and secondary targets. Mattel shows the importance of customer targeting:

Mattel introduced *Barbie* at the 1959 Toy Fair — retail buyer response was negative. Essentially, they told Ruth Handler, Mattel founder and Barbie's originator: "Little girls want baby dolls; they want to pretend to be mommies." Motivational researcher Ernest Dichter advised Handler to launch Barbie with TV advertising. When girls saw TV ads for Barbie, they — and their mothers — stampeded the stores.[28] By targeting the final consumer, Mattel achieved global market leadership in the toy industry.

Japan's Okidata makes office products like fax machines and printers. Its U.S. subsidiary exclusively targeted a small number of geographically focused distributors. These distributors sold products to dealers, who in turn sold to corporate accounts. To speed sales, Okidata reduced focus on distributors, and targeted dealers and corporate customers.

TARGETING SPECIFIC PERSON TYPES/ROLES. Once the firm has selected distribution level, it must decide which specific influencers and/or decision-makers to target. Typically the firm wants to change or reinforce behavior and/or mental states like knowledge, attitudes, and purchase intentions. Recall: Organizations do not make decisions — people in organizations make decisions! For a firm targeting households, potential individual targets are husband, wife, children, grandparents, uncles, and aunts. This choice was very important for College Savings Bank:

College Savings Bank (CSB) offers certificates of deposit (CDs), indexed to college-cost inflation. CSB guarantees sufficient funds to pay college tuition at a specified future date. CSB targets parents and grandparents.[29]

China's one-child policy leads toy firms to target doting grandparents; in the U.S., firms target children directly. Tweens (eight to 12 years) are an increasingly important segment, spending $15 billion annually and *heavily* influencing $30 billion of parental spending. Popular products include privacy doorbells for their rooms, chairs shaped like catcher's mitts, fanciful bed head-boards, and fake-fur computer covers.

B2B firms also make individual-level targeting decisions. A well-known floor-covering firm reaches consumers via distributors and retailers. The firm markets heavily to retailers, but focuses on retail salespeople by providing spiffs (cash incentives). A firm selling raw materials to manufacturers may target operations managers, design engineers, marketing and sales, purchasing agents, and/or general managers.

Creativity is important in customer targeting. The firm should consider:

- **Reachability.** Target customers should be easy to reach — but gaining access may be difficult. In B2B, individual customers like designers, engineers, operations personnel, sales and marketing managers, and senior executives often want customized value. But the procurement system confronts sellers with purchasing professionals who often focus on short-term cost minimization — lower-prices. The creative CEO of one major telecommunications firm took a sales training course. The CEO then pitched the value of his firm's services directly to CEOs of potential customers, essentially bypassing procurement.

- **Obvious versus creative targets.** Some customers are easy to identify and reach, but targeting them can be ineffective, because they are obvious — they may also be competitors' customer targets! Deep customer insight, creativity and a contrarian position can pay great dividends.[30] FedEx's early success came from targeting executives and their secretaries rather than shipping managers, the traditional decision-makers. Much of Michelin's U.S. success in tire sales is due to focusing on parents, primarily mothers, with young children.

- **Influentials.** Customer targets may not be decision-makers, but they should influence the buying decision, like retail sales people for passenger tires and home appliances. Neglecting important influentials can be fatal. In B2B marketing, over-eager sellers often neglect subordinates, who may:
  - Identify specific criteria for supplier selection.
  - Determine which suppliers enter the customer's consideration set.
  - Have *nay* power, even if they don't have *yea* power.
  - Eventually replace their bosses. Firms that treat *the little guy* poorly may later encounter significant obstacles, especially if competitors have been more solicitous.

- **Personally benefits but does not pay.** The ideal customer target has significant influence and personally benefits from the purchase, but does not pay. Examples include:
  - Children influencing parental decisions.
  - Doctors writing prescriptions.
  - Executives whose firms pay travel expenses.
  - Architects, interior designers, and product designers.[31]
  - Accountants, financial advisors, and lawyers for customers with investable funds.
  - Politicians and regulators serving their constituents — they spend taxpayers' money.

Targeting these customers can raise ethical issues. Many people object to children's advertising; others object to targeting government lobbyists.

FRAMING COMPETITOR TARGETS

The firm decides which competitors to compete against. **Competitor targets** can be current and/or potential competitors, direct and/or indirect competitors, and/or supply-chain competitors. Choice of competitor target depends on firm strength in the market segment. For small competitors, choosing the right targets is vital — large and strong firms can be less delicate; Dr. Pepper has less leeway than Coca-Cola. Key issues are:

CATEGORIES OF COMPETITORS. Competitors fall into one of two categories — competitors to avoid and competitors the firm is quite happy (and chooses) to face. This partition helps the firm design its value proposition (next section).[32]

CUSTOMER PERCEPTIONS. Competitive targeting shapes customer perceptions of the firm's offer. Table 9.4's positioning alternatives suggest four competitor framings for 7-Up. Choosing among them has important implications for 7-Up's market opportunities.

TABLE 9.4

FRAMING
COMPETITOR
TARGETS

Claim	Type	Market Opportunities	Customer Implications
"7-Up tastes better than Sprite"[33]	Comparison with direct competitor	One lemon-lime soda substitutes for another	Compare us
"7-Up, the best-tasting lemon-lime soda"	Product form superiority	The whole lemon-lime product form	The best choice when drinking lemon-lime
"7-Up, the uncola"	Out of product form	The cola product form	The alternative to cola. "We're different"
"7-Up, the real thing, the only one," etc.	Implied or claimed uniqueness	All beverages?	There's no other drink quite like it

SUBTLETY IN COMPETITOR TARGETING. The most effective competitor targeting may not be obvious. Who benefits from designating major accounting firms as the Big 3? — Number 3! The Big 3's competitor target is number 4. When Avis *tries harder*, who is the competitor target? Maybe Hertz, but more likely smaller players like National and Budget. Visa advertises that many restaurants globally accept its card, but relatively few accept AmEx. Visa wants customers to believe AmEx is a direct competitor. But Visa's real competitor target is MasterCard.

KEY IDEA

➤ The firm's competitive target can be:

• Current or potential
• Direct or indirect
• Supply chain

➤ Sometimes the targeted competitor is not immediately obvious.

DESIGNING THE VALUE PROPOSITION

A well-designed **value proposition** provides a convincing answer to a deceptively simple question: "Why should target customers prefer the firm's offer to those of competitors?" *Positioning is the heart of the strategy* — the *value proposition* is the heart of positioning. The firm bases its value proposition on functional, psychological, and economic value and related benefits it offers customers. The value proposition defines how the firm gains customers and beats competitors. Related terms are *key buying incentive, differentiated core benefit, core strategy,* and *unique selling proposition,* but *value proposition* best captures the concept.[34]

Examples of Clear and Effective Value Propositions

• Apple's Macintosh computers — *It just works*

• Cosmopolitan — Fun, fearless, female

• Federal Express (now FedEx) delivers on time — *When it absolutely, positively has to get there overnight*

• HSBC — Global reach, local understanding

• iPod — Take your music with you

• Kate Spade — Curious, charming, clever

• Telephone calls made with Sprint are very clear — *You can hear a pin drop*

• Victoria's Secret — Sexy, sophisticated, glamorous, feminine, forever young

• Walmart — Always low prices — *Always*

The firm should base its value proposition on the Principles of Customer Value and Differential Advantage — Chapter 1:

- Focus on satisfying important customer needs,
- Attempt to meet these needs better than competitors and, where possible,
- Offer customer benefits and values that are difficult for competitors to imitate.

In particular, the value proposition should follow the BUSCH system — **b**elievable, **u**nique, **s**ustainable, **c**ompelling, and **h**onest.[35] The value proposition plays two separate but related roles:

- **Externally** — is the firm's major competitive weapon for attracting, retaining, and growing customers. *Value proposition* defines why the firm's benefits and values — functional, psychological, and/or economic — are superior to competition.
- **Internally** — defines the firm's implementation task; provides the organizing framework for implementing all firm activities.

The firm must develop a value proposition for each target customer type. FMCG firms often target both consumers and retailers — they must develop two value propositions:

- **Consumers.** The *value proposition* typically focuses on specific consumer benefits and values. Detergent manufacturers Unilever and P&G offer functional benefits like *clean clothes, stain removal,* and *whiter whites.* They also offer psychological benefits like *caring for the family* and the ability to demonstrate *being a good parent.*
- **Retailers.** The *value proposition* typically focuses on economic benefits like *potential profits* and *promotional support,* or functional benefits like *ease of doing business, one-stop shopping, expertise,* and *product delivery.*

Value propositions for separate customer targets are not independent. Suppose the firm communicates its value proposition for consumers with heavy advertising and promotion. High advertising spending weakens the economic value proposition the firm can offer retailers. By contrast, private-label manufacturers offer retailers a strong economic value proposition based on low price by avoiding heavy advertising and promotion.[36]

ARTICULATING REASONS TO BELIEVE

Declaring the firm's intentions in the *value proposition* is one thing; convincing target customers that the firm will deliver on its promises is quite another. The **reasons-to-believe** statement is an essential component of positioning as it supports the firm's value proposition with compelling facts to make its claims believable — like scientific evidence, independent testing data, testimonials, proven firm competencies and/or prior performance, and/or factual information on product attributes. Examples of possible *reasons-to-believe* statements include:

- **Cisco** — technical expertise in routers and many successful installations worldwide.
- **Citibank** — vast network of branches around the world.
- **CommerceOne** — a convenience bank: Opening hours — 7 a.m. to 7 p.m., 7 days a week.
- **J&J** — Tylenol. Clinical evidence of superior pain relief.
- **P&G** — detergents. P&G's long experience in detergents and a huge commitment to R&D.

DEVELOPING POSITIONING STATEMENTS

"Positioning is not what you do to a product — positioning is what you do to the mind of the prospect."[37]

The capstone of the positioning process is a compelling positioning statement: Positioning is vital for guiding and coordinating the firm's marketing efforts. But developing the positioning statement is complex, difficult, and time-consuming. Many people may be involved. A senior

Marketing Question

Google is the market leader in Internet search; Microsoft's search entry is Bing. How would you advise Microsoft to increase market share? How would you advise Google to resist Microsoft's efforts?

KEY IDEA

➤ The value proposition is the firm's major competitive weapon for *attracting, retaining,* and *growing* customers; it also defines the firm's implementation focus.

➤ The firm must develop a value proposition for each target customer type.

KEY IDEA

➤ "Positioning is not what you do to a product: Positioning is what you do to the mind of the prospect."

Unilever marketing executive alleged that it often takes longer to develop product positioning than to develop the product! When P&G introduced *Whitestrips* (teeth whitener), it delayed expensive TV ads and store testing. Rather, it refined Whitestrips positioning and assessed consumer interest while undertaking a six-month online advertising and sales campaign.

Positioning must clearly distinguish the firm's offer from competitor offers.[38] Positioning should:

Convince	[customer target]
In the context of other alternatives	[competitor target]
That they will receive these benefits and values	[value proposition]
Because we have these capabilities/features	[reasons to believe]

Table 9.5 shows a positioning statement for Cemex (Mexican multinational cement producer). Note the value proposition differs by customer target.

TABLE 9.5

EXAMPLE OF A POSITIONING STATEMENT FOR CEMEX[39]

Task	Focus	Positioning Item
Convince	Builders and contractors; site managers and project investors	Customer Target
In the context of other alternatives	Traditional cement producers	Competitor Target
That they will receive these benefits	Site managers: Consistent delivery within 30 minutes of Cemex receiving an order — versus the three-hour standard Project investors: Additional revenues from early project completion	Value Proposition
Because we have these capabilities	A global positioning satellite system on each truck. Computer software that combines truck positions with plant output and customer orders to calculate optimal destinations. The ability to redirect trucks en route.[40]	Reasons to Believe

Marketing Question

Select your favorite (or least favorite) politician. In his/her most recent political campaign, what segments did s/he target? How did the positioning — customer target, competitive target, value proposition, reasons to believe — differ from segment to segment? How did segment strategies mutually interface?

Marketing Question

Sales of erectile dysfunction drugs — Viagra, Levitra, and Cialis — approximate $5 billion annually. Viagra and Cialis each have about 40 percent market share. How are the three drugs positioned? How, if at all, have their positionings evolved? What recommendations would you make for each drug? How does patent expiration factor into your recommendations?

Positioning statements should be **d**istinct, **c**ompelling, **a**uthentic, **p**ersuasive, and **s**ustainable (DCAPS). Creativity can be crucial. Guinness Stout traditionally served a limited market of older men and women.[41] Guinness repositioned Guinness Stout as a friendly beverage for younger consumers. Guinness also leveraged brand heritage by offering the *Guinness* experience at more than 2,000 Irish pubs worldwide. Sales increased dramatically.

Positioning is especially important for new products. Unilever and P&G *get it*, but many firms launch new products with ineffective positioning. Philips (Dutch electronics firm) has a stellar product innovation record but does not market innovations well. Have you heard of CDI, an easy-to-use CD-based interactive product, superior to early CD-ROMs? Or DCC (Digital Compact Cassette), a backward-compatible, record and playback tape cassette, producing high quality digital sound? Some of Philips' technical successes were marketing failures due to ineffective positioning. Many firms waste millions of advertising dollars because of poorly developed positioning. Positioning statements are not advertising messages, but DCAPS positioning provides excellent guidance for creative personnel at advertising agencies.

IMPLEMENTATION PROGRAMS

Strategic focus and positioning specify the firm's approach to achieve performance objectives. **Implementation programs** — Figure 9.1, p. 223 — describe specific actions the firm must take to execute its approach. Any good market or market-segment strategy must seriously address both the marketing mix and other functional programs. Marketing and associated functions like the sales force are responsible for implementing the marketing mix. Personnel from functions like finance and manufacturing implement other functional programs. Integrating the marketing mix and other functional programs is critical for optimizing the firm's efforts — Figure 9.5. Top executive support is crucial for superb implementation.

IMPLEMENTING THE MARKETING MIX

Three issues are important for implementing the marketing mix:

SUPPORTS THE VALUE PROPOSITION AND EACH OTHER. Table 9.6 shows how marketing-mix elements for Steubenware high-quality glass crystal support its value proposition in the gift segment, and support each other. Consumers receive psychological value from the assurance that recipients will love Steubenware for its high quality, image, and scarcity. Chapters 12 through 20 focus on individual marketing-mix elements.

KEY IDEA

➤ The market segment strategy:
  • Performance objectives
  • Strategic focus
  • Positioning
  • **Implementation programs**

Marketing Mix Element	Steubenware's Implementations
Product	Extremely high quality — Steuben destroys products with imperfections
Service	High-quality pre- and post-sale service
Advertising	High-quality shelter magazines like *Good Housekeeping*
Sales promotion	Brochure material and display racks are high quality
Selling strategy	Focuses on product quality
Distribution	Few retail outlets, but high quality — specialty and upscale department stores
Price	High price — reflecting high image

TABLE 9.6

MARKETING MIX FOR STEUBENWARE IN THE GIFT SEGMENT

BUDGET SIZE AND ALLOCATION. Budgetary issues are critical in designing the marketing mix. The firm must set an overall budget but be prepared for modifications based on corporate priorities, competitor actions, and/or difficult economic times. The firm must allocate the budget across different marketing mix areas. In some areas the firm's budget exceeds competitors; in other areas, competitors spend more.[42] The firm must be sure its efforts are superior in areas supporting the value proposition, and should continually test budget allocation elements:

KEY IDEA

➤ The firm implements market segment strategy via:
  • Marketing mix
  • Other functional programs

Hamfirm (HF) (disguised name) believed that product improvement was the only way to grow sales and profits. Interviews at retail stores carrying its products revealed that HF should moderate product improvement efforts and allocate greater resources to advertising, in-store promotions, promotional giveaways, and salesperson *spiffs*.

Amazon's 16-month test in two cities showed that advertising was not working — it transferred resources to free shipping.

Heinz improved financial performance by reducing incentive payments to retailers and investing in advertising.

ALIGNING CROSS-FUNCTIONAL SUPPORT

Even though marketing may *own* the market strategy, competition is so intense that the entire firm must work together as a competitive weapon by aligning all functional areas — like finance, human resources, legal, operations, and R&D — to support the value proposition — Figure 9.5. Key factors in successful alignment are open and clear leadership, early involvement of key personnel, team-based planning, and interpersonal sensitivity. A leading U.S. business magazine was in crisis when competition challenged its 50-year market dominance. The firm pulled together a cross-functional team to develop and implement a new market strategy. This approach successfully reinforced the magazine's leadership and produced its best-ever financial result![43]

Domino's Pizza provides functional support for its value proposition — delivering hot pizza quickly. Domino's selects locations with easy access to many homes; its customer database saves time taking orders and making deliveries; and R&D produced technology to cook pizza *en route* to the customer. At weekends, Hertz city locations sold out while cars sat idle at airports; Hertz hired *transporters* to move cars back and forth on Thursday and Sunday nights. Disney designs theme parks to implement its value proposition — *the fantasy*; a lot happens behind the scenes:

Marketing Question

What is the iPhone's value proposition? What is its marketing mix? Do the marketing mix elements support the value proposition and one another?

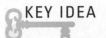

KEY IDEA

➤ Marketing mix programs should support the value proposition, and all elements should support one another.

Customers never see Mickey in the bathroom or two Dumbos at the same time; even street-sweepers are *scripted*. Disney simplified ticket books to *one price* and installed an *easy pass* system to minimize queuing hassles.

If one or more functional areas cannot provide support, the firm must revisit the value proposition. This analysis is critical. Going forward without full support commits the cardinal marketing sin — making promises to customers the firm cannot keep. Customers do not care which individual or department is at fault. They want, and expect, the benefits and values the firm promised. They rightly believe the firm should fix the problem.

FIGURE 9.5

INTEGRATING
THE FIRM'S
FUNCTIONAL
PROGRAMS

KEY IDEA

➤ The firm's functional areas must support the market segment strategy.

Sometimes required support extends beyond various functions in a single business unit to collaboration across several businesses. Cross-business support is increasingly critical in strategic (key) account management, where strategic account managers must design offers that integrate products and services from multiple businesses. Such offers often require one or more businesses to accept reduced profit margins; business leaders may be reluctant!

Wheelwright (disguised medical-products firm) comprised several businesses making products used in hospital operating rooms. Wheelwright's corporate marketing group designed a *one-stop-shop* offer including products from several businesses. Customers were enthusiastic, but some individual businesses refused to make necessary distribution and service changes and price concessions. The initiative failed.

The critical barrier to cross-business collaboration is often the perceived impact on individual business profitability. Top management support and modification of managerial measurement and incentive systems are ways to address this problem.

Test Your Firm's Market Strategy on a Baker's Dozen Items[44]

1. *Clarity* — Is it clear what we *are* going to do and what we *are not* going to do?

2. *External consistency* — Are our offers consistent with the best insight about the market, customers, competitors, and complementers?

3. *Value* — Do our offers deliver significant value to customers?

4. *Advantage* — Do our offers promise greater customer value than the competitors' offers?

CONTINUES ON NEXT PAGE

Test Your Firm's Market Strategy on a Baker's Dozen Items (CONTINUED)

5. *Flexibility* — Do our choices allow us to address expected evolution in the market, customers, competitors, and complementers, and the environment in general?

6. *Financial consistency* — Are our choices consistent with our financial goals?

7. *Focus* — Are our offers consistent with our capabilities and strengths?

8. *Internal consistency* — Are our choices internally consistent?

9. *Focus* — Are our employees able to prioritize their work to deliver our offers?

10. *Learning* — Does the strategy development process build our intellectual capital?

11. *Functionally integrated* — Is the market strategy well integrated with other functional strategies?

12. *Cross-market integrated* — Is the market strategy well integrated with our other market strategies?

13. *Robustness* — Are our choices able to withstand external shocks?

Rate your firm's market strategy on each item: 1 = strongly disagree; 10 = strongly agree.

MANAGING MULTI-SEGMENT STRATEGIES

This chapter shows how to construct a strategy — performance objectives, strategic focus, positioning, and implementation programs — for addressing a target market segment. But the firm often targets several segments simultaneously; hence it must develop several market-segment strategies. Each segment strategy requires its own performance objectives, strategic focus, positioning, and implementation programs. The firm must ensure that each segment strategy is distinct. Pottery Barn Kids' positioning is distinct from Pottery Barn — but Pottery Barn is not well distinguished from its down-market chain, West Elm. Banana Republic is distinct from The Gap and Old Navy — but The Gap and Old Navy are less distinct from each other.

When the firm targets multiple segments, it faces three possible implementation situations:

- **Independence.** Individual segment strategies and implementation programs are unrelated.
- **Positive synergies.** The firm enjoys positive **synergies** from implementation programs across segments. The firm may secure cost efficiencies from using the same sales force, distribution channels, and/or sharing brand equity. The GE brand is so well known and widely respected that new product entries gain enormously.
- **Negative synergies.** The firm suffers negative synergy from implementation programs across segments. Multiple products confuse the sales force; brand extensions confuse customers. Almaden is a strong brand of popularly priced wine, but a $100 Almeden bottle would probably not do well!

The firm's individual market-segment strategies and implementation programs must together form a coherent market strategy. Because of increasing complexity in customer need profiles and related implications for internal coordination, multiple-segment issues are especially intriguing and challenging. Sometimes firms are unable to address two segments simultaneously: *Big pharma* firms seem unable to address low-price segments when drugs come off patent, and no major airline has successfully operated a low-cost carrier. Table 9.7 identifies the sorts of problems that may arise and potential solutions the firm may explore.

KEY IDEA

➤ Together, individual market segment strategies must form a coherent market strategy.

➤ Market segment strategies must be individually distinct, yet the firm should seek positive synergies in implementation programs.

TABLE 9.7

ISSUES IN
TARGETING MULTIPLE
MARKET SEGMENTS

Marketing Mix Element	Potential Problem	Possible Solution
Product	Increased production costs, increased inventory costs, delivery delays	Modular design, just-in-time (JIT) assembly
Service	Alienate customers not receiving premium service package	Try to ensure perceived equity, and maintain physical separation where possible
Advertising	Exposure to different appeals	Ensure that appeals do not conflict and that messages across segments are consistent; use specialized media
Sales force	Salespeople ineffective with multiple products and/or in multiple segments	Extra training or develop specialized sales forces
Distribution	Alienate intermediaries	Secure financial-service package for selected intermediaries; consider different brands and packages
Pricing	Trans-shipment — diversion from one segment to another	Manage price differentials, differentiate elements like brand and package

Marketing Question

What other messages did you glean from this chapter?

KEY MESSAGES

The market strategy has four key purposes:

- Providing strategic direction in the market.
- Securing differential advantage.
- Guiding the effective allocation of scarce resources.
- Achieving cross-functional integration.

The market-segment strategy has four key elements; each element has several constituent parts:

- **Performance objectives**: Results the firm hopes to achieve:
  - **Strategic objectives** — qualitative and directional. Strategic objectives typically fall into one of three categories: growth and market share, profitability, and cash flow.
  - **Operational objectives** — quantitative and time-bound. How much and by when.

- **Strategic focus**: The broad direction of the strategy. Has two main branches — *increase unit sales volume* and *improve margins and investment returns*.
  - **Increase unit sales volume** has two branches:
    - **Current revenue base** — *increase customer retention* and/or *customer use*.
    - **Secure new revenues** — *attract customers from competitors* and/or *new business*.
  - **Improve margins and investment returns** also has two branches:
    - **Increase revenues** — *raise prices* and/or *improve the sales mix*.
    - **Reduce costs and assets** — *reduce operating costs* and/or *improve asset utilization*.

- **Positioning**: How target customers should view the firm's offer. Requires four key decisions:
  - **Select customer targets** — choose the distribution system, level(s) to target, and the specific person types/roles.
  - **Frame competitor targets** — competitors the firm decides to go up against.
  - **Design the value proposition** — why customers should prefer the firm's offer.
  - **Articulate reasons to believe** — supporting evidence for the value proposition.

CONTINUES ON NEXT PAGE

- **Implementation programs**: Actions the firm must take to execute the strategy. Two types:
  - **Marketing mix**: Externally — product, service, promotion, distribution, and price.
  - **Supporting functional programs**: Internally — integrate functional areas to work together.

If the firm targets multiple market segments, each segment strategy must be distinct. The firm should seek positive synergy among its implementation programs.

a901

a902

VIDEOS AND AUDIOS

Marketing Imperative 3 — Market Strategy   a901 🎧
Marketing Imperative 4   a902 🎧

QUESTIONS FOR STUDY AND DISCUSSION

Can you answer the questions implied by this chapter's learning objectives? Check!

1. Apple's iPod is one of the 21st century's most successful consumer products. Using the framework in this chapter, describe Apple's market strategy for the iPod.

2. Better Place (BP) signed agreements with national and local governments — Australia, Canada, Denmark, Israel, California, and Hawaii — to build recharging networks for electric cars. What are BP's strategic marketing challenges? How would you address them?

3. P&G's Tide has led the household detergent market for more than a half-century. Why? What lessons can you draw from Tide's success?

4. The National Basketball Association (NBA) has slumped, whereas the National Football League (NFL) is very successful. Why? How would you turn around the NBA?

5. Quidel manufactures home pregnancy test kits. What segments can you identify in the home-pregnancy test market? How should Quidel position its product in these segments? What implementation programs do you suggest? Hint: Check out your local supermarket.

6. Historically, several competitive battles stand out: Adidas vs. Nike, Bloomberg vs. Thomson-Reuters, Boeing vs. Airbus, Coke vs. Pepsi, GM vs. Ford, Google vs. Facebook, Intel vs. AMD, Microsoft vs. Google, Oracle vs. SAP, Sears vs. Montgomery Ward. Compare and contrast two or more rivalries that interest you. What can you learn about market strategy?

7. What are the challenges of designing an effective market strategy? Use two current examples to explain. Use the Baker's Dozen items to assess the effectiveness of these strategies.

8. Select a product in which you are interested. Alternatively, consider this book — *Managing Marketing in the 21st Century*. Refer to Chapter 8, question 7. Lay out a strategy for a market segment you identified.

v1001

IMPERATIVE 3

*Set Strategic Direction
and Positioning*

CHAPTER 10

MANAGING THROUGH THE LIFE CYCLE v1001

To access O-codes, go to **www.ocodes.com**

*There are risks and costs to a program of action. But they
are far less than the long-range risks and costs of inaction.*

— John F. Kennedy

LEARNING OBJECTIVES

When you have completed this chapter, you will be able to:

- Appreciate the critical importance of pre-emption in developing competitive strategy.
- Use the product life-cycle framework to generate several plausible scenarios.
- Identify and assess business characteristics and strategic considerations for each scenario.
- Generate strategic options for each scenario.
- Recognize effective life-cycle strategies.

OPENING CASE: RYANAIR

Ryanair upset the life cycle for European air travel when it entered the Ireland-England market in 1985 with flights from Waterford (southeast Ireland) to London's Gatwick Airport. In 1986, Ryanair challenged the government-owned British Airways and Aer Lingus duopoly on the Dublin-London route with flights to London's Luton Airport. Ryanair's initial £99 roundtrip price was less than half the £209 duopoly price. In 1986, Ryanair alone carried 82,000 passengers versus route totals of 500,000 annually for the previous several years. Observers believed Ryanair passengers came from three sources: British Airways and Aer Lingus passengers; new air-travel passengers from the 750,000 annually who made the nine-hour trip by rail and ferry for fares as low as £55; and passengers who previously didn't travel because of high airline prices and/or the inconvenience of ferry travel on the often-stormy Irish Sea and British Rail.

In the late 1980s, Ryanair added jet aircraft and rapidly expanded its route network to 15 destinations: from Dublin to other British cities and continental Europe, and from London (Luton) to different parts of Ireland. Ryanair offered conventional airline services including business-class travel and a frequent-flyer club. But intense price competition and new capacity from British Airways and Aer Lingus led to significant accumulated losses and a forced restructuring. Ryanair then adopted Southwest Airlines' model to become Europe's first low-fare airline, offering a single class of service, using a single type of aircraft configured with the maximum number of seats, and high-frequency schedules. Ryanair switched from London (Luton) to Stansted Airport — its new terminal had a direct rail link to London's Liverpool Street station. Dublin Airport became the origin of most Irish flights. Ryanair was profitable by 1991.

To support its low-price strategy, Ryanair obsessively cut costs: Ryanair eliminated free drinks and meals; high-capacity utilization pushed down overhead costs. Airport destinations were a significant distance from the advertised cities; Ryanair promised economic growth and employment benefits to negotiate lower landing fees and other costs, and secure local marketing support. Ryanair revamped its route structure so that typical flights were one hour or less, and organized its hubs to reduce maintenance costs and turn-around times.

Ryanair's major continental European expansion occurred post-1996, following the European Union's Open Skies agreement. Ryanair addressed new markets with its successful low-fares business model. Other airline startups used similar models, but none was as successful as Ryanair. British Airways and KLM formed Go Fly and Buzz, respectively, but sold out to easyJet and Ryanair. Ryanair's most significant competitor was easyJet.

Ryanair's conduct differed from traditional airlines in several ways:

- *Around 20 percent of Ryanair's revenues derived from ancillary activities: Flight attendants used in-flight time to sell snacks, beverages, and duty-free items. Ryanair sold advertising space on seat backs, aircraft exteriors, and in-flight magazines, and earned commissions from hotel bookings and car rental.*

- *Ryanair's advertisements were often racy: one advertisement with the headline "Expensive Bastards!" compared Ryanair with British Airways; another featured a model dressed as a schoolgirl, with the words "Hottest back-to-school fares." Ryanair's advertising frequently led to lawsuits, some won, some lost; regardless, Ryanair secured significant publicity.*

- *Ryanair earned publicity from CEO Michael O'Leary's frequent tirades against Ireland's government ministers, Aer Rianta (Ireland's state-owned airport authority), the European Union, and any person/organization that O'Leary believed interfered with Ryanair's low-airfare strategy.*

- *Passenger convenience was not a high priority: New aircraft did not have reclining seats nor seatback pockets; Ryanair did not refund passengers for missed flights; passengers paid for all checked bags and airport check-in. Other proposed (but not implemented) measures included eliminating some toilets to add more seats, charging for toilet use, redesigning aircraft to allow standing passengers, charging extra for overweight passengers, and asking passengers to carry checked-in luggage to the plane.*

By 2005, Ryanair was Europe's largest airline, carrying 31 million passengers mostly via online booking. To celebrate its 20th birthday, and continuing its practice of airline-seat sales, Ryanair offered 100,000 seats at 99 pence. In 2006 and 2008, Ryanair made unsuccessful hostile takeover bids for the recently privatized Aer Lingus, but retained a significant ownership stake. In 2011, Ryanair flew 250 Boeing 737-800 aircraft on 1,100 routes through 41 bases serving more than 160

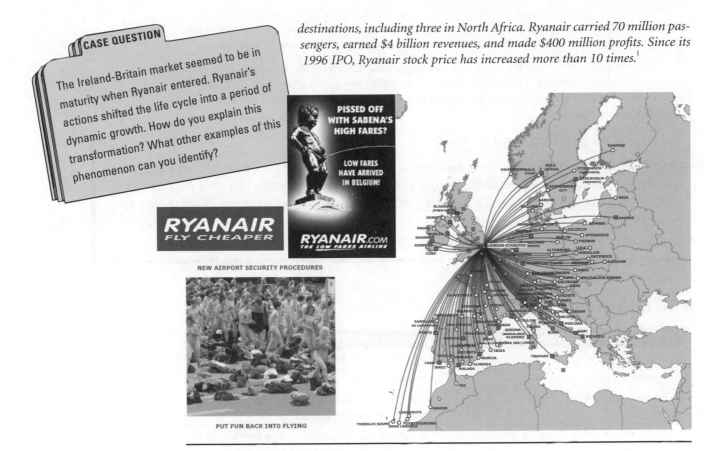

CASE QUESTION

The Ireland-Britain market seemed to be in maturity when Ryanair entered. Ryanair's actions shifted the life cycle into a period of dynamic growth. How do you explain this transformation? What other examples of this phenomenon can you identify?

destinations, including three in North Africa. Ryanair carried 70 million passengers, earned $4 billion revenues, and made $400 million profits. Since its 1996 IPO, Ryanair stock price has increased more than 10 times.[1]

Chapter 10 is the second of three chapters discussing separate facets of Imperative 3: Set Strategic Direction and Positioning. Chapter 9 showed how to develop market segment strategy and market strategy. Earlier in the book, Chapter 3 showed how the **life-cycle framework** can help the firm generate useful market insights. In this chapter, we revisit the life-cycle framework to help the firm make more effective decisions in competitive markets.

By anticipating competitor actions — and sometimes their timing — the firm can develop **pre-emptive** strategies. A pre-emptive strategy means acting before your competitors, perhaps targeting an emerging segment or introducing a new product. Ryanair is a good example of pre-emptive action. Acting pre-emptively often involves risks, and failure may be visible and costly. But the costs of not acting may be significant, particularly for established players. These **opportunity costs** are the market share gains and increased profits the firm did not earn. Opportunity costs are insidious; they do not appear on the firm's income statement, but they may be more significant than costs that do.

Consider Apple and the iPod — many observers counseled caution. They said to Apple: "You are a computer company; you have no experience in digital music. Napster has closed, and downloading music via the Internet faces immense uncertainty. Sony owns portable music players with the Walkman; this is their turf, and they will fight you fiercely." Many would have heeded these arguments, but not Steve Jobs. The iPod launch was an enormous success and even helped Apple sell more Macintosh computers. Think of the opportunity costs Apple would have incurred by not launching the iPod, or the iPhone, or the iPad.

By not acting, the firm opens up potential entry windows for competitors. Firms often fail to address competitive threats because they view competition differently or misunderstand competitive strategy — "we don't really compete" or "we have different strategies." Or firms hesitate because *going out on a limb* is visible and risky. Neither Aer Lingus nor British Airways acted effectively in the face of Ryanair's disruptive change in air travel. Market-leading firms should

KEY IDEA

➤ Firms failing to act pre-emptively may face significant opportunity costs.

view pre-emption as an insurance policy — when change is swift, the costs of inaction escalate rapidly. Firms that will not pay *insurance premiums* should prepare for market share losses.

The life-cycle framework offers a good way to design insurance policies. Understanding how life cycles and competitive strategies evolve is valuable for forecasting and anticipating likely scenarios. With these scenarios, the firm is better equipped to generate good competitive strategic options.

The Value of Pre-emptive Strategy

Meyer Feldberg, Columbia Business School dean, realized that several leading U.S. schools were developing strong international presences. He knew London Business School would be a desirable partner for many U.S. schools, particularly Wharton. Feldberg also knew that a London-Philadelphia axis could marginalize Columbia and would be a PR coup for Wharton. He flew to London, met with London Business School dean John Quelch, and quickly created a strategic alliance for the now highly successful EMBA Global program.

THE CHANGING VIEW

OLD WAY	NEW WAY
Accept low returns and cross-subsidize products	Shareholder value discipline applied rigorously
Commoditization is viewed as inevitable	Innovation is a major strategic weapon
Competition to the death	Merger and consolidation viewed as legitimate strategies in shareholders' interest
Evolutionary change of management approach	Proactively planned change of management approach
Firms cut costs when times are bad	Firms monitor cost efficiency and cut costs continually
Firms hide behind regulatory barriers, often supported by government	Governments work aggressively to increase competition
Firms maximize cash flow by minimizing investment in mature markets	Innovation rejuvenates market growth
Industry structure viewed as fixed	Industry structure viewed as variable
Pre-emptive strategies are rare	Pre-emptive strategies are commonplace
Sequential product development	Concurrent product development
Slow market development with sequential product introductions worldwide	Rapid market development with simultaneous new product launches in multiple countries
Tied to traditional distribution systems and business models	New business models, distribution methods, and technologies to increase efficiencies and add value
Uninformed entry strategies	Entry strategies driven by sophisticated understanding of market development

DEVELOPING COMPETITIVE STRATEGIC OPTIONS

The firm generates **strategic options** by developing scenarios that let it anticipate future competitor actions. The main building block is the classic life cycle — introduction, early growth, late growth, maturity, and decline, typically at the product-form level. The **life-cycle approach** is very powerful because market conditions tend to be similar at the same life-cycle stage across many products and technologies. Each scenario has a limited number of strategic options. These options are valuable input into formulating firm strategy, but creativity is always important. The firm should avoid becoming too predictable, even when it is market leader. This chapter discusses how to generate strategic options from nine scenarios — Figure 10.1.

FIGURE 10.1

LIFE-CYCLE
SCENARIOS

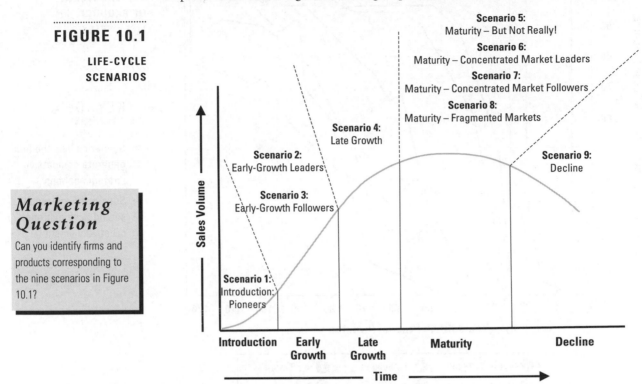

Marketing Question

Can you identify firms and products corresponding to the nine scenarios in Figure 10.1?

John Deere took advantage of market disarray created when farm-implement firm Case merged with New Holland to create CNH Global. Deere offered loyal Case and New Holland customers steep discounts, low interest rates, and $5,000 in cash to swap their products for new Deere products. Deere also slashed trade-in prices, undercutting sales of new CNH products and creating nervousness about trade-in values!

Although the scenarios and strategic options we discuss are valid for many product life cycles, generally life cycles are shortening — Figure 10.2.[2] Implications are:

- When life cycles were longer, firms could enter a market, fail, redevelop products, and re-enter with a reasonable chance of success. Today, re-entry windows are closing.

- Shortening life cycles reduce the time — in early growth — to earn the highest unit margins.

- Good strategic thinking early in the life cycle is more important than ever.

- Faster cycles require proactive management of strategy over the life cycle; evolutionary approaches may be too slow.

Identifying scenarios and developing strategic options is more important than ever. This chapter is designed specifically to improve students' ability to formulate strategic options and design good competitive strategies.[3]

KEY IDEA

➤ Nine scenarios based on
- product life cycle
- competitive position

are the basic building blocks for developing competitive strategic options.

➤ Life cycles are shortening for many products.

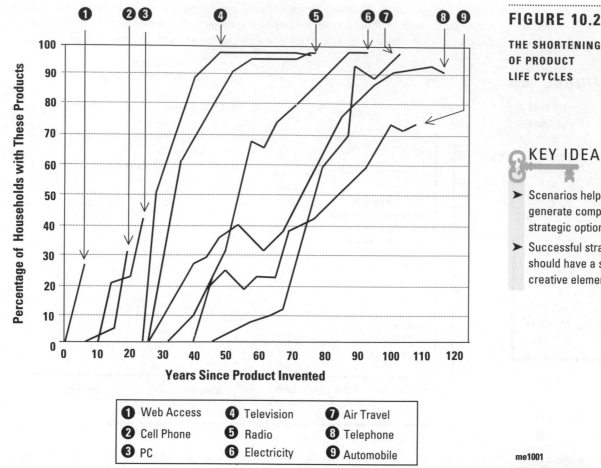

Source Data: W. Michael Cox, Federal Reserve Bank of Dallas (2007)

FIGURE 10.2

THE SHORTENING OF PRODUCT LIFE CYCLES

KEY IDEA

➤ Scenarios help the firm generate competitive strategic options.

➤ Successful strategies should have a strong creative element.

me1001

MARKETING ENRICHMENT

Summary of Strategic Options me1001

Building Product Life-Cycle Scenarios

Let's walk through the nine product life-cycle-based scenarios in Figure 10.1. Each scenario description begins with a brief introduction; then we focus on creating and analyzing alternative objectives and strategies.[4] But we must be very clear about one thing: We cannot tell you what strategy to follow for a given scenario, because your best strategy depends in part on competitor actions. Instead, we give you some strategic options to think about. (Marketing Enrichment me1001 summaries the strategic options.)

SCENARIO 1: INTRODUCTION STAGE: PIONEERS

Gillette spent $1 billion on developing and initially marketing the Mach3 razor. First-year marketing spending was $300 million for a simultaneous launch in 19 countries. Gillette's corporate profits dropped in the launch year due to Mach3's startup expenses.

Most products do not generate profits in the introduction stage. Pioneering firms typically incur significant R&D and market launch expenditures; they must also invest in plant, equipment, and systems before launch. Marketing expenses are high, and revenues may not cover the

firm's ongoing operating costs, much less fixed costs. Early on, cash flows are often negative. Kevin Plank, founder of *Under Armour*, lived in his grandmother's basement for several years before earning profits from launching new athletic wear. Under Armour went public 10 years after founding and now pursues a mission of clothing athletes head to toe, including running shoes. Many other firms like Apple and HP famously started life in garages.

Some firms are better able to sustain new product losses and negative cash flows than others. Large firms typically subsidize new product launches with cash earned from more established products at later life-cycle stages, as part of a long-term product strategy. Tide laundry detergent funds many new ventures for P&G; other examples include operating system software and Windows for Microsoft, and search for Google.

Of course, pioneering firms must have vision, be willing to take risks, to introduce less than perfect product versions for later upgrade (like Google with Android) and, if necessary, cannibalize current products. Despite huge resources, Microsoft initially failed in search. Microsoft shut down its rudimentary Keywords system for fear of cannibalization; later it rejected an opportunity to buy Overture (formerly Goto.com, sold to Yahoo!), the pioneer in combining search with advertising. Google became the dominant search leader.

Small firms typically have fewer resources and often need outside financing. In the very early stages, wealthy individuals — aka **angel investors** — often provide startup funding for new ventures. Later, **venture capitalists** may provide financial backing when the opportunity starts to show promise. If the firm's value proposition is sufficiently compelling, the firm may raise funds from an initial public offering of stock — an **IPO**.[5] Internet firms like Amazon, eBay, Healthion, Priceline, and Yahoo! all got off the ground with venture capital and/or IPOs.

The introduction stage has few **pioneer** firms, often only one. The pioneer should lay the foundation for achieving market leadership and profitability, at least in the short and medium run. The pioneer must develop an appropriate strategy as the life cycle moves toward early growth. The pioneer must demonstrate value to target customers and reduce any market uncertainty that the product is just a *short-term wonder* — it may even work with competitors to agree on technological standards.[6,7] (Chapter 5 and discussion of VHS and Blu-ray technology.) The pioneer must also build a marketing organization and distribution infrastructure.

A critical pioneering task is to keep ahead of competitors by slowing their progress. Some years after introduction, Apple's pioneering iPod has achieved iconic status and held its competitors to small market share. Apple's iTunes breakthrough in commercial music downloading and extending Macintosh compatibility to all PCs were critical factors in cementing its position. Sometimes partnerships and alliances can buttress the firm's position. Apple formed a (short-lived) partnership with HP for the iPod, and with Motorola and Cingular (now AT&T) for a cell phone with iTunes. A particularly effective way of slowing/forestalling competitive entry is to create (or exploit) **entry barriers** — government-imposed, product-specific, and firm-driven.[8]

GOVERNMENT-IMPOSED BARRIERS

Patents are the most common government-imposed barrier. They provide owners with legal monopolies for several years. Firms can petition the courts to enforce these patent monopolies via patent infringement suits, effectively creating long-term barriers for competitors, like Apple's suits against Samsung in smart phones. Even the filing of patents that are not ultimately approved can act as a short-term barrier. Pharmaceutical companies are especially frequent users of patent barriers. Other government impediments include trade barriers, preferential tax treatment, and outright subsidies. Sometimes the pioneer benefits from a barrier or barrier structure already in place; other times, it may lobby the government for a specific benefit. Sun, Netscape, and Novell all encouraged the U.S. government to take action against Microsoft, slowing its entry into various markets.

PRODUCT-SPECIFIC BARRIERS

Product-specific barriers relate directly to the product and include access to capital, raw materials, human resources, and a minimum scale of operations.[9] Sometimes these barriers relate to the product itself so the firm can exploit them; other times, the firm can actively raise barriers. Corning secured differential advantage over Nextel and Lucent in optical-fiber technology by aggressively hiring most of the few optics Ph.D.s graduating each year. Of course, product and/or process innovations cause product-specific barriers to diminish over time. In previous decades, consumers sent film rolls to central laboratories for processing; then storefront mini-labs made the process much more convenient; today, consumers print their own images from digital cameras.

FIRM-DRIVEN BARRIERS

The firm can build *low-cost* barriers via **penetration pricing**. It may also develop and exploit **first-mover advantages**[10]:

LOW-COST BARRIERS AND PENETRATION PRICING. With penetration pricing (PP), the firm plans on low profit margins for a substantial time period, aka *buying* market share. PP is risky and takes significant resolve. PP requires substantial resources as the firm continually reduces costs and prices, builds capacity, and grows quickly. PP also takes significant resolve in the face of large pre-launch and post-launch expenditures and market uncertainty. If successful, low prices built on low costs and experience curve advantages are a significant entry barrier. Figure 10.3 shows the relationship between price and unit cost for a PP strategy.[11]

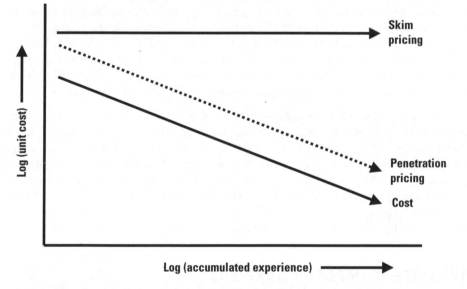

The most advantageous conditions for PP are price-sensitive markets with few government- or product-specific entry barriers.[12] The classic example was Henry Ford's goal to put a Model T in every American garage. Ford invented the assembly line, dramatically lowering production costs; reduced prices continuously; and by the mid-1920s, exceeded 50 percent market share.

PP is particularly attractive if customer-switching costs are high and the after-market for complementary products is significant. Software service providers are good examples. These firms often set initial prices low to generate an *embedded* base of loyal users, but set high prices for upgrades and/or peripherals. Firms selling durable goods and consumables — razors and razor blades, printers and toner, frequently price durables low and consumables high.

FIGURE 10.3

PRICE AND UNIT COST TRAJECTORIES FOR PENETRATION PRICING AND SKIM PRICING

KEY IDEA

➤ When the firm executes a low-price penetration strategy, it must accept low profit margins for a substantial time period. Continual cost reductions are essential to sustain low prices.

MARKETING ENRICHMENT

The Experience Curve me1002

The Experience Curve

Figure 10.3's cost curve is a classic **experience curve** (EC). As accumulated volume (experience) in making, promoting, and distributing a product increases, costs can be made to decline in a predictable manner. The EC is a straight-line relationship when we plot log (unit cost) against log (accumulated experience). Cost reductions result from preferred access to raw materials, and enlightened cost management that makes tough decisions to take advantage of organizational learning, economies of scale, advances in process technology, and product redesign. The EC has an important influence on many marketing decisions, especially pricing. (More on the Experience Curve in Marketing Enrichment me1002.)

PP works only if demand for the basic product remains strong; PP fails when customers demand variation. To continue the Ford example, in the late 1920s, GM identified several market segments where customers wanted additional benefits. While Chevrolet competed with Ford's Model T for price buyers, GM offered Buick, Cadillac, Oldsmobile, and Pontiac to other segments. GM swept past Ford in the late 1920s and early 1930s.

FIRST-MOVER ADVANTAGE. The pioneer may earn advantages because it was first. The pioneer may be able to sustain technological advantage by improving products and/or developing new applications. Examples include DuPont's historic successes with nylon, polyester, and aramid fibers; Citibank's leadership in ATMs; Duracell with alkaline batteries; 7-Eleven with convenience stores (especially in Japan)[13]; and eBay for auction sites where it took advantage of network effects.[14]

If the pioneer's products are high-quality, it may earn a leading reputation among consumers and distributors. Early market entry also gives the pioneer superior market knowledge.[15] But the pioneer must judiciously turn these advantages into buyer switching costs, or a fast follower will surpass it. One key for sustaining first-mover advantage is to build a strong brand, establishing the *standard* against which customers judge subsequent entries.[16] Examples include Jeep (in the U.S.) — four-wheel-drive vehicles; Xerox — high-speed dry copying; Kleenex — paper tissue; Hoover — vacuum cleaners; Cadillac — luxury automobiles; and Apple's iPod, iPhone, and iPad.

KEY IDEA

➤ A *pioneer* can sustain first-mover advantages by producing high-quality products. The firm earns a leading reputation and sets the stage for creating a strong brand.

Indian government regulations that would have forced Coca-Cola to share its secret formula with an Indian partner caused it to leave India from 1977 to 1993. Rival PepsiCo took advantage of Coke's exit. "Pepsi" is now a common synonym for cola drinks in the fast-growing Indian soft-drink market, and outsells Coke by almost 2:1.

Whereas a successful penetration strategy delivers continued price reductions, a firm with first-mover advantages may maintain high prices — **price skimming** (PS).[17] As Figure 10.3 shows, PS keeps prices high, even as the firm reduces costs and earns high profits.[18] PS works if government and/or product-specific entry barriers are high, customer willingness to try is strong, and customers are relatively price-insensitive. The pharmaceutical industry is a good example; patents protect firms from competition, and products deliver significant health benefits. PS strategies fail when entry barriers are low and/or customers are price-sensitive. PS also fails if the firm ignores customer needs and potential competition, as in the J&J example:

Many heart patients undergo balloon-angioplasty procedures. The surgeon inserts a balloon into the artery, inflates it to widen the artery, then implants a wire-mesh device — a *stent* — to stop the artery closing. Three years after entry, J&J stent revenues were $1 billion, profit margins were 80 percent, and market share was 90 percent. Unfortunately, J&J angered cardiologists by not improving stents significantly and refusing price discounts for large purchases.

Guidant entered three years after J&J. Within 45 days, Guidant gained 70 percent market share; one year later, J&J's share was under 10 percent. J&J introduced new products and recovered some market share, but not its early dominance. J&J tried to acquire Guidant but lost out to Boston Scientific.

Generally, new entrants erode first-mover advantages: As product life cycles shorten, advantages erode more quickly. Firms executing PS strategies must be able to shift direction when their advantages disappear. Early in the PC market, Compaq was successful with a high-performance, high-price strategy. Later, it underwent wrenching changes as it tried to compete on price. Ultimately, HP acquired Compaq.[19]

Pioneers face an environment full of risk, but several strategic options can lay the foundation for achieving long-run market leadership and profitability.

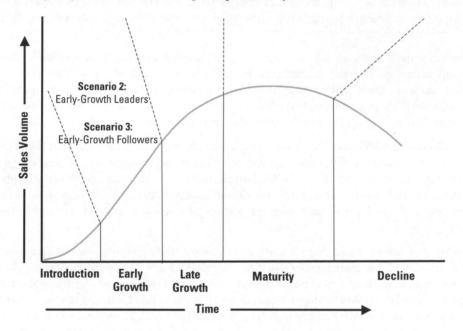

FIGURE 10.4

EARLY-GROWTH-STAGE SCENARIOS

Marketing Question

The iPod and iTunes have gained large shares of the digital music and music download markets. What barriers did Apple erect for potential followers?

KEY IDEA

➤ By the early-growth stage, customers accept the product, and the market leader should be profitable.

SCENARIO 2: EARLY-GROWTH LEADERS

By the early-growth stage — Figure 10.4 — customers have accepted the product form and market demand is growing rapidly. Generally, the market leader has a strong position. The leader has worked out market-entry problems and unit costs are under control. As Figure 10.3 shows, unit costs should reduce as volume builds and the EC takes effect. The firm should be profitable, but cash flows may be negative as it invests to grow the market and adds new capacity.

The leader has four strategic options — two each based on *continuing* and *surrendering* leadership:

- Continue to be leader — enhance position.
- Continue to be leader — maintain position.
- Surrender leadership — retreat to a market segment or segments.
- Surrender leadership — exit the market.

CONTINUE TO BE LEADER: ENHANCE POSITION

The firm leverages its success to seek market dominance. The firm grows and broadens the market by continuously investing in R&D to produce new products, extensive advertising, and personal selling. The firm increases production capacity ahead of market demand and aggressively reduces costs. In India's cell phone market, leader Bharti Airtel reversed the traditional model by outsourcing its network and information technology to European and U.S. providers, so it could concentrate on marketing. In Russia, VimpelCom focused corporate efforts on sales, as cell phone penetration accelerated from 20 percent to 80 percent in two and one half years.

Marketing Question

In the Opening Case in Chapter 7, we examined the car-sharing firm Zipcar. Zipcar has successfully navigated introduction and now faces the early-growth stage. Using the framework in this chapter, and whatever data you can secure, suggest a growth strategy for Zipcar.

As competitors enter, the firm's communications shift from market development to emphasizing superiority over competitors. Regarding the U.S. cell phone market, a senior marketing executive at Nokia told us, "While Motorola and Ericsson were still selling American consumers on switching to digital, we were already selling the superior features and performance of Nokia digital phones to separate customer segments."[20] Leaders may also block competitors by entering emerging market segments, new geographic areas, and new distribution channels — like eBay,[21] Microsoft, Starbucks, Walmart, and Tylenol:

> Tylenol achieved acetaminophen leadership by offering a huge number of product varieties. For adults: Tylenol Regular and Extra Strength, Tylenol Extra Strength Cool Caplets, Tylenol 8 Hour, Tylenol Arthritis Pain Extended Relief, Tylenol PM, Simply Sleep, Women's Tylenol, Tylenol Sore Throat, Tylenol Cold, Tylenol Flu, Tylenol Sinus, and Tylenol Allergy. For children: Children's Tylenol, Children's Tylenol Meltaways, Children's Tylenol Flu, Children's Tylenol plus Cold Daytime, Children's Tylenol Cold, Children's Tylenol Cold and Allergy, Simply Stuffy, and Simply Cough. Tylenol packages products in various forms — tablets, capsules, caplets, and liquid.

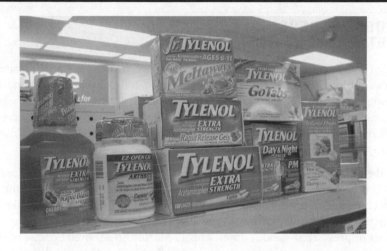

CONTINUE TO BE LEADER: MAINTAIN POSITION

The firm may prefer a more conservative approach and merely try to maintain market position. The firm may enjoy monopoly-like status and be concerned about potential political, legal, and regulatory difficulties, like Microsoft has faced. Alternatively, customers may demand additional sources of supply and/or strong competitors may enter, making it clear they intend to stay.

Sometimes technological standards drive this option. Multiple standards cause uncertainty, prospective customers postpone purchase, and the market develops more slowly. The firm may elect to work with competitors on a single standard rather than go it alone. The early consumer-video, HDTV, and wireless technology markets are all good examples. In consumer video, Sony's Betamax had limited success but VHS quickly surpassed Beta when several producers settled on a single standard and shared the market development effort. Had Sony brought other firms into the *Betamax family*, VHS might have been the also-ran. Apple's early refusal to license its Macintosh operating system undoubtedly stimulated Microsoft to develop its own graphical-user interface (Windows). This phenomenon is currently being played out with the open-source Linux operating system.

Maintaining a leading market position may be more difficult than striving for market dominance. The firm requires good up-to-date competitive intelligence, and must carefully select customer and competitor targets. The firm must have a clear strategy, sufficient resolve to stick to the strategy despite temporary hiccups, and thoughtful contingency and/or scenario planning. Historically, U.S. firms in the automobile, steel, and aluminum industries pursued this objective to mitigate antitrust action and possible breakup.

KEY IDEA

➤ *Early-growth leaders* have four quite different options:

- Continue to be leader — enhance position
- Continue to be leader — maintain position
- Surrender leadership — retreat to a market segment or segments
- Surrender leadership — exit the market

Whether the firm undertakes to *enhance* or *maintain* market position, the broad thrust is the same: to ride the leadership position through the life cycle to maturity. Along the way, the firm shifts focus from selling to first-time users, to selling to repeat users and acquiring competitor customers. To be successful, the firm must broaden and refresh its product line, add services, and build its brand by enhancing communications. Amazon is a textbook example: Amazon began by selling books, and then added recorded music, electronics, and many other product category *stores*, where it personalizes the customer shopping experience. Unfortunately, some leaders become complacent; blinded by early success, they may even treat customers arrogantly (like J&J with stents). As customer needs evolve and they become comfortable with the product, followers may be more adept at listening.

SURRENDER LEADERSHIP: RETREAT TO A MARKET SEGMENT OR SEGMENTS

Unlike market-share loss from competitive pressure, the firm makes a deliberate choice to surrender leadership. The firm may lack resources for fully developing the market and/or funding an ongoing stream of new products. Or a financially stronger competitor sets a market-leadership goal, and the firm knows it cannot win a head-to-head battle. The firm decides to target one or more market segments as a specialized competitor, believing that *discretion is the better part of valor.*

Sometimes, the follower initiates a penetration strategy by building economies of scale and cutting prices. The firm must identify less-price-sensitive segments where it can add value and overcome its cost disadvantage. The firm requires good market research capabilities to identify market segments and the organizational flexibility to address them. Apple, HP, and IBM have all felt this sort of pressure at various times. Apple's Macintosh survived because of strengths in the education and graphic arts segments and new product creativity, but both Compaq and IBM exited the PC business.

SURRENDER LEADERSHIP: EXIT THE MARKET

Leaving a market after being the pioneering leader can seem defeatist, but may be prudent. Throughout the life cycle, as customer needs and markets evolve, the firm should continually assess the value of its market position, based on the projected stream of discounted profits. If the projected value is less than the current sale value, the firm should consider exiting, especially if the product is not central to its mission.[22]

The firm's products may be strategically significant for a potential acquirer, fit well with its current products, and hence be of immense value. The acquirer may also have the resources to invest and drive product growth, like eBay's Skype purchase (widely considered a failure; since divested and acquired by Microsoft). Biotech and other technology firms often face the *sell* decision by inventing products they are ill-equipped to commercialize. Britain's Sinclair Research produced many innovations like amplifiers, radios, high fidelity, calculators, personal computers and peripherals, television, and transportation vehicles — but has an almost legendary inability to commercialize its products. Successful innovators are often better off selling to firms with strong marketing expertise. Colgate's liquid soap and P&G's Crest SpinBrush were both secured from small firms that elected to sell.

Marketing Question

Suppose you have the following information about a market:

- Market growth rate — 15 percent annually
- Leader's market share — 40 percent
- Follower's market share — 10 percent
- Leader's growth rate — 15 percent annually.

Question: How fast must the follower grow annually, to overtake the leader in six years?

Answer: 45 percent.

Marketing Question

SCENARIO 3: EARLY-GROWTH FOLLOWERS

Some firms prefer to be **followers**, entering markets in the early-growth stage. By pursuing a *wait-and-see* strategy, they can better assess market potential and *free ride* on the pioneer's efforts in market development. Followers leverage past successes and learn from the leader's mistakes. But early on, the follower trails the market leader. The follower has lower sales, higher unit costs, and less experience than the leader. Unless the leader is price skimming, followers are often unprofitable, and cash flow is probably also negative.

Followers in early growth have similar strategic options to the leader. But because they start from inferior positions, choosing among them has a different cadence. The options are:

• Seek market leadership.
• Settle for second place.
• Focus on gaining leadership in a market segment or segments.
• Exit the market.

SEEK MARKET LEADERSHIP

The follower can pursue leadership by *imitating* or *leapfrogging* the market leader. In each case, the follower needs good competitive intelligence and entry as soon as possible:

IMITATION. Imitation means what it says. The follower copies the leader but executes more effectively. Successful imitators spend heavily to play *catch-up* on product development and out-spend the leader in promotion. If possible, the follower leverages an existing marketing or distribution infrastructure and clearly highlights its differentiated value. The follower should not confuse imitation with price cutting. Early in the PC life cycle, suppliers offered many designs that earned price premiums, but price competition accelerated as the industry standardized. In search, follower Google eclipsed Overture (formerly GoTo) with a well-executed imitation strategy, but low price was not a factor.

LEAPFROG. The follower improves on the leader. It offers enhanced value by developing innovative and superior products, and/or it enters emerging market segments before the leader. Generally, the leapfrogger avoids head-to-head price competition; it may spend more heavily on R&D than the leader, while marketing spending is also high. In video games, Nintendo and Sega leapfrogged first-mover Atari's original video game. Later, Sony Playstation leapfrogged both Nintendo and Sega by offering 3-D graphics and enhanced digital soundtracks. Playstation 3 and Microsoft's Xbox target a different segment — late teens and early 20-somethings — than Nintendo's young teenager target. But Nintendo leapfrogged both Sony and Microsoft by introducing the Wii, featuring active games for many age groups.

Effective leapfroggers often do an excellent job of anticipating emerging customer needs. They spot segment opportunities before leaders, quickly offering new values and securing differential advantage. The most successful followers *change the rules*.[23] Netflix took advantage of the VHS-to-DVD switch to develop a rent-by-mail option that devastated bricks-and-mortar leader Blockbuster, and ultimately drove it to bankruptcy. More recently, Netflix has been a leader in streaming video — Chapter 3 Opening Case.

For either *imitation* or *leapfrog*, followers must make long-run commitments. Because they must play catch-up, resource requirements can be enormous. Sometimes pioneers make it easy for followers by neither improving products nor investing sufficiently in promotion and distribution, and by keeping prices high. As noted, J&J's actions in the *stent* market helped follower Guidant.

SETTLE FOR SECOND PLACE

Former GE CEO Jack Welch famously mandated that GE be either number *one* or *two* in each of its markets.[24] A follower needs substantial resources to become market leader, so settling for second place may be a reasonable and profitable option. Several situations argue for this alternative. Perhaps the leader is content with current market share and does not seek to increase it; customers may demand a second supplier; multiple competitors may help simplify product standards; and/or the political/legal/regulatory environment may be favorable. Smorgon Industries is a good example of a follower with limited ambition:

> Smorgon set out to become Australia's second domestic steel producer. Smorgon did not challenge market leader BHP but hoped to operate under BHP's price umbrella. Smorgon believed BHP would rather accept its presence than battle for market share. Smorgan was successful in settling for second place and achieving acceptable market position.

FOCUS ON A MARKET SEGMENT OR SEGMENTS

This option may be attractive if the follower has fewer resources than the leader and other followers, and if the segment (or segments) is attractive.[25] When drugs go off patent, pharmaceutical firms often withdraw marketing support, but add services for a narrow physician segment. In Britain, BMS earns sales and profits from anti-cancer drug Taxol, long after patent expiration. BMS provides kits to prepare the drug for patients and replaces these free of charge if patients miss their appointments.[26]

EXIT THE MARKET

If the business sale value is greater than the projected discounted profit stream, the firm should consider exiting the market. Because the product is in early growth, it may have high value for a potential acquirer eager to enter the product's market (market segment).

KEY IDEA

➤ *Imitation* means copying the leader but being more effective in execution.

➤ *Leapfrogging* goes one better than the leader by developing innovative and superior products and/or targeting emerging market segments.

SCENARIO 4: LATE-GROWTH STAGE

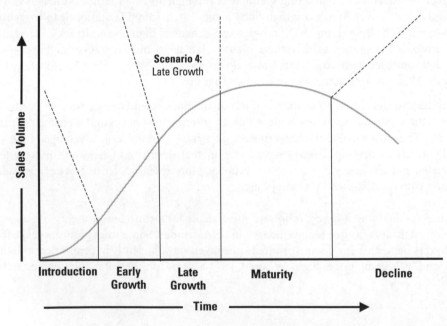

FIGURE 10.5

LATE-GROWTH-STAGE SCENARIOS

Early on, most cell phones offered the same set of basic functions. Later, major players added features like text messaging, music, and color user-interface displays. Some producers offered features like rubberized phones, hybrid phone/PDA organizers, and still- and video-camera phones. Samsung's *Ladyphone* had a biorhythm calculator, a fatness function to calculate height-to-weight ratios, a calorie counter, and a calendar to track menstrual cycles. Nokia offered a platinum-cased handset with a sapphire crystal screen — for only $21,000!

KEY IDEA

➤ By late growth, basic customer benefits and values are still important but may not enter into customers choice decisions. Customers are more likely to base purchase decisions on additional benefits and values.

KEY IDEA

➤ In *late growth*, the firm must decide whether to target *many* segments or just a *few*.

By late-growth — Figure 10.5, the firm receives minimal value from early market leadership or being a fast follower. Although the customer benefits and values that drove purchase in introduction and early growth are still important, they may not enter customer choice decisions. More likely, these elements have become *qualifiers* or *antes*, rather than *determining*. The firm must focus on identifying and offering customers determining benefits and values. Early in the passenger air travel market, safety was critical. Today, most travelers believe major airlines, flying similar airplanes, are equally safe: Safety is an *ante*. Determining benefits and values are frequent-flyer miles, time convenience, and availability of a direct flight.

The firm requires considerable marketing research skills to conduct market segmentation, decide which segment(s) to target, satisfy customer needs in the target segment(s), and monitor evolving segments for new opportunities. Successful firms address target segments with *rifle shot marketing*, and then build defensible positions against competitors.

Even small segments may offer good profit potential. Many local and regional retailers successfully compete against national chains. Think about your own town: What examples can you identify? In the New York area, P.C. Richard is a successful electrical goods retailer; Stew Leonard's, the *Disneyland of Dairy Stores*, has the greatest sales-per-unit floor area of any U.S. food store. More broadly, many U.S. supermarket chains are suffering, but Whole Foods successfully targets a market segment prepared to pay more for higher-quality groceries.

The critical success issue for both leaders and followers boils down to commitment. There are really two broad strategic options — target many segments or settle for a more limited position by targeting just a few. The firm's decision should be based on clear insight about markets and market segments and a rigorous assessment of its ability to serve them successfully.

FIGURE 10.6

MATURITY-STAGE SCENARIOS

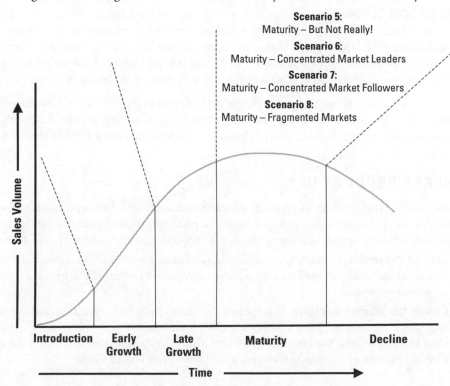

Scenario 5:
Maturity – But Not Really!

Scenario 6:
Maturity – Concentrated Market Leaders

Scenario 7:
Maturity – Concentrated Market Followers

Scenario 8:
Maturity – Fragmented Markets

SCENARIO 5: GROWTH IN A MATURE MARKET

> Former Coke CEO Roberto C. Goizueta used to quote fondly from a 1937 *Fortune* article opining that a typical investor concluded it was too late to make money on Coke stock because the market for its product was saturated!

Before the firm examines strategic options in maturity — Figure 10.6, it must affirm that the life cycle really is in *maturity*. Perhaps there are possibilities for market growth. To make the point succinctly, some authors assert, "There is no such thing as a mature business, there are only mature managers!"[27]

BARRIERS TO GROWTH

When assessing if the lifecycle is in maturity, the firm must analyze barriers to growth:

BEHAVIORAL BARRIERS. Requiring significant behavioral change by customers is often a barrier. *Techies* were early users of PCs and their difficult-to-use operating systems like CPM and MS-DOS. The mass market developed only when Apple, and then Microsoft, launched *easy-to-use* intuitive options. Customer behavior changes can also rejuvenate markets. Bicycles were old-fashioned by the late 1970s, but sales increased dramatically when exercisers used them. And coffee consumption grew outside the home as consumers embraced new and trendier establishments like Starbucks.

ECONOMIC BARRIERS. Economic barriers are often linked to technology. When its Roundup herbicide lost patent protection in the Philippines, Monsanto cut prices to compete with cheaper generics. Monsanto discovered it had vastly underestimated price elasticity[28]; sales grew dramatically when many farmers could afford Roundup.

GOVERNMENT-IMPOSED BARRIERS. When the government removes regulations, competitors often enter, and growth explodes. The U.S. government opened bandwidths to commercial use and wireless-based products expanded rapidly. Deregulation of air transportation spawned rapid growth in airfreight and passenger air travel.

TECHNOLOGICAL BARRIERS. Innovation may obliterate technological barriers to growth. AT&T's transistor technology rejuvenated radios. Improved microprocessors made PCs portable and much cheaper. In-line skates revived the almost-dead roller-skating industry, and Trevor Baylis' new clockwork technology led to the *Freeplay* wind-up radio, flashlights, a global positioning system (GPS) handset, cellular phone chargers, and a landmine detector.

Generally, if the market is not *really* mature, the firm's key strategic objective should be growth. The most serious barrier to growth may be lack of creativity.[29] Creatively generating and analyzing opportunities and approaching seemingly mature markets can spur growth in several ways.

INCREASE PRODUCT USE

The firm may increase product use via reminder and reinforcement communications; promoting different use applications, occasions, or locations; providing incentives and bundling opportunities; and reducing undesirable consequences of frequency. Specific techniques include:

- **Change the model.** Fashion firms make seasonal changes in clothing styles; automobile firms change models annually; and software companies continually introduce new and improved versions.
- **Design the product to expire.** Incorporate devices to indicate product discard dates and encourage repurchase. Read this book quickly ... it was printed with disappearing ink. (Just kidding!) Firms use expiration and *best-if-used-by* dates on beer and soft drinks, and physical indicators on razors, batteries, toothbrushes, and water filters.

Marketing Question

Assume you work for Ford or GM. What barriers to growth exist in the automobile market? Are these barriers different for foreign manufacturers?

KEY IDEA

➤ Creative ways to drive growth in the maturity stage:
- Increase product use
- Improve the product/ service
- Improve physical distribution
- Reduce price
- Reposition the brand
- Enter new markets

- **Develop new product uses.** New product forms replaced baking soda for baking and antacids, leaving Arm & Hammer as the sole surviving brand. Arm & Hammer developed many new uses — removing refrigerator smells and sink odors, treating swimming pools, eliminating underarm perspiration, and sanitizing laundry.

- **Improve packaging for better ease of use.** Examples include single-serving cereals, storage-friendly packages, individual laundry and dishwasher tablets, easy-to-pour condiments, and storage-friendly bulk items like Coke and Pepsi 12-packs for refrigerators

- **Increase quantity per use occasion.** Options include increasing packaging size, like a 20- versus a 12-ounce Pepsi[30]; and/or designing the packaging for dispensing ease, like adding a larger-sized opening for Tabasco hot sauce.

- **Make the product easier to use.** Consumers do not have to clean or disinfect disposable contact lenses. Pharmaceutical firms often redesign injectable drugs as tablets, time-release capsules, and long-lived patches to ease patient burdens and encourage use.

IMPROVE THE PRODUCT/SERVICE

Firms should expect sales to slow if products do not satisfy customer needs. The remedy is simple: *Improve the offer!* In the late 1990s, many analysts believed that Apple, beset by quality problems, would not survive. But it returned to growth and profitability by launching G3 PowerBooks and the popular iMac. More than 25 percent of iMac buyers were new computer users; more than 10 percent switched from the IBM platform.

Sometimes even apparently minor changes can increase sales significantly. Clorox introduced a lemon-fresh version of Pine-Sol household floor and wall cleaner — sales grew by 25 percent. Clorox added a squirt of floral scent or a twist of lemon to Clorox bleach and gained 1 percent market share. Clorox also slightly modified Formula 409, a popular countertop cleaner, and increased market share from 17 to 20 percent. Changes in clothing include availability of wrinkle-free and EKG-monitoring shirts and products containing odor-absorbing micro-granules.

Because product quality has improved significantly in many industries, and gaining product-based advantage is difficult, many firms use services to rejuvenate their brands. IBM based its recent success on a shift from hardware and software to providing services. You've seen the commercials. Today, IBM operates information technology systems and platforms for thousands of major firms like DuPont, Kodak, and Xerox.[31]

IMPROVE PHYSICAL DISTRIBUTION

KEY IDEA

➤ Markets that seem mature may have growth potential waiting to be unlocked via creative approaches.

Sophisticated package delivery and tracking systems helped grow electronic commerce. But Coca-Cola uses whatever distribution works in a given geography — motorcycles, pack mules, or camels — to get Coke to rural backwaters. Traditionally, upscale New York City restaurants secured fish from the local Fulton Fish Market several days after its landing in Maine. Today, buyers in Maine inspect fish at 6 a.m., purchase at 11:15 a.m., pack at 12:15 p.m., and send to New York. Unpacked at 9 a.m. the next day, ready for lunch, the fresher cod earns twice the price. Off the Alaskan coast, Bill Webber e-mails pictures of caught salmon to chefs, packs chosen items in insulated bubble-wrap liners for shipping boxes, then ships by FedEx. The premium-priced fish arrives at restaurants 48 hours after leaving the water.

REDUCE PRICE

Chapter 10's Opening Case shows how Ryanair transformed a seemingly mature airline market into growth with a low-price strategy. Southwest Airlines previously had similar success in the U.S. The author is trying to transform the marketing textbook market via Wessex Press. Of course, low prices demand low-cost operations.

REPOSITION THE BRAND

The firm offers the same product but with new benefits and values for new customers; fine-grained segmentation may reveal growth segments.[32] In a classic example, Honda repositioned motorcycles from a product made for *longhaired guys* and *the police officers chasing them* to *a family activity*. The new mantra, "You meet the nicest people on a Honda," revolutionized the industry. Sears and Cadillac have tried to reposition their brands, but with mixed results.

ENTER NEW MARKETS

When fax capability threatened overnight document delivery, FedEx refocused efforts on shipping physical goods for direct marketers. Customers received products more quickly, and direct marketers gained advantage over brick-and-mortar stores. The changed focus positioned FedEx as an essential part of the new e-commerce industry; UPS quickly followed. More recently, both FedEx and UPS secured retail presence by acquiring Kinko's and Mail Boxes Etc., respectively.

Many firms define new markets by geography — in particular, emerging markets like the BRICI countries (Brazil, Russia, India, China, Indonesia) with millions of low-income customers. To supply sufficiently low-priced products, firms must modify traditional practices. In India, Cummins gained 40 percent share in the low-horsepower power generator market. Cummins created a series of smaller, lower-powered modularized engines with add-ons — ready-to-assemble *gensets* (generation sets) for different segments like farmers and small retailers. Cummins also gained significant new capabilities.[33]

SCENARIO 6: LEADERS IN CONCENTRATED MATURE MARKETS

Historically, Kirin had 60 percent share of the Japanese beer market; Asahi had less than 10 percent. Over time, positions shifted and Asahi's share reached about 50 percent. What happened? Kirin's market dominance led to over-confidence and failure to act on industry trends — the distribution shift from small local shops, where it was strong, to supermarkets and discounters; a slow response as cans replaced bottles; and overemphasis on new, small-volume beers rather than supporting core brands. By contrast, Asahi offered convenience, quality, and value.

Generally, **concentrated markets** support a few substantial competitors whose aggregate market share often exceeds 60 percent[34]; several small players may target market niches. The market leader should have an incumbent's advantage — deeper understanding of customer needs and profitability metrics than followers, and hence be more effective.[35] Profit margins should be high for low-cost leaders; investment should be relatively low (because growth is low); and cash flow should be strongly positive.

The market leader has two strategic options:

- Maintain leadership over the long run.
- Harvest the business.[36]

MAINTAIN LEADERSHIP OVER THE LONG RUN

The core decision for maintaining market leadership is choosing the *right* investment level. Generally, we advocate *cautious* investment. With the *right* investment, in the *right* areas, the

KEY IDEA

➤ Market leaders in concentrated mature markets should have:

• Low costs
• Decent profits
• Positive cash flows

firm may reap profits for many years. *Overinvestment* to gain market share from entrenched competitors often wastes resources. Pressures for overinvestment are:

- **Few alternative opportunities.** The firm fails to develop other growth opportunities like new products or strategic alliances. Success depends on a few products so the firm continues to invest aggressively when it should invest modestly.

- **Internally focused funding criteria.** The firm bases funding on current financial performance. The firm underfunds unprofitable new products and overinvests in mature products.

- **Political power of mature-product champions.** Senior executives directing the firm's large product lines are typically powerful — their products are today's profit-makers. They lobby successfully for large budgets.

Conversely, *underinvestment* can leave the firm vulnerable to aggressive competitors, perhaps by setting overly ambitious profit targets, and the firm loses market share. The author identified one firm whose major product increased revenues at 2 percent annually for five years. Simultaneously, by slashing investment and other costs, annual profit growth increased to 12 percent! Good news? No! Sales imploded due to underinvestment. Increasing short-run profits is not difficult; the trick is finding the right investment level to sustain profits in the medium- and long run.[37] Reasons for underinvestment are:

- **Fear of cannibalization.** The firm could maintain leadership by introducing a lower-profit version(s). The firm fails to act because it fears losing sales of higher profit product(s).

- **Inertia.** Performance is acceptable and the firm sees no reason to change.

- **Limited view of competition.** The firm takes a too-narrow view. For many years, International Paper took little action as disposable plastic cups replaced its market-leading paper cups.

- **Misunderstanding the challenger's strategy.** The firm's competitive data-gathering and analysis is weak; it fails to gain good competitive insight.

Marketing Question

Suppose you managed the Gillette brand for P&G. What actions would you take to secure long-run profits?

Of course, complacency and arrogance can accentuate any or all of these errors, and past success can blind the firm to evolving market realities. To maintain leadership, the firm should be ready to react to follower actions, like Whirlpool's Maytag acquisition to frustrate Haier, and explore the creative options discussed earlier. Generally, the firm can maintain leadership via incremental product improvements; it should also invest in marketing activities that build and sustain brand equity and demonstrate competitive superiority. When a clinical trial showed that Lipitor (cholesterol-lowering drug) reduced heart attack risk by 16 percent, Pfizer widely advertised the result; Lipitor achieved over 40 percent market share.

The firm should speed up product development and invest in process technology for more efficient lower-cost operations. Process technology change can severely affect market leaders that do not adapt. Traditional integrated steel firms like U.S. Steel and Bethlehem Steel were competitively disadvantaged versus Nucor and others with electric arc mini-mills. The firm should also consider *variating* fixed costs — reducing fixed costs and increasing variable costs. Then, if sales slip, costs also reduce. The firm should tightly manage working capital by reducing accounts receivable and inventory and lengthening accounts payable. Dell strives for the lowest possible costs and continually adjusts prices to reflect supplier cost data. Dell only makes-to-order, has minimal inventory, and gets paid before manufacture — hence, negative working capital. Referring to competitors, Michael Dell said, "The industry doesn't have a pricing problem; it has an operating expense problem."[38]

New product innovation should also concern market leaders. Products based on new technology can destroy leadership positions — compact discs versus vinyl records; e-mail versus fax. Kodak continues to struggle with the transition from chemical film to digital cameras. An external orientation is the best protection against this sort of market erosion.[39]

Distribution can also be challenging. Early in the life cycle, the firm may have developed a distribution system to reach end-user customers. But as some end users grow in size and expertise, they demand direct distribution to secure lower prices by cutting out distributor margins. The firm faces a difficult catch-22 situation; if it remains loyal to distributors, it risks losing its sales to powerful end users. If the firm goes direct to end users, it upsets long-standing distributor relationships.[40] Many consumer goods firms face a related problem with electronic commerce. Sony sells computers, cameras, camcorders, TVs, and home audio and video products in big-box *bricks-and-mortar* stores like Best Buy and Sears, sometimes with exclusive designs per store. But consumers can also purchase these products at *www.sonystyle.com*, Sony's website. Of course, presence in multiple distribution channels improves customer *share of mind*.

Addressing Low Price Competitors[41]

Leaders in mature Western markets often face competition from low-price/low-cost competitors. Aldi (Germany — supermarkets), Huawei (China — telecommunications equipment), IKEA (Sweden — furniture), Ryanair (Ireland — airline), and Teva (Israel — pharmaceuticals) have each made life difficult for traditional leaders. Followers' low-cost models drive price competition, but price wars are generally not good responses. Strategic options include:

- **Do nothing.** *Wait-and-see* lets the market leader gain insight into the new entrant's strategy and performance.
- **Enhance value.** Use the creative options discussed in Scenario 5.
- **Develop a dual strategy.** Continue with current products but introduce a low-cost/low-price offer to compete with the follower head-on. This strategy fails if insufficiently aggressive — Go (British Airways), Song (Delta), and Ted (United) are good examples. The firm must set clear customer expectations — low price implies less service — and be prepared to cannibalize the original business. Under attack from low-cost entrants in silicones, global market leader Dow Corning set up Xiameter as a low-price (20 percent less) competitor. Several actions reduced costs: limited product range; website-only orders (extra fees for e-mail/phone); no technical service; shipping 7 to 20 days after order (extra charge for rush); and delivery only in full truck, tank, or pallet loads. Revenues and profits increased.
- **Switch to solutions.** The firm makes price less transparent by bundling the product with services; IBM, HP, Dell, and Xerox each adopted this strategy. Orica (Australia's leading explosives supplier to stone quarries) was in a price war with new entrants. Orica used technical expertise to provide greater flexibility at the blast site (mixing explosives on-site) and improved blasting efficiency by advising on drilling-hole placement. Orica now sets price based on quantity of broken rock — the fundamental customer value.
- **Become a low-cost/low-price competitor.** This option represents a huge change in business model and may be difficult to execute. Ryanair — Opening Case — started out as a traditional airline but transformed to a low-cost/low-price airline, with great success.

HARVEST

The firm is market leader, but a **harvest** strategy may be more important than maintaining sales and market share. Reasons include:

- **Change in firm strategy.** The product becomes less central to the firm. BMS and Pfizer each redefined themselves as pharmaceutical firms and divested over-the-counter products. Financial markets may pressure the firm to focus — eliminate non-core products and *get back to basics*.
- **Desire to avoid specific competitors.** If the firm forecasts tougher competition, harvesting may be the best option. Westinghouse exited traditional markets in electric products where GE was frequently more successful.
- **Government regulations.** The government may restrict the industry or eliminate product use — many governments have banned the use of some pesticides.
- **Investment requirements are too high.** Necessary investment for continued competitiveness, like new product or new process technology, may be too high. British Aerospace (BA) launched the world's first jet aircraft, the de Havilland Comet. But costs to develop

KEY IDEA

➤ *Market leaders* in concentrated mature markets have two major options:

- Long-run leadership
- Harvesting: May be *fast* or *slow*

and produce large commercial jet aircraft rose; BA withdrew, except as a part-owner and subcontractor for Airbus.

- **New technology.** The product will soon become obsolete.

Once the firm decides to harvest, the critical question is *fast* or *slow*? Fast harvesting — divest the product and gain immediate cash. Slow harvesting — the firm should focus on three issues:

- **Cut costs.** Simplify the product line; streamline distribution; reduce advertising, promotion, and services; and eliminate small and unprofitable customers.
- **Minimize investment.** Make little or no further product investment.
- **Raise prices.** Raise prices or eliminate extras like free delivery or extended warranties.

The more aggressive the firm's actions, the more quickly it will exit the market.

SCENARIO 7: FOLLOWERS IN CONCENTRATED MATURE MARKETS

Followers have smaller market shares than the leader; they probably also have higher costs, lower profits, and are weaker financially. But leaders can lose position by poor decisions, and followers may attain leadership by inspired management. Airbus caught up with Boeing in large jet aircraft and for a few years surpassed it. Southwest Airlines is now the leading domestic U.S. airline; Continental, Delta, Northwest, and United Airlines each emerged from bankruptcy to become solid competitors.

Most firms have products that fit scenario 7; hence, this scenario has broad applicability. The follower has three basic strategic options, each with several sub-options:

- Improve market position.
- Keep on truckin'.
- Exit.

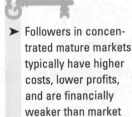

KEY IDEA

➤ Followers in concentrated mature markets typically have higher costs, lower profits, and are financially weaker than market leaders. But they may rejuvenate to become a major threat.

IMPROVE MARKET POSITION

Careful and creative market segmentation, kenneling, and direct attack are three primary alternatives to grow and, perhaps, ultimately dethrone the market leader:

MARKET SEGMENTATION. Options for segmentation typically appear in early growth and become numerous in late growth and maturity. Creative segmentation is the dominant option for counteracting the market leader's advantages.[42] The follower should conduct careful research to identify and target emerging segments. Examples include:

BetterBags (BB) targets upscale and specialty food markets like D'Agostino, Schnucks, and Whole Foods. BB's plastic bags are 20 percent more expensive than traditional bags, but are thicker, can be printed with six colors, and feature fewer defects, a patented pull-down dispenser, and one-at-a-time automatic opening.

Enterprise is the U.S. market leader in automobile rental. Initially Enterprise identified and targeted the *car-under-repair* segment of the rental market.

Jakks Pacific has built a successful video-game business by targeting preteen boys and girls, and price-conscious adults.

MBNA (now part of Bank of America) has been very successful targeting affinity groups like universities, veterans, and fans of sports teams.

Quiksilver built a $2 billion apparel business by focusing exclusively on active sportspeople like surfers, skateboarders, and snowboarders.

Red Bull competes successfully in the global soft-drink market by developing and dominating the energy drink segment.

Firms often identify and target market segments by adding benefits to satisfy customers' ever more fine-grained needs, often at higher prices. But in maturity, there is often one segment that just wants basic product benefits, *getting back to basics* — at a low price. Examples include: automobiles — Citroën 2CV, Mini, Smart cars, and Volkswagen Beetle; airlines — Southwest, Spirit, and Sun Country Airlines (U.S.), and Air Berlin, Baboo, easyJet, and Ryanair (Europe); and cruises — easyCruise. Acer (Taiwan) gained market share on HP and Dell with low-price netbooks. For a low-price strategy to be successful, the firm must have low-cost operations.

KENNELING. Kenneling is a metaphor for bringing several *dog* (seemingly worthless) products together. A follower may acquire several unprofitable (or marginally profitable) low-market-share products, and then do a *roll-up*. By rationalizing operations, distribution, and/or marketing, the follower may become a strong competitor. In commercial banking, JPMorgan Chase resulted from a *roll-up* of Chemical Bank, Manufacturers Hanover, Chase Manhattan, JPMorgan, and Bank One.[43] LKQ *rolled up* dozens of scrap yards that turned junk cars into reuseable parts; Fortress Investments is kenneling U.S. local small-town newspapers. Partnerships like the code-sharing Star Alliance including Air Canada, Air New Zealand, ANA, Asiana Airlines, Austrian Airlines, Lot, Lufthansa, Mexicana, SAS, Singapore Airlines, South African Airlines, Spanair, Swiss Airways, TAP, Thai Airlines, United, and Varig is another form of kenneling. Asea Brown Boveri (ABB) combined segmenting and kenneling globally:

> ABB acquired many small, local, heavy-equipment manufacturers in different countries. Each acquired entity eliminated marginal and unprofitable products so as to specialize in producing a few products. Each national firm offers a full product line, in part by securing products from sister firms, and provides local customer service. ABB secured significant production economies and rates its kenneling strategy as very effective.[44]

DIRECT ATTACK. If the leader has been lazy, underinvested, set prices too high, and/or served customers poorly, direct attack may be the follower's best option. Good market intelligence helps find the leader's weak spots, so the follower can invest to exploit them. In financial information, new-entrant Bloomberg went head-to-head against Dow Jones and Reuters; pre-installed software in custom-made terminals let subscribers do their own financial analyses. Now Bloomberg and Thomson-Reuters share the terminal market. Similarly, Spin Masters' Liv line of girl's dolls is a direct attack on Mattel's Barbie.

In industries as diverse as credit cards and pharmaceuticals, market leaders have lost share to new entrants offering better products and/or lower prices. Firefox, offering greater virus security and faster inter-website speed, has earned roughly 30 percent global market share of web browsers, mostly taken from Internet Explorer.

KEEP ON TRUCKIN'

This adage describes maintaining or rationalizing a firm's current position:

MAINTAIN POSITION. Holding market share roughly constant over the long run can be viable if the firm has a profitable market position and strengths in one or more segments. Harley-Davidson has a relatively small share of the motorcycle market, but design, performance, and community-building have provided a loyal user base.[45] The firm may also leverage its position to other markets and segments, like Harley-Davidson restaurants.

RATIONALIZE POSITION. If profits are marginal or negative, rationalizing operations may be the way to go. The firm should examine all aspects of operations, distribution, and sales with *a fine-tooth comb*, and make tough cost-cutting decisions. The firm may forestall an exit, retain a skilled workforce, and have continued access to raw materials and/or technology — these may be useful in the future.

EXIT

Followers should choose *exit* if profitability is unlikely and/or the product's future is doubtful, perhaps due to negative brand image or slowing market demand. Choices are **divest** or **liquidate**:

DIVEST. By finding a buyer for which the product is a good fit, the firm can secure cash quickly. BMS divested Clairol to P&G and Excedrin to Novartis; Pfizer divested over-the-counter products to J&J; each was a good fit for the acquirer. When the firm divests, it should avoid strengthening a potential competitor. Boeing divested De Havilland Canada, its commuter aircraft operation, to Bombardier. Bombardier upgraded its product line by emphasizing jets and introducing larger aircraft. Boeing later stopped producing its smallest jet, the 717.

LIQUIDATE. If no buyers appear, the only reasonable action may be liquidation — closing down and selling assets.[46] British Aerospace (BAE) was producing 25 jet aircraft annually versus 370 for Bombardier (Canada) and 130 for Empresa Brasileira (Brazil); BA stopped production.

Sometimes the firm faces exit barriers and is unable (or unwilling) to leave a market, despite compelling strategic arguments. Delivery contracts, buyback guarantees, union contracts, and/or potential damage to brand equity may each make exit difficult. Community relations may be important if plant closing would devastate the local economy. Emotional commitments can also be an exit barrier. Ingersoll-Rand continued with rock drilling, despite losses, largely because it was IR's original business. U.S. liquor importer W. A. Taylor sold mostly up-market brands, like B&B (Benedictine and Brandy). Old Smuggler whiskey did not fit. But most top managers had been brand managers for Old Smuggler; they couldn't bear to part with it![47]

Marketing Question

For decades, P&G and Unilever competed fiercely in laundry detergents; P&G has been the market leader for many years. In 2008, Unilever divested its U.S. detergent business to a private equity firm. Why? What five-year strategies would you suggest for P&G and the new private equity owner?

SCENARIO 8: FRAGMENTED MATURE MARKETS

Fragmented markets have many players, but no firm is dominant. Hence leader/follower distinctions have little relevance. An important objective is increasing market share. Two strategic options for restructuring or repositioning offers are acquisition, and standardization and branding:

- Acquisition
- Standardization and branding

Marketing Question

Many service businesses like doctors, dentists, plumbers, electricians, and general contractors are very local. Pick one of these services or another of your choice. How would you increase market share for one of the players?

ACQUISITION

Acquisition is similar to kenneling — p. 262; it can be very successful when geography drives fragmentation. A global firm may acquire many national companies to secure greater market share. AXA, the French insurance giant, built a strong position in the fragmented global insurance industry by acquiring several European insurance firms and Equitable (U.S.). Copart executed a successful domestic *roll-up*:

Copart auctions (including online bidding) totally wrecked vehicles to dismantlers, rebuilders, and used-car dealers. Copart offers insurance-company customers database access to track sales. Copart expanded to 35 percent market share by purchasing dozens of independent auto junkyards. Copart's net margins are 15 to 20 percent.

KEY IDEA

➤ In mature fragmented markets, no firm has a large market share.

STANDARDIZATION AND BRANDING

In fragmented industries, many players typically offer a wide range of products and services. Standardization is a way to reduce variation and improve consistency across various suppliers; branding assures customers that each provider supplies the same value. BASF and ADP both offer lesser-known products in many markets. By promoting the corporate brand, customers have confidence that individual products will deliver the promised value.

Sometimes firms use *franchising* to attract small, independently owned players — Chapter 18. Franchisees maintain independence, but take advantage of the franchisor's brand and other services. Examples include Century 21 — real estate; Holiday Inn — hospitality; and Kampgrounds of America (KOA) — campsites. Alternatively, the firm enters a fragmented industry using wholly owned operations and/or franchising, like KFC, McDonald's, Pizza Hut, and Subway — fast food; and ServiceMaster — cleaning services.

SCENARIO 9: MARKETS IN DECLINE

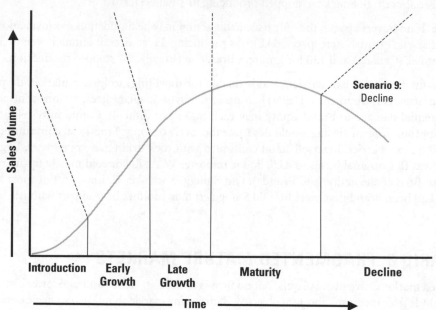

FIGURE 10.7

DECLINE-STAGE SCENARIOS

Figure 10.7 identifies the decline scenario. "So now you've graduated; we're delighted that you've joined us. We're going to throw you in the deep end. You will be in charge of our Deced product where sales have been declining for the past few years." How would you like this assignment? Most new managers would not be happy, yet firms can make good profits from declining products. Table 10.1 shows the results of one study: 21 (8+13) percent of businesses made no profits or had losses. But 78 percent were profitable and almost 40 percent earned over 35 percent ROI.[48]

							Total
Percent of businesses	8%	13%	38%	25%	5%	9%	100%
Return on investment (ROI)	−10%	0%	15%	35%	55%	60%	

TABLE 10.1

PROFITABILITY DISTRIBUTION FOR DECLINE BUSINESSES*

* To be read as, for example, 38% of sample businesses had an average ROI of 15%.

We learned earlier that the pioneer has little competition early in the life cycle. But as the market grows, competitors typically enter. In the decline stage of the life cycle, the reverse occurs — new entry is unlikely and competitors exit. Good examples of declining products are videotape recorders, many canned foods, public telephones, full-service travel agents, and *sake* in Japan. Two dimensions are important: market hospitality and firm business strengths.

MARKET HOSPITALITY. A declining market is **inhospitable** if:
- Decline is rapid and/or uncertain.
- The market is commodity-based; there are no price-insensitive segments.
- Competitors:
  - are viable and credible.
  - are evenly balanced and view the market as strategically important.
  - have high fixed costs and are very sensitive to sales declines.
- Customer switching costs are low.

KEY IDEA

➤ In a declining market, the firm's options depend on market hospitality and its business strengths.

The characteristics of **hospitable** markets are the opposite of these, but declining markets are *especially* inhospitable if, in addition:

- Bankruptcy laws allow failing competitors to return with lower costs, like U.S. airlines.
- Competitors' exit barriers are high — for example, they cannot easily redeploy assets.[49]
- Competitors are emotionally committed to the product.
- The product is part of a vertically integrated supply system.
- The government or the community pressures (or subsidizes) some firms to remain.

BUSINESS STRENGTHS. Firms with good *business strengths* should have low costs, good raw material contracts, and/or be able to keep productive assets running without major investment.

Figure 10.8 shows the four-cell matrix formed by combining market hospitality and business strengths. Each matrix cell suggests a different strategic option.

FIGURE 10.8

STRATEGIC OPTIONS IN DECLINE

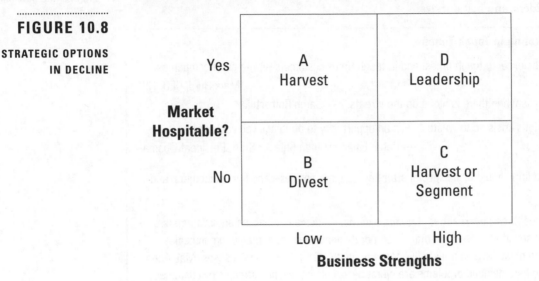

LEADERSHIP

Pursuing leadership (cell D) is a viable option when the market is hospitable and the firm has high business strengths. The firm should publicly recognize the decline, but also demonstrate its commitment. The firm should market aggressively, by adding new products, increasing advertising and promotion, and/or cutting prices. The newspaper industry is a good example:

> Television, the Internet, and other communications have led to circulation declines for many newspapers. But several major U.S. newspapers are showing modest sales gains. These firms offer higher quality — like color pages and later press deadlines to accommodate late-breaking news, door-to-door sales, and earlier delivery. Distribution has improved: *USA Today* sells in corporate cafeterias, university dining halls, hospitals, hotel lobbies, and Starbucks.[50]

Marketing Question

Suppose you were a full-service travel agent. What actions would you take to ensure your survival?

The firm should consider reducing production capacity, like International Paper and international and domestic airlines. White Consolidated (now part of Electrolux) purchased Frigidaire from GM and immediately closed the plant. The firm may also encourage competitors to exit, by offering long-term supply contracts for their customers and/or private-label manufacturing; buying competitors or their assets may be an option.[51]

HARVEST, DIVEST, SEGMENT

Generally, firms in cells A, B, and C should harvest or divest. But for a cell C firm — inhospitable market, high business strengths, well positioned in price-insensitive segments — medium-run viability may be an option. New entry may even be an alternative for attractive market segments: BoltBus, Fung Wah Bus, and MegaBus each offer frequent, low-price bus service with curbside pickup in the Boston–New York–Washington corridor and other routes; new buses have wifi connectivity. We discussed harvesting options earlier.

LEVERAGE THE BRAND

Notwithstanding market decline, and in addition to the above options, the firm may be able to leverage a strong brand in other markets. By diversifying away from its original business, the firm may yet survive and grow. Faced with a decline in cigarette smoking, Zippo, makers of the iconic lighter, introduced life-style products like camping supplies, casual clothing, fragrances, and watches. But this path may be quite difficult; Zippo discontinued earlier entries into tape measures, key holders, and belt buckles.

Managing Marketing in Tough Times

"Great companies excel in tough times, and in tough times customers turn to great companies."
— Mark Hurd, CEO, HP

"The time to buy is when there is blood on the streets." — Baron Rothschild

"Never let a serious crisis go to waste ... it's an opportunity to do things you couldn't do before." — Rahm Emanuel, then Chief of Staff, President Obama

In tough times the firm should focus special attention on three entities – the firm, customers, and competitors.

Firm. The firm faces three new realities: Two are external — demand weakens and customers become very price sensitive; one is internal — corporate demands cuts in marketing and sales budgets. Marketing must develop a laser-like focus on unit sales, prices, and expenses. Marketing should figure out where demand problems are worst by examining revenue streams by customer, product, and market segment — then decide which deserve more effort and which less. Mostly, the firm should invest in its core business, and focus efforts on retaining and growing profitable customers, in part via significant communications — good news and bad news. The firm should be ready to make changes as circumstances evolve, but consider several specific actions:

- Be sure to retain key employees and continue to make R&D investments for the recovery.
- Cut prices by offering short-tem discounts — not permanent price reductions.
- Ensure that incentive compensation drives the right behavior; use recognition as a reward.
- Explore new pricing models, like bundling, unbundling, or mixed bundling; or offer the product benefit rather than the product itself — aircraft engine *power by the hour* versus aircraft engines, and cloud computing.
- Identify inefficiencies: Drop poorly performing products and brands; eliminate marginal value services; withdraw from unproductive market segments; eliminate unproductive sales, service, and support personnel and distributors; reduce advertising not leading to near-term sales.
- Introduce stripped-down products with minimal service at lower prices — Burger King introduced a $1 Whopper (2 versus 2.2 ounce patties), and/or introduce products that focus on value — luxury-goods firm Coach introduced the Poppy accessory line.
- Renegotiate contracts with (or drop) service providers like advertising agencies and marketing researchers.
- Respond to requests for aggregate spending cuts carefully by using zero-base budgeting. Never be *fair* by making equal across-the-board cuts.
- When operations drives use of less expensive raw materials, be sure customers do not react negatively — Campbell's received negative publicity when it reduced the meat quantity in chicken-noodle soup!

CONTINUES ON NEXT PAGE

Customers. B2C and B2B customers face difficult environments. Challenges vary by type and scope but decision-making units, decision-making processes, and purchase requirements may change dramatically. Decision-making takes longer and many B2B purchases receive increased scrutiny from higher-level executives. The firm must identify these changes, take appropriate action, and be creative. GameStop is the market leader in selling used video games (accepted as trade-ins for new-game purchases); in 2008, Hyundai customers could return purchased cars if they lost their job within one year. Other considerations:

- Customers can't afford the firm's products — Can the firm offer new pricing and/or provide leasing options?
- Customers need longer to pay — Can the firm offer attractive credit terms?

Competitors. Competitors behave in new and different ways; the firm should watch carefully for opportunities to make gains. Considerations:

- Competitors sharply cut advertising and sales budgets — Can the firm increase spending and gain market share?
- Competitors lay off marketing and sales executives (or declare bankruptcy) and remaining employees are nervous — Can the firm make attractive hires?
- Competitors may be willing to sell brands, intellectual property, or themselves — Can the firm secure valuable assets from wounded competitors?

The firm must manage through tough times but simultaneously plan for economic recovery.[52]

Marketing Question

What other messages did you glean from this chapter?

KEY MESSAGES

Pre-emption is an important dimension of strategy-making; acting before competitors can put the firm in good competitive position. Using the product life-cycle framework, we constructed nine scenarios for developing pre-emptive strategies:

- Introduction
- Early-Growth Leaders
- Early-Growth Followers
- Late Growth
- Maturity – But Not Really
- Maturity – Concentrated Market Leaders
- Maturity – Concentrated Market Followers
- Maturity – Fragmented Markets
- Decline

These scenarios can help the firm think through its strategy by anticipating, and striving to influence, change. For each scenario, we developed a family of strategic options. Notwithstanding the value of identifying these options, the best competitive strategies are often contrarian. When the firm surprises competitors, it can gain significantly.

VIDEOS AND AUDIOS

Managing through the Life Cycle   v1002 ☜   Ron Boire   Toys R Us

v1002

QUESTIONS FOR STUDY AND DISCUSSION

Can you answer the questions implied by this chapter's learning objectives? Check!

1. Identify the product life-cycle stage for each product. Why did you choose the stages?

Cell phones	Digital cameras	Movies on VHS tapes	Index mutual funds
Desktop PCs	Music on compact discs	Vacation travel	Books on tape

2. Suppose you are the newly appointed marketing VP for the Segway Human Transporter. Identify feasible strategic options. Be prepared to support your choices.

3. How did Nokia rise to global leadership in cell phones? How do you evaluate its current position and strategy? As Nokia's global marketing VP, how would you approach the future?

4. Suppose you own several specialty coffee shops in a mid-sized U.S. urban center. Starbucks enters. What are your options? Be prepared to support your choices.

5. On p. 265, we noted several ways in which U.S. newspapers are addressing flat or declining sales. What options are available for your local newspaper? What action(s) do you recommend?

6. Installations of U.S. pay phones are decreasing by several percentage points each year — pay phone calls are also decreasing. How would you advise an independent payphone firm?

7. Vonage offers low-price voice telecom services; what is the current life-cycle stage? Prepare for a job interview at Vonage by describing current challenges, objectives, strategies, and success measures.

8. Sirius acquired XM Satellite Radio to form Sirius XM Radio. As the incoming marketing VP, lay out your strategy going forward.

9. Select a product in which you are interested. Alternatively, consider this book — *Managing Marketing in the 21st Century*. What is its product life cycle stage? What strategic options does it have? Which do you recommend? Why?

IMPERATIVE 3

*Set Strategic Direction
and Positioning*

CHAPTER 11

MANAGING

BRANDS v1101

To access O-codes, go to **www.ocodes.com**

*If this business were to be split up, I would be glad to take
the brands, trademarks, and goodwill, and you could have
all the bricks and mortar and I would fare better than you.*[1]

— John Stuart, former Chairman of Quaker

LEARNING OBJECTIVES

When you have completed this chapter, you will be able to:

- Understand the nature of brands and the values they provide for buyers and sellers.
- Comprehend the changing role of brands and branding.
- Distinguish between customer brand equity and firm brand equity.
- Measure the monetary value of customer brand equity and firm brand equity.
- Build and sustain a strong brand.
- Construct the firm's brand architecture.
- Make decisions about multi-branding versus umbrella branding, brand broadening, and brand migration.
- Address branding issues for strategic alliances.
- Revitalize struggling brands.

OPENING CASE: SAP

*In the first decade of the 21st century, SAP doubled the value of the SAP brand and moved signifi-
cantly up the global rankings. How did SAP achieve such success?*

In 2000, SAP was the world's largest enterprise systems software firm and third-largest independent software supplier overall.[2] SAP had 12,500 customers and 25,000 software installations in more than 50 countries, mainly with large global firms. SAP's culture was technologically driven and based its success on innovative product development; marketing and branding were not significant. Marketing was decentralized at the national level and multiple advertising agencies produced local campaigns. SAP's branding tagline changed frequently in the previous decade: "We Can Change Your Business Perspective"; "A Better Return on Information"; "The City of 'e'"; "The Time of New Management"; and "You Can, It Does". SAP had one global Internet site, 30 local country sites, many subsidiary sites, and more than 9,000 web pages without a common theme. SAP's brand identity was weak and unclear, and CEO Hasso Plattner concluded its messaging was sprawling, inconsistent, and confusing.

Plattner broke several taboos by bringing in Martin Homlish from Sony Electronics as SAP's new Global Chief Marketing Officer — hiring from outside SAP, outside the software industry, and outside Germany. Homlish's challenge was to transform SAP's marketing and to reposition the SAP brand to have broader, sustainable appeal. Said Homlish, "I saw SAP as a marketer's dream ... great products, strong history of innovation, and a loyal customer base. All we had to do was transform marketing." Homlish faced three core challenges: communicate the brand consistently, align the organization, and create a brand flexible enough to support challenging business objectives in a dynamic industry. Homlish's first decision was to base SAP Global Marketing in New York City, center of media and marketing, rather than at SAP's headquarters in Waldorf, Germany.

Homlish sought a brand identity that could evolve over time. Meeting with customers, Homlish said, "I found a common theme. SAP was considered a mission-critical part of almost every great company." SAP's brand identity became: SAP turns businesses into best-run businesses. *The tagline to convey the new identity was, "The Best-Run Businesses Run SAP."*

Homlish redesigned SAP's brand architecture: SAP became the masterbrand; product brands like my SAP CRM were sub-brands. SAP cut its web pages by two-thirds and aligned national websites with the global site, often by direct translation. Global site changes then triggered changes to local sites using state-of-the-art web content management applications. SAP placed all global advertising with Ogilvy & Mather and reinforced its new brand identity with simple headlines that complemented the tagline: "Lufthansa runs SAP" and "Adidas runs SAP." Large posters in airports around the world helped globalize the SAP brand.

Homlish fended off potential internal challenges to global integration by developing a series of tools to align regional marketing. Regions received incentives for adopting Global Marketing's rules and syndicated tools. Said Homlish, "We drove change through alignment ... working with stakeholders across SAP. [It] takes more time versus strict 'command and control,' but ultimately it results in wider acceptance."

One Voice *was an online resource available to every SAP employee.* One Voice *included information on approved names and trademarks, key messages, and positioning for each of SAP's solutions and products, in customer-friendly language. An SAP Global Marketing team set policy, updated tools, and edited every piece of global collateral and web content before publication. The Sales and Marketing Asset Repository Toolset (SMART) delivered sales and marketing content and assets to field offices, and helped employees search for content, adaptable to local needs. The Sales and Marketing Intranet (SMI) enhanced SAP Global Marketing's efforts by including* One Voice *and SMART, together with branding standards, image library, customer brochures, industry reports, BlackBerry tools, and online customer demos.*

Homlish developed a branding culture by involving local field offices as co-developers of global messaging. He addressed Kick-Off meetings to field organizations in the North America, Europe, Middle East, and Africa (EMEA) regions. SAP Global Marketing created country champions *to roll out each campaign and gain internal support. Said Homlish, "When I arrived at SAP and would ask questions about our company and our products, I would get a lot of jargon ... SAP-anese — it confused me and our customers." SAP Global Marketing distributed pocket-sized brand cards, stating core positioning, attributes, and personality of brands, worldwide to all employees. SAP Global Marketing also selected brand ambassadors to champion the brand locally. "Today if you ask an SAP employee about the company and its products ... they can tell you, 'We help every customer become a best-run business.'"*

To attain growth objectives, SAP targeted small and medium-sized enterprises (SME) with less complex, easy to install new enterprise software. This thrust posed challenges for Homlish's branding strategy as SAP had always supplied large firms. SAP addressed the low awareness of SME products with bold brand-building ads that announced, "Finally, powerful software for the Fortune 500,000." Then, the ads addressed challenges head-on with headlines like, "Companies that thought they couldn't afford SAP run SAP." SAP also incorporated mid-market customers: "Oakley runs SAP" and "The North Face runs SAP."

CASE QUESTION

What core approaches did Marty Homlish use in developing SAP's new brand identity?

Eight years after Homlish joined, SAP showed powerful results. According to BusinessWeek's (BW) annual brand rankings, from 2000 to 2010, SAP's brand value doubled to $12.8 billion. In 2010, BW ranked SAP at number 26, above established brands like Ford, Sony, Volkswagen, and Xerox. SAP's revenues and profits grew from $5.1 billion and $796 million, respectively, in 1999 to $16.7 billion and $2.4 billion in 2010.

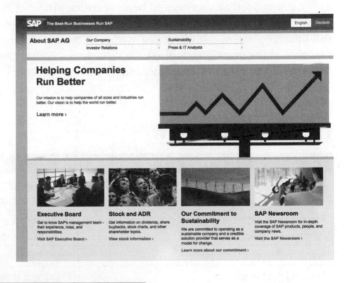

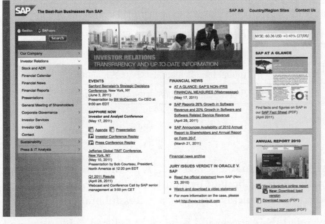

WHERE WOULD WE
BE WITHOUT THEM?

Chapter 11 is the third of three chapters discussing separate facets of Imperative 3: Set Strategic Direction and Positioning. Chapter 9 discussed developing strategy for market segments and markets; in Chapter 10, we focused on pre-emption and used the life-cycle framework to develop scenarios for generating competitive strategic options. In this chapter, we focus on branding and managing brands. As with previous topics, deep insight into markets, customers, competitors, company, and complementers is critical for making good branding decisions.

In recent years, branding has shifted from being a relatively low-level tactical issue concerned with naming products/services to being a critical driver of contemporary marketing practice. Today, the value of many firm brands far outstrips the value of their tangible assets. Accountants and financiers are re-examining the nature of brands as they rethink basic assumptions about the value of the firm. Brands also have value for customers, and branding is now a major decision area for both senior managers and marketing executives alike.

THE CHANGING VIEW

OLD WAY	NEW WAY
Brand management is a junior executive responsibility	Brand management is an important senior management responsibility
Brand owners desire total control over their own brands — co-branding is rare	Brand owners are willing to engage in cooperative strategies — co-branding is increasingly used
Brand proliferation common	Brand rationalization common
Branding is a name	Branding is a multi-sensory memorable experience
Brands tied to products and stock-keeping units (skus)	Brands assets to be managed in their own right
Brands help customers reduce purchase risk	Brands provide customers with many values
Firms add brands haphazardly	Firms carefully consider brand architecture
Local and regional brands are dominant	Global brands increasingly pre-eminent
Only brand owners use brands	Brand licensing increasingly common

WHAT IS A BRAND?

Brands are different from products. A leading marketer once said, "A product is something that is made in a factory; a brand is something that is bought by a customer. A competitor can copy a product; a brand is unique. A product can be quickly outdated; a successful brand is timeless."[3]

Throughout history, sellers have branded their goods and services.[4] Medieval goldsmiths and silversmiths branded their products. The branding iron was an essential tool for U.S. ranchers

*Marketing
Question*

What is your favorite brand? What promise does this brand offer over and above the generic product/service?

(*brand* is an Old Norse word meaning *to burn*); if a rancher had a reputation for high-quality cattle, his brand secured higher prices at market. The traditional definition follows logically: A brand is a "name, term, sign, symbol or design (or letter, number, or character), or a combination of them intended to identify the goods and services of one seller or group of sellers and to differentiate them from the competition."[5] Brands are a part of everyday life for firms and customers — logos, names, package designs, spokespersons, and symbols, trademarks, are on everything we drive, drink, wear, and eat.[6]

The most often used *signifier* is brand name, but other signifiers can be as (or more) important. Target stores are associated with the color red and UPS with brown; the *Financial Times* and fiberglass insulation from Dow Corning (U.S.) and ACI (Australia) are pink. Other well-known *visual* signifiers are the Absolut and Coca-Cola bottles,[7] Gerber baby, Merrill Lynch bull, Nike Swoosh, Pillsbury doughboy, and Volkswagen *Beetle*. *Sound* signifies Harley-Davidson motorcycles and a distinctive perfume *smell* denotes Shanghai Tang (ST) — Shanghai-based designer-wear retail chain.[8]

Today, brands have meaning far beyond these outward manifestations. By offering customers value via its brands, the firm secures value for its shareholders. The brand has become a symbol around which the firm and its customers construct a relationship. We define a **brand** as: *A collection of perceptions and associations that customers hold about a product, a service, or a company. This collection embodies values that create meaning for customers that represent a promise of the experience customers expect when they have contact with the brand.*[9] Important implications are:

- The primary meaning of any brand is carried in customer minds. Great brands are really owned by customers, not by firms — hence Coca Cola's failure with New Coke. The brand's meaning may stay relatively unchanged, but the products/product lines may evolve substantially in terms of attributes, features, underlying technologies, and customer benefits and values.

- The brand makes an implicit or explicit promise of a customer experience.[10] This promise provides value to customers over and above the product/service. By providing this additional value, the firm earns value for shareholders.

KEY IDEA

➤ The firm may brand products at different levels of aggregation.

- Figure 11.1 shows that the term *brand* applies widely to an individual product, a product line, or a group of product lines:

  - **Individual product.** An individual product such as Aveo (Chevrolet), Camry (Toyota), Fiesta (Ford), Leaf (Nissan), Town & Country (Chrysler), or MX-5 Miata (Mazda).

  - **Product line.** A group of closely related products serving a similar function. The Ragu **family or masterbrand** embraces several types of sauces — Cheese, Chunky Garden Style, Light, Old World Style, Pizza, and Robust Blend Hearty.

  - **Group of product lines.** A group of product lines fulfilling many different functions. These **monolithic** brands are often **corporate brands** — Carrefour, Citigroup, GE, Google, IBM, Marks & Spencer, Microsoft, Nike, and Yamaha.

FIGURE 11.1

LEVELS OF BRANDING

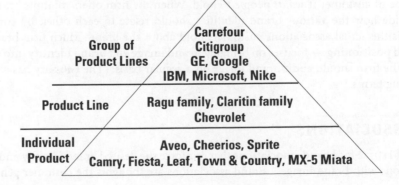

Group of Product Lines	Carrefour, Citigroup, GE, Google, IBM, Microsoft, Nike
Product Line	Ragu family, Claritin family, Chevrolet
Individual Product	Aveo, Cheerios, Sprite, Camry, Fiesta, Leaf, Town & Country, MX-5 Miata

Sometimes a brand's meaning evolves. In the U.S., Honda's original association was motorcycles — today, Honda's associations include automobiles and lawnmowers. Some brands, like Virgin, move away from their origins and become quite abstract:

Virgin — Evolution of a Brand

The original brand associations for Virgin were tied to publishing rock-and-roll records. Expansion into record stores broadened Virgin's brand associations, but Virgin sold its record business and diversified into many product classes — Virgin Atlantic (airlines), Virgin Books, Virgin Bridal Shops, Virgin Cars (retail distribution), Virgin Direct (financial services), Virgin Electronics, Virgin Limousines, Virgin Megastores (retail distribution), Virgin Mobile (cellular phone service), Virgin Sound and Vision (educational computer software), Virgin Vacations, and Radio Free Virgin. More recently, Virgin announced its entry into space travel — Virgin Galactic.

The Virgin brand is now uncoupled from its origins, yet still articulates its original abstract values. Virgin's brand identity is a higher-order sense of fun-loving, hip, irreverent, anti-establishment *underdogness*. Virgin's ongoing battles with British Airways and CEO Sir Richard Branson's personal activities — including attempts at around-the-world balloon flights — strongly support the brand identity. Some observers criticize Virgin's extensions as random and capricious but Branson's response is quite direct: "Branding is everything. I think it's also wise to diversify; this enables you to have a contingency plan when the economy is going through a rough patch."[11]

Firms often combine brand names, like Toyota Corolla or the American Express Personal Card. The firm earns value from the monolithic brand, Toyota and American Express, and additional value from individual product brands. Large retailers also develop brands: Sam's Choice (Walmart) and Michael Graves (Target); even cell-phone service providers like Vodafone offer private-label phones.[12] Other features of brands include:

- Anything can be branded — a product; service; town, city, or country[13]; even yourself![14] Early PC buyers were indifferent to microprocessors; the *intel inside* campaign changed that. Water is the world's most common substance. Compare the prices of Evian, Perrier, and Poland Spring with Budweiser, Coca-Cola, and milk; they demonstrate brand power.

- Brands can provide psychological value: safety and security — ADT, Volvo; caring/nurturing — J&J, Gerber; self-indulgence/reward — Dove, Häagen Dazs; and a winning attitude — Wheaties, Nike.

- Brands may become generic — synonymous with the product class. U.S. examples include Aspirin, Band-Aid, eBay, Google, Kleenex, Lego, Rollerblade, Vaseline, and Xerox. In Britain — Biro and Hoover; in Austria — Walkman.[15]

- Customers' judgments and expectations about brands drive purchase decisions.

- Customers often form communities to demonstrate commitment to brands: Harley-Davidson riders and Macintosh users.[16]

The firm must choose a **brand identity** for each of its brands — associations like personal, lifestyle, or type of customer it *wants* people to hold. When the firm offers multiple brands, it must also decide how the various brand identities should relate to each other. By contrast, **brand image** is the actual associations customers hold about the brand. Much firm branding effort — **brand positioning** — focuses on bringing **brand image** and **brand identity** into alignment. Hence, the firm should audit brand image on a regular basis. (The Glossary has a selection of branding terms.)

BRAND ASSOCIATIONS

The firm should strive for **brand associations** that reinforce the desired brand identity and align these associations with brand image.[18] Brand associations are thoughts the customer generates

---

Marketing Exercise

Find a working friend or relative, and give the Brand Coffee Machine Test. Stand at the coffee machine and ask, "What does your product or company brand stand for?" Then press the *fill* button or lever. If the person cannot give a good answer by the time your cup fills, the brand fails. The organization cannot expect customers to understand the brand's meaning if employees do not.[17]

KEY IDEA

➤ *Brand identity* comprises associations the firm *wants* people to hold.

➤ *Brand image* comprises associations people *actually* hold.

when faced with a stimulus like brand name, logo, message, or spokesperson.[19] **Brand personality** captures the idea of enduring and distinct human or emotional characteristics associated with a brand — Table 11.1.

TABLE 11.1

BRAND PERSONALITY[20]

Dimensions	Descriptors	Examples
Competence	Intelligent — technical, corporate, serious Reliable — hardworking, secure, efficient, trustworthy, careful, credible Successful — leader, confident, influential	*The Wall Street Journal*
Excitement	Daring — trendy, exciting, off-beat, flashy, provocative Imaginative — unique, humorous, surprising, artistic, fun Spirited — cool, young, lively, outgoing, adventurous Up-to-date — independent, contemporary, innovative, aggressive	MTV, Mountain Dew
Ruggedness	Outdoors — masculine, Western, active, athletic Tough — rugged, strong, no-nonsense	L.L. Bean
Sincerity	Cheerful — sentimental, friendly, warm, happy Down-to-earth — family-oriented, small-town, conventional, blue-collar, all-American Honest — sincere, real, ethical, thoughtful, caring Wholesome — original, genuine, ageless, classic, old-fashioned	Hallmark cards, Skippy peanut butter
Sophistication	Charming — feminine, smooth, sexy, gentle Upper class — glamorous, good-looking, pretentious, sophisticated	Chanel, Dior

Effective brand associations are:

- **Strong.** Personally relevant for customers and presented consistently over time.
- **Favorable.** Desired by customers and successfully delivered by the brand.
- **Unique.** Perceived by customers as unique, different from other brands.

Generally, the firm uses implementation tools like communications, distribution outlet, and product design and quality to achieve alignment between brand identity and brand image. Sometimes brand associations (positive and negative) are outside the firm's control. Many people associate Levi's (jeans) and Marlboro (cigarettes) with U.S. cowboy movies. These associations are generally positive but widespread opposition to U.S. policies (Iraq war) has affected some brands negatively. To address such negative associations, McDonald's focuses on local ownership, local suppliers, distinct store designs, and unique menu items — like the *McArabia*, a chicken sandwich on Arabian-style bread.[21]

BRANDING IS NOT JUST FOR CONSUMERS ...

Many people assume that branding is just for B2C marketing. Not so! Branding is also very important in B2B markets, especially for firms with many customers like SAP — Opening Case. Specific industries include banking, capital goods, computing, consulting, office equipment, and shipping; individual firms for which branding is critical are Brother, Canon, Caterpillar, DuPont, FedEx, GE, IBM, Intel, Microsoft, Office Depot, Oracle, Sun, TNT, and Xerox — Figure 11.2.

FIGURE 11.2

BRANDING IS NOT JUST FOR CONSUMERS!

B2C and B2B branding use different languages: B2C firms focus on brand image or associations; B2B firms talk about building relationships, and customer confidence and trust. B2B firms want customers to view them as experienced, risk-free, and trustworthy suppliers, prefer-ably with a solid track record and stellar market reputation. B2B branding is increasingly important as buying decisions in many industries shift from technologists to employees with less technical expertise. Oftentimes, branding is more important than technology — a well-managed brand outlasts many technology changes.

... AND IS NOT JUST ABOUT ADVERTISING

Another common misunderstanding is that branding should focus only on consumers or end-user customers and that advertising is the only approach. Not so![22] Reaching a broad audience for its communications is as important for corporate brands as for many product brands. Communications targets surpass current and potential customers and include:

- Alliance partners
- Intermediaries
- Other government bodies
- Regulators
- Bondholders
- Investment analysts
- Owners/shareholders
- Suppliers
- Employees
- Media
- Prospective employees

In addition to advertising, the firm can build and reinforce brand identity via other com-munication forms like brochures, direct mail, managerial actions and speeches, products and packaging, promotions, publicity and public relations, stationery, physical facilities, telephone interactions, and websites. The CEO can have a major impact on a firm's brand by becoming the *face* of the company; good examples are Richard Branson — Virgin; Steve Jobs — Apple; Mark Cuban — Dallas Mavericks; and Warren Buffett — Berkshire Hathaway.

Firm employees are an important branding audience. Eli Lilly (pharmaceuticals), Verizon (telecommunications), and many others conduct extensive branding programs to ensure that employees internalize the firm's brand identity. Regularly and periodically, these firms measure how employees perceive company brands and then act on the findings. Internal branding is especially important for business services and consulting firms, and B2C firms like retailers, where employees regularly interface with customers. Corrado Passera, CEO of struggling Italian Banca Intesa, even wrote a small book for the 60,000 employees detailing the bank's position, goals, and planned actions.[24] The firm should also conduct branding audits of constituencies like suppliers and affiliates and take appropriate steps to enhance brand commitment.

THE BASIS FOR BRANDING

Historically, the brander and the producer were synonymous. Today, there is no necessary rela-tionship between the brand owner and the producer of the branded product. Most readers know that retailers do not manufacture their private-label products. But as Figure 11.4 shows,

---

KEY IDEA

➤ Brand personality com-prises five important dimensions:

- Competence
- Excitement
- Ruggedness
- Sincerity
- Sophistication

FIGURE 11.3

THE CEO AS BRAND[23]

Marketing Question

Figure 11.3 contains pictures of some well-known current and former CEOs. How many do you recognize? Can you name their firms? How does your view of the CEO affect your associations of the firm and its product brands? For answers, Endnote 23, p. E19.

KEY IDEA

➤ The brand/production relationship may take several different forms.

many traditional manufacturers may not make their branded products either. The brand/production relationship may take many forms:

- **Totally integrated production operations.** Ford's old Rouge River plant is the prototypical example. Ford received iron ore and coal at one end; Model Ts rolled off at the other end. Integrated aluminum and oil producers are also in this category.
- **Subcomponent assembly.** The brand owner assembles components produced by other firms. Examples include contemporary automobile manufacturing and Dell's model for building PCs.
- **No production responsibility.** The brand owner may design the product, set quality control standards, and distribute and market products. The firm does not manufacture but does own the customer experience. Examples include Apple — consumer electronics; Nike — sports shoes; Nintendo — game cartridges; Perdue — chicken; Ralph Lauren and Tommy Hilfiger — designer products; and Xerox — copiers.

FIGURE 11.4

ALTERNATIVE PRODUCTION AND BRANDING RELATIONSHIPS

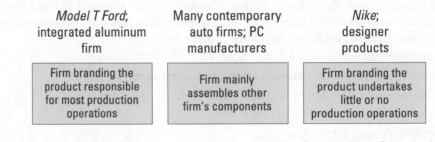

In industries like electronic consumer goods, contract manufacturing is a fast-growing trend. Many brand owners focus resources on customer service, design, marketing, and R&D; they view manufacturing almost as a service function. If the brand does not identify the producing organization, we must ask: What value does a brand deliver?

BRAND EQUITY AND THE VALUE OF BRANDS

By effectively developing and implementing market strategy, the firm creates brand value. The firm may also use brand value to develop and implement market strategy. Excellent branding operates as a virtuous circle, continually employing and enhancing the firm's equity in its brands.

Brand equity captures the idea that brands deliver value, over and above actual products/services. The most widely accepted definition of brand equity is "a set of brand assets and liabilities linked to a brand, its name, and symbol that add to (or subtract from) the value provided by a product or service to a firm and/or that firm's customers."[25] From this definition we see that brand value accrues to both the *firm* and its *customers*. It follows that there are two types of brand equity: **customer brand equity (CBE)** — the value customers receive, and **firm brand equity (FBE)** — the value firms receive.

CUSTOMER BRAND EQUITY

The brand gives customers two types of value: **pre-purchase equity** and **post-purchase equity**.

PRE-PURCHASE EQUITY is the value customers receive from information contained in the brand name and other signifiers via reduced search costs and purchase risks.[26] In overnight package delivery, many business customers believe FedEx offers great *functional* value — packages arrive on time. Many airline passengers believe jetBlue and Southwest Airlines (U.S.), and easyJet and Ryanair (Europe) offer superior *economic* value. Others believe the American Express Platinum card, Air Jordan and Shox sneakers, and fashion items from Armani, Dior,

Marketing Question

You, the reader, are a brand! What is your *brand identity*? What *brand image* and *brand associations* do people hold about you? Do these associations conform to your desired brand identity? Are the image and associations consistent, or do they differ across people — friends, parents, professors, and prospective employers? Are you satisfied with these associations? If so, how will you sustain and enhance them? If not, how will you change them? How do your postings on Facebook support your brand identity?

and Versace provide *psychological* values like status and prestige. The classic pre-purchase CBE example is: "You never get fired for buying IBM."

POST-PURCHASE EQUITY is the value customers receive when the brand enhances the consumption experience. After purchase, brands provide *functional* value — doing the job they were designed to do, and *economic* value — like low cost of ownership. They also provide *psychological* value — like feelings of security from insurance and the assurance of continued *functional* value. Post-purchase psychological value (like status and prestige) can have long-lasting effects, especially if ownership and use are transparent and communicated to others. On a blind taste test, Pepsi (51 percent) scored better than Coke (44 percent); but in an open test, Coke (65 percent) exceeded Pepsi (23 percent), attesting to Coca Cola's brand value.[27]

> **KEY IDEA**
> ➤ Customers may secure significant value from a brand — *before* and *after* purchase.

Sometimes high CBE focuses on a specific product class. Tide *detergent* typically engenders positive customer values, but consumers would probably view Tide *toothpaste* or Tide *cookies* negatively. Other brands provide customer value across several product classes; examples include corporate brands like *Virgin*, and movie brands like *Star Wars* and *Indiana Jones* that earn significant revenues from a wide variety of accessory products in addition to the movies.[28] CBE, either pre- or post-purchase, is generally greater when:

- Comparing alternative products is difficult.
- Customers do not realize value until some time after purchase.
- Customers are inexperienced or unfamiliar with the product class.
- Product quality from some suppliers is variable.
- The product is socially visible.
- There is mental flexibility in portraying the brand.

Table 11.2 shows that a brand can deliver significant CBE for many years.

Product	Leading Brand 1925	Position 2011	Product	Leading Brand 1925	Position 2011
Batteries	Eveready	Leader	Razors	Gillette	Leader
Breakfast cereal	Kellogg	Leader	Shortening	Crisco	Leader
Canned fruit	Del Monte	Leader	Soap	Ivory	Leader
Chewing gum	Wrigley	Leader	Soft drink	Coca-Cola	Leader
Chocolates	Hershey	Leader	Soup	Campbell's	Leader
Cookies	Nabisco	Leader	Tea	Lipton	Leader
Flour	Gold Medal	Leader	Tires	Goodyear	Leader
Paint	Sherwin-Williams	Leader	Toothpaste	Colgate	Leader

TABLE 11.2

LEADING U.S. BRANDS, 1925 AND 2011[29]

FIRM BRAND EQUITY

FBE results from customer responses to firm actions and links directly to CBE. High brand awareness, positive attitudes, high perceived quality, positive word-of-mouth, intention to purchase, purchase, brand loyalty, positive brand image and associations, and satisfaction all enhance FBE.[30] CBE and FBE reflect the trust between the brand and its customers. A former Sony chairman opined: "Our biggest asset is four letters, S-o-n-y. It's not so much our buildings or our engineers or our factories, but our name."[31] Former American Express, RJR Nabisco, and IBM CEO Lou Gerstner had a similar philosophy:

> **KEY IDEA**
> ➤ Brand equity reflects the trust established between the brand owner and its customers.

> Shelly Lazarus, CEO of Ogilvy & Mather Worldwide, said: "I learned a big lesson from Lou. Once you've set a strategy, you never ever violate it. Nobody ever got a free card, a discounted card, or bundled pricing. Lou would say, 'This is a violation of the brand, and we're not doing it.'"[32]

High FBE has many positives. Firms with high FBE:

- Can set higher prices and earn better margins.
- More easily introduce similarly branded items in different product classes and markets.
- Use cross-selling to encourage existing customers to purchase in different product classes.

KEY IDEA

➤ Brand equity generally builds up slowly over time.

- Generate leverage in distribution channels by securing more and better shelf space and more favorable transaction terms. Foot Locker reduced orders from Nike to protest its price and selection terms; Nike significantly cut Foot Locker's allocation. Consumers shopped elsewhere for Nike products and eventually Foot Locker accepted Nike's terms.
- Raise entry barriers for competitors.
- Exploit licensing opportunities.

> Disney acquired Marvel Entertainment, owner of superheroes like Spiderman, the Incredible Hulk, and X-Men. Disney uses Marvel characters for creative activities, but also earns substantial revenues from product licensing.

KEY IDEA

➤ A brand can quickly lose value if not managed properly.

Generally, CBE and FBE build slowly, but new brands sometimes gain strength relatively quickly — eBay, Google, Leapfrog, Red Bull, Ryanair, and Yahoo! Nonetheless, CBE, and hence FBE, are fragile and can dissipate quickly if the firm mis-steps. Many firms unwittingly cause brand equity declines by product proliferation, price-cutting, offering discounts and promotions, using inferior components, squeezing suppliers or channel partners, and simple neglect.[33] Tommy Hilfiger's sales went from red hot to stalled when product proliferation and out-of-control distribution (more than 10,000 department stores and discount outlets) diluted brand value. Quaker Oats experience with Snapple is a salutary lesson:

> Quaker Oats purchased Snapple (fruit and tea soft drinks) from Triarc for $1.7 billion; much of the acquisition price reflected Snapple's brand value. Barely two years later, Triarc repurchased Snapple for $300 million. During the two years, Quaker had $160 million in operating losses — overall, Snapple cost Quaker $2 million per day of ownership. Quaker made several strategic errors: Quaker mistakenly believed it could distribute Snapple in supermarkets and mass markets, even though more than half of Snapple's sales were impulse purchases in convenience stores, gasoline stations, and similar outlets. Quaker also stopped Snapple's quirky, yet memorable, advertising featuring Wendy Kaufman (Snapple employee), and spokespersons Howard Stern and Rush Limbaugh. Snapple lost significant brand equity.[34]

Managerial mishaps can also wreak havoc with FBE. Examples include product recalls by Dow Corning (breast implants), Merck (*Vioxx*), and Perrier (water); product failures by Firestone (*Ford Explorer* tires) and Toyota (unplanned acceleration); and impure products from Schlitz (beer):

> In the early 1970s, Schlitz was a strong second to Anheuser-Busch (AB) in the U.S. beer market. From 1974 to 1976, Schlitz took several actions to reduce costs: Schlitz substituted cheaper corn syrup for barley malt, and introduced *accelerated batch fermentation* that shortened the fermentation process from 12 to four days. These changes caused a slightly lighter taste and spawned a rumor that Schlitz beer was green. AB publicly committed to more expensive ingredients. Schlitz aggressively used discounts and promotions, actions that were inconsistent with its longtime premium positioning. In 1976, Schlitz changed a stabilizer to avoid adding an ingredient required by a new labeling law. The production process was supposed to filter out the new stabilizer, but reaction with other ingredients formed tiny flakes in the beer. One fix removed the stabilizer but the beer went flat; Schlitz *secretly* recalled and destroyed 10 million bottles and cans. In 1974, Schlitz sold 17.8 million barrels; in 1986, it sold less than one million, a stunning destruction of brand equity.[35]

Notwithstanding brand equity's fragility, some brands have greater resilience than others. In 1982, J&J withdrew Tylenol capsules in the face of a cyanide-poisoning scare (six people died; unsolved); sales plummeted to zero. J&J's timely and caring response led to a quick Tylenol rebound when it introduced more secure packaging and ramped up distribution and promotion. By contrast, *Perrier* never really recovered from a recall caused by product impurities. Disgruntled employees, unhappy customers, and aggressive competitors, aided by blogs, Facebook, Twitter, YouTube and third-party websites, can also sabotage the firm's brand(s); planning for damage control and crisis management is increasingly important.[36]

MONETIZING BRAND EQUITY

We just explored the value the brand brings to customers — customer brand equity (CBE), and to the firm — firm brand equity (FBE). Now we focus on the monetary value of brands.

CUSTOMER BRAND EQUITY

Customers receive value from a *generic* product; typically, they receive greater value from a *branded* product. The difference in value — brand less generic — equals CBE. The **dollarmetric** method assesses the monetary value of CBE. The firm asks a customer how much extra she would pay for the branded product versus an unbranded product; this amount is CBE's monetary value. Actually, this figure is *potential* CBE — the customer only receives brand equity after purchase. If the price is higher than she is willing to pay, there is no CBE. The firm can also assess the *marginal* CBE of one brand versus another: How much extra will the customer pay for her favored brand? Conjoint analysis — Chapter 6 Marketing Enrichment `me601, pp. 3–7` — is a valuable methodology for *indirectly* assessing CBE's monetary value.[37]

FIRM BRAND EQUITY

FBE relates directly to the brand's current and future ability to attract paying customers and increase shareholder value.[38] We assess FBE's monetary value at the firm level.[39] Valuation components are:

- **Revenue.** The price difference between the branded product and an identical generic product, multiplied by the branded product's forecast excess sales volume.
- **Cost.** The costs of supporting the brand.

BASIC APPROACH. FBE's monetary value is the sum of the year-by-year differences between revenues and costs, discounted to the present.[40] Unfortunately, this straightforward approach has two inherent problems:

- An unbranded equivalent to the branded product may not exist.
- The approach ignores potential for brand broadening (leveraging) — using the brand to enter a new product form/product class. Brand value is unconstrained by current products, product lines, or customers. Many brands have customer-attracting properties over and above the product (set of products) to which they are currently attached. The brand *Pan Am*, unattached to an aircraft or airline, sold for several million dollars.

MARKET VALUE METHOD. The market provides the best FBE measure; this approach works well for publicly traded corporate brands. FBE equals market value less book value (plus non-brand intangibles like human resources, know-how, and patents). When Ford purchased Jaguar for $2.5 billion, its book value was $0.4 billion. Observers viewed the $2.1 billion difference (2.5 less 0.4) as Jaguar's brand equity.[41,42] When market value does not exist, as for most product brands, the firm must use internal methods.

INTERNAL METHODS. Two internal methods for assessing FBE are:

- **Replacement cost.** The firm multiplies the anticipated brand-replacement cost by the probability of success.[43]

KEY IDEA

➤ Internal approaches for calculating firm brand equity are:
- Replacement cost
- Cash flow methods

**MARKETING
ENRICHMENT**

Interbrand Method for
Calculating Brand Equity
me1101

- **Cash flow.** These approaches are intuitively more appealing, but estimating future cash flows is difficult. Interbrand (brand consultant) uses a proprietary method to estimate firm brand equity based on future cash flows me1101 .[44]

Calculating the *marginal* FBE of one brand versus another is probably easier than calculating an absolute value. New United Motor Manufacturing Inc. (NUMMI) (GM/Toyota joint venture) manufactured two virtually identical cars — Geo Prizm (GM) and Corolla (Toyota). Corolla had a premium price and depreciated more slowly. After five years, Corolla's second-hand value was 18 percent more than Prizm. Figure 11.5 shows Corolla's annual sales were 200,000 @ $11,100; Prizm's annual sales were 80,000 @ $10,700. Clearly, Toyota has greater FBE; operating profit exceeded GM by $128 million, and Toyota dealers earned $107 million more than GM dealers.[45,46]

FIGURE 11.5

THE MONETARY
VALUE OF FIRM
BRAND EQUITY —
AUTOMOBILE EXAMPLE

me1101

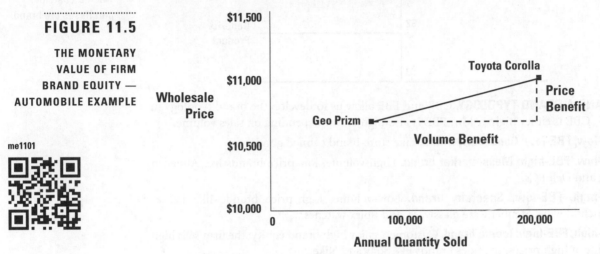

RELATIONSHIP BETWEEN CUSTOMER BRAND EQUITY AND FIRM BRAND EQUITY

We just showed how to assess individual-customer CBE, and firm-level FBE. We now develop a brand typology based on the relationship between CBE and FBE.

CBE AND FBE. For two hypothetical brands, **A** and **B**, Figure 11.6 shows the firm's price and an individual customer's willingness to pay:

- **Brand A.** The customer is willing to pay $8, versus $2 for the generic product. Since brand A's price is $7, she would purchase and gain $6 CBE (8–2=6). (Actually, the customer has a good deal; she receives $6 CBE for $5 additional price over the generic value [7–2=5].) The firm earns revenues and a positive FBE profit contribution.

- **Brand B.** The customer is willing to pay $5, versus the generic product's $2 price. Hence, CBE appears to be $3 (5–2 = 3). But brand B's price is $6, so the customer won't purchase. CBE is zero. The firm earns zero revenues, and zero FBE profit contribution.

Although potential CBE and FBE are positive for both brands, actual CBE and FBE only occurs if customer willingness to pay exceeds the price (and price exceeds cost for FBE).

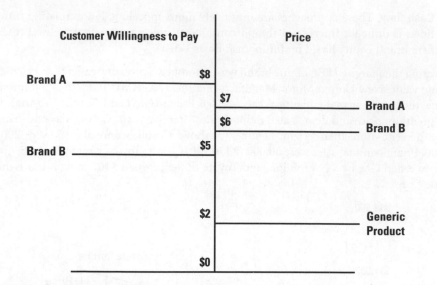

FIGURE 11.6

**MONETARY VALUE
OF BRAND EQUITY**

KEY IDEA

➤ The firm earns a contribution to FBE only when a customer purchases the brand.

CBE, FBE AND A BRAND TYPOLOGY. CBE and FBE allow us to develop the brand typology in Figure 11.7. CBE is either high or low; FBE is also high or low depending on sales volume.

- **CBE-low, FBE-low: Commodity brand.** Like store-brand canned goods.
- **CBE-low, FBE-high: Mass-market brand.** High-volume, low-price brands like Almaden wine and Dell PCs.
- **CBE-high, FBE-low: Specialty brand.** Low-volume, high-price brands like Lafite-Rothschild wine, Steubenware glassware, and Rolex watches.
- **CBE-high, FBE-high: Iconic brand.** Customers enjoy high brand equity; the firm sells high volume at high prices. Includes brands like Sony and Nike.

Monetary Value of Firm Brand Equity

		Low	High
Monetary Value of Customer Brand Equity	**High**	Specialty	Iconic
	Low	Commodity	Mass Market

FIGURE 11.7

A BRAND TYPOLOGY[47]

BUILDING AND SUSTAINING A STRONG BRAND

An important goal of developing and implementing market strategy is to build and sustain a strong brand. Strong brands induce positive responses from customers. In turn, these positive responses enhance brand strength and are a powerful influence on the firm's market strategy.

BUILDING A STRONG BRAND

Strong brands have value for both the firm and its customers. The firm builds a strong brand by making good decisions during the branding process — Figure 11.8.

Marketing Question

Barcelona and Manchester United are the world's leading soccer clubs. How would you suggest they monetize their brand equities? (Or substitute your favorite sports team.)

FIGURE 11.8

BUILDING A STRONG BRAND[48]

Brand Identity

↓

Brand Awareness

↓

Brand Associations and Brand Image

↓

Brand Quality and Value Perceptions

↓

Brand Loyalty

↓

Brand Broadening

BRAND IDENTITY. Brand identity is what the firm wants the brand to mean. Said Eli Lilly CEO Sidney Taurel, "Our brand is our identity. It is who we are in the eyes of our customers ... shareholders, prospective employees, suppliers, and the communities where we operate."[49] Vodafone has a clear vision, a related brand promise, and core values:

"Vodafone's vision is to be the leader of mobile communications in the world, and our brand promise is to go around the world. We back that with five core values — dependability, *can do* (we can solve your problem), practical innovation (we deliver on our promises), empathy, and *joie de vivre*."[50]

Brand identity is the blueprint for many marketing decisions; indeed, brand identity defines the limits on product quality, service, promotion, distribution, and price. Executing on brand identity is critical to customers forming the desired associations and brand image (below).

BRAND AWARENESS. Starting with brand identity, the firm must decide how customers should recognize the brand, including brand name and visual appearance. Choosing a brand name may involve extensive research with considerations of associations, legal availability, length, memorability, and pronounceability. The firm should be especially careful if it plans to use the brand in different countries and cultures with different language systems. Visual appearance requires careful choice of colors, materials, shapes, styles, and themes, and related visuals for advertising and packaging.

Typically, the firm must invest significantly to achieve **brand awareness** at target customers. When the brand is first entrant in a new product form, the pioneer must educate potential customers about the product form, as well as about the brand. Gojo educated consumers, medical professionals, and retailers about its new type of hand-washing liquid — Purell. Launching a new corporate brand is also very costly. Lucent spent $50 million to create corporate brand awareness.[51] But a brand may stay in memory for many years — Datsun, Esso, Master Charge, even after retirement by the brand owner.[52]

BRAND ASSOCIATIONS AND BRAND IMAGE. Brand associations are the meanings the brand has for individual customers — *brand image* is the overall sum of brand associations. Each and every marketing implementation decision the firm takes has a role in developing customers' brand associations and hence brand image — product design, service, communications, distribution outlet, and price. Consistency is critical: Walmart developed guidelines and processes to ensure uniformity among circulars, in-store signage, and TV advertising. Other elements requiring consistency include packaging, stationery, uniforms, vehicles, and websites; and symbols like pictures and graphic illustrations, slogans and jingles, and taglines. A critical firm task is to secure congruence between brand image and brand identity. Multi-level marketer Amway has this problem: Said CEO Dornan, "[People] have dated and incorrect perceptions about the company."[53] Brand equity always suffers when brand identity and brand image are mismatched. Suppose the basis

Marketing Exercise

1. Write down 10 or more associations for each of the brands noted below.
2. For each brand, use the associations to write a one-sentence statement of brand image.
3. Compare your associations and brand image with a fellow student.
4. Write a one-sentence statement of what you believe to be the brand identity.
5. If brand identity and brand image are different, what actions would you take to bring them into alignment?

List of brands: Apple, *Celebrity Apprentice* (TV show), Goldman Sachs, Microsoft, Toyota.

for a product's brand identity is high prestige — yet customers form brand image from inferior product and service quality, poor advertising execution, downscale distribution, and low price. Customer response would most likely be negative, and FBE would suffer:

> For many years under Ford ownership, Jaguar (since acquired by Tata Motors) did not deliver on its luxury identity nor make a profit. Jaguar's entry-level X-type compact car had stale styling, one-size-fits-all marketing, and several thousand dollars in rebates — for a luxury car! Further, Jaguar's slogan, "Born To Perform," was mismatched with U.S. owners — they purchased mostly for style.

BRAND QUALITY AND VALUE PERCEPTIONS. Consistency in communications and customer brand experiences are crucial for developing positive brand quality and value perceptions.

A specific problem for value perceptions is cutting prices and/or offering short-term price promotions. Sales may spike in the short run but cause long-term brand damage as customers hold off buying until the next promotion. Vlasic discounted pickle prices so far that despite volume increases, margin declines eventually forced it into bankruptcy. Clorox faced a similar problem, but reduced discounting and increased television advertising led to higher long-run revenues and profits.[54]

Many global 100 firms have *brand police* or a *brand czar* to oversee branding consistency. These executives make sure the brand name, logos and symbols, and all messaging — including advertising, brochures, and websites — retain consistency. Brand czars provide specific guidance on colors, font size, graphics, signs, stationery, uniforms, vehicles, and words; they also ensure conformity to consistent standards. We saw this consistency in the SAP Opening Case.

Achieving consistency is always difficult, but organizational practices can make it impossible. To explain: Many firms frequently rotate brand managers. New brand managers wanting to make their mark on a product (product line) reformulate brand identity. Each reformulation sacrifices consistency, brand quality, and customer value perceptions. This problem may diminish as branding grows in importance and, as responsibility moves up the managerial hierarchy, the traditional brand manager's role diminishes. The firm should also be wary of advertising agencies, communications specialists, consultants, and design and identity firms. By striving for creativity, these organizations may sacrifice brand identity and consistency, and confuse customers. It's no accident that market leader L'Oreal has maintained the same tagline — "Because you're worth it" — for over a quarter-century.

BRAND LOYALTY. Consistency in brand quality and value perceptions lead to **brand loyalty**, which inspires positive word of mouth, referrals, and repeat purchase.[55] Vertical marketers (own retail outlets) like Starbucks (coffee) and Ben & Jerry's (ice cream) know the importance of consistency. They build brand coherence through personnel and the design and decor of retail facilities. By contrast, most car firms have difficulty providing brand-enhancing experiences in independently owned dealerships. A serious problem for hotel management firms like Hilton, Holiday Inn, and Sheraton is *off-message* execution by individual franchised hotels; inconsistency in the customer experience affects loyalty to the entire chain.

The firm earns high brand loyalty by:

- Selecting the *right* brand identity for target customers and consistently executing on that identity.
- Ensuring that firm employees and third-party organizations (like advertising agencies) are motivated to deliver on the brand identity.
- Continuously measuring customer satisfaction with the brand and making the necessary course corrections. (Following section: Sustaining a Strong Brand.)[56]

BRAND BROADENING. The firm may broaden (leverage) a strong brand to other product forms (and classes). (Following section: Managing Brand Architecture.)

KEY IDEA

➤ A well-structured process for building a strong brand embraces:

- Brand identity
- Brand awareness
- Brand associations and brand image
- Brand quality and value perceptions
- Brand loyalty
- Brand broadening

KEY IDEA

➤ Carefully chosen brand identity and consistent execution are critical to developing brand loyalty.

Marketing Question

Major retailers like 7-Eleven, Costco, Supervalu (Albertsons, Jewell-Osco) and Walgreens have introduced private-label beer. Do you think they will be successful? Why or why not?

KEY IDEA

➤ Firm brand equity represents the brand balance sheet.

➤ Brand health checks compare the brand against historic trends and benchmark competing brands.

SUSTAINING A STRONG BRAND

The key to sustaining a strong brand for the long run is continual assessment of *brand health*. Many firms measure brand managers on short-term revenues, profits, and/or market share; these metrics often lead to cutting prices for short-term results. Focusing exclusively on such measures is rather like examining the firm's income statement but neglecting its balance sheet. FBE is really the brand balance sheet. **Brand health checks** use metrics indicating FBE changes.

Typical brand health checks use a *balanced-scorecard* approach — Chapter 22. Four popular types of measures — Table 11.3 — and sources are:

- **Purchasing and sales** — firm accounting and CRM systems and industry-focused research suppliers.
- **Perceptual** — survey research.
- **Marketing support** — firm accounting and business intelligence systems and industry-focused suppliers.
- **Profitability** — firm accounting system.

Brand-health checks are not one-time events. Brand-health checks should occur regularly — quarterly or bi-annually. The firm should compare current brand health to historic trends and benchmark competing brands.[57] Results from brand health checks should lead to appropriate changes in market strategy and execution.

TABLE 11.3

REPRESENTATIVE SELECTION OF BRAND HEALTH CHECK MEASURES

me01

Type of Measure	Measure	Description of Measure
Purchasing and sales	Market breadth	Number and type of customers purchasing the brand
	Market depth	Extent of repeat purchase
	Market share	Brand sales as a percentage of total market sales (units and/or dollars)
Perceptual	Awareness	Degree of brand awareness
	Brand image	Brand associations, congruence with brand identity
	Quality	Perception of brand quality (from blind tests)
	Uniqueness	Extent of differentiation from competition
	Value	Extent to which the brand provides good value for money
Marketing support	Advertising	Market share/advertising share
		Advertising/total marketing spend
	Distribution	Extent of distribution coverage in target outlets
		For retail goods, quality of display, especially key accounts
	Relative price	Price compared to competitive brands
Profitability	Profit	Gross margin earned from the brand
		Economic value added (EVA) of the brand (Marketing Enrichment me01, pp. 16–17)

KEY IDEA

➤ The firm should carefully manage evolution of the brand portfolio.

➤ Firms adjust brand portfolios in response to shifting customer trends, competitor action, and mergers and acquisitions.

MANAGING BRAND ARCHITECTURE

Many firms maintain multiple brands — a brand portfolio — each with its own brand identity. The LVMH (global luxury goods leader) corporate brand offers *Louis Vuitton* tan and brown monogrammed bags for several hundred dollars, *Murakami* bags at $1,000, and *Suhali* goatskin bags averaging $2,000. The firm's **brand architecture** — its organizing structure for multiple brands — is an important decision area.

Because firm brands have a major impact on shareholder value, branding decisions should have high priority. The firm should carefully consider what to brand, brand identities, and desired brand associations. The firm should also carefully plan brand additions (internally developed and secured by acquisition) and deletions.[58] The firm must also consider interrelationships among the corporate brand, product class brands, and individual product brands.

The firms' brand portfolio should evolve as markets evolve. Anheuser-Busch changed its portfolio as customers switched to different beers, from low-end to higher-end, and from fuller to lighter. The firm should avoid drastic action like P&G's phasing out of 1,000 brands in five years, and Unilever's Path-to-Growth program that dramatically cut its 1,600-brand portfolio.[59] We now discuss several brand architecture decisions, but defer global branding to Chapter 23.

MULTI-BRANDING VERSUS UMBRELLA BRANDING

In **multi-branding** — aka *House of Brands* strategy — the firm uses multiple brands for its various products.[60] The firm seeks target-customer loyalty to individual brands, but not necessarily to the parent-company brand. Do you know the corporate owner of Aguila, Coors, Cristal, Foster's, Hamm's, Henry Weinhard, Icehouse, Keystone, Leinenkugel, Miller, Milwaukee's Best, Mickey's, Molson, Olde English 800, and Tyskie?* More consumers know of Procter & Gamble than SABMiller, but many would not associate P&G with all the following brands — Always, Ariel, Bounty, Braun, Charmin, Crest, Dawn, Downy/Lenor, Duracell, Fusion, Gain, Gillette, Head & Shoulders, Iams, Mach3, Olay, Oral-B, Pampers, Pantene, Tide, and Wella.**

By contrast, a firm using **umbrella branding** emphasizes a monolithic brand for several products (or product lines). Consumers know Yamaha for electronic musical instruments (keyboards and guitars), traditional musical instruments (pianos), home audio products, computer peripherals, motorcycles, and even Grand Prix engines. The *One Ford* strategy led Ford to drop Aston Martin, Jaguar, Land Rover, and Volvo. A single firm may have several monolithic (master) brands: Toyota offers Toyota, Lexus, and Scion; Chrysler provides Chrysler, Dodge, and Jeep. Each master brand may offer finer-level sub-brands, like Caravan, Dakota, Dodge Neon, Durango, Magnum, SRT-4, Stratus, and Viper. Table 11.4 shows factors favoring multi-branding and umbrella branding.

In Favor of Umbrella Branding	In Favor of Multi-Branding
Company culture. Enhances the firm's ability to deliver a consistent message.	*Transfer of negative associations from an umbrella brand.* Customers may transfer negative associations across products. In the 1980s, several women contracted toxic shock syndrome, and some died, after using P&G's ultra high-absorbent tampon, *Rely.* P&G withdrew *Rely* and suffered a financial impact; but far less than had the product been *P&G* tampons. In 2010, Lexus largely avoided the negative impact from Toyota's quality problems.
Intra-firm competition. Reduces the likelihood of intra-firm competition.	*Intra-firm competition.* Some firms favor enhanced intra-firm competition, particularly those in FMCG and pharmaceuticals.
Scale economies. By promoting a single brand, the firm secures economies in advertising, labeling, logos, and other communications efforts.	*Targeting and positioning.* The firm can better target and position products in multiple market segments. Stanley Black & Decker offers power tools under the company name for do-it-yourselfers, DeWalt for construction, and Porter-Cable for woodworking.
Transfer of positive customer experiences across products. A positive customer experience with one product benefits similarly branded products in a different product form (class). Apple's success with the iPod and iPhone helped MacIntosh; Yamaha pianos help sales of electric guitars, and vice versa.[61]	*Inability to transfer positive customer experiences across products in umbrella branding.* Customers may not transfer positive brand associations across product forms (classes). A Yamaha piano experience may transfer to electric guitars, but to motorcycles? An umbrella brand can even cause problems within the same product class. Gallo's association with inexpensive wines led it to a multi-brand approach for higher price points.

* South Africa's SABMiller
** P&G's billion dollar brands

Marketing Question

How do you assess the branding strategy for your college, school, or university? Does your institution pursue a multi-branding strategy or an umbrella branding strategy? How could your college, school, or university improve its branding?

TABLE 11.4

FACTORS FAVORING MULTI-BRANDING AND UMBRELLA BRANDING

KEY IDEA

➤ Both *multi-branding* and *umbrella branding* enjoy pros and cons.

Marketing Question

In the mid-2000s, Starbucks acquired Seattle's Best Coffee (SBC). As SBC's incoming brand manager, how would you position SBC? Would you relate SBC to the Starbucks brand? Why or why not? What marketing decisions would you make to support the new positioning?

BRAND BROADENING (LEVERAGING)

Brand broadening (leveraging) occurs when the firm undertakes a brand extension — attaching an existing brand to a different product (form [class]) to address a new opportunity. Table 11.5 shows several approaches to brand extensions or leveraging.[62]

TABLE 11.5

APPROACHES TO BRAND LEVERAGING

Brand Extension	Examples
A. Common benefit or attribute	Deodorizing: Lysol for the air, toilet bowl, tile Mildness: Ivory in soap and shampoo
B. Companion product	Cameras: Kodak batteries for cameras Pancake mix: Aunt Jemima pancake syrup
C. Customer franchise	Harley-Davidson: restaurants, armchairs Coca-Cola: clothing, fishing lures
D. Designer/ethnic image	Ralph Lauren: clothing, sunglasses Ferrari: automobile, watches
E. Distinctive component/ingredient	Baking soda: Arm & Hammer cat litter Cream cheese: Philadelphia cream cheese salad dressing
F. Expertise	Electronics: Sony Walkman and Discman Low-cost manufacturing: Bic disposable razors and pens
G. Same raw material, different product form	Cranberries: Ocean Spray cranberries to cranberry juice cocktail Pineapples: Dole pineapples to pineapple sauce

Marketing Question

Using well-known brands, suggest some brand extensions. Why do you think they would succeed? Suggest brand extensions you think would not succeed. Why?

For approaches A, B, E, F, and G the brand owner generally retains control of the marketing effort. In C and D, the brand owner typically makes licensing agreements with third parties — the licensee has primary marketing responsibility, subject to the brand owner's guidelines.[63] A single brand may cross scores of product classes. Harley-Davidson has more than 100 licensing agreements — including armchairs, restaurants, and toys; Coke's licensed products include baby clothes, beach towels, boxer shorts, earrings, and fishing lures; and New York's Radio City Music Hall has licensees for coloring books, costumes, DVDs, high-end dolls, holiday ornaments, jewelry, and wallpaper.

Brand leveraging reduces launch costs and/or increases profits for small investments.[64] A new product with a leveraged brand gains automatic brand awareness.[65] Before leveraging, the firm must consider potential opportunities and obstacles, and several branding issues.

OPPORTUNITIES AND OBSTACLES. The firm must address the following sorts of questions:

- Is there sufficient demand for the new venture?
- Is the firm sufficiently strong to succeed in the face of competition?
- Can the firm access the new market through current distribution channels?
- Is the firm capable of satisfying potential demand?
- Does the firm have access to raw materials and other production inputs?
- Does the firm possess other competencies necessary for success?

BRANDING ISSUES. These concern brand associations held by customers and their fit with the extension[66]:

- Do customers perceive a fit between the original product form (class) and the new product form (class) in terms of product features and concepts?
- What are customers' brand image and associations for the core product? Will these associations *transfer* to the new product?
- What is the reverse relationship? How will customer associations for the new product *back transfer* to brand associations for the core product?
- How does the corporate and/or monolithic brand relate to these associations?

Marketing Question

In 1984, Bulgari sold Bulgari brand luxury products in five Bulgari stores. By 2003, Bulgari had 180 stores; 600 outlets also sold Bulgari watches, and 14,000 outlets sold Bulgari perfumes. Bulgari formed Bulgari Hotels and Resorts in a joint venture with Marriott. Do you think Bulgari hotels will succeed? Why or why not? Do you think Bulgari's acquisition by LVMH will affect its hotel venture?

Once the firm has addressed opportunities, obstacles, and several issues, the brand must meet two baseline conditions for an extension to be viable:

- The brand must have strong positive associations.

- Brand associations and the product extension should not be incongruous. How do you rate the likely success for *Tide* candies? *Mercedes-Benz* orange juice? *Microsoft* floor cleaner? *Calvin Klein* mutual funds? *Victoria's Secret* soup?

Brand extensions tend to fail when:

- Associations between the brand and the extension are not obvious.
- The brand has a unique image and associations that do not transfer.
- The new product form (class) has a dominant competitor.
- The positioning is confusing and/or inconsistent.
- The extension's quality does not match customer expectations for the brand.[67]

Brand dilution is a potentially serious issue: The brand extension fails, FBE reduces, and overall sales fall. Trouble![68]

HOW BRAND BROADENING (LEVERAGING) FITS IN. Figure 11.9 shows brand leveraging as one of a family of strategies relating brands and product forms (classes).

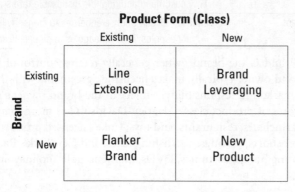

We showed that brand broadening (leveraging) takes an existing brand to a new product form (class). Other options are line extensions, **flanker brands**, and new products:

- **Line extension.** The firm adds a new but similar product to its product line and uses the same brand name. Jello comes in various colors and flavors, all under the Jello brand; J&J offers Tylenol in several sizes, shapes, and physical forms — capsules, caplets, and liquid. *Sports Illustrated* added *Sports Illustrated for Kids.*[70]

- **Flanker brand.** The firm adds a new yet similar product, but develops a new brand, or a distinguishing sub-brand.

- **New product.** The firm adds a new product class or product form and develops a new brand.

Fighter Brands

Firms often introduce *fighter brands* (lower-price *flanker brands*) when existing brands face strong price competition. The fighter brand's job is to *protect* the core brand and secure sales and profits from customers who would otherwise purchase from competitors. Celeron successfully protected Intel's Pentium brand against AMD's K6; P&G's Luvs protected Pampers from private-label diapers. Many fighting brands fail, like Ted (United Airlines), Song (Delta Airlines), and Saturn (GM). Pharmaceutical firms are introducing fighter drug brands — branded generics — when patent protection ends. When introducing a fighter brand, the firm must set clear customer and competitor targets, minimize premium-brand cannibalization, keep management focused on the firm's core business, and be profitable.[71]

KEY IDEA

➤ Firms that leverage brands secure automatic brand awareness for the new product. These firms avoid new brand introduction costs and may increase profits for little additional investment.

FIGURE 11.9

BRANDING CHOICES[69]

KEY IDEA

➤ For an extension to be viable, the brand must have strong positive associations. The difference between these brand associations and the product extension should not be incongruous.

BRAND MIGRATION

We noted earlier that firms sometimes retire individual brands. Perhaps the target market/ segment has contracted, competition may be severe, and/or brand identity may no longer fit with evolving customer needs. Sometimes brand support is expensive, and/or a brand may have lost value because of managerial neglect, a lost internal battle for resources, and/or harvesting for profits and cash.[72] Other times, the firm may decide to refocus efforts on fewer, stronger brands and/or seek economies of scale in marketing. Federated Department Stores retired Abraham & Strauss, L.S. Ayers, Bon Marché, Bullocks, Burdines, Famous-Barr, Filene's, Foley's, Goldsmith's, Hecht's, Jordan Marsh, Kaufmann's, Lazarus, I. Magnin, Marshall Field's, Meier & Frank, Rich's, Robinsons-May, Stern's, Strawbridge's, and The Jones Store in favor of Macy's.

Sometimes the firm secures brands via acquisition and then retires them. Citicorp retired Schroder Salomon Smith Barney; Morgan Stanley retired Dean Witter. Also, the firm may be contractually obligated to stop using the brand. B&D acquired GE's small appliance (housewares) business but could use the GE brand for only five years.[73] In these cases, the challenge is to retain the brand equity being retired by transferring it to another brand — **brand migration**. Most approaches have two main stages:

- Associating the brand to be retired with the surviving brand;
- Dropping the retired brand.

Vodafone, the world's largest cell-phone-service provider, previously comprised many strong domestic brands. Vodafone migrated these brands to *Vodafone* (Vo - voice, da - data, fone - phone). Said Vodafone's global-branding director, "Vodafone uses a dual branding strategy designed to give all constituents — employees, customers, and trade partners — a period of time so people can intellectually *get it*. In Germany we did *D2/Vodafone*, then *Vodafone/D2*, and then we just dropped the *D2* to become *Vodafone*. In various markets, we've done it in one month, nine months, and 15 months. It all depends on the local market situation."[74]

STRATEGIC ALLIANCES

KEY IDEA

➤ The firm can enhance brand equity with effective strategic alliances.

Strategic alliances can extend the firm's brand into new market segments. Alliances can range from informal or contractual working relationships to new entities structured as legal joint ventures. Most alliances focus on competency — one firm's strengths compensate for the other firm's weaknesses, and vice versa. Strategic alliances have important **co-branding** implications when the co-branding partner can transfer positive customer attitudes. Co-branding between customers and suppliers is increasingly common. Two major steel companies, OneSteel and Corus, successfully co-branded with customers,[75] and many PC manufacturers co-brand with Intel. Ruth Owades, founder of Calyx and Corolla (C&C) (direct marketer of fresh flowers), believed the FedEx brand was essential to establish C&C's credibility for service excellence. She asserted she would not have founded C&C without the alliance. But co-branding is no panacea; if the firm does not manage the process well, customers become confused and brand equity suffers.

When firms co-brand with themselves they must ensure that brand associations are appropriate for the product and target segment. In Asia, Holiday Inn closely associates its parent brand with Crowne Plaza hotels; Crowne Plaza is an **endorsed brand**. By contrast, in the U.S., Crowne Plaza is a **standalone brand**; Holiday Inn associations negatively affect Crowne Plaza's brand image.

AGING AND DEFUNCT BRANDS

Some aging brands, like those in Table 11.2 (p. 278), have loyal customers and survive for many years. But these are exceptions. The marketing landscape is littered with the corpses of once-valuable and famous brands. As markets evolve, brands may develop negative reputations and/or be weakly positioned and economically unviable, despite enjoying high brand awareness. Rebranding may be an option, like GMAC's name change to Ally Financial; Chapter 10 identified a second option for improving sales in mature markets — *repositioning the brand*.

Brand reintroduction and/or brand revitalization is the key objective for *repositioning*. Key options are:

- **Target new market segment(s).** Colgate-Palmolive, Avon, and *Reader's Digest* each increased sales by targeting new geographic segments outside the U.S. To its surprise, Sears found that core U.S. customers were *not* male hardware buyers, but 25- to 50-year-old women with children. Sears successfully repositioned by refocusing promotion and expanding clothing and cosmetics products. When P&G acquired Old Spice (OS), OS was mainly known for aftershave and cologne and a graying customer base — OS deodorant was tenth in market share. P&G focused on first-time deodorant users, aged 18 to 34. OS is now the top-selling deodorant and anti-perspirant among male teenagers (Chapter 8).[76] Sales of Memorex (audio cassettes), TDK (stereo products), and Imation (floppy discs) fell substantially but each now targets new market segments with new products.

- **Change brand associations.** Successful examples are Honda's classic motorcycling repositioning from *long-haired guys and the police officers chasing them* to *a family activity* — "you meet the nicest people on a Honda" (Chapter 10). Britain's Labor government changed the country's associations from backward-looking and tradition-based to future-oriented youthfulness, excitement, and opportunity.[77] Some firms develop nostalgic (retro) associations for the *good old days* — Ovaltine powdered drink mix, Burma-Shave shaving cream, and British motor racing at Goodwood.[78]

- **Alter the competitive target.** Bacardi successfully repositioned its light rum to compete against vodka and scotch whisky, rather than other rums.

The firm can avoid the necessity for revitalization by continually innovating, adding new products, and keeping the brand vital and relevant.[79] Intel continually introduces new products for its corporate brand — *Intel*, and its sub-brand — *Pentium*.

Sometimes firms rediscover brands they dropped years earlier or inherited in acquisitions. If such a brand has high awareness, straightforward reintroduction may be an option, like Eagle Snacks, Metrecal, and Silkience.

Marketing Question

What other messages did you glean from this chapter?

KEY MESSAGES

- The nature of brands has changed from signifiers of goods and services to symbols for constructing relationships between the firm and customers.

- A positive relationship between the brand and customers can significantly enhance shareholder value.

- The firm can brand individual products, product lines, and/or product groups.

- The firm should choose a brand identity and supporting associations.

- Brand image represents the associations customers hold about the brand. The firm should strive to achieve alignment between brand image and brand identity.

- Some important items about brands and branding are:
  - Branding is important in both B2C and B2B.
  - Branding is much more than advertising.
  - Customers are only one of several audiences for brand messages.
  - For product brands, we cannot assume that the brand owner is also the manufacturer.

- Customer brand equity (CBE) and firm brand equity (FBE) are two distinct constructs. Each can be monetized.

- To build a strong brand, the firm must execute a process through which it establishes brand identity, creates brand awareness, forms brand associations and brand image, develops consistent brand quality and value perceptions, builds brand loyalty and, possibly, leverages brand strength to new products/services.

- To sustain a strong brand, the firm should regularly measure brand health and act on results.

- To secure the best results from branding efforts, the firm should make serious decisions about various facets of brand architecture.

VIDEOS AND AUDIOS

| Branding | v1102 📹 | Schmitt | Columbia Business School |
| Brand Management | v1103 📹 | Barton Warner | Bayer HealthCare |

| Marketing Imperative 3 — Branding | a1101 🎧 | | |

v1102

v1103

a1101

QUESTIONS FOR STUDY AND DISCUSSION

Can you answer the questions implied by this chapter's learning objectives? Check!

1. Bring to class an example of a B2C branding campaign. Using the positioning statement format (Chapter 9), write what you believe to have been the advertisers' desired positioning. How well does the advertising reflect this positioning?

2. Bring to class an example of a B2B branding campaign. Think hard about who is the target of the advertising. Using the positioning statement format (Chapter 9), write what you believe to have been the advertisers' desired positioning. How well does the advertising reflect this positioning?

3. The text quotes a leading advertising executive as saying: "A successful brand is timeless." Do you agree or disagree? Should the statement be modified in the context of young consumers valuing change, innovation, and unique choice? Explain your answer with current examples.

4. Select a well-known brand and track its brand history. How have brand identity and brand image evolved? Did the brand owner attempt to change brand identity to keep the brand contemporary? Or was the brand owner trying to broaden the market?

5. Identify a firm that provided you with a good customer experience; call the central number and ask for the CEO by name to offer your congratulations on firm performance. Keep a written record of the interactions. What impact does this experience have on your feelings about the corporate brand? If you reach the CEO — highly unlikely — pass on your reactions on how you were treated.

6. The American Red Cross comprises many local chapters that develop their own marketing strategies and communications. As marketing director of the national organization, how would you go about developing a consistent brand identity and brand image for the American Red Cross overall?

7. Contact a firm you know and determine if it measures brand health. Ask about the metrics the firm uses and be prepared to report them in class. If there is no system, ask how the firm ensures that striving for short-term performance does not damage the brand in the long run.

8. Identify an example of poor brand architecture and be prepared to explain your assessment. The example could include multi-branding versus umbrella branding, unwise brand extensions or attempts at broadening (leveraging), brand migration, strategic alliances, and aging brands.

9. Select a product in which you are interested. Alternatively, consider this book — *Managing Marketing in the 21st Century*. Using the concepts and ideas in this chapter, recommend an approach to branding.

SECTION IV
IMPLEMENTING THE MARKET STRATEGY vs4

To access O-codes, go to **www.ocodes.com**

SECTION IV — IMPLEMENTING THE MARKET STRATEGY — COMPRISES 11 CHAPTERS, Chapter 12 through Chapter 22. The section embraces the second three Marketing Imperatives: Imperative 4 — Design the Market Offer; Imperative 5 — Secure Support from Other Functions; and Imperative 6 — Monitor and Control.

The largest group of chapters — Chapters 12 through 20 — address Imperative 4. We organize the material on designing the market offer into four parts.

Part A, *Providing Customer Value*, comprises three chapters. Chapter 12, Managing the Product Line, considers the firm's products as elements in a product portfolio, each with specific roles, together with several product-related issues. Chapter 13, Managing Services and Customer Service, focuses on product/service differences and highlights the importance of customer service. Chapter 14, Developing New Products, introduces the stage/gate process for developing new products.

Part B, *Communicating Customer Value*, also comprises three chapters. Chapter 15, Integrated Marketing Communications, frames an integrated communications strategy. Chapter 16, Mass and Digital Communications, focuses on advertising and other non-personal communications approaches. Chapter 17, Directing and Managing the Field Sales Effort, discusses six core tasks for developing and implementing the sales strategy.

Part C, *Delivering Customer Value*, comprises a single chapter. Chapter 18, Distribution Decisions, focuses on how the firm's products reach end-user customers.

Part D, *Getting Paid for Customer Value*, comprises two chapters: Chapter 19, Critical Underpinnings of Pricing Decisions, and Chapter 20, Setting Prices.

Imperatives 5 and 6 each merit a single chapter. Chapter 21, Ensuring the Firm Implements the Market Offer as Planned, addresses Imperative 5 and focuses on building an externally oriented firm. Chapter 22, Monitoring and Controlling Firm Functioning and Performance, considers Imperative 6 and shows how to maintain the firm's planned trajectory.

Managing Marketing in the 21ˢᵗ Century

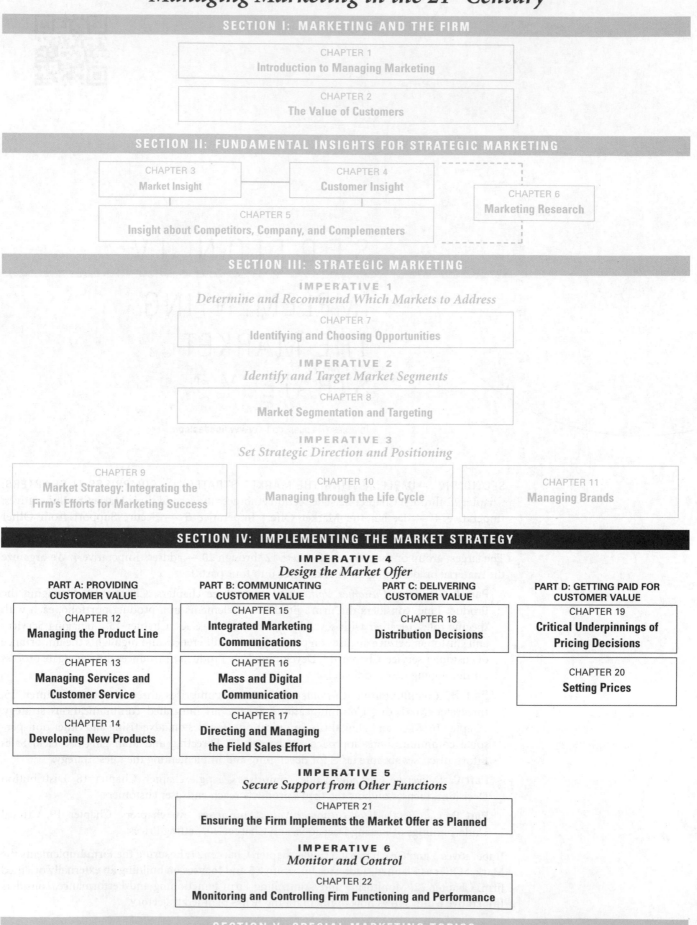

SECTION I: MARKETING AND THE FIRM

CHAPTER 1
Introduction to Managing Marketing

CHAPTER 2
The Value of Customers

SECTION II: FUNDAMENTAL INSIGHTS FOR STRATEGIC MARKETING

CHAPTER 3
Market Insight

CHAPTER 4
Customer Insight

CHAPTER 6
Marketing Research

CHAPTER 5
Insight about Competitors, Company, and Complementers

SECTION III: STRATEGIC MARKETING

IMPERATIVE 1
Determine and Recommend Which Markets to Address

CHAPTER 7
Identifying and Choosing Opportunities

IMPERATIVE 2
Identify and Target Market Segments

CHAPTER 8
Market Segmentation and Targeting

IMPERATIVE 3
Set Strategic Direction and Positioning

CHAPTER 9
Market Strategy: Integrating the Firm's Efforts for Marketing Success

CHAPTER 10
Managing through the Life Cycle

CHAPTER 11
Managing Brands

SECTION IV: IMPLEMENTING THE MARKET STRATEGY

IMPERATIVE 4
Design the Market Offer

PART A: PROVIDING CUSTOMER VALUE	PART B: COMMUNICATING CUSTOMER VALUE	PART C: DELIVERING CUSTOMER VALUE	PART D: GETTING PAID FOR CUSTOMER VALUE
CHAPTER 12 Managing the Product Line	**CHAPTER 15** Integrated Marketing Communications	**CHAPTER 18** Distribution Decisions	**CHAPTER 19** Critical Underpinnings of Pricing Decisions
CHAPTER 13 Managing Services and Customer Service	**CHAPTER 16** Mass and Digital Communication		**CHAPTER 20** Setting Prices
CHAPTER 14 Developing New Products	**CHAPTER 17** Directing and Managing the Field Sales Effort		

IMPERATIVE 5
Secure Support from Other Functions

CHAPTER 21
Ensuring the Firm Implements the Market Offer as Planned

IMPERATIVE 6
Monitor and Control

CHAPTER 22
Monitoring and Controlling Firm Functioning and Performance

SECTION V: SPECIAL MARKETING TOPICS

CHAPTER 23
International, Regional, and Global Marketing

v1201

IMPERATIVE 4
Design the Market Offer

PART A – PROVIDING CUSTOMER VALUE

CHAPTER 12
MANAGING THE PRODUCT LINE v1201

LEARNING OBJECTIVES

When you have completed this chapter, you will be able to:

- Understand the importance of managing the product line as a portfolio.
- Apply alternative approaches to managing the product portfolio.
- Manage key interrelationships among products.
- Address the pressures for product proliferation and product-line simplification.
- Manage both diverse and complementary product lines.
- Deal with important product issues like bundling, counterfeiting, evolving the product line, extending product life, product quality, and secondary market products.
- Anticipate concerns about product safety, packaging, and disposal of products and packaging.

OPENING CASE: SWIFFER

Introduced by P&G in 1999, the Swiffer Sweeper (SS) was not just a new product; it was the first in a new product class — a line of products for cleaning surfaces. The Swiffer product line now comprises several different cleaning products for a variety of surfaces. The Swiffer design includes both hardware *and* disposables. *The hardware is a pole and attachment that grips the disposable, typically a dry or wet cloth. The choice of disposable depends on the surface being cleaned; regardless, the consumer discards the cloth after cleaning. P&G provides refills in various scents: SS dry cloths — 16-count refills, in unscented, Lavender Vanilla & Comfort, or Sweet Citrus & Zest; wet cloths — 24-count refills, in Open Window Fresh, Lavender Vanilla & Comfort, or Sweet Citrus & Zest. Some products are available as starter kits.*

Swiffer comprises the following products:

- **Swiffer Sweeper.** *Cleans hard-surface floors. Dry cloths compete with brooms and dustpans; wet cloths compete with mops and pails of water.*

- **Swiffer SweeperVac.** *Combines the SS dry cloth with a vacuum cleaner. The dry cloth picks up fine debris like dirt, dust, and pet hair; the vacuum picks up larger objects.*
- **Swiffer Dusters.** *Reaches into nooks and crannies. Has an extendable handle and lockable pivoting head; a special version cleans automobile interiors.*
- **Swiffer Sweeper Professional.** *Similar to the SS but with a larger head; cloths are about one and a half times the size of two regular SS cloths.*
- **Swiffer WetJet.** *Replaces mops for difficult-to-clean floors. Premixed cleaning solutions are available — Multipurpose Floor Cleaner, Wood Floor Cleaner, and Antibacterial Floor Cleaner.*
- **Swiffer Dust & Shine.** *Wax-free formula cleans and shines wood furniture and other surfaces like leather and granite.*

Most Swiffer products have differently designed hardware and disposables, but P&G has a consistent business model. The hardware has a low price and generates little profit; P&G makes its money on refills. The premium-priced Swiffer line is part of P&G's Household Care business, roughly 50 percent of total firm revenues.

P&G now has 23 billion-dollar brands. Swiffer is one of 16 brands with revenue between $500 million and $1 billion with the potential to become a billion-dollar brand.

CASE QUESTION

How do you assess P&G's development of the Swiffer product line? What are the critical elements in Swiffer's success?

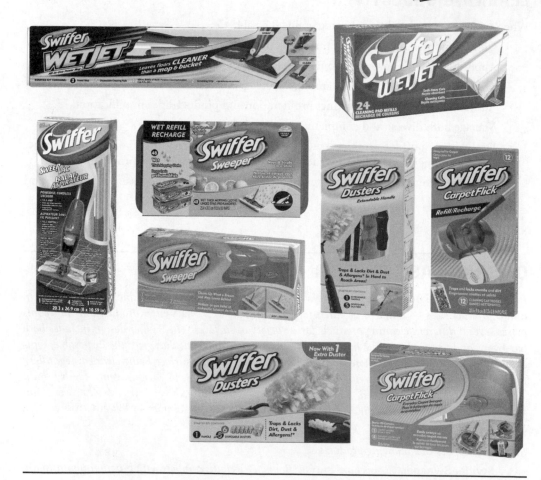

Chapter 12 is the first of three chapters in Part A of Imperative 4 — *Design the Market Offer*. Part A focuses on *Providing Customer Value*. Chapter 12 addresses *Managing the Product Line*.

Products and services are central to the firm's marketing mix. Since decisions about products and services cross functional lines, they have a broader impact on the firm's operations than other marketing-mix variables like promotion, distribution, customer service, and pricing. Firms also face difficult issues allocating limited resources across product portfolios. Optimal product-line breadth is a critical issue; product proliferation and product-line simplification can each have dramatic effects on shareholder value. Introducing new products (Chapter 14), bundling, counterfeiting, evolving the product line, extending product life, packaging, product quality, and secondary market products are important related issues. Product safety can embroil the firm in legal and ethical problems; increased societal expectations regarding health (like fast food and obesity) and environmental concerns (like pesticides and packaging and product disposal) highlight the importance of product decisions.

THE CHANGING VIEW

OLD WAY	NEW WAY
Caveat emptor (buyer beware)	*Caveat venditor* (seller beware)
Ethical considerations relatively rare	Ethical considerations recognized as vital
Focus on profits	Focus on shareholder value
Judgments made exclusively with financial criteria	Judgments based on market and financial criteria
Product managers on pedestals	Product managers subject to executive control
Product profitability data rare	Product profitability data becoming ubiquitous
Product proliferation common, rationalization rare	Product line breadth carefully managed, rationalization common
Products and brands often treated similarly	Products and brands carefully discriminated
Products viewed independently	Products managed as a portfolio
Quality variable	Total Quality Management (TQM)
Reluctance to cannibalize products	Cannibalization as part of product line renewal
Uniform business objectives by product	Business objectives tailored by product and segment
Waste products and packaging ignored	Environmental concerns important

THE PRODUCT PORTFOLIO CONCEPT

GE's business-unit portfolio includes Appliances, Aviation, Capital, Healthcare, Industrial Systems, Lighting, and Transportation. The product portfolio for GE's Appliances (GEA) business unit includes (among others) air conditioners, dehumidifiers and air purifiers, dishwashers, disposers and compactors, microwave ovens, ranges, refrigerators and freezers, wall ovens, washers and dryers, and water systems. GEA must allocate resources among these products and decide which, if any, to add and/or drop.

The firm's **product portfolio** is a collection of products.[1] Large firms offer thousands of products, often grouped by business unit (GE example). Corporate leaders allocate resources among business units. Business-unit heads make resource allocations among products based on their assessments of potential growth and profitability.[2]

The firm does *not* optimize overall profits by maximizing short-run profits from each individual product. Rather, the firm should use a **portfolio approach** to product management, balancing objectives and resource allocations across all products. For example, the firm's new products require investment in R&D, plant and equipment, and promotional activities; these products consume cash. The firm typically believes that securing market position is more important than earning profits, at least in the short run when the market is growing. By contrast, when growth slows and investment requirements diminish, established products become more profitable and generate cash. The firm uses this cash to develop and support new and younger products. The cycle continues.

The firm optimizes shareholder value when the **product portfolio** is **balanced**; an **imbalanced** portfolio puts shareholder interests at risk. Imbalances occur when the firm funds too many new products and creates shortages of cash and other resources.[3] Imbalances also occur when the firm has too many old products; good short-term financial results may mask a failure to invest sufficiently in the future. Securing the *right* balance of successful new products and profitable established products is important for enhancing shareholder value. If the firm has a seriously imbalanced product portfolio, it may become an acquisition candidate for firms seeking either growth or cash flow.

The key to a successful product strategy is setting objectives and allocating resources based on each product's role in the portfolio. The firm should manage some products to achieve growth objectives, and other products to maximize profits or cash flow. The firm's challenge is to allocate the *right* financial and human resources such that each product achieves its objectives. Of course, within the firm, the various products compete for scarce resources.[4]

This chapter shows portfolio analysis methods used by many firms to make these difficult resource allocation decisions. But first we describe traditional financial analysis methods for making these types of decisions, then discuss their advantages and disadvantages.

FINANCIAL ANALYSIS METHODS

Superior financial performance is critical for delivering increased shareholder value. Hence, a **financial analysis** perspective for assessing potential financial return from products is both important and proper.[5] Approaches include[6]:

- **Return on investment (ROI).** ROI calculations project future accounting data. They compare the product's forecast rate of return with a target (or *hurdle*) rate. If the forecast rate exceeds the target rate and resources are available, the firm invests.[7]

- **Payback.** Payback is the forecast time to pay back the investment. In general, shorter paybacks are better than longer paybacks. Payback's problem is ignoring profits earned after the payback period.

Neither **ROI** nor **payback** distinguishes among time periods. They treat financial flows similarly regardless of when they occur. Because of this defect, most firms use approaches that account for the time value of money:

- **Net present value (NPV)** and **internal rate of return (IRR)**. NPV and IRR are the most common financial analysis methods for assessing investment opportunities. Discount factors account for the time value of money. Both methods use actual cash flows rather than financial and cost accounting data. They assess cash inflows (like sales revenues) when earned and cash outflows (like costs and investments) when paid out.[8]
  - **NPV** uses a predetermined discount factor, typically the firm's cost of capital. The firm calculates NPV for various opportunities, then ranks by monetary value.
  - For **IRR**, the firm calculates the discount rate that equalizes cash inflows and cash outflows. IRR typically ranks opportunities whose IRR exceeds the hurdle rate.[9]

KEY IDEA

➤ The firm's products have important resource-related interrelationships.

➤ The firm does not optimize its overall profits by maximizing profits from individual products. It must consider the entire product portfolio.

➤ Firms with imbalanced portfolios are vulnerable to acquisition.

Marketing Question

How would you convince a skeptical finance vice president she should enhance her approach to investment assessment with portfolio analysis?

More recently, firms use **economic profit** or **economic value added (EVA)**. EVA equals the firm's annual profit less an explicit charge for capital.[10] A summary of approaches:

Financial Analysis Approaches

1. **Forecast Return on Investment (%) (ROI)** — (Sales Revenues less Costs)/Investment = Profits/Investment (based on forecast accounting data).

2. **Payback (years, months)** — time to pay back the initial investment.

3. **Net Present Value (NPV)** — the dollar value of an opportunity. Discounts all cash outflows and inflows by a predetermined factor, typically the firm's cost of capital.

4. **Internal Rate of Return (IRR)** — the discount rate that equalizes cash inflows and cash outflows.

5. **Economic Profit** — the opportunity's annual profit less an explicit charge for capital.

🔑 KEY IDEA

➤ Financial analysis methods rely on forecasts — these can be highly uncertain.

➤ Financial analysis does not consider strategic issues and ignores marketing considerations.

➤ Too much reliance on financial analysis can lead to misallocation of resources across products and markets.

Marketing Question

Suppose the products in your business unit span the range from introduction to decline. Corporate has sent a finance VP to assess your business unit and to *help you*! What would you be most concerned about?

ADVANTAGES OF FINANCIAL ANALYSIS (FA). Pluses for FA are:

- **Clarity.** Decisions flow clearly from FA. So long as opportunities exceed a target number, the firm makes selections in attractiveness order.

- **Conceptual simplicity.** Calculations may be complex, but each approach is conceptually simple. The inputs — investments, revenues, costs — are generally readily available.

- **Comparable results.** Each approach ultimately produces a single figure — the firm can easily compare several opportunities.

DISADVANTAGES OF FINANCIAL ANALYSIS. Problems with FA are:

- **Internal political dynamics.** FA can lead to organizational game-playing. Figure 12.1 shows how opportunity-champions may *hockey-stick* sales revenue estimates up, and costs and investments down — marginal opportunities become spectacular performers! Of course, hardnosed financial managers make *realistic adjustments* — sales revenues down, cost estimates up! Because managers can change projected financial performance with *the stroke of a pen*, choosing opportunities often reflects political power, rather than intrinsic value.

- **Potential misallocation of investment funds.** FA leads some firms to allocate investment funds based on historic profitability. These firms invest in mature, low-growth products but starve high-growth products, where current profits are low and uncertainty is high.[11] Also, some firms use larger discount factors for new products — forecasting errors are typically greater.[12] Insufficient investment in new products helps competitors, especially when environmental change requires major shifts in products and markets.[13]

- **Silence on strategic issues.** FA ranks opportunities by financial performance but generally does not consider strategic imperatives. Suppose projected IRR for two opportunities are 22 percent and 18 percent; the hurdle rate is 12 percent, so both are viable. Using IRR, 22 percent is always more attractive than 18 percent. But suppose the 18 percent opportunity is central to the firm's strategy and the 22 percent option is peripheral. Strategically, the 18 percent opportunity makes more sense, but IRR concludes differently. Also, FA does not consider marketing issues like brand building.

- **Uncertainty in the estimates.** FA relies on estimates of sales units, prices, costs, and investments. Estimating short-term investment requirements for even well-defined opportunities is difficult; predicting sales units and prices several years in the future is daunting.

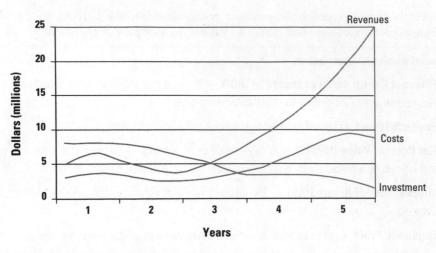

FIGURE 12.1

HOCKEY-STICK ADJUSTMENTS TO SALES REVENUE, COSTS, AND INVESTMENT FORECASTS

> *Marketing Question*
>
> Suppose you were GE's marketing manager for refrigerators. How would you address assumptions underlying your financial analysis, like target market share, technological change, future competitive structure, competitor strategies, and the role of government?

Today, many firms modify/augment financial analysis by examining the assumptions underlying financial projections, and requiring managers to think more deeply about them. Typically, precise answers are not possible, but the process leads to a more externally oriented approach — like portfolio analysis — for allocating resources. Critical questions include:

What is the expected future market growth rate?	Against which companies will the firm compete?
What is the target market share?	How is technology expected to evolve?
What is the likely future market structure?	What will be the government's role?
In what ways is the market changing?	Are there legal/regulatory issues to consider?

PORTFOLIO ANALYSIS

Portfolio analysis (PA) is central to many firms' strategic planning processes. PA is best viewed as an *additional* tool for allocating resources, not as an *alternative* to FA. PA is a systematic, organized, and easily communicable way of assembling, assessing, and integrating important information about products and markets with the goal of constructing a balanced portfolio. PA helps the firm set strategic direction, establish investment priorities, and allocate resources.[14] The firm can use portfolio analysis to evaluate both businesses and products.

PA has dramatically affected many firms' resource allocation processes; PA includes factors traditional financial analysis ignores. Table 12.1 illustrates several differences between FA and PA.[15] Using FA and PA together leads to better investment decisions than either approach alone.

> **KEY IDEA**
>
> ➤ Portfolio analysis is a systematic, organized, and easily communicated way of assembling, assessing, and integrating important information about product/market opportunities.

Variable	Financial Analysis	Portfolio Analysis
General approach	Financial- and budget-oriented	Market- and competitive-oriented
Investment decision focus	Technologies/facilities	Products/markets/customers/ applications
Key concerns	Derived profit and cash flow numbers	Market and competitive factors underlying the financial numbers
Tools	Capital budgeting	Growth-share and multifactor matrices
Typical measures	ROI, payback, NPV, IRR, EVA	Market — size, growth, competitive strength

TABLE 12.1

FINANCIAL AND PORTFOLIO ANALYSIS — INVESTMENT DECISIONS AND STRATEGIC DIRECTIONS

>  **KEY IDEA**
>
> ➤ Portfolio analysis addresses many problems with financial analysis.

Two important PA methods are the growth-share matrix and the multifactor matrix.

THE GROWTH-SHARE MATRIX. The Boston Consulting Group (BCG) developed the original PA. As the name implies, core dimensions are growth and share: *forecast long-run market growth and relative market share.*[16] Figure 12.2 shows each dimension bisected to produce a four-cell classification. Matrix entries represent products (or businesses). Typically, each circle's size is proportional to sales revenues or invested assets.

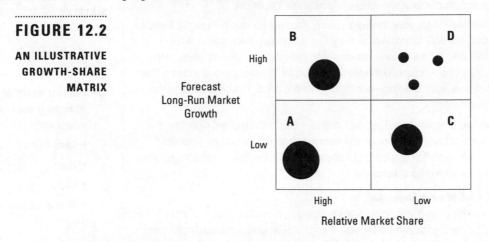

FIGURE 12.2

AN ILLUSTRATIVE GROWTH-SHARE MATRIX

Growth-Share Matrix Dimensions

Long-run market growth. An estimate of future market growth over a three-to-five-year time horizon.[17] Typically, forecasts are for physical units such as pounds, meters, or tons. If price competition is severe, using revenues may be appropriate. All things equal, high-growth opportunities are more attractive.

Relative market share (RMS). The firm's market share divided by its largest competitor's market share. RMS indicates the dominant player directly: RMS > 1. RMS focuses directly on the firm's competitive strength. Consider two situations, I and II. In each case, the market leader has 40 percent market share:

I.   Few competitors — No. 2 firm has 30 percent market share: RMS = 40/30 = 1.33

II. Many competitors — No. 2 firm has 15 percent market share: RMS = 40/15 = 2.67

A focus on market share alone does not distinguish between these two situations; in each case the leader has 40 percent market share! RMS shows that the leader's position is much more favorable in II — RMS = 2.67, than in I — RMS = 1.33.[18] In general, firms with high relative market share have lower costs, stronger positions in customers' minds, and other marketing advantages.

A practical question concerns placement of the dividing line (cut-point) between high- and low-growth markets. Placement is arbitrary, but many firms find a choice rule helpful. An *external* benchmark like growth in **gross domestic product (GDP)** is far superior than an *internal* standard, like the firm's current growth rate. To explain: If the firm's annual growth rate were 1 percent, an aggressive internal cut-point might be 4 percent. Any opportunity with growth greater than 4 percent would appear attractive. But if annual GDP growth were 8 percent, a 4 percent standard would imply the firm is willing to shrink relatively. Based on 8 percent GDP growth, a better cut-point would be 10 percent, or even 12 percent. A good rule of thumb is forecast GDP growth plus a few additional percentage points based on firm goals. The RMS cut-point is typically 1.0; market-leading products to the left, all others to the right.

The growth-share matrix places heavy emphasis on the financial characteristics of products in each cell. High-share products are typically more profitable than low-share products. Growth products typically require significant investment in fixed assets, working capital, and market

KEY IDEA

➤ Portfolio analysis is best viewed as an additional tool for setting investment priorities — not as an alternative to financial analysis.

Cash Cows. Low Market Growth/High Market Share (Cell A)
Classic characteristics of cash cows are:

- Low costs. From experience curve effects — Chapter 10.
- Premium prices. As market leader, cash cows may command premium prices.
- Low reinvestment. Low-growth, mature products require relatively low investment.

Cash cows should be highly profitable and are often the firm's primary internal cash source. Examples include Microsoft Office, IBM mainframes, and P&G Tide detergent. If the firm successfully holds market share, it can *milk* a cash cow and generate cash for many years. Environmental changes like regulatory shifts, patent expiration, innovative competitors, or new technology threaten cash cows by changing demand patterns. Then the firm may *harvest* the product to increase short-term cash flow — raising prices, reducing or eliminating services, and/or cutting promotional support.

Firms with cash cows can make two types of errors. First, they *over-milk* their cash cows and cash flow *dries up*. Starved of investment, the product trails in technology and loses cost leadership and market position.[20] U.S. and European car and steel firms are good examples. In a second scenario, the firm over-invests, reducing financial return, and leaving little cash for other opportunities.

Stars. High Market Growth, High Market Share (Cell B)
Stars are relatively rare; few products enjoy dominant positions in high-growth markets. Stars are often profitable in accounting terms, but use significant cash because their growth requires substantial investment.[21] Groupon and Twitter are good examples. Despite the firm's best efforts, market growth eventually slows. If the firm invests appropriately and retains good market share, profits and cash flow improve, and the star transforms into a *cash cow*. The major error firms make with stars is to cut back investment too early. The star loses dominance and transforms into a *dog* — cell C.[22]

Dogs. Low Market Growth, Low Market Share (Cell C)
Dogs is a pejorative term for products with unfavorable characteristics:

- High costs relative to the leader; dogs do not enjoy the same economy-of-scale or experience curve advantages.
- Prices may be lower than the market leader.

Dogs are often unprofitable or earn only low profits; they are also often the focus of top management attention. Better-positioned dogs often generate positive cash flow but may still be a drag on firm resources. Dogs are the most numerous of all products in any economy. Examples include Lenovo's personal computers and U.S. Airways.[23] Firms with dogs should consider:

- Developing new segmentation approaches that strengthen their positions.
- Refreshing products with additional value from new features.
- Maximizing short-run cash flows by liquidating or divesting. IBM sold its *barely profitable* PC business to Lenovo.
- Implement a *kennel* strategy (Chapter 10) by acquiring similar products to achieve viable scale.

Problem Children (aka Lottery Tickets, Question Marks, Wildcats). High Market Growth, Low Market Share (Cell D)
Problem children combine the uncertainties of high-growth markets with non-dominant market shares. Examples include iRiver, RCA, and M-Pio MP3 players; each has less than 10 percent market share versus well over 50 percent for Apple's iPod. Problem children that grow with the market consume substantial investment capital. Such investment may be risky, as growth does not guarantee future profits. Growing with the market moves the problem-child from cell D to cell C. Hence the key choice for problem children is often *double or quit!*

- *Double.* Large strategic investments can move the product to market leadership. Sony successfully overtook Nintendo in video games with high spending in product development and promotion. By contrast, Philips' CD-Interactive (CDI), a user-friendly interactive CD system, launched when CD-ROM was in its infancy, was quickly overtaken. A less risky approach seeks dominance in a defensible market segment(s).
- *Quit.* Exit, immediately or gradually. The product may command a good price from an aggressive follower. Small biotech firms often sell their new drugs to big pharma.

FIGURE 12.3

PRODUCT CHARACTERISTICS IN THE GROWTH-SHARE MATRIX[19]

KEY IDEA

➤ Product labels derived from the growth-share matrix are:

- Cash Cows
- Stars
- Dogs
- Problem Children

Marketing Question

Identify all Disney businesses — like amusement parks, movies, retail stores, and character licensing — and place them in a growth-share matrix. (You may have to guess a bit.) Which businesses are Cash Cows? Dogs? Stars? Problem Children? How do you think Disney should allocate resources? What additional factors should Disney consider in examining new wholly owned or alliance opportunities?

development. Figure 12.3 describes conventional labels and classic strategic recommendations for products in each cell. Simply:

• **Cash Cows.** Low market growth, high market share (Cell A) — generate cash.
• **Stars.** High market growth, high market share (Cell B) — invest.
• **Dogs.** Low market growth, low market share (Cell C) — critically analyze to retain or divest.
• **Problem Children.** High market growth, low market share (Cell D) — invest cautiously in a limited number of entries.

The experience curve (Chapter 10) and PIMS research (Chapter 9) generally support the characteristics in Figure 12.3. Table 12.2 shows the positive relationship between market share and profitability. ROI for products with less than 10 percent share is 14 percent. In contrast, ROI for products with over 40 percent share is 33 percent.

TABLE 12.2

MARKET SHARE AND PROFITABILITY RELATIONSHIPS FROM THE PIMS STUDY

Market Share	< 10%	10–20%	20–30%	30–40%	> 40%
ROI	14%	18%	23%	24%	33%

Table 12.3 shows a related analysis for a diversified *Fortune* 500 firm. The firm's low market share products (MS < 10%) are 46.5 percent of products, 27.5 percent of revenues, and 34.2 percent of assets, but they generate just 4 percent of profits. Conversely, the firm's high market share products (MS > 40%) are 21.1 percent of products, 17.6 percent of revenues, and 26.7 percent of assets; but they generate fully 56.7 percent of the firm's profits. Market share matters!

TABLE 12.3

INDIVIDUAL FIRM EXAMPLE: DISTRIBUTION OF THE NUMBER OF PRODUCTS, SALES REVENUES, ASSETS, AND PROFITABILITY BY MARKET SHARE

Market Share	< 10%	10–20%	20–30%	30%–40%	> 40%
Number of Products (%)*	46.5	14.8	10.6	7.0	21.1
Sales Revenues (%)**	27.5	15.8	7.9	31.2	17.6
Assets (%)	34.2	16.1	7.4	15.6	26.7
Profits (%)	4.0	8.1	9.1	22.3	56.5

*To be read as: 46.5% of the firm's products are in markets where the firm has < 10% market share.

**To be read as: 31.2% of the firm's sales revenues are in markets where the firm has 30% – 40% market share.

The firm should consider the generalized recommendations from Figure 12.3 carefully, because they are widely advocated and applied. Firms typically view high-growth markets as attractive. Yet, if many firms enter and build excess capacity, and prices drop sharply, all competitors may lose. The best way to view the growth-share matrix is as a device for raising and discussing *what-if* or contingency questions. Like any decision-making aid, the matrix has value only if its assumptions are valid. Issues include:

• **Long-run market growth** is the exclusive measure for market attractiveness. Problems may arise because the framework ignores other factors.
• **Relative market share** captures the firm's competitive strength. The firm can usually validate RMS in mature markets, but this is more difficult in growth markets.[24]
• **Market share/profitability relationship.** Tables 12.2 and 12.3 show a strong relationship between profitability and market share.[25] But this relationship may not be universal, in part because market boundaries may not be clear-cut.[26] Also, market definition affects measures of long-run market growth and RMS, and hence placing products in the matrix.
• **Downward-sloping experience curves** imply an inverse relationship between RMS and unit costs. The matrix assumes comparable cost curves across competitors, but small focused firms often have lower costs than relatively well-managed major players.

THE MULTIFACTOR MATRIX. The growth-share matrix spawned many other portfolio approaches, some public and some proprietary.[27] The most popular is the **multifactor matrix**, aka GE/McKinsey screen.[28] The multifactor matrix redefines the growth-share axes: *Long-run* *market growth* becomes *market attractiveness; relative market share* becomes *business strengths.* The user identifies several factors to measure each dimension. (To see how to develop this matrix — Chapter 8, pp. 208 to 212, where a similar approach assesses market segments.)

Figure 12.4 illustrates the multifactor matrix.[29] The most attractive cell, C, is empty but the firm has some small entries in two other attractive cells, B and F; it should probably invest in these products. The large entries in cells A and E are questionable; the firm should examine them carefully. Finally, the firm should make tough — retain or remove, decisions about the poorly positioned large cell G product:

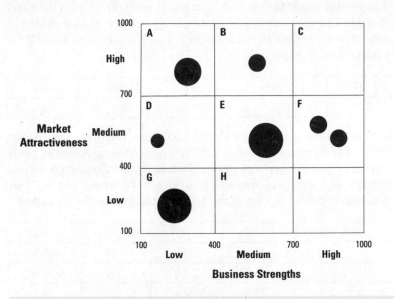

FIGURE 12.4

AN ILLUSTRATIVE MULTIFACTOR MATRIX

Siemens classifies products as green, yellow, or red. Green — invest and grow; yellow — consider; and red — target for improvement. Classification is fluid. In the last recession, Siemens reclassified several yellow products as red.

THE GROWTH-SHARE AND MULTIFACTOR MATRICES. Each method helps the firm make resource allocations, in part by visual display. Table 12.4 shows advantages and disadvantages.

The *growth-share matrix* has only two criteria: long-run market growth and RMS. Once managers agree on market definition, the firm can measure these objectively. Reasonable people may disagree about forecast market growth, but RMS is relatively simple to measure. Hence, managers have limited ability to manipulate entries for their favorite products. But two criteria can also be a weakness; forecast long-run market growth and RMS may not capture all relevant issues. By contrast, the *multifactor matrix* addresses the realism issue by using several criteria, and so embraces many factors that the growth-share matrix omits. But reasonable managers may disagree about the criteria, and their weightings and ratings are often highly subjective. Hence, political and organizational power issues can enter the analysis.

In sum, it is generally easier to evaluate and communicate about a firm's diverse products using the *growth-share matrix* than the *multifactor matrix.* Also, refinements to the *growth-share matrix* can analyze product trajectories and test results from various resource allocations. But the *multifactor matrix* can assess both current products *and* potential new products. The *growth-share matrix* is really useful only for current products; by definition, all new products have zero RMS and are points on the matrix's right side.[30] The *multifactor matrix* can address risk by choice of criteria — the *growth-share matrix* cannot. And because market definition is often difficult, the *growth-share matrix* does not deal well with fragmented markets; this issue is no problem for the *multifactor matrix.* Neither approach assesses the cost to change matrix positions, but the *multifactor matrix* does address business strengths directly.

KEY IDEA

➤ The firm can use the multifactor matrix for resource allocation among products.

➤ The growth-share and multifactor matrices have advantages and disadvantages that impact the viability of strategic recommendations they generate.

TABLE 12.4

COMPARISON OF THE PORTFOLIO APPROACHES

Comparison Criteria	Growth-Share Matrix	Multifactor Matrix
Ability to manipulate entries	Difficult	Easy
Accommodates new businesses	Not well	Yes
Application across firm	Single set of criteria	Multiple sets of criteria
Appropriate for fragmented markets	No	Yes
Communicability	Easy	More difficult
Criteria	Limited but unambiguous	Unlimited but disputable
Explicit consideration of risk	No	Yes, if required
Grouping tendency of entries	Low market growth/low market share (bottom right)	High/high, high/medium, medium/high, medium/medium (top right)
Implementability	Easy	More difficult
Measures	Basically objective	Highly subjective
Realism	May be limited	May have more
Sensitivity to basic assumptions	Yes	Yes
Sensitivity to market definition	Yes	Yes
Underlying focus	Cash flow	ROI

Many firms use these matrices to examine their various products, communicate options, and even select managers skilled in specific strategic situations. But, we repeat: Each method is an aid for strategy development, not a substitute. Executives gain insight *in the process* of developing the matrices, particularly the criteria and weightings for the multifactor matrix. Some portfolio matrices link market performance and financial performance. Figure 12.5 shows the portfolio for a healthcare business specializing in chemicals and laboratory equipment and how it links business-unit position and pre-tax return on assets (ROA). Firms have also used equipment age, human resources spending, investment requirements, and advertising and promotion in portfolio models.[31]

FIGURE 12.5

A PORTFOLIO EXAMPLE

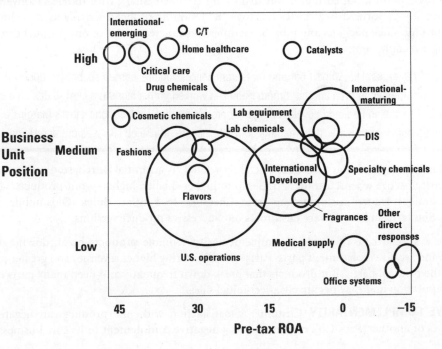

OTHER IMPORTANT PRODUCT INTERRELATIONSHIPS

Products compete for resources; they may also be interrelated in other strategic ways.

INTERRELATIONSHIPS AT THE CUSTOMER

Some products are directly complementary, like razors and razor blades, printers and toner, satellite dishes and program content, and hardware and disposables — as with Swiffer, Opening Case. When each product needs the other, the firm can be successful by placing either or both in its portfolio. If the firm offers both products, like HP printers and toner, pricing becomes particularly crucial. Sometimes product interrelationships at the customer are positive, as in the Bloomberg example, but they can also be negative.

> Bloomberg terminals support the investment community. A Bloomberg executive said: "We surround people with information. They watch TV [Bloomberg channel] when they're having breakfast. They drive into the city and listen to the [Bloomberg] radio station. Then they work on their Bloomberg terminals. Our products complement each other. We always have something for our customer."[32]

POSITIVE COMPLEMENTARITY. In many markets, customers who buy one type of product are more likely to buy a related product — **positive complementarity**.[33] Michelin sells passenger tires and the *Michelin Guide* book. The *Michelin Guide* encourages car travel; when travel increases, tire wear is greater and tire sales rise. Positive attributes associated with the *Michelin Guide* also carry over to Michelin tires, and vice versa. Verizon knows that traditional local wire-based telephone service is declining (but not dead yet!), so it offers customers long-distance, DSL, and wireless services. Satisfied customers for Apple's iPod are favorably disposed to buy Macintosh computers, and Lou Gerstner drove IBM's turnaround integrating customer hardware, software, and services. Motion pictures and derivative products are positive complements; sales of accessory products, like Harry Potter toys and DVDs, often eclipse box office revenues. And at movie houses, popcorn and soft drinks are complementary with movies. Conversely, when Toys "R" Us formed Babies "R" Us, Toys "R" Us traffic dropped sharply as it no longer stocked products like pacifiers and bibs. Sometimes firms increase sales of one product directly by adding a complement:

> HMS Host, the largest U.S. airport bar and restaurant concessionaire, carried six bottled beers. To accept Heineken Lite, Host would have to drop another brand. Heineken worked with a signature chef to design a calamari dish to complement Heineken Lite, and developed a major promotion for Host locations. Host's margins on Heineken Lite plus the calamari dish were greater than margins on Michelob Lite: Michelob Lite was out and Heineken Lite was in.

Sometimes a complementary product is closely related to an initial purchase. Positive complementarity occurs when customers trade up to higher-quality, higher-profit products. GM's historic strategy traded customers up from Chevrolet to Pontiac, Buick, Oldsmobile, and Cadillac. Similarly, many software customers buy successive product versions.

Parts are a special case of product complementarity. Durable products break down, suffer damage, and require replacement parts. Parts sales often bring higher revenues and greater profits than the original part.[34] But products that break down frequently and need many parts earn a poor reputation and may negatively affect initial sales.[35]

NEGATIVE COMPLEMENTARITY. Customer dissatisfaction with one product can negatively affect sales of another. PepsiCo's expansion was a **negative complement** to its core business:

> PepsiCo acquired Pizza Hut, Taco Bell, and Kentucky Fried Chicken for growth and guaranteed sales of Pepsi products. Coca-Cola convinced McDonald's, Burger King, Wendy's, and other fast-food chains that selling Pepsi helped competitors (Pepsi subsidiaries) — they agreed to sell Coke products exclusively. PepsiCo spun off its restaurant businesses.

KEY IDEA

➤ The firm's products may have important interrelationships both at *customers* and within the *firm*.

Marketing Question

Movie theaters offer popcorn and soft drinks as complements. How would you design a new movie house to enhance service and offer a broader variety of complementary products and services?

KEY IDEA

➤ Sometimes one product helps another — *positive complementarity*.

➤ Sometimes one product hurts another — *negative complementarity*.

Before passage of the Sarbanes-Oxley Act, investment banks knew that critical equity research reports negatively affected their ability to sell investment banking services. Professional services and accounting firms knew that company audits exposing financial problems might cut off lucrative consulting contracts. Arthur Andersen failed to acknowledge and address Enron's irregular accounting because it feared such negative complementarity. More generally, spreading attention over multiple products may leave the firm vulnerable to highly focused competitors. Further, negative complementarity at one customer may negatively affect relationships with other customers:

> Tradebank (disguised name) offered leasing products for capital equipment purchases. When customer York (disguised name) had financial problems and missed a lease payment, Tradebank placed a lien on its assets. Several other Tradebank customers did business with York; the lien caused significant problems. Some stopped doing business with Tradebank.

INTERRELATIONSHIPS AT THE FIRM

Sometimes firm products have important internal interrelationships with each other.

STRATEGIC ROLES. Different products may have separate yet mutually reinforcing strategic roles. The Swatch Group (TSG) markets watch brands in five price ranges:

- Prestige and Luxury range: Breguet, Blancpain, Glashütte Original, Jaquet Droz, Léon Hatot, Omega;
- High range: Longines, Rado, Union Glashütte;
- Middle range: Tissot, Calvin Klein, Balmain, Certina, Mido, Hamilton;
- Basic range: Swatch, Flik Flak;
- Private label: Endura.

Each range targets a different market segment and has a different strategic role. TSG earns most profit from products in the top two ranges and less from the middle range. Basic range and private-label products are profitable, but act as **firewalls**. They drive down costs and stop competitors offering low-price watches, thus protecting TSG's middle-, high-, and prestige- and luxury-range products.[36] Similarly, many supermarkets offer private-label products to attract price-sensitive shoppers; Best Buy sells private-label electronic cases and accessories, flash drives, GPS, radios, televisions, and video cables.[37]

In many industries, leading U.S. firms made critical strategic errors in abandoning low-price segments to competitors. They retreated upmarket, unwilling to accept low profits from potential firewall products. Xerox and auto firms allowed Japanese companies to gain footholds in the U.S. Similarly, Nucor and others entered steel making with electric-arc mini-mills and dethroned once-powerful integrated steel firms. Once established, these competitors eventually added higher-profit products.[38]

MULTIPLE BUSINESS UNITS. Interrelationship issues occur with products from different business units when they address (or could address) the same market. The firm has three options:

- **Develop separate missions.** Products from different business units have different missions — Chapter 7. The firm does not *squander* resources by having multiple business units address a single market opportunity.
- **Intra-firm collaboration.** The firm develops processes for separate business units to work together. At J&J, corporate account managers integrated products from several units to form a single offering for operating rooms: Ethicon — sutures and topical products to stop bleeding; Ethicon Endo Surgery — cutters, staplers, and electro-surgery devices; Codman — surgical instruments and shunts to relieve pressure on the brain; Dupuy — orthopedic implants; and Cordis — peripheral stents. When business units do not work together, the firm may miss significant opportunities. Sony was late to follow Apple into

---

Marketing Question

What approach best captures P&G's philosophy of product-line management:

- Separate mission
- Intra-firm competition
- Intra-firm collaboration?

Answer the same question for Marriott. Describe possible conflicts for each firm.

digital music, in part because it could not resolve conflicts between its electronics and content divisions. Bertelsmann had a joint venture with AOL. Yet *Stern*, Bertelsmann's biggest magazine, placed a CD-ROM on its cover offering access to T-Online, Deutsche Telekom's Internet service and AOL's principal competitor!

- **Intra-firm competition.** This Darwinian approach allows products from different business units to pursue overlapping missions. As long as one business unit seizes the opportunity, the firm accepts efficiency losses in product development and promotion. Chapter 5 showed that Citibank undertook parallel initiatives to develop electronic letters of credit for foreign trade. At one point, Citibank Asia-Pacific was selling its system to U.S. customers; simultaneously, Citibank North America was developing its own system!

KEY IDEA

➤ When making product decisions, the firm should carefully consider current and potential interactions with its other products.

PRODUCT LINE BREADTH: PROLIFERATION VERSUS SIMPLIFICATION

Firms often face conflicting pressures for product line size: pressures for *broadening* and pressures for *narrowing*. The firm must trade off these pressures. Since return on investment (ROI) is the operating financial goal for most firms, decomposing ROI can provide insight:

$$ROI = Profit/Investment$$

By adding *sales* as both a numerator and divisor:

$$ROI = Profit/Sales \times Sales/Investment$$
$$ROI = Return\ on\ Sales\ (ROS) \times Investment\ Turnover$$

Competition often shrinks *ROS*, and only high-volume products generate sufficient *investment turnover* to meet ROI targets. Many firms avoid (or withdraw from) low-ROS products, believing volumes will be too low to compensate for slim profit margins. But firms can lower the costs of product variety by integrating information technology into product design, systems, and manufacturing. Investment turnover can also be critical:

KEY IDEA

➤ Firms face conflicting pressures for broad versus narrow product lines.

➤ ROS and ROI measure very different things.

Relating ROS and ROI

FMCG firm PGA (disguised name) faced price pressure from supermarket customer SMC (disguised name). SMC complained that its profit margin — *ROS* — on PGA products was only 1 percent; SMC pressed PGA for price reductions. PGA confirmed that SMC's key performance measure was ROI and that most SMC investment was in inventory. PGA implemented a new logistics system that cut SMC's average inventory from two weeks to one week. SMC's data were:

Current
- Profit Margin = ROS = 1%
- Current investment turnover = Sales/Investment = 52 weeks/2 weeks = 26
- Current ROI = Profit/Investment = ROS × investment turnover = 1% × 26 = **26%**

New
- New investment turnover = Sales/Investment = 52 weeks/1 week = 52
- New ROI = Profit/Investment = ROS × investment turnover = 1% × 52 = **52%**

SMC was very pleased with these results!

PRODUCT PROLIFERATION

Variety in customer needs often drives **product proliferation** as firms add products to fill product-line gaps. Time Inc. traditionally published male-oriented magazines, like *Time*, *Sports Illustrated*, *Money*, and *Fortune*. Time sought growth by targeting new audiences like women, children, teenagers, and minorities, and broadened its product line to include *Entertainment*

Marketing Question

Visit the toiletries aisle at your local supermarket or drugstore. How many toothpaste skus can you identify? Do you think Colgate and/or Crest should reduce the number of product items?

Weekly, In Style, People, People en Español, Teen People, Parenting, Sports Illustrated for Kids, Sunset, Baby Talk, and *Martha Stewart Living.*[39]

Sometimes firms tap different customer needs by offering products in different versions or variations. Common version differentiators are[40]:

- **Access and functionality.** Some firms offer differing versions of information or media products for different audiences based on: user interface — simple for casual users, complex for serious users; speed of operation — slow for casual users, fast for professional users; and access to features or functionality, like limiting types or time of use, or varying the ability to copy or download products or information.

- **Product performance.** Some firms, like plastics producers, make high-quality products for high prices and *degraded* products for price-sensitive customers. Production economics makes this approach more viable than manufacturing lower-value versions directly.[41] The IBM LaserPrinter Series E was identical to the standard LaserPrinter, but contained a chip that slowed printer speed from 10 to five pages per minute.[42] Mathematica offers software as a professional version and as a degraded student version.

- **Time availability.** Package delivery firms like FedEx and UPS offer next-day delivery before 10 A.M., after 10 A.M., and second-day delivery. Publishers initially offer hardcover books and sell paperback copies later. Hollywood launches movies in theaters, then releases them later on DVD or as Internet downloads. Airlines make multiple ticket offers for the same flight; prices differ based on booking time and available capacity.

Firms seeking market dominance in FMCG frequently offer multiple products to maximize display space. They also offer **firewall products** (p. 307) to defend profitable products and deter competitive entry. P&G maintains market leadership in laundry detergents by offering six brands, embracing 53 versions and 122 skus — Table 12.5; Coca-Cola offers Coke in 7.5-, 16-, and 20-ounce, and 2 liter sizes; many firms package individual products, like batteries, razors, and ballpoint pens in multiple-unit packs. Packs may contain a single product type or multiple types; regardless, the firm provides consumers with the perception of greater value.

KEY IDEA

➤ Firms often differentiate individual products by:
- Access and functionality
- Product performance
- Time availability

➤ Implementing a firewall strategy can lead to product proliferation.

TABLE 12.5

PROCTER & GAMBLE'S U.S. OFFERINGS OF LAUNDRY DETERGENT (NUMBER OF PACKAGE SIZES)[43]

Brand	Powder	Liquid
Tide	Tide Powder (4) Tide Clean Breeze (scented) (2) Tide Mountain Spring (scented) (4) Tide Powder with Bleach (5) Tide Clean Breeze with Bleach (scented) (3) Tide Mountain Spring with Bleach (scented) (1) Tide Free (unscented) (1) Tide High Efficiency (2) Tide Lavender (scented) (2) Tide with Febreze (scented) (2) Tide with Dawn Stain-Scrubbers (1) Tide with a Touch of Downy (3) Tide Cold Water (1)	Tide Liquid (6) Tide Clean Breeze (scented) (2) Tide Mountain Spring (scented) (5) Tide with Bleach Alternative (6) Tide Clean Breeze with Bleach Alternative (scented) (4) Tide Mountain Spring with Bleach Alternative (scented) (2) Tide Free (unscented) (3) Tide High Efficiency (3) Tide High Efficiency Clean Breeze (scented) (1) Tide High Efficiency Free (unscented) (2) Tide Loads of Hope (1)
Cheer	Cheer (5) Cheer for Darks (1) Cheer Free & Gentle (1) Cheer Fresh Linen (scented) (1)	Cheer with Colorguard (5) Cheer for Darks (1) Cheer Free & Gentle (3) Cheer Fresh Linen (scented) (1)
Dreft	Dreft (1)	Dreft (6); Dreft High Efficiency (3)
Gain	Gain Original Fresh (2) Gain (four scented versions) (6) Gain with baking soda (1)	Gain Original Fresh (2) Gain (four scented versions) (6) Gain with baking soda (1)
Ivory Snow	Ivory Snow Powder (1)	Ivory Snow Liquid (1)
Era	NO PRODUCT ENTRY	Era Liquid (5); Era Crystal Springs (scented) (2) Era with Oxi Booster (3); Era Free (2) Era High Efficiency (2)

When product proliferation is excessive, costs spiral out of control and the firm loses market position. Motorola lost global leadership in cell phones in part because of a large product line. Fifteen teams of 20 people each supported 128 separate phone types, often with little parts commonality. Purchasing, manufacturing, administrative, and marketing costs were very high.

Product proliferation looks different on the Internet. Shelf space constraints virtually disappear and inventory costs are very low; variable production costs are zero for digital products. Hence, sellers can offer very long product lines. Walmart.com offers 1.2 million skus versus 132,000 in a typical store; Amazon has 3.7 million book titles versus 100,000 for a typical Barnes & Noble bookstore; Netflix has more than 100,000 DVD titles versus 3,000 for a typical Blockbuster; and online music retailer Rhapsody inventories 5 million music tracks versus 55,000 for Walmart. Correspondingly, these firms earn significant revenues from the *long tail* of products not offered in regular stores: Amazon 25 percent, Netflix 21 percent, and Rhapsody 40 percent.[44]

PRODUCT PROLIFERATION AND MARKET SEGMENTATION. The difference between product proliferation and market segmentation confuses many students. *Product proliferation* refers to product variety. *Market segmentation* explores differences in customer needs and developing strategies for market segments. The firm may not require a broad product line to target multiple segments. A single product generates multiple offers by varying brand name, packaging, distribution, and price; the firm secures R&D, manufacturing, and service economies:

- Merck sells *finasteride* as Propecia for hair loss and as Proscar for enlarged prostate. GSK sells *bupropion hydrochloride* as Wellbutrin for depression and as Zyban for smoking cessation.[45]

- Monsanto sells Roundup herbicide to hobby gardeners and commercial farmers. The active ingredient, glyphosate, is identical, but Monsanto uses different packaging, distribution, and promotion, and sets different prices.

- Ricoh developed its copier portfolio by purchasing Savin, Gestetner, Lanier, and other brands. Each brand targets market segments where it is strong — Savin to government and education and Gestetner to hospitals. But the products are identical.

- Some private-label FMCG brands are identical to manufacturer brands, often made on the same production lines.

Generally, product variations do not target different market segments; they just offer variety.[46] Customers for cereals, fasteners, jams and jellies, salad dressings, spices, and even water (flavors, vitamins) demand a wide choice assortment. Sometimes firms provide variety through packaging, like Tylenol in caplet, cool caplet, EZ tab, geltab, and liquid versions.

SIMPLIFYING THE PRODUCT LINE

The late Peter Drucker famously posed the question, "If you weren't already in your business, would you enter it today?" If the answer is no, the firm must answer a second question: "What are you going to do about it?" One answer is to slim down its brand and product portfolios. Unilever reduced its brand portfolio to 400 global and regional brands (from 1,600) — approximately 90 percent of its then $27 billion revenues — and exited the U.S. detergent market. Unilever then sold, reduced support for, and/or consolidated its remaining national and local brands into stronger brands.[47] Firms typically streamline product lines due to pressure from increased competition. In B2C, distribution-channel consolidation and store brand growth are important factors.

Pressures for product-line simplification also result from supply-chain initiatives. **Efficient consumer response (ECR)**, developed by food manufacturers and distributors, drives out excess inventory by focusing on consumer demand-pull, rather than supplier-push. **Direct product profitability (DPP)** uses direct costing to identify a product's true net margin.[48] These initiatives mean less shelf space for many brands and lead firms to streamline their offerings.

KEY IDEA

➤ *Product proliferation* and *market segmentation* are quite different constructs. Product proliferation refers to product variety. Market segmentation explores differences in customer needs.

➤ The firm can develop multiple offers based on a single product, targeted at several segments.

Marketing Question

What was Unilever's marketing objective? How has Unilever performed since brand consolidation? Did Unilever's approach work? Why or why not? With hindsight, would you have taken similar actions had you been leading Unilever's marketing efforts?

Many global B2B firms rationalize product lines. Historically, suppliers' foreign subsidiaries often developed tailored products to meet local needs for multinational customers. These customers now want standard products to execute global contracts. BetzDearborn (U.S.-based global manufacturer of chemicals for treating wastewater) standardized specifications and cut product lines by over 50 percent.[49] Customers for information technology products want standard hardware and software so they can better control processes and data around the world. UPS has a central tracking system for global shipments requiring the same scanning and sorting process in every country. Many global customers ask IBM to send products to a central location, load and test the software, and then *shrink wrap* the configuration for shipment anywhere in the world, ready to run. Both EMI and Warner Music Group dropped large numbers of artists to refocus efforts on high potentials.[50]

KEY IDEA

➤ Beware deleting products without considering all relevant issues.

The firm may reap significant benefits from simplifying the product line, but should make product deletion decisions carefully. Firms often use a single criterion for dropping products — *bottom-line* profits. This is not always wise. When firms eliminate high-volume *loss-making* products, they often discover that these products were carrying a large share of overhead. The remaining products must assume this overhead; their costs increase and overall profits fall! Note the Gillette example and the product-deletion illustration (below), and Table 12.6:

> Gillette's Brazilian subsidiary concluded that its personal-care product line was unprofitable, and divested. Gillette later realized that it still had to assume many fixed costs previously allocated to personal care. Furthermore, without those allocated costs, personal care had been quite profitable.

Illustration of a Poor Product Deletion Decision

Delco (fictional firm) has two products, A and B. Table 12.6 rearranges Delco's traditional cost breakdown — cost of goods sold (COGS), selling, and general and administrative costs (SG&A)— into three categories:

- **Variable costs.** Vary directly with the number of units sold — include raw materials, direct labor, and transportation costs associated with producing and selling individual products.
- **Direct fixed costs.** Do not vary directly with the number of units sold, but are associated with individual products; include salaries for product managers, supervisors, and technicians.
- **Indirect fixed costs.** Not directly related to individual products; include corporate functions like R&D and legal. Delco allocates costs between A and B, based on percentage of sales revenues.

TABLE 12.6

ILLUSTRATION
OF A POOR PRODUCT
DELETION DECISION
($millions)

	1 Overall Firm	2 Product A	3 Product B	4 Firm less Product A
Sales Revenues	$35	$15	$20	$20
Variable Costs	$19.5	$ 8.5	$11	$11
Contribution Margin	$15.5	$ 6.5	$ 9	$ 9
Direct Fixed Costs	$ 8	$ 4.5	$ 3.5	$ 3.5
Indirect Fixed Costs	$ 7	$ 3	$ 4	$ 7
Profit	$ 0.5	($ 1)	$ 1.5	($ 1.5)

KEY IDEA

➤ A simplified product line can make the firm more competitive. But the firm should use appropriate criteria for deletion decisions.

We make several observations:

- Delco's profit is $0.5 million (column 1): ROS is poor; $0.5 million/$35 million = 1.4 percent.
- Delco's $0.5 million profit comes from Product A — $1 million loss (column 2), and Product B — $1.5 million profit (column 3).
- Suppose Delco eliminates its loss-making Product A. Delco's bottom line goes from $0.5 million profit (column 1), to $1.5 million loss (column 4).
- Previously, Product A carried $3 million of indirect fixed costs (column 2). With Product A eliminated, Product B must now absorb these costs.[51]

Firms that simplify their product lines should make product-deletion decisions using a well-developed set of elimination criteria. Table 12.7 lists candidate criteria.

• Availability of new product	• Product elimination effect (PEE) on capacity utilization
• Component interchangeability	• PEE on customer/ distribution
• Contribution to profit center	• PEE on firm image
• Likely competitive reaction	• PEE on firm sales volume
• Market potential	• PEE on fixed capital
• Reallocation of executive and salesperson time	• PEE on full-line policy
	• PEE on other products (sales/profits)
• Reallocation of resources	• PEE on overhead recovery
• Substitute available	• PEE on working capital

TABLE 12.7

EVALUATION CRITERIA FOR PRODUCT DELETION DECISIONS[52]

Sometimes the firm can reverse a product elimination decision, as at Avon. "We have a partial issue when we replace products consumers are used to. Particularly for foundations and lipsticks, and where people have a favorite color. Sometimes we get a lot of noise from customers saying, 'I miss this certain product.' Then we will bring it back and say in the brochure, 'Back by popular demand.'"[53]

KEY IDEA

➤ Sometimes the firm can successfully resurrect deleted products.

Other times firms reduce product lines by divesting, but this approach can lead to problems:

- **Competition.** Divestiture helps the firm refocus efforts, but sale to a potential competitor may upset its plans.

- **Insufficient investment.** The firm starves the product of marketing support and earns good short-run profits. But investment to rebuild the brand may be too high for potential acquirers.

Marketing Question

Think about firms where you have worked or those you have read about. Can you identify examples of ill-advised product eliminations?

OTHER PRODUCT-LINE ISSUES

Now we examine several other issues for managing the product line:

BUNDLING

The firm can sell products as single **unbundled** items; it may also combine products or products and services as **bundled** offers. Typical types of bundled offer include:

- Alternative products and services.[54]
- Complementary products.
- Product plus after-sales service.
- Product plus parts or consumables.

Sometimes firms bundle attractive products with less-attractive products to increase overall sales and profits. Performing arts organizations often sell series subscriptions that combine popular and less-popular events. In **mixed bundling**, the firm sells products both unbundled and bundled. Rooms to Go designs and packages complete rooms, but also sells individual furniture items. Microsoft bundles Word, Excel, Outlook, and PowerPoint into Microsoft Office, but also sells them individually.[55]

Bundling and unbundling decisions are difficult. If the firm shifts from bundling to unbundling, customers may reject less-attractive items. But continued bundling risks losing sales to more focused competitors. Major airlines emphasize round-trips — bundled, but often lose sales to discounters offering low-price one-way fares — unbundled. Weak competition allows the firm to bundle for longer, but it should develop contingency plans for unbundling.

Bundling to Unbundling — Changing Wall Street

Traditionally, Wall Street firms bundled research and trading. Customers paid an *all-included* price based on trading volume. Giant mutual fund Fidelity, a major customer for brokerage firms, told suppliers it was unbundling its purchases — Fidelity would pay for trading and research separately.

COUNTERFEITING

Illegal product copying and brand piracy are increasingly prevalent globally.[56] Counterfeiters and pirates offer a broad range of products including automobiles, ball-point pens, cigarettes, car parts, deodorant, fashion items, medicines, mobile phones, movies, printer ink cartridges, recorded music, soap, shoe polish, software, pharmaceuticals, and toothbrushes.[57] U.S. Customs and Border Protection seizes and destroys about one million electrical items displaying fake safety labels like Underwriters Laboratories annually. In Shanghai, Starbucks competes with *Xing Ba Ke* — loosely translated as *Shanghai Starbucks*, upscale coffee shops with waiters and higher prices![58] In the U.S., consumers can buy equipment for pirating satellite TV signals.

Customer desires for branded products and increasing sales on eBay and other websites fuel **counterfeiting**. British police arrested counterfeiters shipping inexpensive table wine disguised as expensive Rioja Spanish wine. Hard-to-copy features like holograms, special inks, watermarks, and invisible features help authenticate products; Spanish winemakers now attach metallic refractive labels to their bottles, guaranteeing Spanish provenance. The best protection is continual vigilance regarding trademark, copyright, and design patents. The firm should keep tight control over suppliers and distributors and work with local law enforcement, but problems multiply when counterfeiters operate internationally.[59]

In rare cases, counterfeiting and piracy may provide firm benefits like market awareness and trial. Brazil banned Monsanto's genetically modified soybean seeds, so local farmers secured pirated seeds from Argentina. When Brazilian restrictions ended, Monsanto entered a well-developed market. For many years, most copies of Microsoft products sold in China were counterfeit; Microsoft's *market share* was high but revenues were low. Microsoft revenues and *real* market share improved only when China's anti-piracy enforcement grew and Microsoft cut prices by over 90 percent, invested in local R&D, and worked with the Chinese government on software security.[60]

KEY IDEA

➤ The firm should be vigilant about organizations counterfeiting its products.

EVOLVING THE PRODUCT LINE

The firm must address several key issues in evolving the product line: extending product life, improving the product mix, product cannibalization, product replacement, and limitations on product availability.

EXTENDING PRODUCT LIFE. Firms often try to extend product life. We show the typical practice of pharmaceutical firms when their patents expire. Firms in other industries apply variations of these approaches:

- Add additional services to support customers.
- Combine the drug with another drug having a complementary effect.
- Develop new dosage formulations.
- Devise a different method of drug delivery — like patch versus pill.
- Get FDA approval for other *indications* — that is, additional disease states.
- Persuade more physicians to prescribe the product and educate pharmacists.
- Switch the drug from prescription to over-the-counter.

IMPROVING THE PRODUCT MIX. Firms can increase profits by introducing higher-margin products, possibly by replacing lower-margin products. Gillette is a great example — Chapter

9, p. 228. Nissan and Toyota entered the U.S. market with low-price cars and then moved upmarket, eventually introducing the Infiniti and Lexus, respectively. Monsanto introduced genetically modified soybean seed Roundup Ready 2, which offered higher crop yields than its highly popular Roundup Ready 1.

PRODUCT CANNIBALIZATION. To pre-empt (or stave off) competitive threats and/or address new market segments, firms often introduce lower margin products that may **cannibalize** sales of higher-margin products. FedEx complemented air package delivery by purchasing several ground package firms to form FedEx Ground. FedEx risked cannibalizing air package delivery, but believed FedEx Ground would compete strongly with UPS and USPS. When contemplating cannibalization, the firm should consider three important issues:

- **Balancing effects.** A new product entry may cannibalize existing product sales and cause an immediate profit reduction. But the firm should enjoy incremental value from improved market share and brand presence.

- **Fear of lower profits.** When the firm introduces a new-price (lower-profit) product, customers may switch from the original high-price (high-profit) product to the new entry, reducing overall firm profits. Fear of this scenario may generate internal pressures against a new entry and immobilize the firm. Before J&J introduced Tylenol, Bayer Aspirin was so central to Sterling Drug's growth that it refused to introduce its leading European non-aspirin pain reliever (Panadol) in the U.S. This cannibalization fear ultimately led to Sterling Drug's acquisition by Kodak.[61]

- **How to decide.** Many firms make product entry decisions by comparing their most recent history with forecast results after introducing the new product. This practice is incorrect. The firm should always compare *forecast* profits *with* the new product to *forecast* profits *without* the new product. In many markets, some customers want low-priced products. If they cannot buy from the firm, they will buy from competitors. The firm is generally better off accepting limited cannibalization and selling lower-profit products, than losing sales to competitors. Intel's Pentium chips faced growing price competition from AMD — Intel introduced lower-priced Celeron as a *fighting* brand to stem market-share loss.

KEY IDEA

➤ Product managers should address several product-line issues:

- Extending product life
- Improving the product mix
- Product cannibalization
- Product replacement
- Limitations on product availability

Failure to Cannibalize in the U.S. Automobile Industry

Datsun (Nissan), Toyota, Volkswagen, and other foreign firms entered the U.S. with small cars. Because of low profit margins on small cars, U.S. firms did not respond aggressively. Essentially, U.S. firms ceded the small-car market segment, frequently entry-level buyers, to foreign entrants.

In the 1980s, lobbying by U.S. carmakers forced Japanese automakers to accept *voluntary* import quotas. Japanese firms behaved logically; they introduced higher-value, higher-priced models, with greater profit margins. They also started producing cars in the U.S.!

If U.S. firms had successfully entered the small-car segment, foreign entrants would have been less successful, and expansion would have been more difficult. Today, GM, Ford, and Chrysler would likely have higher market shares and better financial results.

Note

Ivan Seidenberg, Verizon CEO, transformed and grew Nynex/Verizon from $13 billion (1995) to $108 (2009). Said Blair Levin, former FCC Chief of Staff, "One of Ivan's greatest strengths is he is not afraid to cannibalize his own business."[62]

PRODUCT REPLACEMENT. When the firm secures differential advantage with a better product, competitors often imitate and reduce price. The best approach is to replace the older product with an innovative successor. Ideally, the firm introduces a higher-value replacement shortly before the competitor's launch. Successful pre-emption weakens competitor resolve to compete against the incumbent. Good competitive intelligence and appropriate timing is critical for managing the replacement cycle:

AstraZeneca (AZ) protected $6 billion revenues from stomach-drug Prilosec, which was losing patent protection. AZ launched Nexium, a Prilosec derivative containing a separately patented compound. Eli Lilly (EL) protected revenues from anti-depressant Prozac. EL introduced newly patent-protected Prozac products — a once-a-week formula and a version for premenstrual disorder.[63]

LIMITATIONS ON PRODUCT AVAILABILITY. Some firms deliberately under-produce so as to create customer value via scarcity. This practice is common in sneakers where Adidas, Converse, Diesel, Nike, and Vans each offer limited editions; Harley Davidson and others offer limited-edition eyeglass frames. Limited editions can also help generate interest in a brand. In Japan, PepsiCo significantly increased market share, in part by offering limited quantities of soft drinks like Ice Cucumber soda; similarly, Nestlé produces special KitKat flavors like Cantaloupe Melon and Koshian Maccha (green tea with red-bean filling).

PRODUCT QUALITY

Product quality is very important to customers and has improved in many industries. Increasingly, any serious competitor must offer high quality products. Table 12.8 shows PIMS results demonstrating that higher quality leads to higher profitability. *BusinessWeek* showed that the share price of Baldridge winners, the well-known U.S. quality award, consistently outperformed the S&P 500 index by a factor of 3:1.[64]

TABLE 12.8

THE RELATIONSHIP BETWEEN QUALITY AND PROFITABILITY DEMONSTRATED BY PIMS[65]

Market-Perceived Quality Ratio	less than 0.76	0.76 to 0.92	0.92 to 1.08	1.08 to 1.24	more than 1.24
Return on Sales (%)	4%	7.2%	8.3%	10.3%	12.5%

Leading firms work hard to produce high-quality products. They avoid problems from poor design by working simultaneously on new products and manufacturing processes. Poor design can lead to customer dissatisfaction and ultimately product withdrawal — *The New York Times* reported that expensive U-shaped bicycle locks could be picked in a few seconds with a simple ballpoint pen. Maintaining high quality is an ongoing challenge for even the best companies. Mercedes, once a symbol for quality cars, had to postpone delivery of 30,000 cars for faulty diesel pumps and recalled 1.3 million cars for braking problems.

Sometimes even well-designed products are poorly made. Historically, received wisdom believed product quality and unit cost were positively correlated — high quality, high cost. The quality movement demonstrated a negative correlation. Waste, rework, servicing and repairs, and loss of customers lead to higher costs. Figure 12.6 outlines four key steps in total quality management.

FIGURE 12.6

THE TOTAL QUALITY CHART[66]

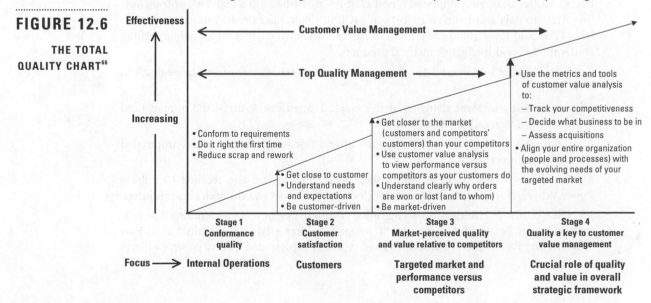

Unfortunately, some firms falsify product quality. Meat Hope (Japan) mixed ground pork and chicken with ground beef — but sold the mixture as 100 percent ground beef. Other food-product mislabelling involves sell-by dates.[67] Product quality declines may lead to product safety issues:

Product Quality at Toyota

Founded in 1937, Toyota Motors emphasized product quality, revolutionized manufacturing, and grew consistently to become the world's largest automobile firm. In 2010, a major scandal arose over reports that, occasionally, Toyota cars accelerated unintentionally, causing more than 30 fatalities. The U.S. National Highway Transportation Safety Administration (NHTSA) opened eight separate investigations. Toyota recalled millions of its eight most popular automobiles including Camry, Lexus, and Prius globally. Toyota even received complaints from owners of *repaired* vehicles.

Toyota was severely criticized for responding slowly to NHTSA information requests, issuing false statements, being late with apologies, misdiagnosing the problem as relating solely to floor mats (accelerator pedals [and possibly the electronic control system] were also involved), and issuing conflicting statements. Some observers believed Toyota's ambitious growth goals and pressure on suppliers to reduce costs and weight for each generation of parts by 10 percent ($10 billion over six years) led to quality declines.

Product Quality at Otis Elevator

Otis had 16,700 elevator installations in the region affected by Japan's 2011 earthquake/tsunami. Most elevators were equipped with seismic detectors that return elevators to the ground floor, where they allow passengers to exit and stay switched off until checked. Despite the enormous devastation, no elevator passengers were injured or trapped.

PRODUCT SAFETY

In many jurisdictions, regulatory bodies like the FDA and CPSC (U.S.) enforce laws protecting consumers from product hazards. Regardless, producers have a special responsibility to ensure their products do not harm customers. Unfortunately, some firms do not behave properly. Chinese firms added toxic melamine (protein powder) to animal feed so as to mimic protein in laboratory tests. Several children died, thousands were hospitalized, and tens of thousands sickened from ingesting tainted milk/milk products. Following legal trials, China executed two producers and jailed fifteen others. In the U.S. and other countries, *whistle-blowers* increasingly highlight safety concerns. Related examples are:

KEY IDEA

➤ Product quality and product safety have critical marketing implications.

- American Airlines continued to fly a Boeing 767 aircraft after finding a mouse infestation.

- Bayer's Cutter Biological unit sold blood-clotting medicine with a high risk of transmitting AIDS to Asia and Latin America, while selling a new, safer product in western countries. GSK paid $750 million to settle U.S. criminal and civil charges for knowingly selling contaminated and ineffective medical products.

- Guidant allegedly sold heart defibrillators it knew might short-circuit and cause death in some patients.

- Hallmark/Westland Meat slaughtered sick cows: Tainted beef entered the human food chain; the USDA recalled 143 million lbs.

- Maclaren USA recalled one million strollers after a side hinge on its strollers amputated 12 children's fingertips.

- Mattel withdrew one million China-made lead-painted toys; it also recalled 10 million Power Wheels ride-on cars and trucks for electrical problems and children's burn injuries.

- McNeil Consumer Healthcare (J&J subsidiary) suffered eight recalls, including 136 million bottles of Benadryl, Motrin, and St. Joseph's children's Tylenol, produced at its Fort Washington, Pa., factory. Management had replaced experienced quality control officers with lower-cost inexperienced employees, and reduced performance standards to enhance production efficiency.

- Merck withdrew top-selling arthritis drug Vioxx because of heart attack and stroke risks. Merck allegedly knew about Vioxx's safety problems, but bullied outside researchers and taught salespeople to *dodge* tricky questions from physicians.

- Mister Donut shops sold 13 million dumplings containing a banned additive.

- Peanut Corporation supplied peanut butter that caused salmonella poisoning in hundreds of people and led to recalls of many peanut brands.

- Snow Brand (Japan) recycled milk through pipes and poisoned 15,000 people.

- Universal Studios (Japan) falsified labels and served beef, caviar, and salami nine months after the sell-by date. It also supplied untreated wastewater to a drinking fountain.[68]

Poor product and/or service design can harm or kill customers. Many motorists died when Ford Explorer SUVs fitted with Firestone tires overturned. Barriers collapse at sporting events, and in many subways passengers can fall or be pushed onto the tracks. How firms respond to product safety issues affects customer perceptions and buying behavior — and product survival. GM and J&J behaved very differently in situations involving death. Restoring faith, trust, and credibility in a damaged brand can take years, if at all:

GM. In *Unsafe at Any Speed*, Ralph Nader alleged that GM's first rear-engine car, the Corvair, was unsafe.[69] Nader alleged that several people died when their Corvairs went out of control. GM denied the problem and hired private detectives to investigate Nader's private life. Nader won a defamation suit against GM — it withdrew the Corvair.

J&J. Several people died when Tylenol capsules were laced with cyanide. J&J withdrew Tylenol capsules throughout the U.S. Reintroduced several months later, with triple packaging, Tylenol quickly regained market leadership.[70]

SECONDARY MARKET PRODUCTS

Owners of durable products like automobiles often resell in the **secondary market**.[71] For customers purchasing new cars, the forecast resale price is often an important product attribute. In the U.S., Toyota gains because its resale prices are typically relatively high. Toyota enhances resale prices by certifying previously owned Toyotas and Lexuses and by limiting sales to fleets and car rental firms, hence restricting used-car supply. Most financial markets are secondary markets; the firm's share price is important for raising capital and measuring shareholder value. Secondary markets in sports tickets — *scalping* — were traditionally illegal, but Internet ticket exchanges like StubHub have driven the shift to legality.

PACKAGING

Packaging is important for guaranteeing product integrity in storage and distribution. But packaging can also communicate information, represent a significant brand statement (like the hourglass Coke bottle), and/or provide convenience benefits. Yoplait is successful with Go-Gurt in-a-tube yogurt for on-the-go kids; and Riverwood's 12-can Fridgepack improved soft drink sales by increasing consumers' cold-can inventories. In India, Hindustan Lever achieved success by selling many products in single-use packages for cash-strapped customers. J&J invests in a special design unit that devises new packaging (and displays) for products launched many years previously.

DISPOSAL: PRODUCTS AND PACKAGING

Most packaging is worthless when the product reaches the end customer. Traditionally, customers were responsible for disposing of packaging and used products — these issues did not concern producers. But governments, particularly in Europe, have passed environmentally friendly laws focused on disposal. In Germany, federal authorities can restrict or ban materials with problematic toxicity or waste volume. Municipalities charge volume-based garbage fees, and using large trash bins carries a social stigma in some communities.[72] A California law mandates safe disposal of toxic materials in PC monitors and circuit boards.

To address disposal issues, cost concerns, and the potential impact on brand image, many firms promote recycling. Mainetti (garment hangers), Van Leer (oil drums), and others recycle products. Because their products contain expensive (and often dangerous) components, electronics firms like Dell, HP, and Sony manage recycling programs as profit centers. Some firms make new products with parts from discarded products. Good examples include auto parts, car batteries, computers, and toner cartridges. *Remanufacturing* is a $50 billion industry — firms can achieve 40 to 65 percent cost savings and also please customers. Fuji and Kodak resell refurbished single-use cameras up to ten times before final discard. Some firms build remanufacturing into their product development processes. Packaging and product disposal are not pressing issues for all firms, but they should be aware of growing environmental concerns and potential government action.

KEY MESSAGES

Managing the firm's product line is a major challenge. The firm must make decisions in four areas:

- **The product portfolio.**

  - The firm should construct a balanced portfolio where some products generate growth and market share, some products earn profits, and some deliver cash flow.
  - The firm's key challenge is allocating resources across the portfolio. Financial analysis methods have advantages and disadvantages. The firm should supplement financial analysis with portfolio analysis, using the growth-share and/or multifactor matrix.

- **Other product interrelationships.** The firm's products may be interrelated at the customer — the firm should seek positive complementarity and avoid negative complementarity. Products may also be interrelated at the firm, playing different strategic roles.

- **Product-line breadth: proliferation versus simplification.** The firm faces conflicting pressures for *product proliferation* and *product simplification*. Variety in customer needs drives proliferation, and many firms offer similar versions of the same product. The reader should not confuse product proliferation with market segmentation. Industry consolidation often drives simplification, but the firm should make product deletion decisions carefully, using well-thought-through criteria.

- **Other product-line issues.** The firm should address many other product management issues, including bundling; counterfeiting; evolving the product line; product quality; product safety; secondary market products; packaging; and disposal of products and packaging.

VIDEOS AND AUDIOS

Luxury Goods   v1202 📹 Ketty Maisonrouge   Columbia Business School

> *Marketing Question*
>
> What other messages did you glean from this chapter?

v1202

QUESTIONS FOR STUDY AND DISCUSSION

Can you answer the questions implied by this chapter's learning objectives? Check!

1. Table 12.9 shows market research data for PortCo's (fictional firm). Develop a growth-share matrix. How do you assess PortCo's product portfolio? What do you recommend?

TABLE 12.9

PORTCO DATA FOR QUESTION 1

Product	Long-run (5-year) Market Growth Rate (%)	PortCo Market Share (%)	Market Share of Leading Competitor (%)*	PortCo Sales Revenues ($ millions)
A	5%	15%	30%	$100
B	7%	30%	12%	$150
C	15%	40%	15%	$ 20
D	1%	50%	10%	$200
E	15%	10%	40%	$ 30
F	20%	20%	20%	$ 40

* If the firm has leading market share, this is the competitor with second-highest market share.

2. The World Health Organization estimates 5.4 million people annually die prematurely of tobacco-related causes like lung cancer, mainly in low- and middle-income countries. Suppose you were offered product manager jobs, with opportunities for extensive overseas travel, at leading cigarette manufacturers Altria and R.J. Reynolds. Starting salaries are 20 percent higher than your other offers. Which, if any, will you accept? Why? What challenges would you face if you did accept?

3. Review cereal product lines at your local supermarket. How do you assess General Mills, Kellogg's, and Quaker? What are their strategies? What recommendations can you offer them?

4. The president of Sony Electronics put the problem this way: "If we're selling a $200 DVD player, we may want to give away Sony DVD software. But that's not in the best interest of Sony Pictures. And Sony Music may want to sell a Springsteen box set for $80 with a coupon that says, 'Get $20 off your Sony CD Player.' Why would Sony Electronics want to do that?" How would you advise the president of Sony Electronics? How would you advise the president of Sony Corporation?[73]

5. Some service providers bundle services — amusement parks and ski hills provide unlimited use for a single price. Others unbundle services, like restaurants with a la carte menus. Prepare guidelines for a service provider making bundling/unbundling decisions.

6. Your electronic components firm contemplates offering a new high-quality device, *Super Great*, to its current product, *Super*. Market research and internal cost data reveals:
   - **Super.** Average price = $25; variable cost = $15; fixed costs = $850,000; expected next year sales = 250,000.
   - **Super Great.** Fixed costs = $1.6 million; variable cost = $20; *Super* fixed costs reduce to $750,000 due to resource sharing. Expected sales at two price points:
     - Price = $30: sales = 200,000. Source: 30% from new customers; 30% from competitors; 40% from Super customers.
     - Price = $35: sales = 150,000. Source: 20% from Super customers; 80% from elsewhere.

   Should you introduce Super Great? If so, at what price?

7. AT&T, Sprint, and Verizon offer many usage plans to address target segment needs. How would you determine the *right* number of plans? What are the marketing challenges of offering many plans?

8. Select a product line in which you are interested. How do the various individual products relate to each other?

IMPERATIVE 4

Design the Market Offer

....

PART A – PROVIDING CUSTOMER VALUE

CHAPTER 13

MANAGING SERVICES AND CUSTOMER SERVICE v1301

To access O-codes, go to **www.ocodes.com**

LEARNING OBJECTIVES

When you have completed this chapter, you will be able to:

- Distinguish among products, services, and customer service.
- Understand why services are becoming increasingly important to firms and customers.
- Identify critical dimensions across which products differ from services.
- Discriminate among different types of services.
- Diagnose quality-related problems and opportunities in service delivery.
- Specify key dimensions of customer service.
- Appreciate the strategic role of customer service.

OPENING CASE: CELEBRITY CRUISES

Celebrity Cruises (11 ships) is a subsidiary of Royal Caribbean Cruises Ltd., positioned upscale of Holland America and Carnival Cruise lines. At 91,000 tons, Celebrity Constellation is a member of the Millennium class with a 940-person crew and capacity for 2,450 passengers. Serving mostly U.S. guests, Celebrity Constellation and sister ships cruise Alaska, Bermuda, the Caribbean, Canada/New England, the Mexican Riviera, Hawaii, Transcanal (Panama), Northern Europe, the Mediterranean, and South America. Celebrity Constellation typically spends November to April in the Caribbean, summers in Europe, and late spring and early fall in Canada and New England. Celebrity fleet itineraries minimize downtime — each ship has a two- to three-week complete dry dock overhaul every five years.

Key officers are Chief Engineer, Staff Captain, and Hotel Director. The Hotel Director is responsible for the entire guest experience, from embarkation to disembarkation. He described how Celebrity optimizes every guest's experience: "Celebrity has made sure that the ship's design and craftsmanship are first rate — from the guest staterooms to all public areas like the Celebrity Theater, San Marco restaurant, and the pools. We maintain that excellence by systematic maintenance on each of our 12 floors. For example, we shampoo carpets every two weeks. If there is a stateroom issue, we can do a complete overhaul when the ship is not completely full. Constellation spends little time in port, so maintenance in the public areas can be challenging, but we keep them at 100 percent with minimal or no guest inconvenience.

"We make an important distinction between port-intensive and non-port-intensive cruises. Generally, port-intensive cruises take seven to ten days — we travel at night, and most guests spend a lot of time off the ship. The routing for this seven-day cruise is San Juan (Puerto Rico), St. Maarten, Dominica, St. Lucia, Margarita Island, Aruba, and San Juan. We offer various land-based tour packages but guests can explore on their own. For 14-day cruises, transatlantic crossings, and some other cruises, we spend more time at sea. We change the on-board activity mix and give guests more options.

"Many guest options are continuously available. We have over a dozen restaurants, cafés, and bars. There's a show every night in the Celebrity Theater — our own Celebrity Singers and Dancers do four shows a week, but we also have comedians and a capella singers. There's a library, casino, Internet café, swimming pools, whirlpools, a shopping arcade, and a fully equipped gym and schedule of classes. On the day at sea from Aruba to San Juan, we have an art auction, bingo, karaoke, shuffleboard, bridge, ping-pong, and many other activities. Then there are special children's programs. We provide guests with many options — they can partake of them or not — and we change them from time to time, based on feedback. All guests have a card that acts as identification, room key, and credit card.

"The crew is the most important factor in delivering the guest experience; we call them Celebrity Family Members (CFMs). We think of ourselves as a family and believe very strongly that happy employees lead to happy guests. We carefully select the entire staff. Agents in many countries around the world source CFMs from the many applications they receive for positions we need filled. Celebrity Constellation has CFMs from 58 different countries. That makes for a more interesting guest experience. We encourage guests to get to know the CFMs they interact with most closely — like waiters and stateroom attendants — but CFMs must not cross the line and become too familiar.

"All CFMs are on contracts, ranging from eight months for waiters to four months for officers, with two months off. Fleet-wide, staff retention is 60 to 70 percent. Our on-board training and development manager puts a lot of effort into training, especially the first week of a contract, to set clear expectations. Many CFMs don't interact with guests regularly, but we want to make sure they behave appropriately when they do. We continue training throughout the person's contract — some about the current job, but also for different jobs. Inevitably we lose people — for health reasons, home emergencies, and sometimes we just let people go — then we need CFMs to pick up different jobs. They can also advance, so we train for the next position.

"There's a lot of management by walking around and a systematic staff-appraisal system. The CFMs work hard for long hours — that's partly the reason for the two-month break between contracts. Each month we give the Shining Star award for outstanding service. We select five CFMs from a host of nominations — the winners earn cash and other prizes. We also make things pretty comfortable; mostly CFMs live two to a room, and they have TVs and Internet access. There are smoking and non-smoking bars, a game room, and exercise facilities. Sometimes our entertainers put on special shows for the staff.

"If we provide a great guest experience, we get customer loyalty. On this cruise, about 800 of our 2,000 guests are repeaters from Celebrity cruises. On European cruises, the loyalty rate is often more than 50 percent. We have three levels of the Captain's Club customer loyalty program: Classic — 1 to 5 cruises, Select — 6 to 10 cruises, and Elite — 11 + cruises. Each level offers rewards like stateroom upgrades, interaction with the captain and senior officers, preferential treatment for

embarkation and disembarkation, and restaurant seating. Guests can book future cruises on board, and we keep in touch after the cruise.

"We use a comprehensive formal system for guest evaluations, including CFM performance — both scaled and open-ended responses, at the end of each cruise. They go to the head office in Miami, and we get the results in a couple of days. These are very important — they are the raw material for appraising our crew and making changes in the guest experience."

Celebrity **X** Cruises ®

Used with permission of Celebrity Cruises Inc.

Chapter 13 is the second of three chapters in Part A of Imperative 4 — *Design the Market Offer.* Part A focuses on *Providing Customer Value.* Chapter 13 addresses *Managing Services and Customer Service.*

Some firms produce and sell *tangible* products like cars, computers, kitchen equipment, and TVs. Much of *Managing Marketing in the 21st Century* focuses on these firms and their approach to markets. But many other firms produce and sell *intangible* services like beauty treatments, information technology services, retail distribution, tax preparation, and transportation. But the product/service distinction is often fuzzy, as many products also have service components. Car companies offer financing, insurance, and warranties; Sony provides delivery, extended warranties, and installation. Further, technology advances allow some products to morph into services as customers purchase the benefits and values the product delivers as a service, rather than the product itself. They may lease (service), rather than buy, an automobile (product); or hire IBM or EDS to support and manage their information systems (service), rather than buy hardware and software (product) directly. Services account for more than 70 percent of employment and GDP in developed countries. Walmart, the world's largest firm, is a service organization that sells products.

Because they are intangible, services can pose a real managerial challenge. Yet well-designed and well-delivered services create customer satisfaction and loyalty, differential advantage, high profits, and positive word of mouth. *Customer service* is a special type of service, a key way for the firm to augment its **core product** or **core service** and differentiate from competitors. Dell and many other firms sell electronic products, but offer customer service in the form of online and phone support.

THE CHANGING VIEW

OLD WAY	NEW WAY
Customer expectations ignored	Customer expectations crucial to satisfaction
Customer service an afterthought	Customer service a key competitive weapon
Customer service separate from marketing	Customer service crucial to customer retention
Low tech	High tech
Management of peak demand rare	Management of peak demand ubiquitous
Mass services, common to all customers	Customized (or personalized) services
Most services provided internally	Many services provided via outsourcing
Narrow view of service	Broad view of service
Products important — services relatively unimportant	Services critical sources of revenues and profits
Relatively narrow range of services available	Explosive growth in service variety
Service performance unmeasured	Service performance carefully tracked
Services and customer service blurred	Services and customer service distinct parts of the marketing offer
Services distinct from products	Products morphing into services

PRODUCTS, SERVICES, AND CUSTOMER SERVICE

> GE is a leader in patient diagnostic products like X-rays and CAT scanners. Traditionally, GE provided after-sales customer service to hospitals and clinics to ensure that products performed well. Today, GE services *any* diagnostic machine, even competitor machines. GE service provides real value — a single source for all equipment servicing. GE even manages all diagnostic operations — including maintaining, upgrading, and replacing existing equipment. Some hospitals and clinics no longer purchase equipment outright — they pay GE on a per-image basis.

The distinction between *products* and *services* remains one of marketing's great confusions. Some people use the term *product* to describe any core offering — including both *physical products* and *services*. We use this convenient shorthand in much of the book. In Chapter 13, we separate a tangible **physical product**, one that can be touched and perhaps kicked or sat upon, from a service. A **service** is *any act or performance that one party can offer another that is essentially intangible and does not result in the ownership of anything.* Or, "*anything that cannot be dropped on your foot!*"[1] Most services concern people — education, medical treatment, restaurants, theater, and transportation[2]; products — car repair, house cleaning, real estate, and retail distribution; or information — financial and legal services, marketing research, and tax preparation.

Fundamental to marketing is a core underlying notion: *Customers do not want your products or services; they want the benefits and values your products and services provide!* Sometimes customers receive benefits and values from a physical product like a car, clothing, food, house, or washing machine.[3] Other times, they receive benefits and values from a service like a haircut, Internet provider, medical procedure, sporting event, or travel.[4] Products are morphing into services as increasing numbers of firms promote the benefits and values their products provide as services (boxed insert above), rather than the products themselves. GE and Rolls-Royce sell jet engines, but traditionally they made significant profits from spare parts and maintenance. As engine quality and performance have improved, customer needs for spare parts and maintenance have decreased. Rolls-Royce offers *TotalCare* (now more than 50 percent of revenues), a program where customers pay a fee *per hour of flight* — a service. Today, firms offer many products like

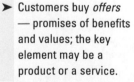

KEY IDEA

➤ Customers buy *offers* — promises of benefits and values; the key element may be a product or a service.

automobiles, computers, copiers, furniture, light bulbs, locomotives, railroad cars, and software as services. Customers lease, rent, or subscribe to products and avoid capital outlays.

The firm can enhance the benefits and value inherent in its product or service by adding **customer service** like delivery, information, repair, sales support, technical support, and warranties. Honda offers the Accord as a core physical product, but also provides customer service before, during, and after purchase. FedEx core service is overnight package delivery, but it surrounds the core with billing statements, documentation, information, logistical advice, order-taking, package-tracking, pickup, and supplies. Finally, a core service for one firm can be customer service for another. Delivery may be *customer service* for your local pizza parlor, but for a chain that only delivers pizza, delivery is part of its *core service.*

GROWTH IN THE SERVICE SECTOR

The service sector of advanced economies has grown dramatically in recent years, making product, service, and customer-service distinctions increasingly important. Services account for upward of 70 percent of total employment and GDP in developed countries.[4] Many service firms now populate the *Fortune* 500,[5] and social enterprises like government and non-profit organizations (NGOs) almost exclusively offer services.[6] Prime examples are education, garbage collection, health and human services, and policing. Rising incomes and age-related demographic shifts are driving services growth. Other important private-sector growth factors are:

• **Customer behavior changes.** Customers preference for purchasing is decreasing. Many consumers want to avoid ownership responsibilities; firms want to remove investments from balance sheets to increase return-on-investment (ROI). Correspondingly, financial services like credit, leasing, and rental are growing.[7]

• **Deregulation.** Deregulation in service industries like electricity, financial services, natural gas, telecommunications, and transportation eases market entry; entrants with innovative strategies fuel growth.

• **Franchising. Franchising** is the backbone of the hospitality, restaurant, and tax preparation industries; leading brands include Hilton, McDonald's, and H&R Block respectively. But businesses like closet installation, commercial property restoration, onsite computer repairs, and window-cleaning are also growing via franchising.[8]

• **Globalization.** Innovations in technology and communications make products and services accessible to global markets. Firms conduct business across the world using many service strategies to meet the diverse needs of new customers.

• **Leveraging core competence.** Some firms find that in-house activities are valuable to other firms, so they repackage and sell them as services. Florida Light and Power, winner of Japan's prestigious Deming quality award, offers quality workshops; Xerox also consults on quality management. Disney offers executive programs in leadership and customer service. Shell provides information technology and other support services to firms outside the oil and gas industry; Amazon's Web Services' offerings use spare computing capacity (cloud computing) from retail operations. SAS trains flight crews from other airlines, maintains planes, and helps Swedish firms prepare employees for relocation.[9]

• **Outsourcing.** Many firms narrow their missions and downsize to focus on core competencies; hence, they **outsource** activities and processes previously performed internally, and often secure better value/cost ratios. Examples include call-center customer-service support, financial transactions, HR functions (benefits, payroll), legal advice, security, technology, telephony, and manufacturing. Outsourcing provides suppliers with service opportunities and potentially higher profit margins than physical products. EDS, IBM, and Unisys design, install, and operate customers' computer and information systems;

Xerox runs imaging centers; and firms like Accenture manage various transactional and transformational business processes.[10]

- **Technology.** Technological advances allow firms to connect with customers and deliver ongoing and complementary services.[11]

CHARACTERISTICS OF SERVICES

Physical products differ from services in several important ways:

INTANGIBILITY

Service focusing on *people* generally requires the customer's physical presence or interactivity; service focusing on *products and information* generally does not. The location for services like factory maintenance, gardening, and house cleaning is necessarily fixed. Other services can occur in various places: We may see a movie in a theater or at home, and receive medical services at a doctor's office, hospital, or perhaps also at home.

Some services like restaurant meals and in-store product purchases are more tangible than others, but the core experience is still intangible. In general, **intangibility** makes customer evaluation of services more subjective than for physical goods. Hence, tangible service elements often play an important role in forming expectations of (and evaluating) the service experience. Service tangibles include equipment, facilities, and personnel.[12] Some firms provide additional tangibility via service guarantees.

SERVICE FACILITIES. Where the firm delivers the service comprises an:

- **Exterior.** Includes the location, outside view, and signage. Provides information about the interior where the firm provides the service; the exterior either attracts customers to, or detracts from, the service experience.
- **Interior.** Has two dimensions:
  - **Offstage.** Out of customer sight.
  - **Onstage.** Where customers experience deeds, efforts, and performance.[13]

The type and quality of onstage facilities significantly affects the service experience — a small intimate theater versus New York's Radio City Music Hall, or servicing your car in a clean versus a dirty and messy facility. The firm can redefine a service by moving offstage activity onstage (or vice versa). To enhance the customer experience, some restaurants shift cooking from offstage to onstage. Although generally out of sight, offstage facilities can provide important clues to service quality.

SERVICE EQUIPMENT. Generally, a service requires physical products: air travel — airplane; haircut — scissors and a mirror. **Service equipment** quality often influences the service experience. Many passengers choose airlines with new planes (Singapore Airlines) versus those with older fleets.

SERVICE PERSONNEL. Some work offstage; others work onstage. Airline mechanics and baggage handlers generally work offstage; ticket agents and flight attendants are onstage. The customer experience depends on how well all **service personnel** — offstage and onstage, perform their functions. Because appearance, demeanor, and manner of onstage personnel offer important quality cues, many service personnel wear uniforms. Bringing offstage personnel onstage can enhance the customer experience. David Letterman frequently brings crew members onstage for his late-night TV talk show. Airline pilots make frequent announcements and often converse with deplaning passengers.

KEY IDEA

➤ Key service characteristics are:
- **Intangibility**
- Inseparability
- Variability
- Perishability
- Divisibility
- Lack of acquisition
- Role of customers

KEY IDEA

➤ Customers often focus on tangible aspects of intangible services:
- Service facilities
- Service equipment
- Service personnel
- Service guarantees

Marketing Question

Think about the last time you purchased a computer. During the purchase, how important to you was the product? How important was the associated service?

Customers have many interactions with onstage service personnel. Jan Carlzon (former SAS airline president) used the phrase **moment of truth** to emphasize their importance. At each *moment of truth*, customers can be satisfied or dissatisfied.[14] Customers make judgments about their own interactions, and about the interactions of service personnel with other customers. Managing customer/service personnel interactions is a major firm challenge. Disney's elaborate training and management program carefully controls employee response behavior so that each customer has a *magical* and consistent experience. Even more difficult is managing customer interactions with distributor and franchisee employees.

A serious concern for service firms like advertising agencies, beauty salons, and those offering professional services is the relative strength of employee versus firm relationships with customers. When the service person-to-customer relationship is strong, employees may resign and take customers with them — Chapter 5. Better company communications can strengthen firm-customer bonds. The firm can also bind critical employees more closely by enlightened contractual provisions that make employees happy but also place barriers to working for (or as) competitors.

SERVICE GUARANTEES. Guarantees about the service experience provide tangible elements of value if the firm does not keep its promises. Good **service guarantees** are unconditional, painless to invoke, and easy and quick to collect.[15] Cort Furniture Rental guarantees on-time delivery and pickup, showroom-quality products, upgraded replacement if substitution is necessary, exchange of any item within two days, and a total refund if any problem cannot be fixed. The service agreement should be simple to understand and communicate, and meaningfully related to the service it guarantees. Good guarantees work because customers have positive experiences with the guarantee. Also, employees improve service quality by working hard to avoid customers invoking the guarantee. Guarantees are most appropriate when:

- Customer ego is involved.
- Customers have little experience with the service.
- Customers make frequent purchases.
- Firm and customer display a lack of trust.
- Industry image for service quality is poor.
- Sales are strongly affected by word of mouth.
- Service failure has significant negative consequences.
- Service price is high.

INSEPARABILITY

Firms manufacture, sell, ship, and store physical goods. Firms deal with demand and supply fluctuations and imperfect forecasting via inventory. For services, provider and customer are inexorably linked — production and consumption are innately **inseparable**. Because firms cannot inventory services, demand forecasting is critical. Crowded restaurants, long ski-lift lines, and standing-room-only on public transportation all result from excess demand. To address supply/demand imbalances the firm must modify supply and/or demand.

MODIFY SUPPLY. The firm can *increase* short-run supply by stretching capacity like working longer hours, outsourcing, renting or sharing extra facilities and equipment, and adding full-time or part-time workers.[16] The critical challenge is maintaining service quality; an upscale hair salon should not hire temporary stylists unless their skills meet the salon's standards. The firm can *decrease* supply by scheduling employee training, maintenance, and renovations.

MODIFY DEMAND. The firm should analyze demand patterns, answering questions like:

- Does service demand follow a regular, predictable cycle? If so, is the cycle length daily, weekly, monthly, or annual?

- What causes these fluctuations — climate, paydays, school vacations, or work schedules?
- Are there random demand fluctuations — births, crime, or weather?
- Can we disaggregate use patterns by market segments or profitability?

Based on the answers, the firm must decide which segments to target — then increase/decrease demand as necessary. To *increase* demand, the firm may improve service offerings, provide better time and place convenience, communicate more effectively with potential customers, and/or reduce prices.[17] To *decrease* demand — demarketing, the firm can offer customers incentives to switch to lower demand periods or reduce marketing activities — cut advertising/promotion spending and service availability, and increase price.[18] To discourage certain types of visitors, some tourist destinations advertise capacity limitations; others emphasize banned activities and inappropriate tourist behavior.

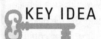

KEY IDEA

➤ Reducing variability is more difficult for services than for products.

The annual demand pattern for many resort hotels has *peak*, *shoulder*, and *low* seasons. In peak season, demand often outstrips supply at standard prices. Possible actions include minimizing vacancies via effective scheduling, raising prices, and switching customers to shoulder seasons. In low season, supply outstrips demand: The hotel may target non-traditional segments, like offering corporate discounts for conventions. In shoulder seasons, effective marketing and sales promotions can even out supply and demand.[19]

VARIABILITY

In general, **variability** in service delivery implies reduced customer satisfaction. Lack of consistency follows directly from human involvement in service delivery. Firms address variability in product manufacturing using quality tools,[20] but these are more difficult for services. Nonetheless, approaches like **six sigma**, a data-driven methodology that eliminates defects in any process, can be effective for service systems.[21]

KEY IDEA

➤ Key service characteristics are:

- Intangibility
- **Inseparability**
- **Variability**
- Perishability
- Divisibility
- Lack of acquisition
- Role of customers

FOCUS ON HUMAN CAPITAL. Employee selection and training are important for improving employee performance and reducing service variability. Treating employees appropriately is also important. Virgin puts employees ahead of customers under the philosophy that "happy employees mean happy customers."[22] Virgin believes that poorly treated employees will not deliver high customer satisfaction.

Sometimes service variability is positive; service providers enhance satisfaction by tailoring actions to individual customers and responding to their needs in real time. To secure such behavior, reward systems should encourage employees *to go the extra mile* to serve customers, not penalize them for innovating or for breaking rules to provide a better customer experience. Ritz Carlton allows each employee up to $2,000 to remedy customer service issues on the spot — no questions asked. Many firms identify and applaud company heroes who deliver exceptional service.

"We seek a highly motivated and skilled group of people. Our corporate culture encourages entrepreneurial thinking, as well as the ability to react quickly and creatively in light of market developments. Recruitment, training, and job evaluation and promotion procedures are designed to ensure we select and treat individuals on the basis of their merits and abilities." — Virgin Mobile

Bob Catell, chairman and CEO of KeySpan (gas utility) regularly delivers appreciation messages to employees whose managers identify their contributions. KeySpan is widely recognized for valuing human capital: No. 1 in Brand Keys *Energy Provider* category for six straight years; top gas utility in the American Customer Satisfaction Index; and *Brandweek's* 2004 Customer Loyalty Award.[23]

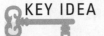

KEY IDEA

➤ Service variability can be positive when service providers tailor behavior for individual customers.

➤ The firm can reduce human variability via automation.

KEY IDEA

➤ Because they cannot be inventoried, services are perishable.

SUBSTITUTE CAPITAL FOR LABOR. The firm can remove human variability via automation like using dispensing machines for cash, drinks, sandwiches, and subway cards. Cost reduction objectives often drive these innovations, but they reduce variability nonetheless. The downside: Machines break down and customers may desire human contact. Some bank customers prefer human tellers to ATMs, and many people object to quasi-personal communication (voice-recognition systems) in call centers; they want human interaction. Do you?

PERISHABILITY

Perishability is tightly linked to inseparability and the inability to inventory services, but focuses on situations where supply is committed but demand is not. Two situations are important:

- **Demand apparently sufficient but unpaid.** Customers agree to purchase the service but default on their obligations. When patients miss doctors' appointments or restaurant patrons are no-shows for reservations, expected revenues are lost forever.

- **Demand insufficient.** As discussed earlier, the firm has several options for increasing demand; lower prices is a favorite approach. New York and London theaters sell full-price tickets at the theater and via ticket-ordering services; they also sell discounted tickets shortly before the performance at TKTS booths in theater districts.

Many services like airlines, hotels, telecommunications, and theaters have high fixed costs but low variable costs. Hence, profit contribution per customer is very high. Coach fares on trans-Atlantic flights are $700–$1,000, but the marginal cost per passenger is minimal — a little fuel, meals, and sundries. Hence, airlines often steeply discount some tickets.[24] But they must be careful that discount customers do not switch from a higher price ticket at a different time.[25] Many airlines optimize profitability via complex computer-based yield management systems.

KEY IDEA

➤ Key service characteristics are:
  - Intangibility
  - Inseparability
  - Variability
  - **Perishability**
  - **Divisibility**
  - Lack of acquisition
  - Role of customers

DIVISIBILITY

Shouldice Hospital (near Toronto) has a long waiting list of prospective U.S. and Canadian patients with uncomplicated hernias awaiting repair. Shouldice does not advertise and receives few physician referrals, but prices are one-third lower than U.S. hospitals. Shouldice has a highly focused strategy and service design with ample customer participation. Patients fill out pre-registration forms, shave their groins and abdomens, and conduct physical therapy by walking and climbing stairs. Assigned roommates have similar background and interests; frequent social activities include post- and pre-operative patients to minimize anxiety. Many former patients attend Shouldice alumni events![26]

We view most products as single entities: An automobile is a single unit, not a collection of components like an engine, seats, transmission, and wheels. **Divisibility** is a key service characteristic; many core and surrounding services comprise a sequence of activities conducted over time, like those at Shouldice. Figure 13.1 illustrates an activity sequence for an evening adult education course.[27]

The activity sequence functions as a service *blueprint* for identifying and addressing service problems. The service blueprint can help redesign service delivery by adding, subtracting, or reorganizing service elements. Many airlines redesigned ticket counters by adding machines for issuing boarding passes — ticket-counter agents deal only with passengers needing luggage check-in or other assistance.[28]

KEY IDEA

➤ Services are divisible — the *service blueprint* is the sequence of activities comprising the service.

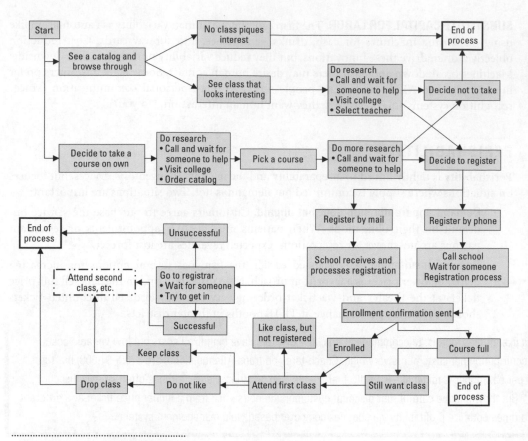

FIGURE 13.1

**A SERVICE BLUEPRINT
FOR AN EVENING ADULT
EDUCATION COURSE**

> *Marketing
> Question*
>
> Think about a recent positive
> service experience. Did you
> buy the service again?
> Did you tell friends, family,
> and colleagues? Did they
> buy the service?
>
> Think about a recent nega-
> tive service experience. Did
> you buy the service again?
> Did you tell friends, family,
> and colleagues? Did they
> buy the service?

LACK OF ACQUISITION

People acquire and frequently own products, but not services. They *experience* the physical manifestation of services like a smoother-running car, a dashing haircut, or a department store purchase. But typically the service is, at best, a set of associations in memory. Yet a service experience can be highly salient, and related associations very influential. Positive associations drive repurchase and positive word of mouth. Negative associations lead customers to avoid the service provider and dissuade others.

ROLE OF CUSTOMERS

Firms rarely refuse to sell products to customers because of the effect on other customers. But customers experience many services in group settings, so customer-customer interaction is a critical issue for many service firms. The drunken airline passenger, the sleeping student in a finance class, and the baseball fan behind home plate shouting out pitches — each affects other customers' experiences. The firm must not unthinkingly believe *the customer is always right*. Some organizations have systems for rejecting customers — like college admission departments, nightclub bouncers, and restaurant maitre d's.

SERVICE QUALITY

In general, high customer satisfaction drives customer loyalty, repurchase, and positive word of mouth, and enhances shareholder value.[29] The converse is also true. Figure 13.2 shows the

KEY IDEA

➤ Key service
characteristics are:

• Intangibility
• Inseparability
• Variability
• Perishability
• Divisibility
• **Lack of acquisition**
• **Role of customers**

SERVQUAL model: Customer satisfaction relates to service quality via **expectations disconfirmation**, **Gap 5** is the *difference* between perceived quality and expected quality[30]:

- **Customer satisfaction.** Perceived service is better than expected service.[31]
- **Customer dissatisfaction.** Perceived service is worse than expected service:

> Two computer hardware firms (disguised) competed fiercely. Firm **A** promised service visits within four hours of a request; firm **B** promised eight hours. **A** averaged five and a half hours; **B** averaged seven hours. **A**'s service performance was better, but **B**'s satisfaction ratings were higher!

Gap 5 depends on four other gaps:

- **Gap 1.** The firm does not understand the customer's service expectations.
- **Gap 2.** Service quality specifications do not reflect firm beliefs about service expectations.
- **Gap 3.** Service delivery performance does not meet service specifications.
- **Gap 4.** External communications about service quality do not reflect service performance.

SERVQUAL identifies a dilemma. The firm may increase short-run sales by advertising high service quality, but if *perceived* quality is lower than *expected* quality customers will be dissatisfied. Yet, if the firm under-promises on service quality, sales may be low. Also, rising customer expectations make it increasingly difficult to deliver greater-than-expected service.

FIGURE 13.2

THE SERVQUAL MODEL FOR DIAGNOSING SERVICE QUALITY

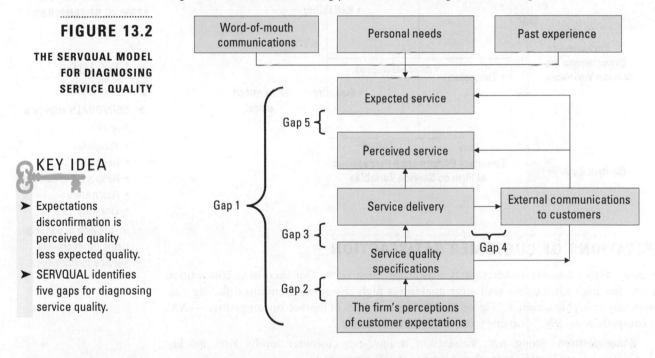

KEY IDEA

➤ Expectations disconfirmation is perceived quality less expected quality.

➤ SERVQUAL identifies five gaps for diagnosing service quality.

Marketing Question

Think about your favorite coffee shop. How do you perceive service quality? Evaluate tangibles, reliability, responsiveness, assurance, and empathy.

MEASURING AND MANAGING SERVICE QUALITY

In SERVQUAL, five key variables influence perceived service quality[32]:

- **Tangibles.** Appearance of communication materials, equipment, personnel, and physical facilities.
- **Reliability.** Ability to perform the promised service accurately and dependably.
- **Responsiveness.** Willingness to help customers and provide prompt service.
- **Assurance.** Employee courtesy, knowledge, and ability to convey confidence and trust.
- **Empathy.** Provision of caring, individualized attention to customers.[33]

Table 13.1 shows the 22-item SERVQUAL scale. Respondents provide service quality expectations data QE[34]; and service perceptions data for providers — QP. The provider's total SERVQUAL score comprises QP minus QE differences, summed over all 22 items. Subscale scores for tangibles, reliability, responsiveness, assurance, and empathy provide finer-grained data and offer action recommendations. Figure 13.3 plots hypothetical scores for one provider: *Reliability* and *empathy* are fine, but the firm may be overemphasizing *empathy*. The firm should focus on *assurance* — high expectations but low perceived performance, and *tangibles*. The provider should also keep an eye on *responsiveness*.[35]

Scott's (disguised name) expensive capital goods were integral to customer production lines; many customers ran factories 24/7/365. But Scott was only marginally profitable. The CEO reduced costs by cutting the field-service force in half. The following year, Scott's service performance rated worst in the industry. The CEO believed the survey results would be bad for morale, so he kept the findings confidential!

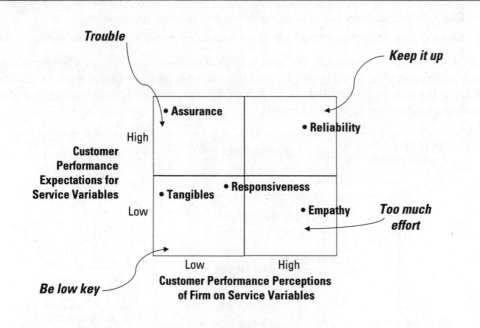

FIGURE 13.3

**CUSTOMER
EXPECTATIONS
AND PERFORMANCE
PERCEPTION ON FIVE
SERVICE DIMENSIONS**

KEY IDEA

➤ SERVQUAL's subscale scores —

• Tangibles
• Reliability
• Responsiveness
• Assurance
• Empathy

— provide actionable items for improving service performance.

LIMITATIONS OF CUSTOMER SATISFACTION

Achieving high customer satisfaction is critical for most firms. But increasing competition implies that high satisfaction no longer guarantees high customer retention; defecting customers may be highly satisfied![36] Figure 13.4 depicts two types of market: uncompetitive — **AA'**, and competitive — **BB'**.[37] Starting from the low/low position:

• **Uncompetitive.** Along **AA'**, satisfaction is low, but customer loyalty rises quickly. Customers are loyal because they have few, if any, alternatives.

• **Competitive.** Along **BB'**, satisfaction increases, but loyalty stays low! Customers have many alternatives and switch suppliers, even though currently satisfied. Moderate satisfaction is insufficient. The firm should strive for high satisfaction by delighting customers with exceptional service.

....
TABLE 13.1

THE SERVQUAL SCALE

SERVQUAL Dimensions	SERVQUAL Expectations Item, QE	SERVQUAL Perception item, QP
Tangibles	1. Excellent_____companies will have modern-looking equipment.	XYZ has modern-looking equipment.
	2. The physical facilities at excellent _____ companies will be visually appealing.	XYZ's physical facilities are visually appealing.
	3. Employees at excellent _____ companies will be neat-appearing.	XYZ's employees are neat-appearing.
	4. Material associated with the service (such as pamphlets or statements) will be visually appealing in an excellent _____ company.	Material associated with the service (such as pamphlets or statements) are visually appealing at XYZ.
Reliability	5. When excellent _____ companies promise to do something by a certain time, they will do so.	When XYZ promises to do something by a certain time, it does so.
	6. When a customer has a problem, excellent _____ companies will show a sincere interest in solving it.	When you have a problem, XYZ shows a sincere interest in solving it.
	7. Excellent _____ companies will perform the service right the first time.	XYZ performs the service right the first time.
	8. Excellent _____ companies will provide their services at the time they promise to do so.	XYZ provides its services at the time it promises to do so,
	9. Excellent _____ companies will insist on error-free records.	XYZ insists on error-free records.
Responsiveness	10. Employees in excellent _____ companies will tell customers exactly when services will be performed.	Employees in XYZ tell you exactly when services will be performed.
	11. Employees in excellent _____ companies will give prompt service to customers.	Employees in XYZ give you prompt service.
	12. Employees in excellent _____ companies will always be willing to help customers.	Employees in XYZ are always willing to help you.
	13. Employees in excellent _____ companies will never be too busy to respond to customers' requests.	Employees in XYZ are never too busy to respond to your requests.
Assurance	14. The behavior of employees in excellent _____ companies will instill confidence in customers.	The behavior of employees in XYZ instills confidence in you.
	15. Customers of excellent _____ companies will feel safe in their transactions.	You feel safe in your transactions with XYZ.
	16. Employees in excellent _____ companies will be consistently courteous with customers.	Employees in XYZ are consistently courteous with you.
	17. Employees in excellent _____ companies will have the knowledge to answer customers' questions.	Employees in XYZ have the knowledge to answer your questions.
Empathy	18. Excellent _____ companies will give customers individual attention.	XYZ gives you individual attention.
	19. Excellent _____ companies will have operating hours convenient to all their customers.	XYZ has operating hours convenient to all its customers.
	20. Excellent _____ companies will have employees who give customers personal attention.	XYZ has employees who give you personal attention.
	21. Excellent _____ companies will have the customer's best interests at heart.	XYZ has your best interests at heart.
	22. The employees of excellent _____ companies will understand the specific needs of their customers.	Employees of XYZ understand your specific needs.

a. All questions answered on a 1-to-7 scale: 1 = Strongly disagree, 7 = Strongly agree.

b. The blank line in the Expectations items is for the particular industry, sub-industry, or department being studied.

c. XYZ in the Perception items stands for the company being studied.

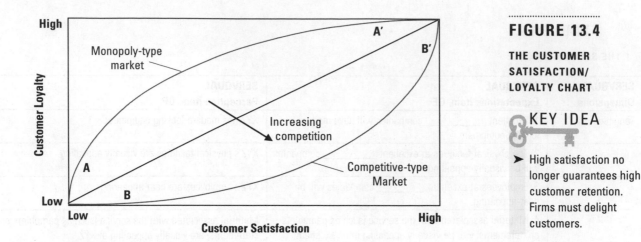

FIGURE 13.4

THE CUSTOMER SATISFACTION/ LOYALTY CHART

KEY IDEA

➤ High satisfaction no longer guarantees high customer retention. Firms must delight customers.

Most insurance firms believe stable policyholders are better risks — *time at current address* is a popular stability measure. Military officers move frequently, hence securing insurance was difficult and expensive. USAA believed *time at current address* made no sense for military officers; they have stable careers. USAA introduced policies designed for military careers, and developed a nationwide distribution system — mail, telephone, and Internet. Military officers are very satisfied and highly loyal — less than 2 percent defect voluntarily each year.[38]

Of course, customers sometimes trade off satisfaction for low price. Discount carriers Ryanair (Europe) and Spirit Airlines (U.S.) receive low customer satisfaction ratings but fill their planes via low prices.

KEY IDEA

➤ All firms experience service failures; how the firm addresses them is key.

ISSUES IN IMPROVING SERVICE QUALITY

To improve service quality, the firm should consider several issues:

- **Customer co-production.** Some firms improve service quality via customer participation in service delivery. Examples include self-service restaurants and self-checkout supermarkets. Previously, FedEx customers tracked packages by phoning customer service representatives; today they track packages via the Internet. Customers enjoy better service and FedEx cuts costs. Nirvana! Some firms promote co-production via differential pricing like airlines, whose Internet prices are often lower than telephone reservations.

- **Improving the offer.** The firm enhances service quality by adding customer service. FMCG firms provide retailers with *plan-o-grams* (layouts) for arranging shelf space. Private banks offer money management seminars for children of high-net-worth clients. Additional customer service is particularly important in mature industries:

KEY IDEA

➤ A drive for service efficiency can lead to inflexible systems that cannot deal with idiosyncratic customer behavior.

Bandag sells truck tire retreads to more than 500 U.S. dealer/installers. Bandag products have no price/quality advantage over competitors, so Bandag offers additional services:

- Helps dealers file/collect on warranty claims from tire manufacturers.[39]
- Offers comprehensive fleet management services to its largest national accounts.
- Embeds computer chips in newly retreaded tires — measures pressure and temperature and counts revolutions.
- Advises the optimal time to retread — reduces downtime caused by blowouts.

Sometimes firms improve quality by removing services! Popular and profitable Southwest Airlines (SWA) uses secondary airfields, on-board ticketing, and non-assigned seats; and has no interline baggage transfer with other airlines. By reducing costs, SWA can offer low fares; high-frequency flights and high on-time performance lead customers to rate service quality high.[40]

- **Maintaining the service environment.** The output from some services negatively affects the physical environment: dirty plates and glasses in restaurants and bars, dirty towels in health clubs, and hair on the barber's floor. Quickly restoring the environment improves service quality.

- **Service performance and information.** Customers want high service quality, but they also want to know when they will receive the service. London's Heathrow Express provides passengers with accurate estimates of train arrivals and departures — on the platform and on the train: New York City's subway has a similar system for train arrivals. In many cities, clocks advise motorists and pedestrians when traffic lights will change. And when customers line up for services, some firms provide queue-time expectations.[41]

- **Service quality failures and service recovery.** Service failure has several potential customer-focused costs — allowances, complaints, liability, loss of goodwill, product recall, returned materials, servicing and repair, and warranty claims. Despite the firm's best efforts, service errors do occur. Some may be *critical incidents* (CI) — extraordinary events that customers perceive and recall as unusually negative.[42] "Our wagons were loaded, but we didn't get a locomotive. When the locomotive finally arrived, we didn't get a locomotive driver. Our transport was delayed for 12 hours."[43] (Of course, some CIs may be positive.) Service failures also happen when the firm's drive for efficiency leads to inflexible systems that cannot deal with idiosyncratic customer behavior:

Jack parked in a lot next to Townbank (disguised name): the sign read, "Free Parking for Townbank Customers." Jack cashed a check and asked the teller to validate his parking ticket. The teller refused, saying that Jack had not made a deposit. Jack explained that he had a long-time relationship at another Townbank branch, including several million dollars in deposits. Neither teller nor bank manager would budge. Jack drove 40 blocks to his regular branch. He told the manager he would close all accounts unless he received a phoned apology by the end of the day. No phone call was made. Jack closed all his accounts![44]

To minimize customer defection, the firm should deal swiftly with service failure and aggressively manage service recovery. Done well, the firm may benefit from the *recovery paradox* — formerly unhappy customers become loyal, even advocates. The firm should address both the immediate customer issue and the underlying cause by upgrading products, services, and/or customer service, as necessary. Failure to fix the cause leads to enhanced customer dissatisfaction on the next occasion and morale loss among front-line employees. Overall, few aggrieved customers complain — they just defect. But complaints are an opportunity to learn customer *pain points* and enhance service delivery overall.[45] Firms should make complaining easier but should follow up swiftly and aggressively:

IBM receives around 100,000 complaints annually, ranging from "My computer won't work" to "Did you think about adding an XXX to your software?" IBM assigns a complaint owner for each complaint: 95 percent are completely addressed in five to seven business days.

Some firms dig deeply to address customer complaints:

Ben & Jerry's (B&J) noticed increased customer complaints about Cherry Garcia ice cream — too few cherries. B&J matched complaints against shipments — the problem was not regional. Manufacturing analysis showed the recipe and ingredients were normal and also ruled out other causes. Finally, B&J identified the problem. The picture on the container was not ice cream but frozen yogurt. Frozen yogurt had more cherries. B&J changed the picture; customer complaints ceased.

Increasingly, customers complain in public, especially on the Internet. They post stories on bulletin boards, Twitter, and YouTube, or set up attack websites: AOL, The Gap, JPMorgan Chase, McDonald's, Microsoft, and United Airlines have all been targets.[46] Some firms employ web watchers to monitor complaints and answer questions. Sears tested a web answer line and received "a couple of hundred" questions per day. It abandoned the effort — too many questions to answer!

A severe ice storm hit New York City, jetBlue's home base. Over six days, jetBlue canceled 1,000 flights and stranded many passengers on runways for hours — a service quality and public relations disaster. jetBlue took several service recovery actions: It quickly apologized and introduced a passenger Bill of Rights, including a service guarantee; proactively made personal apologies to all inconvenienced passengers, seeking opinions on problem causes and fix-it ideas. jetBlue implemented many operational changes. CEO David Neeleman made a YouTube video addressed to customers and gave many high-profile interviews including *BusinessWeek* and *David Letterman*.

CUSTOMER SERVICE

A Glimpse of the Future

It's 6:30 p.m.; Joe is leaving his office. He remembers it's his turn to prepare dinner. He accesses the Pillsbury website; it recognizes Joe's address and queries the corporate database. Joe was here six days ago, and two weeks before that. Both times he wanted data on meals he could prepare with a minimum of fuss. Bet he's back for the same thing.

The computer accesses another database — it identifies popular meals with time-sensitive professional males (research-based). What's on the menu? — Garlic Pasta Chicken Salad? No! He had that last time — on a Saturday. Joe picked it the last three times. Something else in poultry? Ah! Fiesta Chicken. Quick, simple to prepare, spicy — Joe picks spicy meals every time he downloads a recipe. They're popular with males in his age range.

By the time Joe has finished clicking on "What's new in main dishes," an entire meal has been planned — including recipes, suggested side dishes, and even the wine. Joe looks at the Fiesta Chicken page and sees a lovely picture of the dish, recipe beside it.

Now, where is Joe located? Last time he requested data on stores carrying the Green Giant brand along Route 128 near the Mainfair intersection. A quick check of the MapInfo business-oriented geographic information system shows light industry populated by R&D startups. Joe is probably at work — he's going to pick up his dinner items on the way home. A map flashes on the screen, identifying stores where he can most easily pick up Green Giant products for Fiesta Chicken and Pillsbury baked goods for dessert![47]

Marketing Question

Joe's scenario with Pillsbury is feasible with today's technology. Do you regard it favorably or unfavorably? Why or why not?

At the start of this chapter, we showed that core services differ from customer services. Core services like an airline trip or a theater production are central to the offer; all other services are *customer service*. Customer service is any act, performance, or information that enhances the firm's core product or service. Customer service is critical for **customer relationship management (CRM)** — Chapter 2, and can be as important as the core product. IBM did not dominate mainframes because of superior technology or lower prices; IBM's differential advantage was customer service: "You never get fired for buying IBM."[48]

GE Power Systems (GEPS) focused on improving customer service when electric utility deregulation spawned severe price pressure. GEPS reduced replacement time for old or damaged parts from 12 to six weeks, and advised U.S. customers on doing business in Europe and Asia. GEPS provided maintenance staff for equipment upgrades and moved one-third of its engineers from new product development to new service development.

Positive word of mouth follows from great customer service. Financial terminal provider Bloomberg is very clear: "One of the reasons for our heavy customer service emphasis is referrals. The person who's really going to sell you a terminal is the guy sitting next to you, not

KEY IDEA

➤ Customer service can be more central to customer decision-making than the core product or service.

necessarily our sales person."[49] Negative word of mouth can be devastating. Customers receiving bad customer service tell more people than recipients of good customer service.[50] Company-sponsored clubs, like Mac User and Harley Owners Group (HOG), are increasingly important for positive word of mouth. Clubs create strong product affinity, provide positive group experiences, and validate purchase decisions. Sometimes members share experiences on sponsored websites — like physicians reporting experiences with J&J products — and help with more effective product use.[51]

TYPES OF CUSTOMER SERVICE

Figure 13.5 shows the **flower of customer service**, embracing eight dimensions for augmenting the core product or service.[52] We illustrate the information dimension:

CIS, a leading U.S. computer-based information supplier to professional firms, faced tough pressure. CIS' major competitor, seeking increased market share, offered a more comprehensive and easier-to-access database, and annual contracts at 30 percent of CIS' prices! CIS leveraged corporate contacts to provide clients with insight into current and potential customers, and maintained prices. Customer information value far exceeded the 70 percent price differential and CIS retained market share.

FIGURE 13.5

THE FLOWER OF CUSTOMER SERVICE

Marketing Question

Recall when you ordered something over the phone, like a product or airline reservation. Where did the provider do well — billing, consultation, exceptions, hospitality, information, order-taking, payment, or safekeeping? Where could it improve?

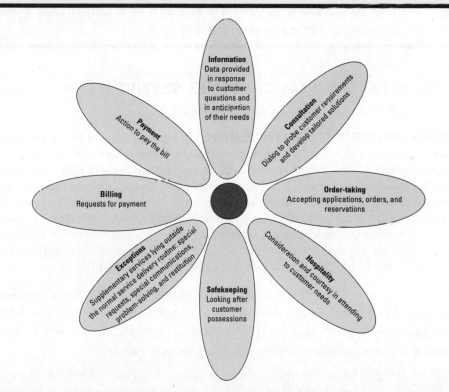

KEY IDEA

➤ Customer service has eight *flower-of-service* dimensions:
- Billing
- Consultation
- Exceptions
- Hospitality
- Information
- Order-taking
- Payment
- Safekeeping

We can also classify customer service by phase of the purchase process — pre, during, and post. Customers have different requirements at each phase; hence, different customer services are appropriate.[53] Of course, first-time versus repeat purchasers typically have different requirements:

- **Pre-purchase.** Assist customers preparing for purchase, including help identifying needs. Also, promotional activities providing information about products and purchase locations.
- **During purchase.** Includes help with selection, customization agreements, financing, personal selling, product assortments, product trial, and quality assurance.

At The Musician's Planet, customers can try out a guitar and make a demo tape. At REI (Seattle), consumers can attempt a 64-foot climbing wall, examine a water pump in an indoor river, or test a Gore-Tex jacket in a rainstorm. Some clothing stores use advanced imaging technology to portray dresses with different styles and fabrics. Levi-Strauss' imaging machine takes precise customer measurements for custom jeans.

- **Post-purchase.** Most marketing activity occurs pre- and during purchase; most customer service occurs after purchase. Post-purchase service (PPS) helps customers pay for, transport, receive, install, use, return and exchange, repair, service, and dispose of products.[54] PPS addresses problems and complaints and includes remanufacturing, spare parts availability, technical service, toll-free service telephone numbers, training, warranties, and websites. The firm may provide some PPS (for some customers) at no charge, but with astute segmentation and pricing, PPS can be very profitable.[55] PPS can also act as an early-warning system for detecting quality problems; hence, PPS raises repurchase rates, enhances cross-selling, and increases customer retention. By tracking buyers after purchase, customer-service leader Pulte Homes doubled repeat and referral business.

KEY IDEA

➤ Customer service differs in relationship to purchase:
- Before
- During
- After

The GE Answer Service handles over four million calls annually for GE's entire product range — from dishwashers to jet engines. Bloomberg provides extensive training on using its terminals — experienced users find it very difficult to switch.[56] Caterpillar has built a profitable business disassembling and rebuilding customers' used engines — Caterpillar also sells rebuilt engines at a discount in the aftermarket.

DELIVERING EXCEPTIONAL CUSTOMER SERVICE[57]

The firm has several levers for delivering outstanding customer service:

TOP MANAGEMENT SUPPORT AND INVOLVEMENT. Top managers should over-communicate that serving customers well is crucial — they should build a culture where all employees emphasize customer service. It's one thing to *talk the talk*, but top managers should also *walk the walk* by *getting their hands dirty* interacting with customers. In B2C firms, they might spend a day or so a month in customer service, like senior Toyota executives when introducing the Lexus. They should identify and reward customer service *heroes* and publicly acknowledge their successes. In B2B firms, top managers should support strategic account managers by serving as *Executive Sponsors* for strategic customers — Chapter 17. CEO Steve Ballmer is Microsoft's *Executive Sponsor* for Walmart; CEO Larry Ellison is Oracle's executive sponsor for GE.

KEY IDEA

➤ Customers requiring *similar* products and services may have *differing* customer service needs, and vice versa.

Nordstrom's is well known for exemplary customer service. Nordstrom's accepts returned merchandise, no questions asked; employees perform above reasonable expectations to serve customers. Top managers and the reward system foster this culture — Chapter 21. Quik Trip (QT) convenience store chain (500 stores, nine U.S. states) trains employees to acknowledge customer presence, no matter how busy they are.[58]

ExxonMobil works hard on customer service. "A elderly woman was parked in the lot next to one of our stations. She had no family in the area, had locked her keys in her car, and didn't know what to do. The store manager had her come in, gave her a cup of coffee, flipped through the yellow pages to find a locksmith, and just paid the guy off on the side because the woman didn't look like she was very well-to-do."[59]

CUSTOMER SERVICE STRATEGY. In developing its market strategy, the firm identifies customer *product- or service-based needs*, then develops a value proposition to satisfy those needs — Chapter 9. In formulating a **customer service strategy**, the firm focuses on customer *needs for customer service*. Customers with similar product- or service-based needs may have very different customer service needs, and vice versa.[60] Wells Fargo did not understand this basic issue:

San Francisco-based Wells Fargo (WF) acquired First Interstate Bancorp (FIB) in a hostile takeover. FIB offered traditional handholding and personal service. WF focused on lowering customer transaction costs, closing branches, and firing employees. Customer service degraded — competitors took advantage. One handed out business cards to customers queuing at former FIB branches. Another advertised for former FIB customers to call 1-800-FED-UP. They heard: "We have just bought your old bank. For a summary of the ways we will be jerking you around, press one. For a list of employees you like who have been fired, press two." Customers outside California defected at 1 percent per month.

Standard marketing research techniques provide insight about customer service needs. At retail, mystery shopping programs examine customer experiences with the firm and competitors. Generally, the firm should strive to surpass competitor service levels. Setting customer expectations slightly below the firm's ability to deliver leads to positive expectations disconfirmations. Because it can be expensive to provide, some firms offer customer service at varying levels. All customers receive a basic customer service backbone; additional service depends on customer importance.[61]

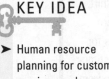

KEY IDEA

➤ Human resource planning for customer service employees requires special attention to:

- Recruiting
- Selecting
- Training and development
- Appraisal
- Recognition
- Reward
- Retention

HUMAN RESOURCE MANAGEMENT (HRM). Human resource (HR) planning — especially for onstage personnel — is integral to superior customer service.[62] Many *front-line* positions, particularly in retail, are low skill and low pay. The firm should develop good HR policies that may include improving work conditions to enhance employee attitudes, and apply them rigorously. Said AMEX CEO Ken Chenault, "Great service starts with the people who deliver it."[63]

When the firm is under cost pressure, indiscriminately cutting customer service personnel reduces service quality; a better approach is cross-training employees for multiple tasks.[64] Traditional recruiting, selecting, training and development, appraisal, recognition, reward, and retention tools are important to ensure a good employee/firm fit. The firm may recruit well-trained customer service personnel (low training costs); or the firm may prefer to hire candidates that meet recruitment criteria, but need extensive training. In Hong Kong, major hairdressing salons Le Salon Orient and Rever operate their own schools, carefully selecting the most promising graduates for their own salons.

Australian chemical firm Orica has a stellar reputation for high-quality telephone-based B2B customer service. Orica uses HRM tools imaginatively. Customer service reps rarely meet customers face-to-face, but they work hard to develop personal relationships. Each Christmas they send greeting cards, photos attached, and a personal note.

High costs lead many firms to outsource customer service call-centers to India, Kenya, Malaysia, and the Philippines. Although well-educated and English-speaking, candidates typically require training in products/services and in speaking with a U.S. accent. Costs often drive outsourcing decisions, but the firm must balance cost reductions with service quality.[65]

Customer service needs drive the knowledge, skills, and abilities (KSAs) that customer service personnel require. KSAs vary by specific customer service, but a general list includes competence, courtesy, credibility, responsiveness, and commitment. Of course, required competence varies widely; compare the average Service-Master (SM) employee (box below) with the GE Answer Service employee who advises on maintaining jet engines.

$6 billion Service-Master's (SM) 250,000-person work force specializes in low-skill, low-pay services that few people like doing — shampooing carpets, spraying pesticides, and stripping hotel beds. SM's training program ranges from enhancing *social graces* to remedial reading. Annual turnover is 30 percent versus 40 percent at competitors.

ExxonMobil (EM) trains gas station personnel at company-owned and franchised dealerships. EM's area personnel make frequent visits to ensure gas stations operate to its standards and deliver good customer service.

The firm must ensure that customer service personnel do their jobs effectively and consistently; a single poorly executed interaction can lose a customer. Significant investment in ongoing coaching and best-practice sharing enhances organizational performance.[66] And individual performance feedback tied to creative and well-designed reward programs can encourage employees to go the extra mile.[67]

> Wachovia Bank's Personal Service Feedback (PSF) process measures customer satisfaction for interactions with bank employees. Weekly reports allow managers to coach and counsel employees on well-performed and under-performed areas. Customer satisfaction scores increased, customer attrition decreased, and shareholder returns increased.[68]
>
> At Vinataxi in Ho Chi Minh City, founder Alan Ho installed a rigorous driver selection program — only 3 percent of applicants passed. Failed, yet determined, applicants could take a two-week driving course and retake the test. All Vinataxi drivers take a personal grooming course. On-duty drivers wear Vinataxi-provided uniforms — white T-shirt, yellow cap with Vinataxi logo, dark trousers, and shoes.[69] Ho placed drivers in teams — high-revenue teams earn bonuses. In Ho's motivational system, each driver is awarded 20 points — Vinataxi awards and subtracts points for on-the-job behavior. *Good deeds* like returning passengers' wallets or personal belongings, and for customer testimonials to excellent service, earn extra points. Ho deducts points for customer complaints and damage that results from driver carelessness. When a driver's score falls below 10 points, he is fired; high point levels earn drivers bonuses.[70]
>
> Madrid's TelPizza (TP) had 185 stores and 40 percent market share (double Pizza Hut's) five years after launch. TP focused on managing and rewarding 4,000-plus delivery men. Each *ambassador* has a small geographic area, so he can get to know customers. Ambassadors spend up to 20 percent of time on pre-sales customer service — handing out coupons and menus. TP rewards ambassadors when territory revenues increase.

SERVICE INFRASTRUCTURE. The firm must design the appropriate infrastructure, like technology and human resources, to support the customer service strategy. Some customer services — like repairs, depend heavily on people; others — like web-based reservation systems, depend on technology. Paradoxically, some highly people-intensive service systems — like airline passenger and baggage check-in, require the highest technology investments.

> France's Supervox (SV) distributes electrical, gardening, and sanitary products to 10,000 mom-and-pop stores in Europe. SV enhanced customer service infrastructure by purchasing cheap PCs — *too primitive for schools*. SV placed PCs at customer locations, complete with web browsers and basic software. Retailers access SV's catalog on the web and place orders. SV confirms orders by fax or e-mail, and cuts order-fill time by more than 20 percent.

Customer interfaces are crucial. Most customers want simple interfaces and a single customer service representative; customers dislike being passed around. Many firms generate customer dissatisfaction by creating specialists (for cost reasons) and making one-stop calls impossible. Other firms outsource customer service to third-party providers, but create serious problems. The author purchased an HDTV and related accessories from BestBuy. The store experience was excellent and an automated phone call provided installation information. But then the customer service experience fell apart: a half-hour spent on the telephone waiting to speak to a human — a third-party installer. And of course, we're sharing the experience with *you*.

Many firms use web-based technological solutions to reduce personnel costs. Well-designed systems — like some airline reservations — guide customers seamlessly; they improve customer service *and* reduce costs. Poorly designed systems can be intensely annoying and highly dissatisfying. Automated telephone systems are some of the worst offenders. How often have you been transferred to out-of-service extensions, trapped in voice-mail hell, or tormented by inadequate voice recognition systems? Consider the message from a $5 billion New Jersey-based firm one weekday at 4:35 p.m. "This is the World Headquarters of XYZ Company. Our switchboard is open from 9:30 a.m. to 4:30 p.m. Eastern Standard Time. In an emergency, please contact

KEY IDEA

➤ Critical elements in delivering exceptional customer service are:

- Top management support and involvement
- Customer service strategy
- Human resource management
- Service infrastructure
- Measuring customer service quality

KEY IDEA

➤ Customer service infrastructure combines the technological and human resources necessary to deliver high-level customer service.

security at [telephone number]." Compare this experience with Fidelity Investments' 24/7/365 service to buy, sell, and transfer mutual funds.

Reporting relationships and customer service interfaces with other firm functions are important infrastructure issues. At global delivery firm TNT, a driver running behind schedule called the control center, which called customer service, which called the customer. By this time, the driver had made the delivery; the call annoyed the customer and embarrassed the driver. TNT solved the problem by allowing drivers to call customers directly. Xerox customers interfaced with sales, service, and business operations. Commissioned salespeople strove to place machines, but were difficult to find when customers needed information or wanted to switch to better-suiting products. (Salespeople were seeking more commission opportunities.) Customer service had to clean up many problems created by the sales force. Xerox eventually teamed up sales, service, and business operations to share responsibility in districts and regions. Districts were responsible for resolving customer problems, exploiting business opportunities, and advertising locally. Xerox harmonized reward systems.[71]

KEY IDEA

➤ Customer defection rate is a more valuable performance measure than customer satisfaction. The firm should identify and measure critical elements driving customer satisfaction.

MEASURING CUSTOMER SERVICE QUALITY. *If you can't measure it, you can't manage it.* Customer satisfaction is a good measure of service quality, but across-the-board quality improvements by many firms have made it somewhat less useful. Customer defection rate is better.[72] Identifying defectors is easy when customers must terminate a formal relationship like banking, insurance, and telephone service, but difficult when individual customer records do not exist. Regardless, the firm should be careful not to rely exclusively on easy-to-collect hard measures, while ignoring difficult-to-collect soft/qualitative measures that capture customer perceptions.

Indeed, analyzing the causes of defection provides valuable information for improving service delivery. The firm should identify and regularly measure critical elements of customer service against performance standards. Differences between standards and actual performance should form the basis for modifying customer service. The firm should also design employee-reward programs based on performance against standards.

Amazon periodically measures customer satisfaction by randomly sampling customers contacting the customer service department. Performance measures include total contacts, cost per contact, and response time by e-mail and telephone. Amazon measures representative performance by customer contacts per day and average turnaround time per contact. Amazon also captures all interaction details about unhappy customers.

AmEx believes *length of time to answer the phone* is an important customer-service measure. AmEx monitors this measure assiduously. Waiting time is prominently and continuously displayed for all customer service operators. Supervisors monitor employee behavior by listening to customer-employee conversations. Other measures focus on time to replace lost cards and speed in customers receiving bills.

Xerox's *sense-and-respond* Sentinel Satisfaction Assurance System regularly emails 130,000 registered customer contacts at 300 major customers, in 12 countries (multiple languages). Customers may reply with a comment, suggestion, or problem. Sentinel enables Xerox to detect, appropriately route, and visibly track all unresolved reported problems.[73]

KEY MESSAGES

- Sometimes the firm's core offering is a service — sometimes a physical product.

- Customer service complements either a core product or a core service.

- Some products are transitioning to services as customers purchase the benefits that physical products deliver, rather than purchase the products.

- Several characteristics distinguish services — core services and customer service, from physical products. Each has important marketing implications:
  - Intangibility
  - Variability
  - Divisibility
  - Role of customers
  - Inseparability
  - Perishability
  - Lack of acquisition

- SERVQUAL is an important diagnostic tool for understanding and improving services.

- High service quality generally leads to greater customer satisfaction, but greater competition and increased quality are weakening the customer satisfaction/loyalty relationship.

- The firm can deliver customer service pre-, during, and post-purchase.

- Well-designed and well-delivered customer service allow the firm to reap significant benefits from repurchase and positive word of mouth.

> ### *Marketing Question*
>
> What other messages did you glean from this chapter?

QUESTIONS FOR STUDY AND DISCUSSION

Can you answer the questions implied by this chapter's learning objectives? Check!

1. Use the SERVQUAL scale to assess service quality for some aspect of your school or college, like the admission process or a finance class. How does your institution rate on tangibles, reliability, responsiveness, assurance, and empathy?

2. The human interface is critical for many service firms. Sometimes customer loyalty to employees is greater than loyalty to the firm. How would you minimize customer defections to departing employees?

3. A mid-size U.S. city wants to address rush-hour problems. Streets are clogged with traffic and public transportation — bus, rail, and subway — are heavily overcrowded. What actions would you suggest the city consider?

4. Select a local restaurant or bar. How could this institution improve customer service and enhance customer loyalty? What advice would you give the proprietor?

5. Many airlines are roundly criticized for poor customer service. Chart out your interactions with the airline on your most recent trip, from the time you decided to take the flight until you exited your destination airport. Identify the various touch-points. At each touch-point where service was poor, develop a system to improve customer service.

6. Select a product/service that you purchased recently, or this book — *Managing Marketing in the 21st Century*. What types of customer service surrounded the product/service? How do you assess customer service quality? How would you improve customer service — pre-, during, and post-purchase?

IMPERATIVE 4

Design the Market Offer

PART A — PROVIDING CUSTOMER VALUE

CHAPTER 14

DEVELOPING
NEW PRODUCTS v1401 💻

To access O-codes, go to **www.ocodes.com**

The best way to predict the future is to invent it.

— Alan Kay, Xerox PARC scientist, 1971

LEARNING OBJECTIVES

When you have completed this chapter, you will be able to:

- Distinguish among different types of innovation for developing and marketing new products.
- Identify critical success factors for consistent innovation.
- Understand and explain the relationship between marketing and innovation.
- Contrast the different ways firms approach the innovation challenge.
- Explain how innovative firms develop successful new products.
- Understand the marketing significance of being an innovative firm.
- Implement the stage-gate, new product development process.
- Understand the factors driving successful new product adoption.
- Classify product adopters into various categories by speed of adoption.

OPENING CASE: THOMSON FINANCIAL — BOARDLINK

Thomson Financial (TF) provides information and decision tools for the financial market. TF successfully launched BoardLink, a product that facilitates information flow between firms and their boards of directors.[1] BoardLink's launch was consistent with TF's focus on informing and building front-end customer strategy (FECS) throughout the organization. The Corporate Communications Broadcast Network Inc. (CCBN), a Boston-based provider of web-based corporate and investment solutions with 3,000 customers, generated the idea that became BoardLink. TF acquired CCBN, formed Thomson Corporate Executive Services (TCES), and supported BoardLink's continued development and launch.

Prior to the Thomson acquisition, Greg Radner, CCBN's marketing head, was responsible for identifying CCBN's next generation of products. Radner leveraged CCBN's traditional customer touch points like sales and service calls to understand the challenges clients were facing. These informal customer discussions, many with corporate secretaries, identified a common pain point — providing board members with information they needed for board meetings in a timely manner.

With this customer need in mind, Radner and CCBN's sales and support teams conducted in-depth informal customer discussions. They sought a deeper understanding of the difficulties firms faced in executing timely and effective board communications. They generated solution ideas and tested them with potential customers. Radner believed that anecdotal findings from informal customer discussions typically had limited value — they often raised more questions than they answered. Radner's new product development team took detailed notes of every customer conversation and shared these data with every team member. This circulation process demonstrated a broad consensus among customers about the problem — it also increased team members' convictions about the new product ideas they were developing.

Radner asserted the core underpinning of his new product development effort was securing a deep understanding of customer needs. "Because this was a new space for us, we couldn't make the assumption that we knew what our customers wanted," he said. Radner's group found that many corporate secretaries were frustrated with preparing information for board meetings, sometimes held monthly. To produce a board book was a time-consuming process involving multiple revisions, often with last-minute changes. Board books had to be professional-looking, but corporate secretaries also had to ensure that board members received them in adequate time for preparation. Said Radner, "We knew from anecdotal evidence that there was significant pain; our question was, 'Can we alleviate that pain?' Because of our strong customer focus, we let the client drive product development, its features and functionalities, rather than letting our idea of the product guide decision-making."

Business school graduate Jeron Paul joined Radner and CCBN's clients in developing the concept. Paul leveraged his personal contacts, CCBN clients, and attendees at corporate secretary conferences. Concept development quickly morphed into concept validation as potential customers became excited at the prospect of solving a significant problem. By this time, CCBN had joined Thomson — BoardLink also generated significant internal excitement because of the potential for organic growth. Senior TF management gave BoardLink the green light, allowing Radner to leverage Thomson's resources to execute on the product concept and move into development.

Radner quickly built a 15-person product development team spanning technology, sales, quality assurance, and product developers in the U.S. and Bangalore, India. Radner and Paul also worked with market research professionals from Client Insight LLC (CI), a market research firm specializing in financial markets. CI implemented a three-phase marketing research plan that included: (1) a real-time concept test with a small sample of board members in several industries, (2) a more quantitative, concept test with a large sample of potential customers; and, once the prototype was developed, (3) a usability study to understand potential users' ability to execute common tasks. Throughout development, Radner ensured that each team member heard every potential customer voice as they gave feedback and interacted with the evolving prototype. Hence, internal pushback to design and user interface changes was minimal. Because the prototype continually reflected feedback from potential users, TF minimized time to launch and optimized development time spent with hard-to-reach board members.

CI made three particularly important findings in developing and launching BoardLink: (1) the sales cycle is long and complex, (2) the original price point was too high, and (3) the product had to be very easy to use. TF successfully launched BoardLink with significant efforts by its small sales force and advertisements in Corporate Secretary *magazine and on the corporate secretary organization website. Within a few months, BoardLink was the solution of choice for board members in 12 organizations. Between 75 percent and 85 percent of the 100-plus board members who signed up to access BoardLink were regular users.*

Radner said BoardLink's success was due to two key factors: First, the strong focus on product usability throughout the development process ensured that customers could easily make BoardLink part of their workflow. "This was especially important because board members have a wide disparity in abilities and willingness to try the product. Indeed, some board members don't have access to a PC. Regardless, we could market our product as 'Director-tested'; by working with customer organizations and their board members, we can drive and track usage of BoardLink." Second, Thomson launched BoardLink at an acceptable price.

At TCES, BoardLink sales teams continue to work with clients and prospective clients. They listen for additional pain points and common challenges across organizations and groups. Said Radner, "Our customers are telling us what our next thing will be, and we're listening."

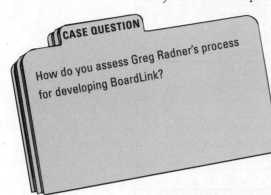

CASE QUESTION

How do you assess Greg Radner's process for developing BoardLink?

THOMSON

THOMSON BOARDLINK™

KEY IDEA

➤ Successful new products enhance shareholder value.

Chapter 14 is the third of three chapters in Part A of Imperative 4 — *Design the Market Offer.* Part A focuses on *Providing Customer Value.* Chapter 14 addresses *Developing New Products.*

New products are crucial for delivering customer value, earning profits, and enhancing shareholder wealth. As globalization pressures drive increasing competition, innovation success is ever more important. Whether developed internally, acquired, or generated from a strategic alliance, successful new products beat competitors and drive growth. Winning firms in the 21st century will have much greater expertise than competitors in **innovation**, developing and launching new products, and providing customers with new and improved product choices. Today, many firms are dissecting and improving internal processes and culture to increase innovation capabilities, and sharpening external searches for new products. New technologies and development processes improve new product success rates and help firms reduce time to market. Both business and academia now pay great attention to managing innovation and developing new products as a critical way to achieve differential advantage.[2]

THE CHANGING VIEW

OLD WAY	NEW WAY
Bureaucratic and slow	Entrepreneurial and fast
Financial criteria only	Market and financial criteria
Functional orientation	Cross-functional teams
Ideas generated internally	Ideas encouraged from many sources
Innovation seen as risky	Managing innovation and risk critical to success
Innovation strategy unfocused	Innovation strategy clearly focused
Innovation viewed as secondary importance	Innovation seen as primary importance
Not-invented-here (NIH) syndrome	Best-in-class benchmarking
Poor risk assessment	Risk profiles assessed
Poor support tools	Advanced support tools, like quality function deployment (QFD), computer-aided design (CAD), rapid prototyping processes (RPS)
Sequential processing	Parallel processing

WHERE AND HOW INNOVATION OCCURS

If we are to achieve results never before accomplished, we must employ methods never before attempted.

— Sir Francis Bacon

The late Peter Drucker asserted that marketing was one of the firm's two basic functions, but:

> ... *Marketing alone does not make a business enterprise. The second function of a business, therefore, is innovation. In the organization of the business enterprise, innovation can no more be considered a separate function than marketing. It is not confined to engineering or research, but extends across all parts of the business. Innovation can be defined as the task of endowing human and material resources with new and greater wealth-producing capacity.*[3]

> *Marketing Exercise*
>
> Select two modern-day successful entrepreneurs. Use the Internet and your analytic skills to assess why each has been successful.

Dell is a distribution innovator; L.L. Bean, Virgin, and Nordstrom are customer service innovators; Apple is a technology and retail innovator.

Chapter 14 focuses on new product innovation and its impact on developing and managing the firm's products. In general, successful innovation provides better, cheaper, and/or faster benefits and values to customers.

Some innovation requires significant R&D effort by highly trained scientists in expensive facilities for long time periods. But much innovation consists of bringing together, in a different way, ideas that are already known.[4] Consider the perspectives of several leaders:

Drucker: "[The best opportunities] are visible, but not seen."

Thomas Edison: "Genius is one percent inspiration and 99 percent perspiration."[5]

Steve Jobs: "Creativity is just connecting things. When you ask creative people how they did something, they feel a little guilty because they didn't really do it, they just saw something. It seemed obvious to them after a while. That's because they were able to connect experiences they've had and synthesize new things."[6]

KEY IDEA

➤ Innovation embraces new products, but also new processes and technologies.

Two good examples are Microsoft and Apple:

> In 1975, at a Harvard Square newsstand, Bill Gates and Paul Allen saw the cover of *Popular Electronics* showing the Altair, a new $400 desktop computer. They related the Altair and its Intel 8080 chip with their experience programming a PDP-8 mini-computer (DEC) in BASIC. Gates and Allen secured the Altair software contract; later they won contracts for IBM and other PCs. Microsoft has dominated the PC operating system market ever since.
>
> In 1979, Steve Jobs visited Xerox's Palo Alto Research Center (PARC); he saw a graphical user interface (GUI) with a *mouse* on a refrigerator-size computer. Jobs realized he could use GUI on a PC — Macintosh.

KEY IDEA

➤ *Sustaining* innovations improve products and processes on existing performance dimensions.

➤ *Disruptive* innovations offer different value propositions.

➤ Leading firms often invest in sustaining versus disruptive innovations.

KEY IDEA

➤ The firm should serve current, especially loyal, customers — the firm must also *create* new customers.

Chapter 3 (p. 78) introduced the ideas of *sustaining* and *disruptive* technologies. Sustaining technologies spawn innovations that improve established products on performance dimensions valued by major customers. Innovations driven by disruptive technologies offer new and very different value propositions. Initially, these innovations may underperform existing products or processes, but a few fringe customers recognize value. Later, as cost-benefit ratios improve, disruptive technologies surpass the old technology and broaden their appeal.[7] Researchers believe that leading firms often miss **disruptive innovations** because they are committed to an existing way of doing business via *cultural lock-in*.[8] One well-respected researcher asserts:

> *[G]ood management was the most powerful reason they [leading firms] failed to stay atop their industries. Precisely because these firms listened to their customers, invested aggressively in new technologies [to] provide their customers more and better products of the sort they wanted, and because they carefully studied market trends and systematically allocated investment capital to innovations that promised the best returns, they lost their positions of leadership.*[9]

Is this heresy? Not at all! Listening to customers can actually lead to failure? Yes! Firms typically design marketing efforts to satisfy existing customer needs. Yet, in a world where change is constant, marketing must also *create* customers, especially for really new products where currently there are only *prospective* customers. Serving existing customers is fine in the short run, but creating new customers is essential for the long run. Many firms focus on existing customers by investing in *sustaining innovations*, but they ignore *disruptive innovations* where entrenched interests may place roadblocks.[10] Because *sustaining* and *disruptive* innovations are so different, when firms pursue both, they should do so in separate organizational units.[11] Relatedly, firms that focus too heavily on operational excellence may have difficulty with their innovation program. As Sam Walton said, "Incrementalism is innovation's worst enemy! We don't want continuous improvement, We want radical change."[12]

WHAT FOSTERS PRODUCT INNOVATION

> In the 1960s, Dalsey, Hilbloom, and Lynn learned that ships anchored outside Hawaii harbour were waiting for bills of lading to clear U.S. Customs. In 1969, they formed document courier DHL; DHL delivered shipping documents days before ships arrived, and other time-sensitive material. DHL is now a major global package delivery and logistics firm (owned by Deutsche Post) — Chapter 23, Opening Case.

Marketing Question

Your CEO has asked why General Mills and P&G are successful innovators. What will you tell her? Use your competitive insight skills.

Firms vary widely in their abilities to develop innovative new products. A Columbia Business School study classified less than one-third of a *Fortune* 500 sample as *product innovators*, but these firms earned the best returns on capital. Three factors were most important for success:

- **Market selection.** High-growth markets stimulate innovation.
- **Organization.** Formal structures to foster R&D efforts; supportive cultures.
- **R&D.** Significant and consistent R&D spending, especially applied versus fundamental.

Supportive factors are in Table 14.1[13,14]:

Appropriate personnel	Idea generators, coaches, mentors, and sponsors
	Boundary spanners for internal/external boundaries
	Product champions/internal entrepreneurs
Right type of support	Top management commitment
	Selective top management involvement
Well-designed system	Multiple new product development efforts
	Continuous project evaluation
	High importance to cross-functional communications
	Measurement system rewards creativity and innovation

TABLE 14.1

FACTORS THAT ENCOURAGE INNOVATION

Funding and business objectives are critical innovation issues. Some firms worry that business units focus too narrowly on short-term profits; hence investments to create disruptive innovations and/or new businesses are insufficient. P&G's Corporate Innovation Fund (CIF) and HP's Innovation Program Office (IPO) are alternative devices for funding innovation teams. Team members from different businesses search widely for technologies to focus on specific opportunities. Innovation occurs in structures like P&G's Future Works or DuPont Ventures. Increasingly, major firms seek innovation both inside and outside corporate structures. Over 50 percent of P&G's initiatives involve at least one external partner.

NEW PRODUCT DEVELOPMENT

KEY IDEA

➤ Critical factors for successful new product development are:
- Market selection
- Organization
- R&D

➤ Supportive factors are:
- Appropriate personnel
- Right type of support
- Well-designed system

Approaches to innovation and new product development are deeply embedded in the firm's culture. If innovation performance is unsatisfactory, the firm's culture may have to change:

In the 1990s, Whirlpool had limited competitive advantages and faced declining appliance prices; Whirlpool evolved its culture by trial and error. First, consultants trained select employee groups in innovation techniques: Most new product ideas were useless and unrelated to Whirlpool's business. Next, top managers urged all Whirlpool's 61,000 employees to innovate: Ideas poured in, but had poor fit with Whirlpool's business. Then Whirlpool added discipline: Ideas had to enhance Whirlpool's products and brands, and went through a formal evaluation and funding process. Promising ideas were thoroughly vetted; businesses had annual revenue and pipeline targets. Whirlpool's culture changed, and innovation revenues quadrupled annually.[15]

New product success is critical for the many firms that introduce thousands of new products annually.[16] These firms often set aggressive product-development targets like: 30 percent annual revenues from products launched in the previous four years. HP earns over 50 percent revenues from products introduced in the previous two years; Reckitt Benckiser earns 35–40 percent revenues from products launched in the previous three years. Some firms benchmark product development processes to identify global best practices, then make appropriate changes in their own processes. Other firms speed development by re-engineering existing systems and processes. And some firms encourage broad employee experimentation by allowing unapproved *skunkworks* projects. Google encourages employees to spend up to 20 percent of work time on their own ideas[17]; W.L Gore (Gore-Tex) nurtures many small projects, often started by employees who convince peers their ideas have merit.

Many firms adopt new technologies for their development processes, like computer-aided design/computer-aided manufacturing (**CAD/CAM**); rapid prototyping systems (**RPS**); cross-functional teamwork; quality function deployment (**QFD**); and conjoint analysis — Chapter 6 Marketing Enrichment `me601, pp. 3–7`.[18] Conferences, executive training, job-changing employees, trade associations, and trade publications all help diffuse new methodologies. The firm may improve innovation processes but standards of excellence have risen and sustaining differential advantage is difficult.[19]

One widespread problem is that product developers are sometimes indifferent to the potential marketability of their discoveries.

> *The New York Times* reviewed the new Chevy Silverado Hybrid pickup. The Hybrid delivered significantly better fuel economy than the equivalent gas-only model but had a much higher price and towed two tons less. When asked who would buy the product, John Turzewski, lead development engineer said, "That is a good question."[20]

The firm can address this issue by using market-oriented criteria in the development process. At BASF, scientists write marketing plans for products they expect to develop. At GE, scientists regularly meet with marketing and business-unit executives to ensure their projects are linked to the businesses. At Philips, research is no longer funded solely at the corporate level; product divisions pay two-thirds of budgets for research projects.

> Traditionally, BMS researchers secured FDA approval for pharmaceuticals and then turned them over to brand teams to develop market strategies. Today, marketers work with researchers early in the drug development process and lend expertise to development decisions.

Four approaches to new product development, each with its own financial return, risk, and time characteristics, are:

KEY IDEA

➤ Product development trade-offs include:

- Time
- Risk
- Financial return

- **Basic technology research.** Typically aimed at disruptive innovations rather than immediate new products. Examples: DNA mapping, finding new chemical entities for pharmaceuticals, and electrical super-conductivity.
- **Applied technology research.** Uses basic technology to develop new products. Examples: pharmaceutical research adapting new chemical entities to treat specific medical conditions; electrical super-conductivity researchers seeking easy-to-make and easy-to-use materials.
- **Market-focused development.** Focuses on marketable products, often by improving ease of use or developing complementary products. Example: pharmaceutical firms developing new delivery methods like pills, patches, or injections. Electrical super-conductivity has not progressed this far.
- **Market tinkering.** Makes minor modifications to current products. Examples: new dessert flavors or different scents for a floor cleaner.[21]

Basic technology research generally takes a long time, can generate profitable new products for many applications, but is risky. Indeed, risk-taking is a given in new product development. When a Google vice-president made a several-million-dollar error, co-founder Larry Page said, "I'm so glad you made this mistake, because I want to run a company where we are moving too quickly and doing too much, not being too cautious and doing too little. If we don't have any of these mistakes, we're just not taking enough risk."[22] But note also comments by Talleyrand and George Santayana, respectively: "Any man may make a mistake once, but only a fool makes the same mistake twice," and "Those who cannot remember the past are doomed to repeat it."

By contrast, **market tinkering** is relatively quick, much less risky, but generally less profitable. Regardless, speeding the process and reducing risk typically improve financial returns for all approaches. From the firm's perspective, these four approaches lead to five new product types — **new-to-the-world products**, **new product lines**, **additions to existing product lines**, **improvements/revisions of existing products**, and **repositioning existing products to new segments.**[23]

The way the firm incurs costs strongly influences the approach to new products. For many FMCG firms, distribution and promotion (for commercialization) may consume up to one half of product development budgets — hence, much market tinkering and market-focused development. By contrast, many B2B products like commercial airplanes and other durable goods incur most costs in actual product development — hence, greater focus on basic and applied technology research. When approaching new product development, marketers should think carefully about several areas:

- **Problem focus.** New product development should address important customer needs. Customers trying to solve problems provide tangible evidence of real needs. Furthermore, supply-chain entities like distributors, wholesalers, and resellers may provide insightful *voice-of-the-customer* perspectives. The firm should also be aware of the costs to customers of switching from the firm's current products.

- **Market knowledge.** Market knowledge is always valuable. Sometimes innovative firms ignore market information and overestimate the value of technological novelty. Regardless, the firm should treat data cautiously. Although customers typically provide data to be helpful, sometimes their contributions have little value — especially for *really new products*. As Henry Ford and Steve Jobs said, respectively, "If I'd asked people what they wanted, they would have asked for a better horse!" and "A lot of times people don't know what they want until you show it to them."[24]

- **Firm competence.** A new product must be made, distributed, sold, and serviced. The firm must possess (or acquire) the appropriate competencies.[25]

- **Complementer products.** During product development, the firm should consider complementer products. When initially launched, Microsoft's Vista lacked drivers for many printers, scanners, and other peripherals; hence they did not work.

- **Effectiveness measures.** The firm should measure the effectiveness of its new product development process; three types of measure are relevant:
  - *Inputs* — R&D spending, number of projects in active development
  - *Intermediates* — percent of idea/concepts commercialized, time/cost budgets versus actuals
  - *Outputs* — revenue growth, percent of sales from new products — see also Chapter 22.

  Specifically, the firm should isolate where it performs well in new product development and where it performs poorly. Intuit CEO Steve Bennett identified great idea generation but poor ability to choose ideas to pursue. P&G CEO Art Laffley evolved a not-invented-here (NIH) organization into one that actively and successfully sources ideas outside the firm.[26]

KEY IDEA

➤ Four new product development approaches are:
- Basic technology research
- Applied technology research
- Market-focused development
- Market tinkering

Marketing Question

Using the four approaches to new product development, how would you classify Apple's iPod, a new MP3 player from Sony, the BlackBerry, Coke Zero, Starbucks Frappuccino, *The Apprentice*, *The Apprentice: Martha Stewart*? Why?

- **Stage-gate process (next section).** Successful new product development requires tough go/no go decisions at several stages in the process. The firm requires product champions that bring enthusiasm to projects, but should beware a collective belief in ultimate success that blinds it to setbacks. The firm may need an exit champion to stop failing projects from consuming excessive resources.[27]

The Stage-Gate Process for New Product Development

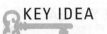
The **stage-gate process** is a systematic way of generating, then pruning, a large number of ideas into a small number of products the firm successfully launches. Figure 14.1 shows a *gate* after each *stage* where the firm must make a go/no-go decision.[28] At each gate, two errors are possible:

TYPE I ERROR. Investing in a project that ultimately fails; these errors occur when such a project is allowed to move from one stage to the next. All firms make Type I errors. Type I errors at the commercialization stage include a host of dotcom failures like Pets.com and Webvan; business-class-only airlines like Eos, Maxjet, and Silverjet; and GM Saturn brand automobiles.

TYPE II ERROR. Rejecting a project that would have succeeded. These errors are difficult to isolate as, typically, the firm cannot know the results from investments that didn't happen! Sometimes we gain insight from independent inventors; examples include:

- Beatles — rejected by Decca Recording Company
- Cellular telephony — not exploited by AT&T
- Personal computers — initially rejected by Atari and HP
- Telephone — rejected by Western Union
- Xerography — rejected by IBM, GE, and Eastman Kodak

FIGURE 14.1

THE STAGE-GATE NEW PRODUCT DEVELOPMENT PROCESS

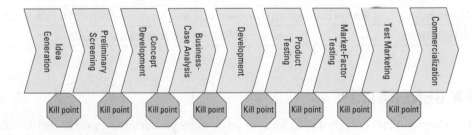

Firms that minimize **Type I errors** accept only the safest alternatives. Failure is low, but developing products with significant financial returns is unlikely. Firms that minimize **Type II errors** develop many products that fail, but some may succeed. The firm must balance these two error types in setting criteria for passing through each *gate*. Type I errors are ultimately highly visible and measurable. Type II errors are more difficult to identify, but are no less real!

Figure 14.2 shows that resource commitments increase dramatically as a project moves from idea to new product launch. Dismissing an idea is inexpensive, but the costs of a failed launch are substantial. Each *gate* is a place to stop, a **kill point**. The firm should clearly specify criteria for each *gate*; only projects that meet the criteria pass though the *gate* and enter the following *stage* — Table 14.2. Since each subsequent stage typically involves greater investment and risk, projects should not pass kill points lightly.[29]

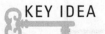

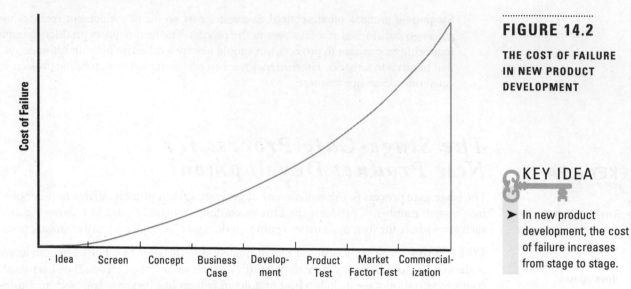

FIGURE 14.2

THE COST OF FAILURE IN NEW PRODUCT DEVELOPMENT

KEY IDEA

➤ In new product development, the cost of failure increases from stage to stage.

Stage in the Process	Typical Criteria
Idea generation	Provides incremental customer value; makes sense as a potential product
Preliminary screening	Technologically feasible; likely market need; fits with firm strategy
Concept development	Well-defined product concept; continues to meet previous criteria
Business-case analysis	Fits firm strategy; coherent business plan; forecasts meet market and financial goals
Development	Fulfills concept definition
Product testing	Performs as planned in business-case analysis
Market-factor testing	Customer attitudes and purchasing as anticipated in business-case analysis
Test marketing	Positive customer response; revenues, market position, and profitability as anticipated
Commercialization	Revenues, market position, and profitability as anticipated

TABLE 14.2

TYPES OF CRITERIA FOR MOVING FROM ONE STAGE TO ANOTHER IN THE STAGE-GATE PROCESS

IDEA GENERATION

It takes a large number of high-quality ideas to create a new product development portfolio that drives long-term growth. Customers are often a good source of new product ideas, but the firm should use any possible idea source — Hyatt.[30] The firm should document and assess the most promising ideas. Typically, the firm quickly discards many ideas, but discarded ideas may help generate others with greater promise.

> In 1957, Jay Pritzker waited for a flight at Los Angeles International Airport. He noticed that Fat Eddie's coffee shop, in Hyatt Von Dehn's hotel, was unusually busy and the hotel had no vacancies. Pritzker bet that executives would want to stay in quality hotels near large airports. He wrote out a $2.2 million offer for the hotel on a napkin. In 2012, Global Hyatt Corporation owned, operated, managed, or franchised 365 hotels and resorts in 45 countries.

NUMBER OF IDEAS

Firms that generate only a few marginal-quality ideas have few new product successes. Successful firms eliminate many ideas during the development process. Hence, they must identify a large number of ideas to find the one idea that produces a successful product. In many studies, the average ratio of new product ideas to successful products is about 100:1; in agricultural chemicals the ratio is 10,000:1. Figure 14.3 shows *universal* success data for substantially new products.

FIGURE 14.3

UNIVERSAL INDUSTRIAL SUCCESS DATA FOR SUBSTANTIALLY NEW PRODUCTS[31]

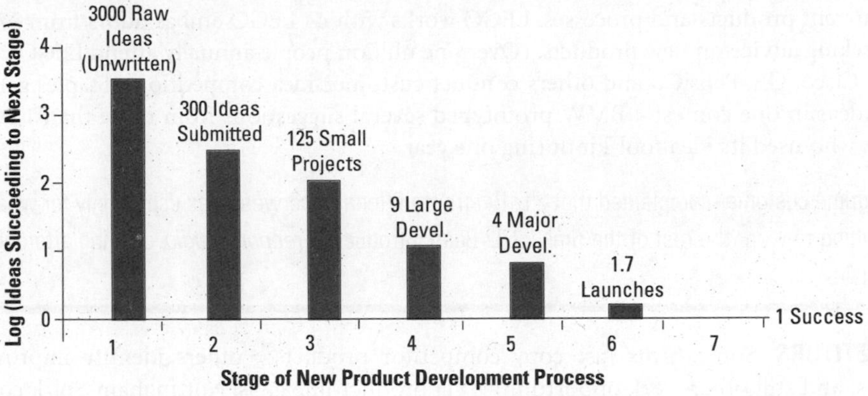

Stage of New Product Development Process

SCOPE OF SEARCH

Focused search within the firm's mission (Chapter 7) typically generates better ideas than unfocused search. (Whirlpool boxed insert, p. 348.)[32] As the firm's mission evolves, so should its scope of search.

> Most ski resorts focus resources on ski hills. But skiers and snowboarders spend only 20 percent of their time on the hill; the rest is spent in restaurants, après-ski bars, and shops. Vail Resorts (Colorado) understands; Vail manages six hotels, 72 restaurants, 40 shops, and more than 13,000 condominiums, in addition to its ski slopes.

NEW IDEA SOURCES[33]

The firm should secure ideas from many sources, both inside and outside the organization. The firm must resist the *not-invented-here* (NIH) syndrome that denigrates ideas from outside sources. P&G embraces a *reapplied-with-pride* (RWP) approach via its successful *Connect and Develop* program. P&G deploys 70 *technology entrepreneurs* globally to participate in external networks, seek ideas, and generate innovations from outside the firm.[34] Specific sources include:

INTERNAL GENERATION. R&D is often a major idea source. Success rates depend on factors like budget and type of people hired, and motivations. Kellogg's Institute for Food and Nutrition Research invests heavily in food laboratories and restaurant-quality kitchens. Researchers are diverse in education and training (from 22 countries). They are also very productive; in one month they generated 65 new product concepts and 94 new packaging ideas.

The sales force, customer service, and manufacturing and operations also generate new product ideas. Many firms conduct employee competitions[35]; in one competition, Cisco received 1,100 submissions from 104 countries. Some firms form employee brainstorming groups (below); Best Buy Studio (web design consulting for small business) resulted from putting four groups of salespeople into an apartment complex for 10 weeks. Starbucks developed 15th Ave. Coffee & Tea when CEO Howard Schultz challenged an employee group to open a store to compete with Starbucks. Some firms even offer employees seed capital to pursue their own ideas. The *GameChanger* panel at Shell's Exploration and Production division can allocate $20 million to unconventional business ideas. In three years, the process generated 300 ideas, some for entirely new businesses; most did not surface in the conventional management system.[36]

Multinational firms may take successful ideas from one country and implement them in others. Häagen-Dazs Argentina added a new flavor, *dulce de leche*, in its single Buenos Aires store. *Dulce de leche* became the store's leading seller, and Häagen-Dazs rolled it out globally.

KEY IDEA

➤ New product development stages are:
- **Idea generation**
- Preliminary screening
- Concept development
- Business-case analysis
- Development
- Product testing
- Market-factor testing
- Test marketing
- Commercialization

CUSTOMERS. In some industries, many key innovations start with customers. Kraft used insight from customer focus groups to launch new variations of Oreo cookies. Sometimes firm employees spend time with customers to observe their likes, dislikes, difficulties, and *pain points* with current products and processes. LEGO works with 44 LEGO ambassadors from 27 countries seeking advice on new products. (Over one million people annually attend LEGO conventions.) Cisco, GE, PepsiCo and others conduct customer-idea competitions: Staples generated 8,300 ideas in one contest[37]; BMW prototyped several suggestions from more than 1,000 customers who used its idea tool-kit during one year.

> A longtime customer complained that L.L. Bean's traditional outerwear was useful only for weekends: "I need something to wear the rest of the time." L.L. Bean introduced *Freeport Studio*, offering affordability, low maintenance, and style.

COMPETITORS. Some firms just copy competitor products[38]; others identify improvement options; and still others seek opportunities via product-line gaps. Nottingham-Spirk conducts Walmart reconnaissance trips looking for product category omissions. One such trip led to the development of P&G's highly successful Crest SpinBrush.

INDEPENDENT INVENTORS. These persons can be a vital source of ideas. Inventors and outside firms now provide 35 percent of P&G's new product ideas. Table 14.3 shows some **independent inventors** and the ideas they successfully developed and marketed.

Product Innovation	Circumstances of Creative Recognition
Kitty Litter 1947	Kaye Draper's cat sandbox froze. Neighbor Edward Lowe gave her kiln-dried, highly absorbent, granulated clay his father sold to mop up grease spills. Kaye returned for more. Then Lowe marked five-pound bags of *Kitty Litter* and sold them through a local pet shop at 65 cents per bag (versus sand @ 1 cent per pound).
Velcro 1948	Swiss engineer George de Mestral saw a connection between burrs sticking on clothing and a new way of fastening.
Zebco late 1940s	Fisherman R.D. Hull knew the *backlash* problem — the spool turned faster than the fishing line. A grocery clerk pulling string from a spool to wrap meat gave him the idea for an improved fishing reel. Zebco has sold over 300 million reels based on Hull's prototype.
Matchbox Toys 1952	In 1952, Jack Odell of Lesney (small London die-casters) made a small brass road roller for his daughter — friends were envious. In 1953, Lesney sold one million miniature versions of Queen Elizabeth II's coronation coach. Lesney expanded into cars, and by 1962 was making 50 million annually — 1/64th size. Mattel now makes Matchbox Toys.
Gang-Nail Plate early 1950s	John Calvin Jureit imagined the Gang-Nail plate (GNP) in church while meditating; he named it in the shower. The GNP, made of galvanized steel, is machine-pressed into two adjoining pieces of wood, typically in a roof truss. The GNP transformed home building.
Dental Implants mid-1960s	Swedish researcher Dr. Per-Ingvar Branemark discovered, serendipitously, that titanium fused to bone. This discovery led to modern-day dental implants.
Gatorade 1965	A University of Florida football coach asked why players didn't urinate after games. J Robert Cade developed a drink to rehydrate athletes, replenish carbohydrates, and was drinkable.
Cuisinart 1971	At a French cookery show, Carl Sontheimer saw an ungainly but versatile machine for processing food in restaurants. This idea led to his Cuisinart invention for the home.
Nike early 1970s	University of Oregon track coach Bill Bowerman developed a running-shoe outsole by pouring rubber compound into his wife's waffle iron. From this experiment, Bowerman and athlete Phil Knight formed Nike.
SuperSoaker water gun, 1982	Aerospace engineer Lonnie G. Johnson conceived the SuperSoaker water gun at home while working on a different project. When he compressed air into a separate chamber, water squirted at far greater velocities than traditional water guns.

TABLE 14.3

EXAMPLES OF IDEAS TURNED INTO PRODUCTS BY INDEPENDENT INVENTORS

Marketing Exercise

Four Wharton graduates founded Warby Parker (WP), an Internet eyewear retailer. WP operates through a mail-order, home-trial program. Get together with a few classmates; can you generate some new product ideas on which to found a business?

TABLE 14.3

CONTINUED

Product Innovation	Circumstances of Creative Recognition
PowerBar 1986	World-ranked marathoner Brian Maxwell had a stomach ailment near the end of a race. Maxwell mixed low-fat, easily digestible potions in his kitchen, then worked with a bio-chemist and food scientist to produce PowerBar. In 2000, he sold to Nestlé for $375 million.
Nature Boy & Girl diapers late 1990s	Swedish mother and lawyer Marlene Sandberg quit her job to launch environmentally friendly diapers — 70 percent biodegradable (versus 20-30 percent for regular diapers). By 2002, *Nature Boy & Girl* diapers gained 1 percent of the Swedish and British markets.

In addition to employee and customer contests (above), some firms harness the power of independent innovators to generate new product ideas. Using a sharing approach, Cisco received 1,200 distinct ideas from 2,500 innovators in 104 countries.[39]

Netflix awarded a $1 million prize for improving its movie-recommendation system. Thousands of teams (more than 50,000 people) from 186 nations took part. Toward the contest conclusion, many teams merged in an attempt to improve performance. Netflix CEO Reed Hastings termed the contest a great success.[40]

3M is well known for its systematic approach to idea generation. 3M identifies **lead users** — individuals and organizations who think up (and may even prototype) products before producers. 3M secures these inventions, completes development, and markets the products[41]:

3M focused development effort on surgical drapes — thin adhesive-backed film that sticks to patients' skin at the incision site prior to surgery. 3M lead users were surgeons in developing countries, specialists at leading veterinary hospitals, and Hollywood make-up artists. Lead users generated concepts for six new product lines and a radical new approach to infection control.[42]

REGULATIONS. Regulations often cause market inefficiencies that stimulate ideas to build businesses. Leased lines, satellites, and voice-over-Internet protocol (VOIP) each helped circumvent local monopolies for international telephone calls. Government regulations concerning global warming, product safety, and healthy lifestyles are good recent examples. In response to calorie-labeling required in New York City stores, Starbucks introduced smaller, lower-calorie pastries.

Strong German shopping laws mandated store closing times: weekdays – 6 p.m., Saturdays – 2 p.m., Sundays – all day, but gas stations were exempt. BP developed an electronic shopping kiosk. Consumers enthusiastically use screens to view short videos, secure advice, and select merchandise for next-day collection or delivery.[43]

Removal of regulations can also stimulate ideas. When the U.S. Supreme Court abolished resale price maintenance (price-setting by manufacturers), Alex Grass started a discount drug store that became Rite Aid — now with 5,000 stores in 30 states.

SERENDIPITY. New product ideas sometimes arise unexpectedly. Pfizer was testing sildenafil citrate for angina when it discovered the unexpected side effect of treating erectile dysfunction. Pfizer developed Viagra, also useful for pulmonary hypertension, a rare disease mainly affecting women. (See dental implants — Table 14.3 — for another serendipity example.)

An Orthovita scientist left for lunch with his work on modified calcium drying in the sun. Upon return, he found a sponge-like substance, riddled with microscopic holes, that allowed passage of nutrients and bone-building cells. Orthovita markets *Vitoss* for helping broken bones in the spine, extremities, and pelvis to re-knit faster. Twelve weeks after it is inserted in a fracture, doctors cannot distinguish broken bone from healthy bone.

IDEA LIBRARIES. Ideas have their own right time. The environment changes and ideas with no value at time A may have great value at time B. AT&T's video telephone failed, but reappeared many years later as video conferencing and Skype. Whirlpool has a library of more than 700 shelved ideas; the 2011 Ford Explorer incorporates previously discarded ideas like lightweight steel body parts, direct injection engine technology, stop-start (engine switches off at traffic lights/in traffic), and turbocharging. Firms should develop **idea libraries** that they search periodically and systematically.[44]

NEW IDEA PROCESSES

The two main approaches for generating new product ideas are[45]:

- **Structured thinking.** Uses logical methods to generate new product ideas — can be very effective for generating ideas to improve current products.
- **Unstructured thinking.** Comprises a family of approaches that attempt to *break the mold* and develop totally new ideas by thinking *outside the box*.

Structured Thinking for Generating New Product Ideas[46]

- **Attribute listing.** Write down all product attributes: For a ballpoint pen, these might include casing material and color, ink quality and color, point width, weight, and price. Construct a table with attributes as column heads. Identify attribute variations, focusing on ways to improve.

- **Idea generator.**[47] Use innovation templates; the two stages are:

  1. List essential elements of a current product, like physical characteristics and attributes such as color and expected useful life. Repeat for the product's environment, like ambient temperature and user type.

  2. Manipulate these elements to identify something new, using one or more of five innovation templates — subtraction, multiplication, division, task unification, and attribute dependency change — Table 14.4.

  Select one or more templates to generate virtual products and explore potential customer value. Most products will not *make the cut*, but several repeats can lead to breakthroughs.

- **Morphological analysis.** Builds on attribute listing. Combine items in each column to develop new and interesting new product ideas.

Unstructured Thinking for Generating New Product Ideas

- **Brainstorming.** Focus on a problem and seek radical solutions.[48] Brainstorming helps participants break everyday patterns and find new ways to look for solutions. Ideas should be as broad and odd as possible. Because judgment and analysis stunt idea generation, brainstorming prohibits discussion and/or evaluation until the idea flow is exhausted — evaluation occurs in a second stage. Because it avoids production blocking (inability to articulate in a group setting), evaluation, and free-riding, individual brainstorming tends to produce a wider range of ideas; group brainstorming tends to be more effective because of the experience and creativity of all members. Incentives can improve idea generation. In **reverse** brainstorming, participants seek ideas on how to cause or enhance the problem, then reverse the process to solve the original problem.[49]

- **Mind mapping.** Write the problem in the center of a page and draw a circle around it. Write associations with the problem in circles elsewhere on the page and draw links to the problem. Each *association* is the focus for another linked set of associations. Seek a solution by examining local clusters of associations.

- **Provocation.** Uses a stupid untrue statement to shock participants from established patterns. A *provocation* in the ballpoint pen example might be: "Ballpoint pens cannot write."[50]

CONTINUES ON NEXT PAGE

Unstructured Thinking for Generating New Product Ideas (CONTINUED)

- **Random input**. Used to regenerate brainstorming sessions. The facilitator selects a random noun from book titles, a prepared word list, or a random picture to help generate ideas. In the ballpoint pen example, random words might be cars, trees, factories, or carpets.

- *Six Thinking Hats.* Each of six different-colored real or imaginary *hats* represents a different nature of thought. *Green* — creative ideas; *red* — emotions, by expressing feelings about an idea or process; *white* — analytic; *black* — pessimistic; *yellow* — optimistic; *blue* — procedural.[51]

TABLE 14.4

EXAMPLES USING THE IDEA GENERATOR

Innovation Template	Definition	Example	Action	Result
Subtraction	Remove components that are particularly desirable or even indispensable	Child's high chair	Remove legs	Seat that attaches to table
		DVD player	Remove control buttons	Philips (award-winning) Slimline Q-series
Multiplication	Make one or more copies of an existing component	Builders' level — vial filled with liquid and air bubble	Vials set at different angles such as one or two degrees	Levels for builders laying floors with small slopes such as for draining water
		Conventional Gillette razor	Add extra blades blades at different angles	Razor cutting action improved
Division	Divide an existing product into its component parts	Typewriter	Forming letters and printing letters	Word processor
		Musical instruments	Making notes and creating sound	Yamaha's Silent Series — piano, violin, cello, trumpet, tuba and drums — do not produce sound. Electronic sensors make sounds via headsets.
Task unification	Assign a new task to an existing element	Radio reception in automobiles	Use defrosting element as radio receptor	No longer need separate radio antenna
		Separate instruction sheet for product assembly	Print instructions on packaging	Saves costly booklet, simplifies packaging, reduces chances of lost instructions
Attribute dependency change	Involves dependent relationships among product attributes and attributes of the immediate environment	Eyeglasses and external lighting conditions	Eyeglass lenses that change color when exposed to sunlight	No need for two pairs of glasses
		Identical razors for men and women	Women's line of razors	Product better suited to women

---

Marketing Question

Select one of the *unstructured thinking* processes. Work with some fellow students to generate ideas to keep people cool in summer.

Marketing Question

A standard portable oscillating fan has three speeds. Use the Innovation Templates to *subtract* something — what actions and results do you get? Try *multiplication, division, task unification,* and *attribute dependency change*. What were the actions and results? How will you decide which ideas to pursue?

KEY IDEA

- ➤ The firm should tap multiple sources for new ideas.
- ➤ "The best way to get a good idea is to get *a lot* of ideas."[52]

PRELIMINARY SCREENING

The goal of **preliminary screening** is to create a balanced portfolio of high-potential new product ideas. For most firms, a balanced portfolio includes ideas ranging from low-return/low-risk to high-return/high-risk, with revenue generation in both the short and long run.[53] Screening decisions for high-risk, high-return, long-time-to-revenue ideas are quite difficult. Figure 14.4 shows a balanced portfolio on return and risk. (Also New Product Development Portfolio, p. 366.)

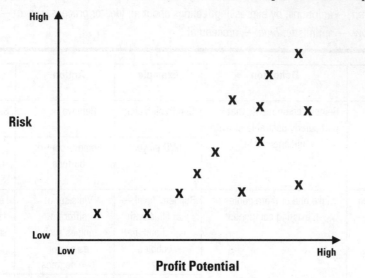

FIGURE 14.4

RISK AND RETURN IN NEW PRODUCT IDEAS — A BALANCED PORTFOLIO

KEY IDEA

➤ New product development stages are:

- Idea generation
- **Preliminary screening**
- Concept development
- Business-case analysis
- Development
- Product testing
- Market-factor testing
- Test marketing
- Commercialization

KEY IDEA

➤ Preliminary screening seeks a balanced portfolio of new product ideas by varying screening criteria across idea types.

Preliminary screening typically involves securing opinions from knowledgeable marketing and/or technical personnel, customers, and even suppliers.[54] The exact mix depends on the idea. Preliminary screening is the first stage for eliminating new product ideas. Typical criteria for preliminary screening include:

Fits with business unit strategy	Uses firm core competencies
Complements existing products	Likely to meet or exceed growth targets
Seems to meet customer needs	Likely to meet/exceed profitability targets

Because return and risk profiles differ markedly among ideas, the firm should use several sets of criteria. For example, criteria for ideas leading to new-to-the-world products should differ from those for additions to existing product lines. A useful way to assess new ideas is the *spider web* diagram — Figure 14.5. Each 10-point-scale spoke represents a screening criterion; poor scores are near the center, good scores near the periphery. The firm has assessed an idea on eight criteria; it scores relatively well on several criteria, but poorly on two.[55]

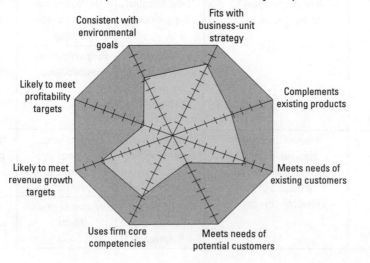

FIGURE 14.5

ASSESSING NEW PRODUCT IDEAS

Marketing Question

Collect the ideas you developed for one of the Marketing Questions, p. 357. Develop a set of screening criteria and select the most promising idea.

CONCEPT DEVELOPMENT

The **product concept** (**concept definition**) describes the product idea. Good concepts detail deliverable customer benefits. FMCG firms take pains to express new product ideas as robust product concepts. The process is highly iterative. Some examples (status) are:

- Breath fresheners for dogs (successful new product)
- Inexpensive four-passenger business jet (under development at Honda and GE)
- Diet baby foods (not under development)
- Global positioning satellite (GPS) locator for children (launched and doing well)
- Rechargeable laptop using energy from typing on the keyboard (not under development)
- SUV Smart car (under development by Smart for the U.S. market)

Criteria for product concept approval should be similar to preliminary screening. Understanding customer needs, particularly unmet needs, is very helpful in crafting and testing concept definitions. Market research tools like conjoint analysis may also be helpful — Chapter 6 Marketing Enrichment me601:

Developing a Product Concept Using Conjoint Analysis

NBV successfully screened its idea for a narrow-band video telephone. The four critical design attributes were accessibility, hard copy, resolution, and transmission time. NDV used conjoint analysis to assess their relative importance to customers and to develop a product concept. Figure 14.6 shows customer utility (y-axis) for the four design attributes. Interpretations are:

- **Accessibility** — very important: Increasing accessibility from 30 minutes to every office raises customer utility significantly – 0.42.

- **Hard copy** — quite important: Hard copy availability has reasonable customer utility – 0.27.

- **Resolution** — unimportant: Increasing from home TV to 4x home TV raises customer utility only marginally – 0.09.

- **Transmission time** — can be very important: Reduction from 30 to 20 seconds adds only 0.04. Reduction from 20 to 10 seconds adds significant utility – 0.38 (0.42 – 0.04).

FIGURE 14.6

RESULTS FROM A CONJOINT ANALYSIS STUDY FOR A NARROW-BAND VIDEO TELEPHONE

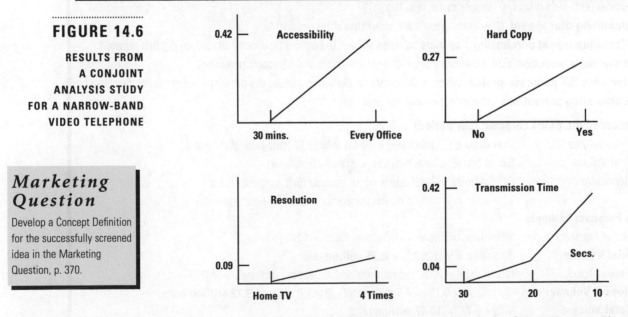

Marketing Question

Develop a Concept Definition for the successfully screened idea in the Marketing Question, p. 370.

Product concepts must appeal to customers and should guide development teams. Firms get in trouble when concepts drift during development. Pontiac's concept for the Aztek was a small, youth-oriented sport utility. But to launch the car quickly and economically, Pontiac used GM's minivan frame. Aztec's appearance received mixed reviews and its $22,000 – $27,000 price was too high for the youth market; Aztec sold poorly. New market data may force firms to rethink product concepts during development and may lead to midstream changes. But serious design compromises may result in products that customers will not buy.

KEY IDEA

➤ The product concept should appeal to customers and guide development.

BUSINESS-CASE ANALYSIS

Business-case analysis (BCA) sits between *concept approval* and *development*. BCA assesses the concept's financial viability and considers various risk factors. Xerox carries out incremental BCA — worldwide with the new product versus worldwide without the new product. Projects must meet minimum financial targets to move forward. The heart of BCA is a draft marketing plan; the firm lays out its market strategy, given successful development. The firm must think through market segmentation, choose target segments, and prepare positioning — including a value proposition for securing differential advantage (Chapters 8, 9, 10). The firm faces significant uncertainty but should base the future market strategy on best available market, customer, competitor, and complementer insight. Financial and human resource commitments jump significantly in development and far too many firms develop their own versions of the Ford Edsel!

Forecast financial performance depends on estimates of sales revenues, costs, and investment. Typically, revenue estimates (unit volumes x prices) are the most uncertain, especially for new-to-the-world products. **BASES** is a popular yet sophisticated way to forecast unit sales. The firm makes pre-market forecasts via simulated test markets; forecasting repeat purchase is critical.[56] For consumer packaged goods and durables, BASES *improves* pre-market sales forecasts using a databank based on past experience[57]:

KEY IDEA

➤ New product development stages are:
- Idea generation
- Preliminary screening
- Concept development
- **Business-case analysis**
- Development
- Product testing
- Market-factor testing
- Test marketing
- Commercialization

The BASES Approach

Sales Forecasting Questions. The firm secures data from a survey instrument:

- **Generating awareness**. How many people will seek information about the product? How many people will know about the product? (Based on advertising quantity and quality.)
- **Estimating distribution**. Can interested customers find the product? (Based on number of outlets and placement in stores [end-aisle displays, number of facings, height].)
- **Calculating trial appeal**. How many people are interested in the product?
- **Calculating repeat purchasing**. Are triers satisfied enough to become repeaters? (Based on product quality.)
- **Estimating transaction size**. How many product units will triers and repeaters purchase?
- **Estimating the purchase period**. When is the customer likely to purchase the product — first month, first year?
- **Incorporating promotions**. How effective will the deals be?

Constructing the Sales Forecast (per period)

Total Volume	=	Trial volume (1st purchase) + repeat volume (2nd and later purchases)
Trial Volume	=	No. of households x trial rate x quantity purchased
Repeat Volume	=	(No. of triers = [trial rate x no. of households]) x repeat rate x
		no. of repeat purchases x quantity purchased

Sales Forecast Example

No. of households	=	30 million; trial rate = 15%; trial units = 1.5
Trial Volume	=	30 million x 0.15 x 1.5 = **6.75 million** units
Repeat Triers	=	repeat rate = 30%; repeat units = 1.8; repeat purchases = 4.0
Repeat Volume	=	(30 million x 0.15 = 4.5 million) x 0.30 x 1.8 x 4.0 = **9.72 million** units
Total Volume	=	6.75 + 9.72 = **16.47 million** units

Marketing Question

Many drivers use cars as on-the-road offices. Show how you would design any mid-size model for office use. Would this change if the car were also the family vehicle?

Four considerations underlie forecast financial performance:

• **Sales revenues.** As discussed; these forecasts can be highly uncertain.
• **Cost of goods sold (COGS).** All ongoing costs to make and sell the product. **Gross profit** equals sales revenues less COGS. The firm may incur losses in the launch phase.
• **Investment costs.** Include all costs to develop the product, plus fixed investment for factories and equipment. The firm incurs many of these costs before it earns any revenues.
• **Discounting.** The firm must discount all future cash flows to the present.

The firm can combine these figures in several ways to forecast financial results. If forecast results exceed the firm's financial criteria, the concept enters development; if not, the firm shelves the concept, at least temporarily. Some firms use varying discount rates to adjust for risk.

DEVELOPMENT

A successful business-case analysis sets the stage for **development**. Development typically occurs deep in the firm and consumes significant resources. Design, engineering, and R&D focus initially on product design and functional performance, but other groups must also be involved.[58] When suppliers share in the development effort, the firm must ensure they are fully capable. Boeing ran into trouble with its technologically advanced 787, *Dreamliner*, because it outsourced design and construction of the wings, one of the most exacting aircraft parts. Development delays are always expensive (lost revenues and increased costs); Dreamliner delays resulted from the inability of a few suppliers to produce sufficient quantities of parts, ranging from small metal fasteners to entire sections of the aft fuselage. Input from manufacturing and service helps ensure the product can be made and serviced efficiently.[59] Development also benefits from customer involvement. Earlier, when Boeing designed the 777, it worked closely with major airlines to address design trade-offs promptly and thoroughly.[60] The firm should also consider complementers; the 777 refueling orifice was 18 inches higher than on other aircraft, and airports had to re-rig equipment. Avoiding complementers may be beneficial: Apple has greater flexibility with Macintosh because it designs both hardware and software; most other PC makers use Microsoft software.

Sometimes concerns about trade secrets deter firms from involving customers in designing functional characteristics. But the firm should always seek customer input for aesthetic, ergonomic, and use characteristics. The emergency brake on one American sports car was between the driver's seat and the door; a woman wearing a skirt could neither enter nor exit gracefully. Table 14.5 highlights other poor designs.

TABLE 14.5

PRODUCTS THAT WENT WRONG

Product	Type of Customer Dissatisfaction
Audio and video systems	Controls (remote or others) labeled in gold on a black casing — virtually impossible to read in low-lighting conditions.
Controls for electronic products	Markings wear off when used normally.
Horn button on American-made car with airbags	Button initially on the steering wheel perimeter but moved to the center; then required greater force. Moving controls around is a hazard.

To route 350 miles of bundled electric wiring in each 500-plus seat Airbus 380 took several weeks. But the wires came up short when connecting aircraft sections. The cause of the problem: Airbus Hamburg (Germany) engineers used a two-dimensional computer program; Toulouse (France) engineers worked in 3D!

Development by multifunctional teams, including *voice of the customer*, helps avoid time-consuming back-and-forth interactions that slow linear, sequential processes. Achieving consensus may be difficult, but teams often produce better products. Caution: Using teams may lead to loss of specialist expertise. Functional experts — designers, developers, manufacturing experts, and service personnel, can become organizationally disconnected from their specialties. Development by autonomous project teams also inhibits standardization across the firm. Requiring clear written reports, intensive problem-solving meetings, good direct supervision, and standard work procedures can mitigate these problems.[61] New project management software and communications technologies can also help, especially when team members work in different locations.

Sometimes, new product development proceeds best by *breaking the rules*, as at Motorola. Apple's CEO Steve Jobs echoed this sentiment when he said, "Remember that 'Think Different' ad campaign that we ran? It was certainly for customers, but it was even more for Apple."

> Motorola charged engineer Ron Jellico with creating the thinnest cell phone ever. Jellico's engineering team (ultimately 20 strong) met daily at 4 p.m. for one-hour meetings (often lasting until 7 p.m.). The team flouted Motorola's development rules by keeping the project secret, even from close colleagues, and using materials and processes never before tried. Engineers made breakthroughs like putting the antenna in the mouthpiece and the battery alongside the circuit board. Originally planned as a niche product, the RAZR sold more than 20 million units in the first year.

PRODUCT DESIGN

As product quality improves, design becomes increasingly important for customer satisfaction:

- **Sony Electronics, President Consumer Sales.** "I think one of the true powers of Sony is great design. We think about the human interface, not just from a 'how do things work' standpoint, but 'how do they fit and feel in human contact.' This is a human strategic advantage. Its something we've invested in for decades, in our design centers, R&D, and product planners, and we're very good at it."[62]

- **Samsung, Chief Marketing Officer.** "We have invested very, very heavily in design for several years. Right now, we're the second most awarded design company in our category. Our products are not simply consumer products, but lifestyle products. We put a very strong emphasis on understanding our consumers and their lifestyles."[63]

Dell has a laser-like focus on cost reduction but now uses design as a competitive weapon. Like Converse and Nike (sneakers), Freddyandma.com (handbags), Oakley (sunglasses), and Steve Madden (shoes), Dell uses choiceboard approaches where customers design their own products. Design is also important for packaging: Opening ease (*frustration-free packaging*) and eye-catching display are especially important in B2C. Figure 14.7 shows examples of superb design.[64]

> **Product Design at Sony**
>
> A senior Sony Electronics executive said: "The most exciting thing about Sony to me is when you're in a line-up review and they're showing you a product and you get this 28-year-old product planner and this 30-year-old designer and they walk into a room and they pull back a piece of cloth and they show you a product that you've been working together on for a year and you go 'Oh my God, it's perfect.' And when you get into those moments, you know, it's about the passion that Sony has for great products. This is a passionate organization that really believes in creating the best possible product that you can create, and the designers, product planners and senior marketers just love what they're doing.
>
> "There's this one designer in Tokyo. He's in his 30s now, but when you see this guy! He's going to walk into the room and you're going to think, 'Oh my God, a street person has escaped and he's loose in the building.' And his pants are four sizes too big and his clothes just hang on and he looks like he hasn't slept in a week … Most products you'll look at and you'll say, 'OK, I could give you 20 comments on how to improve the design.' But when he pulls back the drape, you're not going to have anything to say. On this one occasion I was in Tokyo and he showed us a CD player, and the stuff was perfect. It was just perfect. That line of CD players sold six million units in the U.S. alone. And we didn't have to touch it. So that's the strength of Sony, people like that … somebody with passion designed that thing."

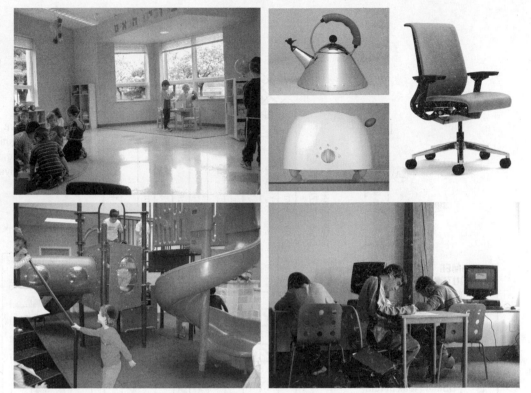

FIGURE 14.7

SUPERB DESIGN HAS ALWAYS BEEN A PART OF PRODUCT DEVELOPMENT

Marketing Exercise

Identify three examples of superb design. Bring visuals or the actual product to class.

During development, the firm must make performance trade-offs among product attributes, but it should always keep the value proposition squarely in mind. The firm must also address negative side effects, possibly with creative design approaches. Clozapine is an effective anti-schizophrenic drug for a small subset of patients who are unresponsive to other medications. Unfortunately, 1 percent of clozapine users suffer a potentially fatal drop in white blood cell counts. Novartis, clozapine's manufacturer, designed a revolutionary solution by offering cloza-pine users a 24-hour service for blood testing at home.[65]

Many pharmaceutical firms spend 15–20 percent of sales on R&D. *Research* seeks out new chemical entities to meet patient needs. *Development* tests promising entities for patient benefits and drug delivery methods. Pharmaceuticals are a good example of synthesizing *research-based discovery* and *customer-sensitive development*.

QUALITY FUNCTION DEPLOYMENT

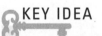

KEY IDEA

➤ Many firms make very large investments in product development.

➤ Multi-functional teams and customer involvement aid the development process.

➤ Design is an increasing-ly important part of the development process.

Quality function deployment (QFD) brings producers and users together. QFD maps customer needs into design, development, engineering, manufacturing, and service functions. QFD helps firms identify spoken and unspoken needs and translates them into actions and designs. QFD also helps various business functions to communicate and focus on achieving a common goal.[66] Figure 14.8 shows QFD's basic design tool, the **House of Quality**.[67] Steps in the process are:

1. **Collect customer requirements as customer attributes** — CAs.[68] Organize CAs into bundles of higher-level requirements — primary, secondary, tertiary. For a car door:

   • **Primary CAs.** One primary CA for car door is *good operation and use*.[69]

   • **Secondary CAs.** For *good operation and use*, secondary CAs include *easy to open and close the door* and *isolation* — inside the car from outside the car.

   • **Tertiary CAs.** Tertiary CAs for *good operation and use* are secondary CAs for *easy to open and close the door*. They include *easy to close from outside*, *stays open on a hill*, *easy to open from outside*, and *doesn't kick back*.

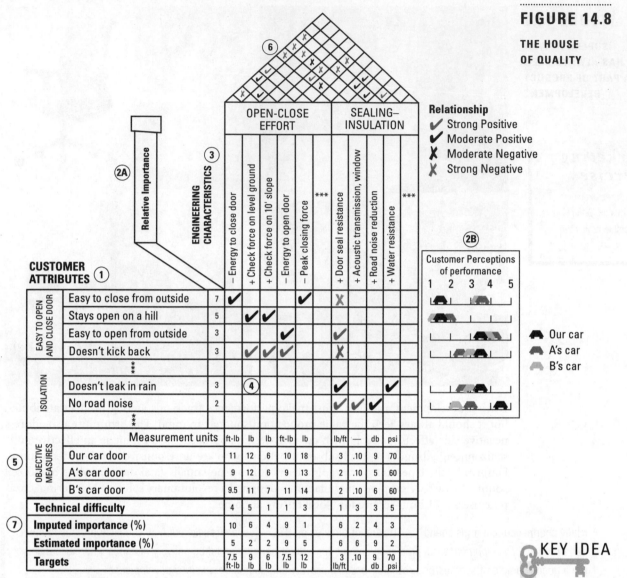

FIGURE 14.8

THE HOUSE OF QUALITY

2. **Measure each tertiary CA:**

   • **2A Relative importance.** Importance weights sum to 100 across all CAs.

   • **2B Firm performance.** Customer perceptions versus competing suppliers on a 1 (worst) to 5 (best) scale.

3. **Translate CAs to engineering characteristics — ECs:** The firm uses ECs to design and modify products. The firm may identify more CAs and/or redundant ECs. Positive and negative signs show direction. The negative sign on *energy to close door* means a hoped-for reduction of energy.

4. **Identify CA/EC relationships and their strengths:** Complete the sparse matrix — an EC may affect more than one CA; several ECs may affect a single CA.

5. **Assess objective performance measures for ECs:** Relate to current performance of firm and competitor products. Act as the basis for eventually establishing target levels.

6. **Identify interrelationships among ECs.** The sparse matrix in the *roof* identifies engineering trade-offs. *Energy to close door* is negatively related to *door seal resistance, acoustic transmission-window,* and *road noise reduction.* If the firm makes the door easier to close, road noise might get worse. The firm may require creative engineering solutions.

KEY IDEA

➤ The House of Quality maps *customer needs* into *product design.*

7. **Design conclusions.** The *basement* identifies technical difficulty, importance to customers, estimated costs, and EC targets.

The firm may link design specifications developed in the House of Quality to parts deployment, process planning, and production planning. Some design elements are more fundamental than others and form *platforms* for designing other elements. The firm must make platform decisions early in development. Other elements are more flexible; the firm can redesign these as it collects more market data.[70]

Development is typically the most time-consuming stage in new product development. Faster development helps gain first-mover advantage and enhance revenues. Approaches include:

- **Continuous development.** Working on a 24/7 cycle, Bechtel and other firms place development teams in London, U.S., and Japan. Teams take over from each other as the day ends/begins.

- **Parallel development.** GE, Toyota, and others form competitive teams that work in parallel toward the same goal. At some point in the development process, the firm selects one approach for completion.

- **Successive development.** Some firms use multiple teams to develop separate successor products. At Intel, different development teams worked simultaneously on P5, P6, and P7 chips.

Firms may also secure significant economies by integrating development across products rather than focus on one product at a time. Traditionally, LEGO used 90 percent of new bricks or elements just once; new toys had on average 13,000! Designers now reuse parts and new toys have less than 7,000 elements. Relatedly, the firm should ensure that pursuing multiple projects does not create bottlenecks and slow the development process.

Quality Is Not Just for Products

Safeway was *stuck in the middle* between price-oriented Walmart and specialty retailers like Whole Foods. Safeway's first annual loss spurred a remodeling of all 1,775 stores — the largest by a U.S. supermarket chain. Safeway continued offering low-priced popular food brands but upgraded perishables by adding products like more tender beef, sweeter grapes, and fresher bread. Same-space sales increased by 90 percent; Safeway returned to profitability.

CO-CREATION

Some firms form collaborative relationships with customers and independent individuals/organizations to increase the number, and broaden the scope, of new product development. LEGO and others extend customer collaboration beyond idea generation into co-creating and co-design, even providing toolkits for product design.[71] Wikipedia, Linux, and Firefox are other good collaboration examples. Open collaboration (OC) requires tight rules for community involvement but volunteer control may be significant. OC generates lots of ideas but screening and selecting may be cumbersome. Threadless (T-shirts) operates a 600,000-member innovation mall that submits (and evaluates) proposals for about 800 new designs weekly. Threadless pays for selected and launched designs; other OC rewards are social/psychological — altruism, fame, fun, and sense of achievement. By contrast, closed collaboration (CC) relies on selected collaborators whose ideas are generally more focused. IBM chose Freescale, Infineon, Samsung, Siemens, and STMicroelectronics as CC partners for a Microelectronics Consortium for developing semiconductor technologies.[72]

NEW PRODUCT DEVELOPMENT PORTFOLIO

For most firms, the new product development portfolio is a critical element in the entire venture portfolio, along with insourcing, outsourcing, acquisition, strategic alliance, licensing and technology purchase, and equity investment — Chapter 7. Regardless, the new product development portfolio is especially critical because of the ongoing large quantity of firm resources involved. Further, environmental change, strategy evolution, and development successes, failures, advances, retreats, and new entries from successful business case analyses, require the firm to update the portfolio periodically. Successful new product firms display top management commitment selective top management involvement, and multiple efforts. Specifically, four goals are important:

- **Portfolio value.** The firm should consider forecast profits, risk, timing, and required resources.

- **Portfolio balance.** Ensure projects are appropriately dispersed among high/low risk, short/long term; across various product forms, markets, and technologies; and across types of development efforts — basic technology research, applied technology research, market-focused development, and market tinkering.

- **Strategic alignment.** The product innovation strategy should be directly linked to the business strategy via resource allocation into *strategic buckets*.

- **Right number of projects.** Resources are limited. Too many projects and the entire product development process slows leading to missed deadlines including product launches. The firm should rank projects and make tough decision to cull projects that don't make the cut.[73]

PRODUCT TESTING

The firm should test new products for aesthetic, ergonomic, functional, and use characteristics. There is no single test or type of test. Rather, development follows a series of *develop → test → develop* feedback loops until the product is ready for market-factor testing.

The two major types of product test are:

- **Alpha tests — in-company.** For most new products, firm employees provide critical feedback. Several alpha tests may run simultaneously; alpha tests often lead to further development. Automakers test new cars on northern Sweden's frozen lakes; new Otis elevator models complete several alpha tests, including drops, electrical sabotage, fire and flooding, and simulated earthquakes.

- **Beta tests — with customers.** Beta tests typically follow successful alpha tests. But firms sometimes conduct beta tests on product features before they finish development.[74] The firm may also conduct several beta tests as development is concluding. Beta tests give customers an early look at developing/soon-to-be-introduced new products. Microsoft's eight-million-user beta test for Windows 7 was the largest ever, and helped avoid problems that plagued Vista. Beta tests also generate word of mouth about the new product.

Speedy testing has many advantages,[75] but inadequate testing can cause major problems. During a moose-avoidance test in a sharp turn at 38 mph, a Swedish journalist tipped over Daimler-Benz's (DB) first subcompact (Mercedes A-Class). DB had invested $1.5 billion in the car; DB spent $171 million to solve the problem. Executives responsible for choosing coffee for the merged United/Continental Airlines did not test their selection in everyday use; hence, they did not realize that coffee pot designs differed across airlines, leading to many customer complaints. P&G's Gillette successfully tested a razor designed for Indian men on Indian students at MIT, but the razor failed in India: Problem — differential regular access to running water.

KEY IDEA

➤ The firm should conduct *in-company alpha tests* throughout development. The firm should conduct *customer beta tests* in latter phases.

➤ Failure to test products sufficiently can have serious marketing and financial consequences.

KEY IDEA

➤ New product development stages are:
- Idea generation
- Preliminary screening
- Concept development
- Business-case analysis
- Development
- **Product testing**
- **Market-factor testing**
- Test marketing
- Commercialization

MARKET-FACTOR TESTING

The product is only one element in the firm's market offer. First-rate products fail if the firm poorly designs and/or implements the rest of the marketing-mix. Conversely, the firm may be successful with marginal products if other marketing-mix elements are superior. The firm should evaluate implementation elements like advertising and distribution via **market-factor testing**. Generally, the firm tests other market factors when product development is complete, but sometimes market-factor and product testing occur in parallel. The firm can test using simulated environments or virtually on the Internet.

SIMULATED ENVIRONMENTS

In B2C, the firm can test advertising messages via split-cable TV or in movie houses. The firm can test packaging, pricing, and shelf placement in mock-up store displays in trailers adjacent to shopping malls. Consumers selecting the test product receive a trial sample; later they report experiences, repurchase intentions, and/or usage rates. Alternatively, consumers may select products from mock-up brochures and magazines when researchers visit them at home. Coach offers bags, wallets, and other fashion accessories in a wide variety of colors, materials, shapes, and styles, then focuses on those that sell best and discontinues the others.

In many tests, critical measures are *trial* and *repeat*. These variables are input into analytic procedures that predict sales volume and market share. BASES (discussed previously) is one approach; ASSESSOR is a second.[76] (Many practitioners use the Bass model and extensions for new product forecasts — Marketing Enrichment me1401.[77])

ASSESSOR

The **ASSESSOR** approach has the important feature of incorporating both a **preference** model and a **trial-and-repeat** model. Each model predicts market share and sales volume. If the results converge, the researcher has greater confidence in the predictions. Divergent results act as a diagnostic; they suggest further analyses to identify sources of discrepancies and reconcile findings. For new products entering *established product classes*, market share from the preference model multiplied by total product class sales provides the sales volume estimate. The firm compares this estimate to the long-term sales volume estimate derived from the trial-and-repeat model. For a *new product class*, the preference model is not useable, so the trial-and-repeat model alone provides the sales estimate.

VIRTUAL TESTING

Virtual testing is a new approach to customer testing. The firm creates an online shopping display and customers shop as in a real store, with all the distracting clutter. An important benefit of virtual testing is the ability to modify displays quickly and analyze results instantaneously:

In a Goodyear study, 1,000 recent and potential passenger-tire purchasers shopped in virtual tire stores; several brands/models had various prices and warranties. Goodyear identified strong and weak competitors, gained insight into brand equity, and developed re-pricing ideas.[78]

Both virtual testing and simulated testing are artificial. Test marketing provides greater realism.

TEST MARKETING

Test marketing simulates actual market conditions. Typically, the firm selects two geographic areas with similar market and customer profiles, considering issues like seasonality. The firm implements the full market launch program in one geography; the other geography acts as a control to isolate product launch results. Global firms often speed time to commercialization by test marketing simultaneously in several countries. P&G test marketed Swiffer in France and the U.S.; Swiffer reached global distribution within 18 months versus the typical five years. For any test market, measurement is crucial and includes:

- **Input measures** — advertising, training, sales effort
- **Intermediate measures** — customer awareness, interest
- **Output measures** — sales, profits, customer satisfaction

FMCG firms collect point-of-sales data from supermarket scanners; *value shopping* cards measure repeat purchase. Consumer panels and/or independent surveys provide intermediate measures and customer satisfaction.

Test marketing has pros and cons.[79] *Pros* include:

- **Fine-tunes launch.** Test marketing provides invaluable data for fine-tuning actual launch.
- **Provides unexpected insight.** Test market failures may provide unexpected data:

Febreze, P&G's laundry product for removing cigarette and other noxious odors from dry-clean-only fabrics, failed in test market — only 10 percent of consumers were *extremely pleased*. But test consumers found additional uses like odor removal from sofas, carpets, car interiors, and other household furnishings. In a second test market, Febreze had a broader "odor neutralizer" positioning. This test was a huge success; initial demand exceeded forecast tenfold.

- **Saves launch costs.** The firm can withdraw products that perform poorly in test market and avoid spending resources on new products that would have failed.

Cons for test marketing include:

- **Alert competitors.** The test market may show firm intentions and reduce its time-to-market advantage.
- **Competitor actions.** Competitors can interfere with the firm's test market by increasing promotion or offering cut-price deals. These actions reduce the test's predictive power.
- **Excessive attention.** The firm may make a test market successful by putting in special effort. If the firm cannot duplicate this effort at launch, it may introduce a product it should have cancelled:

Coca-Cola encouraged Burger King to invest in *Frozen Coke*. When a legitimate test market was going poorly, fountain-division employees paid a Virginia man $10,000 to take hundreds of children to Burger King to buy value meals and Frozen Coke. Several Coke executives lost their jobs, and Coke paid Burger King $21 million to settle lawsuits.

- **Expense and time.** Test marketing is expensive and may take a long time. Also, the firm forgoes revenues from an otherwise successful launch.

COMMERCIALIZATION

Successful completion of the stage-gate process results in a product ready for launch and **commercialization**.[80] The firm assigns resources to construct facilities and expend marketing effort. The launch strategy must consider issues like forecast sales, time to bring facilities on line, production and inventory requirements, adherence to planned launch date,[81] competitive lead

KEY IDEA

➤ New product development stages are:

• Idea generation
• Preliminary screening
• Concept development
• Business-case analysis
• Development
• Product testing
• Market-factor testing
• Test marketing
• **Commercialization**

Marketing Question

The Segway is a battery-driven personal-transportation vehicle developed by Dean Kamen. Launched in 2002, the Segway has been less successful than its inventor predicted. What barriers to adoption did the Segway face? Could Segway have done a better job in addressing these barriers?

KEY IDEA

➤ A useful classification for timing of new product adoption is:

• Innovators
• Early adopters
• Early majority
• Late majority
• Laggards

---

time, expected competitive response, patent or trade secret protection, and available resources. Launch delays can be very costly; further, the firm should synchronize communications and distribution to avoid the sort of problem Under Armour encountered when it introduced cross-training shoes: Super Bowl advertisement ran months before shoes reached the stores. Early launch announcements may also inhibit customers from buying the firm's current products.

All marketing-mix elements are important for launch. Pricing and distribution decisions are critical, but are more difficult the newer the product. Regarding communications, B2C firms often use celebrity spokespersons and advertising to promote new products. They also use *product placement*, working with directors and producers so that actors use products in movies and TV shows. B2B firms focus on good distribution and support programs, including getting key opinion leaders to use new products — medical device and pharmaceutical firms target leading specialists at university teaching hospitals. **Word-of-mouth** is often critical for adoption; prospective buyers reduce purchase risk by learning from trusted sources. In its early days, Starbucks rarely advertised, but gained enormously from positive word-of-mouth. Today, firms try to manage word-of-mouth and social-media communications, rather than just leaving the task to customers.

Traditionally, firms launched new products domestically, then later in foreign markets. Today, many firms launch in multiple national markets simultaneously; Mattel introduced Rapunzel Barbie in 59 countries. Information products where copying is a problem are a special concern; 20th Century Fox launched *X2: X-Men United* in 93 territories within 48 hours.

The firm should not confuse completing product development (or even satisfactory test marketing) with commercial success. Extensive testing is no guarantee against commercial failure. After 10 years of development, S.C. Johnson (SCJ) introduced Allercare to remove dust mites (leading cause of childhood asthma) from carpets/upholstery. SCJ tested Allercare in tens of thousands of homes and launched with a $10 million national TV campaign. But consumers with severe allergies and asthma reported negative reactions; SCJ withdrew Allercare after one year.[82]

The best companies learn from commercialization mistakes.[83] Corning failed with a DNA chip designed to print all 28,000 human genes onto slides for research, but identified the drug-discovery market and now sells Epic for testing potential drugs. British Airways' flat beds upstaged Virgin's new reclined sleeper seats, but Virgin used its learning to develop a *leapfrog* innovation, the *upper-class suite*, that helped improve business-class market share.

PRODUCT ADOPTION

The goal of commercialization efforts is customer product adoption. But not all customers adopt at the same time. As part of product planning, the firm should anticipate five categories of customer adoption behavior[84]:

• **Innovators** (2.5 percent) — *Explorers*.[85] The first to adopt the innovation but are only a small part of the population. Take pride in being first, are considered *experts*, and proactively seek opportunities to try new things. Typically, other customers do not emulate these *venturesome* risk-takers.

• **Early adopters** (13.5 percent) — *Visionaries*. Follow the innovators. Seek understanding of future possibilities and are willing to take risks and break with the past. Are more *respected* in their communities and are opinion leaders for others.

• **Early majority** (34 percent) — *Pragmatists*. Motivated by current problems and make decisions *deliberately*, based in part on the experience of early adopters. Look for proven track records; prefer to buy recognized brands and from market leaders.

• **Late majority** (34 percent) — *Conservatives*. A *skeptical* group that adopts only when half the population has adopted. Tend to be price sensitive.

- **Laggards** (16 percent) — *Critics*. These *traditionalists* gain utility by sticking to the old, are suspicious of change, averse to novelty, and only adopt when most customers have adopted and use is widespread.

Identifying potential customers by adoption category for a new product innovation is a critical marketing challenge. In B2C, early adopters tend to be better educated, socio-economically advantaged, and younger. Avon maintains a database on innovators and early adopters for cosmetics and targets them for new product launches. But innovators and early adopters for one product may be early or late majority for another. Figure 14.9 shows that a product innovation must **cross the chasm** from early adopters to the early majority and the mainstream market to be successful.[86] Many new products fail to cross the chasm; for others, it takes a long time.

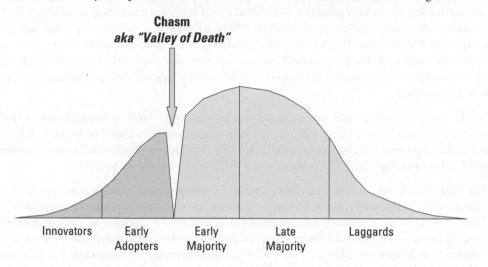

Marketing Question

Talk to an executive about her firm's new product development process. How does it compare with the process described in this chapter? Where is it better? Worse?

FIGURE 14.9

THE ADOPTION CURVE AND CHASM

Marketing Question

What products can you identify that never *crossed the chasm*? What products took a long time to cross the chasm?

Factor (direction of effect)	Meaning
Advantage (increase)	Extent of benefits offered compared to existing alternatives
Compatibility (increase)	Relationship with past experience and current lifestyle
Complexity (decrease)	Implies greater learning requirements
Observability/Communicability (increase)	Extent to which the relative advantage is easily observed and communicated
Risk (decrease)	Financial, physical, and psychological/social risk
Divisibility/Reversibility (increase)	Ability to try on a limited basis and revert to previous product

TABLE 14.6

FACTORS AFFECTING THE SPEED OF ADOPTION (ACCORD)

The **ACCORD** acronym summarizes several factors affecting speed of adoption and commercial success — Table 14.6.[87] Consider the successful introduction of EZ Pass on toll roads and bridges. The EZ Pass device attaches to a vehicle windshield. An electronic signal at the tollbooth recognizes the device, allows passage, and deducts payment from an account linked to a credit card. The account automatically replenishes when the balance falls to a pre-set level:

- **Advantage.** Saves time at tollbooth; automatic bill payment more convenient than cash.
- **Compatibility.** Driver behavior largely unchanged; initiating the credit-card account is trivial.
- **Complexity.** Learning minimal: driver attaches the device; drives through the tollbooth.
- **Observability** (Communicability). Benefits easy to understand and communicate.
- **Risk.** Little risk to trying the EZ Pass system — no upfront payment.
- **Divisibility** (Reversibility). Driver can easily switch back to cash.

KEY IDEA

➤ ACCORD is a useful acronym for factors influencing the speed of new product adoption:
- Advantage (+)
- Compatibility (+)
- Complexity (−)
- Observability (+)
- Risk (−)
- Divisibility (+)

Marketing Question

What other messages did you glean from this chapter?

KEY MESSAGES

- Successful new products are a major factor in creating shareholder wealth.

- Innovations can be either sustaining or disruptive.

- The most important factors for innovation success are market selection, R&D spending, and organization.

- Four approaches to new product development are: basic technology research, applied technology research, market-focused development, and market tinkering.

- The stage-gate process is a systematic approach to new product development. Key stages are:

  1. Idea generation
  2. Preliminary screening
  3. Concept development
  4. Business-case analysis
  5. Development
  6. Product testing
  7. Market-factor testing
  8. Test marketing
  9. Commercialization

- At each stage, the firm should be concerned about two types of error: Type I — investing in a project that eventually fails; Type II — rejecting a project that would have succeeded.

- The cost of failure increases as a project moves through the new product development process. Hence, each gate should be a *kill point*.

- New product success depends on *crossing the chasm* from early adopters to early majority.

- The speed of adoption for a successful project depends on the ACCORD factors. (Do you know what they are?)

VIDEOS AND AUDIOS

Innovation   v1402 ▼ William Duggan Columbia Business School

v1402

QUESTIONS FOR STUDY AND DISCUSSION

Can you answer the questions implied by this chapter's learning objectives? Check!

1. Customer dissatisfaction is an opportunity for firms to learn. When were you dissatisfied with a purchase experience? Why? What new product or service ideas would you suggest?

2. Consider a common product that you use frequently — like a newspaper, fast food outlet, computer, or cell phone. Work with two or three friends to develop new product ideas using the five innovation templates — subtraction, multiplication, division, task unification, and attribute dependency change.

3. Take the product you selected for Question 2 and develop a House of Quality.

4. Suppose that, on graduation, you accept a position as new product director for a medium-size firm with a poor new product innovation record. The CEO has set a three-year goal for 20 percent of sales to come from new products. What actions will you take in your first 100 days?

5. Apple has been successful with its G4 series of desktop and laptop computers and with the iPod, iTunes, iPhone, and iPad. But Apple withdrew the Newton and G4 Cube computer (now in New York's Museum of Modern Art). How do you assess Apple's new product performance? How does your assessment reconcile with Apple's profit performance?

6. Describe the marketing significance of new product innovation. What challenges and opportunities face firms that introduce new products in competitive markets?

7. Select a product in which you are interested. Alternatively, consider this book — *Managing Marketing in the 21st Century*. What related new product ideas do you have?

IMPERATIVE 4
Design the Market Offer

....

PART B – COMMUNICATING CUSTOMER VALUE
....

CHAPTER 15

INTEGRATED MARKETING COMMUNICATIONS

To access O-codes, go to **www.ocodes.com**

LEARNING OBJECTIVES

When you have completed this chapter, you will be able to:

- Understand the communications challenges and opportunities firms face.
- Articulate the causes of miscommunication problems.
- Enumerate the various communications tools the firm can use.
- Integrate communications tools into a communications strategy.
- Distinguish between *push*, *pull*, and combination *push/pull* communication strategies.
- Set communications objectives.

OPENING CASE: CALIFORNIA CHEESE

California's dairy industry faced a significant problem that would likely become more severe — milk surpluses caused by increasing milk productivity. The California Milk Advisory Board (CMAB) evaluated several options and selected cheese, in part because 1 pound of cheese required 10 pounds of milk.

Californians annually consumed 23.3 pounds of cheese per capita (national average — 19.7 pounds). Demographic growth in the heavy-cheese-using Hispanic population would increase that demand. But California's cheese-making reputation paled beside Wisconsin and Vermont. Hence, California was a net cheese importer: 80 percent of natural U.S.-produced cheese, and nearly all processed cheese, came from out of state. For California to become a pre-eminent cheese producer, CMAB had to design and implement an effective communications strategy.

To meet its challenge, CMAB implemented a three-part strategy:

- **Certification mark.** *The mark (seal) showed California with a rising sun and rolling plains on a golden, cheese-colored background: "Real California Cheese" was at the periphery. CMAB* *had this mark placed on as many cheese packages as possible; in all advertising, coupons, and promotional literature; and on restaurant menus and table tents.*

- **Advertising campaign.** *CMAB implemented the Real California Cheese campaign, "California cheese is great cheese," in newspapers, magazines, outdoors, and on radio and TV. The primary target was women aged 25-54, married with children, income slightly above the national average. The copy strategy avoided more traditional, rational, tangible claims of cheese superiority. Rather, the tone and manner tried to create an emotional bond of fondness and affection for California cheese. The advertising used human, intelligent, and humorous messages; but no superiority claim.*

- **Promotional campaign.** *CMAB used in-store cross-promotions with instantly redeemable coupons, product sampling, and self-liquidating offers, like high-quality coffee table books about cheese, that reinforced the advertising campaign. Cross-promotional partners were products frequently consumed with cheese, like bread, crackers, pizza crust, tortillas, poultry, champagne, and wine. CMAB also placed cross-brand coupons on Real California Cheese-identified cheeses.*

After ten years of its three-part strategy, CMAB introduced, "It's the cheese." This campaign made the exaggerated claim that people came to California for the cheese. The tagline appeared adjacent to the Real California Cheese seal on TV spots, at retail, in print, on outdoor executions, on coupons, and all other promotional materials.

Several years later, CMAB introduced "Happy Cows," with the tagline, "Great cheese comes from Happy Cows. Happy Cows come from California." The advertisements showed cows talking, enjoying, and thinking like people about California's best-known features — sunny skies, lack of snow (versus the Midwest), earthquakes (portrayed positively), and beautiful scenery.

CMAB used spot TV advertising in markets outside California where Real California Cheese had a major presence, supplemented by outdoor, bus and bus-shelter, and radio advertising. Later, when Real California Cheese was sold in many major U.S. markets, CMAB introduced national cable advertising. In 2004 and 2005, a Real California Cheese spot aired during the Super Bowl. In 2011, CMAB continued its emotional appeals by launching the Family Farms *campaign featuring website documentaries and shorter versions for television advertising.*

California cheese achieved spectacular awareness levels. Three out of four Californians reported seeing the Real California Cheese seal where they shopped and 95 percent purchased Real California Cheese. Sales increased 600 percent over a 20-year period beginning in the mid-1980s. Cheese production increased dramatically: Before the first campaign, 17 percent of California's milk produced 281.2 million pounds of cheese; 20 years later, 45 percent of California's milk produced 1,994 billion pounds of cheese. CMAB predicts that by 2013, over half of California's milk will be used for cheese.

CASE QUESTION

What factors account for CMAB's successful performance?

Chapter 15 is the first of three chapters in Part B of Imperative 4 — *Design the Market Offer.* Part B focuses on *Communicating Customer Value.* Chapter 15 addresses *Integrated Marketing Communications.*

We've all heard the popular saying: "If we build a better mousetrap, customers will come." Rubbish! Customers will not *come* unless they know about the mousetrap; that's the purpose of communication. To be successful, the firm must communicate the offer's benefits and value to target customers. Also, good communication by itself has value in its impact on customers.

Many communications tools and techniques are available for the firm. We consider four rough categories: **Personal** — face-to-face personal selling, telemarketing/telesales, and service; **mass communications** — traditional advertising, direct marketing, packaging, publicity & public relations, sales promotion (including product placement and trade shows); and **digital communications** — online advertising and public relations, websites, blogs and microblogs (like Twitter and Tumblr), quasi-personal communication, and mobile marketing. Traditionally, firms also planned for some **word-of-mouth** communications to enhance the value of their messages. Via social networking, digital media has changed the paradigm; communications options between and among customers are now much greater. For marketing professionals, the vast array of communications options is both a blessing and a curse. *Blessing:* The firm has many more communications alternatives. *Curse:* To coordinate multiple messages to multiple targets and produce a coherent, consistent, and integrated whole is very difficult.

Integrated marketing communications captures the idea of coordinating all communications messages with the right communication tools and techniques to the right audiences at the right times. This chapter reviews communications strategies and tactics for reaching target audiences and achieving firm objectives.

THE CHANGING VIEW

OLD WAY	NEW WAY
Broad appeal	Targeted messaging
Customers are sole communications target	Multiple communications targets — including complementers, customers, employees, governments, influencers, shareholders, and suppliers
Limited media/vehicle choices	Proliferating media/vehicle choices
Mass communication	Interactive communication
Siloed communications effort	Integrated communications effort
The firm communicates with customers	The firm communicates with customers; customers also communicate with the firm
Word of mouth may provide relevant communications	Managing Internet-based word of mouth a critical managerial challenge

COMMUNICATIONS CHALLENGES

In its first 10 years, Starbucks spent less than $10 million on advertising yet gained high brand awareness. Starbucks clustered retail outlets in highly visible urban locations, was zealous about good coffee, visibly branded all products and materials, had consistent brand positioning, invested smartly in public relations, used the emerging Internet to its advantage, and enjoyed strong word-of-mouth. Starbucks is a good example of how integrated communications can establish and sustain a brand.[1]

An integrated communications program is critical for successfully implementing the firm's market strategy and achieving its objectives. But it's not easy to do. The firm must address many challenges from both outside and inside the organization.

EXTERNAL CHALLENGES

As the firm tries to determine the right mix of tools and techniques for communicating with various audiences, it must address several external challenges:

- **Competitive communications.** Competitors and the firm have similar communications targets. Competitors use varied communications approaches to promote their products and disadvantage the firm. Airbus tried to slow advance orders for the Boeing *Dreamliner* by suggesting Airbus might revamp the A330. By attacking government loans to Airbus for aircraft development, Boeing questioned future Airbus products. Some firms suffer attacks by third-party interest groups like Greenpeace and animal-rights activists.

- **Evolving communications technologies.** Communications choices are expanding rapidly. Growth in digital media allows firms to modify product placement, and promotions for different audiences through different communications channels, even inserting virtual products into movies and TV shows. But digital video recorders allow consumers to opt out of traditional advertising.

- **Multiple information sources.** Customers receive information about the firm and its products from many sources — advocacy groups, competitors, governments, intermediaries, other customers, testing and other third-party organizations, and the media. Communications may be negative, neutral, or helpful to the firm; they can also be very powerful.[2] Reports that Nike used child labor in Indonesia, and that PepsiCo India used excessive amounts of groundwater and sold contaminated products, were negative. Media coverage of AFL-CIO asking Verizon's customers to switch telephone carriers during angry union negotiations were equally problematic. Conversely, many positive press and analyst reports have helped firms like Apple and Google.

Examples of Public Communications

Positive. Ben and Jerry's and The Body Shop generally receive favorable press coverage, in part because they endorse social causes.

Positive. Pharmaceutical firms gain positive public perceptions when the press reports FDA approval of new drugs.

Negative. Accounting firm Arthur Andersen received such negative press coverage for negligent business practices related to the Enron scandal that it collapsed.

Negative. U.S. firms like Accenture, Stanley Works, and Tyco received negative publicity when they attempted to reincorporate abroad. Many believe these actions exploit loopholes in U.S. tax laws and are unethical. Stanley Works remained in the U.S., but Accenture and Tyco shifted incorporations to Ireland and Switzerland respectively.

- **Noise.** Customers and other audiences live in information-rich environments. Myriad messages (*clutter*) bombard them daily; few messages are relevant to customer needs or firm products. Effective communications must cut through the clutter so firm messages resonate with intended targets.

- **Public perception.** Sometimes firms face public criticism for communications activities and feel compelled to change. NBC accepted liquor advertising on a trial basis ... it ended the three-month experiment. NBC received such criticism from the American Medical Association, members of Congress, federal regulators, and public advocacy groups that it voluntarily reinstituted its ban.[4]

- **Regulators.** Firms are biased information providers; hence, government agencies review communications to ensure fairness and accuracy. Many countries have *truth-in-advertising* laws.[5] Some countries (not the U.S.) ban comparative advertising. The U.S. main regulator is the FTC; entities like the National Advertising Review Board are self-regulating industry

Marketing Question

The FDA approves drugs for specific indications — medical conditions. Physicians can *use* an approved drug for different indications, but drug firms cannot *promote* such *off-label use* without FDA approval. The FDA approved Natrecor (J&J) for *short-term* treatment of heart-failure patients with breathing problems. Nurse practitioner Regina Massaro worked closely with Dr. Altschul, the physician who pioneered Natrecor use for *longer-term* treatment of heart-failure patients — an off-label use. J&J paid Massaro to make nationwide trips to discuss heart-failure management. Massaro couldn't promote Natrecor for off-label use, but she could answer questions about her experiences — many physicians ask about *longer-term* Natrecor treatment.[3] How do you assess J&J's actions in arranging and funding Massaro's trips?

KEY IDEA

➤ In formulating an integrated communications program, the firm faces significant *external* and *internal* challenges.

bodies.[6] Because self-regulators have no enforcement power, some advertisers ignore them; Ryanair routinely ignores the British Advertising Standards Authority.

> A U.S. federal district court ordered Philip Morris (PM) to pay $10 billion damages. PM did not tell customers that *light* cigarettes were as harmful as *full-tar* cigarettes.
>
> H&R Block faced lawsuits over *rapid refunds* of taxes. Block hid the fact that rapid refunds were actually high-interest-rate loans — over 500 percent annually.

- **Social media.** The explosion of social media on the Internet has vastly increased the volume of unmanaged communications about the firm and its brands. Positive communications can help the firm, but negative communications from these sources may severely damage the firm's reputation.

INTERNAL CHALLENGES

Communication challenges occur inside the firm as well as outside. Often-heard internal opinions about firm communications are:

- **We don't need it.** Many technically oriented firms assume the *best* product, as defined by their engineers, will *win*. "Our product will sell itself." But customers must believe that the *entire offer* (including the product) provides the best value. Communications play a major role in forming this belief.
- **We've already done that.** The firm believes it has already communicated enough. Perhaps the firm published technical papers or gave literature to the sales force. The firm may underestimate both the communications effort required to get the message across to customers, and competitor efforts. Hence, the firm under-funds communications, then wonders why customers don't know about its products.
- **It's an unnecessary expense.** Many firms prefer to spend resources for tangible assets like land and plant and equipment. Communications provide difficult-to-measure intangible benefits, and firms minimize communications expenses. As we shall see, measuring the impact of communications initiatives can be very challenging.
- **We need different messages for different audiences.** The firm has multiple communications targets like current and potential customers, complementers, employees, suppliers, and shareholders — sometimes even competitors. When different groups inside the firm have responsibility for communicating with these varied audiences, achieving communications consistency is very difficult.

🔑 KEY IDEA

➤ Critical external communications challenges include:
- Competitive communications
- Evolving communications technologies
- Multiple information sources
- Noise
- Public perception
- Regulators
- Social media

COMMUNICATIONS: PROCESS AND TOOLS

> P&G's demographic and psychographic research identified *chatters* — consumers who influence others about new products. P&G launched the Physique brand of hair-care products by targeting *chatters* with direct-to-consumer samples. P&G's website encouraged visitors to tell a friend and generated one million referrals in six months.[7]

THE COMMUNICATIONS PROCESS

Figure 15.1 shows the basis for any **communication process**. The *sender* sends a *message* to a *receiver*; the *receiver* receives the message. The dotted line shows that, in some communication processes, the *receiver* also communicates with the *sender*. Ideally, the receiver receives the message the sender *intended* to send. If this does not occur, there is **miscommunication** — typically not a good outcome. Three main sources of miscommunication are:

- **Encoding error.** Typically, some person or organizational entity decides on the intended message, but this message is not sent. Perhaps the advertising agency misinterprets product positioning and does not craft an appropriate message. Or salesforce training is ineffective, and they don't communicate the *right* message.

- **Distortion.** The firm sends the intended message, but communication is distorted; the receiver does not receive the sent message. Consumers receive similar print and TV advertisements differently: They may receive a TV advertisement running on *The Daily Show* differently from an identical message on *60 Minutes*. Or the salesperson's accent may affect the received message.

- **Decoding error.** Communications targets have selective attention, perception, and/or retention, related to individual perception, memory, and/or belief systems. Hence, the message is misperceived and/or misunderstood.

A critical marketing challenge is understanding and minimizing the causes of miscommunication.

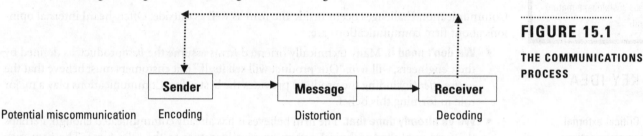

FIGURE 15.1

THE COMMUNICATIONS PROCESS

COMMUNICATIONS TOOLS

Communications tools are the ways marketers interface with target audiences. Two traditional categories driven by the firm are **personal communication** and **mass communication**. We embrace two extra categories — **digital communication** and **word-of-mouth communication** (**WOM**). Figure 15.2 shows how these tools interrelate from a marketer's perspective.

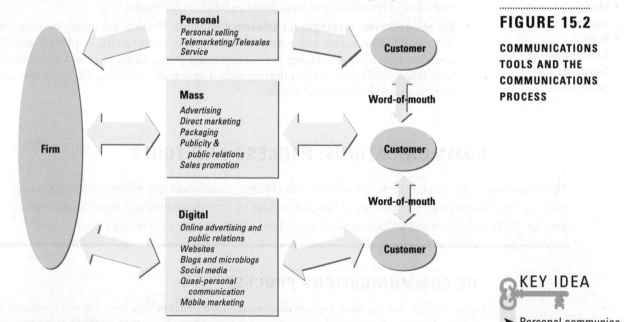

FIGURE 15.2

COMMUNICATIONS TOOLS AND THE COMMUNICATIONS PROCESS

PERSONAL COMMUNICATION. Interpersonal (often *face-to-face*) communication occurs among individuals or groups. Most personal communication in marketing occurs when sales-

KEY IDEA

➤ Mass communication occurs without interpersonal contact between sender and receiver.

Marketing Question

When you last contemplated acquiring a cell phone: How did potential suppliers communicate with you? What personal communication methods did they use? What mass communications methods? Was any digital communication involved? Did any supplier encourage WOM? Which communication method(s) were credible and engaging? Which methods had the greatest impact on your selection of cell phone and cellular service? Did communication methods change during your buying process?

KEY IDEA

➤ Digital communication embraces all forms of communication enabled by the Internet.

people and other firm representatives, like technical- and customer-service personnel, interact with customers individually or as team members. In B2B marketing, salespeople typically visit customer locations; much face-to-face B2C communication occurs in fixed locations like retail stores. In many firms, **telemarketing/telesales** supplements and/or replaces field salespeople. Some firms script personal communications, but most interpersonal communication evolves spontaneously during the interaction.[8]

MASS COMMUNICATION. Much marketing communication occurs without interpersonal contact between sender and receiver, particularly in B2C marketing.[9] Typically, the firm has greater control over message content in mass communication than in personal communication:

- **Advertising.** The firm pays for communications directed at a mass audience. Advertising embraces different modes, typically visual and audio, and types of media.[10] *Visual-static media* — printed matter — includes billboards, brochures, magazines, newspapers, point-of-purchase displays, signage, and trade journals. *Visual-dynamic media* includes television, movies, and online advertising. *Audio* includes radio and newer communications types like podcasts.[11]

- **Direct marketing.** Includes all paid and sponsored communications directed at individuals. Most direct marketing is printed mail, but more modern versions include audio/video tapes, DVD, CD-ROM, and e-mail.

- **Packaging.** Packaging's main value is to protect the product. But packaging is also a communications vehicle, delivering information and visual appeal.

- **Publicity & public relations (P&PR).** Publicity is communication for which the firm does not pay directly. Typically, the firm provides or *places* information like a photograph, press release, story, or video with a third-party transmitter. The transmitter, like an industry analyst, magazine, or news organization incorporates the material in its own communications. PR embraces publicity but is broader; PR includes other ways of gaining favorable responses for the firm. Typical PR activities include sponsoring events, giving speeches, participating in community activities, donating money to charity, and other public-facing activities.

- **Sales promotion (SP).** SP communications provide extra value for customers; firms often design SP to induce immediate sales. Consumer promotions include contests, coupons, games, point-of-purchase materials, premiums, rebates, and samples. Distributor (reseller) promotions include contests, merchandising allowances, special price deals, rebates, and volume buying. Special forms of SP are:

  - **Product placement.** The firm places products in movies and TV shows. Placement can be real, or virtual via electronic insertion of products, logos, and signs.[12] Three major types of placement are:
    - Product used by actors
    - Product integrated into the plot
    - Product associated with a character[13]

  - **Trade shows.** In many industries, suppliers (vendors) display and/or demonstrate products to large numbers of current and potential customers, at one time, in one convenient location. In turn, customers can communicate with large numbers of suppliers offering similar products and services.[14]

DIGITAL COMMUNICATION. The Internet has provided firms with many additional options for communicating with customers. Some methods are electronic analogues of traditional communication tools like various types of advertising on third-party websites and direct marketing via e-mail.

Other methods are specific to the medium, like firm websites, blogs and microblogs, social media, quasi-personal communications, and mobile marketing. Traditional and digital communications can also be linked via technologies like O-codes and QR codes for print media (used in *Managing Marketing in the 21st Century*) and TV ads containing web URLs, Facebook pages, and Twitter hashtags. In contrast to many types of communications, at firm websites customers frequently self-select the communications they receive. Some websites are morphing into *quasi-personal communication (QPC)*, embracing interaction and feedback without human involvement, usually via artificial intelligence. Customers talk on the telephone to computer servers via voice recognition software. QPC allows firms and customers to communicate on a one-on-one basis.[15] Amazon's repeat customers receive book recommendations based on prior purchases; Netflix subscribers receive movie tips.

> **Marketing Question**
>
> Identify a creative approach to quasi-personal communication.

> *The New York Times* reported positively on traveler responses to Julie: "Julie will remain unshakably courteous and tirelessly chipper. 'Hi, this is Amtrak. I'm Julie,' she says in a perky tone. 'O.K., let's get started.' She is casual: 'You'll want a pen and paper handy.' She is exacting: 'I think you said you want a 5 o'clock Acela to New York, am I right?' She is reassuring, interjecting 'Got it!' after each of the caller's answers. Occasionally, she is even apologetic: 'I'm sorry, I didn't get that.' Julie is not your normal telephone representative. Julie is more than an automated ticket agent. She offers a sympathetic ear and reassuring guidance."[16] Julie is Amtrak's computerized voice.

Further, the Internet is shifting from a computer-only medium onto TV sets (and TV programs onto computers), and to cell phones and tablet computers — mobile marketing.

WORD-OF-MOUTH (WOM) COMMUNICATION. Communication among customers and potential customers can impact many purchase elements like brand choice, distribution channel, and timing. Communications about a firm or product can be positive or negative, depending on the customer experience. Because customers typically have no commercial interest in the firm or product, they often have higher credibility than paid communicators.[17] Generally, firms have little control over **WOM** but increasingly they orchestrate **buzz-marketing**, **guerilla-marketing**, and **viral-marketing** campaigns to encourage positive communications.[18] Philips gave 33,000 samples of its new Sonicare Essence power toothbrush plus five $10 rebates to U.S. consumers. Microsoft gave Halo 2 (new version of popular video game) to an inner circle of committed players 18 months before launch; first-day sales, largely from pre-orders, were over $100 million.

> **Marketing Question**
>
> In the past month, have you recommended a product or service to someone — or did someone give you a recommendation? Did the firm take any action to encourage WOM?

Word-of-Mouth Communications

- Ford supplied 155,000 of its 400,000 workers with home PCs and Internet connections to encourage them to join chat groups and be ambassadors for Ford products.[19]
- Half.com launched its website by persuading citizens of Halfway, a small town in Oregon, to rename itself *Half.com*.[20]
- Pharmaceutical firms identify key opinion leaders in the medical community. They map physicians' social networks, focusing especially on individual physicians who link separate sub-networks.[21]
- P&G enrolled 600,000 moms, *connectors* with extensive social networks, in its Tremor program. Selected via an Internet screening site, each mom receives a handful of coupons and carefully crafted messages for specific P&G products.
- Salesforce.com CEO Marc Benioff, said: "We don't have a couple of hundred salespeople, we have a couple hundred thousand salespeople. They're called our customers. And it would be really cool if they were out there chatting it up, telling their friends, because it takes a really long time to go out and visit all the customers."[22]
- *The Big Tease* producers invited hundreds of hairdressers to previews in New York, Los Angeles, San Francisco, and London, hoping for word-of-mouth with customers.[23]
- Toyota used a multi-million-dollar *ride-and-drive* guerrilla marketing campaign to introduce the Scion in California. Scion team members on busy San Francisco street corners frequented by Generation Y encouraged passers-by to take a test drive.

> **Marketing Question**
>
> How can firms encourage positive word-of-mouth communication about their products? How would you use word of mouth to increase viewership for a new movie?

Some firms tap into established groups to take advantage of *social networking*. Cheerleaders are often popular students in high school: P&G and PepsiCo provide information and samples to organizations that promote high school cheerleading camps and competitions. *Bunco* is a three-

KEY IDEA

➤ Word-of-mouth communication occurs among customers and potential customers.

dice game increasingly popular among suburban women: P&G sponsored the Prilosec (heartburn medicine) OTC Bunco World Tour to encourage word-of-mouth for Prilosec. Marketers are increasingly evaluating social media on the Internet — Chapter 16, pp. 416–418.

DEVELOPING THE COMMUNICATIONS STRATEGY

Stainmaster advertises carpets directly to consumers. Stainmaster does not manufacture carpets, just the fiber, but successfully convinces consumers that Stainmaster carpets are stain-resistant. Stainmaster's effective communications drive high consumer awareness and demand for Stainmaster carpets — and also for its fibers.

Table 15.1 depicts critical questions for developing communications strategy.[24]

TABLE 15.1

CRITICAL QUESTIONS FOR DEVELOPING A COMMUNICATIONS STRATEGY

Basic Questions	Subsidiary Questions
1. Who are our communications targets?	Specifically, with what entities shall we communicate?
2. What are our communications objectives?	How do communications objectives vary by communications target?
3. What key message do we want to get across?	How should our message vary across communications targets?
4. What communications tools shall we use?	What combination of personal, mass, digital, and WOM communications is appropriate?
5. What communications budget shall we set?	How shall we apportion the communications budget among the different communications tools?
6. When is the *right* time to communicate?	What is the appropriate timing for the various targeted messages, considering seasonality and other factors?

KEY IDEA

➤ The firm has two major types of communications targets:

• *Directly related* to firm products

• *Not directly related* to firm products

COMMUNICATIONS TARGETS

The firm has two major types of communication targets: *directly related* to firm offers and *not directly related* to such offers. We focus mainly on *directly related* targets, but briefly consider *not directly related* targets. Some targets are decision-makers; others are influencers.

DIRECTLY RELATED COMMUNICATIONS TARGETS. The firm should be most concerned with reaching customers specified in the positioning statement of its market strategy — Chapter 9. These include current and potential customers, direct and indirect customers, and third-party specifiers and advisors. Figure 15.3 illustrates the situation for a hypothetical subcomponent manufacturer.

FIGURE 15.3

POTENTIAL COMMUNICATIONS TARGETS FOR A SUBCOMPONENT MANUFACTURER

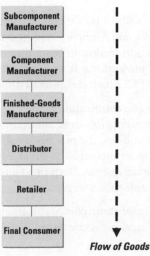

Flow of Goods

Broadly speaking, communications strategies are either **push** or **pull** — Figure 15.4:

- **Push strategy.** Communications focus on *direct* customers. In the illustration, the sub-component manufacturer (SM) places efforts on component manufacturers (CMs). The SM expects CMs to communicate with finished-goods manufacturers and other indirect customers further down the channel. Many B2B firms use *push* communications strategies, most effectively delivered by the sales force.

> Diamond Foods developed a *push* strategy to encourage retailers to carry its full snack food product line and secure better shelf placement and in-store marketing support. Diamond advertised in *Supermarket News* and in e-newsletters distributed by the Grocery Manufacturers Association and Food Retailing Institute. Diamond's message conveyed profitability and brand growth. Sales increased 70 percent.

- **Pull strategy.** Communications focus on *indirect* customers further down the channel, like final consumers or other end-user customers. By encouraging these customers to request and purchase finished goods, the firm generates *pull* and drives its own sales. In the illustration, final consumer demand impacts each channel entity back to the CMs and SM.

  This process can be *resultant* — the firm generates strong consumer demand, leading intermediaries to purchase products. The process may also be *anticipatory* — the firm plans a high-spending promotional campaign, and convinces indirect customers to purchase sufficient product volume to satisfy anticipated demand.

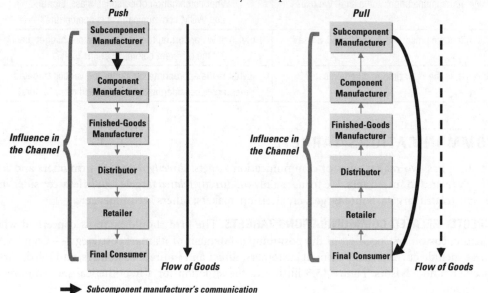

FIGURE 15.4

COMMUNICATIONS TARGETS IN PUSH AND PULL STRATEGIES

Most firms use *either* push or pull strategies, but resource-rich firms often use a combination. FMCG firms like P&G and Unilever rely heavily on *pull*-based advertising directed at consumers. Because of concentration in retail distribution and the emergence of powerful chains, they also place major *push* efforts at retailers. P&G's budget for *push* is roughly the same as for *pull* strategies. Figure 15.5 illustrates Intel's communications.

Regulations influence communications targets in some industries. The FDA previously banned direct-to-consumer prescription-drug advertising but has relaxed this prohibition in recent years (many countries still ban the practice); pull strategies now encourage patients to "ask your doctor." Firms may also be successful by breaking with traditional practice, like the Stainmaster carpet and *intel inside* campaigns. Both product-ingredient campaigns achieved success selecting innovative communications targets.

Competitors can be important communications targets. Frequently, formal communication with competitors is illegal, so some firms *signal* preferred competitor behavior — Chapter 5.

KEY IDEA

➤ Most firms use one of two communications strategies:
- Push
- Pull

Resource-rich firms often use combination *push/pull* strategies.

When American Airlines (AA) introduced *value pricing*, it aimed full-page advertisements in *The Wall Street Journal* at Delta, United Airlines, and other major carriers. AA wanted competitors to follow its lead; most did so within a couple of days. Of course, firms also send messages to confuse competitors. Suppliers and complementers may also be communications targets.

FIGURE 15.5

ILLUSTRATION OF PUSH AND PULL STRATEGIES WORKING TOGETHER

KEY IDEA

➤ Firms have many communications targets other than customers.

KEY IDEA

➤ Core considerations for the communications strategy are:
- Communications targets
- Communications objectives
- Communications messages
- Communications tools
- Budgeting and timing

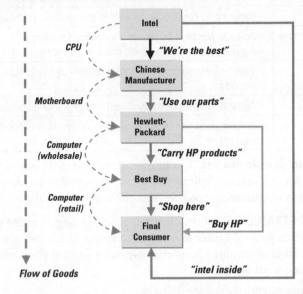

Finally, marketing may have various internal communications targets. Sometimes there is a disconnect between sales and marketing. A critical marketing challenge is ensuring that salespeople use the *right* communications when addressing customers. Marketing may also communicate with all employees so they internalize the firm's brand identity — Chapter 11.

NOT DIRECTLY RELATED COMMUNICATIONS TARGETS. Illustrated by Compaq, firms have many communications targets *not directly related* to products. Capital markets are a special case; firms or their agents (like investment banks) target investors to secure debt and equity financing. They also target specific investor types, like long-term investors, to influence shareholder composition.[25] Many firms also *lobby* legislators and special-interest groups.

> Following poor profit results and the firing of CEO Eckhard Pfeiffer, Compaq chairman Ben Rosen published a full-page letter in *The New York Times* extolling Compaq's virtues to "valued customers, shareholders, and partners."

Although *not directly related* to firm products, communications to these targets can have a serious impact on customers. Help-wanted advertisements for highly trained personnel may indicate technological leadership and that firm products are worth buying. A firm that lobbies against environmentally friendly legislation may lose sales to *green* consumers.

COMMUNICATIONS OBJECTIVES

Typically, long-run marketing communications objectives are to increase sales units and/or revenues. Prior requirements may be securing awareness, knowledge, liking, trial, and repeat purchase of firm products. When we consider objectives for *directly related* customer targets, major considerations are the type of target and the firm's market strategy.

COMMUNICATIONS TARGET. The firm typically has direct and indirect customers, and competitors and complementers.

- **Direct or indirect customers.** Figure 15.3 (p. 381) highlights several direct and indirect customers for a subcomponent manufacturer. Table 15.2 shows that communications objectives for each customer type would likely be quite different:

Marketing Question

Develop a communications plan for your favorite local restaurant. How does your plan improve on the restaurant's current actions?

Type of Customer	Communication Objectives for Customers
Component manufacturer	– Learn how to assemble firm subcomponents into customer components – Purchase subcomponents for use in components – Inventory sufficient components to satisfy finished-goods manufacturers
Third-party advisor	– Recommend firm subcomponents to component manufacturers
Finished-goods manufacturer	– Agree to purchase components for finished products – Agree to place subcomponent brand on finished product
Distributor	– Train salespeople to communicate benefits and sell finished products to retailers
Retailer	– Agree to budget co-op advertising funds for finished products
Consumer	– Become aware, understand, like, try, and continue to purchase finished products

TABLE 15.2

ILLUSTRATIVE COMMUNICATION OBJECTIVES FOR A SUBCOMPONENT MANUFACTURER

Marketing Question

Using the Table 15.2 framework, identify target customers and short- and long-term communications objectives for a firm making global position satellite (GPS) systems for pleasure boats.

- **Competitors and complementers.** Communications objectives are very different from firm objectives for customers. Typically, the firm tries to influence competitor and complementer actions so customers perceive firm offers more favorably.

THE FIRM'S MARKET STRATEGY. The firm identifies customer targets in the positioning statement of the market strategy — Chapter 9. Because customer targets are also communication targets, the firm must align communications objectives with selected alternatives in the *strategic focus* to increase unit sales volume:

- Increase customer retention (reduce defection)
- Increase customer use
- Attract customers from competitors
- Secure new business

Table 15.3 shows how market objectives and corresponding customer targets translate into specific communications objectives.

Market Objective	Customer Target for Increasing Unit Sales Volume	Communications Objective
Increase customer retention (reduce defection)	Current customers	– Reinforce customer beliefs that they made the best decision
Increase customer use	Current customers	– Persuade customers to purchase and use in larger quantities
Attract customers from competitors	Competitor customers	– Establish head-to-head trial against the competitor product
Secure new business	Non-users	– Secure new leads – Qualify potential customers – Increase awareness, knowledge, interest, liking, or trial as appropriate

TABLE 15.3

ILLUSTRATIVE COMMUNICATION OBJECTIVES BY CUSTOMER TARGET

Marketing Question

Identify a firm(s) that relies heavily on a *pull* strategy. Is the firm successful? If so, why? If not, why not?

Of course, communications objectives depend on the age and type of the firm's business and market conditions. In new markets, the firm must necessarily focus on identifying, qualifying, communicating, and selling to *non-users*. Conversely, if the firm is well-placed in a mature market, its objectives probably focus more on retaining *current customers*.

COMMUNICATIONS MESSAGES

Constructing the appropriate message for a customer target is central to developing the communications strategy. The core underlying principle is that message design should reflect the value proposition (positioning element) in the firm's market strategy. If the firm has multiple customer targets, each with different value propositions, then the firm must design multiple messages. Firms spend heavily to develop messages, especially advertising messages; hence we defer discussion of message design to Chapter 16.

Marketing Question

What are the benefits and challenges of using a *pull* strategy?

COMMUNICATIONS TOOLS

Communications objectives and messages drive firm choice of communication tools. Selecting the *right* tool(s) is critical in developing effective communications to reach target audiences. Suppose the communications objective is to build awareness for a new product among a broad consumer group; common sense tells us that advertising is probably more effective than sending salespeople door-to-door. But if the objective is selling sophisticated capital goods to large industrial companies, personal selling would likely be more productive in delivering messages and answering customer questions. Table 15.4 helps firms match communication tools to communications objectives and target customers. In the illustration, a wholesaler is trying to distribute and sell a new product. The wholesaler decides to:

- *Identify* potential retailers via direct marketing.
- *Qualify* retailers by telemarketing.
- *Sell* to qualified retailers via personal selling and its website.
- *Provide* retailers with ongoing sales and service via a sales and service team.

TABLE 15.4

MATCHING COMMUNICATIONS TARGETS, OBJECTIVES, AND TOOLS

Communication Tools	Communications Targets and Objectives			
	Identify potential retailers	Qualify retailers	Sell to qualified retailers	Provide retailers with ongoing sales and service
Personal selling			****	
Telemarketing/telesales		****		
Individual service personnel				
Sales and service teams				****
Advertising				
Direct marketing	****			
Publicity & public relations				
Sales promotion				
Online advertising and public relations				
Website			****	
Blogs and microblogs				
Social media				
Mobile marketing				

KEY IDEA

➤ Communications objectives and timelines drive the choice of communication tools.

The wholesaler chooses *not* to use advertising, publicity & public relations, sales promotion, individual service personnel, or digital approaches other than its website. The wholesaler should develop a similar chart for each customer target.

BUDGETING AND TIMING

The budgeting and timing of firm communications efforts are critical for determining the most effective communications strategy. Both budgeting and timing relate directly to communications objectives and selected communication tools.

A critical budgeting issue concerns the firm's choice of *push* versus *pull* communication strategies; they have very different cost parameters:

- **Pull strategies.** Firms generally spend heavily on advertising to generate *pull*. These *fixed-cost* expenditures require large cash outflows for uncertain revenues. Hence pull strategies are generally more popular with well-financed large firms than with small firms.

- **Push strategies.** Firms generally incur high *variable costs* from margins, discounts, and sales commissions earned by intermediaries like wholesalers and retailers. Payments directly relate to firm sales, limiting upfront cash outflows. Smaller firms favor push strategies.

Chapter 16 discusses budgeting in greater detail in an advertising context. Timing issues are especially critical in developing and executing integrated communications campaigns using multiple communications tools.

INTEGRATING COMMUNICATIONS EFFORTS

By now, you should understand the communications process, know the key questions for developing a communications strategy, and be familiar with communications tools. The firm's core challenge is to develop an effective **integrated marketing communications** program to maximize the impact of its strategy and achieve objectives. Figure 15.6 shows four types of integration for which the firm should strive:

A. Communications for all targets in a single market segment.

B. Communications with other marketing implementation variables — product, service, distribution, price.

C. Communications for all targets in several market segments.

D. Communications for all targets — market segments, markets, businesses, corporate.

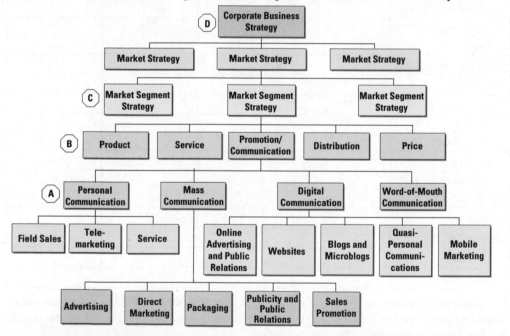

FIGURE 15.6

COORDINATING AND INTEGRATING COMMUNICATIONS

An electrical components supplier had marginal success with radio advertising, and also had little success with its website. When it advertised the website on drive-time radio, the results were spectacular — a real synergistic result.

Glidden's interior paint market share was declining and the brand was losing relevance. Glidden relaunched its website so visitors could paint virtual rooms (walls, ceiling, trim), share creations via social media, and make a shopping list. Newspaper and TV ads offered the first 300,000 website registrants a free quart of paint; later registrants received coupons. Social media accelerated the promotion and Glidden increased market share by 1.5 percent.

A — INTEGRATE COMMUNICATIONS FOR ALL TARGETS, IN A SINGLE MARKET SEGMENT
STRATEGY. This communications integration is fundamental. The firm should blend various communications campaigns (using different tools) to be mutually reinforcing and, if possible,

synergistic. Figure 15.7 shows the core message from a well-known B2B communications execution, featuring a procurement professional, that integrated advertising with personal selling. The critical pitfall is sending discrepant messages in the firm's personal and mass communications. Message consistency improves firm credibility.

FIGURE 15.7

CORE MESSAGE FROM A
PRINT ADVERTISEMENT
INTEGRATED WITH
PERSONAL SELLING

I don't know who you are.	**I don't know your company's customers.**
I don't know your company.	**I don't know your company's record.**
I don't know your company's product.	**I don't know your company's reputation.**
I don't know what your company stands for.	**Now, what was it you wanted to sell me?**

Sales starts before you call — with business-to-business advertising

As digital media becomes more important, many firms are spending significant effort to effectively integrate various digital communication options, as well as integrating digital communications with conventional mass and personal communications.

B, C, AND D — REFLECT HIGHER LEVELS OF INTEGRATION. In each case, the firm must ensure its messages are consistent and even strive for *synergy*. Corporate-level advertising like GE's "Imagination at Work" may be a helpful door-opener for salespeople. But to achieve good corporate-to-market integration, for example with GE's jet engines, the content and timing of product communications must coordinate with corporate advertising.[26]

Of course, communications to different groups — customers, competitors, complementers, shareholders, and government entities, typically have different purposes. But a single individual may belong to multiple groups and be a target for multiple communications. At a minimum, these communications should not be inconsistent.

Increasingly sophisticated segmentation and *mass customization* practices, along with proliferation of communication tools, are creating more opportunities for marketers to deliver targeted and relevant messages in a granular way. But as 21st-century customers move easily among the many communication channels, they expect ever more timely, relevant, and compelling (and even entertaining) marketing communications. The firm must construct a clearly defined communications strategy that seamlessly integrates its entire set of communications.

CONTINUES ON NEXT PAGE

---

*Marketing
Question*

Can you identify a firm that confused customers by sending discrepant messages?

KEY IDEA

➤ Communications integration occurs at several levels.

➤ Integration ensures maximum communications impact to achieve firm objectives.

*Marketing
Question*

What other messages did you glean from this chapter?

KEY MESSAGES

The firm's communications program is critical for implementing the market strategy. To develop a successful program, the firm must address many external and internal challenges.

Three sources of miscommunication are:

- Encoding error. The firm does not send the *intended* message.
- Distortion. The communication process distorts the *sent* message.
- Decoding error. The receiver misperceives and/or misunderstands the *received* message.

The firm has four categories of communications options:

- Personal — mainly salespeople, telemarketing/telesales, and service personnel
- Mass — including advertising, direct marketing, packaging, publicity & public relations, and sales promotion
- Digital — including online advertising and public relations, websites, blogs and microblogs, quasi-personal communication, and mobile marketing
- Word-of-mouth — among customers/potential customers, traditional/digital social media

To develop a communications strategy, the firm must answer six critical questions:

- Who are our communications targets? — *directly related* to firm offers; *not directly related*
- What are our communications objectives? — vary by target and the firm's market strategy
- What key messages do we want to get across? — vary by customer target — Chapter 16
- What communications tools shall we use? — examine the effectiveness of many options
- What communications budget shall we set? — Chapter 16
- When is the *right* time to communicate? — consider seasonality and other factors

The firm's core challenge is to integrate the various elements of its communications strategy to form a coherent whole. Four types of integration are:

A. Communications tools for all targets in a single market segment.
B. Communications with other marketing implementation variables — product, service, distribution, price.
C. Communications for all targets in several market segments.
D. Communication tools for all targets — market segments, markets, businesses, corporate.

QUESTIONS FOR STUDY AND DISCUSSION

Can you answer the questions implied by this chapter's learning objectives? Check!

1. Identify a personal communication that you sent but the receiver did not receive as intended. Was this an encoding, distortion, or decoding problem? How could you improve the communication?

2. Suppose you were marketing VP for Rolls-Royce Aero Engines. Who are your communications targets? What are your communications objectives for each target?

3. For many years, U.S. commercial banks could issue only MasterCard and Visa cards. That changed, and banks can now also distribute both AmEx and Discover cards. Use the Table 15.3 framework to identify new target customers and communications objectives for AmEx and Discover. Explain how and why target customers and communications objectives differ between AmEx and Discover.

4. Many firms have shareholder-relations departments. What do these departments do? Compare and contrast their activities to the advertising department in a business unit.

5. Sketch out an integrated communications program for Samsung's newest cell phone, or for a product that interests you, or this book — *Managing Marketing in the 21st Century*.

6. Repositioning by a regional bank involves longer weekday hours, weekend opening, and extensive online banking services. What steps would you take to develop an effective communications strategy for the *new* bank?

IMPERATIVE 4
Design the Market Offer

PART B – COMMUNICATING CUSTOMER VALUE

CHAPTER 16

MASS AND DIGITAL COMMUNICATION v1601

To access O-codes, go to **www.ocodes.com**

LEARNING OBJECTIVES

When you have completed this chapter, you will be able to:

- Articulate how advertising works.
- Define and measure advertising objectives.
- Design an advertising campaign.
- Know when to use each of the firm's major mass communication options — advertising, direct marketing, publicity & public relations, and sales promotion.
- Understand various digital communications options — advertising and public relations, websites, blogs and microblogs, social media, quasi-personal communications, and mobile marketing.
- Evaluate the mass and digital communications mix.

OPENING CASE: MASTERCARD INTERNATIONAL

MasterCard (MC), a credit card company owned by member banks, was in trouble in the late 1990s. Market share had declined for ten straight years and competitive pressures from Visa, AmEx, and Discover were intensifying. MC enjoyed the same retail acceptance as Visa, but top-of-mind awareness was ten percentage points inferior. MC was also losing support from member banks, both domestic and international: In the U.S., MC's share of direct-mail solicitations trailed Visa significantly.

MC conducted an extensive advertising agency review and selected McCann-Erickson (ME). ME concluded that this once-dominant brand had lost emotional relevance with consumers. MC had also lost credibility with critical member banks that claimed brand ownership, and MC was losing power. Worse, not only did the MC brand have different campaigns in almost every international market, Visa and AmEx consistently spent more.

ME's research in the U.S. and key international markets indicated consumers viewed MC as a stodgy, functional, everyday brand, with little aspirational relevance. AmEx was professional, worldly, and responsible; Visa was sociable, stylish, and on-the-go. By contrast, MC was unassuming, unpretentious, and practical. ME saw its task as shifting MasterCard from an emotionally neutral generic card to a card that consumers felt good about using.

ME's secondary data analysis revealed a shift away from the materialistic and outer-directed consumer culture of the 1980s and early 1990s. Success symbols like wearing designer clothes, shopping at prestigious stores, staying at luxury hotels, owning expensive cars, and using a prestigious credit card had been replaced. The new success symbols were being in control of, and satisfied with, one's life; having a good home and family; and being able to afford what was really important. The vast majority of consumers believed an unpaid credit card balance was "necessary and justified." ME dubbed this emerging mindset as good revolving *and set out to target* good revolvers, *by helping them lead* rich lives. *ME's selling idea was: MasterCard is* The Better Way to Pay for Everything That Matters.

Armed with this insight and direction, ME's three-person creative team — Joyce King Thomas, Jeroen Bours, and Jonathan Cranin — brainstormed extensively for a month. Cranin generated the tag line "Some things money can't buy" in the shower. A couple of weeks later, over Sunday morning coffee and bagels, Thomas and Bours conceived the first advertisement — set at a baseball game featuring some ordinary transactions. In the ad, voice-over actor Billy Crudup intoned, "Two tickets, $28; hot dogs, popcorn and soda, $18; autographed baseball, $45; real conversation with 11-year-old-son, priceless ... there are some things money can't buy. For everything else, there's MasterCard."

ME crafted more than 300 TV commercials, in 50 languages, shown in 108 countries. Globally, ME's work for MasterCard is the largest single campaign ever and won well over 100 creative awards. In the ultimate accolade, numerous comics and satirists parodied the Priceless campaign, incorporating impressions of Bob Dylan, Kenneth Lay, Bill Clinton, and George W. Bush, among others.

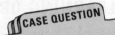

CASE QUESTION

How do you account for MasterCard's success? What other advertising campaigns do you consider memorable? Why?

Most important, the Priceless *campaign delivered impressive results for MasterCard. MasterCard's gross dollar volume increased by well over 250 percent; banks issued more than one trillion cards; brand awareness rose significantly; and the gap with Visa narrowed.*[1] *In May 2006, MasterCard's initial public offering (IPO) changed its status from a partnership of member banks to a public company. In 2011, MasterCard's share price reached $380, significantly higher than its $40 IPO.*

Chapter 16 is the second of three chapters in Part B of Imperative 4 — *Design the Market Offer.* Part B focuses on *Communicating Customer Value.* Chapter 16 addresses *Mass and Digital Communication.* Chapter 15 showed the firm has many ways of reaching audiences with mass and digital communications. We partition Chapter 16 into two sections, commencing with traditional forms of mass communications, devoting most attention to advertising. Then we switch direction to consider the newer forms of digital communications.

Advertising is the most visible form of mass communications and consumes the largest percentage of many FMCG firms marketing budgets. Advertising is also becoming increasingly important for a growing number of B2B firms. No matter what communications approaches the firm chooses, it must set objectives, select specific tools, execute the program, and measure results. This chapter explores the advertising process, then focuses most discussion on advertising strategies and methodologies. We also address other traditional marketing communications tools like direct marketing, publicity and public relations (P&PR), and sales promotion. In the chapter's second section, we focus on the newer form of digital communication. Advertising and public relations are also important in these media, but we focus here on websites, blogs and microblogs, social media, and mobile marketing.

THE CHANGING VIEW

OLD WAY	NEW WAY
Creativity desirable in messaging	Creativity essential in everything
Direct response methods are rare	Direct response methods are ubiquitous
Exposure-driven	Impact-driven
Intermediaries are usually involved	Movement to direct marketing
Intuition	Measurement/tracking
Local/national advertising strategies	Regional/global advertising strategies
Media scheduling is pedestrian	Media scheduling creativity is essential
Passive audience	Active/interactive audience
Short-term promotions common	Long-term brand equity a key concern

Half the money I spend on advertising is wasted; the trouble is I don't know which half.

— John Wanamaker[2]

Mass Communications

ADVERTISING FOUNDATIONS

At its essence, advertising is a service. When you pay attention to an advertising message, you receive the functional value of information and sometimes even find it entertaining — many of us look forward to Super Bowl advertisements. You may also receive psychological and economic value, but you rarely ever pay for them! From the customer's point of view, TV advertising (and TV) is free. When you purchase products like newspapers or magazines, you pay only a fraction of the product cost because the advertisements are part of the offer. What's going on?[3]

Figure 16.1 explains how this system works. Mostly, you (as a customer) receive advertising messages together with some content you desire, like a newspaper/magazine story or a TV show. The advertiser pays the media company to *bundle* its advertising with this content, but receives nothing *directly* in return. The advertiser receives its value *indirectly*, from the attention of your eyes and ears and, hopefully, your switched-on brain. Customers receive value from highly subsidized or free content; advertisers receive value from customer attention to their messages. These customers have immense value to advertisers.[4] Google's high market valuation is based on the sheer number of people who visit its website and then click through to advertiser websites.

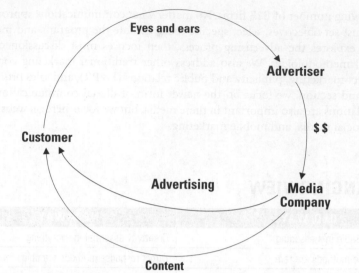

FIGURE 16.1

THE ADVERTISING
PROCESS

In many industries, particularly FMCG, advertising is central to implementing market and communications strategies. (Opening Case — MasterCard.) Table 16.1 shows critical questions for developing an **advertising strategy** and the relevant links to market and communications strategies. Similar questions help develop strategy for other mass and digital communications options.

Element	Question	Link to Market and Communications Strategies
Target audience	Whom are we trying to influence?	Customers in target segments (market strategy)
Advertising objectives	What are we trying to achieve?	Directly related to strategic and operational objectives (market strategy)
Messaging	What content should the target audience receive?	Related to the value proposition (market strategy)
Execution	How shall we communicate the message?	The most effective way to target customers
Media selection and timing	Where and when shall we place our advertising?	Select media to reach target customers at the appropriate time
Advertising budget	How much shall we spend on advertising?	Advertising budget is one element of the entire communications budget
Program evaluation	How shall we test our advertising and measure its effectiveness?	Choose from a variety of measurement methodologies

TABLE 16.1

ELEMENTS OF
AN ADVERTISING
STRATEGY

KEY IDEA

➤ Advertising is critical
for both market and
communications
strategies.

*Marketing
Question*

Table 16.2 shows reasons
that advertising can fail.
Identify some *ineffective*
advertising. Why did this
advertising fail?

Firms make investments today for financial returns tomorrow. In implementing market strategy, the firm should consider advertising as an *investment*; Today's advertising should achieve short-term results, but may also have long-run impact. Advertising may contribute to building the brand and lead to future customer purchases. Unfortunately, advertising spending is an expense on the firm's income statement and counts against this year's revenues. Hence, many firms under-fund advertising. Table 16.2 shows other reasons why advertising can fail.

Unclear or non-specific target	Weak creative content
Does not create a unique, ownable space	Creative does not support message
Mismatched message and advertising vehicle	No way to measure effectiveness
Too much information	Too many people involved
Inconsistent messages to multiple targets	Short-lived campaigns

TABLE 16.2

WHY ADVERTISING
CAN FAIL

The Advertising Program

TARGET AUDIENCE: WHOM ARE WE TRYING TO INFLUENCE?

Chapters 8 and 9 taught us that a key element in formulating the market strategy is deciding which segments to target. For each target segment, the positioning statement identifies customer targets with whom the firm wishes to communicate. For a *push* strategy, the firm focuses on direct customers; for a *pull* strategy, the firm focuses on indirect customers. The firm must also decide whether to reach decision-makers, influencers, and/or other entities in the purchase decision process. Because advertising funding is limited, the firm must carefully select its target audience before making advertising budget allocations.

FIGURE 16.2

HIERARCHY-
OF-EFFECTS
ADVERTISING
MODELS

How Advertising *Works*

Advertising effectiveness is perhaps the most-studied marketing topic.[5] **Hierarchy-of-effects** models are central to understanding how advertising works. Figure 16.2 shows models for high-involvement and low-involvement products.[6] Typically, the ultimate firm goal is to reinforce the brand and encourage *purchase* and *repeat purchase*. Note particularly the intermediate steps between *awareness* and *repeat purchase* in each model.[7,8]

High involvement. The customer believes the purchase, like a new automobile, involves financial and/or psychosocial risks. The customer engages in a staged learning process[9]:

- **Awareness.** Learning the product is available for purchase
- **Knowledge.** Understanding product features, benefits, and values
- **Liking or preference.** Developing favorable/positive feelings about the product
- **Trial.** Testing the product before purchase and use
- **Purchase.** Exchange money or other resources for the product
- **Repeat purchase.** Purchasing the product again. Advertising can reinforce positive feelings that lead to repeat purchase

Low involvement. Customers see little risk and require little pre-purchase knowledge — FMCG categories such as soda or cereal. Because risk is low, the hierarchical process is quite different. Advertising's role is to create high *awareness* and motivate customers to *trial*.[10] If customers like the product, they purchase and repurchase.[11]

🔑 **KEY IDEA**

➤ Hierarchy-of-effects models for high involvement and low involvement products are central to understanding how advertising works.

Marketing Exercise

Apply a hierarchy-of-effects model to your purchase of a HDTV set.

ADVERTISING OBJECTIVES: WHAT ARE WE TRYING TO ACHIEVE?

Once the firm has validated advertising as the appropriate communications vehicle, it should formulate **advertising objectives**. Two considerations are:

- **Output objectives** — what the firm ultimately wants to achieve, like sales, repeat purchase, market share, and brand loyalty.

- **Intermediate objectives** — relate to hierarchy-of-effects models and include awareness, knowledge, liking (preference), trial, and emotional commitment (to a brand). For a new product launch, the firm may initially focus on *awareness* as the crucial advertising objective. The importance of other intermediate objectives depends on the particular hierarchy-of-effects model governing purchase.

To achieve output objectives, the firm takes many actions, like delivering and servicing products, in addition to advertising. Hence, a failure to achieve an output objective like sales may be little related to success or failure in advertising. By contrast, well-chosen *intermediate objectives* provide excellent feedback on advertising effectiveness. The firm must choose specific output and/or intermediate advertising objectives for its particular strategic situation. Then it decides on numerical performance targets and when to measure actual performance.[12]

Illustrative Advertising Objectives

- To secure *90 percent awareness* of antioxidant toothpaste Wiz-klene among dentists within *one month of launch*.

- To increase *repeat purchase* of Munchee candy bars *from 30 to 50 percent* among 10- to 16-year-old boys *by end of June*.

MESSAGING: WHAT CONTENT SHOULD THE TARGET AUDIENCE RECEIVE?

The firm's advertising message derives directly from the market strategy — Chapter 9. Look back at that chapter, especially the four positioning elements:

Convince	[customer target]
In the context of other alternatives	[competitor targets]
That they will receive these benefits	[value proposition]
Because we have these capabilities/features	[reasons to believe]

The firm's advertising message should follow directly from the positioning statement, with special emphasis on the value proposition. The message should focus upon core benefits and values and reflect unique claims where the firm has a differential advantage. Clear positioning statements provide excellent guidance for creative personnel in advertising agencies to develop effective messages. By contrast, poor positioning often leads to unsatisfactory and/or confusing messages. The messaging must also reflect the amount of time the audience may be exposed to advertisements. The life span for newspapers is usually part of a day; for magazines maybe one week; for television a few seconds. Messages must also evolve and resonate with the audience over time, but support consistent positioning (like the Opening Case — MasterCard). Table 16.3 shows how FedEx's objective and core message evolved.[13]

KEY IDEA

➤ The firm should set two types of advertising objectives — output and intermediate.

➤ *Output objectives* are what the firm ultimately wants to achieve:
- Purchase
- Repeat purchase

➤ *Intermediate objectives* relate to hierarchy-of-effects models and include:
- Awareness
- Knowledge
- Liking (preference)
- Trial

TABLE 16.3

ADVERTISING
OBJECTIVES AND
MESSAGING —
FEDEX (FEDERAL
EXPRESS)

Year	Objective	Core Message	Slogan
1972	Awareness	Who are we? How do we work?	"Take away our planes and we'd be just like anybody else."
1978	Knowledge	How do we compare?	"When it absolutely, positively has to be there overnight."
1980–1987	Trial and repeat purchase	Try us! Don't switch	"Why fool around with anybody else?"
1995 and later	Repeat purchase	Don't switch	"Don't be a dope."

Firms active in multiple countries must decide whether, and to what extent, they should *standardize* messages globally or *localize* them for national/regional markets. National markets differ in cultural norms, living patterns, and income distribution, so these variables provide useful *hooks* for developing messages. But standardization can provide cost and efficiency savings. Also, by exerting quality control centrally, the firm can avoid problems like those that Coke faced when it relinquished corporate control of its message. If the firm standardizes, it should still seek local input to avoid potential translation problems.[14]

As part of a decentralization initiative, Coke gave power to regional marketers who previously relied on corporate expertise. Some advertising was unCoke-like. In one U.S. advertisement, a grandmother is angry that Coke is not served in a restaurant — she knocks over a table with her wheelchair. In Germany, a scantily clad couple is shown groping while enjoying a Coke.[15]

Marketing Question

Can you think of advertising messages or slogans that would not work globally?

Recently, standardization has become easier as advertising agencies have *gone global*. Large firms increasingly rely on single agencies for communications around the world. HSBC placed all global advertising and marketing with WPP; a 600-person WPP team from 21 local agencies manages the $600 million account. Exxon shot commercials for its advertising campaign, "We're drivers too," in two locations, but used more than 20 different casts to make it seem local wherever it aired. Of course, the *right* degree of standardization depends on the product form, target customers, and competition. Some messages may not work well in different countries.

EXECUTION: HOW SHALL WE COMMUNICATE THE MESSAGE?

🔑 KEY IDEA

➤ Creating advertising is an enigma, more art than science, mysterious, and unexplainable.

Execution focuses on the method (style) firms use to turn core messages into effective advertising. This task is daunting and challenging. Columbia colleague, branding guru Schmitt, explains: "Creative output [is] the most visible part of advertising. Although judging creative output may be easy, the creative process is an enigma, more art than science, mysterious and unexplainable. The essence of creativity seems to be a willingness to alternate between divergent and convergent thinking, between brainstorming and analytic reasoning, between pushing the limits and being reasonable and practical. [The result, ideally,] culminates in an illumination — the Big Idea."[16]

In the Opening Case, we saw how a *Big Idea* drove MasterCard's highly successful advertising campaign. Another creative success was Absolut vodka's print campaign. Absolut's share of imported vodka increased from 1 percent to over 60 percent. Figure 16.3 shows typical Absolut ads, beginning with a two-word headline, or *tag line*, starting with Absolut, then adding carefully chosen words to reinforce the imagery, like Absolut Perfection, Absolut Appeal, Absolut Original, in the context of the bottle shape. Absolut's campaign, featuring several hundred executions on a single theme, won many awards for elegance, simplicity, and effectiveness that set it apart from competition.[17]

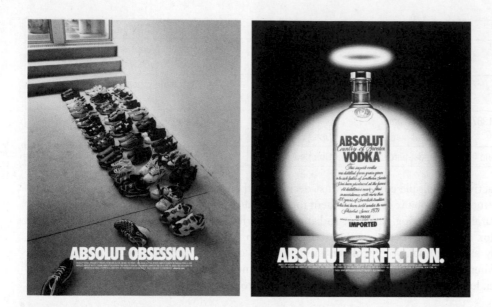

FIGURE 16.3

EXAMPLES OF ABSOLUT ADVERTISEMENTS

HSBC ran a print campaign based on a similar premise, a core message with multiple executions. HSBC's value proposition was global reach and local knowledge. The headline, "Never underestimate the importance of local knowledge," appeared two-thirds of the way down the page followed by six short paragraphs that elaborated the local knowledge claim. The top part of the page showed two or three objects identified by country.

HSBC used two types of execution:

- Type 1 — same objects: *Identical* objects were labeled *differently* in different countries. Figure 16.4 (LHS) shows the *grasshopper* advertisement (top part): USA — pest; China — pet; Northern Thailand — appetizer. Other similar advertisements were: *hand position*: Egypt — "Be patient"; Italy — "What exactly do you mean?"; Greece — "That's just perfect"; and *foot position*: USA — relaxed; Thailand — rude.

- Type 2 — different objects: *Different* objects were labeled *similarly* — Table 16.4 (RHS). Table 16.4 shows how HSBC supported its local claim by using examples from many countries. HSBC continued its *glocal* message by placed locally themed advertising on jet bridges, in baggage claim, and many other locations at major international airports.

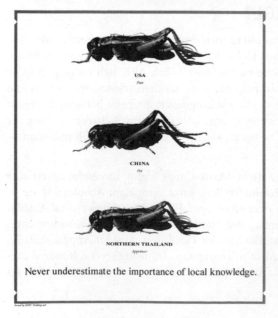

Never underestimate the importance of local knowledge.

Type of Object	Countries
Football	USA, UK, Australia
Lucky charm	Egypt, UK, Turkey
Delicacy	China, Mexico, France
Bagpipes	Scotland, Ireland, England
Married	India, USA
Gift to newborn	UK, China, Turkey
Dancing shoes (boots)	USA, UK, South Africa
Rugby team (mascot)	USA, South Africa, Argentina
Formal wear	Scotland, Malaysia, Philippines
Unlucky number	China, Japan, USA
Mousetrap	USA, Malaysia
Robot	Japan, South Africa

FIGURE 16.4 (LEFT)

EXAMPLE OF HSBC ADVERTISEMENT: IDENTICAL OBJECTS

TABLE 16.4 (RIGHT)

EXAMPLE OF HSBC ADVERTISEMENT: DIFFERENT OBJECTS

Sometimes audience characteristics drive executional variety. A Unilever brand manager explained how a strategy change at Sony influenced Unilever: "PlayStation had 19 different executions last year because Sony knows young consumers get bored easily. Three years ago we ran three Lynx (deodorant for boys) executions a year; we raised this to 10, with more to come."[18]

Advertising executions come in two major forms — **rational** and **emotional:**

RATIONAL APPEALS

Rational appeals appeal to people's sense of logic. Five main styles are:

- **Comparative (Attack).** Successful comparative advertising focuses on demonstrating superiority over competition. Small market share firms often compare products to the leader, so as to enter the customer's consideration set. Well-known examples are Avis ("We try harder"), the "Pepsi Challenge," and multiple executions of Mac versus PC with actors Justin Long and John Hodgman, respectively.[19]

> Virgin Atlantic Airways chairman Sir Richard Branson makes a point of exploiting gaffes by arch-rival BA. BA's CEO referred to Hollywood stars as "gutless cowards" for refusing to fly after 9/11. Virgin advertised in *Variety* and the *Hollywood Reporter* featuring the "gutless cowards" remark and providing Virgin Atlantic's phone number.

- **Demonstration.** Shows the product in use and focuses on performance. Many B2B communications use **demonstration ads**; they are also common in sales force materials.[20]
- **One-sided and two-sided.** **One-sided advertising** focuses only on positive product attributes; **two-sided advertising** presents both positive and negative messages. One-sided appeals are most effective when the target audience is less educated and feels positive about the product. Two-sided appeals are more effective when the initial audience opinion is not necessarily positive and the audience is educated and/or skeptical. Two-sided appeals enhance advertiser credibility because they present opposing viewpoints. They may also inoculate target audiences against competitor communications by making them more likely to resist counterclaims.[21]
- **Primacy or recency.** Research shows that items at the beginning of a message — **primacy** — and at the end — **recency** — are more effective than those in the middle.[22] When the audience is less interested in a product, or has an unfavorable prior impression, primacy advertising is generally more effective in gaining attention and/or minimizing objections. When the audience is initially favorable, and disinterest and/or objections need not be overcome, recency advertising generally reinforces a favorable product impression.
- **Refutational.** A special case of two-sided advertising explicitly mentions competitor claims, but then directly refutes them — beef advertisement alludes to the implication that red meat may be less healthy than other choices, then refutes that proposition. Refutational appeals may also succeed by inoculation.[23]

Firms often use high-credibility sources to enhance rational appeals. When battling Oracle's takeover bid, PeopleSoft placed full-page advertisements in *The Wall Street Journal, The Washington Post*, and other major papers. These ads quoted major U.S. newspapers and analysts, suggesting an Oracle-PeopleSoft merger would harm PeopleSoft customers and should be defeated (Oracle prevailed). Firms also use employees — both CEOs and shop-floor workers — as credible sources.

EMOTIONAL APPEALS

These advertising approaches appeal to emotions. Four main styles are:

- **Celebrity endorsement.** Advertisers often use well-known people to endorse products, especially on TV. A good celebrity/product match creates product awareness and credibil-

Marketing Exercise

Use available resources like print media and YouTube to identify advertisements using each of the rational and emotional appeals discussed. Bring to class.

KEY IDEA

➤ Rational-style advertising includes:

- Comparative
- Demonstration
- One- and two-sided appeals
- Primacy or recency
- Refutational

ity. Houston Rockets basketball star Yao Ming endorsed Disney, Gatorade, McDonald's, and Reebok. Coty offered a Jennifer Lopez fragrance; Elizabeth Arden countered with Britney Spears.[24] Celebrity endorsements reached a new level when former heavyweight champion George Foreman sold his name and image to grill manufacturer Salton for $137.5 million.[25]

Celebrity endorsement is not a *slam dunk*. To be effective, the audience must attend to the product, not just the celebrity! A celebrity can lose credibility by endorsing too many products. Former basketball star Michael Jordan endorsed AMF Bowling, Ball Park Franks, Bijan, CBS Sportsline, Chicagoland Chevrolet Dealer Association, Gatorade, Hanes, MCI Worldcom, Nike, Oakley, Rayovac, Wheaties, and Wilson Sporting Goods! Also, negative publicity for the celebrity can affect the product. O.J. Simpson's murder trials hurt Hertz. A Beef Industry Council campaign featuring Cybill Shepherd and James Garner used the tag line, "Real food for real people." Shepherd was later quoted in *Family Circle* as "trying to cut down on red meat"; Garner had a quadruple bypass! Coca-Cola, McDonald's, and Spalding dropped Kobe Bryant (sexual assault accusations); Haynes dropped Charlie Sheen (felony assault and menacing charges); Nike dropped sprinter Justin Gatlin (performance-enhancing drugs) and football player Michael Vick (illegal dogfighting); Phonak dropped Tour de France "winner" Floyd Landis (performance-enhancing drugs); and Accenture, AT&T, Gillette, and PepsiCo dropped Tiger Woods (extramarital affairs).[26] Sometimes CEOs become celebrities by endorsing firm brands, like Charles Schwab (investments) and Frank Perdue (chicken), but there can be problems: Pete Coors (Coors Chairman) strongly promoted responsible drinking, yet was arrested for DUI (driving under the influence).

- **Fear.** Fear appeals create anxiety; behaving as the advertising suggests removes the anxiety. *Physical danger* is common in insurance advertising; *social disapproval* for personal hygiene products; *monetary loss* for security products and credit cards; and *female insecurities* for cosmetic creams. A famous fear appeal shows a baby sitting in a Michelin tire with the tagline "So much is riding on your tires." Developing effective fear appeals is not easy: Too mild and they lack impact; too strong and they may be blocked or rejected by audience defense mechanisms.[27]

- **Humor.** Humor is widespread in advertising but should be used carefully. Humor helps create awareness, sets a positive tone, and enhances memory, but if improperly crafted may distract from the core message. The result: The audience remembers the ad but not the product. Worse, the audience may *mis-index*, linking the humor with a competitive product. Further, humor can be tedious if not varied, and humor for one person may be unfunny for another. Many people found Go Daddy's 2005 Super Bowl ad very funny — a well-endowed dancer struggled with her top while explaining a commercial to a stuffy Congressional committee.[28] Fox ran the ad early in the game, but canceled a planned second airing.[29]

- **Storytelling.** Storytelling can be a very effective way of appealing to people's emotions. MasterCard's *Priceless* campaign and Nike's *Just Do It* are good storytelling examples.

In practice, many firms combine/blend these pure-form message approaches. Regardless of appeal type, advertisers must understand the language of target customers. Bankers talk of "spreads" and "basis points." Urban teenagers talk of "gangstas" and "y'all wordupbra." Understanding word meanings is critical, especially when firms target customers abroad. A British firm whose product is great for "knocking you up" might be surprised at its reception in the U.S.!

KEY IDEA

➤ Emotional-style advertising includes:
- Celebrity endorsement
- Fear
- Humor
- Storytelling

Marketing Question

Identify an advertisement using a fear appeal. What is the objective and the advertiser's anticipated outcome? Do you think the ad works?

Marketing Question

View Go Daddy's *Censorship Hearing* advertisement (www.godaddy.com). Do you think it is funny? Why or why not? Bring your favorite humorous advertisement to class.

Marketing Question

Select three of your favorite advertisements. Describe their message styles. Were they *rational* — comparative, demonstration, one- or two-sided appeals, primacy or recency, refutational? Or *emotional* — celebrity endorsement, fear, humor, storytelling? Or a combination of styles?

MEDIA SELECTION AND TIMING: WHERE AND WHEN SHALL WE PLACE OUR ADVERTISING?

In 2011, global advertising spending exceeded $460 billion; U.S. spending was $165 billion.[30] Figure 16.5 shows global spending by major media class. Media choices are expanding; Internet advertising is growing fastest.

FIGURE 16.5

GLOBAL ADVERTISING SPENDING BY MAJOR MEDIA CLASS 2011 ($ BILLIONS)[31]

Marketing Exercise

Redraw Figure 16.5 with your forecast of advertising spending ten years in the future.

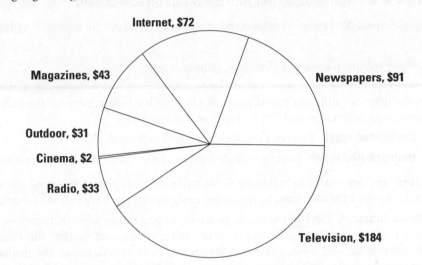

To select the appropriate media, the firm must answer five related questions:

- **Media objectives.** What should our media strategy accomplish?
- **Type of media.** Which media classes shall we use — print, broadcast, outdoor?
- **Specific media.** Which media vehicles shall we use — *Vanity Fair, Survivor*, bus stops?
- **Timing.** When will our advertising appear?
- **Media schedule.** Specifically, where and when shall we place our ads?

MEDIA OBJECTIVES

KEY IDEA

➤ Critical media selection and timing decisions:

Media objectives
↓
Type of media
↓
Specific media
↓
Timing
↓
Media schedule

WHAT SHOULD OUR MEDIA STRATEGY ACCOMPLISH? Key concerns are **reach**, **frequency**, and **impact**:

- **Reach.** Number of target individuals exposed to the advertising at least once.
- **Frequency.** Average number of times a target individual is exposed to the advertising.
- **Reach and frequency.** Reach and frequency calculate **gross rating points** (**GRPs**).

Gross rating points (GRPs) = Reach × Frequency

Generally, advertisers trade off reach and frequency. GRP objectives are popular, but may cause problems. For example, to secure 250 GRPs:

- 100 percent of the audience receives, on average, 2.5 exposures.
- 10 percent of the audience receives, on average, 25 exposures.

Many advertisers require a minimum number of exposures; hence, they set GRP objectives subject to a minimum required frequency. For complex messages, messages in competition with others, and/or messages for new products, advertisers typically require high frequency, but they should also be concerned about diminishing returns. Of course, media objectives should relate directly to advertising objectives.

Illustration of Media Objectives

- *Reach* 50 percent of the target audience five times in the next six months — *frequency.*
- Deliver 250 *GRPs* subject to a minimum 70 percent *reach.*

Illustration of Advertising Objectives (AO) and Media Objectives (MO)

AO: Increase repeat purchase of Munchee candy bars from 30 to 50 percent among 10- to 16-year-old boys by end of June.

MO: Deliver 1,500 GRPs, subject to a minimum 60 percent reach.

When the firm uses different media types, duplication is an issue. Suppose the firm decides to advertise on both radio and TV; two relevant measures are:

- **Duplicated reach:** Receive a message from *both* radio and TV.
- **Unduplicated reach:** Receive a single message, *either* radio or TV, but not both.

Sometimes the firm wants to maximize *duplicated reach* by exposure to several media types. Alternatively, the firm may want to maximize *unduplicated reach* regardless of media type.

- **Impact.** Impact is directly related to creativity in generating advertisements — indeed, many *creatives* view the media department's job as boring and routine. But mass media has fragmented and consumer media habits are more varied; hence, the media task is increasingly challenging. Thirty years ago, an FMCG firm could reach 70 percent of women aged 25 to 54 with less than 10 advertising spots on network TV; today it takes more than 100 spots. The best media executives are highly creative; an innovative media strategy, embracing novel use of existing media, first use of a new medium, or highly targeted messaging can generate enormous impact. Some firms achieve objectives with fewer GRPs and with lower expenditures by placing a single basic advertisement in several media like using varying length videos for TV, movie theaters, and the Internet. Creative media strategies spawned advertising-supported bus shelters in New York and colorful buses and taxis in many other cities.[32]

> **KEY IDEA**
>
> ➤ Important media objectives include:
>
> - Reach
> - Frequency
> - Impact

Häagen-Dazs successfully launched super-premium ice cream in Britain, using only black-and-white newspaper ads, for just £375,000. This unexpected copy gained significant publicity and the creatives won a major advertising award.

TYPE OF MEDIA

WHICH MEDIA CLASSES SHALL WE USE? A **media class** is a group of closely related media. Media classes differ from one another on dimensions like time availability and intrusiveness. A common category system (with examples) is:

- **Broadcast** — television and radio. Exist for short time periods — significantly intrusive.
- **Online** — e-mail and web alerts. Delivered in real time. Read at leisure — more intrusive than print.
- **Outdoor** — billboards and in-store. Long presence — relatively non-intrusive.
- **Print** — newspapers and magazines. Read at leisure — relatively non-intrusive.

Table 16.5 shows advantages and disadvantages of selected media classes[33]:

>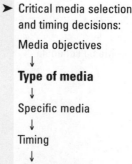
>
> **KEY IDEA**
>
> ➤ Critical media selection and timing decisions:
>
> Media objectives
> ↓
> **Type of media**
> ↓
> Specific media
> ↓
> Timing
> ↓
> Media schedule

TABLE 16.5

**ADVANTAGES AND
DISADVANTAGES
OF SELECTED
MEDIA CLASSES**

Media Class	Advantages	Disadvantages
Direct mail	High information content High selectivity Opportunities for repeat exposures Reader controls exposure	High cost per contact High level of in-store clutter Poor image (junk mail)
In-store	Customers ready to buy Location specific Many options — special displays, packaging, TV	Difficult to measure impact
Internet	Measurement by click-through Multiple options Segmented audiences	Less understood than others
Magazines	High information content Longevity Multiple readers (high pass-along) Quality reproduction Segmentation potential	Lack of design flexibility Long lead time for placing advertising Visual only
Newspapers	Ads can be placed in interest sections Can be used for coupons High coverage Low cost Reader controls exposure Short lead time for placement Timely (current ads)	Clutter Low attention-getting capabilities Poor reproduction quality Selective reader exposure Short life
Outdoor	Easily noticed High repetition Location specific	Local restrictions Poor environmental image Short exposure time requires short ad
Radio	Flexible High frequency Local coverage Low cost Low production costs Well-segmented audiences	Audio only Clutter Fleeting message Low attention-getting
Television	Attention-getting Favorable image High prestige High reach Impact of sight, sound, and motion Low cost per exposure Mass coverage	Clutter High absolute cost High production costs Low selectivity Short message life

*Marketing
Question*

You are launching an
Internet security system for
large and small businesses.
Identify your communica-
tions targets. Identify media
classes. Why these?

Figure 16.5 (p. 399) shows that the most-used media classes are direct mail, newspapers, and television, but firms try to avoid clutter by using less-conventional approaches. Technological advances, low prices, and increased driving make outdoor advertising attractive — airport signs, billboards, blimps, buses, bus shelters, malls, racing cars, soccer jerseys, subways, street furniture, and stadium displays. Ford purchased $50 million of billboard advertising, gaining exposure on hundreds of U.S. billboards. Some firms base their success on outdoor advertising:

At the Taj Mahal, a sign reads, "Only 10,728 miles to Wall Drug." Wall Drug (Wall, South Dakota [population 800]) has $10 million annual revenues. Wall's initial growth came from signs on nearby Route 16. Later, it put signs on every South Dakota highway and in neighboring states, stating the distance to Wall Drug. Wall spent $300K annually on a global outdoor campaign, including London buses and every train station in Kenya. Wall gained publicity from many newspaper and magazine articles and from U.S. GIs placing "xxx miles to Wall Drug" signs around the world.

Firms also use unusual outdoor advertising placements. Consider urinals: Brut placed print ads at eye level mostly in bar bathrooms; some firms use video advertising. Kentucky Fried Chicken paid to repair 350 Louisville potholes; "Re-freshed by KFC" advertisements sprayed on the spots lasted about one month. In Beijing, groups of 15 teenagers, wearing identical Ai Jia ("love home") neon-yellow warm-up jackets and matching baseball caps, ride bicycles in formation along set street routes.[34] In rural China, HP advertises by sending flashy buses with TVs to country schools and towns. Detroit Pistons player Richard Hamilton advertised for Goodyear by wearing his hair in the shape of a tire tread. Hotels.nl, a Dutch online reservations firm, displayed its corporate logo on waterproof blankets worn by sheep. McDonald's placed signs at street-sign posts in Bariloche, Argentina.

SPECIFIC MEDIA

WHICH MEDIA VEHICLES SHALL WE USE? A **media vehicle** is a specific entity in a media class. The *newspaper* media class includes *The New York Times*, *The Boston Globe*, and *The San Francisco Examiner*. The *magazine* media class includes *Good Housekeeping*, *Time*, and *Vanity Fair*. The *television* media class includes *60 Minutes*, *American Idol*, *Days of Our Lives*, and in-store (e.g., Walmart, Tesco). How do you select which vehicle is right for your product or service? Critical issues in choosing media vehicles are:

- **Audience size.** How many readers/viewers/listeners are there? Audited readership, listenership, or viewership statistics are available for most media vehicles; audited figures drive advertising costs.[35] Of course, the firm must assess the proportion of total audience with *target* audience characteristics. The firm must also consider behavioral attributes affecting audience size: Multiple readerships from magazines in professional offices and TV viewers leaving the room, changing channels, or using *time-shifting* digital-video recorders (DVRs) to avoid advertising. Listenership/viewership in group settings like college dormitories, hospitals, and prisons is a difficult measurement issue.

- **Audience type.** Does the audience fit with the communications target? Specifically, does it have the right demographics — age, gender, lifestyle, marital status, and product-use characteristics? If not, the media vehicle is inappropriate.

- **Cost.** Two costs are important in assessing advertising vehicles:
  - **Absolute cost.** Total out-of-pocket cost — the price for one advertisement in *The New York Times* or a 30-second commercial on *60 Minutes*.
  - **Cost per audience member.** A breakdown cost for comparing media vehicles, based on audience size.[36] A popular measure for print media is:
    Cost per thousand (CPM) = Total cost of advertising space × 1000/Circulation[37]

- **Nature of the media vehicle.** How does the message interact with the media vehicle? Readers generally pay more attention to advertisements in magazines than in newspapers. A *good* ad may be ineffective in a particular media vehicle, even with a good audience fit and favorable costs — like a serious, fear-provoking ad in a TV comedy show. Said one influential media buyer, "I've got a number of advertisers who have told me: 'Don't put me next to negative coverage of the economy.'"[38]

TIMING

WHEN WILL OUR ADVERTISING APPEAR? The four main timing patterns are:
- **Concentration.** Commit all expenditures at one time.
- **Continuous.** A regular periodic advertising pattern.
- **Flighting.** Repeated high advertising levels followed by low (or no) advertising.
- **Pulsing.** Combines continuous and flighting. Pulsing can occur within a media vehicle, within a media class, or across multiple media vehicles and classes.[39]

KEY IDEA

➤ Critical media selection and timing decisions:

Media objectives
↓
Type of media
↓
Specific media
↓
Timing
↓
Media schedule

TABLE 16.6

ILLUSTRATION OF A MEDIA PLAN FOR A CONSUMER PRODUCT

Generally, advertising experts believe **continuous advertising** is most effective for products purchased throughout the year. **Flighting** and **pulsing** are more effective when demand varies as for seasonal products — cruises and air travel.[40] Advertising carryover effects — the extent to which advertising in one period has value in subsequent periods — may be important.[41]

MEDIA SCHEDULE

SPECIFICALLY, WHERE AND WHEN SHALL WE PLACE OUR ADS? In selecting its media schedule, the firm tries to optimize media objectives like reach, frequency, and GRPs, subject to a budget constraint. Securing the best media buy in one media class is a complex task. Designing a campaign embracing multiple media classes is even more difficult. Major advertisers use computer models, modified by managerial judgment, to develop optimally effective **media schedules**. Table 16.6 shows a typical media plan.

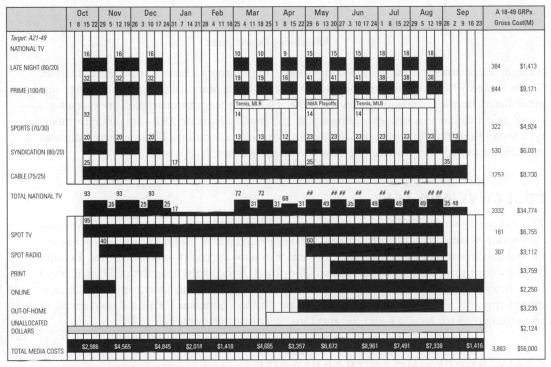

a. Online comprises promotions, microsites, and rich media
b. Read "80/20" as 80% — 15-second slots, 20% — 30-second slots; 100% is all 15-second slots
c. Read 16 as gross rating points (GRPs) per week. The blocks indicate numbers of weeks.
d. All spot television is 30-second slots.
e. All spot radio is 60-second promotional spots.
f. Out-of-Home comprises aerial banners, king-size bus posters, 8-sheet posters, indoor billboards, and coasters.

KEY IDEA

➤ The advertising message must appear in the right place at the right time.

➤ Major timing options are:
  • Concentration
  • Continuous
  • Flighting
  • Pulsing

ADVERTISING BUDGET: HOW MUCH SHALL WE SPEND ON ADVERTISING?

The **advertising response function (ARF)** relates advertising spending to advertising objectives like sales. The ARF is crucial for setting the **advertising budget** but its shape is typically not known. The firm faces two questions in deciding its advertising budget:

• **What shape is the ARF?** Figure 16.6 shows alternative ARFs, A and B. Each has some intuitive appeal and research support.[42] Spending implications are different for low and moderate spending.

- **Where is the firm currently operating?** If the firm were at I on ARF **A**, it would probably increase spending modestly; if the firm were at II, it would probably hold or reduce spending. At I' on ARF **B**, the firm should increase spending dramatically.

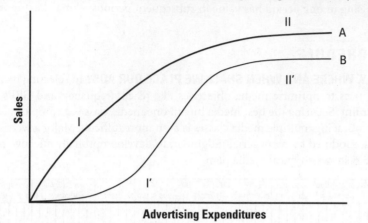

FIGURE 16.6

**ALTERNATIVE
ADVERTISING
RESPONSE
FUNCTIONS**

If the firm can answer these two questions, budgeting is simply a matter of marginal analysis: Set the budget where marginal revenue equals marginal cost. Marginal analysis underpins computer-based, decision-calculus models like ADBUDG.[43] Managers estimate sales, or other advertising objectives, at various advertising levels; the models estimate ARFs for different media vehicles and calculate optimal spending levels and media allocations. Because these estimates are difficult to make, in practice firms use several approaches:

OBJECTIVE AND TASK

This *bottom-up* approach focuses on advertising objectives like *achieving 80 percent awareness* by a specified time, then identifies the necessary tasks. The firm uses historical and/or experimental data to estimate the budget for each task, then sums the costs to calculate a total. Because linking advertising spending to advertising objectives is difficult, the objective and task method is not broadly popular. But as pressures grow to justify marketing and advertising expenditures, more firms will use the approach, if only to get *ballpark* estimates.[44] Firms should invest in advertising research to gain better insights into advertising relationships.

> ### *Marketing Question*
> The price of advertising on the U.S. Superbowl is around $3 million for 30 seconds. Is it worth it?

OTHER BUDGETING METHODOLOGIES

Firms sometimes use *top-down* methods to calibrate budgets they develop by *objective and task*:

- **Percentage of sales.** The advertising budget is a **percentage of sales (A/S)**; *sales* is current sales, anticipated next-year sales, or some combination.[45]

Illustration of the Percentage of Sales Method for Setting the Advertising Budget

- Sales = $50 million

- Firm's advertising to sales ratio = 5%

- Advertising budget = $50 million x 5% = $2.5 million

Percentage of sales is simple to implement but is logically inconsistent. First, the firm figures out *sales*, then it calculates the *advertising*. This logic implies that sales generate advertising. But the firm advertises because it believes *advertising leads* to sales! Practical problems include:

- **Advertising new products.** Because sales are low, the firm is biased against advertising spending even though it may be vital.

- **Basing the budget on anticipated sales.** The firm would reduce advertising when it expects sales to dip, yet maintaining or increasing advertising may be the best strategic action.
- **Basing the budget on last year's sales.** Suppose sales would grow if the firm increased advertising; the firm would not increase its budget.
- **Seduction.** The firm makes competitive comparisons based on **A/S** ratios; but these ratios do not specify actual advertising spending. Firm B's A/S ratio is twice Firm A's — yet Firm B's advertising is only $1 million, versus $5 million for Firm A.

Illustration of the Peril of Advertising-to-Sales A/S ratios		
	Firm A	**Firm B**
A/S ratio	5%	10%
Sales	$100 million	$10 million
Advertising	$5 million	$1 million

- **Competitive parity.** The firm bases advertising on competitor actions. The firm may decide to match the competitor dollar-for-dollar or use competitor spending as a benchmark. Some firms base their budgets on competitor spending per market share point.[46] This method makes several implicit, and probably erroneous, assumptions:
  - The firm and competitors have similar communications objectives.
  - The firm's competitors make good budgeting decisions.
  - Different campaigns are equally effective at similar spending levels.

Illustration of the Competitive Parity Method

- Competitor advertising = $3 million   • Competitor's market share = 25%   • Firm market share = 15%

  Hence, firm advertising = $ 3 million × 15%/25% = $1.8 million

- **What the firm can afford.** There is no rational basis for this approach. Unfortunately, it is not that uncommon.[47]

After several good years, Carter Inc. (disguised name) suffered losses in a cyclical business downturn. Desperate for profits, the new CEO cut costs — starting with the entire advertising budget. Guess what happened to Carter?

PROGRAM EVALUATION: HOW SHALL WE TEST OUR ADVERTISING AND MEASURE ITS EFFECTIVENESS?

Now we have answered the who, what, how, where, when, and how much to spend advertising questions, we must evaluate advertising relative to objectives. The firm may test individual advertisements, different levels and types of spending, and/or evaluate the entire advertising program.

TESTING INDIVIDUAL ADVERTISEMENTS

The firm tests ads with target customers (subjects), individually or in groups; in a laboratory or experimental field setting. Some examples of testing techniques are:

- **Laboratory/print.** Show several advertisements or mock publications with advertising inserted; subjects view these at home or at a central location.
- **Laboratory/broadcast.** Insert advertisements in a TV program or movie; subjects view these in a theater or shopping mall.

- **Field setting.** Similar to the laboratory but with real publications and TV programs; a test might involve two or more publications or TV programs. Subjects see only one advertising vehicle. The firm often confines these tests to a limited geographic area.[48]

Laboratory testing lets researchers manipulate several advertising elements, exercise tight control over subject interaction with the ad, and limit costs. The major downside is lack of realism. Field settings reverse these pros and cons. **Advertising effectiveness measures** for both field and laboratory tests include:

- **Recognition.** Widely used for print advertising. The researcher asks subjects which advertisements they recognize. In the *Starch* system, researchers visit respondents at home.[49]
- **Unaided recall.** Widely used for broadcast advertising. The researcher asks subjects what advertising they remember, *without* prompting.[50]
- **Aided recall.** Widely used for broadcast advertising. The researcher asks subjects what advertising they remember, *with* prompting.
- **Purchase.** Used in field settings. Customer panel members present ID cards at grocery stores when they make purchases.[51]

Some observers argue that these methods are too rational and verbal. Although they prefer nonverbal methods like galvanic skin response and pupil dilation, significantly higher expense limits their use.[52]

TESTING DIFFERENT LEVELS AND TYPES OF SPENDING

The firm tests alternative spending patterns using experimental design procedures. The firm sets advertising objectives, then selects appropriate advertising effectiveness measures. Each of several different geographic test areas receives a different spending pattern. The firm compares results across test areas, using sophisticated analytic techniques to account for test-area differences.

EVALUATING THE ENTIRE ADVERTISING PROGRAM

Over and above testing individual advertisements and spending levels, the firm may wish to evaluate an entire advertising program. **Tracking studies** measure customer responses over time, using either a customer panel or randomly selected respondents. Suppose the firm's objectives mirror the high-involvement, hierarchy-of-effects model: Awareness → liking → trial → purchase → repeat purchase; the firm should base advertising objectives and actions on these stages. In a tracking study, the results from one period help define the advertising program for the following period.[53] Table 16.7 shows market research results; what follows shows firm actions in four quarterly periods.[54] (Boxed insert, opposite page, shows an example.)

Time Period	I	II	III	IV
Awareness	25%	70%	70%	70%
Knowledge	20%	60%	60%	60%
Liking	20%	20%	40%	40%
Trial	20%	20%	20%	30%
Purchase	18%	18%	18%	25%
Repeat purchase	15%	15%	15%	20%

- **Time Period I.** The firm has *awareness* and *knowledge* problems; only 25 percent of target customers are aware of the product. The firm aims to increase awareness and knowledge.
- **Time Period II.** The campaign raised awareness to 70 percent and knowledge to 60 percent. But *liking* and *trial*, each at 20 percent, remain too low. The firm focuses on liking.

KEY IDEA

➤ The firm should test both individual advertisements and the entire advertising program.

➤ Important advertising effectiveness measures are:

- Recognition
- Unaided recall
- Aided recall
- Purchase

KEY IDEA

➤ Evaluating advertising effectiveness is a complex task. The firm must choose among various types of tests and measures.

TABLE 16.7

ILLUSTRATIVE EVALUATION OF AN ADVERTISING PROGRAM: PERCENTAGE OF TARGET AUDIENCE (%)

- **Time Period III.** The *liking* campaign was moderately successful, doubling to 40 percent, but *trial* stayed at 20 percent. The firm runs a new campaign to increase trial.
- **Time Period IV.** The new campaign increased trial to 30 percent, purchase to 25 percent, and repeat purchase to 20 percent.

Example of a Tracking Study[55]

Campaign: "Pork: The Other White Meat." A six-month TV campaign in 17 major metropolitan markets, supplemented by national magazine advertising.

Customer target: Primarily women (25–54) with children, purchasing for the family.

Test: Three different media exposures, each in two different cities:
- Cleveland and Sacramento — double TV exposure plus magazine
- Pittsburg and Denver — normal TV plus magazine
- Baltimore and San Diego — magazine only

Measurements:
- **Wave I. Benchmark.** Two months before the campaign; 1,200 men and women surveyed in the six test markets. Major findings:
  a. White meat preferred over red meat 42 versus 28 percent
  b. Most commonly recognized white meat — chicken
  c. Awareness of pork as white meat — 9 percent
- **Wave II. Post Campaign.** Phone survey of 1,800 consumers (25–54) in the six test cities:

  Goal A. Unaided association of pork and white meat
    – *Findings A.* Increases: double TV markets — 10 to 35 percent; normal TV markets — 12 to 29 percent

  Goal B. Recall of advertising message
    – *Findings B.* Double TV — 72 percent; normal TV — 56 percent; no TV — 35 percent

  Goal C. Changed attitudes toward pork
    – *Finding C.* Preference for white meat over red meat increased from 42 to 50 percent

Revenue Result. Revenues increased $500 million

THE ADVERTISING AGENCY SYSTEM

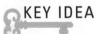

KEY IDEA

➤ The advertising agency system is in a continuous state of flux.

Most major U.S. advertisers outsource advertising program development to advertising agencies, but some firms like The Prudential and Ryanair running simple advertisements in print media conduct advertising activities in-house.[56] Large in-house advertisers may secure superior access to low-price media deals but, by outsourcing, firms have better access to creative talent and greater flexibility. These firms can demand refreshed creative teams and switch agencies on short notice. The firm usually works with three agency groups:

- **Account/relationship managers** — the key agency interface and help craft the strategy;
- **Creative department** — develops the advertising messages and executions;
- **Media department** — prepares the media schedule and provides supporting data.

Traditionally, firms paid advertising agencies a fixed percentage (often 15 percent) of advertising spend or commitment. More recently, firms and agencies negotiate fees, often making *value-based* arrangements. Coke and P&G cover agency costs but also pay bonuses based on performance against agreed metrics. Such arrangements more closely align firm and agency interests. Similarly, firms are starting to pay public relations agencies (below) by metrics like number of press mentions. In a further evolution, firms like LG and Nokia hire one agency for creative work and a second larger agency for advertising placement.

The agency's core job is to translate firm market strategy into an advertising message, and execute on that message. Firm and agency personnel should jointly develop a **creative brief** (boxed insert) — a *contract* between firm and agency, particularly with *creatives*. Each messaging initiative should have a creative brief — for advertising, but also for visual aids like displays and sales force materials. Sometimes an advertising campaign requires two creative briefs: one for the campaign idea, one for execution of the idea.[57] When the brand competes in multiple product classes, like Unilever's Dove products — anti-perspirant/deodorant, bar/body wash, face care, hair care, and hair styling — the brand brief frames the creative briefs for individual products.

Core Elements of the Creative Brief

Marketing objective. What the firm wants to achieve — output and intermediate objectives.

Assignment. The type of campaign including media type, timing, and approval process.

Customer insight. Informs the creative process — critical insight into target market; identifies rational and emotional factors that drive product purchase/use.

Competitive insight. Informs the creative process — includes barriers to achieving firm objectives.

Target audience. Whom the firm wishes to influence — customer types and segments, includes demographics, psychographics, and current products.

Key benefit. The most important benefit or value the firm wishes to emphasize.

Reasons to believe. Why the target customer should believe firm claims.

Brand identity. How the firm wants the target audience to feel about its product. Should be important to the audience, deliverable by the firm, and unique to the brand.

Mandates. Elements outside the advertiser's control — must or must not be included, like corporate and/or legal requirements advertising must meet.

Measurement. How the firm will know if the campaign has been successful.

Some important institutional changes are occurring in the advertising agency industry. These have major implications for advertisers:

- **Formation of large groups.** Many well-known individual agencies are now part of four major groups: Interpublic and Omnicom (U.S.), WPP (Britain), and Publicis (France).
- **Globalization.** Advertising agencies have developed global scopes to serve clients globally.
- **Broadening of services.** Advertising agencies are taking a more holistic view of communications by expanding to include direct marketing, Internet marketing, P&PR, sales promotion, marketing research, and market strategy development.

Regardless, creatives continue to leave large firms to form new agencies.

> ***Marketing Question***
>
> Suppose your school, college, or university plans advertising to increase student applications. Develop a creative brief for developing a campaign idea.

Other Mass Communications Options

DIRECT MARKETING

Direct marketing is a fast-growing communications tool embracing many ways of requesting a customer response. Today, direct marketing includes traditional print and broadcast advertising, packaging, package inserts, warranty cards, take-ones, and newer digital options like fax, e-mail, and the Internet.[58] Direct mailing brochures, catalogs, and statement inserts is a major category. Firms like L.L. Bean, Lands' End, and Lillian Vernon develop and refine demographic and product preference customer databases to fine-tune product development, product assortments, and communications programs. Low bulk postal rates, online shopping, and widespread credit card use help to grow direct marketing. Other factors are:

- **Delivery systems.** Package delivery firms like FedEx and UPS increasingly offer greater service variety.
- **Demographics and lifestyles.** The growth of dual-income families facing increasing time pressures, especially in developed countries, has reduced available shopping time. Direct marketing is attractive because consumers can shop from home.
- **Internet.** The Internet allows far greater personalization/customization and immediacy than other direct marketing methods.
- **Product quality.** The generalized increase in product quality has reduced customer risk when buying products remotely.
- **Professionalism.** Direct marketing firms are more professional and sophisticated, especially in segmenting, targeting, and communicating.
- **Technology.** Using advances in computer- and telecommunications technologies, firms can develop, manage, and mine customer databases.

Although direct marketing may be more expensive than advertising on a CPM basis, it offers several advantages:

- **Ability to identify prospects.** By relating customer profiles to purchase patterns, direct marketers can identify high-quality prospects.
- **Ability to tailor the offer.** Direct marketers know the products customers purchase; hence, they can tailor messages and offers to individuals.
- **Action-oriented customer response.** Advertising programs typically work via an effects hierarchy; purchase often occurs after awareness, knowledge, and liking. By contrast, direct marketing is more action-oriented and typically requests purchase.
- **Better customer knowledge.** Many direct marketing firms have extensive information on customers. But they must be sensitive to privacy concerns and act appropriately.
- **Better measurement.** The firm can test program elements like message, price, incentives, and/or type of direct marketing to assess their impact on sales and adjust accordingly.
- **Flexibility.** The firm can develop some direct marketing campaigns, like e-mail, much more quickly than mass advertising.
- **Predictability.** Because direct marketing typically requests purchase, sales forecasts for direct marketing programs can be fairly accurate. Budgeting for direct marketing is simpler than for advertising.

PUBLICITY AND PUBLIC RELATIONS

German condom manufacturer Condomi received significant press coverage in Europe and overseas for its plan to test condoms with British university students. Advertisements in college newspapers asking, "Want to get paid for having sex?" led respondents to a website asking questions like, "Who would you most like to do it with?"

Publicity and public relations (P&PR) are closely related; publicity is really a subset of public relations. **Publicity** focuses on securing neutral or favorable short-term press coverage. **Public relations (PR)** is broader in scope and more multifaceted. PR embraces corporate reputation, crisis management, government relations (lobbying), internal relations, press relations, product publicity, and shareholder relations. P&PR generally relies on intermediaries to transmit messages (hopefully positive) to target audiences. The advantage for P&PR is that the audience may view the intermediary as impartial, and the firm need not pay for media space and time!

The first modern PR example was the famous *Torches of Freedom* campaign. In 1929, a small group of women walked down New York's Fifth Avenue smoking cigarettes; newspapers nation-wide carried the story. Subsequently, women in many cities smoked on the street. Figure 16.7 shows Edward L. Bernays' simple model of how PR could promote a product or a cause.[59]

FIGURE 16.7

BERNAYS MODEL

Many firms focus communications efforts on P&PR.[60] Pharmaceutical firms use news releases to encourage patients to ask physicians about products. Mutual fund giant Vanguard does little advertising, but gets favorable press for low expense ratios. College Saving Bank launched the CollegeSure CD by focusing initial communication efforts on news releases and press confer-ences. Within one month, more than 300 news stories were written or broadcast. Articles and editorials appeared in all major U.S. newspapers; weekly news magazines like *Time, Newsweek,* and *U.S. News and World Report*; major business magazines; and local newspapers.[61] The agency responsible for the Aflac talking duck commercial tried, unsuccessfully, to hire actor Ben Affleck. But on the *Tonight* show, Affleck said, "Everywhere I go, no matter what I do, there is always some drunk lady screaming, 'Aflac!'"[62] Firms can also use P&PR and advertising syner-gistically. Victoria's Secret (VS) spends several million dollars advertising its annual fashion show; the extensive publicity sends millions of visitors to the VS website.

For difficult situations in the public eye, P&PR can be negative or positive.

- **Negative.** *The Social Network* movie caused problems for Facebook because of the unflat-tering portrait of founder Mark Zuckerberg. When 200 Coke drinkers suffered nausea, headaches, and diarrhea, and several children were hospitalized, observers criticized Coke for "forget[ing] the cardinal rule of crisis management — to act fast, tell the whole truth, and look as if you have nothing to hide." *The Economist* concluded that "Coca-Cola has made a big mess of what should have been a small public-relations problem."[63]

- **Positive.** J&J received considerable praise for handling the mid-1980s Tylenol poisoning scare. CEO James Burke took charge and J&J focused its concern on customers.[64] J&J tem-porarily withdrew Tylenol tablets, then relaunched in tamper-free packaging. J&J's actions and related P&PR campaign put senior executives, including Burke, on many U.S. talk shows; they explained J&J's actions and commitment to customers. J&J turned a major debacle into a major coup. More recently, jetBlue reacted quickly and extensively following a flight-cancellation crisis related to a severe ice storm at its New York hub — Chapter 13, p. 336; Quantas received favorable publicity following a mid-air engine explosion on an Airbus A380; and in the face of negative publicity over its role in the 2008–9 economic crisis, Goldman Sachs earned plaudits for its *10,000 Women* initiative. Walmart earned credibility with environmentalists for work on a sustainability index.

P&PR has several drawbacks. The firm cannot select the audience, except as it selects interme-diaries like editors, journalists, and media personalities. Also, the intermediary may ignore, modify, or shorten the message. And it may portray the firm inconsistently or even negatively.

P&PR can generate unintended consequences. Three examples:

- Canongate (small British firm) published 12 paperback *Pocket Canons*. These biblical texts included introductions by celebrities like Australian rock star Nick Cave (Mark's gospel) and feminist writer Doris Lessing (Ecclesiastes). Traditionalists angrily protested, generating significant press coverage; sales of *Pocket Canons* soared.

- Phillip Morris' Czech subsidiary announced findings from a study of smokers: The Czech Republic benefited financially from smokers' premature deaths by saving money on healthcare, housing, and pensions!

Marketing Question

In 2010, BP (Gulf oil spill), Goldman Sachs (banking crisis), and Toyota (product quality) each received significant negative publicity. How do you assess their responses? What would you have done differently?

Marketing Exercise

Three African countries — Mozambique, Swaziland, and South Africa — formed the *East3Route* initiative to attract European tourists. *East3Route* has issued an RFP (request for proposal) to develop a P&PR campaign to support the initiative. Prepare a proposal.

KEY IDEA

➤ Publicity & public relations relies on an intermediary, typically the press, to transmit a message to a target audience.

- P&G's P&PR campaign for *Scope* released a kissing survey on Valentine's Day naming the most-kissable and least-kissable celebrities in several TV categories. The campaign ranked Rosie O'Donnell as the least-kissable talk show host. That morning, O'Donnell prominently displayed a bottle of *Listerine* (Warner Lambert [WL]) on her show. WL ran full-page "Love Letter to Rosie" ads in *The New York Times* and *USA Today*. WL sent O'Donnell thousands of bottles of Cool Mint Listerine that she gave to audience members; she kept a mouthwash bottle on her desk for several weeks. Starting in March, each time a celebrity guest kissed O'Donnell, WL donated $1,000 to her favorite charity. Each kiss highlighted a Listerine bottle and a banner showing the running total of kisses. Many guests also gargled with Listerine. Two months and 500 kisses later, WL presented O'Donnell with $500,000 — equivalent to the cost of 13 30-second commercials.

SALES PROMOTION

Marketing Question

Identify a recent sales promotion. What was the firm's objective? Was the firm successful? Why or why not?

Sales promotion (SP) is a complex blend of communications techniques providing extra customer value, typically for trial to stimulate immediate sales. Sometimes SP has longer-run objectives like increasing awareness. The three main SP types are:

- **Consumer promotion** — manufacturer to consumer
- **Trade promotion** — manufacturer to retailer
- **Retail promotion** — retailer to consumer

Consumer and retail promotions include cash refunds, contests, coupons, deals, games, rebates, point-of-purchase displays, premiums, prizes, samples, and sports sponsorships. *Trade promotions* include advertising and merchandising allowances, contests, deals and prizes, special price deals, *spiffs*, and trade shows.[65] Firms are continually creating new SP techniques.

Before selecting an SP device, the firm should set clear objectives. Table 16.8 shows several SP techniques and related possible objectives. Cash refunds, *cents-off* coupons, and point-of-purchase displays may generate short-term sales. Sports sponsorships and naming educational facilities, sports stadiums, and theaters are options for long-term image building. A particular sales promotion technique may help achieve several objectives — Table 16.9 shows the ubiquitous *cents-off* coupon.

TABLE 16.8

ILLUSTRATIVE
SALES PROMOTION
TECHNIQUES AND
OBJECTIVES

Sales Promotion Technique	Possible Objectives
Cash refund	Purchase by reducing risk
Cents-off coupon	Table 16.9
Custom publishing	Awareness, interest, knowledge by personalization
Deals	Increase use; pre-emptive inventory building
Events	Interest, knowledge, trial
Games	Trial, repeat purchase, increase use
Infomercials	Awareness, interest, knowledge
Point-of-purchase displays	Knowledge, trial, increase use, repurchase
Premiums	Trial, repeat purchase, increase use
Product literature	Interest, knowledge, increase use
Product placement	Awareness, interest, knowledge via association
Sampling	Trial (for new product)
Spiffs	Customer salesperson effort, pull-through sales
Sports sponsorship	Corporate image building, awareness, community building
Building and stadium naming	Corporate image building, awareness
Trade shows	Awareness, interest, liking, intention to buy, trial, repurchase

Objective	Action
Encourage consumers to increase personal product inventories, create sense of urgency	Include expiration on coupon; publicize approaching expiration
Encourage repeat purchasing	Include coupon in product package
Induce trial among non-users	Distribute coupon in a magazine

TABLE 16.9

ALTERNATIVE OBJECTIVES AND ACTIONS FOR A CENTS-OFF COUPON

Generally, SP is not a good standalone approach; the firm should tightly integrate SP with other communications. Firms often advertise several sales promotions simultaneously, but these should all support (or be supported by) the firm's advertising and/or personal selling efforts. Rarely is SP the central element in the firm's communications strategy, but may be a large portion of the budget. Examples are:

- **Product placement.** Increasingly popular in movies, music videos (and lyrics), TV shows, and video games. The James Bond movie *Die Another Day* featured Aston Martin Vanquish (automobile), Ballantine (turtleneck sweaters), Brioni Roman Style (suits), British Airways (airline), Finlandia (vodka), Kodak (camera), Omega Seamaster (watch), Philips (mobile phone), Revlon (makeup), and Samsonite (luggage).[66] *The Italian Job* (movie) vastly increased awareness for the Mini Cooper.[67]

- **Skateboard parks, events, and films.** Shoe manufacturer Vans Inc. has 140 stores nationwide targeting skateboarding fanatics. Vans builds skateboard parks in malls, sponsors skateboarding events, and made a documentary film celebrating skateboarding.

- **Sports stadiums.** Philips Electronics paid $180 million to name home arenas for the Atlanta Hawks (baseball) and the Thrashers (ice hockey).[68] Goldman Sachs, Merrill Lynch, and Morgan Stanley funded *named* classrooms at Columbia Business School.

The firm should always keep in mind SP's long-term impact, particularly if SP involves short-term price reductions. Regular discounts may lead to competitive escalation; also, customers may accumulate inventory and never pay the *regular* higher price.[69,70] For trade promotions, manufacturers must be concerned that intermediaries pass on price savings to customers, and do not divert products.[71] Pass-through at the trade level frequently depends on issues suppliers cannot control, like retailer profit margins, inventory turns, and retail competition.

Further, volume fluctuations from frequent price changes may lead to mismatched production schedules, inventory build-up, and higher costs. Also, multiple SP programs are costly to manage. In the past, P&G conducted many special promotions and price changes; one in four orders from retailers contained errors. P&G's 150-person department corrected 27,000 orders per month, costing $35–$75 per order. These problems led many FMCG firms to switch to *everyday low pricing.*

The firm should always cost out the financial impact of SPs.

> Hoover's British division launched a consumer sales promotion — £100 Hoover purchases earned two free airline tickets for travel to continental Europe. Encouraged by this promotion success, Hoover introduced a second airline promotion: two free tickets for travel to the U.S. for £250 purchases. Sales skyrocketed — more than 200,000 customers applied, but profits plunged. Hoover took an earnings charge of £48.8 million and fired many senior executives.[72] A word of advice for marketers: **Don't develop a sales promotion you can't deliver on!**

Marketing Question

Why would Minute Maid sponsor a sports stadium? What are the benefits of this promotion? What are drawbacks and risks of this investment?

KEY IDEA

➤ Sales promotion comprises a potpourri of techniques, mostly for short-term objectives.

➤ Poorly designed sales promotion programs hurt profits and brand image.

Digital Communications[73]

The first section of this chapter focuses on traditional mass communications approaches for the firm to reach customers and other audiences, but heavies up on advertising. Section 2 addresses digital communications options. In addition to offering alternative communication

approaches, the Internet does three things that traditional communication methods do not —
Figure 16.8. The Internet:

- Communicates globally 24/7/365;
- Makes it easy for customers to communicate with the firm;
- Makes it easy for customers to communicate with each other.

On the Internet, the firm can follow customers as they visit websites, blogs and microblogs, view advertisements, and make purchases. The firm can combine these data with bricks-and-mortar purchases and telephone and other interactions to increase sales, enhance customer satisfaction, and strengthen brand image. We discuss five digital communications topics: online advertising and public relations, websites, blogs and microblogs, social networking, and mobile marketing.

FIGURE 16.8

INTERNET IMPACT ON COMMUNICATION OPTIONS

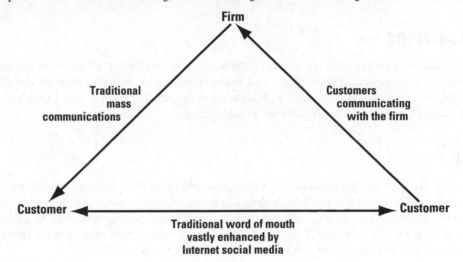

ONLINE ADVERTISING AND PUBLIC RELATIONS

As a communications tool, the Internet offers many ways for marketers to communicate with customers, each with its own characteristics:

SEARCH

Generic search, exemplified by Google and Bing, has two important facets for marketers — **paid search** and **search engine optimization**:

PAID SEARCH. Advertisers pay to appear next to, and be associated with, search results based on keywords. An electronics retailer may pay to appear next to searches for HDTV or digital cameras. Typically, the advertiser pays only when a searcher actually clicks on the advertisement. Advertisers bid for position; higher bids and higher click-through rates earn higher page listings.[74]

SEARCH ENGINE OPTIMIZATION. Success in appearing at higher page positions (free) is a somewhat arcane process. To be successful requires understanding the mechanics of search engines and *optimizing* the firm's website by selecting significant key words.[75]

Vertical search focuses on specific topics like hotels (Tripadvisor), automobiles (Edmunds), and jobs (Monster). For both generic and vertical search, advertisers generally pay-per-click; sometimes they pay flat fees for inclusion in directories.

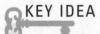
KEY IDEA

➤ Online advertising and public relations embraces:

- Search
- Display
- Classifieds
- Video
- E-mail

DISPLAY

Display advertising comprises banner ads on websites. Originally based on a magazine model, banner ads come in standard sizes; hence, they are easy to develop, purchase, track, and measure. The basic banner ad has been standard for many years but new sizes include tall, skyscraper-like and medium-rectangle ads.[76] (Facebook [more than 800 million global users] is the largest source of online display advertising.) Clicking on a banner ad directs the user to the advertiser's website. Measuring advertising effectiveness by click rate or other customer action like download, enquiry, registration, sale, sales lead, or sign-up is straightforward and often forms the payment basis. Increasingly, firms use data-mining techniques to identify web-surfing patterns for advertising targeting.

CLASSIFIEDS

Online classifieds are typically text listings for specific types of products and services like automobiles, jobs, real estate, yellow pages, and time-sensitive auctions. Migration of classifieds from offline to online has been swift and devastating for newspapers. The free Craigslist network of local community sites commands a huge audience.

VIDEO

Internet video is increasing dramatically. Firms place videos on their own and other firm websites, and on public sites like YouTube. Videos can be advertising focused, or public relations in nature like jetBlue's YouTube response to its winter-storm flight-cancellation crisis. As TV-show episodes migrate to the Internet (Hulu and others), and content providers produce Internet-only shows, the firm's advertising choices will increase dramatically.

E-MAIL

Out-bound e-mail communication is a popular way for firms to maintain contact with current customers. Retailers like Amazon and Netflix regularly send e-mails to stimulate purchase and maintain relationships, often including recommendations based on previous purchases. Many community-oriented sites and content publishers regularly send e-mail news alerts to keep customers returning and maintain their user bases for advertising. For acquiring new customers, the firm may buy e-mail lists or develop its own behavioral targets based on customer website visits learned from *cookies*; of course, *spam* filters may reject unsolicited e-mail. To avoid the spam problem, many firms encourage prospective customers to provide e-mail addresses, then allow *opting out*. The firm may also send news releases and other publicity for inclusion on news sites (Yahoo! News, CNN Digital Network), blogs and microblogs, and non-firm websites.

E-mail is a two-way street. *In-bound* e-mail allows the firm to deal with customers on a personal basis, but it must develop processes to address in-bound communications fully and promptly. Some firms develop automated response systems like frequently asked questions (FAQ) so as to cut costs and minimize the need for human responders.

A key benefit of digital advertising is the firm's targeting ability, based on user location, search engine keywords, online behavior, expressed interests, and social network ties to other customers or brands.

> **Marketing Question**
>
> Many firms have developed creative approaches to using the Internet as a communications device. What is your favorite example of an Internet campaign? Was it successful? Why or why not?

KEY IDEA

➤ Important digital
options include:

- Online advertising
and public relations
- Websites
- Blogs and micro-
blogs — Twitter
- Social media
- Mobile marketing

WEBSITES

At a minimum, the firm's website is a form of mass communications (brochureware); it can also enable sales promotion by offering free samples and discounts. The website's true potential is its ability to engage customers and build brand equity. Websites allow the firm to generate product awareness, provide product information, and explain and demonstrate products. Websites comprise words and pictures and videos, but may also host webinars and podcasts, and offer branded games and mobile apps. Websites often allow customers to register (for later communications) and secure access; customers can post responses to a blog, download content, upload videos and photos, review or recommend products and distribution outlets, or enter contests. Customers form links to the brand and can join with like-minded customers to form online communities. At Netflix's website, customers order movies, rate movies, see movie ratings (from other customers), and discuss movie choices on bulletin boards.

Nestlé builds highly targeted consumer communities. Nespresso is a several-million-person club whose members "treasure quality coffee as part of the simple moments of pleasure in everyday life." Club Buitoni members (Italian culture lovers) click on favorite Italian recipes made with Buitoni pasta and may win a trip to Buitoni's testing kitchens in Tuscany.

Simple websites are inexpensive to establish and take down, but complex websites may be more cost-effective. Websites are increasingly important for marketers; they help customers recognize needs — customers may even help the firm develop product specifications. Websites are often potent during evaluation and choice; in e-detailing events, pharmaceutical reps make drug presentations and offer samples. Websites can also generate feedback on product performance.

Some firms encourage customers to use the Internet for routine tasks like product information search, placing orders, and checking delivery status. Sometimes websites replace communication forms like telephone operators and on-the-road salespeople. Other firms integrate websites with different communication vehicles.

Dell links its website and telephone sales reps by tracking customers who explore the website. Dell can take control of the search process to help customers find products faster than by searching alone. Dell's website can initiate telephone conversations between customer and sales reps. Also, customers can place innovative ideas for Dell to consider, view others' ideas, vote for favorites, and track the progress of ideas Dell selects. Dell has several blogs, sponsors online communities and owners' clubs, and has significant followings on Twitter, Facebook, and YouTube.

Many firms use the Internet to generate sales directly. (For potential conflicts with existing distributors, see Chapter 18.) Included are most major traditional B2C retailers like Kmart, Macy's, Nordstrom's, Target, and Walmart, and catalog retailers like Brooks Brothers and Lands' End. Many merchants, like Amazon and Netflix, exist only on the Internet. The Internet also supports many tiny specialty merchants like Germany-based Wurzburger — selling sheet music for accordion players, and Wessex Press — publisher of North American, European, Chinese, Latin American Spanish, and Russian editions of *Managing Marketing in the 21st Century*. Check out **www.axcesscapon.com**.

Whereas most media targets domestic audiences, website visitorship knows no geographic boundaries. Websites for *The Times, Sunday Times, Guardian, Daily Mail, Independent* and other British newspapers generate 50 percent or more of their traffic from the U.S. Such shifts from conventional domestic media challenges advertisers that organize communications efforts geographically.

BLOGS AND MICROBLOGS – TWITTER

Originally online diaries, blogs (from web logs) are platforms to offer opinionated comments; sometimes bloggers allow readers to comment on their blogs. Blogs are often highly specialized (celebrities, food, travel, wine); some bloggers have enormous followings and are important opinion leaders. Hence, bloggers offer marketers the ability to target specialized audiences. Technology firms often provide bloggers with advance versions of new products, hoping for favorable comments. Other firms start their own blogs.

Brandweek reported, "Nike, Dr Pepper, Mazda, SBC, and others have ... found blogging an easy, cheap way to appear hipper and keep customers engaged with the brand."[77] Microsoft let 1,000 developers set up personal blogs to build relationships, but not to release commercially sensitive information. Microsoft also hosts a site where developers talk with other community members — around one million unique visitors per month.

But blogging can backfire. Dr Pepper/7-Up launched Raging Cow, a *milk-based product with an attitude*. 7-Up tried to reach a hip young audience turned off to traditional media by setting up a blog run by a cow. Some bloggers viewed the blog as commercial interests invading a non-commercial domain and called for a product boycott. Whole Foods' co-founder/CEO John Mackey posted many comments to Internet bulletin boards anonymously, and was highly criticized when unmasked. Laura and Jim drove an RV across the U.S., staying overnight in Walmart parking lots. Their trip blog pictured a host of happy Walmart employees, but when Laura was exposed as a freelance writer hired with company funds, Walmart's reputation suffered.

Twitter is a microblogging service; users send and read other users' messages — *tweets*, text posts of up to 140 characters displayed on the author's profile page. Users send tweets to friends' lists and subscribe to other authors' tweets. Some users direct Twitter readers to their blogs. Advertising on Twitter includes *Promotional Tweets* — look like regular tweets; *Promotional Trends* — advertisement appears on top of a list of hot topics on Twitter's home page; and *Promoted Accounts* — Twitter recommends users *follow* a particular account's tweets.

> **Marketing Question**
>
> Firms are increasingly using blogs for commercial purposes. Search the Internet. Which company blog do you think is most effective? Why? What are the benefits and limitations of blogs?

SOCIAL MEDIA

Social media (SM) are online tools and platforms that allow Internet users to share insights and experiences for business or pleasure,[78] share content (words, pictures, audio, video), entertain each other, offer reviews and opinions, and collaborate. SM communications are very powerful: Customers often find strangers' opinions more credible than paid spokespeople![79]

THE BRIGHT SIDE OF SOCIAL MEDIA

SM include blogs and microblogs, Internet forums, networks, photo and video sharing, podcasts and webinars, and wikis for meeting like-minded people.[80] Many firms engage in community building by bringing together users, like Nespresso and Club Buitoni (above), HOGs (Harley Owners Group), and Mac users. These communities offer excellent opportunities to stimulate positive word of mouth, gain awareness, enhance brand image, build brand equity, and drive sales.[81] Microsoft formed offline partnerships with Burger King (Halo Whopper), Mountain Dew, Doritos, and Pontiac to launch its new video game Halo 3. Microsoft also built an event-planning website that invited journalists, bloggers, and fans to a pre-launch party. Party attendees uploaded photos to their blogs and discussed the anticipated launch; Internet users planned strategies to secure the game at online and offline retailers.[82]

Many firms like EBags use customer reviews for product redesign; other firms engage customers in new product development — Chapter 14. Gardening retailer Burpee asks customers to post product reviews online; very positive reviews lead to immediate sales. Heinz's "Top This TV"

Bom Chicka Wah Wah. To promote Axe deodorant, Unilever developed the bom-chicka-wah-wah campaign featuring TV ads, bom-chicka-wah-wah Girls band, YouTube videos showing girls chasing men using Axe, and online games where young men received fragrance recommendations for their chosen type of young woman. YouTube videos went viral as millions of people sent them to friends. Axe earned significant market share in many countries.

Back Dorm Boyz. In China, Motorola introduced a new line of youth-oriented mobile phones by hiring two Guangzhou college students (well-known Internet lip-synchers) to lip-synch *As Long as You Love Me* (Backstreet Boys). The related lip-synching and song re-mixing contest garnered 14 million page views and 1.3 million voters. Motorola's new phone sales soared.

KEY IDEA

➤ Social media offers the firm many opportunities to interface positively with current and potential customers. But the firm must also consider the *dark side* of social media.

contest, promoted on ketchup labels, challenged customers to design its advertising. Heinz received 6,000 YouTube submissions and 10 million views. During the contest, ketchup sales increased substantially.

Other communities that bring together like-minded users include *Tripadviser.com* (hotel and vacation destinations), *Inthemotherhood.com* (mothers), and many disease-specific sites. Community members are often attractive targets for coupons, online and offline conversations, product previews, and samples. But many of these sites discourage or ban advertising.

Individual use of Internet sites designed specifically for social networking is fast growing. Facebook dominates general sites where the goal is to see and be seen; professional sites include LinkedIn and Plaxo. Large memberships and high traffic volume make these sites attractive for marketers to interact with users via advertising, fan pages, and other means. Many firms have Facebook pages.

THE DARK SIDE OF SOCIAL MEDIA

Much social media activity by firms aims to create favorable mentions about the firm and its brands among customers and other third parties. But customer-to-customer communications can also be negative. Defecting customers may encourage network members to defect also.[83] Disenchanted customers can broadcast dissatisfactions widely using websites, blogs and micro-blogs, and YouTube.

Former Pfizer marketing VP Peter Rost blogs about healthcare (peter-rost.blogspot.com). Drug industry whistleblowers provided him information that led to Congressional investigations of AstraZeneca (Arimidex marketing irregularities) and Pfizer (marketing irregularities).[84]

Jeff Jarvis (unhappy Dell customer) blogged (BuzzMachine) about his negative experience with Dell customer service. Comments included: "The machine is a lemon and the service is a lie," and "DELL SUCKS. DELL LIES." BuzzMachine visits doubled to 10,000 daily and Dell's customer service rankings dipped.

Increasingly, firms are training employees to monitor the Internet for negative communications and implement ways to mitigate brand damage. Dell now proactively looks for unhappy customers. By searching Twitter for "Comcast" (and "Comcrap"), Comcast can address customer problems before they become formal complaints. jetBlue, General Motors, Kodak, Whole Foods, and others also track Twitter and blogs.

The firm's response to negative communications should depend on the situation. Dell added more call centers and increased phone rep training. Some general options are: Correct misinformation; do not respond but allow loyal customers to address negative issues; use customer comments as a form of marketing research; and fix the problem and advise the unhappy customer. Sometimes the firm should bring in the lawyers but generally this is not a worthwhile option. Regardless, the firm should be ready to act quickly: Domino's Pizza suffered considerably when it waited over 48 hours to respond to a prank YouTube video by two employees — by the time it acted, there had been one million views.

In general, the firm's social media strategy should commence by becoming aware of, and continually updating, the main sources of communication about the firm and its brands, markets, and industry. The firm should develop creative approaches to enhance the positives and mitigate the negatives, both by acting directly and by engaging community members to implement its approaches. Measurement is crucial: The many alternative measures include website visits and duration, community membership, blog and microblog followers and mentions, and sales.

MOBILE MARKETING

Not long ago, if people used mobile devices at all, they made phone calls. Nowadays, hand-held personal digital assistants (PDAs), smart phones (like the iPhone and Android phones), and tablet computers (like the iPad) free web surfers from personal computers. Digital communications can now be done *on the go* 24/7/365. Mobile marketing will increase in importance as *mobile*-device sales exceed PC sales.

Mobile devices offer new options for marketers:

- **Short message service (SMS)** — short text messages (up to 160 characters) that remain stored until the user opens the mobile device.
- **Multimedia message service (MMS)** — similar to SMS but may include graphics, video clips, and sound files.

Marketers may send permission-based or unsolicited messages. For permission-based (*opt in*) options, users subscribe to a service like *foursquare* or *shopkick*, perhaps for a benefit like free calls, or to send an advertised code. They receive advertisements, *coupons of the day*, loyalty points, or other benefits like feedback options, games, mini-dramas, music, polls, quizzes, ringtones, sports, and videos. Unsolicited messages include coupons and other offers, especially when users are in close geographic proximity to specific retail outlets. Opt-in communications are preferable in many situations; regardless, consumers should have the ability to *opt out*. Interactivity and entertainment seem the most important factors for successful mobile marketing. Future mobile communications will only be limited by designer creativity.

Sony sent 600,000 SMS messages to people aged 12–25. A singing *Santa Claus* called each respondent who also received a second text message offering to place a Christmas wish for a Play Station 2 (PS2) with a "loved one." Loved ones (mostly parents) received a call from Santa Claus saying their son/daughter had requested a PS2: 36 percent requested; 70 percent of those received.

Marketing Question

As book publishers have embraced electronic publishing (iPad, Kindle, Nook), some are assessing the opportunity to secure additional revenues by placing advertising in both electronic and printed books. As a publishing marketing executive, how would you approach an assignment to investigate this opportunity?

Marketing Question

What is your favorite example of a mobile marketing campaign? Why is this campaign your favorite?

Marketing Question

What other messages did you glean from this chapter?

KEY MESSAGES

- Advertising *works* via hierarchy-of-effects models incorporating awareness, knowledge, liking, trial, purchase and repeat purchase as major variables.
  - High-involvement and low-involvement products have different hierarchies.

- A well-developed advertising strategy requires answers to seven critical questions:
  - **Target audience**. Whom are we trying to influence?
  - **Advertising objectives**. What are we trying to achieve?
  - **Messaging**. What content should the target audience receive?
  - **Execution**. How shall we communicate the message?
  - **Media selection and timing**. Where and when shall we place our advertising?
  - **Advertising budget**. How much shall we spend on advertising?
  - **Program evaluation**. How shall we test our advertising and measure its effectiveness?

- The core of the advertising message should reflect the positioning statement in the market segment strategy.

- Advertising messages embrace many rational and emotional approaches.

- Key issues for media selection are reach, frequency, and impact.

- The firm should approach the marketing budget from a marginal analysis perspective and limit rule-of-thumb approaches.

- The creative brief is the critical interface between the firm and advertising agency.

- Direct marketing (DM), publicity and public relations (P&PR), and sales promotion (SP) are mass communications approaches that supplement or replace advertising.

- The Internet is fast becoming an important communications medium. Critical areas for marketers to explore include online advertising and public relations, websites, blogs and microblogs, social networking, and mobile marketing.

VIDEOS AND AUDIOS

Advertising	v1602 🎥	Joseph T. Plummer	Columbia Business School
Internet Marketing	v1603 🎥	Jeremy H. Kagan	Columbia Business School
Social Media	v1604 🎥	Peter Propp	
Buzz Marketing	v1605 🎥	Mark Hughes	Buzzmarketing

v1602

v1603

v1604

v1605

QUESTIONS FOR STUDY AND DISCUSSION

Can you answer the questions implied by this chapter's learning objectives? Check!

1. Many social critics attack advertising in general and specific advertising programs in particular. What are the major arguments against advertising? How would you respond? Why is it difficult to measure advertising effectiveness?

2. Suppose GM is about to launch a new car powered by fuel cells — suggested retail price about $30,000. Mileage is 80 mpg city, 100 mpg highway. Use Table 16.10 to develop a consumer advertising campaign.

Advertising Element	Question
Target audience	Whom are we trying to influence?
Advertising objectives	What are we trying to achieve?
Messaging	What content should the target audience receive?
Execution	How shall we communicate the message?
Media selection and timing	Where and when shall we place our advertising?
Advertising budget	How much shall we spend on advertising?
Program evaluation	How shall we test our advertising and measure its effectiveness?

TABLE 16.10

ADVERTISING STRATEGY

3. Identify and bring to class examples of three recent advertising campaigns you believe were outstanding. Use Table 16.10 to analyze their success. What commonalities can you identify among these campaigns that will help you develop great advertising?

4. Identify and bring to class examples of three recent advertising campaigns you believe were ineffective. Use Table 16.10 to analyze why they failed. What commonalities can you identify among these campaigns that will help you avoid making truly bad advertising?

5. Identify a direct marketing campaign to which you responded. Why did you respond yet ignore so many others?

6. Suppose your friend is planning to open a new retail seafood restaurant in your hometown but cannot afford to advertise. Develop a P&PR campaign. Alternatively, complete this task for a product in which you are interested, or this book — *Managing Marketing in the 21st Century*.

7. Develop a creative new sales promotion device you will sell to a major national advertiser.

8. Table 16.11 shows firm sales by quarter. The firm ran a sales promotion in Q3 of 20XY+2. What is your estimate of baseline sales? What impact did the promotion have?

	20XY	20XY+1	20XY+2
Quarter 1	150	165	180
Quarter 2	190	207	165
Quarter 3	210	231	375
Quarter 4	120	132	135

TABLE 16.11

SALES PROMOTION EXAMPLE

9. What is your favorite commercial website? Why is it a good communications device?

10. Message execution includes rational styles — comparative, demonstration, one-sided and two-sided appeals, primacy, recency, and refutational; and emotional styles — celebrity endorsement, fear, humor, and storytelling. Bring to class an example of each advertising style. Is the advertisement effective? Why or why not?

11. In 2011, Facebook revenues were less than $5 billion, yet its IPO valued Facebook in excess of $100 billion. Why? What actions should Facebook take to increase revenues and profits. (Or replace Facebook with Linked-in.)

IMPERATIVE 4
Design the Market Offer

CHAPTER 17

DIRECTING AND MANAGING THE FIELD SALES EFFORT v1701

To access O-codes, go to **www.ocodes.com**

LEARNING OBJECTIVES

When you have completed this chapter, you will be able to:

- Understand marketing's role in the field sales effort.
- Lead a field sales force.
- Implement the six tasks of sales management.
- Develop a sales strategy: Set sales objectives, determine and allocate selling effort, and design sales approaches.
- Design and staff the sales organization to implement the sales strategy.
- Manage critical organizational processes to support sales strategy implementation.
- Integrate market strategy and sales strategy.
- Design a strategic (key) account management program.

OPENING CASE: HONEYWELL BUILDING SOLUTIONS

Honeywell Building Solutions (HBS) provides building automation, security, and fire and life safety solutions and services to public- and private-sector facilities. HBS is also a global leader in energy services, helping organizations conserve energy, optimize building operations, and leverage renewable energy sources. HBS has a storied history as a Honeywell business unit. Chances are that when you adjust your heat or air conditioning at home or in the office, you are using a Honeywell product.

HBS addresses three market segments for commercial buildings:

- **Installation.** *Mostly for new buildings where the decision-making unit frequently includes owners, architects, and mechanical and electrical contractors.*

- **Service.** *Making sure that customer installations and equipment perform optimally.*
- **Energy.** *Retrofitting current buildings to improve energy efficiency. HBS acts as project designer and general contactor, but most work is sub-contracted.*

In 1999, Honeywell merged with AlliedSignal to form Honeywell International Inc. In 2000, United Technologies held merger talks with the new firm, but these broke down when GE attempted to buy Honeywell. The U.S. Justice Department approved the GE acquisition; but in 2001, the European Commission refused and Honeywell continued as an independent firm.

Following months of turmoil, when its employees were preparing for the expected GE acquisition, HBS did not perform well: Sales declined 20 percent annually. In an attempt to save the business, Honeywell's CEO Dave Cote appointed a new leadership team for HBS including a President and VPs of operations, marketing, and sales. Kevin Madden became worldwide VP of sales. Cote gave the team 90 days to develop a turnaround plan, and to "get rid of their ancestors" — the cause of the poor performance.

Madden, a 20-year Honeywell veteran, described the situation he inherited. "Not only were sales declining, internally a victim mentality was pervasive. Because of the turmoil, 35 to 40 percent of the intellectual capital had left and the business unit was in a tailspin. The entire organizational focus was on productivity and cost, and most sales were to current HBS customers; we were securing a minimal number of new customers. We had dismantled most of the sales teams that focused on the installations of our systems. HBS had outsourced this activity to transaction-oriented partners who had little interest in building deep relationships or delivering complete solutions. Quite frankly, customers had lost confidence in HBS to do an installation and we no longer had any competitive advantage."

Madden said that energy and many installation projects were make *businesses. Sales reps had to be proactive in getting in front of customers and writing specifications. But that was not happening, for several reasons:*

- *HBS had lost many of its good salespeople.*
- *Current salespeople were generalists; they sold in all three lines of business. Yet the nature of the challenges and the skills required tended to be quite different by market segment.*
- *The first-line sales leaders'* **span of control** *averaged 25 to 1. They were too preoccupied with administrative tasks, and gave little guidance and coaching to salespeople.*

Madden said that the turnaround plan focused on five key areas:

- **Marketing and sales alignment.** *Marketing and sales became tightly integrated. The sales force not only agreed on all new marketing initiatives, but often stimulated new ideas.*
- **Customer coverage model.** *When Madden arrived, the Americas region had 192 generalist salespeople. Seven years later, it had over 400 salespeople, many hired from competitors with the challenge to be part of the build, focused in individual market areas. Many new salespeople displaced outsourced partners as HBS returned to the installation marketplace.*
- **Sales planning.** *The five-stage sales process — HBS' playbook was tightly linked:*
  - **First calls.** *The salesperson figures out the customer's decision-making unit, what needs to be done, and secures agreement to develop a list of requirements.*
  - **Requirements definition.** *The salesperson prepares the list of requirements — technical, financial, legal — and gets the customer to agree.*
  - **Commitment.** *The salesperson identifies HBS resources meeting customer requirements, and gets agreement from the customer.*
  - **Solutions development.** *The salesperson brings in Honeywell engineers to design the installation.*
  - **Final negotiation.** *The customer and HBS sign the contract.*

For all jobs over $750,000, HBS conducts an impact review with senior sales executives. The review team focuses on the customer's best competitive alternative and HBS' next move. At these reviews, the team may telephone the customer to check its understanding and probe additional ways to add value. HBS also rigorously qualifies all sales opportunities and only allocates expensive sales support manpower where it believes it can win. HBS rigorously debriefs all wins and losses.

- **Roles and responsibilities.** *HBS reduced first-line sales manager spans from 25 to 1, to an average 10 to 1, to increase salesperson coaching.*

- **Performance management.** *HBS implemented a rigorous performance measurement system and pays for results. Base pay is comparable to competition, but HBS designs incentive compensation and rewards to be among the most lucrative in the industry.*

Madden said an important investment was in a sales force data system. The sales process also functions as a funnel and HBS knows, for example, that a certain number of agreements to prepare a list of requirements will lead to a certain number of contracts. HBS manages the funnel aggressively and salespeople must update their funnels continuously. If ten days have lapsed without a salesperson updating, Madden sends that salesperson a letter.

Since the new leadership team took over, sales have turned around; HBS is now a multi-billion-dollar business and a strong member of the Honeywell portfolio. The renewed HBS has beaten the industry's 4- to 5-percentage growth rate every year. Sales growth rates have ranged from 6 percent to 30 percent, doubling the business.

CASE QUESTION

To what extent do HBS sales force initiatives generalize to other sales forces?

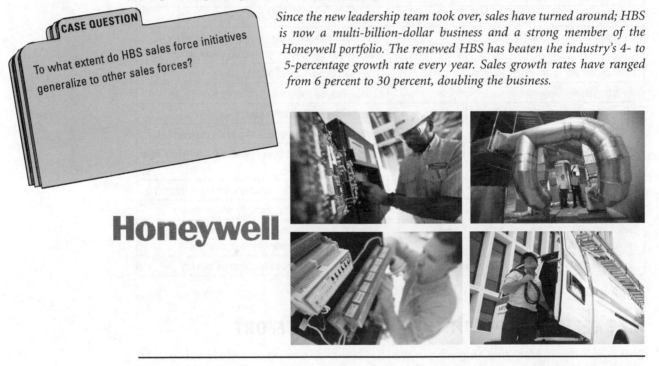

Honeywell

Chapter 17 is the third of three chapters in Part B of Imperative 4 — *Design the Market Offer.* Part B focuses on *Communicating Customer Value.* Chapter 17 addresses *Directing and Managing the Field Sales Effort.*

In many firms, the sales force is the only group specifically charged with making sales and securing revenues. Field salespeople efforts are the firm's critical persuasive component. Some sales forces are huge. Several U.S. life insurance firms employ more than 10,000 salespeople; GE, IBM, and Pfizer have respectively, 40,000, 50,000, and 35,000 salespeople and sales managers around the world; Avon has close to one half million independent representatives in the U.S. alone.[1]

In B2B marketing, the field sales force has always been critical; salespeople typically introduce firm products and services to customers. By contrast, in B2C marketing, advertising is often the main communication channel to consumers — the sales force has played a supporting role. But as the retail industry concentrates in many countries, and a few large retailers or distributors secure significant power, B2C field sales efforts are increasing. Some FMCG firms now spend more heavily on direct selling to wholesalers and retailers than on advertising to consumers! At P&G, more than 400 persons work exclusively with Walmart.

Chapter 17 addresses four main topics: the marketing/sales interface, leading the selling effort, the tasks of sales force management, and managing key (strategic) accounts.

THE CHANGING VIEW

OLD WAY	NEW WAY
Firms seek profits by cost reduction	Firms seek profits through revenue growth
Focus on making sales	Focus on building long-term, profitable customer relationships
Salesperson as seller	Salesperson as educator and problem-solver
Transactions-based sales	Relationship-based partnerships
Salespeople individualism emphasized	Salespeople increasingly team players
Salespeople undervalued in the firm	Salespeople increasingly valued — the only firm function responsible for generating revenues
Salespeople act in an ad hoc fashion	Salespeople developing planning skills
Salesperson skill requirements relatively low	Salesperson skill requirements increasingly high
Many low-powered sales personnel	Fewer high-powered sales personnel
Evaluation based on sales volume	Evaluation increasingly based on profit contribution
Salesperson the sole interface with customers	Salesperson manages the organizational interface with many personnel
Sales efforts managed domestically	Sales efforts for global customers managed globally
Sales and marketing clearly separate	Sales and marketing increasingly intertwined
Sales force organization and processes are fixed for long periods of time	Sales force organization and processes are modified to reflect environmental and strategic changes
Sales force/service linkages poor or loose	Sales force closely linked to customer service

MARKETING'S ROLE IN THE FIELD SALES EFFORT

This book's title is *Managing Marketing in the 21st Century*, so why do we include a chapter on directing and managing the field sales effort? Aren't there enough dedicated books on sales management? Of course! But throughout Chapter 17, we discuss the importance of aligning firm **selling efforts** with marketing. This alignment is ever more crucial as many firms evolve field sales efforts — to key (strategic) account management, to address their most important customers and to telesales and lower-cost alternatives to secure efficiencies and lower costs. Salespeople's actions can *make or break* the market strategy:

> At SalesCo (disguised name), marketing's job was to develop sales leads. Marketing worked hard but salespeople often did not follow up and leads languished in files. A new management team harvested 3,000 dormant leads and assigned a special group to work them. Within six months, 250 new customers were providing $5 million in new revenues.

Old-fashioned stereotypes pose a serious problem in some firms: Marketing — "Salespeople don't understand the complexities involved in developing a market strategy"; Sales — "Marketing is full of *ivory-tower* types, removed from the market with limited understanding of

Marketing Exercise

Interview a senior marketing executive and ask two core questions:

- What works well in your relationship with the sales force? Why do these things work?
- What works poorly in your relationship with the sales force? Why do these things not work?

customer needs and unwilling to *get their hands dirty* fighting competitors." As at SalesCo, lead generation can also be a fraught area: Marketing complains about poor follow-up on leads; sales complains of lead quality.[2] As competition increases, these perceptions just don't cut it. Marketing and sales must be on the same team, each performing its own critical functions.

We do not pretend this is easy. Marketing and sales often have different perspectives on budget allocations; also, marketing tends to have a long-term view; sales must deliver short-term performance.[3] Regardless, creative tension may be beneficial to firm performance.[3] (Perceived compensation inequities can also cause problems.) The focus of market and sales strategies is also quite different. Marketing typically develops market strategy for various firm products — Chapter 9. A multi-product firm has several product-market strategies; each product-market strategy comprises several market-segment strategies. The sales strategy must integrate these market strategies; typically, sales strategies focus on selling a range of products to a variety of market segments. Badly coordinated or ill-formed sales strategies can lead to distracting internal competition among product managers[4]:

> Salespeople at FMCG Co (disguised name) sold the firm's entire product line to retail customers. Some brand managers devised incentive schemes to secure disproportionate sales force effort on their products. These actions caused considerable internal dissension.[5]

Marketing Exercise

Interview a senior sales executive and ask two core questions:

- What works well in your relationship with marketing? Why do these things work?
- What works poorly in your relationship with marketing? Why do these things not work?

FMCG Co's practice is inexcusable. Marketing and sales must work hand-in-hand; when they coordinate poorly, the sales force fights competitors *with one hand tied behind its back.* Many firms use a well-worked metaphor to capture the different responsibilities for marketing and sales: Marketing — architect; designs the overall approach to the market. Sales — builder; executes marketing's design. In construction, the architect/builder interface should be seamless; in business, the marketing/sales interface should also be seamless.

As leading firms adopt strategic (key) account management programs, the architect/builder metaphor is breaking down. The sales force is increasingly responsible for securing deep understanding of customer needs, proposing actionable solutions, and securing firm resources to solve customer problems. When the sales person is in the driver's seat at a specific customer, marketing must play a supportive role.

In many firms and business units, separate VPs head up marketing and sales. Although members of the same team, their different approaches, backgrounds, objectives, and philosophies may create separate cultures leading to inter-group discord. Some firms pointedly address this issue by creating a combined position — VP of Sales and Marketing (Chief Revenue Officer), to whom both sales and marketing VPs report. Other alignment processes include integrating marketing and sales metrics, or even sharing revenue and profit targets, and reward systems.[6]

Well-managed firms implement processes that tightly coordinate marketing and sales efforts. They encourage disciplined (not just more) communications, create joint assignments, rotate jobs, co-locate marketing and sales personnel, and improve sales force feedback. Marketing develops market plans in good time, with significant sales force input; sales strategy work starts when market plans are well developed but not yet complete.[7] Senior marketing and sales managers meet frequently to hammer out realistic and coordinated marketing and sales objectives and priorities in a spirit of cooperation. Some firms even appoint sales/marketing coordinators whose job is to build effective senior marketing and sales manager relationships.[8]

KEY IDEA

➤ Effectively managing the sales/marketing interface is critical for achieving sales excellence.

LEADING THE SALES EFFORT[9]

Sales receives short shrift in many firms. "Most CEOs have financial, science, marketing, legal, or manufacturing backgrounds — and no sales experience. So they don't identify with the people who interact with customers."[10] These CEOs don't realize the firm will fail if the sales force generates insufficient revenues. This stark reality places a premium on leadership at each level in the sales organization. After all, the sales management job is to make salespeople successful; the sales force is no better than its management. All sales managers, junior and senior, should *lead from the front*, spending time in the field with their salespeople — coaching, inspecting, observing, teaching, and selling. They should empower salespeople to take initiative by fostering a culture of acting like "it's your own business." The most effective sales managers lead by example, encouraging two-way communication with customers, and collaborating with other organizational functions, by emphasizing teams and teamwork. These managers innovate new ways of delivering customer value, drive entry into attractive markets, and spearhead the evolution of new sales models and sales organizations.

To secure the best results, sales leaders treat human resource expenditures as an investment and view selling as a training ground for general management.[11] The sales force gets *tough love*: Performance expectations are challenging and very clear, but support is plentiful. Managers empower salespeople to succeed via day-by-day focus on their activities. Managers devote substantial effort and ingenuity to reward and recognition programs, and align individual salesperson financial incentives with required organizational performance.

The most effective sales leaders *advance the science of sales and the art of the customer relationship* by making fact-based decisions, like allocating sales resources — salespeople, strategic (key) account managers, telesales, across customer segments and sales channels. They match sales models — like generalist versus specialist salespeople, to emerging customer needs, and leverage sophisticated intellectual capital by:

- Supplementing firm products with advisory services to offer customer solutions.

- Building specialist expertise by industry/market/product to fashion and develop customer solutions.

- Working with specialists to install and implement customer solutions; and with customers to refine installed solutions, identify opportunities for additional solutions, and provide feedback to marketing.

Sales leaders understand viscerally that customer success drives firm success. They continually improve sales information, sales analytics, sales processes, and sales operations.

Sales leaders create a *risk-taking* culture where failed experiments for delivering customer value are *accepted* and *expected*. They celebrate and reward learning from honest mistakes, but penalize repeated mistakes. They hire and develop people willing to try, fail, and learn; and ensure cost-effective experimentation by coaching. Sales leaders' operating mantra is *fail quickly*, but aggressively transfer lessons from failed experiments and pilot programs to new efforts. By anticipating changes in market conditions and customer needs, sales leaders identify opportunities for new experiments with sales models and sales processes. Sales leaders discover and develop best practice by following the *fail* or *scale* principle.

Perhaps the most critical leadership function is encouraging sales people to *live the mission* — to provide a rationale for the sales job over and above financial rewards. Salespeople who internalize a greater purpose build credibility and trust with customers and develop a powerful differentiator for defeating competitors. A well-articulated sales purpose aids aligning resources with customer needs, attracts the best sales talent, and accelerates training and development. A sales purpose also motivates above and beyond the call-of-duty performance, and enhances innovation by cultivating openness to new opportunities for serving customers profitably.

KEY IDEA

➤ Effective leadership is critical for developing a successful sales force.

KEY IDEA

➤ Successful sales managers:
- Lead from the Front
- Practice tough *love* with the sales force
- Advance the science of sales and the art of customer relationship
- Develop a risk-taking culture
- Encourage salespeople to *Live the Mission*

Marketing Question

Interview one or more senior sales executives. Ask how they do their jobs. Do they exhibit the leadership characteristics discussed in this chapter?

Marketing Question

Two truths: Car salesmen are the least trusted of all salespeople; many people don't like haggling over car prices. As sales director for a regional car dealership with many outlets, you are responsible for changing the selling model from haggling to fixed prices. What challenges do you anticipate? How will you proceed?

The Tasks of Sales Force Management

To mount an effective selling effort, sales managers must focus on six tasks. Three sales force management tasks address *developing* sales strategy; three deal with *implementing* sales strategy. The chapter discusses the six tasks sequentially but shows how each task relates to the others. A new sales approach (task 3) may require new sales staffing (task 6).[12]

Developing the sales strategy	Implementing the sales strategy
Task 1: Set and achieve sales objectives.	Task 4: Design the sales organization.
Task 2: Determine and allocate selling effort.	Task 5: Create critical organizational processes.
Task 3: Develop sales approaches.	Task 6: Staff the sales organization.

TASK 1: SET AND ACHIEVE SALES OBJECTIVES

In 1973, Sidney Frank became U.S. distributor for Jägermeister, an odd-tasting golden German liqueur. Frank hired hundreds of provocatively dressed young women — Jagerettes — to offer bar patrons free shots. Today, their male counterparts, Jager Dudes, visit gay clubs. Case sales increased globally from 600 (mid-1970s) to 2.7 million (2010).

KEY IDEA

➤ Sales objectives are the firm's desired results. Achieving sales objectives is the sales force central task. Sales objectives turned into specific performance requirements are called quotas.

Sales objectives are the firm's desired results. Broad categories derive from the strategic focus in the market segment strategy — Chapter 9: Retain current sales, increase customer use, attract sales from competitors, and secure new business.[13] Achieving sales objectives is the sales force central task. The firm makes profits, survives, grows, and enhances shareholder value only by selling products/services to customers. Achieving sales objectives takes precedence over all other activities like collecting payments, delivering goods, entertaining, and gathering information. Sales objectives turned into specific performance requirements are **sales quotas**.

DEFINING SALES OBJECTIVES

The firm can choose among several sales performance measures. Most firms set sales objectives in terms of volume like gross sales revenues (dollars) or gross sales units. But focusing solely on volume can short-change profits, so profitability objectives like profit contribution — gross profits less direct sales force costs — are also popular.[14] Well-set objectives specify *how much* and *by when* the sales force must meet targets. We illustrate sales objectives for Essex (fictional firm)[15]:

KEY IDEA

➤ Gross sales revenues are the traditional basis for sales objectives. Sometimes firms base sales objectives on profit contribution.

Essex, Inc.: Overall Sales Objectives

In 20xy, sales revenue objectives — $40 million.

In 20xy, gross profit contribution objectives — $14.5 million.

RELATING SALES OBJECTIVES TO MARKETING OBJECTIVES

KEY IDEA

➤ Sales objectives integrate firm market strategy and sales strategy.

As noted, integrating market strategy with sales strategy is a difficult problem for many firms. A useful way of driving integration is to rigorously translate marketing objectives into sales objectives.[16] Essex offers three products (I, II, III) to three market segments (A, B, C). Table 17.1 shows several ways to view Essex's sales revenue objectives:

- Overall objectives — $40 million.
- Objectives by market segment: A — $10 million, B — $20 million, C — $10 million.
- Objectives by product: I — $26 million, II — $5 million, III — $9 million.

- Individual cells show objectives by product/market segment. Essex sets revenue objectives for IA, IB, IC, IIB, IIC, IIIA, and IIIB, but zero revenue objectives for IIA and IIIC.[17]

Although each approach to Essex's sales revenue objectives has value, only product/market segment objectives really integrate market and sales strategy perspectives.

		Product			Totals
		I	II	III	
Market Segment	A	$7	$0	$3	$10
	B	$13	$1	$6	$20
	C	$6	$4	$0	$10
	Totals	$26	$5	$9	$40

TABLE 17.1

ESSEX, INC. SALES
REVENUE OBJECTIVES
BY PRODUCT AND
MARKET SEGMENT
($ MILLIONS)

To illustrate objectives/performance relationships, Table 17.2 focuses on product I. Essex:

- Exceeded overall objective by $2 million (28 minus 26),
- Performed $6 million better than expected in segment B (19 minus 13), but
- Fell short by $2 million in both segments A (5 minus 7) and C (4 minus 6).

Market Segment	Sales Objectives	Actual Sales Performance
A	$7	$5
B	$13	$19
C	$6	$4
Totals	$26	$28

TABLE 17.2

ESSEX, INC. ACTUAL
SALES PERFORMANCE
VERSUS SALES
OBJECTIVES FOR
PRODUCT I BY MARKET
SEGMENT ($ MILLIONS)

What does this analysis tell us about sales force performance for product I? Exceeding the overall objective was great and segment B performance was stellar. But Essex's sales force failed in segments A and C. If these were high profit and/or high growth segments, this sales force failure could be a severe problem and would outweigh the positive result in segment B. (Note we only focus on revenue objectives.) Translating market segment objectives into sales objectives by product is complex. (Marketing Enrichment me1701 shows a simplification by partitioning products and customers into existing and new.)

BREAKING DOWN SALES OBJECTIVES

Typically, the sales force breaks down overall sales objectives into **control units** like sales regions, sales districts, and individual sales territories. Senior sales managers gain significant insight by comparing actual sales performance versus sales objectives for individual control units; they see if a particular region, district, or territory is performing well or poorly.

Table 17.3 illustrates control-unit breakdowns for Essex in the San Francisco district (Western region). Essex set these objectives using a top-down/bottom-up process — Chapter 6.

- **Top-down.** Senior sales managers partitioned the overall $40 million revenue objective among sales regions. The Western region manager partitioned her objective among districts, including San Francisco.
- **Bottom-up.** The San Francisco district manager asked each salesperson to commit to certain sales levels by product and segment. Rolling up these figures across salespeople produced San Francisco's bottom-up objectives.
- **Integrating top-down and bottom-up.** Surprise! The top-down figures were higher than the bottom-up figures. Discussions among Essex sales managers and salespeople ironed out differences. San Francisco's final overall revenue objective ended up at $5 million.

MARKETING ENRICHMENT

Illustration of Setting Objectives
and Allocating Selling Effort by
Product and Customer Status —
Old versus New me1701

me1701

KEY IDEA

➤ The firm should break down sales objectives by control unit — sales regions, sales districts, and individual sales territories. The firm should also calendarize sales objectives — quarterly, monthly, and possibly weekly.

Across the sales force, if each district met or exceeded its performance objectives, the entire firm would meet or exceed its targets.

		Products			Totals
		I	II	III	
Market Segment	A	$1,300	$ 0	$ 250	**$1,550**
	B	$1,420	$ 80	$ 500	**$2,000**
	C	$ 280	$1,170	$ 0	**$1,450**
	Totals	**$3,000**	**$1,250**	**$ 750**	**$5,000**

Firms also establish sales objectives in time units like quarterly, monthly, and sometimes even weekly. **Calendarizing** allows the firm to monitor performance continuously and sets the stage for making course corrections when performance deviations are negative.[18] Table 17.4 shows the San Francisco district's overall sales revenue objectives by quarter.

Quarter 1	Quarter 2	Quarter 3	Quarter 4	Total
$1,100	$1,450	$950	$1,500	**$5,000**

ALTERNATIVE SALES PERFORMANCE MEASURES

Sales and profit-type objectives are the most popular performance measures, but there are many others. The firm should choose carefully based on the nature of the business and its strategic situation:

- **Customer retention.** The proportion of customers from the start of the year who are still customers at the end of the year — the opposite of customer defection (churn). (This measure speaks to customer lifetime value issues — Chapter 2.)
- **Market share.** This measure focuses on firm performance versus competitors.
- **Price realization.** The extent to which the firm achieves planned price levels.
- **Close rate.** The proportion of sales attempts that results in actual sales.
- **Customer satisfaction.** Specific metrics focusing on the customer experience.

KEY IDEA

➤ The firm can set sales objectives related to:

- Close rate
- Customer satisfaction
- Customer retention
- Market share
- Price realization

ACHIEVING SALES OBJECTIVES

The remainder of this chapter focuses on *right* and *appropriate* actions for achieving sales objectives. Most salespeople are ethical and positively motivated to sell products and services to target customers. But some salespeople engage in illegal and/or unethical practices in pursuit of sales. Although relatively uncommon, sometimes firms pressure salespeople to make sales by any method — including giving customers improper payments, kickbacks, and/or all-expenses-paid trips.[19] Ultimately, unethical and illegal behavior tends to come to light, damaging the firm's reputation and reducing shareholder value. A *win-at-all-costs* strategy can be very expensive:

TAP Pharmaceuticals paid $885 million to settle U.S. government allegations that salespeople paid kickbacks and bribes to physicians for prescribing Lupron, and persuaded them to charge Medicare patients for free drug samples. AstraZeneca settled a similar free-sample suit for $355 million. J&J paid $70 million in civil and criminal fines for bribing surgeons in Greece to use its products. Both AstraZeneca ($520 million) and J&J ($75 million) were fined for promoting pharmaceutical products for unapproved uses.

TASK 2: DETERMINE AND ALLOCATE SELLING EFFORT

The best way to determine and allocate **selling effort** is by examining four interrelated decisions:

- **Sales force size.** How much selling effort should the firm expend in total? In particular, how many salespeople should sell its products?
- **Sales force activities.** What activities should salespeople do? What proportion of total time should salespeople spend actually *selling*?
- **Selling effort allocation.** How should salespeople allocate selling time among firm products and segments?
- **Telesales.** What proportion of overall selling effort should the firm allocate to telesales? What should telesales people do?

KEY IDEA

➤ The firm should consider four key issues in determining and allocating selling effort:
- Sales force size
- Sales force activities
- Selling effort allocation
- Telesales

SALES FORCE SIZE

For effective selling effort, the firm must have the *right* number of well-trained, motivated salespeople. Managing *headcount* is typically a crucial HR function and sales managers often wage difficult internal battles to optimize sales force size. Figure 17.1 shows an underlying conceptual framework for deciding sales force size — the **sales response function**.[20] When selling effort is low, the firm makes few sales. As selling effort increases, sales increase. Ultimately, sales *top out* at a maximum level, even if the firm adds extra salespeople. The firm should continue hiring until the marginal revenue from adding a salesperson equals that salesperson's marginal cost. Many sales managers find this curve intuitively reasonable, but do not know their sales force position. Approaches to the sizing decision are either experimental or analytic.

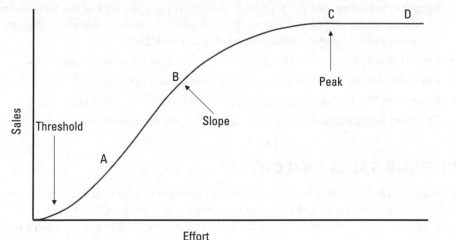

FIGURE 17.1

THE SALES RESPONSE FUNCTION

EXPERIMENTAL METHOD. Sales managers change sales force size and see what happens. Two broad hypotheses follow from Figure 17.1:

1. The sales force is too small, perhaps at B.
2. The sales force is too large, perhaps at D.

Sales managers should decide what criteria would support/reject each hypothesis. Then they select one or more sales districts/regions for a trial and comparable districts/regions as controls. Sales managers increase/decrease sales force size in the trial geography for a predetermined period. If the experimental data supports hypothesis 1, the firm should add salespeople; if the data support hypothesis 2, the firm should reduce sales force size.

ANALYTIC METHOD. The analytic approach has three steps:

1. Estimate the total number of selling hours required to achieve sales objectives.
2. Calculate the number of available selling hours per salesperson.
3. Calculate the required sales force size — divide (1) by (2).

KEY IDEA

➤ The firm should develop a hypothesis about the shape of, and its position on, the sales response function.

1. Total number of selling hours required to achieve sales objectives. Two broad approaches for calculating *required number of selling hours* are **single-factor models** and **portfolio models**:

- **Single-factor models.** Table 17.5 illustrates the single-factor model. The firm classifies current and potential customers into A, B, C, and D categories (I) by a value measure like sales potential (II). Then:

  i. Identify the number of customers in each category (III).

  ii. Estimate the required selling hours annually for customers per category (IV).

  iii. Multiply III and IV to secure the required selling hours annually per category (V).

  iv. Sum the results across customer categories (VI).

TABLE 17.5

ILLUSTRATION OF
SINGLE-FACTOR
MODEL FOR
CALCULATING
REQUIRED SELLING
TIME

Customer category, I	Sales potential, II	Number of customers, III	Selling time per customer annually, IV	Required selling time annually, III × IV = V
A	>$2M	100 accounts	100 hours	10,000 hours
B	$250K to $2M	250 accounts	50 hours	12,500 hours
C	$10K to $250K	800 accounts	12 hours	9,600 hours
D	<$10K	3,000 accounts	4 hours	12,000 hours
Total				44,100 hours **(VI)**

Single-factor models are simple to use, but may not fully capture the complexity of selling to various customers. Portfolio models can do a better job.

- **Portfolio models.** The firm classifies customers on multiple dimensions. Figure 17.2 uses *customer potential* and firm share of customer business — *customer share*. The firm partitions each dimension into low, medium, and high. The firm identifies the number of customers in each matrix cell (III); and the required selling time per customer (IV). The analysis proceeds as with single-factor models (above).

FIGURE 17.2

PORTFOLIO MODEL
FOR DETERMINING
REQUIRED SELLING
TIME

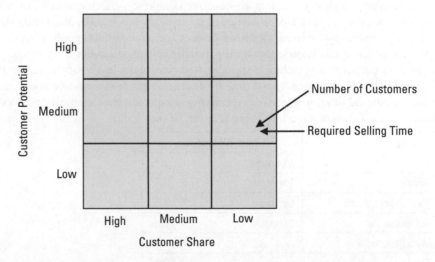

KEY IDEA
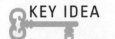

➤ Salespeople conduct several activities. In many firms, they spend less than 20 percent of time face to face with customers trying to make sales.

From this point on, calculations for single-factor and portfolio models are identical.

2. Number of available selling hours per salesperson. Salespeople conduct many activities (next section). Sales managers must calculate the time available for selling. Suppose this is 30 percent of total time.

3. Required sales force size. Continuing the Table 17.5 illustration:

  i. Total available salesperson time per annum (hours)
     = (365 days less 104 [weekends] less 30 [holidays/vacations])
     = 231 × 10 hours per day = **2,310 hours**

ii. Actual selling time per salesperson
= Total available salesperson time × 30% (assumed)
= 2,310 × 30% = **693 hours**

iii. Number of salespeople required
= Total number of selling hours required/Actual selling time per salesperson
= 44,100/693 = **64 salespeople**

In practice, this calculation provides a *ballpark* estimate for sales force size. The firm should expect some variation from the actual size, but significant variation demands action.[21]

SALES FORCE ACTIVITIES

The sales force's main job is to make sales. But claims on salespeople time include checking credit and inventories, collections, customer service, delivering products, education and training, gathering market intelligence, internal communications, meetings, qualifying sales leads, receiving payments, record-keeping, report writing, sales planning, and travel. In many firms, even the best salespeople spend less than 20 percent of their time (the equivalent of one day per week) face to face with customers trying to make sales. Many firms increase salesperson **face time** by using less-critical personnel for time-consuming sales-support activities; Xerox pairs on-the-road salespeople with inside sales resources to increase selling time.[22] Other firms employ technological solutions:

> Textile Inc. (disguised name) sold products to department stores and specialty clothing stores. The stores continually called for order status reports. Salespeople spent many hours making phone calls to answer these requests. Textile developed a barcode system to identify each order and posted status updates on a customer portal. Satisfaction improved and Textile's salespeople had more time for selling.

Firms regularly deploy technology to improve salesperson effectiveness. Most salespeople use cell phones, e-mail, iPads, laptop computers, smart phones, standardized slide show presentations, voice mail, and/or websites. Other devices and applications enable advertising coordination, best practice and knowledge sharing, reseller training and virtual meetings, sales training, trade show participation, technical support, well-designed sales literature, and working models. Cisco's TelePresence reduces travel time by allowing remote face-to-face sales meetings.[23] Sales managers should develop guidelines specifying salesperson time commitment to various activities. A general classification like Table 17.6 can be very useful.

Activity	Time Allocation	
Selling	Minimum	25%
Traveling	Maximum	30%
Servicing customers	Minimum	30%
Administration	Maximum	10%
Miscellaneous		5%
Total		**100%**

Time allocations differ from one sales territory to another. Salespeople in urban areas need less travel time than those in rural areas, hence greater face time. Salesperson activities also evolve. In growth markets, salespeople should make many sales calls to potential customers; they may also forecast product volumes, gather competitive intelligence, and train distributor salespeople. In decline markets, salespeople may consolidate distribution; dispose, liquidate, or reassign inventory; and collect unpaid invoices.

Marketing Question

If you, a friend, or a colleague have worked in sales, what percentage of time was *face time* with customers? What other activities were part of the job? Were the time allocations good? Why or why not? What were the challenges of increasing face time?

KEY IDEA

➤ Sales managers should develop guidelines specifying how salespeople should spend their time.

TABLE 17.6

TIME ALLOCATION GUIDELINES BY ACTIVITY FOCUS

IBM had a face-time problem. Senior managers wanted data from the field; salespeople wanted advice, decisions, information, and resources from managers. Internal communications were sporadic and time-consuming. IBM developed guidelines for communications within the sales organization — Table 17.7; salespeople and sales managers at all levels had to adhere to these guidelines. Salesperson face time increased considerably.

TABLE 17.7

GUIDELINES FOR COMMUNICATIONS WITHIN THE IBM SALES FORCE

Day	Time Allotted	Type of Communication
Monday	30 minutes	Salespeople and first-line sales managers
Tuesday	60 minutes	First-line sales managers and regional sales managers
Wednesday	60 minutes	Regional sales managers and zone sales managers
Thursday	60 minutes	Zone sales managers and sales vice presidents
Friday	2 hours	Sales vice presidents and executive management

SELLING EFFORT ALLOCATION

The firm's selling effort (selling time allocation) should mirror the *structure* of sales objectives. For sales objectives by product, the firm should allocate selling effort by product. For sales objectives by product and market segment, the firm should allocate selling effort by product and market segment. Sales objectives by old versus new products require a similar selling effort allocation. Two important issues are:

- **Percentage allocations.** Although the *structure* of selling effort allocations and sales objectives should be identical, generally the *proportions* are different. Suppose sales revenue objectives required 70 percent of sales from existing products and 30 percent from new products. Most likely new product sales would require greater selling effort, maybe 60 percent versus 40 percent for existing products. After all, repeat sales are generally easier. Table 17.8 reproduces Table 17.1 (Essex's sales revenue objectives by product and market segment) but illustrates Essex's selling effort allocation for each product, market segment, and product and market segment.[24]

  If Essex set sales objectives only by product: I — $26 million; II — $5 million; III — $9 million, it would allocate selling effort by product (not by segment). If Essex set sales objectives only by segment: A — $10 million; B — $20 million; C — $10 million, Essex would allocate selling effort by market segment (not by product). Since Essex set sales objectives by product and market segment, it must similarly allocate selling effort by product and market segment.

TABLE 17.8

ESSEX, INC. SALES REVENUE OBJECTIVES ($ MILLIONS AND [PERCENT]), AND PERCENTAGE SELLING EFFORT BY PRODUCT, BY MARKET SEGMENT, AND BY PRODUCT AND MARKET SEGMENT[25]

		Products						Totals	
		I		II		III		$	%
		Sales objectives	% Selling Effort	Sales objectives	% Selling Effort	Sales objectives	% Selling Effort	Sales objectives	% Selling Effort
Market Segments	A	$ 7 (18%)	20%	$0 (0%)	0%	$3 (8%)	15%	$10 (25%)	35%
	B	$13 (33%)	20%	$1 (3%)	15%	$6 (15%)	10%	$20 (50%)	45%
	C	$ 6 (15%)	10%	$4 (10%)	10%	$0 (0%)	0%	$10 (25%)	20%
Totals		$26 (65%)	50%	$5 (13%)	25%	$9 (23%)	25%	$40 (100%)	100%

- **Actual time allocations.** Suppose Essex believes the sales force can expend 50,000 hours selling effort annually. Table 17.9 translates Table 17.8's percentage allocations into hours.

Product (% allocation)	Selling Time	Market Segment (% allocation)	Selling Time	Product/Market Segment (% allocation)	Selling Time
I (50%)	25,000 hrs.	A (35%)	17,500 hrs.	IA (20%)	10,000 hrs.
II (25%)	12,500 hrs.	B (45%)	22,500 hrs.	IB (20%)	10,000 hrs.
III (25%)	12,500 hrs.	C (20%)	10,000 hrs.	IC (10%)	5,000 hrs.
Total	50,000 hrs.	Total	50,000 hrs.	IIA (0%)	0 hrs.
				IIB (15%)	7,500 hrs.
				IIC (10%)	5,000 hrs.
				IIIA (15%)	7,500 hrs.
				IIIB (10%)	5,000 hrs.
				IIIC (0%)	0 hrs.
				Total	50,000 hrs.

TABLE 17.9

ESSEX, INC. HOURLY SELLING EFFORT ALLOCATION BY PRODUCT, BY MARKET SEGMENT, AND BY PRODUCT AND MARKET SEGMENT (HOURS)

Similar to sales objectives, the firm should break down selling effort allocations by individual control units — sales regions, sales districts, and sales territories. Table 17.5 shows how firms group customers into categories, based on required selling effort. Table 17.10 illustrates calling norms by customer category, based on Table 17.5 data.[26]

Customer Type	Selling time per customer (hours/year)	Calling time per call	Number of calls per year	Call Frequency
A	100 hours	2 hours	50	1 x per week
B	50 hours	1 hour	50	1 x per week
C	12 hours	30 minutes	24	2 x per month
D	4 hours	20 minutes	12	1 x per month

TABLE 17.10

ILLUSTRATION OF CALLING NORMS BY CUSTOMER CLASS

Sales managers must make these selling effort allocations and ensure that salespeople stick to guidelines. If managers do not lead, salespeople will set their own priorities. Individual salesperson decisions are unlikely to optimize firm performance:

- Product managers tasked with meeting sales objectives will compete for salespeople time, perhaps by offering idiosyncratic rewards (boxed insert p. 425, FMCG Co).
- Some sales tasks, like selling current products to current customers, are generally more *comfortable* than others. Without direction, salespeople gravitate to their *comfort zones*.[27]

TELESALES

In recent years, many firms have reduced sales costs by adding telesales departments. Telesales functions differ markedly from firm to firm:

- **Lead generation.** Some firms use telesales to make cold calls and appointments for on-the-road salespeople.
- **Potential customers.** Telesales may be more effective than impersonal communication methods for contacting potential customers. Xerox's 1,000-person telesales operation (Canada) calls on small/mid-size organizations. Wessex employs Indian telesellers to persuade faculty to adopt its textbooks.
- **Current customers.** Some firms assign small current customers to telesales. In Scandinavia, Reebok stopped serving mom-and-pop shoe retailers with a field sales force

KEY IDEA

- ➤ Selling effort allocation guidelines must mirror the structure of sales objectives.
- ➤ Typically, selling effort allocation is not proportional to sales objectives.
- ➤ The firm must break down selling effort allocations by individual control units like sales regions, sales districts, and sales territories.
- ➤ The firm should allocate selling effort by customer category.

and switched to telesales. Costs reduced and customer satisfaction *increased* because telesales people were always available to take customer calls.

- **Partner with field sales.** Some firms pair field sales and telesales. Less-expensive telesales conducts many customer-facing activities as well as field sales, hence raising overall sales effectiveness.

Pearson assigned schools and school districts where sales were below a threshold level to a new (typically female) U.S.-based telesales force. Benefits included positive group dynamics, no relocation for promotions, easy availability of temporary replacements, and training by listening to top reps. Sales performance improved substantially.

TASK 3: DEVELOP SALES APPROACHES

The value proposition is central to the firm's market-segment strategy — Chapter 9. Hence, the value proposition anchors the **sales approach** — the central message the salesperson delivers to customers. Because customer needs differ by segment, the firm should offer a different value proposition for each market segment. It follows that salespeople selling multiple products to multiple segments must have multiple sales approaches — one per market segment.[28] Aided by sales managers and product managers, salespeople should develop messages for specific customers and competitive threats. In particular, they should:

- Secure insight into specific needs and competitive threats at individual customers. Typically, salespeople must develop trusting relationships before customers will fully articulate problems.
- Understand the various perspectives of customer decision-makers and influencers.
- Develop sales approaches that address critical customer needs, answer objections, and counter competitor sales approaches.
- Secure support from sales managers and bring in senior executives as necessary to interface with customer executives.[29]

KEY IDEA

➤ The value proposition anchors the sales approach — the central message the salesperson delivers to customers.

The traditional sales approach has two major components:

- Tailoring the sales message for different customer targets, and
- Designing a process to explain values and benefits in the firm's offer.

TAILORING THE SALES MESSAGE FOR DIFFERENT CUSTOMER TARGETS

Customer needs and competitive offers drive the value proposition and the sales approach. Of course, individual decision-makers and influencers often have different perspectives. Salespeople must decide whom to target and how to tailor sales messages for each person. Procurement personnel are typically interested in price, engineers focus on product design, and manufacturing personnel are concerned about production efficiency.[30] The salesperson must orchestrate the value proposition into a sales approach for each customer role (and individual), recognizing that customer needs may evolve as the buying process proceeds.

Enterprise is now the largest car rental firm in the U.S. Starting in 1964, Enterprise provided temporary replacement cars for drivers whose cars were being repaired. One key customer target was garage mechanics. Salespeople made morning calls and always carried donuts. This sales approach got garage mechanics' attention very quickly![31]

In designing the sales approach, salespeople should sharpen competitive focus. Table 17.11 shows firms I, II, and III, each trying to sell to a customer requiring four benefits — A, B, C, and D. A consultant explored sales approaches for each firm.

Customer Benefits	Relative Importance	Firm I		Firm II		Firm III	
		Benefit	Rank	Benefit	Rank	Benefit	Rank
A	1	A	1	A	2	A	3
B	2			B	1		
C	3			C	1	C	2
D	4	D	2			D	1

TABLE 17.11

FORMULATING SALES APPROACHES

Marketing Question

Based on Table 17.11 and the boxed insert, what marketing research and product development would you suggest for Firm I? Firm II? Firm III?

Developing the Sales Approach: Sharpening Competitive Focus

- The customer seeks four benefits in importance order: Benefit A > B > C > D.
- The three firms — I, II, III — each offer different benefit packages.
- Each firm performs better on some benefits than on others:
  - Benefit A: All three firms offer — firm I > II > III
  - Benefit B: Only firm II offers
  - Benefit C: Firm II > III; firm I does not offer
  - Benefit D: Firm III > I; firm II does not offer

- **Firm I.** Should focus on the customer's most important benefit — A. Firm I dominates on this benefit but is vulnerable on the other benefits.

- **Firm II.** Dominates firm III on benefits A, B, and C and is inferior only on the least important benefit — D. Hence, firm II's major challenge is from firm I. Firm II's major problem is that firm I ranks best on the customer's most important benefit — A. Further insight and possible sales approaches for firm II are to persuade the customer that:
  - Competitive ranking on benefit A is incorrect; actually, firm II > I. Firm II should persuade the customer it offers the best benefit A. Firm II then dominates both competitors on the three most important benefits — A, B, and C.
  - Customer benefits are incorrectly ordered; actually, B > A > C > D. By persuading the customer of its error, firm II dominates both competitors on the now most important benefit, B, and also on benefit C.
  - Customer should base its decision on the benefit set. Firm II's offer is superior; it provides all of the most important benefits — A, B, and C.

- **Firm III.** Has little hope of making the sale. Firm III's best sales approaches focus on benefit D and the combination — A, C, and D. More importantly, why is firm III spending time with this customer when its benefits are so inferior?

No firm offers all of the desired benefits, so each is vulnerable to competition.

When Xerox launches a new product or product upgrade, it makes sure that salespeople have in-depth knowledge about competitive products. Xerox provides easy-to-use charts and a professional video showing key strengths and weaknesses versus *face-off* products. Xerox's laboratories create courses for salespeople including hands-on experience with competitive products and techniques to combat competitive threats.

DESIGNING A PROCESS TO EXPLAIN THE FIRM'S BENEFITS

Selling is a process to facilitate customer buying. A completely standardized process is undesirable, but sales managers should guide salespeople via coaching, counseling, and well-designed training programs. Teaching employees to *sell* is daunting; good sales managers break the selling task into discrete easy-to-learn steps like:

- **Call objectives.** Know the desired results from each sales call and at each stage in the buying process. A pre-call planning process can help.

- **Sales interviews tone.** Decide how strident or aggressive to be in different situations.
- **Need elicitation.** Develop procedures to elicit customer needs.[35]
- **Presenting product benefits.** Present product benefits in the context of customer needs.[36]
- **Handling objections.** Anticipate customer objections and know how to address them. Objections differ from product to product and from customer to customer.
- **Communications timing and closing the deal.** Communicate in a strategic sequence. For example, do not elicit customer needs after presenting product benefits. Learn how to close a sale and ask for the order. Learn when to accept rejection and move to another customer and learn to better qualify prospects.

> In Bose's retail stores, customers relax and enjoy exquisite sound from a large TV and huge speakers. When the show concludes, the salesperson executes *the reveal*. She removes the *fake* speakers to show baseball-sized Bose speakers.

Specific influence principles that may help persuade customers include: *liking* (people buy from people they like), *reciprocity* (if you give, people give back), *social proof* (people follow the lead of others), *consistency* (people fulfill commitments [especially public and written]), *authority* (people defer to experts), and *scarcity* (people value what is scarce).[37]

TASK 4: DESIGN THE SALES ORGANIZATION

Tasks 1, 2, and 3 address *developing* the sales strategy. Tasks 4, 5, and 6 focus on *implementing* the sales strategy, ensure the sales force delivers the planned levels and types of selling effort. Task 4 covers sales organization design; firm choices should reflect strategic realities. For example, if the firm's product line is complex and heterogeneous, perhaps it should have multiple sales forces. Three critical issues are:

- Should firm employees conduct selling effort? Or should the firm outsource selling?
- How should an employee-based sales force be organized? Or reorganized?
- How should the firm design sales territories?

SHOULD FIRM EMPLOYEES CONDUCT SELLING EFFORT? OR SHOULD THE FIRM OUTSOURCE SELLING?[38]

Today, many firms outsource functions like call centers, computer systems, financial processes, legal, payroll, production operations, and security. Should the firm outsource selling effort? Three issues are important:

- **Control.** Employee-based sales forces are more likely to follow managerial direction. Outsourced agents, brokers, and reps earn commissions; hence, the firm may exercise little control, particularly if the outsourcer sells other firm (even competitor) products.
- **Cost.** Employee-based sales forces typically incur substantial fixed costs like salaries, travel and entertainment, sales management, and other overhead, regardless of sales volume. By contrast, third-party sellers on commission are a variable cost: No sales, no costs!
- **Flexibility.** To modify an employee-based sales force takes time and almost always involves HR. Third-party sellers typically work with strict performance criteria and short-term contracts; hence, relatively easy termination.

> Direct sales costs were too high for software firm Altiris so it fired the entire sales force. Altiris partnered with Compaq, Dell, Microsoft, IBM, and others to sell its products. Altiris customized partner relationships, like making communication materials partner-specific. In less than 10 years, Altiris grew from $1 million sales to an acquisition value of $830 million (by Symantec).

SALES OPERATIONS

A common feature of modern-day sales organizations is sales operations (SO). Historically, SO was a low-level function charged mainly with producing sales reports and ensuring salespeople were paid appropriately. Today, SO enhances the *science of sales*.[32] SO identifies and assesses sales potential via customer segmentation, and ensures alignment of sales resources to sales opportunities. SO also makes sales processes more fact-based, reliable, and predictable. Activities vary across firms, but mature SO departments form a flexible interface between sales and marketing and in-house sales and support processes. SOs strive for both continuous improvement and transformational change.[33]

As a *front office*, SO drives top-line sales growth by improving sales productivity. SO works with marketing to ensure programs and events are effective. SO enhances the sales experience by developing and continually updating a central database of firm-wide sales knowledge. SO draws data from R&D, product divisions, marketing, local competitive intelligence, and sales force best practice and success stories. SO shapes and segments these data for specific sales roles and steps in the sales process. SO produces *playbooks*, comprising specific customer solutions for individual salespeople. SO innovates with new sales tools, and gets deeply involved when sales roles change, like developing key account managers.

As a *back office*, SO focuses on efficiency by handling repetitive, scaleable tasks like[34]:

- **Approval processes.** Develops processes and guidelines to help salespeople navigate their own organization.
- **Bids and contracts.** Provides price information and drafts bid proposals and contracts.
- **Complaint management.** Ensures the firm expeditiously addresses customer issues.
- **Executive sponsor program.** Manages the executive sponsor program for high-value customers, including recruiting, selecting, assessing, and replacing.
- **Experiments.** Conducts experimental pilots to push the envelope on selling effectiveness.
- **Lead generation.** Interfaces with marketing to ensure sales leads have value to salespeople.
- **Low value activities.** Develops alternative processes to minimize salesperson time.
- **Monitor and control.** Develops metrics, creates standards, and designs dashboards to assess sales pipeline performance. Designs and manages customer and sales employee satisfaction surveys.
- **Pipeline management.** Constructs a system and ensures consistent/complete data entry.
- **Reward and recognition.** Designs salespeople and sales management compensation and recognition programs that drive required behavior.
- **Role clarity.** Constructs position descriptions for different selling roles, sets quotas, and structures career paths.
- **Sales planning.** Provides frameworks and templates for salespeople to prepare sales territory, account, and pre-call plans.
- **Sales time management.** Defines optimal sales-time profiles for various roles. Balances time among sales, service, and administration; measures sales time against standards.
- **Training.** Designs and implements training programs for salespeople and sales managers.

The firm must allocate resources between *front office* and *back office*. HP operates 20:80 in mature markets but increases *front office* allocation in uncertain developing markets.

Sometimes the balance favors employee-based selling; sometimes it favors outsourcing the selling effort. There is no right or wrong answer. If the firm has insufficient salespeople for a new market entry, third-party sellers may take up the slack. Conversely, long lead times and/or high market share in mature markets with predictable sales may favor employee-based selling.

HOW SHOULD AN EMPLOYEE-BASED SALES FORCE BE ORGANIZED?

> Avon's sales organization has a group vice president of sales, three regional vice presidents, seven regional sales directors, 85 division sales managers, and 2,500 district sales managers. In some geographies, district sales managers have several hundred reps. Avon also aligns its sales force ethnically in terms of language and culture.

KEY IDEA

➤ The employee-based or outsourced sales force decision involves trade-offs among:

- Control
- Cost
- Flexibility

Avon has a classic geographically organized sales force (boxed insert). Three interrelated variables for choice of organizational design are:

- **Degree of centralization/decentralization.** Extent to which sales management directs salespeople versus allows/encourages individual freedom and initiative.
- **Number of management levels.** Avon has five: group, regional (VP), regional (sales manager), division, district.
- **Managerial span of control.** A manager's number of direct reports; the most critical is the first-line sales manager.

As many firms have downsized, sales forces have decentralized, with fewer management levels and larger managerial spans of control, especially for first-line sales managers. Such *hollowing out* makes directing and coaching salespeople more difficult (Opening Case — Honeywell Buildings Solutions).

Specialization is one of the most important design variables. Should the firm specialize its selling effort? And if so, how?[39] Table 17.12 defines several **pure-form sales organizations**, shows conditions for their use, and presents pros and cons. Essentially, sales organizations can be unspecialized or specialized:

- **Unspecialized.** Two organization forms are generally considered unspecialized:
  - No geographic bounds on a salesperson's search for sales opportunities.
  - Territories organized by geography where salespeople sell all products, to all customers, for all applications, in specified geographic areas.
- **Specialized.** Specialization can be by product, maintenance/new business, distribution channel, market segment, and/or customer importance (strategic accounts). Generally, specialized selling effort leads to higher sales, but selling costs are also higher.

KEY IDEA

➤ Key sales organization design variables are:

- Degree of centralization/decentralization
- Number of management levels
- Managerial span of control

➤ Specialization may lead to higher sales but also higher costs. Specialization may also cause problems when several firm salespeople sell to the same customer.

Specialization simplifies effort allocation; individual managers, like product and/or segment, do not compete for salespeople's time. The firm assigns salespeople consistent with planned selling effort. Referring to the Essex illustration in Table 17.8, a sales force specialized by product may assign salespeople to products I, II, and III in the ratio 50:25:25. If Essex organized the sales force by market segment, it may assign salespeople to segments A, B, and C in the ratio 35:45:20.[40]

Specialization can cause problems when two or more salespeople sell to the same customer. British Aerospace Regional Aircraft's (BARA) Asset Management Division (AMD) disposed of secondhand planes recovered from bankruptcies. AMD competed vigorously with BARA's new plane sales division. This competition frequently drove down prices![41]

Some firms combine different types of specialized organizations. Salespeople specialized by product are often effective in urban areas where travel times are low. In rural areas, customer density is low, travel times are high, and generalist (unspecialized) sales forces often work better. Product specialists sometimes back up generalist sales forces. At Wachovia Bank, cash management, commercial finance, and leasing specialists supported account managers.[42] In a variant of the product-based organization, some pharmaceutical firms use *mirroring* organizations in which multiple salespeople call on each doctor with the same products.[43]

TABLE 17.12

SALES FORCE ORGANIZATION

	Organizational Form	Definition	Conditions	Pros	Cons
UNSPECIALIZED	**No Geographic Bounds**	Salespeople free to make sales calls with no geographic constraints	• Difficult to identify customers • Relationships important (e.g., life insurance, stock brokering)	• No artificial barriers to salespersons' entrepreneurial drive	• Potential multiple calling on same customer • Little managerial control
	Geographic	Salesperson has full responsibility in a specific geographic area	• Customer requirements and applications similar, product complexity low • Sales force sometimes backed up by product specialists	• Maximizes selling time • Minimizes travel and admin. costs • Close supervision • Minimizes confusion for customer and salesperson	• Salesperson may be unable to understand full complexity of customer requirements and product line • Salesperson must be *jack of all trades*; may be *master of none*
SPECIALIZED	**Product**	Different salespeople responsible for different product lines	• Product line large and heterogeneous and/or at different life-cycle stages • Product sold to different market segments • Firm attempts to increase *face time* with critical customers	• Sales force deployment decisions for products made at policy level • Sales force becomes product experts through close relationships with product-oriented personnel • Customers value the sales force's knowledge	• Increased travel and admin. costs (vs. geographic sales force) • Multiple calling on individual customers
	Maintenance/ New Business	Different salespeople responsible for: • Finding new business • Maintaining existing business	• Significant new business opportunities available, especially for new products	• Optimizes use of more-difficult-to-find new-business salespeople	• Increased travel and admin. costs (vs. geographic sales force) • Difficult handover from new business to maintenance sales force
	Distribution Channel	Different salespeople responsible for different types of intermediaries and end users	• Products move through an extended channel structure • Different selling activities required at each channel level	• Sales force deployment decisions for intermediaries made at policy level • Clarity of focus for salesperson	• Increased travel and admin. costs (vs. geographic sales force) • Potential for confusion among neighboring intermediaries
	Market Segment	Different salespeople responsible for different market segments (e.g., by industry buying center, customer application)	• Selling problems differ by market segment • Specific *types* of salesperson likely to be successful in different market segments	• Sales force deployment decisions for segments made at policy level • Greater flow of new product ideas from closer customer relationships • Customer offered *best* solution • Salespeople matched to market segments	• Increased travel and admin. costs (vs. geographic sales force) • Potential *feast or famine* with market segments • Some segments may be more lucrative than others
	Customer Importance (Strategic/ Key Account)*	Specific salespeople responsible for the firm's most important customers	• Small number of customers (current and/or potential) responsible for a high proportion of revenues — 80/20 rule	• Focuses attention on customers most critical to firm's future • Greater ability to identify opportunities for the firm	• Increased travel and admin. costs (vs. geographic sales force) • Difficulties interfacing with the regular sales force

* Technically a form of market segment organization.

... OR REORGANIZED?

As the firm's environment evolves, so must its market and sales strategies evolve. The sales organization must also evolve:

- **From a geographic-based sales force to a sales force with no geographic boundaries.** Manhattan-based Stuart Dean sells cleaning services to apartment and office buildings via

KEY IDEA

➤ The firm should implement sales force reorganizations *very carefully.*

a four-person, geographic-based sales force. Historically, building managers spent many years at a single building, but increasingly they move from building to building. Salesperson/building manager relationships are critical to capture and retain business. Stuart Dean abandoned its geographic structure. Each salesperson is free to seek business throughout the city.[44]

• **From a product-based sales force to strategic account managers (SAMs).** Traditionally, P&G sold its wide variety of products — dental care, deodorants, detergents, floor-care items — via specialized sales forces. Supermarket chains complained about the interface costs of many different salespeople. P&G appointed SAMs for each supermarket chain. SAMs direct customer teams responsible for meeting strategic account needs.

• **From a geographic-based sales force to a product-based sales force.** Sales growth of Oracle's new application software was unacceptable. The product was very complex; salespeople found it difficult to demonstrate and sell. Oracle reorganized its global sales team into two separate product-based sales forces: applications and databases.

• **From a geographic-based sales force to a distribution-level-based sales force.** Okidata's geographic-based sales force sold imported electronic goods to companies via regional distributors and local dealers. Okidata discovered that selling challenges for distributors, dealers, and creating customer pull were all different. Okidata split its sales force into three: one each for distributors, dealers, and business customers.

• **From an undifferentiated account-based sales force to a strategic account-based sales force.** Merrill Lynch's (ML) U.S. retail brokerage provided the same costly service to clients with $100,000 to invest (67 percent of customers) as to multimillionaires. In a reorganization, wealthy clients continued with their own brokers, but ML served other customers through a call center. Regardless, each customer, however small, could talk to a broker by phone once per quarter.

Designing a new sales organization responsive to environmental and/or strategic change is one thing; implementing the new design is quite another. Reorganizations typically mean that some salespeople have to do different jobs; others may have to relocate. Ill-planned changes can have serious consequences:

> Incoming Xerox CEO Rick Thoman shifted Xerox's sales organization from a product and geographic focus to an industry focus. Thoman saw the salesperson job as analyzing an entire customer business and identifying the best way to manage complex flows of data, graphics, and images. Thoman believed salespeople's intellectual capital would generalize among firms in an industry. But Xerox changed to an industry organization before salespeople were trained, and did a poor job of switching accounts among salespeople. Xerox *orphaned* previously well-served accounts. Many salespeople left rather than relocate. Competitors hired disgruntled Xerox salespeople, and Xerox fired Thoman.

Apple's shift to an employee-based sales force was also less than stellar:

> Apple's CEO Steve Jobs said: "We were very straightforward and told these third-party salespeople that, 'Hey, in four months we're going to switch [the sales force organization] and you're going to be out of a job.' Obviously these folks did everything they could to sell as much as they could by June 30, when we let them go, and did absolutely nothing to build for sales in the July quarter. So when our folks got there, they found there was no pipeline work at all: They had to start from scratch. And, duh, this was during the *peak buying time for schools* [emphasis added]. It was just stupid on our part to do this then, and that was my decision. It was a train wreck, and it was totally my fault."[45]

HOW SHOULD THE FIRM DESIGN SALES TERRITORIES?

Within the sales organization structure, the firm must design (redesign) **sales territories**. Of course, frequent territory design changes are undesirable as they disrupt customer-salesperson relationships. The two key variables are **sales potential** (available sales); and **salesperson workload** — time to complete required activities. The four sales territory design steps are:

- **Initial design by sales potential.** The firm identifies geographically contiguous territories with roughly equal *sales potential.* Some trial territories are geographically larger than others. Equivalent potential territories for Xerox might be a few blocks of midtown Manhattan or several Western states.

- **Calculate workload.** Use sales-effort allocation decisions (Task 2) to determine *workload.* Based on the initial design, in some territories, salespeople may have time left over; in other territories, they may have insufficient time.

- **Adjust initial design for workload.** Make territory design adjustments to optimize sales potential and salesperson workload. Ensure that all salespeople can cover their territories effectively.

- **Continuous monitoring.** Sales managers must monitor salespeople and their territories and continually adjust. Some customers may grow faster or slower than expected; new customers may emerge; others may go out of business. Aggressive young salespeople may be frustrated with insufficient sales potential; experienced salespeople may *cherry-pick* (select) the best short-term accounts and avoid difficult sales. Sales management must continually optimize territory design:

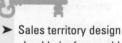

> ### KEY IDEA
>
> ➤ Sales territory design should aim for roughly equal:
> - Sales potential
> - Workload

ConstructCo's (disguised name) analysis showed that market share by territory ranged from 8 to 50 percent. Also, many high-revenue salespeople had low territory shares. ConstructCo redesigned sales territories to take advantage of untapped potential and added salespeople. Revenue decline turned into revenue growth.

TASK 5: CREATE CRITICAL ORGANIZATIONAL PROCESSES

All sales organizations employ a variety of organizational processes to implement the sales strategy. We focus on sales planning, pipeline analysis and sales forecasting, evaluation methods, and reward systems to help implement planned selling effort.

> ### KEY IDEA
>
> ➤ The firm should actively engage salespeople in the sales planning process.

SALES PLANNING

The firm should actively engage salespeople in a detailed sales planning process. As discussed earlier, senior sales managers work with regional and district sales managers to decompose overall firm sales objectives into individual control units like sales regions, districts, and territories. They also decide on broad selling effort allocations by product and market segment. In bottom-up planning, salespeople analyze their individual territories, work with district sales managers to agree on territory objectives, and develop sales action plans. Time is the salesperson's critical scarce resource; the sales action plan drives selling effort by specifying where the salesperson will place effort in the upcoming year plus identify shorter-term action steps. Sales managers must ensure the firm implements planned selling effort at each control unit and achieves its sales objectives. Deviating from the sales strategy can cause problems:

A startup medical device firm, specialized in hemodialysis treatments (blood cleansing for failed kidneys), decided to focus selling effort on major teaching hospitals. The sales approach required salespeople to provide customers with high service levels to ensure proper use. But in implementation, salespeople made sales to more hospitals than they could service. The product was widely misused and the firm suffered serious credibility problems.

PIPELINE ANALYSIS AND SALES FORECASTING

The sales pipeline comprises stages in the selling process that customers traverse in moving from prospects (potential customers) to buyers. **Pipeline analysis** tracks firm success in moving customers through these stages and is particularly important for sales forecasting. IBM's pipeline comprises:

- **Discover.** The salesperson believes the customer is intending to buy.
- **Identify.** The customer is interested in working with IBM.
- **Validate.** The customer states a need and buying vision. The customer allows IBM access to project sponsors — customer personnel responsible for the purchase.
- **Qualify.** Project sponsors and an IBM team work on a preliminary solution.
- **Conditional agreement.** Project sponsors conditionally approve IBM's proposed solution.
- **Business won.** The customer and IBM team sign a contract.
- **Customer expectations met.** The customer is satisfied as purchase and installation move forward — and IBM receives payment as scheduled.

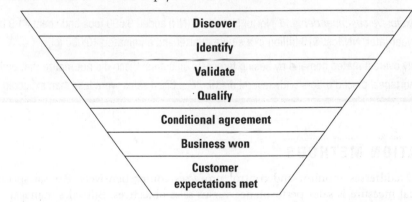

IBM salespeople enter each potential opportunity into the pipeline and estimate potential sales revenues. Periodically, salespeople update each opportunity with a refined sales forecast. If plans change or the customer eliminates IBM as a potential supplier, the opportunity exits the pipeline. IBM aggregates pipeline data and constantly tracks opportunities by sales territory, district, and region. IBM also tracks percentage of opportunities moving from stage to stage, starting with *total sales leads*. Hence, IBM can project expected revenues by territory, district, and region, and identify where performance is on track and where it needs improvement. (Also Opening Case for Honeywell's system.)

To achieve organizational consistency, the firm should implement a single pipeline system across its many sales territories.[46] For various reasons, salespeople often resist entering pipeline data, but the firm must make this mandatory.[47] Many firms use software applications to track and manage sales pipelines and decide where and when to apply additional selling resources — like securing leads or validating opportunities.[48] These applications have many tools: For salespeople to better analyze customer data; and for sales managers to gain greater insight into sales force performance so they can make appropriate interventions. Table 17.13 illustrates typical pipeline data for a single sales territory.

	Total Sales Leads Discovered	Opportunities Identified	Opportunities Validated	Opportunities Qualified	Conditional Agreements Made with Customer	Business Won
Territory total	$76 million	$28 million	$17 million	$13 million	$10 million	$8 million
Percentage of total pipeline leads	100%	37%	22%	17%	13%	11%
Percentage success from previous stage	100%	37%	61%	76%	77%	80%

TABLE 17.13

ILLUSTRATION OF PIPELINE ANALYSIS

We cannot overstate the importance of good sales forecasting. At a minimum, good forecasts are important for financial budgeting, production planning, and reporting future firm prospects to shareholders and financial analysts (public companies). Pipeline analysis is a fundamental tool for improving forecast accuracy. Poor forecasting can lead to significant problems:

To meet *explosive customer demand*, Nortel Networks (NN) added 9,600 jobs and spent $1.9 billion to boost production. One year later, NN lost $19 billion in a single quarter and eliminated 10,000 jobs.

Cisco vastly overestimated demand by basing forecasts on orders. Cisco did not realize that end users, worried about product shortages, placed orders with several distributors. Cisco sales were less than expected, and inventory swelled.

EVALUATION METHODS

Chapter 22 addresses monitor-and-control processes comprehensively. For salespeople, the most critical measure is sales performance versus sales objectives. But sales managers should also assess the quantity and quality of selling effort. Are salespeople working hard? Are they working smart? Only by enhancing these *input* behaviors will salespeople improve *output* sales performance. Table 17.14 shows candidate input behavior measures and their limitations.

Sales managers should use several measures to evaluate selling effort as a single measure can be misleading. Suppose a salesperson has high sales per existing account; seems like great performance. Not so fast: The salesperson could have few existing accounts and overall territory sales may be low. Sales managers at every level — district, regional, and national —should receive regular data on direct reports and access selective data deeper in the sales force as needed.

Measure	Value	Limitations
Calls per day	Identifies level of calling effort	Measures quantity of calls, not quality
Calls per account	Identifies level of calling effort	Measures quantity of calls, not quality
Calls per new account	Identifies where time is spent; links to sales strategy	Should be used together with calls per existing account
Calls per existing account	Identifies where time is spent; links to sales strategy	Should be used together with calls per new account

TABLE 17.14

MEASURES FOR ASSESSING A SALESPERSON'S EFFORT

REWARD SYSTEMS

Reward systems are powerful motivators for salespeople. To establish a truly motivating system, salespeople should answer "yes" to the following questions[49]:

- Can I *achieve* my sales objectives?
- Do I *value* the rewards I will earn for meeting my sales objectives?

- Do I believe I will truly *receive* the rewards I earn?
- Is the reward system fair?

Pharma Inc.'s (disguised name) reps were paid salary and incentive to sell to physicians. The incentive portion was based on achieving sales goals and adhering to planned calling patterns. Pharma's marketing group discovered that, in some therapeutic areas, nurses and nurse practitioners influenced the medications patients received; sometimes they actually prescribed medications. Marketing devised a plan for salespeople to call on nurse practitioners, but Pharma did not change its compensation system. Salespeople were not paid for these calls and the initiative failed.

Sales reward systems can have several components:

- **Financial compensation.** The firm combines three financial rewards in various ways:
  - **Base salary.** Paid to the salesperson regardless of sales performance (in the short run).
  - **Bonus:** Reward paid for achieving quota — typically a target sales or profit level.
  - **Sales commission.** Variable compensation based on sales or profits. In some industries, like life insurance, salespeople earn no base salary and work strictly on commission.

KEY IDEA

➤ The firm's reward system should motivate salesperson behavior. Primary components are:
- Financial incentives
- Recognition
- Promotions and work assignments

➤ The primary ways to pay salespeople are:
- Salary
- Commission
- Bonus

- **Recognition.** This important reward is relatively inexpensive but can be a powerful motivator. Creative sales managers recognize salespeople for performance like highest revenues, best sales growth, most profitable sales, most new accounts, and/or most lost accounts retrieved. Many sales forces recognize high performers with membership in a President's club, often associated with an annual trip (with spouse) to an exciting destination. Amica Mutual Insurance introduced a point-based system to motivate 900 sales and service reps to sell more policies. The online reward catalogue, formed in part from salespeople's suggestions, embraces products like airfares, gift cards, luggage, and PCs. To stimulate internal competition and provide recognition, Amica presents prizes in office ceremonies.[50]

- **Promotions and work assignments.** Promotions and more interesting and responsible job possibilities are highly motivating for some salespeople. Others may not value such advancement or change. They may prefer to be career salespeople and/or lack the necessary skills to move to other positions in the firm.

Generally, financial compensation is a salesperson's most important motivator. The firm should decide the take-home target pay range, then decide the particular combination of salary, commission, and/or bonus for reaching the target. Each component can have drawbacks:

- High salary — may not motivate salespeople to put in high selling effort
- High commissions and established customers — rewards historical rather than current efforts
- High bonuses — may lead to reduced effort after attaining quota and/or persuading customers to hold off placing orders until the next period, as salespeople try to beat the system.[51,52]

The amount of incentive pay — commissions and bonus — should be proportionate to the role of selling effort in making sales.[53] A recent U.S. trend is to put more salespeople pay *at risk* by increasing the incentive portion.

By developing a fair and consistent compensation plan, the firm drives the behavior it desires. Commissions based on sales volume motivate sales but can ignore profits. LG's Kwang-Ro Kim says, "[We make] our salespeople responsible not just for sales but for profits too… [We make] the costs of the business readily available to them…. Our people know … that they have to control their marketing expenses and other costs."[54] Previously, Computer Associates paid its 2,500 salespeople with upfront commissions; salespeople focused on renewing old contracts. A new compensation plan paid higher commissions for additional product sales; by paying over the contract's life, salespeople also focused on customer satisfaction.

Marketing Question

Think about jobs you have had. How were you compensated? What types of incentives did the employer provide? What did you find demotivating?

Every six months, 400–500 customers provide Siebel Systems with satisfaction data on its various departments and individual salespeople. These data drive bonuses and commissions. Salespeople do not receive full commissions until one year after a sale, and then only if customer satisfaction scores are up to par.

A well-designed compensation system can be highly motivating, but a poorly designed system can be highly demotivating. Firms should avoid systems where: Compensation and sales performance are not linked, the incentive portion is too low, and compensation is capped so that increased sales do not earn increased compensation. Of course, the higher the incentive portion, the less predictable are the firm's selling costs. Whenever the firm contemplates a change in its sales compensation mix, it should simulate total sales force costs under various scenarios to avoid surprises for management and salespeople.

The firm should be especially concerned that the financial compensation system does not encourage aberrant behavior:

Dan & Bradstreet (D&B) paid credit-report salespeople salary and bonus. Base salary was low, and the bonus didn't take effect until sales exceeded the previous year plus 15 percent. In order to reach this difficult target, several salespeople sent to customers (and billed for) credit reports they hadn't ordered! When D&B unearthed this practice, it made substantial payments to customers including six-figure amounts to AT&T and IBM. Said a senior D&B executive, "We were a cesspool."[55]

Sears Auto Centers shifted the compensation system for 3,500 service advisors from salary to salary plus commission — based on product-specific sales quotas. Investigation by the California's Bureau of Automotive Repairs revealed that automobiles brought in for simple repairs typically received unnecessary expensive repairs. After many months negotiating and numerous lawsuits, Sears settled with California and 41 other states by distributing $46.6 million in coupons to dissatisfied customers, plus fines totaling $15 million.[56]

TASK 6: STAFF THE SALES ORGANIZATION

Salespeople are the sales force most important resource. Today, few sales professionals compare to Arthur Miller's classic Willy Loman stereotype in *Death of a Salesman* or David Mamet's manipulators in *Glengarry Glen Ross*.[57] But only salespeople can *bring home the bacon* by making sales. Sales managers must ensure the sales force is fully staffed and all territories filled, at all times. Far too often, sales managers do not plan for natural attrition, transfers, promotions, and/or dismissal, and are forced to scramble when a salesperson leaves. Sales managers should *inventory* salespeople and have their own *pipeline* of candidates ready to move to a territory when one opens up.

If the firm has a policy of recruiting salespeople internally, it can create a career path in related departments like sales support or customer service. These employees are committed to customers, know the firm's products, and are ready to transfer into the sales force as needed. If the firm recruits externally, sales managers should continually interview candidates, develop short lists, and be ready to hire when needed. Staffing trade-offs include:

- **Availability.** If experienced competent salespeople are not available, as in new and growing industries, the firm must be ready to provide significant training.
- **Hiring philosophy.** The firm may require salespeople *uncontaminated* by *bad habits* from previous selling experiences.
- **Time.** If a new hire must perform effectively and immediately, there may be no time for a broad search and significant training.
- **Tolerance for failure.** Hiring only the best salespeople may be critical. In other cases, a sink-or-swim approach can be more effective.

Marketing Question

What are the challenges of consistently motivating a sales team? How would you address these challenges?

KEY IDEA

➤ Important trade offs in populating the sales force include:

- Availability
- Hiring philosophy
- Time
- Tolerance for failure

The staffing process to hire and prepare effective salespeople involves several steps:

- **Recruiting.** Sizing and defining the pool from which the firm will select salespeople.
- **Selecting.** Using selection criteria to choose salespeople from the recruitment pool.
- **Training.** Ensuring salespeople have the knowledge, skills, and abilities (KSAs) to be effective.
- **Coaching.** Continuous efforts by first-line sales managers to improve selling effectiveness.
- **Retaining.** Maintaining high-performing salespeople.
- **Replacing.** Weeding out and replacing poorly performing salespeople.

RECRUITING

The recruitment pool reflects the firm's hiring philosophy. Two broad approaches are:

- **Experience.** Hire experienced sales professionals. Sales managers should monitor the job market for successful salespeople in their industries and/or geographies. A West Coast stock brokerage firm stated: "We'll recruit anyone with more than five years experience at Merrill Lynch!"[58]
- **Inexperience.** Hire high-potential individuals with zero (or limited) sales experience. The firm may focus on recent college graduates or employees in telesales or non-sales functions.

In either case, the firm should continually monitor success with its current recruitment pool. If the firm seeks experienced salespeople, yet its yield of high performers is unsatisfactory, it should broaden the pool or shift to a new pool.[59] Many pharmaceutical firms believe their salespeople need two skills: selling skills and scientific skills. Historically big pharma recruited high-potential science majors direct from college, then focused training on selling skills. Today, many pharma firms recruit successful salespeople from any industry, then provide science training and back-up support.[60]

CEO Joe Galli hired 500 high-achieving recent college graduates to help turn around Newell Rubbermaid (NR). The special *Phoenix* sales force worked directly with major U.S. retailers like Home Depot, Lowe's, and Walmart. Phoenicians stocked shelves, demonstrated products, and organized in-store scavenger hunts; they also exchanged ideas online. Phoenicians generated double-digit year-over-year sales growth. NR promoted successful members to mid-level sales and marketing positions — more than 100 promotions in two years.[61]

SELECTING

Selection criteria can be loose or tight. Loose criteria imply a *sink-or-swim* philosophy, prevalent in the life insurance industry. Of 100 salespeople hired, after five years only five are contributing performers (on average). For firms with an established customer base, criteria should be tight and salesperson selection rigorous. The firm should use previously developed selection criteria, including psychometric tests, but evolve these criteria as the environment and/or firm strategy changes.[62] Popular generalized criteria for salesperson selection are empathy, ego drive, and ego strength[63]; other important criteria are affability, credibility, sensitivity, and trustworthiness. In the selection process, several managers should interview each successful candidate. The firm must minimize two key selection errors:

- **Type I Error** — Hiring a salesperson who eventually fails.
- **Type II Error** — Not hiring a salesperson who would have succeeded had they been hired.

The firm soon learns about Type I errors. To detect Type II errors, sale managers should follow up on rejected candidates to assess their performance with other firms. By identifying and tracking hiring errors, the firm can sharpen its recruiting and selecting policies.

TRAINING

Successful training turns newly hired salespeople into effective performers by making their KSAs congruent with the selling job. Training requirements depend on the firm's recruiting and selecting policies. If the firm hires inexperienced salespeople, training in selling skills is an absolute requirement. If the firm hires experienced salespeople, it should focus training on firm business practices, culture, products, and support services. Some training may be useful regardless of background — like advanced selling skills, negotiating, sales-action planning, and time-management skills. Learning development groups may prepare individualized training programs but, more typically, firms offer standardized programs for all new hires. As firm strategy evolves, salesperson success requirements also evolve. Hence, sales training is not a one-time event; sales force development programs should be ongoing. Even experienced salespeople need continuing education, but trainers should be sensitive to their experience.

Newell Rubbermaid (NR) has a well-developed training process for 1,500 salespeople in 90 countries. *Sales Excellence 101* for entry-level reps focuses on consumer-driven innovation and brand building; *Sales Excellence 201* for mid-career salespeople teaches how to be a value-added supplier; and *Sales Excellence 301* for senior salespeople integrates sales and strategic planning. NR also administers online training and audiocasts.

Sam Abdelnour, Whirlpool's VP U.S. Sales, described the *Real Whirled* program comprising several classes annually of fresh college graduates. "Each Real Whirled class has an average of eight people and has to be a minimum of 50 percent diverse. They live in a house together for eight weeks. They do their own cooking, their own cleaning, and they get their training there. They have to entertain Whirlpool people every night and cook them a meal. That's how they get to know people from different parts of the company. We change the appliances every week so that not only do they use all of our appliances but they also use our competitors' appliances as well. At the end of the eight weeks, they know not only what products are available from the appliance industry but also how they all work."[64]

COACHING

Training typically occurs intermittently; coaching is ongoing. First-line sales managers should work with their salespeople to ensure they are being as effective as possible and not making classic salesperson mistakes.[65] Although sales results are critical, effective sales managers know that salespeople only achieve outstanding results by engaging in the right behaviors.[66] A particular concern in many sales forces is a tendency for salespeople to pick *low-hanging fruit* rather engage in deep customer penetration. Sales managers should coach all areas of the sales job, like territory analysis, call planning, identifying and gaining access to the *right* customers, and understanding customer behavior.[67] They make joint calls to provide feedback and help salespeople develop sales networks and negotiate with customers and with their own organizations (to gain support).[68]

KEY IDEA

➤ Coaching salespeople is perhaps the sales manager's most important job.

RETAINING

High-performing salespeople are valuable assets, and the relationships they forge with customers are often vital for long-term firm success. When a high-quality salesperson moves to new responsibilities or to a different company, firm/customer relationships become vulnerable. Succession planning and measured hand-overs mitigate these problems; but unexpected vacancies and minimal succession planning can spell disaster.

Successful salespeople are vulnerable to *poaching* by competitors. They face switching costs and risks in moving to new employers, but firms that lag the market in reward systems will surely lose critical personnel. Sales force retention is an important measurement criterion for sales managers; they must ensure firm rewards are competitive. One useful device is a database for departing salespeople that tracks why they left and where they went.

me1702

REPLACING

The firm should plan for replacing high-performing salespeople who are promoted, transferred, or leave. The firm should also quickly replace underperforming salespeople. Sometimes the firm makes a hiring error; sometimes a previously high-performing salesperson cannot adjust to a new strategy like being unable/unwilling to sell new products to new customers. When the *status quo* is unacceptable, sales managers must fire or reassign poor performers and secure better-equipped salespeople.

> PrintCo's (PC) sales force analysis revealed that its top 15 (of 50) salespeople accounted for 71 percent of gross margin; the bottom few salespeople actually lost the firm money. PC implemented a three-fold plan: Top performers — focus on retention; worst performers — replace; mid-level performers — design and implement a new mandatory training program.

KEY IDEA

➤ First-line sales managers may have the most important role in the sales force; securing effective first-line sales managers is crucial.

MARKETING ENRICHMENT

Improving Sales Performance at DHL  me1702

Marketing Question

How would you go about identifying potential candidates for first-line sales manager positions?

SALES MANAGEMENT

Securing effective salespeople is one thing; finding effective sales managers is quite another. First-line sales managers may have the most critical role in the entire sales force; they require very different KSAs than successful salespeople. Regrettably, many firms thoughtlessly promote their best salespeople to be sales managers. The firm may lose a great salesperson and gain a poor sales manager![69] The firm should implement a rigorous recruiting, selecting, and training process for sales managers by developing a clear set of job competencies. A particularly serious problem is the minimal training often given to new sales managers. At one leading life insurer, first-level sales managers often directed 50 or more salespeople. Said one newly appointed district manager, "The company brought us to New York for a two-day *dog-and-pony show*. That was it. Essentially no training for my new position."[70] The appropriate training mix varies by firm, industry, and management level but is too important to be haphazard.

To improve sales performance, sales managers must carry out the six tasks of sales management. Senior sales managers must be able to drive required change through the sales organization, and also have the skills to interface with marketing and other firm functions. All sales managers must be leaders, developing a sales culture, using heroes, rituals, symbols, and values that shape and reinforce appropriate salesperson behavior. (Section on *Leading the Sales Force* earlier in the chapter. Marketing Enrichment me1702 for sales performance actions at DHL.)

KEY/STRATEGIC ACCOUNT MANAGEMENT

Realizing that the 80:20 rule (or 80:20:120 [Chapter 2]) applies to their revenue and profit distributions, many firms are implementing strategic account (SA) programs.[71] These firms identify the most important current and potential customers, then invest in them by providing additional resources and generally lavishing greater attention than on *regular* customers. To lose a current strategic account (customer) or win a new strategic account that the firm anticipates will deliver many years' revenues, is a significant organizational event.[72]

In most SA programs, **strategic account managers** (**SAMs**) are responsible for building and sustaining relationships with individual strategic accounts.[73] Generally, SAMs have many fewer customers than regular salespeople. Traditionally, the average UPS salesperson managed 100 large accounts; when UPS introduced strategic account management, the average customer number dropped to about ten. For the firm's most important customers, individual SAMs may focus on single accounts and be responsible for many millions of revenue dollars annually.

KEY IDEA

➤ Strategic account managers are responsible for individual major customer.

Vivek Gupta is a star IBM salesman. As strategic account manager for wireless telco Bharti Mittal (BM), Gupta persuaded his fast-growing customer to outsource most back-office operations to IBM while BM focused on strategy, branding, and operations. The $750 million, 10-year contract grew to $1 billion after five years. When Gupta became strategic account manager for Vodafone, the managing director told him, "I don't do any business with IBM, and I don't intend to." Gupta persuaded IBM to provide Vodafone employees with laptop computers; he secured his first server order one year later. After three years, Vodafone awarded IBM a $600 million contract to handle operations — from customer service to finances. Gupta's success relates to his ability to work both customer and IBM bureaucracies, deep client knowledge — specifically identifying *pain points*, deep knowledge of IBM capabilities, and forming personal and professional relationships.[74]

SAMs spend significant time working closely with customer corporate offices and typically locate in that vicinity. Walmart is a strategic account for many FMCG firms; P&G and others base team members in Bentonville, Arkansas, Walmart's head office location.[75] SAMs develop and execute plans to optimize firm revenues and profits at the account. SAMs direct teams that may include local sales and customer service personnel, and others from product and brand management, finance, HR, logistics, market research, operations, and trade marketing. Firms often form partnerships with their most important accounts. These customers have input into product development and other key decisions, and may even embrace shared risk/return agreements for target cost savings.

Successful strategic account programs adopt the *congruence model*, requiring critical decisions in four areas:

- **Strategy.** Includes deciding firm commitment to the strategic account program, overall resource allocation, number of SAs and revenue and profit targets, nominating and selecting criteria for SAs, and types of firm/SA relationships.

- **Organization structure.** Concerned with organizational placement of the SA program, reporting structure, and interfaces with other functions, notably the sales force.

- **Human resources.** Securing the appropriate personnel to be SAMs; includes other classic HR functions like training, retaining, and compensation.

- **Systems and processes.** Methodologies for helping SAMs do their jobs like SA planning systems, customer profitability, benchmarking, and best practice sharing.

In recent years, SA programs have evolved in two important ways:

- **Managing global accounts.** Increasingly, multinational firms are making their procurement decisions on a global (and/or multi-country regional) basis.[76] To better serve these customers, suppliers are adopting SA practices at a global level. As a senior 3M executive opined, "The fact that we are a multi-product, multi-business, multi-national company should not be the customer's problem." **Global account managers** (**GAMs**) develop plans for multinational accounts and manage global account teams that implement their strategies. IBM has about 150 global accounts, each with a GAM; for its top 40 customers, IBM GAMs are senior executives. GAMs function similarly to domestic SAMs but their job scope is much greater. GAMs must develop significant understanding of the global business environment, have comprehensive knowledge of global supply chains, and be sensitive to local cultural differences. Sometimes the firm's top executive acts as account manager or *point person* for the most global critical accounts: Oracle's Larry Ellison — GE; Nestlé's U.S. head — Walmart; and its French head — Carrefour. At Merck, IBM wrested an important contract from Accenture when CEO Sam Palmisano came calling, and Cisco's John Chambers reviews and summarizes critical accounts around the world each night before going to bed.

- **Customer tiers.** Rather than classify major customers as either strategic accounts or regular accounts, leading firms partition SAs into several tiers based on current and potential revenues — like Tier I (platinum), Tier II (gold), and Tier III (bronze) — and allocate

---

Marketing Question

How does the SAM job differ from the salesperson's job?

KEY IDEA

➤ Successful strategic account management requires critical decisions in:

- Strategy
- Organization structure
- Human resources
- Systems and processes

KEY IDEA

➤ Global account managers are responsible for multinational customers that want to make global purchases.

KEY IDEA

➤ Firms often group major customers into separate tiers, like

• Tier I (platinum)
• Tier II (gold)
• Tier III (bronze)

and address each differently.

➤ Tier I customers typically provide the highest levels of sales and profits.

v1702

resources accordingly. Microsoft uses a three-tier system for its most important customers — 40 *global* accounts, 250 *strategic* accounts, and 1,000 *corporate* accounts. Some firm tiering is more complex, based on profits and potential revenues, and more tiers. Whatever the basis, the firm has few Tier I, more Tier II, and many more Tier III customers, and addresses each tier differently.

Designing and implementing an SA program is not a simple matter. The firm improves its chances of success by focusing on nine critical success factors:

- Establish the scope — size and boundaries — of the SA program
- Secure senior management commitment
- Select the *right* strategic accounts
- Design the line organization for managing SAs
- Secure effective SAMs
- Develop effective SA plans
- Establish the supporting organizational infrastructure
- Deliver and document the creation of incremental value
- Put it all together — align the success factors in SA management

Many salespeople are responsible for individual customers. They may also be local contacts for strategic accounts. Typically, such salespeople report to a first-line sales manager but also have dotted-line relationships to one or more SAMs (or GAMs).

Marketing Question

What other messages did you glean from this chapter?

v1703

v1704

v1705

KEY MESSAGES

- The marketing/sales interface should be seamless. Successful sales managers are true leaders.

- Effective sales managers must successfully complete six tasks.

- The first three sales management tasks address developing sales strategy:
  - **Task 1.** Set and achieve sales objectives.
  - **Task 2.** Determine and allocate selling effort.
  - **Task 3.** Develop sales approaches.

- The second three tasks focus on implementing the sales strategy:
  - **Task 4.** Design the sales organization.
  - **Task 5.** Create critical organizational processes.
  - **Task 6.** Staff the sales organization.

- Many firms are developing strategic account and/or global programs for their most valuable customers.

VIDEOS AND AUDIOS

Consultative Selling	v1702 ▼	Eric Baron	The Baron Group
Sales Force Compensation	v1703 ▼	Dave Cichelli	The Alexander Group
Managing Strategic (Key) Accounts	v1704 ▼	Hajo Rapp	Siemens AG
Becoming a Strategic Partner	v1705 ▼	Gus Maikish	IBM

QUESTIONS FOR STUDY AND DISCUSSION

Can you answer the questions implied by this chapter's learning objectives? Check!

1. A close friend has just become national sales manager for a small firm with 25 salespeople as direct reports. What advice can you offer for the first 100 days on the job?

2. Which of the six sales management tasks are the most important? Why? Interview a sales manager to develop your answer.

3. "Good salespeople are born, not made." Discuss! What are the most important skills and abilities for an effective salesperson?

4. Aco (disguised names) sells adhesives for a high-end printing application. Printfirm is a major customer, but its specifications are difficult to meet. Historically, Aco was Printfirm's sole supplier, but Bco has started to supply Printfirm with similar adhesives. Aco believes Bco is a low-cost producer that sometimes cuts corners. Last year, Aco's plant flooded and closed for one week. Aco halted all deliveries and Printfirm is adamant that it wants a second supplier. Aco's top management has set a goal of retaining 80 percent of Printfirm's business. How would you advise Aco's sales and marketing managers?

5. PrdCo's (fictional firm) recent sales growth has mirrored the industry — the incoming CEO is demanding improved performance. She wants to implement forced ranking evaluation like Jack Welch introduced at GE. In the sales force, 20 percent would be rated superior, 70 percent average, and 10 percent inferior. Inferior salespeople would be fired. PrdCo's salesforce comprises a national sales manager (NSM), three regional sales managers (RSM), 12 district managers (DSM), and 110 salespeople. Assume you are the NSM; how do you respond to the CEO's ideas?

6. What are the most important changes occurring in sales force management? How will these changes affect firms' future market and sales strategies?

7. Select a product in which you are interested, or this book — *Managing Marketing in the 21st Century*. How would you complete the tasks for developing a sales strategy?

IMPERATIVE 4
Design the Market Offer

....

PART C – DELIVERING CUSTOMER VALUE

CHAPTER 18

DISTRIBUTION
DECISIONS

To access O-codes, go to **www.ocodes.com**

LEARNING OBJECTIVES

When you have completed this chapter, you will be able to:

- Understand the nature and function of distribution systems.
- Develop and implement effective distribution strategies.
- Trade off alternative forms of direct and indirect distribution.
- Identify challenges and opportunities in ongoing management of distribution channels.
- Manage power and conflict in distribution systems.

OPENING CASE: CISCO

Cisco is the world's leading supplier of products to power the Internet. A small portion of Cisco's more than $40 billion revenues goes though direct channels, well over 85 percent through 28,000 channel partners in 160 countries.[1] Previously Cisco sold direct to end-user customers, but in the late 1990s shifted its major efforts to three types of intermediaries:

- **Tier 1 partners.** *Systems integrators including global players like EDS and Accenture, but also well-established local partners. Tier 1 partners integrate Cisco products with technology products from other firms to provide end-user customers with complete solutions.*

- **Tier 2 resellers.** *Intermediaries that sell to smaller end-user customers than Tier 1 partners. Reseller sales range from a few thousand to several million dollars; they secure Cisco products from distributors. Distributors hold inventory and provide logistics value to Cisco. Cisco may have thousands of resellers in a particular geography, but only a few distributors.*

- **Service provider partners.** *Mainly telecommunications firms that supply Cisco equipment to their customers. These channel partners may also make customer-service agreements to relieve customers of the management burden of operating Cisco equipment.*

Cisco's sales force works hand-in-hand with channel partners to serve large end-user customers. Salespeople develop end-user customer relationships and make joint sales calls with channel-partner salespeople. Channel partners are responsible for local relationships, developing business solutions, consultancy assistance, product delivery, after-sales support, and financing customer purchases. Cisco develops and monitors joint business plans with channel partners.

Channel partners provide significant value to Cisco. Most importantly, channel partners leverage the efforts of Cisco's salespeople, enabling much greater coverage and customer intimacy for Cisco products. Channel partners deliver and install Cisco products and provide significant after-sales service. Since Cisco insists on 30-day payment, channel partners supply their own working capital.

Cisco channel-partner relationships have evolved. An initial concern for partner growth developed into making money for partners, using measures like return on invested capital. Today, Cisco focuses on partner ability to grow and differentiate themselves in their markets. Cisco policy places all relevant business through partners; Cisco does not cherry-pick attractive business to serve directly.

Cisco classifies channel partners as Premier, Silver, or Gold, based on partner investment in securing capabilities to provide value to end-user customers. Higher value levels earn greater recognition from customers and greater resources and support from Cisco. This classification does not consider revenues, so some gold accounts are smaller than other premier accounts. Cisco's incentive system considers three performance categories:

- **VIP** — *Developing advanced technological expertise*
- **OIP** — *Seeking out new opportunities and/or new customers*
- **SIP** — *Developing new and innovative solutions*

Cisco encourages channel partners to earn VIP, OIP, and SIP incentives; an individual partner may earn incentives in more than one category.

In the mid-2000s, Cisco introduced an innovative structure that placed all emerging market countries, regardless of geographic location, into an emerging-markets organization. Hence, a country like Saudi Arabia, formerly part of the Europe, Middle East, and Africa (EMEA) region, no longer had to compete for resources with advanced western countries like France and Germany. The emerging-market organization contained channel partners from 140 developing countries around the world. Cisco's tasks in these markets were:

- *Develop sufficient channel partners to have good coverage. Cisco hired country managers and salespeople and identified partners in each country.*

- *Develop replicable channel-partner models by industry vertical to transfer across countries — like tourism, and oil and gas. Partners could be non-traditional — like Schlumberger in oil and gas markets.*

- *Work with country-level policy makers to encourage investment in information technology infrastructure and spur economic growth.*

More than ninety-five percent of emerging markets revenues go through channel partners (100 percent in many countries); annual growth rates exceed 40 percent. Cisco's challenge is to increase its channel partner capacity by adding channel partners, increasing existing partner capabilities, or both. Having successfully established itself in many emerging markets, in 2011, Cisco folded emerging market countries into a new global organization comprising three geographic regions.

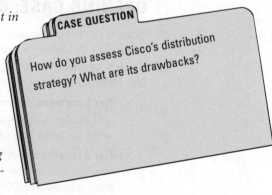

CASE QUESTION

How do you assess Cisco's distribution strategy? What are its drawbacks?

Chapter 18 is the sole chapter in Part C of Imperative 4 — *Design the Market Offer*. Part C focuses on *Delivering Customer Value* via Chapter 18, *Distribution Decisions*. Firm products reach customers via distribution channels. Distribution can be direct from supplier to customer, but may also be highly complex involving many intermediaries. Intermediaries fulfill many different functions and frequently enjoy mutually beneficial relationships with suppliers. But supplier and distributor goals rarely overlap completely; hence, distribution systems are riddled with conflict and power inequalities. FMCG firms like Colgate, Nabisco, and P&G work hard to secure good shelf positions in supermarkets. But they often compete with chains like Albertsons, Royal Ahold, and Walmart who put store brands in the best positions, and want suppliers to reduce prices and pay *slotting fees* for shelf space.[2]

Power inequalities may prevent firms from making distribution innovations. Yet no distribution system lasts forever; new approaches that add value and reduce costs can unseat market leaders. Consider video-rental: Traditionally, consumers rented from retail outlets like Blockbuster or Hollywood Movies, but Netflix (Chapter 3 — Opening Case) allows consumers to order movies online, initially delivered by mail but now also available as video-on-demand.

THE CHANGING VIEW

OLD WAY	NEW WAY
Conflict models dominate	Cooperative models ascendant
Customers patient	Customers impatient
Direct marketing rare	Direct marketing common
Distribution arrangements fixed	Distribution arrangements changeable
Distribution — local/regional	Distribution — regional/national/global
Fast delivery rare	Delivery speed highly valued
Information technology poorly used	Information technology essential
Manufacturer as channel captain	Retail power increasing
Overnight distribution unavailable	Overnight distribution increasing
Push inventory systems (loading intermediaries common)	Pull inventory (efficient consumer response systems)
Slow progression: exclusive → selective → intensive	Fast progression: exclusive → selective → intensive
Telecommunications infrequent	Telecommunications ubiquitous

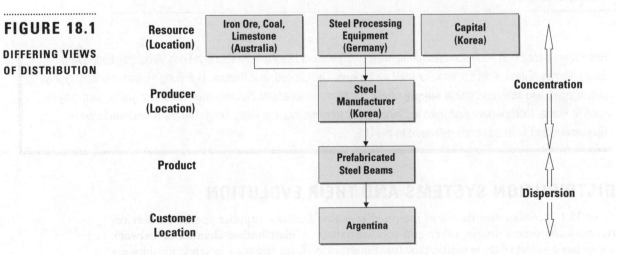

FIGURE 18.1

DIFFERING VIEWS OF DISTRIBUTION

Two Views of Distribution — Broad and Narrow

Inputs like raw materials, sub-assemblies, and assemblies undergo changes in *state*, *physical location*, and/or *time* before the firm delivers a finished product to an end-user customer.[3] The **broad view of distribution** includes all of these changes. Figure 18.1 shows changes for delivery of prefabricated steel beams to an Argentinean builder.

- **Raw materials**. Iron ore, coal, and limestone are mined in Australia and separately shipped to an integrated steel manufacturer in Korea.
- **Processing equipment**. Sourced in Germany for use in Korea.
- **Capital**. Bank loans to finance equipment purchasing and working capital for manufacturing based on bank deposits made by Korean citizens.
- **Steel beams**. Manufactured in Korea.
- **Completed steel beams**. Shipped to a distributor in Argentina.
- **Finishing**. The Argentine distributor does minor finishing operations and delivers beams to the building site.

Major changes that these activities embrace include:

- **Change of state**. Iron ore, coal, and limestone into prefabricated steel beams.
- **Change of physical location**. Australian raw materials and German processing equipment shipped to Korea. Completed steel beams shipped to Argentina.
- **Change in time**. This process takes time to accomplish.[4]

Along with most marketers, we adopt a **narrow view of distribution**. We focus on changes in *physical location* and *time* of *finished* products. Marketing also addresses minor *state* changes like final processing and repackaging. Major state changes like turning iron ore, coal, and limestone into steel beams are the concern of manufacturing; procurement secures raw material and capital equipment; and finance secures capital.

Most people understand that firms create value by making *state* changes. Firms also create value by making *physical location* changes and in the *timing* of those changes. The Korean manufacturer creates value by forming steel beams from iron ore, limestone, and coal. But the Argentinean builder receives no value if the beams are in Korea or on a ship; they have value only at the building site. And unless they arrive on time, the entire construction project will stop. Delays may cost millions of dollars.

Hong Kong-based Li & Fung supplies garments to U.S. retailers like Abercrombie and Fitch, American Eagle, Ann Taylor, Disney, Guess, Kohl's, Laura Ashley, Levi Strauss, The Limited, and Reebok. Li & Fung's intranet-based, highly coordinated, and seamless global **supply chain** comprises hundreds of discrete links. For Guess jeans, yarn may be spun in Korea, fabric woven and dyed in China, and fastenings made in Hong Kong. The jeans are then sewn in Guatemala, and finished goods delivered to the U.S.[5]

DISTRIBUTION SYSTEMS AND THEIR EVOLUTION

Table 18.1 identifies and describes intermediaries that facilitate supplier goods and services reaching consumers and/or other end-user customers. A **distribution channel or network** comprises a subset of these entities; the functions they perform and their interrelationships are continually in flux. Table 18.2 shows selected changes as customer needs, competitor actions, and environmental forces exert pressure. Leading indicators of impending change include unhappy consumers, end-user customers, and/or suppliers; complacent intermediaries; deteriorating system economics; market coverage gaps; new technology; outdated system interfaces; poor logistics; and unexplored channels.[6]

TABLE 18.1

DEFINITIONS
OF SELECTED
DISTRIBUTION
ENTITIES*[7]

* Developed in part from
the American Marketing
Association Glossary of Terms

DISTRIBUTION ENTITY	DESCRIPTION OF DISTRIBUTION ENTITY
Agents, brokers, manufacturers' representatives	These entities have similar functions. Generally, they sell products but do not take title or physically handle goods. They may work for the supplier or the customer, or be impartial between supplier and customer.
Banks and finance firms	Provide financing for customers to aid in purchasing products.
Distributors	Provide promotional support for suppliers, especially for selective or exclusive distribution (discussed later). Often a synonym for wholesaler.
Retailers	Display and sell products to consumers. May operate at a fixed location — bricks-and-mortar stores, as traditional direct marketers, or on the Internet.
Shipping companies	Transport products.
Warehouse operators	Receive and inventory products, arrange product pickup, often break bulk.
Wholesalers	Primarily buy, take title to, store, and physically handle goods in large quantities. Usually break bulk — resell to retailers or industrial businesses.

TABLE 18.2

SELECTED CHANGES
AFFECTING
DISTRIBUTION
SYSTEMS

CHANGE CATEGORY	TYPE OF CHANGE
Customers	Increasing expectation of multi-channel access.
Direct marketing	Continuing growth.
Distributor concentration	Powerful intermediaries emerging.
Internet purchasing	B2C — accelerating as home access to broadband communication increases. B2B — growing popularity of reverse auctions. Spurring **disintermediation** — direct-to-customer — and **intermediation** — intermediary placed between supplier and customer.
Production	Product-build times shortening, permitting widespread mass customization and inventory reductions throughout the supply chain.
Retailer sophistication	In B2C, industry concentration and better management shifts power to retailers.
Supplier focus	Greater attention to supply-chain management and working capital reduction.
Technology	Advances in capturing, transferring, and analyzing point-of-sale data drive supply-chain efficiencies. In B2C, purchasing behavior insights enhance retailer power.
Transportation	Speedy, reliable, inexpensive ways to transport goods globally increasingly available.

Ultimately, customer needs drive distribution arrangements. Early in the life cycle, products are often unreliable and service needs are high; customers require help to make choices and support to use the new technology. These requirements diminish as customers become more self-sufficient. Customers may no longer require the benefits intermediaries provide, and early market leader distribution strategies become increasingly outdated:

When VHS technology drove home video, mom-and-pop stores initially dominated retail distribution; later, Blockbuster emerged as the leading national chain. Video technology shifted to DVD and Netflix became leader with a direct-to-home distribution system via U.S. mail; Redbox similarly grew but with an alternative distribution system via automatic dispensers in supermarkets and drug stores. Video streaming from content providers like Netflix is direct-to-consumer distribution, bypassing intermediaries like U.S. mail.

In the 1890s, 70 percent of Americans lived on farms, miles from the nearest general store. Sears Roebuck (SR) revolutionized purchasing with a new distribution system — the catalog. SR offered practical hard goods — *Prairie-Breaking plows* and *Mark-Your-Poultry leg bands*, and luxuries — ladies' *kidskin-opera slippers* and *ostrich-plume hat trimmings*. Buyers no longer drove buggies for hours to reach the store; the store came to them, and everyone had access to the same goods at the same price. Across the U.S., people kept up with changing fashions and accessed the escalating product variety — the *money-back* guarantee reassured wary customers. In five years, SR's sales went from $750,000 (1895) to over $10 million (1900), as it surpassed retail leader Montgomery Ward.[8]

The effectiveness of any distribution system changes over time, but suppliers often have difficulty making appropriate adjustments. Suppliers can revise prices overnight and, in the short run, develop new promotions or even add/delete products and services. By contrast, the firm's distribution arrangements often remain unchanged for many years, in part because of end-user customer loyalty to distributors. The average tenure of Caterpillar's 186 dealer relationships worldwide exceeds 50 years!

Developing a Distribution Strategy

To develop distribution strategy, the firm must make several critical decisions[9]:

- **Distribution functions.** What exactly must be done in the distribution channel?
- **Distribution channel: direct or indirect?** Should the firm deal directly with consumers and/or end-user customers? Or should the firm use intermediaries, and if so, which ones?
- **Distribution channel breadth.** How many intermediaries should there be at each distribution level? For example, how many wholesalers and/or retailers? Should there be selectivity or exclusivity?
- **Criteria for selecting and evaluating intermediaries.** How should the firm decide whether a particular intermediary is appropriate for handling its products?

We focus largely on physical goods but distribution is also important for services. Our focal concern is sometimes with manufacturers, sometimes with other entities. Consider Whirlpool and Nike: Whirlpool manufactures kitchen appliances but Nike outsources production.

DISTRIBUTION FUNCTIONS

By completing many functions, distribution closes gaps in physical location and time between factory-finished products and consumers/end-user customers. Sometimes the supplier undertakes a particular function; other times intermediaries or end users do so. In a complex distribution channel, some functions, like physical movement, must be done several times. Table 18.3 shows various distribution functions.

Physical Product	Information	Ownership
Assortment[11]	Information-sharing[14]	Financing
Bulk-breaking	Marketing research	Impartiality[15]
Inventory	Order collection	Risk-shifting[16]
Physical movement[12]	Selling and promotion	Service
Physical-state changes[13]		Title Transfer
Quality assurance		

Increasingly, channel members, especially retailers, work at enhancing the customer buying experience. Product display is critical but at Forum shops in Las Vegas, Atlantis rises and falls on the hour. The Mall of America (Minneapolis) attracts consumers to its 400 retail stores with Camp Snoopy (indoor amusement park) and Underwater World (walk-through aquarium). At Wizards stores (owned by toy manufacturer Hasbro) a game room occupies one-third of retail space. (Conversely, Costco and Sam's Club offer minimal services and compete on price.)

The firm should align incentives to motivate distribution channel entities to perform required functions. Actions that improve firm sales and profits should also benefit channel members.

Unfortunately, distribution channels often contain significant inefficiencies and misaligned objectives.

> Coca-Cola CEO Roberto Goizueta was widely hailed for improving Coke's share price by spinning off bottlers into an independent firm, Coca-Cola Enterprises Inc. (CCE). CCE controls 80 percent of Coke U.S. distribution; Coke has 39 percent ownership. In the mid-2000s, CCE switched objectives from revenue growth to improving profit margins and raised prices sharply. This action caused significant conflict between Coke and CCE, and Coke volume growth dropped.

KEY IDEA

➤ Direct distribution methods, combined with database marketing, are powerful alternatives to indirect distribution.

FIGURE 18.2

REACHING CONSUMERS: DIRECT AND INDIRECT CHANNELS

Marketing Question

Fingood (disguised name) distributed products to consumers via distributors and retailers. To spur consumer demand, Fingood cut prices to distributors by 20 percent, but Fingood's leading distributor held prices firm so as to increase its margins. The price reduction failed. What were Fingood's mistakes? How should Fingood proceed?

DISTRIBUTION CHANNELS: DIRECT OR INDIRECT?

Figure 18.2 shows alternative channel designs for conducting various distribution functions:

*   **Direct channels.** Suppliers manage most contact with consumers and end users.
*   **Indirect channels.** Intermediaries like distributors, wholesalers, and retailers play a major role in transferring products to consumers and end users. Some indirect channels have a single intermediary; others have multiple intermediaries.

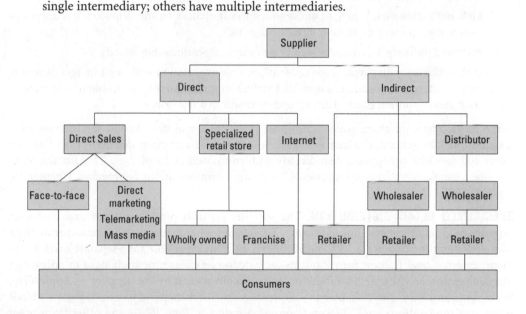

REACHING CONSUMERS THROUGH DIRECT CHANNELS

Direct distribution, combined with database marketing,[17] is a serious alternative to indirect distribution. In B2C, **direct distribution** has several forms:

FACE-TO-FACE DIRECT SALES. Direct customer contact can give suppliers intimate insight into customer needs. In advanced economies, direct selling and distribution costs are often too high for consumer goods. Regardless, Avon, Mary Kay, and Tupperware successfully sell and deliver products direct to consumers. In less-developed countries, lower incomes make personal selling more viable. When Citibank launched credit cards in India, face-to-face sales were quite successful.[18]

> In Japan, salespeople sell automobiles by visiting consumers at home. In Britain, Malaysian-based automaker Proton supplements car showrooms with salespeople; they visit consumer homes with demonstration vehicles. In the U.S., Handtech.com sells PCs via technology consultants who target friends, neighbors, and small businesses.

DIRECT SALES VIA DIRECT MARKETING, MASS MEDIA, AND TELEMARKETING. The firm makes contact with individual consumers; they receive products directly by package delivery from remote locations.[19] The firm may initiate contact to target customer lists via **outbound** communications — firm-to-customer — or the customer may initiate via **inbound** communications — customer-to-firm. Regardless of communications mode, message centralization gives the firm greater control and cost efficiencies in addressing customers. The high cost of face-to-face selling drives telemarketing; QVC (quality, value, convenience) and the Home Shopping Network (HSN) are effective means of selling some product classes directly via television.

INTERNET. The Internet is the fastest-growing *inbound* communications method for many product forms, even including luxury goods. Firms use various business models:

- **Consumers pick up products.** At Chronodrive (supermarket [France]), consumers order online, then pick up goods at easily accessible warehouses. At Best Buy, 30 percent of customers ordering online make in-store pickups.

- **Direct delivery.** Firms deliver many digital products like books, music, videos, and financial services directly to customer cell phones, computers, and tablets.

- **Link with telesales.** When a Landsend.com visitor clicks on the *help* icon, a salesperson uses instant messaging to help navigate the site.

- **Package delivery.** Consumers receive products at locations they specify.

- **Link with visual displays.** Tesco covered Seoul subway station walls with images of supermarket shelves. Consumers assembled virtual shopping carts by scanning product codes with smart phones; home delivery occurred within a few hours.[20]

Some newspapers are abandoning traditional production and distribution for Internet-only distribution.[21] In general, the Internet reduces search costs and often *disintermediates* wholesalers and retailers so suppliers deal directly with consumers and end-users.[22,23] Also, the *long-tail* effect enables very large inventories. (For digital communications approaches, Chapter 16, pp. 412–418)

SPECIALIZED RETAIL DISTRIBUTION. The supplier controls product display and customer experience in retail outlets. Bulgari, Coach, Tiffany and other luxury goods firms operate their own upscale stores; Coach's factory outlets offer a different experience for a separate market segment. International fashion firm Zara makes twice-weekly assortment changes to encourage frequent customer visits. Retail outlets are either **wholly owned** by the supplier — Apple, Gap, Body Shop, and Starbucks (Chapter 1 — Opening Case); or **franchised** to a third party — H&R Block (tax preparation) and 7-Eleven (convenience stores). Toys "R" Us and other firms open *Pop-Up* (temporary) stores during holiday seasons.

The first Apple store opened in 2001, four years after Steve Jobs' return to Apple. Initial press reaction was negative: "What does Apple know about retail?" "Apple will upset its retail distributors." But Apple received little attention from retailers as its market share was so small. Over the years, store design evolved but Apple maintained the *genius bar*. Apple's product line also evolved from Macintosh computers to include the iPod, iPhone, and iPad. Apple has around 400 stores globally, earning well over 10 percent corporate revenues, and earning the highest sales per square foot of any retail chain — $5,600 (versus Tiffany [2nd — $3,000] and Coach [3rd — $1,800]).

Many fast-food brands like KFC, McDonald's, and Taco Bell use franchising. Typically the franchisor develops the business model and seeks entrepreneurs to invest capital. The franchisee agrees to implement the franchisor's strategy and pays an initiation fee and ongoing fees.[24] Franchisors often limit franchisees to a fixed number of outlets so as to retain more control.[25] Sometimes firms use franchising to grow their brands, but later buy back successful franchises to secure wholly owned outlets. Luxury-goods supplier LVMH purchased its franchisees to gain greater control and cultivate a more upscale consumer experience.[26]

Marketing Question

Review the websites for L.L. Bean, Lands' End, or a direct marketer of your choice. Phone your firm and order a product. In a couple of days, order another product. What data did the firm request on each occasion? Did the firm remember you from the first order to the second order?

KEY IDEA

➤ Advantages for wholly owned retail distribution are greater operational control and earning the entire retail margin.

➤ Disadvantages for wholly owned retail distribution are capital required for growth, and operating risk.

KEY IDEA

➤ Advantages for franchising are leveraging firm financial resources for faster growth, and harnessing franchisees' entrepreneurial drive.

KEY IDEA

➤ Disadvantages for franchising are loss of control and smaller profit margins.

Innovative Distribution Methods to Reach Consumers

- **Banana Republic.** Sets up makeshift stores in corporate offices for several days at a time.
- **Banco Popular.** Serves Hispanic immigrant laborers with check-cashing vans. On Fridays, vans travel to factories, hospitals, nurseries, plants, and other locations where Hispanic immigrants (many illegal) congregate.[27]
- **Fifth Third Bank, Cincinnati, OH.** All employees are potential salespeople. They earn profit-sharing, bonuses, and stock options — up to 125 percent above base salary — for attracting new clients. Fifth Third Bank also places retail outlets in supermarkets. At a Kroger's branch, the manager makes frequent loudspeaker announcements about special loan rates and other services. She patrols grocery aisles, identifying prospective customers to discuss financial needs.
- **P&G.** In countries like Mexico and Venezuela, P&G faces serious cultural problems in marketing tampons. Religion and beliefs about health risks and loss of virginity from using tampons hamper sales. P&G focuses marketing efforts on *bonding* sessions in women's homes, much like *Tupperware* parties. Female hosts educate friends and neighbors about tampon benefits and provide free samples. Forty percent of attendees later become hosts.
- **Sogebank.** Aggressively markets to small, independent business owners in Haiti.[28] Loan officers sell from street-corner *offices*; they also make home visits to discuss client needs and assess collateral.
- **Walgreen.** Maintains several hundred health centers in corporate offices.

REACHING CONSUMERS THROUGH INDIRECT CHANNELS

Many B2C firm products reach consumers via **indirect distribution**: Distributors, wholesalers, and/or retailers provide *physical location* and *time* value. By constructing product assortments from many suppliers, indirect channels reduce customer search costs and provide an entire shopping experience. Indirect channels may also add brand value to supplier products, like Macy's (U.S.) or Harrods (Britain).[29] New technology products like Kindle, Nook, and iPad offer distribution alternatives for book, magazine, and newspaper publishers.

KEY IDEA

➤ Intermediaries offer value-added benefits like providing:

- Product assortments
- Shopping experience
- Market access

Also, they often reduce the costs of conducting various distribution functions.

Intermediaries may provide market access that would otherwise be very expensive (or impossible) for the firm to secure. By gaining U.S. distribution in BestBuy (700 stores) and The Home Depot (1,800 stores), Korean white-goods producer LG has earned over five percent U.S. market share and is No. 3 globally behind Whirlpool and Electrolux. Individuals and organizations in Amazon's Associates program send millions of customers to Amazon's website. Market access is particularly important when venturing abroad. Many products fail because firms do not understand local cultures, customers, and markets; local partners can be invaluable. Efficiencies from using channel partners also reduce costs for suppliers:

- Agents, manufacturers' representatives, and brokers — selling economies.
- Banks and financial institutions — financing economies.
- Independent warehouses — inventory economies.
- Package delivery and transportation companies — transportation economies.
- Distributors, wholesalers, and retailers — inventory, selling, and transportation economies.

The U.S. Postal Service (USPS) and FedEx are direct competitors in overnight and ground package delivery. Yet USPS allows 10,000 FedEx drop boxes at post offices nationwide; FedEx ships Express, Priority, and First Class mail.

REACHING ORGANIZATIONAL CUSTOMERS

B2B firms use both direct and indirect distribution to reach organizational customers:

- **Direct distribution.** Firms sell directly to end-user customers via on-the-road sales forces, telemarketing, direct marketing, and/or the Internet. (Few B2B firms operate retail stores.) Suppliers use various transportation methods to deliver products to customers.
- **Indirect distribution.** Some suppliers reach customers, especially small businesses, through retail stores like Office Depot and Staples for office supplies. Plumbing, electrical, and home building firms purchase from Home Depot and Lowe's. More generally, many firms reach customers via distributors and wholesalers.

Machine tool builder Okuma America requires each of 46 distributors to inventory a minimum number of machine tools and select repair parts. When customers order out-of-stock items, the distributor contacts Okumalink — a shared information technology system. Okumalink keeps distributors informed about parts availability/location in Okuma warehouses. If a part is unavailable, the distributor contacts other distributors online and arranges delivery direct to the customer.[30]

Table 18.4 shows factors favoring, respectively, direct and indirect distribution.[31]

Direct Distribution	Indirect Distribution
Complex end-user customer purchasing decisions — multiple functions and high-level executives	Simple end-user purchasing decision — often by low-level purchasing agents
Custom-tailored products	Stockable items, manufactured in large quantities but sold in small quantities
Delivery speed not critical	Rapid delivery and service important
Large quantity sales	Small quantity sales
Small potential customer base	Large potential customer base

Distribution speed is increasingly important as firms use **just-in-time (JIT)** inventory systems to increase operating efficiencies. Industrial distributors must provide customers with complex product assortments in a timely manner. Typically, some requirements are predictable but others are not. Holding sufficient inventory to satisfy both predictable and unpredictable demand can be very expensive. Okuma America (above) has one approach; Volvo has another:

Volvo GM (VGM) Heavy Truck Corporation sells replacement parts via commercial truck dealers; VGM supplies dealers from regional warehouses. Parts inventories in Volvo warehouses were rising, but sometimes dealers could not secure needed parts because of stockouts! VGM worked with FedEx Logistics to set up a warehouse in Memphis (FedEx's hub). Dealers with emergencies call a toll-free number; FedEx ships the required parts and delivers to dealer offices, holds for airport pickup, or drops off at the required site. VGM closed three warehouses, reduced total inventory by 15 percent, and regained much business previously lost to stockouts.[32]

DISTRIBUTION CHANNEL BREADTH

Distribution channel breadth refers to the number of channel members the firm uses at a particular distribution level — like wholesalers or retailers. The firm can increase/decrease:

In France, Norwegian furniture manufacturer J.E. Ekornes distributed to consumers via 450 furniture dealers. Ekornes believed this was too many. Dealers put in little selling effort, in part because they carried small product selections. Ekornes dropped 300 dealers; the remaining 150 received exclusive territories. These dealers increased local advertising for Ekornes' furniture and dropped competing lines. Ekornes sales increased threefold.[33]

TABLE 18.4

B2B CUSTOMERS: FACTORS FAVORING DIRECT AND INDIRECT DISTRIBUTION

KEY IDEA

➤ For B2B suppliers, conditions typically favor either direct or indirect distribution. In each case, several options are available.

The firm should also consider different types of distributor. Adding a new distributor type can be important when customers have preferred outlets. In the Pacific Northwest, consumers prefer *either* marine *or* forest-products distributors depending on their interests; each distributor type relates to specific problems and issues. Many firms use both types of distributor.

Adding new distributor types can be positive or negative. Tupperware halted a 15-year revenue slide by placing booths in shopping malls and selling over the Internet; later Tupperware added distribution in Target. With ready product availability, consumers no longer had a reason to go to Tupperware parties. Sales dropped 17 percent, profits 47 percent, and Tupperware's sales force by 25 percent as many "good, solid performers" left. Tupperware stopped distributing at Target; profits doubled.

> An average Staples store carries 8,000 office-supply items; an average shopper spends $600–$700 annually. Staples.com offers 200,000 items; an average store *and* catalog shopper spends $1,200–$1,400. Staples installed in-store computer kiosks linked to Staples.com; sales jumped to $2,500 per store *and* catalog shopper. Each of Staples' 1,000 retail outlets has at least four online computer kiosks.

Marketing Question

Best Buy discovered that many customers were examining products in its stores, then searching the Internet for better prices and placing orders online. How would you advise Best Buy?

When the firm distributes through multiple channels, channel crossing becomes an issue — customers secure product information and/or try the product in one (or more) channels (showrooming), but purchase from a third channel. The first channel(s) provides free service — only the third channel earns revenues.[34] As Internet commerce grows, this problem will increase for traditional channels. The firm benefits from the sale, but some channel partners receive no revenues for their services. In the long run, this practice may lead to channel breakdown.

Firms have three broad channel-breadth options:

INTENSIVE DISTRIBUTION. When customers minimize search, products should be easily available. The firm maximizes the number/type of outlets where customers buy. Intensively distributed consumer products include convenience goods like cigarettes and soft drinks. In emerging markets, intensive distribution is a critical strategic thrust for firms like Coca Cola and P&G.

> WD-40, developed for the space industry as a rust-prevention solvent, is present in 80 percent of U.S. homes and has more than 2,000 uses. A major success factor is intensive retail distribution via well over 10,000 wholesalers.[35]

EXCLUSIVE DISTRIBUTION. When customers are willing to search and travel, the firm should be very careful in selecting outlets. When retailers provide brand equity and positive shopping experiences, a B2C firm may choose a few prestigious outlets. Fine china and crystal firms distribute products in high-class department stores like Saks Fifth Avenue and Macy's, or specialty stores like Tiffany. Relatedly, successful bands like AC/DC, the Eagles, and Journey made exclusive distribution arrangements with Walmart.

KEY IDEA

➤ Suppliers should select distribution channel(s) that are appropriate for their target segment(s) and perform the required functions.

➤ Providing customer benefits and values, rather than traditional industry practice, should guide supplier distribution choices.

SELECTIVE DISTRIBUTION. Selective distribution is a compromise between intensive and exclusive distribution. Too many outlets can lead to excessive competition; too few outlets and the firm's products are difficult to find. Sony and Samsung distribute products selectively, making careful outlet decisions. Samsung repositioned its products upmarket and for a few years withdrew from Walmart and Kmart.

Distribution breadth is equally important in B2B and B2C marketing. Under competitive pressure from Dell, Compaq (now HP) shifted distribution efforts from 40 distributors to four large wholesalers. Distribution breadth raises three related exclusivity issues:

DISTRIBUTORS — GEOGRAPHIC EXCLUSIVITY. Should the supplier give distributors geographic exclusivity? (Within limits, most suppliers can enforce such restrictions.) Exclusivity eliminates *free riding* and intra-brand competition by providing geographic monopolies, but may breed complacency. Regardless, exclusivity motivates distributors to invest in promotion and improved service. When Canon USA's copier market share declined, it removed geographic restrictions so the strongest dealers could better compete with Xerox.

DISTRIBUTORS — PRODUCT EXCLUSIVITY. Product exclusivity may reduce conflict, satisfy channel partners, and better meet end-customer needs. Sometimes firms offer different product designs and/or brands to different distribution channels. Black & Decker sells the *Black & Decker* brand at Kmart and similar outlets, *Quantum* for serious enthusiasts at Home Depot, and *DeWalt* for professional contractors/builders at trade dealers. Panasonic, Samsung, and Sony produce separate models for major retail chains like Best Buy. Product exclusivity may also be important for market entry when suppliers require focused attention from intermediaries. Hence, Apple's iPhone was initially available only on AT&T's wireless network.

SUPPLIER EXCLUSIVITY. Some suppliers require that intermediaries focus entirely on their products; others insist on exclusivity within a product category. Pepsi and Coke each have exclusive agreements with airlines, restaurants, and retailers; Anheuser-Busch InBev has similar arrangements with beer distributors; and Visa and MasterCard with some restaurants.[36] IBM's Authorized Assembly Program commits distributors to use only IBM original parts.

> Suppliers seeking exclusivity should avoid the appearance of anti-competitive behavior. European Commission officials seized internal documents in dawn raids on Coca-Cola offices across Europe. Italy's competition authority alleged that Coke designed a complex system of exclusivity bonuses and discounts to "oust . . . Pepsi from the market." Regulators alleged Coke offered rebates and volume discounts only to retailers that regularly increased shelf space for Coke products and made in-store promotions and special offers.[37]

CRITERIA FOR SELECTING AND EVALUATING INTERMEDIARIES

Clear and unambiguous criteria for selecting channel partners favor both suppliers and distributors. The firm should clearly specify the functions and performance standards distributors must meet. Would-be distributors can then fairly assess their capabilities versus supplier requirements. IBM prevailed in a court case because it set and applied clear standards:

> When IBM launched its personal computer, computer retailers who were denied the IBM franchise banded together to sue IBM. The courts ruled that IBM had not discriminated among retailers and that its selection criteria were clear and fairly applied.

Both the firm and distributors should recognize their separate obligations before making an agreement. To improve success probabilities, the supplier should ask several questions[38]:

- Does the distributor have adequate market coverage?
- How competent is distributor management?
- How does the distributor rate on aggressiveness, enthusiasm, and taking initiative?
- Is the distributor the appropriate size to do business with us?
- What is the distributor's credit and financial condition?
- What is the distributor's general reputation among suppliers and customers?
- What is the distributor's selling capability? What is its historic sales performance?
- Will the distributor forgo competitive products? Does it welcome the supplier's products?

The answers drive the supplier's decision to accept/reject a potential distributor.

KEY IDEA

➤ Critical distribution strategy decisions include:

- Functions to be performed
- Direct versus indirect channels
- Distribution channel breadth
- Criteria for selecting intermediaries

PUTTING IT ALL TOGETHER: THE DISTRIBUTION STRATEGY

Figure 18.3 shows an eight-step method for developing distribution strategy.[39] In the boxed insert, a small candy supplier develops distribution strategy for three market segments. This illustration shows the complexity of distribution in a simple case; for large firms with many products targeting several segments, distribution can be very complex.

FIGURE 18.3

A STEP-BY-STEP APPROACH TO DEVELOPING AND IMPLEMENTING DISTRIBUTION STRATEGY

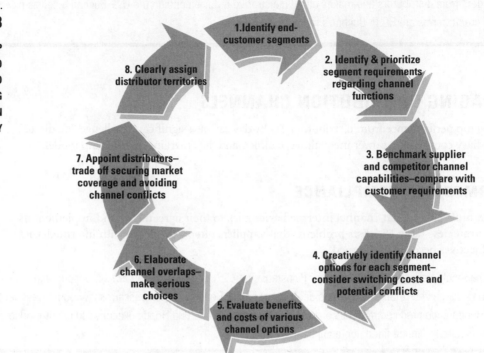

1. Identify end-customer segments
2. Identify & prioritize segment requirements regarding channel functions
3. Benchmark supplier and competitor channel capabilities—compare with customer requirements
4. Creatively identify channel options for each segment—consider switching costs and potential conflicts
5. Evaluate benefits and costs of various channel options
6. Elaborate channel overlaps—make serious choices
7. Appoint distributors—trade off securing market coverage and avoiding channel conflicts
8. Clearly assign distributor territories

Distribution Strategy for a Small Candy Manufacturer

Buchan Inc. (fictional firm) is a small U.S. candy manufacturer. Buchan targets the domestic consumer mid-price candy market for family consumption. Buchan distributes products through supermarkets and small retailers that add value by offering product assortments. Buchan does not sell direct to consumers; it believes that channel intermediaries can more efficiently finance, inventory, sell, and transport its products. Buchan evolved its market strategy by targeting two additional segments: domestic U.S. firms for employee consumption, and consumer markets in Latin America. Buchan now has several distribution arrangements:

- **Domestic consumer middle market.** Consumers purchase candy from supermarkets and small retailers.
  . Major supermarkets are regional and national chains; other retail chains are small regionals and locals.
  - **Major chains.** Buchan's strategic account sales force sells direct. Buchan delivers to retailer warehouses direct from its factory warehouse via third-party truckers. Chains are slow payers, so Buchan discounts its accounts receivable to a factor.[40]
  - **Small regional and local retail chains.** Buchan uses food brokers for selling effort. Buchan fills orders from geographically dispersed, independently owned warehouses. Third-party truckers, hired by Buchan, supply these warehouses from Buchan's factory warehouse; independent warehouses make store deliveries.
  - **Small stores.** Buchan sells to a national distributor, delivers to the distributor's main warehouse in its own trucks, and holds accounts receivable until payment. The distributor makes its own arrangements to ship products to the stores.

continues on next page

- **Domestic U.S. firms:** Buchan sales force sells direct to corporate purchasing groups and ships candy from independently owned warehouses (above).

- **Latin American consumer markets:** Buchan has an export agent with good Latin American contacts. Distributors in each country identify retail outlets and make all local arrangements. The export agent combines orders from distributors and makes all administrative arrangements in the U.S. Buchan receives payment by letter of credit; terms are F.O.B. Buchan's factory warehouse.[41]

MANAGING DISTRIBUTION CHANNELS

Ensuring top performance from distributors day by day can be a significant challenge. We discuss intermediary compliance, power inequalities, conflict, and the emerging-partnership model.

INTERMEDIARY COMPLIANCE

The firm must ensure that channel intermediaries stick to their agreements and implement its market strategies. Table 18.5 lists problems that suppliers often experience with intermediaries when objectives become misaligned.

Honda had multiple retail dealers in major Pakistani cities: 27 in Lahore, 16 in Karachi. Despite agreements to adhere to Honda's suggested retail prices, some dealers cut prices. Dealers with significant showroom investments were very upset. Honda appointed committees consisting of two dealers and one Honda executive to monitor price compliance in each major city. Honda fined non-compliant dealers.[42]

• Apply insufficient effort to consumers/end-user customers the supplier has targeted
• Are inadequately financed
• Are overloaded with products from competing and non-competing suppliers
• Can't or won't meet supplier goals
• Carry insufficient inventory
• *Cherry-pick* the supplier product line
• Do an inadequate job of solving consumer and end-user problems
• Do not allow the firm to contact their sales forces
• Do not follow supplier suggested pricing
• Do not pass on promotional programs and rebates to consumers and end users
• Do not stress the supplier brand — in the extreme, push private-label or competitor brands
• Do not use supplier promotional materials
• Get very close to end-user customers and will not provide the supplier with customer data
• Make ineffective use of supplier sales managers
• Primarily sell on price, not on value
• Require fixed payments to carry the supplier's products

TABLE 18.5

SUPPLIER OPERATING PROBLEMS WITH RESELLERS

Marketing Question

Have you or a friend or colleague ever been involved in distribution? Which issues in Table 18.5 posed problems? How did you solve them?

When firms compensate intermediaries with standard commissions for all products and customers, they may encounter compliance problems. The firm can better direct distributors by varying commissions by product and customer type. The firm can also tie evaluation and compensation directly to contract requirements like maintaining inventory levels, providing customer service, and ensuring customer satisfaction.[43] Table 18.6 shows a partial list of performance measures for evaluating distributors.[44]

TABLE 18.6

**CHANNEL MEMBER
PERFORMANCE
EVALUATION**[45]

Criterion	Frequently Used Operational Performance Measures	
Sales performance	Gross sales Sales by product, market segment Sales growth over time	Actual sales/sales quota Market share Realized prices
Inventory maintenance	Average inventory maintained Inventory/sales ratio	Inventory turnover On-time delivery
Selling capabilities	Total number of salespeople Salespeople assigned to supplier's products	Salespeople assigned by geography Account managers assigned to strategic customers
Information provision	Sales data by customer[46] Information on end-user needs	Information on inventories and returns

KEY IDEA

➤ A well-designed compensation system can help the supplier direct distributor efforts.

The firm should continuously evaluate intermediary performance. But the firm must remember that intermediary relationships are a two-way street. Distributors also evaluate supplier performance. Are the supplier's products selling? Are consumers and/or end-users complaining about supplier products? Are supplier deliveries prompt? Is the supplier easy to do business with?

A specific compliance problem occurs when the supplier sets different prices in different segments. Distributors in low-price segments may engage in arbitrage by reselling products in high-price segments — *diversion*.[47] Diversionary activity can play havoc with the supplier's market strategy.

POWER IN DISTRIBUTION SYSTEMS[48]

Amazon initially set $9.99 as the price for many Kindle books. Macmillan (publisher) objected to Amazon's Kindle pricing and Amazon suspended sales of Macmillan books. One week later, Amazon backed down and allowed Macmillan to set its own Kindle prices — $12.99 and $14.99.

KEY IDEA

➤ Power is one channel member's ability to get another channel member to do what it wants it to do.

KEY IDEA

➤ Power distribution among channel members is typically asymmetric.

Power and conflict are endemic in distribution systems. **Power** is one channel member's ability to get another member to act as it wants. Typically, some channel members have more power than others; they also have different objectives. When a supplier is more powerful, it can impose demands. Some suppliers pressure intermediaries to carry large inventories under the premise that *a loaded dealer is a loyal dealer*. Microsoft sets many conditions for PC manufacturers. Similarly, powerful intermediaries may exert power when they enjoy strong market positions. Walmart pressures suppliers for low prices, takes control of product delivery, and demands adherence to supply-chain guidelines and sustainability initiatives.

Over time, power tends to shift from one channel member to another. Sometimes firms seek greater control over supply chains by forward (FI) or backward (BI) integration. Suppliers acquire customers (FI) — Coca-Cola and PepsiCo each purchased large bottlers; GM purchased parts supplier Delphi Automotive. Customers acquire suppliers (BI) — Boeing purchased a factory from aircraft fabricator Vought; steelmaker Nucor purchased a major scrap-metal processor. Table 18.7 identifies conditions for greater or lesser power for suppliers — **upstream** — and distributors/end users — **downstream**.

Upstream — Suppliers	Downstream — Distributors or End Users
Demand greater than supply	Supply greater than demand
Distributor has high switching costs	Distributor has few switching costs
Few substitute products available	Many firms can supply
Few substitute suppliers available	Few substitute distributors available
Individual distributors unimportant to supplier success	Distributor purchases are large percent of supplier output
Proprietary technology	Products/services undifferentiated
Supplier enjoys monopoly-like position	Distributor enjoys monopsony-like position
Supplier has extensive end-customer contact	Supplier has little end-customer data
Supplier products important to distributor success	Supplier products unimportant to distributor success
Supplier poses credible threat of forward integration — to cut out distributors	Distributor poses credible threat of backward integration — to make supplier unnecessary

TABLE 18.7

CONDITIONS THAT INCREASE OR DECREASE POWER UP AND DOWN THE DISTRIBUTION CHANNEL

Figure 18.4 shows several entities in a distribution system. We explore power relationships among manufacturers/brand owners, distributors/wholesalers, retailers, and end-user customers.

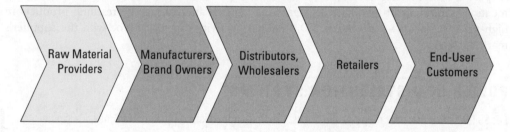

Raw Material Providers | Manufacturers, Brand Owners | Distributors, Wholesalers | Retailers | End-User Customers

FIGURE 18.4

POWER IN DISTRIBUTION SYSTEMS

MANUFACTURERS AND BRAND OWNERS. In the early 20th century, manufacturers grew and increased power over distributors and wholesalers. Manufacturers researched customer needs, designed good products, and reduced costs and prices via mass production. Firms like Budweiser, Campbell's, Coca-Cola, Frito-Lay, Gillette, Kellogg's, Kodak, Levi's, and PepsiCo used consumer advertising to build powerful brands and become *channel captains*. Not all brand owners are manufacturers: Calvin Klein, Nike, and Polo outsource production but carefully manage distribution. Sometimes raw material/ingredient providers like NutraSweet (artificial sweetener) and Intel (chip maker) earn significant distribution power.

DISTRIBUTORS AND WHOLESALERS. In the late 19th century, full-line, full-service wholesalers like Alexander T. Stewart and H.B. Claffin (long defunct) were *channel captains*. Wholesalers dominated U.S. consumer goods distribution, linking distant manufacturers with retailers and consumers.[49] Economic changes and growth in manufacturer and retailer power diminished these once-powerful intermediaries, but they still play a major role in many industries. As depicted in the movie *Blood Diamond*, De Beers buys nearly all of the world's raw diamonds and virtually sets diamond prices worldwide. **Value-added resellers (VARs)** are a new type of intermediary, building software modules on other firms' platforms and modifying computer hardware for niche markets. **Systems integrators** like Accenture and EDS add value by installing/servicing software and hardware from many vendors and making them work together.

KEY IDEA

➤ Over time, power shifts from one type of channel member to another.

Intermediaries often provide information value. Insurance brokers dominate business insurance by identifying and analyzing business risks and helping firms secure coverage from insurers. Intermediaries provide end-user customers with product choices and reduce the necessary number of supplier relationships. Consider the time you would spend to buy groceries from individual specialists: milk from a farm, produce from various growers, and meat from a butcher. Dairies, grocers, and butchers were once valuable intermediaries, but today supermarkets provide their products in one convenient location.

Today, many supplier websites offer customers greater product variety than traditional retail distribution. But intermediaries are also successful. Amazon's product assortment encompasses books, CDs, prescription drugs, and many other products from manufacturers *and* retailers. eBay is also a powerful intermediary, using online auctions to link sellers and buyers. Expedia, Orbitz, Priceline, and Travelocity broker sales of airline tickets and hotel rooms online.[50]

An investor diversified in several mutual funds has many interactions — multiple calls to purchase/sell individual funds and check fund balances, deposit/receive checks, and receive multiple statements. By combining multiple funds (intermediation), Schwab's OneSource decreases the hassle and keeps funds continuously invested.[51]

Via intermediation, OpenTable (OT) allows consumers to make online reservations 24/7 at more than 20,000 restaurants in the U.S. and abroad. OT is free to diners; restaurants pay a one-time installation fee and one dollar per reservation (for diner reward points). Since its 1998 founding, OT restaurants have seated more than 200 million guests.

KEY IDEA

➤ Intermediaries add value by reducing the number of relationships a supplier and end-user customer must have.

➤ Intermediaries occupy the nexus between suppliers and end-user customers.

RETAILERS. Strong retail chains have evolved via industry concentration. In the U.S., *category killers* like Best Buy, Home Depot, and Toys "R" Us virtually dictate industry direction. Tesco, ASDA, and Sainsbury's dominate British supermarkets; Walmart, Royal Ahold, Kroger, and Safeway also play a similar role in the U.S. National warehouse clubs like Costco and Sam's Club place significant pressure on grocery suppliers. Retailing has trailed many industries in globalization, but Carrefour (France), Walmart (U.S.), and vertically integrated Zara (Spain) have significant global operations.

Major retailers are often price leaders. They use buying power and efficient logistics to drive down costs, but must trade off cost efficiencies from standardized product assortments against more customer-responsive local variations. More sophisticated chains study customer needs and use powerful information technology to tailor assortments and offer consumers customized promotions. Organization is also important: Starbucks placed U.S. stores in time-zone-defined divisions; performance improved when Starbucks realized coffee-drinking habits varied by geography (Northeast, Pacific Northwest, Sun Belt) and reorganized on that basis.

Planograms

Consumers make many purchase choices in stores; hence, display is critical. The strategic retail decision concerns product category selection and space allocation. The planogram is a visual diagram specifying physical placement of products/brands within a product category. The retailer (corporate) and/or category captain (Chapter 21) develops planograms; store managers are responsible for implementation. Sophisticated retailers develop multiple planograms per product category to account for local market variation; *planogram police* ensure compliance.

Major retailers force suppliers to make direct payments to secure shelf space — aka **slotting fees**.[52] In 2001, slotting fees for five major food companies — Campbell's, Coca-Cola, Kellogg's, Kraft, PepsiCo — were 14 percent of sales at retailers that sold their products. Coca-Cola spent $2.6 billion, Kraft $4.6 billion, and PepsiCo $3.4 billion just to get products placed on retailer shelves.[53] At Christmas, to enhance its own highly profitable battery sales, Walmart *persuaded* Kodak to stop supplying batteries with its cameras. An important trend is the introduction of smaller stores: Traditional Best Buy stores average 38,750 square feet; Best Buy Mobile stores average 1,420 square feet. Office Depot, Walmart, and Britain's Tesco also have multiple formats.

END-USER CUSTOMERS. In B2C markets, individual consumers seldom have significant power, but consumer groups can profoundly influence producers. European consumers boycotted genetically modified products like Roundup Ready corn, and local groups protesting McDonald's presence have vandalized restaurants. In Germany, environmentally minded consumer coalitions encourage strict recycling laws. In B2B, mergers and acquisitions have left the

Marketing Question

National retailers must balance the efficiency benefits of national purchasing with greater market responsiveness from decentralized buying. How would you advise Macy's?

remaining customers in several industries with significant power. The few global automobile firms and aircraft manufacturers Boeing and Airbus are good examples.

CONFLICT IN DISTRIBUTION SYSTEMS

Because distribution channel members have multiple organizational relationships, the potential for conflict is high. **Operational conflict** occurs daily due to late shipments, invoice errors, unfulfilled promises, unacceptable product quality, supplier attempts to *load* channels by *forcing* unwanted inventory on intermediaries, and price and margin disagreements. ESPN distributors (cable companies) continually complain about price increases but don't dare stop distributing ESPN. These conflicts are annoying, frustrating, and channel disrupting, so most members try to minimize them. Sometimes supplier and distributor are unable to work out their differences and the relationship stops, at least temporarily:

> When ABC's (supplier) largest cable distributor Cablevision balked at a requested price increase, ABC stopped transmitting its signal for the Academy Awards and other shows.
>
> Upset with Unilever price increases, major Belgian supermarket Delhaize removed 300 Unilever products from shelves in well over 700 stores.

Strategic conflict is more serious and may lead to significant change in channel relationships. Sometimes conflict emerges from downstream customers; other times from upstream suppliers. Sometimes strategic conflict develops slowly; other times, specific actions precipitate strategic conflict. Figure 18.5 shows a simple distribution channel we use for illustration.

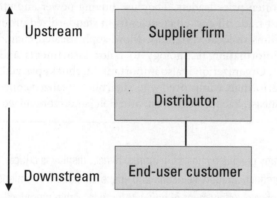

FIGURE 18.5

A SIMPLE DISTRIBUTION CHANNEL

KEY IDEA

➤ Distribution channel members have high conflict potential:
- Operating conflict
- Strategic conflict

STRATEGIC CONFLICTS INITIATED BY DOWNSTREAM CUSTOMERS. We discuss four conflicts:

- **End-user customers grow and desire direct-to-supplier relationships.** Many suppliers start out using distributors to reach end-users (especially small businesses). As these customers grow, they believe that distributors provide insufficient value for their margins. End users believe they can secure lower prices from direct supplier relationships.

> Jco (disguised names) supplies disposable tableware for parties. Jco reaches retailers like Playstore through Disco, a major national distributor. Founded as one store in the early 1980s, Playstore now has more than 500 outlets. Playstore's new management team told Jco that it wanted to cut out Disco and buy direct from Jco.

If the supplier agrees to these requests, it risks harming its distributor relationships. After all, the distributor played an important role in growing the supplier's business. But if the supplier remains loyal to the distributor, it risks losing valuable end-user customers.

> Norton was a large-scale producer of grinding wheels to U.S. industry. Norton became market leader by forging strong relationships with industrial distributors. Norton earned high market share with small business customers, like local machine shops. But market share dropped precipitously at large customers, like auto manufacturers. These customers bypassed industrial distributors and formed direct relationships with other grinding wheel suppliers.[54]

- **Distributors become large and change the power balance.** When small single-location retailers characterized U.S. automobile retailing, manufacturers like GM, Ford, and Chrysler were very powerful. But the emergence of multiple-location mega-dealers like AutoNation, CarMax, and Potemkin, selling huge volumes from several producers, has shifted the power balance from manufacturers to retailers.[55]

- **Distributors supply private-label products.** In B2C, many supermarkets, department stores, and other retail chains increasingly offer private-label products. In B2B, innovative distributors disrupt channel relationships by offering their own branded products in competition with (or instead of) supplier products. Distributors may secure products from other suppliers or backward integrate to make products they formerly only distributed. Nucor began as a steel distributor; dissatisfaction with suppliers led it to manufacture steel. Nucor is now the most profitable U.S. steel producer.

- **New buying influences enter the distribution channel.** In some industries, independent buying groups amass buying power for members. The Independent Grocers Association (IGA) and TruValue have long served small grocery and hardware stores respectively. In hospital supply, Novation and Premier purchase for many small and large hospitals.

STRATEGIC CONFLICTS INITIATED BY UPSTREAM SUPPLIERS. We discuss three conflicts:

- **To reach end-user customers more efficiently, the supplier goes direct.** Sometimes suppliers believe they can be more effective than distributors. Suppliers bypass distributors and sell direct to end-user customers. Distributors typically resent these initiatives:

> British brewer Bass Ale piloted a home-delivery service. Cash-and-carry warehouses and convenience stores carrying Bass Ale products feared they would lose business. Leading cash-and-carry firm Nurdin and Peacock stopped carrying several Bass beers and encouraged customers to avoid Bass products. Bass abandoned the pilot.[56]

The Internet has enhanced suppliers' ability to sell direct to end-users and hence increased the likelihood of conflict with intermediaries. Some firms place major efforts on Internet sales, but others restrict Internet activity to directing website visitors to distributors so as to avoid conflict.

Sometimes suppliers go direct in a limited way that minimizes conflict. Hershey, Mars, and Nike (NikeTown) have their own retail stores. Wholesalers and retailers believe these stores enhance supplier brands, so there is little conflict. Mattel sells a wide range of toys and apparel over the Internet, but avoids conflict by never undercutting distributor retail prices and not offering some popular items.

- **The supplier addresses a new market and competes with its distributor.** The supplier/distributor relationship may be fine, but the supplier introduces products that compete with its distributor, and strains the relationship. IBM (distributor) resells $3 billion of Cisco (supplier) products annually but Cisco server products compete directly with IBM in the data-center market.

- **For better market penetration, the supplier adds new distributors and/or distributor types.** Suppliers sometimes initiate *horizontal conflict* by adding additional distributors and/or new distribution channels. Current distributors are often unhappy with these initiatives and reduce their efforts. Hill's Science Diet pet food experimented with a store-within-a-store pet-shop concept in grocery channels, but lost support from pet shops and feed stores.[57] By contrast, when Goodyear distributed through mass merchandisers like Walmart, it kept independent Goodyear dealers happy by working to increase market demand for replacement tires.[58]

PLANNING FOR POWER CHANGES

All things equal, the firm is better off having a stronger (versus weaker) power position relative to other channel intermediaries. If the firm initiates strategic conflict, it must assess the likely impact on other channel members and anticipate how they may respond. To continue the Norton illustration (boxed insert, p. 470): Norton eventually addressed market share loss at large customers by going direct. Industrial distributors were upset, but remained loyal; there were no viable alternative suppliers. Similarly, major U.S. airlines eliminated travel-agent commissions and encouraged passengers to purchase flights at their websites. Travel agents had few options and continued to sell airline seats. Tables 18.8 and 18.9 show possible actions for upstream suppliers and downstream customers, respectively, to improve power positions.

TABLE 18.8

ILLUSTRATIVE ACTIONS TO IMPROVE SUPPLIER POWER

Type of Action	Examples
Become central to distributor success	• Develop joint marketing strategies with distributors. • Develop value-added services like sales training, field technical support, field selling support, inventory control systems, and product manuals, both directly and indirectly related to its own products.[59] • Hire a sales and marketing group to research end user needs, then pass sales opportunities to distributors. • Innovate new products and (perhaps more importantly) develop expectations of continuous innovation. Strong supplier relationships assure the distributor of early access to these innovations. • Strongly support current products, especially in market downturns where such support may differentiate the supplier from competitors.
Broaden the scope of supplier options	• Broaden the distribution base by adding distributors. • Demonstrate the folly of backward integration by distributors. • Develop an information base on end users. Initiate direct communication, for example, by a technical support force or via e-mail. • Explore limited forward integration by adding a few wholly owned distributors.[60]
Improve bargaining power	• Integrate disparate product lines.[61]
Raise distributor switching costs	• Develop customized products needing customized equipment and specialized training. • Develop dedicated online access for information and simplified order placing. • Improve supplier reputation by enhancing relationship quality. • Increase number of contact points within the distributor. • Offer benefits to concentrate purchases.[62] • Work to secure end-user/testing agency qualification by brand, rather than generic product.

KEY IDEA

➤ Suppliers and distributors each have various ways to improve power positions.

KEY IDEA

➤ When suppliers attempt to improve power positions, they should try to anticipate the actions of other distribution channel members.

TABLE 18.9

ILLUSTRATIVE ACTIONS TO IMPROVE DISTRIBUTOR POWER

Type of Action	Examples
At end-user customers	• Add value to end-user customers. • Build loyalty with end-user customers. • Consider branding service packages. • Introduce additional services.
At suppliers	• Increase contact points with the supplier. • Persuade the supplier to outsource activities to the distributor. • Work to minimize supplier costs.
Broaden the scope of distributor options	• Explore limited backward integration. • Secure additional suppliers. • Show the disadvantages of forward integration by the supplier.
Improve bargaining power	• Centralize purchasing operations.

Marketing Question

Walmart is well known for driving tough bargains with suppliers to secure low prices. Yet Walmart has a partnership agreement with P&G. Why? Why does P&G partner with Walmart?

THE PARTNERSHIP MODEL

When firms exercise power and generate strategic conflict, the underlying assumption is a *zero-sum game*. If the firm *wins*, another channel member *loses*, and vice versa. The **partnership model** assumes the possibility of a *positive-sum game*. By developing trust and working together, several channel members win; there are no losers.[63] Supplier-customer partnerships are at the heart of strategic account management — Chapter 17.

P&G sells billions of dollars of consumer products annually through Walmart; the two firms have developed have a highly effective distribution partnership. Walmart captures point-of-sale data for P&G products and transmits to P&G in real time using state-of-the-art information systems. By combining these data with seasonal purchasing trends, P&G improves forecast accuracy; gains purchasing, manufacturing, and packaging efficiencies; reduces inventory; and cuts costs. P&G codes products by store destination and places them directly on Walmart trucks at warehouse interchange points (cross-docking). Full trucks leave frequently for store-to-store deliveries.[64] P&G and Walmart also use paperless systems for receiving goods and managing payables/receivables.[65] JCPenney has a similar relationship with Hong Kong shirt maker TAL Apparel. JCPenney sends TAL point-of-sale data from all 1,040 North American stores; TAL forecasts JCPenney's requirements and replenishes each store, sometimes shipping by air.[66]

By developing partnerships, channel members can establish joint strategic goals like cutting costs and reducing supply chain inventory while limiting stockouts.[67] Better forecasting allows retailers to offer more efficient product sets, conduct more effective promotions, and eliminate heavy discounts on unwanted merchandise. By working with retailers, suppliers can achieve lower production and distribution costs and better use promotional funds. Macy's used a re-engineering approach to cost-cutting[68]:

Macy's traditional garment-distribution practice involved several steps:

- **At the manufacturer.** Make the garment; add a hang tag; press the garment; place on a wire hanger and cover with polyethylene; put several garments in a box; ship the box to a Macy's facility.

- **At Macy's.** Remove the garment from the box; remove the polyethylene; throw out the wire hanger; put the garment on a floor-ready hanger; put the garment in new polyethylene; add a price tag; place the garment in a shipping container; ship to a Macy's store. This activity averaged 20 minutes per box.

Macy's gave garment producers floor-ready hangers and barcodes for each item. Macy's cut the average time to process new inventory from 4.5 days to 2.5 days and significantly reduced working capital.

LEGAL ISSUES IN DISTRIBUTION

Other than pricing, distribution issues are more subject to legal concerns than any other marketing-mix variable. The legality of various distribution practices varies by industry and legal jurisdiction. What is illegal in the U.S. may be normal business practice elsewhere. We provide an introduction to U.S. issues to provide a general sense for all readers.[69] Many **antitrust** lawsuits focus on distribution; many violations occur when firms with significant market power take action that reduces competition. Sometimes offended competitors file lawsuits; other times the federal government initiates legal action.[70] Critical U.S. issues are:

- **Exclusive territories.** Generally, the courts look unfavorably on arrangements that give distributors exclusive territories when this reduces competition.

- **Price discrimination.** The Robinson-Patman Act prohibits suppliers from setting different prices for different buyers, where this would reduce competition.

- **Resale price maintenance (RPM).** Suppliers set *retail* prices. RPM used to be illegal in the U.S., but a 2007 Supreme Court decision allowed its reestablishment in many situations.[71]

- **Selecting and terminating distributors.** Generally, suppliers are free to select and terminate distributors. IBM example, p. 464.

- **State and local laws.** Many local laws focus on distribution. Some states tightly regulate alcohol sales — especially type of outlet and opening hours. In some localities, *blue laws* prohibit certain types of store from opening on Sunday.

- **Tying agreements.** Strong suppliers force resellers to sell their entire product line. **Full-line forcing** is illegal if it reduces competition. Overstating the firm's revenues by overloading distributors — **channel stuffing** — can initiate legal problems.

KEY MESSAGES

- A broad view of distribution embraces *changes in state, physical location*, and *time*. Marketing generally takes a narrow view — distribution includes *changes in physical location* and *time of finished products*.

- Distribution channels continuously evolve; the firm can gain competitive advantage by innovating its distribution arrangements.

- In developing distribution strategy, the supplier firm must make crucial decisions in four areas:
  - **Distribution functions.** What exactly must be done in the distribution channel?
  - **Distribution channels: direct or indirect?** Should the firm deal directly with consumers and/or end-user customers? Or should the firm use intermediaries? If so, which?
  - **Distribution channel breadth.** How many intermediaries at each distribution level? For example, how many wholesalers and/or retailers? Should there be exclusivity?
  - **Criteria for selecting and evaluating intermediaries.** How should the firm decide whether a particular intermediary is appropriate for handling its products?

- Implementing strategy through distributors can be very challenging. The supplier must clarify each channel member responsibilities, understand potential distributor problems, and take steps to gain compliance.

- Typically some channel members have more power than others, but each has options to improve its position. Distributors/wholesalers, manufacturers/brand owners, retailers, and consumers or end-user customers may each become *channel captains*. Many firms are moving to partnership models where each member gains.

- Operating conflict is endemic in distribution channels but most firms work at reducing it. Strategic conflict is more serious and may lead to significant change in channel relationships.

- The Internet is driving many changes in distribution.

Marketing Question

What other messages did you glean from this chapter?

VIDEOS AND AUDIOS

The Future of Retailing   v1802 🎞   Mark Cohen   Columbia Business School

v1802

QUESTIONS FOR STUDY AND DISCUSSION

Can you answer the questions implied by this chapter's learning objectives? Check!

1. Your friend operates a highly successful *loose-meat* sandwich restaurant (regional specialty) in his hometown in Iowa. He wants to expand nationally. What are his options and the pros and cons? How would you advise him to proceed? Why? What pitfalls should he look out for?

2. Alasdair MacLean wanted a high-speed bicycle. He gathered information about several bicycles from a department store. He test-rode several models at a local bicycle store. Then he purchased his favorite model from the manufacturer's website. Several major department stores and a trade association of local bicycle stores have complained about this kind of customer behavior to BikeCo, a leading bicycle manufacturer. How would you advise BikeCo?

3. U.S.-based Detha (disguised names) produces wire harnesses to protect electric wires in automobiles. Detha sells to a distributor; the distributor sells to CarSup, a Tier 1 supplier to U.S. auto firms. Also, Detel, one of Detha's sister businesses, sells significant quantities of electric wire direct to CarSup. Last year, Detha's sales to the distributor dropped by 20 percent. Detha discovered that auto firms were demanding local supply in various geographic areas globally. CarSup was enforcing compliance; 40 percent of requirements were now sourced in Asia, hence the drop in Detha's business. How should Detha proceed?

4. Refer to the Jco, Playstore, and Disco example, p. 470. The retailer, Playstore, told Jco it would no longer purchase Jco products from the distributor — Disco. Playstore would *either* purchase direct from Jco *or* find a new supplier. Disco also distributes products for several Jco sister business units. Playstore owns roughly half its 500 outlets; the others are franchisees. Some franchisees are unhappy with Playstore's new management; one half have formed an independent federation. Jco expects the federation to assume greater control of shelf selection and purchasing. What should Jco do?

5. Select a product in which you are interested, or this book — *Managing Marketing in the 21st Century*. What are the key distribution decisions? What actions would you take?

IMPERATIVE 4

Design the Market Offer

PART D – GETTING PAID FOR CUSTOMER VALUE

CHAPTER 19

CRITICAL UNDERPINNINGS OF PRICING DECISIONS v1901

To access O-codes, go to **www.ocodes.com**

LEARNING OBJECTIVES

When you have completed this chapter, you will be able to:

- Discriminate between pricing strategy and pricing tactics.
- Recognize the key role of price in capturing customer value.
- Analyze the role of costs in pricing decisions.
- Incorporate competitor objectives and strategies in determining your prices.
- Relate strategic objectives to your pricing decisions.

OPENING CASE: SOUTHWEST AIRLINES

Southwest Airlines (SWA) is a major U.S. domestic airline. But in 1973, SWA was a puny upstart battling Braniff, a significant national/international carrier (based in Texas). That SWA survived a harrowing period was due in no small part to astute pricing decisions by CEO Lamar Muse.[1]

SWA was formed in the mid-1960s to fly among three major Texas cities — Dallas, Houston, and San Antonio. Flight distances ranged from 190 to 250 miles; flight times were about 45 minutes. Because SWA's proposed routes were within Texas, the Texas Railroad Commission, rather than the Civil Aeronautics Board (CAB), was its regulator. To start flying, SWA fought an extensive legal battle with Braniff and Texas International Airlines (TI) that went to the U.S. Supreme Court, but SWA prevailed.

In June 1971, SWA started flying from Dallas to Houston and San Antonio. Initial advertising positioned SWA as "The Love Machine." SWA had new Boeing 737s, attractive hostesses in hot pants, *and quick ticketing. Braniff and TI fares from Dallas were $27 to Houston and $28 to San Antonio. SWA entered at $20 on both routes. Braniff and TI immediately met SWA prices. In November 1971, SWA added San Antonio–Houston, also $20, and shifted some flights from Houston Intercontinental airport (HI) to the close-in Hobby airport (HH). In late 1972, SWA abandoned HI.*

During the next few months, SWA made several pricing moves. In November 1971, SWA experimented with $10 on weekend evening flights; in May 1972, SWA extended the $10 fare to all flights after 9 p.m. Load factors were higher than full-fare flights. In July, facing a deteriorating financial condition, SWA raised its basic fare to $26, increased leg room, and provided free drinks. In one week, TI matched SWA's fares; Braniff followed two days later and increased onboard service. Now flying into Hobby (as well as HI), Braniff started a $10 evening fare at 7:30 p.m.

SWA devised numerous publicity stunts — SWA held onboard parties, decorated aircraft cabins, and hung posters in lounges and on aircraft. By July 1972, SWA's market share on the important Dallas-to-Houston route was 40 percent. Braniff's share dropped from 75 to 48 percent and TI's from 25 to 11 percent. But Braniff's passenger load was roughly the same as before SWA's entry.

In October 1972, SWA replaced its $10 fares with $13 fares after 8 p.m. on weekdays and all weekend, supported with heavy advertising; traffic increased. SWA was now profitable on Dallas–Houston, but was unprofitable on Dallas–San Antonio where Braniff had four times as many flights. On January 22, 1973, SWA announced a "60-Day Half-Price Sale" from Dallas to San Antonio. Passenger loads increased threefold almost immediately and SWA reached an 85 percent load factor. On February 1, Braniff responded with a 60-day half-price "Get-Acquainted" sale at $13 for all Dallas-HH (but not HI) flights.

Lamar Muse reported his initial reaction to Braniff's price move: "Them bastards." He said Braniff knew that Dallas to Houston was SWA's one profitable route; he thought Braniff expected SWA to eliminate its $13 fares on Dallas-to-San Antonio. Muse also believed Braniff's move was a predatory action, designed to put SWA out of business. If Braniff were successful, Muse believed it would raise prices back to $26 or higher, close HH, and force passengers back to HI.

Muse said he believed the public should realize that SWA's highly reliable hourly service was worth $26, and that it should be disgusted at Braniff's action. SWA ran double-truck advertisements in Dallas and Houston newspapers with a picture of Muse, a statement — "Nobody's Goin' to Shoot Southwest Airlines Out of the Sky for a Lousy $13" — and all the reasons the public should not let that happen. SWA also printed 50,000 brochures with even stronger language. SWA gave these to all passengers, and off-duty hostesses handed them out at lunch hour in downtown Dallas and Houston.

CASE QUESTION

How do you assess Southwest Airlines' pricing actions? How do you assess Braniff's pricing actions?

SWA also offered a premium. It told passengers that the flight was worth $26; SWA would like them to pay $26. But if they felt they had to fly Braniff because of the $13 price, Southwest would also take them for $13. Those who paid the full fare received a gift — a fifth of Chivas Regal or Crown Royal, or a nice leather ice bucket. These items cost SWA around $7 to $8, but each had a retail value of around $13. Businessmen, in particular, put $26 on their expense reports and took a fifth of Chivas Regal home! On April 1, Braniff ended its "Get-Acquainted" sale; SWA also went back to $26. February 1973 was SWA's best month, and in March it made its first profit. SWA has not looked back.[2]

Chapter 19 is the first of two chapters in Part D of Imperative 4 — *Design the Market Offer*. Part D focuses on *Getting Paid for Customer Value*. Chapter 19 addresses *Critical Underpinnings of Pricing Decisions*.

Pricing is critical for earning profits and creating shareholder value.[3] Pricing is also pivotal for entering new markets, introducing new products, and changing firm objectives and/or strategy. Figure 19.1 shows that price decisions have a greater profit impact than other profit levers. Reasons include:

- Price affects profit margin since margin equals price *less* cost.
- Price affects unit volume via the demand curve.
- Because price affects volume, it also affects costs via economies of scale.
- Price often affects customer quality and value perceptions.

> Henry Ford understood the critical role of price. Ford's vision was "a car in every garage"; the challenge was to design, build, and distribute a $250 car at a profit. Ford's Model "T" assembly line kept costs down and brought automobiles to the masses. Ford became the leading U.S. car firm by understanding what customers valued and pricing accordingly.

FIGURE 19.1

HOW PRICING VERSUS OTHER FACTORS AFFECTS PROFITS[4]

1% improvement in:	Creates operating profit improvement of:
Price	11.0%
Variable cost	7.8%
Volume	3.3%
Fixed cost	2.3%

KEY IDEA

➤ Price has a larger impact on profits than any other lever. Price affects:

- Margins
- Unit volumes
- Costs
- Customer value perceptions (often)

Table 19.1 shows how price could affect International Paper (IP), a leading *Fortune* 500 firm. Let's make the assumption for this illustration that IP's unit sales remain constant while overall prices go up or down by 1 percent.[5] (Since unit sales are constant, none of the cost items change.)

- **1 percent price increase.** Profits *increase* 39 percent, to $896 million.
- **1 percent price decrease.** Profits *drop* 39 percent, to $392 million.

TABLE 19.1

HOW PRICING AFFECTS PROFITS AT INTERNATIONAL PAPER

	Year 2010	1% price increase	1% price decrease
Net Sales ($millions)	$25,179	$25,431	$24,927
Net Earnings ($millions)	$ 644	$ 896	$ 392

THE CHANGING VIEW

OLD WAY	NEW WAY
Customer ill-informed	Customer well-informed
Focus on costs	Focus on perceived customer value
Full-cost systems pervasive	Activity-based costing becoming prevalent
Inflation permitted easy price increases	Low inflation/foreign competition hold prices down
Perceived customer value ignored	Perceived customer value measured and tracked
Prestige sometimes ahead of value perceptions	Value consciousness pervasive among customers

Chapter 19 focuses on the fundamental underpinnings for developing price strategy. In Chapter 20, you learn how to set actual prices.

Pricing strategy is the firm's overall approach to setting price. Figure 19.2 shows four critical underpinnings of pricing decisions: **perceived customer value, costs, competition**, and **strategic objectives**. Too much emphasis on a single element leads to suboptimal pricing, like the destructive, downward pricing spiral that can follow from an excessive focus on competitors. Skilled pricing executives assess all factors before developing pricing strategy.[6]

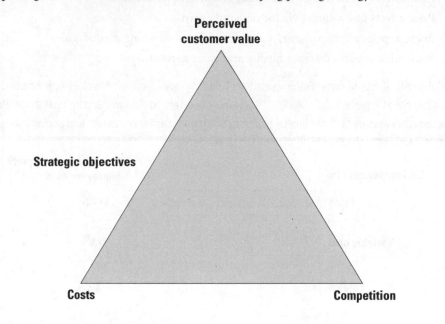

FIGURE 19.2

CRITICAL
CONSIDERATIONS
IN SETTING
PRICING STRATEGY

 **KEY IDEA**

➤ In setting prices, the firm should consider:

- Perceived customer value
- Costs
- Competition
- Strategic objectives

Excessive focus on a single element leads to suboptimal pricing decisions.

PERCEIVED CUSTOMER VALUE

When increased competition brings more customer options, they invariably seek lower prices. As customers turn elsewhere, the firm may believe it has a pricing problem. More likely, it has a **perceived value** problem — the firm delivers insufficient value, or has not established a good price/value relationship. We focus on three value-related issues — creating, measuring, and capturing value; then we turn to a closely associated issue — price sensitivity.

CREATING VALUE

Chapter 9 showed that the value proposition is central to market strategy. The firm creates value in its offer primarily through non-price elements in the marketing mix — Chapters 12–18:

- **Product.** Typically delivers the major portion of the value proposition.

KEY IDEA

➤ What seems to be a pricing problem may be a perceived value problem.

KEY IDEA

➤ Critical topics in per-
ceived customer value
are:

• Creating value
• Measuring value
• Capturing value

• **Service.** Adds additional value to the core product.

• **Promotion.** Conveys information about value, but sometimes provides value in its own right — like reassuring customers they made a good purchase.

• **Distribution.** Provides value through time and place convenience.

Price may also create value by contributing to brand image. Products like Bentley, Ferrari, and Rolls-Royce automobiles; Rolex; and Apple's iPod are all perceived as quality brands. Factors outside the firm's control also affect customer value perceptions. On a hot day, you may value a can of Coke at $3 if that is your only option, but if you could also obtain Pepsi and 7-Up, Coke's value would be less.

MEASURING VALUE

Measuring the value customers perceive in firm and competitor offers is critical. If you don't know customer value perceptions, you'll never make good pricing decisions. Some approaches are:

DIRECT VALUE ASSESSMENT. The firm simply asks customers what they would pay for various products. Downward response bias is a concern, but carefully phrased questions can provide helpful data. In launching the original Ford Mustang, Lee Iacocca asked customers to estimate its price. Estimates were much higher than Ford's planned price, so Iacocca knew it would be a winner. The Mustang was the U.S.' best-selling new car ever.

DOLLARMETRIC METHOD. This method compares each option with the others. For each pair of options, customers say which they prefer and how much extra they would pay. Summing positive and negative differences reveals the relative value of the options. Table 19.2 shows the responses for four products: A, B, C, and D.

Marketing Question

The price for *Managing Marketing in the 21st Century* is 80 percent less than the price of competitor books. How should Wessex Press address a potential concern with price/quality perceptions?

TABLE 19.2

ILLUSTRATIVE DATA FROM THE DOLLARMETRIC METHOD

Options Compared	Preferred Option	Extra Price for Preferred Option
A and B	B	$10
A and C	C	$13
A and D	A	$5
B and C	C	$3
B and D	B	$8
C and D	C	$12

We calculate the customer's relative value for these options as follows:

• The *extra price* is positive for the preferred option, negative for the non-preferred option.

• Each option has three comparisons. Sum these *extra prices* for each option.

• Divide the sums of *extra prices* by three to calculate the average *extra price*.

The average extra prices customers are prepared to pay for the four options are:

$$A = -10 - 13 + 5 = -18/3 = \mathbf{-6} \qquad B = 10 - 3 + 8 = 15/3 = \mathbf{+5}$$

$$C = +13 + 3 + 12 = 28/3 = \mathbf{+9.3} \qquad D = -5 - 8 - 12 = -25/3 = \mathbf{-8.3}$$

• Using the least valued option as a base, find the difference between the base and the average *extra price* for each option. This figure is what the customer would pay over the base.

D is the least valued option so the base is –8.3. The *extra prices* for the other options are:

$$A = (-6) - (-8.3) = \mathbf{\$2.3} \qquad B = 5 - (-8.3) = \mathbf{\$13.3} \qquad C = 9.3 - (-8.3) = \mathbf{\$17.6}$$

PERCEIVED VALUE ANALYSIS. Table 19.3 identifies five steps for measuring an offer's perceived value. Data are best secured directly from customers, but sometimes experienced managers provide *best-guess* data that marketing research can validate.

Step	Description
1. Identify customer-required benefits and values	Identify the key benefits and values customers require — typically 5 to 8 — but exclude price.
2. Weight relative value of benefits and values to customers	Weight each benefit or value by allocating 100 points based on its importance to customers. Weights sum to 100.
3. Rate each offer from the various suppliers	Rate each offer based on how well customers believe it delivers the required benefit or value (1 = poor; 10 = excellent).
4. Develop benefit/value scores	For each offer, form individual benefit/value scores by multiplying the results of step 2 and step 3 for each benefit or value. Benefit/Value score = Weighting x Rating.
5. Develop the perceived value scores	For each offer, sum the individual benefit/value scores.

TABLE 19.3

MEASURING THE PERCEIVED VALUE OF AN OFFER

The perceived value scores, Step 5 in Table 19.3, are a measure of each supplier's value, as perceived by customers. Note that price does *not* enter into the analysis, but is important for interpretation. Table 19.4 shows a numerical illustration: A, B, and C represent three different suppliers of easy chairs. (We note prices in the table.) The results and interpretation are:

- **Perceived value.** Supplier B — 820 offers the greatest perceived value, followed by A — 665, and C — 580.

- **Price.** Supplier A has the highest price — $500, followed by B — $450, and C — $300.

Supplier C has the lowest perceived value and the lowest price, but A and B are misordered. Supplier B has the greatest perceived value — 820 versus 665 for supplier A. But supplier A's price is higher — $500 versus $450. Since supplier B provides greater value for a lower price, it should be gaining market share.

Marketing Question

The prices for printed and pdf versions of *Managing Marketing in the 21st Century* (600 pages) and *Capon's Marketing Framework* (300 pages) are identical. Do you agree with this pricing decision? Why or why not?

Benefits Required	Relative Importance Weighting	Supplier A Price = $500		Supplier B Price = $450		Supplier C Price = $300	
		Rating (1–10)	Total	Rating (1–10)	Total	Rating (1–10)	Total
Chair design	20	5	100	7	140	6	120
Comfort	30	6	180	8	240	4	120
Fabric quality	15	10	150	9	135	8	120
Fabric design	15	5	75	7	105	4	60
Ease of purchase	20	8	160	10	200	8	160
Grand Total	**100**		**665**		**820**		**580**

TABLE 19.4

ILLUSTRATION OF PERCEIVED VALUE ANALYSIS FOR SUPPLIERS OF EASY CHAIRS

The **customer value map** is a useful approach for displaying value/price (V/P) positions — Figure 19.3.[7] These positions relate directly to Table 19.4 and are good predictors of likely market share changes in most product markets. Exceptions are markets where higher prices lead to greater sales, like prestige products or luxury goods. Other exceptions are inefficient markets, like new product forms, and complex products like insurance.

FIGURE 19.3

CUSTOMER VALUE MAP

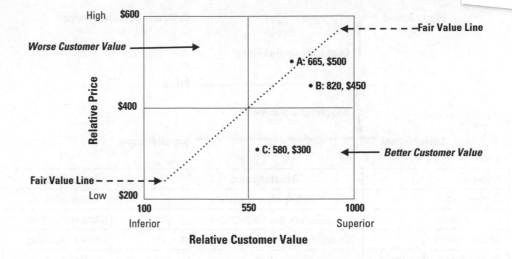

ECONOMIC ANALYSIS — ECONOMIC VALUE FOR THE CUSTOMER (EVC). Many B2B firms use EVC — the maximum price customers will pay — to calculate the economic value of new products. EVC analysis depends critically on competitive products in the customer's choice set.[8] EVC helps clarify firm options: Should the firm add more value for a higher price or provide less value for a lower price? Chapter 4, pp. 97–98 shows an EVC calculation.

Value/Price Options

Higher value for higher price. Alcoa's new press makes very wide metal and alloy sheets. For customers building airplane wings, wide sheets mean less time and fewer materials (rivets). Rivets add weight, so fewer rivets mean lower fuel costs. Fewer rivets also mean lower inspection and maintenance costs. Alcoa has lead market share for aircraft wings and enjoys premium prices.[9]

Lower value for lower price. ChemX (disguised name) supplied chemicals for extracting oil from wells; it also studied customer operations and advised on usage quantities. A small customer did not follow ChemX's advice; it simply pumped a few gallons of chemicals into each well when ChemX's truck came by. By mutual agreement, the customer discontinued the monitoring service. ChemX reduced prices to that customer by 7 percent, but profitability increased from minus 6 percent to plus 32 percent because it no longer provided monitoring![10]

PRICE EXPERIMENT. The firm offers the test product at different prices in different market areas, like geographic locations. Sales levels at different prices reflect customer value. The Internet offers many possibilities for systematically changing price when customers visit the firm's website. The experimental approach has the advantage of securing real market data, but higher-paying customers may be upset if they discover the experiment! Several years ago, Amazon received negative publicity for a price experiment and immediately stopped the practice.[11,12]

CAPTURING VALUE

The firm incurs many costs to develop an offer; it creates value if these costs are less than the value customers perceive. Figure 19.4 shows how price apportions the created value: The firm retains some value; customers receive some value. High prices imply that the firm retains most value; low prices imply that the firm transfers most value to customers. A critical firm decision is the degree to which it retains/transfers value. Table 19.5 suggests conditions that favor retaining and transferring value.

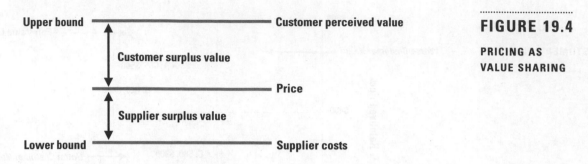

Criteria	Transfer Value	Retain Value
Competitors	Strong and aggressive	Weak or lax
Firm objectives	Growth and market share	Profit and cash flow
Market conditions	Growth market — firm well positioned	Mature or declining
Potential competitive entry	Likely	Unlikely
Response to price changes	Customers highly responsive	Customers non-responsive

TABLE 19.5

CONDITIONS
FOR THE FIRM
TO RETAIN AND
TRANSFER VALUE

Most firms develop new products, then set prices based on costs or some value estimate using a method like we just discussed. By contrast, Avon starts with the value it wants a new product to deliver to customers, then sets a target price. Avon translates this price into cost parameters that enable it to meet profit targets. Engineering and manufacturing must then design a product/production process that delivers desired customer value within the cost parameters.[13] P&G used this approach to develop Naturella (feminine hygiene pads) for the Mexican market[14]; Zara (Spain-based international clothing manufacturer/retailer) operates similarly.

CUSTOMER PRICE SENSITIVITY

Reducing price a little (increasing customer value a little) may lead to a major increase in customer purchase volume. Other times, customers only buy more if the price reduction is large (major increase in value). (Equivalent effects hold for price increases.) Sometimes customers are **price sensitive**; other times they are **price insensitive**. Classical microeconomics focuses on price sensitivity at the market level; we also discuss individual price sensitivity.

MARKET-LEVEL PRICE SENSITIVITY. Figure 19.5 shows elastic and inelastic **demand curves:**

- **Price elasticity.** When price goes down a little, volume increases significantly; when price goes up a little, volume decreases significantly. Includes products like many grocery items.
- **Price inelasticity.** Volume does not change much, even with significant price changes.[15] Includes products like critical raw materials, electricity, and heart pacemakers.

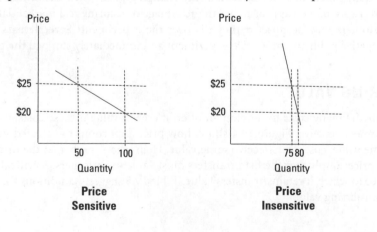

KEY IDEA

➤ Price apportions value — some to the firm, some to customers.

Marketing Question

How should firm marketing efforts differ between price-elastic versus price-inelastic markets?

KEY IDEA

➤ Price elasticity of demand (PED) helps estimate market demand when price changes.

FIGURE 19.5

MARKET DEMAND
CURVES

Marketing Question

Are airline tickets, theater tickets, health club memberships, milk, and HIV medication price elastic or price inelastic? How did you decide?

We quantify price sensitivity via the price elasticity of demand.

Price elasticity of demand (PED) = Percentage change in demand/percentage change in price.

Because volume typically increases when price decreases, PED has a negative sign. Conventionally, when PED's absolute value (ignoring the minus sign) is less than one, the market is price inelastic; when PED is greater than one, the market is price elastic.

Table 19.6 shows illustrative PED calculations for three products — A, B, and C; in each case, current demand = 1,000 units; current price = $100. The markets for B and C are inelastic; the market for A is elastic. Table 19.7 shows how to estimate the effect of price changes on sales volume for products X, Y, and Z, knowing current sales and price elasticity.

TABLE 19.6

CALCULATING
PRICE ELASTICITY

New Price ($)	Absolute Price Change ($)	Percent Price Change (%)	Sales Volume (units)	Absolute Volume Change (units)	Percent Volume Change (%)	Price Elasticity Calculation	**Price Elasticity (PED)**
A $ 99	−$1	−1%	1030	+30	+3%	+3%/−1%	**−3.0**
B $ 98	−$2	−2%	1010	+10	+1%	+1%/−2%	**−0.5**
C $105	+$5	+5%	990	−10	−1%	−1%/+5%	**−0.2**

TABLE 19.7

CALCULATING
SALES VOLUME
FROM PRICE
ELASTICITY

Original Price ($)	Original Sales Volume (units)	New Price ($)	Percent Price Change (%)	Price Elasticity	Sales Volume Calculation	Percent Sales Volume Change (%)	Sales Volume Change (units)	**New Sales Volume (units)**
X $50	300	$55	+10%	− 4.0	+10% x − 4.0 =	− 40%	−120	**180**
Y $80	200	$75	−6.3%	− 0.3	−6.3% x − 0.3 =	+ 1.9%	+ 3.8	**204**
Z $90	150	$95	+5.6%	− 2.0	+5.6% x − 2.0 =	−11.2%	−16.8	**133**

A final related item: Pundits often advise marketers to set prices at what *the market will bear*. This advice is *useless.* All markets *bear* many prices; each price produces a different volume. The firm should decide what volume it wants to sell, then set the appropriate price. Understanding customer value and price sensitivity helps the firm do just that.

INDIVIDUAL CUSTOMER PRICE SENSITIVITY. Markets are rarely homogeneous. Some customers place high value on an offer; other customers value the offer less. Some consumers are price sensitive because disposable income is low and/or they face financial demands. Some business customers are price sensitive because competitors are cutting prices, and profits are under pressure. Customers with full information on alternatives, benefits, values, and prices tend to be more price sensitive than those with less information. Other factors affecting willingness to pay include brand loyalty, frequency of use, past experience, product availability, and seasonality. Timing may also be important: Customers are generally less price sensitive for unplanned, immediately required services than for planned purchases — hence, higher same-day and rush-order prices. Table 19.8 provides a fairly comprehensive list of factors affecting price sensitivity.

KEY IDEA

➤ Pricing at *what the market will bear* is not useful advice; the market *will bear* many prices.

TABLE 19.8

FACTORS AFFECTING
INDIVIDUAL CUSTOMER
PRICE SENSITIVITY

Factors	Related Questions
Competitive comparison	Can customers easily and fairly compare alternative offers? Without purchasing? Are experts required? Do customers know how to use firm and competitor products? Are prices directly comparable, or must customers make calculations to understand differences?
Education	Do firms educate customers to focus on price by fierce price competition?
End benefit	What end benefit/value does the offer deliver? How price sensitive are end-user customers? What percentage of the end benefit's price does the firm's offer represent? Can the firm reposition its offer to deliver an end benefit to price-insensitive customers?

CONTINUES ON NEXT PAGE

Factors	Related Questions
Expenditures	How significant are absolute purchase expenditures? What percentage of annual spending, income, or wealth does the purchase represent?
Fairness	How does the current price compare to customer experience with similar products? What do they expect to pay? Is the price justified?
Inventory	Do buyers hold inventory? Do they expect current prices to be temporary?
Non-monetary costs	What effort, time, and/or risk must customers expend to make a purchase?
Perceived substitutes	What competitive offers and prices do customers consider? Can the firm influence customer price expectations via positioning decisions?
Price/quality	Are price and quality related for competitor products?
Shared cost	Do customers pay the full cost? If not, what portion do they pay?
Switching costs	What costs/investments would customers incur if they switched suppliers? Are they locked into current suppliers? For how long? Can the firm encourage switching?
Terms	Are financing options available and clearly communicated?
Unique value	How do customers weigh elements of the firm's offer that influence their decisions? Is the firms' offer differentiated from competitors? Can the firm persuade customers some offer elements are more important than others?

TABLE 19.8

(CONTINUED)

> **Marketing Question**
>
> As the newly appointed marketing director for a chain of movie houses, you find that prices are identical for all seats for all movies. How might you improve profits by adopting a different pricing approach?

Mike Smith is a salesman for component supplier MachinCo; Mike earns a low salary but can make a high bonus based on quarterly sales versus quota. In mid-March, Mike realizes he will not make quota for Q1 (quarter 1), but he knows that Bill typically places a major order early in each quarter. Mike calls Bill:

Mike: "Bill, how would you like to place your regular order next week, instead of mid-April?" Bill demurs — he is concerned about inventory and payment timing. Mike calls again: "Bill, I've got you a great deal. If you place your order next week, I can get you $18 per unit instead of the regular $20 and you can defer payment by a couple of weeks." Bill places the order. In mid-June, and mid-September, Mike and Bill play out the same scenario. In early December, Bill calls Mike.

Bill: "I've been thinking about my quarterly order: I'm ready to place an order for mid-December delivery. I'll pay $16 per unit!"

> **Marketing Question**
>
> Mike caused Bill to become sensitive to price. What industries or firms *educate* customers to be sensitive to price?

Price-sensitive customers feel pain when prices are high; Marketing Enrichment me1901 shows four scenarios formed from customer value assessments in the context of price *pain*.

> **MARKETING ENRICHMENT**
>
> Customer Value and Price Pain me1901

me1901

COSTS

Costs are important for setting prices.[16] After all, costs represent one-half of the profit equation: **Profit = sales revenues – costs.** In practice, many firms use costs for setting prices, but often do so inappropriately. Because you must understand these issues, we start with them. Then we show how the firm *should* use costs in pricing decisions.

THE INAPPROPRIATE ROLE FOR COSTS: COST-PLUS PRICING

Cost-plus pricing is a pricing methodology used by most firms, harkening back to our earlier discussion of an *internal* orientation — Chapter 1. Despite its popularity, it is the wrong way to set prices.[17] Cost-plus pricing proceeds simply by identifying product costs, then adding a pre-determined profit margin (mark-up). Table 19.9 shows how this works:

TABLE 19.9

ILLUSTRATION OF COST-PLUS PRICING FOR CAPITAL EQUIPMENT ITEM

Variable costs	$400,000
Total fixed costs	$300,000
Total costs	$700,000
Standard mark-up: 15% of costs	$105,000
Price	**$805,000**

KEY IDEA

➤ The firm creates value for customers primarily via non-price elements in its offer — the marketing mix.

➤ Many factors affect the value customers perceive in the firm's offer.

KEY IDEA

➤ In cost-plus pricing, the firm identifies its costs and adds a profit margin.

➤ Cost-plus pricing does not consider customer value.

KEY IDEA

➤ Disadvantages of cost-plus pricing include:

• Profit limitations
• Inappropriate treatment of fixed costs
• Arbitrary overhead calculations
• Mismatch with market realities

➤ Firms often determine fixed costs per unit arbitrarily by assuming some level of sales or production.

Advantages of cost-plus pricing are:

• **Profitability.** All sales seem profitable as price must, by definition, be above cost.

• **Simplicity.** If the firm knows its costs, pricing is simple. Anyone can do the math.[18]

• **Defensibility.** Legally acceptable and often required for government and other cost-plus contracts.

Regardless, cost-plus pricing has four main disadvantages:

PROFIT LIMITATIONS. Customer value has no role in price-setting:

• **Prices are too low.** Customers value the offer at more than the cost-plus price. Table 19.9: Suppose customers value the product at $900,000. By setting price at $805,000, the firm forgoes $95,000 profit on each item sold: $900,000 less $805,000 = $95,000.

• **Prices are too high.** Customers value the offer at less than the cost-plus price. Table 19.9: Suppose customers value the product at $750,000; they will not purchase at $805,000. The firm forgoes $50,000 profit on each item it could have sold at $750,000: $750,000 − $700,000 = $50,000.

In both cases, the firm sets prices incorrectly because it has not assessed customer value. Cost-plus pricing leads to over-pricing in price-sensitive markets and under-pricing in price-insensitive markets. Cost-plus pricing also leaves the firm vulnerable to competitors. By estimating firm costs, competitors can predict firm prices.

INAPPROPRIATE TREATMENT OF FIXED COSTS. Firms frequently classify costs as fixed and variable — Table 19.9[19]:

• **Variable costs.** Vary directly with the volume of sales and production. Variable costs increase as volume increases, and decrease as volume decreases. What costs are variable depends on the specific product and technology. For manufactured products, variable costs usually include raw materials, utilities to power production machines, direct labor, and sales commissions.

• **Fixed costs.** Do not vary with the volume of sales or production, over a reasonable range. Fixed costs include overhead and allocated items like depreciation, rent, salaries, and SG&A (selling, general, and administrative).

As noted, the firm's cost-plus price equals costs plus a predetermined margin. Using the fixed and variable cost distinction:

Cost per unit = *variable* cost per unit plus *fixed* cost per unit

Variable cost per unit is relatively straightforward, but calculating fixed cost per unit is illogical:

1. Fixed cost per unit equals fixed costs divided by number of units sold.

2. But the number of units varies with the price.

3. Hence, to set the price, price is an input to the calculation; this makes no sense!

In practice, many firms arbitrarily assume some sales level to calculate fixed costs per unit.

ARBITRARY OVERHEAD ALLOCATIONS. Suppose a firm has two business units, A and B; A is comfortably profitable but B is not. Corporate may reduce B's overhead allocation and increase A's. B's fixed costs are reduced, but A's are increased. Such financial machinations are typical of firms striving to even out profits across products. But they can be highly demotivating to A's managers! (Also, Marketing Enrichment `me01`, p. 10.)

> Industrial parts maker Parker Hannifin (PH) traditionally set prices based on cost (manufacturing and delivery) plus a target markup (35 percent). Following an extensive study, PH classified products based on degree of competition: A — at least one large competitor helps shape prices; through B and C to D — *specials* and *classics* that only PH produced. PH raised many prices, some as much as 60 percent, but reduced others. In three years, net income rose from $130 million to $673 million; return on invested capital increased from 14 to 21 percent; and PH's share price doubled.

MISMATCH WITH MARKET REALITIES. When demand falls, logic suggests the firm should lower prices. Pure cost-plus pricing does not allow such action. As sales fall, and the firm spreads fixed costs over lower volumes, fixed costs per unit increase — and so must price! When demand surges, logic suggests the firm should raise prices. But it spreads fixed costs over larger volumes, and fixed costs per unit decrease. And so must price! Variable mark-ups based on demand can partially solve this problem.

APPROPRIATE ROLES FOR COSTS

Cost-plus pricing is the lazy way to set prices. But we should not underestimate the role costs play in price-setting. Costs are important in three critical situations:

BIRTH CONTROL. Costs are particularly important for new product introduction. Typically, a new product must meet or exceed financial criteria like the firm's hurdle rate to receive go-ahead approval.[20] The firm bases cash flow estimates on target prices, volumes, and costs. The relevant costs are **fully loaded costs**, meaning they include all incremental costs related to the new product, *including* incremental overhead.

DEATH CONTROL. Costs are also important when the firm is considering dropping a product. The relevant cost is the **marginal cost** — the cost to make and sell one additional unit. Marginal cost includes all variable costs plus some incremental fixed costs,[21] but *excludes* all allocated overhead. Suppose product Z's costs are:

Marginal cost (to produce and sell each unit) = $4 per unit

Overhead allocation   = $2 per unit

Fully loaded cost   = $6 per unit

Let's examine two situations:

- **Situation A.** Price = $7. Product Z makes a bottom-line *profit* of $1 (7 − 6 = 1).
- **Situation B.** Price = $5, Product Z makes a bottom-line *loss* of $1 (5 − 6 = −1). Many would consider dropping the product; after all a *loss* is a loss. But if we consider only the marginal cost, product Z makes a $1 profit contribution (5 − 4 = 1). This *contribution* helps cover overhead costs like rent, top manager salaries, and the corporate jet. The firm incurs these costs anyway; if the firm dropped product Z, other products would have to carry this burden.

The marginal cost is the **floor price**; only in rare circumstances should the firm set prices below the floor price.[22] Returning to the illustration; at prices less than $4, the firm loses money on every unit it makes and sells — it should drop the product. At prices greater than $6, the firm earns bottom-line profit — it should retain the product. At prices between $4 and $6, the product makes a positive contribution to covering fixed costs; if this price range is sustainable, generally the firm should continue with the product, at least in the short run.

> *Marketing Question*
>
> What would be the implications for Apple and Verizon if they based prices for the iPod and cell phone service, respectively, on cost?

> **KEY IDEA**
>
> ➤ Costs have three important price-setting roles:
>
> • Birth control
> • Death control
> • Profit planning

PROFIT PLANNING. Birth control and death control are special cases; the major role for costs is profit planning. Table 19.10 shows a simple illustration. The firm explores various possible prices and estimates unit volumes and unit costs. The firm uses these data to calculate sales revenues and profits. In the illustration, the optimal price is $12.

TABLE 19.10

ROLE OF COSTS IN PROFIT PLANNING

MARKETING ENRICHMENT

The Relationship between Customer Value and Firm Costs me1902

me1902

Price a	Estimated Unit Sales Volume b	Sales Revenues c = a × b	Estimated Costs d	Profits e = c − d
$ 8	650	$5,200	$4,800	$400
$10	500	$5,000	$4,500	$500
$12	400	$4,800	$4,100	$700
$14	300	$4,200	$3,700	$500

(Marketing Enrichment me1902 for the relationship between customer value and firm costs.)

COMPETITION

The firm should always consider competitor prices. Basing the firm's price on competitor prices is legal and ensures price parity, but focusing too heavily on competitor pricing strategies has distinct disadvantages:

- *Price parity* with competitors devalues features, benefits, and values and tends to *commoditize* products. Customers then focus buying decisions on price.

- An *excessive price focus* may lead to losses for everyone, both the firm and competitors.

Generally, the firm should not focus on beating the competitor's *price*. Rather, the firm should beat the competitor's *offer* — product, service, and other marketing-mix elements. The firm should attempt to make offers with greater value per unit price than competitors. *Offer* superiority is crucial, not *price* superiority. Of course, price plays a critical balancing role. Two issues are crucial:

- How will competitors respond to firm price changes?

- How should the firm respond to competitor price reductions?

KEY IDEA

➤ The firm should seek *offer* superiority, not *price* superiority.

HOW WILL COMPETITORS RESPOND TO FIRM PRICE CHANGES?

When making price changes, the firm should always consider likely competitor responses. Although pricing tactics can be quite complicated, basically competitors have three pricing options — *raise, hold,* or *lower.* Whether or not the firm's price moves are successful depends on competitors' response choices. Table 19.11 summarizes common scenarios, firm actions, and likely competitor responses. We revisit some questions the firm should be able to answer:

- Has the competitor been raising or lowering prices?

- How comparable are the various competitive offers in terms of perceived customer value?

- How many firms are competing? What are their market shares?

- What are the competitor's costs and profits?

- How is the competitor's product positioned relative to the firm's?

Current Situation	Firm Action	Likely Competitor Response
Few competitors and marginal profits Firm is market share leader Market demand inelastic	Raise prices	Accept the firm's price leadership; also raise prices
All competitors make similar offers Market demand moderately elastic No competitor dominant	Lower prices	Follow suit
Competitors profitable Market demand moderately elastic Marketing offers highly differentiated	Raise prices	Hold prices constant (High-quality restaurants do not typically raise prices to follow other restaurants.)

TABLE 19.11

LIKELY COMPETITIVE RESPONSES TO FIRM ACTIONS UNDER VARIOUS SCENARIOS

KEY IDEA

➤ In high fixed cost/ low variable cost oligopolies, competitors often cut prices to gain extra volume. Prices can spiral downward and profits vanish.

Assessing likely competitor response is always important, but is vital in oligopolies with few major competitors, high fixed costs, and low variable costs (airlines and many highly capital-intensive industries). When several competitors have poor profits, sometimes one firm cuts price to gain volume and better cover fixed costs. Competitors follow and prices spiral downward. Sometimes firms launch *trial balloons*, strategic pre-announced price intentions to gauge likely competitor response. Warnings and other signals (Chapter 5) may pre-empt competitors, but can raise antitrust issues. Successful and unsuccessful price leadership examples are:

Oligopoly Pricing

Successful price leadership. Coca-Cola raised concentrate price by 7 percent, twice the usual rate. Two weeks later, PepsiCo announced a similar increase.

British Aluminum Company (BACO) competed fiercely against Alcoa and Alcan in the low-growth, barely profitable British aluminum oligopoly. BACO divided the market into three: BACO's long-term contract customers — *ours*; competitors' long-term contract customers — *theirs*; and switchers — *up-for-grabs*. BACO resolved not to lose any *our* business on price. If it did lose, BACO *punished* the competitor by pricing low at one of *theirs*. BACO effectively executed this *tit-for-tat* strategy; Alcoa and Alcan *got the message*.[23]

Unsuccessful price leadership. American Airlines (AA) attempted to change the pricing structure for domestic U.S. airlines. American West, Continental, Delta, Northwest, United, and USAir quickly followed AA's lead. But TWA undercut AA's prices by 10 to 20 percent, and the attempt failed.[24]

HOW SHOULD THE FIRM RESPOND TO COMPETITOR PRICE REDUCTIONS?

The firm's response depends on its market position. Generally, strong firms should match price cuts only after exhausting other options. But weak firms with minimal sustainable differential advantage may have to respond right away. Only the low-cost producer wins when price-cutting is rampant; how that firm uses its cost advantage determines other competitors' fates.

Firms with dominant market shares often face severe price competition from small competitors and/or new entrants. These competitors may believe the leader:

- Has not carefully managed costs, and assumes its own costs are lower.
- Does not know individual product costs because of difficulties allocating overhead.
- Will not retaliate directly because it would sacrifice profits on its much larger volume.

Unless demand is *price elastic*, the firm should minimize direct price-cutting responses.[25] The nature of competitive price reductions governs the firm's price and non-price options:

KEY IDEA

➤ Rampant price-cutting is disastrous for all but the low-cost producer.

PRICE OPTIONS. Price retaliation can range among indirect and direct actions:

- **Indirect price retaliation.** The firm signals disapproval by cutting prices in the competitor's strong markets. Suppose firm A is a strong supplier in segment 1, and firm B is a strong supplier in segment 2. Firm A enters segment 2 with low prices that significantly undercut firm B. In response, firm B visits firm A's loyal customers in segment 1, presents its offer, and the following conversation ensues:

    Firm B: "Thanks for listening to our offer, but we know you can't buy from us."
    Firm A's loyal customer: "Why not?"
    Firm B: "Firm A just visited some of our customers and we can't meet its low prices."
    Firm A's loyal customer: "We'll have to have a conversation with firm A!"

  This scenario was played out by InfoX (disguised name); InfoX provided premium data services to select private universities. InfoY(disguised name) made similar offerings to public universities. In an aggressive move, InfoY offered low prices to InfoX's customers (private universities). InfoX responded like firm B (above); InfoY withdrew its offers.[26] Similarly, America West's (AW) hub is in Phoenix; AW introduced new low-fare flights from Houston. Continental (dominant Houston airline) cut prices on flights from Phoenix. AW withdrew its low fares in Houston; Continental withdrew its low fares in Phoenix.[27]

- **Selective price competition.** If the competitor attacks part of the firm's product line with low prices, the firm has two sorts of options:

    - **Selective price cuts.** The firm may cut prices directly against the attack and/or offer lower prices in selected channels like the Internet. Siebel Systems sells discounted software; hotels and airlines distribute low-price products via Priceline.com and other consolidators.

    - **Introduce a *fighting* brand.** The firm cuts prices against the attack but with a specially designed *fighting* brand. To compete with store brands, P&G offers low-price brands to supermarkets meeting strict volume-based criteria — like *Tide Basic* in 100 southern U.S. stores where market share was poor. Delta and United introduced Song and Ted, respectively (now abandoned) to compete with low-priced carriers like Southwest Airlines and jetBlue.

- **Cut prices across the board.** Ultimately the firm may have to cut prices broadly.[28] But this approach will not succeed unless the firm also cuts costs, especially variable costs. Typically, the highest variable cost producer *blinks first* when prices fall. Some firms, notably U.S. airlines, use bankruptcy filings to reduce costs.

NON-PRICE OPTIONS. The firm uses its creative abilities to compete in areas other than price. Alternatives for defending its position across the board include:

- **Change the basis of competition.** Rather than compete product versus product, the firm changes the type of competition. Specifically, it may bundle products to remove a competitor's price advantage, like McDonald's successful *Value Meals*.

- **Clarify and reinforce the price/value relationship.** Goodyear prices tires based on expected miles driven; Orica prices explosives based on degree of rock fragmentation.[29] The firm may be able to sensitize customers to the value it offers by creating price/value expectations — higher/ lower prices imply higher/lower value. By stressing that packages "absolutely positively" get there overnight, FedEx implies superiority to other carriers.

- **Invest in fixed-cost marketing expenditures.** The firm reinforces its position and builds switching costs by making marketing expenditures like advertising, better quality and delivery, customer service, and loyalty programs. The firm spreads these fixed costs over large volume. During Asian economic crises, some luxury Malaysian hotels compete on price. By contrast, Ritz-Carlton increases service. Each hotel's general manager greets arriving guests with music, drinks, and personalized items; occupancy rates improved. Relatedly, major airlines use loyalty programs to defend against low-priced airlines.

Marketing Question

Select a product and then search the Internet for different prices. Do the prices vary? Why? If you were to purchase, which supplier would you use? Why?

Marketing Question

Identify several examples of non-price actions that firms took when competitors cut prices. Were these actions successful? Why or why not? What was the rationale for the firms' actions?

- **Make pricing opaque.** Price transparency increases customers' bargaining power, so the firm may make pricing opaque. The firm shifts from traditional schemes, like pricing by the yard to pricing by the meter; or uses discounts/rebates without changing list prices.[30]
- **Signal the firm's position.** Communicate the firm's capabilities and/or intentions — Chapter 5. Sara Lee (SL) is low-cost supplier for several products but it sets prices relatively high. SL lets competitors know its low-cost position to deter price cutting.

If none of these actions work and the firm is in severe trouble, it may seek help. U.S. airlines regularly appeal to unions for wage reductions and simplified work rules. Firms facing foreign competition lobby government for tariff protection. Britain's sugar giant Tate & Lyle receives large government subsidies for export competition; U.S. steel firms frequently seek protection.

If it cannot withstand competitive attack, the firm may withdraw, partly or totally:

- **Partial withdrawal.** The crucial decision is which market segment(s) to cede to competitors and which to retain. The firm must develop a razor-sharp focus on retained segments and take appropriate actions — redesign products, add services, and/or offer long-term contracts.
- **Total withdrawal.** When facing a competitor with significant cost advantage pursuing a low-price strategy, discretion may be the better part of valor. The firm withdraws and plays a different game. Faced with intense Taiwanese price competition, Intel withdrew from memory chips but successfully refocused on microprocessors.

STRATEGIC OBJECTIVES

Choosing strategic objectives is a major component of developing market strategy. The three major options are increase volume and/or market share, maximize profits, and maximize cash flow. Generally, each strategic objective relates to a particular pricing strategy:

MAXIMIZE GROWTH IN VOLUME AND/OR MARKET SHARE. The firm must offer high customer value — a value/price (V/P) ratio superior to competitors. Appropriate conditions are:

- Deep pockets to absorb initially low profit margins
- Desire to deter competitors
- Good ability to cut costs in the future
- Price-elastic market
- Sufficient capacity to fulfill increased demand

Ryanair's price leadership in European air travel and P&G's aggressive price strategy in disposable diapers follow this **penetration-pricing** approach.

MAXIMIZE PROFITABILITY. When the firm's paramount objective is maximizing profits, it provides less value to customers and retains more for itself. Firms use this **skim-pricing** approach when products have patent protection — like pharmaceuticals or offer high value like pioneering high technology products.

KEY IDEA

➤ The firm has various price and non-price actions for responding to price competition.

KEY IDEA

➤ The firm should link pricing strategy to its strategic objectives.

Penetration Pricing and Skim Pricing

Here we review *penetration pricing* and *skim pricing*, introduced in Chapter 10. These pricing strategies correspond to different strategic objectives: maximizing growth and/or market share, and maximizing profits, respectively.

Penetration pricing. The firm provides significant customer value by setting prices close to costs. Volume increases, unit costs fall, the firm reduces price, and volume increases ... in a virtuous spiral. The firm forgoes high profits today in favor of achieving high volumes and ultimately earning profits from high unit volumes, but low profit margins.

Skim pricing. The firm retains value for itself by pricing high. It earns high profit margins, but provides less value to its relatively few customers. The firm reduces prices periodically — sequential skimming, to attract increasing numbers of customers. These customers experience greater value in part because of the original higher-price framing.[31]

Apple used a skim-pricing strategy for the iPhone. Introduced at $599, Apple reduced price to $399 after just two months.[32] Less than one year later, Apple priced the new iPhone 3G at $199.

MAXIMIZE CASH FLOW. If the firm plans market withdrawal, maximizing cash flow is often a good short-term strategic objective. In Chapter 10, we discuss *harvesting* products as the approach to short-term cash-flow maximization.[33]

KEY MESSAGES

- Pricing is a big deal. Pricing decisions have a major impact on profitability.

- Four critical considerations should enter firm pricing decisions: perceived customer value, costs, competition, and strategic objectives.

  - **Perceived customer value**. The firm must make key decisions about creating, measuring, and capturing value. The firm must understand customer price sensitivity.

  - **Costs**. Many firms use cost inappropriately by implementing cost-plus approaches to setting price. Costs have three proper roles: birth control, death control, and profit planning.

  - **Competition.** Critical firm issues are predicting how competitors will respond to price changes, and deciding how to respond to competitor price reductions. The firm can take a variety of price and non-price actions.

  - **Strategic objectives**. The firm should link strategic objectives — growth in volume and/or market share, maximizing profits, and maximizing cash flow, to pricing actions.

VIDEOS AND AUDIOS

Pricing   v1902 🎥   Reed Holden   Holden Advisors

QUESTIONS FOR STUDY AND DISCUSSION

Can you answer the questions implied by this chapter's learning objectives? Check!

1. Merck priced prescription hair-growth drug, Propecia, at $50 per month's supply. Over-the-counter competitor Rogaine (topical liquid) was about $30 per month. Merck's drug for enlarged prostate, Proscar, has the same active ingredient — finasteride — as Propecia. Merck's price for 30 Proscar tablets was $70 — one Proscar tablet equals five daily doses of Propecia. Some physicians write Proscar prescriptions for balding men, who slice the pills into five parts. Hence, they pay about $14 per month ($70/5) for hair-loss treatment, versus $50 for Propecia. Merck defends Propecia's price premium by citing research costs including clinical trials — $450 million. Most insurance policies cover Proscar, but not Propecia. The makers of Rogaine launched an $80 million advertising campaign for extra-strength Rogaine, applied twice daily. An Italian website offers Proscar tablets for U.S. delivery at $63 per 36 tablets. Suggest actions for:
   - Merck's director of marketing.
   - The compliance director for a national HMO.
   - Rogaine's marketing director.

2. Develop a customer value map for soft drinks (or a product form of your choice). Interpret the map. What pricing options do the several competitors have?

3. Large competitors frequently have cost structures with a high proportion of fixed costs. Why? What pricing alternatives would you recommend to one of their small competitors? Why?

4. In 1958, Kaplan, Dirlam, and Lanzillotti showed that cost-plus pricing was the most common pricing method. In 1995, Shim and Sudit found essentially the same result. This chapter argues that cost-plus pricing is deeply flawed. Why does this apparent incongruity exist? What should firms do about it?

v2001

IMPERATIVE 4

Design the Market Offer

....

PART D – GETTING PAID FOR CUSTOMER VALUE

CHAPTER 20

SETTING

PRICES v2001

To access O-codes, go to **www.ocodes.com**

LEARNING OBJECTIVES

When you have completed this chapter, you will be able to:

- Set price for a new product.
- Change price for an existing product.
- Manage and monitor pricing tactics.
- Use the pricing toolkit and price waterfall concept for price setting.
- Assess several approaches to setting prices.
- Address several pricing issues.
- Design a system for price management.
- Converse about legal and ethical issues in pricing
- Integrate pricing with other marketing implementation elements.

OPENING CASE: ORACLE CORPORATION

Led by its famously aggressive CEO, Larry Ellison, Oracle is a world leader in enterprise software. Oracle develops, manufactures, distributes, and services databases and middleware software, application software, and hardware systems worldwide. Oracle's 2011 $36.6 billion revenues and 24 percent net profit margins were a sharp improvement from a decade earlier.

In the late 1990s and early 2000s, Oracle competed strongly with Microsoft and IBM in the small- and medium-size business (SMB) software market. Oracle pursued a clear pricing strategy, placing its list prices online for customers, implying pricing rigidity and fair pricing for all. But in the early 2000s, IBM and Microsoft lowered prices for enterprise databases for SMB customers. Oracle reacted strongly by offering large discounts to close deals. Oracle's price aggressiveness became well known in the industry. Many customers delayed purchase commitments until the end of the quarter, anticipating that Oracle salespeople would offer heavily discounted prices to make their numbers. As competition between IBM, Oracle, and Microsoft heated up, Oracle adopted price competition as a strategic weapon. Jacqueline Woods, Oracle vice-president of global practices and pricing, stated: "Now we are saying that it is time to lower our prices to penetrate broader markets." But Oracle's pricing actions led to significant margin erosion and did not impede IBM and Microsoft's determination to fight for revenues.

To address decreasing margins, Oracle pursued an aggressive acquisition strategy so as to offer customers a more compelling value proposition. Between 2005 and 2009, Oracle acquired more than 50 software firms (2005 — 13; 2006 — 13; 2007 — 11; 2008 — 13; 2009 — 5), including BEA, Hyperion, PeopleSoft, and Siebel, together with server manufacturer Sun Microsystems. Oracle invested more than $30 billion in this effort.

By pursuing acquisition in the context of a deep understanding of customer needs, Oracle could offer customers very attractive product bundles (especially software), and incentivize them to purchase additional software for integration with database software. Oracle's acquisitions also brought an extensive customer base to which it then offered integrated solutions. Oracle secured innovation and revenue growth, and constructed a software ecosystem whose constituent products worked well together.

In addition to offering integrated solutions, Oracle's ecosystem created high customer switching costs and allowed it to ease out of the price war with IBM and Microsoft. Oracle's new strategy even allowed it to raise prices by 20 percent in the 2009 economic slowdown. Oracle became a one-stop shop for many customers, keen to avoid the high financial and organizational costs and risks of migrating databases from one software supplier to another. Correspondingly, Oracle secures significant revenues from maintenance and service contracts.

CASE QUESTION

How do you assess Oracle's strategy and performance? What other approaches could Oracle have attempted? As an Oracle customer, how do you feel about being locked in? Is Oracle's strategy sustainable over the long run?

Oracle's financial results demonstrated the success of its strategy. Gross profit margins increased from 70 percent in 2002 to 80 percent by 2009, outperforming industry rivals. Revenues increased from $9.6 billion in 2002 to $35.6 billion in 2011. The stock market reacted favorably: Oracle's stock price increased from $11 in 2003 to $36 in 2011.

THE CHANGING VIEW

OLD WAY	NEW WAY
Antitrust considerations minimal	Growing enforcement in U.S. and European Union
Destructive pricing tactics common	Growing sophistication in using the pricing toolkit
Inefficient product markets	Efficient product markets — role of the Internet
List-price mentality	Varied pricing tactics
Price and offer homogeneity	Price and offer heterogeneity
Pricing complexity limited by human factors	Pricing complexity driven by software
Standard pricing	Customized pricing
Pricing decisions disorganized	Intellectual capital development in pricing

When Ryanair launched Ireland-to-Britain routes in the 1980s, it chose a low-price strategy. Ryanair was initially successful because incumbents British Airways and Aer Lingus held a **price umbrella** over the market. In the early 1990s, Aer Lingus cut prices and almost forced Ryanair into bankruptcy. Ryanair then buttressed its low-price strategy with a sustained effort to cut costs and considerably expanded its route structure. Despite low prices, today Ryanair is comfortably profitable.

Chapter 20 is the second of two chapters in Part D of Imperative 4 — *Design the Market Offer.* Part D focuses on *Getting Paid for Customer Value.* Chapter 20 addresses *Setting Prices.*

Using Chapter 19 as background, Chapter 20 shows the mechanics of price setting. The firm should use the four factors we discussed — *perceived customer value, costs, competitors,* and *strategic objectives* — to approach price-setting holistically, not independently. The firm starts with perceived customer value, considers costs, then factors in competitors and its strategic objectives. Chapter 20 shows how to approach strategic price setting for a new product, change price for an existing profit, and avoid price changes. Then we turn to tactical pricing decisions, including elements in the pricing toolkit, the pocket price, and the price waterfall. We continue with pricing approaches, setting the actual price, and special topics in setting prices; and conclude by discussing pricing management, and legal and ethical issues in pricing.

SETTING PRICE FOR A NEW PRODUCT

Ace (fictional firm) is setting price for a new manufacturing furnace. Ace believes the furnace offers superior value versus competitor Beta. Table 20.1 shows data that Ace collected. Customer startup costs and post-purchase costs are the same for both Ace and Beta. To frame the *right* approach for setting price, we first show improper methods — cost-plus and competitive-equivalence approaches. Then we introduce the correct method:

TABLE 20.1

DATA FOR PRICE-SETTING COLLECTED BY ACE FURNACE

Beta	Furnace price	$260,000
Ace	Economic value to the customer (EVC)	$360,000
Ace	Direct out-of-pocket cost: variable and fixed	$100,000
Ace	Fully loaded cost, including overhead allocations	$160,000

IMPROPER APPROACHES

COST-PLUS PRICING. Since the pricing decision concerns a new product, Ace must consider the fully loaded cost — $160,000. Commonly used mark-ups in the furnace industry are 75 percent and 50 percent. Price options are:

75 percent mark-up: Price = $160,000 × 1.75 = **$280,000**

50 percent mark-up: Price = $160,000 × 1.5 = **$240,000**

Note that at 75 percent mark-up, Ace's price exceeds Beta's — $280,000 versus $260,000. At 50 percent mark-up, Ace's price is less than Beta's — $240,000 versus $260,000. We do not know which is a *better* price for Ace.

COMPETITIVE EQUIVALENCE PRICING. Strict competitive equivalence suggests that Ace set a $260,000 price, the same as Beta. But Ace offers considerable extra value. If Ace sets price at $260,000, it should sell lots of furnaces. But does a $260,000 price represent appropriate value-sharing between Ace and its customers? Note: this approach does not consider Beta's response.

THE *RIGHT* WAY TO SET PRICE

Figure 20.1 diagrams the recommended three-step approach:

- **Step 1: Determine the maximum price.** The maximum price is the EVC from Ace's furnace — $360,000.[1] At $360,000, rational customers should be indifferent between furnaces from Ace and Beta. (Of course, customers may believe Ace's furnace poses a greater risk because the new product has no track record — we ignore this factor in the illustration.)

termine the minimum price. The minimum price is Ace's fully loaded cost — Ace earns profit contribution at any price above direct out-of-pocket cost — $100,000, but this is an incorrect figure for the minimum price of a new product.)

- **Step 3: Set the price based on Ace's strategic objectives and Beta's likely competitive response.** From steps 1 and 2, Ace's price should be between $360,000 and $160,000 — the crucial question is where. Ace should consider its strategic objectives and its forecast of Beta's likely response — probably correlated factors. Possible strategic objectives are:

  - **Toehold.** Ace wants a market presence but has little other ambition. Perhaps Ace identified a small high-price segment. Ace sets price around **$320,000**. Sales will be low, but profit margins will be high. Beta is unlikely to respond.

  - **Short-term profit.** Ace has greater ambition than the toehold option, so price is closer to Beta's $260,000. Because Ace offers greater customer value, it may set the price between **$260,000** and, say, **$280,000**. Ace will probably take some volume from Beta — the closer Ace's price to $260,000, the more likely Beta will reduce price. Prices significantly above $260,000 signal Beta that Ace wishes to avoid price competition.

  - **Market share.** Ace is ready to battle Beta for market share. At $260,000 and below, Ace offers customers significant value. Between **$200,000** and **$220,000**, Ace may sell many furnaces with good profit margins. But these prices will encourage a strong response from Beta. Ace must plan how to address Beta's likely actions.

When setting price, Ace should also consider customer *potential lifetime value*. Ace should ask several questions. Is this a one-time purchase, or will customers purchase more furnaces? Can Ace sell furnace parts and accessories and/or multi-year service contracts? Can Ace sell complementary products and services? Will customers recommend Ace to others? Responses should influence Ace's price setting decision.

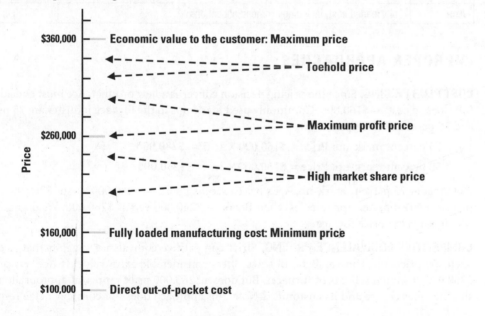

FIGURE 20.1

PRICING ANALYSIS FOR A NEW ITEM OF CAPITAL EQUIPMENT

CHANGING THE PRICE OF AN EXISTING PRODUCT

The firm has many reasons to change price. Sometimes external competitive pressures are critical, but other pressures may be internal. Financial managers may want increased profit margins by raising prices. Seeking increased volume, the sales force may lobby for price decreases. Critical questions are:

- Can the firm *increase price* without losing significant volume? How much volume will it lose? Will the incremental profit margin offset the lost volume?

- If the firm *decreases price*, will it gain significant volume? How much volume will it gain? Will the extra volume offset the reduced profit margin?

To answer these questions, the firm must calculate the volume of sales necessary at the proposed price in order to make the same profit it earns at the current price. Figure 20.2 shows a five-step process for considering price changes. Before tackling this section, you should become familiar with Marketing Enrichment me01 .

FIGURE 20.2

A PROCESS FOR DETERMINING PRICE CHANGES

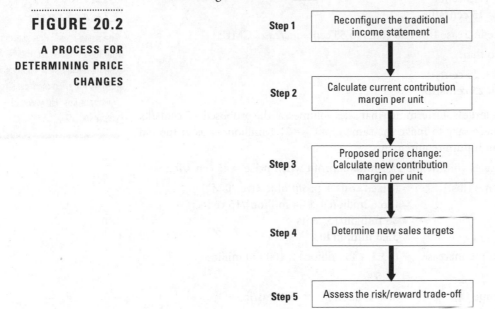

Step 1 Reconfigure the traditional income statement

Step 2 Calculate current contribution margin per unit

Step 3 Proposed price change: Calculate new contribution margin per unit

Step 4 Determine new sales targets

Step 5 Assess the risk/reward trade-off

Step 1: Reconfigure the traditional income statement. We partition costs into two categories: variable costs and fixed costs.[2] Table 20.2 is a simplified version of Marketing Enrichment me01 Table ME4 (derived from the traditional income statement — Table ME2).

TABLE 20.2

EXAMPLE OF PRODUCT INCOME STATEMENT ($000s)

Sales Revenues (SR) (40 million lbs. @ 50 cents/lb. selling price [SP])	$20,000
Variable Costs (VC)	$12,000
Contribution Margin (CM)	$ 8,000
Fixed Costs (FC)	$ 6,600
Net Profit before Taxes (NP)	$ 1,400

KEY IDEA

➤ **Changing Price for an Existing Product**

The firm must calculate required sales at the new price to make the same profit as at the current price.

Step 2: Calculate current contribution margin per unit. Contribution margin (CM) is an important concept. CM must cover fixed costs; any remainder is profit. CM equals (is identical to) sales revenues (SR) less variable costs (VC). (Hence, variable costs do not enter future CM calculations.)

Restated: $SR - VC \equiv CM$ On a per-unit basis, $SP - VCU \equiv CMU$

And: $SR \equiv CM + VC$ On a per-unit basis $SP \equiv CMU + VCU$

Table 20.3 shows that **contribution margin per unit (CMU)** is simply CM on a per-unit basis — similarly for **variable cost per unit (VCU)**:

TABLE 20.3

CONTRIBUTION MARGIN PER UNIT (CMU) CALCULATION

	Total Revenue	Unit Sales (000s)*	Per Unit (lb.)	
Sales revenue (SR) *less*	$20 million	40,000	Price per unit (SP)	50 cents
Variable costs (VC) *equals*	$12 million	40,000	Variable cost per unit (VCU)	30 cents
Contribution margin (CM)	$ 8 million	40,000	Contribution margin per unit (CMU)	20 cents

* lbs.

Step 3: Proposed price change: Calculate new contribution margin per unit. Suppose the firm is considering two options: Raise price by 5 cents, and lower price by 5 cents. VCU does not change. But:

- **Decrease price.** A price reduction from 50 cents to 45 cents *decreases* CMU:

  SP ≡ VCU + CMU   so that:

    45 cents ≡ 30 cents + 15 cents
    Hence, new CMU = **15 cents/lb.**

- **Increase price.** A price increase from 50 cents to 55 cents *increases* CMU:

  SP ≡ VCU + CMU   so that:

    55 cents ≡ 30 cents + 25 cents
    Hence, new CMU = **25 cents/lb.**

Step 4: Determine new sales targets. Determine what sales volumes, at the proposed 45 cents/lb. and 55 cents/lb. prices, are necessary to make the same profit — $1.4 million — as at the old 50-cent/lb. price. These are minimum requirements:

- **Decrease price.** Unit sales volume for $1.4 million profit when price = 45 cents/lb.:

Target sales volume (lbs.)	= (Fixed costs + profit objective)/CMU
	= ($6.6 million + $1.4 million)/15 cents
	= $8 million/15 cents
	= **53.3 million lbs.**
Percent sales volume increase	= (53.3 – 40 million) × 100 /40 million
	= **32.5%**
Target sales revenue ($)	= 53.3 million lbs. × 45 cents/lb.
	= **$24 million**

If the firm *reduces* price to 45 cents/lb., it must sell **53.3 million pounds** (32.5% increase) to make the same profit as previously.

- **Increase price.** Unit sales volume for $1.4 million profit when price = 55 cents/lb.:

Target sales volume (units)	= (Fixed costs + profit objective)/CMU
	= ($6.6 million + $1.4 million)/25 cents
	= $8 million/25 cents
	= **32 million lbs.**
Percent sales volume decrease	= (32 – 40 million) × 100 /40 million
	= **20%**
Target sales revenue ($)	= 32 million lbs. × 55 cents
	= **$17.6 million**

If the firm *increases* price to 55 cents/lb., it must sell **32 million pounds** (20% decrease) to make the same profit as previously.

We summarize these results in Table 20.4.

Price	CMU	Target Volume	Sales Volume Percentage change	Target Revenues
50 cents	20 cents	40 million lbs.	—	$20 million
45 cents	15 cents	53.3 million lbs.	+ 32.5%	$24 million
55 cents	25 cents	32 million lbs.	– 20%	$17.6 million

Step 5: Assess the risk/reward trade-off. The results from Step 4 *do not make* the pricing decision. The firm must assess the likelihood it can meet (or exceed) the new volume targets: 53.3 million lbs. @ 45 cents/lb., or 32 million lbs. @ 55 cents/lb. The answer depends, in part, on

Marketing Question

The sales force is pressuring you to cut prices, so they can increase sales. Finance pushes for price increases to raise margins. How would you respond?

KEY IDEA

➤ Many firms make a fixed offer, then vary price when under pressure. The firm may avoid price changes via a price menu of variable offers with fixed prices.

TABLE 20.4

SUMMARY OF PRICING CALCULATIONS

me2001

competitive response. Considering all factors, the firm must decide whether or not to change price and take the chance of meeting or exceeding its volume targets. (Marketing Enrichment me2001 for a short-cut approach to assessing price changes.)

AVOIDING PRICE CHANGES

Many firms address pricing issues by assessing the value they offer customers, and then decide on the price. This approach often leads to considerable customer pressure to reduce price — *fixed offer, variable price.* An alternative approach for mitigating this pressure is to design several offers, each at a fixed price — *variable offer, fixed price.* The firm presents a **price menu**, including two or more product alternatives, and different delivery and/or service options like employee training, guaranteed supply, and special packaging. Figure 20.3 illustrates five separate price-menu options. IBM and Oracle each have web-based à la carte menus that salespeople and customers can access through password-protected portals.

The price-menu approach has two significant benefits. First, firms often add services to a base product and then charge higher prices. The price menu tests the value of extra services; if customers do not value the extra service, they will continue to buy the base product. Second, by pricing the product and service together in a single offer, the firm averages; some customers overpay (don't want services) and some underpay (use the service). With a price menu, each customer selects the offer that best meets its needs. Information technology facilitates managing a price menu, but the firm should ensure its price menu is understandable.

ChemX (disguised name) sold additives for improving plant productivity, together with employee training and technical support. Sophisticated customers resented paying for unneeded services and purchased from low-price, low-service suppliers. Other customers bought sufficient additives to qualify for the support, but purchased large volumes from low-price suppliers. ChemX developed an à la carte price menu with services priced separately (except for long-term contracts). ChemX also cut prices to be more competitive with lower-priced suppliers.[3]

FIGURE 20.3

ILLUSTRATION OF A PRICE MENU

	Offer 1	Offer 2	Offer 3	Offer 4	Offer 5
Product version 1	*	*			*
Product version 2			*	*	
Delivery option 1	*	*	*		
Delivery option 2				*	*
Service 1		*	*	*	*
Service 2			*	*	*
Service 3					*
Price	$150	$155	$165	$175	$180

TACTICAL PRICING

Tactical pricing is the ongoing stream of pricing decisions the firm makes on a daily basis. Generally, robust strategic pricing drives good tactical pricing, but tactical pricing has a major impact on firm performance. A common misconception is that a product has a single price; in fact, single prices are rare. Table 20.5 shows the **pricing toolkit**, the variety of tools the firm can use to make price adjustments, often for individual customers. Undisciplined use of the toolkit can lead to **price waterfall** problems (p. 503).

Acceptable currency	Credit terms	Guarantees and warranties	Price stability	**TABLE 20.5**
Allowances	Discounts	Inventory carrying costs	Slotting fees**	**A SELECTION OF TOOLS IN THE PRICING TOOLKIT**
Barter	Company shares	Leasing	Returns	
Buy-backs	Freight	List price	Unbundling and bundling	
Credit availability		Markdown money*		

* Agreements by suppliers to make payments to retail customers if products are discounted

** Payments by suppliers to retailers to put products in stores

THE PRICING TOOLKIT

Sometimes the firm wants a price change to be highly visible to customers and competitors; other times, the firm wants to keep it secret. Firms often set highly visible list prices (rate cards), but make minimal sales at list price. Rather, list price is the basis for discounts and rebates; actual prices may be 20 or 30 percent off list. The firm can base discounts on many factors like firm/customer relationship, inventory, matching competitors, quantity, selling effort, and timing.[4] Less visible ways to change price include allowances — for advertising, selling effort, trade-ins, and returns. Credit availability and terms (time to pay and interest rates) can be potent pricing tools, especially during inflation.

Freight or shipping charges are important price-changing mechanisms. For C.I.F. (cost, insurance, freight) prices, the supplier pays; for F.O.B. (free on board) prices, the customer pays.[5] The firm can change price by modifying customer inventory arrangements: JIT (just-in-time) systems cut customer inventory holding costs; selling on consignment (pay when used) reduces inventory costs to zero. Leasing versus purchasing offers customers the ability to reduce capital employed; and product guarantees and warranties reduce prices by protecting customers from repair costs. The firm should recognize that *toolkit* elements are differentially important across customers. For an equivalent price reduction, one customer may prefer a larger discount; another may prefer an advertising allowance. In B2B, the reward system for purchasing staff may be important: Some customers incentivize staff based on price reductions off the invoice price. A cash discount applied when the firm receives the order may be very attractive! Sometimes firms and customers prefer barter and buy-backs to money transactions:

> ### Barter
>
> - British Aerospace earned $20 billion revenues from Saudi Arabia for Tornado fighters, Hawk trainers, and backup services. Most payments were in oil.
>
> - During an Argentine recession, consumers acquired food and clothing, psychological counseling, and dental work, all by barter.
>
> - In Siberia's Altai territory, over 50 percent of economic transactions are bartered; some large firms transact 90 percent of business by barter.
>
> - A Polish organization contracted with Norton to erect a turn-key grinding wheel factory. Part payment was a buyback of products made in the plant.[6]

The firm can also modify prices by shifting between **unbundling** — pricing items separately (like an à la carte restaurant meal), and **bundling** — each offer has a single price (like a prix-fixe meal). **Mixed bundling** combines bundled and unbundled prices — Chapter 12.

Marketing Question

Identify six specific pricing tools you have observed. Why do you think they were used?

KEY IDEA

➤ Single product prices are rare in the real world.

➤ Pricing actions vary between highly visible and opaque.

THE POCKET PRICE AND PRICE WATERFALL

Some firms use toolkit items appropriately, but many others have poor systems for tracking use. List price and invoice price are transparent, but other pricing elements are often deeply buried in myriad financial accounts: early payment discounts — interest-expense account; cooperative advertising allowances — promotion and advertising accounts.[7] Hence, these firms do not know their **pocket prices** — the money they actually receive (in their pockets). When firms conduct pocket-price analysis, they are often surprised to find a broad price range, but little rationale — Figure 20.4. Small-volume customers may receive large discounts; high-volume customers do not. The most aggressive, clever, or persistent customers get the best prices, aka the *squeaky wheel* syndrome. These customers manipulate supplier management systems for extra discounts; firm salespeople often cooperate:

Knowing Oracle's concern with end-of-quarter results, customers waited for salespeople to offer larger discounts. Oracle booked most sales at the end of the quarter. To address the problem, Oracle started rejecting last-minute deals with large discounts. (See also Opening Case.)

FIGURE 20.4

HYPOTHETICAL POCKET
PRICE BAND FOR AN
INDUSTRIAL PARTS
MANUFACTURER

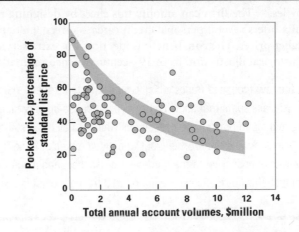

The **price waterfall** — Figure 20.5 — illustrates how pricing toolkit elements cumulate to produce the pocket price. Customers can earn 27.6 percent reductions from four separate discounts (1 to 4) to make the invoice price 72.4 percent of the standard list price. They can also earn 15.3 percent reductions from seven other toolkit items (5 to 11) to make the pocket price 57.1 percent of list price.[8]

FIGURE 20.5

HYPOTHETICAL PRICE
WATERFALL FOR A
CONSUMER DURABLES
MANUFACTURER
AVERAGED OVER ALL
ACCOUNTS. AVERAGE
DISCOUNT FROM
STANDARD LIST PRICE
(PERCENT)[9]

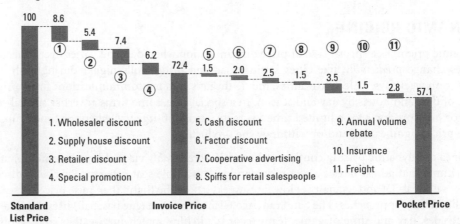

To optimize pricing, the firm must understand the pocket price for each customer and the way these prices developed. This task may not be easy; the firm may have to modify its accounting systems. Agricultural firm Syngenta's Brazilian subsidiary built a software program to estimate currency shifts, employee commissions, freight charges, and other costs for calculating pocket prices for proposed sales. Another firm took several initiatives to address price-waterfall problems:

- Acted aggressively to bring over-discounted customers into line with other customers.
- Delivered specific benefits to profitable customers to increase sales volumes.
- Brought price-setting under control by improving the accounting system.
- Tightened up on discounts and based sales force compensation on the pocket price.

DESIGNING PRICING APPROACHES

Several pricing methods are available:

PRICE DISCRIMINATION AND VARIABLE PRICING

The firm optimizes profits by setting different prices for different customers/segments — some pay more, others pay less.[10] The firm can amplify this effect by designing multiple offers with different values: AmEx offers several personal credit cards — green, gold, platinum, and black — at successively higher prices. The core benefit is identical, but extra services differentiate the offers. Consider an historical illustration from 19th-century French railroads:

> "It is not because of the few thousand francs which would have to be spent to put a roof over the third-class carriages or to upholster the third-class seats that some company or other has open carriages with wooden benches ... What the company is trying to do is to prevent the passengers who can pay the first-class fare from traveling third-class: it hits the poor, not because it wants to hurt them, but to frighten the rich ... And it is again for the same reason that companies, having proved almost cruel to the third-class passengers and mean to the second-class one, become lavish in dealing with first-class passengers. Having refused the poor what is necessary, they give the rich what is superfluous."[11]

Regardless, the firm may benefit from an inflexible single price. When salespeople have no **price discretion**, aggressive customers cannot negotiate price discounts (Oracle boxed insert, p. 503). Also, a single price is simpler to understand and provides a perception of fairness, like CarMax's *no haggle* pricing policy for automobiles.

DYNAMIC PRICING

Dynamic pricing is a special case of price discrimination when demand varies over time. Some prices change *predictably*, like cities setting road and bridge tolls higher during rush hours and/or on weekdays.[12] Electric utilities, movie theaters, and telecommunications firms price by time of day; and hotels by day and season. In a special case, some firms advertise special prices and/or offer products for a limited time to create a sense of urgency; when the time is up, they raise prices significantly, and/or withdraw the product.

Airlines use dynamic pricing continuously and *less predictably* via **yield management** systems, algorithms that adjust fares based on demand and available seat capacity. European discount airlines like easyJet and Ryanair set low fares weeks before the flight, then raise prices as seats fill and flight time approaches. The San Francisco Giants (major league baseball) uses data like past ticket sales, day and time of game, team records, pitching match-up, weather, and secondary market prices to set prices for individual games.

KEY IDEA

➤ The firm needs good systems to track elements in the pricing toolkit.

➤ The pricing toolkit produces the pocket price via the price waterfall.

➤ Pricing toolkit elements are differentially important to customers.

Marketing Exercise

Compare and contrast pricing in 19th-century French railroads with 21st-century passenger air travel.

Marketing Exercise

Next time you fly, ask fellow travelers what fare they paid. What is the basis for the price differences? Be prepared for them — or you — to be disgruntled!

KEY IDEA

➤ Important approaches to pricing include:
- Price discrimination — variable pricing
- Dynamic pricing
- Variable rate versus flat rate
- Customer-driven pricing
- Auction pricing

Customers seem to accept variable pricing for airlines, hotels, and restaurants, but sometimes they believe dynamic pricing is unfair. Coke announced the pending installation of new vending machines that would increase price as temperatures rose; the storm of protest led Coke to back off.[13]

VARIABLE-RATE VERSUS FLAT-RATE PRICING

Firms selling services can price by use — **variable-rate**, or by time period — **flat-rate**. Variable prices may earn greater revenues, but flat-rate prices are generally easier to administer.[14] Previously, ski hills charged for chair lifts by the ride — variable rate; today, most charge per day, week, or season — flat rate. Commuter rail travelers and season ticket holders for sporting and cultural events pay a flat-rate price per season; others pay by the trip or event. Some firms combine flat rates and use fees, like cell phone providers.

CUSTOMER-DRIVEN PRICING

In many markets, sellers set a price and buyers accept it or not.[15] In customer-driven pricing, the customer names the price; the firm can accept it or not. At Priceline.com, customers *name their own price* for automobiles, hotel reservations, mortgages, and airplane tickets. If the product is available, customers *must* complete the purchase. Customer-driven pricing has significant potential in services where products cannot be inventoried.

AUCTION PRICING

A form of customer-driven pricing where customers compete with other potential buyers to purchase a product. Alternative types of auction are:

ENGLISH AUCTION. Used especially for secondhand items. Prices start low, and potential buyers bid up the price. Auctioneers seek the buyer willing to pay the highest price. Typically, the seller sets a **reserve price**; if the price does not reach the reserve, the seller withdraws the product. eBay and Amazon.com use English auctions; similarly, Ticketmaster auctions the best seats to concerts.

VICKREY AUCTION. A **sealed-bid** English auction where the winning bidder pays the price of the second-highest bid.[16] Google uses Vickrey auctions for online advertising.

DUTCH AUCTION. Prices start high; the seller reduces price until a buyer bids. Google used a Dutch auction for its IPO.

REVERSE AUCTION. This type of auction is for suppliers. The customer states its requirements; suppliers bid to provide the product. Prices go down and the lowest bidder wins the business[17]:

> An auto firm authorized 25 suppliers to bid in a 20-minute reverse auction for plastic automobile parts. The benchmark (starting) price was the most recent price — $745,000. The first bid was $738,000; after 10 minutes the price was $612,000. Thirty seconds before planned closing, the price was $585,000; each extra bid added one minute of bidding. After 13 more minutes, bidding concluded at $518,000.

Marketing Question

In your educational institution, the most popular courses are oversubscribed; some students are forced to take less popular courses. One proposal calls for a two-tier pricing system; more popular courses have a higher price. How do you react to this suggestion?

Marketing Question

Why did the Chilean firm come off so badly? What makes for a successful reverse auction for the customer? For the supplier?

Many suppliers worry that reverse auctions lead to lower prices, but there are exceptions. A Chilean firm used a reverse auction to purchase a mining chemical. Two profitable suppliers competed. Each roughly knew the other's prices, but neither had sufficient capacity to satisfy the full requirement. Also, each supplier had a *most-favored-nation* clause with its major customer; these customers received the lowest price offered to any other customer. The reverse auction took five minutes; the final price was 45 percent above its previous price. The Chilean firm tried to nullify the auction, but the suppliers refused.

SETTING THE ACTUAL PRICE

Several issues are important when setting the actual price:

FEES AND SURCHARGES

Many firms use **fees and surcharges** to increase pocket prices, especially in difficult economic times. Banks charge for ATM use and bounced checks; telecoms charge fees for directory assistance, set-up, change of service, number portability, and service termination; airlines charge fees and surcharges for checked bags, flight changes, fuel, pillows, and preferred seats (aisle, extra legroom [exit rows], and front of the plane). Revenues and profits increase, but overly aggressive fees may lead customers to go elsewhere — they don't like being nickel-and-dimed.

ING Direct (banking) and Virgin Mobile USA (cell phone service) are examples of successful firms that make pricing simple and transparent.[18]

PROMOTIONAL PRICING VERSUS STEADY PRICING

In many situations, sales are sensitive to short-term price promotions — Chapter 16. Firms often execute price promotions by comparing the sale price with the regular (or reference) price. In **loss-leader pricing**, retailers deliberately take losses on some products to build customer traffic and sell other products. Despite sales increases, promotions can have negative effects:

- **Brand image.** The promotion negatively affects the brand, especially upscale brands.
- **Diversion.** Retailers and/or distributors may *divert* the product to non-competing outlets, often in different geographic areas.
- **Hidden costs.** Frequent price promotions can be difficult and costly to administer.
- **Poor forecasting.** Demand exceeds forecast and customers are upset. Hong Kong Disneyland's one-day discounted tickets were not valid on *special days* like Chinese New Year. Chinese New Year was four days in Hong Kong but longer in mainland China. When Chinese New Year was over in Hong Kong but still continued on the mainland, mainlanders flooded into Hong Kong, and Disneyland had to close its gates.
- **Time-shifting.** Customers buy for inventory to avoid paying the full price later.

Some firms have abandoned promotional pricing. P&G introduced *everyday low pricing*, and Burger King stopped using promotional devices like coupons and discounts.

PSYCHOLOGICAL PRICING

For many customers, the psychological distance from $9.95 to $10.00 is greater than from $10.00 to $10.05; hence, many firms set prices to end with 95 cents.[19] Price framing is also important. An $8 product discounted to $7 is typically viewed more favorably than a $6 product with a $1 surcharge.[20] Firms also use price to *frame* offers. Apple framed the iPhone's value with a $599 initial price; its subsequent $399 price seemed like a great deal. Relatedly, Nook, a neighborhood restaurant in Manhattan's Hell's Kitchen, added an expensive filet mignon dish to its menu.

Louis Vuitton (LV) creates high-priced limited-edition *products of the year;* LV priced the *Theda* bag at $5,550. Said factory director Stephen Fallon, "The aim of the fashion bags isn't to make money, but to make envy." Compared to the *product of the year,* LV's other bags are inexpensive, so they seem like bargains.[21]

Marketing Question

Your firm's revenue goal for a service offering is $50. Various managers have suggested the following communication and pricing approaches:

- Advertise and price the service at $50.
- Advertise a $45 price, then add a $5 surcharge at the time of purchase.
- Advertise a $55 price with a $5 discount.

Which option will you choose?

KEY IDEA

➤ Considerations in setting actual prices include:

- Fees and surcharges
- Promotional pricing versus steady pricing
- Psychological pricing
- Pricing bases

PRICING BASES

Most industries have accepted bases for setting prices, typically by individual product, but changing the price basis may be a way to secure advantage. Some firms sell individual medical diagnoses rather than diagnostic machines; some software firms price per use rather than by software package. Japan's Viking chain of buffet restaurants sets prices in *yen per minute* to increase customer turns; Zipcar prices by annual membership fee plus a per hour charge versus daily or weekly prices like most car-rental firms. Relatedly, customers pay $79 annually for Amazon Prime, then receive unlimited free 2-day shipping. In Africa, Asia, and Latin America, fast-growing Millicom International Cellular charges customers per second (versus per minute). Some B2B firms share risk with customers by receiving partial payment in customer profits earned with their products; customers pay advertising agencies by results rather than percentage of billings (traditional).[22] Auction firms Christie's and Sotheby's offer customers price guarantees for artwork, but share differences in price above the guarantee (plus sales commissions).

> TelServ (TS) (disguised name) sold, installed, and maintained telephone switch boxes containing various numbers of switches; installation costs drove prices for maintenance service. TS found customer value was more related to number of maintained switches. TS then priced by switch, lowering some prices and raising others; profitability improved.

SPECIAL TOPICS IN SETTING PRICES

We examine several special pricing topics:

COMPLEMENTARY PRODUCT PRICING

Complementary products are used together — hot dogs and buns, automobiles and spare parts, vacuum cleaners and bags, printers and cartridges, and movies and popcorn. The firm must make a two-part pricing decision. Gillette is well known for pricing razors low and blades high, but strong differential advantage from recent innovations lets Gillette price each component high. HP prices printers low and cartridges high, but faces strong competition from low-price cartridge refills; by contrast, Kodak prices printers higher and cartridges lower. In the U.S., wireless carriers heavily subsidize cell phones in exchange for multiyear contracts.

Timing can be a critical issue. Sometimes it makes sense to lock in customers with an initial sale, then up-sell later — like selling a car and later offering a special-deal options package. Other times, it may be more advantageous to offer additional items simultaneously with the main purchase.[23]

> **FREE.** Sometimes firms set a price of zero — FREE. FREE may be useful in several situations[24]:
>
> • **Cross-subsidies.** One product is FREE; a second product is not free. To encourage increased purchases, Amazon provides FREE shipping for orders more than $25; cell phone carriers provide FREE phones for multi-year-subscription contracts. Also, some clubs offer FREE entry to women, but men must pay.
>
> • **Multiple versions.** The firm offers a limited product version FREE. The firm hopes some portion of FREE customers will upgrade to enhanced versions and pay. FREE is common for software and on the Internet: Monty Python launched a free channel on YouTube; sales of the group's movies and TV shows increased by 23,000 percent. Earlier, the Grateful Dead allowed fans to tape concerts; merchandise and ticket sales increased.
>
> • **Non-financial goals.** Psychological motives like personal achievement and altruism may drive organizational member goals. Craigslist, Wikipedia, and Linux fall into this category.
>
> CONTINUES ON NEXT PAGE

- **Public image.** Many people and organizations criticize prescription drug firms for high prices. Merck has a long-standing program to provide FREE drugs to combat river blindness (endemic in parts of Africa and Latin America); in the 2008 recession, Pfizer provided drugs FREE to people who lost jobs.

- **Trial.** The firm provides free samples, or allows service access for a limited time, so customers enjoy the experience. Many FMCG firms and retailers use this approach.

- **Two-sided markets.** The firm offers its product FREE in one market — subsidy side; and secures revenues from the second market — money side. Consumers enjoy Internet search, radio, TV, and websites FREE; advertisers pay for consumer attention. Relatedly, employers pay, job seekers do not; home sellers pay, home buyers do not.[25] Google provides the Android operating system FREE to handset makers (more than 300) and software development kits FREE to app makers; Google earns revenues from increased advertising on mobile devices.[26]

GRAY MARKET PRICING

Gray markets undercut the firm's strategy.[27] Gray markets develop when the firm sells a similar product in different markets at different prices. Customers purchase the product in a low-price market, then ship it for resale to a high-price market — *diversion*. Suppliers can avoid gray markets by reducing price dispersion.[28] Goodyear gave large discounts to regional tire distributors; some resold tires in other regions; Goodyear reduced discounts to stop the practice.

U.S. textbook publishers set high U.S. prices and significantly lower foreign prices — an average 42 percent difference between U.S. and foreign online booksellers in one study. A $500 package of books at Amazon.com had a $350 price at Amazon.co.uk (including one-to-three-day expedited shipping). Student entrepreneurs, please note!

PAY-WHAT-YOU-WANT PRICING

In October 2007, British rock band Radiohead released *In Rainbows* as a digital download; customers chose their own prices! Many charitable organizations traditionally offer services on this basis, and restaurants in several countries have adopted similar pricing approaches.[29] These organizations rely on customers' sense of fairness and satisfaction to earn revenues.[30] Wessex, publisher of *Managing Marketing in the 21st Century* and other textbooks, similarly offers read-online versions.

TOPSY-TURVY PRICING

Suppliers and customers exchange value. The firm provides product/ service value; the customer provides monetary value via the price. But sometimes the customer provides additional value and the supplier, not the customer, pays the price — **topsy-turvy pricing**. Sports teams typically pay medical practitioners to treat players, but some hospitals and medical practices receive value by calling themselves *official medical providers*. They pay sports teams up to $1.5 million annually to treat players.

Typically, airlines pay airport authorities for gate access and other services. But Ryanair makes agreements with small cities it selects as destinations. These cities often pay Ryanair significant subsidies for landing and ground-handling fees, funds for hiring staff, marketing new routes, office space, and hotel accommodations.[31]

> *Marketing Question*
>
> How do you assess the pay-what-you-think-it's-worth pricing approach for *Managing Marketing in the 21st Century*? As incoming marketing director, what prices would you set for printed and pdf versions of *Managing Marketing in the 21st Century*? Why?

TRANSFER PRICING

Firms set **transfer prices** among business units and geographic subsidiaries — a firm in Australia shipping to a sister subsidiary in Italy. Of course, transfer prices affect subsidiary profits and, internationally, the firm's tariff and tax liabilities. Thousands of U.S. firms legally avoid income taxes by converting U.S. sales to paper profits in countries with lower tax rates.[32]

PRICING MANAGEMENT

"At Alcoa, we have pricing responsibility clearly delineated by the customer. For example, Airbus pricing comes through a system. It doesn't matter where the product is made; individual plants do not quote prices. The same is true for automotive. We assign one individual to make sure we offer the best price, best cost, best delivery, best everything — at any given time. The most senior marketing manager for mill products is responsible for pricing all aerospace products anywhere in the world. But he cannot offer Airbus a contract without a few of us reviewing it at the market sector/lead team level."[33]

Now that you have learned about critical underpinnings of pricing decisions — Chapter 19, and actually setting prices — Chapter 20, you probably have several questions: How should the firm create a **pricing management** structure? How should the firm set prices? Who should be responsible? Generally, centralized pricing provides greater control; decentralized pricing offers greater market sensitivity. But decentralized pricing may also have long-run negative effects[34]:

- **Information sharing.** Customers talk to each other about prices; those paying higher prices exert pressure for price reductions.
- **Limited perspective.** A local decision-maker like a salesperson is unlikely to consider the potential long-run impact of a local price reduction on the firm's entire customer base.
- **Negotiation.** Customers learn to place end-of-period orders when suppliers are anxious about revenues and may reduce prices. They also learn to play off multiple vendors against one another.

For these reasons, many firms develop pricing policies via a governance process that addresses long-run strategic questions like pricing new products, as well as short-term tactical decisions. These policies set guidelines for addressing multi-person buying decisions like those involving purchasing agents (tend to focus on price), and engineers, operations, and marketing personnel (other concerns). To enforce strategic pricing (and avoid slippage to cost-plus behavior), Parker Hannifin (PH) (Chapter 19 boxed insert, p. 488) appointed a series of divisional pricing specialists.

KEY IDEA

➤ The firm should develop pricing policies at high levels in the firm.

➤ Price-setting can be a strategic capability.

Some experts argue that price-setting is a strategic capability, comparable to new product development and advertising.[35] Most firms have significant capabilities for creating customer value, but less expertise in measuring and capturing value. Far too often, managers with pricing responsibility do not understand price-volume-profit trade-offs. They lack good analytic skills and rely instead on gut instinct, hearsay, responding to competitors, and rules of thumb. Polaroid failed to exploit an early lead in digital-imaging technology because it did not know how to capture value.[36] When Sun Country Airlines suspended operations, the CEO complained it had insufficient expertise to price routes effectively. Even GE Chairman Jeffrey Immelt fessed up; "[we] did an analysis of our pricing in appliances and found that about $5 billion is discretionary [by the sales force] … with the prices we charge, we're too sloppy."[37]

As competition increases globally and earning profits becomes more difficult, successful firms will develop human, systems, and social capital for improving pricing decisions — Roche Marketing University (box below). One industrial goods firm set up a *war room* with wall charts and complex graphs. Cross-functional teams met daily to monitor the flow of leads, quotes, and signed deals; targeting customers; and watching the win rate. Teams updated a dashboard weekly so executives had a clear view on sales revenues, discounting trends, and key account behavior. The war room helps the firm price competitively and gives the sales force the best possible advantage when bidding against competitors.[38] Firms that develop the appropriate capabilities and focus significant effort on pricing make better pricing decisions.

Roche Marketing University

Pharmaceuticals giant Roche builds pricing knowledge and teaches three areas of pricing capability:

- **Human capital.** Broad pricing knowledge at decision-makers' command.

- **Social capital.** The ability to negotiate agreements on prices among firm decision-makers. Marketing may want *low steady* prices to demonstrate *good value*; salespeople may want high prices with discount flexibility so they can make sales and be heroes, and/or if they know buyers earn rewards for securing discounts off list price.

- **Systems capital.** Supports pricing decisions by:
  - Assembling accurate information on customer purchase history, including actual prices paid.
  - Managing price changes.[39]
  - Providing product and customer profitability.
  - Quickly responding to requests for price quotations.
  - Testing different prices.
  - Tracking competitors' prices and discounts.
  - Tracking firm prices, discounts, and reasons for different customer discounts.

LEGAL AND ETHICAL ISSUES IN PRICING

Most firms engage professionals to advise on legal implications of pricing decisions; we only scratch the surface. Marketers should have a working knowledge of three broad topics: anti-competitive pricing, fairness in consumer pricing, and dumping.[40]

ANTI-COMPETITIVE PRICING

Several pricing approaches are anticompetitive:

DISCRIMINATORY PRICING. Under the U.S. Robinson-Patman Act, firms cannot sell identical products to different customers at different prices when the effect is to lessen competition or create a monopoly. Defenses against Robinson-Patman are cost-justification and meeting a competitive threat.

PREDATORY PRICING. The U.S. defines predatory pricing as pricing below average variable costs, with the intention of putting the competitor out of business. Dominant firms sometimes engage in **predatory pricing** by temporarily pricing very low to thwart a competitive threat.

PRICE CONSPIRACIES. A firm and competitors overtly collude to fix prices, make implicit agreements to price in parallel, and/or exchange price information. Higher prices and customer harm typically occur. A high-level U.S. businessman, secretly recorded by an FBI whistleblower, summed up the **price-fixing** philosophy: "Our competitors are our friends; our customers are the enemies!" Two senior executives at Archer Daniels Midland (large U.S. agribusiness firm) earned long jail terms for price collusion.[41] Recent price-fixing cases won by governmental bodies include[42]:

- **Air cargo** – price fixing: BA and Korean Air — fined $300 million each; Air France-KLM — fined $350 million; China Air — fined $40 million (U.S.).
- **Airlines** – collusion on fuel surcharges: BA — fined £121.5 million (Britain); fined $300 million (U.S.)

> **KEY IDEA**
>
> ➤ Important legal and ethical pricing issues include:
> - Anti-competitive pricing, including:
>   - Discriminatory pricing
>   - Predatory pricing
>   - Price conspiracies
> - Dumping
> - Fairness in consumer pricing, including:
>   - Bait and switch
>   - Deceptive pricing

- **Auction houses** – price collusion: Sotheby's — fined $45 million (U.S.) for collusion with Christie's, plus a $512 million civil settlement (both firms)
- **Dynamic random access memories (DRAMs)** – price fixing: Samsung, Hynix Semiconductor, Infineon Technologies, and Elpida — fined $730 million in total; 11 executives went to jail (U.S.).
- **Elevators** – cartel for installing/maintaining elevators: Kone, Mitsubishi, Otis, Schindler, and Thyssen Krupp —fined € 992 million (European Union)
- **LCD screens** – price fixing: Chunghwa, LG, Sharp — fined $585 million (U.S.)
- **Paraffin wax** – price fixing: Exxon Mobil, Reposol, Sasol, Shell, YPF, and five other firms — fined € 675 million (European Union)
- **Synthetic rubber** – cartel: Bayer and Zeon — fined more than € 870 million (European Union)
- **Vitamin ingredients** — set production quotas, market shares, prices, and distribution: Roche — fined $500 million; BASF — fined $225 million (U.S.).[43]

In **resale price maintenance (RPM)**, manufacturers set prices for retailers. This *vertical price fixing* is illegal in many countries. Previously illegal in the U.S., a 2007 Supreme Court decision allowed its reestablishment in many situations.

PRICING FOR GOVERNMENTS. Many governments require that their programs, like Medicaid (U.S.), pay the lowest prices. The U.S. government fined Bayer (Cipro) and GSK (Paxil, Flonase) $257 million and $87.6 million, respectively, for shipping products to Kaiser for relabeling as Kaiser drugs, at lower than Medicaid prices.

DUMPING

Some firms **dump** products in foreign markets at "less than fair market value," below home market prices, and often below average costs. Dumping prices are often higher than variable costs, so the firm's contribution margin is positive. This practice may be illegal in the receiving country if it causes or threatens material harm to the domestic industry.

FAIRNESS IN CONSUMER PRICING

Two important fairness issues for consumers are:

BAIT AND SWITCH. Retailers advertise a low price product but have only limited availability. The *bait* sells quickly, then retailers offer most customers a higher price product, the *switch*.

DECEPTIVE PRICING. False prices or prices that may confuse or mislead customers are deceptive. If the firm advertises a product, price = $X, but the product cannot function without other critical elements, the $X price is deceptive. (That's why many products carry the disclaimer "batteries not included.") Difficult-to-understand prices and price information in *fine print* may also be deceptive.

KEY IDEA

➤ Many governments scrutinize prices for illegal activity.

KEY MESSAGES

- To set price for a new product, the firm should start with perceived customer value, consider costs, then factor in competitors and its strategic objectives.

- When contemplating changing price for an existing product, the firm should use a contribution margin approach to assess volumes needed to meet various profit targets.

- The firm may avoid making frequent price changes by implementing a price menu system.

- The firm has many pricing toolkit elements available for setting the actual price.

- Undisciplined use of pricing toolkit elements leads to price waterfall problems. Appropriate systems and pricing discipline can address these problems.

- The firm should consider many issues in designing pricing approaches and setting actual prices.

- To set prices well, the firm must invest in human, systems, and social capital.

- Price-setting is fraught with legal and ethical issues.

Summary questions for making better pricing decisions are in Table 20.6.[44]

1. What is the pricing objective, as stated in the market strategy?
2. What value do customers place on the firm's product/service?
3. Is there variation in the way in which customers value the firm's product? Search for segments.
4. How price sensitive are customers?
5. How are competitors likely to respond to firm prices?
6. What is the optimal approach to setting prices? — variable pricing, dynamic pricing, variable-rate pricing, flat-rate pricing, customer-driven pricing, or an auction.
7. What pocket price does the firm receive?
8. What are customers' emotional reactions to prices?
9. How do factors like brand preferences, demand shifts, and seasonality affect price?
10. Which firm customers are profitable to serve?[45]

VIDEOS AND AUDIOS

Segmented Pricing   v2002 🎬 Hitendra Wadhwa   Columbia Business School

TABLE 20.6

SUMMARY QUESTIONS FOR SETTING PRICES

v2002

QUESTIONS FOR STUDY AND DISCUSSION

Can you answer the questions implied by this chapter's learning objectives? Check!

1. A British entrepreneur is testing variable prices for movies. Do you think he will succeed? Why or why not?

2. Select a product in which you are interested. What price would you set? Why? Does your recommended price differ from the current price? Why?

3. Table 20.7 shows Printfirm's (disguised name) inkjet printer- and cartridge prices:

TABLE 20.7

PRICING FOR PRINTFIRM INKJET PRINTERS AND CARTRIDGES

	Price	Variable Cost	Unit Sales	Price Elasticity
Printer	$400	$300	100,000	−2.5
Cartridges	$ 25	$ 10	10 per printer	−1.0

Printfirm is considering three pricing options:
- Increase printer price by 10 percent
- Increase cartridge price by 10 percent
- Reduce printer price by 5 percent and increase cartridge price by 10 percent

What advice would you offer Printfirm?

4. Identify three examples of unfair or deceptive pricing practices. Why is each practice unfair or deceptive? How can customers protect themselves?

5. How would you go about setting price for a subscription-based online specialized news site, an automobile repair shop, and an accounting service?

6. Canon distributes digital cameras to many retail chains. These chains compete, in part by differentiating on price. What are the implications for a retail chain and for Canon?

IMPERATIVE 5

Secure Support from Other Functions

CHAPTER 21

ENSURING THE FIRM IMPLEMENTS THE MARKET OFFER AS PLANNED v2101 📹

To access O-codes, go to **www.ocodes.com**

It is amazing what you can accomplish if you do not care who gets the credit.

— Harry S. Truman

LEARNING OBJECTIVES

When you have completed this chapter, you will be able to:

- Understand how several externally oriented firms became successful via functional excellence.
- Recognize the challenges of creating an externally oriented firm.
- Deploy an organizational development model to facilitate becoming externally oriented.
- Explain the pros and cons of traditional and newer approaches of organizing for marketing.
- Appreciate the critical role of systems and processes, and human resources in developing and implementing market strategy.
- Realize the importance of other functions in contributing to marketing as a philosophy.
- Understand the importance of integrating many organizational functions and business units.
- Take steps to ensure your firm maintains an external orientation.

OPENING CASE: BRISTOL-MYERS SQUIBB

Senior executives at Bristol-Myers Squibb (BMS) (multinational pharmaceutical/healthcare) concluded BMS needed greater market focus and greater consistency in marketing processes and application among its therapeutic franchises and across the organization. The CMO, Marketing SVP, and senior marketing leaders formulated and implemented a Marketing Excellence *initiative. The two main elements were:* marketing system — *a systematic and analytic approach to marketing;* talent system — *an approach to career and talent development for all marketers. BMS also implemented a formal development program to educate and train marketers worldwide so as to embed marketing excellence within the culture.*

NEW MARKETING APPROACH. *The new vision reflected the importance of marketing to BMS success. Marketers should strive and aspire to create a premier marketing firm, not just a premier pharmaceutical marketing firm. To achieve the vision, BMS studied marketing programs/frameworks at successful marketing firms like P&G and Starbucks.*

The primary impact of Marketing Excellence *was implementation of a specific marketing process across BMS. Previously, brand managers planned in an ad-hoc fashion; senior management presentations reflected this individuality. Hence, making comparisons across brands, pharmaceutical franchises, and geographic regions, was difficult for BMS.* Marketing Excellence *provided a disciplined, systematic, and analytic approach that gave BMS a philosophy, consistent framework, and application tools to enable and empower marketers. The new approach facilitated better performance measurement and cross-brand comparisons. BMS grounded core elements of the new approach in several marketing principles, brand management choices, and application tools:*

- **Marketing principles.** *BMS wanted to guide marketer thinking in three areas: customer focus, value and brand creation, and their collective strategic implementation. To illustrate, principle 1: "Marketers should secure deeper insights into customers and their interactions." This principle was critical to BMS because of the many customer types it faced. Principle 3: "BMS should anticipate and out-maneuver competitors' activities." This principle reflects increasing levels of competition and the relatively short time to establish differential advantage.*

- **Brand management choices.** *To be successful, marketers must make strategic choices from a set of options. BMS created a set of choices categorized as strategic, planning, and execution. Strategic choices: deciding what the market definition is now and will be in the future, how BMS will differentiate the brand, what specific business opportunities are available for the brand, and what future data are needed to support those opportunities. Planning and execution choices: How to implement the strategic choices by considering customer segmentation and messaging, specific brand tactics, and measurement systems for plans and tactics. Marketers also had to establish alternative strategies and plans.*

- **Marketing application tools.** *BMS supported each choice with a specific set of tools, guiding questions, and worksheets to assist BMS marketers' thought processes.*

ENHANCE MARKETING COMPETENCE. *BMS believed that embedding Marketing Excellence worldwide would require a sustainable infrastructure to develop and train marketers. In the first three years, around 400 BMS marketing executives of all levels attended programs directed and taught by Columbia Business School marketing faculty, approximately 25 participants per program.*

BMS marketers developed experience with the principles and choices, BMS developed a unique, innovative, and sustainable training program. The program comprises a mix of delivery methods to train new marketers and those transitioning into marketing. The curriculum is case-driven learning accessed online with interactive software or through workshops facilitated by experienced BMS marketers designated as coaches.

THE RESULTS. Marketing Excellence *benefited BMS in three important areas:*

- **Cross-functional integration.** *The new approach encourages cross-functional teamwork and strongly recommends that marketers consult, inform, and align with functions like R&D, market research, and medical affairs. The common framework provides a way to educate non-marketers on marketing fundamentals, and provides a familiar approach across brands.*

- **International operations.** *BMS substantially changed its approach to international operations. Previously, regional and country heads had significant autonomy. Local executives made positioning decisions for new pharmaceuticals, including choice of brand names; BMS might position a specific product in several different ways, including different brand names. BMS now makes core positioning decisions for new drugs centrally; local executives cannot change positioning.*

- **Marketing culture.** Marketing Excellence *fostered a strong marketing culture within BMS. Brand managers around the world follow the same process, and vocabulary is common. Plans are easily shared for cross-brand comparisons and best-practice sharing.*

Marketing Excellence *has embedded a sustainable and consistent approach to marketing within BMS; industry experts rate three consecutive product launches among the top ten in pharmaceuticals.*

CASE QUESTION

How do you assess BMS' Marketing Excellence initiative? How would you improve on the design?

✳ **Bristol-Myers Squibb**
Together we can prevail.™

In previous chapters, we focused on gaining insight into markets, customers, competitors, the company, and complementers; developing market strategy; and designing implementation programs around product, promotion, distribution, service, and price. People with marketing titles tend to do much, but not all, of this work. By contrast, executing implementation programs involves many people throughout the firm, in a variety of functional areas.

To execute well, the firm must practice the Principle of Integration and seamlessly align various implementation programs with its market strategies. All employees must recognize that customers are central to the firm's success and act accordingly. Vision, mission, and strategy form the superstructure within which they do their jobs; the firm's values underpin its culture. Much of the hard implementation effort relates to organization structure, systems and processes, and human resource practices. Unfortunately, these elements tend to evolve slowly and lag both environmental changes and the firm's market strategies.

Chapter 1 showed that securing appropriate alignment is much easier when the firm has customer-focused values leading to a true external orientation. Chapter 21 presents a model for creating and maintaining an external orientation, including specific action steps. To frame the chapter, we show how several externally oriented firms became successful by achieving excellence in particular functional areas. We should all try to emulate these exemplars.

THE CHANGING VIEW

OLD WAY	NEW WAY
Customer satisfaction and loyalty are low priority	Customer satisfaction and loyalty are high priority
Hierarchy-based organization	Knowledge-based organization
Human resource factors neglected	Human resource factors highlighted
Internally oriented structures, and systems and processes	Externally oriented structures, and systems and processes
Marketing as a separate function	Marketing as everybody's business
Marketing seen as a department	Marketing seen as a philosophy
Market-share oriented	Shareholder and customer-value oriented
No customer information systems	Highly developed customer information systems
Operational focus	Strategic focus
Rigid, inflexible structures	Flexible, adaptive structures
Rules-driven	Values-driven
Sales and marketing discrete	Sales and marketing merging
Selection, training, and rewards driven by bureaucracy	Selection, training, and rewards driven by strategy

FUNCTIONAL EXCELLENCE IN SUCCESSFUL EXTERNALLY ORIENTED FIRMS

What does it take to deliver customer value and secure differential advantage? Successful firms deploy various resources and expertise to build core competence. Expertise areas include customer service, finance, human resources, operations and the supply chain, research and development, and even sales. Table 21.1 shows firms that leveraged such expertise into success.[1]

Functional Area	Company	Capability	Customer Benefit
Customer Service	Amazon	Collaborative filtering; one-click	Ease purchasing
	Fidelity	24/7/365 availability	Convenience
	Nordstrom	Values and reward system	Attentive personalized service
Finance	GE Capital	Sophisticated financial engineering	Innovative financing to leverage shareholder returns of clients
	Monsanto	Accepts barter payment	Able to purchase without cash
	Praxair	Flexible billing system	Site-based bills to facilitate project management

Marketing Question

When you place an order online, many supplier functions are involved in getting the product to you. Chart out the supplier process.

TABLE 21.1

DELIVERING CUSTOMER VALUE AND SECURING DIFFERENTIAL ADVANTAGE VIA FUNCTIONAL EXCELLENCE

TABLE 21.1

CONTINUED

Functional Area	Company	Capability	Customer Benefit
Human Resources	Google	Employee quality of life	Innovative products/services
	In-N-Out Burger	Training and benefits	Superior service
	Ritz Carlton/ Singapore Airlines	Selection and training	Superior service
Operations and the Supply Chain	Alcoa	Integrated operations and supply chain	Just-in-time delivery
	Dell	Design/build to order	Customization
	FedEx	System ownership	Reliability
	Walmart	Logistics and inventory management	Low prices
Research and Development	3M	Many new technologies	Innovative products
	Apple	Design skills	Aesthetically pleasing, functional, trendy products
	DuPont/Monsanto	Research skills in chemistry	Productivity increases
Sales	Avon	*Avon Lady* sales force	Close personal relationships between buyer and seller
	Direct Line	Direct sales of insurance	Lower prices
	IBM	Global account management program	Partnership relationship with leading technology firm

Marketing Question

Think about your cell phone supplier. With what functions or departments have you had contact — mail, e-mail, retail store, or customer service rep? Did one area provide a good experience? Is this part of the supplier's differential advantage?

Marketing Question

Select three firms from Table 21.1. What investments in resources are they making to maintain their differential advantages?

CUSTOMER SERVICE

We revisit aspects of customer service discussed in Chapter 13. Increased competition has made customer service very important for delivering customer value, securing differential advantage, and attracting, retaining, and growing customers. Yet, in many firms, customer service does not report to marketing. This may not matter when an external orientation is the firm's dominant philosophy. But we have witnessed many cases where the *customer service* job focused on collecting payments against invoices, or when customers desiring service had long telephone waits (forced to hear musac or an endlessly repeated message), then finally reached a clueless employee — *non-customer service.* Poor customer service generates significant customer dissatisfaction, especially if expectations are high, and can destroy an otherwise effective market strategy.

Amazon is a notably successful Internet retailer; CEO Jeff Bezos is dedicated to Amazon customers. Without follow-through and superlative service, Amazon could have suffered the fate of so many Internet start-up failures. Amazon's website is easy to navigate, acknowledges orders immediately, personalizes the customer experience, remembers basic ordering information, and makes purchasing suggestions based on past behavior. Delivery performance is also excellent. Amazon's expansion well beyond books is fulfilling Bezos' vision of being the leading Internet retailer.

Fidelity is the U.S. market leader in mutual funds. Fidelity's key insight was that investors preferred to interact with brokers on their personal schedules, not just when the market was open. Fidelity's innovation was to become the first financial services firm open 24/7/365. Many other factors contributed to Fidelity's leadership, but customer confidence and trust in the Fidelity brand and the customer service convenience it offered were critical. Today, online brokerage competitors offer similar convenience and Fidelity has lost some ground.

Some externally oriented firms differentiate their offers from tough competitors via customer service excellence. Nordstrom's (department store) is rightly famous for employees' customer service zeal. Careful employee selection, enlightened management, and supportive incentive

Marketing Question

Which firm has provided you personally with the best customer service? What was so great about it? How could your selected firm improve its performance?

systems encourage the *right* behavior. Nordstrom's accepts returned goods without question, sometimes from competitor stores!

FINANCE

Clearly, financial skills are a key success factor in financial services, but financial decisions and controls play a critical role in managing the operations of any successful firm. Financial engineering is central to marketing major capital goods and services, from aircraft and earth-moving equipment to business systems. Externally oriented firms galvanize their finance and accounting functions; they contribute to the firm's marketing efforts in many ways.

GE is an excellent example; GE Capital provides a substantial share of GE's profits. Its origins gave GE unique insight into home appliance purchases. GE recognized it could meet the working capital needs of appliance dealers and the credit needs of consumers better than financial services firms could. From humble beginnings, GE Capital has become an innovative, diversified, financial services firm.

Getting paid is a critical part of any firm's business model but sometimes that's not so easy. Monsanto provides genetically modified seeds to large growers in many countries. When growers have difficulty in paying cash, Monsanto accepts finished crops in payment (barter); later, Monsanto sells these crops at market prices to realize cash.

Billing systems can be a major customer problem, but a good place to seek differential advantage. After all, the bill is one supplier communication that customers always read! Praxair (industrial gases) has many construction customers that work simultaneously on different projects; they must account for costs by site and project. Praxair created a flexible billing system that offers customers this service; they appreciate it.

> ### *Marketing Question*
> Can you think of a firm whose finance operations made doing business with it easier? What specifically did you like? How could the firm improve?

HUMAN RESOURCES

Human resources (HR) is a vital function for any business, but some firms create differential advantage by developing unique approaches to developing and motivating the work force to achieve high levels of excellence. Many consultants claim HR advantages are the most sustainable since they are difficult to copy and *talent management* is a key driver in many firms. GE is well known for developing successive generations of business leaders and many former GE executives become CEOs of major corporations.

Google encourages its innovative culture via employee benefits. Many are free — Wi-Fi-equipped shuttles to/from San Francisco and its Mountain View campus, doctors, meals, clothes washers and driers (and detergent), and flu shots. Other conveniences include car wash, oil change, climbing wall, lap pool, volley ball, ping pong (and other table games), massages, scooters, language study, lecture series, notaries, and an annual ski trip (all expenses paid). Google also makes payments for referring hires, having babies, and buying hybrid cars.

Firms as different as HCL Technologies (outsourced software developer) and In-N-Out Burger (INOB) (200+ outlets/southwest U.S.) succeed by putting employees first. INOB emphasizes employee training; above-market pay; and retirement, healthcare, and other benefits to earn greater per-store sales than McDonald's and Burger King.

Managing human resources is especially important in services firms, where employee/customer interaction is constant and ongoing. Major hotel chains like Four Seasons, Marriott, and Ritz-Carlton place particular emphasis on their employees.[2] Singapore Airlines 40-year leading reputation among long-distance air travelers is primarily based on cabin service delivered by *Singapore Girls*. Virgin Atlantic has a similar capability and has achieved considerable success on North Atlantic routes. CEO Sir Richard Branson firmly believes that employees come first; if Virgin treats its employees right, they will treat Virgin's customers right.

> ### *Marketing Question*
> In your experience, which firms do the best job of managing human resources? How did this translate into marketplace success? Define key objectives and success for HR.

OPERATIONS AND THE SUPPLY CHAIN

Internal operations and the supply chain are important areas for the firm to improve its external focus, especially in services where it touches the customer most often. All contemporary approaches to teaching operations systems design work back from the marketplace. The operations system is a great place for the firm to secure differential advantage.[3]

Alcoa innovated its operating processes, including forecasting customer needs, and created advantages unlike other sheet metal providers. A senior executive explained how Alcoa integrates operations and the supply chain:

> "We spent a great deal of time trying to get accurate bills of material from our customers. It's very difficult in aerospace because customers don't think of airplanes in terms of extruded feet or pieces of sheet [metal]. They think in terms of tail assemblies, or speed brakes, or section 39 on a fuselage. After four years, we now have a bill of materials that is probably 80 percent accurate. So I can push a button and tell you how much product goes into a 757. We can tell the revenues and profitability. We supplement with an array of outside data to get a handle on billed rates and forecasting. We use five different sources, and supplement with a couple of good consultants to alert us to potential changes in the bills of material. Airplanes are not static. Even if they are specified and the airworthiness certificate is built on a certain structure, the structure can change. We then pull together a five-year estimate by quarter — volume, product types, Alcoa share, and so forth. Then we can do facilities planning and capacity planning and get ahead on investments. Our investment cycle is rarely less than 12 to 24 months.

> "To make the system work day-by-day, we bring customer personnel into our plant, and we go to their plant. We see how their process is constructed and what information they're using. We usually do a lot of work to match the systems. We use a combination of electronic and paper kanbans. Our best illustration is the system we constructed for Ford, American Axle, General Motors, and Dana for drive shafts for rear-wheel drive cars. They give us a piece-by-piece pull signal Monday morning. We build the requirement in truckload quantities. They send trucks in, starting at 2:00 on Wednesday. We have the exact piece of every spec; there could be 30, 40, or 50 specs in 48 hours. Their truck can't wait more than 30 minutes. We're the only guys in the world that can do it. It used to take us 29 operations and about 9 weeks. Now we do it in 48 hours or less."[4]

KEY IDEA

➤ The most successful externally oriented firms seek functional excellence in:

- Customer service
- Finance
- Human resources
- Operations and the supply chain
- Research and development
- Sales

Integrating these efforts helps implement the market strategy.

Dell started out with a services model, modifying IBM and IBM-compatible PCs, then back-integrated into manufacturing. Michael Dell believed the traditional model — forecast demand, build PCs to meet demand, persuade customers to buy PCs — was ineffective. Dell created an entirely new business model for building customized computers users had already agreed to buy. The demand-driven, direct-to-customer model is very successful. The Dell model minimizes costs and investment throughout the system: No finished goods inventory and just-in-time delivery minimizes supply-side inventory. Dell's high efficiency focus allowed low prices and won Dell a leading global position in PCs. Federal Express (FedEx) also constructed a unique model for shipping time-sensitive packages. FedEx formed its own airline and constructed a giant sorting facility in Memphis that provided consistent overnight package delivery in the continental U.S.

Walmart became the world's largest firm by offering everyday low prices, built on maintaining low costs throughout the supply chain. Walmart partners with suppliers to transmit point-of-sale data to improve forecasting. Walmart benefits from purchasing, manufacturing, and packaging efficiencies, and reduced inventory. Walmart also introduced cross-docking: The supplier drives its truck through a facility containing many Walmart store-delivery trucks and loads them directly. Systems for receiving goods and for managing receivables and payables are paperless and highly efficient. Walmart is renowned for high stock-turns in most product categories and earns significant profits, despite low prices.[5]

RESEARCH AND DEVELOPMENT

R&D breakthroughs have given birth to many great firms. 3M, Apple, DuPont, GlaxoSmithKline (GSK), HP, Intel, Medtronics, Monsanto, and Xerox are just a few that achieved and maintained pre-eminence based on technological strengths. When the firm manages its R&D/Marketing interface well, the impact can be dramatic.

3M has a formidable record for innovation combined with successful, even ingenious, marketing; 3M survived a period of excessive focus on internal process improvement under CEO James McNerney, and has racheted up its innovation performance. Apple has become one of the U.S.'s most valuable firms based on innovation. For many years, Macintosh computers have offered elegant design and functionality. More recently, Apple's innovation machine has produced the iPod, iTunes, iPhone, and iPad. Over the years, DuPont and Monsanto have demonstrated a consistent ability to build markets for many chemical industry products. Today, they compete vigorously in the high-growth genetically modified seed market.

SALES

The sales function rarely reports to marketing yet, as with customer service, selling is critical for implementing the market strategy. Innovation in sales can be the key to success. In B2C, several firms have gained differential advantage via selling efforts. Avon sells cosmetics differently from most cosmetics firms. Avon Ladies are independent businesswomen who have close personal relationships with customers. They consult on cosmetics issues, help customers select the most relevant products, and personally deliver orders. The traditional agency system for selling insurance products is very costly; in Britain, Direct Line's (DL) direct-selling Internet approach for automobile, business, home, and pet insurance allowed it to capture large market shares. In B2B, Chapter 17 shows many B2B firms like IBM and DHL are driving successful growth by innovating with strategic (key) account and global account programs.

INTEGRATED SYSTEMS

Specific functional areas bring success to externally oriented firms. These firms succeed, not because of a single strong suit, but because they integrate efforts from many functions. Toyota is an outstanding example of high performance based on three integrated systems:

- **Research and development.** Toyota's process begins with extensive research into customer demographics and lifestyle trends. These data feed into Toyota's four research and design studios in Japan (1), U.S. (2), and Europe (1). These studios compete for the best design in a target market.

- **Manufacturing.** Toyota's process is perhaps the world's best-known, most-discussed, and most-praised industrial operation. The Toyota system has spawned many books and is a model of Total Quality Management (TQM). Boeing and Airbus copied the Toyota system.

- **Dealer management and customer service.** Toyota invests heavily in its dealers and customer service. All Toyota's franchised dealers must adhere to a strong set of guidelines; if not, Toyota does not renew agreements. When Toyota introduced the Lexus, it set up a completely independent dealer system. The first Lexus cars had a minor quality problem; for every car, Toyota fixed the problem, filled the gas tank, and returned a clean car. For Lexus' first ten years, each management employee telephoned four customers per month to gain real-time data on the car and dealer.[6]

Notwithstanding problems with unexpected acceleration in some cars, Toyota's excellence on multiple integrated dimensions made it the world's most profitable carmaker. Toyota products span the entire range of automotive offerings.

A FRAMEWORK FOR DEVELOPING AN EXTERNAL ORIENTATION

"Culture eats strategy for breakfast." — Peter F. Drucker

To achieve success in increasingly competitive markets, the firm must focus resources on delivering customer value and securing differential advantage. In the final analysis, nothing else matters. The firm must keep resources aligned with the ever-changing environment. Continual realignment is difficult, but some firms do it better than others. The most successful develop a culture of an **external orientation**.

Chapter 1 introduced the idea of organizational orientations; we described the external orientation and various **internal orientations**.[7] Firms with internal orientations focus on various internal functional needs, and are often excessively regimented and rule-based. But the externally oriented firm looks outward, focusing on customers, competitors, and broader environmental variables. This firm knows that current products and processes are the key reasons for past and present success. But it also knows the external environment is always changing and that it must make internal changes in organization structure, systems and processes, and human resources to adjust to new market realities.[8] Rather than fearing change, the externally oriented firm knows that change is inevitable. The externally oriented firm welcomes change as a challenge and understands new opportunities are the firm's *lifeblood*.

It's one thing to recognize the value of an external orientation; it's quite another to change the organization over objections by those preferring the *status quo*. To successfully make the transformation requires committed leadership, typically fewer management layers, new systems and processes and ways of working (like empowering customers in product development),[9] building new capabilities, and changes in mind-sets and behavior.[10] Top management exhortations are insufficient; successful implementation of an external orientation demands middle management support and work-group experts with informal power.[11]

Some successful corporate leaders believe instilling an external orientation is a critical part of their job and institute change-management processes to accomplish the task.[12] Intel owes its success to addressing environmental discontinuities, like legal and regulatory issues, and competitive challenges. When asked about his most important achievement, former CEO Andy Grove said: "It's that I've played a significant part in developing the work environment and culture at the company and with the directors."[13]

We demonstrate how to develop an external orientation. Figure 21.1 shows the inverted-pyramid used by externally oriented firms like SAS and Nordstrom's. This framework places customers at the top of the pyramid and reinforces their critical role in firm success.

External Orientation. A senior executive of Valeo (French car-parts manufacturer) stated: "Customers expect seamless delivery, and they don't care how we are organized. We have to work as more of a team and forget our internal battles." Crossing divisional lines, Valeo developed seven principal *domains* — product areas broadly related to automobile functions. Valeo's new organization provided customer coherence in a highly complex structure.[14]

Internal Orientation. Three decentralized business units of a major U.S. healthcare firm separately sold products for use in hospital operating rooms. A corporate group decided the firm should develop a single integrated offer to better satisfy customer needs. Senior business-unit managers agreed with the rationale but could not make it work — too many entrenched interests, especially around pricing.

Marketing Question

If you had been on the U.S. healthcare firm's management team, how could you have made this initiative successful?

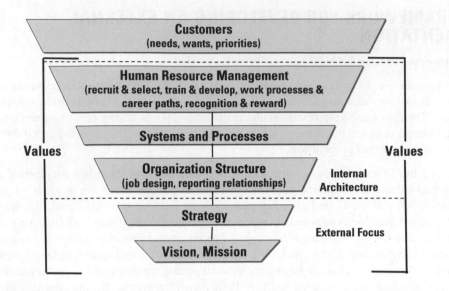

FIGURE 21.1

A FRAMEWORK FOR DEVELOPING AN EXTERNAL ORIENTATION (EO)

VALUES

A company's values — what it stands for and what it believes in — are crucial to its competitive success.

— Robert Haas, Chairman and former CEO Levi Strauss[15]

Values are a common set of beliefs that guide the behavior of all organization members. Some values are **hard**, like profitability and market share; other values are **soft**, like customer pre-eminence, integrity, respect for others, and trust. Many firms use customer-focused value statements to emphasize the importance of building a customer-focused culture.

Values can be integral to firm success: Investment firm KKR (Kohlberg, Kravis, Roberts) employs accountability, excellence, fortitude, innovation, integrity, respect, sharing, and teamwork. Certainly, misplaced (or absent) values can lead to firm failures. Arthur Andersen, Enron, HealthSouth, Tyco, and Worldcom are recent examples of firms losing their way. Previously, firm values were often unstated; today, many firms are rethinking corporate values and making them explicit and public (advertising, annual reports, websites). Many firms' values explicitly emphasize customers[16]:

- **Apple.** "Apple values are the qualities, customs, standards, and principles that the company believes will help it and its employees succeed. They are the basis for what we do and how we do it. Taken together, they identify Apple as a unique company. The values that govern our business conduct [are]: *Empathy for Customers/Users, Aggressiveness/ Achievement, Positive Social Contribution, Innovation/Vision, Individual Performance, Team Spirit, Quality/Excellence, Individual Reward, Good Management.*"

- **Procter & Gamble.** "We show respect for all individuals; the interests of the company and the individual are inseparable; we are strategically focused in our work; innovation is the cornerstone of our success; we are externally focused; we value personal mastery; we seek to be the best; mutual interdependency is a way of life."[17]

- **Seagate.** "People, customer success, excellence, innovation, teamwork, openness, social responsibility and sustained profitability — focus on our long-term perspective for leadership and prosperity. These values should inspire us to a level of excellence that maximizes value for customers, business partners, and shareholders, while supporting our employees and the communities in which our employees live and work. These values are intended to be a foundation to guide our decisions. They are reflected in our business objectives and they represent the global standard by which all of our individual and collective actions will be measured."

- **Williams-Sonoma.** "We are in the business of enhancing the quality of our customers' life at home. To succeed, we live by a short, but important list of values — people first, customers, quality, shareholders."

Merrill Lynch and L'Oreal show the importance of values, but with different results.

Winthrop H. Smith Jr., son of a Merrill Lynch founder, blames Merrill's billions of dollars in subprime related losses on CEO Stan O'Neal's failure to embrace or articulate five core principles underlying Merrill's culture — primacy of client's interests, respect for colleagues, teamwork, responsibility to the community, and integrity.[18]

L'Oreal is highly successful: "At L'Oreal, everyone shares a few common values — that's the heart of our culture. Everyone is passionate. We obsess with product, like touching products, feeling products. We're all very flexible, because we really change. We say that everyone's a product manager, even the CEO. The product only becomes successful by confronting opinions ... and changing the concept 25 times and the packaging 25 times. If you're not flexible, you'll be miserable here. We all share the same values but there's a very high premium placed on diversity, of different personality types and quirks. Our people are not stamped out of a mold."[19]

FIGURE 21.2

THE JOHNSON & JOHNSON CREDO

We believe our first responsibility is to the doctors, nurses and patients,
to mothers and fathers and all others who use our products and services.
In meeting their needs everything we do must be of high quality.
We must constantly strive to reduce our costs
in order to maintain reasonable prices.
Customers' orders must be serviced promptly and accurately.
Our suppliers and distributors must have an opportunity to make a fair profit.

We are responsible to our employees,
the men and women who work with us throughout the world.
Everyone must be considered as an individual.
We must respect their dignity and recognize their merit.
They must have a sense of security in their jobs.
Compensation must be fair and adequate,
and working conditions clean, orderly and safe.
We must be mindful of ways to help our employees
fulfill their family responsibilities.
Employees must feel free to make suggestions and complaints.
There must be equal opportunity for employment, development
and advancement for those qualified.
We must provide competent management,
and their actions must be just and ethical.

We are responsible to the communities in which we live and work
and to the world community as well.
We must be good citizens — support good works and charities
and bear our fair share of taxes.
We must encourage civic improvements and better health and education.
We must maintain in good order the property we are privileged to use,
protecting the environment and natural resources.

Our final responsibility is to our stockholders.
Business must make a sound profit.
We must experiment with new ideas.
Research must be carried on, innovative programs developed
and mistakes paid for.
New equipment must be purchased, new facilities provided
and new products launched.
Reserves must be created to provide for adverse times.
When we operate according to these principles,
the stockholders should realize a fair return.

Values statements are more likely to *stick* if employees actively participate in their development; they are worthwhile only if embraced by the entire firm. Figure 21.2 shows J&J's credo: The credo epitomizes an external orientation that focuses on customer well-being and drives executive behavior. When Tylenol tablets were laced with cyanide, J&J followed its credo by immediately withdrawing Tylenol to protect customers from potential harm.[20]

An important component for installing an external orientation is developing *artifacts* that exemplify an external orientation. Included are *stories* — examples of employees performing exceptional behavior like providing *over-the-top* customer service; *arrangements* — like "an open and friendly entrance and welcome area"; *rituals* — like customer events and awards for employees' customer-oriented behavior; and *language* — externally versus internally focused.[21]

VISION, MISSION, STRATEGY

All framework elements must reflect and reinforce firm commitment to an external orientation. Many organizational transformations start at the bottom of the pyramid, developing (or reworking) external elements discussed in Chapter 7:

- **Vision.** A description of the firm's ideal future state — an impressionistic picture of what the future should be. Good vision statements set a broad direction — they should inspire employees for the long run. A good vision statement is not too broad, nor is it too specific nor easily achievable.
- **Mission.** Guides the firm's search for market opportunities more directly. A well-developed mission keeps the firm focused in a limited arena where success is likely.
- **Strategy.** The firm's game plan for the market, pointing the way to firm actions. The market strategy specifies what the firm is trying to achieve, which segments it will target for effort, and how it will position itself in those segments.

Decisions about vision, mission, and strategy are very important; hence, *Managing Marketing in the 21st Century* has spent considerable space on them. Active involvement and/or communications about change sends powerful signals throughout the firm. But communication is one thing; behavior is another. Senior managers must exercise leadership with their behavior — they must *talk the talk*, but also *walk the walk*. The firm's integrity and credibility is at stake and managers must follow through; if not, employees will see hypocrisy.[22]

The more difficult work of culture change lies in aligning the firm's **internal architecture** — organization structure, systems and processes, and HR practices — with vision, mission, and strategy. Customer-oriented values are a good start; unless the culture is externally focused, desire for the *status quo* will undermine firm efforts. Architectural elements must also reflect and shape the culture, but alignment must be systemic. Changing one element, say organization structure, is not enough. Change must pervade all areas. Bob Joss, a serious marketer and former Westpac (large Australian firm) CEO, said, "Too often the popular conception is that strategy and vision are all that matters, 'just get the strategy right and success follows.' Nothing could be further from the truth. In business, execution is the major management challenge. Disciplined daily execution of myriad details must be done correctly to deliver a strategy."[23]

ORGANIZATION STRUCTURE

The firm must design the marketing organization's **internal architecture** so it can make effective and timely decisions. Some traditional structures still have great value, but contemporary approaches are breaking new ground.[24] Table 21.2 is a guide to figures showing traditional and new approaches.

KEY IDEA

➤ Well-thought through vision, mission, and strategy are critical for developing an external orientation.

KEY IDEA

➤ An EO framework comprises:

Values
↓
Vision, Mission, Strategy
↓
Organization Structure
↓
Systems and Processes
↓
Human Resource Management

TABLE 21.2

TRADITIONAL AND
NEWER APPROACHES
TO ORGANIZING
MARKETING

Traditional Approaches	Figure	Newer Approaches	Figure
Functional	21.3	Inclusion	21.7
Product/brand management	21.4	Business process	21.8
Segment-based	21.5	Customer management	21.9
Combined product/brand management-market segment	21.6		

***TRADITIONAL:* FUNCTIONAL MARKETING ORGANIZATION.** In Figure 21.3, the firm places activities like advertising and promotion, distribution, marketing administration, marketing research, and new product development in a marketing department. Marketing is usually separate from the sales force and functions like accounting, human resources, production, and R&D.

Reporting relationships vary by firm and industry. Most commonly, heads of sales and marketing report to a Marketing and Sales SVP. One variant is separate sales and marketing VPs reporting to a more senior level. But conflict between marketing — long-term focus — and sales — short-term focus — may result; it is only resolvable at high organizational level (C-Suite). One CEO commented: "The trouble with this company is that the functional elevators don't stop until they reach the 20th floor. I'm going to make sure that they stop much lower down!"

Functional organizations tend to work best when markets and products are homogeneous (like many small firms). Sometimes, functional organizations linger too long in growing firms. As the firm becomes more complex, it needs specialized responsibility for either products or markets. Firms structured as product/brand management, and market segment, organizations (below) try to solve this problem.

FIGURE 21.3

THE FUNCTIONAL
MARKETING
ORGANIZATION

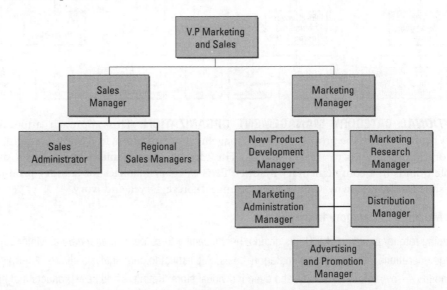

***TRADITIONAL:* PRODUCT/BRAND MANAGEMENT ORGANIZATION.** P&G developed the original product management organization to provide a product/brand focus.[25] Figure 21.4 shows a well-documented example at General Foods (Altria). Product/brand managers develop market plans for products and brands; they are responsible for volume, market share, and/or profits, but do not control all inputs. In many FMCG firms, product/brand managers compete for resources like promotional dollars and sales force time. Sometimes firms view internal brand-manager competition as healthy because it spurs extra effort, but it may undermine a coherent product-line strategy.

Product/brand managers' general management orientation provides a clear career path, but this organization structure has two significant problems: Potentially destructive internal brand manager competition (as noted) and brand manager turnover. Many firms move brand managers rapidly so they gain experience; also, well-trained brand managers are attractive hires for many firms. But incoming brand managers often want to make their *mark* on the brand by modifying brand strategy. Lack of coherence and a disjointed long-run strategy may result:

> One year, P&G's *Bounty* (paper towel) lost 1.8 market share points — $49 million revenues — in supermarkets, drugstores, and major discounters. Newly aggressive Kimberly Clark (KC) had introduced softer, more absorbent Scott *with ridges*. KC increased advertising in target markets; Bounty reduced advertising by 30 percent; KC prices increased 6 percent, Bounty increased 9 percent. KC also ran more frequent price promotions and had greater salesperson presence in supermarkets. The core problem (acknowledged by P&G): Bounty had four brand managers in 18 months.

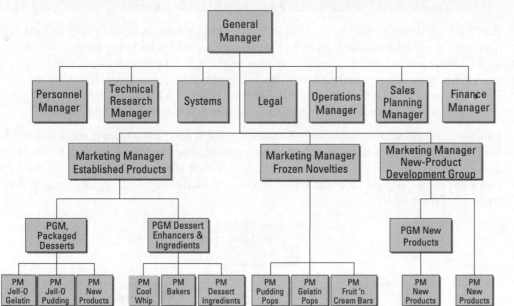

FIGURE 21.4[26]

THE PRODUCT/BRAND MANAGEMENT MARKETING ORGANIZATION

KEY IDEA

➤ An EO framework comprises:

Values
↓
Vision, Mission, Strategy
↓
Organization Structure
↓
Systems and Processes
↓
Human Resource Management

TRADITIONAL: CATEGORY MANAGEMENT ORGANIZATION. This approach attempts to address problems with the product/brand management organization, in part by leveraging success from strong brands to weaker brands. The **category management** organization directs multiple brands in a complementary manner. P&G category manager for laundry products is responsible for Tide, Downy, Gain, Cheer, Bounce, Febreze, Dryel, and Ivory.

New Meaning to Category Management

Increasing retailer power in FMCG has given a new meaning to *category management*. Major supermarkets now manage operations on a category-by-category basis. Sophisticated data analysis allows determining individual product profitability — by region, state, city, and even individual store. Retailers add new products and brands only if they help achieve category goals.

In the U.S., some retailers outsource product category management to suppliers. Retailers charge the chosen supplier with increasing category revenues and profits. Mostly (but not always) the retailer appoints the market-leading supplier as *category captain*. This supplier gains privileged access to retail sales data for all category suppliers, including competitors. Appointments are typically for several years.[27]

TRADITIONAL: MARKET SEGMENT ORGANIZATION. The market segment organization is more externally focused than the preceding options; managers are responsible for individual market segments. The market segment organization may overlie other marketing and sales functions. (Typically, the rest of the firm is functionally organized.) IBM organizes by industry:

Business sector managers are responsible for broad industry categories like manufacturing, banking and financial services, transportation, and retailing. Figure 21.5 shows Ciba Chemicals' evolution from a product management organization to a market segment organization.

FIGURE 21.5

**THE MARKET
SEGMENT
ORGANIZATION**

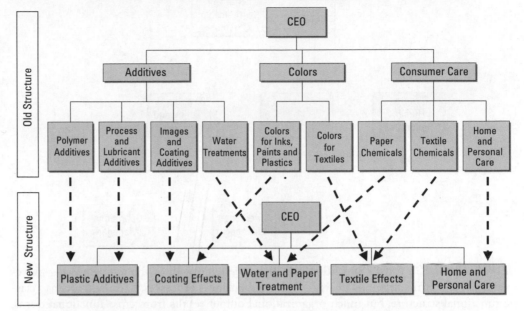

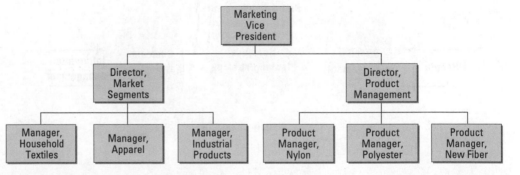

***TRADITIONAL:* COMBINED PRODUCT/BRAND MANAGEMENT AND MARKET SEGMENT ORGANIZATION.** Product/brand and market segment organizations each omit a crucial dimension. In product/brand organizations, no one is specifically responsible for market segments: In the market segment organization, no one is specifically responsible for individual products/brands. Figure 21.6 shows how a synthetic fibers firm incorporated both dimensions. Segment managers were responsible for end-use markets like household textiles, apparel, and industrial products. Product managers were responsible for individual product lines like nylon, polyester, and new fibers.[28]

FIGURE 21.6

**THE COMBINED
PRODUCT/BRAND
MANAGEMENT-
MARKET SEGMENT
ORGANIZATION**

***NEWER:* INCLUSION ORGANIZATION.** Figure 21.7 shows the newer inclusion organization; the firm groups many activities under marketing. As one marketing practitioner said, "Marketing is everything, and everything is marketing." Pillsbury adopted this organization early, but found *brute force* unsatisfactory for developing an external perspective.[29] British Airways (BA) adopted a similar approach; BA recognized that Operations controlled two critical customer requirements — safety and schedule reliability. BA restructured so that Operations reported to Marketing; indeed, 80 percent of employees reported through Marketing. The **inclusion organization** may work well in service businesses, where marketing and operations are difficult to distinguish, but is not appropriate for all firms.

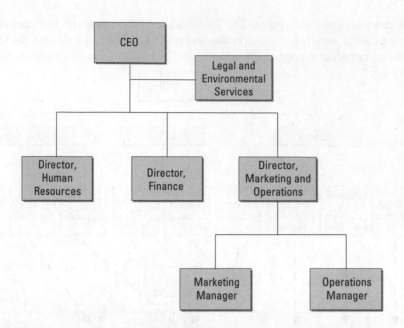

FIGURE 21.7

THE INCLUSION ORGANIZATION

NEWER: **BUSINESS PROCESS ORGANIZATION.** One outgrowth of the re-engineering movement was some firms' attempts to organize around **business processes.**[30] The firm retains a classic functional structure, but much organizational output results from cross-functional teams. Figure 21.8 shows how a British-based Unilever subsidiary reorganized on this basis. Marketing's major responsibilities are brand development, innovation, and related strategic tasks. The sales force conducts operational marketing tasks like trade promotions.

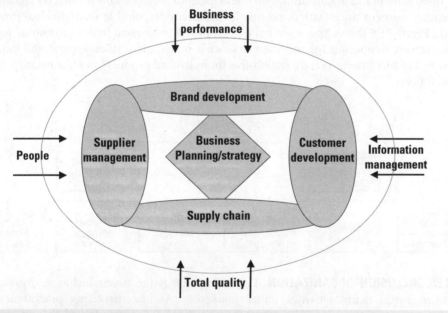

FIGURE 21.8

THE BUSINESS PROCESS ORGANIZATION — EXAMPLE FROM A UNILEVER SUBSIDIARY

Statements by senior executives at leading firms[31]**:**

Consumer durables. "The key to our organizational transformation has been the reorganization of our business units around distinct teams that serve our various customer segments. Each team is cross-functional and has full P&L responsibility. ... it hasn't been easy, but ... it has meant the difference between failure and success."

Global package goods. "Getting cross-functional coordination right has been our biggest go-to-market objective. We managed around key processes ... Then we embedded those processes into our organization's culture. ... all our incentives are aligned around one strategic plan. ... [W]hen you work in silos, it's tough to be nimble. You need to build your organization around core processes rather than core functions."

NEWER: **CUSTOMER-MANAGEMENT ORGANIZATION.** This organization focuses specifically on customers. We expect this organizational form to become more popular as firms become increasingly aware of the customer lifetime value (CLV) concept and the importance of customer retention — Chapter 2. CRM systems that allow firms to identify customers by name, buying patterns, and history support this organization.[32]

Figure 21.9 shows how the **customer management organization** (CMO) turns the product/brand management organization (PBMO) on its side.[33] In PBMO, brands (B1 ... B4 ... Bn) are pillars; all other functional activities serve the brands. In CMO, customer portfolios (CP1 ... CP4 ... CPn) are pillars; brands and other functions like customer service, marketing research, and R&D serve customer portfolios. Customer managers, reporting to a chief customer officer (CCO), have responsibility and authority for customer portfolios; brand management is almost a staff function.[34] Product/brand managers continue to manage brand assets, but support customer managers by developing products/brands to increase customer lifetime value. In CMO, traditional metrics shift: Product profitability to customer profitability; current sales to customer lifetime value; brand equity to customer equity; and market share to customer equity share.[35]

A specific CMO advantage is increased customer contact; hence, customer managers gain significant customer insight. The blinders that occur in PBMOs diminish,[36] but implementing CMO typically requires significant organizational change[37]:

Jorgen Centerman, ABB's incoming CEO, restructured ABB to respond more quickly to customer needs. Within weeks, Centerman replaced four industrial divisions with four new customer segments — process industries; manufacturing and consumer industries; utilities; oil, gas, and petrochemicals, two product-based divisions, and a new organization to manage the corporate transformation. Based on his vision of *collaborative commerce* between suppliers, manufacturers, and customers, Centerman's goal was to achieve "highly flexible mass customization," by creating flexible links with customers, through the Internet and traditional channels. Centerman also strove for a seamless and coherent flow of internal information-technology systems within ABB.[38]

Faced with a serious performance crisis, British Gas (BG) found significant profitability variation by customer; BG formed a new segment-driven organization. *Premier Energy* focused on good paying, heavy users by offering additional services and relocation assistance. *Energy First* addressed cost reduction in serving lower-use customers who settled bills with pre-paid cards. *Pay-As-You-Go Energy* served late payers by developing expertise in managing receivables. BG improved financial performance by increasing customer retention and reducing bad debts.[39]

Microsoft faced several problems — slow decision-making, defection of talented employees, and increasingly tough competition. Microsoft redeveloped its vision and shifted to a customer-focused organization. Individual organizational units became responsible for customer groups — corporate customers, knowledge workers, home PC buyers, game players, software developers, web surfers, and cybershoppers. Said founder Bill Gates: "The new structure puts the customer at the center of everything we do by reorganizing our business divisions by customer segment rather than along product lines."[40]

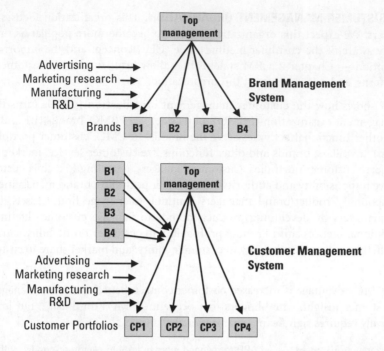

FIGURE 21.9

THE TRANSITION FROM BRAND MANAGEMENT TO CUSTOMER MANAGEMENT

More B2C firms will adopt the CMO as they become able to identify and understand individual customers. Most B2B firms already identify customers; hence, customer management is becoming more widespread. Many firms build strategic (key) account management programs; strategic (key) account managers (SAMs [KAMs]) develop and manage relationships with the most important current and potential customers — Chapter 17. Initially these programs were domestic.[41] Today, firms with global customers are developing global account programs; global account managers (GAMs) develop and manage relationships with key global customers.[42]

The firm may implement CMO at the corporate level or in individual business units, but there are trade-offs. At corporate, customer management may be ineffective because account managers do not have deep understanding across the firm's many businesses. Focus at the business level only, and the firm may be unable to develop an integrated corporate-wide offer:

> Lucent's business-unit organization pushed authority and responsibility deep in the firm. But getting business units to cooperate was difficult. Several businesses developed variations of the *softswitch* telecommunications product.[43] One customer said that he was "confused on what Lucent is actually offering, because I've heard different descriptions of the same solution from different Lucent teams."[44]

SYSTEMS AND PROCESSES

All organizations use systems and processes to produce organizational outputs; we can array them along a continuum. One pole embraces **hard systems**. Hard systems typically require capital equipment and are often computer-based, like automatic teller machines, Internet portals, and auction sites. At the other pole are human-resource-intensive **soft systems**, like retail customer service desks. Many customer interactions involve a combination of hard and soft systems. All systems can be improved.

HARD SYSTEMS. Hard systems improve operational efficiency and reduce costs. But they can also contribute to creating an external orientation, improve marketing effectiveness, optimize sales force efforts, and help secure differential advantage. Perhaps the most popular hard systems in major firms are enterprise resource planning (ERP). ERP software contains customer-focused modules and attempts to integrate many departments and functions across the firm.

KEY IDEA

➤ The firm's organizational structure should support an integrated marketing approach.

KEY IDEA

➤ Systems and processes help produce organizational outputs and provide consistency to customers.

ERP uses a single computer platform serving each department's needs and makes information available to others. Hard systems are also the core of supply-chain management, leading to better supply/demand matching, reduced inventories, fewer stockouts, and reduced customer disappointment. Benefits from hard systems are:

- **Customer information.** Customer information is more readily available and widely distributed; hence, employees better understand customer needs. At insurance firms like USAA, hard systems are essential to success. USAA's service associates have access to full client records and are prompted to ask customers about other financial services. A customer telephone call about homeowner insurance for a new home triggers a change of address for auto insurance and a profile update.

- **Customer intimacy.** Customer relationship management (CRM) systems — Chapter 2 — provide significant information about customers, including purchase histories, buying patterns, and other firm interactions. These data alleviate the soul-less anonymity of transaction-based markets. Large firms can emulate the high-touch personal service that small firms offer, like the local grocer who knew customers by name and built his business on that basis.

- **Customer effort.** User-friendly computer systems are not just for employees. Many firms use externally facing systems for customers to access product information and order online; customers save time, effort, and risk in purchasing. These systems help the firm get closer to customers and reinforce the brand. FedEx package tracking and customer portals, and customer-managed check-in kiosks at many major airlines, are good examples.

> At Dell's website, customers design computers to meet their needs, place orders, and pay. Dell builds the product to order and delivers it promptly. Apple, HP, and IBM have emulated Dell's ordering and production systems.

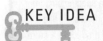
SOFT SYSTEMS. People-based soft systems can also help the firm become more externally oriented. Consider the planning process.[45] Good planning is externally driven: Planning commences by emphasizing insight into the market, customers, competitors, complementers, and the environment in general. Well-developed situation analyses, based on the precepts in Chapters 3, 4, and 5, can force an external orientation, and help deliver solid planning assumptions for developing market strategy. Firms that build market strategy using the Chapter 9 framework necessarily become more externally focused. Try it yourself: Use *The Virgin Marketer* (companion volume) to develop a market strategy for an organization of your choice.

Good planning is collaborative-participative. Good planning involves all functional areas and several management levels. Planning brings people across the firm face-to-face with external realities. Outputs from market planning set firm direction; they also play a critical role in driving an external orientation via monitor and control processes — Chapter 22. A good planning system produces measures that encourage organizational members to look beyond their narrow silos. Marketing executives have a major responsibility to be sensitive to issues concerning sister organizational functions, and behave accordingly. To illustrate, many firm operations departments develop extreme frustration with marketing: "Marketing is hesitant to make predictions and/or makes inaccurate predictions, and provides poor customer feedback; marketing makes unrealistic customer promises about delivery, product features, and new product introductions; and marketing seems indifferent to costs, manufacturing loads, and working capital requirements." Such complaints do not auger well for inter-functional collaboration; if such complaints are justified, marketing must shape up.[46]

MAKING FIRM SYSTEMS AND PROCESSES THE BEST THEY CAN BE. More important than any individual system are methodologies for evolving and integrating systems and processes to drive an external orientation[47]:

- **Best practice transfer.** For any process, some business units, departments, or functions are probably more effective than others. Unfortunately lateral communication within firms is generally poor: Underperforming units may know little about their more effective cousins. A **best practice** system helps identify and transmit superior expertise, knowledge, and processes across the firm. Multi-business, multi-national firms offer rich terrain for identifying best practices. Samsung's system communicates hundreds of best practice examples company-wide. An extensive annual evaluation process identifies the *best of the best*; the winners personally receive awards from Samsung's CEO.

Starbucks shares best practices among U.S. operations and international partners. Founder and CEO Howard Schultz opines, "In some cases the international partners are better than we are, and they're teaching us some things. At our first global conference, 30 countries were represented. We had a mini controlled Starbucks trade show where each country set up a booth to show its best practice."[48]

Pantene entered P&G's portfolio as a shampoo. Later, P&G's Taiwan office made several product changes and successfully repositioned Pantene as a high-end beauty product. Sales took off in Asia Pacific, Latin America, Europe, and the U.S. as P&G's geographic regions adopted Taiwan's best practice. Pantene is now a $3 billion brand.[49]

Some firms assign specific employees as *thought leaders* to identify and promote best practices throughout the organization. At Intel, the *data czar* identifies best-known methods and places them in a knowledge repository. Bain employees write up each consultancy project as a *knowledge module*; these are stored electronically so employees don't *reinvent the wheel* when they encounter similar challenges. Any firm's market success or failure is an opportunity to identify best practices and barriers to best practices.[50] Some firms institutionalize this process by analyzing every customer *win* and *loss*.

Disseminating best practices, expertise, and knowledge across the firm can be a major challenge. Contemporary methods include specially tagged databases for easy search, and collaborative *communities of practice* where experts share information. Other options include regular e-mail communications, *virtual meeting technology* for spur-of-the-moment knowledge-sharing, and meetings designed to break down barriers and facilitate transfer. Other ways to encourage internal communications are physical organization of workspaces and frequent personnel transfer from one organizational unit to another.

Chevron's best practices discovery team identifies groups of people sharing best practices in grassroots networks; the team publicizes their efforts using a *best practice resource map*. Process masters (PMs) identify and disseminate best practices. PMs have no formal authority, but their broad experience generally commands respect.[51]

Xerox shares knowledge through an online *Knowledge Universe* housing a catalog of best practices and at an annual *Teamwork Day*. Xerox uses chat rooms to disseminate best practices and publishes a *Xerox Yellow Pages* to facilitate employee interaction.

- **Benchmarking.** Best practices frequently occur in other firms. **Benchmarking** competitors, customers, suppliers, and firms in other industries, like Xerox's *best-in-class* concept, can improve firm processes.[52] Global fast-food firm Yum! Brands (KFC, Pizza Hut, Taco Bell) identified internal best practice and benchmarked its fierce rival McDonald's. Yum! identified three improvement areas — more healthy food, greater drink variety, and menus matched to time of day. Target implemented *Horizontal Councils* in each merchandising and functional area. Council members meet regularly to share best and worst practices, but senior managers always ask them: "What did you find out from other firms about this?" They must have answers to these questions! The Columbia Initiative in Global Account Management enabled 3M, Citibank, Deloitte & Touche, HP, Lucent, Milliken, Saatchi and Saatchi, and Square D-Schneider to benchmark one another's global account management programs.

- **Re-engineering.** The **re-engineering** approach examines fundamental assumptions about firm systems and processes and seeks alternative approaches for redesign and

Marketing Question

Identify a specific customer service process — like buying a product in a store. Visit several establishments to examine their processes. What improvement suggestions do you have?

improvement. Many organizational processes have a long history, but changes in customers, competitors, technology, and other environmental factors may make them obsolete. The critical question is: Can a new process reduce costs and/or increase customer value? The Internet has driven change in many business processes, like supplier-customer relationships where online communication has superseded telephone calls and faxes for purchase orders, invoices, and shipping notices. Most successful firms have made major commitments to process-based re-engineering:

> IBM Credit's (IBMC) process for financing major computer system sales traditionally involved several steps: A salesperson provided purchase and customer data to a *logger*; the logger created a file and sent it onward; credit specialist — conduct credit check; business practices — request changes in standard loan covenants; pricer — decide the interest rate; administrator — develop formal quote, sent overnight to the salesperson for presentation to the client.
>
> To deliver a quote averaged six days, but sometimes took two weeks. Salespeople could not access application status, and anxious customers switched to competitors. IBMC researched actual work time per application — average, 90 minutes! The file spent much time at in- and out-boxes. IBMC's new *deal structurers* averaged four hours for 90 percent of requests; specialists did the rest. Today, customers input data via the Internet; credit scoring, agreeing on terms and conditions, setting the interest rate and payment terms, and sending out contracts takes a few minutes.[53]

HUMAN RESOURCE MANAGEMENT

KEY IDEA

➤ Hiring experienced marketers, including those at the highest levels, can play a major role in developing an external orientation.

➤ Marketing education helps marketers learn new behaviors that can instill an external perspective.

Many firms trying to become more externally oriented believe the simple mantra — *Happy employees make happy customers*. **Human resource management (HRM)** tools like recruiting, selecting, training, measuring and rewarding, career development, and talent management provide many opportunities to emphasize the importance of an organization-wide external focus. An external orientation should follow from hiring the *right* people and developing and managing career transitions effectively. Chapter 17 discusses HRM tools in the sales management context. Here we focus on two additional areas: marketing executives and non-marketing employees who have critical customer interactions.

MARKETING EXECUTIVES. The ideal marketer is multifaceted, possessing a blend of analytic, creative, and leadership skills. Other positive traits include committed, energetic, hardworking, inspiring, passionate, and talented. A McKinsey study identified several undesirable traits: expensive, faddish, inconsistent, narrow, self-important, uncommercial, undisciplined, and not accountable.[54] The firm should search for individuals with desirable traits (avoiding undesirable) and place them in key marketing roles. Ways to enlarge marketing talent pools are:

KEY IDEA

➤ If the firm hires the *right* people and develops and manages them appropriately, an external orientation should follow.

• **Recruiting and selecting.** Successful hires can play a major role in developing an external orientation. Many internally oriented firms striving for change use this approach. Citibank hired experienced marketing professionals from well-known FMCG firms like P&G and General Mills; these hires had a major impact on Citibank. Intel hired Eric Kim, architect of Samsung's brand growth; Vodafone hired Lance Batchelor, Amazon's chief marketing officer (CMO); Prudential hired Rodger Lawson, driver of Fidelity's growth; HP hired Marty Homlish, architect of SAP's brand improvement; and Sears hired Ron Boire, former President, Consumer Sales Company, Sony Electronics (via Best Buy, Toys "R" Us, and Brookstone). Hiring from direct competitors can be advantageous, but the firm must be concerned about non-compete clauses in executive contracts.

CMOs typically have broad authority to take action but face high performance expectations and increasingly active boards of directors. Whereas internally promoted CMOs are typically familiar with firm culture, organization, and systems and processes, outside hires face a steep learning curve. Outside hires may also face internal resistance when they attempt to change the status quo. The most effective new CMOs *hit the ground running*, starting day 1 with a clear sense of strategic direction (if not fully worked out plans), a new team, and a good understanding of potential internal challenges.[55]

For many years, the marketing job at GE comprised (at best) sales support, trade shows, and advertising and promotional materials — marketing was not involved in strategic discussions. In the 2000s, seeking internal growth, GE developed a new marketing framework comprising principles, people, and process. GE recognized four key roles for marketing leaders: *instigator* — think strategically and challenge the status quo; *innovator* — identify opportunities to move GE forward; *integrator* — work across multiple organizations and functions; and *implementer* — make stuff happen (typically without line authority). GE established CMO positions in all businesses and at corporate, sourced CMOs from both within and outside GE, and doubled the number of marketers to 5,000. GE identified eight major capability areas for marketing — strategy & innovation, branding & communications, sales force effectiveness, new world skills, market knowledge, segmentation & targeting, value creation & pricing, and commercial activation — each with detailed definitions requiring specific skills. Each marketing team completes an annual self-assessment on 35 skills embracing 140 definitions to identify areas of strength and improvement opportunities.[56]

- **Training and development.** In-depth marketing education, for new hires and the full cadre of senior and middle managers, can help embed an external orientation throughout the firm — BMS (Opening Case). Well-designed professional education helps build and embed new behaviors, orients executives to firm culture, and facilitates team building. The author has directed many **action-learning** programs for marketing executives; participants bring their own marketing problems, then hammer through analysis, alternatives, and solutions in a collaborative atmosphere.

  Pfizer augments education and leadership training via a sophisticated computer-based human relations information system (HRIS) including a learning-management component accessible through an easy-to-use portal. Any marketer (new or experienced) anywhere in the world, can click on a personal development plan comprising job roles, competencies, and online tools. The plan offers a recommended stream of training information about Pfizer's many marketing processes, from "How do I execute a plan of action for sales material?" to "How do I do DTC [direct-to-consumer] advertising?" Pfizer employees can access the full set of learning, guidance, principles, and prophecies. (And managers can check progress!)[57]

> **Marketing Question**
>
> What firms should have customer-focused training for employees? What sort of training do you think they should have?

From a *McKinsey Quarterly* interview: "What would be your advice to a new chief marketing officer?"

Alex Myers, Senior Vice President, Carlsberg: "Measurement and accountability, not creativity, should be at the core. And before you talk, listen to other functions, to other people internally, to consumers, to customers. Before you start driving in a new direction, make sure the fact base is solid. But don't forget to be passionate about brands and about what the consumer wants."[58]

NON-MARKETING PROFESSIONALS. To become a truly externally oriented organization, all employees (not only marketers) must become externally focused. Customer-responsive employees are critical for managing the customer experience, especially in services:

- **Recruiting and selecting employees.** Firms as diverse as L.L. Bean, Hyatt, Nordstrom's, Singapore Airlines, and Walmart work hard at selecting and *onboarding* new employees. Southwest Airlines even includes loyal customers in the new-hire interviewing process. Some B2B firms allow customers to choose their strategic account managers from several qualified candidates; others regularly recruit customer employees to gain greater customer insight.

- **Training and development.** Training and development present great opportunities for shaping employee perspective, including addressing customer concerns and complaints. SAS and British Airways were widely praised for educating *all* employees on how to treat customers. Better employee/customer-interaction improved market share and profits; when each firm's focus shifted to cost reduction, performance deteriorated on both

> **KEY IDEA**
>
> ➤ An EO framework comprises:
>
> Values
> ↓
> Vision, Mission, Strategy
> ↓
> Organization Structure
> ↓
> Systems and Processes
> ↓
> **Human Resource Management**

measures. Yum! broke down barriers among brands and secured implementation of three initiatives (p. 534) by training top managers, then subordinates, right down the chain of command. Many firms modify training courses to include customer participation; others implement internal branding programs — Chapter 11. Customers serve as participants, speakers, and/or facilitators in the learning process; they may even participate in the annual employee review process.[59] More broadly, Google and P&G employees participate in each other's training programs.

> In-N-Out Burger, a 200-plus restaurant chain in the southwest U.S., exceeds Burger King and McDonald's in per-store sales. In-N-Out pays employees more than the going rate; managers earn over $100,000 annually. Employees with over one year's service are eligible to attend In-N-Out University.[60]

KEY IDEA

➤ Critical human resource practices for developing an external orientation include:

- Recruiting and selecting employees
- Training and development
- Measurement and reward systems
- Work processes

- **Measurement and reward systems.** Measurement and reward systems are critical for aligning employees to the firm's external thrust. Asking employees to be externally oriented is insufficient; the firm must hold them accountable. Nordstrom's entered the Cleveland market and was immediately successful, mainly because it outshone competitors in customer service. But many employees had previously worked for competitors like Dillard's, Kaufman's, JCPenney, and Sears! A major part of Nordstrom's success is due to an HRM development model that inculcates values and sets high standards for employee behavior.

Measurement systems should be tightly linked to reward systems. When customer-focused measures drive incentive compensation, the external orientation effort has real teeth. Managers are often skeptical about basing take-home pay on survey findings, but Microsoft and Xerox each report excellent results using customer satisfaction measures. Good survey design, rigorously tested items, and competent and independent data collectors reduce skepticism. At Bloomberg, every employee, including the janitor and the person who stocks the kitchen, receives incentive compensation based on terminal sales. *Equity equivalence certificates* get everyone's attention; they know Bloomberg's core objective is to sell terminals.

As a caution, required performance must be attainable. If targets are set too high, executives may engage in unethical and possibly illegal actions:

> Sunbeam chairman "Chainsaw" Al Dunlap was widely criticized for setting excessively high performance targets. Required revenues and profits were "so outrageous, they were ridiculous." To retain their jobs and stock options, managers used several types of aberrant behavior — withheld commissions from independent sales representatives, did not pay bills, and forced vendors to accept partial payment. They also booked future orders early by offering heavily discounted prices and extended credit.[61] Dunlap was fired and settled SEC charges for $700K.

KEY IDEA

➤ Managers at all functions and levels should have consistent and regular contact with customers.

- **Work processes.** Except for very small organizations, most firms specialize by function. Some managers making critical customer-based decisions are far removed from the market, like financial managers deciding on credit. Service firms like Avis, Disney, and Hyatt instill a learning culture and ensure that all executives retain customer focus by planning consistent and regular customer contact, regardless of function and position. Some bankers spend a half-day per month as tellers; insurance executives answer policyholder inquiries. Some firms participate in short- and long-term job exchange with customers, like shipping department employees working in customer receiving departments. Many firms sponsor user groups or customer advisory boards where executives hear directly from customers, customers talk to each other, and the firm advises on strategy and product planning decisions. Some firms creatively seek insight into customer lives. At Unilever, cross-functional teams gain simultaneous exposure to customers. Gessy-Lever (Brazil) uses ethnographic research; employees live for several weeks in Rio de Janeiro's favelas (shantytowns).

Top management exposure to customers is especially important. Sir Terry Leahy, former Tesco CEO (world's second most valuable retailer) had a hands-on approach. Two days per week, Leahy visited branches, often unannounced. One week a year, Leahy and other senior executives spent time in stores, working checkouts and stocking shelves. Many B2B firms are introducing *executive-sponsor* programs so that senior executive interface with major customers.

SUSTAINING AN EXTERNAL ORIENTATION

Many industry leaders have stumbled badly and lost their pre-eminent positions. Why? The stories are strikingly similar: The firm originally gained industry leadership by delivering customer value and securing differential advantage. The firm developed and focused resources, core competencies, and expertise. The firm was externally oriented ... but then things changed. Past success began to hold the firm back; it could not sustain an external orientation and adjust to the new reality. We can find old and new leaders in many industries: air freight (Emery, FedEx), automobiles (General Motors, Toyota), home video (Blockbuster, Netflix), imaging systems (Xerox, Canon), and PCs (IBM, Dell, and HP). The original leader had superior technology, scale economies, substantial buying power, and well-established brands. But the new leader introduced a new business model, technology, and/or product design.

Getting everything right is difficult, and a chain is only as strong as its weakest link. For perfect integration of the marketing offer, the firm should execute every *moment of truth* flawlessly. The firm must not merely satisfy customers, it should delight them. Poor performance on some dimensions can overwhelm world-class performance on others. Even Dell has problems:

> Dell sells notebook computers to incoming college students, preconfigured to institutional specifications. One year, a demand spike caught Dell unprepared. Dell broke delivery promises and could not provide accurate delivery information. The recorded voice at customer service insisted that Dell was really concerned about the caller's time. Maybe once or twice, but 40 times!

Sustaining an external orientation is a little easier if the firm understands its challenges:

- **Accounting systems.** The firm must produce data in a form that supports an external perspective. Many firms collect profit only by product; they should also measure profits by customer and/or customer group.

- **Bureaucracy.** As firms grow, departmentalization and task specialization are efficient ways to complete repetitive tasks. But rules and behaviors, reinforced by day-to-day work pressures, become embedded in the organization.[62] As customers, we have all dealt with employees who tell us, "That's not my department" or "You'll have to talk to XYZ about that." Firms must complete day-by-day tasks, but they must also build the agility to serve customers well. Flattening organization structures, increasing employee empowerment, and introducing sensing mechanisms to identify and address market opportunities are proven ways to defeat bureaucracy.

- **Centralization versus decentralization.** Centralizing and standardizing can have great value, especially for cost reduction. But excessive centralization leads to standardized actions, rather than customer *responsiveness*. Key decision-makers are distant from the customer; those with detailed market, customer, and competitor insight play less significant decision-making roles. But excessive decentralization can leave the organization without a clear focus. Deciding which activities are better centralized and which are better decentralized (closer to the customer) is a critical firm challenge.[63]

Multi-business and/or multi-product firms like Sony face a special challenge. Sony's myriad units often act like *warring tribes,* each pursuing its own agenda, rather than cooperating as *Sony United* to better serve customers. Broadly speaking, the firm can break down silos and improve customer focus in three complementary ways: *Coordination* — establish internal structural mechanisms and processes; *cooperation* — use cultural

🔑 **KEY IDEA**

➤ The firm must clearly understand the implications for developing and sustaining an external orientation. Many elements can get in the way.

means, incentives, and power allocation; and *capability* — encourage skill development and define clear career paths for employees.[64]

> Home Depot secured a dominant position in home-improvement retailing by catering to customer needs. Incoming CEO Nardelli consolidated nine regional purchasing centers into a centralized buying operation; costs reduced, but store-level inventory was often mismatched to customer needs. In response, Home Depot recreated a regional merchandising team scattered throughout the U.S., to take into account local requirements in store-level buying decisions.

- **Excessive focus on organizational efficiency.** Many firms work extremely hard to reduce costs by improving organizational efficiency. They use techniques like *Six Sigma* to make continuous incremental improvements in processes — operations and customer service. An organizational culture dominated by *Six Sigma* can become internally focused, less innovative, and drive out behavior addressing external changes.

- **Functional divisions.** Firms develop specialized functions to increase expertise in key areas. But specialization can lead to silo thinking and divisiveness among specialties. Functional heads must recognize the importance of cross-functional cooperation to firm success. Merck's recovery after the Vioxx scandal owes much to *One Merck*, introduced by CEO Clarke. Said Clarke at the time, "We need a more integrated approach. From the time we begin talking about a particular drug franchise, I want researchers, marketers, and manufacturing people sitting in the same room."[65]

- **Functional view of marketing.** The firm must distinguish between marketing as a *philosophy* and marketing as a *department.* The firm that delegates all marketing problems to a marketing department will neither create nor deliver fully integrated offers. Achieving integration demands coordination among many different functional departments.

- **Internal politics.** The CEO and/or business head must actively support institutionalizing an external orientation and frequently communicate this support. If not, some functions will be suspicious of customer-focused initiatives. Jockeying for power and position occurs in all firms; leaders must not allow political concerns to override customer centricity.

- **Inward-oriented marketing departments.** Marketing departments are sometimes their own worst enemies. They implement a not-invented-here (NIH) syndrome that quashes *foreign* ideas and initiatives to *protect their turf.* This problem tends to be most serious in firms with good reputations for marketing expertise, where the marketing department has great political power.

- **Misaligned incentives.** People in organizations do what is *inspected* of them, not what is *expected* of them! They behave in ways that earn rewards. Conflicting and function-specific performance objectives and rewards make it difficult to integrate across functions. The result is often internal conflict and division.

- **Social fabric of institutions.** Firm employees know each other and interact daily. Customers, competitors, and suppliers are occasional *intruders* who interrupt daily life! How often have employees ignored you, the customer, as they chat together, seemingly oblivious of your presence? Or preferred to interrupt their conversation with you to answer a telephone call?

For long-run success, the firm must be responsive yet initiating, learning but not forgetting, understanding of human resources yet demanding of high performance, customer-sensitive yet competitive, and shareholder-value-creating but not short-sighted. Jack Welch lifted performance at an already highly regarded GE to an entirely new level. In one of his more famous exhortations, he stated, "I want managers who manage with their face to the customer and their backside to the CEO!" Jeff Bezos, founder of famed dotcom Amazon describes himself and his organization as "customer obsessed!" And at IBM, customer-focused Lou Gerstner restored the fallen computer giant to its former glory with a *services* vision. Leadership counts! Leaders must spread an external orientation throughout the firm.

KEY IDEA

➤ Yesterday's and today's success sow the seeds of tomorrow's defeat.

KEY MESSAGES

- For long-run success, the firm must develop and sustain an external orientation.

- Firms with an external orientation often build success on functional excellence — customer service, finance, human resources, operations and the supply chain, research and development, and sales.

- The model for developing an external orientation contains external elements — vision, mission, and strategy; and internal architectural elements — organization structure, systems and processes, and HRM practices. Customer-focused values help achieve the necessary alignment.

- The firm can achieve an external orientation only if employees in various functional areas do their jobs with a keen understanding that customers are central to firm success.

- Most action in developing an external orientation rests in the firm's internal architecture.

- Sustaining an external orientation can be very difficult. Past and current firm success contains the seeds of future failure. Inability to adapt leads many previously successful firms to fail.

- The firm must beware of several impediments to sustaining an external orientation: accounting systems, bureaucracy, centralization versus decentralization, excessive focus on organizational efficiency, functional divisions, functional view of marketing, internal politics, inward-oriented marketing departments, misaligned incentives, and the social fabric of institutions.

VIDEOS AND AUDIOS

Developing the Marketing Organization	v2102 🎥	Samuel Moed	Bristol-Myers Squibb
Marketing at GE	v2103 🎥	Steve Liquori	GE
Leading the Marketing Organization	v2104 🎥	William Klepper	Columbia Business School
Marketing Imperative 5	a2101 🎧		

v2102

v2103

v2104

a2101

QUESTIONS FOR STUDY AND DISCUSSION

Can you answer the questions implied by this chapter's learning objectives? Check!

1. Identify three firms that do a great job of being externally oriented — what makes you think they really are externally oriented?

2. Identify three firms that are internally oriented — what makes you think they really are internally oriented? What recommendations do you have for these firms?

3. Think about a time when you decided you would no longer be a customer of a business or other organization. Why did you quit? How could the organization have acted for you to have stayed? How would the organization have to change for you to become a customer again?

4. What markets does your school or college address? How does your school or college organize to address these markets? Is the organization structure appropriate? How would you change it?

5. Go to a local restaurant. Map out the process for addressing customers. Re-engineer this process and develop a better one. Alternatively, complete this task for a product in which you are interested, or this book — *Managing Marketing in the 21st Century*.

IMPERATIVE 6

Monitor and Control

CHAPTER 22

MONITORING AND CONTROLLING FIRM PERFORMANCE AND FUNCTIONING

To access O-codes, go to **www.ocodes.com**

LEARNING OBJECTIVES

When you have completed this chapter, you will be able to:

- Describe critical elements in the monitor-and-control process.
- Implement key principles of the monitor-and-control process.
- Measure input, intermediate, and output variables.
- Monitor and control firm performance versus objectives.
- Monitor and control firm functioning.
- Understand and recognize success factors.

OPENING CASE: SONY ELECTRONICS

Sony has been a consumer electronics leader for many years. Ron Boire, President Sony Electronics Sales, talked about Sony's careful focus on well-chosen measures and how it uses them to secure the behavior it requires. "Sony is really driven by the concept of, 'If you can't measure it, you can't do it.' Sometimes that's straightforward; sometimes it's very complicated. Interactions that Sony sales-people have with our retail trade channel customers are a good example.

"With national customers like Best Buy, Sears, Target, and Walmart or a strategically important regional chain, we used to do classic sales compensation. Each salesperson had a sales budget, and we measured salespeople performance against budget. If you had a budget target of $1 million for a product category, and you sold at $1.1 million, you did a great job and you made a good bonus. Regardless of what was stuck in the barn at the end of the month or the end of the year. Regardless of whether or not they could pay for it. Regardless of whether you delivered it to them on time.

"*Today, we base up to 70 percent of our inventory management/asset management group's compensation, and 50 percent of our salespeople's compensation, on customer scorecards. We agree on metrics individually with each national and strategic customer. Most focus on simple things like on-time delivery, percent in-stock, forecast accuracy, and gross margin return on inventory [GMROI] — the key retail performance metric. To set these metrics we ask each customer: 'What's important to you? What are your targets? What are your strategic concerns?' Best Buy's current target is 90 percent on-time delivery, plus or minus one day, and 95 percent in stock. We may or may not hit that metric due to a variety of reasons, but everybody has the same goal in mind. Depending on their size, we track retailers either monthly or weekly. And our salespeople are bonus compensated twice a year based on their customer scorecards.*

"*As the saying goes, 'People do what they're paid to do.' When you change the basis of people's paychecks, it really is remarkable how fast they change their behavior. We've seen a tremendous shift in the behavior of the organization, and a very positive reaction from the marketplace. No one else in the consumer electronics industry is doing this. And in most industries that our customers do business in — appliances, software, consumer electronics, or computers — all sales forces are compensated on sell-in. It's revolutionary in consumer electronics for a salesperson to say, 'No, I won't take your purchase order, because you have too much inventory.' Everybody talks about aligning with your customers, but if you're paying your salespeople to stuff the box you can't be aligned — it's impossible.*"

Sony wants to know customer profitability. Boire continued, "*We measure customer profitability from a contribution margin perspective. Once you get past that sell-in mentality, you can focus on simple measurements like contribution margin; incremental contribution margin is the best ongoing measure of a marketing relationship with our trade channel customers. Marketing holds the P&Ls on these major customer accounts, but the only thing we load in are direct costs attributable to that customer; we include the sales team and all its funding, but we take nothing from headquarters. We look at the contribution margin in dollars per customer; we project mid-range contributions some years ahead, and we calculate a net present value [NPV] with a conservative termination value.*

"*Sometimes we have one or two customers that are in financial difficulties. And we ask, what's the contribution margin of this customer? If they go away, the fixed cost at headquarters doesn't go away. But there may be $30 million in contribution margin that goes away. The contribution dollars and the NPV give you the measures to say, 'What should we invest in this customer to try to help them stay healthy?' We have one of those customers now. We've hired outside consultants to go in as a crisis management team to work with them on process re-engineering. We're working with them on inventory and supply-chain management. We're working with them on advertising productivity. And the at-risk number in our minds is this annual contribution margin. If we invest up to that point and the customer turns the corner, we're not going to claim sole credit for saving them, but we certainly didn't help them go down, right? On a day-to-day basis, this grounds management as to the relative value of any customer. Because we can say, 'You know what? The net present value of this customer is $600 million. That's what this relationship is worth.'*

"*Outside the consumer electronics channel we have less influence. A major national multi-category retailer that's in difficulties, we're such a small percentage of their total business that it wouldn't matter what we did. What we can do in those cases is manage our risk well, as we did with Kmart. We called the day Kmart would file for bankruptcy protection. We predicted it well in advance. We took some losses, but we managed our receivables with Kmart probably better than anyone in the trade.*"[1]

CASE QUESTION

Compare and contrast Sony's old measurement-and-control system with its new system. Suppose a firm with which you are familiar made this sort of change. What implementation problems would you anticipate? How would you deal with them?

Lack of a monitor-and-control system can put the most successful firm at risk. Starbucks (Opening Case: Chapter 1) was a highly successful fast-growing firm: 2007 — net profits, $673K; share price high, $40. In 2008, net profits dropped to $316K, share price reached $7. Said a Starbucks executive, "When the numbers went south, we couldn't even make an educated guess about why. We had no way to get details about sales, no way to capture customer opinion, no good way to get information from the baristas."

In recent years, the Marketing Science Institute placed marketing measurement on its agenda.[2] For many years, most firms measured brand, marketing, and product managers solely on sales, market share, and/or profit contribution. Firms did not explore the factors that drove these results, nor question if sales and profits came at the expense of long-term harm to brand equity. Today, many firms use brand health-check measures — Chapter 11 — but monitoring and controlling marketing performance is a broader issue.

Marketing and business managers take many actions — enter new markets and segments, introduce new products, increase and reduce advertising, add and cut salespeople, shift distribution channels, and raise and lower prices. Typically, the firm hopes to increase sales, market share, and/or profits, and create shareholder value. But the firm must also know if its actions lead to intended results. A good monitor-and-control system tells if firm actions, individually and collectively, improved performance; leading indicators help the firm assess if it is on track, or should change direction.

THE CHANGING VIEW

OLD WAY	NEW WAY
Accounting profit	Shareholder value creation
Backward looking	Forward looking
Bottom-line oriented	Variety of measures
Fact finding	Learning and improvement
Financial focus	Business focus
Focus on firm success	Focus on firm and customer success
Internally oriented	Externally oriented
Measurement and control based on accounting performance measures	Measurement and control based on marketing performance measures
Output measures only	Emphasis also on input and intermediate measures
Post-action control	Steering control
Punitive philosophy	Analytic philosophy
Unbalanced scorecard	Balanced scorecard

KEY PRINCIPLES OF MONITOR-AND-CONTROL PROCESSES

A popular management saying: *"If you can't measure it, you can't manage it."* People in organizations tend to do what is *inspected* of them, not what is *expected* of them. Hence, good monitor-and-control processes are critical for ensuring that people do what they are supposed to do, so the *right* actions lead to the *right* results. *Monitoring* focuses on measuring how well the firm is doing in various business aspects. *Control* is concerned with making changes or adjustments so it does better. Monitor-and-control processes are the most powerful means of changing individual behavior and enhancing long-term results.[3] Chapter 22 focuses on two complementary areas: firm performance and **firm functioning**:

- **Firm performance.** *Is the firm achieving planned results?* Planned results are the **standards** against which the firm measures actual results. All things equal, if actual results meet or exceed standards, performance is satisfactory and the firm continues to operate as planned. If actual results are below standards, the firm should modify its actions.[4]

- **Firm functioning.** To achieve desired results, the firm allocates resources and takes actions. *Is the firm functioning well?* For greater insight, we decompose this question into three:
  - **Implementation.** Did the firm implement planned actions?
  - **Strategy.** Is the firm's market strategy well conceived and on target?
  - **Managerial processes.** Are the firm's managerial processes the best they can be?

Monitor and control should not occur as managerial whim; the firm should build a monitor-and-control philosophy into its DNA. This is not simple; it may take considerable time and effort to assemble the infrastructure for an effective system. Measurement is crucial; in this chapter we discuss many types of measures. But the best-designed measures have no impact unless the firm also implements a process for developing standards and assessing results against those standards. Effective monitor-and-control processes rest on five key principles:

- Focus on market levers and develop alternative plans.
- Implement steering control rather than post-action control.
- Use the right performance measures at the right organizational levels.
- Model the relationship between input, intermediate, and output measures.
- Tie compensation to performance.

FOCUS ON MARKET LEVERS AND DEVELOP ALTERNATIVE PLANS

Market levers flow from the firm's market strategy and implementation plans; they include actions like introducing new products, increasing/decreasing advertising, adding/replacing salespeople, and enhancing training. The firm allocates resources and takes actions to achieve planned performance. The firm's actual performance versus standards tell if firm resource allocations and actions were successful. Monitor-and-control efforts should focus on market levers. If actual results fall below standards, the firm should be ready with alternative plans.

> Pfizer built experimentation with marketing levers into its DNA. Pfizer continually tests different advertising and promotion strategies and ways of allocating selling effort. Pfizer spends millions of dollars on experiments as it searches for optimal actions. Said a senior Pfizer executive, "We're measurement-intense. So 'metrics are us.' We believe in it. We measure everything. That is the root of our business."[5]
>
> Historically, Samsung focused on low-price, high-volume products so production managers could optimize capacity utilization. Samsung's new monitor-and-control system measures market price position and encourages sales of higher-price products.

Marketing Question

Consider your personal objectives and strategy: Have you thought through these rigorously? Are you achieving your planned objectives? Are you functioning well in trying to achieve your objectives?

KEY IDEA

➤ Monitor-and-control processes are the most powerful means of changing individual behavior in firms.

➤ Monitor-and-control processes focus on firm results:
- Is the firm achieving planned results?

And on firm functioning:
- Is the firm functioning well?

KEY IDEA

➤ The firm should plan contingent actions for actual performance falling below standards.

KEY IDEA

➤ Post-action control means waiting for a *pre-set* time before comparing actual results against performance standards.

IMPLEMENT STEERING CONTROL RATHER THAN POST-ACTION CONTROL

Steering control and **post-action control** are different monitor-and-control approaches. Firms using post-action control wait a pre-set time period, then compare actual results against standards. If results are unsatisfactory, they take corrective action. Firms exercising post-action control typically develop annual marketing plans and set standards by quarter, but increased environmental change and complexity are driving reduced time periods.

By contrast, steering control is dynamic, continuous, and anticipatory. Firms using steering control set standards for measures like sales, market share, and profit, then calendarize by month, week, or even day. These firms set control limits for performance and continually compare actual results against standards.[6] Because they also track leading indicators, these firms are more market responsive.

Amazon conducts web-based promotions by sending millions of e-mails during two or three days. Amazon tests multiple legs of each message for click-throughs and sales. Within a couple of hours, Amazon knows what's working and what's not, and then sends only those messages providing the best results.[7]

Historically, Gillette consolidated sales every quarter; now these figures are available daily. Cisco can close its books in a single day by converting 50 different ledgers in a single global system. Managers can view revenues, margins, backlog, expenses, and other data by region, business unit, channel, and account manager daily and take appropriate actions.[8] Dell focuses heavily on short feedback cycles. Discussing salespeople, a senior Dell executive opined, "We drive to develop a meritocratic environment where people have a profit-per-minute mentality."[9] At Zara's Spanish headquarters, sales managers sit at terminals monitoring sales at every store around the world, thus enabling twice-per-week restocking.

Based on early data from many stores, by 8 a.m. on the Friday after Thanksgiving Walmart knew that sales would not reach expectations. Between Friday and Sunday, Walmart executives decided which items to mark down. New prices took effect nationwide on Tuesday; on Thursday Walmart broadcast a video promoting the newly discounted items. New advertising began on Friday with revamped displays in all stores. Walmart rebounded, and quarterly earnings were within the expected range.

KEY IDEA

➤ Steering control allows the firm to be more market responsive. Steering control *continually* compares firm results to performance standards.

➤ Feedback cycles — time between firm actions and measured results — should not be too short.

Internet-related technologies have made frequent performance monitoring more viable. But **feedback cycles** — time between firm action and measured results — should not be too short. Otherwise, measured results may be due to random fluctuations. A leading pharmaceutical firm mistakenly made major changes in a new product launch four weeks after introduction, long before it could make a decent assessment of results. On returning as Starbucks CEO, Howard Schultz stopped reporting monthly growth in same-store sales as he believed this drove short-term thinking by store managers.

USE THE RIGHT PERFORMANCE MEASURES AT THE RIGHT ORGANIZATIONAL LEVELS

If possible, the firm's monitor-and-control process should use objective measures like sales, market share, and profits.[10] When less concrete measures like customer satisfaction are appropriate, the firm should use validated scales.[11] Regardless, the firm should use the *right* measures:

Kellogg's CEO, Carlos Gutierrez, introduced a *volume-to-value* strategy to shift resources to higher-margin products. Gutierrez altered Kellogg's daily tracking systems to record dollar sales — not pounds — and overhauled bonus plans to reward profits and cash flow — not volume. In meetings, Gutierrez interrupted executives who gave results in weight sold rather than dollars.

CONTINUES ON NEXT PAGE

Many life insurance firms compensate agents on the number and value of new policies. But agents often receive little/no compensation for maintaining existing policies. Hence, agents *roll over* existing policyholders into new policies. But new policies must be in force for several years before the firm profits. Failure to measure and reward agents for serving existing policyholders creates serious profit problems.

The firm should measure performance at multiple organizational levels, like corporate, geographic region, business unit, market segment, marketing function, customer, sales region, sales district, and/or sales territory. Alcoa measures profitability by market sector, business, and customer and, in its aerospace division, by airplane program.[12] *De-averaging* performance via finer-grained analysis may allow the firm to identify particularly well-performing areas that warrant greater investment, and poorly performing units whose problems need addressing.

The Bowen example illustrates the **iceberg principle** — Figure 22.1 — by showing that opportunities and problems may lie hidden beneath the surface. Organizational position should largely drive the data employees receive. Senior managers do not typically require performance variances by salesperson, but they should have the ability to do deep dives. Salespeople do not need to know performance variances of peers in other sales regions.

KEY IDEA

➤ The firm should use objective measures for monitor-and-control purposes; if scales are appropriate, these should be validated.

FIGURE 22.1

THE ICEBERG PRINCIPLE

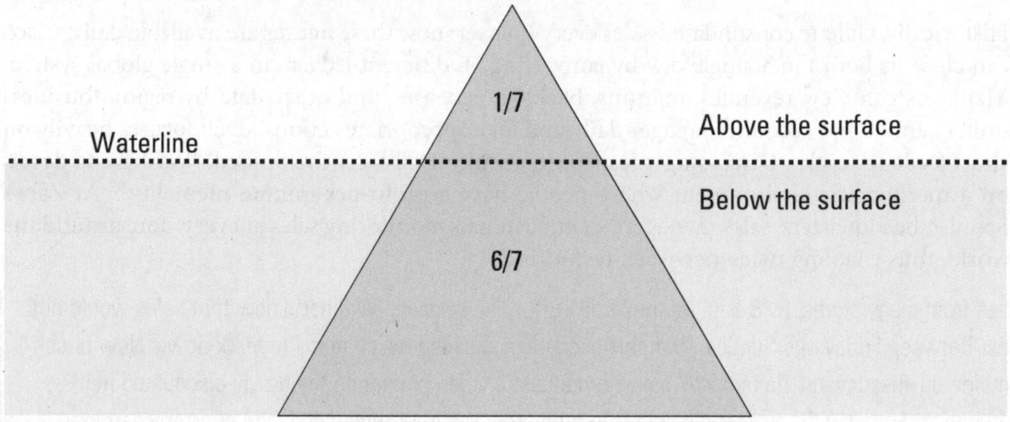

Waterline

1/7

Above the surface

Below the surface

6/7

Bowen Inc.

Bowen Inc. (disguised name) sells tools through retail stores. We illustrate the iceberg principle via Bowen Inc.'s sales force structure — national, regional, district, and territory — Figure 22.2. Bowen's performance was satisfactory overall, and in each of its four geographic regions. But the Northeast region's results comprised strong performance in the New York and New Jersey/Pennsylvania districts and very poor performance in Capitol (New England performance is acceptable). Even in Capitol, two salespeople — Mapes and Hornig — performed exceptionally well; Grant and Canatos pulled the district down.

KEY IDEA

➤ The firm should measure performance at multiple organizational levels.

➤ Good performance in a unit or sub-unit can hide poor performance elsewhere. The firm must isolate problem areas.

FIGURE 22.2

THE ICEBERG PRINCIPLE IN A NATIONAL SALES FORCE

Key

Excellent	Superior	Acceptable
Needs Improvement	Unacceptable	

National

Sales Regions

Northeast | South | Midwest | West

Sales Districts

Capitol | New York | New Jersey/Pennsylvania | New England

Sales Territories

Williams | Busch | Grant | Mapes | Canatos | Hornig

MODEL THE RELATIONSHIP BETWEEN INPUT, INTERMEDIATE, AND OUTPUT MEASURES

Monitor-and-control systems must disentangle cause and effect. Suppose we observe that advertising spending increases and sales also increase. One interpretation is that advertising was effective: Increased advertising spending led to increased sales. The alternative interpretation is that increased sales led to increased advertising spending: The advertising budget is a fixed percentage of sales! To ensure the firm makes valid inferences, it must distinguish among:

- **Input measures** — actions the firm takes.
- **Intermediate measures** — customer actions or changes in their state of mind.
- **Output measures** — performance variables like sales and profits.[13]

Figure 22.3 shows input measures leading to intermediate measures; in turn, intermediate measures lead to output measures, in a cause-and-effect relationship. Market levers provide the input measures; they affect intermediate steps that must occur before customers purchase products and provide the firm with outputs. Generally, collecting data on input and output measures is relatively easy; securing data on intermediate measures is often more resource-intensive.

Regarding numbers of measures, the firm is generally better off choosing a limited number of *good* measures than just a lot of measures. At Home Depot, CEO Nardelli used an excessive 30 store-manager measures (since reduced to eight) but omitted customer satisfaction. The firm must have confidence in the presumed relationships between inputs and intermediates and between intermediates and outputs. Many marketing researchers spent significant effort investigating these relationships.[14] To illustrate, when the firm takes advertising and sales force actions, input, intermediate, and output measures may be:

- **Input measures.** Financial resources spent on advertising, number of sales calls per day
- **Intermediate measures:**
  - **Customer actions.** Number of customers agreeing to a product trial, number of customers placing deposits for future purchases.
  - **Customer mental states.** Product awareness, associations, attitudes, product interest, intention to purchase.
- **Output measures.** Sales, market share, profits.

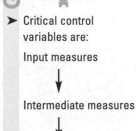

KEY IDEA

➤ Critical control variables are:

Input measures

↓

Intermediate measures

↓

Output measures

Output measures are **lagging indicators** — *rearview mirror*, what has happened. Intermediate and input measures are **leading indicators** — *dashboards*, what should happen.[15]

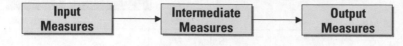

FIGURE 22.3

RELATIONSHIPS
AMONG CONTROL
MEASURES

TIE PERFORMANCE TO COMPENSATION

The performance-to-compensation linkage is the final but critical piece of the monitor-and-control puzzle. In the Opening Case, we saw how Sony dramatically changed sales force behavior by linking compensation to a new set of performance measures. In 2004, Lego had a $344 million loss; in recessionary 2008, profits were $355 million. An important contributing factor to the $700 million turnaround was tying employee pay to newly developed key performance indicators (KPIs).

Developing the performance-to-compensation linkage is not easy. If compensation design is poor, employees may optimize individual performance and compensation. But they may harm the firm by failing to cooperate across functional boundaries and business units — Chapter 21.

KEY IDEA

➤ Generally, people in organizations do what they are paid to do.

CRITICAL ELEMENTS OF THE
MONITOR-AND-CONTROL PROCESS

> McDonald's customer satisfaction rankings dropped considerably; it experienced its first quarterly loss in 40 years, and share price hovered around a ten-year low. A major factor: To avoid bothering powerful franchisees, McDonald's decided not to seek detailed store-by-store information. McDonald's lacked a good system to monitor performance against outlet standards.
>
> Coach CEO Lew Frankfort receives many reports: daily and weekly sales broken down by product category and store (around 450 full-price and factory outlets); number of people entering the store; percent who purchased; what they purchased; and how much they spent.

Figure 22.4 shows nine repeatable yet distinct stages for any monitor-and-control process[16]:

1. **Identify the process to control.** Clarify the control system's focus.

2. **Decide and define measures.** Options include input, intermediate, and/or output variables. The firm must also decide *when* to measure, and devise a process for developing standards.

3. **Develop a measurement system.** Figure out a system to collect, integrate, and analyze relevant data and distribute results.

4. **Set standards.** Decide what standards to apply for each measure. Generally, standards flow from action programs related to the market strategy. Of course, standards likely differ by market segment.

5. **Measure results.** Using the measurement system from step 3, collect, integrate, analyze, and distribute results.

6. **Compare results against standards.** Compare results — step 5, against standards — step 4, to identify **performance gaps**/variances.

7. **Understand and communicate performance gaps.** Communicate data and interpretation of performance gaps to executives responsible for taking action. Some gaps will be positive — results exceed standards. Other gaps will be negative — results inferior to standards.

8. **Generate and evaluate alternatives.** Executives identify alternative corrective actions to close negative gaps. Large positive gaps may indicate higher performance standards are in order. Executives should always question if the original standards were appropriate.

9. **Select alternative and take action.** Executives select a course of action, then develop and implement an action plan.

Monitor-and-control processes are not one-time events. After completing the nine stages, the firm should confirm that stages 1, 2, and 3 are well developed. Then, completing step 9 leads directly to step 4 — confirm or reset standards. Table 22.1 illustrates for individual salespeople.

The firm must recognize the impact of monitor-and-control systems on employee motivation. The firm optimizes motivated behavior when standards are moderately challenging. Participation in standard setting also enhances motivation. Standards that are too easy or too difficult reduce motivation. Perceived fairness in setting standards is very important.[17]

FIGURE 22.4

THE MONITOR-AND-CONTROL PROCESS

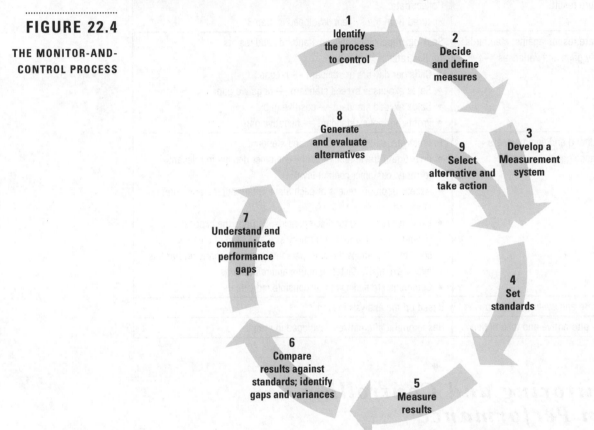

TABLE 22.1

ILLUSTRATING THE MONITOR-AND-CONTROL PROCESS FOR INDIVIDUAL SALESPEOPLE

Process Step	Managerial Focus
1. Identify the process to control	Actions and performance of individual salespeople
2. Decide and define measures	What measures? • Input measures: total number of calls per day, number of calls to new accounts per day, sales expenses per call • Intermediate measures: number of factory trials, number of formal customer planning meetings • Output measures: sales revenues, profits, sales revenues from new accounts When to measure: monthly How to develop standards: individual salesperson with district sales manager; regional sales manager approves standards

CONTINUES ON NEXT PAGE

Process Step	Managerial Focus
3. Develop a measurement system	Develop a coding system for existing/new accounts. Develop systems to secure data for individual salespeople: • Call data and intermediate measures from salesperson call reports • Sales expense data from T&E (travel and entertainment) reports • Sales revenue data from the order entry process • Profit data from the accounting department Develop system to aggregate data at district, regional, and national levels.
4. Set standards	Specific input, intermediate, and output standards vary by salesperson experience and sales territory characteristics (sales opportunity and workload).
5. Measure results	Collect data. Secured from the system developed in step 3
6. Compare results against standards; identify gaps and variances	Seek discrepancies between standards and results. To illustrate: • Calls per day are at standard — no gap • Sales expenses exceed standard — negative gap • Sales exceed standard — positive gap • Profits are below standard — negative gap
7. Understand and communicate performance gaps	To illustrate, sales expenses exceed standard. • Investigate travel requirements, customer density in relevant territory, customer contact level • Assess appropriateness of each input, intermediate, and output standard • Establish reason(s) for discrepancies. Perhaps the expense budget is too low for the territory size and level of customer contact. Or perhaps the salesperson plans trips poorly and/or has overly expensive tastes in hotels and restaurants • Communicate findings to responsible individuals
8. Generate and evaluate alternatives	Based on the analysis in step 7
9. Select alternative and take action	Based on the alternatives developed in step 8

TABLE 22.1

(CONTINUED)

Monitoring and Controlling Firm Performance

What performance should the firm monitor and control? The Figure 22.3 framework — **input → intermediate → output** — helps answer this question (reverse order).[18]

OUTPUT MEASURES

Output measures are the *final* results the firm wants to achieve. These results can be **hard**, objectively assessed measures, or **soft** measures like rating scales requiring more interpretation. **Internal** hard measures include sales volume, product profitability, and customer profitability; **external** (market-based) hard measures include market share and market-occupancy ratio. Soft measures include brand health checks and customer satisfaction.[19]

THE SALES INFORMATION SYSTEM

The sales information system is fundamental to managing a business. In good systems, the firm captures each sale on multiple dimensions like customer; product item; order, delivery, and payment date; price; terms; and delivery location. When the firm enjoys such disaggregated data, it can develop summary reports by aggregating across products, customers, and other variables. Some firms develop their own proprietary systems to address specific issues, others use publicly available software from firms like Oracle and SAP. Developing a sales information system may seem conceptually straight forward, but faces several issues:

- **Timing.** The frequency with which managers require information depends on the decisions they have to make. When Amazon sends a 24-hour e-mail blast, it requires reports every few minutes so it can improve message effectiveness. Walmart shares sales data with suppliers every 24 hours so as to optimize store delivery; Cisco closes its books every 24 hours. For other firms, hourly or daily data may be overkill and weekly or even monthly data may be sufficient. The firm must select the *right* periodicity for its decisions.

- **Organizational complexity.** Many firms comprise multiple business units. Each business may have a sales information system sufficient for its own activities, but system incompatibility makes integrating across businesses difficult, if not impossible. For many multinational firms, aggregating product sales data across countries and geographic regions is a real problem. Relatedly, aggregating sales by customer across product divisions and/or geographic regions is similarly challenging.

> When Lou Gerstner arrived as IBM's new CEO, he asked a senior executive: "How much business do we do annually with Ford around the world?" The response: "Give us a couple of days and we'll get back to you." IBM had no system to capture global sales by customer (much less profitability). Today, IBM has a sophisticated system that produces this information.

- **Distribution.** Typically, sales information systems capture sales to direct customers, but the firm may be more interested in sales to distributor customers. The firm must seek these data from distributors, but they may not wish to share. Many firms have to be content with estimates of end-customer purchases.

- **Profitability.** Sales information systems provide sales data, not profitability data. To secure product and customer profitability, the firm must take the extra steps of subtracting out variable costs and various fixed cost allocations. This process can be quite complicated.

INTERNAL HARD MEASURES — SALES VOLUME

Sales volume includes sales units, sales revenues, and their growth rates.[20] Overall measures are important, but breaking these down to identify components provides greater insight. Two alternative revenue breakdowns are:

REVENUE PREDICTABILITY. We may classify revenue in three ways:

- **Continuous.** The firm expects to receive revenues on a week-by-week or month-by-month basis. Examples are raw material sales and long-term contractual payments.
- **Periodic.** Sales are infrequent but can be forecast; capital equipment sales are a good example.
- **Episodic.** Occur because of unanticipated events and cannot be forecast, like building materials sales following a hurricane.

Some firms develop strategies to shift *periodic* revenues to *continuous*, like technology firms replacing product sales by service sales on a usage basis.

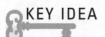

KEY IDEA

➤ Important internal *hard* measures are:
- Sales — units and revenues
- Product profitability
- Customer profitability

The Iceberg Principle in Practice

Gross analysis. Figure 22.5: Overall sales revenue standard is $160 million; actual sales revenues are $150 million; performance is $10 million below standard (total/total). This comparison provides zero information about reasons for the discrepancy, nor options for solving the problem.

First-level breakdown (marginals). We examine firm performance by product and market.

- **Product analysis**: Current products did fine: $135 million actual versus $125 million standard (+ $10 million). New products did poorly: $15 million actual versus $35 million standard (– $20 million).

- **Market analysis**: Current markets did fine: $130 million actual versus $120 million standard (+ $10 million). New markets performed poorly: $20 million actual versus $40 million standard (– $20 million).

- **Conclusion**: The firm has problems with both new products and new markets.

Second-level breakdown.

1. Good performance — current products and current markets: $120 million actual versus $100 million standard (+ $20 million).

2. Poor performance — all other market/product combinations:
   - Current markets/new products: $10 million actual versus $20 million standard (– $10 million).
   - Current products/new markets: $15 million actual versus $25 million standard (– $10 million).
   - New products/new markets: $5 million actual versus $15 million standard (– $10 million).

FIGURE 22.5

ILLUSTRATING MONITORING AND CONTROLLING SALES REVENUES

Products		Markets — Current	Markets — New	Total
New		Standard: $20 million / Actual: $10 million	Standard: $15 million / Actual: $5 million	Standard: $35 million / Actual: $15 million
Current		Standard: $100 million / Actual: $120 million	Standard: $25 million / Actual: $15 million	Standard: $125 million / Actual: $135 million
Total		Standard: $120 million / Actual: $130 million	Standard: $40 million / Actual: $20 million	Standard: $160 million / Actual: $150 million

Assuming standards were well set, these performance gaps are very troubling; the firm is failing with new products and new markets. The results demand even deeper analysis. Breakdowns by market segment or sales region/district/ territory may provide clues to causes of poor performance.

Finally, suppose overall actual sales revenue total had been $161 million versus the $160 million standard. Despite this apparently satisfactory performance, some product/market combinations would probably have performed below standard. The firm must always consider the iceberg principle; overperformance in one area often masks underperformance somewhere else. Only by isolating underperforming areas and taking appropriate action can the firm improve overall performance.

PENETRATION VERSUS GROWTH. Many firms want to distinguish between sales based on current business — *penetration*, and sales from new business — *growth*. Retail organizations gain deeper insight by partitioning sales into *same-store* sales (penetration) and *new-store* sales (growth). Figure 22.5 (boxed insert) illustrates the iceberg approach to monitoring and controlling sales revenues. We examine firm performance in each cell of the 2×2 matrix formed from current and new products, and current and new markets.[21] For a deeper analysis, see Marketing Enrichment me2201 .

ISSUES WITH SALES MEASURES. We consider three topics:

- **Different sales volume measures.** At a minimum, the firm should measure both sales units and sales revenues. Both measures are necessary to distinguish between revenue growth based on sales units and revenue growth based on price increases.

- **Sales quality.** Some firms focus on specific types of sales. General Mills measures sales of products meeting certain nutritional targets and sets goals on that basis.

- **Accuracy and consistency of sales volume measures.** The firm must ensure that sales units and sales revenue measures are accurate, and are derived consistently from period to period. Some growth-seeking firms abuse these sound business practices, forcing the SEC to demand earnings restatements:

Used in moderation and tightly managed, **vendor financing** is sound business. But some firms abuse the practice by excessive lending to customers; effectively, they purchase from themselves to meet unrealistic sales goals. **Factoring** (selling) the firm's accounts receivable is also acceptable practice, but inconsistent factoring practice to *improve* financial statements is not. Finally, retailers do not typically account for **slotting fees** separately from product revenues, yet slotting fee revenues often rival overall profits.[22] Lack of transparency can easily lead to unsound decision-making.

> **Are sales real?**
>
> - Software firm MicroStrategy booked incomplete sales as revenues.
>
> - BMS booked sales to wholesalers early to meet quarterly targets.
>
> - Several firms heavily discount prices, effectively shifting future sales to the current period. *Channel stuffing* (*loading*) created trouble for Brocade, Coca-Cola, Computer Associates, Dial, Lucent Technologies, PepsiCo, Peregrine Systems, Symbol Technologies, and Warnaco.

Marketing Question

As a senior MicroStrategy manager, what measures could you have taken to identify and control questionable practices?

INTERNAL HARD MEASURES — PRODUCT PROFITABILITY

Marketing Question

What is the overhead allocation problem? Why do firms face this issue?

Achieving good sales volume performance is important, but management is generally more interested in profits. Unfortunately, the most common profit measure — *bottom-line profit*, may not be terribly useful for assessing marketing effectiveness. Failure to meet profit targets may result from lack of promised resources or *unfair* corporate overhead allocations, rather than poor marketing. (Marketing Enrichment me2202 illustrates the overhead allocation problem, and a solution.)

The firm should focus on measures that exclude allocations, like **profit contribution** and **direct product profit**.

PROFIT CONTRIBUTION equals sales revenues less variable costs. To earn positive net profits, profit contribution must exceed fixed costs.

DIRECT PRODUCT PROFIT assesses profit performance after taking into account fixed costs. The firm separates fixed costs into two parts: costs *directly related* to the product (would disappear if the product were dropped) — **direct fixed costs**, and *allocated* costs — **indirect fixed costs**. Direct product profit equals profit contribution less direct fixed costs.[23]

Direct product profit is an excellent measure for marketers:

- Sales revenue is a key determinant of profit contribution.

- Marketing-expenses — advertising, promotion, field sales, are a major portion of direct fixed costs. Marketers must ensure that individual marketing expenses help the firm achieve sales volume, market share, and profit targets.

PROFIT RETURN MEASURES. Some firms prefer **profit return** measures to absolute measures like profit contribution or direct product profit. Two popular measures are **return on sales (ROS)** and **return on investment (ROI)**.[24] But an exclusive focus on either, especially ROS, can lead to poor decisions.[25]

> ### KEY IDEA
> ➤ Be careful with return-on-sales (ROS) as a performance measure.

Illustrating the ROS and ROI Problem

At VW, the key brand performance measure was ROS. VW marketed Seat and Skoda as strategically low-price brands, but meeting ROS targets was difficult. To improve ROS, Seat and Skoda introduced larger, higher-price (higher profit) cars. But these cars destroyed VW's low-cost strategic positioning. VW switched to ROI measures.

INTERNAL HARD MEASURES — CUSTOMER PROFITABILITY

Most firms have systems to measure product profitability; some are rudimentary, others are highly sophisticated. By contrast, relatively few firms measure customer profitability. Yet customers provide firm revenues and are its core assets. Conceptually, translating product profitability to customer profitability is straightforward, but financial system design and implementation may be challenging and expensive. When firms do secure customer profitability (fully accounting for direct service and shipping costs), they often identify unprofitable customers.

> ### KEY IDEA
> ➤ Most firms measure product profitability; fewer firms measure customer profitability.

Table 22.2 shows an income statement comprising three products; Table 22.3 shows the same economic reality presented as an income statement comprising three customers.[26]

	Product X	Product Y	Product Z	Total
Sales Revenues	$4,330	$6,400	$7,001	$17,731
less Cost of Goods Sold	3,175	4,120	5,213	12,508
Gross Margin	1,155	2,280	1,788	5,223
less Other Operating Costs				4,023
Net Profit				1,200

TABLE 22.2

PRODUCT INCOME STATEMENTS ($000s)

	Customer* A	Customer* B	Customer* C	Total
Sales Revenues	$9,380	$4,351	$4,000	$17,731
less Cost of Goods Sold	4,452	4,353	3,703	12,508
Gross Margin	4,928	(2)	297	5,223
less Other Operating Costs:				
Sales Force	425	225	225	875
Field Service	224	325	224	773
Technical Assistance	285	285	380	950
Order Processing	275	162.5	112.5	550
Delivery	437	233	205	875
Other Operating Costs	1,646	1,230.5	1,146.5	4,023
Net Profit	3,282	(1,232.5)	(849.5)	1,200

TABLE 22.3

CUSTOMER INCOME STATEMENTS ($000s)

> ### KEY IDEA
> ➤ Sales volume and profitability measures have serious shortcomings; they don't show firm performance relative to competitors.

* Instead of *customer*, the column headings could equally well be market segments or distribution channels.

When customers purchase directly from the firm, the accounting system provides sales revenues and cost assignments. Difficulties arise when individual product data reside on different systems, and these systems do not *talk to each other*; similarly for customer profitability.

> An experienced marketing executive at HP reported: "We measure profitability by customer, geographic territory, and lines of service (products). We don't get every piece of data on every customer, but we get 70–80 percent of global data so we get a very good indication of profit contribution. Achieving customer profitability is very important to us. Some countries don't have the data, some don't put product codes in their systems, and some don't care if it's right or wrong. So we must deal with data capture and data quality issues."

Sales volume and profit measures provide good data on firm performance, but lack an external benchmark. Firm sales and profits may be happily growing at 10 percent per annum, but simultaneous 20 percent market or competitor growth would suggest a serious problem. Market-based measures address this issue.[27]

EXTERNAL HARD MEASURES — MARKET SHARE

Marketing Question

What are the challenges of setting standards and measuring performance against them?

Market share compares firm performance directly with competitors and is the most common *market-based* measure. The firm should measure market share in both units and revenues. These measures are identical when the firm's price equals the market average. When price exceeds the average, revenue share exceeds unit share (and vice versa). When he became GE's CEO, Jack Welch required that each business be No. 1 or No. 2 in its market.[28] **Market occupancy ratio** measures the breadth of the firm's market activity. MTV has an important 60-country *footprint*, even though many countries operate at breakeven. Table 22.4 shows several market-based measures.

TABLE 22.4

EXTERNAL MEASURES OF FIRM PERFORMANCE

Measure	Calculation	Information Provided
Market share (MS) (%)	Firm sales/sales of all competitors	Market position versus all competitors
Relative market share (RMS) (%)	Firm sales/sales of major competitor(s)	Market position versus the firm's major competitor(s)
Market occupancy ratio (MOR) (%)	Number of firm customers/ Total number of customers	Fraction of potential customers with which the firm does business

KEY IDEA

➤ Important external *hard* measures are:
- Market share
- Relative market share
- Market occupancy ratio

SOFT MEASURES

The firm should regularly take its customers' pulse. Customer satisfaction and attitudes are widely employed *soft* output measures. Soft measures help track how customers are responding to the firm and competitors. Because many soft measures are tied to hard measures, like **customer satisfaction** to sales, they can be valuable intermediate measures.[29]

> IBM's chief marketing intelligence officer said: "IBM hired me because the CEO couldn't get reliable marketing information. Each business unit invented its own customer satisfaction survey, chose its own sample, did its own survey, and reported results. Guess what? Every customer was totally satisfied — no dissatisfaction! Meanwhile, market shares were falling like a rock. Marketing played the role of honest broker. We had incredible battles to get consistent measures that people would believe in. Remember, people get paid on these numbers, so they would *game* the system."[30]

KEY IDEA

➤ Customer satisfaction and attitudes are widely used *soft* measures.

A well-structured, validated, independently administered customer survey provides the best soft data. Generally, the firm takes measures of both itself and competitors. At Siebel, each six months, an independent firm measures satisfaction with Siebel's departments and personnel at 400–500 of its 2,500 customers. Siebel bases salespeople's bonuses and commissions on these results. Salespeople don't receive full commissions until one year after the sale, and then only if their scores are up to par. Microsoft bases performance-based stock awards for its top 600 managers mainly on customer satisfaction ratings.[31]

Enterprise car rental surveys one in 15 customers for the Enterprise Service Quality Index (ESQi). Enterprise aggregates responses to just two questions:

- On a scale ranging from "completely satisfied" to "completely unsatisfied," how would you rate your last Enterprise experience?
- Would you rent from Enterprise again?

Each Enterprise branch receives its ESQi score; branch managers scoring under the company average are not promoted. Similarly, GE (and many other firms) use **Net Promoter Score** to gauge customer sentiment.[32] Marketing research provider Burke developed a customer loyalty index; brand health checks are another popular example of soft measures — Chapter 11, p. 285.

Popular Soft Measures

Net Promoter Score (NPS). The firm derives its net promoter score from answers to a single question measured on a 0 to 10 scale;

"How likely is it that you would recommend XXXX to a friend or colleague?,"
0 = not at all likely; 5 = neutral; 10 = extremely likely.

Net Promoter Score = percentage of customers scoring 9 or 10 (promoters) minus percentage of customers scoring 0 to 6 (detractors).

Firms using net promoter score also probe for the reasons behind the score.[33]

Burke's Secure Customer Index (SCI). Burke's index is based on five equally weighted components:

- Overall *customer satisfaction* with the firm
- Likelihood of *repeat business* for the firm
- Likelihood to *recommend* the firm to others
- *Preference* for the firm versus others
- Extent to which the firm has *earned loyalty*

Burke measures customer responses on five-point scales: *agree completely — disagree completely*: Scores range from 0 to 100. Burke recommends tracking the SCI index over time and making comparisons with competitors and best-in-class performers.[34]

KEY IDEA

➤ A well-structured, validated, independently administered customer survey provides the best soft data.

➤ Net Promoter Score is a widely used soft measure.

Marketing Question

Why is Net Promoter Score so popular? What are the pros and cons of using this performance measure?

INTERMEDIATE MEASURES

The firm takes actions — *inputs*, to improve *outputs*. *Intermediate* measures sit between inputs and outputs. Success on intermediate measures does not guarantee output performance. But the firm only achieves good output performance by securing good intermediate performance. Intermediate measures have two characteristics:

- **Input effect.** The firm's marketing effort must affect the intermediate measure.
- **Output effect.** The intermediate measure must influence another intermediate measure and/or an important output measure(s).

The distributor of inexpensive Fleischmann's gin developed a new retail distribution strategy; shelve products next to high-quality Gordon's and Gilbey's. The theory: Consumers would reach Gordon's and Gilbey's displays, see less expensive Fleischmann bottles, then select Fleischmann's. The key intermediate measure: number of stores accepting Fleischmann's shelf placement.

Marketing Question

BMS introduced Abilify, a new drug for people with schizophrenia and bipolar disorder. BMS promotional strategy is twofold: sales representatives detailing Abilify to physicians and consumer advertising. What output measures would you suggest for Abilify?

> The sales cycle for Jostens high school yearbooks (delivered June) starts early fall. Salespeople ask high school decision-makers to agree to a formal presentation. Jostens' predictive sales model estimates the probability of a sale, conditional on a presentation. Number of signed agreement cards is an important intermediate measure for Jostens.

KEY IDEA

➤ Success on intermediate measures *does not guarantee* firm output performance. But the firm can achieve good output performance *only by achieving* good intermediate performance.

➤ Intermediate objectives are particularly important in long-cycle sales.

The best intermediate measures are leading indicators of output performance; they should result from a tested customer purchase model: inputs → intermediates → outputs. Columbia Business School Executive Education models promotional spend — *input*; number of enquires — *intermediate*; and number of participants — *output*, for open-enrollment programs. Pfizer's marketing-process model for prescription pharmaceuticals comprises 32 distinct steps. Markers indicate the type of return Pfizer needs from each specific marketing input. Pfizer's extensive historical database provides good information on relationships among input measures and intermediate measures. Pfizer knows that a given type and amount of advertising — *input* — will generate a certain number of physician requests — *intermediate* — and that those requests will lead to a certain number of prescriptions — *output*.

Intermediate measures are particularly important in long-cycle sales processes, like major capital goods. Many months or even years may pass between an initial customer contact and the actual sale. Many firms manage sales pipelines — Chapter 17 — using intermediate measures. Pipeline management can help sales managers close unfavorable intermediate performance gaps by requiring salespeople to change input actions.[35]

INTERMEDIATE SALES FORCE MEASURES

The firm should base these measures on a sales pipeline model. Intermediate sales force measures differ from firm to firm. For one firm, factory trials may be a good measure; for another, dollars of co-op advertising agreed — Table 22.5.

TABLE 22.5

POSSIBLE INTERMEDIATE MEASURES FOR THE SALES FORCE

Measure	Rationale
Commitments to co-op advertising	Customers place resources at risk and make best efforts
Customer's subjective impression of salesperson interaction — telesales	Indicator of future sales
Distribution breadth for products	Securing distribution is a necessary step to making sales
Entry on approved supplier list	Customers purchase only from fully qualified suppliers
Factory trials agreed	Customers will not buy without factory use experience
Proposals accepted	Necessary step to winning business
Retail displays accepted	Good shelf positioning leads to sales

INTERMEDIATE ADVERTISING MEASURES

The firm should base measures on an advertising effectiveness model geared to the market situation. For a newly launched product, *awareness* may be appropriate; for an established product, *quality perception* — Table 22.6.

TABLE 22.6

POSSIBLE INTERMEDIATE MEASURES FOR ADVERTISING

Measure	Information Provided
Awareness	Degree of product/brand awareness
Liking	Indicates positive feeling toward the product/brand
Interest	Indicates likelihood of product/brand purchase
Product quality perception	Perception of product/brand quality
Number of press mentions	Indicates customer awareness
Message recall	Indicates advertising effectiveness

Monitoring and Controlling Firm Functioning

In a well-developed monitor-and-control system, input measures are closely and explicitly linked to intermediate measures. In turn, intermediate measures are closely and explicitly related to output measures.

INPUT MEASURES

Input measure performance depends on three aspects of firm functioning:

- Implementation control. Did the firm implement planned actions?
- Strategy control. Is the firm's market strategy well conceived and on target?
- Managerial process control. Are the firm's processes the best they can be?

IMPLEMENTATION CONTROL

The firm's market strategy spawns many implementation programs; these programs generate action plans in marketing-mix areas like product, service, promotion, distribution, and price. The market strategy may also generate action plans in functional areas like engineering, operations, R&D, and technical service. Marketing and other functional managers are typically responsible for ensuring these action plans are executed. Table 22.7 and Table 22.8 respectively illustrate possible input measures for the sales force and new product development.

Measure	Measure Focus
Implementation of sales planning system	Ensure sales force plans time allocations
New product knowledge training	Ensure sales force is competent to sell new products
Sales calls per day	Ensure sales force is working hard
Sales calls on new accounts	Ensure sales force spends time with target accounts
Sales territories vacant	Ensure sales managers plan for attrition
Total expenses	Manage sales force discretionary costs

TABLE 22.7

POSSIBLE INPUT MEASURES — SALES FORCE

Measure	Measure Focus
Qualified new product ideas generated	Creativity in generating high-quality ideas
New concepts tested	Success in developing new ideas
Licenses/technology purchases checked out	Success in looking outside the firm
Products completing beta tests	Success in moving ideas through the new product development system
Test markets conducted	Success in developing products for market readiness
New products launched	Entire new product development process

TABLE 22.8

POSSIBLE INPUT MEASURES — NEW PRODUCT DEVELOPMENT

Home Depot (HD) measures store associate time use. HD reschedules tasks that take associates away from customers; HD receives deliveries at night. HD schedules demonstrations of pneumatic nail guns on Mondays and Tuesdays from 7 a.m. to 9 a.m. when sales are highest. ExxonMobil's Hal Cramer is very clear: "Operationally, you've got to start with measuring, monitoring, and helping your own employees. Because, unless your employees *get it*, they can't deliver on your brand promise. If they get it, then you can reach through them to customers."[36]

KEY IDEA

➤ Monitoring and Controlling firm functioning comprises:
- Implementation control
- Strategy control
- Managerial process control

STRATEGY CONTROL

Strategy control answers the question: **Is the firm's market strategy well conceived and on target?** The firm typically sets strategy for the medium or long run; it should not overreact to poor output performance by making hasty changes. For strategy control, post-action control is generally superior to steering control.

Figure 22.6 shows how to integrate strategy control and implementation control to isolate causes of firm output performance.[37] Performance is good in Cell A, but less so in the other cells:

MARKET STRATEGY GOOD/IMPLEMENTATION GOOD (CELL A). A well-developed and well-implemented strategy should drive good output performance. The firm must monitor customers, competitors, and the general environment to ensure the strategy remains on track.

MARKET STRATEGY GOOD/IMPLEMENTATION POOR (CELL B). Poor implementation of a good strategy will probably lead to poor output performance. Sometimes an especially robust strategy can survive poor implementation, but this is unusual. Cole National (CN) targeted hardware and other small stores for key-making machines and key blanks; CN succeeded despite poor sales force execution. The firm should focus on improving execution.

MARKET STRATEGY POOR/IMPLEMENTATION GOOD (CELL C). Rarely does excellent implementation overcome a poor strategy. If the firm fails to provide customer value, successfully implementing other marketing elements will not compensate. Some years ago, Frito-Lay failed with a new cookie despite legendary sales force implementation.

MARKET STRATEGY POOR/IMPLEMENTATION POOR (CELL D). Output performance is likely disastrous. The firm's challenge is to isolate the cause: poor strategy or poor implementation?

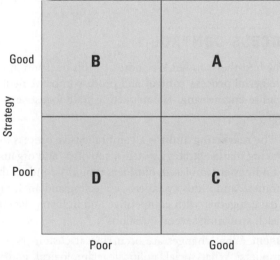

This framework explicitly recognizes that good output performance requires both good strategy *and* good implementation. Poor output performance has many authors; the challenge for management is isolating the cause. Deep analysis across many business aspects may be necessary:

- **Market strategy foundations** — market, customer, competitor, company, and complementer insight — Chapters 3, 4, 5, 6
- **Market segmentation and market strategy** — Chapters 8, 9, 10, 11
- **Action plans** — Chapter 9
- **Measures for monitoring and controlling implementation** — Chapter 22
- **Actual performance versus input, intermediate, and output standards** — Chapter 22 (Marketing Enrichment me2203 shows how to separate out planning and performance variances.)

No matter where the firm isolates problems — strategy or implementation — some things must change. But some changes are more difficult to make than others. This can be a special problem when the environment evolves quickly and managers cling to outdated strategies, and implementation programs outlive their usefulness. Advertising is relatively easy to change; indeed, most firms undertake reviews annually if not more frequently. Distribution arrangements are more difficult to alter due to logistical, contractual, and interpersonal relationships. Figure 22.7 suggests inertia levels for different marketing-mix implementation areas.[38]

KEY IDEA

➤ Distinguishing between strategy and implementation problems is crucial.

FIGURE 22.7

INERTIA IN MARKETING-MIX IMPLEMENTATION

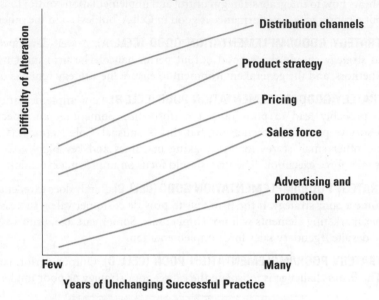

MANAGERIAL PROCESS CONTROL

Are the firm's processes the best they can be? We addressed this question in Chapter 21. Three broad approaches to **managerial process control** and process improvement are best practice transfer, benchmarking, and re-engineering. The marketing audit focuses explicitly on improving marketing functioning.[39]

THE MARKETING AUDIT. The **marketing audit** is a comprehensive process for evaluating firm marketing practices embracing market strategy systems, activities, and organization. To ensure confidences are kept and findings are unbiased, outsiders typically conduct the audit. Auditors meet with managers, customers, and industry experts, collecting and analyzing internal financial, sales, and operating data, together with competitive and industry data. A useful auditing framework has six parts, each spawning several questions[40]:

- **Marketing environment.** What changes are occurring at customers, competitors, complementers, and suppliers? What social, political, technological, and regulatory trends affect the industry? How do these changes and trends affect the firm? What are the performance implications?

- **Market objectives and strategy.** Are the firm's market objectives and strategy realistic given the environment and firm strengths? Do managers understand the objectives and strategy?

- **Marketing implementation.** How do firm offers compare to competitor offers in terms of product, service, promotion, distribution, and price? Does the firm's marketing mix implement the market strategy? Are they mutually consistent?

- **Marketing organization.** Are job roles and responsibilities clear and consistent? Is recruiting, hiring, training, and development on track? Is senior management engaged with major customers? Do measurement and reward systems motivate performance?

KEY IDEA

➤ Managerial process control: Are the firm's processes the best they can be?

- **Marketing systems.** How effective are the firm's marketing systems, including competitor intelligence, customer advisory boards, customer database design and update, marketing research, measuring customer satisfaction, new product development, sales forecasting and pipeline management, and sales lead generation?

- **Marketing productivity.** How profitable are the firm's product lines? How profitable are the firm's customers and segments? Do some products or customers merit additional effort? Should some products be repriced or discontinued? Should some customers be dropped? Should other customers be pursued more vigorously? Is the firm's focus appropriate, given the market environment? How should the firm allocate resources across the marketing mix? Does it need more or less product improvements, trade incentives, and sales or service personnel?

Marketing audits can be a very effective diagnostic tool. The firm should look out for[41]:

- **Considering marketing only as the marketing department's job.** Customers are the firm's critical assets. Marketing is everybody's business, not just the marketing department's responsibility.[42]

- **Cutting prices rather than increasing value.** The sales force complains and the firm cuts prices. The firm earns insufficient profit to enhance customer value.

- **Failure to invest for the future, especially in human resources.** The firm views marketing and HR as expenses, not investments. The firm under-funds marketing and training and development.

- **Failure to segment markets effectively.** Firms form simple geographic or demographic segments; they do not probe deeply enough to gain good insight.

- **Insufficient knowledge of customer attitudes and behavior.** Firms collect customer data too infrequently. Even with frequent collection, senior managers are often ill-informed and the data do not drive marketing decision-making.

- **New product development delegated to the developers.** Technical employees develop new products with little marketing input and insufficient customer insight.

Many of these concerns mirror issues discussed in Section I — Marketing and the Firm. We reinforce them here because firms find it so difficult to be truly externally oriented. No matter how noble the intentions, following through requires attention to detail, hard work, and the right mind-set. The marketing audit is a useful tool to keep the firm on track.

KEY IDEA

➤ The marketing audit is a comprehensive process for evaluating the firm's marketing practices.

THE BALANCED SCORECARD

The **balanced scorecard** is an increasingly widespread approach for monitoring and controlling firm performance and firm functioning. The balanced scorecard seeks a middle ground between using too few measures and too many. Each extreme leads to problems:

TOO FEW MEASURES. Managers may *game* the system to optimize performance on those measures, especially if they drive compensation. Such behavior may cause unintended consequences. When short-term profit is the only standard, performing well is very easy: Cut back on advertising and R&D. Of course, such actions hurt the firm in the long run. Previously, U.S. airlines competed by advertising shorter flight times; when on-time performance data became widely available, airlines lengthened advertised flight times and improved *on-time* performance! When incoming Home Depot CEO Robert Nardelli focused on *inventory velocity* (inventory turns) some managers ordered fewer products; *inventory velocity* improved, but customers couldn't find products they wanted.

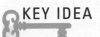

KEY IDEA

➤ The balanced scorecard reflects a steering control philosophy, balancing input, intermediate, and output marketing measures.

TOO MANY MEASURES. Multiple measures cause problems if they are unclear or conflicting. Employees have difficulty discerning required behavior and may focus efforts on actions that do not further firm goals.[43]

Many firms address these problems via the balanced scorecard.[44] Well-balanced scorecards reflect a steering control philosophy by *balancing* input, intermediate, and output measures. PepsiCo's marketplace profit and loss system, used to decide managers' bonuses, includes:

- Customer attitudes
- Financial profit and loss
- Quality
- Employee motivation
- Market share

Perhaps the most commonly used measures for balanced scorecards are:

- **Market share** — hard output measure
- **Customer satisfaction relative to competition** — soft output measure
- **Customer retention versus industry averages** — hard output measure
- **Investment as a percentage of sales** — hard input measure
- **Employee attitudes and retention** (especially customer-facing employees) — soft and hard input measures

Many balanced scorecards focus on four measurement categories — financial, customer, internal business processes, and learning and growth. To illustrate, Table 22.9 shows candidate measures for a global account management program — Chapter 23. Table 22.10 shows key elements in a balanced scorecard for gasoline marketing.[45] This scorecard is noteworthy for many *soft* measures; financial measures are weighted 10 percent versus 90 percent for non-financial measures.

Financial	Internal Business Process
• Year-on-year revenue and profit growth • Sales expense as a percentage of revenues	• Percentage of customers with long-term contracts • Percentage of customers with *solutions* contracts • Process improvements from collaboration — summary billing, product development
Customer	**Learning and Growth**
• Customer satisfaction and loyalty • Access to customer at the C-level — CEO, CFO, CIO, and COO	• Number of best practices adopters • Improved management practices

TABLE 22.9

CANDIDATE VARIABLES FOR A BALANCED SCORECARD APPROACH TO MEASURING THE GLOBAL ACCOUNT PROGRAM

Perspective	Weighting	Objective	Measure
Financial	10%	Service operating efficiency	Budget variance
Client	30%	Evaluate organizational effectiveness	Client satisfaction service agreement feedback (5-point scale) • Gasoline marketing • Retail dealer operations • Franchise re-engineering • Training • Retail dealer operations • Fuels support • Leadership development • Real estate • Strategy implementation
Internal	40%	Excel in channel management	Tracking versus channel strategy • Retail • Wholesale • Fuels support • Training • Real estate
		Optimize sales force management development	Area manager development index
		Service integration/alignment	Quality service forums

TABLE 22.10

A BALANCED SCORECARD FOR MOBIL GASOLINE MARKETING

> *Marketing Question*
>
> In your educational institution, each instructor has his or her own way of measuring student performance. Can you suggest a balanced-scorecard framework that all instructors could use to measure student performance?

TABLE 22.10

CONTINUED

Perspective	Weighting	Objective	Measure
Learning and Growth	20%	Core competencies and skills	Personnel development • 360 feedback on all employees • Competency plan on employees executed
		Organizational involvement/ scorecard understanding	Idea generation index Quarterly climate survey

The firm should closely align scorecards for different functional areas and managerial levels — like brand and category managers, and district, regional, and national sales managers. Carefully designed and aligned sets of measures improve firm chances of securing high performance. Well-designed scorecards help minimize deviant behavior like accounting manipulation and channel loading that can cause significant problems.

Marketing Question

What other messages did you glean from this chapter?

KEY MESSAGES

The purpose of monitor-and-control systems is to improve firm performance. Four key principles are:
- Focus on market levers and develop alternative plans.
- Implement steering control rather than post-action control.
- Use the right performance measures at the right organizational levels.
- Model the relationship between input, intermediate, and output measures.

Critical stages in developing a monitor-and-control process are:
- Identify the process to control
- Decide and define measures
- Develop a measurement system
- Set standards
- Measure results
- Compare results against standards; identify gaps and variances
- Understand and communicate performance gaps
- Generate and evaluate alternatives
- Select alternative and take action

The firm should monitor and control three sorts of measures:
- Output measures — final results the firm wants to achieve; can be *hard* or *soft*.
- Intermediate measures — sit between input and output measures, affect other intermediate measures and/or output measures.
- Input measures — concerned with firm functioning, explicitly linked to intermediate measures. Input measures concern three types of control:
  - Implementation control
  - Strategy control
  - Managerial process control
- The balanced scorecard typically embraces input, intermediate, and output measures.

VIDEOS AND AUDIOS

Monitor and Control	v2202 🎥	Alan Fortier	Fortier & Associates
Monitor and Control	v2203 🎥	Ron Boire	Toys R Us
Marketing Imperative 6	a2201 🎧		

v2202

v2203

a2201

QUESTIONS FOR STUDY AND DISCUSSION

Can you answer the questions implied by this chapter's learning objectives? Check!

1. Chapter 22 discusses several output measures. Develop six other output measures that a firm might use. How did you choose them? Why is each measure valuable? What does it add to the output measures in the chapter?

2. Many managers are distrustful of *soft* performance measures like customer satisfaction. How would you convince managers that *soft* measures have value?

3. Use the input → intermediate → output framework to identify alternative measures for the marketing executive responsible for Apple's iPad. Using these measures, develop a balanced scorecard to assess executive performance. Alternatively, complete this task for a product in which you are interested, or this book — *Managing Marketing in the 21st Century*.

4. How can a marketing audit enhance brand value? What do you expect to learn from the audit process?

5. How would you justify the investment in capturing timely customer data?

SECTION V

SPECIAL

MARKETING TOPICS vs5

To access O-codes, go to **www.ocodes.com**

SECTION V — SPECIAL MARKETING TOPICS — COMPRISES A SINGLE CHAPTER. Chapter 23 focuses on a topic appearing in various places throughout *Managing Marketing in the 21st Century* — International, Regional, and Global Marketing. Globalization is one of the major trends facing practically all firms in practically all industries today. Chapter 23 helps firms decide whether or not to enter foreign markets, which foreign markets to enter, and which entry options to choose. Further, the chapter discusses designing, implementing, and organizing for international, regional, and global marketing.

Managing Marketing in the 21ˢᵗ Century

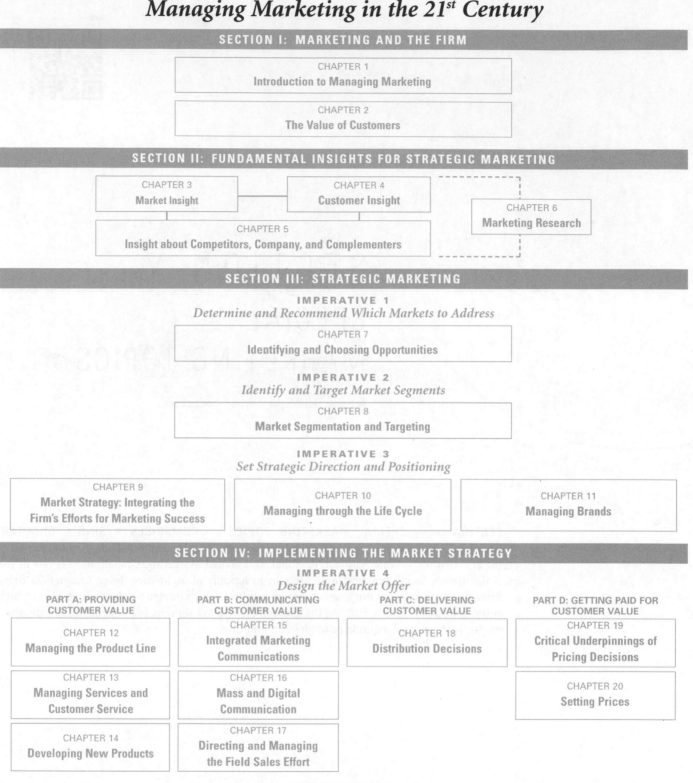

SECTION I: MARKETING AND THE FIRM

CHAPTER 1
Introduction to Managing Marketing

CHAPTER 2
The Value of Customers

SECTION II: FUNDAMENTAL INSIGHTS FOR STRATEGIC MARKETING

CHAPTER 3
Market Insight

CHAPTER 4
Customer Insight

CHAPTER 6
Marketing Research

CHAPTER 5
Insight about Competitors, Company, and Complementers

SECTION III: STRATEGIC MARKETING

IMPERATIVE 1
Determine and Recommend Which Markets to Address

CHAPTER 7
Identifying and Choosing Opportunities

IMPERATIVE 2
Identify and Target Market Segments

CHAPTER 8
Market Segmentation and Targeting

IMPERATIVE 3
Set Strategic Direction and Positioning

CHAPTER 9
Market Strategy: Integrating the Firm's Efforts for Marketing Success

CHAPTER 10
Managing through the Life Cycle

CHAPTER 11
Managing Brands

SECTION IV: IMPLEMENTING THE MARKET STRATEGY

IMPERATIVE 4
Design the Market Offer

PART A: PROVIDING CUSTOMER VALUE

PART B: COMMUNICATING CUSTOMER VALUE

PART C: DELIVERING CUSTOMER VALUE

PART D: GETTING PAID FOR CUSTOMER VALUE

CHAPTER 12
Managing the Product Line

CHAPTER 15
Integrated Marketing Communications

CHAPTER 18
Distribution Decisions

CHAPTER 19
Critical Underpinnings of Pricing Decisions

CHAPTER 13
Managing Services and Customer Service

CHAPTER 16
Mass and Digital Communication

CHAPTER 20
Setting Prices

CHAPTER 14
Developing New Products

CHAPTER 17
Directing and Managing the Field Sales Effort

IMPERATIVE 5
Secure Support from Other Functions

CHAPTER 21
Ensuring the Firm Implements the Market Offer as Planned

IMPERATIVE 6
Monitor and Control

CHAPTER 22
Monitoring and Controlling Firm Functioning and Performance

SECTION V: SPECIAL MARKETING TOPICS

CHAPTER 23
International, Regional, and Global Marketing

CHAPTER 23

INTERNATIONAL, REGIONAL, AND GLOBAL MARKETING v2301

LEARNING OBJECTIVES

When you have completed this chapter, you will be able to:

- Decide whether or not to enter foreign markets.
- Assess alternative foreign markets and decide which to enter.
- Become familiar with global and regional government-type organizations aspiring to enhance foreign trade and investment.
- Decide how to enter foreign markets.
- Develop market strategy for approaching global markets.
- Segment global markets and develop global branding strategies.
- Implement international and global market strategies.
- Develop the *right* organization for managing the firm's activities in foreign markets.
- Manage global customers.

OPENING CASE: DHL

*DHL (**Dalsey, Hillblom, and Lynn**) was founded in 1969 as a document courier in the Asia-Pacific region several years before Federal Express (now FedEx).[1] During the next 30 years, DHL expanded throughout Asia Pacific, Europe, and the Americas. In 2002, Deutsche Post (DP) acquired DHL. Subsequently, DP acquired more than 100 firms in related fields, including Danzas-AEI (Europe's largest freight forwarder) and leading domestic parcel firms in Britain, France, Spain, and the Benelux countries. (In 2008, DHL withdrew from the U.S. domestic market.) By 2009, DHL had annual revenues approaching $100 billion and employed 285,000 people worldwide.*

DHL serves the express delivery and logistics business segments for its parent DP. DHL's express service links 120,000 destinations in more than 220 countries and territories. DHL provides delivery services from a network of 5,000 offices with a fleet of more than 70,000 vehicles and 400 aircraft. DHL maintains 3.5 million square meters of warehouse space at over 1,000 distribution centers and provides freight forwarding, logistics, and supply-chain-management services.

DHL's vision states: "Customers trust DHL as the preferred global express and logistics partner, leading the industry in terms of quality, profitability, and market share. DHL enhances the business of our customers by offering highest quality express and logistics solutions based on strong local expertise combined with the most extensive global network presence."

To serve customers, DHL's four major brands (businesses) have profit and loss responsibility:

- *DHL Express: same-day, time-definite, day-definite express delivery services*
- *DHL Supply Chain CIS: contract logistics and industry solutions — supply-chain management, warehousing, distribution, value-added services, logistics outsourcing, and lead logistics supplier*
- *Global Forwarding Freight Air Freight and Ocean Freight Services: air freight, ocean freight, industrial projects, and customer program management*
- *Global Forwarding Freight Road and Rail Freight: flexible and customized road and inter-modal transport network*

DHL customers comprise three tiers. Tier 1 — top 100 customers, managed by Global Customer Solutions (GCS) globally. Tier 2 — other multinational customers, managed by individual business units globally. Tier 3 — thousands of local customers, managed by individual business units locally.

***Global Customer Solutions.** DHL organizes GCS by nine industry sectors (Aerospace; Automotive; Chemical; Consulting; Fashion; Industrial, Engineering, and Manufacturing; Life Sciences; Retail; and Technology). Each Tier 1 customer has a dedicated global customer manager (GCM) who reports into one of the industry sectors. GCMs are responsible for global revenues and profits at their customers. They enjoy three types of support:*

- *Local Key Account Managers (KAMs). Individual KAMs work for one of the brands in a specific country but are assigned to GCMs on a dotted-line basis.*

- *Regional Customer Managers (RCMs). RCMs are responsible for certain areas of the world — Asia Pacific; Europe, Middle East, Africa; and the Americas. They report to the GCMs but have more direct everyday contact with KAMs.*

- *Staff Support. Various types including program management, supply-chain consultants, pricing, information technology, tender management, and legal/risk expertise.*

CASE QUESTION

How do you assess DHL's approach to addressing increasing globalization?

Opportunities for firms to engage in **international and global marketing** are large and growing.[2] Since the 1950s, inter-country trade has increased dramatically — Figure 23.1. Of all responsible factors, one is critical: Individual firms seek opportunities beyond their domestic markets. The purpose of this chapter is to help you think through approaching foreign markets.

Note that Chapter 23's title is deliberate — international, regional, and global marketing. Some firms engage in *global marketing* by entering many foreign markets in different continents; some focus on specific geographic regions — *regional marketing*; and others on just a few foreign countries — *international marketing*. This chapter has value for each type of firm.

Each firm must decide whether foreign market entry makes sense. Many firms seek overseas revenues but many more do not. At home, customers speak the same language; they use the local currency; and governmental, legal, and cultural imperatives are familiar. The firm avoids the risks and uncertainties from addressing new customers and new competitors, and having to acquire the skills to operate in foreign markets. Most small- and medium-size businesses and some large firms are purely domestic: Check your local telephone directory — electric, gas, and water utilities, and perhaps your local supermarket. Target and Virgin America are U.S. domestic firms; Indigo and Kingfisher airlines fly only within India, and Azul in Brazil.[3]

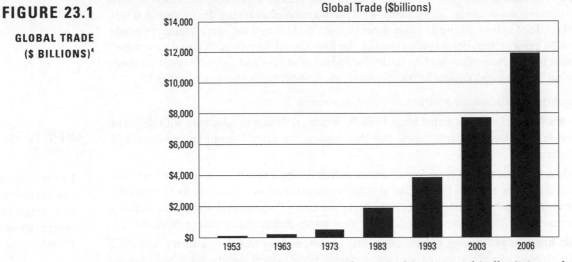

FIGURE 23.1

GLOBAL TRADE ($ BILLIONS)[4]

Chapter 23 focuses on key marketing issues for expanding geographically. (We touch on production issues only when necessary.) Specifically, we address marketing across borders but also draw on material from the previous 22 chapters. We ask and answer seven questions:

- Should the firm engage in marketing outside its domestic borders?
- How should the firm choose which foreign markets to enter?
- What foreign-market-entry options are available?
- What marketing strategy should the firm choose for foreign markets?
- What global market strategy issues must the firm address, and how should it do so?
- How should the firm organize for global markets?
- How should the firm address global customers?

THE CHANGING VIEW

OLD WAY	NEW WAY
Brand decisions made locally and regionally; supported by myriad advertising and PR agencies	Strategic brand decisions made centrally; single agency acts as global partner
Intercountry agreements on economic issues fragmented and limited in scope	Intercountry agreements on economic issues becoming the norm
International and global marketing mainly for large firms	International and global marketing an increasing option for small- and medium-size firms
International trade conducted in multiple languages	English emerging as the lingua franca of international and global business
Many international marketing decisions made at country and regional levels	Firms struggle over which decisions to centralize at head office and which to place in countries and regions
Most firms group countries by geographic proximity for international and global marketing	Leading firms group countries in ways other than geographic proximity
Product and geography dominate organizational design for international marketing	Global customer organizations are increasingly important for B2B firms
Technology not a major factor in international and global marketing	Global package delivery and the Internet critical growth drivers for international and global marketing

SHOULD YOU ENTER FOREIGN MARKETS?

Historically, large firms were more likely to venture abroad than medium-size and small firms. Firms like Citibank, Ford, General Motors, Heinz, IBM, Nestlé, Shell, and many others have operated overseas for decades. Today, firms of all sizes contemplate taking the plunge into foreign markets. IBM earns two thirds of revenues outside the U.S. and the much younger Google earns over 50 percent. But, before going abroad, the firm should be very clear about its reasons. Why should it trade home-market familiarity for the uncertainties and risks of venturing overseas?[5] Unless it has a good answer to this question, the firm probably shouldn't bother.

Generally, firms go abroad for a variety of different reasons:

- **Diversify risk.** Domestic firms spread risk by seeking revenues in countries with different local and regional business cycles. But they assume currency, foreign government, and other risks.

- **Follow customers.** When an important customer enters a foreign market, the firm may have little choice but to follow, like Toyota's suppliers. Following customers is especially common when transportation costs are high: Van Leer (The Netherlands) places facilities for making storage drums (oil/chemicals) close to oil-company customer refineries.

- **Gain knowledge.** Foreign market entry may be the best way to enhance firm intellectual capital, especially if the industry's most demanding customers are abroad. The firm may also learn serendipitously: Cemex adopted English as a common language, rotates managers internationally, and gained access to international consultants.

> **KEY IDEA**
>
> ➤ Before entering foreign markets the firm should make sure it has good reasons for venturing abroad.

In recent years, many Indian firms entered foreign markets (often via acquisition) to enhance scale, gain technology, and improve competitiveness, as foreign competitors entered India. Tata Motors acquired Jaguar Land Rover; by purchasing European steelmaker Corus, Tata Steel gained 80 U.S. patents and 1,000 researchers. Chinese firms are also expanding abroad: Lenovo acquired IBM's PC business; Geely acquired Volvo (from Ford); and Haier invested in several domestic appliance firms.

- **Growth opportunities.** Revenue and profit opportunities seem greater abroad than at home. An opportunity may arrive randomly, like an unsolicited request for the firm's products from a foreign market, or derive from a broad search process the firm conducts. Fierce home-market competition can drive such a search: Many small Italian firms, like wedding-dress maker Giovanna Sbiroli, lost business to Asian imports, but successfully entered foreign markets with distinctively Italian products.

- **Keep competitors honest.** Sometimes a foreign competitor subsidizes entry in the firm's domestic market with profits earned at home. To *keep the competitor honest* and deny it such funding, the firm may enter the aggressor's home market.

To enter the U.S. market, European home-appliance leader Electrolux acquired third-place White Consolidated. Then, U.S. market leader Whirlpool acquired Philips' home appliance business (Europe No. 2); GE (U.S. No. 2) acquired a stake in Britain's GEC. Later, Maytag (U.S. No. 4) acquired Hoover, and Whirlpool acquired Maytag.

When leading European cement producer Holcim invested in Mexico, Mexican cement maker Cemex entered Spain where Holcim had significant investments.

- **Reduce costs.** Sometimes firms base success on low-cost operations that allow low prices. By entering foreign markets, the firm may be able to tap international capital markets and secure lower capital costs. It may also enhance scale economies and secure access to low-cost labor. (Sometimes venturing abroad increases costs, like bringing employee pay up to international standards.)

me2301

Marketing Question

In Kenya, sugar was sold in 50 and 100 kg. bags for both industrial and consumer markets. Trade liberalization and common market protocols led to severe price competition from imported sugar. How should Kensug Inc. (disguised name), a major Kenyan sugar producer, address this challenge?

- **Small home market.** For firms based in small countries, going abroad may be the only reasonable way to grow. Both Switzerland and Sweden have relatively large numbers of firms competing in foreign markets.

When the firm enters foreign markets, the many unknowns increase risks. The firm should only go abroad if it believes that profits from foreign market entry outweigh the risks. Conversely, it should not hesitate to withdraw from a foreign market(s) if entry is unprofitable, like Carrefour exiting Southeast Asia, and Walmart leaving Germany and Korea. Of course, never venturing abroad, but rather competing with aggressive domestic and foreign competitors, may be even more risky!

HOW TO CHOOSE WHICH FOREIGN MARKETS TO ENTER

The firm should decide which foreign market(s) to enter similarly to other market entry decisions. Key considerations are expected financial return, risk, and timing of profits — Chapter 7; these factors depend on foreign market attractiveness for firm products and services and the firm's ability to compete.

FOREIGN MARKET ATTRACTIVENESS

To assess foreign market attractiveness, we adapt the PESTLE framework — Chapter 3. PESTLE factors affect market attractiveness in different ways. Critical considerations are economic and political/legal issues domestically in the foreign market, and internationally from the foreign market's perspective. We also consider sociocultural and geographic distance from the home market.

ECONOMIC AND POLITICAL/LEGAL: DOMESTIC

Economic. The crucial economic issue is current and potential market size for firm products and services. A critical determinant is often country wealth: Wealthier countries' greater spending power implies larger markets for many products and services. (Of course, some firms target low-income consumers and societies.) The most important wealth measures are **gross domestic product (GDP)** and **GDP per capita.**[6]

GDP is the annual market value of all final goods and services made within a country's borders. For intercountry comparisons, economists typically convert local-currency GDP into U.S. dollars using one of two approaches — **current currency exchange rate (nominal)** or **purchasing power parity (PPP)**. Economists often prefer PPP because it better indicates living standards in less-developed countries.[7] Marketing Enrichment me2301 shows individual country data for population and GDP (PPP) per capita organized by various (mainly geographic) regions. Despite widespread use, GDP measures ignore potentially important economic factors, especially for less-developed countries:

- Barter
- Gifts, loans, and debt forgiveness from international organizations and wealthy countries
- Nonmarket transactions — like subsistence farming
- Remittances from country nationals living abroad[8]
- Underground economy — includes tax-avoiding activities like undocumented immigrant labor, home business, and freelancing,[9] and illegal trade like drug trafficking; and other criminal businesses
- Uneven wealth distribution — significant concentration among a small elite group

In less-developed countries, the population exceeding certain thresholds may be better market potential measures for some products than GDP per capita. At US$1,000 per year, family diets shift from vegetables to meat; at US$10,000 per year, people purchase automobiles. Many firms keep a close watch on thresholds, especially in the large emerging BRICI countries — Brazil, Russia, India, China, and Indonesia.[10]

Political/legal. The political/legal environment often has an important impact on market attractiveness. Many countries develop governmental and institutional processes to benefit local firms. Some give exporters financing and tax advantages; others impose tariffs and quotas on imported goods. Sometimes countries get into spats: In 2009, the U.S. imposed a 25 percent tariff on tires imported from China; the following year, China responded with increased import duties on U.S.-sourced chicken parts. Governments may use administrative procedures like inspections, delayed approvals, and the courts to restrict foreign firms' products. Of course, restricting imports negatively affects consumers, but on safety issues governments often act to protect citizens; in pharmaceuticals, some countries ignore patents, but Thailand invoked compulsory drug licensing.

> Many Western firms complain that China uses unfair standards, conflicting regulations, and buy-local policies to discriminate against foreign firms — both exporters to China and local subsidiaries. Some standards effectively eliminate foreign products, and China's indigenous-innovation policy gives preference to local firms for state contracts.

International marketers sometimes adapt systems and processes to address disadvantageous decisions by foreign governments. Many firms avoid high tariffs on finished products by importing parts for local assembly — like the Segway personal transporter. *Commercial vans* imported to the U.S. face a 25 percent tariff, so auto firms import *wagons* from Asian factories, then remove the seats and windows before sale.

Regulation is often a critical entry variable. Many French entrepreneurs start businesses in Britain because the regulatory environment is friendlier; in Germany, firms must abide by strict environmental laws. Britain's largest train operator, the First Group, entered the U.S. market (by acquiring the largest operator of yellow school buses and Greyhound intercity coaches) because it believed geographically proximate countries like France and Germany were too tightly regulated. Corruption is a serious problem in many countries — Marketing Enrichment `me2301`.

Marketing Question

Segway is considering entry into Asia. Which countries should Segway enter? Why? What additional data would you require to appropriately advise Segway?

> Increasingly, firms with international aspirations are targeting emerging markets, especially **BRICI** — Brazil, Russia, India, China, and Indonesia. As these economies grow, large numbers of consumers who previously lived at subsistence levels become able to afford higher-value products.[11] PepsiCo is making major multibillion-dollar investments in China and Russia (acquiring Russia's largest juice maker, OAO Lebedyansky — $2 billion) and $500 million in India. Of course, the firm may have to conduct significant marketing research to understand these markets. In China and Russia (accounting for over half of all global soup consumption — mostly homemade), where tastes vary by region, Campbell's conducted thousands of consumer interviews and offers many soup varieties.

ECONOMIC AND POLITICAL/LEGAL: INTERNATIONAL

In addition to domestic economic, political, and legal factors, the firm must also consider the impact of global and regional organizations.

Global organizations. Several global government-type organizations enhance foreign-market attractiveness by securing intercountry agreements to increase trade and investment:

- **International Monetary Fund (IMF).** The 186-country member **IMF** works to foster global monetary cooperation, secure financial stability, facilitate international trade, promote high employment and sustainable economic growth, and reduce poverty.

KEY IDEA

➤ Important global organizations impacting international trade include:

- International Monetary Fund (IMF)
- World Bank (WB)
- World Trade Organization (WTO)

- **World Bank (WB).** 188 member countries own the **WB**, which provides financial and technical assistance to developing countries via the **International Bank for Reconstruction and Development (IBRD)** and the **International Development Association (IDA)**. The IBRD concentrates on middle income and creditworthy poor countries; the IDA focuses on the world's poorest countries.[12]

- **World Trade Organization (WTO).** The 153-country member **WTO** succeeded the General Agreement on Tariffs and Trade (**GATT**). Formed after World War 2, GATT sought agreements to reduce trade barriers around the world. The WTO encompasses GATT but addresses a broader scope of international agreements to liberalize trade via trade rules and dispute resolutions. The WTO is working on trade-barrier reductions from the Doha (Qatar) negotiations, begun in 2001.

Relatedly, many governments cooperate in investigating and prosecuting bribery. German prosecutors received significant help form other countries in their successful prosecution of Siemens AG (fined more than $250 million) for bribing customers around the world.

Regional organizations. Several regional organizations focus on increasing member-country trade by reducing trade barriers. Some work on reducing administrative barriers to trade and investment; some form free-trade areas and customs unions; others aspire to substantial economic and political integration — Table 23.1. The most important country groupings include the European Union (EU), North American Free Trade Association (NAFTA), Mercosur, and the Association of South East Asian countries (ASEAN)[13]:

- **European Union (EU).** The EU's 27 member countries comprise an economic and political union of 500 million people generating 30 percent of global world product. Only six individual countries have a larger territory size; the EU has the world's second longest coastline, and borders 21 nonmember states. People, goods, services, and capital move freely and all EU countries apply a common external tariff. EU citizens elect the European Parliament every five years. Most EU countries use the euro; Great Britain and Denmark opted out and some newly admitted countries have yet to qualify. The EU is a great market opportunity for many firms.

- **NAFTA.** In 1994, Canada, Mexico, and the U.S. formed NAFTA as a three-country trading area. In contrast to the EU, NAFTA focuses almost exclusively on trade and investment but its population of 450 million generates similar economic activity.

- **Mercosur.** Founded in 1991, Mercosur has four members — Brazil, Argentina, Paraguay, and Uruguay — and several associate members. Like NAFTA, Mercosur is a free-trade zone; population exceeds 260 million.

- **ASEAN.** ASEAN is a 10-member group promoting economic growth and cultural development. Six members — Brunei, Indonesia, Malaysia, Philippines, Singapore, and Thailand — formed AFTA, a free-trade area dedicated to reducing tariffs among members; Cambodia, Laos, Myanmar, and Vietnam are scheduled to join in 2012. ASEAN's population is 600 million; unlike the EU, AFTA does not have a common external tariff.

In addition, many countries form bilateral trade agreements. Australia has free-trade agreements with New Zealand (ANZERTA), Singapore (SAFTA), Thailand (TAFTA), and the U.S. (AUSFTA). The U.S. and South Korea have free-trade agreements with Peru and the EU respectively.[14]

When contemplating foreign market entry, the firm should understand the type and scope of the country's international relationships — with individual countries, regional groupings, and global institutions. The firm should also become familiar with the scope, rules, and regulations of relevant regional and global organizations, and predict how these may evolve. Today's bilateral trade relationships may become tomorrow's free-trade areas or even economic/political unions.

Intercountry relationships can have a major impact on foreign market attractiveness. Exports to a free-trade-group country enter other countries duty free, so the firm can make logistics decisions regionally. Political unions allowing free movement of labor and capital affect production-facility and many other decisions.

Organization	Current Members
AMERICAS	
North American Free Trade Agreement (NAFTA)	3: Canada, Mexico, U.S.
Andean Community (CAN)	5: Bolivia, Columbia, Ecuador, Peru, Venezuela
Common Market of the South (MERCOSUR)[15]	4: Argentina, Brazil, Paraguay, Uruguay
Caribbean Community (CARICOM)[16]	15: Antigua and Barbuda, Bahamas,[17] Barbados, Belize, Dominica, Grenada, Guyana, Haiti, Jamaica, Montserrat, St Kitts and Nevis, St. Lucia, St. Vincent and the Grenadines, Suriname, Trinidad and Tobago
ASIA PACIFIC	
Asia Pacific Economic Cooperation (APEC)	21: Australia, Brunei Darussalam, Canada, Chile, China, Hong Kong, Indonesia, Japan, Malaysia, Mexico, New Zealand, Papua New Guinea, Peru, Philippines, Russia, Singapore, South Korea, Taiwan, Thailand, U.S., Vietnam
Association of Southeast Asian Nations (ASEAN)	10: Brunei Darussalam, Cambodia, Indonesia, Laos, Malaysia, Myanmar, Philippines, Singapore, Thailand, Vietnam
EUROPE	
European Union (EU)	27: Austria, Belgium, Bulgaria, Cyprus, Czech Republic, Denmark, Estonia, Finland, France, Germany, Great Britain, Greece, Hungary, Ireland, Italy, Latvia, Lithuania, Luxembourg, Malta, Netherlands, Poland, Portugal, Romania, Slovakia, Slovenia, Spain, Sweden
European Economic Area (EEA)	EU members plus Iceland, Liechtenstein, Norway[18]
AFRICA	
Common Market for Eastern and Southern Africa (COMESA)	20: Angola, Burundi, Comoros, Democratic Republic of the Congo, Djibouti, Egypt, Eritrea, Ethiopia, Kenya, Madagascar, Malawi, Mauritius, Namibia, Rwanda, Seychelles, Sudan, Swaziland, Uganda, Zambia, Zimbabwe
Council of Arab Economic Unity (CAEU)	12: Egypt, Iraq, Jordan, Kuwait, Libya, Mauritania, Palestine, Somalia, Sudan, Syria, United Arab Emirates, Yemen
East African Community (EAC)	5: Burundi, Kenya, Rwanda, Tanzania, Uganda
Economic Community of Central African States (ECCAS)	10: Angola, Burundi, Cameroon, Central African Republic, Chad, Democratic Republic of the Congo, Equatorial Guinea, Gabon, Republic of the Congo, Sao Tome and Principe
Economic Organization of West African States (ECOWAS)	15: Benin, Burkina Faso, Cape Verde, Ivory Coast, Gambia, Ghana, Guinea, Guinea-Bissau, Liberia, Mali, Niger, Nigeria, Senegal, Sierra Leone, Togo

....

TABLE 23.1

SELECTED COMMON MARKETS AND TRADE ZONES

> *Marketing Question*
>
> Your firm manufactures inexpensive consumer goods. Management has asked you to identify the most attractive countries to enter taking regional organizations into account. How would you proceed?

GEOGRAPHIC AND SOCIOCULTURAL DISTANCE

Geographic. *Geographic distance* concerns the ease/difficulty of transporting people and goods and communications between the home and target country. Technology and the physical environment are key issues. In addition to physical distance, important factors include the presence/absence of physical land borders, separation by land/water, time zones, transportation and communication alternatives, topography, and climate. Reduced geographic distance implies increased market-entry attractiveness. Of course, within-country geographic dimensions are also important.

Sociocultural. Countries often differ from each other on multiple dimensions — language, religion, values and attitudes, education, social organization, technical and material, politics, law, and aesthetics — Table 3.6, p. 76. Hofstede's five-dimensional framework is a useful approach for assessing culture.[19] Hofstede's framework comprises:

- **Individualism versus collectivism.** The extent to which people develop and display individual personalities versus conducting themselves primarily as members of family or religious groups.

- **Long-term versus short-term orientation.** The extent to which people value attitudes and actions that affect the future, like persistence and thrift, versus attitudes and actions that are affected by the past or present, like stability, tradition, and reciprocity.

- **Masculinity versus femininity.** The relative value placed on competitiveness, assertiveness, ambition, and wealth accumulation — *masculinity*, versus relationships and quality of life — *femininity*.
- **Small versus large power distance.** The extent to which people accept and expect power relations to be consultative versus based on formal hierarchies.
- **Strong versus weak uncertainty avoidance.** The extent to which people are anxious about the unknown and prefer explicit rules and formally structured activities versus preferring flexible rules, guidelines, and informal activities.

Sociocultural distance varies widely from one country pair to another. Typically, low sociocultural distance occurs among colonizing and colonized nations — Britain and British Commonwealth countries; France and many African countries; Spain and Spanish Latin America; Portugal and Brazil; and the Netherlands and Indonesia. Foreign diasporas also display small sociocultural distance from their home countries, like Irish, Italian, and Mexican Americans; Turks in Germany; and Chinese in southeast Asian countries.[20]

Low sociocultural distance between the home and target countries implies reduced firm risk; high sociocultural distance can lead to failure despite other promising factors. When sociocultural distance is high, the firm may improve its chances of success by hiring people and organizations from the target country and seeking common ground among various sociocultural imperatives. Anecdotes about cultural insensitivity and business failure are legion:

> A U.S. technology firm was well placed to win a major contract from a Chinese firm. But at a banquet given by the Chinese company, a senior U.S. manager started eating before the host, a cultural no-no. A French firm won the contract: Its technology was inferior, but the Chinese felt more comfortable.

Firms can get in trouble with seemingly straightforward dimensions like language; Table 23.2 shows problems caused by poor translation that could have been avoided via rigorous and independent back translation. Because translation mistakes are easy to make, leading firms work with established language service providers.

TABLE 23.2

GLOBAL MARKETING MISHAPS: UNFORTUNATE TRANSLATIONS*

*Secured from the Internet

Company	Product	English name/slogan	Geographic area	Translation
American Airlines	air travel	"Fly In Leather"	Latin America	"Fly Naked"
Chevrolet	automobile	Nova	Latin America	"No va": doesn't go
Clairol	curling iron	"Mist Stick"	Germany	Mist is slang for manure
Coca-Cola	cola drink	Coca-Cola	China[21]	The Chinese pronunciation "Kekoukela" translates to "Bite the wax tadpole," or "Female horse stuffed with wax"
Colgate	toothpaste	"Cue"	France	Sounds like "cul," slang for "ass"
Coors	beer	"Turn It Loose"	Latin America	"Suffer From Diarrhea"
Dairy Association	milk	"Got Milk?"	Mexico	"Are you lactating?"
Electrolux	vacuum cleaner	"Nothing sucks like an Electrolux"	United States	
Parker	pens	"It won't leak in your pocket and embarrass you"	Mexico	"It won't leak in your pocket and make you pregnant"
Pepsi	cola drink	"Come Alive with the Pepsi Generation"	China	"Pepsi Brings Your Ancestors Back From the Grave"
Perdue	chicken	"It takes a strong man to make a tender chicken"	Latin America	"It takes an aroused man to make a chicken affectionate"

BALANCING COUNTRY ATTRACTIVENESS FACTORS

When assessing foreign market attractiveness, the firm must consider various economic, political/legal, sociocultural, and geographic issues.[22] In general, positive economic and political/legal factors and low sociocultural and geographic distance imply attractive opportunities, but typically the firm must balance positives and negatives. Consider a U.S. firm evaluating Australia: Many political, legal, and sociocultural factors are positive, but the relatively small population and large geographic distance may be negatives. Relatedly, South Korean firms conduct little business with North Korea despite geographic proximity and a common language!

Table 23.3 illustrates a simple approach to securing an attractiveness score for several individual countries. Possible scores range from 100 (very low attractiveness) to 1,000 (highly attractive).

Criteria	Importance Weight (I)	Great Britain Rating (RA) (1 to 10 scale)	Australia Rating (RB) (1 to 10 scale)	Mexico Rating (RC) (1 to 10 scale)	Great Britain I × RA	Australia I × RB	Mexico I × RC
1 Market Size	30	8	3	5	240	90	150
2 Growth Potential	20	5	7	8	100	140	160
3 Communications Ease	10	10	10	3	100	100	30
4 Travel Ease	10	5	2	9	50	20	90
5 Currency Stability	10	7	7	4	70	70	40
6 Firm Learning	10	3	3	8	30	30	80
7 Degree of Corruption	10	8	8	5	80	80	50
	100				**Σ670**	**Σ530**	**Σ600**

TABLE 23.3

ASSESSING COUNTRY ATTRACTIVENESS – ILLUSTRATION FOR A U.S. FIRM

THE FIRM'S ABILITY TO COMPETE

Foreign-market attractiveness is important but the firm must also consider its ability to compete. Put starkly, what are the firm's chances of attracting, retaining, and growing customers in the face of current and potential competitors, in the proposed foreign market? A new market entrant may secure differential advantage on the basis of technological expertise or brand strength, but also from an ability to execute projects and political and networking skills.

> Bus-service firm Automóviles Luarca SA (ALSA) grew in Spain's highly regulated transportation market. ALSA became adept at navigating the often highly complex process of securing licenses by forging personal connections and managing relationships with local officials. In the 1980s, ALSA became a minority partner in a joint venture offering taxi service near Hong Kong, and started building relationships in China. In 1990, when regulations allowed, ALSA formed a joint venture offering bus service from Beijing to Tianjin. Many other joint ventures followed: providing bus services (regular schedules and modern comfortable coaches — innovations in China), building bus stations, assembling buses, and managing maintenance facilities. ALSA's success derived from political skill and expertise in licenses.[23]

The firm should pay close attention to both foreign competitors and strong domestic competitors. Generally, local firms are effective in catering to local tastes, use local resources efficiently, and know how to address local obstacles. In less-developed countries, competitors often enjoy low labor costs, but may also use the latest technology. Baidu (China: search engine), Bharti-Airtel (India: cell phone service), Ctrip (China: online travel service), Focus Media (China: out-of-home advertising), Gol (Brazil: budget airline), Grupo Positivo (Brazil: PCs), Titan Industries (India: wristwatches), Wimm-Bill-Dann Foods (Russia: dairy products), and many others succeed at home despite facing strong multinational competitors.[24]

KEY IDEA

➤ Regardless of foreign market attractiveness, before entry, the firm should assess its ability to compete.

Increasingly, firms from less-developed countries are making significant inroads in mature advanced-economy markets. Frequently, domestic firms seek high profit margins by adding customer value and targeting up-market segments, but are less effective in cost control. The foreign entrant serves an unfilled market need for a basic low-price product, then later adds higher-value, higher-priced products. Japanese automobile firms secured high market shares in many developed countries using this approach. More recently, Giant (bicycles) took advantage of low-cost labor in Taiwan (later mainland China) to enter the global bicycle market. Giant has moved up-market and now offers bicycles at many different quality and price levels.

Today, many firms from low-wage Asian countries offer outsourcing services in developed countries, often competing with their customers' internal organizations. Indian technology firms like Tata Infotech and Wipro are major technology players; Indian firms run many customer service operations, and Indian law firms secure significant revenues from developed countries.

OPTIONS FOR ENTERING FOREIGN MARKETS

When contemplating foreign-market entry, firms start from many different places. A firm with regional or global ambitions may have already entered many foreign markets and have significant international experience, perhaps with several different entry approaches. By contrast, a domestic firm going abroad for the first time starts from scratch.

KEY IDEA

➤ When entering foreign markets, the firm can choose among several *passive* and *active* entry modes.

In this section, we focus on alternative ways to enter foreign markets. For *all* foreign-entry decisions, the core marketing issue is the firm's planned investment and involvement in the target country. We distinguish between *passive* entry and *active* entry: The firm may enter some markets passively and others actively — it may also switch from passive to active as it achieves success and/or learns about the new foreign market. Of course, the firm must also make important location decisions like production, design, finance, and human resources, but we focus on customer-facing marketing issues.

The firm must also consider how many foreign markets to enter, how quickly, and in what order. Increased number of entries expand the firm's opportunities and permit better fixed-cost amortization; but they require more resources and imply greater risk. Speed of entry involves several trade-offs. Simultaneous or fast-sequential entries earn profits more quickly, preempt competition, and erect entry barriers. When Citibank launched credit cards in Asia Pacific, it entered, in order, Indonesia, Singapore, Taiwan, Thailand, Australia, India, and Malaysia, within 18 months. Taking it more slowly is less risky and allows the firm to learn so that later entries may be more effective; it also mitigates the strain on managerial talent. When the firm makes sequential entries, order is important; early failure may cause the firm to push back, or even abort, other planned foreign market entries.

PASSIVE ENTRY

The firm allows another organization to do all or most of the work and has little control over marketing and sales efforts. Correspondingly, risk and financial return are lower than for active entry. Options include:

EXPORTING

KEY IDEA

➤ Major options for *passive* entry into foreign markets are:

• Exporting
• Licensing

The firm exports products but outsources most activities by:

• Simply responding to orders arriving from abroad.
• Appointing an export agent to sell products in foreign markets.[25] The firm may not know (or care about) destination countries; it simply fills export orders.

- Deciding which foreign markets to address, then appointing local sales agents and/or distributors (exclusive or nonexclusive) to conduct marketing and sales efforts.

> Wessex Press entered the Russian and Spanish Latin American markets via *passive entry*. Piter Publishing (St. Petersburg) produces, sells, and distributes the Russian version of *Managing Marketing in the 21st Century*. For Spanish Latin America, Wessex employs a Mexico-based sales agent and distributor; it ships Shanghai-printed books on consignment. When the agent makes sales, the distributor ships books and pays Wessex.

LICENSING

The firm has an asset — like product or process technology (patent or trade secret), brand name, or trademark — with value in foreign markets. The firm (licensor) agrees that another firm (licensee) can use the asset; in return, the licensee typically pays *minimum* royalties (right to use the asset) and *earned* royalties (based on sales or profits) to the licensor. Brand licensing is very common in B2C: Product scope includes clothing; food; movie-, comic-, and sports-related merchandise; and toys. In B2B markets, international licensing agreements are largely technology based. The licensee is typically responsible for marketing, sales, and production. The licensor gains foreign-market access and financial returns with minimal short-term risk. But licensing is no panacea; the licensor must consider:

- **Brand image.** Are the licensee's products/services consistent with the firm's brand identity?
- **Potential competitor.** Well-managed licensees become very familiar with the licensor's operations. Aggressive licensees have the potential to become serious competitors in the licensor's home or other markets. This problem is significant for patent-based licenses when the patent expires. The firm can minimize potential competition by continually providing new and additional value to its licensees.

ACTIVE ENTRY

The firm plays a major role in marketing and sales, but greater profit potential comes with higher risk. The firm should be especially careful in projecting from domestic experience but can reduce uncertainty via marketing research. Many foreign countries, especially emerging markets, lack a local market research infrastructure, but this should not be a barrier. By conducting its own research, the firm may secure differential advantage. Essentially, the firm has two major active-entry options: importing to the foreign market or producing locally.

IMPORTING

Traditional. Products enter the foreign market as imports from the firm's home country and/or third countries.[26] The firm actively markets and sells products via traveling home-based sales representatives and/or local salespeople based in foreign branches/subsidiaries. Both Boeing (U.S.) and Airbus (France) conduct vigorous marketing and sales efforts using these methods: Airlines around the world import finished airplanes from these firms. Zara designs and produces most products in Spain, then imports goods into foreign markets. Zara sells to local consumers via its own marketing efforts and wholly owned stores.

Many firms earn significant revenues from foreign markets but are virtually unknown outside their home countries. They supply customer firms with raw materials, parts, and even finished products. Have you heard of Foxcom? If you own an Apple iPod or iPhone, Sony Playstation, Dell PC, or some other electronic product, Foxcom probably made it. With many factories in Taiwan and China, Foxconn's more than one million employees produce and export many electronic products.

Marketing Question

Tasks Everyday <*www.taskseveryday.com*>, based in Mumbai, India, offers virtual assistants for small, midsize, and large businesses and busy professionals. Tasks Everyday has a ready supply of university educated graduate assistants and is seeking rapid expansion. What actions would you advise Tasks Everyday to take?

KEY IDEA

➤ Major options for *active* entry into foreign markets are:
- Importing
- Local production
- Franchising

Marketing Question

On the opening day of the 2008 baseball season, the Boston Red Sox beat the Oakland Athletics by six to five. But they did not play in Massachusetts or California; the game was in Japan. Develop an international marketing strategy for Major League Baseball.

Many firms address foreign markets by importing products *from* their home country and/or third countries. By contrast, many services firms *import* customers to their home countries. Tourism is a classic example. Today, *medical tourism* is a fast-growing facet of both the medical and tourism industries. Low prices, state-of-the-art hospitals, and well-trained physicians in Brunei, China, Hungary, India, Mexico, Singapore, Thailand, Turkey, and other countries attract American and Western European patients for a wide range of medical procedures. Some U.S. firms even offer employees reduced insurance premiums for accepting treatment abroad.

Facilitated by the Internet. The Internet and growth in air-courier transportation have helped many firms identify and serve customers in foreign markets. Using various techniques, the firm drives customers to its website where they select products and pay by credit card. An air courier or other transportation service delivers the purchase.

For many years, Boston-based Lobster Trap (LT) sold live lobsters to U.S. restaurants and European wholesalers. In 2008, after working with government officials, LT entered the Chinese market. LT ships specially packed lobsters via FedEx; they arrive in China 30 hours after leaving Boston.

Extreme Outdoors, a Florida provider of elaborate outdoor kitchens, lists products on eBay and sells to customers in Canada, France, Germany, Israel, Norway, and Sweden.

Wessex Press reaches foreign-market customers via **www.axcesscapon.com**. Many firms host foreign language websites. Amazon reaches customers in Canada — amazon.ca; China — amazon.cn; France — amazon.fr; Germany — amazon.de; Great Britain — amazon.co.uk; Japan — amazon.co.jp; and Spain — amazon.es.

The firm can *export* any digital product — book, video game, movie, recorded music — without traditional import arrangements. Wessex offers all products as pdf e-books; customers pay by credit card and can *import* to any geography. TutorVista (India) uses voice-over-Internet telephony, instant messaging, and electronic blackboards to provide online tutoring and educational content in more than 30 subjects to students in many foreign countries.

LOCAL PRODUCTION

The firm has several options for offering products locally:

ACQUISITION

The firm acquires a firm/business unit in the foreign market. Marketing, sales, and other functions are already in place, together with local business and personal relationships. The firm surmounts many political/legal and sociocultural barriers. Entry can be fast, but acquisition may be more expensive than greenfield investment. Further, governmental bodies may delay, modify,[27] or even prohibit some acquisitions, like the EU blocking GE's Honeywell purchase.

GREENFIELD

In a *greenfield* **project**, the firm constructs local facilities from scratch. Factors driving this option include high tariff barriers, high transportation costs, local content rules, and wanting to be close to customers. Some firms enter foreign markets via imports and build local marketing and sales organizations. When revenues reach a threshold, they switch to local production. Trade liberalization, transportation cost reductions, and outsourcing have reduced greenfield's attraction but it remains popular.

⚷ **KEY IDEA**

➤ Firms that set up production operations in a foreign country may choose among:
- Greenfield
- Acquisition
- Joint venture

➤ Sometimes host countries insist that foreign firms form joint ventures with local firms.

Greenfield Market Entry

Tesco is the world's third largest supermarket, Britain's largest and most successful retail chain, and the global leader in Internet grocery. Tesco entered the U.S market in 2007 — Sainsbury's and Marks & Spencer (Britain), Carrefour (France), and many European food retailers had failed. Years of marketing research and planning preceded Tesco's entry. Tesco conducted many focus groups and surveys and a senior executive team lived with 60 U.S. families for two weeks; Tesco even built a mock store in a California warehouse. Tesco opened several *Fresh & Easy* stores in Phoenix neighborhoods to gain more data. At 10,000 square feet, *Fresh & Easy* supermarket/convenience store hybrids are quite different from Tesco's mammoth British stores. But they similarly promise "Every Day Low Price" and build on Tesco's British convenience store experience in product assortment and operational efficiency. *Fresh & Easy* stores offer a wider food selection (including ready meals) than typical U.S. convenience stores. Using customer data from its Clubcard loyalty program, Tesco modifies product assortments and sends customers discount offers tailored to shopping behavior. Within three years, Tesco was operating 150 *Fresh & Easy* stores in Arizona, California, and Nevada.

JOINT VENTURE

A joint venture with a local partner helps the firm reduce political/legal and sociocultural risks, but degree of ownership can be a critical issue. Some governments require foreign entrants to have domestic partners, and may limit percentage ownership — the U.S. insists foreign interests can have only minority ownership in U.S. airlines. Conversely, some foreign market entrants desire majority control, but they may be surprised: GE's wholly owned Korean subsidiary was unsuccessful, but its newer minority-stake joint ventures with Hyundai Motors are very successful. Overall, results from international joint ventures are mixed; problems arise when investment requirements and results differ from expectations, partner objectives change, and parent-firm problems negatively affect the joint venture.

Local relationships are important for various aspects of entering foreign markets. In 2004, Cemex and other Mexican producers used various import-blocking tactics to prevent the *Mary Nour* from unloading 27,000 tons of Russian cement at Mexican ports. After six frustrating months, the *Mary Nour* left Mexican waters.

Local production requires host-country investment but strengthens local institutional and customer ties. The firm becomes part of the host country's administrative and cultural fabric as supplier, customer, employer, and taxpayer. Local production also avoids quotas and tariffs — Toyota and Nissan initially produced automobiles in the U.S. to avoid quotas. Challenges for firms producing in foreign markets are exposure to local labor laws, safety and security, and currency and expropriation risk.

Increasingly, firms make production-location decisions on regional or global bases; they may shift operations to low-wage countries or outsource to third-parties. Many U.S. service firms place call centers in India, Pakistan, and African English-speaking countries. Some firms site production to gain marketing and sales advantage. Boeing enhances Dreamliner sales efforts to Japanese airlines by securing complete wing assemblies from Japan's Fuji Heavy Industries.

Swedish/Swiss engineering firm ABB's various country subsidiaries specialize in producing certain products, then ship them to sister subsidiaries. ABB's specialization increases efficiency, lowers production costs, and vastly offsets increased transportation costs.

FRANCHISING

Franchising is a popular foreign-entry mode when the firm's value proposition requires local production and/or delivery. Fast food is the outstanding example; brands like Burger King,

KFC, McDonalds, Pizza Hut, Subway, and Wendy's mostly expand in foreign markets via franchising. Other international franchises include hotel brands like Hilton, Holiday Inn, Hyatt, and Sheraton; Curves (women's fitness centers); and Home Instead (senior care). The franchisor secures franchisees, conducts marketing and brand building, enforces standards, and may supply raw materials. The franchisee invests in local operations, local marketing and sales, and pays fees to the franchisor.

Because many franchisees are local entrepreneurs, market entry can be fast. Franchisors often appoint master franchisees for a country or geographic region. These established businesses are knowledgeable about local laws, customs, and consumer needs; they often act as mini-franchisors in their geographic areas. For the franchisor, securing strict adherence to standards from independent franchisees can be difficult, and failure may negatively affect the brand. In the hotel market, customers expect brand consistency from property to property around the world. Yet, many different hotel operators manage major global brands.

Sometimes franchisors allow local market variation to better address local needs — KFC Japan offers egg sandwiches for breakfast, specially flavored chicken, and special packaging.

> Wessex Press entered Europe via active entry. To identify potential faculty adopters, Wessex advertises in European marketing journals, sends its sales director to academic conferences, and e-mails marketing instructors. Wessex prints books in Shanghai and England; a local distributor maintains inventory and ships books throughout Europe.

KEY IDEA

➤ When firms expand internationally, they often follow a trajectory of:

• Limited international marketing
• Regional marketing
• Global marketing

STRATEGIES FOR INTERNATIONAL, REGIONAL, AND GLOBAL MARKETING

Globalization is driving increased numbers of firms to expand outside their home countries. They must decide on the scope of their foreign activities, then make serious strategic international and global marketing decisions. The basis for these decisions should be the six marketing imperatives at the heart of *Managing Marketing in the 21st Century*. Specifically, they must make decisions about objectives, and consider segmentation and branding decisions.

SCOPE

Firms engage in **international marketing** when they expand outside their domestic markets. The major differences across firms concern the *scope* of their efforts in foreign markets and the challenges they face — Figure 23.2. We identify three broad approaches to international marketing.

FIGURE 23.2

APPROACHES TO ADDRESSING FOREIGN MARKETS

Limited international marketing. These firms limit operations outside their domestic markets. A typical exemplar enters a few geographically proximate countries: U.S. firms in Canada

Product Innovation and International Growth

The international product life cycle (IPLC) model dates to the 1960s. The four-stage, time-bound, IPLC attempted to describe the international trade cycle for most products. Stage 1: U.S.-developed products launched domestically, then beyond the U.S. to dominate the world market. In stages 2, 3, and 4, producers from other developed countries became stronger in their markets, then in third-country markets and, finally, in the U.S.[28]

The IPLC was a useful descriptive device in the mid-20th century and may still describe some product evolution today. But many changes have decreased its utility[29]:

- **Innovation locus.** The IPLC assumed that innovation occurred in the U.S. Although the U.S. still produces much global innovation, many firms in other advanced economies like Western Europe, Japan, and Korea also produce significant innovation.

- **Global launch.** Enhanced global competition means that product innovators can no longer wait months and years to go abroad. Increasingly, innovative firms launch simultaneously in many countries and regions. Easily copied digital products like movies are a special case: Three weeks after release, *Avatar*'s $1 billion box-office revenues made it the all-time most successful movie — international revenues approached $700 million.[30]

- **New products and developing economies.** The IPLC assumed that developing economies received the product last and never innovated. But as multinationals mature, they transfer ideas and products among subsidiaries, even bypassing head office. Walmart's international failures relate to local insensitivity, but it is evolving. In India, Walmart modeled *Best Price Modern Wholesale* stores for small merchants on successful *Maxxi* stores (Brazil); in China, *Smart Choice* discount supermarkets derive from *Todo Dia* stores (Brazil); Walmart is successful in Japan with private-label wines, cookies, and other products developed by *Asda* (Britain). McDonald's Australia pioneered McCafé; *Big Tasty* burger was developed in Germany and test marketed in Sweden; sales are high in Europe, Latin America, and Australia.

GE, John Deere, P&G, and Unilever and others now develop products for customers in low-income countries.[31] GE Healthcare developed the MAC 800 electrocardiograph for doctors in China and India. Reversing the *hand-me-down* IPLC, GE pursued a *hand-me-up* strategy by launching MAC 800 in the U.S. Nestlé sells low-cost South Asian Maggi noodles in Australia.

Emerging markets can act as idea generators. Obopay (Silicon Valley startup) offers consumers and small businesses money transfer via cell phone.[32] Millions of Africans and Indians now have access to financial services. Obopay's system is also available in the U.S. Worldwide estimates of one billion bank accounts and four billion cell phones suggest a large potential global market.

- **Emerging market multinationals.** Until recently, virtually all multinationals were based in the U.S., Western Europe, and Japan. But as emerging economies spawn strong domestic firms, many are becoming multinationals (by organic growth and acquisition).[33] China's Hisense and Haier compete in the global home appliance market; Lenovo and Taiwan's Acer are PC leaders[34]; BYD is world leader in nickel-cadmium batteries. Brazil's Embraer is a world leader in regional jet aircraft; Sadia and Perdigão are global players in pork, poultry, and grain; and InBev is a global beer leader. Mexico's Cemex is a world leader in ready-mix concrete. India's Tata is a global conglomerate; ArcelorMittal (steel), Wipro (information services) and Ranbaxy (generic drugs), are also major players. Frequently these firms have cost advantages from domestic labor and economies of scale from large home markets; also, they may not have costly *legacy systems*. They may have strong local competencies like addressing hard-to-reach, price-sensitive customers, and standardize these approaches for foreign markets.[35,36]

Marketing Question

You have been appointed Tata Motors' Marketing Vice President for North America. Your immediate task is to launch the *Nano,* a four-door, four-passenger vehicle that sells in India for about $2,200. What will be the core elements in your three-year launch plan? Make sure you ask and answer critical strategic questions.

and/or Mexico and Caribbean countries — like State Farm (insurance) and Alaska Airlines; Belgian firms in Holland and Luxembourg, or New Zealand firms in Australia. These firms generally face five core challenges:

- Which countries to enter
- In what order
- How to enter
- What market strategy to employ
- How to implement the market strategy

Regional marketing. These experienced international marketers focus their efforts on a relatively large group of countries typically, but not exclusively, within a single continent — like Europe, Latin America, or Asia Pacific. Many airlines focus on geographically proximate countries, like Ryanair and easyJet (Europe) and Air Asia. By contrast, Brazilian bus maker Marcopolo concentrates on less-developed markets (Argentina, China, Colombia, Egypt, India, Mexico, South Africa). The regional marketer's strategic anchor may be its domestic market, but the firm allocates resources broadly across the region and attempts to optimize performance across the various countries.

Global marketing. Like regional marketers, global marketers have extensive international experience, but set their sights more broadly. Rather than focus on a single region, they seek opportunities globally. The typical global marketer has multicountry presence in several continents, and faces the challenge of optimizing performance across regions and countries.

Regional and global marketers are serious about foreign markets; each firm type must carefully manage its country portfolio. Sometimes the firm *fills out* geographic scope by adding countries; other times it may withdraw — some countries may be less attractive than they appeared before entry. Walmart's stated goal is to be a global retailer yet it withdrew from both the German and South Korean markets (but entered Africa by acquiring Massmart). Regional marketers may contemplate forging a global strategy by entering countries in additional regions.

OBJECTIVES

The firm should consider objectives at two levels: international business overall, and its partition by region and country. In general, relevant measures are similar to those for domestic markets — revenues, profits, and market share — Chapter 22. The firm should also set goals for the speed with which it ramps up international activity.

SEGMENTING MULTIPLE COUNTRY MARKETS

International and global marketers should answer two critical questions:

- How should we form segments for developing international market strategy? The firm can either group countries or form across-country segments.
- How should we decide which segments to address?

Segmentation also has important implications for organizing for international and global markets (below).

SEGMENTATION BY GROUPING COUNTRIES

Approaches to country grouping include:

- **Common markets and trade zones.** Related to geographic proximity but omits non-member geographically proximate countries. Examples: EU,[37] AFTA, Mercosur, and NAFTA.

- **Cultural closeness.** The firm may group countries based on various attitudinal dimensions. Table 23.4 shows country clusters based on a synthesis of research studies.[38]

Anglo	Arab	Far Eastern	Germanic	Latin American	Latin European	Near Eastern	Nordic	Independents
Australia	Bahrain	Indonesia	Austria	Argentina	Belgium	Greece	Denmark	Brazil
Canada	Kuwait	Hong Kong	Germany	Chile	France	Iran	Finland	India
Great Britain	Oman	Malaysia	Switzerland	Colombia	Italy	Turkey	Norway	Israel
Ireland	United Arab Emirates	Philippines		Mexico	Portugal		Sweden	Japan
New Zealand	Saudi Arabia	Singapore		Peru	Spain			
South Africa		Taiwan		Venezuela				
United States								

TABLE 23.4

CLUSTERING COUNTRIES BY ATTITUDINAL DIMENSIONS

- **Geographic proximity.** Options include grouping by continent — Africa, Asia, Australasia, Europe, North America, South America; or by subcontinent — Scandinavia, Central America. Southeast Asia, Indian subcontinent.[39] Reduced physical distance via geographic proximity has many benefits.

- **Historical relationships.** Examples are the British Commonwealth (former British possessions), the Commonwealth of Independent States (CIS) (formerly members of the Soviet Union), Spain and Spanish Latin America, and Portugal and Brazil.

- **Income:**[40]
  - **Organisation for Economic Co-operation and Development (OECD) members (high income):** 34 countries — includes Australia, Italy, U.S.
  - **Other high income:** 39 countries — includes Andorra, Israel, United Arab Emirates
  - **Upper middle income:** 46 countries — includes Algeria, Lithuania, Venezuela
  - **Lower middle income:** 55 countries — includes Albania, Kosovo, West Bank and Gaza
  - **Low income:** 43 countries — includes Afghanistan, Madagascar, Zimbabwe

- **Language.** Has elements of geographic proximity and historical relationships but focuses specifically on language. Examples are English- and Spanish-speaking countries.

- **Specific purpose.** Examples are OPEC (oil production) and NATO (defense).

KEY IDEA

➤ Many firms form segments by grouping countries. Geographic proximity is the most common method but other approaches may be more useful.

ACROSS-COUNTRY SEGMENTATION

The firm may form market segments regardless of geographic location:

- **Demographic characteristics.** Traditional demographic variables alone or in combination — Chapter 8 — can form segments. B2C variables include age, education, gender, income, and religion. Company size, growth, industry, and profitability are useful B2B variables. In the Opening Case, DHL employs a fairly typical B2B global segmentation:
  - **Tier 1:** top 100 customers
  - **Tier 2:** other multinational customers
  - **Tier 3:** thousands of local customers

- **Values.** Roper Starch Worldwide (RSW) identified six global B2C segments by interviewing 1,000 consumers in 35 countries about core values. Generally, consumers in different segments were different in activities, media use, and product purchase[41]:
  - **Strivers.** Place greater emphasis on material and professional goals than other groups
  - **Devouts.** Tradition and duty very important
  - **Altruists.** Interested in social issues and society welfare
  - **Intimates.** Value close personal family relationships
  - **Fun seekers.** Frequent restaurants, bars, and movies
  - **Creatives.** Strong interest in education, knowledge, and technology

KEY IDEA

➤ Some firms develop international segments by grouping countries; other firms form segments that cross country boundaries.

Three examples of targeting market segments regardless of geographic location: Swiss-based Phonak markets personal communication assistants (hearing aids) to baby boomers. Clinique offers products to particular skin types and skin tones. P&G discovered that teenage girls around the world have the same questions about puberty, hence Always/Whisper brands use similar targeting approaches everywhere.

In the automobile industry, firms like BMW and Toyota make automobiles for specific market segments regardless of geographic location. By contrast, Ford traditionally made separate models for regional markets like the U.S., and Europe, in part because differing managerial perspectives made global collaboration difficult. But the *One Ford* initiative is a global approach, starting with the Ford Fiesta. To support Ford's global efforts, advertising agency WPP formed regional hubs for North America (Detroit), Asia Pacific (Shanghai), Europe, and Latin America, comprising individual WPP agencies. Team Detroit includes JWT, Mindshare, Ogilvy & Mather Worldwide, Wunderman, and Y&R; a senior WPP executive signs off on all Ford global launches.

Marketing Question

Over many years, Toyota earned an enviable record for high-quality products. But in 2009, Toyota was forced to recall over seven million automobiles because of unintended acceleration. What actions would you suggest that Toyota take to repair the damage to its brand image?

BRANDING IN GLOBAL MARKETS

The firm's core branding choice is between *local* and *global*. When the firm provides the same or similar products in multiple countries, should it offer a single brand — **global branding**, or multiple **local brands**? The branding decision follows directly from the firm's segmentation choices. Global brands are now ubiquitous. Arguments for **global branding** include:

- **Cross-border travel.** Increased travel drives demand as consumers seek out their favorite brands while traveling.
- **Growth.** The firm may be able to leverage brand equity to new geographic markets.
- **Homogeneity of customer tastes across countries.** Global media and global product availability shape consumer tastes for global brands. Sweden's H&M operates 500 stores in 12 European countries. Eighty percent of sales are outside Sweden; operating profits are growing at 20 percent annually. H&M attributes its success to global fashion trends driven by satellite television, movies, music, and the Internet. Relatedly, many B2B firms are introducing global standardization for parts and raw material purchases.
- **Increased global media reach and lower costs.** Television — like Star TV (Asia), CNN, ESPN, BBCWorld News, and the Internet reach multinational audiences. The firm can achieve scale economies in advertising, perhaps by dubbing in different languages.

Global brands offer specific advantages:

- **Aspirational values.** Only global brands deliver aspirational values for products like cosmetics, and associate them with global events — Olympic Games and World Cup.
- **Brand image.** A global brand promotes a consistent brand image.
- **Best practice.** Global branding eases best-practice transfer across geographies.
- **Competitive advantage.** Global brands often signify quality and innovation.
- **Global appeal.** Some brands like BMW, Rolls-Royce, and Marlboro have global appeal from many years of international exposure.
- **Human capital.** A global brand can help recruit and retain better people worldwide.

Firms that adopt global branding make branding decisions at corporate headquarters.[42] Typically, the firm must make an affirmative global branding decision as, traditionally, it probably made branding decisions locally, almost by default. Most multinationals vest substantial decision-making authority in country managers and regional vice presidents; these executives attempt to optimize performance in their countries and regions. In such cases, the firm may brand its products quite differently from one country/region to another.

Unilever is the second largest detergent firm globally (after P&G) based on ALA, OMO, Persil, Skip, and other brands. Traditionally, these brands operated as a loose confederation embracing 25 different positionings, names, and packaging designs in various countries around the world. Unilever's *Dirt Is Good* (DIG) umbrella provides a single global positioning for its brands by invoking the universal social mission of human development focused on children. The underlying notion: When children are

CONTINUES ON NEXT PAGE

learning and developing sometimes their clothes get dirty — DIG takes care of the dirt. To develop this positioning, Unilever embraced several core principles the DIG team implemented:

- **Build.** Unilever dramatically increased resources to the global approach and provides tools and practical tips to operating teams around the world.

- **Connect.** Each brand stakeholder had a voice in developing a new vision that emphasized similarities (not differences) across geographic markets.

- **Focus.** Address underlying differences but make clear choices.

- **Inspire.** Inspire consumers, customers, and internal stakeholders with the new positioning.

- **Organize.** Demonstrate new ways of working by agreeing to new roles.

Unilever achieved double-digit growth and market share increases in key markets.[43]

For many years, Samsung and LG located branding responsibility with dozens of individual country agencies. In shifting to global branding, Samsung ($600 million) and LG ($350 million) placed their entire advertising budgets with single global agencies. Sometimes internal roadblocks inhibit this evolution: Unilever decided to manage its Dove soap brand globally — but only top management intervention secured cooperation from German and French subsidiaries.

Global branding does not imply identical implementation programs across countries.[44] Differing national tastes often drive product design variations; MTV is a global brand with local and regional adaptations. Pricing should reflect what local customers can pay; promotional activities should be appropriate for the market, and the firm should base distribution on local options. *Think global, act local — glocal —* guides many firms. Petit Bateau (PB) is a good example:

PB makes and sells high-quality clothing for babies and children. PB has a consistent global brand image for comfort and quality. Designs and fabrics are fairly standard; all products bear PB's trademark blue-and-yellow logo. PB's websites, posters, and hangtags are identical except for text translations. Yet in the U.S., young women (20s and 30s) wear PB's tee-shirts. PB raises prices and dedicates the front half of its stores to *Les Grands* (for adults); posters depict young women wearing PB products.

In practice, global firms have global, regional, and local brands. Coca-Cola offers 500 brands in 200 countries: Four brands are global — Classic Coca-Cola/Coca-Cola, Diet Coke/Coke Light, Sprite, and Fanta. Many soft drink brands — fruit juice, bottled water, and sports drinks — are only available regionally, sometimes in a single country. Local bottlers support these brands as they often·outsell global brands. Table 23.5 displays selected Coke brands.

Americas		Europe, Middle East, Africa		Asia/Pacific
Barq's	Mello Yellow	Cherry Coke	Sensun	Ambasa
Cherry Coke	Minute Maid	Kinley	Tab	Kin Cider
Citra	Mr. Pibb	Lilt	Tab X-tra	Krest
Delaware Punch	Nordic Ginger Ale	Mezzo Mix	Urge	Lemon & Paeroa
Fresca	Quatro	Schizan		Lift
Kinley	Surge			Mello
Kuat	Tai			Sarsi

TABLE 23.5

SELECTED COCA-COLA SOFT DRINK BRANDS BY REGION

Nestlé has 10 worldwide corporate brands, 45 worldwide strategic brands, 140 regional strategic brands, and 7,500 local brands. Nestlé evolves its brand portfolio. Nestlé redefined Chambourcy and Findus from worldwide strategic brands to regional strategic brands, and used the German Maggi brand to expand into Eastern Europe with prepared foods — Figure 23.3 for Nestlé's branding tree.

Building a Company without Borders: Reckitt Benckiser[45]

Reckitt Benckiser (RB) resulted from the 1999 merger of two FMCG firms — Reckitt Coleman (Britain) and Benckiser (the Netherlands). Since the merger, net revenues have more than doubled; operating profits have quintupled. Post merger, RB deliberately placed top managers in new territories; most country managers and many direct reports are foreigners. All 400 top managers have the same employment contract and compensation structure; hence, relocation is relatively easy. RB's global mobility supports taking a successful product from one country to another, like Dettol (British antiseptic disinfectant) to Chile. RB seeks ideas in all markets, supports minority positions, and takes risks. A Korean brand manager identified a potential new air freshener; most evaluating group members believed it would fail in Europe, but two members were passionate advocates and RB went ahead — the Air Wick Freshmatic, launched in 85 countries, is RB's most successful new product ever. In 2010, RB acquired SSL International; its Durex (condoms) and Scholl's (foot products) brands offer good expansion opportunities in China and Russia.

FIGURE 23.3

THE NESTLE BRANDING TREE[46]

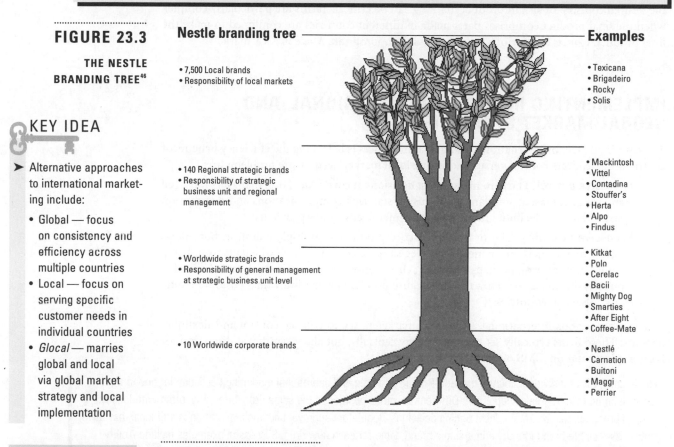

Nestle branding tree

- 7,500 Local brands
- Responsibility of local markets

- 140 Regional strategic brands
- Responsibility of strategic business unit and regional management

- Worldwide strategic brands
- Responsibility of general management at strategic business unit level

- 10 Worldwide corporate brands

Examples

- Texicana
- Brigadeiro
- Rocky
- Solis

- Mackintosh
- Vittel
- Contadina
- Stouffer's
- Herta
- Alpo
- Findus

- Kitkat
- Polo
- Cerelac
- Bacii
- Mighty Dog
- Smarties
- After Eight
- Coffee-Mate

- Nestlé
- Carnation
- Buitoni
- Maggi
- Perrier

KEY IDEA

➤ Alternative approaches to international marketing include:

- Global — focus on consistency and efficiency across multiple countries
- Local — focus on serving specific customer needs in individual countries
- *Glocal* — marries global and local via global market strategy and local implementation

---

Marketing Question

In the aftermath of WWII, Western customers viewed Japanese goods as cheap and poor quality; today, many customers have positive associations with Japanese products. How would you advise a Russian firm seeking to export to the U.S.?

COUNTRY OF ORIGIN

Country-of-origin (COO) effects add to (or subtract from) firm brands, forming customer attitudes and intentions and securing purchase.[47] Country of origin researchers identify three effects[48]:

- **Cognitive.** COO signals product quality but can be positive or negative depending on the product. German engineering and French wine have positive quality perceptions but French cars and computers are negative.

- **Affective.** COO has symbolic and emotional meaning for customers and confers attributes like authenticity, exoticness, and status. Many second-generation Italian-American women are strongly attached to Italian products, especially food-related — *Italy* has a strong emotional and symbolic connotation for these consumers. Many Asian consumers have positive attitudes toward Western brands.

- **Normative.** Customers view purchasing from certain countries as doing the *right* thing — domestic products to help the national economy[49] or products from a developing country to help alleviate poverty; or the *wrong* thing to do — British consumers avoiding Argentine beef during the Falklands/Malvinas war, European antiwar consumers avoiding U.S. products after the Iraq invasion, and Chinese consumers boycotting Japanese products because of economic and military rivalry.[50]

The extent of cognitive, affective, and normative effects varies across products, across countries being evaluated, and across evaluators.[51] Some COO effects are long lasting, like individualism and democracy for the U.S., but others change over time. South Africa's image improved dramatically when it abolished apartheid and adopted majority rule; perceptions of Japanese goods evolved from cheap and nasty in the 1940s–1950s to high quality today.

Because of COO-related branding issues and differential tariff rates across countries, securing the desired country-of-origin product marking can be critical. Tariffs are particularly complex when the final product comprises parts made in different countries are combined to make the final product. Courts use various tests to assess the appropriate *Made in XXX* mark.[52]

IMPLEMENTING INTERNATIONAL, REGIONAL, AND GLOBAL MARKET STRATEGIES

The core challenge for international and global marketers is balancing the efficiency benefits of centralized corporate control versus addressing local market needs. Core problems are:

- **Excessive control.** The firm makes most decisions at corporate. Local managers must sell standard products, at standard prices, using standard communications and distribution systems. Lack of flexibility in meeting customer needs causes problems.

- **Excessive flexibility.** The firm offers a core product in multiple countries but allows country managers to make most other decisions. The firm gains few benefits from being a multinational firm, perhaps branding, cost economies, or intellectual capital transfer. Country-specific approaches may also cause problems when individual customers purchase in several countries.

Today, most serious international and global marketers try to balance control and flexibility benefits. These firms typically set market strategy centrally, but allow significant discretion for local implementation. BMS offers a good example:

Historically, BMS' individual country managers made strategic and operational marketing decisions for new drugs after securing local regulatory approval. Different countries positioned the same drug differently, often with locally chosen brand names, and made local pricing decisions. Regulatory approval and implementation is still local, but BMS now uses a single brand identity and a single brand name for each new drug. Successful examples include Abilify (schizophrenia, bipolar disorder) and Reyataz (HIV).

For marketing mix implementation decisions, we assume the firm has set market strategy centrally but provides significant autonomy to meet local needs.

PRODUCT

Degree of product standardization is the critical *product* decision for international, regional, and global marketers. Product standardization across national markets reduces costs and may allow the firm to offer lower prices. Conversely, standardization ignores local requirements and makes it easier for gray markets to form by shipping a standard product across national borders. Alternatively, the firm may develop a core product appropriate for many foreign markets but allow local variations. Some variations are trivial, like local language translation for books, movies, and packaging, but others are more substantial. Firms offering food and body care products frequently use different formulation to match local requirements; FMCG firms should select packaging colors and shapes sensitively.

> Disney understands the need to localize. Hong Kong's Disneyland sells local food and gift items; Main Street parades focus on Chinese themes and music; Mickey and Minnie dress in red Chinese outfits; and visitors take photos with Cai Shen Ye, the bearded Chinese god of wealth.

In B2B markets, where multinational customers are shifting to global procurement, suppliers often standardize product lines to reduce costs. Conversely, in large foreign markets, customer needs may differ by geographic region. Consumer needs in China's coastal cities are often quite different from interior cities; consumers in large Indian cities like Delhi, Kolkata, and Mumbai may have different needs from rural areas. To address Indian disparities, Nokia offers cell phones that double as flashlights (for power outages) and for multiple-person use.

Frequently, firms with successful domestic products enter foreign markets by focusing on its diaspora. Coca-Cola Russia created a new version of a traditional Russian drink — Kvass; Krushka & Bochka now sells in New York targeting Russian immigrants.

Marketing Question

Successful Spanish restaurant chain 100 Montaditos (inexpensive sandwiches and beer) entered the U.S. with a goal of opening 4,000 outlets in five years, via a combination of company-owned and franchised stores. Do you think 100 Montaditos will be successful? Why or why not? How would you advise 100 Montaditos?

COMMUNICATIONS

Firms expanding internationally may have to adapt communications approaches to local conditions. In Brazil, Nestlé's barge, *Nestlé Até Voce a Bordo* (*Nestlé Takes You on Board*), travels the Amazon to showcase Nestlé products to river-port inhabitants. Citibank launched credit cards in India using door-to-door salespeople — an unthinkable practice in developed economies. Hindustan Lever's *Shakti* program trains rural women (over 45,000) as entrepreneurial salespeople (and distributors) of consumer products in small villages.

Language differences across countries imply different communications. But the firm must be careful about translations; poor translations can cause problems — Table 23.3. Also, in low-literacy countries, the firm should emphasize visuals, including graphs and diagrams, rather than words, but must be careful how customers interpret images and symbols (including logos). Color is an important issue. In Western Europe and the U.S., white implies birth, peace, and purity; in China, death, mourning, and spirits. In Western Europe and the U.S., blue implies authority, coldness, and conservatism; in Islamic countries, honesty, trust, virtue, and wealth. Of course, media decisions depend on local options.

> Exxon gains globalization benefits while localizing its message. Typically, Exxon develops TV advertising campaigns with expensive visuals, but uses multiple groups of local actors to tailor these campaigns to local markets.

Communications are also critical in face-to-face situations. Different negotiating styles are more or less successful in different cultures. *Individualistic* cultures like the U.S. favor direct *to-the-point* approaches; *collectivist* cultures like China favor an emphasis on developing personal relationships. Further, English is fast becoming the lingua franca of international business but true bilingual fluency is relatively rare. Communications with customers and internal to the firm can each pose significant problems. An Indonesian national may give a competent English *presentation*, but be unable to understand and implement decisions *proposed* in English.

DISTRIBUTION

The firm's distribution efforts should be appropriate to the local market. In China, Gucci and Louis Vuitton prosper with large stores that offer wide product variety with prices as low as a few hundred dollars — attracting luxury entrants and gift buyers. By contrast, Tiffany has done less well with small stores and limited high-end product selection. In the U.S., Walmart focuses distribution in very large stores — Supercenters and Sam's Clubs, but in Mexico it also operates small convenience stores — *Bodega Aurrera Express.*

Domestic-type distribution systems from developed countries may not be available in foreign markets, so creativity is critical. In Russia, P&G secured distribution to 80 percent of the population by funding 32 regional distributors and 68 subdistributors. In Eastern Europe, P&G's *McVan* model provides significant competitive advantage by funding distributors to secure information technology, training, vans, and working capital. Coca-Cola distributes products in over 200 countries by doing *whatever it takes.* In less-developed countries, individuals deliver Coke using handcarts, motorcycles, and small boats, depending on topography. In Russia, Coke's own vehicles stock half a million stores.

PRICE

The firm should gear prices to target market segment(s) in specific countries. Firms may successfully offer mass-market products at similar prices in several developed countries. But in less-developed countries, similar product/price combinations may only address wealthy elites. To reach broader customer segments with the same product, the firm may have to reduce prices.

In setting prices in multiple countries, the firm must consider arbitrage and **gray markets**. If the price difference between two countries is significantly greater than transportation, import duty, and other costs, entrepreneurs may purchase in Country A for resale in Country B. Such gray market activity typically plays havoc with firm marketing efforts in foreign markets. Of course, the firm must keep its eye on exchange rates as actual prices necessarily diverge from planned prices as exchange rates evolve.[53]

When exporting products, the firm must ensure it does not run afoul of antidumping regulations. **Dumping** occurs when the firm exports goods to a foreign country below its home market price or production cost. Typically, governments initiate antidumping investigations to protect local industries. In 2010, the U.S. government initiated an antidumping investigation of aluminum extrusions from China; in 2010, China imposed antidumping duties on U.S. chicken products. In the 10 years from 1998 onwards, the EU initiated over 300 antidumping investigations.

When the firm targets multinational B2B customers, price differences by country are a special problem. Historically, many firms set markedly different prices for similar products in different countries. These differential prices did not pose a serious problem when multinationals made procurement decisions locally. Today, many multinationals use global procurement for many inputs. They do not understand why they should pay widely different prices from country to country and so pressure suppliers for price equivalence around the world.[54]

Transfer pricing is a special issue for international marketers. Transfer prices are internal to the firm — between one subsidiary and another. Generally, firms set high transfer prices when exporting from low tax-rate countries (low transfer prices when exporting from high tax-rate countries). Taxes are lower, but high transfer prices may lead to increased import duties.

ORGANIZING FOR INTERNATIONAL, REGIONAL, AND GLOBAL MARKETS

Firms entering foreign markets must make critical organizational decisions. In part, organization structure depends on the number of foreign markets entered and firm investment. Many international efforts start with export departments and international divisions but evolve to more advanced forms where segmentation plays an important role in organizational design.[55]

EXPORT DEPARTMENT

Typically, an export department at head office directs the firm's initial efforts in foreign markets. This department interfaces with agents and brokers and develops intellectual capital about international marketing and sales. When the firm transitions to local marketing and sales directed by country managers, the export department often continues as the key organizational link to head office.

KEY IDEA

➤ As firms increase participation in foreign markets, they typically evolve their organizational structures.

INTERNATIONAL DIVISION

As foreign sales increase, the firm replaces its export department with an international division; country managers report to the international division head. The relationship between country managers and corporate varies widely from firm to firm: Corporate may impose critical decisions on the countries, or assign them broad decision-making autonomy. Local autonomy promotes entrepreneurship, initiative, and speedy adaptation to local needs. Kraft successfully introduced Vegimite iSnack 2.0 in Australia and New Zealand; this Vegimite brand extension went from concept to launch in 10 months! Between the control/autonomy extremes, corporate decisions may allow some local autonomy; or local managers make decisions within a broad corporate policy framework and/or coordination.[56]

Many firms augment local marketing and sales with additional functions like production, technical service, finance, and even R&D. Country manager responsibility morphs from marketing and sales to general management, with P&L responsibility. Country managers often become very powerful individuals within the firm. Using this model, IBM local country operations were, for many years, a series of mini-IBMs.

Export departments and international divisions are appropriate organizational devices when the firm has limited entry in foreign markets. At some point, when international revenues become a significant part of corporate revenues and/or the firm enters a substantial number of foreign markets, more advanced organizational forms become appropriate.

GEOGRAPHIC REGION

The firm places individual countries in a regional structure, typically based on geographic proximity, and manages P&L at the country level. A typical structure comprises four regions: U.S. and Canada; Latin America; Europe, Middle East, and Africa (EMEA); and Asia Pacific (APAC).[57] There are many variations: Some firms split the Indian subcontinent from the rest of Asia Pacific; BMS treats Japan as a region; previously, the French electrical firm Schneider treated France as a region; in 2011, Starbucks evolved from an international division to three geographic regions — Asia, the Americas, and EMEA. Country managers are responsible for country performance, reporting to regional VPs with region-wide responsibility.

*Marketing
Question*

How do you assess Starbucks' organizational shift?

Advantages of the geographic-region organization over the international division are:

- Allows the firm to integrate functions across countries, within regions
- Avoids duplication costs
- Offers greater ability to manage performance across several countries, and
- Provides promotion opportunities for upwardly mobile executives.

The geographic (and international) division structure is appropriate when customer needs are *heterogeneous* across geography; country managers have significant autonomy.[58] Observers attribute McDonald's success to country franchises' ability to tailor offerings to local tastes. In Vienna, McCafés offer blended coffee; Indonesian customers can have French fries or rice; and a South Korean option is roast pork on a bun, with a garlicky soy sauce.

Swiss packaging firm Tetrapak operates globally through 41 market companies and 78 sales offices. Tetrapak manages global marketing efforts through 11 geographically proximate country clusters: North America, Central and South America, North Europe, Central Europe, South Europe, East Europe & Central Asia, Greater Middle East, Sub-Saharan Africa, Greater China, South & Southeast Asia, and Northeast Asia & Oceania. Each cluster head is country manager for Tetrapak's most important country in that cluster. Hence, the Japanese country manager heads the Northeast Asia & Oceania cluster encompassing Japan, Korea, Australia, and New Zealand.

FUNCTIONAL

In the functional structure, all firm functions globally, report directly to corporate; corporate controls decision-making around the world. The downside may be unresponsiveness to local conditions like offering inappropriate products, pricing, and service in various countries. Toyota was very successful with a functional structure, but was unresponsive to U.S. dealer complaints about unintended acceleration prior to the 2009 recall crisis. Complaints were adjudicated by a special committee in Japan, then routed back to the U.S.!

"Consistent with managing the ExxonMobil (EM) brand globally, we changed our organizational structure. We went from a geographic organization to a global functional organization. Previously, EM was organized as six geographically based operating companies held together by a logo. Each operating company was largely autonomous, had its own marketing staff, and developed its own advertising campaigns. Now, all the strategy development occurs at corporate. EM develops advertising campaigns globally; it operates with three guiding principles — consistency, improve communications quality, and efficiency. The operating companies execute locally. Corporate provides all advertising material and allows local variation in music background."[59]

GLOBAL PRODUCT DIVISION

The international-division and geographic-region structures place heavy focus on geographic diversity. By contrast, the global product-division (brand, business unit) focuses on global consistency and cost efficiency, and is appropriate when customer needs are *homogeneous* across geography.[60] The global product-division structure promotes production rationalization and is popular among FMCG firms with large product lines. This organization usually overlies a geographic structure where regional and/or country organizations have sales and distribution responsibility. Headquarters provides regions with standardized advertising programs for adaptation to local markets. The firm manages P&L at the product-division level; because it firm concentrates organization expertise by product, making global product variations is relatively straightforward. Conversely, the structure fragments international expertise, and product managers tend to favor large developed-country markets over emerging markets.

KEY IDEA

➤ Firms operating in many countries often develop matrix organizations where the two major axes are product and geography.

"L'Oreal is the most amazing global company. It's really global in the truest sense of the word. Inherent in our structure for the past 15 years has been a desire to truly integrate global development and have global brands. We have a system called the Affair d'Marc, according to the brand's origin. So, L'Oreal and Lancôme are Parisian brands; Redken and Maybelline are U.S. brands. In those countries, each Affair d'Marc has a development team for the basic brand strategy, brand image, and brand health, globally. Now L'Oreal is a Paris brand, so it has an Affair d'Marc in Paris, a 60-person group responsible for the L'Oreal brand. But because the U.S. is the largest and most competitive country for L'Oreal business, in spite of that structure, we must be 100 percent integrated into L'Oreal development. So we are considered co-developers; we have video-conferences every week, meetings once a month, and we debate a lot. We're the lead on several projects. We have a lot of ownership on practically all hair color projects. For the latest hair color launch we were the lead country. We had many meetings with the international team in France, working on brand international expansion. If we took a U.S. brand to Latin America, we would work with that team."[61]

GEOGRAPHIC REGION/PRODUCT DIVISION MATRIX

As previously discussed, advanced organization structures focus on a single dimension — Figure 23.4. Geographic-region organizations emphasize customer diversity in national markets; product-division organizations emphasize consistency, efficiency, and cost reduction. Matrix organizations attempt to balance both geographic and product concerns.[62] Some firms, like P&G, have moved beyond the matrix:

> P&G evolved slowly from a geographic-regional structure to a product/geographic matrix, but found this too unwieldy. In P&G's new structure, the product and geographic axes have different roles:
>
> - **Product.** Global business units (GBUs) have P&L responsibility.
>
> - **Geography.** Geographic market development organizations (MDOs) develop local go-to-market strategies and direct local sales forces — shared across GBUs.
>
> This organization works via a series of tables that produce protocols for deciding GBU/MDO conflicts, an elaborate review system, and flexibility to treat distinct areas like emerging markets outside the framework.

me2302

MARKETING ENRICHMENT

A Primer on Managing Global Customers me2302

GLOBAL CUSTOMER MANAGEMENT

When firms expand operations to multiple countries they often evolve their procurement operations. They prefer to source some inputs locally, but global procurement is often more effective and efficient. To enable global contracts, these firms want global supplier relationships. Hence, suppliers must develop organizational structures to interface with their global customers — global customer management, the third axis in Figure 23.4. The centerpiece of global customer management organizations is the global account manager (GAM). GAMs have full customer responsibility, but balancing customer priorities with product-division and geographic imperatives is often difficult.[63] Marketing Enrichment me2302 provides a primer on managing global customers.

> Previously, IBM had strong country managers reporting to powerful regional executives. Today, IBM operates with an industry-based structure where senior executives head up customer industries like financial services, manufacturing, and retail. In each industry organization, GAMs manage IBM's relationships with major global customers. Domestic salespeople report through the industry organization.[64] Geographic organizational structures remain intact for government relations, corporate advertising, and the care and feeding of locally employed personnel, but country heads no longer have budget responsibility.

FIGURE 23.4

ORGANIZATIONAL DESIGN DIMENSIONS FOR GLOBAL MARKETING

KEY IDEA

➤ Many B2B firms adopt global customer management organizations to address multinational customers.

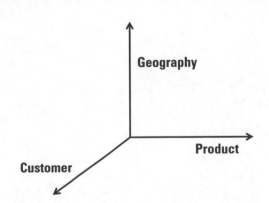

KEY MESSAGES

- Before your firm enters one or more foreign markets, make sure you have a good answer to the question — why are we doing this?

- In assessing a country's attractiveness for market entry, you should consider economic, political/legal, sociocultural, and geographic factors.

- Many international organizations take actions that affect foreign markets. Some organizations are global, like the WTO and World Bank; others are regional, like the EU, NAFTA, and ASEAN. The firm should monitor their activities, and individual bilateral agreements between countries.

- Passive entry strategies for entering foreign markets include exporting and licensing.

- Active entry strategies for entering foreign markets include importing — traditional and Internet-facilitated; local production — greenfield, acquisition, joint venture, and franchising.

- Many firms follow a strategy of progressive commitment to international markets via limited commitment to international marketing, regional marketing, then global marketing.

- When firms address the global market they may segment by country group or identify across-country segments.

- Many factors are driving firms to develop global marketing strategies.

- Many firms offering products globally also provide products for specific regions and countries.

- A *glocal* approach combines global strategy and local implementation.

- International and global marketers may choose among a variety of organizational forms.

VIDEOS AND AUDIOS

Global Marketing   v2302 📹   Spencer Pingel   Colgate-Palmolive

> ### Marketing Question
>
> What other messages did you glean from this chapter?

v2302

QUESTIONS FOR STUDY AND DISCUSSION

Can you answer the questions implied by this chapter's learning objectives? Check!

1. Wessex Inc. has secured a manuscript entitled *The Song of Hiroshima* by Atsuhiro Ozaki. Ozaki was working at a radio station in Hiroshima on August 6, 1945, the day the atom bomb dropped. *The Song of Hiroshima* is a personal account of his experience on that day and the following few days. How would you advise Wessex to proceed with publishing the book?

2. You recently joined Maxpleasure Inc., the well-known European condom manufacturer, as regional marketing manager for Africa. CEO Jennifer Major selected you from several well-qualified candidates. Major believes that a growing desire for family planning and the ravages of AIDS offer Maxpleasure an important opportunity to improve sales and profits in Africa. (USAID and the European Union will heavily subsidize condom production costs.) How will you approach this new assignment? What decisions must you make within the first three months?

3. As the CEO of a successful budget-hotel firm in the U.S., you have decided to expand operations to Spanish-speaking Central and South America. In the U.S., all hotels are company run but you are willing to contemplate a franchise business model. Either way, there are significant entry costs for any new foreign market and you must choose the countries very carefully. How would you go about developing an ordered list of countries by market attractiveness? Pick half a dozen countries to test your approach.

4. To solve an unexpected vacancy, Citibank has made a rush appointment. You have been promoted from a regional sales manager position in the midwest U.S. to become global account manager (GAM) for German electrical giant Siemens. You will be based in Siemens' headquarters in Munich, Germany. On Monday morning you are due to meet with your new boss, the global account director, for the first time. Prepare a list of questions that you would like him to answer.

5. Select a product in which you are interested. Alternatively, consider this book — *Managing Marketing in the 21st Century*. Develop a strategy and action plans for improving its global sales and the global sales of all Wessex's books.

ENDNOTES

To access O-codes, go to **www.ocodes.com**

CHAPTER 1

1 Based in part on an interview with Howard Schultz; N. Capon, *The Marketing Mavens*, New York: Crown Business, 2007 `e101`.

2 Day part means part of the day, like breakfast, mid-morning, or lunchtime.

3 Stephan Haeckel, Director of IBM's Advanced Business Institute, summed up the marketing philosophy: "Marketing's future is not as a function of business, but as the function of business." S.H. Haeckel, "Adaptive Enterprise Design: The Sense-and-Respond Model," *Planning Review*, (May–June 1995).

4 A.G. Lafley, "What Only The CEO Can Do," *Harvard Business Review*, 87 (May 2009), pp. 54–62, at p. 57 `e104`.

5 For a new chief marketing officer's (CMO) experience, see F.M. Jacques, "Even Commodities Have Customers," *Harvard Business Review*, 85 (May 2007), pp. 110–119 `e105`.

6 Marketing gains internal stature and greater resources when it demonstrates value to the firm. Many marketing researchers try to show positive relationships between marketing, profit, and shareholder value: R.T. Rust, T. Ambler, G.S. Carpenter, V. Kumar, and R.K. Srivastava, "Measuring Marketing Productivity: Current Knowledge and Future Directions," *Journal of Marketing*, 68 (October 2004), pp. 76–89 `e106a`; D. O'Sullivan and A.V. Abela, "Marketing Performance Measurement Ability and Firm Performance," *Journal of Marketing*, 71 (April 2007), pp. 79–93 `e106b`; S. Srinivasan and D.M. Hanssens, "Marketing and Firm Value: Metrics, Methods, Findings, and Future Directions," *Journal of Marketing Research*, 46 (June 2009), pp. 293–312; and "Commentaries and Rejoinder," pp. 313–329 `e106c`.

7 Marketing ideas and concepts have broad applicability. We focus on for-profit firms but other domains include: public and not-for-profit organizations — for customers and funders; politicians — for votes; nations, states, and cities — for tourists and business investment; ideas and causes — for individuals to exert political pressure. At some level, marketing is a technology to encourage people to behave in a desired fashion; hence, marketing relates to the exercise of power — reward, coercive, legitimate, referent, and expert power. J.R.P. French and B. Raven, "The Bases of Social Power," in D. Cartwright and A. Zander, *Group Dynamics*, New York: Harper & Row, 1959 `e107`.

8 Some firms extend the customer-value/shareholder-value link to employees. Virgin CEO Richard Branson said: "I am convinced that companies should put their staff first, customers second, and shareholders third — ultimately that's in the best interests of customers and shareholders." D. Sheff, "The Virgin Billionaire," *Playboy*, February 1995. A senior Citibank executive described his firm's customer relationship managers: "Our critical assets walk in the door at 9:00 A.M. and walk out at 6:00 P.M."

9 Firms that do not understand these linkages and try raising stock price by other means often get in trouble, like Enron.

10 R. Martin, "The Age of Customer Capitalism," *Harvard Business Review*, 88 (January–February 2010), pp. 58–65 `e110a`, makes important distinctions among managerial capitalism (A.A. Berle and G.C. Means, *The Modern Corporation and Private Property*, New York: Macmillan, 1932 `e110b`), shareholder-value capitalism (M.C. Jensen and W.H. Meckling, "Theory of the Firm: Managerial Behavior, Agency Costs, and Ownership Structure," *Journal of Financial Economics*, 3 (October 1976), pp. 305–360 `e110c`), and customer-driven capitalism. Customer-driven capitalism focuses on delivering customer value and satisfaction.

11 In *CFO* magazine. Also Martin, *op. cit.* `e110a`

12 "At Alibaba, Investors Come Last," *BusinessWeek*, August 17, 2009, p. 49 `e112`.

13 In money economies, customers typically offer financial resources. In non-money economies and sometimes in money economies, customers

barter goods and services. *Managing Marketing in the 21st Century* focuses on output markets for firm product/services. The firm also participates in other important markets — as customer in raw material and capital goods markets, human resource markets, and financial markets.

14 IBM's earnings were: 1990 — $6.02 billion; 1991 — $2.82 billion; 1992 — ($4.96 billion); and 1993 — ($8.10 billion). L.V. Gerstner, *Who Says Elephants Can't Dance?* New York, Harper Business, 2002 **e114**.

15 P.F. Drucker, *The Practice of Management*, New York, Harper and Row, 1954, pp. 37–38 **e115**.

16 Wroe Alderson, Theodore Levitt, and other early marketing thinkers had a similar point of view.

17 "The customer is the most important in our business. The customer is not dependent on us; we are dependent on him. The customer is not an interruption of our work; he is the purpose of it. A customer does us a favor when he comes to see us; we aren't doing him a favor by waiting on him. A customer is part of our business, not an outsider. He is not just money in the cash register; he is a human being with feelings like our own. He comes to us with his needs and wants; it's our job to fill them. A customer deserves the most courtesy we can give him. He is the lifeblood of this and every business. He pays your salary. Without him we would have to close our doors. Don't ever forget it." Reputedly developed by Mahatma Gandhi and hung in his South African law office.

18 W.I. Huyett and S.P. Viguerie, "Extreme Competition," *The McKinsey Quarterly*, 1 (2005), pp. 47–57 **e118**.

19 For marketing's historical development, see R.S Tedlow, *New and Improved: The Story of Mass Marketing in America*, New York: Basic, 1990 **e119a**; F.E. Webster, "The Changing Role of Marketing in the Corporation," *Journal of Marketing*, 58 (October 1992), pp. 1–17 **e119b**.

20 Returns to shareholders combine dividends and capital gains from increasing share prices.

21 Periodically, influential academics and politicians attack the shareholder-value perspective. Thoughtful observers believe the more serious issue is less shareholder value per se, but using short-term stock-price as a measurement proxy.

22 When the firm purchases shares in the stock market it reduces the number of shares outstanding; the share price should increase. Share repurchase rewards shareholders when capital gains are less heavily taxed than dividends. Stock options give beneficiaries the right, but not the obligation, to buy shares at a specified price within a specified time period. Firms generally provide stock options to senior executives.

23 Managerial mindsets can also be liabilities. Polaroid's instant-photography demise is a good example: M. Tripsas and G. Gavetti, "Capabilities, Cognition, and Inertia: Evidence from Digital Imaging," *Strategic Management Journal*, 21 (2000), pp. 1147–1161 **e123**.

24 Cost of capital combines cost of equity and cost of debt. Multi-business firms should make appropriate adjustments for risk and may set different target rates of return for each business: J.C. Van Horne and J.M. Wachowicz, *Fundamentals of Financial Management* 13th Ed., Englewood Cliffs, NJ: Prentice Hall, 2008, Chapter 15 **e124a**. Many firms, like Herman Miller (office furniture), have adopted Economic Value Added (EVA) to manage and measure investment success. EVA is operating net income on a cash basis (or operating net income excluding amortization of goodwill and certain intangibles) less an explicit capital charge (debt plus equity): G. B. Stewart III, "EVA: Fact, and Fantasy," *Journal of Applied Corporate Finance*, 7 (Summer 1994), pp. 72–84 **e124b**. Also A.K. Sharma and S. Kumar, "Economic Value Added (EVA) — Literature Review and Relevant Issues," *International Journal of Economics and Finance*, 2 (May 2010), pp. 200–220 **e124c**. Three ways to increase EVA are: (1) increase profits without increasing capital, (2) invest in projects that earn more than the cost of capital, (3) withdraw from projects earning unattractive returns; Marketing Enrichment **me01**.

25 M.W. Johnson, C.M. Christensen, and H. Kagerman, "Reinventing Your Business Model," *Harvard Business Review*, 86 (December 2008), pp. 51–59, identifies four business-model components — customer value proposition, profit formula, key resources, and key processes **e125**.

26 P.F. Drucker, *Management: Tasks, Responsibilities, Practices*, New York, Harper & Row, 1973, p. 63 **e126**.

27 Personal communication from David Haines, Director of Global Branding, Vodafone.

28 Gerstner, *op. cit.*, p. 72 **e114**.

29 *Ibid*, p. 189 **e114**.

30 This term is taken from military usage.

31 We prefer **external orientation** to related terms like marketing culture, customer orientation, and market focus. First, *marketing* is historically associated with a function; hence, marketing may generate opposition from other functions. Second, firms often misidentify marketing with customer focus or even customer service — at a minimum, **external orientation** embraces competitors as well as customers. Third, **external orientation** connotes a broader environmental concern — firms, suppliers, customers, competitors, complementers, and the environment in general. Fourth, a firm may be customer oriented but not market oriented. Market-oriented firms select markets well but may serve customers poorly — customer-oriented firms do the reverse. External orientation subsumes good market selection and excellence in delivering customer value.

This perspective is virtually identical to Narver and Slater (**market orientation**) and is commonly employed by academics and practitioner-scholars at the Marketing Science Institute (MSI): J.C. Narver and S.F. Slater, "The Effect of a Market Orientation on Business Profitability," *Journal of Marketing*, 54 (October 1990), pp. 20–35 **e131a**. Kohli and Jaworski place more emphasis on using market intelligence and less on environmental understanding: A.K. Kohli and B.J. Jaworski, "Market Orientation: The Construct, Research Propositions and Management Implications," *Journal of Marketing*, 54 (April 1990), pp. 1–18 **e131b**; B.J. Jaworski and A.K. Kohli, "Market Orientation: Antecedents and Consequences," *Journal of Marketing*, 57 (July 1993), pp. 53–70 **e131c**. Also B. Shapiro, "What the Hell Is 'Market-Oriented'?," *Harvard Business Review*, 67 (November–December 1989), pp. 119–225 **e131d**, and R. Deshpandé, *Developing a Market Orientation*, Thousand Oaks, CA: Sage, 1999 **e131e**.

Slater and Narver also differentiate between expressed needs — the customer is aware, and *latent* needs — not consciously understood. *Market-oriented* firms try to satisfy both types of need. S.F. Slater and J.C. Narver, "Customer-Led and Market-Oriented: Let's Not Confuse the Two," *Strategic Management Journal*, 19 (1998), pp. 1001–1006 **e131f** and "Market-Oriented Is More Than Being Customer-Led," *Strategic Management Journal*, 20 (1999), pp. 1165–1168 **e131g**; B. Jaworski, A.K. Kohli, and A. Sahay, "Market-Driven Versus Driving Markets," *Journal of the Academy of Marketing Science*, 28 (2000), pp. 45–54, distinguish between market driven — doing a good job of serving current customers, and market driving — influencing market structure and customer behavior **e131h**. Also G.S. Carpenter, R. Glazer, and K. Nakamoto, *Readings on Market-Driving Strategies: Towards a New Theory of Competitive Advantage*, Reading, MA: Addison-Wesley, 1997 **e131i**.

32 A.J. Slywotsky and B.P. Shapiro, "Leveraging to Beat the Odds: The New Marketing Mind-Set," *Harvard Business Review*, 71 (September–October 1993), pp. 97–107 **e132**. Rahm Emmanuel, President Obama's first chief of staff, captured this perspective cogently by paraphrasing Nico Machiavelli (*The Prince*): "You never want a serious crisis to go to waste."

33 "The World's Most Admired Companies," *Fortune*, March 16, 2009, p. 77 **e133**.

34 "As Antidote to Slowdown, Intel Will Spend, Not Cut," *The New York Times*, February 28, 2001 `e134`.

35 Because advertising time and space rates decreased significantly, Sara Lee's actual benefit was greater than 25 percent.

36 "Don't Cut Back on Innovation," *Fortune*, April 22, 2009, p 69 `e136`.

37 Unfortunately, many firms *don't get it*. Ed Zander, Motorola CEO, said: "I think we ought to get back to putting the customer first … [it's something that] every corporation around the world takes for granted." "Motorola's Modernizer," *The Wall Street Journal*, June 23, 2005.

38 "Wachovia Bank and Trust Company," in N. Capon, *The Marketing of Financial Services*, Englewood Cliffs, NJ: Prentice Hall, 1992 `e138`.

39 Seven people died; the perpetrator was never caught.

40 Personal communication from Pat Kelly, Senior Vice President Worldwide Marketing, Pfizer Pharmaceuticals.

41 Many researchers found positive correlations between external orientation and organizational performance: C.R. Cano, F.A. Carrillat, and F. Jaramillo, "A Meta-Analysis of the Relationship between Market Orientation and Business Performance: Evidence from Five Continents," *International Journal of Research in Marketing*, 21 (2004), pp. 179–200 `e141`.

42 Haeckel, *op. cit.* `e103`, and S.H. Haeckel, *Adaptive Enterprise: Creating and Leading Sense-and-Respond Organizations*, Cambridge, MA: HBS Press, 1999 `e142`.

43 The Tylenol and stent examples show the easy slip from external orientation to internal orientation. J&J's actions in the stent market appear to have violated its credo — Chapter 21.

44 In his successful-small-company sample, Simon found intensive customer interaction: H. Simon, *Hidden Champions: Lessons from 500 of the World's Best Unknown Companies*, Boston, MA: Harvard Business School Press, 1996 `e144`.

45 D. Brass, "Microsoft's Creative Destruction," *The New York Times*, February 4 2010, p. A27 `e145`.

46 Personal communication from a senior Nabisco executive.

47 Perhaps best exemplified at ITT in the 1970s under CEO Harold Geneen. H. Geneen, *Managing*, Garden City, NY: Doubleday, 1984 `e147`.

48 Private firms are often less vulnerable to short-term profit pressures.

49 J. A. Byrne, *Chainsaw: The Notorious Career of Al Dunlap in the Era of Profit-at-Any-Price*, New York: Harper Business, 1999 `e149`.

50 For *really new products*, customers may be unable to articulate their needs. Regardless, as the new product development process gains momentum, there is typically plenty of opportunity to secure customer feedback.

51 Also E.S. McKay, *The Marketing Mystique*, New York: Amacom, 1979, revised by A.M. Rittenberg, Amacom, 1994 `e151a`. Some firms operate with a *legal orientation* — spend extensive effort on avoiding legal action, rather than viewing legal issues in a broader framework of business decisions. Some firms view legal as the *sales prevention department*. Intel shows that a properly aligned legal department can play an important role in business strategy. T. Jackson, *Inside Intel*, New York: Dutton, 1997 `e151b`.

52 Responsibility for some imperatives may fall elsewhere, like a business development group focusing on Marketing Imperative 1.

53 In Chapter 13, we expand on the critical distinction between *services* and *customer service*.

54 FMCG firms understand this value — far too many executives see only marketing communication expenses.

55 "Less Than the Sum of Its Parts," *The Economist*, June 23, 2001 `e155`.

56 K. Simmonds, "Removing the Chains from Product Strategy," *Journal of Management Studies*, 5 (1968), pp. 29–40 `e156`.

57 J. Welch, *Jack: Straight from the Gut*, Warner: New York, 2001 `e157`.

58 Personal communication from Pat Kelly, *op. cit.*

59 This principle is also fundamental to military strategy: "The secret of strategy is concentration of firepower on the right battlefield" (Napoleon); "The heart of all strategy is concentration of strength" (Von Clausewitz); "The essence of strategy is concentration of strength against enemy weakness" (Liddell-Hart). Important examples are the Inchon landings in the Korean War and Allied use of air power and mobility in the first Gulf War.

60 Other important selectivity dimensions are product portfolio choices; distribution system decisions; whether to focus on non-users, current customers, or competitors' customers; and which members of customer decision-making groups to target.

61 The firm should not discard market opportunities because it does not currently possess the required competencies; perhaps it can secure them.

62 Personal communication from Eric Kim, Executive Vice President, Global Marketing Operations, Samsung Inc.

63 Personal communication from Michael George, Chief Marketing Officer and Vice President, Corporate Strategy, Dell.

64 "A Cheerleader, for a Company in a Midlife Funk," *The New York Times*, June 23, 2002 `e164`.

65 In the 1992 U.S. presidential election, a critical statement was, "It's the economy, stupid."

66 Personal communication from Stew McHie, Global Brand Manager, Exxon Mobil Fuels Marketing.

67 Differential advantage is similar to monopolistic competition — firms earn a return greater than the going interest rate.

68 Simon, *op. cit.* `e144` Also J.R. Williams, "How Sustainable is Your Competitive Advantage," *California Management Review*, 34 (Spring 1992), pp. 29–52 `e168a`; P. Ghemawat, "Sustainable Advantage," *Harvard Business Review*, 64 (September–October 1986), pp. 53–94 `e168b`.

69 For other approaches to developing differential advantage: G. Stalk, P. Evans, and L.E. Shulman, "Competing on Capabilities: The New Rules of Corporate Strategy," *Harvard Business Review*, 70 (March–April 1992), pp. 57–69 `e169a`; D.J. Collis and C.A. Montgomery, "Competing on Resources: Strategy in the 1990s," *Harvard Business Review*, 73 (July–August) 1995, pp. 118–128 `e169b`; M. Reeves and M.S. Deimler, "New Bases of Competitive Advantage: The Adaptive Imperative," *The Boston Consulting Group*, 2009 `e169c`. For knowledge assets in securing competitive advantage, see D.J. Teece, "Capturing Value from Knowledge Assets," *California Management Review*, 40 (Spring 1998), pp. 55–78 `e169d`.

70 R. D'Aveni, *Hypercompetition*, New York: The Free Press, 1994 `e170`.

71 Tide has been the market-leading detergent for more than 50 years; in this period, Tide made more than 50 product and packaging changes.

72 R.L. Foster, *Innovation: The Attacker's Advantage*, New York: Summit, 1986 `e172`.

73 Some data suggest any difference may have value: G.S. Carpenter, R. Glazer, and K. Nakamoto, *Readings on Market-Driving Strategies: Towards a New Theory of Competitive Advantage*, New York: Addison Wesley Longman, 1997 `e131i`.

74 Personal communication from Michael Francis, Senior Vice President of Marketing, Target Stores.

75 R.W. Ruekert and O.C. Walker, "Marketing's Interaction with Other Functional Units: A Conceptual Framework and Empirical Evidence," *Journal of Marketing*, 51 (January 1987), pp. 1–19 `e175`.

76 Personal communication from Marty Homlish, senior marketing executive, Sony Electronics. Also H. Krohmer, C. Homburg, and J.P. Workman, "Should Marketing Be Cross-Functional? Conceptual Development and International Empirical Evidence," *Journal of Business Research*, 55 (2002), pp. 451–465, for a study of functional integration `e176`.

CHAPTER 2

1 L. Selden and G. Colvin, *Angel Customers & Demon Customers*, New York: Portfolio, 2003; used by permission `e201`.

2 Many life insurance firms do not treat customers as assets. Policyholders whose agents leave the firm are *orphans*. They frequently receive no agent attention.

3 This chapter benefited considerably from discussions with colleagues Sunil Gupta and Don Lehmann: S. Gupta, D.R. Lehmann, and J. Ames Stuart, "Valuing Customers," *Journal of Marketing Research*, 41 (February 2004), pp. 7–19 `e203a`; S. Gupta and D.R. Lehmann, "Customers as Assets," *Journal of Interactive Marketing*, 17 (Winter 2003), pp. 9–24 `e203b`; and S. Gupta and D.R. Lehmann, *Managing Customers as Investments*, Philadelphia, PA: Wharton, 2004 `e203c`.

4 Personal communication from Ron Boire, President Consumer Sales, Sony Electronics.

5 The firm applies the sum of net margins across all customers to its fixed costs to identify overall gross margin. Net margin equals gross margin less specific costs for retaining customers.

6 In each successive year, the value of money decreases — $100 earned next year is worth less than $100 earned this year. Hence, we discount all future margins to the present as in net present value (NPV) calculations. We treat the original acquisition cost for current customers as a sunk cost. Also P.D. Berger and N.I. Nasr, "Customer Lifetime Value: Marketing Models and Applications," *Journal of Interactive Marketing*, 12 (Winter 1998), pp. 17–30 `e206`.

7 Type of defection is important. Customers that defect to competitors may be recoverable if the firm offers greater value. By contrast, a customer that leaves the market may be lost forever.

8 Deciding if a customer has defected is not simple. Amazon, eBay, and L.L. Bean treat customers who haven't purchased within the prior year as having defected. This judgment varies with the purchase cycle.

9 The CLV formulation applies to contractual relationships — cell phone plans, household utilities, magazine subscriptions; and non-contractual relationships — most bricks-and-mortar and online purchases. For non-contractual relationships, the firm must infer if a particular customer is still active.

10 Margin = revenues less costs; most firms do not track costs by customer. Marketing Enrichment `me01` shows customer profitability calculations.

11 Strictly speaking, the margin-multiple formula applies to a series of terms summed to infinity. Hence, we avoid arbitrary assumptions about actual customer lifetime. Assuming reasonable values for retention rate (r) and discount rate (d), after a few years the impact of all terms is very small. You can check this out for yourself.

12 By convention, we apply both retention and discount factors to first-year margins.

13 Note that the term *discount* in *discount rate* has a quite different meaning from selling at a *discount* from list price.

14 R. G. McGrath, "How the Growth Outliers Do It," *Harvard Business Review*, 90 (January–February 2012), pp. 111–116, shows that 10 growth-outlier firms (5 percent growth in revenues and net profits, each year for 10 years) (from a 4,793 sample) reported customer satisfaction and customer retention in excess of 90 percent `e214`.

15 S. Gupta and C.F. Mela, "What Is a Free Customer Worth," *Harvard Business Review*, 86 (November 2008), pp. 102–109 `e215`.

16 *Customer Referral Value* (CRV) measures the value of customer referrals, V. Kumar, J.A. Petersen, and R.P. Leone, "Driving Profitability by Encouraging Customer Referrals: Who, When, and How," *Journal of Marketing*, 74 (September 2010), pp. 1–17 `e216`. Intention to recommend (refer) is central to Net Promoter Score, see Chapter 22.

17 F.F. Reicheld, *The Loyalty Effect*, Boston, MA: Harvard Business School Press, 1996, p. 51 `e217`.

18 Reicheld, *op. cit.*, p. 38 `e217`.

19 Empirical studies on customer profitability relationships show mixed results. Reicheld, *op. cit.* supports the propositions in this chapter `e217`. W.J. Reinhartz and V. Kumar, "On the Profitability of Long-Life Customers in a Noncontractual Setting: An Empirical Investigation and Implications for Marketing," *Journal of Marketing*, 64 (October 2000), pp. 17–35 `e219a`; W. Reinartz and V. Kumar, "The Mismanagement of Customer Loyalty," *Harvard Business Review*, 80 (July 2002), pp. 86–94 `e219b`; and W. Reinartz and V. Kumar, "The Impact of Customer Relationship Characteristics on Profitable Lifetime Duration," *Journal of Marketing*, 67 (January 2003), pp. 77–99 `e219c`, report some contrary findings.

20 Gupta and Lehmann, *op. cit.*, pp. 35–39 `e203c`, also show the impact on CLV when: (a) Margins grow at a decreasing rate, (b) Retention rates increase with length of customer tenure, (c) Time horizon is finite versus infinite.

21 Reicheld, *op. cit.*, p. 36 `e217`. Also F.F. Reicheld, *Loyalty Rules*, Boston, MA: Harvard Business School Press, 2001 `e221a`; B.J. Pine II, D. Peppers, and M. Rogers, "Do You Want to Keep Your Customers Forever?," *Harvard Business Review*, 73 (March–April 1995), pp. 103–154 `e221b`; R.C. Blattberg and J. Deighton, "Manage Marketing by the Customer Equity Test," *Harvard Business Review*, 74 (July–August 1996), pp. 136–144 `e221c`; R.C. Blattberg, G. Getz, and J.S. Thomas, *Customer Equity*, Boston, MA: Harvard Business School Press, 2001 `e221d`; and R.T. Rust, V.A. Zeithaml, and K.N. Lemon, *Driving Customer Equity*, New York: Free Press, 2000 `e221e`.

22 Steady state market shares are independent of starting positions. Jane's and Joe's initial division of the 1,000 customers does not affect the long run.

23 Reicheld's work also demonstrates the importance of employee and shareholder loyalty.

24 "Customer Acquisition Cost — A Key Marketing Metric," *National Petroleum News*, April 2003. These costs are averages and may vary widely depending on complexity of the selling process.

25 In the credit card industry, a good response rate for new-customer direct mail campaigns is 2 to 3 percent. To secure 1,000 applications, the firm must send 30,000 to 50,000 solicitations. Factoring in costs for credit evaluation, card issuance, and entering customer data into its system, the cost to acquire each new customer ranges from $50 to $100.

26 To maximize CLV, marketing must calculate optimal budget allocations across different spending categories, D.M. Hanssens, D. Thorpe, and C. Finkbeiner, "Marketing When Customer Equity Matters," *Harvard Business Review*, (May 2008), pp. 117–123 `e226`.

27 For empirical studies: W. Reinartz, J. Thomas, and V. Kumar, "Balancing Acquisition and Retention Resources to Maximize Customer Profitability," *Journal of Marketing*, 69 (January 2005), pp. 63–79 `e227a` and J. Thomas, W. Reinartz, and V. Kumar, "Getting the Most out of All Your Customers," *Harvard Business Review*, 82 (July–August 2004), pp. 116–123 `e227b`.

28 V. Mittal and W.A. Kamakura, "Satisfaction, Repurchase Intent, and Repurchase Behavior: Investigating the Moderating Effect of Customer Characteristics," *Journal of Marketing Research*, 38 (February 2001), pp. 131–142 `e228`.

29 In B2C industries like banking, credit cards, and retailing, and in much B2B, customers frequently patronize multiple suppliers. The critical issue is often not loyalty *versus* defection, but *share* of wallet.

30 Personal communication from Dave Goudge, senior vice president for marketing, Boise Office Solutions (now OfficeMax).

31 Some firms use CLV to make decisions on the most effective way of communicating with customers: V. Kumar, R. Venkatesan, T. Bohling, and D. Beckmann, "The Power of CLV: Managing Customer Lifetime

Value at IBM," *Marketing Science*, 27 (July–August 2008), pp. 585–599 `e231a`. Also R. Venkatesan, V. Kumar, and T. Bohling, "Optimal Customer Relationship Management Using Bayesian Decision Theory: An Application for Customer Selection," *Journal of Marketing Research*, 44 (November 2007), pp. 579–594 `e231b`.

32 When evaluating customer acquisition efforts, the firm should estimate potential CLV, including the option value of abandoning customers that become unprofitable, M. Haenlein, A.M. Kaplan, and D. Schoder, "Valuing the Real Option of Abandoning Unprofitable Customers When Calculating Customer Lifetime Value," *Journal of Marketing*, 70 (July 2006) pp. 5–20 `e232`.

33 Firms that minimize credit losses reject many customers that would have repaid their credit. Credit card firms must strike a balance, recognizing they must accept many customers who won't pay!

34 Also Selden and Colvin, *op. cit.* `e201`

35 Many firms have adopted activity-based costing (ABC) to secure more precise answers to these types of question.

36 Also *Kanthal (A)*, 9-190-002, Harvard Business School `e236`.

37 We ignore the value of the customer in covering fixed manufacturing costs (part of cost of goods sold). We assume that a thorough activity-based costing (ABC) system generated selling, service, and additional expenses. Of course, in some situations, selling and service are shared activities across businesses. For a more detailed example of assessing customer profitability, see Marketing Enrichment `me01`.

38 Selden and Colvin, *op. cit.*, pp. 54–55 `e201`. Selden and Colvin suggest the profit skew is even more extreme than we suggest — 150 percent of profit from 20 percent of customers.

39 V. Kumar and D. Shah, "Expanding the Role of Marketing: From Customer Equity to Market Capitalization," *Journal of Marketing*, 73 (November 2009), pp. 119–136 `e239a`. Also R. Niraj, M. Gupta, and C. Narasimhan, "Customer Profitability in a Supply Chain," *Journal of Marketing*, 65 (July 2001), pp. 1–16 `e239b`.

40 Credit card firms are experts in removing unprofitable customers. Others also slim their portfolios; AOL fired 350,000 deadbeat customers.

41 For this discussion, overhead comprises costs not directly assigned to customers, like long-run R&D and corporate assessments for advertising, legal services, and government relations.

42 M. Hanlin and A.M. Kaplan, "Unprofitable Customers and Their Management," *Business Horizons*, 52 (2009), pp. 89–97 `e242a` and V. Mittal, M. Sarkees, and F. Murshed, "The Right Way to Manage Unprofitable Customers," *Harvard Business Review*, 86 (April 2008), pp. 95–101 `e242b`. Of course, predicting future customer profitability may be difficult: E.C. Malthouse and R.C. Blattberg, "Can We predict Customer Lifetime Value?," *Journal of Interactive Marketing*, 19 (Winter 2005), pp. 2–16 `e242c`.

43 "Minding the Store: Analyzing Customers, Best Buy Decides Not All Are Welcome," *The Wall Street Journal*, November 8, 2004 `e243`. Relatedly, *wardrobers* purchase garments for events, then return them afterwards; *closeters* purchase products like tools, computers, or video cameras for a specific use, then return them after completing the task.

44 Mittal, Sarkees, and Murshed, *op. cit.* `e242b`, suggest a *reassess, educate, renegotiate, migrate* process with customers prior to termination.

45 The fast growth of blogs and Twitter is raising this concern to new levels.

46 An important factor in PepsiCo's divestiture of Kentucky Fried Chicken, Taco Bell, and Pizza Hut was Coca-Cola's success in persuading many fast-food chains that selling PepsiCo drinks was aiding a competitor.

47 These customer types and non-payers (deadbeats) are *jaycustomers*: C. Lovelock and J. Wirtz, *Service Marketing: People, Technology, Strategy*, 7th Ed., Upper Saddle River, NJ: Prentice-Hall, 2011 `e247`.

48 I. Gordon, *Relationship Marketing: New Strategies, Techniques and Technologies to Win the Customers You Want and Keep Them Forever*, Ontario: Wiley, 1998, p. 9 `e248`.

49 "Every Little Helps Tesco to £1.6 Billion Record," *The Daily Telegraph*, April 21, 2004. For background on Tesco, see *Tesco PLC: Getting to the Top... Staying at the Top?* Fontainebleau, France: INSEAD, 1999 `e249`.

50 Chapter 19 shows how to build this type of organization.

51 M. Ebner, A. Hu, D. Levitt, and J. McCrory, "How to Rescue CRM," *The McKinsey Quarterly*, 4 (2002), pp. 49–57 `e251a`; also D.K. Rigby, F.F. Reicheld, and P. Schefter, "Avoid the Four Perils of CRM," *Harvard Business Review*, 80 (February 2002), pp. 101–109 `e251b`.

52 The firm may apply CRM techniques to other firm stakeholders like suppliers, shareholders, and employees.

53 Peter Heffring, President CRM Division, Teradata, 2002.

54 Gordon, *op. cit.*, p. 30 `e248`.

55 Excerpted from a presentation by M. Atkinson, Managing Director, Tequila Asia Pacific (Singapore) Pte. Ltd.

56 R. Glazer, "Strategy and Structure in Information-Intensive Markets: The Relationship between Marketing and IT," *Journal of Market-Focused Management*, 2, (1997), pp. 65–81. Glazer believes firms should organize key IT functions — information acquisition, distribution and interpretation, and organizational memory — into *departments* within decision teams. Also R. Winer, "A Framework of Customer Relationship Management," *California Management Review*, 43 (2001), pp. 89–105.

57 From granular database modeling, BlackRock discovered that people living near IBM offices frequently prepaid mortgages early (for company relocation).

58 Also A. Agarwal, D.P. Harding, and J.R. Schumacher, "Organizing for CRM," *The McKinsey Quarterly*, 3 (2004), pp. 81–91 `e258`.

59 Personal communication from Lance Batchelor, Head Worldwide Marketing, Amazon.com.

60 Do not confuse *event-driven* marketing with event marketing. Event marketing comprises promotional activities like trade shows that firms design and implement for current and potential customers.

61 Thanks to Mark Holtom, Eventricity, for insight on events `e261`.

62 Immediacy is critical for Austra; sales drop dramatically for even a two- or three-day delay in making customer contact.

63 J. Fox-Greene, A.J. McCarthy, and P.S. Simone, "How U.S. Banks Can Attract Middle-Market Customers," *McKinsey on Corporate & Investment Banking*, 7 (September 2008), pp. 9–15 `e263`.

64 S. Coyles and T.C. Gokey, "Customer Retention Is Not Enough," *The McKinsey Quarterly*, 2 (2002), pp. 81–89, distinguish among different types of loyalty: *emotive loyalists* — committed customers who rarely reassess chosen suppliers; *inertial loyalists* — rarely reassess due to high switching costs or low involvement, and *deliberative loyalists* — frequently reassess on rational criteria `e264a`. A loyalty ladder in B2B markets embraces: *cynic* — won't buy; *skeptic* — willing to be convinced; *switcher* — will buy if the price is right; buys a bundle of products; invests in the relationship; actively seeks to expand the relationship; *enthusiastic advocate*; and willing to pay a premium, D. Narayandas, *Customer Management Strategy in Business Markets*, N9-503-060, 2003, Harvard Business School `e264b`. An alternative loyalty scheme identifies: *negative advocates* — strongly negative and persuade others not to buy; *negative status* — strong negative, would never use; *occasional users* — buy very occasionally; *switchers non-preferred* — purchase from time to time; *switchers-preferred* — prefer the product but will buy others with sufficient inducement; *truly loyal* — will always purchase if available;

super loyal — undertake significant search cost to find and purchase; *ultra loyal* — like *super loyal* but also enthusiastic advocates to others.

65 T. Wagner, T. Hennig-Thurau and T. Rudolph, "Does Customer Demotion Jeopardize Loyalty?" *Journal of Marketing*, 73 (May 2009), pp. 69–85 `e265`.

66 *Hilton Honors Worldwide: Loyalty Wars*, 9-501-010, Harvard Business School `e266`.

67 G.R. Dowling and M. Uncles, "Do Customer Loyalty Programs Really Work?," *Sloan Management Review*, (Summer 1997), pp. 71–82 `e267a`; L. O'Brien and C. Jones, "Do Rewards Really Create Loyalty?," *Harvard Business Review*, 73 (May–June 1995), pp. 75–82 `e267b`; J.C. Nune and X. Drèze, "Your Loyalty Program Is Betraying You," *Harvard Business Review*, 84 (April 2006), pp. 124–131 `e267c`.

68 R. Kivetz, O. Urminsky, and Y. Zheng, "The Goal-Gradient Hypothesis Resurrected: Purchase Acceleration, Illusionary Goal Progress, and Customer Retention," *Journal of Marketing Research*, 43 (February 2006), pp 39-58 `e268`.

69 Loyalty programs are a vigorous research area in marketing: R. Kivetz and I. Simonson, "The Idiosyncratic Fit Heuristic: Effort Advantage as a Determinant of Consumer Response to Loyalty Programs," *Journal of Marketing Research*, 40 (November 2003), pp. 454–467 `e269a`; R. Kivetz and I. Simonson, "Earning the Right to Indulge: Effort as a Determinant of Customer Preferences Toward Frequency Program Rewards," *Journal of Marketing Research*, 39 (May 2003), pp. 155–170 `e269b`; R. Kivetz, "The Effects of Effort and Intrinsic Motivation on Risky Choice," *Marketing Science*, 22 (2003), pp. 477–502 `e269c`; R. Kivetz, "Promotion Reactance: The Role of Effort-Reward Congruity," *Journal of Consumer Research*, 31 (March 2005), pp. 725–736 `e269d`. For a review, see T.H.A. Bijmolt, M. Dorotic, and P.C. Verhoer, "Loyalty Programs: Generalizations on Their Adoption, Effectiveness, and Design," *Foundations and Trends in Marketing*, 5 (2010), pp. 197–258 `e269e`.

70 These data from *Sonik CD: Future Growth Strategy*, Columbia Business School, by permission of Professor Sunil Gupta. Ignore differences in fixed costs across alternatives.

CHAPTER 3

1 Rent the Runway uses the Netflix postal model to provide high-end fashions for four-night loans `e301`.

2 For a good discussion of market definition, see *Note on Market Definition and Segmentation*, 9-579-083, Harvard Business School `e302`.

3 T. Levitt, "Marketing Myopia," *Harvard Business Review*, 53 (September–October 1975), pp. 26 *et seq.* `e303`

4 R.K. Srivastava, M.I. Alpert, and A.D. Shocker, "A Customer-Oriented Approach for Determining Market Structures," *Journal of Marketing*, 48 (Spring 1984), pp. 32–45 `e304`.

5 Some use *product category* instead of *product class*; *product sub-category* instead of *product form.*

6 Sometimes new words reflect this merging — cosmeceuticals, nutraceuticals, and edutainment!

7 Since B2C market demand drives B2B market demand, we focus on key indicators of B2C market size.

8 India's population growth rate — 1.31 percent — is more than twice China's — 0.48 percent, CIA Factbook 2012 `e308`.

9 The required fertility rate to sustain the population globally is 2.3 — 2.1 in advanced countries. More than 70 countries have fertility rates less than 2.1 — up from 24 in the 1970s.

10 Data from U.S. Census Bureau, International Data Base, 2012 `e310`.

11 *International Migration Report 2002*, New York: United Nations, 2002 `e311`.

12 *Ad Budget Alignment: Maximizing Impact in the Hispanic Market*, Washington, DC: Association of Hispanic Advertising Agencies (AHAA), 2004 `e312`.

13 2010 data from World Economic Outlook Database — September 2011, International Monetary Fund `e313`.

14 The *Gini* coefficient, measuring the inequality of a distribution, provides similar results to EPIR.

15 United Nations Population Database `e315`. Estimates of population percentages over age 65 in 2050 are Italy and Spain — 70 percent, Germany — 57 percent, France — 53 percent, Sweden and Britain — 49 percent, and Ireland — 48 percent: *The Economist*, December 23, 2000.

16 The related *technology life cycle* encompasses many product classes — usually presented as an S-curve of technological performance versus time. A technology may take a considerable time to get off the ground, but once established, performance increases rapidly. Then the technology reaches its limits. Successive technologies follow similar patterns.

17 For an excellent review of product life cycle research, see S. Klepper, "Entry, Exit, Growth, and Innovation over the Product Life Cycle," *American Economic Review*, 86 (June 1996), pp. 562–583 `e317`.

18 S.L. Holak and Y.E. Tang, "Advertising's Effect on the Product Evolutionary Cycle," *Journal of Marketing*, 54 (July 1990), pp. 16–29 `e318`.

19 The first hybrids were built between 1899 and 1920. The Electric and Hybrid Vehicle Research, Development and Demonstration Act of 1976 spurred development of gas-electric hybrid cars. Development accelerated when California adopted *zero emission vehicle* (ZEV) rules in 1990. The first commercial prototypes were built in 1996. The first commercially available hybrid was the 2000 Honda Insight, followed by the 2000 Toyota Prius. L.E. Hall, *Back to the Past: The History of Hybrids* `e319`.

20 E.M. Rogers, *Diffusion of Innovations*, 5th Ed., New York: Free Press, 2003. We address this topic in Chapter 12 `e320`.

21 Andy Grove (former Intel CEO) initially dismissed the Macintosh computer as a toy. He believed the graphical interface was a nuisance and absence of a hard disk a severe limitation. A.S. Grove, *Only the Paranoid Survive*, New York, Doubleday, 1996 `e321`.

22 *Xerox Corporation: The Customer Satisfaction Program*, 9-591-055, Harvard Business School `e322`.

23 The U.S. banking industry restructured in the 1980s and 1990s. A combination of federal and state regulation had led to considerable overbanking. The U.S. still has several thousand banks. By comparison, Great Britain (about one-fifth the U.S. population) had four major banks until deregulation increased the number somewhat.

24 Fragmentation and concentration is often in the eye of the beholder. A British firm examining its home market may identify just a few major competitors — a concentrated oligopoly. Similar markets in various European countries may also appear to be oligopolies. But a European perspective would see a single fragmented market. What appears as an oligopoly at the lower level seems fragmented at a higher level. This perspective change has important strategic implications.

25 R.W. Olshavsky, "Time and the Rate of Adoption of Innovations," *Journal of Consumer Research*, 6 (March 1980), pp. 425–428 `e325a`; W. Qualls, R. W. Olshavsky, and R.E. Michaels, "Shortening of the PLC–An Empirical Test," *Journal of Marketing*, 45 (Fall 1981), pp. 76–80 `e325b`. Some life cycles, like fads, start and end quickly; when product use changes — like bicycles and motorcycles from transportation to recreation — the life cycle has multiple distinct elements.

26 M. E. Porter, *Competitor Strategy: Techniques for Analyzing Industries and Competitors*, New York: Free Press, 1980 `e326a` . B. Greenwald and J. Kahn, *Competition Demystified*, New York: Portfolio, 2005, builds on Porter's model but focuses attention on barriers to entry `e326b` .

27 Bankruptcy laws often prolong marginal players and negatively affect industry profitability.

28 Historically, many industries comprised relatively insulated national oligopolies. As national barriers fall, global oligopolies are developing in several industries.

29 AmBev (Brazil), Interbrew (Belgium) and Anheuser-Busch (U.S.) joined to become Anheuser-Busch InBev (ABI), the leading global brewer.

30 Management buyouts (MBOs) are a special case of LBOs; existing management executes the purchase. In recent years, LBOs have rebranded as *private equity*.

31 C. Zook with J. Allen, *Profit from the Core: Growth Strategy in an Era of Turbulence*, Boston, MA: Harvard Business School Press, 2001, pp. 26–28 `e331` .

32 See M. Corstjens and J. Merrihue, "Optimal Marketing," *Harvard Business Review*, 81 (October 2003), pp. 114–121, for Samsung's decisions to invest in various global product/markets `e332` .

33 R.M. Kanter, "Collaborative Advantage: The Art of Alliances," *Harvard Business Review*, 72 (July–August 1994), pp. 96–108 `e333` .

34 In pyramid sales forces, salespeople earn commissions from direct sales. They also earn *overrides* on sales of salespeople they recruit. They may also earn overrides on sales from their recruits' recruits, and so on.

35 When indirect competitive threats are high, political forces may impel governments to remove/amend offending regulations.

36 Some firms address large commodity price swings by *hedging* purchases. Some multinationals, like Caterpillar, strive to match production and sales by country to avoid currency swing problems.

37 K. Harrigan, *Strategies for Vertical Integration*, Lexington, MA: Lexington Books, 1983 `e337` .

38 H. Simon, *Hidden Champions: Lessons from 500 of the World's Best Unknown Companies*, Boston, MA: Harvard Business School Press, 1996 `e338` .

39 Pricing is crucial in two-sided markets — Chapter 20; T. Eisenmann, G. Parker, and M.W. Van Alstyne, "Strategies for Two-Sided Markets," *Harvard Business Review*, 84 (October 2006), pp. 92–101 `e339` .

40 To manage potential frictions, Samsung's component business negotiates with consumer-product businesses on the same basis as outside firms.

41 This section draws on P. Fitzroy, A. Ghobadian, and J.M. Hulbert, *Strategic Management: The Challenge of Creating Value*, London: Routledge, 2012 `e341` .

42 Used mainly in Australia: Mulesing protects sheep from blowfly infestation by removing skin folds from hind quarters, typically without anesthetic.

43 Prices are typically 30–50 percent less than regular supermarkets.

44 *The New Shorter Oxford English Dictionary*, Oxford: Clarendon, 1993 `e344` .

45 For tips on dealing with different cultures, see R.E. Axtell (ed.), *Do's and Taboos around the World*, New York: Wiley, 1993 `e345` .

46 J. Garreau, *The Nine Nations of North America*, Boston, MA: Houghton-Mifflin, 1981, classifies North America (Canada and U.S.) into nine subcultures `e346` .

47 Taken in part, and modified, from V. Terpstra, *The Cultural Environment of International Business*, Cincinnati, OH: Southwestern Publishing, 1978, Figure 1 `e347a` . Also V. Terpstra and K. David, *The Cultural Environment of International Business*, 3rd Ed. Cincinnati, OH: Southwestern, 1991 `e347b` .

48 *Baby Boomers* — 77 million persons born in the U.S. between 1946 and 1964; *Generation X* — 50 million persons born between 1965 and 1976; *Generation Y* (echo boomers, millennium generation) — 77 million persons born between 1977 and 1995.

49 United Nations' membership: End 1940s — 59; end 1960s — 126; 2011 — 192 (total number of countries — 196).

50 Protesters targeted McDonalds in some European countries including France. McDonald's operating profit in France is second only to the U.S.!

51 Blinded by its brilliant science, Monsanto did not foresee negative consumer reaction to genetically modified crops, especially in Europe.

52 Thanks to Alan Fortier for this demonstration.

53 C. M. Christensen, *The Innovator's Dilemma: When New Technologies Cause Great Firms to Fail*, Boston, MA: Harvard Business School Press, 1997 `e353` .

54 L. Downes and C. Mui, *Unleashing the Killer App: Digital Strategies for Market Dominance*, Boston, MA: Harvard Business School Press, 1998, pp. xix, 243 `e354a` . George Washington University Forecast of Emerging Technologies identified several future technologies and dates: 2005 — fuel-cell-powered cars introduced; 2008 — virtual assistants common and genetically modified food widely accepted; 2010 — smart robots in homes and factories; 2012 — children genetically designed; 2030 — average life span 100 years; 2050 — humans travel to nearby star systems. See also The World Future Society `e354b` .

55 C. M. Christensen, *op. cit.* `e353` Disruptive technologies that damaged incumbents include: handheld calculators — slide rule manufacturers; overnight package delivery — freight forwarders; TV — radio, jet aircraft — turbo-props and ocean liners.

56 Downes and Mui, *op. cit.* `e354a`

57 We expect increased concern with data security to counteract threats from external hackers and internal staff abusers. Data security is a significant obstacle to e-commerce development — advances in encryption systems will be critical.

58 D. A. Beck, J. N. Fraser, A. C. Reuter-Domenech, and P. Sidebottom, "Personal Financial Services Goes Global," *The McKinsey Quarterly*, 3 1999, pp. 39–47 `e358` .

59 Consistent with Metcalfe's law — a network's value to an individual user is proportional to the number of users squared. K. Kelly, *New Rules for the New Economy: 10 Radical Strategies for a Connected World*, New York: Viking Press, 1998, notes that the basis of Metcalfe's law is point-to-point connections like telephone and fax networks. Because Internet connections can be made simultaneously with groups, the potential value is n^n, where n is the number of people connected `e359` .

60 J.H. Dessauer, *My Years with Xerox: The Billions Nobody Wanted*, Garden City, NJ: Doubleday, 1971 `e360` .

61 *Doing a Dyson (A), (B), (C)*, 599-051-1BW, European Case Clearing House. Most major vacuum cleaner manufacturers have since copied Dyson's invention.

62 Batteries are too expensive for the world's poor; the impact has been dramatic.

63 K. O'Neill Packard and F. Reinhardt, "What Every Executive Needs to Know About Global Warming," *Harvard Business Review*, 78 (July–August 2000), pp. 129–135 `e363` .

64 For P&G's struggles to address environmental issues in Germany, see *Procter & Gamble Company: Lenor Refill Package*, 9-592-016, Harvard Business School e364.

65 J. Elkington, *Cannibals with Forks: The Triple Bottom Line of 21st Century Business*, Oxford, UK: Capstone, 1997, pp. xiv, 402, believes firms should adopt the triple bottom line and pursue social, environmental, and economic objectives e365.

66 Over two-thirds of South Korean households subscribe versus U.S. — 15 percent — and Western Europe — 8 percent.

67 Paradoxically, many consider GE, one of the world's most successful firms, a conglomerate.

68 Some highly successful private equity firms like the Blackstone Group and Kohlberg Kravis Roberts (KKR) resemble conglomerates.

69 N. Capon, J.U. Farley, and J. Hulbert, "International Diffusion of Corporate and Strategic Planning Processes," *Columbia Journal of World Business*, 15 (Fall 1980), pp. 5–13.

70 N. Capon, J.U. Farley, and J.M. Hulbert, *Corporate Strategic Planning*, New York: Columbia University Press, 1987 e370.

71 I. Nonaka and H. Takeuchi, *The Knowledge-Creating Company*, New York: Oxford University Press, 1995 e371.

72 F. Broetzmann and J. Goetz, "The Revival of Scenario Planning: An Integral Part of Reliable Corporate Management," Ernst & Young, 2010 e372a; and C. Roxburgh, "The Use and Abuse of Scenarios," *The McKinsey Quarterly*, (November 2009), pp 1–10 e372b.

CHAPTER 4

1 This and the preceding example are from *Selling Power*.

2 In some societies, and at certain times, people prefer barter to paying money for products.

3 In advanced Western societies, individual, family, and organizational customers increasingly avoid purchase — they often prefer to rent or lease. We use the term *purchase* loosely to encompass these methods.

4 Typically, indirect customers are all customers in the customer channel beyond direct customers.

5 Firms with both **paying** and **free** customers must decide how to balance marketing efforts among them. Firms must consider both *direct* and *indirect* network effects and assess whether they are positive or negative. For an auction house, *direct* effects concern how buyers attract (or not) more buyers and how sellers attract (or not) more sellers. *Indirect* effects concern how buyers attract (or not) more sellers and how sellers attract (or not) more buyers. S. Gupta and C. Mela, "What Is a Free Customer Worth," *Harvard Business Review*, 86 (November 2008), pp. 102–109, shows how to value *free* customers e405.

6 In many nation states, government is the largest organizational purchaser. The annual budget for the U.S. Defense department is between $600 billion and $700 billion.

7 T.V. Bonoma, "Major Sales: Who Really Does the Buying," *Harvard Business Review*, 60 (May–June 1982), pp. 111–120 e407.

8 UPS's mid-2000s advertising, "What Can Brown Do For You?"

9 See M.H. Morris, P. Berthon, and L.F. Pitt, "Assessing the Structure of Industrial Buying Centers with Multivariate Tools," *Industrial Marketing Management*, 28 (1999), pp. 263–276, for a study of role structure in organizational buying e409.

10 University of Washington, University of Southern California, Georgia Tech, MIT, and Purdue.

11 Personal communication from Richard L. Melville Jr., Vice Chairman, Aerospace Market Sector Lead Team, Alcoa Inc.

12 "Serving Your Customer's Customer: A Strategy For Mature Industries," *The McKinsey Quarterly*, 2 (1997), pp. 81–89 e412.

13 This example shows the importance of branding. Without a brand, the product has no identity — indirect customers see it as generic. Consider: If Intel's product works, the indirect customer never sees it!

14 Personal communication from Dale Hayes, Vice President Brand Management and Customer Communications, UPS.

15 Sometimes the firm wants customers to purchase products; sometimes to influence other customers. Some marketing seeks other behavioral responses like voting. We focus on mainstream marketing. Some influence techniques, such as force and threats of force, are not part of marketing — organizations, like protection rackets, specialize in these techniques to encourage purchase of their services!

16 In addition to *communicating* value, the communications process may also *create* value.

17 This watermelon has a thin rind, no seeds, and tastes delicious.

18 From the president of Stanley Works.

19 Personal communication.

20 A. Maslow, *Motivation and Personality*, New York: Harper, 1954 e420. Maslow's framework raises the question, discussed extensively by Freud: Are all needs fully conscious?

21 Related work from J. Guttman, "A Means-End Chain Model Based on Consumer Categorization Processes," *Journal of Marketing*, 46 (Spring 1982), pp. 60–72 e421a; B.A. Walker and J.C. Olson, "Means-End Chains: Connecting Products with Self," *Journal of Business Research*, 22 (1991), pp. 111–118 e421b; T.R. Graeff, "Comprehending Product Attributes and Benefits: The Role of Product Knowledge and Means-End Chain Inferences," *Psychology and Marketing*, 14 (March 1997), pp. 163–183 e421c; J.C. Olson and T.J. Reynolds, "The Means-End Approach to Understanding Consumer Decision Making," in *Understanding Consumer Decision Making: The Means-End Approach to Marketing and Advertising Strategy*, T.J. Reynolds and J.C. Olson, Eds., Hillsdale, NJ: Erlbaum, 2001, pp. 3–20 e421d.

22 For customer-based definitions of competition: G.S. Day and R. Wensley, "Assessing Advantage: A Framework for Diagnosing Competitive Superiority," *Journal of Marketing*, 52 (April 1988), pp. 1–20 e422.

23 A separate system has two categories: *rational* — subsuming functional and economic; and *emotional* — psychological. These value-laden terms may obscure the often vital importance of psychological benefits.

24 Example from Systematic Inventive Thinking (SIT).

25 Alternative value models embrace more value types — conditional, emotional, epistemic, functional, social: J.N. Sheth, B.I. Newman, and B.L. Gross, "Why We Buy What We Buy: A Theory of Consumption Value," *Journal of Business Research*, 22 (1991), pp. 159–170 e425a; emotional, price/value for money, quality/performance, social: J.C. Sweeney and G.N. Soutar, "Consumer Perceived Value: The Development of a Multiple Item Scale," *Journal of Retailing*, 77 (2001), pp. 203–220 e425b. Also S.E. Beatty, L.R. Kahle, P. Homer, and S. Misra, "Alternative Measurement Approaches to Consumer Values: The List of Values and the Rokeach Value Survey," *Psychology and Marketing*, 2 (Fall 1985), pp. 181–200 e425c. Of course, the firm must assess which value type — functional, psychological, or economic — is most important in the specific purchase decision.

26 R. Friedmann, "Psychological Meaning of Products: Identification and Marketing Applications," *Psychology and Marketing*, 3 (Spring 1986), pp. 1–15 e426.

27 Since 1982, 99 Cents Only has grown to about 300 stores.

28 Of course, working-capital issues like inventory turns and time to pay are also important.

29 GE's *at-the-customer, for-the-customer* initiative sends six-sigma squads to improve processes at customers like Southwest Airlines.

30 Transactions costs derive from search, information, bargaining, decision, policing, and enforcement: L. Downes and C. Mui, *Unleashing the Killer App: Digital Strategies for Market Dominance*, Boston, MA: Harvard Business School Press, 1998 e430a ; based on R.H. Coase, "The Nature of the Firm: Origin," *Economica*, 4 (1937), pp. 368–405 e430b .

31 J.L. Forbis and N.T. Mehta, "Value-Based Strategies for Industrial Products," *Business Horizons*, 24 (1981), pp. 32–42 e431 .

32 Personal communication from Jackson's (disguised name) regional sales manager. Chapter 20 includes further discussion of economic value. *Value-in-use* captures the same idea.

33 This calculation does not include savings from avoiding costs to repair cotton-based conveyor belts, nor downtime costs of more frequently replacing cotton conveyor belts.

34 Customers may receive some value items over time; hence, time value may be important.

35 In *Wild Man Blues*, Woody Allen explains his love for New York City: He can always get duck wonton soup at 3:30 A.M., but would never want to!

36 For value in scarcity, secrecy, amplification, entertainment, and tricksterism: S. Brown, "Torment Your Customers (They'll Love It)," *Harvard Business Review* 79 (October 2001), pp. 83–88 e436 .

37 A. Pettigrew, *Politics of Organizational Decision Making*, London: Tavistock, 1973, p. 266 e437 .

38 Some *real* experiences focus on today; *recollection* experiences focus on memories.

39 C. Meyer and A. Schwager, "Understanding Customer Experience," *Harvard Business Review*, 85 (February 2007), pp. 117–126 e439 .

40 *Outside*'s Go: Travel & Style for Men e440 .

41 In Brazil, Colombia, and Kenya, coffee farmers earn around $1 per pound, fractions of a cent per cup of coffee. In grocery stores, Nestlé and Folgers sell the same beans for 5 to 25 cents per cup. In the *Starbucks* scene in the movie *You've Got Mail*, the coffee price is $5 a cup! Director Nora Ephron explained she chose to shoot part of the film in Starbucks because it is a *third place*, after home and work. N. Ephron, director's commentary on *You've Got Mail*, DVD Special Feature, 1998. R. Oldenburg, *The Great Good Place: Cafes, Coffee Shops, Bookstores, Bars, Hair Salons and Other Hangouts at the Heart of a Community*, New York: Marlowe and Co., 1999 e441 . Oldenburg believes we all need a *third place* — our homes are the first, and our places of work the second. Other frequented places become that *third place* of socialization — local pubs in England, tavernas in Greece, and sidewalk cafés in France. For many people, the Internet is becoming the *third place*, albeit a virtual place.

42 B.J. Pine II and J.H. Gilmore, *The Experience Economy*, Boston, MA: Harvard Business School Press, 1999 e442 .

43 B. Schmitt, *Experiential Marketing: How to Get Customers to Sense, Feel, Think, Act and Relate to Your Company and Brands*: New York: Free Press, 1999 e443a ; and B. Schmitt, "Experience Marketing: Concepts, Frameworks, and Consumer Insights," *Foundations and Trends in Marketing*, 5 (2010), pp. 55–112, for a review e443b . Also B.J. Pine II and J.H. Gilmore, "Welcome to the Experience Economy," *Harvard Business Review*, 76 (July–August 1998), pp. 97–105 e443c .

44 H. Stern, "The Significance of Impulse Buying Today," *Journal of Marketing*, 26 (April 1962) pp. 59–62 e444 .

45 Other purchase-decision process models include: J.A. Howard and J. Sheth, *The Theory of Buyer Behavior*, New York: Wiley, 1969 e445 . Mapping the purchase decision is similar to process mapping in reengineering — Chapter 7.

46 Of course, customers can only acquire information if available. Governments often require firms to provide information — food ingredients and finance charges on loans. When smart electric meters advise consumers of intra-daily price changes, consumers modify consumption patterns. The Internet makes information more readily available.

47 Marketing scholars have paid more attention to evaluating alternatives than any other stage.

48 Thanks to Paul Capon and Peter Capon for help with this illustration.

49 Aka cognitive algebra. The firm can also use conjoint analysis to explore customer value trade-offs — Chapter 6.

50 Formally,

$$\text{Value of an alternative} = \sum_{i=1}^{i=n} A_i B_i$$

A_i = importance weight for attribute "i"; B_i = belief that the alternative possesses attribute "i"; and n = the number of salient attributes.

51 For *cognitive algebra* research: J.R. Bettman, N. Capon, and R.J. Lutz, "Multi-attribute Measurement Models and Multi-attribute Attitude Theory: A Test of Construct Validity," *Journal of Consumer Research*, 1 (March 1975), pp. 1–15 e451a ; J.R. Bettman, N. Capon, and R.J. Lutz, "Cognitive Algebra in Multi-attribute Attitude Models," *Journal of Marketing Research*, 12 (May 1975), pp. 151–164 e451b ; and J.R. Bettman, N. Capon, and R.J. Lutz, "Information Processing in Attitude Formation and Change," *Communication Research*, 2 (Fall 1975), pp. 267–278 e451c .

52 B2B customers use similar processes to evaluate suppliers.

53 E.J. Johnson and D.G. Goldstein, "Do Defaults Save Lives?," *Science*, 302 [2003], pp. 1338-1339 e453a . Defaults can be *mass* — presented to all customers, or *personalized* — tailored to individuals. D.G. Goldstein, E.T. Johnson, A. Herrmann, and M. Heitman, "Nudge Your Customers toward Better Choices," *Harvard Business Review*, 86 (December 2008), pp. 99–105 e453b .

54 Consumers who travel for the book but not the home-entertainment system are probably making proportional judgments, consistent with the Weber-Fechner law of psychophysics: R. Thaler, "Toward a Positive Theory of Consumer Choice," *Journal of Economic Behavior and Organization*, 1 (1980), pp. 39–60 e454 .

55 This section relies heavily on I. Simonson, "Get Closer to Your Customers by Understanding How They Make Choices," *California Management Review*, (Summer 1993), pp. 74–84 e455 .

56 I. Simonson and A. Tversky, "Choice in Context: Tradeoff Contrast and Extremeness Aversion," *Journal of Marketing Research*, 29 (1992), pp. 281–295 e456a ; also R. Kivetz, O. Netzer, and V. Srinivasan, "Alternative Models for Capturing the Compromise Effect," *Journal of Marketing Research*, 41 (August 2004), pp, 237–257 e456b , and G.E. Smith and T.T. Nagle, "Frames of Reference and Buyers' Perception of Price and Value," *California Management Review*, 38 (1995), pp. 98–116 e456c .

57 J. Huber, J. W. Payne, and C. Puto, "Adding Asymmetrically Dominated Alternatives: Violations of Regularity and the Similarity Hypothesis," *Journal of Consumer Research* 9 (1982), pp. 90–98 e457 .

58 I.P. Levin and G.J. Gaeth, "How Consumers Are Affected by the Framing of Attribute Information Before and After Consuming the Product," *Journal of Consumer Research*, 15 (1988), pp. 374–378 e458 .

59 I. Simonson, Z. Carmon, and S. O'Curry, "Empirical Evidence on the Negative Effect of Product Features and Sales Promotions on Brand

Choice," *Marketing Science*, 13 (Winter 1994), pp. 23–40 e459a. Also, when customers learned the *irrelevant* reason for another customer's choice, they were less likely to make the same choice: G.S. Carpenter, R. Glazer, and K. Nakamoto, "Meaningful Brands from Meaningless Differentiation: The Dependence on Irrelevant Attributes," *Journal of Marketing Research*, 31 (August 1994), pp. 339–350 e459b; C.L. Brown and G.S. Carpenter, "Why Is the Trivial Important? A Reasons-Based Account for the Effects of Trivial Attributes on Choice," *Journal of Consumer Research*, 26 (March 2000), pp. 372–385 e459c.

60   R. Dhar and I. Simonson, "The Effect of the Focus of Comparison on Consumer Preferences," *Journal of Marketing Research*, 29 (November 1992), pp. 430–440 e460.

61   I. Simonson, S. Nowlis, and K. Lemon, "The Effect of Local Consideration Sets on Global Choice Between Lower Price and Higher Quality," *Marketing Science*, 12 (Fall 1993), pp. 357–377 e461a; also J. Gourville and D. Soman, "Pricing and the Psychology of Consumption," *Harvard Business Review*, 80 (September 2002), pp. 90–99 e461b.

62   T. Levitt, "After the Sale is Over," *Harvard Business Review*, 61 (September–October 1983), pp. 87–93 e462.

63   Firm responses include: Ignore, try to address customer concerns, buy the sites, build sites to refute charges, supply data to competitor hate-site sponsors, and/or register sites like IhatefirmX.com or FirmXsucks.com before disgruntled customers can do so.

64   D.C. Edelman, "Branding in the Digital Age," *Harvard Business Review*, 88 (December 2010), pp. 62–69, shows that 60 percent of facial-skin-care customers sought information online *after* purchase e464.

65   The firm may use a few well-chosen questions to gain customer insight like: Who are they? What, where, when, and how do they buy? Why do they buy? How do they choose?

66   A.J. Slywotzky and D.J. Morrison, *The Profit Zone*, New York: Times Business, 1997 e466.

67   Based in part on Howard and Sheth, *op. cit.* e445, Columbia Business School, and Robinson, Faris, and Wind (RFW), Wharton: P.J. Robinson, C.W. Faris and Y. Wind, *Industrial Buying and Creative Marketing*, Boston, MA: Allyn and Bacon, 1967 e467. RFW use different terms: routinized-response behavior — *straight rebuy*; limited problem-solving — *modified rebuy*; extended problem-solving — *new buy*.

68   R.D. Blackwell, P.W. Miniard, and J.F. Engel, *Consumer Behavior*, 10th Ed., Ft. Worth, TX: Thomson/South-Western, 2005, for psychological processes in consumer behavior e468.

69   E. Hall, *The Silent Language*, Garden City, NY: Anchor, 1973 e469.

70   500 companies produce more than 2,000 kretek brands.

71   W. Chan Kim and R. Mauborgne, *Blue Ocean Strategy*, Boston, MA: Harvard Business School Press, 2005, pp. 71–74 e471.

72   A condensed version of Coleman-Rainwater: R.P. Coleman and L.P. Rainwater, with K.A. McClelland, *Social Standing in America: New Dimensions of Class*, New York: Basic Books e472, from Blackwell, Engel, and Miniard, *op. cit* e468.

73   Groups an individual consciously wants to avoid — *dissociative* groups.

74   Typically, buying books at Amazon.co.uk and shipping to the U.S. is less expensive than buying from Amazon.com!

75   Information about time is also important: consider traffic lights displaying time to change, telephone holding times, and queue-time information at Disneyland.

76   K.L. Milkman, T. Rogers, and M.H. Bazerman, "Harnessing Our Inner Angels and Demons," *Perspectives on Psychological Science*, 3 (2008), pp. 324–338 e476.

77   Occupation is related to lifecycle stage.

78   Table 4.10 summarizes VALS2 — SRI International, Menlo Park, CA. Name changes from the previous version include: Innovators — formerly Actualizers; Thinkers — formerly Fulfilleds; and Survivors — formerly Strugglers.

79   For discussion of organizational politics: P. Block, *The Empowered Manager: Positive Political Skills at Work*: San Francisco, CA: Jossey Bass, 1991 e479.

80   Mostly marketers consider B2B and B2C purchasing decisions separately. Regardless, in some domains, like PCs, tablet computers, and smart phones, employee experiences as consumers drive changes in organizational procurement decisions.

81   Chapter 3 discussed broad environmental influences — globalization, industry concentration, and increased competition. This section is based on N. Capon, *Key Account Management and Planning*, New York: The Free Press, 2001 e481a, and N. Capon, D. Potter, and F. Schindler, *Managing Global Accounts*, Bronxville, NY: Wessex, 2008 e481b.

82   Personal communication.

83   Marriott Corporation has highly sophisticated sourcing systems and significant procurement expertise. Marriott performs over half its purchasing and distribution activities for non-Marriott clients!

84   When Jose Lopez, GM procurement czar, joined Volkswagen, GM alleged he took a 3,350-page printout listing 60,000 parts and suppliers for GM Europe, exact prices, and delivery schedules.

85   For example, component suppliers have production facilities in various areas of Volkswagen's Brazilian plant.

86   Xerox uses a fivefold *customer relationship triangle* — supplier, authorized supplier, preferred supplier, sole supplier, and quality partner.

87   See J.D. Burdett, "A Model for Customer-Supplier Alliances," *Logistics Information Management*, 5 (1992), pp. 25–31, for contrasting approaches to buyer/seller relationships e487.

CHAPTER 5

1   Based on material from Boeing and Airbus websites and Wikipedia.

2   Boeing switched from traditional in-house manufacture to an outsourced model, assembling components from other manufacturers. Boeing lost control of the process and purchased some subcontractors.

3   Personal communication from Michael George, Chief Marketing Officer and Vice President, Corporate Strategy, Dell.

4   "Detroit Motor Show," *Telegraph Motoring*, January 15, 2005. Ford since sold Jaguar to Tata Motors.

5   *Groupthink* refers to drawing conclusions based on the shared, and poorly examined, assumptions of group members: Wikipedia e505a; I.L. Janis, *Groupthink: Psychological Studies of Policy Decisions and Fiascoes* (2nd ed.), Boston: Wadsworth, 1972 e505b.

6   J. Urbany, D.B. Montgomery, and M. Moore, "Competitive Reactions and Modes of Competitive Reasoning," Cambridge, MA: Marketing Science Institute, 2001 e506a. Also B.H. Clark and D.B. Montgomery, "Managerial Identification of Competitors, *Journal of Marketing*, 63 (July 1999), pp. 67–83 e506b.

7   For this example and more on *strategic intuition*: W. Duggan, *Strategic Intuition: The Creative Spark in Human Achievement*, New York: Columbia Business School, 2007, p. 94 e507.

8   In *Winning*, New York: HarperBusiness, 2005, former GE CEO J. Welch and S. Welch focus on five competitively oriented sets of questions as the basis for developing strategy: 1. What does the playing field look like now? — identifying and describing competitors; 2. What has the competition been up to? — strategy and actions; 3. What have you been up

to? — the firm's strategy and actions; 4. What's around the corner? — potential competitor actions; 5. What's your winning move? — actions the firm can take `e508`.

9   Of course, firms may use legal, political, and/or regulatory means to remove (or weaken) competitors.

10 Prepared in part by Françoise Simon, SDC Group. Reproduced by permission.

11 *Citibank N.A.*, in N. Capon, *The Marketing of Financial Services: A Book of Cases*, Englewood Cliffs, NJ: Prentice Hall, 1992 `e511`.

12 M. Tushman and C. O'Reilly, "Ambidextrous Organizations: Managing Evolutionary and Revolutionary Change," *California Management Review*, 38 (1996), pp. 8–30 `e512`.

13 For the steel division as a whole, structural steel was the more profitable building technology. But, reinforced concrete used a considerable amount of steel.

14 For a good source, see L.M. Fuld, *Competitor Intelligence: How to Get It — How to Use It*, New York: Wiley, 1985 `e514`.

15 L.M. Fuld, *The Secret Language of Competitive Intelligence*, New York: Crown Business, 2006, pp. 40–41 `e515`. For a good example of gaining insight from a competitor's production process, pp. 123–134.

16 Fuld 2006, *op. cit.* pp. 51–56 `e515`.

17 "How Companies Respond to Competitors: A McKinsey Global Survey," *The McKinsey Quarterly*, 2008 `e517`.

18 Based on L. Fahey, *Outwitting, Outmaneuvering and Outperforming Competitors*, New York: Wiley, 1999, Table 5.3, p. 133 `e518`, by permission.

19 In general, the firm should conduct competitive analysis close to the market. In multi-business firms, a corporate-level competitive analysis department may provide some economies of scale.

20 For a good description of a war game, see Fuld 2006, *op. cit.*, pp. 69–118 `e515`.

21 According to Andy Grove, then CEO of Intel: "There is a tendency to walk away from failure and leave it buried. There's an enormous amount of institutional learning that gets lost because failures don't get analyzed," in "Introduction" to *Forbes, Great Minds of Business*, New York: Wiley, 1998, p. xviii `e521`.

22 "A Pretext for Revenge," *Fortune*, June 11, 2007, p. 103 `e522`. HP was involved in a pretexting scandal when its agents investigated information leaks from the board of directors; HP's chairman and several board members resigned.

23 When the author proctored a graduate-school standardized test at Columbia Business School (as a Ph.D. student), he identified Stanley Kaplan writing questions on scraps of paper, presumably to improve his test-prep products.

24 China, Cuba, France, Iran, Israel, and Russia were named as particularly aggressive. Other countries have also been targeted.

25 Based on a competitor analysis framework in Fahey, *op. cit.* `e518`, by permission.

26 The firm should conduct this analysis with a more general objective including opportunities and threats: SWOT — strengths, weaknesses, opportunities, threats.

27 M.E. Porter, *Competitive Advantage: Creating and Sustaining Superior Performance*, New York: Free Press, 1985 `e527`.

28 To reinforce this point, around 500 B.C., Chinese warrior Sun Tzu said: "All men see the tactics whereby I conquer, but none see the strategy out of which victory evolved." *The Art of War*, Wikidepia `e528a`; Oxford; Oxford University Press, 1963 `e528b`.

29 Reproduced from Fahey, *op. cit.* `e518`, Table 4.1, p. 90, by permission.

30 Portfolio analysis may also provide insight — Chapter 12.

31 Nobel Prize-winner John Nash was a pioneer of game theory — Academy Award-winning film, *A Beautiful Mind* `e531a`. Other influential pioneers were: J. von Neumann and O. Morgenstern, *Theory of Games and Economic Behavior*, New York: Wiley, 1964 [c1944] `e531b`.

32 This illustration is the prisoner's dilemma. Two persons are alleged to have committed a crime but the police have insufficient evidence to convict either without a confession. The police separate the prisoners and offer each a deal. If both confess, each receives a medium-length sentence; if neither confesses, each receives a short sentence; if only one confesses and implicates the other, the confessor goes free but the implicated prisoner receives a long sentence. Should a prisoner confess or not? Marketing applications often involve pricing, but also new product introduction, service delivery, and advertising.

33 Personal communication from a former J&J executive.

34 This section based on Fahey, *op. cit.* `e518`, Chapter 16, by permission.

35 G. Stalk Jr., "Curveball: Strategies to Fool the Competition," *Harvard Business Review*, 84 (September 2006), pp. 115–122 `e535`.

36 For an excellent discussion of signaling, see Fahey, *op. cit.* `e518`, Chapter 4.

37 In China, Unilever paid a $300,000 fine for discussing impending price raises and "disrupting market order." Intel paid AMD $1.25 billion for antitrust violations; relatedly, it agreed to refrain from paying customers *not* to use competitor chips, nor to design chips to harm competitor chips. See Chapter 20 on reacting to competitors' price moves.

38 "AMD Sets a Course for 2008," *ZDNet News*, June 1, 2006 `e538`.

39 H. Gatignon and D. Reibstein, "Formulating Competitive Strategies," *Wharton on Dynamic Competitive Strategies*, G. Day and D. Reibstein (eds.), New York: Wiley, 1997 `e539`.

40 Of course, a strong competitor with high market share should be concerned with running afoul of antitrust laws.

41 Now part of the French multinational Schneider Electric.

42 This section based in part on A. Brandenburger and B.J. Nalebuff, *Co-opetition*, New York: Doubleday, 1996 `e542`. Broadly, complementarity includes relationships by which the firm secures needed resources. Formal agreements include co-branding; joint production, marketing, and distribution; joint ventures; R&D partnerships; and supply agreements; but formality is not a requirement for complementarity.

43 Sony's Blu-ray defeated HD-DVD, backed by a rival consortium.

44 These products are not strictly competitors. General Mills has several such delivery arrangements.

45 A major exception is Southwest Airlines — it has no interline agreements.

46 Reilly's Law of Retail Gravitation formalized the power of stores to draw consumers; Wikipedia `e546`.

47 For many years, the U.S. basketball team beat all comers. Fierce competition in the NBA made U.S. players the best.

....
CHAPTER 6

1   Note: *Data* is a plural word; *datum* is singular.

2   Case material from Client Insight, LLC, Boston.

3   Personal communication.

4   Personal communication from Michael Francis, Executive Vice President of Marketing, Target Stores.

5   *Stratified random sampling:* Draw random samples from each group. *Cluster sampling:* Randomly select groups; *area* (*geographical cluster*) sampling is a special case for groups selected by geography.

6   *Boston Fights Drugs (A)*, 9-588-031, Harvard Business School e606.

7   Personal communication from Stephen Cunliffe, President, Nestlé Prepared Foods, U.S.

8   "Vince Camuto: Nine West's Founder Looks Back," *Fortune*, June 29, 2011 e608.

9   C.M. Christensen, S.D. Anthony, G. Berstelll, and D. Nitterhouse, "Finding the Right Job for Your Product," *Sloan Management Review*, 48 (Spring 2007), pp. 38–47 e609.

10 Thanks to Andrew Gershoff for this example.

11 G. Zaltman and R.A. Higie, "Seeing the Voice of the Customer: The Zaltman Metaphor Elicitation Technique," Working Paper 93-114, Cambridge, MA: Marketing Science Institute, 1994 e611a. Patent e611b.

12 The picture approach derives from the Thematic Apperception Test (TAT), widely used in psychology.

13 Attributed to Yogi Berra, baseball player and manager — New York Yankees and New York Mets e613.

14 Mystery shopping is a form of observational research where the researcher participates in the behavior being studied.

15 Technological innovations, like tracking in-store shopping behavior with eye cameras, add rigor to the observational methodology.

16 Example from The Michael Allen Company.

17 F. Gouillart and F. Sturdivant, "Spend a Day in the Life of Your Customers," *Harvard Business Review*, 72 (January–February 1994), pp. 116–125 e617.

18 As Kellogg's CEO, Carlos Gutierrez used to spend an hour each Sunday morning watching consumers buy cereal in supermarkets.

19 A.G. Laffley and R. Charan, *The Game-Changer: How You Can Drive Revenue and Profit Growth with Innovation*, New York: Crown Business, 2008 e619a. Also R.J. Harrington and A.K. Tjan, "Transforming Strategy One Customer at a Time," *Harvard Business Review*, 86 (March 2008), pp. 62–72 e619b.

20 Probability sampling approaches include simple random, stratified random, multistage clustering, and systematic. Convenience sampling is not recommended for projecting results to the population. For a good overview: N.K. Malhotra, *Marketing Research: An Applied Orientation*, Upper Saddle River, NJ: Pearson, 2006, Chapter 11 e620.

21 E. Ofek and O. Toubia, "Marketing and Innovation Management: An Integrated Perspective," *Foundations and Trends in Marketing*, 4(2009), pp. 77–128, reports a professionally administered online survey in which more than 50 percent of respondents reported awareness of at least one *fictitious* oral-care brand e621.

22 Closed-end response questions typically allow for "other."

23 Chapter 8 uses these scales to assess market segments on market attractiveness and business strengths criteria.

24 Numbers of brands/comparisons are: 3 brands/3 comparisons; 4 brands/6 comparisons; 5 brands/10 comparisons; 6 brands/15 comparisons; 7 brands/21 comparisons; etc.

25 Panel members may be subject to the Hawthorne effect. Because someone is observing, they behave differently.

26 *Repeated measures* on the same individuals is a problem for panel data. Special statistical techniques typically take care of this issue.

27 Scanner data have largely superceded other services to secure sales data, like audits for retail store sales and warehouse withdrawals.

28 S.A. Brasel and J. Gipps, "Breaking through Fast Forwarding: Brand Information and Visual Attention," *Journal of Marketing*, 72 (November 2008), pp 31–48 e628.

29 S.M. McClure, J. Li, D. Tomlin, K.S. Cypert, L.M. Montagu, and P.R. Montague, "Neural Correlates of Behavioral Preferences for Culturally Familiar Drinks," *Neuron*, 44 (October 2004), 379–387 e629.

30 T.H. Davenport, "How to Design Smart Business Experiments," *Harvard Business Review*, 87 (February 2009), pp. 69-76 e630.

31 D.T. Campbell and J.C. Stanley, *Experimental and Quasi-Experimental Designs for Research*, New York: Houghton Mifflin, 1963 e631.

32 J. Surowiecki, *The Wisdom of Crowds*, New York: Doubleday, 2004 e632.

33 For a glossary of marketing research terms e633.

34 Attributed to Yogi Berra, *op. cit.* e613

35 More fine-grained analyses use a segment-by-segment approach.

36 Other forecasting methods include BASES and ASSESSOR — Chapter 14. The classic non-durable forecasting model is L.A. Fourt and J.N. Woodlock, "Early Prediction of Market Success for New Grocery Products," *Journal of Marketing*, 25 (October 1960), pp. 31–38 e636a. For a review of the seminal Bass model for consumer durables and other new product forecasting models: V. Mahajan, E. Muller, and F.M. Bass, "New Product Diffusion Models in Marketing: A Review and Directions for Research," *Journal of Marketing*, 54 (January 1990), pp. 1–28 e636b. For a more contemporary application: F.M. Bass, K. Gordon, T.L. Ferguson, and M.L. Githens, "DirecTV: Forecasting Diffusion of a New Product Technology Prior to Product Launch," *Interfaces*, 31 (May–June 2001), pp. 582–593 e636c, e636d. Also Marketing Enrichment me1401.

....

CHAPTER 7

1   Response to a question asked by R. Rumelt (1998). D. Lovallo and L.T. Mendonca, "Strategy's Strategist: An Interview with Richard Rumelt," *The McKinsey Quarterly*, August 2007 e701.

2   Zipcar and Flexcar commenced in the mid-2000s with similar business models; they merged as Zipcar in late 2007.

3   Relatedly, many European cities provide bicycle sharing. For a $30 membership fee, customers access bicycles from bike stands around the city. Paris — 20,000 bicycles, 1,450 stations — has the largest system. In 2011, Paris introduced electric car rental.

4   C. Zook with J. Allen, *Profit from the Core*, Boston, MA: Harvard Business School, 2001 e704a; C. Zook, *Beyond the Core*, Boston, MA: Harvard Business School, 2004 e704b; and C. Zook, *Unstoppable*, Boston, MA: Harvard Business School, 2007 e704c. For a shortened version of the 2007 book: C. Zook, "Finding Your Next Core Business," *Harvard Business Review*, 85 (April 2007), pp. 66–75 e704d.

5   O. Gadiesh and J.M. Gilbert, "Profit Pools: A Fresh Look at Strategy," *Harvard Business Review*, 76 (May–June 1998), pp. 139–147 e705.

6   *White space* is also called *blue ocean*. W.C. Kim and R. Mauborgne, *Blue Ocean Strategy: How to Create Uncontested Market Space and Make the Competition Irrelevant*, Boston, MA: Harvard Business School Press, 2005 e706.

7   B. Chakravortu, "Finding Competitive Advantage in Adversity," *Harvard Business Review*, 88 (November 2010), pp, 103–108 e707.

8   A.S. Grove, *Only the Paranoid Survive*, New York: Doubleday, 1996 e708.

9   In May 1961, President John Kennedy developed a vision for NASA. "Achieving the goal, before this decade is out, of landing a man on the moon and returning him safely to Earth."

10 J.C. Collins and J.I. Porras, "Building Your Company's Vision," *Harvard Business Review*, 74 (September–October 1996), pp. 65–77 e710a — *vision* is closely related to *BHAGs* — Big Hairy Audacious Goals. Terms like *vision*, *mission*, and *strategic objective* (Chapter 9) often have multiple definitions and confuse managers; readers should clarify each author's definition. Specifically, *mission* is neither a firm/business unit charter or motherhood statement, nor *strategic objectives*. Also D.J. Collis and M.G. Rukstad, "Can You Say What Your Strategy Is?" *Harvard Business Review*, 86 (April 2008), pp. 82–90 e710b.

11 Google CEO Eric Schmidt estimated this vision will take 300 years to achieve.

12 J.B. Quinn, *The Intelligent Enterprise: A New Paradigm*, New York: Free Press, 1992 e712.

13 A focused mission is contrary to conglomeration. Conglomerates diversify risk by operating multiple different businesses. In the West, conglomerates have generally lost favor, but current exemplars are VEBA (Germany), GE (U.S.), Keiretsu (Japan), Chaebol (Korea), and large family-owned firms in smaller Asian countries.

14 Some business missions define organizational boundaries — they avoid resource waste from multiple businesses addressing the same market. Conversely, when the firm writes business missions loosely, internal Darwinian competition helps ensure that at least one business addresses a market opportunity.

15 *BYD Company, Ltd.*, 9-606-139, Harvard Business School e715. Berkshire Hathaway (Warren Buffett) purchased 10 percent ownership in BYD.

16 This insight underlay the famous article: T. Levitt, "Marketing Myopia," *Harvard Business Review*, 53 (September–October 1975), p. 26 *et seq.* e716

17 Otis Elevator is a unit of United Technologies.

18 J.M. Brion, *Corporate Marketing Planning*, New York: Wiley, 1967, pp. 155–156 e718a. For a simpler version: H. I. Ansoff, *Corporate Strategy*, New York: McGraw-Hill, 1965, p. 109 e718b. Ansoff labels the four cells in his 2x2 matrix — market penetration, market development, product development, and diversification.

19 The growth path does not address all types of risk. We address various risk types later in the chapter.

20 Day shows that Cell A entries have a 25–40 percent failure probability; Cells C, F, and I have 75–90 percent. In general, Cells D and G have higher failure probabilities than Cells B and C. G.S. Day, "Is It Real? Can We Win? Is It Worth Doing? Managing Risk and Reward in an Innovation Portfolio," *Harvard Business Review*, (December 2007), pp. 110–120 e720.

21 Related to an earlier-used term — *distinctive competence*, that, in some ways, better captures the underlying idea.

22 Withdrawal from unprofitable product/markets also increases profits.

23 We take the producer's position. Retailers incur mainly working-capital risk from product-line extension and expansion.

24 Zook, 2007, *op. cit.* e704c

25 Research suggests that interrelationships among market opportunities may be more important than technological competencies and synergies. N. Capon, J.U. Farley, J. Hulbert, and L.E. Martin, "Corporate Diversity and Economic Performance: The Impact of Market Specialization," *Strategic Management Journal*, 9 (January–February 1988), pp. 61–74 e725.

26 Quaker's Snapple acquisition is probably better viewed as a business extension. Cadbury Schwepps purchased Snapple (plus Mistic [teas and soft drinks] and Stewart's root beer) for $1.03 billion plus assuming $400 million debt. In 2010, Kraft Foods acquired Cadbury Schwepps.

27 Based in part on H.I. Ansoff and J.M. Stewart, "Strategies for a Technologically-Based Business," *Harvard Business Review*, 45 (November–December 1967), pp. 71–83 e727.

28 T. Levitt, *Marketing for Business Growth*, New York: McGraw-Hill, 1974 e728.

29 G.J. Tellis and P.N. Golder, *Will and Vision: How Latecomers Grow to Dominate Markets*, New York: McGraw-Hill, 2002 e729.

30 Tellis and Golder, *op. cit.* e729

31 *We've Got Rhythm! Medtronic Corporation's Cardiac Pacemaker Business*, 9-698-004, Harvard Business School e731.

32 Dell has more than 500 patents on business processes.

33 Chapter 10 discusses strategic options in evolving markets. For capability development — *dynamic capabilities*; P. Fitzroy and J.M. Hulbert, *Strategic Management: Creating Value in Turbulent Times*, Hoboken, NJ: Wiley, 2005 e733.

34 R.G. McGrath and I.C. MacMillan, *Discovery-Driven Growth*, Boston: Harvard Business School, 2009 e734.

35 Chapter 12 describes systematic methods for incorporating such market factors into an evaluation scheme. For definitions of terms — the glossary and any good finance textbook.

36 T. Kuczmarski, *Managing New Products*, Englewood Cliffs, NJ: Prentice Hall, 1988 e736a. Most firms base financial return calculations on discounted cash flow analyses, using higher discount rates for higher risk ventures. More recently, firms also use *real options* analysis to account for large potential upsides and the ability to abandon a venture before making the entire investment; A.B. van Putten and I.C. MacMillan, "Making Real Options Really Work," *Harvard Business Review*, 82 (December 2004), pp. 134–141 e736b.

37 Management fashion plays a role in selecting growth paths. In the late 1960s and early 1970s, many U.S. firms chose *conglomeration*; today, firms generally prefer more-focused approaches. Research shows that *related* growth strategies — markets/customers or products/technologies — are generally more successful; R.P. Rumelt, *Strategy, Structure, and Economic Performance*, Cambridge, MA: Harvard University Press, 1974 e737a; R.P. Rumelt, "Diversification and the Market Share Effect," *Strategic Management Journal*, 3 (October–December 1982), pp. 359–369 e737b; and C.H. Christensen and C.A. Montgomery, "Corporate Economic Performance: Diversification Strategy versus Market Structure," *Strategic Management Journal*, (October–December 1981), pp. 327–343 e737c.

38 Toyota's non-auto business would be in the top 200 of the S&P 500.

39 Losses from the CAT scanner were largely responsible for EMI's subsequent merger with Thorn PLC. *EMI and the CT Scanner (A) and (B)*, 9-383-194/195, Harvard Business School e739. Innovator Geoffrey Hounsfield received the Nobel Prize. (Thorn later divested EMI.)

40 F. Webster, "The Changing Role of Marketing," *Journal of Marketing*, 56 (1992), pp. 1–17 e740.

41 The seminal article: C.K. Prahalad and G. Hamel, "Core Competence of the Corporation," *Harvard Business Review*, 68 (May–June 1990), pp. 79–91 e741a. K.P. Coyne, S.J.D. Hall, and P.G. Clifford, "Is Your Core Competence a Mirage?," *The McKinsey Quarterly*, 1 (1997), pp. 40–54, proposes a formal definition: "A core competence is a combination of complementary skills and knowledge bases embedded in a group or team that results in the ability to execute one or more critical processes to a world-class standard" (p. 43) e741b. Also P. Leinwand and C. Mainardi, "The Coherence Premium," *Harvard Business Review*, 88 (June 2010), pp. 86–92 e741c.

42 Intel improved once-abysmal manufacturing yields to become the industry leader.

43 The Carlyle Group (private equity) grew by acquiring disparate businesses from "larger companies that were looking [to pare their holdings] to find their core competencies"; "Carlyle Changes Its Stripes," *BusinessWeek*, February 12, 2007, at p. 58 e743 .

44 "Virgin in the Oil Patch," *Fortune*, February 6, 2006 e744 .

45 Ansoff, *op. cit.* e718b ; M. Goold and A. Campbell, "Desperately Seeking Synergy," *Harvard Business Review*, 76 (September–October 1998), pp. 131–143 e745 .

46 Alcoa and others sometimes provide expertise as a free service to current and potential customers.

47 Of course, the portfolio the firm selects has important implications for individuals and organizations that become shareholders.

48 G.E. Blau, J.F. Pekny, V.A. Varma, and P.R. Bunch, "Managing a Portfolio of Interdependent New Product Candidates in the Pharmaceutical Industry," *Journal of Product Innovation Management*, 21 (2004), pp. 227–245 e748 .

49 A contributing factor to Enron's collapse was the absence of a risk assessment for the entire venture portfolio, K. Eichenwald, *A Conspiracy of Fools*, New York: Broadway, 2004 e749 .

50 N. Capon and R. Glazer, "Marketing and Technology: A Strategic Co-Alignment," *Journal of Marketing*, 51 (July 1987), pp. 1–14 e750 . Pharmaceutical giant Merck focuses largely on internal development but has had problems with product failure.

51 N. Capon, J. U. Farley, and J. Hulbert, *Corporate Strategic Planning*, New York: Columbia University Press, 1988 e751a ; and N. Capon, J.U. Farley, and S. Hoenig, *Toward an Integrative Explanation of Corporate Financial Performance*, Norwell, MA: Kluwer Academic Publishers, 1997 e751b .

52 Personal communication from Pat Kelly, Senior Vice President, Worldwide Marketing, Pfizer Pharmaceuticals.

53 To aid in acculturation, some Japanese firms require employees to wear firm uniforms, sing corporate songs, and learn corporate mantras.

54 Large R&D spenders include life science and information-science firms — R&D spending at Microsoft exceeds 15 percent of sales!

55 Some firms post research problems on Eli Lilly's InnoCentive website — problem solvers earn cash payments.

56 A.J. Slywotzky and D.J. Morrison, *Value Migration*, New York: Times Business, 1996 e756a ; and *The Profit Zone*, Times Business: New York, 1998 e756b . Also R. Wise and P. Baumgartner, "Go Downstream: The New Profit Imperative in Manufacturing," *Harvard Business Review*, 77 (September– October 1999), pp. 133–141 e756c .

57 Offshoring is a controversial political issue in the U.S.

58 B. Arruñada and X.H. Vázquez, "When Your Contract Manufacturer Becomes Your Competitor," *Harvard Business Review*, 84 (September 2006), pp. 135–144 e758 .

59 McKinsey showed that successful acquirer goals are: adding capabilities, expanding geographically, and buying growth; rarely is diversification a goal. *The McKinsey Quarterly* Chart Focus Newsletter, July 2007 e759 .

60 L.V. Gerstner, Jr., *Who Says Elephants Can't Dance*, New York: Harper-Business, 2003, p. 222 e760 . Gerstner adds that IBM often accelerated technology development through highly focused acquisitions.

61 eBay's Skype acquisition was widely considered a failure; in 2010, eBay sold most of its Skype investment to an investor group, since acquired by Microsoft.

62 Personal communication from Pat Kelly, *op. cit.*

63 Pharmaceutical examples include Roche purchasing Genentec and GSK purchasing Sirtis.

64 M.A. Hayward and D.C. Hambrick, "Explaining the Premiums Paid for Large Acquisitions: Evidence of CEO Hubris," *Administrative Science Quarterly*, 42 (1997), pp. 103–127 e764 .

65 M. Bradley, A. Desai, and E.H. Kim, "Synergistic Gains from Acquisitions and Their Division between the Stockholders of Target and Acquiring Firms," *Journal of Financial Economics*, 21 (1988), pp. 3–40 e765a ; E. Berkovitch and M.P. Narayanan, "Motives for Take-overs: An Empirical Investigation," *Journal of Financial and Quantitative Analysis*, 28 (1993), pp. 347–362 e765b ; M.L. Sirower, *The Synergy Trap: How Companies Lose the Acquisition Game*, New York: Free Press, 1997 e765c .

66 Capon, Farley, and Hoenig, *op. cit.* e751b

67 Gerstner, *op. cit.* e760

68 W.H. Bergquist, *Building Strategic Relationships: How to Extend Your Organization's Reach through Partnerships, Alliances and Joint Ventures*, San Francisco, CA: Jossey-Bass, 1995 e768 .

69 For licensing issues, *Amicon Corporation (A,B,C,D)*, 9-574-093/4/5/6, Harvard Business School e769 .

70 At PARC, Xerox pioneered the Ethernet, the graphical user interface, the mouse, and Alto, an early personal computer.

71 P.A. Gompers and J. Lerner, "Can Corporate Venture Capital Work?," Working Paper, Harvard Business School, 1998. Xerox replaced XTV with Xerox New Enterprise (XNE) (mid-1990s) and took a more aggressive ownership approach. Xerox closed XNE in 1999. Internal corporate venturing seems to follow a cycle of 10 years or less; typically, the firm closes the program and later restarts in a different form: R.A. Burgelman and L. Välikangas, "Managing Internal Corporate Venturing Cycles," *Sloan Management Review*, (Summer 2005), pp. 26–34 e771 .

72 M. Tushman and C.A. O'Reilly III, "Ambidextrous Organizations: Managing Evolutionary and Revolutionary Change," *California Management Review*, 38 (Summer 1996), pp. 8–30 e772 .

CHAPTER 8

1 Marriott brand properties include Marriott Hotels & Resorts, JW Marriott, and Marriott Vacation Club.

2 By contrast, when Cendant added Budget to its Avis subsidiary, it combined back-office operations like accounting and maintenance, but kept front offices separate. Similarly, upscale handbag-maker Coach factory outlets are normally one hour's drive from full-price stores.

3 An exception often occurs early in the product life cycle when the pioneer's technological benefits may overshadow all others.

4 Ideally, segments are mutually exclusive and collectively exhaustive.

5 Segmentation is a way of escaping the commodity trap. F.M. Jacques, "Even Commodities Have Customers," *Harvard Business Review*, 85 (May 2007), pp. 110–119 e805 .

6 SMSA is a Bureau of the Census definition of urban agglomerations, regardless of political boundaries.

7 *Daypart* — like morning, afternoon, evening — is an oft-employed *use occasion* variable.

8 For a life-stage segmentation scheme based on birthdates: Baby Boomers — 1946 to 1965, Generation X — 1966 to 1980, Generation Y — 1981 to 1999, and Tweens — 2000 to 2004. As one senior marketing executive confided, "If you want to know where the next profitable client base is going to be, just watch that pig moving through the python!"

9 Y. Atsmon, A. Keretsz, and I Vittal, "Is Your Emerging Market Strategy Local Enough," *The McKinsey Quarterly* (April 2011), advocates addressing the China market via 22 geographically proximate and relatively demographically homogeneous urban clusters e809.

10 "Taxonomy at the Pump: Mobil's Five Types of Gasoline Buyers," *The Wall Street Journal*, January 30, 1995.

11 R.J. Harrington and A.K. Tjan, "Transforming Strategy One Customer at a Time," *Harvard Business Review*, 86 (March 2008), pp. 62–72 e811.

12 "Mirabella Told Summer Issue to Be its Last," *The New York Times*, April 28, 2000 e812.

13 An Internet-shopper study identified eight segments — shopping lovers (11.1 percent), adventurous shoppers (8.9 percent), suspicious learners (9.6 percent), business users (12.4 percent), fearful browsers (10.7 percent), fun seekers (12.1 percent), technology muddlers (19.6 percent), and shopping avoiders (15.6 percent).

14 Macy's identifies four female lifestyles among core customers (it also has male lifestyles): Katherine — traditional, classy dresser, takes risks, likes quality; Julie — neo-traditional, slightly more edgy, but still classic; Erin — contemporary, loves newness, shops by brand; and Alex — fashion consumer, wants the latest and greatest. Walmart also identified a handful of segments like *loyalist*, *selective shopper*, and *skeptic*; it addresses segments by modifying skus and department placement by store.

15 *The Wall Street Journal, op. cit.* A two cents price increase would have led to a 20 percent increase in Mobil's profits.

16 A *lifestage* formulation has 11 groups: Midlife Success, Young Achievers, Striving Singles, Accumulated Wealth, Young Accumulators, Mainstream Families, Sustaining Families, Affluent Empty Nesters, Conservative Classics, Cautious Couples, and Sustaining Seniors e816a. An alternative approach based on technology adoption, income, and children in the household has 53 clusters comprising 11 groups. Other commercially available segmentation schemes include VALS (Chapter 4), Mosaic (Experian) e816b, Acorn (ESRI) e816c, and PSYTE (MapInfo) e816d.

17 C.K. Prahalad, *The Fortune at the Bottom of the Pyramid*, Philadelphia PA: Wharton School, 2004 e817a. Of course, the base of the pyramid should also be segmented: V.K. Rangan, M. Chu, and D. Petkoski, "Segmenting the Base of the Pyramid," *Harvard Business Review*, 89 (June 2011) , pp. 113–117 e817b.

18 C.P. Beshouri, "A Grassroots Approach to Emerging-Market Consumers," *The McKinsey Quarterly*, 4 (2006), pp. 61–71 e818.

19 M. Yunus, *Banker to the Poor: Micro-Lending and the Battle against World Poverty*, Jackson TN: PublicAffairs, 1999 e819.

20 Similar insurance is available for farmers. Insurance protection enables herdsmen and farmers secure credit.

21 In addition to segmenting product markets, the firm may also segment the investor market. Shareholder Relations departments use descriptor variables like current/previous firm and/or competitor holdings, assets under management, average holding period, and investment style.

22 D.K. Rigby and V. Vishwanath, "Localization: The Revolution in Consumer Markets," *Harvard Business Review*, 84 (April 2006), pp. 82–92 e822.

23 Platform engineering is very important in the automobile industry.

24 B.J. Pine II, B. Victor, and A.C. Boyton, "Making Mass Customization Work," *Harvard Business Review*, 71 (September–October 1993), pp. 108–119 e824a; B.J. Pine II, D. Peppers, and M. Rogers, "Do You Want to Keep Your Customers Forever?," *Harvard Business Review*, 73 (March–April 1995), pp. 103–114 e824b; and E. Feitzinger and H.L. Lee, "Mass Customization at Hewlett-Packard: The Power of Postponement," *Harvard Business Review*, 75 (January–February 1997), pp. 116–121 e824c.

25 A.J. Slywotzky, "The Age of the Choiceboard," *Harvard Business Review*, 78 (January–February 2000), pp. 40–41 e825.

26 Some heavy users in the single-male segment visit fast-food restaurants upwards of 20 times per month, spending in excess of $40 per day!

27 M.J.A. Berry and G. Linoff, *Data Mining Techniques for Marketing, Sales and Customer Support*, New York: Wiley, 1997 e827.

28 *TESCO PLC: Getting to the Top ... Staying at the Top?* 599-037-1BW, European Case Clearing House e828. Tesco's loyalty card comes in gold, silver, and bronze tiers, reflecting customer profitability.

29 In 2005, Stock Building Supply acquired Siegle's. In 2009 the Siegle family reacquired the cabinetry operation to become the largest distributor of kitchen and bath products in the Chicago area.

30 The firm may also evaluate segment opportunities via financial analyis (FA). FA typically embeds assumptions about the segment and the firm. The multifactor analysis makes assumptions explicit and is an excellent complement to financial analysis.

31 H. Simon, *Hidden Champions: Lessons from 500 of the World's Best Unknown Companies*, Boston, MA: Harvard Business School Press, 1996 e831.

32 We use a linear compensatory model with correlated variables — at best, the variables have interval-scale properties. In practice, these theoretical concerns cause little difficulty. Parallel analyses typically report high convergence of relative positions. But the firm should be careful not to attach too much importance to absolute (versus relative) factor scores.

33 When all rating scores are 1, the total factor score is 100 ; when all rating scores are 10, the total factor score is 1,000.

34 We assume market segments are independent — targeting one segment has no effect on targeting others. If the firm contemplates targeting multiple segments, it should consider potential synergies among segments. The firm must also consider the complexity of designing and delivering individual marketing offers. Chapter 9 addresses this issue.

35 The firm typically develops dimensions from customer survey data and an analytic process like multidimensional scaling — Marketing Enrichment me601. For scaling procedures to develop perceptual maps, see any good marketing research text — for example, D.R. Lehmann, J. Steckel, and S. Gupta, *Marketing Research*, Reading, MA: Addison-Wesley, 1997 e835. Most firms use two-dimensional maps, but three dimensions may be useful. If three dimensions (A, B, C) best describe the market, three separate two-dimensional maps (AB, AC, BC) typically suffice.

36 Prescription medicines that sought to combine these benefits — Cox-2 inhibitors — were initially very successful. But Merck withdrew Vioxx; Pfizer stopped consumer advertising for Celebrex.

37 This map does not capture other possibly important customer-need dimensions like toy size or willingness to pay.

38 An ideal point is the *center of gravity* of customer needs. *High* is not necessarily better than *low*, *more* is not necessarily better than *less*! Consider aero-engines for a 50-seat aircraft. Low-power engines cannot fly the airplane; high-power engines are too heavy. *Ideal* power is between high and low. Also, the perceptual map shows segment size, but neither growth nor potential size.

39 The firm may also shift segment ideal points by persuading customers to modify their needs — this tends to be difficult.

40 Whirlpool based all design variations on extensive consumer research.

41 Stockbroker Edward D. Jones grew with a focused strategy — offering personal service in rural areas and small towns.

42 "Wish I'd Thought of That!" *Fortune*, May 15, 2000 e842.

43 Sometimes the large company elects to acquire rather than fight; small firm owners may reap large financial rewards.

44 Aquilisa Quartz: Simply a Better Shower, Harvard Business School, 9-502-030 e844 .

CHAPTER 9

1 Personal communication.

2 For more on Mayo Clinic: L.L. Berry and N. Bendapudi, "Clueing in Customers," *Harvard Business Review*, 81 (February 2003), pp. 2–7 e902 .

3 Note: *market* strategy, not *marketing* strategy. Many functional areas, not just marketing, should help develop and implement the strategy.

4 Sometimes people use the terms *strategy* and *plan* interchangeably and present their plans as a set of figures. A set of figures is *not* a strategy!

5 For Harvard Business School's perspective on marketing strategy: *Note on Marketing Strategy*, 9-598-061, Harvard Business School. For an important perspective on strategy: M.E. Porter, "What Is Strategy?," *Harvard Business Review*, 74 (November–December 1996), pp. 61–78 e905 .

6 Strategies do not always exist before the fact. Sometimes a firm is successful, then after-the-fact analysis reveals a pattern of actions. Someone designates this pattern as a strategy. Generally, researchers cannot tell whether a pattern existed as an idea or concept before the fact; H. Mintzberg, *The Rise and Fall of Strategic Planning*, New York: Free Press, 1994 e906a . Also N. Capon, "Review of *The Rise and Fall of Strategic Planning* by Henry Mintzberg," *Academy of Management Review*, (January 1996), pp. 298–301 e906b .

7 For an interesting perspective on strategy: B.D. Henderson, "The Origin of Strategy," *Harvard Business Review*, 67 (November–December 1989), pp. 139–143 e907 . Also *Marketing Strategy — An Overview*, 9-579-054, Harvard Business School.

8 J.R. Williams, "How Sustainable Is Your Competitive Advantage?," *California Management Review*, 34 (Spring 1992), pp. 29–52 e908a ; P. Ghemawat, "Sustainable Advantage," *Harvard Business Review*, 64 (September–October 1986), pp. 53–94 e908b ; and M.E. Porter and V.E. Millar, "How Information Gives You Competitive Advantage," *Harvard Business Review*, 63 (July–August 1985), pp. 149–159 e908c .

9 To ensure the firm seriously considers competition, re-label *Market Strategy* as *Competitive Market Strategy*.

10 An approach sometimes favored by high-market share firms. By contrast, low-market-share competitors often gain by cutting prices in price-inelastic markets — high-share leaders are reluctant to follow because they earn lower profit margins on much higher volumes.

11 Sometimes the firm must work closely with third-party organizations like joint-venture partners.

12 Behavioral economics suggests several reasons firms may develop poor strategies: *overconfidence* — unrealistic belief in their abilities; *mental accounting* — categorizing money differently depending on its origin, where it's kept, and how it's spent; *status quo bias* — keeping things the way they are; *anchoring* — basing actions on what is known; *sunk cost* — throwing good money after bad; *herding instinct* — following others; *misestimating hedonic states* — inability to estimate pleasure/pain if things change quickly; and *false consensus* — overestimating the extent to which others share views: C. Roxburgh, "Hidden Flaws in Strategy," *The McKinsey Quarterly*, 2 (2003), pp. 1–9 e912a . D.P. Lovallo and O. Sibony, "Distortions and Deceptions in Strategic Decisions," *The McKinsey Quarterly*, 1 (2006), pp. 19–29, identify three cognitive distortions — overoptimism, loss aversion, and overconfidence; and four deceptions resulting from organizational interactions — misaligned time horizons,

misaligned risk aversion profiles, overacceptance of the champion's views (champion bias), and overacceptance of top management's views (*sunflower* management) e912b .

13 Options for resolving inter-functional conflict in the absence of a market strategy include: *big stick* — one function is more powerful and imposes its will; *send it up* to senior managers — may be unhappy that lower levels cannot resolve issues; *compromise* — the competition wins.

14 Positioning is typically more familiar in B2C than B2B, but the same basic principles apply.

15 R.D. Buzzell, B.T. Gale, and R.G.M. Sultan, "Market Share — a Key to Profitability," *Harvard Business Review*, 53 (January–February 1975), pp. 97–106, was the first paper in a stream of research on the relationship between market share and profitability e915 . In general, the relationship is positive, but may break down at high market share levels.

16 If the firm is well positioned in a growing market segment, short-term profits (or cash flow) could be the appropriate strategic objective: A.J. Slywotsky and B.P. Shapiro, "Leveraging to Beat the Odds: The New Marketing Mind-Set," *Harvard Business Review*, 71 (September–October 1993), pp. 97–107 e916 .

17 We present a detailed exposition of *cash cows* and other product portfolio members in Chapter 12.

18 PIMS (Profit Impact of Market Strategy) measures the relationship between business actions and results. PIMS was developed at GE in the mid-1960s; in the early 1970s, PIMS moved to the Marketing Science Institute. The Strategic Planning Institute has maintained this research since 1975 e918 .

19 Figures are averages of more than 1,000 businesses pooled across time periods and industries.

20 Generally, operational objectives set in real numbers — units, dollars, are more useful than objectives stated as percentages. Units have direct capacity implications, and the firm takes dollars to the bank, not percentages. Further, the *base* for percentage calculations is often disputable.

21 The strategic-focus-alternatives tree is loosely based on the famous DuPont formula; Wikipedia e921 .

22 Pepsi offered large soft-drink bottles to remove Coke's *hourglass* bottle advantage in supermarkets: J. Sculley with J.A. Byrne, *Odyssey: Pepsi to Apple . . . A Journey of Adventure, Ideas and the Future*, New York: Harper & Row, 1987 e922 .

23 Some price promotions merely time-shift purchases without securing product-use increases.

24 Citibank also reduced costs as fewer customers called for explanations.

25 Working capital = accounts receivable *plus* cash *plus* inventories *less* accounts payable.

26 End-user customers are individuals, family, or formal organizations.

27 Some finished-goods manufacturers, like Avon and Amway, sell products direct to consumers.

28 H. Evans, *They Made America*, New York: Little Brown, 2004, pp. 391–392 e928 .

29 College Savings Bank (A) and (B) in N. Capon, *The Marketing of Financial Services: A Book of Cases*, Englewood Cliffs, NJ: Prentice Hall, 1992 e929 .

30 P. M. Nattermann, "Best Practice Does Not Equal Best Strategy," *The McKinsey Quarterly*, August 18, 2004 e930 .

31 In B2B marketing argot — a *specification sell*. By tightly specifying product/service attributes, the purchaser has little choice of suppliers.

32 Generally, the firm should avoid head-to-head competition with stronger competitors — who may respond strongly, and concentrate on

weaker firms. But competing against strong competitors may lead to a more adept organization, better equipped to face competition elsewhere. Porter showed that countries whose firms together earned the highest global market shares in many product classes experienced fierce domestic competition: M. E. Porter, *The Competitive Advantage of Nations*, New York: Free Press, 1990 `e932`.

33 In the U.S., the firm can use comparative claims in advertising if supported statistically — not so in other countries.

34 "Achieving Market Focus," Chapter 7, in F.J. Gouillart and J.N. Kelly, *Transforming the Organization*, New York: McGraw-Hill, 1996 `e934`.

35 Thanks to Mary Murphy, Impact Planning Group, for this acronym.

36 As supermarkets consolidate, FMCG firms place increasing resources on large retail chains.

37 A. Ries and J. Trout, *Positioning: The Battle for Your Mind*, New York: McGraw-Hill, 1993 `e937`.

38 Robert Christian, formerly of Impact Planning Group, Old Greenwich, CT, developed this structure.

39 Developed by the author from published data.

40 With these capabilities, Cemex saves on fuel, maintenance, and payroll, and uses 35 percent fewer trucks. Cemex secures higher prices by delivering a perishable item within minutes of receiving an order. Customers use the Internet to place orders, secure delivery information, and check payment records.

41 Marketing researchers spend significant effort in modeling the impact of marketing implementation variables. The seminal paper is: J.D.C. Little, "BRANDAID: A Marketing-Mix Model, Part 1: Structure," *Operations Research*, 23 (July–August 1975), pp. 628–655 `e941`.

42 In Britain and Ireland, doctors frequently recommend Guinness for pregnant women!

43 The CEO fully backed the cross-functional team. As the team developed creative ideas, the finance executive ran back-of-the-envelope calculations to assess viability.

44 Based on an earlier version developed by the Impact Planning Group.

CHAPTER 10

1 Michael O'Leary, Ryanair's CEO, specializes in four-letter-word abuse against anyone who comes in range. O'Leary notes that "Business books are bullshit and are usually written by wankers." A. Ruddock, *Michael O'Leary: A Life in Full Flight*, London: Penguin, 2007 `e1001`.

2 Note the slope differences between older inventions like the automobile and the telephone, and newer inventions like web access and the cell phone. Some analysts measure life-cycle duration from birth to death. An alternative is from take-off until the onset of maturity — the critical strategic period when firms often establish long-run competitive positions. Well-supported products entering maturity in dominant position are difficult to dislodge. Most observers believe life cycles are shortening: R. Olshavsky, "Time and the Rate of Adoption of Innovations," *Journal of Consumer Research*, 6 (March 1980), pp. 425–428 `e1002a`; and W. Qualls, R. Olshavsky, and R. Michaels, "Shortening of the PLC — an Empirical Test," *Journal of Marketing*, 45 (Fall 1981), pp. 76–80 `e1002b`. Other observers dispute this view; B.L. Bayus, "Are Product Life Cycles Really Getting Shorter," *Journal of Product Innovation Management*, 11 (1994), pp. 300–308 `e1002c`; B.L. Bayus, "An Analysis of Product Lifetimes in a Technologically Dynamic Industry," *Management Science*, 44 (June 1998), pp. 763–775 `e1002d`; and R. Agarwal and B.L. Bayus, "The Market Evolution and Sales Take-Off of Product Innovations," *Management Science*, 48 (August 2002), pp. 1024–1041 `e1002e`.

3 Other approaches to developing competitive strategy include three generic strategies — low cost, focus, and differentiation: M.E. Porter, *Competitive Advantage: Creating and Sustaining Superior Performance*, New York: Free Press, 1985 `e1003a`; and three value disciplines — *operational excellence*, *customer intimacy*, and *product leadership*, M. Treacy and F. Wiersema, *The Discipline of Market Leaders*, Reading, MA: Addison-Wesley, 1997 `e1003b`. Other strategy literature has focused on more internally focused perspectives like core competencies and strategic resources: G. Hamel and C.K. Prahalad, "The Core Competence of the Corporation," *Harvard Business Review*, 68 (May–June 1990), pp. 79–91 `e1003c`. In Chapter 10, these approaches appear in different forms as strategies at various life-cycle stages. Despite some merit, prescriptions from the approaches noted here are too simplistic for today's competitive, complex, and global environments. An external focus should play a major role in strategy development — the scenario approach does just that.

4 A separate but related issue: At what stage should the firm enter the market? We address this question in Chapter 7.

5 Many observers associate the U.S. high level of new firm formation with its historically strong venture capital market.

6 Classically, RCA licensed color TV patents to spread the *catch-22* market-development burden: Demand for color TV sets was weak without large numbers of color TV programs; production of color TV programs was difficult to spur without a large installed base of color TVs!

7 GSM is the standard wireless phone technology in Europe and many other countries, but not the U.S. Because the U.S. has multiple incompatible technologies, European cell phones and services are more advanced.

8 Entry barriers retard firm market *entry*; exit barriers retard firm market *exit*. The general term for inhibiting firm movement is *mobility barriers*. For entry barriers: T.S. Gruca and D. Sudharshan, "A Framework for Entry Deterrence Strategy: The Competitive Environment, Choices, and Consequences," *Journal of Marketing*, 59 (July 1995), pp. 44–55 `e1008a`; and B. Greenwald and J. Kahn, *Competition Demystified: A Radically Simplified Approach to Business Strategy*, New York: Portfolio Hardcover, 2005 `e1008b`.

9 Product-specific barriers evolve. Historically, entry barriers for mainframe computers were capital and human resources. Today, entry into PCs is relatively straightforward.

10 Many marketing textbooks address penetration and skim pricing in the pricing chapter. We believe the fundamental issues these strategies represent make them appropriate for Chapter 10.

11 For theoretical underpinnings of the experience curve: *Perspectives on Experience*, Boston, MA: Boston Consulting Group, 1972 `e1011`.

12 Penetration pricing relies on three simple relationships. When demand is price-elastic, low prices drive high volumes; high volumes reduce unit costs; lower unit costs permit price reductions, *et seq.*

13 7-Eleven Japan was so successful, it acquired 7-Eleven US, the original parent!

14 eBay is more valuable to sellers when there are more buyers; it is more valuable to buyers when there are more sellers.

15 In the 1980s, Pepsi displaced Coke as the leading cola in supermarkets by introducing large plastic bottles and aggressively tying up bottle-producing capacity. J. Sculley and J.A. Byrne, *Odyssey*, New York: Harper & Row, 1988 `e1015`.

16 G.S. Carpenter and K. Nakamoto, "Consumer Preference Formation and Pioneering Advantage," *Journal of Marketing Research*, 26 (August 1989), pp. 285–298 `e1016a`. Research supporting the success of pioneering firms includes: G. Urban, T. Carter, S. Gaskin, and Z. Mucha, "Market Share Rewards to Pioneering Brands: An Empirical Analysis

and Strategic Implications," *Management Science*, 32 (June 1986), pp. 645–659 e1016b; and M. Song, C.A. DiBenedetto, and Y. L. Zhao, "Pioneering Advantages in Manufacturing and Service Industries: Empirical Evidence from Nine Countries," *Strategic Management Journal*, 20 (1999), pp. 811–836 e1016c.

17 The term *price skimming* is derived from the practice of skimming the cream from unhomogenized milk.

18 J. Dean, "Pricing Policies for New Products," *Harvard Business Review*, 28 (November–December 1950), pp. 28–36 e1018.

19 On some measures, No. 2 firms perform better than leaders — Lowes versus Home Depot, AMD versus Intel, and Target versus Walmart.

20 Personal communication from former senior Nokia marketing executive Richard Geruson.

21 eBay has more than 500 million registered users.

22 Peter Drucker famously posed the question: "If we were to decide now, would we still enter the businesses we are in today? And if not, what are we going to do about it?" P. Drucker, *Managing for the Future*, New York: Truman Talley/Dutton, 1992 e1022.

23 R. Buaron, "New Game Strategies," *The McKinsey Quarterly* (Spring 1981), pp. 24–30 e1023.

24 Hence the sobriquet *Neutron Jack*, referring to empty buildings after GE sold businesses in number *three* position or below.

25 Frequently, the U.S. leader does not lead abroad. Outside the U.S., Ford and Heinz are larger than GM and Campbell's, respectively. Followers often target foreign geographic segments early in the product life cycle.

26 Patients receive Taxol (paclitaxel) intravenously. Because it is not water-soluble, doctors mix Taxol with castor oil and alcohol (Cremophor).

27 G. Stalk Jr., D.K. Pecaut, and B. Burnett, "Breaking Compromises, Breakaway Growth," *Harvard Business Review*, 74 (September–October 1996), pp. 131–139 e1027a; and Y. Moon, "Break Free from the Product Life Cycle," *Harvard Business Review*, 83 (May 2005), pp. 77–94 e1027b.

28 Price elasticity = percentage change in quantity demanded divided by percentage change in price = dQ/Q ÷ dP/P.

29 Productive ways to identify creative opportunities include — analogous situations in other industries, deep insight into customer purchase and use, industry diseconomies, latent dissatisfactions, and performance anomalies; Stalk, Pecaut, and Burnett, *op. cit.* e1027a

30 An informal survey of plumbers revealed that clean dishes require less than 50 percent of the amount of dishwashing soap recommended by dishwasher manufacturers.

31 For interesting approaches to securing growth in mature markets: W.C. Kim and R. Mauborgne, "Creating New Market Space," *Harvard Business Review*, 77 (January–February 1999), pp. 83–93 e1031a; and *Blue Ocean Strategy*, Boston, MA: Harvard Business School, 2005 (same authors) e1031b.

32 M. Baghai, S. Smit, and P. Viguerie, "Is Your Growth Strategy Flying Blind?" *Harvard Business Review*, 87 (May 2009), pp. 86–96 e1032.

33 J.S. Brown and J. Hagel III, "Innovation Blowback: Disruptive Management Practices from Asia," *The McKinsey Quarterly*, 1 (2005), pp. 35–45 e1033.

34 Economists refer to concentrated markets as oligopolies. J.N. Sheth and R.S. Sisodia, *The Rule of Three: Thriving and Surviving in Competitive Markets*, New York: Free Press, 2002, suggest many mature industries follow *The Rule of Three* — three generalist firms have most market share e1034a. Empirically, leading firms and small specialists are more profitable than those *stuck in the middle*: C. Uslay, Z.A. Altintig, and R.D. Winsor, "An Empirical Examination of the "Rule of Three": Strategy

Implications for Top Management, Markters, and Investors," *Journal of Marketing*, 74 (March 2010), pp. 20–39 e1034b.

35 I.C. Macmillan and L. Selden, "The Incumbent's Advantage," *Harvard Business Review*, 86 (October 2008), pp. 111–121 e1035.

36 Managers often confuse *harvesting* with *milking*. Milking focuses on securing resources for use elsewhere in the firm — *the cow must be fed so the milk continues to flow*. Harvesting implies a decision to exit, sooner or later.

37 A focus on incremental avoidable costs is often a better approach than relying on traditional accounting measures.

38 "Technology; Earnings Are Down a Bit at Dell," *The New York Times*, May 18, 2001 e1038.

39 For maintaining current business while preparing for discontinuous change: M.L. Tushman and C.A. O'Reilly III, "Ambidextrous Organizations: Managing Evolutionary and Revolutionary Change," *California Management Review*, 28 (Summer 1996), pp. 8–30 e1039.

40 For further discussion — Chapter 17 and *Norton Company (A)*, 9-570-001, Harvard Business School.

41 Based in part on N. Kumar, "Strategies to Fight Low-Cost Rivals," *Harvard Business Review* 84 (December 2006), pp. 104–112 e1041.

42 D.J. Bryce and J.H. Dyer, "Strategies to Crack Well-Guarded Markets," *Harvard Business Review*, 85 (May 2007), pp. 84–92 e1042.

43 In the 1980s and 1990s, BancOne (later Bank One) grew by acquiring many Midwestern banks.

44 A.J. Slywotzky and D.J. Morrison, *The Profit Zone*, New York: Times Business, 1997 e1044a; also A.J. Slywotsky and B.P. Shapiro, "Leveraging to Beat the Odds: The New Marketing Mind-Set," *Harvard Business Review*, 71 (September–October 1993), pp. 97–107 e1044b.

45 Viable options are similar to long-run market leadership.

46 Many firms hang on too long before exiting: J.T. Horn, D.P. Lovallo, and S.P. Viguerie, "Learning to Let Go: Making Better Exit Decisions," *The McKinsey Quarterly*, 2 (2006), pp. 65–75 e1046.

47 Personal communication from W. A. Taylor executive.

48 K. Harrigan, "Strategies for Declining Industries," *Journal of Business Strategy*, 1 (Fall 1980), pp. 20–34 e1048. Of course, investment may be extremely low if the firm has depreciated most capital equipment. Table 10.1 contains rounding errors.

49 A faulty accounting system obscures financial performance; it may create a serious exit barrier if the competitor does not know products are unprofitable.

50 Newpapers have lost classified advertising revenues to free websites like Craigslist, and are struggling to monetize Internet content.

51 R. Adner and D.C. Snow, "Bold Retreat: A New Strategy for Old Technologies," *Harvard Business Review*, 88 (March 2010), pp. 77–81 e1051.

52 R. Gulati, N. Nohria, and F. Wohlgezogen, "Roaring out of Recession," *Harvard Business Review*, 88 (March 2010), pp. 63–69 e1052.

CHAPTER 11

1 J. Sampson, "Brand Valuation: Today and Tomorrow," Chapter 20 in *Brand Valuation*, R. Perrier and P. Stobart (eds.), London: Premier Books, 1997 e1101.

2 Adapted from B.H. Schmitt and D. Rogers, "SAP: Building a Leading Technology Brand," Center on Global Brand Leadership, Columbia Business School, and personal communication from Marty Homlish. In 2011, Homlish joined HP as executive vice president and chief marketing officer.

3   S. King, *Developing New Brands*, London: J. Walter Thompson Co. Ltd., 1984 `e1103`.

4   Branding dates to brickmakers in ancient Egypt and guilds in medieval Europe.

5   American Marketing Association, from K.L. Keller, *Strategic Brand Management*, Upper Saddle River, NJ: Prentice-Hall, 2003, Chapter 1 `e1105`.

6   In Romeo and Juliet (ll, 11, 1-2), Juliet says, "What's in a name — that which we call a rose by any other name would smell as sweet." In *Positioning: The Battle for Your Mind*, New York: McGraw Hill, 2001, Ries and Trout say: "Shakespeare was wrong. A rose by any other name would not smell as sweet ... which is why the single most important decision in the marketing of perfume is the name." `e1106`

7   The shape of a fragrance bottle was critical to Calvin Klein's trademark-infringement lawsuit against Ralph Lauren.

8   Apparently *irrelevant attributes* may have important differentiating properties. G.S. Carpenter, R. Glazer, and K. Nakamoto, "Meaningful Brands from Meaningless Differentiation: The Dependence on Irrelevant Attributes," *Journal of Marketing Research*, 31 (August 1994), pp. 339–350 `e1108`.

9   J. M. Hulbert, N. Capon, and N. Piercy, *Total Integrated Marketing: Breaking the Bounds of the Function*, New York: Free Press, 2003 `e1109`.

10 B.H. Schmitt, *Experiential Marketing*, New York: Free Press, 1999 `e1110a`; and *Customer Experience Management*, Hoboken, NJ: Wiley, 2003 `e1110b`.

11 www.virgin.com `e1111`

12 Most retailers outsource manufacturing, typically to producers of product brands — 20 percent of U.S. retail goods are store-branded.

13 Granville, N.D., won a $100,000 contest from the distributor of McGillicuddy Schnapps for being branded McGillicuddy City for five years. Several leading chefs brand themselves and become spokespersons for chef attire, food types, kitchen equipment, and tableware. In the Czech Republic, Dedra launched "Ordinary Laundry Detergent," similar in concept to Brand X products in the U.S.

14 T. Peters. *The Brand Called You: Or: Fifty Ways to Transform Yourself from an 'Employee' into a Brand That Shouts Distinction, Commitment, and Passion!*, New York: Fast Company, 1997 `e1114`.

15 Under trademark law, a brand's registration may be revoked if the brand name is judged to have become generic.

16 A. Muniz, Jr. and T.C. O'Guinn, "Brand Community," *Journal of Consumer Research*, 27 (March 2001), pp. 412–432 `e1116`.

17 Thanks to David James, Henley Management College.

18 D.A. Aaker, *Brand Portfolio Strategy*, New York: Free Press, 2004 `e1118`.

19 Aaker, *op. cit.* `e1118`, offers seven categories to classify associations — product category, product attribute/functional benefits, application, technology, channel, user, and brand personality/self-expressive benefits.

20 J. Aaker, "Dimensions of Brand Personality," *Journal of Marketing Research*, 34 (August 1997), pp. 334–356 `e1120`. Based on data from 1,000 U.S. respondents: 60 well-known brands and 114 personality traits.

21 D.A. Aaker, *Managing Brand Equity*, New York: Free Press, 1991 pp. 114–128, identifies 11 types of associations — product attributes, intangibles, customer benefits, relative price, use/application, user/customer, celebrity/person, life style/personality, product class, competitors, and country/geographic area `e1121`.

22 E. Joachimsthaler and D.A. Aaker, "Building Brands without Mass Media," *Harvard Business Review*, 75 (January–February 1997), pp. 3–10 `e1122`.

23 From the top left — Sir Richard Branson (Virgin), Bill Gates (Microsoft), Larry Page (Google), Jamie Dimon (JPMorgan Chase), Shelly Lazarus (Ogilvy & Mather Worldwide); second row — Meg Whitman (HP), Michael Dell (Dell), Mark Zuckerberg (Facebook), Philippe Wolgen (Clinuvel), and Warren Buffett (Berkshire Hathaway).

24 G. Ghislanzoni and J. Shearn, "Leading Change: An Interview with the CEO of Banca Intesa," *The McKinsey Quarterly*, 3 (2005), pp. 73–80 `e1124`.

25 Aaker, 1991, *op. cit.*, p. 15 `e1121`; *Building Strong Brands*, New York: Free Press, 1995 `e1125a`; and *Brand Leadership* (with E. Joachimsthaler), New York: Free Press, 2000 `e1125b`.

26 If a product is unbranded, the supplier is completely substitutable — customers purchase a commodity.

27 L. de Chematony and M.H.B. McDonald, *Creating Powerful Brands*, Oxford: Butterworth-Heinemann, 1992 `e1127`.

28 Reputedly, the majority of *Star Wars*' $20 billion revenues resulted from non-movie merchandise. For more on customer brand equity: K.L. Keller, "Conceptualizing, Measuring, and Managing Customer-Based Brand Equity," *Journal of Marketing*, 57 (1993), pp. 1–22 `e1128`.

29 T.S. Wurster, "The Leading Brands," Perspectives, Boston, MA: The Boston Consulting Group, 1987; and research by Ting Wu, Columbia University. Also G.J. Tellis and P.N. Golder, *Will and Vision: How Latecomers Grow to Dominate Markets*, New York: McGraw-Hill, 2002, Chapters 1 and 11 `e1129`.

30 Aaker's 1991 *op. cit.* original brand equity notion encompassed brand awareness, brand associations, perceived quality, brand loyalty, and other proprietary brand assets `e1118`. FBE components are not necessarily positive for customers: Brand loyalty may impede the search for more attractive options, and branded products have higher prices than generics.

31 Norio Ohga, Chairman and CEO, Sony, quoted in *Fortune*, June 12, 1995 `e1131`.

32 "Big Blue," *Fortune*, April 14, 1997 `e1132`.

33 P. Berthon, J.M. Hulbert, and L.F. Pitt, "Brand Management Prognostications," *Sloan Management Review*, 40 (Winter 1999), pp. 53–65 `e1133`.

34 Triarc returned Snapple to its roots; Cadbury Schweppes acquired Snapple for $1 billion.

35 Aaker, 1991, *op. cit.*, pp. 80–85 `e1118`.

36 For a detailed examination of *brand resilience*: J.R. Copulsky, *Brand Resilience: Managing Risk and Recovery in a High-Speed World*, New York: Palgrave Macmillan, 2011 `e1136`.

37 Sometimes customers prefer a generic product to the branded product; then CBE's monetary value is negative.

38 M.E. Barth, M.B. Clement, G. Foster, and R. Kasznik, "Brand Values and Capital Market Valuation," *Review of Accounting Studies*, 3 (1998), pp. 41–68 `e1138`.

39 Sears created KCD IP (Kenmore, Craftsman, DieHard) to issue $1.8 billion worth of bonds backed by the intellectual property of its three largest brands. Sears pays KCD royalty fees to license the brands; KCD uses the fees to pay interest on the bonds.

40 D.A. Ailawadi, D.R. Lehmann, and S.A. Neslin, "Revenue Premium as an Outcome Measure of Brand Equity," *Journal of Marketing*, 67 (October 2003), pp. 1–17 `e1140`.

41 The average ratio of market value to book value for the S&P 500 rose from 1.2 to 2.8 during the past 35 years. Firm brand equity accounts for much of this increase.

42 Ford booked the $2.1 billion as *goodwill*. Historically, U.S. firms had to amortize *goodwill* booked in acquisitions or write off the amount against reserves. In 2002, the U.S. Financial Accounting Standards Board (FASB) allowed companies to record values of acquired brands as identifiable intangible assets on their balance sheets. Each year, the firm must

test goodwill for impairment and mark it down if necessary. U.S. practice followed Australia, France, Great Britain, and New Zealand.

43 The cost to create a successful mid-size B2C brand is about $100 million. At a 15 percent success rate, brand value = $670 million (100/0.15).

44 An alternative approach for consumer brands is Young & Rubicam's *Brand Asset Valuator* (BAV) `e1144`. In the BAV, brand value comprises brand vitality and brand stature. In turn, brand vitality comprises *energized differentiation* — standing apart from competitors — and *relevance* — the importance of the brand in a large consumer market. Brand stature comprises *esteem* — perceived quality and consumer perceptions about the growing/declining brand popularity, and *knowledge* — awareness and understanding of the brand's identity.

45 Boston Consulting Group (John Lindquist), reported in "What's in a Name?," *The Economist*, January 6, 1996 — profit figures not discounted. In Britain, Hitachi and General Electric (GEC) (British, since acquired) jointly owned a factory that made TV sets. Hitachi sold twice as many identical TVs at a $75 premium over GEC sets: P.H. Farquhar, "Managing Brand Equity," *Marketing Research*, (September 1989), pp. 24–33.

46 From NUMMI, GM learned important lessons about automobile manufacturing. Key metrics and performance at GM, NUMMI, and Toyota, respectively, were: assembly hours per vehicle — 31, 19, 16; defects per 100 vehicles — 130, 45, 45; assembly space per vehicle (sq. feet/vehicle/year) — 8.1, 7.0, 4.8; average parts inventory — 2 weeks, 2 days, 2 hours.

47 From P. Berthon, M.B. Holbrook, and J.M. Hulbert, "Understanding and Managing the Brandspace," *Sloan Management Review*, 44 (2003), pp. 49–55, by permission `e1147`.

48 Developed from G. Gordon, A. di Benedetto, and R. Calantone, "Brand Equity as an Evolutionary Process," *The Journal of Brand Management*, 2 (1994), pp. 47–56 `e1148`.

49 "Bringing a Corporate Brand to Life Using the Principles of Experiential Marketing," Presentation by C.P. Lange and S. Tollefson at *True Love or One-Night Stand? Conference on Brand Relationships and Experiences*. Columbia Business School, May 29-30, 2001.

50 Personal communication from David Haines, Director of Global Branding, Vodafone.

51 Alcatel acquired Lucent (formerly part of AT&T) to form Alcatel-Lucent.

52 Nissan dropped Datsun in 1986; Esso changed to Exxon in 1973; Master Charge became MasterCard in 1979.

53 Amway became Quixtar, then returned to Amway.

54 L.M. Lodish and C. Mela, "If Brands Are Built over Years, Why Are They Managed over Quarters?," *Harvard Business Review*, 85 (July–August 2007), pp. 104–112 `e1154`.

55 Repeat purchasers often act with significant intentionality (brand loyalty), but may exhibit habitual behavior with little or no connection to the brand. For an ethnographic brand loyalty study: S. Fournier and J.L Lao, "Reviving Brand Loyalty: A Reconceptualization within the Framework of Consumer-Brand Relationships," *International Journal of Research in Marketing*, 14 (1997), pp. 451–472 `e1155`.

56 Some brand customers demonstrate *extreme* loyalty — 99 pairs of the same Nike shoe, 150 Canon cameras in four years, and lunch at the same restaurant every day for five years! Extreme customers identify with their brands, defend them against attacks, and tirelessly advocate via blogs, fan websites, YouTube, and word of mouth: A.B. Eisinerich, G. Bhardwaj, and Y. Miyamoto, "Behold the Extreme Consumers and Learn to Embrace Them," *Harvard Business Review*, 88 (April 2010), pp. 30–31 `e1156`.

57 K.L. Keller, "Conceptualizing, Measuring, and Managing Customer-Based Brand Equity," *Journal of Marketing*, 57 (January 1993), pp. 1–

22 `e1157a`; and "The Brand Report Card," *Harvard Business Review*, 78 (January– February 2000), pp. 147–157 `e1157b`.

58 The stock market reacts favorably to brand acquisitions when the acquirer has strong marketing capabilities and identifies cost synergies, and when the acquired brand raises the firm's average price/quality positioning: M.A. Wiles, N.A. Morgan, and L.L. Rego, "The Effect of Brand Acquisition and Disposal on Stock Returns," *Journal of Marketing*, 76 (January 2012), pp. 38–58) `e1158`.

59 S.J. Carlotti Jr., M.E. Coe, and J. Perrey, "Making Brand Portfolios Work," *The McKinsey Quarterly*, 4 (2000) `e1159`. Many remaining P&G brands are market leaders; 21 have annual revenues in excess of $1 billion.

60 M. Ritson, "Should You Launch a Fighter Brand?," *Harvard Business Review*, 87 (October 2009), pp. 87–94 `e1160`.

61 Aaker, 1991, *op. cit.* `e1118`

62 M.J. Hatch and M. Schultz, "Are the Strategic Stars Aligned for Your Corporate Brand?," *Harvard Business Review*, 79 (February 2001), pp. 129–134 `e1162`.

63 In one study, 80 percent of all new grocery products extended or leveraged existing brands; E. Tauber, "Brand Leverage: Strategy for Growth in a Cost Conscious World," *Journal of Advertising Research*, (August–September 1988), pp. 26–30.

64 V.R. Lane, "Brand Leverage Power: The Critical Role of Brand Balance," *Business Horizons*, (January–February 1998), pp. 75–84 `e1164a`; and D.A. Aaker, "Brand Extensions: The Good, The Bad and The Ugly," *Sloan Management Review*, (Summer 1990), pp. 47–56. `e1164b`

65 S. K. Reddy, S. L. Holak, and S. Bhat, "To Extend or Not to Extend: Success Determinants of Line Extensions," *Journal of Marketing Research*, 31 (May 1994), pp. 243–262 `e1165`.

66 FMCG firms build and manage brands for the long run. By contrast, pharmaceutical firms must build a brand for each new drug, M. Corstjens and M. Carpenter, "From Managing Pills to Managing Brands," *Harvard Business Review*, 78 (March–April 2000), pp. 20–21 `e1166`.

67 R. Batra, P. Lenk, and M. Wedel, "Brand Extension Strategy Planning: Empirical Estimation of Brand-Category Personality Fit and Atypicality," *Journal of Marketing Research*, 47 (April 2010), pp. 335–347, develop an approach to measure brand fit `e1167`.

68 Retailers typically merchandise products by category rather than by brand — hence, consumers may face higher search costs for new products.

69 D.A. Aaker and K.L. Keller, "Consumer Evaluation of Brand Extensions," *Journal of Marketing*, 54 (January 1990), pp. 27–41 `e1169a`; S.M. Broniarczyk and J.W. Alba, "The Importance of the Brand in Brand Extension," *Journal of Marketing Research*, 31 (May 1994), pp. 214–228 `e1169b`; S.J. Milberg, C.W. Park, and M.S. McCarthy, "Managing Negative Feedback Effects Associated With Brand Extensions: The Impact of Alternative Branding Strategies," *Journal of Consumer Psychology*, 6 (1997), pp. 119–140 `e1169c`; D.R. John, B. Loken, and C. Joiner, "The Negative Impact of Extensions: Can Flagship Products Be Diluted?," *Journal of Marketing*, 62 (January 1998), pp. 19–32 `e1169d`; and V. Swaminathan, R.J. Fox, and S.K. Reddy, "The Impact of Brand Extension Introduction on Choice," *Journal of Marketing*, 65 (October 2001), pp. 1–15 `e1169e`.

70 E.M. Tauber, "Brand Franchise Extension: New Product Benefits from Existing Brand Names," *Business Horizons*, 24 (March–April 1981), pp. 36–41 `e1170`.

71 *Flanker products* are quite different from *flanker brands*.

72 For brand revitalization: D. Desmet, L. Finskud, M. Glucksman, N.H. Marshall, M.J. Reyner, and K. Warren, "The End of Voodoo Brand Management," *The McKinsey Quarterly*, 2 (1998), pp. 107–117 `e1172`.

73 B&D's most serious problem was strong customer associations with GE. In five years, B&D spent more than $100 million to migrate GE to B&D — consumers still believed GE was the housewares market leader. When Enron wanted to supply retail electricity, it asked consumers: "If your current electricity provider could not supply you, which supplier would you choose?" The favored choice was GE — GE last produced electricity more than 100 years previously! Personal communication from Jeffrey Skilling, CEO Enron.

74 Personal communication from David Haines, *op. cit.*

75 Formerly BHP Steel (Australia) and British Steel, respectively.

76 Oldsmobile failed in its attempt to abandon its aging owner base for younger customers. Ultimately GM abandoned the Oldsmobile brand.

77 Nigeria also attempted rebranding but failed due to wrenching social problems.

78 *The Goodwood Conundrum*, Columbia Business School, by J.M. Hulbert and M.M. Lyman. Also *www.goodwood.co.uk* e1178 .

79 Polaroid filed for bankruptcy in 2001. Polaroid still has a multi-million-dollar instant photography business with some pockets of growth, and is the fourth-largest seller of portable DVD players and plasma TVs, with outsourced production.

CHAPTER 12

1 We use *product* to include both physical products and intangible services.

2 Portfolio approaches are appropriate for resource allocation at both the business unit and corporate levels.

3 Many startups face this situation. Of course, the capital markets may be an option for securing cash. Regardless, maintaining a balanced portfolio is better than having to seek funds when liquidity is insufficient.

4 ABC faced a late-night television crisis. ABC's serious news program *Nightline* did not attract the younger viewers most desired by advertisers. Hence, ABC bid for the David Letterman show to replace *Nightline* in the crucial 11.35 p.m. weekday slot. This crisis reflected a long-running battle between ABC's news and entertainment divisions for resources for their respective programs (products).

5 J.L. Bower, *Managing the Resource Allocation Process*, Boston, MA: Harvard Business School Press, 1970 showed that real-world behavior did not conform to academics' convenient, simplifying assumptions e1205 . Today, *behavioral finance* examines how actual behavior often differs from simplistic assumptions.

6 For a detailed treatment of financial analysis techniques: J.C. Van Horne and J.M. Wachowicz, Jr., *Fundamentals of Financial Management*, 13th ed., Englewood Cliffs, NJ: Prentice Hall, 2008 e1206 .

7 Most firms try to maximize shareholder value by improving return on shareholder equity (ROE). They often use return-on-investment (ROI) as a proxy for ROE, N. Capon, J.U. Farley, and J. Hulbert, *Corporate Strategic Planning*, New York: Columbia University Press, 1988 e1207 .

8 A simple principle underlies discounting — the future value of $1 is less than today's value of $1.

9 IRR is the rate of return when NPV = 0; IRR assumes the firm invests surplus funds at the IRR. NPV assumes the firm reinvests at the discount rate.

10 Stern Stewart trademarked EVA; J. M. Stern, J. S. Shiely, and I. Ross, *The EVA Challenge*, New York: Wiley, 2001 e1210 . Also me01, pp. 16–17 .

11 Even EVA is vulnerable to this problem — early-stage new ventures typically appear to destroy shareholder value.

12 Some firms use risk-analysis or simulations to address this issue.

13 R.L. Foster, *Innovation: The Attacker's Advantage*, New York: Summit, 1986 e1213 .

14 Portfolio analysis helps set priorities among market segments — Chapter 8.

15 P. Haspeslagh, "Portfolio Planning: Uses and Limits," *Harvard Business Review*, 60 (January–February 1982), pp. 58–74 e1215 .

16 The visual appearance of portfolio matrices — 2x2, 3x3 — is arbitrary. Regardless, by placing products in the matrix, the firm can assess potential return and risk and gain insight into strategic options. "A picture is worth 1,000 words" captures much of portfolio models' appeal — senior managers can assess the firm's products in two simple dimensions.

17 The Delphi approach is a good way to secure agreement — Chapter 6.

18 Typically, firms use a linear scale for market growth, and a logarithmic scale for RMS. Further, the RMS scale is typically high to low, versus the more common low-to-high x-axis scaling.

19 This framework focuses on internal cash flows; it does not consider cash inflows from, or outflows to, external constituencies.

20 R. Vernon, "Gone Are the Cash Cows of Yesteryear," *Harvard Business Review*, 58 (November–December 1980), pp. 150–155.

21 Firms typically expense capital investments over several years. Hence, a profitable growth product may be cash flow negative.

22 A less common error is overinvestment to drive out all competitors; this approach rarely succeeds.

23 Top management often focuses greater than average attention on *dogs*; and managerial turnover is high. GE's former CEO Jack Welch required that each GE business be No. 1 or No. 2 in their market. Welch recognized that strong No. 2s could reach GE's demanding profit performance standards, but less competitively placed product lines could not!

24 Also, generally in accord with growth/share matrix predictions, cash flows are not always accurate, D.C. Hambrick, I.C. MacMillan, and D.L. Day, "Strategic Attributes and Performance in the BCG Matrix — A PIMS-Based Analysis of Industrial Product Business," *Academy of Management Journal*, 25 (September 1982), pp. 510–531 e1224 . PIMS' own studies produced similar results, B.T. Gale and B. Branch, "Cash Flow Analysis: More Important Than Ever," *Harvard Business Review*, 59 (July–August 1981), pp. 131–136.

25 Of course, *market share* refers to *achieved market share* — the process of securing market share may be unprofitable!

26 Key issues are market segmentation and geographic-market boundaries. Choice of market boundary should be strategically significant for the firm and revisited periodically.

27 Examples include Arthur D. Little's *stage of industry maturity* (embryonic, growth, mature, aging) versus *competitive position* (dominant, strong, favorable, tenable, weak); the Shell Chemical Directional Policy Matrix, D.C. Hussey, "Portfolio Analysis: Practical Experience with the Directional Policy Matrix," *Long Range Planning* 11 (August 1978), pp. 2–8 e1227a ; and Mead Paper's system, C.W. Hofer and D.E. Schendel, *Strategy Formulation: Analytical Concepts*, St. Paul, MN: West, 1978 e1227b . In each case, matrix position indicates an investment strategy.

28 Aka the stoplight matrix — three green (invest) cells, three red (don't invest) cells, and three amber (be careful) cells.

29 Note we define the x-axis as low to high, different from the growth-share matrix.

30 Of course, this statement does not apply to new products the firm gains from acquisitions.

31 For an extension of these ideas: N. Capon and R. Glazer, "Marketing and Technology: A Strategic Coalignment," *Journal of Marketing*, 51 (July 1987), pp. 1–14 `e1231`.

32 Personal communication from Judith Czelusniak, Head of Global Public Relations, Bloomberg LP.

33 Chapter 5 discusses complementarity with competitors, customers, and suppliers. For an approach to product policy: *Principles of Product Policy*, 9-506-018, Harvard Business School `e1233`.

34 T. Gallagher, M.M. Mitchke, and M.C. Rogers, "Profiting from Spare Parts," *The McKinsey Quarterly*, (February 2005), pp. 1–6 `e1234`.

35 Many producers face offshore competitors that produce parts if demand and/or prices are high. In some industries, final products are now made from assemblies, like automobile dashboards, rather than parts. Hence, *aftermarket* competition is for assemblies rather than parts.

36 A.J. Slywotzky and D.J. Morrison, *The Profit Zone*, New York: Times Business, 1997 `e1236`.

37 Best Buy bases simple product innovations on customer feedback.

38 Firewall brands are sometimes called *flankers* — Chapter 11. C.M. Christensen, *The Innovator's Dilemma*, HarperBusiness, 2003 `e1238a`; and C.M. Christensen and M.E. Raynor, *The Innovator's Solution: Creating and Sustaining Successful Growth*, Boston, MA: Harvard Business School Press, 2003 `e1238b`.

39 Time's website reveals in excess of 115 separate publications worldwide.

40 C. Shapiro and H.R. Varian, *Information Rules*, Boston, MA: Harvard Business School Press, 1999 `e1240`.

41 Also R. Deneckere and P. McAfee, "Damaged Goods," *Journal of Economics and Management Strategy*, 5 (1996), pp. 149–174 `e1241a`; and G. Taguchi and D. Clausing, "Robust Quality," *Harvard Business Review*, 68 (January–February 1990), pp. 65–75 `e1241b`. Do not confuse deliberate product degradation with low product quality.

42 Shapiro and Varian, *op. cit.*, p. 59 `e1240`.

43 P&G continually evolves product offerings so the table will likely be out of date by the time you read this chapter.

44 C. Anderson, *The Long Tail*, New York: Hyperion, 2006 `e1244a`; and A. Elbese, "Should You Invest in the Long Tail," *Harvard Business Review*, 86 (July-August 2008), pp. 88–96 `e1244b`.

45 This strategy is not always successful. B&L sold identical contact lenses for both high-end and disposable lens markets — when this became public knowledge, B&L received significant negative publicity.

46 J.A. Howard and J.N. Sheth, *The Theory of Buyer Behavior*, New York: Wiley, 1969 `e1246`.

47 In the following few years, Unilever disposed of a large number of businesses, vastly outnumbering acquisitions.

48 Pioneered by Dayton-Hudson, DPP ignores overhead allocations that enter into gross margin calculations, consistent with activity-based costing (ABC).

49 Now part of GE.

50 Warner even dropped Madonna and Nickelback.

51 Firms that cannot classify costs as variable and fixed run the risk of reducing profits by unwittingly eliminating products. Marketing Enrichment `me01` for financial analysis details.

52 G.J. Avlonitis, "'Project Dropstrat': Product Elimination and the Product Life Cycle Concept," *European Journal of Marketing*, (September 1990), pp. 55–67 `e1252a`. Also S.J. Hart, "Product Deletion and the Effects of Strategy," *European Journal of Marketing*, (October 1989), pp. 6–17 `e1252b`; D.M. Lambert and J.U. Sterling, "The Product Abandonment Decision, *Management Accounting*, (August 1998), pp. 8–27; and M.A. Mitchell, R.D. Taylor, and F. Tanyel, "Product Elimination Decisions: A Comparison of American and British Manufacturing Firms," *International Journal of Commerce & Management*, (1998), pp. 8–27 `e1252c`. For classic articles: R.S. Alexander, "The Death and Burial of Sick Products," *Journal of Marketing*, 28 (April 1964), pp. 1–7 `e1252d`; P. Kotler, "Phasing Out Weak Products," *Harvard Business Review*, 43, (March–April 1965), pp. 108–118; and P.W. Hamelman and E.M. Mazze, "Improving Product Abandonment Decisions," *Journal of Marketing*, 36 (April 1972), pp. 20–26 `e1252e`.

53 Personal communication from Bob Bridden, Group Vice President, Global Marketing, Avon.

54 In a more prosaic example, many restaurants offer *à la carte* (*unbundled*) and *table d'hote* or *prix fixe* (*bundled*) menus.

55 "The Joy of Bundling," The Boston Consulting Group, 2008 `e1255`.

56 The OECD estimates that international trade in counterfeit and pirated goods exceeds $250 billion annually. Domestic trade may rival this figure.

57 Types of counterfeit products vary by geography: fashion item in advanced western countries; basic products in Africa. In recorded music, legal alternatives like Apple's iTunes and Spotify (free downloads, advertising supported) have reduced piracy.

58 In 2011, a blogger identified several counterfeit Apple stores in Chinese cities.

59 R.F. Maruca, "Is Your Brand at Risk?," *Harvard Business Review*, 77 (November–December 1999), pp. 22, 25 `e1259a`. For a case study on counterfeiting: P.F. Nunes and N.P. Mulani, "Can Knockoffs Knock Out Your Business?," *Harvard Business Review*, 86 (October 2008), pp. 41–50 `e1259b`. Commercial brand protection services are proliferating.

60 China's Tomato Garden was a major Microsoft pirate. In 2009, CEO Hong Lei received a three-and-one-half-year prison term for piracy; three partners also received jail terms.

61 R. Foster and S. Kaplan, *Creative Destruction: Why Companies That Are Built to Last Underperform the Market — and How to Successfully Transform Them*, New York: Currency/Doubleday, 2001 `e1261`.

62 "The Dream Phone," *Fortune*, November 15, 2010, pp. 129–140 @ p. 131 `e1262`.

63 Some pharma firms whose drugs are going off patent collaborate in introducing *authorized generics* to compete with independent generic producers. Examples include Pfizer's Zoloft (antidepressant) and Merck's Zocor (cholesterol lowering).

64 The American Customer Satisfaction Index (ACSI) measures customer satisfaction with hundreds of products and services annually — National Quality Research Center, Ross School of Business, University of Michigan.

65 B. T. Gale, *Managing Customer Value*, New York: Free Press, 1994, Exhibit 1-3, p. 16 `e1265`.

66 Gale, *op. cit*, taken from Exhibit 1-1, p. 9 `e1265`.

67 *The New York Times'* experience with lying journalist Jayson Blair, Wikipedia `e1267a`; and *The New Republic's* experience with Stephen Glass (*Shattered Glass*), Wikipedia `e1267b`, are good examples for information products.

68 Of course, tobacco products cause many deaths.

69 R. Nader, *Unsafe at Any Speed: The Designed-In Dangers of the American Automobile*, New York: Pocket Books, 1966 `e1269`.

70 On a lighter note, Britain's *Guardian* newspaper introduced a "Corrections and Clarifications" column — prominently presenting *mea culpas*. Observers reacted favorably. The satirical British weekly *Private Eye* commented, "The Grauniad's corrections are far, far more

interesting than the original articles."

71 The firm sells products in *primary* markets; owners resell products in *secondary* markets.

72 *The Procter & Gamble Company: Lenor Refill Package,* 9-592-016, Harvard Business School `e1272`.

73 Personal communication from Ron Boire.

....

CHAPTER 13

1 From *The Economist.*

2 C.H. Lovelock and J. Wirtz, *Services Marketing,* 7th ed., Upper Saddle River, NJ: Prentice Hall, 2011, distinguish between services directed at people's bodies — health care and transportation, and services directed at people's minds — education, radio, TV `e1302`.

3 *The New Shorter Oxford English Dictionary,* Oxford: Clarendon Press, 1993 `e1303`.

4 Lovelock and Wirtz, *op. cit.* `e1302`; C.H. Lovelock, *Product Plus: How Product + Service = Competitive Advantage,* New York: McGraw-Hill, 1994 `e1304`. Government statistics typically count manufacturers' in-house activities as value-added manufacturing. Identical outsourced activity is mostly counted as a service. This statistical quirk has helped fuel reported service growth.

5 From inception, the *Fortune* 500 contained only manufacturing firms; in the mid-1990s, the *Fortune* 500 expanded to include service firms.

6 Services and social behaviors dominate social enterprises (SE). Features differentiating SE from private-sector marketing include: non-financial objectives; need to attract resources from various sources — customers, donors, volunteers, grant agencies; multiple constituencies; tension between strategy implementation and customer satisfaction; public scrutiny; non-market pressures; and tough management problems embracing employees, volunteers, and trustees.

7 Automobile firms finance car purchases; Boeing finances aircraft.

8 Offered by The Franchise Company, *www.thefranchisecompany.com* `e1308` — Chapter 18. *Franchisors* develop strategy; *franchisees* provide capital and entrepreneurial energy.

9 B.G. Auguste, E.P. Harmon, and V. Pandit, "The Right Service Strategies for Product Companies," *The McKinsey Quarterly,* 1 (2006), pp. 41–51 `e1309`.

10 Manufacturers offering services compete with value-added resellers (VARs). VARs assert that manufacturers cannot make impartial product recommendations. Manufacturers disagree.

11 For elaboration of services trends: Lovelock and Wirtz, *op. cit.* `e1302`

12 M.J. Bitner, "Evaluating Service Encounters: The Effects of Physical Surroundings and Employee Responses," *Journal of Marketing,* 54 (April 1990), pp. 69–82, offers an alternative framework `e1312`: *physical evidence* — surroundings and tangible cues; *participants* — human actors like supplier personnel and customers; and *process* — procedures, mechanisms, and activity flow.

13 E. Goffman, *The Presentation of Self in Everyday Life,* New York: Doubleday Anchor, 1959 `e1313`. In financial services, onstage — front office; offstage — back office.

14 J. Carlzon, *Moments of Truth,* Cambridge, MA: Ballinger, 1987 `e1314`.

15 C.W.L. Hart, "The Power of Unconditional Service Guarantees," *Harvard Business Review,* 66 (July–August 1988), pp. 54–62 `e1315`.

16 *Optimum* capacity utilization is preferred; *maximum* capacity utilization is only sustainable for a short time.

17 The firm may temporarily store demand using queues or reservation systems, but queuing may reduce customer satisfaction.

18 P. Kotler and S.J. Levy, "Demarketing, Yes, Demarketing," *Harvard Business Review,* 49 (November–December 1971), pp. 74–80 `e1318`.

19 "The Mass Transit Railroad in Hong Kong," in N. Capon and W. Van Honacker, *The Asian Marketing Case Book,* Singapore: Prentice Hall, 1999, addresses supply/demand imbalances `e1319`.

20 Process control charts, close supervision, and quality control inspections.

21 Firms like Allied Signal, GE, and Motorola adopted six-sigma DMAIC — define, measure, analyze, improve, control — to improve processes. The related DMADV process focuses on product design — Chapter 14.

22 This relationship is fundamental to the service-profit chain: J.L. Heskett, T.O. Jones, G.W. Loveman, W.E. Sasser Jr., and L. Schlesinger, "Putting the Service-Profit Chain to Work," *Harvard Business Review,* 72 (March–April 1994), pp. 164–174 `e1322a`; and G.W. Loveman, "Employee Satisfaction, Customer Loyalty, and Financial Performance: An Empirical Examination of the Service Profit Chain in Retail Banking," *Journal of Service Research,* 1 (August 1998), pp. 18–31 `e1322b`.

23 M. Gilbert, "A Culture that Recognizes the Contributions Made by Unsung Heroes," *Workforce Management,* 83 (November 2004), pp. 82–84 `e1323`.

24 Or reduce prices to specific segments; the challenge is identifying these customers. For many years, the Saturday night stopover fulfilled this function.

25 Compared to major airlines, easyJet sets low fares that generally increase as departure approaches. O. Koenigsberg, E. Muller, and N.J. Vilcassim, "Should easyJet Offer Last-Minute Deals?," *Quantitative Marketing and Economics,* 6 (2008), pp. 279–297 `e1325`.

26 *Shouldice Hospital Ltd.,* 9-683-068, Harvard Business School `e1326`.

27 Developed by Columbia Business School MBA student Cory Linton from R. Schachter and C.H. Lovelock, "The Boston Adult Education Center," in C.H. Lovelock, *Services Marketing,* 3rd. ed., Upper Saddle River, NJ: Prentice Hall, 1996, pp. 254–267.

28 G.L. Shostack, "Service Positioning Through Structural Change," *Journal of Marketing,* 51 (January 1987), pp. 33–34 `e1328`.

29 E.W. Anderson, C. Fornell, and S.K. Mazvancheryl, "Customer Satisfaction and Shareholder Value," *Journal of Marketing,* 68 (October 2004), pp. 172–186 `e1329a`; L. Askoy, B. Cooil, C. Groening, T.L. Keiningham, and A. Yalçin, "The Long-Term Stock Market Valuation of Customer Satisfaction," *Journal of Marketing,* 72 (July 2008), pp. 105–122 `e1329b`.

30 *Not* perceived quality alone. A. Parasuraman, V.A. Zeithaml, and L.L Berry, "A Conceptual Model of Service Quality and Its Implications for Future Research," *Journal of Marketing,* (Fall 1985), pp. 41–50 `e1330a`, and V.A. Zeithaml, A. Parasuraman, and L.L. Berry, *Delivering Quality Service: Balancing Customer Expectations and Perceptions,* Free Press, 1990 `e1330b`. Some expectations' models include a *tolerance zone*: Service quality below expectations but still acceptable.

31 Customers may be *delighted* if *perceived* service greatly exceeds *expected* service. But if the firm significantly under-promises (sets expectations too low), it may not secure the opportunity to provide service at all!

32 V.A. Zeithaml, A. Parasuraman, and L.L. Berry, "Ten Lessons for Improving Service Quality," Boston, MA: Marketing Science Institute, 2003, pp. 61–77, expand five key variables into ten lessons for improving service quality `e1332`. Reliability and listening overarch eight items: basic service, service design, service recovery, surprising customers, fair play, teamwork, employee research, and servant leadership.

33 The firm must be very clear about what these terms mean for individual customers. High responsiveness may mean two hours for some customers but two minutes for others. Related service quality dimensions include access, communication, courtesy, and competence.

34 V.A. Zeithaml, L.L. Berry, and A. Parasuraman, "The Behavioral Consequences of Service Quality," *Journal of Marketing*, 60 (April 1996), pp. 31–46 e1334.

35 The SERVQUAL model is general. Many firms develop models for their specific circumstances.

36 Ogilvy and Mather data show that: 85 percent of automobile purchasers are satisfied, but only 40 percent repurchase the brand; two-thirds of consumers identifying a favorite packaged goods brand purchased another brand most recently; and 65 percent to 85 percent of B2B defectors were satisfied/very satisfied with former suppliers.

37 T.O. Jones and W.E. Sasser, "Why Satisfied Customers Defect," *Harvard Business Review*, 73 (November–December 1995), pp. 88–99 e1337.

38 Personal communications from Lisa Gray, MBA student, Columbia University and Captain Paul Capon (USAF); also F.F. Reicheld, *The Loyalty Effect*, Boston, MA: Harvard Business School Press, 1996, p. 71 e1338.

39 B.J. Pine II, D. Peppers, and M. Rogers, "Do You Want to Keep Your Customers Forever?," *Harvard Business Review*, 73 (March–April 1995), pp. 103–114 e1339.

40 To achieve ground efficiency, Southwest Airlines benchmarked Indy 500 pit crews.

41 W. Whitt, "Improving Service by Informing Customers about Anticipated Delays," *Management Science*, 45 (February 1999), pp. 192–207 e1341.

42 I. Roos, "Methods of Investigating Critical Incidents: A Comparative Review" *Journal of Service Research*, (February 2002), pp. 193–204 e1342.

43 J. van Doorn and P. C. Veroef, "Critical Incidents and the Impact of Satisfaction on Customer Share," *Journal of Marketing*, 72 (July 2008), pp. 123–142 e1343.

44 C.W.L. Hart, J.L. Heskett, and W.E. Sasser Jr., "The Profitable Art of Service Recovery," *Harvard Business Review*, 68 (July–August 1990), pp. 148–156 e1344.

45 Technical Assistance Research Program (TARP), Consumer Complaint Handling in America: An Update Study, Parts I and II, Washington, DC: TARP and U.S. Office of Consumer Affairs, April 1986. Consumer reasons for not complaining include: They don't think it's worth the time or effort; no one would be concerned about (or act upon) the problem; and/or they don't know how or where to complain.

46 Some web devices allow unhappy customers to secure e-mail addresses and personal phone numbers of senior executives.

47 Excerpted and abridged from M.J. Tucker, "Poppin' Fresh Dough," *Datamation*, (May 1997), pp. 50–58.

48 For poor customer service and commentaries: D. Ariely, "The Customers' Revenge," *Harvard Business Review*, 85 (December 2007), pp. 31–43 e1348.

49 Personal communication from Judith Czelusniak, Head Global Public Relations, Bloomberg L.P.

50 TARP and Blockbuster video-store chain respectively. E.W. Anderson, "Customer Satisfaction and Word of Mouth," *Journal of Service Research*, 1 (August 1998), pp. 5–17, finds only slightly greater word of mouth from highly dissatisfied customers than from highly satisfied customers, contrary to popular belief e1350.

51 Also Blogs and Microblogs — Twitter, Chapter 15, p. 416.

52 Lovelock and Wirtz, *op. cit.* e1302.

53 H. Takeuchi and J.A. Quelch, "Quality is More than Making a Good Product," *Harvard Business Review*, 61 (July–August 1983), pp. 139–145 e1353. We can decompose extended purchase decisions into finer-grained pre-purchase customer service.

54 M.M. Lele and U.S. Karmarkar, "Good Product Support is Smart Marketing," *Harvard Business Review*, 61 (November–December 1983), pp. 124–132 e1354a; I.C. MacMillan and R.G. McGrath, "Discovering New Points of Differentiation," *Harvard Business Review*, 75 (July–August 1997), pp. 133–145 e1354b.

55 R.G. Bundschuh and T.M. Dezvane, "How to Make After-Sales Services Pay Off," *The McKinsey Quarterly*, 4 (2003), pp. 116–127 e1355.

56 Personal communication from Judith Czelusniak, Head Global Public Relations, Bloomberg L.P.

57 W.H. Davidow and B. Uttal, *Total Customer Service*, New York: Harper & Row, 1989 focuses on six elements — leadership, strategy, personnel, design, infrastructure, and metrics, for delivering outstanding customer service e1357a. Also Heskett, Jones, Loveman, Sasser, and Schlesinger, *op. cit.* e1322a and R.T. Rust, A.J. Zahorik, and T.L. Keiningham, "Return on Quality (ROQ): Making Service Quality Financially Accountable," *Journal of Marketing*, 59 (April 1995), pp. 58–70 e1357b.

58 QT's employee turnover is less than 15 percent (average retail turnover exceeds 100 percent) and financial performance is stellar. Wawa (500 stores, five U.S. states) has similar results. N. Bendapudi and V. Bendapudi, "Creating the Living Brand," *Harvard Business Review*, 83 (May 2005), pp. 124–132 e1358.

59 Personal communication from Hal Cramer, President Fuels Marketing, ExxonMobil.

60 Davidow and Uttal, *op. cit.* e1357a.

61 T. Baumgartner, R.H. John, and T. Nauclér, "Transforming Sales and Service," *The McKinsey Quarterly*, 4 (2005), pp. 81–91 e1361.

62 B. Donaldson and T. O'Toole, *Strategic Market Relationships: From Strategy to Implementation*, Chichester, UK: Wiley, 2002 e1362.

63 "American Express: Happy Workers Mean Happy Customers," *Fortune*, August 16, 2010, p. 14 e1363.

64 *Accor: Global Excellence Through People*, Lausanne, Switzerland: IMD for an excellent example e1364.

65 L.L. Berry and A. Parasuraman, *Marketing Services: Competing through Quality*, New York: Free Press, 1991, p. 16 e1365a, and K.A. Gibson and D.K. Khandelwal, "Getting More from Call Centers," *The McKinsey Quarterly*, April 2005 e1365b.

66 A. Braff, Z.H.M. Gaibi, and J.C. Garcia, "A Call Center's Last Line of Defense," *The McKinsey Quarterly*, (2006), pp. 12–14 e1366.

67 *The Ritz-Carlton: Using Information Systems to Better Serve the Customer*, 9-395-064, Harvard Business School, for Ritz-Carlton's legendary service.

68 K. McSwain-Campbell and D. Jacobe, "Wachovia Takes Customer Engagement to the Bank," *Gallup Management Journal*, July 8, 2004 e1368. gmj.gallup.com. Wells Fargo acquired Wachovia in 2008 and finally retired the Wachovia brand in 2011.

69 Many Vietnamese wear sandals; Ho considered sandals a driving danger.

70 "Vinataxi," in N. Capon and W. Van Honacker, *The Asian Marketing Case Book*, Singapore: Prentice Hall, 1999 e1319.

71 *Xerox Corporation: The Customer Satisfaction Program*, 9-591-055, Harvard Business School e1371.

72 F.F. Reichheld and W.E. Sasser Jr., "Zero Defections: Quality Comes to Services," *Harvard Business Review*, 68 (September–October 1990), pp.

105–111 e1372a; T.O. Jones and W.E Sasser Jr., "Why Satisfied Customers Defect," *Harvard Business Review*, 73 (November–December 1995), pp. 88–99 e1372b; and F.F. Reicheld, "Learning from Customer Defections," *Harvard Business Review*, 74 (March–April 1996), pp. 56–69 e1372c. Some firms use net-promoter score: the percentage of people who would recommend the firm, minus those who wouldn't. F.F. Reicheld, "The One Number You Need to Grow," *Harvard Business Review*, 81 (December 2003), pp. 46–54. Also Chapter 21 e1372d.

73 D. McGarry and F. Heller, "Agile to Adaptive: Making Organizations More Responsive to Customers — A Xerox Case Study," Chapter 9 in N. Pal and D. Pantaleo (eds.), *The Agile Enterprise: Reinventing Your Organization for Success in an On-Demand World*, New York: Springer, 2005 e1373.

CHAPTER 14

1 Based on material provided by Client Insight (CI), LLC, Boston, MA. CI principals work extensively with Thomson businesses.

2 Marketing *really new products* is high on The Marketing Science Institute's placed research priority list.

3 P.F. Drucker, *The Practice of Management*, New York: Harper and Row, 1956, pp. 65–67 e1403.

4 W. Duggan, *Strategic Intuition*, New York: Columbia Business School, 2007 e1404.

5 As reported in *Harper's Monthly Magazine*, September 1932.

6 Duggan, *op. cit.* p. 102 e1404. In a different field, T.S. Elliot said, "Immature poets imitate. Mature poets steal." Duggan, *op. cit.*, pp. 101–102 e1404.

7 Disruptive technologies (existing) include personal computers (mainframes and mini computers), small off-road motorcycles (powerful on-road bikes), and transistors (vacuum tubes). Henry Ford's assembly line was a disruptive process innovation; previously, many small firms produced automobiles one by one. Ford's low costs put them out of business.

8 R. Foster and S. Kaplan, *Creative Destruction: Why Companies That Are Built to Last Underperform the Market — and How to Successfully Transform Them*, New York: Currency/Doubleday, 2001 e1408.

9 C.M. Christensen, *The Innovator's Dilemma*, Boston, MA: Harvard Business School Press, 1997 e1409.

10 A mid-level employee pushed IBM's entry into the Internet against significant internal resistance. G. Hamel, "Waking Up IBM: How a Gang of Unlikely Rebels Transformed Big Blue," *Harvard Business Review*, 78 (July–August 2000), pp. 137–146 e1410.

11 Christensen, *op. cit.* e1409 Also M. Tushman and C. O'Reilly, "Ambidextrous Organizations: Managing Evolutionary and Revolutionary Change," *California Management Review*, 38 (1996), pp. 8–30 e1411a; and C.A. O'Reilly and M.L. Tushman, "The Ambidextrous Organization," *Harvard Business Review*, 82 (April 2004), pp. 74–81 e1411b.

12 Innovation leader 3M's new product performance reportedly suffered when incoming CEO James McNerney rigorously implemented *six sigma*.

13 N. Capon, J.U. Farley, D.R. Lehmann, and J.M. Hulbert, "Profiles of Product Innovators Among Large U.S. Manufacturers," *Management Science*, 38 (February 1992), pp. 157–169 e1413a. Also Synectics Corporation, *Succeeding at Innovation*, Cambridge, MA, 1993; and *Managing Innovation: A Primer*, Stamford, CT: Gartner, 2006 e1413b. Individual firms develop their own approaches to innovation. Amazon — measures everything, keeps development teams small, is unafraid of weird ideas, opens up to outsiders, and watches customers rather than competitors.

14 Conventional wisdom argues that competition spurs innovation. Research at Columbia Business School suggests that in some industries monopoly generates greater innovation: Increased profits provide greater resources for R&D, and advancing technology spurs demand. R. Goettler and B. R. Gordon, "Does AMD Spur Intel to Innovate More?", *Journal of Political Economy*, forthcoming, 2012 e1414.

15 Also *Change at Whirlpool Corporation (A), (B), (C)*, 9-705-463, Harvard Business School e1415.

16 U.S. supermarkets introduce 20,000 to 40,000 new skus annually.

17 At 3M, Art Fry developed Post-It notes in this system.

18 One successful commercial development process has five stages: 1. **Observation** — cognitive psychologists, anthropologists, and sociologists try to understand the customer experience. 2. **Brainstorming** — intense idea-generating sessions analyzing data gathered in stage 1. 3. **Rapid Prototyping** — Mocking up working models to help visualize possible solutions. 4. **Refining** — narrowing down choices to a few possibilities. 5. **Implementation** — use engineering, design, and social-science capabilities to create an actual product/service. "The Power of Design," *BusinessWeek*, May 17, 2004, pp. 86–94 e1418.

19 D.L. Liebermann and D.B. Montgomery, "First-Mover Advantages," *Strategic Management Journal*, 9 (1988), pp. 41–58 e1419.

20 "Chevy Builds a Hybrid to Haul," *The New York Times*, April 26, 2009 e1420.

21 E.A. Roth and K.D. Sneader, "Reinventing Innovation at Consumer Goods Companies," *The McKinsey Quarterly*, 2006, report that less that seven percent of new U.S.-launched FMCGs offer significant new or added benefits e1421. The authors argue that firms should concentrate insight gathering on focus groups, rely on internal resources, and secure as many ideas as possible.

22 "Chaos by Design," *Fortune*, October 2, 2006 e1422.

23 From Booz Allen Hamilton. Some development projects lead to cost reductions. New-to-the-world products — aka *really new products* — let customers do new things, but at the cost of greater uncertainty about benefits and cost-benefit tradeoffs, and requiring greater behavior changes for successful use.

24 "Back to the Future at Apple," *BusinessWeek*, May 24, 1998 e1424.

25 Research at Columbia Business School suggests that market-based synergies may be as important as technological synergy; N. Capon, J.U. Farley, J. Hulbert, and L.E. Martin, "Corporate Diversity and Economic Performance: The Impact of Market Specialization," *Strategic Management Journal*, 9 (January–February 1988), pp. 61–74 e1425.

26 M.T. Hansen and J. Birkenshaw, "The Innovation Value Chain," *Harvard Business Review*, 85 (June 2007), pp. 121–130 e1426.

27 I. Royer, "Why Bad Projects Are so Hard to Kill," *Harvard Business Review*, 81 (February 2003), pp. 48–56 e1427.

28 For discussion of stage-gate process issues, G.L. Urban and J.R. Hauser, *Design and Marketing of New Products*, Englewood Cliffs, NJ: Prentice Hall, 1993 e1428a; *www.prod-dev.com/stage-gate.shtml* e1428b; and *Product Development: A Customer-Driven Approach*, Harvard Business School e1428c. Some research suggests too rigorously applying the stage-gate process may restrict organizational learning and negatively affect development of novel products; R. Sethi and Z. Iqbal, "Stage-Gate Controls, Learning Failure and Adverse Effect on Novel New Products," *Journal of Marketing*, 72 (January 2008), pp. 118–134 e1428d.

29 Generaly, new *service* development receives less funding than new *product* development, but some service firms invest significantly. S. Thomke, "R&D Comes to Services," *Harvard Business Review*, 81 (April 2003), pp. 71–79 e1429.

30 Sony's honorary chairman Masaru Ibuka had the original Walkman idea; CEO Akio Morita championed development despite internal opposition. The Walkman was not successful with its initial teenager target — initial customers were yuppies for jogging and commuting. J. Mingo, *How the Cadillac Got Its Fins*, New York: Harper Business, 1994 e1430.

31 G.A. Stevens and J. Burley, "3000 Raw Ideas = 1 Commercial Success," *Research Technology Management*, 40 (May–June 1997), pp. 16–27 e1431.

32 From Booz Allen and Hamilton — improved performance relates to attention to core competence and focused innovation.

33 Jack Welch (GE) had a simple mantra: "The operative assumption is that someone, somewhere, has a better idea, and the operative compulsion is to find out who has that better idea, learn it, and put it into action."

34 L. Huston and N. Sakkab, "Inside Procter & Gamble's New Model for Innovation," *Harvard Business Review*, 84 (March 2006), pp. 58–86 e1434.

35 O. Toubia, "Idea Generation, Creativity, and Incentives," *Marketing Science*, 25 (September–October 2006), pp. 411–42, shows the positive impact of financial incentives on the number and quality of new ideas e1435.

36 J.I. Cash, Jr., M.J. Earl, and R. Morison, "Teaming Up to Crack Enterprise Innovation: Enterprise Integration," *Harvard Business Review*, 86 (November 2008), pp. 90–100 e1436.

37 E. von Hippel, *The Sources of Innovation*, New York: Oxford University Press, 1988 e1437.

38 O. Shenkar, "Imitation Is More Valuable than Innovation," *Harvard Business Review*, (April 2010), pp. 28–29 e1438.

39 In Cisco's sophisticated creation-net process, individual innovators often formed teams to improve on one individual's idea. G. Jouret, "Inside Cisco's Search for the Next Big Idea," *Harvard Business Review*, 87 (September 2009), pp. 43–45 e1439a; and J.S. Brown and J. Hagel III, "Creation Nets: Getting the Most from Open Innovation," *The McKinsey Quarterly*, (2006), pp. 41–51 e1439b.

40 Formed after the Netflix contest, Kaggle runs similar contests for firms that supply data sets and prize money.

41 E. von Hippel, S. Thomke, and M. Sonnack, "Creating Breakthroughs at 3M," *Harvard Business Review*, 77 (September–October 1999), pp. 47–57, at p. 54 e1441a, and E. von Hippel, *Democratizing Innovation*, Cambridge, MA: MIT Press, 2005 e1441b. Free download e1441c at *http://web.mit.edu/evhippel/www/*. The author was a lead user for gas phase chromatography.

42 von Hippel, Thomke, and Sonnack, *op. cit.* e1441a

43 L. Downes and C. Mui, *Unleashing the Killer App: Digital Strategies for Market Dominance*, Boston, MA: Harvard Business School Press, 1998 e1443.

44 S.D. Anthony, *The Silver Lining: An Innovation Playbook for Uncertain Times*, Boston, MA: Harvard Business School Press, 2009 e1444.

45 Independent consulting organizations like Synectics (Cambridge, MA) have proprietary idea-generation processes. Research shows that creativity training (visualization) plus extrinsic rewards increase creativity in new product development. J.E. Burroughs, D.W. Dahl, C.P. Moreau, A. Chattopadhyay, and G.J. Corn, "Facilitating and Rewarding Creativity During New Product Development," *Journal of Marketing*, 78 (July 2011), pp. 53–67 e1445.

46 Based in part on *www.mindtools.com* e1446a; also J. Goldenberg, *Creativity in Product Innovation*, Cambridge, UK: Cambridge University Press, 2002 e1446b.

47 J. Goldenberg, R. Horowitz, A. Levav, and D. Mazursky, "Finding Your Innovation Sweet Spot," *Harvard Business Review*, 81 (March 2003), pp. 3–10 e1447. Goldenberg et al.'s work is the basis for this section.

48 A.F. Osborn, *Applied Imagination: Principles and Procedures of Creative Problem Solving*, New York: Scribner, 1953 e1448.

49 A different type of *reverse brainstorming* focuses on group process. Rather than generate ideas in groups, participants meet periodically but bring with them ideas they generated between meetings.

50 Also E. De Bono, *Lateral Thinking: Creativity Step by Step*: New York, Harper & Row, 1970 e1450.

51 E. De Bono, *Six Thinking Hats: An Essential Approach to Business Management from the Creator of Lateral Thinking*, Boston, MA: Little Brown, 1985 e1451.

52 From Nobel prize-winning (twice) scientist Linus Pauling.

53 *New-to-the-firm* products are generally riskier — but are more important if successful, T.D. Kuczmarski, *Managing New Products: Competing through Excellence*, Englewood Cliffs, NJ: Prentice Hall, 1988 e1453.

54 O. Toubia and L Florès, "Adaptive Idea Screening Using Consumers," *Marketing Science*, 26 (2007), pp. 342–361 e1454.

55 The firm may earn royalty income from attractive screened-out ideas (incompatible with its mission) by securing patents.

56 G.L. Urban, J.R. Hauser, and J.H. Roberts, "Prelaunch Forecasting of New Automobiles," *Management Science*, 36, No. 4 (April 1990), pp. 401–421 e1456.

57 BASES, the Booz Allen Sales Estimation System, from A.C. Nielsen.

58 Allied Signal, GE, Motorola, and other major firms embrace the five step six-sigma-DMADV approach — define, measure, analyze, design, verify. The related DMAIC process focuses on process improvement.

59 W.H. Davidow and B. Uttal, *Total Customer Service: The Ultimate Weapon*, New York: Harper & Row, 1989 e1459.

60 The 777 is a favorite example: All Regional Project Directors attended Columbia Business School's executive *Marketing Management* Program, like previous generations of Boeing executives.

61 D.K. Sobek II, J.K. Liker, and A.C. Ward, "Another Look at How Toyota Integrates Product Development," *Harvard Business Review*, 76 (July–August 1998), pp. 36–49 e1461.

62 Quotation and boxed insert: Personal communication from Ron Boire, President Consumer Sales Company, Sony Electronics.

63 Personal communication from Eric Kim, Executive Vice President Global Marketing Operations, Samsung Electronics, and "Samsung: Design Strategy at Samsung Electronics: Becoming a Top-Tier Company," Boston, MA: Design Management Institute 2008. Samsung has six design centers around the world; in 2010, Samsung was 19 on Interbrand's global brand valuation (versus Sony, 34). For insight on design, R. Verganti, "Innovating through Design," *Harvard Business Review*, 84 (December 2006), pp. 114–122 e1463.

64 Some firms design using the cradle-to-cradle (C2C) philosophy; Steelcase's new *Think* chair is 99 percent recyclable: W. McDonough and M. Braungart, *Cradle to Cradle: Remaking the Way We Make Things*, New York: North Point, 2002 e1464.

65 A.J. Slywotzky and D.J. Morrison, *The Profit Zone*, New York: Times Business, 1997 e1465.

66 From the QFD Institute website, *www.qfdi.org* e1466.

67 J.R. Hauser and D. Clausing, "The House of Quality," *Harvard Business Review*, 66 (May–June 1988), pp. 63–73 e1467a; and J.R. Hauser, "How Puritan-Bennett Used the House of Quality," *Sloan Management Review*, 34 (Spring 1993), pp. 61–70 e1467b.

68 From consumers, distributors, and/or regulators.

69 For simplicity, we omit other primary CAs like *good appearance*.

70 A. Ward, "The Second Toyota Paradox: How Delaying Decisions Can Make Better Cars Faster," *Sloan Management Review*, 36 (Spring 1995), pp. 43–61 `e1470`.

71 S. Thomake and E. von Hippel, "Customers as Innovators: A New Way to Create Value," *Harvard Business Review*, 80 (April 2002), pp. 74–81 `e1471`.

72 G.P. Pisano and R. Verganti, "Which Kind of Collaboration Is Right for You?," *Harvard Business Review*, 86 (December 2008), pp. 78–86 `e1472a`; V. Ramaswamy and F. Gouillart, "Building the Co-Creative Enterprise," *Harvard Business Review*, 88 (October 2010), pp. 100–109 `e1472b` and *The Power of Co-Creation*, New York: Free Press, 2010 `e1472c`; J. Grönlund, D.R. Sjödin, and J. Fishammar, "Open Innovation and the Stage-Gate Process," *California Management Review*, 52 (Spring 2010), pp. 106–131 `e1472d`.

73 R.G. Cooper, S.J. Edgett, and E.J. Kleinschmidt, "Portfolio Management for New Product Development: Results of an Industry Practices Study," *R&D Management*, 31 (2001), pp. 361–380 `e1473a`; R.G. Cooper and S.J. Edgett, "Portfolio Management for New Products: Picking the Winners," Product Development Institute, Reference Paper 11, 2008 `e1473b`; and S. Kavadias and R.O. Chao, "Resource Allocation and Product Portfolio Management," in C.H. Loch and S. Kavadias (eds.), *Handbook of New Product Development Management*, Oxford: Elsevier/Butterworth, 2007, Chapter 6, pp. 135–163 `e1473c`.

74 Coinstar (Redbox video rental) consistently places primitive versions of new kiosk concepts in public spaces to assess customer reaction.

75 Gleevec (Novartis) addresses chronic myeloid leukemia by halting the body's production of the abnormal "Philadelphia chromosome." Gleevec's clinical trials took half the normal time and was the fastest-ever FDA approval — 72 days. *Gleevec: Success by Design in Oncology*, Columbia Business School.

76 More on ASSESSOR, G.L. Urban and J.R. Hauser, *Design and Marketing of New Products*, Englewood Cliffs, NJ: Prentice Hall, 1993, pp. 461–467 `e1476a`; and *www.mktgeng.com* `e1476b`. Both BASES and ASSESSOR may be useful for concept testing and prior to product launch. The Bass model (endnote 77, `me1401`) is another valuable tool.

77 F. Bass, "A New Product Growth Model for Consumer Durables," *Management Science*, 15 (1969), pp. 215–227) `e1477`, and/or later formulations to forecast new product sales.

78 R.R. Burke, "Virtual Shopping: Breakthrough in Marketing Research," *Harvard Business Review*, 74 (March–April 1996), pp. 120–131 `e1478`.

79 N.D. Cadbury, "When, Where, and How to Test Market," *Harvard Business Review*, 52 (May–June 1975), pp. 96–103 `e1479`.

80 Also *New Product Commercialization: Common Mistakes*, 9-594-127, Harvard Business School `e1480`.

81 Scholastic worked hard to avoid early availability of Harry Potter novels.

82 Also J. Schneider and J. Hall, "Why Most Product Launches Fail," *Harvard Business Review*, 89 (April 2011), pp. 21–23 `e1482`.

83 Some authors even advocate making deliberate mistakes. P.J.H. Schoemaker and R.E. Gunther, "The Wisdom of Deliberate Mistakes," *Harvard Business Review*, 84 (June 2006), pp. 109–115 `e1483`.

84 E.M. Rogers, *Diffusion of Innovations* (5th Ed.), New York: Free Press, 2003 `e1484a`; E. Ofek and O. Toubia, "Marketing and Innovation Management: An Integrated Perspective," *Foundations and Trends in Marketing*, 4 (2009), pp. 77–128 `e1484b`.

85 Size percentages, based on standard deviations from the mean, have not been empirically validated.

86 G.A. Moore, *Crossing the Chasm — Marketing & Selling High-Tech Products to Mainstream Customers*, New York: HarperBusiness, 2002 `e1486`.

87 J.T. Gourville, "Eager Sellers, Stony Buyers," *Harvard Business Review*, 84 (June 2006), pp 99-106, argues that several factors may slow new product adoption: *Status quo bias* — the tendency to continue with current products; *endowment effect* — valuing products they already possess; and *loss aversion* — a focus on potential loss in benefits from adopting a new product versus potential gains from new benefits (Prospect Theory) `e1487`.

CHAPTER 15

1   H. Schultz and D.J. Yang, *Pour Your Heart Into It*, New York: Hyperion, 1997, p. 245 `e1501`. Aka McDonald's for yuppies.

2   Following independent tests, Mercedes redesigned the A Class; Suzuki withdrew the Samurai; and Toyota recalled the 2010 Lexus GX 460.

3   Some physician spokespeople place *shills* in the audience to ask questions about off-label uses.

4   Many local TV stations continue to air liquor ads.

5   The U.S. allows *puffery* — unbelievable exaggerated claims.

6   Judges and juries play important roles in lawsuits for false or misleading advertising. U.S. consumers can sign up to avoid telemarketing calls.

7   Less than 15 percent of launch costs went to TV advertisements!

8   Alternative categories are: *broadcast media* — television, radio, newspapers; and *addressable media* — e-mail, direct mail, telephone; *Note on Marketing and the World Wide Web*, Harvard Business School.

9   G.E. Belch and M.A. Belch, *Advertising and Promotion: An Integrated Marketing Communications Perspective*, 9ᵗʰ ed., Homewood, IL: McGraw-Hill/Irwin, 2011 `e1509`.

10 Welch's grape juice print ads tapped into a different sense by incorporating lickable strips to stimulate taste buds.

11 J. Hulbert and N. Capon, "Interpersonal Communication in Marketing: An Overview," *Journal of Marketing Research*, 9 (February 1972), pp. 27–34 `e1511`.

12 Product placement addresses the problem of consumers skipping TV advertisements using DVR technology. Virtual placement allows the firm to insert different communications in different geographic areas; C.A. Russell and M. Belch, "A Managerial Investigation into the Product Placement Industry," *Journal of Advertising Research*, 45 (March 2005), pp. 73–92 `e1512`.

13 *Branded entertainment* derives from product placement; the content provider and advertiser jointly develop content.

14 S. Gopalakrishna, G.L. Lilien, J.D. Williams, and I.K. Sequeira, "Do Trade Shows Pay Off?," *Journal of Marketing*, 59 (July 1995), pp. 75–83 report an interesting study `e1514`.

15 D. Peppers and M. Rogers, *The One-to-One Future: Building Relationships One Customer at a Time*, New York: Currency Doubleday, 1993 `e1515`.

16 "Your Train Will Be Late, She Says Cheerily: Voice of Amtrak Computer Works on Frayed Nerves," *The New York Times*, November 24, 2004 `e1516`.

17 Word of mouth can be highly valuable; it comes in various forms:
    • **Persuasive** — explicit person-to-person recommendation
    • **Casual** — positive mention but not an explicit recommendation, typically oral

- **Visual** — unconscious non-verbal recommendation based on behavior, like wearing clothes with a designer label
- **Artificial** — produced by computer algorithms like Amazon and Netflix recommendations

V. Kumar, J.A. Petersen, and R.P. Leone, "How Valuable is Word of Mouth?," *Harvard Business Review*, 85 (October 2007), pp. 139–146 e1517 .

18 *Buzz marketing* focuses on getting people talking about the firm's products. *Guerilla marketing* is a subset of buzz marketing that typically uses stunts. Buzz marketing relies on the six buttons of buzz — taboo (sex, lies, bathroom humor), unusual, outrageous, hilarious, remarkable, and secrets (kept and revealed) — to get people talking. Five popular types of media story enhance *buzz* — David & Goliath, unusual and outrageous, controversy, celebrities, and what's currently hot in the media; M. Hughes, *Buzz Marketing*, New York: Portfolio, 2005 e1518 . BzzAgent and Buzzador use social networking to pair consumers wth products and give them Internet tools to share opinions.

19 C. Locke, "Smart Customers, Dumb Customers," *Harvard Business Review*, 78 (November–December 2000), pp. 187–191 e1519 .

20 Hughes, *op. cit.* e1518 Within six months of launch, eBay acquired Half.com for $300 million.

21 R. Iyengar, C. Van den Bulte, and T.W. Valente, "Opinion Leadership and Social Contagion in New Product Diffusion," *Marketing Science*, 30 (2011), pp. 195–212 e1521 .

22 "The Big Benioff," *Fortune*, December 13, 2004 e1522 .

23 Film producers used similar strategies for *Crouching Tiger, Hidden Dragon* and *X-Men: The Movie*.

24 Also *Communications Policy*, 9-576-086; *Integrated Marketing Communications*, 9-599-087; *Marketing Promotions*, 9-506-028, Harvard Business School.

25 Berkshire Hathaway shares trade at over $100,000 per share. CEO Warren Buffett (Columbia Business School alumnus) refuses to split the stock; he believes the high share price generates a more stable shareholder base.

26 The purpose of corporate advertising is not always clear: Options include umbrella for marketing activities, persuading investors to become shareholders, and CEO self-aggrandizement.

CHAPTER 16

1 Visa rejected several banks' requests to place bank logos on its cards; they switched all new card acquisitions (and replacements) to MasterCard.

2 Founder of Wanamaker department store, Philadelphia, circa 1870. Statement also attributed to Lord Leverhume, founder of Unilever.

3 Newspapers like *Financial Times*, *The New York Times*, and *Wall Street Journal* have dropped this model for web versions and charge directly for content.

4 H.E. Krugman, "What Makes Advertising Effective?," *Harvard Business Review*, 53 (March–April 1975), pp. 96–103, is the classic advertising effectiveness article.

5 For a fine discussion of hierarchy-of-effects models: G.E. Belch and M.A. Belch, *Advertising and Promotion: An Integrated Marketing and Communications Perspective*, 8th ed., Homewood, IL: McGraw-Hill/Irwin, 2011 e1605 .

6 Customers exhibit differing (self-explanatory) awareness levels. In order, recall dominance, top of the mind, unaided recall, aided recall, and recognition (from a list).

7 D. Vakratsas and T. Ambler, "How Advertising Works: What Do We Really Know?," *Journal of Marketing*, 63 (January 1999), pp. 26–43 e1607 .

8 Although advertising effects are generally short-term, researchers also observe long-term effects; R.P. Leone, "Generalizing What Is Known about Temporal Aggregation and Advertising Carryover," *Marketing Science*, 14 (1995), G141–150 e1608a ; L.M. Lodish, M. Abraham, S. Kalmenson, J. Livelsberger, B. Lubetkin, B. Richardson, and M.E. Stevens, "How Advertising Works: A Meta-Analysis of 389 Real World Split Cable TV Advertising Experiments," *Journal of Marketing Research*, 32 (May 1995), pp. 125–139 e1608b and "A Summary of Fifty-Five In-Market Experimental Estimates of the Long-Term Effects of Advertising, *Marketing Science*, 14 (1995), G133–140 e1608c .

9 Several high-involvement models are based on a learning hierarchy; Belch and Belch, *op. cit.* e1605

10 Sampling customers to induce trial is more cost-effective than advertising in some product categories.

11 Some use different terminology: awareness and knowledge — *think*; liking — *feel*; trial — *act*. The two hierarchies then become: high-involvement: *think → feel → act*; low involvement: *think → act → feel*.

12 For classic work on advertising objectives: R.H. Colley, *Defining Advertising Goals for Measured Advertising Results*, New York: Association of National Advertisers, 1961 e1612 .

13 Thanks to Professor Gita Johar for this example.

14 Chapter 23, Table 23.2, p. 575.

15 Both campaigns were dropped within weeks of introduction.

16 B.H. Schmitt, "Advertising and Mass Communications," in N. Capon (Ed.), Section 7, *Marketing*, in AMA Management Handbook (3rd ed.), J. Hampton (Ed.), AMACOM, 1994, 2-108 – 2-115, p. 2-112 e1616 . Creativity is different from impact. Advertising campaigns may earn creativity prizes yet fail to achieve objectives.

17 More recently, Absolut lost market share to other imported vodkas.

18 "Elida Returns to Its Youth to Find Secrets of Success," *Financial Times*, November 5, 1999. PlayStation ads mostly show different games, demonstrating that Sony had the broadest variety.

19 Some countries ban comparative advertising. B. Buchanan and D. Goldman, "Us vs. Them: The Minefield of Comparative Ads," *Harvard Business Review*, 67 (May–June 1989), pp. 38–50, reviews the legal status e1619a . For *deceptive advertising*: G.V. Johar, "Consumer Involvement and Deception from Implied Advertising Claims," *Journal of Marketing Research*, 32 (August 1995), pp. 267–279 e1619b .

20 Humor, often using exaggeration, can make a demonstration advertisement more effective.

21 E.J. Faison, "Effectiveness of One-Sided and Two-Sided Mass Communications in Advertising," *Public Opinion Quarterly*, 25 (Fall 1961), pp. 468–469; R.E. Settle and L.L. Golden, "Attribution Theory and Advertiser Credibility," *Journal of Marketing Research*, 11 (May 1974), pp. 181–185 e1621 .

22 H.E. Krugman, "On Application of Learning Theory to TV Copy Testing," *Public Opinion Quarterly*, 26 (1962), pp. 626–639 e1622 .

23 A.G. Sawyer, "The Effects of Repetition of Refutational and Supportive Advertising Appeals," *Journal of Marketing Research*, 10 (February 1973), pp. 23–37 e1623a ; G.J. Szybillo and R. Heslin, "Resistance to Persuasion: Inoculation Theory in a Marketing Context," *Journal of Marketing Research*, 10 (November 1973), pp. 396–403 e1623b .

24 Cosmetic companies use many celebrities. Ms. Spears ceased being effective when she shaved her head!

25 In a six-year period, Salton sold more than 40 million George Foreman grills — revenues increased twelvefold. Venus and Serena Williams annually earned $20 million and $16 million, respectively, promoting brands like Avon, Nortel Networks, Reebok, Sega, and Wilson's The Leather Experts. Muhammad Ali sold an 80 percent stake in his name, image, and likeness for $50 million.

26 The Davie Brown celebrity index evaluates awareness, appeal, and relevance of a celebrity to brand image. The seven key attributes are appeal, notice, trendsetter, influence, trust, endorsement, and aspiration.

27 M.L. Ray and W.L. Wilkie, "Fear: The Potential of an Appeal Neglected by Marketing," *Journal of Marketing*, 34 (January 1970), pp. 54–62 `e1627a`; and B. Sternthal and C.S. Craig, "Fear Appeals Revisited and Revised," *Journal of Consumer Research*, 1 (December 1974), pp. 12–18 `e1627b`.

28 *http://videos.godaddy.com/candice-michelle.aspx*. `e1628a` Go Daddy is an Internet domain registry. For other banned ads, *http://www.youtube.com/watch?v=PRiYkwtBK34* `e1628b`.

29 For more on humor: B. Sternthal and C.S. Craig, "Humor in Advertising," *Journal of Marketing*, 37 (October 1973), pp. 12–18 `e1629`; and T.J. Madden and M.C. Weinberger, "Humor in Advertising: A Practitioner View," *Journal of Advertising Research*, 24 (August–September 1984), pp. 23–26. For a taxonomy: P.S. Speck, "The Humorous Message Taxonomy: A Framework for the Study of Humorous Ads," *Journal of Current Issues and Research in Advertising*, 22 (1993), pp. 1–44.

30 Insider's Report, McCann Worldgroup.

31 Source: *ZenithOptimedia*. Advertising expenditure breakdown by geographic area ($billions): North America — 165; Western Europe — 104; Asia/Pacific — 121; Central/Eastern Europe — 25; Latin America — 33; Middle East/North Africa — 4; rest of world — 11.

32 In somewhat of an overstatement, Robin Kerr, former chairman of media giant Universal McCann, said: "The media planner is becoming the most important person on the planet." *The Economist*, April 2, 2005 `e1632`.

33 Belch and Belch, *op. cit.* `e1605`

34 Ai Jia pays $1,200 per month for a 15-person team (excluding uniforms and bicycles). By contrast, a one-time 15-second commercial on local TV costs $2,800; a large, prominently located billboard costs $3,000 to $8,000 per month.

35 Advertisers must exercise caution regarding audited figures as media companies may try to artificially enhance their viewership/readership. Concerning TV: In a low-viewership week, ABC labeled several days of *Good Morning America*, as specials — *Good Morning Amer*, so they wouldn't count in the ratings. Conversely, other networks run popular shows one or two minutes after the hour/half hour, so the weaker following show gains the advantage of high ratings from the strong show.

36 Audience certification is crucial for establishing good comparable cost data. Independent agencies like Mediamark Research Inc. (MRI), Nielsen, and Simmons Market Research Bureau certify audiences for various advertising vehicles. Total circulation typically provides print media data; projections from samples provide radio and TV data. Paper-and-pencil diaries for estimating listeners/viewers has largely given way to electronic measurement systems, but simple on/off measures do not capture who or how many listeners/viewers; DVR use poses special challenges for TV advertising measurement.

37 The firm should adjust circulation by proportion of target audience — a better measure is *CPM target customer*, but this is difficult to calculate. The *M* in CPM represents thousand, MM represents million.

38 "In Vogue," *The Economist*, September 21, 2002. Some firms build program-engagement measures based on survey data.

39 The classic paper is H.A. Zielske, "The Remembering and Forgetting of Advertising," *Journal of Marketing*, 23 (January 1959), pp. 239–243 `e1639a`. Also J.A. Simon, "What Do Zielske's Real Data Show about Pulsing," *Journal of Marketing Research*, 23 (March 1979) pp. 415–420 `e1639b` and L.M. Lodish, Empirical Studies on Individual Responses to Exposure Patterns," *Journal of Marketing Research*, 8 (May 1971), pp. 214–216 `e1639c`.

40 The firm should also consider the timing of competitive advertising.

41 K.S. Palda, *The Measurement of Cumulative Advertising*, Upper Saddle River, NJ: Prentice Hall, 1964 `e1641`.

42 J.A. Simon and J. Arndt, "The Shape of the Advertising Response Function," *Journal of Advertising Research*, 20 (1980), pp. 11–28; P.B. Luchsinger, V.S. Mullen, and P.T. Jannuzzo, "How Many Advertising Dollars Are Enough," *Media Decisions*, 12 (1977), p. 59. Also D.A. Aaker and J.M. Carman, "Are You Overadvertising?," *Journal of Advertising Research*, 22 (1982), pp. 57–70; and G. Assmus, J.U. Farley, and D.R. Lehmann, "How Advertising Affects Sales: Meta Analysis of Econometric Results," *Journal of Marketing Research*, 21 (1984), pp. 65–74 `e1642`.

43 J.D.C. Little, "Models and Managers: The Concept of a Decision Calculus," *Management Science*, 50 (December 2004), pp. 1841–1853 `e1643`.

44 J.N. Sheth and R.J. Sisodia, "Feeling the Heat," *Marketing Management*, 4 (1995), pp. 8–23. Direct marketing more precisely measures results.

45 According to Schmitt, *op. cit.*, two-thirds of major advertisers use this method `e1616`. Our colleague Joe Plummer estimates that 85 percent of marketers use last year's sales to budget current year's spending.

46 The underlying model is: Share of spend → share of voice → share of mind → market share. Firms like TNS Media and ComScore help firms benchmark advertising spending versus competitors.

47 For advertising budgeting models: Little, *op. cit.* `e1643`; M.L. Vidale and R.H. Wolfe, "An Operations Research Study of Sales Response to Advertising, *Operations Research*, (June 1957), pp. 370–381 `e1647a`; J.D.C. Little, "A Model of Adaptive Control of Promotional Spending," *Operations Research*, (November 1966), pp. 1075–1097 `e1647b`; G.L. Lillien, P. Kotler, and K.S. Morthy, *Marketing Models*, Upper Saddle River, NJ: Prentice Hall, 1992, Chapter 6 `e1647c`.

48 Split-cable TV systems show identical programming in a confined geography — different ads appear on each half.

49 The Starch Readership Report compares specific advertisements with a large historic database.

50 Commercial entities offering this service are Information Resources Inc. (IRI), Burke Marketing Research (the Burke day-after recall test), and ASI Market Research.

51 IRI's BehaviorScan service uses customer panels in 25 U.S. markets in conjunction with split-cable TV systems.

52 R.I. Haley, J. Stafforini, and A. Fox, "The Missing Measures of Copy Testing," *Journal of Advertising Research*, (May–June 1994), pp. 46–56.

53 The firm may also use recognition and recall measures in conjunction with overall advertising program analysis.

54 For a full discussion of advertising testing: Belch and Belch, *op. cit.* `e1605`

55 Thanks to colleague Gita Johar for this example, Quirk's Marketing Research Review, 1988.

56 The top five U.S. agencies account for 60 percent of advertising expenditures, up from 30 percent in 2000. Several agencies, like WPP, earn more fee revenue from marketing services than advertising.

57 Absolut and HSBC (earlier) are good examples of a campaign idea and various executions of that idea.

58 For a synopsis: M. Kalter and E. Stearns, "Direct Marketing," in N. Capon (Ed.), Section 2, Marketing, in *AMA Management Handbook* (3rd ed.), J. Hampton (Ed.), New York: AMACOM, 1994, 2-116 — 2-121 e1616.

59 Bernays, Sigmund Freud's nephew, is often known as the *father* of public relations. L. Tye, *The Father of Spin: Edward L. Bernays and the Birth of Public Relations*, New York: Random House, 1998 e1659.

60 Successful P&PR campaigns are legion. James Sterling Moran hatched out an ostrich egg to publicize *The Egg and I*, a best-selling book. He opened a Washington embassy for a mythical country to publicize the movie *The Mouse that Roared*. To promote a Broadway show, he rigged a taxi so a chimpanzee seemed to be driving.

61 *College Savings Bank (A) and (B)* in N. Capon, *The Marketing of Financial Services: A Book of Cases*, Englewood Cliffs, NJ: Prentice Hall, 1992, pp. 93–121 e1661.

62 "The New Pitch," *The New Yorker*, March 28, 2005 e1662.

63 "Bad for You," *The Economist*, June 19, 1999 e1663. Two bottling-system failures emerged: "bad" carbon dioxide at one plant and fungicide contamination from wooden pallets at another.

64 The author believes that in crisis, the firm's decision-makers should reject arguments from legal (admitting guilt attracts lawsuits) and finance (repair actions reduce profits) in favor of doing what is right!

65 *Spiffs* are direct cash payments from a firm to customer salespeople, contingent on sales success.

66 The producers earned $120 million in sponsored advertising, product tie-ins, promotions, and sweepstakes. Relatedly, Bulgari paid Fay Weldon for highlighting the firm in her novel.

67 Chapter 15, endnote 12. Product placement ranges from background items to an integral part of the storyline. Using TV, some firms integrate product placement with product advertising in commercial breaks. Products placed more than 1,000 annually in U.S. TV shows include Coca-Cola Classic, Everlast (apparel and sporting equipment), Nike (apparel) and Gatorade. For contrasting views on product placement: E.M. Peebles, "And Now, a Word from Our Sponsor," *Harvard Business Review*, (October 2003), pp. 31–41 e1667.

68 Philips placed video monitors throughout the arena and created a retail showroom. For research on sponsorship effectiveness: G.V. Johar and M.T. Pham, "Relatedness, Prominence and Constructive Sponsor Identification," *Journal of Marketing Research*, 36 (August 1999), pp. 299–312 e1668. Stadium owners have problems when they make bad partner choices. New England Patriots — CMGI (failed dot-com); Tennessee Titans — Adelphi Communications (former CEO jailed for corporate looting and accounting fraud); Houston Astros — Enron Field!

69 FMCG firms' spending on consumer and trade promotion often exceeds 50 percent of total marketing budgets.

70 C.F. Mela, S. Gupta, and D.R. Lehmann, "The Long-Term Impact of Promotion and Advertising on Consumer Brand Choice," *Journal of Marketing Research*, 34 (May 1997), pp. 248–261 e1670a. M. Tsiros and D.M. Hardesty, "Ending a Price Promotion: Retracting It in One Step or Phasing It Out Gradually," *Journal of Marketing*, 74 (January 2010), pp 49–64 shows that *steading decreasing discounting* (SDD) is more effective than returning to the pre-discounted price in one step e1670b1, e1670b2.

71 To divert is to resell products to other retailers, typically in a different geographic area.

72 "Maybe Maytag Should Give Away Cash?," *The New York Times*, March 31, 1993 e1672a and S. Gupta and D.R. Lehmann, *Managing Customers as Investments*, Philadelphia: Wharton, 2005, pp. 3–4 e1672b. Hoover is a Maytag subsidiary. *The Times* commented: "In the United States, top executives lose their jobs when their companies sell too little. In Britain, it can happen when their companies sell too much." The promotion was such a good deal that many consumers used their airline tickets, but sold their Hoovers! Relatedly, P&G underestimated the popularity of its sales promotion, "Pampers Perks" — Fisher-Price toys for consumers who collected *points* on diaper packages. After two months, consumers had not received their toys.

73 Thanks to Jeremy Kagan, Lyn Maize, Peter Propp, and Judy Strauss for assistance in preparing this section.

74 Click fraud is an ongoing problem for paid search — the paid-search advertising network simulates clicks on the ads it features. Of course, all major search engines work hard to detect and combat click fraud. A second problem is inflated measures from search engine robots and other automated software.

75 Google reputedly uses more than 200 variables to determine rank.

76 Ad sizes in pixels (wide × tall) are: standard banner – 468 × 60; skyscraper – 160 × 600; medium rectangle – 300 × 250.

77 "Blogs: Fad or Marketing Medium of the Future?," *Brandweek*, November 24, 2004.

78 BzzAgent (U.S.), Buzzador (Scandinavia), TRND (Germany) are word-of-mouth media networks. They pair consumers with products and give them digital tools to share opinions.

79 J. Strauss, "Marketing Communication Strategies," in *The Handbook of Technology Management*, Vol. 2, H. Bidgoli (Ed.), Hoboken, NJ: Wiley, 2010, pp. 449–461 e1679.

80 A. Beale and J. Strauss, *Radically Transparent: Monitoring and Managing Reputations Online*, Indianapolis, IN: Wiley, 2008 e1680.

81 P. Manchanda, G.M. Packard, and A. Pattabhiramaiah, "Social Dollars: The Economic Impact of Customer Participation in a Firm-Sponsored Online Community," January 12, 2012. Available at SSRN e1681.

82 Success factors for a viral marketing campaign are: memorable message; structure of the social network; behavioral characteristics of recipients and incentives to share the message; and a seeding strategy that determines the initial set of target consumers; O. Hinz, B. Skiera, C. Barrot, and J.U. Becker, "Seeding Strategies for Viral Marketing: An Empirical Comparison," *Journal of Marketing*, 75 (November–December 2011), pp. 55–71 e1682a, e1682b.

83 I. Nitzan and S.B. Libal, "Social Effects on Customer Retention," *Journal of Marketing*, 75 (November 2011), pp. 24–38 e1683.

84 Other industries face similar challenges: airlines (*planebuzz.com*), finance (*wallstreetfolly.com*), media (*tvnewser.com*), retail (*walmartwatch.com/blog*), and tech (*fakesteve.net*).

....

CHAPTER 17

1 Sales force costs are a large part of Pfizer's marketing and sales expenses — around 40 percent of sales revenues. Thomas Friedman (*New York Times* columnist) labels professional service workers who bring in business as the new *untouchables* — will not be laid off.

2 T.M. Smith, S. Gopalakrishna, and R. Chatterjee, "A Three-Stage Model of Integrated Marketing Communications at the Marketing-Sales Interface," *Journal of Marketing Research*, 43 (November 2006), pp. 564–579 e1702.

3 C. Homburg and O. Jensen, "The Thought Worlds of Marketing and Sales: Which Differences Make a Difference?" *Journal of Marketing*, 71 (july 2007), pp. 124–142 e1703.

4   Part of the problem may be historic: Marketing evolved from the sales force to become its own entity. Marketing and sales may also lack effective interpersonal and conflict-resolution skills.

5   The author of a well-known psychology textbook attended her publisher's annual sales conference. In explaining their books to the sales force, individual editors (product managers) focused on securing more sales effort on their books than on colleagues' books. Also, marketing may mislead sales by inflating objectives on certain products as a way to secure greater sales force effort. W.M. Strahle, R.L. Spiro, and F. Acito, "Marketing and Sales: Strategic Alignment and Functional Implementation," *Journal of Personal Selling & Sales Management*, 16 (Winter 1996), pp. 1–20 e1705.

6   D. Rouzies, E. Anderson, A.K. Kohli, R.E. Michaels, B.A. Weiss, and A.A. Zoltners, "Sales and Marketing Integration: A Proposed Framework," *Journal of Personal Selling and Sales Management*, 25 (Spring 2005), pp. 113–122 e1706a. P. Kotler, N. Rackham, and S. Krishnaswamy, "Ending the War between Sales & Marketing," *Harvard Business Review*, 84 (July–August 2006), pp. 68–78, contains a multi-item scale for measuring marketing and sales alignment and integration e1706b.

7   Five specific planning problems we have come across are:
   • The sales force receives the finished marketing plan late, far beyond end-of-period deadlines.
   • The sales force starts and finishes its planning early, before marketing delivers its plans.
   • Sales and marketing do not share either plans or *voice of the customer* feedback.
   • The sales force has no input into marketing and views marketing as irrelevant to daily issues.
   • Marketing believes the sales force is *sandbagging* the sales forecasts to make it easier to earn incentive compensation.

8   C. Homburg, O. Jensen, and H. Krohmer, "Configurations of Marketing and Sales: A Taxonomy," *Journal of Marketing*, 72 (March 2008), pp. 133–154, identifies five empirical archetypes of the marketing-sales interface. The most successful archetypes demonstrate strong structural linkages between marketing and sales e1708.

9   Material sourced from N. Capon and G. Tubridy, *Sales Eats First*, Bronxville, NY: Wessex, 2011 e1709.

10 Fred Hassan (Schering-Plough CEO) in T.A. Stewart and D. Champion, "Leading Change from the Top Line," *Harvard Business Review*, 84 (July–August 2006), pp. 90–97 e1710.

11 Seven of IBM's nine CEOs, including current CEO Virginia Rometty, had sales backgrounds.

12 See *www.sellingpower.com/video* for a series of short videos about selling e1712.

13 R.C. Dudley and D. Narayandas, "A Portfolio Approach to Sales," *Harvard Business Review*, 84 (July–August 2006), pp. 16–18, classify sales but omit retention e1713. The authors split *new business* into two categories: *expansion* — serve customer needs not currently being satisfied; and *innovation* — identify and serve new customer needs.

14 Direct costs typically include sales force costs, but exclude costs not controllable by sales managers — plant overhead and R&D allocations. For a detailed discussion of financial analysis, see Marketing Enrichment me01.

15 We use fictional firm Essex throughout the chapter.

16 If marketing and sales objectives are not integrated, sales is likely to set its own objectives disconnected from marketing; Strahle, Spiro, and Acito, *op. cit.* e1705.

17 Where *not to* allocate resources may be as important as where *to* allocate. Marketing should advise the sales force on *go* and *no-go* areas.

18 Calendarization is especially important when sales patterns are seasonal.

19 Physicians can use approved drugs for any indication (disease state) but the FDA prohibits promoting drugs for non-approved indications. Allergan, Astra Zeneca, Bristol-Myers Squibb, Eli Lilly, Forest Laboratories, and Novartis each made settlements with the U.S. Justice Department concerning unapproved uses and other infractions.

20 The firm may assume alternative sales response functions; viz. advertising response functions — Chapter 16.

21 For an alternative but more complex process: A.A. Zoltners, P. Sinha, and S.E. Lorimer, "Match Your Sales Force Structure to Your Business Cycle," *Harvard Business Review*, 84 (July–August 2006), pp. 81–89 e1721.

22 When store traffic is heaviest, Home Depot employees cease all non-customer-facing activities; many airlines are following Ryanair's innovation of making sales to *captive* airline passengers.

23 Cisco CEO John Chambers reputedly made 200 CEO sales calls in one month using TelePresence.

24 In Table 17.3, cells IIA and IIIC have zero revenue objectives and zero effort. Sometimes firms allocate zero effort, yet set positive revenue objectives — like a declining product with a core of loyal customers. Conversely, the firm may place selling effort on a segment but not expect sales revenues in the current period.

25 This table contains rounding errors.

26 Many firms incorrectly use current revenue-based classes (ignoring potential) to allocate effort. Decision calculus models use managerial judgment of likely sales responses, then solve for optimal allocations; L.M. Lodish, "CALLPLAN: An Interactive Salesman's Call Planning System," *Management Science*, 18, Part II. (December 1971b), pp. 25–40 e1726.

27 Of course, some salespeople thrive on seeking new opportunities — we are speaking of general *comfort* tendencies.

28 V. Kumar, R. Venkatesan, and W. Reinhart, "Performance Implications of Adopting a Customer-Focused Sales Campaign," *Journal of Marketing*, 72 (September 2008), pp. 50–68, found that multi-product firms that orchestrated selling efforts across products secured better results than those focusing on products individually e1728.

29 P. Lay, T. Hewlin, and G. Moore, "In a Downturn, Provoke Your Customers," *Harvard Business Review*, 87 (March 2009), pp. 48–56 e1729.

30 Much psychological research suggests people use relatively few criteria to process information and make decisions. G.A. Miller, "The Magical Number Seven, Plus or Minus Two," *Psychological Review*, 63 (March 1956), pp. 81–97 e1730a; J.M. Hulbert, "Information Processing Capacity and Attitude Management," *Journal of Marketing Research*, 12 (February 1975), pp. 104–106 e1730b. Incorporating too many benefits in a sales approach may confuse customers and/or create credibility gaps.

31 Boeing's sales approach to airlines includes attractive pricing, financing and leasing arrangements, and service and training packages.

32 D. Ledingham, M.Kovac, and H. Locke Simon, "The New Science of Sales Force Productivity," *Harvard Business Review*, 84 (September 2006), pp. 124–133 e1732.

33 The firm must trade-off efficiency gains from standardization and transformational change.

34 *Front office/back office* distinction from HP.

35 Many *how-to-sell* books on consultative selling and other systems teach these procedures.

36 Like primacy/recency decisions: Should the salesperson present more powerful arguments earlier or later in the sales call?

37 R. Cialdini, *The Psychology of Persuasion*, New York: William Morrow, 1993, developed these principles from extensive field research including going *undercover* as a used-car salesman e1737.

38 For outsourced sales forces, E. Anderson and B. Trinkle, *Outsourcing the Sales Function*, Mason, OH: Thomson, 2005 e1738.

39 We focus on employee-based sales forces.

40 Actual ratios deviate for operational reasons like workload.

41 N. Adams, J. Gillibrand, D. Treinish, K. Woodberry, and B. Zaldivar, "British Aerospace Regional Aircraft: Addressing the Need for Key Account Management," Term Paper for Developing and Managing Strategic Customers, B8699-02, New York: Graduate School of Business, Columbia University.

42 Wachovia deliberately understaffed product specialist functions to motivate account managers to understand their products; Wachovia Bank and Trust Company in N. Capon, *The Marketing of Financial Services: A Book of Cases*, Englewood Cliffs, NJ: Prentice Hall, 1992 e1742.

43 Some pharmaceutical firms abandoned this organization under pressure from physician organizations.

44 Stuart Dean instituted a process to avoid multiple calling on individual customers.

45 "Steve Jobs: The Graying Prince of a Shrinking Kingdom," *Fortune*, May 14, 2001 e1745.

46 This is not simple; HP took three years to secure organizational agreement for its global pipeline system.

47 HP does not credit salespeople for sales resulting from opportunities *not* entered into the pipeline.

48 Like Siebel Systems and www.salesforce.com e1748.

49 Based on the expectancy/value model for securing motivated behavior; J.W. Atkinson, "Motivational Determinants of Risk Taking Behavior," *Psychological Review*, 64 (1957), pp. 359–372 e1749.

50 Other motivators include special bonuses, prizes, evaluation points, stamp schemes, and training awards.

51 Two potential problems relate to bonuses: Successful salespeople may slack off after earning the bonus; and salespeople who believe they will not earn the bonus may shift sales to a subsequent period. Over achievement commissions address the first problem; calendarizing the bonus addresses the second. Notwithstanding mixed perspectives and empirical results on the value of bonuses, T.J. Steenburgh, "Effort or Timing: The Effect of Lump-Sum Bonuses." *Quantitative Marketing and Economics*, 6 (2008), pp. 235–256, shows that bonuses drive greater salesperson effort e1751.

52 At Microsoft, a salesperson and customer escalated the decision for significant discounting on a potential sale several managerial levels. Robert Youngjohns, President North America Sales, said: "I asked one question. What is the impact of this sale on the salesperson's attainment of quota?" The answer: "Without this sale the salesperson is at 98.2 percent of quota: with the sale, the sales person is at 102.2 percent of quota!"

53 Some firms employ product-mix incentives to avoid a narrow focus on easy-to-sell products.

54 P. R. Sinha, "Premium Marketing to the Masses: An Interview with LG Electronics India's Managing Director," *The McKinsey Quarterly*, (Special Edition 2005), pp. 52–61 e1754.

55 *BusinessWeek*, November 27, 1989.

56 Sears Auto Centers (A), (B), and (C), 9-394-009/10/11, Harvard Business School e1756.

57 A. Miller, *Death of a Salesman*, 1949 e1757a; D. Mamet, *Glengarry Glen Ross*, 1984 e1757b.

58 Personal communication.

59 Some firms reward salespeople for recruiting new salespeople.

60 M.E. Elling, H.J. Fogle, C.S. McKhann, and C. Simon, "Making More of Pharma's Sales Force," *The McKinsey Quarterly*, (2002), pp. 86–95, suggests pharmaceutical reps are inadequately trained! e1760

61 K.A. Allredge, T.R. Griffin, and L.K. Kotcher, "May the sales force be with you," *The McKinsey Quarterly*, (3 - 1999), 110–121 for the importance of retail execution e1761.

62 The firm should use validated psychometric tests for salesperson selection.

63 Empathy and ego drive (need to persuade) from D. Mayer and H.M. Greenberg, "What Makes a Good Salesman," *Harvard Business Review*, 42 (July–August 1964), pp. 119–125 e1763. Ego strength embraces the self-confidence and ability to handle rejection, accept criticism, and *bounce back.*

64 Capon and Tubridy, *op. cit.*, pp. 36–37 e1709.

65 In order: Don't follow the customer buying process; don't listen to customer needs; don't follow up; be pushy, aggressive, or disrespectful; don't explain solutions adequately; make exaggerated or inaccurate claims; don't understand the customer's business; act too familiar; and don't know or respect the competition; T. Atkinson and R. Koprowski, "Sales Rep's Biggest Mistakes," *Harvard Business Review*, 84 (July–August 2006), p. 20 e1765.

66 E. Anderson and V. Onyemah, "How Right Should the Customer Be?," *Harvard Business Review*, 84 (July–August 2006), pp. 59–67 e1766.

67 Gaining access is critical. Of 100 pharmaceutical reps calling on physicians, only eight see the doctor and are remembered! Elling, Fogle, McKhann, and Simon, *op. cit.* e1760

68 T. Üstüner and D. Godes, "Better Sales Networks," *Harvard Business Review*, 84 (July–August 2006), pp. 102–112 e1768.

69 The firm can develop alternative career tracks for career salespeople, involving increased responsibility, income, and recognition.

70 Personal communication.

71 *Key* and *strategic* are interchangeable. Generally, European use is *key*; U.S. use is *strategic.* Firms making excessive price concessions to large customers may find smaller customers are more profitable.

72 For critical factors driving key/strategic account management N. Capon, *Key Account Management*, New York: Free Press, 2001, Chapter 2 e1772.

73 D. Narayandas and V.K. Rangan, "Building and Sustaining Buyer-Seller Relationships in Mature Industrial Markets," *Journal of Marketing*, 68 (July 2004), pp. 63–77 e1773.

74 "IBM's All-Star Salesman," *Fortune*, September 29, 2008 e1774a. For building sales networks: T. Ustuner and D. Godes, "Better Sales Networks," *Harvard Business Review*, 84 (July–August 2006), pp. 102–112 e1774b.

75 Walmart has a large percentage share of some suppliers' sales — Playtex (28%), Clorox (27%), Hasbro (24%), Revlon (24%), Tootsie Roll Ind. (24%), Spectrum Brands (18%), Russell (18%), P&G (16%), General Mills (16%), and J. M. Smucker (16%).

76 N. Capon, D. Potter, and F. Schindler, *Managing Global Accounts* (2nd ed.), Bronxville, NY: Wessex, 2008 e1776.

CHAPTER 18

1 From interviews with Cisco executives and data from V.K. Rangan, *Transforming Your Go-To-Market Strategy*, Boston, MA: Harvard Business School Press, 2006 e1801.

2 Some observers believe that P&G acquired Gillette to improve its power position versus large supermarket chains.

3 An end-user customer is where the product loses its identity; both consumers and firms can be end-user customers. Consumer advertising may push end-user customers down the channel. Previously, end-user customers for microprocessors were PC manufacturers; *intel inside* turned consumers into end-user customers. Sometimes we use *end user* instead of *end-user customer*.

4 The broad view includes *concentration* and *dispersion*. Inputs are concentrated in Korea, and prefabricated steel beams are dispersed to Argentina. Relatedly, natural resources are randomly distributed — *meaningless heterogeneity*; customers require disparate resource bundles — *meaningful heterogeneity*. All distribution systems transform *meaningless heterogeneity* into *meaningful heterogeneity*. For example, a New York restaurant serves patrons a delicious salad of California lettuce, Mexican tomatoes, and Arizona carrots.

5 Many supply chains have global scope via technological advances in communications and transportation, and reduced trade barriers. Hides from Argentinean cows are tanned in China, sewn into flight jackets in Korea, then sold in Japan.

6 C.B. Bucklin, S.P. DeFalco, J.R. DeVincentis, and J.P. Levis III, "Are You Tough Enough to Manage Your Channels?," *The McKinsey Quarterly*, (1996), pp. 105–114 e1806.

7 *Distribution* encompasses all these functions — **logistics** is about getting the product from A to B.

8 When increasing numbers of consumers began shopping online, Sears dropped its catalog; D.V. Fites, "Make Your Dealers Your Partners," *Harvard Business Review*, 74 (March–April 1996), pp. 84–95 e1808.

9 *Going to Market*, 9-599-078, Harvard Business School.

10 Many *physical distribution* functions are irrelevant for services and information products.

11 Developing a product range to satisfy customers; especially important for wholesalers and retailers.

12 Aka outbound logistics. *Drop shipping* — manufacturer ships products direct to customers, often in retailer packaging — has grown along with direct marketing and Internet commerce. Products needing repair are returned via inbound (reverse) logistics. Annually, suppliers spend $40 billion handling over $60 billion returned goods; personal communication from John Beystehner, senior VP Worldwide Sales and Marketing, UPS.

13 Includes finishing, fitting, shaping, and sizing — also, paint-mixing and product assembly.

14 Includes data on financing, inventory, ownership changes, product availability, product location, and sales.

15 When purchases are difficult and complex, advisors, agents, and brokers often provide impartiality.

16 Channel members often shift risks relating to title transfer and financing via insurance, warranties, and guarantees.

17 Chapter 2 — customer relationship management.

18 Some direct sales approaches involve pyramid schemes. Salespeople earn commissions on their own sales; they also earn commissions on the sales of salespeople they recruit, sometimes *ad infinitum*. Handtech.com reps earn 10 percent commission on their sales, half the $145 fee of salespeople they recruit, and 2–5 percent of recruits' sales.

19 For factors driving direct marketing growth; pros and cons — Chapter 16.

20 D. Rigby, "The Future of Shopping," *Harvard Business Review*, 89 (December 2011), pp. 64–73 e1820.

21 *Christian Science Monitor, Kentucky Post, Seattle-Post Intelligencer.*

22 Most Internet action is from start-up firms and traditional retailers adding Internet capability; some successful Internet start-ups like T-shirt firm Threadless build on their brand equity to open retail stores.

23 Firms that sell products through multiple websites (third-party and their own) should take care to ensure consistency in product availability, model numbers, product reviews, and visuals.

24 Disputes between franchisees and the franchisor are not uncommon; they typically concern high fees and insufficient customer demand.

25 Franchising does not imply the presence of physical retail outlets.

26 Ford traditionally distributed products through franchised dealerships but purchased its Salt Lake City franchises. Ford superstores offer Ford, Lincoln, and Mazda brands.

27 Banco Popular is the largest U.S. Hispanic bank.

28 These customers account for 80 percent of Haiti's economy. Sogebank is Haiti's leading commercial bank.

29 Some department stores emphasize *store brands* — Kohl's (U.S.) and Marks & Spencer (Britain). *Showcase* stores focus on manufacturer brands — vendors are responsible for inventory, staff, and selling space.

30 J.A. Narus and J.C. Anderson, "Rethinking Distribution," *Harvard Business Review*, 74 (July–August 1996), pp. 112–120 e1830.

31 J.D. Hlavacek and T.J. McCuistion, "Industrial Distributors — When, Who and How?," *Harvard Business Review*, 61 (March–April 1983), pp. 96–101 e1831.

32 Narus and Anderson, *op. cit.* e1830

33 Ekornes also changed salesperson pay from commission to salary plus bonus — based on retailer-service; N. Kumar, "The Power of Trust in Manufacturer-Retailer Relationships," *Harvard Business Review*, 74 (November–December 1996), pp. 92–106 e1833.

34 P.F. Nunes and F.V. Cespedes, "The Customer Has Escaped," *Harvard Business Review*, 81 (November 2003), pp. 96–105 e1834. In response to *showrooming*, in 2012 Target stopped distributing Amazon's Kindle.

35 Among WD-40's more esoteric uses are: Freeing a person's tongue stuck to cold metal, cleaning ostrich eggs for craft uses, preventing squirrels from climbing into a birdhouse, and removing a python coiled around an Asian bus undercarriage.

36 Distributor agreements involve preferred credit terms, cash payments, and other benefits; sometimes distributors forgo exclusivity in favor of new opportunities.

37 Coke denied allegations of abusive practices.

38 From Pegram, *Selecting and Evaluating Distributors*, reproduced in B. Rosenbloom, *Marketing Channels: A Management View*, 7th ed., Tampa, FL, Internal Thomson, 2003 e1838.

39 L.W. Stern and F.D. Sturdivant, "Customer-Driven Distribution Systems," *Harvard Business Review*, 65 (July–August 1987), pp. 34–41 e1839a; V.K. Rangan, A.J. Menzes, and E. Maier, "Channel Selection for New Industrial Products: A Framework, Method and Application," *Journal of Marketing*, 56 (July 1992), pp. 69–82 e1839b; V.K. Rangan, *Designing Channels of Distribution*, Boston, MA: Harvard Business School, 1994, 9-594-116 e1839c; J.M. Hulbert, *Marketing: A Strategic*

Perspective, Katonah, NY: Impact Publishing, 1985; E. Anderson, G.S. Day, and V.K. Rangan, "Strategic Channel Design," *Sloan Management Review*, (Summer 1997), pp. 59–69 e1839d .

40 Factoring firms buy accounts receivable at a discount.

41 F.O.B. (free on board) — price at the factory/warehouse; C.I.F (carriage, insurance and freight) — price delivered to the customer.

42 Atlas Honda Ltd.: Communication Plan 1993; N. Capon and W. Van Honacker, *The Asian Marketing Casebook*, Singapore: Prentice Hall, 1998 e1842 . Anti-competitive practices, like Honda's, are illegal in many countries.

43 In the U.S., *functional-discount* structures must be objectively measurable to ensure they are fair and non-discriminatory. The Supreme Court condemned discounts that create exclusivity, or promote anti-competitive behavior. D. A. Balto "Networks and Exclusivity: Antitrust Analysis to Promote Network Competition," *George Mason Law Review*, 7 (Spring 1999), pp. 523–576 e1843 .

44 Also Rosenbloom, *op. cit.* e1838 and A. Coughlan, E. Anderson, L.W. Stern, and A. El-Ansary, *Marketing Channels*, 7th ed., Englewood Cliffs: Prentice Hall, 2006 e1844 .

45 Reproduced with permission from Rosenbloom, *op. cit.*, p. 439 e1838 .

46 Some suppliers require extensive information on each sale — by product item, customer, and delivery and billing location.

47 In *U-boat* diversion, the *diverter* loads merchandise purchased for export onto a cargo ship. The ship sails but returns to the same or neighboring port; the diverter resells products in the home (higher-price) market.

48 This section benefited from D. Ford, L.E. Gadde, H. Hakansson, A. Lundgren, I. Snehota, P. Turnbull, and D. Wilson, *Managing Business Relationships*, Chichester, UK: Wiley, 1988 e1848a . The seminal work on power identified five bases — coercive, reward, legitimate, referent, and expert; J.R.P. French and B. Raven, "The Bases of Social Power," in D. Cartwright and A. Zander, *Group Dynamics*. New York: Harper & Row, 1959 e1848b .

49 A.P. Chandler, Jr., *The Visible Hand: The Managerial Revolution in American Business*, Cambridge, MA: Harvard University Press, 1977 e1849 .

50 Amazon works with tens of thousands of commissioned affiliates who direct traffic to its website.

51 Of course, mutual fund suppliers no longer have direct contact with investors; A. J. Slywotzky and D. J. Morrison, *The Profit Zone*, New York: Times Business, 1997 e1851 .

52 A 2002 Financial Accounting Standards Board (FASB) rule required that manufacturers restate 2001 revenues by subtracting incentive payments from reported sales. This one-time event revealed these payments.

53 Shelf position is important for both bricks and mortar and virtual displays; A. Valenzuela and P. Raghubir, "Position-based Beliefs: The Center-Stage Effect," *Journal of Consumer Psychology*, 19 (2009), pp. 185–196 e1853 .

54 *Norton Company (A) and (B)*, 9-570-001/2, Harvard Business School.

55 In the 1990s, the U.S. had more than 15,000 car dealerships. Today, the top 250 firms sell over 50 percent of industry volume.

56 C.B. Bucklin, P.A. Thomas-Graham, and E.A. Webster, "Channel Conflict: When Is It Dangerous?," *The McKinsey Quarterly*, (1997), pp. 36–43 e1856 .

57 Bucklin, Thomas-Graham, and Webster, *op. cit.* e1856

58 Bucklin, Thomas-Graham, and Webster, *op. cit.* e1856

59 The *Merck Manual* comprises 3,000 pages on disorders and suggested therapies. Parker Hannifin's "O-Ring Handbook" e1859 helps design

engineers specify solutions for preventing oil/air system leakage, Hlavacek and McCuistion, *op. cit.* e1831

60 Suppliers learn about distribution challenges and opportunities — hence, the firm can better serve third-party distributors. This action also sends distributors a message about supplier options. Dealer concentration led Ford and GM to acquire equity positions in some automobile dealers. Power equipment manufacturer Cummins acquired many distributors. Global leader Claas sells combine harvesters to farmers through local distributors; in each major country, Claas owns at least one retail outlet to gain first-hand experience of farmer problems/needs. H. Simon, *Hidden Champions: Lessons from 500 of the World's Best Unknown Companies*, Boston, MA: Harvard Business School Press, 1996 e1860 .

61 Heinz (U.S.) placed food, pet food, and food service into a single unit — distribution improved and Heinz secured greater bargaining power with retail chains.

62 Armstrong World Industries offers educational benefits to distributors that place 100 percent of business with Armstrong.

63 For trust in partnership relationships: J.C. Anderson and J.A. Narus, "A Model of Distributor Firm and Manufacturing Firm Working Partnerships," *Journal of Marketing*, 54 (January 1990), pp. 42–58 e1863a ; and Kumar, *op. cit.* e1833 Also J. Lewis, *Trusted Partners: How Companies Build Mutual Trust and Win Together*, New York: Free Press, 1999 e1863b .

64 *Cross-docking* removes the need for regional warehouses.

65 G. Stalk, P. Evans, and L.E. Shulman, "Competing on Capabilities: The New Rules of Corporate Strategy," *Harvard Business Review*, 70 (March–April 1992), pp. 57–69 e1865 .

66 JCPenney previously held up to nine months' inventory. M.L. Fisher, A. Ramam, and A.S. McClelland, "Rocket Science Retailing Is Almost Here — Are You Ready?," *Harvard Business Review*, 78 (July–August 2000), pp. 115–124, for a thoughtful article on getting the *right product* in the *right place* at the *right time* at the *right price* e1866 . Based on research at Japan-based World Company and Spain-based Zara fashion retailers.

67 J.D. Sterman, "Modeling Managerial Behavior: Misperceptions of Feedback in a Dynamic Decision Making Experiment," *Management Science*, 35 (March 1989), pp. 321–339, addresses trade-offs in *beer-game* simulations e1867 .

68 M. Hammer and J. Champy, *Re-engineering the Corporation: A Manifesto for Business Revolution*, New York: Harper Business, 1994 e1868a . A narrow view of supply-chain management focuses on product flow. A broad view includes customer relationship management, customer service management, demand management, order fulfillment, manufacturing flow management, procurement, product development, commercialization, and returns, M.C. Cooper, D.M. Lambert, J.D. Pagh, "Supply Chain Management: More Than a New Name for Logistics," *The International Journal of Logistics Management*, 8 (1997), pp. 1–13 e1868b .

69 For a more in-depth presentation: Rosenbloom, *op. cit.* e1838 ; Coughlan, Anderson, Stern, and El-Ansary, *op. cit.* e1844

70 Similar bodies play these roles in other countries.

71 Some firms evade RPM restrictions by using exclusive territories.

CHAPTER 19

1 Personal communication from Lamar Muse. Also J.H. Gittell, *The Southwest Airlines Way*, New York: McGraw Hill, 2003 e1901 , and *Southwest Airlines (A)*, 9-575-060, Harvard Business School.

2 By 2011, Southwest Airlines operated 550 Boeing 737 jet aircraft serving 75 cities in 40 states, making more than 3,100 flights daily. SWA was the largest U.S. domestic airline. Annual revenues exceeded $12 billion and SWA had been consistently profitable for almost 40 years. In 2011, SWA acquired AirTran.

3 Good pricing texts include T.T. Nagle, J. Hogan, and J. Hale, *The Strategy and Tactics of Pricing: Growing More Profitably*, 5th ed. Upper Saddle River, NJ: Pearson Prentice Hall, 2010 `e1903a`; and R. Holden and M. Burton, *Pricing with Confidence: 10 Ways to Stop Leaving Money on the Table*, Hoboken, NJ: Wiley, 2008 `e1903b`. Important articles include P.E. Green and Y. Wind, "New Way to Measure Consumers' Judgments," *Harvard Business Review*, 53 (July–August 1975), pp. 107–118 `e1903c`; R.J. Dolan and A.P. Jeuland, "Experience Curves and Dynamic Demand Models: Implications for Optimal Pricing Strategies," *Journal of Marketing*, 45 (Winter 1981), pp. 52–73 `e1903d`. For classic pricing works, A.D.H. Kaplan, J.B. Dirlam, and R.F. Lanzillotti, *Pricing in Big Business*, Washington, DC: Brookings Institution, 1958 `e1903e`; and J. Dean, "Pricing Policies for New Products," *Harvard Business Review*, 28 (November–December 1950), pp. 28–36 `e1903f`.

4 Based on 2,463 companies in the Compustat database; M.V. Marn and R.L. Rosiello, "Managing Price, Gaining Profit," *Harvard Business Review*, 70 (September–October 1992), pp. 84–94 `e1904`. More recently, percentage reductions in operating profit from a 1 percent price decrease were: food and drug stores — 23.7 percent; airlines — 12.9 percent; computers and office equipment — 11 percent; tobacco — 4.9 percent; semiconductors — 3.9 percent; and diversified financial — 2.4 percent, *Fortune*, May 14, 2001. Fortier & Associates report similar findings for a 2 percent improvement: price — 20 percent; variable costs — 11 percent; volume — 9 percent; fixed costs — 7 percent.

5 Of course, we expect unit volume to change with price — the illustration just shows the magnitude of the effect.

6 *Principles of Pricing*, 9-506-021, Harvard Business School `e1906`.

7 Also B.T. Gale, "How Much Is Your Product *Really* Worth?," Boston: Customer Value Inc., 2002; and B.T. Gale, *Managing Customer Value*, New York: Free Press, 1994 `e1907`.

8 Aka *value in use* (VIU). Industry-specific terms include: *systems cost analysis* — defense; *outcomes research* — health care; *total distribution cost analysis* — logistics and transportation; and *total cost of ownership* — electronics.

9 J. Zale and W. Wise, "Pricing When Sales Slow," *The Professional Pricing Society Journal*, 10 (3rd Quarter 2001), pp. 1–9. Note that many aircraft components are now bonded rather than riveted — indirect competition!

10 J.C. Anderson and J.A. Narus, "Business Marketing: Understand What Customers Value," *Harvard Business Review*, 76 (November–December 1998), pp. 5–15 `e1910`.

11 Personal communication from Lance Batchelor, Head of Worldwide Marketing, Amazon.com.

12 Conjoint analysis is a powerful method for measuring the perceived value (*utility*) of various product attributes and the **disutility of price**. Marketing Enrichment `me601` shows a research design including product attributes and three price levels — current price, and 125 percent and 150 percent of current price.

13 P.C. Browne, N. Capon, T.S. Harris, H.N. Mantel, C.A. Newland, and A.H. Walsh, *The Ratemaking Process for the United States Postal Service*, New York: Institute of Public Administration, 1991. Also R. Cooper and R. Slagmulder, "Develop Profitable New Products with Target Costing," *Sloan Management Review*, 40 (Summer 1999), pp. 23–33 `e1913`.

14 A.O. Laffley and R. Charan, *Game-Changer*, New York: Crown Business, 2008, pp. 88–90 `e1914`.

15 **Positive sloping** demand curves are relatively rare — volume increases as price increases! They occur with luxury products like perfumes and fragrances. Price conveys information about product and/or service quality.

16 Before tackling this section, students should become familiar with Marketing Enrichment `me01`, Section 1.

17 E. Shim and E.F. Sudit, "How Manufacturers Price Products," *Management Accounting*, (February 1995), pp. 37–39 report that more than 80 percent of U.S. manufacturers use cost-plus pricing — 7 percent use *fully allocated costs* (Marketing Enrichment `me01`).

18 Cost-plus pricing can be useful when the firm must set prices for many products, like in supermarkets.

19 Advances in activity-based costing (ABC) provide firms with superior knowledge of cost dynamics.

20 The hurdle rate is the minimum return for a new investment. Typically hurdle rate is tied to the firm's cost of capital.

21 For example, if the firm adds fixed capacity or a new shift.

22 A price below $4 may be acceptable when demand is cyclical and stopping and starting production is very costly.

23 N. Capon, J.U. Farley, and J. Hulbert, "Pricing and Forecasting in an Oligopoly Firm," *Journal of Management Studies*, 12 (1975), pp. 133–156 `e1923`.

24 American Airlines attempted to simplify the complex pricing system by combining price increases and reductions; *American Airlines (A) and (B)*, 9-594-001 and 9-594-019, Harvard Business School `e1924`.

25 This section draws on A.K. Rao, M.E. Bergen, and S. Davis, "How to Fight a Price War," *Harvard Business Review*, 78 (March–April 2000), pp. 107–116 `e1925`.

26 Zale and Wise, *op. cit.* `e1909`

27 S. Jayachandran, J. Gimeno, and P.R. Varadarjan, "The Theory of Multimarket Competition: A Synthesis and Implications for Marketing Strategy, *Journal of Marketing*, 63 (July 1999), pp. 49–66 `e1927`.

28 H.J. Van Heerde, E. Gijsbrechts, and K. Pauwels, "Winners and Losers in a Major Price War," *Journal of Marketing*, 45 (October 2008), pp. 499–518, show how a retail market leader stopped market share losses and increased share price when forced to initiate a price war `e1928`.

29 M. Bertini and L. Wathieu, "How to Stop Customers from Fixating on Price," *Harvard Business Review*, 88 (May 2010), pp. 84–91 `e1929`.

30 Forty percent of consumer rebates are never redeemed, in part because some firms make redemption difficult.

31 *Polaroid, The First Thirty Years, 1948–1978: A Chronology of Polaroid Photographic Products*, Cambridge, MA: Polaroid Corporation, 1979, provides a classic description of sequential skimming `e1931`.

32 Steve Jobs apologized for such a swift price reduction; affected customers received $100 store credit.

33 For problems of inappropriate actions, *We've Got Rhythm! Medtronic Corporation's Cardiac Pacemaker Business*, 9-698-004, Harvard Business School.

CHAPTER 20

1 We omit time value of money issues to simplify the illustration.

2 Traditional income statements partitions are cost of goods sold (COGS) and all other costs — mostly marketing and SG&A. Table 19.12 gathers variable costs and fixed costs from these traditional categories:

- *Variable costs* — raw materials, direct labor, electricity (for production), freight, and sales commissions.
- *Fixed costs* — indirect labor, manufacturing overhead, and depreciation; also advertising, field sales (salary, expenses), and product and marketing management.

We assume variable costs per unit and fixed costs are constant over the volume range we consider.

3   T. Nagle, "How to Pull It Off," *Across The Board*, (March 1999), pp. 53–56.

4   Annual volume discounts based on matching/exceeding last year's volume may repel aggressive new competitors.

5   For more on these terms, see *http://www.investopedia.com/terms/f/fob.asp* e2005a and *http://www.investopedia.com/terms/c/cif.asp* e2005b.

6   *Norton Company*, 9-581-046, Harvard Business School.

7   M.V. Marn and R.L. Rosiello, "Managing Price, Gaining Profit," *Harvard Business Review*, 70 (September–October 1992), pp. 84–94 e2007.

8   More detailed analysis calculates the pocket margin for each account: hence, a *pocket-margin* distribution and *pocket-margin* waterfall; M. V. Marn, E.V. Roegner, and C.C. Zawada, "The Power of Pricing," *The McKinsey Quarterly*, (2003), pp. 1–8 e2008.

9   For real examples of a price band and price waterfalls, Marn, Roegner, and Zawada, *op. cit.* e2008.

10 Similar products sold to different customers at different prices may run afoul of anti-price discrimination legislation — like the U.S. Robinson-Patman Act.

11 18th-century economist quoted in R.B. Ekelund, "Price Discrimination and Product Differentiation in Economic Theory: An Early Analysis," *Quarterly Journal of Economics*, 84 (1970), pp. 268–278 e2011.

12 Examples include Singapore, Sweden (Trondheim, Bergen, Oslo), Netherlands (Amsterdam, Rotterdam, Utrecht, The Hague), and London.

13 When commodities represent a significant portion of product cost, the firm may link price to commodity price indices. Customers may secure price predictability by hedging the relevant commodity.

14 Some electric utilities are shifting to hourly pricing and installing smart meters so customers can monitor use and time-shift activities.

15 The profusion of price information on the Internet is encouraging consumers to haggle with retailers. National stores like Best Buy, The Home Depot, and Ralph Lauren allow salespeople to negotiate prices.

16 Bidders avoid the *winner's curse* of paying far too much.

17 S.D. Yap, "An Exploratory Study of the Introduction of Online Reverse Auctions," *Journal of Marketing*, 67 (July 2003), pp. 96–107 e2017.

18 G. McGovern and Y. Moon, "Companies and the Customers Who Hate Them," *Harvard Business Review*, 85 (June 2007), pp. 78–84 e2018.

19 E. Anderson and D. Simester, "Mind Your Pricing Cuts," *Harvard Business Review*, 81 (September 2003), pp. 97–103 e2019.

20 G.E. Smith and T.T. Nagle, "Frames of Reference and Buyers' Perception of Price and Value," *California Management Review*, 38 (1995), pp. 98–116 e2020.

21 "The Magic Touch," *Fortune*, September 6, 2004 e2021.

22 Some law firms are shifting from prices based on billable hours to flat payments plus success fees. In American Express' winning case against MasterCard and Visa, winning lawyer fees exceeded $150 million.

23 G. Antorcha and J. Schürmann, "Just-in-Tome Pricing," *The Boston Consulting Group*, 2010 e2023.

24 C. Anderson, *FREE*, New York: Hyperion, 2009 e2024a. K. Pauwels and A. Weiss, "Moving from Free to Fee: How Online Firms Market to Change Their Business Model Successfully," *Journal of Marketing*, 72 (May 2008), pp. 14–31, discuss the challenges of shifting from FREE to a non-zero price on the Internet e2024b.

25 Sometimes the subsidy implies a zero price — like network TV; other times the subsidy side pays something — like most newspapers.

26 Ways to respond to competition from FREE offerings include: Introduce a FREE basic product, gain widespread use, then: a. Charge for a premium version; b. Sell other products; c. Charge third parties for access to customers; and/or d: Offer a FREE product with a paid offering; D.J. Bryce, J.H. Dyer, and N.W. Hatch, "Competing against FREE," *Harvard Business Review*, 89 (June 2011), pp. 104–111 e2026.

27 **Black markets** occur when demand is greater than supply. Buyers resell products at higher prices. Tickets for popular concerts/sporting events are often *scalped* at prices higher than list. Producers of the hit Broadway show *The Producers* (top price $100) offered 50 seats per night at $480 per ticket.

28 Some jurisdictions prohibit imports of *gray market* products.

29 Der Wiener Deewan — Vienna; Just Around the Corner — London; Lentil As Anything — Melbourne; One World Café — Salt Lake City.

30 J-Y. Kim M. Natter, and M. Spann, "Pay What You Want: A New Participative Pricing Mechanism," *Journal of Marketing*, 73 (January 2009), pp. 44–58 e2030 and Y. Chen, O. Koenigsberg, and Z.J. Zhang, "Pay-as-You-Wish-Pricing," Working Paper, Columbia Business School, 2011.

31 Ryanair has fallen afoul of European Union regulators who view such arrangements as illegal subsidies. Small U.S. cities make guaranteed-revenue arrangements with airlines in exchange for air service.

32 The firm should set transfer prices at *arms' length* to avoid potential legal entanglements. In 2006, Britain's GSK settled a transfer-pricing case with the U.S. for $3.6 billion.

33 Personal communication to the author from Dick Melville, vice chairman of Alcoa's Aerospace Market Sector Lead Team.

34 J. Zale and W. Wise, "Pricing When Sales Slow," *The Professional Pricing Society Journal*, 10 (3rd Quarter 2001), pp. 1–9.

35 S. Dutta, M. Bergen, D. Levy, M. Ritson, and M. Zbaracki, "Pricing as a Strategic Capability," *Sloan Management Review*, 43 (Spring 2002), pp. 61–66 e2035a; and S. Dutta, M. Zbaracki, and M. Bergen, "Pricing Process as a Capability: A Resource-Based Perspective," *Strategic Management Journal*, 24 (2003), pp. 615–630 e2035b1, e2035b2. Also *Organizing for Pricing*, Perspectives, Boston Consulting Group, 2002 e2035c.

36 Dutta, Bergen, Levy, Ritson; and Zbaracki, *op. cit.* e2035a; Dutta, Zbaracki, and Bergen, *op. cit.* e2035b; and M. Tripsas and G. Gavetti, "Capabilities, Cognition, and Inertia: Evidence from Digital Imaging," *Strategic Management Journal*, 21 (2000), pp. 1147–1161 e2036.

37 J.R. Immelt interviewed by T.A. Stewart, "Growth as a Process," *Harvard Business Review*, 84 (June 2006), pp. 60–70, at pp. 64–65 e2037.

38 S. Duranton and J-M. Izaret, "Crisis Pricing for the Downturn and After," Boston: *The Boston Consulting Group*, 2009 e2038.

39 Traditionally, firm data on orders, promotions, revenues, and inventory levels were kept in separate locations. Some firms now collect these data in a single place and use complex algorithms to modify prices. The Internet allows instant price changes; without automation, the cost to change prices can be significant. And it can take months for price adjustments to filter down to distributors, retailers, and salespeople — hence, sub-optimal pricing. An Internet problem is pricing accuracy. An incorrect price can lead to high sales volume before a mistake is identified. For example, $588 Hitachi computer monitors listed at $164, a $299 MP3 player listed for $26.89, and United Airlines offered $27 U.S.-to-Paris flights!

40 For a fuller discussion and bibliography: G.W. Ortmeyer, "Ethical Issues in Pricing," in N.C. Smith and J.A. Quelch, *Ethics in Marketing*, New York: McGraw Hill, 1993, Chapter 5.1 e2040 . If unsure about pricing actions, consult a knowledgeable attorney.

41 K. Eichenwald, *The Informant*, New York: Broadway, 2000 e2041 .

42 Many jurisdictions have *leniency* policies. In the U.S. and Britain, the *whistle-blowing* firm receives immunity.

43 In the landmark *phases of the moon* case in steam turbine generators, Allis-Chalmers, GE, and Westinghouse were found guilty of price fixing. This case was significant because, for the first time, U.S. executives went to jail. R.G.M. Sultan, *Pricing in the Electrical Oligopoly, Vols. 1 and 2*, Cambridge, MA: Harvard University Press, 1974 e2043 .

44 Also R.J. Dolan, "How Do You Know When the Price Is Right?," *Harvard Business Review*, 74 (September–October 1995), pp. 4–11 e2044 .

45 To conclude this chapter, a pricing anecdote. When George Bernard Shaw first visited the U.S., several New York society women, knowing his reputation for wit, sought to outwit him. Said one, "Mr. Shaw, would you sleep with me for one million dollars?" Shaw responded, "How about ten dollars?" The woman was taken aback, "Mr. Shaw, what do you take me for? A whore?" Shaw replied, "Madam, we've already established what you are, we're just trying to figure out the price."

CHAPTER 21

1 J. M. Hulbert, N. Capon, and N. Piercy, *Total Integrated Marketing: Breaking the Bounds of the Function*, NY: Free Press, 2003 e2101 .

2 Ritz-Carlton's CEO even carried bags as a bellhop — a fellow employee admonished him for turning down a tip!

3 B.F. Shapiro, "Can Marketing and Manufacturing Coexist?," *Harvard Business Review*, 55 (September–October 1977), pp. 104–112 e2103 .

4 Personal communication from Richard L. Melville Jr., Vice Chairman Aerospace Market Sector Lead Team, Alcoa.

5 Apple considers its supply chain a critical success factor for the iPod, iPhone, and iPad.

6 New York City mayor Mike Bloomberg received this call regarding his new Lexus — he introduced the customer-calling system for Bloomberg terminals.

7 For important work on market orientation: B. J. Jaworski and A.J. Kohli, "Market Orientation: Antecedents and Consequences," *Journal of Marketing*, 57 (July 1993), pp. 53–70 e2107a ; S. F. Slater and J. C. Narver, "Market Orientation and the Learning Organization," *Journal of Marketing*, 59 (July 1995), pp. 63–74 e2107b , and other work by these authors.

8 Also G.S. Day, "The Capabilities of Market-Driven Organizations," *Journal of Marketing*, 58 (October 1994), pp. 37–52 e2108 .

9 C. Fuschs and M. Schrier, "Customer Empowerment in New Product Development," *Journal of Product Innovation Management*, 28 (2011), pp. 17–32 e2109 .

10 J. Claret, P. Mauger, and E.V. Roegner, "Profiting from Proliferation: Managing a Marketing and Sales Transformation," *The McKinsey Quarterly*, (2006), pp. 111–121 e2110 .

11 S.K. Lam, F. Krauss, and M. Ahearne, "The Diffusion of Market Orientation Throughout the Organization: A Social Learning Perspective," *Journal of Marketing*, 74 (September 2010), pp. 61–79 e2111 .

12 J. Garten, "Andy Grove Made the Elephant Dance," *BusinessWeek*, April 11, 2005, p. 26 e2112 .

13 J.P. Kotter, *Leading Change*, Boston: Harvard Business School Press, 1996, identifies eight principles of change management: Establish a sense of urgency, form a powerful guiding coalition, create a vision, communicate the vision, empower others to act on the vision, plan for and create short-term wins, consolidate improvements and produce still more change, and institutionalize new approaches e2113 .

14 "Less Than the Sum of its Parts," *The Economist*, June 23, 2001, pp. 73–74 e2114 .

15 R.R. Ellsworth, *Leading with Purpose*, Stanford, CA.: Stanford University Press, 2002, p.115 e2115 .

16 *www.amanet.org/research/pdfs/2002_corp_value.pdf*. Satisfying customers was essential in 77 percent of firms value statements e2116 .

17 From P&G's *Purpose*: "We will provide branded products and services of superior quality and value that improve the lives of the world's consumers, now and for generations to come. As a result, consumers will reward us with leadership sales, profit and value creation, allowing our people, our shareholders, and the communities in which we live and work to prosper" — and *Values*: integrity, leaderhsip, ownership, passion for winning, trust.

18 "Win Smith on the Exit of Merrill CEO Stan O'Neal," *BusinessWeek*, November 12, 2007, pp. 25–26 e2118 . Bank of America acquired Merrlll as losses increased, less than one year after O'Neal's 2009 ouster.

19 Personal communication from Michael Tangui, Senior Vice President of Marketing for the L'Oreal Paris brand in the U.S.

20 Senior employees affirm that J&J frequently resolves difficult management decisions by reference to the credo. Regardless, recent problems at J&J, including significant fines, suggest that continued vigilance is critical or values may take second place to business pressures.

21 C. Homburg and C. Pflesser, "A Multiple-Layer Model of Market-Oriented Organizational Culture: Measurement Issues and Performance Outcomes," *Journal of Marketing Research*, 37 (November 2000), pp. 449–462 e2121 .

22 P.F. Drucker, "The Coming of the New Organization," *Harvard Business Review*, 76 (January–February 1998), pp. 45–53 e2122a ; J.B. Quinn, *Intelligent Enterprise*, New York: Free Press, 1992 e2122b .

23 B. Costock, R. Gulati, and S. Liguori, "Unleashing the Power of Marketing," *Harvard Business Review*, 88 (October 2010), pp. 90–98 for developing the marketing function at GE. e2123 .

24 R.S. Achrol, "Evolution of the Marketing Organization," *Journal of Marketing*, 55 (October 1991), pp. 77–93 e2124a . J.P. Workman Jr., C. Homburg, and K. Gruner, "Marketing Organization: An Integrative Framework of Dimensions and Determinants," *Journal of Marketing*, 62 (July 1998), pp. 21–41 e2124b ; L.P. Katsanis, "Some Effects of Changes in Brand Management Systems: Issues and Implications," *International Marketing Review*, 16 (1999), pp. 518–532. C. Homburg. J.P. Workman Jr., and O. Jensen, "Fundamental Changes in Marketing Organization: The Movement Toward a Customer-Focused Structure, *Journal of the Academy of Marketing Science*, 28 (2000), pp. 459– 478 e2124c .

25 P&G is organized into business areas like Personal Beauty, House & Home, Health & Wellness, Baby & Family, and Pet Nutrition & Care. The brand management organization is essentially a *matrix*. Individuals charged with marketing activities, like salespeople, execute various brand manager plans, yet report to their sales organizations.

26 From *General Foods Corporation: The Product Management System*, 5-587-053, Harvard Business School. Also J.A. Quelch, P.W. Farris, and J.M. Olver, "The Product Management Audit: Design and Survey Findings," *Harvard Business Review*, 65 (March–April 1987), pp. 30, 32, 36; also *Journal of Consumer Marketing*, 4 (1987), pp. 45–58 e2126 .

27 Research shows that both retailers and category captains gain from this relationship, and that category captains do not discriminate against competitors; R.A. Gooner, N.A. Morgan, and W.D. Perreault, "Is Retail Category Managment Worth the Effort (and Does a Category Captain Help or Hinder)?" *Journal of Marketing*, 75 (September 2011), pp.18–33 e2127 .

28 When an individual product targets a single end-use market, product/brand and market segment managers overlap.

29 R.J. Keith, "The Marketing Revolution," *Journal of Marketing*, 24 (January 1960), pp. 35–38 e2129 .

30 M. Hammer and J. Champy, *Reengineering the Corporation: A Manifesto for Business Revolution*, New York: Nicholas Brealy, 1993 e2130 .

31 "Go-to-Market Advantage: The New Battlefield for Consumer Companies," *The Boston Consulting Group*, 2007 e2131a . J.M. Hulbert and L. Pitt, "Exit Left Center Stage? The Future of Functional Marketing," *European Management Journal*, 14 (1996), pp. 47–60 e2131b .

32 R.C. Blattberg and J. Deighton, "Interactive Marketing: Exploiting the Age of Addressability," *Sloan Management Review*, 33 (Fall 1991), pp. 5–14 e2132a ; D. Peppers and M. Rogers, *The One-to-One Future: Building Relationships One Customer at a Time*, New York: Century Doubleday, 1993 e2132b .

33 Like Tom Peters' suggestion to turn the organization on its head; T. Peters, *Thriving on Chaos*, New York: Bantam, 1987 e2133 .

34 This thinking has influenced terminology in Blattberg and Deighton, *op. cit.* e2132a and Peppers and Rogers, *op. cit.* e2132b Wachovia Bank (merger of First Union and Wachovia) has long managed retail customers like this. N. Capon, "Wachovia Bank and Trust Company," *The Marketing of Financial Services*, Englewood Cliffs, NJ: Prentice Hall, 1992 e2134 .

35 R.T. Rust, C. Moorman, and G. Bhalla, "Rethinking Marketing," *Harvard Business Review*, 88 (January–February 2010), pp. 94–101, notes that such diverse firms as Chrysler, Oracle, Samsung, Sears, United Airlines, and Wachovia have CCOs e2135 .

36 J.K. Johansson and I. Nonaka, "Market Research the Japanese Way," *Harvard Business Review*, 65 (May–June 1987), pp. 16–19 e2136a ; L.P. Carbone and S.H. Haeckel, "Engineering Customer Experience," *Marketing Management*, 3 (1994), pp. 8–1 e2136b 9; G.A. Churchill, R.H. Collins, and W.A. Strang, "Should Retail Salespersons Be Similar to Their Customers?," *Journal of Retailing*, 51 (Fall 1975), pp. 29–42 e2136c ; A.G. Woodside and W.J. Davenport, "The Effect of Salesman Similarity and Expertise on Consumer Purchasing Behavior," *Journal of Marketing*, 11 (May 1974), pp. 198–202 e2136d .

37 Peppers and Rogers, *op. cit.* e2132b For research on aligning the organization with the market, G.S. Day, "Aligning Organizational Structure to the Market," *Business Strategy Review*, 10 (1999), pp. 33–46, and G.S. Day, "Aligning the Organization with the Market," *MIT Sloan Management Review* (Fall 2006), pp. 41–49 e2137 . AMEX has separate marketing groups focused of different customer types: *acquisition* — secures new cardmembers; *early engagement* — focuses specifically on different aspects of new membership (activation; day 1 post activation to day 90; day 91 to day 180; day 180 to day 360); *loyalty* — increase spend and cardmember engagement; *retention* — monitor cardmembers close to attrition.

38 "A Great Leap, Preferably Forward," *The Economist*, January 20, 2001 e2138 .

39 M.W. Blenko, M.C. Mankins, and P. Rogers, "The Decision-Driven Organization," *Harvard Business Review*, 88 (June 2010), pp. 54–62 e2139 .

40 "Visionary-in-Chief," *BusinessWeek*, May 17, 1999 e2140 .

41 N. Capon, *Key Account Management and Planning*, New York: Free Press, 2001 e2141 .

42 N. Capon, D. Potter, and F. Schindler, *Managing Global Accounts*, (2nd ed.), Bronxville, NY: Wessex, 2008 e2142 .

43 A communications switch programmable by outsiders.

44 "The Genesis of a Giant's Stumble," *The New York Times*, January 21, 2001. In 2006, Lucent merged with Alcatel.

45 N. Capon, J.U. Farley, and J. Hulbert, *Corporate Strategic Planning*, New York: Columbia University Press, 1988 e2145 .

46 Shapiro, *op. cit.* e2103

47 J&J's *process excellence* approach rests on six principles — customer focus, fact-based management, alignment to strategy, process management across functions, continuous assessment and renewal, and innovative improvement. *Process excellence* rests on a set of structured methodologies and tools — lean thinking, six sigma (DMAIC), design excellence (DMADV), business assessment, dashboards (scorecards), and preferred (best) practices. J&J has trained process improvement professionals to coach or lead applications of these techniques. Note: Six sigma processes have less than 3.4 defects per million.

48 Personal communication from Howard Schultz.

49 A.O. Laffley and R. Charan, *Game-Changer*, New York: Crown Business, 2008, pp. 112–113 e2149 .

50 "I Think of My Failures as a Gift," Interview with A.G. Lafley, former P&G CEO, *Harvard Business Review*, 89 (April 2011), pp. 86–89 e2150a ; and R. G. McGrath, "Failing by Design," *Harvard Business Review*, 89 (April 2011), pp. 76–83 e2150b .

51 ExxonMobil has Centers of Excellence/Expertise (COE) responsible for sharing best practices around the world via meetings and an automated e-mail system. COE personnel are available to address specific problems.

52 R.C. Camp, *Benchmarking: The Search for Industry Best Practices that Lead to Superior Performance*, Milwaukee, WI: American Society for Quality, 1989 e2152 .

53 Hammer and Champy, *op. cit.* e2130 Business processes often cut across existing functional departments. Internal *political opposition* to change may be widespread, contributing to the failure of many well-intended re-engineering projects.

54 F. Cassidy, A. Freeling, and D. Kiewell, "Credibility Gap for Marketers, *The McKinsey Quarterly*, 2005, no. 2 e2154 .

55 Executive-search firm Spencer Stuart reports average tenure for CMOs as less than two years.

56 B. Comstock, R. Gualati, and S. Liguori, "Unleashing the Power of Marketing," *Harvard Business Review*, 88 (October 2010), pp. 1800–1808 e2156 .

57 Personal communication from Pat Kelly, Senior Vice President, Worldwide Marketing, Pfizer Pharmaceuticals.

58 T.R. Knudsen, "Confronting Proliferation ... in Beer. An Interview with Carlsberg's Alex Myers," *The McKinsey Quarterly*, (May 2007) e2158 .

59 R.W. Revans, *Developing Effective Managers: A New Approach to Business Education*, New York: Praeger, 1971 e2159a . L. Fortini-Campbell, *Hitting the Sweet Spot*, Chicago: The Copy Workshop, 1992 e2159b ; and F.J. Gouillart and F.D. Sturdivant, "A Day in the Life of Your Customers," *Harvard Business Review*, 72 (January–February 1994), pp. 116–125 e2159c .

60 S. Perman, *In-N-Out Burger*, San Francisco: Collins, 2009 e2160 .

61 J.A. Byrne, *Chainsaw: The Notorious Career of Al Dunlap in the Era of Profit-at-Any Price*, New York: HarperBusiness, 1999 e2161 .

62 Weber's original bureaucracy concept was much more positive. M. C. Weber, C. Wright Mills (ed.), and H. H. Gerth (ed.), from *M. Weber: Essays in Sociology*, Oxford, UK: Oxford University Press, 1958 e2162 .

63 Additional organizational dimensions requiring decisions are: *Formalization* — the extent to which the firm enacts formal rules and procedures for decisions and working relationships, and *specialization* — the degree to which the firm divides up tasks and activities.

64 R. Gulati, "Silo Busting: How to Execute on the Promise of Customer Focus," *Harvard Business Review*, 85 (May 2007), pp. 98–108 e2164 .

65 "From Scandal to Stardom: How Merck Healed Itself," *Fortune*, February 18, 2008, p. 96 e2165 .

CHAPTER 22

1 Personal communication from Ron Boire.

2 The Marketing Science Institute (MSI) is a research-based, industry/academic collaboration headquartered in Cambridge, MA.

3 The reward system should reinforce appropriate behavior if performance meets or exceeds standards; it should change behavior if performance fails to reach standards. Former Columbia professor J.O. Whitney identifies several inappropriate behaviors leading to poor performance: vacillation, paralysis, bravado, intransigence, impatience, hand-wringing, breast-beating, rage, withdrawal, and flight!

4 Note the use of *performance* in this chapter. Suppose the performance measure is sales dollars; actual sales were $12 million versus a standard of $10 million. Performance refers to the variance between actual sales and the standard, in this case a positive $2 million (12–10). Performance does *not* refer to the actual sales, $12 million.

5 Personal communication from Pat Kelly, Senior Vice President, Worldwide Marketing, Pfizer Pharmaceuticals.

6 Control limits ensure that random fluctuations do not cause firms to act too hastily.

7 Personal communication from Lance Batchelor, Head of Worldwide Marketing, Amazon. Amazon feeds sales data directly to its supply chain. Suppliers dispatch products within hours.

8 A side benefit is happier, more motivated salespeople. Previously, salespeople complained about the time to fill out expense reports and the long wait for reimbursement. Cisco now calculates and pays sales commissions in real time, as orders arrive.

9 Personal communication from Steve Larned, VP of Marketing, Dell Americas.

10 A non-trivial issue is standardization of terms across business units and across the firm. Profit numbers can vary widely depending on when the firm recognizes revenues and how it allocates costs. For effective analysis, the firm should compare *apples with apples*.

11 For a comprehensive set of performance measures: P.W. Faris, N.T. Bendle, P.E. Pfeifer, and D.J. Reibstein, *Marketing Metrics: 50+ Metrics Every Executive Should Master*, Upper Saddle River, NJ: Pearson, 2006 e2211 .

12 Said Dick Melville, Vice Chairman Alcoa's Aerospace Market Sector Lead Team, "If you want to push a button and say, 'What does the entire Alcoa profit look like on a Canadaire CRJ-70?' or 'What is the profitability of all of our castings in the new Pratt & Whitney jet engine?' we can tell you." Personal communication.

13 Sometimes it may be valuable to measure the results of actions the firm did not take! ... like an investment bank that measures the outcomes of deals it turned down and counts as successes those that failed.

14 D. Bowman and H. Gatignon, "Market Response and Marketing Mix Models: Trends and Research Opportunities," *Foundations and Trends in Marketing*, 4 (2009), pp. 129–207 e2214 .

15 P. Lapoint, *Marketing by The Dashboard Light*, New York: Association of National Advertisers, 2005 e22151 , e22152 .

16 W. Edwards Deming is widely credited as the founder of the Quality movement. The famous Japanese quality prize is named after Deming. An anecdote: In the early 1990s, the author attended a small meeting of Columbia faculty with then 90-year-old Deming. During the conversation, some of us were surprised to hear Deming say, "... when I turned around Japan. ..." Then we thought about it. He actually did! The following system elaborates the Deming Cycle:

   Plan. Design/revise business process components to improve results.
   Do. Implement the plan and measure performance.
   Check. Assess measurements; report results to decision makers.
   Act. Decide on changes needed to improve the process.

17 R. Simons, *Levers of Control*, Boston, MA: Harvard Business School Press, 1994 e2217 .

18 Note that this framework is equally effective for overall performance, and for sub-elements like advertising, innovation, and sales force.

19 Marketers have typically lacked the political power or technical ability to question traditional performance measures like sales and profits. Fortunately, leading thinkers in accounting and finance are increasingly moving toward more appropriate measures that look outward and forward rather than inward and backward. Activity-based costing is making a significant dent in traditional costing approaches. Kaplan has called for measures that include stock market, operations, and customer data. R.S. Kaplan and D.P. Norton, "Putting the Balanced Scorecard to Work," *Harvard Business Review*, 71 (September–October 1993), pp. 134–142 e2219 . Some firms set social and/or environmental measures — GE requires business units to cut carbon dioxide (CO_2) emissions, each with different targets.

20 Attempting to focus employee attention on innovation, some firms adopt related business-unit measures. These measures often focus on percentage of operating period sales revenues derived from products not in the product line several years previously, along with customer retention and its opposite — customer churn.

21 M. Treacy and J. Sims, "Take Command of Your Growth," *Harvard Business Review*, 82 (April 2004), pp. 127–133 e2221 .

22 Illustrative supplier payments/profit margins as a percentage of sales are: Albertsons — 6.2 percent/5.0 percent, Kroger — 5.3 percent/5.2 percent, and Safeway — 6.5 percent/5.2 percent, "Accounting Games in the Grocer's Aisle," *BusinessWeek*, April 14, 2003 e2222 .

23 After subtracting indirect fixed costs from direct product profit, the residual is bottom-line profit.

24 Return on equity (ROE) derives from ROI by focusing on the equity portion of the firm's capital structure. In good times, the firm can increase ROE by increasing debt and decreasing equity, but in bad times profits may be insufficient to make interest payments on debt. Bankruptcy may ensue, as with Lehman Brothers.

25 Some firms assess various marketing programs via return on marketing investment (ROMI) — incremental revenue (profit) generated by the program divided by the program's cost. For a critique of these and other return measures: T. Ambler and J. Roberts, "Assessing Marketing Performance: Don't Settle for a Silver Metric," *Journal of Marketing Management*, 24 (2008), pp. 733–750 e2225 .

26 Activity-based costing (ABC) — Marketing Enrichment me01 is very helpful in making the conversion.

27 To measure and reward senior managers, P&G uses operating TSR (total shareholder return) comprising sales growth, profit margin growth, and increased capital efficiency. P&G believes improved operating TSR leads to increased stock price.

28 Later, when Welch became concerned about growth, he told business leaders they had *low market share*. Hence, a business leader's job was to identify growth opportunities — Chapter 3, p. 61.

29 E.W. Anderson, C.G. Fornell, and D.R. Lehmann, "Customer Satisfaction, Market Share, and Profitability," *Journal of Marketing*, 58 (July 1994), pp. 53–66 `e2229`. Brand health checks (Chapter 11) fall into this category.

30 Personal communication.

31 Previously, Microsoft based stock-bonus awards on meeting sales and profit targets.

32 J.R. Immelt interviewed by T.A. Stewart, "Growth as a Process," *Harvard Business Review*, 84 (June 2006), pp. 60–70 `e2232`.

33 Research on 400 companies in 28 industries showed a median Net Promoter Score of 16 percent. Leading companies like Amazon, eBay, and USAA scored from 75 percent to 80 percent; F.F. Reichheld, "The One Number You Need to Grow," *Harvard Business Review*, 81 (December 2003), pp. 46–54 `e2233a`. Although it is widely used, writers have criticized the simplicity of Net Promoter Score and whether a single *recommendation* measure can fully predict loyalty behavior; N.A. Morgan and L.L. Rego, "The Value of Different Customer Satisfaction and Loyalty Metrics in Predicting Business Performance," *Marketing Science*, 25 (September–October 2006), pp. 426–439 `e2233b`; T.L. Keiningham, B. Cooil, T.W. Andreassen, and L. Askoy, "A Longitudinal Examination of Net Promoter and Firm Revenue Growth," *Journal of Marketing*, 71 (July 2007), pp. 39–51 `e2233c`.

34 *www.burke.com/Services* `e2234`

35 As digital media has increased in importance, many web-based intermediate measures have been developed, like *hits*, *page views*, and *unique visitors*.

36 Personal communication from Hal Cramer, President Fuels Marketing, ExxonMobil.

37 T.V. Bonoma, "Making Your Strategy Work," *Harvard Business Review*, 62 (March–April 1984), pp. 68–78 `e2237`.

38 T.V. Bonoma, "Market Success Can Breed 'Marketing Inertia'," *Harvard Business Review*, 59 (September–October 1981), pp. 115–121.

39 Former Columbia Business School professor Abe Shuchman, mentor to the author, was one of the first writers on the marketing audit. A. Shuchman, "The Marketing Audit: Its Nature, Purposes and Problems," Management Report No. 32, *Analyzing and Improving Marketing Performance*, New York: American Management Association, 1959.

40 W.H. Rodgers, G.A. Osborne, and P. Kotler, "Auditing the Marketing Function," in N. Capon, (Ed.), Section 7, *Marketing*, in AMA Management Handbook (3rd ed.), J. Hampton, (Ed.), AMACOM, 1994 `e2240a`. This section is heavily based on this material. Also P. Kotler, W.T. Gregor, and W.H. Rodgers III, "The Marketing Audit Comes of Age," *Sloan Management Review*, 30 (Winter 1989), pp. 49–62 `e2240b`.

41 Rodgers, Osborne, and Kotler, *op. cit.* `e2240a`

42 For detailed discussion of functional integration to serve customers, J. Hulbert, N. Capon, and N. Piercy, *Total Integrated Marketing*, New York: Free Press, 2003 `e2242`.

43 Other performance measurement problems include only comparing against internal referents like prior years' performance. A. Likierman, "The Five Traps of Performance Measurement," *Harvard Business Review*, 87 (October 2009), pp. 96–101 `e2243`.

44 Kaplan and Norton, *op. cit.* `e2219` For a more thorough and recent treatment: R.S. Kaplan and D.P. Norton, *Strategy Maps: Converting Intangible Assets into Tangible Outcomes*, Boston, MA: Harvard Business School Press, 2004 `e2244`.

45 Reproduced with permission from *Mobil USM&R (D): Gasoline Marketing*, N9-196-151, Harvard Business School; Anderson, Fornel, and Lehmann, *op. cit.* `e2229` Brand health checks (Chapter 11) fall into this category.

CHAPTER 23

1 For DHL's founding and biography of the *H* (Larry Lee Hillblom): J.D. Scurlock, *King Larry: The Life and Ruins of a Billionaire Genius*, New York: Simon & Schuster, 2012 `e2301`.

2 Source: World Trade Organization: International Trade Statistics 2007, `e2302`.

3 David Neeleman, jetBlue founder and former CEO, raised a record $235 million to inaugurate Azul.

4 For a thoughtful analysis of globalization: T.L. Friedman, *The World Is Flat: A Brief History of the Twenty-First Century* (*expanded edition*), New York: Farrar, Strauss & Giroux, 2006 `e2304`.

5 W.J. Henisz and B.A. Zelner, "The Hidden Risks in Emerging Markets," *Harvard Business Review*, 88 (April 2010), pp. 2–8 `e2305`.

6 GDP per capita source: Wikipedia, from The World Bank `e2306`.

7 PPP accounts for currency weakness in world markets. For example, India ranks 12th by nominal GDP but 4th by PPP, *Wikipedia*.

8 Annual remittances globally are about $300 billion. Leading recipients: India — $45 billion; China — $34 billion; Mexico — $26 billion; the Philippines — $18 billion; and Poland — $12 billion. Source: The World Bank.

9 Estimates of percent GDP range from U.S. — 9 percent to Bolivia and Georgia — 70 percent

10 Goldman Sachs originally coined the term *BRIC*; it also identified the *Next 11 (N11)* — Bangladesh, Egypt, Indonesia, Iran, Korea, Mexico, Nigeria, Pakistan, Philippines, Turkey, and Vietnam, poised to rival the G7 — Canada, France, Germany, Great Britain, Italy, Japan, United Kingdom, and United States (adding Russia formed the G8), in economic influence in the 21st century. In 2010, Indonesia received a *promotion: BRIC* became *BRICI*.

11 The Boston Consulting Group, "Decoding the Next Billion Consumers," Boston, MA: The Boston Consulting Group, 2007 `e2311`.

12 Additionally, leaders of the world's wealthiest countries meet annually to discuss global economic issues. The G8 comprises the following countries:

	Population (millions)	GDP per capita (US $billions)
Canada	32	29.3
France	60	26.0
Germany	82	26.2
Great Britain	60	25.5
Italy	58	25.1
Japan	127	28.7
Russia	145	9.7
U.S.	290	36.3

A.K. Vaidya, Ed., *Globalization: Encyclopedia of Trade, Labor, and Politics*, 2006, p. 600 `e2312`. The G20 is an outgrowth of the G8 and comprises 19 nations plus the EU — 85 percent of global GDP, 80 percent of global trade, and two thirds world population. Member countries are Argentina, Australia, Brazil, Canada, China, France, Germany, Great Britain, India, Indonesia, Italy, Japan, Mexico, Russia, Saudi Arabia, South Africa, Korea, Turkey, and the U.S.

13 GDPs of these regional groups are roughly: EU — $16 trillion; NAFTA — $17 trillion; Mercosur — $3 trillion; ASEAN — $1 trillion.

14 Some economists argue that growth in bilateral arrangements hinders prospects for global agreements.

15 Venezuela has applied for full membership; Bolivia, Chile, Columbia, Ecuador, and Peru are associate members

16 Associate members: Anguilla, Bermuda, British Virgin Islands, Cayman Islands, Turks and Caicos Islands.

17 The Bahamas is a member of the Community but not of the Common Market.

18 Formerly members of the European Free Trade Area; Switzerland declined to join.

19 G. Hofstede, *Culture's Consequences: Comparing Values, Behaviors, Institutions and Organizations Across Nations* (2nd ed.), Thousand Oaks, CA.: Sage, 2001 e2319a. An alternative framework embraces seven dimensions: *Universalism* versus *particularism, collectivism* versus *individualism, affective* versus *neutral* relationships, *specificity* versus *diffuseness, achievement* versus *ascription, orientation toward time,* and *internal* versus *external control;* F. Trompenaars, "Resolving International Conflict," *Business Strategy Review,* 7 (1996), pp. 51–68 e2319b.

20 Of course, many countries also harbor subcultures; in China, vast cultural differences exist between coastal and inland cities, and between urban and rural populations.

21 Chinese confuse General Electric (GE) with General Motors (GM). *General* translates to *Tongyong.* That's the name for both firms in China!

22 Adapted from the CAGE framework in P. Ghemawat, *Redefining Global Strategy: Crossing Borders in a World Where Differences Still Matter,* Boston, MA: Harvard Business School Press, 2007 e2322.

23 M.F. Guillén and E. Garcia-Canal, "How to Conquer New Markets with Old Skills," *Harvard Business Review,* 88 (November 2010), pp. 118–112 e2323. ALSA expanded into Europe in the 1960s; today, an ALSA subsidiary helps multinationals operate in China.

24 A.K. Bhattacharya and D.C. Michael, "How Local Companies Keep Multinationals at Bay," *Harvard Business Review,* 86 (March 2008), pp. 85–95 e2324.

25 Some agent organizations, like Japanese trading houses, are huge and represent many producers.

26 The firm exports, customers import. Because increasing numbers of firms are outsourcing production activities abroad, we believe it makes more sense to focus the discussion on imports by customers rather than on exports by the firm.

27 A typical government concern is to preserve competition. Sometimes governments allow acquisitions to proceed only if the acquiring firm divests one or more competitive business units.

28 R. Vernon, "International Investment and International Trade in the Product Life Cycle," *Quarterly Journal of Economics,* 80 (May 1966), pp. 190–207 e2328a; and I.T. Wells, "A Product Life Cycle for International Trade," *Journal of Marketing,* 5 (July 1968), pp. 1–6 e2328b.

29 I. Ayal, "International Product Life Cycle: A Reassessment and Product Policy Implications," *Journal of Marketing,* 45 (Fall 1981), pp. 91–96 e2329.

30 D.J. Isenberg, "The Global Entrepreneur," *Harvard Business Review,* 86 (December 2008), pp. 107–111 e2330.

31 J.R Immelt, V. Govindarajan, and C. Trimble, "How GE Is Disrupting Itself," *Harvard Business Review,* 87 (October 2009), pp. 56–65 e2331.

32 N.T. Washburn and B.T. Hunsaker, "Finding Great Ideas in Emerging Markets," *Harvard Business Review,* 89 (September 2011), pp. 115–120 e2332.

33 Bhattacharya and Michael, *op cit.* e2324 Also The Boston Consulting Group's biennial publication on the 100 New Global Challengers.

34 For Haier's approach to foreign markets: Y. Wu., "China's Refrigerator Magnate," *The McKinsey Quarterly,* 3 (2003) pp. 107–115 e2334a; and H. Liu and K. Li, "Strategic Implications of Emerging Chinese Multinationals: The Haier Case Study," *European Management Journal,* 20 (December 2002), pp. 699–706 e2334b.

35 Some observers believe that competition from emerging-market multinationals will increase: The markets for managerial talent and capital are increasingly liquid; emerging markets are very large; ever-stronger domestic firms are developing international and global ambitions; and Western firms are dispersing R&D to these countries. *The Economist,* Special Report on Innovation in Emerging Markets, April 2010 e2335.

36 Ghemawat's AAA Triangle framework embraces *Adaptation* — focus on local customer needs, *Arbitrage* — focus on global economies, and *Aggregation* — achieving scale and scope economies via international standardization: P. Ghemawat, "Managing Differences: The Central Challenge of Global Strategy," *Harvard Business Review,* 85 (March 2007), pp. 58–68 e2336.

37 Several European countries like Iceland, Lichtenstein, Norway, and Switzerland are not members of the EU.

38 Studies of country clusters are limited by the number included and their variation across studies; many parts of the world seem to be ignored, especially Africa. Table 23.4 is based on eight studies, mostly completed in the 1970s: S. Ronen and O. Shenker, "Clustering Countries on Attitudinal Dimensions," *The Academy of Management Review,* 10 (July 1985), pp. 435–454 e2338.

39 For organizational purposes, many multinationals group Europe, the Mid-East, and Africa as the EMEA region.

40 Source: The World Bank.

41 Young & Rubican (Y&R) developed a western-European based 4Cs (Cross Cultural Consumer Characterization) lifestyle segmentation from several basic values — survival, escape, security, status, control, discovery, and enlightenment. Y&R labeled its segments Resigned, Struggler, Mainstream, Aspirer, Succeeder, Explorer, and Reformer.

42 M. Schultz and M.J. Hatch, "The Cycles of Corporate Branding: The Case of the LEGO Company," *California Management Review,* 46 (Fall 2003), pp. 6–26 e2342.

43 Based on an online bulletin from EffectiveBrands.

44 D.A. Aaker and E. Joachimsthaler, "The Lure of Global Branding," *Harvard Business Review,* 77 (November–December 1999), pp. 137–144.

45 B. Becht, "Building a Company without Borders," *Harvard Business Review,* 88 (April 2010), pp. 103–106 e2345.

46 A.J. Parsons, "Nestlé: The Visions of Local Managers," *The McKinsey Quarterly,* (1966-2), pp. 5–29 e2346.

47 P. Kotler and D. Gertner, "Country as Brand, Product, and Beyond: A Place Marketing and Brand Marketing Perspective," *Brand Management,* 9 (April 2002), pp. 249–261 e2347a; and N. Papadopoulos and L. Heslop, "Country Equity and Country Branding: Problems and Opportunities," *Brand Management,* 9 (April 2002), pp. 294–314 e2347b.

48 P.W.J. Verlegh and J.-B. E.M. Steenkamp, "A Review and Meta-Analysis of Country of Origin Research," *Journal of Economic Psychology,* 20 (1999), pp. 521–546 e2348.

49　Likely driven by ethnocentrism: T.A. Shimp and S. Sharma, "Consumer Ethnocentrism: Construction and Validation of the CETSCALE," *Journal of Marketing Research*, 24 (August 1987), pp. 220–289 `e2349`.

50　J.G. Klein, R. Ettenson, and M.D. Morris, "The Animosity Model of Foreign Product Purchase: An Empirical Test in the People's Republic of China," *Journal of Marketing*, 62 (January 1998), pp. 89–100 `e2350`.

51　Z. Gürhan-Canli and D. Maheswaran, "Cultural Variations in Country of Origin Effects," *Journal of Marketing Research*, 37 (August 2000), pp. 309–317 `e2351`.

52　I. Clarke III, M. Owens, and J.B. Ford, "Integrating Country of Origin into Global Marketing Strategy: A Review of U.S. Marketing Statutes," *International Marketing Review*, 17 (2000), pp. 114–126 `e2352`.

53　The firm may be able to fix its selling price by hedging foreign currencies and other financing mechanisms.

54　Contract terms are an important issue: FOB (free on board) — customer responsible for shipping; CIF (carriage, insurance, freight) — supplier responsible for shipping.

55　N. Capon, J.U. Farley, and J. Hulbert, *Corporate Strategic Planning*, New York: Columbia University Press, 1988, for empirical data concerning organization structure for international business `e2355`.

56　G. Ghislanzoni, R. Penttinen, and D. Turnbull, "The Multi-local Challenge: Managing Cross-Border Functions," *The McKinsey Quarterly*, 2008 `e2356`.

57　A geographic-region arrangement within the international division may precede birth of the full-scale geographic region structure.

58　S. Douglas and Y. Wind, "The Myth of Globalization," *Columbia Journal of World Business*, (Winter 1987), pp. 19–29.

59　Personal communication from Stewart McHie, Global Brand Manger, ExxonMobil Fuel Marketing Company.

60　T. Levitt, "The Globalization of Markets," *Harvard Business Review*, 61 (May–June 1983), pp. 92–102 `e2360a`. J.A. Quelch and E.J. Hoff, "Customizing Global Marketing," *Harvard Business Review*, 64 (May–June 1986), pp. 59–68 provides a more integrative view `e2360b`.

61　Personal communication from Carol Hamilton, President, L'Oreal Paris USA.

62　Some corporations base one branch of their matrix organizations on a functional structure.

63　N. Capon, D. Potter, and F. Schindler, *Managing Global Accounts* (2nd ed.), Bronxville, NY: Wessex, 2008 `e2363a`; and N. Capon and C. Senn, "Global Customer Management Programs: How to Make Them Really Work," *California Management Review*, 52 (Winter 2010), pp. 32–55 `e2363b`. For alternative approaches: P. Cheverton, *Global Account Management: A Complete Action Kit of Tools and Techniques for Managing Key Global Customers*, London: Kogan Page, 2008 `e2363c`; and G. Yip and A.J.M. Brink, *Managing Global Customers*, Oxford: Oxford University Press, 2007 `e2363d`.

64　This organization is matrixed with a brand management organization focused on IBM products.

GLOSSARY

80:20 rule. 80 percent of a firm's revenues come from 20 percent of its customers. An extension is the **80:20:120 rule** — these 20 percent of customers earn the firm 120 percent of its profits.

20:80 rule. This rule follows directly from the 80:20 rule: 20 percent of a firm's revenues come from 80 percent of its customers. An extension is the **20:80:20 rule** — these 80 percent of customers are responsible for reducing the firm's profits by 20 percent.

ACCORD. An acronym for factors that affect the speed of new product adoption: **A**dvantage, **C**ompatibility, **C**omplexity, **O**bservability, **R**isk, and **D**ivisibility.

Acquisition. A firm purchases another firm or business.

Acquisition cost (AC). The cost of attracting a new customer to the firm.

Action-learning. An approach to organizational development that focuses on learning by doing.

Activity-based costing (ABC). A costing system based on identifying the causes of cost behavior and associating each cost with its cause.

Adoption categories. Describe consumer behavior in adopting innovations — innovators, early adopters, early majority, late majority, and laggards.

Adoption curve. The sales trajectory for a new product or product form.

Advertising. Paid communications directed at a mass audience.

Advertising agency. A third-party organization to which many firms outsource the development and execution of their advertising.

Advertising budget. The monetary amount to be spent on advertising. Approaches to budget setting are:
    Objective and task. A *bottom-up* approach focusing on advertising objectives and the tasks to be accomplished.
    Percentage of sales. A rule-of-thumb approach that sets the budget as a percentage of sales: current sales, anticipated next-year sales, or some combination.
    Competitive parity. An approach that bases the budget on competitors' spending.

Advertising effectiveness measures. Used to test advertising effectiveness. Options include:
    Recognition. Advertising that respondents recognize.
    Aided recall. Advertising that respondents remember with prompting.
    Unaided recall. Advertising that respondents remember without prompting.

Advertising objectives. What the firm is trying to achieve with its advertising:
    Output objectives. What the firm ultimately wants to achieve, like sales, repeat purchase, market share, and brand loyalty.
    Intermediate objectives relate to the hierarchy-of-effects models and include awareness, knowledge, liking or preference, trial, and emotional commitment (to a brand).

Advertising response function (ARF). Relates advertising spending to an objective like sales.

Advertising strategy. Specifies how the firm will spend resources to achieve advertising objectives and includes decisions about target audience, advertising objectives, messaging, execution, media selections and timing, advertising budget, and program evaluation.

Alliances. Formal economic relationships between the firm and other entities (partners) — suppliers, customers, and distributors.

Alpha test. A new product test within the firm by company employees.

Angel investors. Wealthy individuals who provide funding for new business ventures at a very early stage. Angel investors typically invest before venture capitalists.

Antitrust. U.S. laws that prohibit actions to reduce competition.

ASSESSOR. A new-product-forecasting model based on trial and repeat.

Auction pricing. A product's price resulting from competition among potential buyers:
    English auction. Prices start low and potential buyers bid up the price.
    Vickrey auction. A form of **sealed-bid** English auction where the winning bidder pays the price of the second-highest bid.
    Dutch auction. Prices start high; the seller reduces price until a buyer bids.
    Reverse auction. The buyer states product requirements; suppliers bid to provide the product, and prices go down.

B2B — Business-to-business. This acronym generally describes marketing where customers are other organizations — business, public, and not-for-profit.

B2C — Business-to-consumer. This acronym generally describes marketing where customers are consumers.

Backward integration. A customer undertakes activities currently performed by its suppliers.

Bait and switch. Retailers advertise a low price for a product with limited availability. The *bait* sells quickly. Retailers offer most customers a higher-priced product — the *switch*.

Balanced scorecard. A performance measurement system that balances input, intermediary, and output variables.

BASES. A new-product-forecasting model that uses an historical database to improve forecast accuracy.

BDI. See brand development index.

Behavioral targeting. An Internet-based technique that uses information collected from a users online activity to present (on a website visit) or send by e-mail specific messages to motivate purchase or other goals.

Benchmarking. The practice of securing best practices from outside the firm at other organizations.

Benefits and values, categories of:
    Functional. Follow from the product's design.
    Psychological. Satisfy customer needs like status, affiliation, reassurance, risk, and security.
    Economic. Result from financial considerations of purchasing a product or service.
    Search. Customers can gain good information before they purchase.
    Use. Customers do not know the value at the time of purchase.
    Credence. Customers do not know the value until long after the purchase.

Best practice transfer. An approach to identifying and transmitting superior processes across the firm.

Beta test. A new product test by cooperating customers.

Blog. An Internet vehicle for individuals to offer opinions and receive feedback from others.

Brand. The traditional definition is: *a name, term, sign, symbol, or design (or letter, number, or character), or a combination of them intended to identify the goods and services of one seller or group of sellers and to differentiate them from competition.* A more customer-focused definition is: *a collection of perceptions and associations that customers hold about a product, a service, or a company. This collection embodies values that create meaning for customers that represent a promise of the experience customers expect when they have contact with the brand.*

Brand architecture. The organizing structure for the firm's brand portfolio.

Brand associations. The meanings the brand has for customers.

Brand attachment. The strength of the bond connecting the brand with the self (cognitive and emotional) including positive feelings and memories (related to brand attitude strength).[1]

Brand attitude strength. Positive or negative feeling (valence) about the brand factored by the confidence that the feeling is valid (related to brand attachment).

Brand awareness. The extent to which customers know that the brand exists.

Brand broadening/leveraging. A branding approach for extending an existing brand into a new product form/class.

Brand coherence. The extent of agreement between brand identity and the experience a customer has with the brand.

Brand commitment. Often used as a synonym for brand loyalty.

Brand development index (BDI). A U.S.-based measure of brand strength used in B2C. BDI in a specific geographic area is percentage of brand sales divided by percentage of the U.S. population, converted to a percentage.

Brand earnings. That portion of a firm's earnings that is attributable to the brand.

Brand equity. The classic definition is: *a set of brand assets and liabilities linked to a brand, its name, and symbol that add to (or subtract from) the value provided by a product or service to a firm and/or that firm's customers.* There are two types of brand equity:

> **Customer brand equity** is the value customers receive from a brand, less the value they receive from a generic product. Customer brand equity comprises value received before purchase — **pre-purchase equity**, and value received after purchase — **post-purchase equity**.
>
> **Firm brand equity** derives directly from customer brand equity when the firm secures in its customers brand awareness, positive attitudes, high perceived quality, positive word-of-mouth, intentions to purchase, purchase, brand loyalty, positive brand image and associations (or brand personality), and satisfaction.

Brand equity protection. Actions the firm takes to reduce the negative effects on its brand(s) from actions like counterfeiting, diversion, tampering, and theft.

Brand essence. The brand's fundamental promise reflected in its brand identity.

Brand experience. Customers' subjective internal (sensations, feelings, cognitions) and behavioral responses evoked by brand-related stimuli that are part of its design and identity, packaging, communications, and environment.[2]

Brand extension. Broadening (leveraging) the brand to a new product form (class).

Brand harmonization. The extent to which the firm positions the brand consistently in different product/markets.

Brand health check. A way of measuring the overall health of the brand.

---

1 C.W. Park, D.J. MacInnis, J. Priester, A.B. Eisingerich, and D. Iacobucci, "Brand Attachment and Brand Attitude Strength: Conceptual and Empirical Differentiation of Two Critical Brand Equity Drivers," *Journal of Marketing*, 74 (November 2010), pp. 1–17 **eg1**.

2 J.J. Brakus, B.H. Schmitt, and L. Zarantonello, "Brand Experience: What Is It? How Is It Measured? Does It Affect Loyalty?" *Journal of Marketing*, 73 (May 2009), pp. 52–68 **eg2**.

Brand identity. What the firm wants the brand to mean to customers, including brand personality and the brand promise.

Brand image. The overall meaning that the brand has to customers.

Brand licensing. The practice of making agreements with third-party organizations to attach the brand to their products.

Brand loyalty. The extent to which customers are predisposed to make repeat purchases of the brand.

Brand management. The practice of developing and/or sustaining brand identity by designing and executing marketing actions.

Brand migration. The process of transferring the equity in a brand being retired to a surviving brand.

Brand parity. The extent of similarity or difference of various brands (typically in a product form [class]).

Brand personality. A set of enduring and distinct human characteristics associated with a brand.

Brand positioning. The process by which the firm attempts to align brand image with brand identity.

Brand prominence. The extent to which the brand is top of mind; the ease and frequency with which the brand and feelings about the brand are brought to mind.

Brand promise. A synonym for brand essence.

Brand resilience. The ability of a brand to recover from negative information.

Brand revitalization. An approach designed to rejuvenate under-performing brands.

Brand strategy. The firm's game plan for developing and achieving objectives for the brand.

Brand trust. The willingness of the average customer to rely on the ability of the brand to perform its stated function.

Brand valuation. The process of putting a monetary value on brand equity, typically firm brand equity (FBE).

Branding. The attachment of a symbol to a product, service, and/or organization that uniquely identifies the supplier and/or owner. The symbol may consist of words, a concept, or an auditory or visual signal.

Breakeven analysis. The approach for calculating the breakeven point.

Breakeven point (BE). The level of sales required to cover fixed costs.

Bundling. The firm sells a product and sets a price only in combination with other products and/or services. **Unbundling**. The firm sells products and sets prices for each item individually. **Mixed bundling**. The firm offers its products as part of a bundle, but also individually.

Business-case analysis. Assesses the financial viability of a project, including various risk factors.

Business model. The way the firm creates value, generates revenues, and incurs costs.

Business strengths. Capabilities, competences, and resources the firm needs to be successful.

CAD. An acronym for computer-aided design. CAD uses computer systems to design detailed two- or three-dimensional models of physical objects like mechanical parts, buildings, and molecules.

Calendarize. Partitioning sales objectives by time period like quarter, month, or week.

CAM. An acronym for computer-aided manufacturing: CAM is a manufacturing process that uses specialized computers to control, monitor, and adjust tools and machinery in manufacturing.

Candidate descriptor variables — segmentation variables. Used to identify segments; typically fall into one of four categories: geography, demography, behavioral, and socio-psychological.

Capabilities, resources, competences. Three related terms that embrace several factors the firm can use as the basis for securing differential advantage. Often called business strengths.

Category development index (CDI). A U.S.-based measure of category strength used in B2C. CDI in a specific geographic area is percentage of category sales divided by percentage of U.S. population, converted to a percentage.

CDI. See category development index.

Channel stuffing. The firm overloads distributors and hence overstates its revenues. Can lead to legal problems.

Chasm. The transition between making sales to innovating and early-adopting customers, and to the mainstream market. Products failing to **cross the chasm** do not realize their potential.

Co-branding. An approach to branding typically involving cooperation between two brands from different firms.

Cognitive algebra. Embraces various mental approaches customers might use to integrate information about alternatives to make purchase decisions. These include:

> **Linear compensatory.** The customer chooses the alternative with the highest value. An alternative's value comprises the values from each attribute such that high value on one attribute balances out poor value on another.

> **Lexicographic.** The customer chooses the alternative that performs best on the most important attribute. To resolve ties, the customer moves to the second most important attribute.

> **Conjunctive.** The customer sets a performance cut-off for each attribute. The chosen alternative must meet or exceed each cut-off.

> **Disjunctive.** The customer sets a performance cut-off for each attribute. The chosen alternative must meet or exceed a cut-off for at least one attribute.

Cognitive resources. Describe the decision-maker's ability to process information. Key features are:

> **Direction.** Are they paying attention?

> **Intensity.** Can they process the information?

Commercialization. The final step in bringing a new product to market.

Commodity brand. A brand with little brand equity. Customers believe the firm's offer has little or no additional value over competitive offers.

Communication process. The activities involved in sending and receiving information.

Communications tipping point. The level above which communications generate customer resentment.

Complementer. Any organization like independents and competitors whose actions can affect the firm's sales.

Competitive assessment analysis. A way of mapping customer needs, required benefits, and values, with the required resources, to assess the competitive position of various suppliers.

Competitive data:

> **Level of.** The organizational level for collecting data — corporate, business unit, market, and market segment.

> **Type of.** The sorts of quantitative and qualitative data the firm can collect.

> **Secondary.** Data that have been collected for another purpose.

> **Primary.** Data that require a focused acquisition effort.

Competitive intelligence department. An organizational unit that collects, analyzes, and distributes competitive information.

Competitive intelligence system. A process to collect, analyze, and distribute competitive information.

Competitor. Any organization whose products and services provide similar or superior benefits and values to the same customers that the firm seeks to attract and retain. They may be:

> **Current.** Competitors that the firm faces *today*.

> **Potential.** Competitors that the firm may face *tomorrow*.

> **Direct.** Offer similar benefits with similar products, technologies, or business models.

> **Indirect.** Offer similar benefits with alternative products, technologies, or business models.

Competitor target. The organizational entity against which the firm decides to compete.

Complementary products. Products that are used together like razors and razor blades, vacuum cleaners and bags, and printers and toner cartridges.

Concentrated market. A market with few substantial competitors.

Concept definition. See product concept.

Contribution margin (CM). Sales revenues less variable costs, and:

Contribution margin per unit (CMU). Contribution margin stated on a per-unit basis.

Contribution margin rate (CMR). Contribution stated per monetary unit of sales revenues.

Control, types of:

Firm functioning. Asks the question, "Is the firm functioning well?" Three sub-areas are:

Implementation. Did the firm implement its planned actions?

Strategy. Is the firm's market strategy well conceived and on target?

Managerial process. Are the firm's managerial processes the best they can be?

Performance control. Did the firm achieve its desired results?

Post-action. The firm waits until a pre-set time, then compares actual results against standards.

Steering. A dynamic, continuous, and anticipatory system. The firm sets control limits for performance standards and compares results against standards on an ongoing basis.

Control unit. An element of the sales force for monitoring and controlling sales activities and performance, like a sales region, sales district, or sales territory.

Cookie. A piece of text stored by a user's web browser for identification and authentication.

Cooperation with competitors:

Back-office. Competitors work together in non-customer-facing activities to reduce costs and improve efficiency for all firms.

Marketplace or front-office. Competitors work together to better satisfy customer needs like developing a new technology standard.

Core product. The central element in the firm's offer of a physical product, like an automobile.

Core service. The central element in the firm's service offer, like overnight package delivery.

Cost of capital. The financial return the firm must earn to recover its capital outlay. The cost of capital is a weighted average of the firm's cost of equity and debt. In evaluating investment opportunities, the firm discounts expected future cash flows at its cost of capital.

Cost per 1000 (CPM). A measure of the advertising cost. CPM = Absolute Cost of Advertising Space × 1000/Circulation.

Costs, types of:

Direct. Occur because a particular product, organizational unit, or activity exists or is being contemplated. Can be identified with, or directly linked to, a product, sales territory, or function. Include all variable costs and at least some fixed costs.

Direct fixed costs. Costs directly related to the product. These costs do not vary directly with the number of units sold, but are associated with individual products.

Fixed. Do not vary with the volume of sales or production over a reasonable range. Usually comprise overhead items like managerial salaries, depreciation, and selling, general, and administrative expenses (SG&A).

Fully loaded. Incremental costs plus overhead charges.

Indirect. Relate to several products, organizational units, or activities. Cannot be identified with a single product, sales territory, or activity. Are always fixed costs.

Marginal. The cost to make and sell one additional unit. Includes all variable costs and some incremental fixed costs, but *excludes* overhead charges.

Programmed. Set and controlled by managers for a planning period.

Standby. Do not change significantly without a major change in operations.

Variable. Vary directly with the volume of sales and production. Increase as volume increases and decrease as volume decreases.

Counterfeiting. Illegal copying of a firm's products.

Creative brief. A *contract* between the firm and its advertising agency that provides parameters and information for translating the firm's market strategy into an advertising message.

Cross-docking. The logistics practice of unloading materials from an incoming truck/railroad car and reloading directly onto outbound trucks/rail cars, with minimal (or zero) storage.

Cross-selling. Selling different products to a customer who has already purchased from the firm.

Customer. Any person or organization in the channel of distribution or decision (other than competitors) whose actions can affect the purchase of the firm's products and services. Categories of customers include:

    Current (today). The firm does business with these customers today.

    Potential (tomorrow). The firm hopes to do business with these customers in the future.

    Direct. Exchange money or other resources with the firm for its products.

    Indirect. Secure the firm's products from intermediaries like manufacturers or distributors.

    Macro-level. Organizational units like manufacturers, wholesalers, retailers, government entities, and families.

    Micro-level. Individuals with influence or decision-making authority within the macro-level customer.

Customer attribute (CA). A characteristic, function, or property of the seller's offer.

Customer experience. A state, condition, or event that consciously affects a customer.

Customer insight. A deep and unique understanding of customers' needs and required benefits and values.

Customer lifetime. The estimated length of time a firm's customer will remain a customer.

Customer lifetime value (LTV). The economic value to the firm from a customer over the lifetime of its relationship. LTV is the discounted future stream of profits the customer generates.

Customer needs. A basis for identifying market segments.

Customer needs, types of:

    Recognized. The customer is consciously aware of these needs; they may be **expressed** to others, or **non-expressed**.

    Latent. The customer is not consciously aware of these needs.

Customer profitability. The profit the firm earns from an individual customer or group of customers.

Customer relationship management (CRM). The ongoing process of identifying and creating new value with individual customers and sharing these benefits over a lifetime of association with them.

Customer segment. A finer-grained group of customers than a market segment. Within a market segment, the firm might identify several customer segments.

Customer service. Any act, performance, or information that enhances the firm's core product or service.

Customer service strategy. An approach to delivering customer service based on understanding customers' needs for customer service.

Customer target. Individuals and/organizations that the firm tries to make its customers.

Customer tiers. A term for classifying customers in terms of importance to the firm. For example:

    Tier I (platinum). The firm's most important current and potential customers.

    Tier II (gold). Important current and potential customers but less so than Tier I.

    Tier III (bronze). Important current and potential customers but less so than Tiers I and II.

Customer value. The utility a customer receives from purchasing the firm's product or service. Value is a higher-level construct embracing several benefits the product offers.

Customer value map. A method of assessing a product's price/value position by plotting relative customer value versus relative price for various competitive products.

Customer value, methods of assessing:

    Dollarmetric method. A method for assessing customer value. For several pairs of alternatives, the customer states which alternative she prefers and how much extra she would pay.

    Direct value assessment. The firm simply asks customers what they would pay for various products.

    Economic value for the customer (EVC). The price the customer pays for a competitive product, plus the net additional value the firm's product provides. EVC is an upper bound for price.

Perceived value analysis. The firm secures data directly from customers, but sometimes experienced managers provide *best-guess* data that can be validated later by marketing research.

Price experiment. The firm offers the test product at different prices in different market areas, like geographic locations.

Data mining. A quantitative approach to gain insight into customers' purchasing behavior as the basis for making specialized offers.

Data warehouse. A place to store data on an individual customer's characteristics and purchase transactions.

Decision-making. Deviations from rationality:

Hyperbolic discounting. As decision time approaches, individuals reverse their preferences from larger rewards received later to smaller rewards received earlier.

Mental accounting. Consumers categorize funds and resources in separate mental accounts and spend differently from these accounts.

Prospect theory. Individuals place greater weight on potential losses than on equivalent value potential gains.

Decision-making process (DMP). The individual stages that members of the decision-making unit complete in making a purchase.

Decision-making unit (DMU). The individuals involved in a purchase decision.

Defection rate (1–r). The rate at which the firm loses customers from one time period to the next (also called *churn*). Sometimes calculated as a probability. The opposite of retention rate.

Demand curve. A graph of the relationship between price and volume showing price sensitivity.

Demarketing. Firm efforts to reduce demand, typically because of a supply/demand imbalance.

Demonstration ad. Shows the product in use and focuses on its performance.

Development. The process of turning a product concept into an actual product.

Direct marketing. A communications tool embracing many ways of requesting a direct customer response. Includes traditional print and broadcast advertising as well as newer digital options like e-mail and the Internet.

Direct product profit. Assesses profit performance after taking into account the fixed costs the product incurs.

Discount rate (d). The rate at which the firm discounts future earnings so as to calculate customer lifetime value. The discount factor is typically set equal to the firm's cost of capital.

Disintermediation. The removal of a layer in a distribution system.

Distribution approaches:

Exclusive. A distribution strategy that focuses on a few well-chosen outlets.

Intensive. A distribution strategy that maximizes the number of outlets.

Selective. A sort of compromise between intensive and exclusive distribution.

Distribution channel or Distribution. Encompasses the entities, interrelationships, and functions that members perform, so that the supplier's products reach customers.

Distribution channel breadth. The number of members at a particular level in the channel system.

Distribution conflict:

Operational. Focuses on day-to-day issues like late shipments, invoicing errors, unfulfilled salesperson promises, unacceptable product quality, supplier attempts to load channels, and price and margin disputes.

Strategic. May change the relationships among distribution channel members.

Distribution exclusivity:

Geographic. The supplier gives the distributor a monopoly on selling products in its territory.

Product. The supplier gives the distributor exclusivity to sell a group of products.

Supplier. The intermediary agrees to distribute only the supplier's products.

Distribution functions. The activities that the distribution channel must perform. Concerned with the physical product, information, and/or ownership.

Distribution, method:
    Direct. The supplier supplies products directly to consumers and end users.
    Indirect. Intermediaries like distributors, wholesalers, and retailers play a major role in transferring products to consumers and end users.

Distribution, view of:
    Broad view. Encompasses changes in *state*, *physical location*, and *time*.
    Narrow view. Encompasses mainly changes in *physical location* and *time*.

Disutility of price. Refers to the fact that whereas customers receive value (utility) from a product's features/attributes, they must *give up* economic resources. Price has negative value or disutility.

Diversion. The practice of purchasing the firm's products ostensibly for sale to one set of customers, then reselling (diverting) those products to a different set of customers. Typically, the firm's strategy is negatively affected.

Divest. Selling a business to another firm.

Dollarmetric method. A method for estimating the monetary value of customer brand equity.

Downstream. The firm's customers and its customers' customers, etc.

Drop shipping. A retailer makes the sale but the manufacturer ships the product direct to the retailer's customer.

Dumping. Selling products in foreign markets below home market prices at "less than fair market value" and often below average costs.

Duration effect. The relationship between customer retention rate and customer lifetime. As customer retention rate increases, customer lifetime increases.

Dynamic pricing. A special case of price discrimination where the price varies over time.

Economic value for the customer (EVC). The price the customer pays for a competitive product, plus the net additional value the firm's product provides. EVC is an upper bound for price.

Efficient consumer response (ECR). An approach to drive out excess inventory by focusing on consumer demand-pull versus supplier-push. Developed by food manufacturers and distributors.

Endorsed brand. The firm uses one firm brand to support — endorse — another.

Engineering characteristics (EC). Engineering parameters to design and modify a product.

Entry barrier. Something that forestalls or slows a firm's entry into a market.

Environmental influences. Factors external to the consumer that affect decision-making, embracing culture, social class, other people, family, and the situation.

Ethnographic research. An observational research technique derived from anthropology.

Exchange. The firm and its customers exchange value. Through its products and services, the firm offers value to customers. Customers typically offer value to the firm via their financial resources. If the firm and customer each accept the value offered by the other, an exchange occurs.

Executional style. The way the firm turns the core message into effective advertising:
    Rational-style advertising appeals to people's sense of logic.
    Emotional-style advertising appeals to the emotions.

Expectations disconfirmation. A key feature of the SERVQUAL model. Customer satisfaction is the *difference* between expected quality and perceived quality.

Experience curve. An empirical relationship between unit product cost and the firm's experience in making and distributing the product.

Experiment. A research approach where the researcher manipulates one or more independent variables to assess the impact on a dependent variable.

External orientation. A firm with this orientation focuses on customers, competitors, complementers, and factors in the external environment that could affect its future health.

Face time. The time a salesperson spends face-to-face with customers.

Factoring. A process by which the firm sells its accounts receivable for cash.

Family or masterbrand. The brand for a group of closely related products serving a similar function.

Feature or attribute. A characteristic, function, or property of the seller's offer.

Feature/benefit/value ladder. A hierarchy that joins the product's features with the benefits and values those features deliver to customers.

Features of services:

  Divisibility. A feature of services emphasizing that they often comprise a sequence of activities.

  Inseparability. A feature of services emphasizing that production and consumption occur simultaneously.

  Intangibility. A feature of services emphasizing that they have no physical presence. They cannot be touched, driven, flown, worn, kicked, batted, squashed, or sat upon.

  Perishability. A feature of services relating to *inseparability*. Services cannot be inventoried.

  Variability. A feature of services emphasizing a lack of consistency because of human involvement in service delivery.

Feedback cycle. The time period between the firm's actions and its measured results.

Financial analysis approaches. Methods for making resource decisions.

  Economic profit or economic value added (EVA). The firm's annual profit less an explicit charge for capital.

  Internal rate of return (IRR). A method of evaluating investment opportunities using future cash flows. IRR is the discount rate that equalizes cash inflows and cash outflows.

  Net present value (NPV). A method of evaluating investment opportunities using future cash flows. **NPV** is the monetary value from discounting cash flows at a predetermined rate, typically the firm's cost of capital.

  Payback. Payback is the forecast time to pay back the investment. In general, shorter paybacks are better than longer paybacks.

  Return on investment (ROI). ROI calculations project future accounting data. They compare the product's forecast rate of return with a target (or *hurdle*) rate.

Financial analysis perspective. Making resource allocations based on financial analysis.

Firewall brands. Brands that defend the firm's profitable products, sometimes termed *fighting brands*.

First-mover advantage. An advantage gained simply by being first. The firm may earn a leading reputation for quality and/or gain superior market knowledge.

Five-forces model. A set of forces impinging on the firm:

  Current direct competitors. Satisfy customer needs by offering similar benefits with similar products, technology, or business models.

  New direct entrants. Offer similar products, but were not previously competitors.

  Indirect competitors. Satisfy similar customer needs by offering alternative products, technologies, or business models.

  Suppliers. Provide the firm's inputs.

  Buyers. Purchase the firm's products.

Flanker brand. A brand introduced to protect an important brand from competition.

Floor price. The price below which a firm should never sell a product, typically the marginal cost.

Flower of customer service. Eight elements of customer service: safekeeping, order-taking, information, consultation, billing, payment, exceptions, and hospitality.

Focus group. A small number of people, typically eight to 12, assembled by a marketing researcher to secure insight into customers' needs and motivations.

Follower. A firm that enters after the pioneer has created a new market.

Forecasts, types of:
  Market. The predicted market-level sales in a future time period.
  Sales. The firm's predicted sales in a future time period:
      Bottom-up. A forecast that starts with customer-by-customer forecasts.
      Synthetic. A forecast that combines top-down and bottom-up forecasts.
      Top-down. A forecast that starts with a market-size forecast.

Forward integration. A supplier undertakes activities currently performed by its customers.

Fragmented market. A market with many competitors.

Franchising. A distribution strategy in which the franchisor develops a business model. Franchisees agree to implement the franchisor's model and typically pay an initiation fee and ongoing fees.

Frequency. The average number of times a targeted individual is exposed to the advertising.

Full-line forcing. See tying agreements.

Game theory. A process that helps marketers think through options available to the firm and its competitors and how pursuing these options may affect these parties.

Global account manager (GAM). A person responsible for the firm's most important global customers.

Global branding. A branding approach that uses a common brand around the world.

***Good* market segments.** Segments that satisfy five criteria: differentiated, identifiable, stable, appropriate size, and accessible.

Gray markets. A reseller offers the firm's product in a market at a price lower than the firm's price in that market.

Gross domestic product (GDP). A measure of the nation's economy based on its production of goods and services.

Gross rating points (GRPs) Combines reach and frequency. GRP = Reach × Frequency.

Growth path. Describes the route the firm or business unit takes to achieve its growth objectives. Nine individual approaches reduce to four basic options:
  Market growth. Engage related and new customers with existing products.
  Market penetration. Focus on existing products in existing markets.
  Product and market diversification. Bring new products to new customers.
  Product growth. Bring related and new products to existing customers.

Growth-share matrix. BCG's portfolio analysis system; dimensions are forecast long-run market growth rate and relative market share. Product types in the growth-share matrix are:
  Cash cows. High market shares in low growth markets; should generate cash.
  Dogs. Low market shares in low growth markets; many *dog* products have poor financial performance, but some are respectable.
  Stars. High market shares in high growth markets; comparatively rare. Many *stars* consume significant cash, but should create generous returns later.
  Problem children, question marks, lottery tickets, or wildcats. Low market shares in high growth markets. Need a lot of investment and are high risk.

Guerilla marketing. Word-of-mouth communication stimulated by the firm.

Harvest. The firm seeks short-term cash flow at the expense of sales and market share.

Hierarchy-of-effects models. Describes how advertising works for different types of products:
  High-involvement products. The purchase involves financial and/or psychosocial risks.
  Low-involvement products. The purchase involves little risk.

Hierarchy of needs. Developed by psychologist Maslow; needs are in five groups, ordered low to high — physiological, safety and security, social, ego, and self-actualization.

Hockey stick. A forecasting practice in which managers make overly optimistic estimates about future revenues and costs so that their projects achieve the required returns.

Hospitable market. A market that is attractive to the firm.

House of Quality. A popular graphical representation of the quality functional deployment process — links customers attributes and engineering characteristics.

Human resource management (HRM). Processes for managing people including recruiting, selecting, training and development, work processes, talent management and career paths, and recognition and reward.

Hurdle rate. A minimum return that any investment opportunity must exceed.

Iconic brand. A brand with high customer brand equity and high firm brand equity.

Iceberg principle. An analogy to the iceberg whereby good aggregate performance in a unit or sub-unit can *hide* poor performance elsewhere in the same unit.

Idea library. A storage medium for ideas that were suggested and/or discussed but not used.

Imitation. Copying a competitor's strategy; often used in early-growth markets to surpass leaders.

Implementation (of growth strategy). Alternative approaches for the firm to achieve its objectives:
　　Acquisition. The firm acquires another firm or a business unit.
　　Equity investment. The firm takes an ownership position.
　　Insourcing. The firm undertakes activities currently done by others.
　　Internal development. The firm develops the opportunity in-house.
　　Licensing and technology purchase. The firm secures access to technology developed by others. License — the original firm maintains ownership. Technology purchase — the firm gains ownership.
　　Outsourcing. The firm secures other firms to undertake activities it previously conducted in-house so it can focus on higher return opportunities.
　　Strategic alliance. Two firms join together to develop a stronger combined entity.

Implementation programs. Alternative approaches for the firm to achieve its objectives. In the context of market strategy, these include the marketing mix and other functional programs.

Independent inventors. Innovators working independently outside any corporate umbrella.

Indicators, types of:
　　Leading. Help managers assess if they are on track to achieve planned results.
　　Lagging. Measure what has already occurred.

Inhospitable market. A market that is unattractive to the firm.

Initial public offering (IPO). A company's first sale of stock to the public. Venture capitalists often sell equity stakes in an IPO.

Innovation. Endowing human and material resources with new and greater wealth-producing capacity.

Innovation, types of:
　　Disruptive innovations. Developed from a new technology offering new and very different value propositions, initially for new applications and a limited number of new-to-the-market customers.
　　Sustaining innovations. An innovation that improves the performance of established products along dimensions valued by mainstream customers.

Innovation, firm types. Four types based on their orientations toward technology and customers:
　　Isolates. Low customer orientation, low technology orientation.
　　Followers. High customer orientation, low technology orientation.
　　Shapers. Low customer orientation, high technology orientation.
　　Interactors. High customer orientation, high technology orientation.

Insight. Securing understanding of strengths and weaknesses in order to gain strategic perspectives. There are three types.
　　Competitive insight is the ability to describe, evaluate, project, and manage competitors.
　　Company insight is the firm's understanding of itself — its advantages and disadvantages compared to the competition.
　　Complementer insight is insight into any organization whose actions affect the firm's sales.

Integrated marketing communications. The integration of the firm's various communications efforts, using various tools, for various communications targets.

Interdependence of opportunities. The extent to which the needed resources and/or the success or failure of one opportunity are related to one or more other opportunities.

Intermediation. The introduction of a layer in a distribution system.

Internal architecture. The firm's organizational structure, systems and processes, and HRM practices.

Internal orientation. A firm with this orientation looks inward. It focuses on internal functions like finance, operations, sales, and technology (R&D), rather than external factors.

Internet communications. Information available electronically on websites, blogs, and other methods.

Intra-firm competition. A type of competition where different firm units compete with each other.

Just-in-time (JIT). An approach to reducing inventory by making raw materials and parts deliveries shortly before use in the production line.

Kenneling. The practice of purchasing low-share businesses in low growth markets and placing them together. The acquirer typically makes profits by rationalizing operations to achieve lower costs.

Kill point. A point where the firm must decide to proceed or drop the project.

Lead users. Organizations and individuals who think up, and may even prototype, new products.

Leapfrog. A way of surpassing the market leader by developing innovative and superior products, and/or entering emerging market segments; often used in early growth markets.

Leveraged buyout (LBO). Formation of a new firm when an existing firm spins off a business to a group of investors and/or management — a management buyout (MBO).

Life cycles. A common means for describing the evolution of markets and products. Product class and product form life cycles are typically partitioned into several stages:

> **Introduction.** The period from product launch until sales take off and grow at an accelerating rate. Total sales during introduction are generally low.
> **Early growth.** The period from sales take-off until the growth rate begins to slow.
> **Late growth.** Sales are still growing, but the rate of growth is slowing.
> **Maturity.** The sales growth rate ranges from flat to growth in gross national product (GNP).
> **Decline.** Overall sales decrease year by year.

Liquidate. Closing down a business and selling its assets.

Lock-in. The situation when customers are committed to buying from the firm. Lock-in customers have high **switching costs**.

Logistics. The process of moving a product from point A to point B:

> **Outbound.** Getting the product from the supplier to the customer.
> **Inbound (reverse).** Getting the product from the customer back to the producer.

Loyalty programs. Methods that firms use to enhance customer retention.

> **Hard rewards.** Denominated in dollars and cents, or translatable points.
> **Soft rewards.** Include toll-free information numbers, restaurant seating, theater ticket availability, hotel room and airline seat upgrades.
> **Probabilistic rewards.** The customer wins a large reward, or zero.
> **Deterministic rewards.** The customer accumulates points, then collects the reward.

Maintenance expenses. Expenses specifically designed to enhance customer retention.

Managerial process environment. The received wisdom that executives use to lead and manage their firms — their intellectual capital.

Margin multiple. A quick way to calculate LTV if customer margin, customer retention rate, and discount rate are constant from time period to time period. LTV equals customer margin multiplied by the margin multiple.

Margins, types of:

> **Unit margin.** A term used by retailers and wholesalers that measures the difference between the product's selling price and its unit cost.

Percent margin on cost. The product's margin divided by the cost, stated as a percentage (not generally used by wholesalers and retailers).

Percent margin on selling price. The product's margin divided by the selling price, stated as a percentage. Wholesalers and retailers generally use this term.

Inventory turnover (stockturn). The number of times the firm sells average product inventory during the year.

Customer margin. Sales revenues less all attributable customer costs.

Market. Customers — people and organizations — who require goods and services to satisfy their needs. Customers must have sufficient purchasing power and a willingness to pay for the products that suppliers offer.

Market-factor testing. A process for exploring the effect of one or more marketing-mix elements on expected sales. Typically performed in a simulated environment.

Market insight. The understanding firms secure about future market changes that lead to an appreciation of opportunities and threats.

Market levers. The actions the firm takes to achieve its performance standards.

Market-segment attractiveness. How attractive a segment is to the firm. An individual segment may be differentially attractive to different firms.

Market segmentation. A conceptual and analytic process for grouping actual and potential customers into market segments.

Market share. The most common market-based performance measure; compares the firm's sales units or revenues directly with competitors.

Market strategy. The firm's game plan for addressing the market.

Market structure. The market, products serving the market, and suppliers offering these products.

Market tinkering. An approach to new product development in which a firm makes minor modifications to its current products.

Marketing. There are several related meanings:

Philosophy. Marketing as a guiding philosophy for the entire organization embraces an external orientation. It recognizes that revenues from customers are the critical source of cash flows.

Imperatives. Marketing as six imperatives describes the specifics of the marketing job. These are the *must dos* of marketing.

Principles. The firm must apply four marketing principles to do the marketing job well. They act as guidelines for making good marketing decisions based on the six imperatives.

American Marketing Association (AMA). The AMA periodically redefines *marketing*. The 2004 definition stated, "Marketing is an organizational function and a set of processes for creating, communicating, and delivering value to customers and for managing customer relationships in ways that benefit the organization and its stakeholders." In 2007, the definition became, "Marketing is the activity, set of institutions, and processes for creating, communicating, delivering, and exchanging offerings that have value for customers, clients, partners, and society at large."

Marketing audit. A comprehensive process for evaluating the firm's marketing practices.

Marketing offer. The package of benefits and values the firm offers to customers.

Marketing mix. The traditional description of the tools marketers use to construct an offer. They are often called the 4Ps—product, place (distribution), promotion, and price. Today, service is often treated separately to form 4Ps and an S.

Marketing myopia. The tendency for firms to have such an overly narrow view of their market that they miss opportunities and/or fail to recognize threats.

Marketing principles. Guidelines for making good marketing decisions:

Selectivity and concentration. Because resources are scarce, the firm should be selective in its choice of market and market segment. It should concentrate its resources against its chosen targets.

Customer value. Success in target market segments depends on the firm's ability to provide customers with value.

Differential advantage. To be profitable, the firm must provide a net benefit, or cluster of benefits, to a sizable group of customers, that they value and are willing to pay for, but cannot get, or believe they cannot get, elsewhere. Competition eventually erodes away any differential advantage—the firm must continually renew its differential advantage.

Integration. The firm must carefully integrate and coordinate all elements in the design and execution of its market strategy. Integration includes elements of the marketing mix and the activities of all functions that play a role in delivering promised benefits.

Marketing research, types of:

Primary. The firm collects data for the specific purpose of the study.

Secondary. Based on data that has already been collected for another purpose.

Qualitative. A flexible and versatile approach comprising several techniques that is not concerned with numbers. Often used for exploratory studies.

Quantitative. A research approach that uses numerical data to test hypotheses.

Marketing research process. A rigorous methodology for improving the probability that investments in marketing research will produce actionable insights.

Market-occupancy ratio. A performance measure defined as the ratio of firm's number of customers to the total number of customers.

Mass customization. Related to segments-of-one. The firm customizes its products to individual requirements on a large scale.

Mass-market brand. A brand the firm targets at the mass market.

Means/ends tree. A diagrammatic method for outlining, assessing, and choosing among various alternatives.

Measures, types of:

Input. Focus on actions taken by the firm — leading indicators.

Intermediate. Focus on actions that customers take — leading indicators.

Output. Focus on performance variables like sales and profits — lagging indicators.

Hard. Objectively measured like sales volume, profit, and market performance.

Soft. Rating scale measures like customer satisfaction or attitudes.

Media class. A group of closely related media — newspapers, TV, and billboards are each media classes.

Media objectives. What the firm wants to accomplish with its media strategy:

Reach. The number of targeted individuals exposed to the advertising message at least once.

Duplicated reach. The portion of the target audience exposed to the advertising message from multiple media sources.

Unduplicated reach. The portion of the target audience exposed to the advertising message from a single source.

Media schedule. The placement and timing of advertisements for the advertising program.

Media vehicle. A specific exemplar of a media class — *The New York Times* and *60 Minutes* are each media vehicles.

Merger. Two firms join together to form a new entity.

Miscommunication. Misperception and/or misunderstanding by a *receiver* of a message the *sender* intended to send. Problems may occur in:

Encoding. Translating and interpreting the intended message into the actual sent message.

Distortion. Receiving a different message from the message that was sent.

Decoding. Misperceiving and/or misunderstanding the received message because of selective attention, distortion, and/or retention.

Mission. Guides the firm's search for opportunity so it can focus on a limited number of areas where it is likely to be successful.

Modularity. A design approach in which the firm uses common components (modules) to produce a broad product line.

Moment of truth. An interaction between a service customer and service personnel.

Monitor-and-control system. A process for measuring whether the firm's actions, individually and collectively, are consistent with its plan. Forms the basis for making adjustments.

Monolithic brand. The brand for a group of products fulfilling many different functions. A **corporate brand** — for the firm as a whole — is a special case of a monolithic brand.

Multi-branding. A brand architecture approach in which the firm uses multiple brands for its entries in various product classes.

Multifactor matrix. A portfolio analysis system that helps the firm decide which segments to target by assessing the attractiveness of market segments and the extent to which the firm possesses the business strengths to succeed.

Negative complementarity. The negative effect on sales of one product caused by customer dissatisfaction with another product.

Negative working capital. Working capital equals current assets minus current liabilities. Negative working capital implies that the firm's suppliers and/or customers are financing its operations.

New idea processes. Methods for generating new ideas:
> **Structured thinking.** Logical ways to create new product ideas.
> **Unstructured thinking.** A family of approaches that attempt to *break the mold* and develop totally new ideas by thinking *outside the box*.

Non-compete agreement. An employee agrees not to work for a direct competitor for a specified period of time after he or she leaves the company.

Non-disclosure agreement (NDA). Aka a confidentiality agreement; a contract promising to protect confidential data disclosed during employment or other business transaction.[3]

Non-personal communication. Communications without interpersonal contact between sender and receiver.

One-on-one interviews. A marketing research approach conducted by interviewing respondents individually.

One-sided advertising. Advertising that focuses only on the product's positive attributes.

Opportunity costs. Costs incurred by not taking a course of action. They are not out-of-pocket costs but represent forgone profits due to inaction.

Organization structures, types of:
> **Business process.** An outgrowth of re-engineering movement, the firm organizes around business processes.
> **Category management.** An evolutionary development of a product/brand management structure in which the firm manages multiple brands in a complementary manner.
> **Combined product/brand management/market segment.** Combines a product/brand focus with a market segment focus.
> **Customer management.** An organization focused specifically on customers.
> **Functional marketing.** The firm places activities like marketing research, distribution, advertising and promotion, marketing administration, and new product development in a marketing department. Other major functional areas are likewise in separate departments.
> **Inclusion.** The firm groups many activities together under marketing.
> **Market segment.** Managers are responsible for individual market segments.
> **Traditional product/brand management.** Product and brand managers develop market plans for their products and brands. They are responsible for volume, share, and/or profit — they compete for resources like advertising dollars and sales force time.

---

3   Definitions of non-compete and non-disclosure from *Everyday Law for Everyday People*, <www.nolo.com> eg3.

Organizational orientations, types of:

    External. A firm with this orientation focuses on customers, competitors, complementers, and factors in the external environment that could affect its future health.

    Internal. A firm with this orientation looks inward. It focuses on internal functions like finance, operations, sales, and technology (R&D), rather than external factors.

        Financial. This firm is *run by the numbers* with scant regard for strategic issues. It avoids expenses with long-term payoff like R&D and marketing, in favor of increasing short-term profits. It often minimizes capital investment.

        Operations. This firm's culture revolves around operational efficiency; there is typically a shared belief that cost reduction and volume maximization will ensure success. The firm does not have a deep understanding of customers' needs.

        Sales. Maximizing short-term sales volume is the over-arching goal. This firm often cuts prices to secure orders, but does little forward planning. As markets evolve, broadly acceptable new products are not available.

        Technological (R&D). "Have technology, will travel—our technology will sell itself." This firm is often technologically sophisticated but rarely understands marketing and makes new product decisions with little or no customer input.

Outsourcing. When the firm engages a supplier to conduct an activity previously done inhouse.

Packaging communication. Communication delivered by the package containing the product.

Paid search. Online advertisers pay to appear next to and be associated with search results based on keywords. For example, an electronics retailer might pay to appear next to searches for HDTVs.

Panel. A group of respondents who agree to provide data over time.

Partnership model. An approach to distribution channel members that involves building cooperation and trust.

Penetration pricing. A long-run low-price strategy to grow a market and secure high market share.

Perceived customer value. The value the customer believes the firm is delivering.

Perceptual map. A way of plotting the various products and market segment ideal points (and sizes) into a two-dimensional (sometimes three) space defined by the most important customer needs.

Performance gap (variance[4]). The difference between performance standards and actual performance.

Performance objectives. Describe the business results the firm hopes to achieve. A performance objective has two components:

    Strategic. The qualitative and directional results the firm wants to achieve. Strategic objectives typically fall into three categories: growth and market share, profitability, and cash flow.

    Operational. Quantitative statements of business results the firm hopes to achieve that relate directly to the strategic objectives. How much is required and by when.

Permission marketing. Presenting marketing messages only to people who agree to receive them; the firm receives permission by asking people to *opt in*. When firms do not have permission they frequently allow people to *opt out* of future messages.

Personal communication. Face-to-face communications with targeted individuals or groups.

PESTLE model. An acronym for identifying the environmental forces acting on an industry — Political, Economic, Sociocultural, Technological, Legal, and Environmental (Physical).

Pioneer. A firm that creates new markets and is the first, or among the first, with a new product form.

Pipeline analysis. A method for tracking the firm's performance at different selling process stages.

Pocket price. The amount of money the firm actually receives — in its pocket.

Portfolio analysis. A method of evaluating investment opportunities that arrays the firm's products in two dimensions.

Portfolio approach. Individual products play different roles in the firm's portfolio. Some products generate growth and market share, some products earn profits, and some deliver cash flow.

---

4 Not to be confused with the statistical term *variance*, as in mean and variance.

Positioning. The heart of the market strategy that should create a unique and favorable image in the minds of target customers. Positioning requires four key decisions: select customer targets, frame competitor targets, design the value proposition, and articulate the reasons to believe.

Potentials, types of:

    Market. The maximum market-level sales that the firm expects in a future time period.

    Sales. The maximum sales that the firm could achieve in a future time period.

Power. The ability of one channel member to get another to do what it wants it to do.

Predatory pricing. Pricing below cost with the intent to eliminate a competitor.

Pre-emptive. Acting before competitors.

Preliminary screening. The first stage for eliminating new product ideas.

Price bases. The ways in which a firm can set prices such as by individual product, by use, or by results.

Price discretion. The firm's ability to use several pricing approaches. Firms that offer high value but also have low costs enjoy the most price discretion.

Price discrimination. Setting different prices for the same product to different segments or customers.

Price elasticity of demand (PED). PED = % change in demand/% change in price.

Price fixing. Competitors collude to set prices.

Price management. Organizing the firm to make its strategic and tactical pricing decisions.

Price sensitivity. Degree of change in volume related to change in price:

    Price-elastic market. Volume *increases/decreases* significantly as price *decreases/increases*.

    Price-inelastic market. Volume is *relatively insensitive* to price changes.

Price setting, types of:

    Competitive-driven pricing. Pricing based on competitors' prices.

    Cost-plus pricing. Setting price by identifying costs and adding a *satisfactory* profit margin.

    Customer-driven pricing. Customers name the prices they are prepared to pay. If the product is available, they must complete the purchase.

    Deceptive pricing. False prices and prices that might confuse or mislead customers.

    Fees and surcharges. Extra charges such as bank fees for ATM use or airline fees for checked bags.

    Flat-rate pricing. Pricing for a fixed time period. **Variable-rate pricing.** Pricing by use.

    Loss-leader pricing. Retailers deliberately take losses to build customer traffic.

    Psychological pricing. A common retail practice of pricing just below a *benchmark* number, like $9.95 or $9.99 versus $10.00.

    Topsy-turvy pricing. The supplier receives additional value from a customer so that suppliers pay a price, rather than customers.

    Transfer pricing. A price set for transactions among a firm's business units.

Price skimming. A strategy of setting high prices even though costs are falling. Often used in the early stages of the product life cycle.

Price strategies. The firm's overall approach to setting prices; should be based on four considerations — perceived customer value, costs, competition, and strategic objectives:

    Penetration pricing. The firm sets prices close to costs as it seeks growth and market share.

    Skim pricing. The firm keeps prices high to secure high margins.

Price umbrella. By setting a high price, a firm relieves competitors of pricing pressure.

Price waterfall. The reduction, by discounts and allowances, from list price to pocket price.

Pricing, and transportation:

    CIF (carriage, insurance, freight). The supplier pays the cost, insurance, and freight.

    FOB (free on board). The customer pays freight, insurance, and other charges.

Pricing information systems. Methods to provide decision-makers with detailed price information.

Pricing menu. An approach to pricing in which the firm designs multiple offers, each at a fixed price.

Pricing toolkit. A set of pricing tactics for the firm to change a product's price.

Product. Sometimes *product* refers to the core offer, both *physical products* and *services*. We use this shorthand in much of the book. But tangible physical products can be touched, worn, kicked, or sat upon; a service cannot.

Product, types of:

Product class. A set of products offered by competing suppliers that serve a set of customer needs in a roughly similar manner.

    Product form. A group of products offered by competing suppliers that are more closely similar in the way they meet customer needs than products in a product class.

    Product item. A uniquely identified product offered by the firm.

    Product line. A group of related products offered by the firm.

Product cannibalization. Sales of the firm's lower margin product decrease sales of a higher margin product.

Product complementarity. Relationships among the firm's products. **Positive complementarity** occurs when one product helps another; **negative complementarity** when one product hurts another.

Product concept. A description of a product idea that details the benefits and values the product should deliver to customers.

Product portfolio. Describes the set of products that the firm or business unit offers.

Product portfolio imbalance. The firm's products are misbalanced between resource generating and resource consuming. In the growth/share matrix, this imbalance refers to cash flows.

Product proliferation. The firm offers a large number of products. Often viewed as undesirable, but can act as a barrier against competitive entry. Sometimes confused with market segmentation.

Profit contribution. The extent to which the product's sales revenues exceed variable costs.

Publicity. Communication for which the firm does not pay, typically via the press.

Public relations (PR). Communication that embraces publicity but is broader — includes other ways of managing the firm's image to gain favorable responses.

Pull. A communications approach that focuses on indirect customers.

Purchase decision categories:

    Routinized-response behavior. A straightforward purchase decision; purchase criteria are well-established, and the alternatives are well known. Aka **straight re-buy**.

    Limited problem-solving. Purchase criteria are well-established, but a new alternative and/or supplier is available; more difficult than a straight rebuy. Aka **modified re-buy**.

    Extended problem-solving. Purchase criteria are not well-developed, and the alternatives are not well known; more difficult than a modified re-buy. Aka **new buy**.

Pure-form sales organization. Specialized and unspecialized ways to organize the selling effort.

Push. A communications approach that focuses on direct customers.

Quality function deployment (QFD). Maps customer needs into design, development, engineering, manufacturing, and service functions. Helps firms seek out both spoken and unspoken customer needs and translate these needs into actions and designs.

Quantitative analyses, types of:

    Cluster. A way of grouping a large number of items, people, or organizations into a small number of groups; popular for forming market segments.

    Conjoint. A way of assessing the value that customers put on individual product attributes.

    Discriminant. A way of identifying variables that discriminate between two or more groups.

    Factor. A way of reducing a large number of variables into a manageable number of factors.

    Multidimensional scaling. A way of developing a perceptual map of a market for use in segmentation and targeting.

    Regression. A research technique for assessing the relationship between one or more independent variables and a dependent variable.

Quasi-personal communication (QPC). Interaction and feedback without human involvement, usually via artificial intelligence software.

Reasons to believe. Claims that support the firm's value proposition. Should provide compelling evidence to make the firm's claims believable.

Recommendation systems. Software that enables a firm to make personal recommendations to customers based on their prior purchases or browsing behavior on the Internet, or personal or social characteristics.

Re-engineering. Examines fundamental assumptions about the way the firm conducts its activities. Seeks alternative approaches for redesigning and improving the firm's processes.

Reference groups. Individuals and groups that influence customers in their decision-making:
    Primary. Include family members and organizational work groups.
    Secondary. Include club and church members and professional organizations.
    Aspirational. Those to which the customer would like to belong.

Relative market share (RMS). A dimensionless ratio used in the growth-share matrix; the firm's market share divided by the nearest competitor's market share.

Retail price maintenance (RPM). A distribution practice where suppliers set the prices at which retailers can sell their products. Following a 2007 Supreme Court decision, RPM is legal in the U.S., but is illegal in many other countries.

Retention rate (r). The rate at which the firm retains customers from one time period to the next. Sometimes calculated as a probability. The opposite of defection rate.

Return measures, types of:
    Return on sales (ROS). Profit expressed as a percentage of sales revenues; may be calculated for net or gross profit.
    Return on investment (ROI). Profit expressed as a percentage of investment; may be calculated for gross or operating profit or net profit.
    Return on stockholder equity (ROE). Profit expressed as a percentage of stockholder equity.
    Return per linear foot (ROLF). Profit divided by the linear feet of shelf space.

Reverse logistics. The process of returning used goods/equipment from the point of use for disposal, refurbishing, or remanufacturing.

Reward system. The way to compensate salespeople for their efforts and performance. Includes elements like financial compensation, recognition, and promotions and work assignments.

RPS. An acronym for rapid prototyping system. RPS is a method for turning three-dimensional computer models into three-dimensional physical objects.

Safety factor. Indicates the extent to which the product's revenues exceed the breakeven point.

Sales approach. The essential message that the salesperson delivers to customers.

Sales force management tasks. Six related jobs that sales managers must complete to be effective.
    Task 1. Set and achieve sales objectives.
    Task 2. Determine and allocate selling effort.
    Task 3. Develop sales approaches.
    Task 4. Design the sales organization.
    Task 5. Create critical organizational processes.
    Task 6. Staff the sales organization.

Sales forecast. The firm's predicted sales in a future time period:
    Bottom-up. A forecast that starts with customer-by-customer forecasts.
    Top-down. A forecast that starts with a market-size forecast.

Sales objectives. The firm's desired results — typically stated in terms of sales revenues, sales units, or profit contribution.

Sales promotion (SP). Activities providing extra customer value, often for immediate sales. Includes:

Trade shows. Products displayed to large numbers of customers at one time.

Product placement. Products placed in movies and TV shows.

Sales quotas. Sales objectives stated in terms of specific performance requirements.

Sales response function. The relationship between selling effort and sales results.

Sales territory. A set of customers or geographic area assigned to an individual salesperson.

Salesperson workload. The effort a salesperson must expend to complete assigned activities; a key variable for designing sales territories.

Scanner data. Purchase data collected electronically at point of sale, typically from bar codes (product/service identifiers).

Scenario. A descriptive narrative of how the future may evolve for a plausible option.

Screening criteria. Aids for evaluating and selecting opportunities. Important screening criteria are:
Objectives. What does the firm seek to achieve by investing in the opportunity?
Compatibility (or fit). Can the firm successfully address the opportunity?
Core competence. Can the firm use its core competencies or gain new core competencies?
Synergy. Can the firm use existing resources and earn greater returns than a standalone entry?

Search engine optimization. An element of search marketing strategy whose goal is to move the firm's website link as high up the ranking list as possible.

Secondary market. Resale of a product or service. Most financial markets are secondary markets.

Segment-of-one. The firm addresses customers individually by developing customized offers.

Selling effort. The demands of the sales job. Methods to estimate required selling effort include:
Single-factor model. Uses a simple classification of customer importance.
Portfolio model. A more complex approach for estimating required selling effort.

Service. Any act or performance that one party can offer another that is essentially intangible and does not result in the ownership of anything. Anything that cannot be dropped on your foot.

Service equipment. Physical products needed to perform the service.

Service facilities. Where the firm produces the service. These facilities can be:
Offstage. Out of the customers' sight.
Onstage. Where customers experience deeds, performances, or efforts.

Service guarantee. A promise about the service experience that includes elements of value if the firm does not keep its promise.

Service personnel. People who provide the service.

Service quality. The extent to which the firm's service performance exceeds customers' expectations.

SERVQUAL. A popular model and measurement device for service quality based on several *gaps*.

Shadow system. Securing competitive information by having executives *shadow* specific competitors.

Shareholder value. The total value to shareholders—market capitalization—is measured by the market price of the firm's shares times the number of shares outstanding. Increasing shareholder value has become a mantra for many firms.

Shareholder-value perspective. Management's job is to maximize returns for shareholders. The shareholder-value perspective is prevalent in many capitalist countries—particularly in the U.S.

Signal. Information the firm sends to competitors, hoping they will process the information and act accordingly. A special type of signal designed to mislead competitors is **misinformation**.

Six sigma. A data-driven methodology for eliminating defects in any process.

SKU. See stock-keeping unit.

Slotting fees. Payments that suppliers make to retailers for providing shelf space for their products.

SMART goals. Goals that are specific, measurable, achievable, realistic, and timely.

Social media. Online tools and platforms that allow Internet users to collaborate on content, share insights and experiences, and connect for business or pleasure. Involves multimedia and includes blogs, wikis, photo and video sharing, forums, and networks for meeting like-minded people.

Spam. Unsolicited and unwanted e-mail messages.

Span of control. The ratio of subordinates to supervisors. For example, a sales manager supervising 10 salespeople would be a span of 10-to-1.

Special relationships. Informal economic relationships between the firm and other entities such as government agencies, political parties, and public interest groups, as well as suppliers and customers.

Specialty brand. A brand providing high customer brand equity but relatively low firm sales.

Stage-gate approach. A systematic process for condensing a large number of ideas to a few products the firm can successfully launch. After each **stage**, the idea or project must pass through a **gate** (meet or exceed a standard) to continue. Each gate is a **kill point** where the firm must decide whether to proceed or drop the project.

Standalone brand. An individual brand with no apparent relationship to any other firm brand.

Standardized segments. Commercially available customer groupings that many firms find useful.

Standards. The firm's planned results; criteria against which the firm measures its performance.

Stock-keeping unit (sku). A unique identifier assigned to a specific product or service.

Strategic account manager (SAM). A person responsible for the firm's most important customers.

Strategic (or key) accounts. Customers that provide the highest levels of current and/or potential sales and profits.

Strategic alliance. A cooperative arrangement that pools the strengths of individual partner firms. Strategic alliances range in formality from a new joint-venture firm to temporary, informal arrangements.

Strategic focus. Selected from a tree of alternatives and states broadly how the firm will achieve its performance objectives.

Strategic options. A variety of alternatives, each requiring significant investment, among which the firm must choose.

Strategic sourcing. A discipline of specially designed systems and processes for reducing the costs of purchased materials and services.

Strategy for growth. A set of frameworks that helps the firm decide which businesses to be in and which businesses not to be in. Includes vision, mission, growth path, and timing of entry.

Supply chain. A coordinated system of organizations, people, activities, information, and resources that move a product or service, physically or virtually, from supplier to customer.

Survey. A common technique for securing data by asking respondents questions.

Switching costs. The costs that a customer must incur to switch from one supplier to another. Customers with high switching costs experience **lock-in**.

Synergy. Occurs when the combined effect of two or more elements is greater than the sum of their separate effects — **positive synergy**. If the combined effect is less than the sum of the separate effects, there is **negative synergy**.

Systems, types of:
>   **Hard.** Based on information technology.
>   **Soft.** Based on employees.

Systems integrators. Firms that install, service, and integrate software from many vendors.

Tactical pricing. The ongoing stream of pricing decisions the firm makes on a daily basis.

Target audience. The audience that the firm is trying to reach with its advertising.

Targeting. Deciding the market segments against which the firm should concentrate its resources.

Technology, types of:

    Disruptive technology. A new technology offering new and very different value propositions, initially for new applications and a limited number of new-to-the-market customers.

    Sustaining technology. A new technology that improves the performance of established products along dimensions valued by mainstream customers.

Telemarketing. Communication by telephone, usually viewed as a subset of personal communication:

    Inbound. Initiated by the customer.

    Outbound. Initiated by the firm.

Test marketing. Tests a full-scale product launch on a limited basis.

Timing of entry. Denotes alternative entry stages in the product form life cycle:

    Pioneer. Creates new markets.

    Follow-the-leader. Enters markets when they are growing rapidly.

    Segmenter. Enters in the late-growth stage by matching offers to emerging customer needs.

    Me-too. Enters mature markets.

Timing pattern. When the advertising will appear. The major options are:

    Continuous. A regular periodic advertising pattern.

    Flighting. Repeated high advertising levels followed by low (or no) advertising.

    Pulsing. Continuous and flighting advertising combined, within a single media vehicle or class or across multiple media vehicles and classes.

Tracking study. A method of securing research data. In a tracking study, aka a longitudinal study, a panel of individuals agrees to provide responses periodically over time.

Two-sided advertising. Presents both pro and con messages for a product as a way of gaining credibility.

Tying agreements. Strong suppliers *force* resellers to sell their entire product line. This practice is illegal in the U.S. if it reduces competition.

Type I error. A false positive error like investing in a project that fails or hiring a salesperson who performs poorly.

Type II error. A false negative error like rejecting a project that would have succeeded or not hiring a salesperson who would have performed well.

Umbrella branding. A brand architecture approach in which the firm uses a monolithic brand for several products, like a corporate brand.

Upstream. The firm's suppliers and its suppliers' suppliers, etc.

VALS2. This framework groups customers based on their **self-orientation** and **resources:**

    Self-orientation. How they pursue and acquire products, services, and experiences to give their identities "shape, substance, and character."

    Resources. The full range of their psychological, physical, demographic, and material assets.

Values, types of. A common set of beliefs that guide the behavior of the firm's employees. Values can be:

    Hard, like profitability and market share.

    Soft, like integrity, respect for others, trust, and customer pre-eminence.

Value-added resellers (VARs). Firms that build additional software modules onto other firms' platforms and modify hardware for niche markets.

Value proposition. The heart of positioning that provides a convincing answer to a deceptively simple question: Why should target customers prefer the firm's offer to competitors' offers?

Vendor financing. The supplier finances the customer's purchase of its products.

Venture capitalists. Individuals and firms that provide funds for new early-stage businesses.

Venture portfolio. The set of opportunities the firm decides to pursue.

Viral marketing. Marketing techniques that use pre-existing social networks to convey marketing messages.

Virtual testing. A new approach to customer testing in which the firm creates an online shopping display that it can modify and secure results from quickly. Customers shop as in a real store with all the distracting clutter.

Vision. A description of an ideal future state; an impressionistic picture of what the future should be:
   Corporate vision. Focuses on the firm
   Business-unit vision. Focuses on the business.

Wiki. A website that allows uses to easily create and edit interlinked websites. Uses include creating collaborative websites, powering community websites, and for knowledge management systems.

Winback. Securing sales from a customer that previously defected.

Word-of-mouth (WOM) communication. Communication between and among current and potential customers.

Yield management. Continuous price adjustments based on demand and available capacity.

IMAGE CREDITS

INDEX

BRAND/COMPANY INDEX

SUBJECT INDEX

*Locators beginning with "G" indicate
terms defined in the glossary.*